THE
KINGDOM
OF THE
CULTS

Other Books by Walter Martin

The Christian and the Cults
Christian Science
Essential Christianity
Herbert W. Armstrong and the Worldwide Church of God
Jehovah of the Watchtower
Jehovah's Witnesses
The Maze of Mormonism
Mormonism
New Age Cults
The New Cults
The Riddle of Reincarnation
The Rise of the Cults
Screwtape Writes Again
Through the Windows of Heaven (Jill Martin Rische, coauthor)
Walter Martin Speaks Out on the Cults
Walter Martin's Cults Reference Bible

THE KINGDOM OF THE CULTS

WALTER MARTIN

RAVI ZACHARIAS
General Editor

BETHANY HOUSE PUBLISHERS

Minneapolis, Minnesota

The Kingdom of the Cults
Revised, Updated, and Expanded Edition, October 2003
Copyright © 1965, 1977, 1985, 1997, 2003
The Estate of Walter Martin

Scripture quotations identified KJV are from the King James Version of the Bible.

Scripture quotations identified RSV are from the Revised Standard Version of the Bible. Copyright 1946, 1952, 1971 by the Division of Christian Education of the National Council of Churches of Christ in the USA. Used by permission.

Scripture quotations identified NKJV are from the New King James Version of the Bible. Copyright © 1979, 1980, 1982 by Thomas Nelson, Inc. Used by permission. All rights reserved.

Scripture quotations identified NRSV are from the New Revised Standard Version of the Bible, copyright 1989 by the Division of Christian Education of the National Council of Churches of Christ in the U.S.A. Used by permission. All rights reserved.

Published by Bethany House Publishers
11400 Hampshire Avenue South
Bloomington, Minnesota 55438
www.bethanyhouse.com

Bethany House Publishers is a Division of
Baker Book House Company, Grand Rapids, Michigan.

Printed in the United States of America

Library of Congress Cataloging-in-Publication Data

Martin, Walter Ralston, 1928–1989
   The kingdom of the cults / by Walter Martin ; Ravi Zacharias, general editor ; Jill Martin Rische and Kevin Rische, managing editors.—Rev. and updated ed.
     p. cm.
Includes bibliographical references and indexes.
   ISBN 0-7642-2821-8 (alk. paper)
   1. Cults—United States. 2. Sects—United States. 3. United States—Religion—1960–
4. Apologetics. I. Zacharias, Ravi K. II. Rische, Jill Martin, 1957–   III. Rische, Kevin.
IV. Title.
  BL2525M366   2003
  209—dc22   2003013905

In Memory of

Peter de Visser

My friend and brother in the common faith.
His help and encouragement
made this volume possible.
If you seek his monument,
consult the libraries of the informed.

About the Author

WALTER MARTIN was fondly and respectfully known as "the father of modern Christian cult apologetics." Many current professional and academic cult apologists credit him with their introduction to the field. He held four earned degrees, having received his Master's from New York University and his Doctorate from California Coast University in the field of Comparative Religions. Author of a dozen books, a half-dozen booklets, and many articles, he founded *The Bible Answer Man,* one of the oldest and most popular nationally syndicated call-in radio shows. Known worldwide as "The Bible Answer Man," he was also the founder of Christian Research Institute and its director for almost thirty years. His work is continued today through Walter Martin Ministries located in Southern California (*www.waltermartin.com*).

About the Managing Editors

KEVIN RISCHE and JILL MARTIN RISCHE are the founders and directors of Walter Martin Ministries located in Southern California. The Risches are the producers of the nationwide radio program *Essential Christianity,* featuring Dr. Walter Martin as "The *Original* Bible Answer Man." Kevin Rische designed and developed the Walter Martin Ministries Web site: *www.waltermartin.com,* including the extensive listening library and tape catalog. He is responsible for conserving hundreds of Dr. Martin's lectures and resources. Jill Martin Rische is the eldest daughter of Dr. Martin and coauthor of *Through the Windows of Heaven: 100 Powerful Stories and Teachings from Walter Martin, the Original "Bible Answer Man."* She is also the author of *Jack Star and the Secret Door* (*www.jackstar.com*), a youth fantasy adventure in the tradition of C. S. Lewis's *The Lion, the Witch, and the Wardrobe.* Jill has been a guest on television and radio programs across the United States and Canada, including Billy Graham's *Decision Today* and Janet Parshall's *America.*

About the Senior Researcher

KURT VAN GORDEN began his work in Christian Apologetics under Dr. Walter Martin's ministry in 1976 as a staff researcher, writer, and missionary. He also filled in as Dr. Martin's teaching assistant and directed his Bible classes. He is currently directing Jude 3 Missions and the Utah Gospel Mission, which began in 1898 as the oldest mission to cults in America. In addition to writing the book *Mormonism* (Zondervan, 1995), he contributed chapters to works by Drs. Walter Martin, Josh McDowell, Alan Gomes, and Ronald Enroth.

About the Research Contributors

Each of the contributors to this updated and expanded edition has years of experience understanding, explaining, and defending the Christian faith, and each is thoroughly competent in the areas for which they provided revising, updating, editing, and/or content for this edition. Kurt Van Gorden, Robert Bowman, Dan Schlesinger, Paul Copan, Alan Gomes, James Beverley, John Morehead, and Everett Shropshire have remained faithful to the vision of Walter Martin while bringing *The Kingdom of the Cults* to the cutting edge of cult apologetics and scholarship today. In addition, we would like to thank the researchers for *The New Cults, The New Age Cults,* and *The Kingdom of the Cults,* 1997 edition, for their contribution to this volume. Most of the contributors regard the late Dr. Martin as their mentor, and all look to his example as an able defender of the faith "once for all delivered to the saints" (Jude 3).

Acknowledgments to the 1985 Edition

I wish to express my deep gratitude to Pierson Curtis, former senior master of the Stonybrook School, who helped edit and correct the original manuscript; the Rev. Anthony Collarile, Messrs. Herbert Jacobsen, Robert Smith, and John Carter, who offered valuable insights and research data; Mr. Walter Bjorck Jr., of the American Tract Society, who made many helpful manuscript suggestions that were adopted in a number of instances; Kurt Van Gorden, whose careful and accurate research was used in the chapters on the Unification Church and the Church of Scientology; editor-researcher Gretchen Passantino, who revised the majority of this present edition; and associate Clark F. Hyman, who also contributed significantly to the revision of this present edition.

Acknowledgments

Special thanks are due Dr. Martin's widow, Darlene Martin, for her faithfulness in preserving her husband's classic text on American cults; Ravi Zacharias for his commitment and support; researcher-author Kurt Van Gorden for his invaluable help on all aspects of this edition; and Bethany House editors Steve Laube and Carol Johnson, whose ideas, encouragement, and support were greatly appreciated.

General Editor's Introduction

Scores of books have a short shelf life; still others endure longer. Yet *The King-dom of the Cults*, now celebrating thirty-five years in print, may legitimately be called "a classic." And it is not without reason, for its author, the late Walter Martin, reveals not only a vast knowledge of the Scriptures and competing world-views, but a profound understanding of how truth is always threatened by subtle distortions and seductive means.

Knowing the truth and having a right understanding of the way we get to truth form the bedrock of the Christian faith. That knowledge and foundation will ever be attacked as long as there is a voice that questions if God has truly spoken consummately and clearly in His revealed Word and through His Son Jesus Christ. G. K. Chesterton once said, "What we need is a religion that is not only right where we are right, but right where we are wrong." Only the Word of God provides that corrective, which Dr. Martin faithfully reminds us. In *The King-dom of the Cults* he wrote,

> It has been wisely observed that "a man who will not stand for something is quite likely to fall for almost anything." So I have elected to stand on the ramparts of biblical Christianity as taught by the apostles, defended by the church fathers, rediscovered by the reformers. . . . It is most significant that those who have written on the cults have only recently stressed the authority of the Scriptures as a criterion for measuring either the truth or falsity of cultic claims. When this book first appeared in 1965, it was the first to make such a stress on such a large scale.

Walter Martin was called "the Bible Answer Man" because the Bible was, in truth, the final authority for him, the Word that breathed life and hope to all who would hear. It is therefore a great privilege to be asked by his family to serve as general editor of this volume. My role is a distinct honor, particularly as I have valued his contribution to my own thinking on the task of apologetics, even when I was a young student. I have listened to his messages over the years and appreciated his sensitivity to those who ask honest questions and to the language barriers that sometimes stand between the questioner and the one providing the answer. Sometimes words themselves can die the death of a thousand equivocations before the listener comes to grasp the true meaning. Walter Martin was a genius in recognizing this chasm.

Indeed, the first and most vital task of apologetics is to clarify truth claims. Dr. Martin identified this as "scaling the language barrier." When asked to define a word such as *truth,* however, many Christians freeze, for they have seldom paused to consider what it means even as they themselves quote Jesus as "the way, the truth and the life." This easy mistake is a costly one.

I remember delivering a lecture in Moscow some years ago at the Lenin Military Academy. It was apparent that I was unwelcome by many of the officers forced to attend, and throughout my talk one officer kept giving me the choke sign. Trying to speak through an interpreter with this constant threat made the task even more daunting. Yet when I finished, I soon realized my blunder and oversight. You see, the officer who was interrupting me immediately stood up and said, "You have been using the word *God* for the last one hour. What do you mean by that term?"

I was thoroughly embarrassed—how disconnected I had been from my audience. Here I was speaking to a group of atheists, and I had neglected to define my fundamental terms. Truth is the verbal coinage by which we exchange concepts of value and engender trust. Yet we often fail to explain what we mean when we reiterate the claims of Christ, and hence, when the cultist acknowledges he or she believes the same, we are left befuddled.

The first reminder in understanding and responding to cults is to remember that the claims of Jesus Christ at their core are exclusive and exclude everything to the contrary. This ought not to surprise us. Truth by definition is exclusive. If truth were all-inclusive, nothing would be false. And if nothing were false, what would be the meaning of *true*? Moreover, if nothing were false, would it be *true* to say that everything is false? It quickly becomes evident that the denial of truth as an absolute either ends up denying itself or else in effect not making any truthful assertion about truth. It is in this very challenge the various cults must be tested. Are they overriding or substantiating the ultimate expression of Truth in the person of Jesus Christ? Oftentimes, on the surface, the follower of a cultic teaching claims to follow nothing more than the teaching of Jesus Christ. But upon close scrutiny, one sees a thin layer after layer of superimposed or distorted teaching. Or to use a different metaphor, what may seem as a small alteration at the starting point becomes more serious as the theology develops in the further reaches of teaching—like the settings on the instruments at ground level that widen the error at higher altitudes.

Of one thing we can be sure: Where we find truth, often in close proximity we also find a way of thinking that distorts and faults. In fact, the philosophical method of the central figures in cults is to take a partial truth—such as a verse used as a proof-text—and blend it with an untruth so that the mix has the appearance of interpretation but in reality is systemically false. Hence we encounter cults that stray from the teachings of Christ by adding other requirements to the Gospel of grace, or by claiming a new revelation or "more accurate word from God," or by exercising inordinate control over its followers.

It is here that the church needs to see its own failing. Biblical scholar Jan Karel van Baalen argued in his *The Chaos of the Cults* (1938) that Christians "can learn from cultists, not only noting what not to believe, but also bearing in mind that 'the cults are the unpaid bills of the church.' " What a profoundly true observation. For regarding "noting what not to believe," it was, after all, the heresy of Marcion's teachings in the second century that prompted a serious effort in the early church to compile the canon. On the other hand, poor teaching and discipleship in many churches have made possible erroneous thought. Even the term

Christian in many parts of the globe today is encountered with prejudice and with more of a perverted view of what it means to be a Christian than the authentic transformation that Christ alone can bring.

The power to deceive is enormous. To this end Paul warned Timothy to cherish the Scripture, for it made him "wise unto salvation," and to "guard both your doctrine and conduct." The Scriptures are meaningful and personal because they are true, and not because we can wrest them to advantage or manipulate them into personal meaning. Meaning and application can be prostituted at the altar of self-gratification, but truth will stand in history when all human dissenters have said their last. The apostle also went on in speaking of Jesus Christ and His work to say, "We are complete in Him." Nothing need be added to the person and work of Jesus in the salvation He has provided and the Word that He has given for our instruction.

This was indeed the firm and right conviction in the mind of Walter Martin as he first penned this extraordinary volume. I applaud all the contributors and editors who have brought up to date the material so well articulated by him. He himself would have been delighted at this effort to keep the truth ever before the seeker and to protect the sincere questioner from the distortions of those who arrogate to themselves a superceding authority over God's Word and gift of salvation through His Son.

Ravi Zacharias

Managing Editors' Preface

In his 1956 book, *The Christian and the Cults,* a twenty-eight-year-old Walter Martin wrote, "The Christian Church in this atomic age is faced with the highly 'fissionable' problem of accelerated cult activities both in the continental United States and on every major mission field throughout the world. Today, as never before, the danger of a 'Cult-Bomb' detonating in the Christian world grows ominously closer as the Church delays unified action against the looming specter of insidious cultism. It is the author's earnest desire to attract attention to this mounting danger and to awaken the Christian public to a spirited defense of the historic faith of the Church of Jesus Christ. This defense can only be effected by informed pastors, teachers, evangelists and laymen who recognize the growing threat of the cults and educate themselves and the Church at large to both the deviations of cult theology and the massive refutation of them which is inherent in the teaching of sound doctrinal theology."[1]

The year 1965 brought the release of *The Kingdom of the Cults,* which has stood for nearly forty years as a sentinel in the field of Christian apologetics. Our intent in editing this volume was to ensure that the voice of Dr. Walter Martin would continue to be heard in the same strong, clear way. In order to guarantee the clarity of his voice in this new revision, the tilde symbol (~) was used at the beginning and ending of paragraphs or sections where significant new editorial material was introduced into the original text. In addition to this, an editor's note was added at the end of some pages where further clarification of authorship was needed.

New chapters were added by different authors only where original material was either significantly outdated or never commented upon in detail by Walter Martin. In some cases, material from other Martin resources, such as audiotapes, books, and articles, was used for continuity and development purposes. Several chapters removed from previous editions were updated and included in this new edition, their facts both accurate and concise—their relevancy still indisputable nearly four decades after they were first written. Chapter titles were reviewed and rearranged to reflect the order present in previous editions originally edited by Walter Martin.

---

[1]Walter Martin, *The Christian and the Cults* (Grand Rapids, Mich.: Zondervan Publishing House, 1956), 5–6.

Early in the editorial process, Dr. Ravi Zacharias eloquently commented, "A man's words are a man's words," and wherever possible, we've tried to follow this advice and preserve Walter Martin's voice—a unique voice called to a unique purpose in the defense of the faith, "once for all delivered to the saints" (Jude 3 NKJV).

> *Rise up, O men of God!*
> *Have done with lesser things;*
> *Give heart and soul and mind and strength,*
> *to serve the King of Kings.*
>
> *Rise up, O men of God!*
> *The Church for you doth wait,*
> *Her strength unequal to her task:*
> *Rise up and make her great!*[2]

In the service of our Lord Jesus Christ,
Kevin Rische
Jill Martin Rische
March 2003

---

[2]William P. Merriall and William H. Walter, "Rise Up, O Men of God."

Contents

Chapter I

The Kingdom of the Cults

It has been said of the United States that it is "the great melting pot" for the people of the world. And the contents of that pot would not be complete unless it also included the religions of those masses that now make up the populace of America. This writer has spent over forty years of his life in research and field-work among the religions of America, and this volume, limited as it is by the vastness and complexity of the problem itself, constitutes his evaluation of that vibrant brand of religion that has come to be recognized by many as the "Kingdom of the Cults."

In his study of modern American cults and minority religious movements as found in his text *These Also Believe*, Dr. Charles Braden, emeritus professor at Northwestern University, and coauthor John C. Schaffer, lecturer and visiting professor at Scripps College, made a number of observations with which this writer agrees. In regard to the term *cult*, for instance, Dr. Braden states:

> By the term cult I mean nothing derogatory to any group so classi-
> fied. A cult, as I define it, is any religious group which differs significantly
> in one or more respects as to belief or practice from those religious
> groups which are regarded as the normative expressions of religion in our
> total culture.[1]

I may add to this that a cult might also be defined as a group of people gath-
ered about a specific person or person's *misinterpretation* of the Bible. For example, Jehovah's Witnesses are, for the most part, followers of the interpretations

---

This chapter updated and edited by Kevin Rische and Jill Martin Rische.
[1]Charles S. Braden and John C. Schaffer, *These Also Believe* (New York: The Macmillan Company, 1949), Preface xii. Dr. Braden NU Emeritus Professor (1954), John C. Schaffer, lecturer (1955), Scripps (1954–56).

of Charles T. Russell and J. F. Rutherford. The Christian Scientist of today is a disciple of Mary Baker Eddy and her interpretations of Scripture. The Mormons, by their own admission, adhere to those interpretations found in the writings of Joseph Smith and Brigham Young. It would be possible to go on citing many others, such as the Unity School of Christianity, which follows the theology of Charles and Myrtle Fillmore. From a theological viewpoint, the cults contain many major deviations from historical Christianity. Yet, paradoxically, they continue to insist that they are entitled to be classified as Christians.

It is my conviction that the reader is entitled to know the theological position from which this volume is written so that there will be no misconceptions as to the ground for my evaluation. I am a Baptist minister, an evangelical holding to the inerrancy of Scripture, and teach in the fields of Biblical Theology, Comparative Religion, and Apologetics.

It is impossible for me to agree with Dr. Braden, "an unrepentant liberal,"[2] or to agree that I "hold no brief for any particular cult, nor am violently opposed to any."[3] While I am in agreement that "in general the cults represent the earnest attempt of millions of people to find the fulfillment of deep and legitimate needs of the human spirit, which most of them seem not to have found in the established churches,"[4] I feel there is still much more to be said. It has been wisely observed by someone that "a man who will not stand for something is quite likely to fall for almost anything." So I have elected to stand on the ramparts of biblical Christianity as taught by the apostles, defended by the church Fathers, rediscovered by the Reformers, and embodied in what is sometimes called Reformed Theology.

It is the purpose of this book, then, to evaluate the so-called cults and isms that today are found in abundance in America and on the great mission fields of the world. My approach to the subject is threefold: (1) *historical analysis* of the salient facts connected with the rise of the cult systems; (2) *theological evaluation* of the major teachings of those systems; and (3) *apologetic contrast* from the viewpoint of biblical theology, with an emphasis upon exegesis and doctrine.

It is not my desire in any sense to make fun of adherents of cult systems, the large majority of whom are sincere, though I am not adverse to humor when it can underscore a point. A study of the cults is a serious business. They constitute a growing trend in America—a trend that is away from the established Christian churches and the historic teachings of the Bible—an emphasis upon autosoteric efforts, or the desire to save one's self apart from biblical revelation.

It is most significant that those who have written on the cults have only recently stressed the authority of the Scriptures as a criterion for measuring either the truth or falsity of cultic claims. When this book first appeared in 1965, it was the first to make such a stress on such a large scale. Since then my example has been followed and the Christian is now in a position to readily find the Scriptures' verdict on the cults. Dr. Marcus Bach, who has written extensively from a

---

[2]Ibid., xi.
[3]Ibid.
[4]Ibid.

liberal viewpoint on the cults, summed up this attitude of tolerance apart from scriptural authority when he wrote:

> Somehow I felt I must become a representative of the average church-goer everywhere in America, whose heart was with me in my seeking. If the Jehovah's Witnesses have some heavenly tip-off that the world is coming to an end in 1973,[5] we want to tell our friends about it in plenty of time! If Father Divine is really God, we want to know about it! If Unity is building a new city down in Missouri, we Americans want to get in on the ground floor! If that man in Moscow, Idaho, talked with God, actually and literally, we have a right to know how it's done! Certainly these modern movements suggest that there was a vital, if not always coherent, moving force back of them, giving luster and drive to their beliefs. I decided that I would not concern myself so much with the rivalry among groups as with their realization. I would devote myself more to the *way* than to the *why* of their doctrine. Let others turn ecclesiastical microscopes on them or weigh them in the sensitive scale of final truth; I would content myself with the age-old verdict of Gamaliel: "If this work be of men, it will come to naught; but if it be of God, we cannot overthrow it."
>
> I decided to set forth on my own with no strings attached and no stipend from any university, no commission from any church, no obligation to any individual or group, no bias, no preconceived judgment, no illusions.
>
> "All roads that lead to God are good." As I began my adventure, the fervor of this naïve and youthful conviction rushed over me once more.[6]

Dr. Bach admits more in this statement than perhaps he intended, for though it is a laudable aim to become "representative of the average churchgoer everywhere in America," his use of the word *if* with reference to the teachings of the cults indicates that the final truth, grounded in the authority of Scripture and the revelation of Jesus Christ, has *not* been obtained by the Christian church, and that other sources must be investigated in order to ascertain the whole truth of the Christian message. We are in full agreement that "these modern movements suggest that there was a vital, if not always coherent, moving force back of them, giving luster and drive to their beliefs." But since the cult systems vigorously oppose the Christian church, particularly in the realm of Christology and soteriology, perhaps it is not at all out of order to suggest "that force" is the same that opposed our Lord and the apostles and has consistently opposed the efforts of the Christian church, the force described by the apostle Paul as "the god of this world."[7]

Liberal scholars, then, have devoted themselves more to *the way* than to *the why* of the doctrines of the cults, and they have adopted the statement of Gamaliel

---

[5]They most recently decided on September of 1975, to their later dismay. This new false prophecy cost them thousands of members.

[6]Marcus Bach, *They Have Found a Faith* (Indianapolis: The Bobbs-Merrill Company, 1946), 19–21.

[7]2 Corinthians 4:4.

as their creed. It will be remembered that Gamaliel counseled the Jews not to oppose the Christians, for "if this counsel or this work be of men, it will come to naught: But if it be of God, ye cannot overthrow it."[8] Let it not be forgotten that Gamaliel's advice is *not* biblical theology; and if it were followed in the practical realm of experience as steadfastly as it is urged, then we would have to recognize Islam as "of God" because of its rapid growth and reproductive virility throughout the world. We would have to acknowledge Mormonism (six people in 1830 to eleven million in 2002)[9] in the same category as Islam, something that most liberals are unwilling to do, though some have not hesitated to so declare themselves.

We do not suggest that we "turn ecclesiastical microscopes" on the cults, but rather that they be viewed in the light of what we know to be divine revelation, the Word of God, which itself weighs them "in the sensitive scale of final truth," for it was our Lord who taught, "If ye believe not that I am he, ye shall die in your sins."[10] And the final criterion today as always must remain, "What think ye of Christ? whose son is he?"[11]

I must dissent from the view that "all roads that lead to God are good" and believe instead the words of our Lord, "I am the way, the truth, and the life: no man cometh unto the Father, but by me."[12] It should be carefully noted that Jesus did not say, "I am one of many equally good ways" or "I am a better way than the others, I am an aspect of truth; I am a fragment of the life." Instead, His claim was absolute, and allegiance to Him, as the Savior of the world, was to take precedence over all the claims of men and religions.

I should like to make it clear that in advancing criticism of some of the views of liberal scholars in the field of cults and isms, I do not discount their many valuable contributions. And no singular study, regardless of the time involved and the thoroughness of the investigation, can review all the data and evaluate all the facts necessary to completely understand the origin and development of cultism. My approach is quite honestly theological in its orientation with the aim of contrast and reaffirmation in view. Dr. Jan Van Baalen is correct when he says that "the cults are the unpaid bills of the church."[13] They are this and more, for they are a challenge to the church to affirm once again the great principles and foundations of the Gospel of Christ and to make them meaningful to the present generation. There can be no doubt that the great trend in religion is syncretistic, or a type of homogenization of religions, such as the great historian Arnold Toynbee has more than once suggested.

We are consistently being told in books, articles, council pronouncements, and ecumenical conclaves that we must play down the things that divide us and emphasize those things that make for unity. This is all well and good if we are speaking about a firm foundation of doctrinal, moral, and ethical truth, and if we are speaking about true unity within the body of Christ. But if, as some sug-

---

[8]Acts 5:38–39.
[9]http://library.lds.org (2001 Statistical Report). See also *www.connect-a.net/users/drshades/stats.htm* and *www.adherents.com/Na_185.html#1056*
[10]John 8:24.
[11]Matthew 22:42.
[12]John 14:6.
[13]Jan Karel Van Baalen, *The Chaos of Cults* (London: Pickering & Inglis Ltd., 1962), 14.

gest, this is broadened to include those who are not in agreement with the essentials of biblical Christianity, we must resolutely oppose it.

It is most interesting to note that the National Council of Churches and the World Council of Churches, which constitute the spearhead of the ecumenical movement throughout the world, have consistently denied membership to the cults under study in this volume on the ground that they do not recognize or worship Jesus Christ as God and Savior. In 1957 *The Christian Century* printed a series of articles on four prominent cults, which were written by Dr. Marcus Bach. Dr. Bach's presentation was so sympathetic that the then editors of *The Christian Century* were compelled to write an editorial, pointing out the differences between the cults and Christianity. Editor Harold Fey and Managing Editor Theodore Gill wrote that the promises of the cults were empty and could not satisfy as Christianity could.[14] We can sympathize with Fey and Gill's concerns, since any series of articles that present the cults in such a favorable light, though appearing to be objective, does little or nothing for Christianity except to encourage weaker Christians to dabble in what is a dangerous hobby.

Biblical Perspectives

The age that saw the advent of Jesus Christ was an age rich in religion, stretching from the crass animism and sex worship of the great majority of the world to the Roman pantheon of gods and the Greek mystery religions. One need only peruse Gibbon's *Decline and Fall of the Roman Empire* to become acutely aware of the multiplicity of gods and goddesses, as well as of philosophical and ethical systems that pervaded the religious horizon in that era of history. Judaism had withdrawn itself from any extensive missionary activity, burdened as the Jews were by the iron rule of an unsympathetic Roman paganism. The Law of God had been interpreted and reinterpreted through commentaries and rabbinical emendations to the place where our Lord had to say to the religious leaders of His day, "Why do ye also transgress the commandment of God by your tradition? . . . Thus have ye made the commandment of God of none effect by your tradition."[15]

Into this whirlpool of stagnant human philosophy and perverted revelation came the Son of God, who, through His teachings and example, revealed that there was such a thing as *divine humanity,* and through His miraculous powers, vicarious death, and bodily resurrection, cut across the maze of human doubts and fears and was lifted up, to draw all men unto Him. It has been wisely observed that men are at liberty to reject Jesus Christ and the Bible as the Word of God; they are at liberty to oppose Him; they are at liberty to challenge it. But they are not at liberty to *alter* the essential message of the Scriptures, which is the good news that God does care for the lost souls of His children, and so loved us as to send His only Son that we might live through Him.

In keeping with this Gospel of God's grace, our Lord not only announced it, but He prophesied the trials and tribulations that would encompass His followers,

---

[14]*The Christian Century,* 551.
[15]Matthew 15:3, 6.

both within the church and without, and one of the greatest of all these trials would, our Lord taught, be the challenge of false prophets and false christs who would come in His name and deceive many.[16] So concerned was Christ in this area that He at one time declared:

> Beware of false prophets, which come to you in sheep's clothing, but inwardly they are ravening wolves. Ye shall know them by their fruits. Do men gather grapes of thorns, or figs of thistles? Even so every good tree bringeth forth good fruit; but a corrupt tree bringeth forth evil fruit. A good tree cannot bring forth evil fruit, neither can a corrupt tree bring forth good fruit. Every tree that bringeth not forth good fruit is hewn down, and cast into the fire. Wherefore by their fruits ye shall know them. Not every one that saith unto me, Lord, Lord, shall enter into the kingdom of heaven; but he that doeth the will of my Father which is in heaven. Many will say to me in that day, Lord, Lord, have we not prophesied in thy name? and in thy name have cast out devils? and in thy name done many wonderful works? And then will I profess unto them, I never knew you: depart from me, ye that work iniquity.[17]

Christ pointed out that the false prophets would come. There was not a doubt in the mind of the Son of God that this would take place, and the history of the heresies of the first five centuries of the Christian church bear out the accuracy of His predictions. Christ further taught that the fruits of the false prophets would also be apparent, and that the church would be able to detect them readily. Let us never forget that "fruits" from a corrupt tree can also be doctrinal, as well as ethical and moral. A person may be ethically and morally "good" by human standards, but if he sets his face against Jesus Christ as Lord and Savior, and rejects Him, his fruit is corrupt, and he is to be rejected as counterfeit. The apostle John understood this when he wrote, "They went out from us, but they were not of us; for if they had been of us, they would no doubt have continued with us: but they went out, that they might be made manifest that they were not all of us."[18]

The Bible, then, does speak of false prophets, false christs, false apostles, and "deceitful workers, transforming themselves into the apostles of Christ. And no marvel; for Satan himself is transformed into an angel of light. Therefore it is no great thing if his ministers also be transformed as the ministers of righteousness; whose end shall be according to their works."[19]

We cannot afford to hold any concept of the purveyors of erroneous doctrines *different* from that held by our Lord and the apostles, and we must, as Paul states, "abhor that which is evil; cleave to that which is good."[20] In the light of this teaching, it is extremely difficult for this writer to understand how

---

[16]Matthew 24:5.
[17]Matthew 7:15–23.
[18]1 John 2:19.
[19]2 Corinthians 11:13–15.
[20]Romans 12:9.

it is possible to cleave to that which is good without an abhorrence of that which is evil.

The biblical perspective, where false teachers and false teachings are concerned, is that we are to have compassion and love for those who are enmeshed in the teachings of the false prophets, but we are to vigorously oppose the teachings, with our primary objective the winning of the soul and not so much the argument. It must never be forgotten that cultists are souls for whom Jesus Christ died, for "he is the propitiation for our sins: and not for ours only, but also for the sins of the whole world."[21]

Today the kingdom of the cults stretches throughout the world, its membership in the millions, with over seventeen million cult members in the United States alone.[22] In the past, the church of Jesus Christ has badly neglected both the evangelizing and refuting of the various cult systems, but there is now cause for some optimism. ~According to recent studies on American Religious Adherents, membership in several Christian denominations is growing rapidly, while the membership growth rate of the Latter-day Saints, Jehovah's Witnesses, and other cults has slowed considerably. Today in the United States, Christianity statistically outpaces the kingdom of the cults, but we are still facing a dangerous exponential rise in numbers in Latin America and Third World countries. Islam and Buddhist religions, as well as the New Age/Pagan movement, also claim increases in membership worldwide, so the problem faces us all the same and continues to grow: The kingdom of the cults is expanding.[23]~

Our purposes in this volume are to further awaken interest in this tremendously important field of Christian missionary effort among the cults, to point out the flaws in the various cult systems, and to provide the information that will enable Christians both to answer cultists and to present effectively to them the claims of the Gospel of Christ, with a deep concern for the redemption of their souls. It is also the aim of this book to so familiarize the reader with the refreshing truths of the Gospel of Christ that he may see the great heritage that is ours in the Christian faith and be challenged more effectively to both live and witness for the Savior.

The American Banking Association has a training program that exemplifies this aim of the author. Each year it sends hundreds of bank tellers to Washington in order to teach them to detect counterfeit money, which is a source of great loss of revenue to the Treasury Department. It is most interesting that during the entire two-week training program, no teller touches counterfeit money. Only the original passes through his hands. The reason for this is that the American Banking Association is convinced that if a man is thoroughly familiar with the original he will not be deceived by the counterfeit bill, no matter how much like the original it appears.[24] It is the contention of this writer that if the average Christian would become familiar once again with the great foundations of his faith, he would be able to detect those counterfeit

---

[21] 1 John 2:2.
[22] *www.Adherents.com/Religions_By_Adherents.html*
[23] *www.Adherents.com/rel_USA.html*
[24] *This training program was discontinued, but the example remains relevant.*

elements so apparent in the cult systems that set them apart from biblical Christianity.

Charles W. Ferguson, in his provocative volume *The New Books of Revelation*, describes the advent of modern cult systems as "the modern Babel." He goes on to state,

> It should be obvious to any man who is not one himself, that the land is overrun with messiahs. I refer not to those political quacks who promise in one election to rid the land of evil, but rather to those inspired fakirs who promise to reduce the diaphragm or orient the soul through the machinery of a cult religion. Each of these has made himself the center of a new theophany, has surrounded himself with a band of zealous apostles, has hired a hall for a shrine and then set about busily to rescue truth from the scaffold and put it on the throne.[25]

Ferguson did the Christian church a great service in the late 1920s by focusing attention upon the rise of the cults. His observations were pithy and to the point, and though they cannot always be endorsed from a biblical standpoint, there can be little doubt that he put his finger on the cults as a vital emergent force in American Protestantism with which the church of Jesus Christ must reckon. It is with this force that we now come to deal, confident that on the authority of the Scriptures, the Christian church has the answers, and in the Gospel of Christ, a Savior who can provide the cultist with something no cult system has ever been able to originate—peace with God and fellowship with the Father and with His Son, Jesus Christ.

The cults have capitalized on the failure of the Christian church to understand their teachings and to develop a workable methodology both to evangelize and to refute cult adherents. Within the theological structure of the cults there is considerable truth, all of which, it might be added, is drawn from biblical sources, but so *diluted* with human error as to be more deadly than complete falsehood. The cults have also emphasized the things that the church has forgotten, such as divine healing (Christian Science, Unity, New Thought), prophecy (Jehovah's Witnesses and Mormonism), and a great many other things that in the course of our study we will have opportunity to observe. But let it never be forgotten that where the Gospel of Jesus Christ is proclaimed in power and with what Dr. Frank E. Gaebelein has called "a compelling relevancy," cults have made little or no headway. This has led Dr. Lee Belford, Professor of Comparative Religions at New York University, to state,

> The problem is essentially theological where the cults are concerned. The answer of the church must be theological and doctrinal. No sociological or cultural evaluation will do. Such works may be helpful, but they will not

---

[25] *Charles W. Ferguson, The New Books of Revelation* (Garden City, N.Y.: Doubleday, Doran and Co., Inc., 1928), 1.

answer the Jehovah's Witness or Mormon who is seeking biblical authority for either the acceptance or rejection of his beliefs.

The problem, then, is complex. There is no simple panacea, but it constitutes a real challenge to Christianity that cannot be ignored or neglected any longer—for the challenge is here and the time is now.

Quick Facts About Scaling the Language Barrier

- Learn the terminology of major cult systems.

- Define key words and standard doctrinal phrases.

- Compare definitions with contexts.

- Review the importance of defining terms.

- Present a clear testimony of regenerative experience with Jesus Christ.

Chapter 2

Scaling the Language Barrier

The scientific age in which we live, in the very real sense of the term, has given rise to a new vocabulary, which, unless it is understood, can create enormous problems in the realm of communication. The revolutions in culture that have taken place in the vocabularies of technology, psychology, medicine, and politics have not left untouched the religions of the world in general and the theology of Christianity in particular.

Writing in *Eternity* magazine, the noted theologian Dr. Bernard Ramm calls attention to this particular fact when evaluating the theological system of the late Dr. Paul Tillich, leading theological luminary of our day and former professor of theology at the University of Chicago's Divinity School. Dr. Ramm charges that Tillich has so radically redefined standard theological terms that the effect upon Christian theology is nothing short of cataclysmic. "Such biblical notions of sin, guilt, damnation, justification, regeneration, etc., all come out retranslated into a language that is foreign to the meaning of these concepts in the Scriptures themselves."[1]

Dr. Ramm is quite right in his observations, for any student of Tillich's theology and, for that matter, the theology of contemporary neoliberalism and neoorthodoxy will concede immediately that in the theological framework of these two systems of thought, the vocabulary of what has been rightly termed by Dr. Edward Carnell as "classical orthodoxy" undergoes what can only be termed radical redefinition. Just how this is effected is worthy of another chapter, but no one informed on the subject seriously questions that this is what has occurred.

It is therefore possible for modern theologians to use the terminology of the Bible and historical theology, but in an entirely different sense from that intended by the writers of Scripture.

This chapter updated and edited by Kevin Rische and Jill Martin Rische.
[1]November 1963: 33.

Before attempting to examine the non-Christian cult systems contained in this volume, one must face the fact that the originators and promulgators of cult theology have done exactly the same thing to the semantic structure of Christian theology as did the modern theologians. So it is possible for a Jehovah's Witness, a Christian Scientist, or a Mormon, for example, to utilize the terminology of biblical Christianity with absolute freedom, having already redesigned these terms in a theological framework of his own making and to his own liking, but almost always at direct variance with the historically accepted meanings of the terms.

The student of cultism, then, must be prepared to scale the language barrier of *terminology*. First, he must recognize that it does exist, and second, he must acknowledge the very real fact that unless terms are defined when one is either speaking or reading cult theology, the semantic jungle that the cults have created will envelop him, making difficult, if not imposible, a proper contrast between the teachings of the cults and those of orthodox Christianity.

On countless occasions, the author has been asked, "Why is it that when I am talking with a cultist he seems to be in full agreement with what I am saying, but when we have finished talking, I am aware of a definite lack of communication, almost as though we were not talking the same language?"

The answer to this question is, of course, that we have not been communicating, because the vocabulary of the cults is not the vocabulary of the Bible by definition. Only the Lord knows how many fruitless hours have been spent attempting to confront cultists with the claim of the Gospel, when five short minutes of insistence upon definitions of the terms employed in conversation (particularly concerning the nature of God and the person, nature, and work of Jesus Christ) would have stripped the cult theology of one of its most potent tools, that of theological term-switching. Through the manipulation of terminology, it is therefore obvious that the cultist has the Christian at a distinct disadvantage, particularly in the realm of the great fundamental doctrines of biblical theology. The question, then, is how can the interested Christian solve that problem, if indeed it can be solved at all? In short, is there some common denominator that one can use when faced with a cultist of any particular variety and, if so, how does one put this principle into practice?

The cults capitalize on the almost total inability of the average Christian to understand the subtle art of redefinition in the realm of biblical theology. Human nature being what it is, it is only natural that Christian ministers as well as laymen should desire a panacea to the irritating and, at times, frustrating problem of cult terminology. Unfortunately, however, no such panacea exists. But lest we become discouraged with the prospect of facing the ever-multiplying bodies of non-Christian cults unprepared for this conflict (and make no mistake, this *is* spiritual conflict), proper usage of definitions as a practical tool will rob the cultist of at least two of his advantages: surprise and confusion.

The Riddle of Semantics

The problem of semantics has always played an important part in human affairs, for by its use or abuse, whichever the case may be, entire churches, thrones, and even governments, for that matter, have been erected, sustained, or overthrown. The late George Orwell's stirring novel *1984*, in which he points out that the redefinition of common political terms can lead to slavery when it is allowed to pass unchallenged by a lethargic populace, is a classic illustration of the dangers of perverted semantics. It should be of no particular surprise to any student of world history that trick terminology is a powerful propaganda weapon. The communist dictatorship of China, which even the Russian theorists rejected as incalculably brutal and inept, dares to call itself the People's Republic of China. As history testifies, the people have very little, if any, say in the actual operation of communism, and if democracy is to be understood as the rule of the people, the Chinese communists have canonized the greatest misnomer of all time!

Both the Chinese communists and the Russians have paid a terrible price for not defining terminology, and for listening to the siren song of Marxism without carefully studying and analyzing the atheistic collectivism through which the music came.

Applying this analogy to the field of cults, it is at once evident that a distinct parallel exists between the two systems. For cultism, like communism, plays a type of hypnotic music upon a semantic harp of terminological deception. And there are many who historically have followed these strains down the broad road to spiritual eternal judgment. There is a common denominator then, and it is inextricably connected with language and the precise definition of terminology. It is what we might call the key to understanding cultism.

Precisely how to utilize the key that will help unlock the jargon of cult semantics is best illustrated by the following facts, drawn from over thirty years of research and practical fieldwork with cultists of every variety.

The average non-Christian cult owes its very existence to the fact that it has utilized the terminology of Christianity, has borrowed liberally from the Bible (almost always out of context), and sprinkled its format with evangelical clichés and terms wherever possible or advantageous. Up to now this has been a highly successful attempt to represent their respective systems of thought as "Christian."

On encountering a cultist, then, always remember that you are dealing with a person who is familiar with Christian terminology, and who has carefully redefined it to fit the system of thought he or she now embraces.

A concrete example of a redefinition of terms can be illustrated in the case of almost any of the Gnostic cult systems that emphasize healing and hold in common a pantheistic concept of God (Christian Science, New Thought, Unity, Christ Unity Science, Metaphysics, Religious Science, Divine Science).

In the course of numerous contacts with this type of cultist, the author has had many opportunities to see the semantic maze in full operation, and it is awesome to behold. Such a cult adherent will begin talking at length about God and Christ. He will speak especially about love, tolerance, forgiveness, the Sermon on the Mount, and, as always, the out-of-context perversion of James' "faith without works is dead."

It should be noted that hardly ever in their discourses will such cultists discuss the essential problem of evil, the existence of personal sin, or the necessity of the substitutionary atonement of Christ as the sole means of salvation from sin, through the agency of divine grace and the exercise of faith. In fact, they conscientiously avoid such distasteful subjects like the proverbial plague and discuss them only with great reluctance. Of course, there are exceptions to this rule, but on the average it is safe to assume that reticence will characterize any exploration of these touchy issues. Both Christian Science and Unity talk of God as Trinity; but their real concept of God is a pantheistic abstraction (Life, Truth, and Love constitute the triune divine principles—Christian Science).

The historic doctrine of the Trinity is seldom, if ever, considered without careful redefinition. If the reader consults the *Metaphysical Bible Dictionary,* published by the Unity School of Christianity, he will see the masterpiece of redefinition for himself. For in this particular volume, Unity has redefined exhaustively many of the cardinal terms of biblical theology, much as Mary Baker Eddy did in her Glossary of Terms in the book *Science and Health With Key to the Scriptures.* The reader will be positively amazed to find what has happened to biblical history, the person of Adam, the concept of human sin, spiritual depravity, and eternal judgment. One thing, however, will emerge very clearly from this study: Unity may use the terminology of the Bible, but by no stretch of the imagination can the redefinition be equated with the thing itself.

Another confusing aspect of non-Christian cultists' approach to semantics is the manner in which they will surprise the Christian with voluminous quotations from no less authority than the Bible, and give the appearance of agreeing with nearly every statement the Christian makes in attempting to evangelize the cultist. Such stock phrases as "We believe that way too; we agree on this point" or the more familiar: "Mrs. Eddy, Mr. or Mrs. Fillmore, Mr. Evans, Dr. Buchman, Joseph Smith, or Brigham Young says exactly the same thing; we are completely in agreement." All such tactics based upon the juggling of terms usually have the effect of frustrating the average Christian, for he is unable to put his finger on what he knows is error and is repeatedly tantalized by seeming agreement which, as he knows, does not exist. He is, therefore, often forced into silence because he is unaware of what the cultist is actually doing. Often, even though he may be aware of this in a limited sense, he hesitates to plunge into a discussion for fear of ridicule because of an inadequate background or a lack of biblical information.

The solution to this perplexing problem is far from simple. The Christian must realize that for every biblical or doctrinal term *he* mentions, a redefinition light flashes on in the mind of the cultist, and a lightning-fast redefinition is accomplished. Realizing that the cultist will apparently agree with the doctrine under discussion while firmly disagreeing in reality with the historical and biblical concept, the Christian is on his way to dealing effectively with cult terminology. This amazing operation of terminological redefinition works very much like a word association test in psychology.

It is simple for a cultist to spiritualize and redefine the clear meaning of biblical texts and teachings so as to be in apparent harmony with the historic Christian faith. However, such a harmony is at best a surface agreement, based upon double meanings of words that cannot stand the test of biblical context, grammar, or sound exegesis. Language is, to be sure, a complex subject; all are agreed on this. But one thing is beyond dispute, and that is that in context words mean just what they say. Either we admit this or we must be prepared to surrender all the accomplishments of grammar and scholastic progress and return to writing on cave walls with charcoal sticks in the tradition of our alleged stone-age ancestors. To illustrate this point more sharply, the experience of everyday life points out the absurdity of terminological redefinitions in every way of life.

An attorney who is retained by his client must know the laws that govern trial procedure, cross-examination, and evidence. But above all else he must believe in the innocence of his client. A client who tells his attorney that he is guilty of a misdemeanor but not a felony is using the vocabulary of law. But if his attorney finds out that his client has perverted that vocabulary so that the terms are interchangeable, he will either refuse to defend him or will clarify the terminology before the court, because by definition a misdemeanor is a misdemeanor and a felony is a felony. A man who says he stole only ninety dollars (petty theft), but who really means ninety dollars more or less, and in reality knows that it was in excess of five hundred dollars (grand theft), is playing a game that the law will not tolerate. He will most certainly be punished for such perversions of standard legal terms. In the realm of medicine, a doctor who announces that he will perform an open-heart operation, then proceeds in the presence of his colleagues to remove the gall bladder, and then attempts to defend his action by the claim that open-heart surgery actually means removal of the gallbladder in his vocabulary, could not practice medicine for long! Open-heart surgery is delicate repair of the heart muscle. Removal of the gallbladder is, by definition, surgery of another type. In law and in medicine, therefore, terms are what they are by definition. On the business and professional level this also holds true. But to the cultists words do not always mean what they have always meant by definition in specific context. And just as the American Bar Association will not tolerate confusion of terminology in the trial of cases, and as the American Medical Association will not tolerate redefinition of terminology in diagnostic and surgical medicine, so also the church of Jesus Christ has every right not to tolerate the gross perversions and redefinitions of historical biblical terminology simply to accommodate a culture and a society that cannot tolerate an absolute standard or criterion of truth, even if it is revealed by God in His Word and through the true witness of His Spirit.

The major cult systems, then, change the definition of historical terms without a quibble. They answer the objections of Christian theologians with the meaningless statement, "You interpret it your way and I'll interpret it mine. Let's be broad-minded. After all, one interpretation is as good as another."

A quick survey of how cults redefine Christian terminology illustrates this important observation.

Cult	Term	Cult Definition	Christian Definition
~Mormonism	God	Many gods	One God
Jehovah's Witnesses	Jesus Christ	Not god, created by Jehovah	God the Son, Creator of all
Christian Science	Sin	Illusion, error, not real	Disobedience to God
New Age	Salvation	Becoming one with the universe/God	Reconciliation with God by means of Christ's atonement[2]~

---

[2]~Cited from Walter Martin, *Kingdom of the Cults*, (Minneapolis: Bethany House Publishers, 1997), 32.

Is it any wonder, then, that orthodox Christians feel called upon to openly denounce such perversions of clearly defined and historically accepted biblical terminology, and claim that the cults have no rights—scholastically, biblically, or linguistically—to redefine biblical terms as they do?

We ought never to forget for one moment that *things are what they are by definition.* Any geometric figure whose circumference is $2\pi r$ is by definition circular. Any two figures whose congruency can be determined by the application of angle-side-angle, side-angle-side, or side-side-side, is by definition a triangle. To expand this, we might point out that any formula that expresses hydrogen to be in two parts and oxygen to be in one part is water; and hydrogen to be in two parts, sulfur in one part, and oxygen in four parts is sulfuric acid. H_2O can never be H_2SO_4. Nor can the Atonement become at-one-ment as the theology of the Gnostic cults (Christian Science, Unity, New Thought) explains it. *It simply cannot be,* if language means anything.

To spiritualize texts and doctrines or attempt to explain them away on the basis of the nebulous word *interpretation* is scholastic dishonesty, and it is not uncommonly found in leading cult literature. Cultists are destined to find out that the power of Christianity is not in its terminology, but in the relationship of the individual to the historic Christ of revelation. The divine-human encounter must take place. One must become a new creation in Christ Jesus, and the emptying of Christian terminology of all its historic meanings serves only the purpose of confusion and can never vitiate the force of the Gospel, which is the Person of the Savior performing the historic function of redeeming the sinner by grace.

The Christ of Scripture is an eternal, divine personality who cannot be dismissed by a flip of the cultist's redefinition switch, regardless of how deftly it is done. The average Christian will do well to remember the basic conflict of terminology that he is certain to encounter when dealing with cultists of practically every variety.

Summary

Whenever a Christian encounters a cultist, certain primary thoughts must be paramount in his mind: (1) He must strive to direct the conversation to the problem of terminology and maneuver the cult adherent into a position where he must define his usage of terms and his authority, if any, for drastic, unbiblical redefinitions, which are certain to emerge; (2) the Christian must then compare these "definitions" with the various contexts of the verses upon which the cultist draws support of his doctrinal interpretations; (3) he must define the words and phrases *interpretation and historic orthodoxy,* and standard doctrinal words and phrases such as *the new birth, Atonement, context, exegesis, eternal judgment,* etc., so that no misunderstanding will exist when these things come under discussion, as they inevitably will; (4) the Christian must attempt to lead the cultist to a review of the importance of properly defining terms for all important doctrines involved, particularly the doctrine of personal redemption from sin, which most cult systems define in a markedly unbiblical manner; and (5) it is the responsibility of the Christian to present a clear testimony of his own regenerative experience with Jesus Christ in terminology that has been carefully clarified regarding the necessity of such regeneration on the part of the cultist in the light of the certain reality of God's inevitable justice. It may be necessary also, in the course of discussing terminology and its dishonest recasting by cult systems, to resort to occasional polemic utterances. In such cases, the Christian should be certain that he is tempered with patience and love, so that the cultist appreciates that such tactics are motivated by one's personal concern for his eternal welfare and not simply to "win the argument."

Let it never be forgotten that cultists are experts at lifting texts out of their respective contexts without proper concern for the laws of language or the established principles of biblical interpretation. There are those of whom Peter warns us, who "wrest . . . scriptures, unto their own destruction" (2 Peter 3:16). This is an accurate picture of the kingdom of the cults in the realm of terminology.

Looking back over the picture of cult semantics, the following facts emerge:

1. The average cultist knows his own terminology very thoroughly. He also has a historic knowledge of Christian usage and is, therefore, prepared to discuss many areas of Christian theology intelligently.

2. The well-trained cultist will carefully avoid definition of terms concerning cardinal doctrines such as the Trinity, the Deity of Christ, the Atonement, the Bodily Resurrection of our Lord, the process of Salvation by Grace, and Justification by Faith. If pressed in these areas, he will redefine the terms to fit the semantic framework of orthodoxy, unless he is forced to define his terms explicitly.

3. The informed Christian must seek for a point of departure, preferably the authority of the Scriptures, which can become a powerful and useful tool in the hands of the Christian, if properly exercised.

4. The concerned Christian worker must familiarize himself to some extent with the terminology of the major cult systems if he is to enjoy any measure of success in understanding the cultist's mind when bearing a witness for Christ.

We have stressed heavily the issue of terminology and a proper definition of terms throughout this entire chapter. It will not have been wasted effort if the reader has come to realize its importance, and will be guided accordingly when approaching the language barrier, which is an extremely formidable obstacle both to evangelizing cultists and to giving a systematic and effective defense of the Christian faith against their perversions.

Quick Facts About the Psychological Structure of Cultism

- Recognize that belief systems of the cults are characterized by closed-mindedness and antagonism on a personal level.

- Understand that all cultic belief systems manifest institutional dogmatism and intolerance for any position but their own.

- Become a source of neutral, objective data.

- Communicate love and sincerity to those in virtual isolation from the Christian message.

- Avoid direct usage of terms certain to evoke a theologically conditioned reflex and sever the lines of communication.

Chapter 3

The Psychological Structure of Cultism

It is extremely difficult, when approaching the study of the field of non-Christian cults, to accurately appraise such groups without some knowledge of the psychological factors involved in both their formation and growth.

Each cult has what might be called its own "belief system" that follows a distinct pattern and, allowing for obvious differences of personality that exist in any group, can be analyzed and understood in relation to its particular theological structure. Since until recently very little, if anything, has been written on this subject relative to the cults, considerable research was necessary in order to bring this matter under discussion. That it must be discussed and understood as an integral part of the whole complex of the development of American cult systems, no thorough student will deny.

In the course of working with cultists, it has been the observation of this writer that each cultist, though different as an individual, does share certain psychological traits in common with his fellow members, and a careful study of these similarities has revealed some interesting trends.

It is not possible in one chapter to cover all of the cult systems, so we have limited our observations to Jehovah's Witnesses, Mormons, and Christian Scientists. The Jehovah's Witnesses represent those cult systems that put strong emphasis upon eschatology and prophecy; the Mormons represent those that emphasize priestly authority, secret rituals, and symbols; and Christian Science, the Gnostic cults, which ground their experience in metaphysical pantheism and physical healing (a fact which contains within itself enough material to merit an entire book on the problem of psychosomatic medicine and healing).

Dr. Milton Rokeach, in his illuminating book *The Open and Closed Mind,* notes that there are three regions or levels that psychologists generally recognize in any belief or disbelief system. The first or central region is that which encompasses

This chapter updated and edited by Kevin Rische and Jill Martin Rische.

the individual's basic primitive outlook on the world in which he lives and asks such questions as, "Is the world a threatening place, or is it an accepting place?"

The second or intermediate region is the area of authority. In other words, whose authority is a person willing to accept in matters pertaining to the functions of life?

Finally, there is the peripheral region, which penetrates into the details of the structure of living. The details may vary or change according to the specific content that the authority, once accepted, may invoke.

There is no doubt in my mind that the belief systems of the cults share much in common, and that some of these common factors are worth noting.

First and foremost, the belief systems of the cults are characterized by closed-mindedness. They are not interested in a rational, cognitive evaluation of the facts. The organizational structure interprets the facts to the cultist, generally invoking the Bible and/or its respective founder as the ultimate source of its pronouncements. Such belief systems are in isolation; they never shift to logical consistency. They exist in what we might describe as separate compartments in the cultist's mind and are almost incapable of penetration or disruption if the individual cultist is completely committed to the authority pattern of his organization.

Second, cultic belief systems are characterized by genuine antagonism on a personal level, since the cultist almost always identifies his dislike of the Christian message with the messenger who holds such opposing beliefs.

The identification of opposing beliefs with the individual in the framework of antagonism leads the cultist almost always to reject the individual as well as the belief, a problem closely linked with closed-mindedness and one that is extremely difficult to deal with in general dialogue with cultists.

Theoretically speaking, if one could drive a wedge between the individual (or the personality of the individual toward whom the cultist is antagonistic) and the theology (which is the real source of the antagonism), it would be possible to deal with the individual cultist by becoming in his or her eyes a neutral objective source of data. The Christian would then become a person who maintains a system of theology opposed to theirs but not necessarily involved on a level of personal antagonism toward the cultist. Experience has shown me that when this is accomplished it is the first step in a systematic undercutting of one of the basic problems all cultists face in interpersonal contact—the problem of hostility toward those who reject their interpretations.

Such a procedure can go a long way toward allaying hostility, for once a cultist, who has been thoroughly "brainwashed" psychologically by his own authority system (the Watchtower Society, Mrs. Eddy's books, the writings of Joseph Smith and Brigham Young), is confronted by a Christian whom he can learn to accept on a personal basis apart from differences of theological opinion, the possibility of communication improves markedly.

In effect, the cultist is faced with a dilemma: "How can this person (the Christian) be such an acceptable personality yet not share my (the cultist's) theology?"

The cultist, then, quite often begins to wonder how it is possible for the Christian to accept him as a person and yet not accept his beliefs. This can be the beginning of rapport in the realm of personal evangelism.

Since almost all systems of authority in cult organizations indoctrinate their disciples to believe that anyone who opposes their beliefs cannot be motivated by anything other than satanic force or blind prejudice and ignorance, a cultist's encounter with Christians who do not fit this pattern can produce startling results. A discerning Christian who gives every indication of being unprejudiced, reasonably learned, and possessed of a *genuine love* for the welfare of the cultist himself (which is easily detectable in the Christian's concern for his soul and spiritual well-being) can have a devastating effect upon the conditioning apparatus of any cult system.

Above all else, Christians must learn that most cults consider that they have freed their adherents from religious exploitation, which they almost always accuse historic Christianity of practicing. In this connection it becomes a vital necessity to demonstrate genuine interest in the cultist as a person for the sake of himself and his personal redemption rather than as a possible statistic for any given denomination.

The prime task of Christians who would be effective witnesses for Christ in the midst of the kingdom of the cults is that they be free from all appearance of guile and ulterior motivation, remembering that our main task is to communicate to those who are by their very adherence to cultic systems of belief in virtual isolation from the Christian message.

This isolationism, which can be extreme, must be considered in preparing one's presentation of the gospel to a cultist. It is a very real mental and emotional chain that has a stronghold on the cultist's ability to discern truth from error, light from darkness. If the tragedy of Jonestown on November 18, 1978, when over 900 cult followers of "Rev." Jim Jones committed forced suicide, has taught us anything, it has taught us the *despair* and *isolationism* of cultists. The following quote from *People's Temple—People's Tomb* illustrates this graphically:

> A sealed note found on the cult commander's body, apparently written by a follower just prior to the ritual suicide, gave additional credence to this theory. "Dad," the note said, "I see no way out. I agree with your decision— I fear only that without you the world may not make it to communism. For my part I am more than tired of this wretched, merciless planet and the hell it holds for so many masses of beautiful people—thank you for the ONLY life I've known."[1]

While this volume deals primarily with traditional American cults and therefore will not treat Jim Jones' People's Temple cult in a separate chapter, it is important for us to remember that the cultic psychological patterns evidenced in manic proportions at Jonestown are present to some degree in every cult.

Third, almost without exception, all cultic belief systems manifest a type of institutional dogmatism and a pronounced intolerance for any position but their own. This no doubt stems from the fact that in the case of non-Christian cult systems that wish to be identified with Christianity, the ground for their claims is almost always supernatural.

We do not wish to imply that there is no such thing as an authoritative dogmatism that is valid and true (such as the teachings of Jesus Christ), but rather

---

[1] Phil Kerns with Doug Wead, *People's Temple—People's Tomb* (Plainfield, N.J.: Logos International, 1979), 205.

that cult systems tend to invest with the authority of the supernatural whatever pronouncements are deemed necessary to condition and control the minds of their followers.

Thus it is that when Joseph Smith Jr., the Mormon prophet, and his successor, Brigham Young, wished to implement doctrines or changes of practice in the Mormon Church, they prefaced their remarks with proclamations that God had revealed to them the necessity of such doctrines or practices among the "saints."

An example of this was Charles Taze Russell's bold claim that his writings were indispensable to the study of the Bible for Jehovah's Witnesses, and that to study the Bible apart from his inspired comments was to go into spiritual darkness. Russell also taught that concentration upon his writings even at the expense of studying the Bible would most certainly lead one into deeper spiritual illumination within two years.

Mary Baker Eddy, the founder of Christian Science, also conformed to this pattern by requiring her followers to regard her book *Science and Health With Key to the Scriptures* as a divine revelation, and her religion as a "higher, clearer, and more permanent revelation than before."[2] Mrs. Eddy did not hesitate to state that she would blush to write of this work as she did, if she were its author apart from God.[3]

The history of cultism generally begins with an authoritarian pronouncement on the part of the founder or founders. This in turn is institutionalized during their lifetime or after their death into a dogmatic system that requires absolute faith in the supernatural authority of those who received the initial revelation and whose writings and pronouncements are alleged to have transmitted it. Some interesting studies of institutional dogmatism can be found in such books as George Orwell's *1984*, Eric Hoffer's *The True Believer*, and Crossman's volume *The God That Failed*.

The problem of intolerance is closely linked to institutional dogmatism or authoritarianism, and those systems that embody this line of reasoning are resistant to change and penetration, since the cults thrive on conformity, ambiguity, and extremeness of belief.

The fourth and final point in any analysis of the belief system of cults is the factor of isolation.

Within the structure of non-Christian cult systems, one can observe the peaceful coexistence of beliefs that are beyond a shadow of a doubt logically contradictory and which, in terms of psychological analysis, would come under the heading "compartmentalization." In *1984*, George Orwell describes this as "double think." Rokeach commenting on this illustrates the point admirably:

> In everyday life we note many examples of "double think"; expressing an abhorrence of violence and at the same time believing it is justifiable under certain conditions; affirming a faith in the common man and at the same time believing that the masses are stupid; being for democracy but also advocating a government run by an intellectual elite; believing in freedom

---

[2]From a personal letter of Mrs. Eddy to a student. Quoted in Georgine Milnine, *The Life of Mary Baker G. Eddy and the History of Christian Science* (Grand Rapids: Baker Book House, 1909, 1937).
[3]Mary Baker Eddy, *The First Church of Christ, Scientist, and Miscellany* (Boston: Trustees Under the Will of Mary Baker Eddy, 1941 [first published in 1913]), 1, 15.

for all but also believing that certain groups should be restricted; believing that science makes no value judgments, but also knowing a good theory from a bad theory and a good experiment from a bad experiment. Such expressions of clearly contradictory beliefs will be taken as one indication of isolation in the belief system. . . . A final indicator of isolation is the outright denial of contradiction. Contradictory facts can be denied in several ways: on grounds of face absurdity ("it is absurd on the face of it"), "chance," "the exception that proves the rule," and "the true facts are not accessible, and the only available sources of information are biased."[4]

Relating this to the belief system of cults, I do not believe it could be stated with greater clarity. Dr. Rokeach has hit the proverbial nail squarely on the head. Jehovah's Witnesses are well aware of the fact that the Watchtower organization under the leadership of Judge Rutherford maintained that Abraham, Isaac, and Jacob would return to earth before the close of the 1920s, and even bought a home for the patriarchs to dwell in (San Diego, California, Beth Sarim, "the house of princes"). At the same time, Jehovah's Witnesses are fully aware of the fact that the patriarchs did not materialize on schedule, yet they cling tenaciously to the same principles of prophetic interpretation that conceived and brought forth the now defunct interpretations of previous Watchtower leaders. How tenaciously they do cling is evident from their latest fiasco, a prediction that the Battle of Armageddon would occur in 1975. It obviously hasn't occurred yet, but faithful Jehovah's Witnesses are still pounding on the doors of America, telling of the "light" they receive through Jehovah's organization.

Well-informed Mormon historians and theologians are equally aware that the first edition of *The Book of Mormon* and the present edition of *The Book of Mormon* are quite different in 3,913 separate instances[5] (over 25,000 including punctuation changes), the first edition having been revised and corrected by Joseph Smith and his successors over the last one hundred fifty years. Yet both errors and revisions of *The Book of Mormon* are heralded by Mormons as divine revelation. This is another example of the peaceful coexistence of logical contradiction within the belief system of Mormonism, which permits the isolation or compartmentalization of conflicting evidence or concepts.

Still another example of contradiction is the fact that the Christian Science Church has known for many years that though Mary Baker Eddy spoke vigorously against doctors and drugs as well as vigorously affirming the unreality of pain, suffering, and disease, she herself was frequently attended in her declining years by doctors, received injections of morphine for the alleviation of pain, wore glasses, and had her teeth removed when they became diseased. However, despite this, the Christian Science Church insists upon the validity of Mrs. Eddy's teachings, which deny the very practices Mrs. Eddy herself exemplified. This is a classic example of isolation, which might justly come under the heading of "Physician, heal thyself!"

It would be possible to point out many other instances of psychological aberration in the belief systems of the major cults, but it is apparent that we are

---

[4]*The Open and Closed Mind*, 36–37.
[5]Jerald Tanner and Sandra Tanner, *3,913 Changes in the Book of Mormon* (Salt Lake City: Utah Lighthouse Ministry, 1996), Introduction. See also *www.utlm.org/onlinebooks/3913intro.htm*.

confronted with those whom the apostle Paul described as victims of the master psychologist and propagandist of the ages, described by our Lord as "the prince of this world" and by the apostle Paul as "the god of this world," the one who by the sheer force of his antagonism to the truth of divine revelation in the person of Jesus Christ has psychologically "blinded the minds" of those who believe not the Gospel, "lest the light of the glorious gospel of Christ, who is the image of God, should shine unto them" (2 Corinthians 4:4).

This, of course, is not only a psychological blindness, but a spiritual blindness brought about by the isolation of man from God through the rebellion of human nature and the repeated violation of divine law. These are factors that cannot be ignored, for they are a direct reflection of the forces that from "the heavenlies" dominate the world in which we live (Ephesians 6:10–12).

The Psychological Conditioning Process

To conclude our observations in this area of cultic analysis, let us consider examples of how the cult systems of Jehovah's Witnesses, Mormonism, and Christian Science condition their adherents to respond to the "outside world" of unbelievers.

In the case of Jehovah's Witnesses, the literature of the Watchtower is replete with examples of a psychological conditioning that elicits a definite pattern of religious reflexes in response to a given stimuli. As Pavlov's dogs salivated at the sound of a bell that represented food, so a true Jehovah's Witness will spiritually and emotionally salivate whenever the Watchtower rings the conditioning bell of Russellite theology. The example that I believe best demonstrates this is taken in context from Watchtower publications and speaks for itself:

> In Christendom, as surprising as it may seem to some, the false religious teachings create traditions, and commands of men are both directly and indirectly responsible for the physical and spiritual miseries of the poor, notwithstanding Christendom's showy display of charity.[6]
> . . . Christendom's pretended interest in the poor is sheer hypocrisy . . . her priests have done violence to my law and have profaned my holy things . . . her princes in the midst thereof are like wolves ravening the prey to shed blood and to destroy souls that they may get dishonest gain . . . and her prophets have daubed them with untempered mortar, seeing false visions in divining lies unto them, saying thus says Jehovah when Jehovah hath not spoken . . . the people of the land have used oppression and exercised robbery, yea they have vexed the poor and needy and have oppressed the sojourners wrongfully . . . oh, wicked Christendom, why have you forsaken God's clean worship? Why have you joined forces and become part of Satan's wicked organization that oppresses the people? Why have you failed to show concern for the poor as Jehovah commands?[7]
> The little charitable help the poor get from Christendom is like the crumbs that beggar Lazarus picked up from the rich man's table while the dog licked his ulcerous sores. Neither the crumbs nor the licking remedied the beggarly condition. Only Jehovah can effect a rescue. How comforting

---

[6] *The Watchtower,* December 1, 1951, 731.
[7] Ibid., 732–33.

then for the dejected, down-trodden people of the earth to learn that there is One higher than the highest of Christendom's moguls . . . yes, Jehovah the Almighty hears the cries of the half-dead ones, and in hearing He answers their prayers and sends His good Samaritans to the rescue, even the witnesses who are despised by Christendom.[8]

Haters of God and His people are to be hated, but this does not mean that we will take any opportunity of bringing physical hurt to them in the spirit of malice or spite, for both malice and spite belong to the devil, whereas, pure hatred does not.

We must hate in the truest sense, which is to regard with extreme and active aversion, to consider as loathsome, odious, filthy, to detest. Surely any haters of God are not fit to live on His beautiful earth. The earth will be rid of the wicked, and we shall not need to lift a finger to cause physical harm to come to them, for God will attend to that, but we must have a proper perspective of these enemies. His name signifies recompense to the enemies.

Jehovah's enemies are recognized by their intense dislike for His people and the work these are doing. For they would break it down and have all of Jehovah's Witnesses sentenced to jail or concentration camps if they could. Not because they have anything against the Witnesses personally, but on account of their work. They publish blasphemous lies and reproach the holy name Jehovah. Do we not hate those who hate God? We cannot love those hateful enemies, for they are fit only for destruction. We utter the prayer of the Psalmist, "How long, oh God, shall the adversary reproach, shall the enemy blaspheme thy name forever? Why drawest thou back thy hand, even thy right hand? Pluck it out of thy bosom and consume them" (Psalm 74:10–11).

We pray with intensity and cry out this prayer for Jehovah to delay no longer and plead that His anger be made manifest; oh Jehovah, God of hosts . . . be not merciful to any wicked transgressors. . . . consume them in wrath, consume them so that they shall be no more (Psalm 59:4–6, 11–13). These are the true sentiments, desires, and prayers of the righteous ones today. Are they yours . . . how we despise the workers of iniquity and those who would tear down God's organization! . . . "Oh, Jehovah. Let them be put to shame and dismayed forever, yea, let them be confounded and perish that they may know that Thou alone whose name is Jehovah art the most high over all the earth" (Psalm 83:9–18).

The near neighbors of Judah . . . have been the opposers of the Israelites right from the time when refusal was given by them to supply provisions to Israel as they journeyed to the promised land. Moab hired Baalam to curse Israel . . . they had much contempt for Jehovah's people and prided themselves in their own lofty city, her counterpart today being that rich, lofty city, the mighty religious organization standing for the whole of Satan's organization. The modern-day Moabites are the professing Christians whose words and actions are as far removed from Christianity and true worship of Jehovah as Moab was removed from true worship in the covenant of Jehovah. Jehovah had warned Moab of His proposed punishment for her iniquity and opposition.

The modern-day Moabites have opposed Jehovah's Witnesses with a hatred not born of righteousness but from the devil and against all

---

[8]Ibid., 733.

righteousness. Their hatred for God's true people increases as they see upon us the very plain evidence of Jehovah's favor in the obvious disfavor they themselves are in. They put forth every effort to prevent the people of good-will from entering the new world. They are richer than Jehovah's Witnesses in material things and with it they have much pride and arrogance.

The modern-day Moabites will be brought low, for Jehovah has completely finished with them. Hear just a part of the punishment:

"For in this mountain will the hand of Jehovah rest and Moab shall be trodden down in his place, even as straw is trodden down in the water of the dung hill. He shall spread forth his hands in the midst thereof as he that swimmeth spreadeth forth his hands to win, but Jehovah will lay low his pride together with the craft of his hands."

It is a sure thing that one cannot have much pride left when one is being pressed down into a manure pile, showing the utter contempt Jehovah has for modern-day Moab, keeping her wallowing in the mire of shame.

"For thou has made of a city a heap, of a fortified city a ruin, a palace of strangers to be no city; it shall never be built."

He hath put down them that dwell on high; the lofty city, he layeth it low, he layeth it low even to the ground, he bringeth it even to the dust. The foot shall tread it down, even the feet of the poor and the steps of the needy.

When this happens, what a tremendous change will take place; the tables will be turned! Brought down will be the lofty from dwelling on high as the great, high influential ones of this world to the lowest possible place imaginable, so low and degraded they can only be compared to being trampled under foot by the poor, like straw in a manure heap. Christendom's lofty looks, boastful words, bragging tongue are her superior attitude toward the holy Word of God, her trust in idols, men and riches, such as belong to this world will not provide her with security or any safety from Jehovah's storm and blast. They have no defense nor disgrace.

Christendom's defenses are of no value, but Jehovah's Witnesses have a strong city and this is something to sing about. There are millions who want a safe place and are in need of security; let them know we have a strong city! "Thou shalt call thy walls Salvation, and thy gates Praise" (Isaiah 60:18). Only God's kingdom offers such protection and salvation, for inside the city one is safe. Those desiring salvation must make for God's organization, and find entrance into it and remain there permanently.

God has been grossly misrepresented by the clergy. If this statement is true, then that alone is proof conclusive that the clergy do not, in fact, represent God and Christ but do represent God's enemy, the devil. . . . If the Bible plainly proves that the doctrines they teach are wrong and their course of action is wrong, then the most that can be said in extenuation of their wrongful teachings and their wrongful course of action is that they have been misled by the evil and seductive influence of Satan, the enemy of God. If the doctrines taught and the course taken by the clergy differ from that which is declared in the Word of God, then the clergy are in no wise safe guides for the people and should no longer be followed by the people.[9]

These doctrines originated with the devil. They have long been taught by his representatives. . . . The clergy have been his instruments freely used to instill these false doctrines into the minds of men. Whether the clergy

---

[9]Judge J. F. Rutherford, *Reconciliation* (Brooklyn, N.Y.: Watchtower Bible and Tract Society, 1928), 85.

have willingly done so or not does not alter the fact. If they have now learned that they are wrong they should be eager to get that false thought out of the minds of the people. They do not take such a course.[10]

The clergy have at all times posed as the representatives of God on earth. Satan overreached the minds of these clergymen and injected into their minds doctrines, which doctrines the clergy have taught the people concerning Jesus and His sacrifice. These doctrines have brought great confusion. The apostles taught the truth, but it was not long after their death until the devil found some clergyman wise in his own conceit who thought he could teach more than the inspired apostles.[11]

[The clergy] are willingly or unwillingly the instruments in the hands of the god of this world, Satan, the devil, who has used them to blind the minds of the people, to prevent the people from understanding God's great plan of salvation and reconciliation.[12]

According to the Watchtower, then, the clergy of Christendom are obviously the villains and are the object of "pure hatred." Just how pure hatred differs from good old-fashioned hatred the Watchtower never gets around to explaining, but it is clear that Christendom (all historic denominations and churches) led by the allegedly corrupt clergy has foisted the "satanically conceived" Trinity doctrine and the doctrines of hell and eternal punishment upon the unsuspecting masses of mankind. Clergymen are, therefore, always suspect, and their theology is to be regarded as untrustworthy and inspired by Satan.

Is it any wonder that the usually calm and detached Stanley High, writing in the *Reader's Digest* of June 1940, could state:

Jehovah's Witnesses hate everybody and try to make it mutual. . . . Jehovah's Witnesses make hate a religion.

The doctrines of hell and eternal punishment that stimulate fear of judgment are "unreasonable" and not in accord with the Watchtower concept of the character of God; therefore, it and the doctrine of the Trinity are satanic in origin, and all must be rejected and hated as false.

What the Watchtower does in essence is attach polemic significance to certain common theological terms (Holy Trinity, Deity of Christ, Hell, Eternal Punishment, Christendom, immortal soul, etc.). Thus, every time these terms are mentioned by anyone, the reflex action on the part of the Jehovah's Witnesses is instantaneous and hostile.

If we couple this with the Watchtower's heavy emphasis upon the fulfillment of prophecy and a distorted eschatology, the sense of urgency they radiate about Armageddon (which they believe will solve all these problems by annihilating the clergy and all organized religion) begins to make sense, and the reason for their actions becomes clear.

When dealing with the average Jehovah's Witness, this entire pattern of preconditioning must be understood so that the Christian can avoid, where possible, direct usage of terms that will almost certainly evoke a theologically conditioned

---

[10]Ibid., 91.
[11]Ibid., 100.
[12]Ibid., 125.

reflex and sever the lines of communication.

Another important point where Jehovah's Witnesses are concerned is the fact that an intricate part of their belief system is the conviction that Christians will always attack Jehovah's Witnesses on a personal as well as a religious level, hence the Witnesses readily assume a martyr or persecution complex the moment any antagonism is manifested toward Russell, Rutherford, their theology, the Watchtower, or themselves. It is apparently a comfortable, somewhat heroic feeling to believe that you are standing alone against the massed forces of "the devil's organization" (a Watchtower synonym for Christendom), and this illusion is made to seem all the more real when unthinking Christians unfortunately accommodate the Witnesses by appearing overly aggressive toward the Watchtower theology or the Witnesses personally.

In the light of Jehovah's Witnesses' insistence upon "pure hatred," one wonders how they live with their own New World Translation of Matthew 5:43–44, which reads,

> You heard that it was said you must love your neighbor and hate your enemy. However, I say to you: continue to love your enemies and pray for those persecuting you; that you may prove yourselves sons of your Father who is in the heavens.

The Watchtower, then, does not hesitate to accuse the clergy and Christendom of provoking all kinds of evil; in fact, they have not hesitated to suggest that Christendom encouraged and did nothing to prevent the two great world wars: "Had Christendom chosen to do so, she could easily have prevented World Wars I and II."[13]

Some of the basic motivations of the Watchtower are clearly seen in stark contrast with the teachings of Holy Scripture and reveal that there is more than a spiritual disorder involved. Indeed, there exist deep psychological overtones that cannot be considered healthy in any sense of the term.

Whereas Jehovah's Witnesses are preoccupied with Armageddon, the theocracy, the end of the age, and "pure hatred," the Mormons have quite different psychological and theological emphases.

At the very core of Mormon theology, there is a tremendous emphasis upon authority as it is invested in the priesthood, rituals, and symbols presided over by the hierarchy of the Mormon Church. Mormons are taught from their earliest days that the priesthood has the key to authority, and that one of the marks that identifies the "restoration" of the true church of Jesus Christ on earth is the fact that this priesthood exists and perpetuates that authority.

A devout Mormon will wear symbolic underclothing, which perpetually reminds him of his responsibility and duties as a Mormon. When this is coupled with Mormonism's tremendous emphasis upon baptism for the remission of sins, tithing, and voluntary missionary service, it is seen to bind its followers into a tight, homogeneous circle, escape from which, apart from severe spiritual as well as economic penalties, is virtually impossible.

Every Mormon is indoctrinated with the concept that his is the true Christian religion, or to use their terms, "the restoration of Christianity to earth." The

---

[13] *The Watchtower,* December 1, 1951, 731.

secret rites in the Mormon temples, the rituals connected with baptism for the dead, and the secret handshakes, signs, and symbols bind the average Mormon and his family into what might be called in psychological terms the "in group." Apart from acceptance by this group the average Mormon can find no peace or, for that matter, community status or prestige.

Instances of discrimination against Mormons who have experienced true Christian conversion are not infrequent in Mormon-dominated areas where a man can lose his business very easily by incurring the disfavor of the Mormon Church.

The social welfare program of the Mormons is another excellent inducement to Mormons to remain faithful, since if the "breadwinner" of the family is injured, loses his job, or dies, the church undertakes the care and support of his family. So effective is this work that during the Great Depression of the 1930s, no Mormon family went hungry, and no soup kitchens or bread lines disfigured the domain of Mormondom.

The Mormons also conscientiously invoke the biblical principle of helping one another. They lend to one another, work for one another, and cooperate toward the common goal of bringing "restored Christianity" to the masses of mankind. These and other forces make Mormonism a family centered religion, which ties the faith of the church to the indissoluble bonds of family unity and loyalty. This forges an incredibly complex system of pressures and intertwining values over which is superimposed the theological structure of the Mormon Church, which stands between the *average* Mormon and the attainment of "exaltation" or progression to godhood. (See chapter on Mormonism for a discussion of this.)

With such great psychological, economic, and religious forces concentrated upon him, it is a courageous person indeed who shakes off these varied yokes and steps into the freedom of a genuine experience with the Son of God. But a growing number are doing just this as the Spirit of God continues to call out the church, which is Christ's body.

Christian Science, unlike the two other cults we have considered, is neither interested in bestowing godhood on its adherents (Mormonism) nor pushing the eschatological panic button of Armageddon (Jehovah's Witnesses).

Christian Science is an ingenious mixture of first-century Gnostic theology, eighteenth-century Hegelian philosophy, and nineteenth-century idealism woven into a redefined framework of Christian theology with an emphasis upon the healing of the body by the highly questionable practice of denying its objective material reality.

In Christian Science there is a complete separation between the objective world of physical reality (matter) and the spiritual world of supernatural existence (mind). Mrs. Eddy taught that "man as God's idea is already saved with an everlasting salvation."[14]

Hence, it is unnecessary for Christian Scientists to think of themselves as sinners in need of a salvation they believe is already theirs by virtue of the fact that "man is already saved" because he is a reflection of the divine mind.

---

[14]Mary Baker Eddy, *Miscellaneous Writings* [Boston: Trustees under the Will of Mary Baker Eddy, 1924 (first pub. 1896)], 261.

However, in Christian Science there are disturbing psychological aberrations. Mrs. Eddy demanded of her followers that they abstain from any critical contact with the nonspiritual elements of the illusory material world. She forbade the reading of "obnoxious literature," lest Christian Scientists become convinced that the physical body and its diseases, suffering, and inevitable death were real.

There is in Christian Science a subconscious repression, a conscious putting out of one's mind certain things that are disconcerting to the entire configuration of psychological patterns of conditioning. Christian Scientists are conditioned to believe in the nonexistence of the material world, even though their senses testify to its objective reality. They continually affirm that matter has no true existence, and thus, in a very real sense, entertain a type of religious schizophrenia. One side of their personality testifies to the reality of the material world and its inexorable decay, while the conditioning process of Christian Science theology hammers relentlessly to suppress this testimony and affirm that the only true reality is spiritual or mental.

In Margaret Mitchell's classic novel *Gone With the Wind,* Scarlett O'Hara, the heroine, when confronted with the harsh realities of life in the wake of the Civil War, repeatedly states, "I'll think about that tomorrow," as if not thinking about it today would eliminate the reality of its claim at that moment.

When working with sensory data, Christian Scientists totally disassociate their religious convictions, for if they did not, they would not continue to feed, clothe, or house their bodies. But in still another sense, they attempt to master the all-too-obvious frailties of the body by the application of a religion that denies the material reality of that body. A psychologist of the behaviorist school in one sense does the same thing. In the office he may talk about "conditioning" and may associate everything, including his home, with mechanistic psychology; however, at home he still loves his wife and children, and doesn't respond in that same manner. This is one of the chief reasons why Christian Scientists sometimes appear to be almost immune to the conviction of personal guilt as a result of sin. Guilt implies the threat of judgment and a standard that is the basis of that judgment; hence the reality of the concept of sin, which is transgression of the law of God. Christian Scientists desperately want only a "good" world, a pleasant place full of happiness, life, love, and security. This they can have only if they deny the empirical evidence of the opposites of those concepts. In effect, they affirm the reality of "good" at the expense of the antithesis of "good," as if by denying the existence of evil one had annihilated evil!

There can be no doubt that there is "selective perception" in the mind of the Christian Scientist, which enables him to select those things that are of a metaphysical nature, disassociate them from the sense perception of the physical world, and still maintain his idealistic philosophy and Gnostic theology. This he accomplishes by repressing or suppressing any evidence to the contrary.

By following Mrs. Eddy's advice and avoiding what she would call "obnoxious literature," i.e., evidence that controverts the idealism of Christian Science philosophy, Christian Scientists avoid facing the damaging data of physical reality. It is, in effect, an act of unconscious suppression, utilized in order to escape the data. Concluding our thoughts in this area we might say that in the kingdom of the cults we are actually seeing a mosaic of abnormal conditioned behavior patterns that express themselves in a theological framework, utilizing Christian terms perverted by redefinition and represented as "new insight," when in truth they are only old errors with new faces. The defense mechanisms on a psychological level are apparent when one considers the background and vocabulary of the cult systems. There exists, beyond a shadow of a doubt, an abnormal behavior syndrome operating in the mentality of most cultists, which causes the cultist (in the case of Christian Scientists) to build his theological system upon a preconditioned and artificially induced criterion of evaluation, i.e., the divine mission and inspiration of Mary Baker Eddy. In the case of other cultists, the names Joseph Smith, "Pastor" Russell, Brigham Young, or any other cult authority figure could be supplied, and the conditioned reflex would be virtually the same.

There are many more observations that could be made, but space will not permit. It is my hope that in observing and analyzing the facets of cult behavior patterns already discussed, the reader may obtain a deeper insight and appreciation of the psychological structure of cultism as it continues to influence a growing segment of professing Christendom, which is ill-prepared for psychological and theological deviations.

Quick Facts About the Jehovah's Witnesses and the Watchtower Bible and Tract Society

- Jesus is not Jehovah God; he is the first and only direct creation of God and the agent through which Jehovah made all other things.

- Jesus' true followers are known by their worship of the true and almighty God, Jehovah, who is not a Trinity.

- Jesus was raised from the dead, not with a physical body, but as a mighty spirit creature.

- The second "coming" of Jesus was an invisible spiritual presence that began in 1914.

- The dead exist only in God's memory: the wicked will not be punished with conscious torment but will be extinguished forever.

Chapter 4

Jehovah's Witnesses and the Watchtower Bible and Tract Society

A Brief History

Charles Taze Russell was the founder of what is now known as the Jehovah's Witnesses cult and the energetic administrator that brought about its far-flung organization. The name "Jehovah's Witnesses," incidentally, was taken at Columbus, Ohio, in 1931, to differentiate between the Watchtower organization run by Judge Rutherford, Russell's successor, and those who remained as true followers of Russell as represented by The Dawn Bible Students and the Laymen's Home Missionary Movement.

C. T. Russell was born on February 16, 1852, the son of Joseph L. and Anna Eliza Russell, and spent most of his early years in Pittsburgh and Allegheny, Pennsylvania, where at the age of twenty-five he was known to be manager of several men's furnishings stores. At an early age he rejected the doctrine of eternal torment, probably because of the severe indoctrination he had received as a Congregationalist, and as a result of this act entered upon a long and varied career of denunciation aimed at "organized religions." In 1870, at the age of eighteen, Russell organized a Bible class in Pittsburgh, which in 1876 elected him "Pastor" of the group. From 1876 to 1878 the "Pastor" was assistant editor of a small Rochester, New York, monthly magazine, but he resigned when a controversy arose over Russell's counterarguments on "the atonement" of Christ.

Shortly after leaving his position, Russell founded *The Herald of the Morning* (1879), which developed into today's *The Watchtower Announcing Jehovah's Kingdom*. From 6,000 initial issues, the publication has grown to 17.8 million copies

---

This chapter updated and edited by Robert Bowman and Jill Martin Rische.

per month in 106 languages. The other Watchtower periodical, *Awake,* has a circulation of 15.6 million per month in thirty-four languages. It is true that this magazine has grown until it has surpassed even Russell's fondest dreams. In the year 1884, "Pastor" Russell incorporated "Zion's Watch Tower Tract Society" at Pittsburgh, Pennsylvania, which in 1886 published the first in a series of seven books (Russell wrote six by himself), now entitled *Studies in the Scriptures* and originally published as *The Millennial Dawn.* The seventh volume was edited from his writings after his death and published in 1917. This seventh volume, *The Finished Mystery,* caused a split in the organization, which culminated in a clean division, the larger group following J. F. Rutherford, the smaller remaining by itself. This smaller group subsequently became the Dawn Bible Students Association. Meanwhile, under Rutherford's leadership, the "Society" became known by its present common name—Jehovah's Witnesses—and its corporate name, the Watchtower Bible and Tract Society, with its international office in Brooklyn, New York.

According to Watchtower statistics, in January 1981, the Watchtower Bible and Tract Society (founded 1896), which is the focal point of the organization, had known branches in more than 100 lands and missionary works and Kingdom preaching in over 250. Its literature is distributed in 110 languages, and the Society's volunteers (called "publishers") numbered 563,453. With its numbers ever increasing as we enter the new millenia, the Society has become a great disseminator of propaganda and a challenge to the zeal of every Christian.

In the year 1908 the headquarters of the movement was transferred to Brooklyn, New York, where property was purchased at 17 Hicks Street and became known as "The Brooklyn Tabernacle." Large tracts of property were purchased by the Society on Columbia Heights Street as it grew and prospered, until today whole blocks are in their possession. Among the other things the Society owns are a large, up-to-date printing plant, which has produced billions of pieces of literature since its inauguration in 1928 and expansions in 1949 and 1957; a modern apartment building and office quarters; one "Kingdom Farm," which supplies food, wood for furniture, etc.; a Bible school, "Gilead"; and many more enterprises of like character. All employees in the factory receive room and board, but no salaries are paid (although workers are given a nominal sum each month for incidental personal expenses and purchases—a few years ago that amount was fourteen dollars).[1]

Russell continued his teachings until his death on October 31, 1916, aboard a transcontinental train in Texas. The former pastor had a remarkable life, highly colored with legal entanglements, but not without success in his chosen field. In fairness to the reader and in the interest of truth, the full account is quoted from *The Brooklyn Daily Eagle,*[2] November 1, 1916 (Obituaries), and has been inserted at this point to authenticate beyond doubt the true history of Russell so that even his most devoted followers might realize the character of the man to whose teach-

---

[1]Assets, employee remuneration, etc., fluctuate with time, and many of these specific details are no longer made public.

[2]*"The Brooklyn Daily Eagle* was a newspaper of local and national importance that ran from 1841–1955." See *http://216.239.53.100/search?q=cache:lp3fdxqV1WUC:www.metro.org/modic/ppt/joy-susan-bpl.ppt+The+Brooklyn+Daily+Eagle+%2B+History&hl=en&ie=UTF–8* for more information. The *Eagle* is a significant historical source in and of itself, but its importance increases even more when we consider that Brooklyn, New York, was an integral part of early Watchtower history. Its headquarters was first established there in 1908.

ings they have entrusted their eternal destiny.

A year after this publication, *The Watch Tower,* had been established, Russell married Maria Ackley in Pittsburgh. She had become interested in him through his teachings, and she helped him in running the Watchtower.

Two years later, in 1881, came "The Watch Tower Bible and Tract Society," the agency through which in later years "Pastor" Russell's sermons were published (as advertisements) in newspapers throughout the world. This Society progressed amazingly under the joint administration of husband and wife, but in 1897 Mrs. Russell left her husband. Six years later, in 1903, she sued for separation. The decree was secured in 1906 following sensational testimony and "Pastor" Russell was scored by the courts.

There was much litigation then that was quite undesirable from the "Pastor's" point of view regarding alimony for his wife, but it was settled in 1909 by the payment of $6,036 to Mrs. Russell. The litigation revealed that "Pastor" Russell's activities in the religious field were carried on through several subsidiary societies and that all of the wealth that flowed into him through these societies was under the control of a holding company in which the "Pastor" held $990 of the $1,000 capital and two of his followers the other $10.

Thus Russell apparently controlled the entire financial power of the Society and was not accountable to anyone.

The *Eagle* column goes on to say:

After the "work" had been well started here, "Pastor" Russell's Watch Tower publication advertised wheat seed for sale at $1.00 a pound. It was styled "Miracle Wheat," and it was asserted that it would grow five times as much as any other brand of wheat. There were other claims made for the wheat seed, and the followers were advised to purchase it, the proceeds to go to the Watch Tower and be used in publishing the "Pastor's" sermons.

The *Eagle* first made public the facts about this new venture of the Russellites and it published a cartoon picturing the "Pastor" and his "Miracle Wheat" in such a way that "Pastor" Russell brought suit for libel, asking $100,000 damages. Government departments investigated the wheat for which $1.00 a pound was asked, and agents of the Government were important witnesses at the trial of the libel suit in January 1913. The "Miracle Wheat" was low in the Government tests, they said. The *Eagle* won the suit.

Prior to entering court the *Eagle* had said,

The *Eagle* goes even further and declares that at the trial it will show that "Pastor" Russell's religious cult is nothing more than a money-making scheme.

The court's decision vindicated the *Eagle's* statement and proved its reliability.

All during this time the "Pastor's" sermons were being printed in newspapers throughout the world, notably when he made a tour of the world in 1912 and caused accounts to be published in his advertised sermons telling of enthusiastic greetings at the various places he visited. It was shown in many cases that the sermons were never delivered in the places that were claimed.

For the benefit of any Jehovah's Witness who may think that the "Miracle Wheat" fraud is an invention of the "jealous religionists" who are trying to defame the "Pastor's" memory, we document the scandal, trial, and verdict as follows:

From originals (now microfilmed in New York) of *The Brooklyn Daily Eagle,* the following articles with dates and pages can be found: "Miracle Wheat Scandal," January 1, 1913, 1–2; "Russellite Beliefs," January 22, 1913, 2; "Testimony on Wheat," January 23, 1913, 3; "Financial Statements Proving Russell's Absolute Control," by Secretary-Treasurer Van Amberg, January 25, 1913, 16; "Government Experts Testify on 'Miracle Wheat' and Ascertain Its Ordinariness," January 27, 1913, 3; "Prosecution and Defense Closing Arguments," January 28, 1913, 2; "Russell Loses Libel Suit," January 29, 1913, 16.

The Watchtower Society has maintained that Russell never made money on the "Miracle Wheat," and that proceeds from its sale were "contributions" to the organization. They fail to note that Russell controlled the Watchtower Society, owning 990 of the 1,000 shares of its stock. Any contributions to it were also to Russell!

The *Brooklyn Daily Eagle* led the fight to expose the hypocrisy of "Pastor" Russell, and nothing could be more appropriate than their on-the-spot testimony as to his many fraudulent claims. The following documentary evidence is taken from *The Brooklyn Daily Eagle,* February 19, 1912, page 18, and is titled "Pastor Russell's Imaginary Sermons—Printed Reports of Addresses in Foreign Lands That He Never Made—One at Hawaii, a Sample." These excerpts concern the Pastor's "World Tour" and are very enlightening with respect to his reliability and truthfulness.

> "Pastor" Russell, who has found the atmosphere of Brooklyn uncongenial ever since the *Eagle* published the facts concerning his methods and morals, is making some new records in the far parts of the world. He is delivering sermons to imaginary audiences on tropical islands and completing "searching investigations" into the missions of China and Japan by spending a few hours in each country.
>
> Following the *Eagle*'s exposure of "Pastor" Russell's "Miracle Wheat" enterprise and its publication of the testimony on the basis of which Mrs. Russell obtained a separation and alimony, the "Pastor" developed the "world tour" idea. He set his printing plant to work to get out advance literature, huge bundles of which were sent to every place where he intended to appear. Then he contracted for advertising space in many American newspapers to print his never-delivered sermons.
>
> His first stop after sailing from the Pacific Coast was Honolulu. And presto!—the newspapers in which advertising space had been engaged printed long cable dispatches that presented the "Pastor's" discourses. In one paper that printed the advertisement the opening sentences read, "Honolulu, Hawaiian Islands: The International Bible Students Committee of Foreign Mission investigation stopped at Honolulu and made observations. Pastor Russell, Chairman of the committee, delivered a public address. He had a large audience and attentive hearing."
>
> Then follows the sermon, full of local color and allusions to the "Paradise of the Pacific": "I can now well understand [the printed report makes the 'pastor' say] why your beautiful island is 'The Paradise of the Pacific.' I

note your wonderful climate and everything which contributes to bring about this Paradise likeness."

And so on for two columns.

It has long been known that "Pastor" Russell has a strong imagination, but now it appears that he is even capable of delivering imaginary sermons. *Pastor Russell never spoke in Honolulu during the few hours that his ship stopped there to take on coal.* In the hope of securing an accurate report of his sermon, the *Eagle* wrote to the editor of the *Hawaiian Star,* which is published in Honolulu.

The following reply was shortly thereafter received:

In answer to your inquiry of December 19, concerning Pastor Russell, I would say that he was here for a few hours with a Bible students' committee of foreign mission investigation, but did not make a public address as was anticipated.—Walter G. Smith, Editor, *Star.*

That this was an isolated occurrence is refuted in other documentation. The following evidence is taken from *The Brooklyn Daily Eagle,* January 11, 1913:

> *Tour of Orient Branded Huge Advertising Scheme*
> As to the "Pastor's" methods of carrying Russellism to the heathen and the speed with which his searching investigations into the missions of the world are being conducted, the *Japan Weekly Chronicle* of January 11 supplies some interesting information. After explaining how the office of the paper had for weeks been bombarded with Russell literature and advance agents with contracts "just as if the Reverend gentleman were an unregenerated theatrical company," the *Chronicle* says:
> "These gentlemen arrived in Japan on Saturday the 30th December. On the following day 'Pastor' Russell delivered a sermon in Tokyo entitled: 'Where Are the Dead?' which, though the title is a little ambiguous, does not seem to have any special connection with the mission work. On Monday it is assumed that the mission work in Japan was begun and finished, for the next day seems to have been devoted to traveling, and on Wednesday 'Pastor' Russell and his coadjutors left Kobe for China in the same vessel in which they had arrived in Yokohama. . . . The truth is that the whole expedition is merely a huge advertising scheme!"

Russell carried on many such advertising stunts, and despite his protestations about earthly governments and laws being organizations of the devil, he was always the first to claim their protection when it was convenient for him to do so.

To mention one instance in addition to the *Eagle* suit, Russell brought suit for "defamatory libel" against the Reverend J. J. Ross, pastor of the James Street Baptist Church of Hamilton, Ontario, when the fearless minister wrote a blistering pamphlet denouncing Russell's theology and personal life. Russell lost this attempt (see *The Brooklyn Daily Eagle,* January 11, 1913), with J. F. Rutherford as his attorney. For the benefit of the interested reader, at this time we recount the facts concerning the libel suit as it actually occurred.

In June 1912, the Reverend J. J. Ross, pastor of the James Street Baptist Church, Hamilton, Ontario, published a pamphlet entitled "Some Facts About the Self-Styled 'Pastor' Charles T. Russell," which minced no words in its denunciation of Russell, his qualifications as a minister, or his moral example as a "pastor." Russell promptly sued Ross for "defamatory libel" in an effort to silence the courageous minister before the pamphlet could gain wide circulation and expose his true character and the errors of his theology. Rev. Ross, however, was unimpressed by Russell's action and eagerly seized upon the opportunity as a means of exposing Russell for the fraud he was. In his pamphlet, Ross assailed Russell's teachings as revealed in *Studies in the Scriptures* as "the destructive doctrines of one man who is neither a scholar nor a theologian" (p. 7). Rev. Ross scathingly denounced Russell's whole system as "anti-rational, anti-scientific, anti-biblical, anti-Christian, and a deplorable perversion of the gospel of God's dear Son" (p. 7).

Continuing his charges in the pamphlet, Ross exposed Russell as a pseudo-scholar and philosopher who "never attended the higher schools of learning, knows comparatively nothing of philosophy, systematic or historical theology, and is totally ignorant of the dead languages" (pp. 3–4). It must be clearly understood at this point by the reader that in a libel suit of the type pursued by Russell, the plaintiff (Russell) had to *prove* that the charges lodged against him by the defendant (Ross) were not true. It is significant to note that Russell lost his suit against Ross when the High Court of Ontario, in session March 1913, ruled that there were no grounds for libel; and "the case was thrown out of Court by the evidence furnished by 'Pastor' Russell himself" (p. 15).[3]

"Pastor" Russell refused to give any evidence to substantiate his "case," and the only evidence offered was Russell's own statements, made under oath and during cross-examination by Ross's lawyer, Counselor Staunton. By denying Ross's charges, Russell automatically claimed high scholastic ascendancy, recognized theological training (systematic and historical), working knowledge of the dead languages (Greek, Hebrew, etc.), and valid ordination by a recognized body.[4] To each part of Mr. Ross's pamphlet (and all was read), Russell entered vigorous denials, with the exception of the "Miracle Wheat Scandal," which he affirmed as having "a grain of truth in a sense" to it.[5] "Pastor" Russell had at last made a serious mistake. He had testified under oath before Almighty God, and had sworn to tell "the truth, the whole truth, and nothing but the truth." He was soon to regret his testimony and stand in jeopardy as a perjurer, an unpleasant experience for the "pastor," which more than explains his aversion to the witness chair.

Jehovah's Witnesses cannot deny this documentary evidence; it is too well substantiated. This is no "religionist scheme" to "smear" the "pastor's" memory; I offer it as open proof of their founder's inherent dishonesty and lack of morals that they may see the type of man to whose doctrines they have committed their eternal souls.

The following reference quotations are taken in part from Mr. Ross's second pamphlet, entitled *Some Facts and More Facts About the Self-Styled Pastor—Charles T. Russell:*

> But now what are the facts as they were brought out by the examination on March 17, 1913? As to his scholastic standing he (Russell) had sworn that what was said about it was not true. Under the examination, he admitted that at most he had attended school only seven years of his life at the public

---

[3] *Some Facts and More Facts About the Self-Styled Pastor—Charles T. Russell,* Mr. Ross's second pamphlet.
[4] Ibid., 18.
[5] Ibid., 17.

school, and that he had left school when he was about fourteen years of age. . . .

The cross-examination of Russell continued for five hours. Here is a sample of how the "pastor" answered. (The following reproduction of the *Russell v. Ross* transcript relative to the perjury charge made against Russell is taken from a copy on file in the headquarters of the cult in Brooklyn and is presented in the interests of thorough investigation.)

> *Question (Attorney Staunton):* "Do you know the Greek alphabet?"
> *Answer (Russell):* "Oh yes."
> *Question (Staunton):* "Can you tell me the correct letters if you see them?"
> *Answer (Russell):* "Some of them; I might make a mistake on some of them."
> *Question (Staunton):* "Would you tell me the names of those on top of the page, page 447, I have got here?"
> *Answer (Russell):* "Well, I don't know that I would be able to."
> *Question (Staunton):* "You can't tell what those letters are? Look at them and see if you know."
> *Answer (Russell):* "My way" [he was interrupted at this point and not allowed to explain].
> *Question (Staunton):* "Are you familiar with the Greek language?"
> *Answer (Russell):* "No."

It should be noted from this record of the testimony that Russell frequently contradicted himself, claiming first to know the Greek alphabet, then claiming under pressure that he might make mistakes in identifying the letters, and then finally admitting that he couldn't read the alphabet at all when confronted with a copy of it.

From this it is easy to see that Russell did not "know" the Greek alphabet in any proper sense of the term, since it is assumed that when we say we "know" the English alphabet, for example, we shall be able upon request to name the letters by their correct titles.

"Pastor" Russell, in failing to name the letters of the Greek alphabet, therefore, proved himself a perjurer, for he had previously stated that he "knew" them, thereby implying the ability to recite them, which he could *not* do.

It makes very little difference, therefore, whether the Watchtower wants to admit Russell's guilt or not, since *their* transcript shows that Russell said he "knew" what was later proved he did not know.

Here is conclusive evidence: The "pastor" under oath perjured himself beyond question. Can one sincerely trust the teachings of a man who thought nothing of such evidence?

This, however, was not all of Russell's testimony, and as Counselor Staunton pressed him further, the "pastor" admitted that he knew *nothing* about Latin and Hebrew, and that he had never taken a course in philosophy or systematic theology, much less attended schools of higher learning. Bear in mind now that Russell a short time before had sworn he *did* have such knowledge by denying Mr. Ross's allegations. But there was no way out now; the "pastor" was caught in a bold-faced fabrication and he knew it. However, all was not over yet. It will be remembered that Russell claimed "ordination" and equal if not superior status to ordained and accredited ministers, who at that time were almost all graduates of at least Bible college if not a graduate program in a seminary. Counselor Staunton next smashed this illusion by demanding that Russell answer "Yes" or "No" to the following questions:

> *Question (Staunton):* "Is it true you were never ordained?"
> *Answer (Russell):* "It is not true."

It was necessary at this point for Counselor Staunton to appeal to the magistrate in order to make Russell answer the question directly. The magistrate presiding ruled that Russell must answer the questions put to him. Here is the result of the cross-examination.

> *Question (Staunton):* "Now, you never were ordained by a bishop, clergyman, presbytery, council, or any body of men living?"
> *Answer (Russell, after a long pause):* "I never was."

Once again Russell's "unswerving" honesty received a rude blow; the situation was out of his hands, and Russell stood helpless as Counselor Staunton wrung statement after statement from him, which established him beyond doubt as a premeditated perjurer. Russell further swore that his wife had not divorced him and that the court had not granted alimony from him, a statement he soon regretted when Counselor Staunton forced him to admit that the court did divorce[6] him from his wife, and did award his wife alimony. The evidence was in; the case was clear. Russell was branded a perjurer by the court's verdict "No bill." As a result of the court's action, Ross's charges were proven true and the real character of Russell was revealed, that of a man who had no scruples about lying under oath and whose doctrines were admittedly based on no sound educational knowledge of the subject in question. Much evidence is available concerning Russell's moral life, but I see no reason to inject lewdness into the text. The character of the man is evident for all to see.

The easily offended "pastor" might have practiced what he preached for once and heeded Christ's injunction concerning the patient enduring of "reviling and persecution" (Matthew 5:11–12), but in Russell's case it is not at all applicable. Russell took every opportunity to make money, and legal clashes were frequent as a result. He maneuvered masterfully just one jump ahead of the law, and had it not been for Rutherford, who was a clever lawyer, the "pastor" might not have been so fortunate. Russell hid, whenever cornered, behind the veil of a martyr for religious toleration, and despite the denunciation of churches and ministers, he somehow succeeded in escaping the effects of damaging publicity. The Christian church fought him openly but without the unified effort needed to squelch his bold approach. Some churches and pastors were united (see *The Brooklyn Daily Eagle,* January 2, 1913, page 18) and called for Russell's silencing as a menace. The "pastor" was also deported from Canada because he hindered mobilization (see *The Daily Standard Union,* November 1, 1916), and in the early stages of World War I he was a prominent conscientious objector, as all of his

---

[6]Neither party, however, obtained an absolute decree.

followers (Jehovah's Witnesses) are today.

As a speaker, Russell swayed many; as a theologian, he impressed no one competent; as a man, he failed before the true God. Russell traveled extensively, spoke incessantly, and campaigned with much energy for "a great awakening" among the people of the world. In the course of his writings and lectures, Russell denied many of the cardinal doctrines of the Bible—the Trinity, the deity of Christ, the physical resurrection and return of Christ, eternal punishment, the reality of hell, the eternal existence of the soul, and the validity of the infinite atonement, to state a few. The honest fact is that Russell had no training or education to justify his interpretation of Scripture. By this it is not meant that great education is a necessary qualification for exegesis, but when a man contradicts practically every major doctrine of the Bible, he ought to have the education needed to defend (if that is possible) his arguments. "Pastor" Russell did not have that knowledge, or even the qualifications for ordination by any recognized body. The title "pastor" was assumed—not earned—and to document this fact we quote from the November 1, 1916, edition of *The Brooklyn Daily Eagle:*

> Although he styled himself a "pastor" and was so addressed by thousands of followers all over the world, he had never been ordained and had no ministerial standing in any other religious sect than his own.

Psychologically, the man was an egotist whose imagination knew no bounds and who is classed (by his followers) along with the apostle Paul, Wycliffe, and Luther as a great expositor of the gospel. These are trite words for a man who proffered his writings as necessary for a clear understanding of the Scriptures and who once declared that it would be better to leave the Scriptures unread and read his books rather than to read the Scriptures and neglect his books.

For the benefit of those so naïve as to believe that the "pastor" did not make such a claim, we document the above assertion from *The Watchtower,* September 15, 1910, page 298, where the "pastor" makes the following statement concerning his *Studies in the Scriptures* and their "indispensable" value when examining the Bible.

> If the six volumes of SCRIPTURE STUDIES are practically the Bible, topically arranged with Bible proof texts given, we might not improperly name the volumes THE BIBLE IN AN ARRANGED FORM. That is to say, they are not mere comments on the Bible, *but they are practically the Bible itself*. . . .
>
> Furthermore, not only do we find that *people cannot see the divine plan in studying the Bible by itself,* but we see, also, that if anyone lays the SCRIPTURE STUDIES aside, even after he has used them, after he has become familiar with them, after he has read them for ten years—if he then lays them aside and ignores them and goes to the Bible alone, though he has understood his Bible for ten years, our experience shows that within two years *he goes into darkness.* On the other hand, if he had merely read the SCRIPTURE STUD- IES with their references, and had *not read a page of the Bible, as such,* he would be in the light at the end of two years, because he would have the light of the Scriptures.[7]

---

[7]Emphasis is ours.

Nowhere is Russell's egotism or boldness better revealed than in that statement. Think of it: According to the "pastor," it is impossible to understand God's plan of salvation independent of Russellite theology. Also, if one's study is of the Bible alone, void of Russell's interpretations, that one will walk in darkness at the end of two years. If all will adopt Russellism as a guide in biblical interpretation, mankind will enter into a "new" Kingdom Age; for then, by virtue of the "pastor's" expositions, true understanding of the Bible's basic doctrines will have been arrived at. To quote the Rev. J. J. Ross: "This inspiration has its origin in the pit." But there is a ray of hope for all those foolish enough to study God's Word alone.

Jehovah's Witnesses pursue this same line of theological interpretation today. Russellism did not die with Charles Taze Russell; it lives under the title *The Watchtower Announcing Jehovah's Kingdom.* The "pastor's" dream has survived its author and remains today a living challenge to all Christians everywhere. Let us recognize it for what it is and unmask the unsound principles upon which it stands.

Upon Russell's death the helm of leadership was manned by Judge Joseph Franklin Rutherford, who acquitted himself nobly in the eyes of the Society by attacking the doctrines of "organized religion" with unparalleled vigor, and whose radio talks, phonograph recordings, numerous books, and resounding blasts against Christendom reverberated down the annals of the organization until his death on January 8, 1942, from cancer, at his palatial mansion, "Beth Sarim" or "House of Princes," in San Diego, California. He was seventy-two. Rutherford's career was no less amazing than Russell's, for the judge was an adversary of no mean proportions, whether in action against "organized religion," which he termed "rackets," or against those who questioned his decisions in the Society.

Throughout the years following Russell's death, Rutherford rose in power and popularity among the "Russellites," and to oppose him was tantamount to questioning the authority of Jehovah himself. An example of this one-man sovereignty concerns the friction that occurred in the movement when Rutherford denounced Russell's pyramid prophecies scheme as an attempt to find God's will outside the Scriptures (1929). Many followers of Russell's theory left the Society as a result of this action by Rutherford, only to be witheringly blasted by the vituperative Judge, who threatened that they would "suffer destruction" if they did not repent and recognize Jehovah's will as expressed through the Society.

Rutherford also approached at times the inflated egotism of his predecessor Russell, especially when in his pamphlet *Why Serve Jehovah?* he declared in effect that he was the mouthpiece of Jehovah for this age and that God had designated his words as the expression of divine mandate. It is indeed profitable to observe that Rutherford, as do all would-be "incarnations of infallibility," manifested unfathomable ignorance of God's express injunctions, especially against the preaching of "any other gospel" (Galatians 1:8–9). It was under the leadership of the judge that the Russellites adopted the name "Jehovah's Witnesses" (1931), partly to distinguish Rutherford's group from the splinter groups that arose after Russell's death.

Fear of retaliation or rebuke was never characteristic of Judge Rutherford, and quite often he displayed complete contempt for all "religions" and their leaders. Lashing out against the persecution of the Witnesses in 1933, Judge Rutherford challenged all of Christendom, especially the Roman Catholic Church, to answer his charges of religious intolerance. Needless to say, he was ignored. Rutherford also battled against the Federal Council of the Churches of Christ in the U.S., and even offered to pay half the time cost for a radio debate on the subject of persecution. When ignored, Rutherford abated for a time. Few things, however, were allowed to dampen the judge's vociferous thundering, and even a term in Atlanta Federal Penitentiary, for violation of the "Espionage Act" in 1918, failed to silence the judge's attacks. Rutherford was released from Atlanta in March 1919 and returned to the Witnesses' fold a martyr-hero, a complex readily appropriated by all Witnesses upon the slightest pretext. Indeed, they greatly enjoy playing the role of persecuted saints. One only regrets that some of our less prudent administrators have so obligingly accommodated them.

The person of J. F. Rutherford, then, in the light of these facts, cannot be ignored in any true evaluation that seeks valid data concerning the Society's history. The great personal magnetism and the air of mystery that surround the man account most probably for his success as a leader, for he was almost a legendary figure even during his lifetime. The judge shunned photographs, although he was most photogenic and presented both an imposing and impressive figure when attired in his familiar wing collar, bow tie, and black suit. Reading glasses, which hung on a string across His Honor's portly profile, accentuated the illusion of dignified importance, along with the title "Judge," which, contrary to popular opinion, he held from the days of his early legal career, when he was a special judge of the Eighth Judicial Circuit Court of Boonville, Missouri. Rutherford also possessed a deep, powerful voice, which was capable of holding large audiences with its crescendo-like effect—but he seldom appeared in public and lived a closely guarded private life. Toward the end of his life, Rutherford's reign was not overly smooth, notably when the deposed head of the Witnesses' legal staff, Mr. Olin Moyle, sued Rutherford and several members of the Watchtower's Board of Directors in 1939 for libel and won his case, a judgment of $25,000, in 1944, two years after Rutherford's demise.

In comparing Russell and Rutherford it must be noted that the former was a literary pygmy compared to his successor. Russell's writings were distributed, some fifteen or twenty million copies of them, over a period of sixty years, but Rutherford's in half that time were many times that amount. The prolific judge wrote over one hundred books and pamphlets, and his works as of 1941 had been translated into eighty languages. Thus, he was the Society's second great champion who, regardless of his many failings, was truly an unusual man by any standard. Russell and Rutherford are the two key figures in the Society's history, and without them it is doubtful that the organization would ever have come into existence. But conjecture never eliminated a problem, and Jehovah's Witnesses are now a problem with which every Christian must cope.

The next president of the combined organization was Nathan Homer Knorr, who was elected president immediately after Rutherford's death. Knorr was responsible for the Gilead Missionary Training School in South Lansing, New York. He followed diligently in the footsteps of Russell and Rutherford, and under his tutelage Christianity saw much opposition. Knorr died in June of 1977, and Frederick W. Franz, a longtime leader and then vice-president of the Society, was elected president and piloted the Watchtower in the pattern of his predecessors.

With each succeeding president, the control of the Society grows stronger.

One of the most distressing traits manifested in the literature and teachings of Jehovah's Witnesses is their seemingly complete disregard for historical facts and dependable literary consistency. At the same time, however, they condemn all religious opponents as "enemies of God"[8] and perpetrators of what they term "a racket."[9]

For some time this author has been considerably disturbed by Jehovah's Witnesses' constant denial of any theological connection whatsoever with "Pastor" Charles T. Russell, their admitted founder and first president of the Watchtower Bible and Tract Society. Since Russell was long ago proven to be a perjurer under oath, a sworn adversary of historical Christianity, and a scholastic fraud, it is obvious why the Witnesses seek to avoid his influence and memory whenever possible. However, some light should be thrown on the repeated self-contradictions that are committed by the Witnesses in their zeal to justify their position and the ever-wavering doctrines to which they hold. It is my contention that they are following the basic teachings of Charles T. Russell in relation to many biblical doctrines that he denied, and from their own publications I shall document this accusation.

In their eagerness to repudiate the charge of "Russellism," the Witnesses dogmatically say, "But who is preaching the teachings of Pastor Russell? *Certainly not* Jehovah's Witnesses! They cannot be accused of following him, for they *neither quote him as an authority nor publish nor distribute his writings.*[10] This is the statement of the Witnesses' magazine. Now let us compare this with history, and the truth will be plainly revealed.

Historically, Jehovah's Witnesses have quoted "Pastor" Russell numerous times since his death in 1916. The following is a token sample of what we can produce as concrete evidence. In 1923, seven years after the "pastor's" demise, Judge J. F. Rutherford, heir to the Russellite throne, wrote a booklet some fifty-odd pages in length, entitled *World Distress: Why and the Remedy.* In this informative treatise, the new president of the Watchtower Bible and Tract Society and the International Bible Students quoted "Pastor" Russell no fewer than *sixteen* separate times; referred to his books *Studies in the Scriptures* at least twelve times; and devoted six pages at the end of the booklet to advertising these same volumes. Further than this, in a fifty-seven-page pamphlet published in 1925, entitled *Comfort for the People,* by the same Rutherford, "His Honor," in true Russellite character, defines clergymen as "dumb dogs (D.D.)," proceeds to quote "Pastor" Russell's prophetical chronology (A.D. 1914),[11] and then sums up his tirade against Christendom universal by recommending Russell's writing in four pages of advertisements at the back of the book.

The dark specter of historical facts thus begins to creep across the previously happy picture of a "Russell-free" movement. As a matter of fact, the Watchtower, its followers, and its publications have *never* been "Russell-free." Jehovah's Witnesses have been forced openly to acknowledge Russell, owing to the effect of my book *Jehovah of the Watchtower,* which gave the true history of Russell's infamous

---

[8]J. F. Rutherford, *Deliverance* (Brooklyn: Watchtower Bible and Tract Society, 1926), 91.

[9]J. F. Rutherford, *Religion* (Brooklyn: Watchtower Bible and Tract Society, 1927), 88, 104, 133, 137, 140–41, etc.

[10]*Awake!* (May 8, 1951): 26.

[11]Jehovah's Witnesses still hold to it today and teach it as dogma.

doings, thus necessitating an answer from the Witnesses, even if their response was unreliable in many respects and highly colored. The historical series was run in *The Watchtower* for some months and was entitled "A Modern History of Jehovah's Witnesses." It was a very weak apologetic. Another history, *Jehovah's Witnesses in the Divine Purpose,* was published still later and gave high praise to Russell as well. The Society's debt to Russell as founder and to his teachings as foundational is still acknowledged in Watchtower publications such as *Jehovah's Witnesses in the Twentieth Century.*[12]

But let us further consult history. In the year 1927, the Watchtower Bible and Tract Society published Judge Rutherford's "great" literary effort entitled *Creation,* which was circulated into the millions of copies, and in which this statement appeared concerning "Pastor" Russell:

> The second presence of Christ dates from about 1874.
> From that time forward many of the truths long obscured by the enemy began to be restored to the honest Christian.
> As William Tyndale was used to bring the Bible to the attention of the people, so the Lord used Charles T. Russell to bring to the attention of the people an understanding of the Bible, particularly of those truths that had been taken away by the machinations of the devil and his agencies. Because it was the Lord's due time to restore these truths, he used Charles T. Russell to write and publish books known as *Studies in the Scriptures,* by which the great fundamental truths of the divine plan are clarified. Satan has done his best to destroy these books because they *explain* the Scriptures. Even as Tyndale's Version of the Bible was destroyed by the clergy, so the clergy in various parts of the earth have gathered together thousands of volumes of *Studies in the Scriptures* and burned them publicly. But such wickedness has only served to advertise the truth of the divine plan.

Concluding this brief historical synopsis of the Watchtower Society's past, we quote the grand finale of J. F. Rutherford's funeral oration over the prostrate remains of "dear brother Russell" who, according to the floral sign by his casket, remained "faithful unto death." Said the judge: "Our brother sleeps not in death, but was instantly changed from the human to the divine nature, and is now forever with the Lord." This episode in Jehovah's Witnesses' history is cited for its uniqueness to show the adoration in which Russell was once held by the theological ancestors of those who deny his influence today.

Leaving the past history of the Witnesses, I shall now answer those who say, "The Society may have quoted him in the past, but that was before Judge Rutherford's death. We do not do it now, and after all, didn't we say 'neither quote . . . publish . . . nor distribute his writings'? This is in the *present* tense, not the past." This would, we agree, be a splendid refutation of our claims if it were true, but as we shall now conclusively prove, it is not! Not only did Jehovah's Witnesses quote the "pastor" as an authority in the past, before Rutherford's death in 1942, but they have done it many times up through the present.

In the July 15, 1950, edition of *The Watchtower* (p. 216), the Witnesses quoted "Pastor" Russell as an authority regarding his chronology on the 2,520-year reign of the Gentiles, which reign allegedly ended, according to his calculations (and

---

[12]The Internet Web Site edition of this booklet is copyrighted 1997.

Jehovah's Witnesses), in A.D. 1914. To make it an even more hopeless contradiction, they listed as their source *The Watchtower* of 1880, of which "Pastor" Russell was editor-in-chief. Now, if they "do not consider his writings authoritative and do not circulate them," why (1) publish his chronology; (2) quote his publication as evidence; and (3) admit his teachings on this vital point in their theology?

To shatter any misconception as to their literary shortcomings, I refer the interested reader to a pamphlet published by the Watchtower entitled *Jehovah's Witnesses, Communists or Christians?* (1953). Throughout the major content of this propaganda, Jehovah's Witnesses defend the thesis that they are not communists (which they are not), but, in their zeal to prove "their skirts clean," they quote "Pastor" Russell's writings no fewer than *five times,* refer to them with apparent pride twice (pp. 4–5), and even mention *two* of his best-known works, *The Plan of the Ages* (1886) and *The Battle of Armageddon* (1897). Further than this, *The Watchtower* of October 1, 1953, quoted "Pastor" Russell's *Studies in the Scriptures* (4:554) (and Judge Rutherford's *Vindication* [2:311])—convincing evidence indeed that the Watchtower still follows the Russellite theology of its much denied founder. All this despite the fact that they say, in their own words, "Jehovah's Witnesses . . . neither quote him [Russell] as an authority nor publish nor distribute his writings." *Jehovah's Witnesses in the Divine Purpose,* a Society history published in 1959, devoted almost fifty pages to Russell and his invaluable contributions to the Society and its doctrines. More recently, the 1973 Watchtower publication *God's Kingdom of a Thousand Years Has Approached* based its assertion of the end of the "Gentile Times" on the studies and declarations of Russell (p. 188).

Through a careful perusal of these facts, it is a simple matter to determine that Jehovah's Witnesses have never stopped being "Russellites," no matter how loudly some have proclaimed the opposite. To those who are enmeshed in the Watchtower's web, we can only say that you are *not* following a "new" theocratic organization; you are following the old teachings of Charles Taze Russell, a bitter antagonist of historical Christianity, who has bequeathed to you a gospel of spiritual confusion. Those who are contemplating becoming members of the Watchtower Society, we ask you to weigh the evidence found here and elsewhere.[13] Judge for yourselves whether it is wiser to trust the plain teachings of the Scriptures and the guidance of the Holy Spirit and the Christian church or to cast your lot with a group of zealous but misled people who are blindly leading the blind down the broad way that leads to destruction. These persons, it should be remembered, have abandoned practically every cardinal doctrine of biblical Christianity for the dogmatic doctrinal deviations of Charles Taze Russell and J. F. Rutherford. In the light of Holy Scriptures, however, Russellism is shown to be a snare from whose grip only Jesus Christ can deliver.

This is the history of Jehovah's Witnesses, the product of Charles Taze Russell, who, because he would not seek instruction in the Word of God, dedicated his unschooled talents to a lone, vain search without the guidance of the Holy Spirit. This attempt has produced a cult of determined people who are persuaded in their own minds and who boldly attempt to persuade all others that the king-

---

[13]See Walter Martin, *Jehovah of the Watchtower* (Minneapolis: Bethany House Publishers, 1975), chapter 1.

dom of God is "present," and that they are Jehovah's Witnesses, the only *true* servants of the living God.

~A look at the Watchtower Bible and Tract Society at the end of the century shows that it is a mixture of tradition, innovation, and contradiction. In some respects, especially doctrinally, the Society is clearly the legacy of Charles Taze Russell and Judge Joseph F. Rutherford. In other respects, such as its far-flung missionary and publishing reach, it is clearly a religion to influence the twenty-first century.

Recent History

Upon the death of President Frederick Franz in 1992, Society Vice-President Milton G. Henschel was elevated to the position of president. Henschel stepped down in 2000, and Don Adams became the sixth president of the Watchtower Society. Under the current corporate leadership of the Governing Body, the Watchtower publications and meetings have exhibited fewer antagonistic denouncements of the less popular Jehovah's Witness distinctives, such as the rejection of birthday celebrations and higher education. The Governing Body has also encouraged a strong evangelistic outreach overseas, the source of the vast majority of the converts. The Governing Body continues the unbroken autocracy of the Society, consistently condemning any dissension, any criticism, and any doubt on the part of rank-and-file members.

Total membership in the Watchtower Bible and Tract Society as of the end of 2001 was 6,117,666.[14] Of that number, 979,637 are members in the United States—a remarkably small increase of 3,808 over a five-year period (1996–2001). During 2001 United States Witnesses baptized only 27,731 U.S. converts, while worldwide the convert baptisms numbered 235,700—down considerably from the 1996 count of 366,579. Since door-to-door "preaching" is an essential part of the works necessary for Witnesses to be saved, it is not surprising that Witnesses in the United States spent 178,831,678 hours "preaching," with the worldwide total of more than 1.1 *billion* hours—a formidable number, if the Watchtower's count is credible, but still down considerably from an estimated 1.4 billion in 1996. "Bible" studies, which are actually *book* studies for Witnesses and potential converts to learn distinctive Watchtower doctrines and practices, are also essential for spiritual progress in this system. In 2001 American Jehovah's Witnesses reported conducting 416,556 "Bible" studies, while Jehovah's Witnesses worldwide accumulated more than 4.5 *million* "Bible" studies. The annual "Memorial" service of Jehovah's Witnesses is their own unbiblical version of the Lord's Supper, and although only a minute fraction of the members, the "spiritual class," or "anointed," partake, *all* Jehovah's Witnesses and as many friends, relatives, and prospective members as possible are encouraged to attend. In 2001 more than *15 million* people attended the Memorial service. This is a prime recruiting tool, exemplifying the "unity" of the Watchtower Society to a watching world.[15]

---

[14]Statistics reported in the *2001 Report of Jehovah's Witnesses Worldwide*, published in the first *Watchtower* issue of 2001 and posted on the official Watchtower Society Web site: *www.watchtower.org/statistics/worldwide_report.htm*.

[15]Ibid.

Publications

Contemporary Watchtower publications are truly impressive regarding their distribution and their carefully targeted objectives of recruiting and then training followers who dare not have any independent questions, doubts, or ideas regarding Jehovah's "theocratic" organization. With magazine publications estimated at 832 million combined issue copies per year, and new book titles enjoying estimated publication runs of three to five million copies each, the power of the written word is well exploited by the Society.

The Watchtower publishes a variety of Bible translations in various languages, as well as its own translation (carefully changed from the originals to support peculiar Watchtower doctrine) in English, the *New World Translation of the Holy Scriptures*. *The New World Translation* was completed in portions between 1950 and 1960, the complete volume being published in 1961. There have been four revisions, the last in 1984. Greek interlinear New Testament publications include *The Emphatic Diaglott* and *The Kingdom Interlinear Translation of the Greek Scriptures* (1969, revised in 1985). These interlinears use the Westcott and Hort Greek text, their own interlinear translations, and, in the case of *The Kingdom Interlinear,* the *New World Translation* as a parallel. One of their most important booklets is *Reasoning From the Scriptures* (1985, revised in 1989), which answers the most commonly challenged Watchtower interpretations and teachings from Scripture.

Since Rutherford's death, all Society publications are issued without any author credit, or anonymously. The Society position is that this preserves the humility of the contributors and focuses attention on God's Word and will rather than on the human agency used to communicate that divine truth. Detractors point out that concealing the identity of the authors makes it impossible for anyone to evaluate the authors' qualifications, expertise, or authority in the areas in which they write.

"Bible Study Aids" include *My Book of Bible Stories* for children, *Revelation—Its Grand Climax at Hand, Mankind's Search for God, Questions Young People Ask—Answers That Work, The Greatest Man Who Ever Lived,*[16] *Life—How Did It Get Here? By Evolution or By Creation*, among many others.

Smaller hardcover books include *Knowledge That Leads to Everlasting Life, The Bible—God's Word or Man's, Let Your Kingdom Come, Happiness—How to Find It, The Secret of Family Happiness, True Peace and Security—How Can You Find It, Listening to the Great Teacher,* and others. Small pamphlets are distributed by the millions and are used to introduce the teachings of the Watchtower to prospective members and for conducting "Bible" studies with interested parties and newly baptized members.

Current pamphlets include *What Does God Require of Us, Look! I Am Making All Things New, Jehovah's Witnesses and Education, How Can Blood Save Your Life, The Divine Name That Will Endure Forever, Should You Believe in the Trinity,* and *Jehovah's Witnesses in the Twentieth Century*.

Two of the many "Bible Reference Aids" Witnesses use to answer objectors'

---

[16]Remember, for the Watchtower Society Jesus was *only* a man. He was not the incarnation of the eternal Son of God, Second Person of the Trinity.

questions are *All Scripture Is Inspired of God and Beneficial* and *Insight on the Scriptures*.[17]

The two signature magazines of the Society, *The Watchtower,* published in 125 languages, and *Awake,* published in eighty-one languages, are published semi-monthly. Figures available for each of the January 1996 issues of *The Watchtower* (18.9 million copies) and *Awake!* (15.7 million copies) indicate the widespread influence of the Society.

Activities

In October 2000, the Watchtower Bible and Tract Society announced a major restructuring in the leadership of the Church. This was viewed by many observers as the most significant change in the organization since Judge Rutherford took over the Watchtower shortly after the death of Charles Taze Russell (*www.cftf.com*). The followers of the Watchtower Bible and Tract Society are still managed in a closely controlled, tightly knit organizational structure that is dictated from the Governing Body in Brooklyn, New York, and is not open to any adaptation or revision from any other authority—but its power is now largely *moral,* the Watchtower Organization having been divided into different corporations with individual presidents who are not members of the Governing Body. The Governing Body is a group of "heavenly class" or "anointed" men (currently numbering twelve) presided over by President Adams. The restructuring has restricted the legal culpability of the Watchtower Organization as a whole—making it more difficult for lawsuits to succeed in gaining large financial settlements (*Christianity Today,* March 5, 2001).

Prospective members are encouraged to commit themselves to the Society as quickly as possible and become members through baptism by immersion at the local congregational level. New members must immediately begin training for "fieldwork" by spending time with older members as they conduct their own fieldwork. In the past, *Publishers* were Witnesses who committed an average of 1,200 hours per year in fieldwork, including door-to-door recruitment, sidewalk soliciting, and "book" studies with prospective and new members. Those who dedicated a significantly greater amount of time than 1,200 hours earned the title *Pioneer,* to distinguish them from mere publishers.

Groups meeting together are called *congregations,* but the places where they meet are called *Kingdom Halls,* not churches. Members appointed from higher up for leadership are called *Overseers* or *Elders.* The person who leads the elder meetings is called the *Presiding Overseer* of the congregation. The *Service Overseer* handles service business within the congregation. *Ministerial Servants* are delegated administrative responsibilities as assistants to the elders.

Circuits are associations of around twenty congregations, supervised by a *Circuit Overseer.* Circuits organize twice-a-year conventions for their member congregations. *Districts* are geographical collections of circuits (twenty-two are in the United States). The *District Overseer* organizes the annual district convention, at

---

[17]*Insight* (1988) replaces the earlier Society Bible encyclopedia, *Aid to Bible Understanding* (1971), after doctrinal changes and the disfellowshipping of some of its contributors made *Aid* unacceptable.

which all new teachings and rules from the Governing Body are announced to the members, and at which new publications are presented. Collections of districts are called *Branches,* collections of branches are *Zones,* and the Brooklyn Society office is called the *Headquarters.*

Jehovah's Witnesses have only one day of ceremony each year, the *Memorial of Christ's Death* at Passover. At this ceremony, held in large auditoriums, all members are expected to be present along with family, friends, and prospective members. The elements of the Lord's Supper are passed through the audience, but only those of the anointed or heavenly class are allowed to partake. (That number is now fewer than nine thousand worldwide, since no one born after 1914 is considered eligible for the class.) Jehovah's Witnesses reject celebration of any other religious, national, or cultural holidays (Christmas, Easter, birthdays, Sabbath or Sunday ceremonies, etc.) as pagan and idolatrous. Those members who are caught participating in such holidays can be disfellowshipped.

Each Kingdom Hall has five meetings per week, which all congregation members are expected to attend. The *Public Talk* is usually held each Sunday, and the *Watchtower Study* normally follows, while the *Theocratic Ministry School* is usually a weekday evening meeting, followed by the *Service Meeting.* Each Witness is also required to attend a weekly *Book Study* in addition to his or her own fieldwork, and these book studies may be conducted by the Witness. The fieldwork cannot be neglected, since "every one of the Witnesses, whether serving at the world headquarters, in branches, or in congregations, does this fieldwork of personally telling others about God's Kingdom."[18]

Society Assets

In past years, the Society has owned several lucrative enterprises, including an eight-story factory building in Brooklyn, seven additional factory buildings, a large office complex, housing for the three thousand resident volunteer workers, a farm (which produces food for the volunteers), and a factory (with approximately one thousand workers) near Wallkill, New York.

The billions of copies of publications are distributed worldwide for a specific "donation" price or, in countries where that practice is not to their tax advantage (such as the United States), on a voluntary donation basis with suggested donation amounts that are far above the negligible cost of printing. Additionally, members and congregations are strongly pressured to ensure that the donations they send to headquarters are at least as much as the suggested amounts, even if some of the materials were distributed on the local level free or at reduced donations. None of the Watchtower workers, even full-time workers, receive any salary for their "Kingdom work," and only a small monthly allowance is given to full-time volunteers for incidental expenses. Extra donations are encouraged by the placement of collection boxes in each Kingdom Hall and by periodic reminders in various publications.

---

[18]Watchtower booklet, *Jehovah's Witnesses in the Twentieth Century.*

Structural Authority

At first glance, Jehovah's Witnesses seem to be the model of religious democracy. In their informational booklet *What Does God Require of Us?*[19] congregational leaders are described: "These men are not elevated above the rest of the congregation (Matthew 23:8–10). They are not given special titles (2 Corinthians 1:24). They do not dress differently from others. Neither are they paid for their work."

However, in reality the Watchtower Society is an absolute autocracy. All authority is vested in the Governing Body, including the authority to understand and teach the Bible.

> So Jehovah's visible organization under Christ is a channel for bringing the divine interpretation of his word to his devoted people.[20]
>
> We acknowledge as the visible organization of Jehovah on earth the Watchtower Bible and Tract Society, and recognize the Society as the channel or instrument through which Jehovah and Christ Jesus give instruction and meat in due season to the household of faith.[21]
>
> If we are to walk in the light of truth we must recognize not only Jehovah God as our father but his organization as our "mother."[22]
>
> Make haste to identify the visible theocratic organization of God that represents his king, Jesus Christ. It is essential for life. Doing so, be complete in accepting its every aspect.[23]
>
> They [Witnesses] must adhere absolutely to the decisions and scriptural understanding of the Society because God has given it this authority over his people.[24]
>
> Avoid independent thinking ... questioning the counsel that is provided by God's visible organization. . . . Fight against independent thinking.[25]
>
> To receive everlasting life in the earthly Paradise we must identify that organization and serve God as part of it.[26]

Dissent is not permitted and, if discovered, is punished swiftly and completely. Jehovah's Witnesses are excluded from membership or disfellowshipped not merely for gross, unrepentant immorality or heresy but also for questioning the teachings and authority of the Society. Should a Witness be disfellowshipped, he learns firsthand what it means to be shunned by the very people he once considered his friends, family, and brothers and sisters in Christ. Witnesses are taught:

> A disfellowshipped person is cut off from the congregation, and the congregation has nothing to do with him. Those in the congregation will not extend the hand of fellowship to this one, nor will they so much as say "hello" or "good-bye" to him. . . . [The congregation members] will not converse with such a one or show him recognition in any way. If the

[19] *What Does God Require of Us?* (Brooklyn: Watchtower Bible and Tract Society, 1997 electronic edition): 2.
[20] *The Watchtower* (June 1, 1938): 169.
[21] Ibid. (April 15, 1939): 125.
[22] Ibid. (May 1957): 274.
[23] Ibid. (October 1, 1967): 591.
[24] Ibid. (May 1, 1972): 272.
[25] Ibid. (January 15, 1983): 22, 27.
[26] Ibid. (February 15, 1983): 12.

disfellowshipped person attempts to talk to others in the congregation, they should walk away from him. In this way he will feel the full power of his sin. . . . The disfellowshipped person who wants to do what is right should inform any approaching him that he is disfellowshipped and they should not be conversing with him.[27]

What if a person cut off from God's congregation unexpectedly visits dedicated [Witness] relatives? What should the [Jehovah's Witness] Christian do then? If this is the first occurrence of such a visit, the dedicated Christian can, if his conscience permits, carry on family courtesies on that particular occasion. However, if his conscience does not permit, he is under no obligation to do so. If courtesies are extended, though, the Christian should make it clear that this will not be made a regular practice. . . . The excommunicated relative should be made to realize that his visits are not now welcomed as they were previously when he was walking correctly with Jehovah.[28]

Witnesses are not only to isolate themselves from those who were once Witnesses and have been disfellowshipped or disassociated but also from anyone who is not a Witness and who attempts to present a view contrary to the Watchtower. No Witness is allowed to read dissenting material, whether it is written by a disgruntled Jehovah's Witness, a disfellowshipped or disassociated Witness, or someone who has never been a Witness:

> Have no dealings with apostates. . . . For example, what will you do if you receive a letter or some literature, open it, and see right away that it is from an apostate? Will curiosity cause you to read it, just to see what he has to say? You may even reason: "It won't affect me; I'm too strong in the truth. And besides, if we have the truth, we have nothing to fear. The truth will stand the test." In thinking this way, some have fed their minds upon apostate reasoning and have fallen prey to serious questioning and doubt.[29]

Surprisingly, prospective Jehovah's Witnesses are told that it is right to question what one believes and to search out God's will for ourselves. In what used to be their standard introductory study for new prospective members, *The Truth That Leads to Eternal Life,* they taught,

> We need to examine not only what we personally believe but also what is taught by any religious organization with which we may be associated. Are its teachings in full harmony with God's Word, or are they based on the traditions of men? If we are lovers of the truth, there is nothing to fear from such an examination. It should be the sincere desire of every one of us to learn what God's will is for us, and then to do it.[30]

However, the Society means by this exhortation that one is supposed to test his own *non-Witness* religion, not the teachings of the Watchtower Society. Jehovah's Witnesses are not allowed to study the Bible on their own, to interpret what they read in the Bible for themselves, or to teach directly from the Bible. Rather, they must teach from approved Watchtower publications *about* the Bible. Concerning the Bible the Society says,

---

[27] *The Watchtower* (July 1, 1963): 411–13.
[28] Ibid. (July 15, 1963): 443–44.
[29] Ibid. (March 15, 1986): 12.
[30] *The Truth That Leads to Eternal Life* (Brooklyn: Watchtower Bible and Tract Society, 1968), 13.

Rather we should seek for dependent Bible study, rather than for independent Bible study.[31]

He does not impart his holy spirit and understanding and appreciation of his Word apart from his visible organization.[32]

The Bible is an organizational book and belongs to the Christian congregation as a whole, not to individuals, regardless of how sincerely they may believe that they can interpret the Bible. For this reason the Bible cannot be properly understood without Jehovah's visible organization in mind.[33]

We all need help to understand the Bible, and we cannot find the scriptural guidance we need outside the "faithful and discreet slave" organization.[34]

They [questioners] say that it is sufficient to read the Bible exclusively, either alone or in small groups at home. But, strangely, through such "Bible reading," they have reverted right back to the apostate doctrines that commentaries by Christendom's clergy were teaching 100 years ago.[35]

The Watchtower Bible and Tract Society has weathered the storms of its inconsistent and turbulent history by enforcing absolute control over its members and by excluding anyone who dares to question anything. It should not surprise us, therefore, that most Witnesses have memorized the basic doctrinal teachings of the Society and will defend them adamantly, even when their defense is irrational, unbiblical, and historically inaccurate. We turn now to the doctrines of Jehovah's Witnesses.[36]~

Some of the Doctrines of Jehovah's Witnesses

Below is a comparison of Jehovah's Witnesses' beliefs "then" (during the 1960s) and "now" (in 1997), from their own publications. Note that although some of the wording has changed, the Witnesses' teachings about the core doctrines of the faith have remained remarkably unchanged over three decades, with a few notable exceptions.

THEN (1960s)	NOW (1997)
I. There is one solitary being from all eternity, Jehovah God, the Creator and Preserver of the Universe and of all things visible and invisible.	~1. People worship many things. But the Bible tells us that there is only one TRUE God. He created everything in heaven and on earth. . . . God has many titles but has only one name. That name is JEHOVAH.

---

[31] *The Watchtower* (September 15, 1911): 4885.
[32] Ibid. (July 1, 1965): 391.
[33] Ibid. (October 1, 1967): 587.
[34] Ibid. (February 15, 1981): 19.
[35] Ibid. (August 15, 1981): 29.
[36] ~Cited from Walter Martin, *Kingdom of the Cults,* (Minneapolis: Bethany House Publishers, 1997), 79–178.

II. The Word or Logos is "a god," a mighty god, the "beginning of the Creation" of Jehovah and His active agent in the creation of all things. The Logos was made human as the man Jesus and suffered death to produce the ransom or redemptive price for obedient men.

2. Jesus lived in heaven as a spirit person before he came to earth. He was God's first creation, and so he is called the "firstborn" Son of God (Col. 1:15; Rev. 3:14). Jesus is the only Son that God created by himself. Jehovah used the prehuman Jesus as his "master worker" in creating all other things in heaven and on earth (Prov. 8:22–31; Col. 1:16–17).

III. The Bible is the inerrant, infallible, inspired Word of God as it was originally given, and has been preserved by Him as the revealer of His purposes.

3. Another mark of true religion is that its members have a *deep respect for the Bible.* They accept it as the Word of God and believe what it says.

IV. Satan was a great angel who rebelled against Jehovah and challenged His Sovereignty. Through Satan, sin and death came upon man. His destiny is annihilation with all his followers.

4. At first, he was a perfect angel in heaven with God. However, he later thought too much of himself and wanted the worship that rightly belongs to God.

V. Man was created in the image of Jehovah but willfully sinned, hence all men are born sinners and are "of the earth." Those who follow Jesus Christ faithful to the death will inherit the heavenly Kingdom with Him. Men of good will who accept Jehovah and His Theocratic Rule will enjoy the "new earth"; all others who reject Jehovah will be annihilated.

5. By disobeying God's command, the first man, Adam, committed what the Bible calls "sin." So God sentenced him to death (Gen. 3:17–19). . . . Adam passed on sin to all his children. . . . Soon Jesus will judge people, separating them as a shepherd separates sheep from goats. The "sheep" are those who will have proved themselves his loyal subjects. They will receive everlasting life on earth. . . . Jehovah has also selected some faithful men and women from the earth to go to heaven. They will rule with Jesus as kings, judges, and priests over mankind. . . . The "goats" are those who will have rejected God's Kingdom. . . . In the near future, Jesus will destroy all goat-like ones.

VI. The atonement is a ransom paid to Jehovah God by Christ Jesus and is applicable to all who accept it in righteousness. In brief, the death of Jesus removed the effects of Adam's sin on his offspring and laid the foundation of the New World of righteousness including the Millennium of Christ's reign.

6. Unlike Adam ... Jesus was perfectly obedient to God under even the greatest test. He could therefore sacrifice his perfect human life to pay for Adam's sin. This is what the Bible refers to as the "ransom." Adam's children could thus be released from condemnation to death. All who put their faith in Jesus can have their sins forgiven and receive everlasting life.

VII. The man Christ Jesus was resurrected a divine spirit creature after offering the ransom for obedient man.

7. Jesus died and was resurrected by God as a spirit creature, and he returned to heaven (1 Pet. 3:18–22).

VIII. The soul of man is not eternal but mortal, and it can die. Animals likewise have souls, though man has the preeminence by special creation.

8. The dead cannot do anything or feel anything. . . . The soul dies, it does not live on after death.

IX. Hell, meaning a place of "fiery torment" where sinners remain after death until the resurrection, does not exist. This is a doctrine of "Organized Religion," not the Bible. Hell is the common grave of mankind, literally *sheol* (Hebrew), "a place of rest in hope" where the departed sleep until the resurrection by Jehovah God.

9. Would a *loving God* really torment people forever? . . . The wicked, of course, are not literally tormented because, as we have seen, when a person is dead he is completely out of existence. . . . And it is also a lie, which the Devil spread, that the souls of the wicked are tormented.[37]

X. Eternal Punishment is a punishment or penalty of which there is no end. It does not mean "eternal torment" of living souls. Annihilation, the second death, is the lot of all those who reject Jehovah God, and it is eternal.

10. Millions of dead ones will be resurrected to human life on the earth (Acts 24:15). If they do what God requires of them, they will continue to live on earth forever. If not, they will be destroyed forever (John 5:28–29; Rev. 20:11–15).

---

[37] *You Can Live Forever in Paradise on Earth* (Brooklyn: Watchtower Bible and Tract Society, 1982), 81–89.

XI. Jesus Christ has returned to earth A.D. 1914, has expelled Satan from Heaven, and is proceeding to overthrow Satan's organization, establish the Theocratic Millennial Kingdom, and vindicate the name of Jehovah God. He did not return in a physical form and is invisible as the Logos.

11. In 1914, Jehovah gave Jesus the authority He had promised him. Since then, Jesus has ruled in heaven as Jehovah's appointed King (Dan. 7:13–14).... As soon as Jesus became King, he threw Satan and his wicked angels out of heaven and down to the locality of the earth. That is why things have become so bad here on earth since 1914.

XII. The Kingdom of Jehovah is Supreme, and as such cannot be compatible with present Human Government ("Devil's Visible Organization"), and any allegiance to them in any way which violates the allegiance owed to Him is a violation of the Scripture.

12. God's Kingdom is a special government. It is set up in heaven and will rule over this earth.... Jesus' disciples must be *no part of this wicked world* (John 17:16). They do not get involved in the world's political affairs and social controversies.~[38]

The Holy Trinity

1. "The doctrine, in brief, is that there are three gods in one: 'God the Father, God the Son, and God the Holy Ghost,' all three equal in power, substance, and eternity" (*Let God Be True,* Brooklyn: Watchtower Bible and Tract Society, 1946 ed., 100).

2. "The obvious conclusion is, therefore, that Satan is the originator of the Trinity doctrine" (*LGBT,* 101).

3. "Sincere persons who want to know the true God and serve Him find it a bit difficult to love and worship a complicated, freakish-looking, three-headed God" (*LGBT,* 102).

4. "The Trinity doctrine was not conceived by Jesus or the early Christians" (*LGBT,* 111).

5. "The plain truth is that this is another of Satan's attempts to keep God-fearing persons from learning the truth of Jehovah and his Son, Christ Jesus. No, there is no Trinity" (*LGBT,* 111).

6. "Any trying to reason out the Trinity teaching leads to confusion of mind. So the Trinity teaching confuses the meaning of John 1:1–2; it does not simplify it or make it clear or easily understandable" (*"The Word," Who Is He? According to John,* 7).

7. "Is Jehovah a Trinity—three persons in one God? No! Jehovah, the Father, is 'the only true God' (John 17:3; Mark 12:29). Jesus is His firstborn Son, and he is subject to God (1 Cor. 11:3). The Father is greater than the Son (John 14:28).

---

[38]All statements above except for #9 are taken from *What Does God Require of Us?* (Brooklyn: Watchtower Bible and Tract Society, 1997, electronic version).

The holy spirit is not a person; it is God's active force (Gen. 1:2; Acts 2:18)" (*What Does God Require of Us,* Brooklyn: Watchtower Bible and Tract Society, 1997, electronic version).

8. "Thus, neither the thirty-nine books of the Hebrew Scriptures nor the canon of twenty-seven inspired books of the Christian Greek Scriptures provide any clear teaching of the Trinity. . . . Thus, the testimony of the Bible and of history makes clear that the Trinity was unknown throughout biblical times and for several centuries thereafter" (*Should You Believe in the Trinity,* Brooklyn: Watchtower Bible and Tract Society, 1997, electronic version).

The Deity of Christ

1. "The true Scriptures speak of God's Son, the Word, as 'a god.' He is a 'mighty god,' but not the Almighty God, who is Jehovah" (*The Truth Shall Make You Free,* Brooklyn: Watchtower Bible and Tract Society, 1943, 47).

2. "In other words, he was the first and direct creation of Jehovah God" (*The Kingdom Is at Hand,* Brooklyn: Watchtower Bible and Tract Society, 1944, 46–47, 49).

3. "The Bible shows that there is only one God . . . greater than His Son . . . and that the Son, as the Firstborn, Only-begotten, and 'the creation by God,' had a beginning. That the Father is greater and older than the Son is reasonable, easy to understand, and is what the Bible teaches" (*From Paradise Lost to Paradise Regained,* Brooklyn: Watchtower Bible and Tract Society, 1958, 164).

4. "Jesus was 'the Son of God.' Not God himself!" (*"The Word," Who Is He?,* 20).

5. "The very fact that he was sent proves he was not equal with God but was less than God his Father" (*TWWIH,* 41).

6. "Certainly the apostle John was not so unreasonable as to say that someone (the Word) was with some other individual ('God') and at the same time was that other individual ('God')" (*TWWIH,* 53).

7. "Thus, Jesus had an existence in heaven before coming to the earth. But was it as one of the persons in an almighty, eternal triune Godhead? No, for the Bible plainly states that in his prehuman existence, Jesus was a created spirit being, just as angels were spirit beings created by God. Neither the angels nor Jesus had existed before their creation" (*Should You Believe in the Trinity?*).

The Holy Spirit

1. "The holy spirit is the invisible active force of Almighty God that moves his servants to do his will" (*Let God Be True,* 108).

2. "As for the 'Holy Spirit,' the so-called 'third Person of the Trinity,' we have already seen that it is not a person, but God's active force" (*The Truth That Leads to Eternal Life,* Brooklyn: Watchtower Bible and Tract Society, 1968, 24).

3. "The Scriptures themselves unite to show that God's holy spirit is not a person but is God's active force by which he accomplishes his purpose and executes his will" (*Aid to Bible Understanding,* Brooklyn: Watchtower Bible and Tract Society, 1969, 1971, 1543).

4. "The Bible's use of 'holy spirit' indicates that it is a controlled force that

Jehovah God uses to accomplish a variety of his purposes. To a certain extent, it can be likened to electricity, a force that can be adapted to perform a great variety of operations" (*Should You Believe in the Trinity?*).

5. "No, the holy spirit is not a person and it is not part of a Trinity. The holy spirit is God's active force that he uses to accomplish his will. It is not equal to God but is always at his disposition and subordinate to him" (*SYBITT?*).

The Virgin Birth

1. "Mary was a virgin. . . . When Joseph learned that Mary was going to have a child, he did not want to take her as his wife. But God's angel . . . said, 'That which has been begotten in her is by holy spirit'. . . . He took Mary his wife home. 'But he had no relations with her until she gave birth to a son' (Matt. 1:20–25)" (*From Paradise Lost to Paradise Regained*, 122–123).

2. "Jesus was conceived by a sinless, perfect Father, Jehovah God. . . . The perfect child Jesus did not get human life from the sinner Adam, but received only a human body through Adam's descendant Mary. Jesus' life came from Jehovah God, the Holy One. . . . Jehovah took the perfect life of his only-begotten Son and transferred it from heaven to . . . the womb of the unmarried girl Mary. . . . Thus God's Son was conceived or given a start as a human creature. It was a miracle. Under Jehovah's holy power the child Jesus, conceived in this way, grew in Mary's womb to the point of birth" (*FPLTPR*, 126–127).

3. "Jesus' birth on earth was not an incarnation. . . . He emptied himself of all things heavenly and spiritual, and God's almighty spirit transferred his Son's life down to the womb of the Jewish virgin of David's descent. By this miracle he was born a man. . . . He was not a spirit-human hybrid, a man and at the same time a spirit person. . . . He *was* flesh" (*What Has Religion Done for Mankind*, 231).

4. "While on earth, Jesus was a human, although a perfect one because it was God who transferred the life-force of Jesus to the womb of Mary" (*Should You Believe in the Trinity?*).

The Atonement

1. "That which is redeemed or bought back is what was lost, namely, perfect human life, with its rights and earthly prospects" (*Let God Be True*, 114).

2. "Jesus as the glorified High Priest, by presenting in heaven this redemptive price, is in position to relieve the believing ones of Adam's descendants from the inherited disability under which all are born" (*LGBT*, 118–119).

3. "The human life that Jesus Christ laid down in sacrifice must be exactly equal to that life which Adam forfeited for all his offspring: it must be a perfect human life, no more, no less. . . . This is just what Jesus gave . . . for men of all kinds" (*You May Survive Armageddon Into God's New World*, Brooklyn: Watchtower Bible and Tract Society, 1955, 39).

4. "Jesus, no more and no less than a perfect human, became a ransom that compensated exactly for what Adam lost—the right to perfect human life on earth. . . . The perfect human life of Jesus was the 'corresponding ransom' required by divine justice—no more, no less. A basic principle even of human justice is that the price paid should fit the wrong committed. . . . So the ransom,

to be truly in line with God's justice, had to be strictly an equivalent—a perfect human, 'the last Adam.' Thus, when God sent Jesus to earth as the ransom, he made Jesus to be what would satisfy justice, not an incarnation, not a god-man, but a perfect man, 'lower than angels' " (*Should You Believe in the Trinity?*).

Salvation by Grace

1. "Immortality is a reward for faithfulness. It does not come automatically to a human at birth" (*Let God Be True*, 74).

2. "Those people of good will today who avail themselves of the provision and who steadfastly abide in this confidence will find Christ Jesus to be their 'everlasting Father' [Isaiah 9:6]" (*LGBT*, 121).

3. "We have learned that a person could fall away and be judged unfavorably either now or at Armageddon or during the thousand years of Christ's reign or at the end of the final test . . . into everlasting destruction" (*From Paradise Lost to Paradise Regained*, 241).

4. "Make haste to identify the visible theocratic organization of God that represents his king, Jesus Christ. It is essential for life. Doing so, be complete in accepting its every aspect" (*The Watchtower*, October 1, 1967: 591).

5. "To receive everlasting life in the earthly Paradise we must identify that organization and serve God as part of it" (*The Watchtower*, February 15, 1983: 12).

The Resurrection of Christ

1. "This firstborn from the dead was raised from the grave, not a human creature, but a spirit" (*Let God Be True*, 276).

2. "Jehovah God raised him from the dead, not as a human Son, but as a mighty immortal spirit Son. . . . For forty days after that he materialized, as angels before him had done, to show himself alive to his disciples" (*LGBT*, 40).

3. "Jesus did not take his human body to heaven to be forever a man in heaven. Had he done so, that would have left him even lower than the angels. . . . God did not purpose for Jesus to be humiliated thus forever by being a fleshly man forever. No, but after he had sacrificed his perfect manhood, God raised him to deathless life as a glorious spirit creature" (*LGBT*, 41).

4. "Usually they could not at first tell it was Jesus, for he appeared in different bodies. He appeared and disappeared just as angels had done, because he was resurrected as a spirit creature. Only because Thomas would not believe did Jesus appear in a body like that in which he had died" (*From Paradise Lost to Paradise Regained*, 144).

5. "Having given up his flesh for the life of the world, Christ could never take it again and become a man once more. For that basic reason his return could never be in the human body that he sacrificed once for all time" (*You Can Live Forever in Paradise on Earth*, Brooklyn: Watchtower Bible and Tract Society, 1982, 143).

The Return of Christ and Human Government

1. "Christ Jesus returns, not again as a human, but as a glorious spirit person" (*Let God Be True*, 196).

2. "Some wrongfully expect a literal fulfillment of the symbolic statements of the Bible. Such hope to see the glorified Jesus coming seated on a white cloud where every human eye will see him. . . . Since no earthly men have ever seen the Father . . . neither will they see the glorified Son" (*LGBT,* 186).

3. "It does not mean that he [Christ] is on the way or has promised to come, but that he has already arrived and is here" (*LGBT,* 198).

4. "Any national flag is a symbol or image of the sovereign power of its nation" (*LGBT,* 242).

5. "All such likenesses [symbols of a national power, eagle, sun, lion, etc.] are forbidden by Exodus 20:2–6 [the commandment against idolatry]" (*LGBT,* 242).

6. "Hence no witness of Jehovah, who ascribes salvation only to Him, may salute any national emblem without violating Jehovah's commandment against idolatry as stated in His Word" (*LGBT,* 243).

The Existence of Hell and Eternal Punishment

1. "Those who have been taught by Christendom believe the God-dishonoring doctrine of a fiery hell for tormenting conscious human souls eternally" (*Let God Be True,* 88).

2. "It is so plain that the Bible hell is mankind's common grave that even an honest little child can understand it, but not the religious theologians" (*LGBT,* 92).

3. "Who is responsible for this God-defaming doctrine of a hell of torment? The promulgator of it is Satan himself. His purpose in introducing it has been to frighten the people away from studying the Bible and to make them hate God" (*LGBT,* 98).

4. "Imperfect man does not torture even a mad dog, but kills it. And yet the clergymen attribute to God, who is love, the wicked crime of torturing human creatures merely because they had the misfortune to be born sinners" (*LGBT,* 99).

5. "The doctrine of a burning hell where the wicked are tortured eternally after death cannot be true, mainly for four reasons: (1) Because it is wholly unscriptural; (2) it is unreasonable; (3) it is contrary to God's love; and (4) it is repugnant to justice" (*LGBT,* 99).

6. "It is . . . a lie, which the Devil has had spread, that the souls of the wicked are tormented in a hell or a purgatory" (*You Can Live,* 89).

Man the Soul, His Nature and Destiny

1. "Man is a combination of two things, namely, the 'dust of the ground' and 'the breath of life.' The combining of these two things (or factors) produced a living soul or creature called man" (*Let God Be True,* 68).

2. "So we see that the claim of religionists that man has an immortal soul and therefore differs from the beast is not scriptural" (*LGBT,* 68).

3. "The fact that the human soul is mortal can be amply proved by a careful study of the Holy Scriptures. An immortal soul cannot die, but God's Word, at Ezekiel 18:4, says concerning humans: 'Behold all souls are mine. . . . The soul that sinneth it shall die' " (*LGBT,* 69–70).

4. "It is clearly seen that even the man Christ Jesus was mortal. He did not have an immortal soul: Jesus, the human soul, died" (*LGBT,* 71).

5. "Thus it is seen that the serpent (the Devil) is the one that originated the doctrine of the inherent immortality of human souls" (*LGBT,* 74–75).

6. "The Scriptures show that the destiny of the sinful man is death" (*LGBT,* 75).

7. "The Holy Scriptures alone offer real hope for those who do seek Jehovah God and strive to follow his ways" (*LGBT,* 75).

8. "At death man's spirit, his life-force, which is sustained by breathing, 'goes out.' *It no longer exists.* . . . When they are dead, both humans and animals are in this same state of complete unconsciousness. . . . That the soul lives on after death is a lie started by the Devil" (*You Can Live,* 77).

9. "The human soul ceases to exist at death. . . . Hell is mankind's common grave" (*Jehovah's Witnesses in the Twentieth Century,* electronic version).

The Kingdom of Heaven (a Heavenly One)

1. "Who and how many are able to enter it [the Kingdom]? The Revelation limits to 144,000 the number that become a part of the Kingdom and stand on heavenly Mount Zion" (*Let God Be True,* 136).

2. "In the capacity of priests and kings of God they reign a thousand years with Christ Jesus" (*LGBT,* 137).

3. "He [Christ] went to prepare a heavenly place for his associate heirs, 'Christ's body,' for they too will be invisible spirit creatures" (*LGBT,* 138).

4. "If it is to be a heavenly kingdom, who will be the subject of its rule? In the invisible realm angelic hosts, myriads of them, will serve as faithful messengers of the King. And on earth the faithful children of the King Christ Jesus, including faithful forefathers of his then resurrected, will be 'princes in all the earth'. . . . Then, too, the 'great crowd' of his 'other sheep' . . . will continue to 'serve him day and night,' and many of them will also be 'princes'. . . . They will 'multiply and fill the earth' in righteousness and their children will become obedient subjects of the King Christ Jesus. And finally the 'unrighteous' ones that are to be resurrected then, to prove their integrity, must joyfully submit themselves to theocratic rule. . . . Those who prove rebellious or who turn unfaithful during the loosing of Satan at the end of Christ's thousand-year reign will be annihilated with Satan, the Devil" (*LGBT,* 318–319).

5. "The Creator loved the new world so much that he gave his only begotten Son to be its King" (*LGBT,* 143).

6. "The undefeatable purpose of Jehovah God to establish a righteous kingdom in these last days was fulfilled in A.D. 1914" (*LGBT,* 143).

7. "Obey the King Christ Jesus and flee, while there is still time, to the Kingdom heights. . . . Time left is short, for 'the kingdom of the heavens has drawn near' " (*LGBT,* 144).

8. "Only a little flock of 144,000 go to heaven and rule with Christ. . . . The 144,000 are born again as spiritual sons of God" (*Jehovah's Witnesses in the Twentieth Century,* electronic version).

Jehovah's Witnesses become intensely disturbed whenever they are referred to as "Russellites" or their theology as "Russellism." After a thorough examination of the doctrines of the Society and a lengthy comparison with the teachings of "Pastor" Russell, its founder, the author is convinced that the two systems are basically the same, and whatever differences do exist are minute and affect in no major way the cardinal beliefs of the organization. I believe, however, that in any research project substantiating evidence should be produced for verification whenever possible. I have attempted to do this and, as a result, have listed below five of the major doctrines of the Jehovah's Witnesses paralleled with the teachings of Charles Taze Russell, their late great "pastor." I am sure that the interested reader will recognize the obvious relationship between the two systems, for it is inescapably evident that Russell is the author of both.

The Teachings of Charles Taze Russell or "Russellism"	**The Doctrines of the Jehovah's Witnesses**

The Triune Godhead

"This view [the Trinity] suited well 'the dark ages' it helped to produce" (*Studies in the Scriptures*, 5:166).	"Does this [John 1:1] mean that Jehovah God (Elohim) and the . . . Son are two persons but at the same time one God and members of a so-called 'trinity' or 'triune god'? When religion so teaches it violates the Word of God, wrests the Scriptures to the destruction of those who are misled, and insults God-given intelligence and reason" (*The Truth Shall Make You Free*, 45).
"This theory . . . is as unscriptural as it is unreasonable" (*Studies*, 5:166).	"The confusion is caused by the improper translation of John 1:1–3 . . . such translation being made by religionists who tried to manufacture proof for their teaching of a 'trinity' " (*The Truth*, 45–46).
"If it were not for the fact that this trinitarian nonsense was drilled into us from earliest infancy, and the fact that it is so soberly taught in Theological Seminaries by gray-haired professors . . . nobody would give it a moment's serious consideration" (*Studies*, 5:166).	"The obvious conclusion is, therefore, that Satan is the originator of the 'trinity doctrine' " (*Let God Be True*, 101).
"How the great Adversary [Satan] ever succeeded in foisting [the Triune Godhead] upon the Lord's people to bewilder and mystify them, and render much of the Word of God of none effect, is the real mystery" (*Studies*, 5:166).	"The testimony of history is clear: The Trinity teaching is a deviation from the truth, an apostatizing from it" (*Should You Believe?*, electronic version).

The Deity of Jesus Christ

"Our Lord Jesus Christ is *a* God . . . still the united voice of the Scriptures most emphatically asserts that there is but one Almighty God, the Father of all" (*Studies,* 5:55).

"Our Redeemer existed as a spirit being before he was made flesh and dwelt amongst men. At that time, as well as subsequently, he was properly known as 'a god'—a mighty one" (*Studies,* 5:84).

"The Logos [Christ] himself was 'the beginning of the creation of God' " (*Studies,* 5:86).

"As chief of the angels and next to the Father, he [Christ] was known as the Archangel (highest angel or messenger), whose name, Michael, signifies 'Who as God' or 'God's Representative' " (*Studies,* 5:84).

"The true Scriptures speak of God's Son, the Word, as 'a god.' He is a 'mighty god,' but not the Almighty God, who is Jehovah—Isaiah 9:6" (*The Truth,* 47).

"At the time of his beginning of life he was created by the everlasting God, Jehovah, without the aid or instrumentality of any mother. In other words, he was the first and direct creation of Jehovah God. . . . He was the start of God's creative work. . . . He was not an incarnation in flesh but was flesh, a human Son of God, a perfect man, no longer a spirit, although having a spiritual or heavenly past or background" (*The Kingdom Is at Hand,* 46–47, 49).

"This One was not Jehovah God, but was 'existing in God's form. ' He was a spirit person . . . he was a mighty one, although not Almighty as Jehovah God is . . . he was a God, but not the Almighty God, who is Jehovah" (*Let God Be True,* 32–33).

"Being the only begotten Son of God . . . the Word would be a prince among all other creatures. In this office he [Christ] bore another name in heaven, which name is 'Michael'. . . . Other names were given to the Son in course of time" (*The Truth,* 49).

The Resurrection of Christ

Our Lord was put to death in the *flesh,* but was made alive in the *spirit;* he was put to death as a *man,* but was raised from the dead *a spirit being* of the highest order of the divine nature" (*Studies,* 5:453).

"In his resurrection he was no more human. He was raised as a spirit creature" (*TKIAH,* 258).

"It could not be that the man Jesus is the Second Adam, the *new* father of the race instead of Adam; for the *man* Jesus is dead, forever dead" (*Studies*, 5:454).

"Having given up his flesh for the life of the world, Christ could never take it again and become a man once more. For that basic reason his return could never be in the human body that he sacrificed once for all time" (*You Can Live Forever in Paradise on Earth*, 143).

"[Christ] instantly created and assumed such a body of flesh and such clothing as he saw fit for the purpose intended" (*Studies*, 2:127).

"Therefore the bodies in which Jesus manifested himself to his disciples after his return to life were not the body in which he was nailed to the tree. They were merely materialized for the occasion, resembling on one or two occasions the body in which he died" (*TKIAH*, 259).

"Our Lord's human body . . . did not decay or corrupt. . . . Whether it was dissolved into gases or whether it is still preserved somewhere . . . no one knows" (*Studies*, 2:129).

"This firstborn from the dead was raised from the grave not a human creature, but a spirit" (*Let God Be True*, 276).

The Physical Return of Christ

"And in *like manner* as he went away (quietly, secretly, so far as the world was concerned, and unknown except to his followers), *so*, in this manner, he comes again" (*Studies*, 2:154).

"Christ Jesus returns, not as a human, but as a glorious spirit person" (*Let God Be True*, 196).

[Russell's idea of what Christ is saying, and his teaching on the matter.] "He comes to us in the early dawn of the Millennial Day. [Jesus] seems to say. . . . 'Learn that I am a spirit being no longer visible to human sight' " (*Studies*, 2:191).

"Since no earthly men have ever seen or can see the Father, they will not be able to see the glorified Son" (*LGBT*, 197).

"[Christ] does not come in the body of his humiliation, a human body, which he took for the suffering of death . . . but in his glorious spiritual body" (*Studies*, 2:108).

"It is a settled scriptural truth, therefore, that human eyes will not see him at his second coming, neither will he come in a fleshy body" (*The Truth*, 295).

The Existence of Hell or a Place of Conscious Torment After Death

"Many have imbibed the erroneous idea that God placed our race on trial for life with the alternative of *eternal torture*, whereas nothing of the kind is even hinted at in the penalty" (*Studies*, 1:127).

"The Bible hell is mankind's 'common grave' " (*Let God Be True*, 92).

"Eternal torture is nowhere suggested in the Old Testament Scriptures, and only a few statements in the New Testament can be so misconstrued as to appear to teach it" (*Studies*, 1:128).

"Hell could not be a place of torment because such an idea never came into the mind or heart of God. Additionally, to torment a person *eternally* because he did wrong on earth *for a few years* is contrary to justice. How good it is to know the truth about the dead! It can truly set one free from fear and superstition" (*You Can Live Forever in Paradise on Earth*, 89).

In concluding this comparison, it is worthwhile to note that as far as the facts are concerned, "Jehovah's Witnesses" is simply a pseudonym for "Russellism" or "Millennial Dawnism." The similarity of the two systems is more than coincidental or accidental, regardless of the Witnesses' loud shouts to the contrary. The facts speak for themselves. Inquisitive persons may ask at this point why the organization assumed the name of "Jehovah's Witnesses." The answer is more than understandable.

After Russell's death, Judge Rutherford, the newly elected president of the Society, saw the danger of remaining "Russellites" and over a period of fifteen years labored to cover up the "pastor's" unpleasant past, which did much to hinder the organization's progress. In 1931 Rutherford managed to appropriate the name "Jehovah's Witnesses" from Isaiah 43:10, thus escaping the damaging title "Russellites." Rutherford thus managed to hide the unsavory background of Russellistic theology and delude millions of people into believing that Jehovah's Witnesses was a "different" organization. Rutherford's strategy has worked well for the Russellites and, as a result, today those trusting souls and millions like them everywhere sincerely believe that they are members of a "New Kingdom Order" under Jehovah God, when in reality they are deluded believers in the theology of *one* man, Charles Taze Russell, who was proven to be neither a Christian nor a qualified Bible student. Jehovah's Witnesses who have not been in the movement any great period of time deny publicly and privately that they are Russellites; and since few, if any, of the old-time members of "Pastor" Russell's personal flock are still alive, the Society in safety vehemently denounces any accusations that tend to prove that Russell's theology is the basis of the entire Watchtower system. Proof of this is found in a personal letter from the Society to the author dated February 9, 1951, wherein, in answer to my question concerning Russell's influence, they stated: "We are not 'Russellites' for we are not following Charles T. Russell or any other imperfect man. Honest examination of our literature today would quickly reveal that it differs widely from that of Russell's, even though he was the first President of our Society."

Further than this, in another letter dated November 6, 1950, and signed by Nathan H. Knorr, the Society's then legal president, the Society declared that "the latest publications of The Watchtower Bible and Tract Society set out the doctrinal views of this organization, and I think any information you want in that regard you can find yourself without an interview." It is therefore evident from these two official letters that we must judge the faith of the Jehovah's Witnesses by their literature.

A Refutation of Watchtower Theology

The Triune Deity[39]

One of the greatest doctrines of the Scriptures is that of the Triune Godhead (*tes theotetos*) or the nature of God himself. To say that this doctrine is a "mystery" is indeed inconclusive, and no informed minister would explain the implications of the doctrine in such abstract terms. Jehovah's Witnesses accuse "the clergy" of doing just that, however, and it is unfortunate to note that they are, as usual, guilty of misstatement in the presentation of the facts and even in their definition of what Christian clergymen believe the Deity to be.

First of all, Christian ministers and Christian laypersons do not believe that there are "three gods in one" (*Let God Be True*, 100), but *do* believe that there are three persons all of the same Substance—coequal, coexistent, and coeternal. There is ample ground for this belief in the Scriptures, where plurality in the Godhead is very strongly intimated if not expressly declared. Let us consider just a few of these references.

In Genesis 1:26 Jehovah is speaking of Creation, and He speaks in the plural: "Let *us* make man in *our* image, after *our* likeness." Now, it is obvious that God would not create man in His image and the angels' images if He were talking to them, so He must have been addressing someone else—and who but His Son and the Holy Spirit who are equal in Substance could He address in such familiar terms? Since there is no other god but Jehovah (Isaiah 43:10–11), not even "a lesser mighty god" as Jehovah's Witnesses affirm Christ to be, there must be a unity in plurality and Substance, or the passage is not meaningful. The same is true of Genesis 11:7, when God said at the Tower of Babel, "Let *us* go down," and also of Isaiah 6:8, "Who will go for *us*? . . ." These instances of plurality indicate something deeper than an interpersonal relationship; they strongly suggest what the New Testament fully develops, namely, a Tri-Unity in the One God. The claim of Jehovah's Witnesses that the early church fathers, including Tertullian and Theophilus, propagated and introduced the threefold unity of God into Christianity is ridiculous and hardly worth refuting. Any unbiased study of the facts will convince the impartial student that before Tertullian or Theophilus lived, the doctrine was under study and considered sound. No one doubts that among the heathen (Babylonians and Egyptians) demon gods were worshiped, but to call the triune Godhead a doctrine of the devil (*Let God Be True*, 101), as Jehovah's Witnesses do, is blasphemy and the product of untutored and darkened souls.

In the entire chapter titled "Is there a Trinity?" (*Let God Be True*, 100–101), the whole problem as to why the Trinity doctrine is "confusing" to Jehovah's Witnesses lies in their interpretation of "death" as it is used in the Bible. To Jehovah's Witnesses, death is the cessation of consciousness, or *destruction*. However,

---

[39]Jehovah's Witnesses take great delight in pointing out that the word *Trinity* does not appear as such in the Bible. They further state that since it is not a part of Scripture, it must be of pagan origin and should be discounted entirely. What the Witnesses fail to understand is that the very word *Jehovah*, which they maintain is the only true name for God, also does not appear as such in the Bible, but is an interpolation of the Hebrew consonants *YHWH* or *JHVH*, any vowels added being arbitrary. Thus it is seen that the very name by which they call themselves is just as unbiblical as they suppose the Trinity to be.

no single or collective rendering of Greek or Hebrew words in any reputable lexicon or dictionary will substantiate their view. Death in the Scriptures is "separation" from the body as in the case of the first death (physical), and separation from God for eternity as in the second death (the lake of fire, Revelation 20). Death never means annihilation, and Jehovah's Witnesses cannot bring in one word in context in the original languages to prove it does. A wealth of evidence has been amassed to prove it does not. I welcome comparisons on this point.

The rest of the chapter is taken up with childish questions—some of which are painful to record: "Who ran the universe the three days Jesus was dead and in the grave?" (death again portrayed as extinction of consciousness) is a sample of the nonsense perpetrated on gullible people. "Religionists" is the label placed on all who disagree with the organization's views regardless of the validity of the criticism. Christians do not believe that the Trinity was incarnate in Christ and that they were "three-in-one" as such during Christ's ministry. Christ voluntarily limited himself in His earthly body, but heaven was always open to Him and He never ceased being God, Second Person of the Trinity. At His baptism the Holy Spirit descended like a dove, the Father spoke, and the Son was baptized. What further proof is needed to show a threefold unity? Compare the baptism of Christ (Matthew 3:16–17) with the commission to preach in the threefold name of God (Matthew 28:19), and the evidence is clear and undeniable. Even in the Incarnation itself (Luke 1:35) the Trinity appears (see also John 14:16 and 15:26). Of course it is not possible to fathom this great revelation completely, but this we do know: There is a unity of Substance, not three gods, and that unity is One in every sense, which no reasonable person can doubt after surveying the evidence. When Jesus said, "My Father is greater than I," He spoke the truth, for in the form of a servant (Philippians 2:7) and as a man, the Son was subject to the Father willingly; but upon His resurrection and in the radiance of His glory taken again from whence He veiled it (vv. 7–8), He showed forth His deity when He declared, "All authority is surrendered to me in heaven and earth" (Matthew 28:18); proof positive of His intrinsic nature and unity of Substance. It is evident that the Lord Jesus Christ was never inferior—speaking of His nature—to His Father during His sojourn on earth.

Jehovah's Witnesses vs. the Scriptures, Reason, and the Trinity

Every major cult and non-Christian religion that seeks to deride orthodox theology continually attacks the doctrine of the Trinity. Jehovah's Witnesses (the Russellites of today) are the most vehement in this endeavor, and because they couch their clever misuse of terminology in scriptural contexts, they are also the most dangerous. Throughout the whole length and breadth of the Watchtower's turbulent history, one "criterion" has been used in every era to measure the credibility of any biblical doctrine. This "criterion" is *reason*. During the era of "Pastor" Russell, and right through until today, reason has always been "the great god" before whom all followers of the Millennial Dawn[40] movement allegedly bow with unmatched reverence. In fact, the "great paraphraser," as Russell was once dubbed, even went so far as to claim that reason—or the ability to think

---

[40]Name originally given to the movement by Russell in 1886.

and draw conclusions—opened up to the intellect of man the very character of God himself! Think of it—according to the "pastor," God's nature is actually openly accessible to our feeble and erring reasoning powers. In the first volume of the *Millennial Dawn* series (later titled *Studies in the Scriptures*), "Pastor" Russell makes God subject to our powers of reasoning. Wrote the "pastor": "Let us examine the character of the writings claimed as inspired (The Bible), to see whether their teachings correspond with the character we have *reasonably* imputed to God" (p. 41). Here it is plain to see that for Russell, man's understanding of God's character lies not in God's revelation of himself to be taken by faith, but in our ability to reason out that character subject to the laws of our reasoning processes. Russell obviously never considered Jehovah's Word as recorded in the fifty-fifth chapter of Isaiah the prophet, which discourse clearly negates man's powers of reasoning in relation to the divine character and nature of his Creator.

> For my thoughts are not your thoughts, neither are your ways my ways, saith the Lord. For as the heavens are higher than the earth, so are my ways higher than your ways, and my thoughts than your thoughts (Isaiah 55:8–9).

By this statement God certainly did not say reason and thought should be abandoned in the process of inquiry, but merely that no one can know the mind, nature, or thoughts of God in all their fullness, seeing that man is finite and He is infinite. The term "reason" and derivatives of it (reasonable, reasoning, reasoned, etc.) are used eighty-eight times in the English Bible, and only *once* in all these usages (Isaiah 1:18) does God address man. Jehovah's Witnesses maintain that since God said, "Come now and let us reason together," He therefore gave reason a high place, even using it himself to commune with His creatures. While this is true, it is only so in a limited sense at best. God never said, "Reason out the construction of my spiritual substance and nature" or "Limit my character to your reasoning powers." Nevertheless, Jehovah's Witnesses, by making Christ (the Logos, John 1:1) "a god" or "a mighty god," but not "Jehovah God," have done these very things. In the reference quoted above (Isaiah 1:18), Jehovah showed man the way of salvation and invited him to be redeemed from sin. God never invited him to explore His deity or probe into His mind. The apostle Paul says, "For who hath known the mind of the Lord? or who hath been his counsellor? Or who hath first given to him, and it shall be recompensed unto him again? For of him, and through him, and to him, are all things: to whom be glory for ever" (Romans 11:34–36).

But now let us examine this typical propaganda from the Watchtower's arsenal and see if they really do follow "Pastor" Russell and his theory of reason. In this article,[41] "The Scriptures, Reason, and the Trinity," the Witnesses constantly appeal to *reason* as the standard for determining what God thinks. The following are quotations that we believe illustrate this point beyond doubt. In addition, we will compare the statements of this article at strategic points with a much more recent publication, *Should You Believe in the Trinity?*[42] to show that the teaching has remained consistent over time.

---

[41] *The Watchtower* (January 1, 1973).

[42] *Should You Believe in the Trinity?* (Brooklyn: Watchtower Bible and Tract Society, 1989), 15–26.

1. "To hold that Jehovah God the Father and Christ Jesus His Son are co-eternal is to fly in the face of reason" (*Watchtower*). Notice that reason is used as the "yardstick" to determine the validity of a scriptural doctrine. The more recent publication remarks concerning the Trinity: "Is such reasoning hard to follow? Many sincere believers have found it to be confusing, contrary to normal reason, unlike anything in their experience" (*Believe*, electronic version, 1).

2. "Jehovah God says, 'Come now, and let us reason together' (Isaiah 1:18). The advocates of the Trinity admit that it is not subject to reason or logic, and so they resort to terming it a 'mystery.' But the Bible contains no divine mysteries. It contains 'sacred secrets.' Every use of the word 'mystery' and 'mysteries' in the *King James Version* comes from the same Greek root word meaning 'to shut the mouth,' that is to keep secret. There is a vast difference between a secret and a mystery. A secret is merely that which has not been made known, but a mystery is that which cannot be understood.

"However, contending that since the Trinity is such a confusing mystery it must have come from divine revelation creates another major problem. Why? Because divine revelation itself does not allow for such a view of God: 'God is not a God of confusion.' In view of that statement, would God be responsible for a doctrine about himself that is so confusing that even Hebrew, Greek, and Latin scholars cannot really explain it?" (*Believe*, electronic version, 3).

Once again the interested reader must pay close attention to the Witnesses' favorite game of term-switching. *The Watchtower* makes a clever distinction between the term *mystery* and the term *secret* and declares that "the Bible contains no divine mysteries." In view of the seriousness of this Watchtower exercise in semantics, we feel obliged to destroy their manufactured distinction between *secret* and *mystery* by the simple process of consulting the dictionary.

Mystery is defined as (1) "secret, something that is hidden or unknown." *Secret* is defined as (1) "something secret or hidden; mystery." Surely this is proof conclusive that the Bible contains "divine mysteries" as far as the meaning of the term is understood. It must also be equally apparent that Jehovah's Witnesses obviously have no ground for rejecting the word *mystery* where either the Bible or the dictionary is concerned. We fail to note any "vast difference" between the two words, and so does the dictionary. The truth is that the Watchtower rejects the Trinity doctrine and other cardinal doctrines of historical Christianity not because they are mysterious, but because Jehovah's Witnesses are determined to reduce Jesus, the Son of God, to a creature or "a second god," all biblical evidence notwithstanding. They still follow in "Pastor" Russell's footsteps, and one needs no dictionary to substantiate that.

3. "Jehovah God by His Word furnishes us with ample *reasons* and logical bases for all regarding which he expects us to exercise faith. . . . We can make sure of what is right only by a process of reasoning on God's Word."

Here indeed is a prime example of what Jehovah's Witnesses continually represent as sound thinking. They cannot produce even one shred of evidence to bolster up their unscriptural claim that God always gives us reason for those things in which He wants us to "exercise faith." Biblical students (even "International" ones)[43] really grasp at theological straws in the wind when they attempt

---

[43]International Bible Students is one of the other names for Russellism.

to prove so dogmatic and inconclusive a statement. A moment of reflection on the Scriptures will show, we believe, that this attempt to overemphasize reason is a false one.

First, does God give us a reason for creating Lucifer and allowing him to rebel against the Almighty? Is such a reason found in the Scriptures? It is not, and yet we must believe that he exists, that he opposes God, and that all references in the Scriptures to Satan are authoritative. God demands that we exercise faith in their objective truth, yet He *never* gives us a reason for it.

Second, does God anywhere give to man a "reasonable" explanation of how it is possible that He exists in Trinity—as three persons while at the same time retaining oneness of nature and essence? No. Never in Scripture is this explained. Here we see a gross inconsistency of Watchtower reliance upon reason in their rejection of the Trinity. When compared to their acceptance of the miracles of Jesus, one wonders what they consider "reasonable." If they can believe that Jesus raised Lazarus from the dead, changed the water into wine, and fed five thousand with only two fishes and five loaves, *without* a "reasonable" explanation as to "how" He did this, should the "how" of the Trinity be of more difficulty in "reasonableness"? Surely the former is every much as mysterious as the latter!

Third, does God anywhere give the grieving parent who has lost a child a "reasonable" explanation as to the "why"? That certain physical catastrophes can be traced to the results of sin upon mankind, no one will argue. But is God under any obligation to furnish the parent with a "reason" as to why his child *in particular* was taken? No. Never do the Scriptures address the issue. Yet, through it all, God asks us to believe that these seemingly indescribable evils will ultimately work out His divine plan, and He asks us at times to believe in Him *against reason* and with the eyes of faith.

Much, much more could be said along the same lines, but enough has been shown to refute adequately the contention of Jehovah's Witnesses that God *always* gives us "reasons and logical bases" for all regarding which He expects us to exercise faith.

Let us also remember the falsity of their other claim in the same paragraph: "We can make sure of what is right only by a process of reasoning on God's Word." But Jesus said, "The Comforter, which is the Holy Ghost, whom the Father will send in my name, he shall teach you all things, and bring all things to your remembrance, whatsoever I have said unto you" (John 14:26). Now if only by a process of reasoning on God's Word we can make sure of what is right, as Jehovah's Witnesses contend, then Jesus and they are at direct variance, for they do not have the guidance of the Holy Spirit, since they deny His person and deity. In a controversy of this nature, we prefer to choose God and His Word as opposed to the Watchtower's jumbled Russellism.

Fourth, "God, through His Word, appeals to our reason. The Trinity doctrine is a negation of both the Scriptures and reason."

~"We also need to keep in mind that not even so much as one 'proof text' says that God, Jesus, and the holy spirit are one in some mysterious Godhead. Not one scripture anywhere in the bible says that all three are the same in substance, power, and eternity. The Bible is consistent in revealing Almighty God, Jehovah, as alone Supreme, Jesus as his created Son, and the holy spirit as God's active force" (*Believe,* electronic version, 12).~

Like so many other of the Watchtower's clever examples of phraseology, these statements from *The Watchtower* contain a mixture of truth and error, with just enough of the former to make good sense and just enough of the latter to confuse the gullible reader. It is unquestionably true that God through His Word appeals to our reason; were it not so, we could not understand His desires. But by the same token, God does not invite our inquiry into His nature or character. Jehovah's Witnesses, however, if their views are rightly understood, assume that human reason is capable of doing just that.

The Watchtower has never failed to echo the old Arian heresy. This was a theory popularized by Arius of Alexandria (in Egypt) in the fourth century A.D., which taught that Jesus was the first creature, a second and created god, inferior to Jehovah, the Father. It is upon this theological myth, banished from the church in A.D. 325 (along with Arius), that Jehovah's Witnesses unsteadily base their whole system.

~Arius was the most popular proponent of the view that Jesus Christ was created, and it was not until the early church Fathers understood exactly what he was saying that he was uniformly condemned, both at the Council of Nicea in A.D. 325 and in subsequent church rulings. He was condemned because he believed and taught that Jesus Christ was not God, but was created. At the Council of Nicea he declared that the Son of God was a created being, created out of nothing. Accordingly, there was a time when He "was not."[44]~

Jehovah's Witnesses know beyond doubt that if Jesus is Jehovah God, every one of them is going to a flaming hereafter; and hell they fear above all else. This no doubt explains a great deal of their antagonism toward the doctrines of the Trinity and hell. The Witnesses, it must be remembered, consistently berate the Trinity doctrine as of the devil and never tire of proclaiming that the hell of the Bible is the grave. The thought of being punished in unquenchable fire for their disobedience to God is probably the strongest bond holding the Watchtower's flimsy covers together.

Let us further pursue the Watchtower's logic. In *The Watchtower's* article, two other terms are repeated constantly by Jehovah's Witnesses. These terms are *equal* and *coeternal.* The terms are used some six times in this particular article, and each time it is denied that Jesus Christ is either equal to or coeternal with God His Father. Says *The Watchtower:*

> We see God in heaven as the Superior One. . . . We see his Son on earth expressing delight to do his Father's will; clearly two separate and distinct personalities and not at all equal. Nothing here (Matthew 28:18–20) to indicate that it (The Holy Spirit) is a person, let alone that it is equal with Jehovah God. The very fact that the Son received his life from the Father proves that *he could not be coeternal with him.* (John 1:18; 6:57). . . . Nor can it be argued that God was superior to Jesus only because of Jesus then being a human, for *Paul makes clear that Christ Jesus in his prehuman form was not equal with his father.* In Philippians 2:1–11 (NWT)[45] he counsels Christians not to be motivated by egotism but to have lowliness of mind, even as Christ Jesus

---

[44]For further information on this important issue in church history, see Bruce L. Shelley, *Church History in Plain Language* (Dallas: Word Publishing, 1995).

[45]NWT stands for the *New World Translation of the Holy Scriptures* (Brooklyn: Watchtower Bible and Tract Society, 1961, revised edition 1984).

had, who, although existing in God's form before coming to earth was not *ambitious* to become equal with his Father. . . . Jesus did not claim to be *The God*, but *only* God's Son. That Jesus is inferior to his Father, is also apparent. . . . The "Holy Ghost" or Holy Spirit is God's active force. . . . There is no basis for concluding that the Holy Spirit is a person. . . . Yes, the Trinity finds its origin in the pagan concept of a multiplicity, plurality, or pantheon of Gods. The law Jehovah God gave to the Jews stated diametrically the opposite. "Jehovah our God is *one* Jehovah" (Deuteronomy 6:4).

Let us briefly examine these statements of the Jehovah's Witnesses and see if they have any rational content where the Bible is concerned. The Watchtower maintains that Christ and His Father are "not at all equal," which has been their boldest insult to Christianity since Russell and Rutherford concocted and promoted the whole Watchtower nightmare. This type of unbelief where Christ's true deity is concerned has gladdened the hearts of non-intellectuals the country over who find it easier to mock the Trinity than to trust God's Word and His Son. Concerning His relationship with the Father, the apostle John in the fifth chapter of his gospel, the eighteenth verse, when speaking of Jesus and the Jews, said, "Therefore the Jews sought the more to kill him, because he not only had broken the sabbath, but said also God was his Father, making himself *equal* with God." The Greek word for equal is *ison*, which according to *Thayer's Greek Lexicon* (p. 307), an acknowledged authority, means "equal in quality as in quantity, to claim for one's self the nature, rank, authority, which belong to God." Dr. Thayer, Jehovah's Witnesses might take notice, was a Unitarian who denied Christ's deity even as they do; yet, being honest, he gave the true meaning of the biblical terms even though they contradicted his views. Thus God's Word directly contradicts Jehovah's Witnesses, and this they cannot deny.

The Watchtower further contends that since Christ received life from His Father: "I live by the Father" (John 6:57), He could not be coeternal with Him. At first glance this seems plausible, especially when coupled with John 5:26: "As the Father hath life in himself; so hath he given to the Son to have life in himself." However, taking this text in its context we readily see that it cannot mean that Christ derived "eternal existence" from the Father. John 1:1 bears witness that "the Word *was* God"; therefore, eternity was inherent in His makeup by nature. The logical conclusion must be that the indwelling "life" of "God the Word" entered time in the form of "the Son of Man," and by this operation the Father, through the agency of the Holy Spirit, gave the "Son of Man" to have "life in himself," the same life that was eternally His as the eternal Word. But it takes more than a glance to support this garbled Watchtower polytheism, as we shall soon see.

Unwittingly, Jehovah's Witnesses answer their own scriptural double-talk when they quote Philippians 2:5–11. In this passage of Scripture, Paul claims full deity for Christ and maintains that in His preincarnate life He existed "in the form of God" and "thought it not something to be grasped" at to be *equal* with God, but took upon himself the "*form* of a servant, being born in the likeness of men" (RSV). The term *equal* here is another form of *ison*, namely *isa*, which again denotes "absolute sameness of nature," thus confirming Christ's true deity. Further, this context reveals beyond reasonable doubt that *all* references to Christ's being subject to His Father (e.g., John 5:26; 6:57) pertain to His earthly existence, during which "he emptied himself" to become as one of us. This in no way affected His true deity or unity with the Father, for Jesus claimed Jehovahistic identity (John 8:58) when He announced himself to the unbelieving Jews as the "I AM" of Exodus 3:14.

Twice, in the same terms, Jehovah's Witnesses deny what the Scriptures specifically testify, that Christ *is equal* with the Father in essence, character, and nature, which truths the Watchtower's term-switching campaigns can never change.

I should also like to call attention to an extremely bold example of misquoting so commonly found in Watchtower propaganda. On page twenty-two, the Russellite oracle declares, "Paul makes clear that Christ Jesus in his prehuman form was not equal to his Father. In Philippians 2:1–11 (NWT), he counsels Christians not to be motivated by egotism but to have lowliness of mind even as Christ Jesus had, who, although existing in God's form before coming to earth, *was not ambitious to become equal with his Father*."

Now, as far as the original Greek text of Philippians 2:1–11 is concerned, this is an absurd and plainly dishonest statement. Paul never even mentions Christ being ambitious to attain anything at all or even his lack of ambition, since no Greek term there can be translated "ambition." Jehovah's Witnesses themselves do not use the word "ambition" in their own *New World Translation,* nor does any other translator that we know of. Despite this, however, they introduce the word that clouds the real meaning of the Greek terms. Further than this, and worse, the Watchtower plainly attempts to use Paul's declaration of Christ's deity as a means of confusing the issue. They maintain that Paul here taught that Jesus was inferior in nature to His Father, when in reality Paul's entire system of theology says the opposite. If we are to believe the Greek text, Paul declares that Jesus did *not* consider equality with God something "to be grasped after," or "robbery" (Greek *arpazo*), since He previously existed as the eternal Word of God (John 1:1) prior to His incarnation (John 1:14) and as such fully shared all the Father's prerogatives and attributes. Hence, He had no desire to strive for what was His by nature and inheritance. Paul elsewhere calls Christ "all the fullness of the Deity . . . in bodily form" (Colossians 2:9, NIV), "our great God and Savior" (Titus 2:13, RSV), and "God" (Hebrews 1:8). These are just a few of the references; there are at least twenty-five more that could be cited from Paul's writings and over seventy-five from the balance of the New Testament. Contrary to the Watchtower, then, Paul never wrote their Russellite interpretational paraphrase as recorded on page twenty-two, since even the Greek text bears witness against them.

Jehovah's Witnesses sum up another blast at the Trinity doctrine by informing us that John 1:1 should be rendered, "In the beginning was the Word, and the Word was with God, and the Word was *a god*." This is another example of the depths to which the Watchtower will descend to make Jesus "a second god" and thus introduce polytheism into Christianity. Needless to say, no recognized translators in the history of Greek exegesis have ever sanctioned such a grammatical travesty as the Watchtower translation, and the Watchtower translators know it. Such a rendition is an indication of markedly inferior scholarship and finds no basis whatsoever in New Testament Greek grammar. Both James Moffatt and Edgar Goodspeed, liberal translators, render John 1:1: "The Word was Divine," while most acknowledged authorities read it as "The Word was Deity." Moffatt and Goodspeed, however, admit that Scripture teaches the full and equal deity of Jesus Christ, something Jehovah's Witnesses vehemently deny. Beyond doubt the Watchtower of Jehovah's Witnesses presents a strange dilemma, "ever learning, and never able to come to the knowledge of the truth" (2 Timothy 3:7). The Russellite movements (there are other small branches) all cry loudly the old Jewish Shema, "Hear, O Israel: the LORD our God *is* one LORD" (or, "The LORD is One," Deuteronomy 6:4), and attempt to use it against the doctrine of the Trinity. But once again language betrays the shallowness of their resources. The term *echod*, "one" in Hebrew, *does not* denote "absolute unity" in many places throughout the Old Testament, and often it definitely denotes "composite unity," which argues for the Trinity of the Deity (Jehovah).

For example, in the second chapter, twenty-fourth verse of Genesis, the Lord tells us that "a man leave[s] his father and his mother, and shall cleave unto his wife: and they shall be one flesh" (in Hebrew, *bosor echod*). Certainly this does not mean that in marriage a man and his wife become one *person,* but that they become one in the unity of their *substance* and are considered as *one* in the eyes of God. Please note, this is true unity, yet *not solitary,* but *composite unity.*

Let us further consider composite unity. Moses sent twelve spies into Canaan (Numbers 13), and when they returned they brought with them a great cluster of grapes (in Hebrew *eschol echod*). Now, since there were hundreds of grapes on the one stem, it could hardly be absolute or solitary unity, yet again *echod* (one) is used to describe the cluster. This shows conclusively that the grapes were considered "one" in the sense of their being of the same origin; hence, *composite unity* is again demonstrated.

Jehovah's Witnesses continually ask, "If Jesus, when on the cross, was truly an incarnation of Jehovah, then who was in heaven?" This is a logical question to which the eighteenth chapter of Genesis gives fourteen answers, each reaffirming the other. As recorded in Genesis eighteen, Abraham had three visitors. Two of them were angels (Genesis 19:1), but the third he addressed as "Jehovah God"— *fourteen times!* Abraham's third visitor stayed and conversed with him and then departed, saying concerning Sodom, "I will go down now, and see whether they have done altogether according to the cry of it, which is come unto me; and if not, I will know" (18:21). And so, "The LORD went his way, as soon as he had left communing with Abraham: and Abraham returned unto his place" (v. 33).

Now, if the apostle John is to be believed without question, and Jehovah's Witnesses agree that he must be, then "No man hath seen God [the Father] at any time; the only begotten Son [Jesus Christ], which is in the bosom of the Father, he hath declared him" (John 1:18). To further confuse the Witnesses' peculiar view of God as a *solitary unit,* Jesus himself said concerning His Father, "You have neither heard his voice at any time, nor seen his shape. God is a Spirit: and they that worship him must worship him in spirit and in truth" (John 4:24; 5:37).

Now then, here is the evidence. Moses declares that God spoke face-to-face with Abraham (Genesis 17:1), and Jesus and John say, "No man hath seen God at any time." But Jesus makes it clear that He is referring to *the Father,* and so does John. The nineteenth chapter of Genesis, the twenty-fourth verse, solves this problem for us once and for all, as even Jehovah's Witnesses will eventually be forced to admit. Moses here reveals a glimpse of the *composite unity* in the Triune God. "Then the Lord rained upon Sodom and upon Gomorrah brimstone and fire *from the Lord* out of heaven." This is unquestionably the only solution to this dilemma. God the Father rained fire on Sodom and Gomorrah, and God the Son spoke and ate with Abraham and Sarah.

Two persons (the third Person of the Trinity is revealed more fully in the New Testament: John 14:26; 16:7–14; etc.) are both called Jehovah—translated LORD in the KJV—(Genesis 18:20; 19:24; cf. Isaiah 9:6; Micah 5:2), and both are *one (echod) with the Holy Spirit in composite unity* (Deuteronomy 6:4). God the Father was in heaven, God the Son died on the cross, and God the Holy Spirit comforts the church till Jesus shall come again. This is the triune God whom Jehovah's Witnesses are committed to ridicule, berate, and blaspheme in the name of "human reason."

God said in Genesis 1:26, "Let us make man in *our* image, after *our* likeness," not in *my* image, after *my* likeness. Here plurality is seen, for obviously, God is speaking to His coeternal Son (Christ) and addressing *Him* as an *equal.* Genesis 11:7, with reference to the Tower of Babel, also lends strong support to the triune God doctrine. Here, God, speaking as an *equal* to His Son, declares, "Let *us* go down and there confound their language"—again, plurality and *equal* discourse. In the face of all these texts, the Watchtower is strangely silent. They, however, rally afresh to the attack on page twenty-three of their article and declare, "There is no basis for concluding that the Holy Spirit is a person." This is so immature and unskilled an attack that it hardly justifies an effort to refute it.

The fact that the Holy Spirit is referred to as a person in the masculine gender throughout the New Testament, that He also is described as possessing an active *will* ("If I go not away, the Comforter will not come unto you" John 16:7), which is the most concrete trait of a distinct personality, and that He is said to exercise the characteristics of a *teacher* (John 16:8), apparently all falls on deaf ears where the Watchtower is concerned. The literature of Jehovah's Witnesses is also consistently filled with nonsensical questions such as, "How could the one hundred and twenty persons at Pentecost be baptized with a person?" (Acts 1:5; 2:1–4). In answer to this, it evidently escapes the ever-zealous Russellites that the fulfillment of Jesus' prophecy as recorded in Acts 1:5 was explained in chapter 2, verse 4. Luke here says, "And they were all filled [Greek *eplesthesan*] with the Holy Ghost." Jesus all too obviously did not mean that the apostles would be "immersed" in a person, but filled with and immersed in the power of His presence as symbolized in the tongues like unto fire. If Jehovah's Witnesses ever studied the Scriptures in the open with good scholars and stopped masquerading as biblical authorities, which they are not, it might be interesting to see the results. Of course, great scholarship is not necessary to obtain a saving knowledge of Jesus Christ from God's Word; even so, when people deny the historical Christian faith and berate those who profess it, they ought to have some scholastic support, and Jehovah's Witnesses have none.

The Watchtower widely cries that they will meet all persons with an open Bible, but to this date not one of their alleged authorities has materialized despite our numerous invitations. We of orthodox Christianity do not desire to maliciously attack anyone's faith merely for the "joy" of doing it, but we must be faithful to our Lord's command to "preach the word and contend for the faith."

As long as the Watchtower continues to masquerade as a Christian movement and attack, without biblical provocation or cause, orthodox Christian theology with such articles as "The Scripture, Reason, and the Trinity," etc., so long will our voice be raised in answer to their consistent misrepresentations. God granting us the grace, we can do no other but be faithful to Him "who is the faithful and true witness, the *source* through whom God's creation came" (Revelation 3:14, Knox Version)—His eternal Word and beloved Son, Jesus Christ, our Lord.

Jehovah's Witnesses and the Holy Spirit

Though it is rudimentary to any study of the Bible, the personality and deity of the Holy Spirit must constantly be defended against the attacks of the Watchtower.

The Watchtower, as has been seen, denies the Holy Spirit's personality and deity, but the following references, only a few of many in Scripture, refute their stand completely:

(1) *Acts 5:3–4.* In verse 3, Peter accuses Ananias of lying *to* the Holy Spirit, and in verse 4, he declares the Holy Spirit to be God, an equation hard for the Watchtower to explain, much less deny. Who else but a person can be lied to?

(2) *Acts 13:2, 4.* In this context the Holy Spirit *speaks* and *sends,* as He does in 21:10–11, where He *prophesies* Paul's imprisonment. Only a personality can do these things, *not* "an invisible active force," as the Jehovah's Witnesses describe Him.

(3) Finally, such references as *John 14:16–17, 26; 16:7–14* need no comment. *He* is a divine person and He is God (Genesis 1:2).

The New World Translation of the Bible

In any dealings one may have with the Watchtower or its numerous representatives, it is a virtual certainty that sooner or later in the course of events the Watchtower's "translation" of the Bible will confront the average prospective convert. This translation of the entire Bible is called the *New World Translation of the Holy Scriptures.* It is usually abbreviated as NWT.

First published in part in 1950 and later revised several times (1951, 1961, 1984), the New Testament version of this translation sold over 480,000 copies before its initial revision, and the entire Bible has now sold tens of millions of copies. This version lies behind a thin veneer of scholarship, which proclaims the Society's daring and boldness in a field into which all informed scholars know Jehovah's Witnesses are almost totally unprepared to venture.

Their translation has had wide distribution on all six continents. Jehovah's Witnesses boast that it is "the work of competent scholars" and further declare that it gives clarity to the Scriptures that other translations have somehow failed to supply. Such stupendous claims by the Watchtower involve the necessity of a careful examination of their work so that it may be weighed by the standards of sound biblical scholarship. An exhaustive analysis of this volume is impossible in this limited space, but we have selected some of the outstanding examples of fraud and deceit from the *New World Translation.* These examples should discourage any fair-minded individual from placing much value upon the Jehovah's Witnesses' Bible.

In their foreword to the *New World Translation of the Christian Greek Scriptures* (NWTCGS—published before the whole Bible appeared in 1950), the translation committee of the Watchtower cleverly claims for itself and its translation a peculiar freedom from what they define as "the misleading influence of religious traditions, which have their roots in paganism" (p. 7). This "influence," the Watchtower insists, has colored the inspired Word of God, so it is necessary for them, Jehovah's chosen theocratic representatives, to set aright the numerous alleged examples of "human traditionalism" (p. 6) evidenced in all translations from John Wycliffe's to the present. Should anyone question that this arrogant attitude is the true Watchtower position regarding other translations, the following quote from the foreword to the NWTCGS will dismiss all doubt:

> But honesty compels us to remark that, while each of them has its points of merit, they have fallen victim to the power of human traditionalism in varying degrees. Consequently, religious traditions, hoary with age, have been taken for granted and gone unchallenged and uninvestigated. These have been interwoven into the translations to color the thought. In support of a preferred religious view, an inconsistency and unreasonableness have been insinuated into the teachings of the inspired writings.
>
> The Son of God taught that the traditions of creed-bound men made the commandments and teachings of God of no power and effect. The endeavor of the New World Bible Translation committee has been to avoid this snare of religious traditionalism. (p. 6)

From this pompous pronouncement it is only too evident that the Watchtower considers its "scholars" the superiors of such great scholars as Wycliffe and Tyndale, not to mention the hundreds of brilliant, consecrated Christian scholars who produced the subsequent orthodox translations. Such a pretext is, of course, too absurd to merit refutation, but let it be remembered that the New World Bible translation committee had no known translators with recognized degrees in Greek or Hebrew exegesis or translation. In fact, Frederick W. Franz, then representing the translation committee and later serving as the Watchtower Society's fourth president, admitted under oath that he could not translate Genesis 2:4 from the Hebrew.

From the Pursur's Proof of the cross-examination held on Wednesday, November 24, 1954 (p. 7, paragraphs A–B), examining Frederick W. Franz, vice-president of the Watchtower Bible and Tract Society and sent as representative of the Society and the Translation Communications:

Q: Have you also made yourself familiar with Hebrew?
A: (Franz) Yes.
Q: So that you have a substantial linguistic apparatus at your command?
A: Yes, for use in my biblical work.
Q: I think you are able to read and follow the Bible in Hebrew, Greek, Latin, Spanish, Portuguese, German, and French?
A: Yes.
Later, during the same cross-examination:
Q: You, yourself, read and speak Hebrew, do you?
A: I do not speak Hebrew.

Q: You do not?
A: No.
Q: Can you, yourself, translate that into Hebrew?
A: Which?
Q: That fourth verse of the second chapter of Genesis.
A: You mean here?
Q: Yes.
A: No.

We asked a Hebrew teacher at Biola University/Talbot Theological Seminary if the fourth verse of the second chapter of Genesis was a particularly difficult verse to translate. After all, the pursur's question would hardly have been fair if it were the hardest verse in the Old Testament to translate. The professor said that he would never pass a first-year Hebrew student who could not translate that verse. This is an example of the "scholarship" backing the NWT.

However, the Watchtower "translation" speaks for itself and shows more clearly than pen can the scholastic dishonesty and lack of scholarship so rampant within its covers. In order to point out these glaring inconsistencies, the author has listed five prime examples of the Watchtower's inaccuracies in translating the New Testament.

The Watchtower's Scriptural Distortions

1. The first major perversion that Jehovah's Witnesses attempt to foist upon the minds of the average reader is that it has remained for them as "God's true Witnesses" to restore the divine Old Testament name *Jehovah* to the text of the Greek New Testament. But let us observe this pretext as they stated it in their own words:

> The evidence is, therefore, that the original text of the Christian Greek Scriptures has been tampered with, the same as the text of the LXX [the Septuagint—a Greek translation of the Old Testament] has been. And, at least from the third century A.D. onward, the divine name in tetragrammaton [the Hebrew consonants *YHWH*, usually rendered "Jehovah"] form has been eliminated from the text by copyists. . . . In place of it they substituted the words *kyrios* (usually translated "the Lord") and *theos*, meaning "God" (p. 18).

The "evidence" that the Witnesses refer to is a papyrus roll of the LXX, which contains the second half of the book of Deuteronomy and which does have the tetragrammaton throughout. Further than this, the Witnesses refer to Aquila (A.D. 128) and Origen (ca. A.D. 250), who both utilized the tetragrammaton in their respective *Version* and *Hexapla*. Jerome, in the fourth century, also mentioned the tetragrammaton as appearing in certain Greek volumes even in his day. On the basis of this small collection of fragmentary "evidence," Jehovah's Witnesses conclude their argument:

> It proves that the original LXX did contain the divine name wherever it occurred in the Hebrew original. Considering it a sacrilege to use some substitute such as *kyrios* or *theos*, the scribes inserted the tetragrammaton at

its proper place in the Greek version text. (p. 12)

The whole case the Witnesses try to prove is that the original LXX and the New Testament autographs all used the tetragrammaton (p. 18), but owing to "tampering" all these were changed; hence, their responsibility to restore the divine name. Such is the argument, and a seemingly plausible one to those not familiar with the history of manuscripts and the Witnesses' subtle use of terms.

To explode this latest Watchtower pretension of scholarship completely is an elementary task. It can be shown from literally thousands of copies of the Greek New Testament that not *once* does the tetragrammaton appear, not even in Matthew, which was possibly written in Hebrew or Aramaic originally, therefore making it more prone than all the rest to have traces of the divine name in it—yet it does not! Beyond this, the roll of papyrus (LXX) that contains the latter part of Deuteronomy and the divine name only proves that one copy did have the divine name (*YHWH*), whereas all other existing copies use *kyrios* and *theos*, which the Witnesses claim are "substitutes." The testimonies of Aquila, Origen, and Jerome, in turn, only show that *sometimes* the divine name was used, but the general truth upheld by all scholars is that the Septuagint, with minor exceptions, always uses *kyrios* and *theos* in place of the tetragrammaton, and the New Testament never uses it at all. Relative to the nineteen "sources" the Watchtower uses (pp. 30–33) for restoring the tetragrammaton to the New Testament, it should be noted that they are all translations from Greek (which uses *kyrios* and *theos*, not the tetragrammaton) back into Hebrew, the earliest of which is A.D. 1385, and therefore they are of no value as evidence.

These cold logical facts unmask once and for all the shallow scholarship of Jehovah's Witnesses, whose arrogant pretension that they have a sound basis for restoring the divine name (Jehovah) to the Scriptures while inferring that orthodoxy suppressed it centuries ago is revealed to be a hollow scholastic fraud. ~The Watchtower itself admits, "But apart from [the use of "Jah" in "Hallelujah" in the book of Revelation], no ancient Greek manuscript that we possess today of the books from Matthew to Revelation contains God's name [the tetragrammaton] in full."[46]~

No reasonable scholar, of course, objects to the use of the term *Jehovah* in the Bible. But since only the Hebrew consonants *YHWH* appear without vowels, pronunciation is at best uncertain, and dogmatically to settle on *Jehovah* is straining at the bounds of good linguistics. When the Witnesses arrogantly claim then to have "restored" the divine name (Jehovah), it is almost pathetic. All students of Hebrew know that any vowel can be inserted between the consonants (*YHWH* or *JHVH*), so that theoretically the divine name could be any combination from JoHeVaH to JiHiViH without doing violence to the grammar of the language in the slightest degree. So much then for this, another empty claim of the Watchtower's pseudoscholars.

2. *Colossians 1:16.* "By means of him all [other][47] things were created in the heavens and upon the earth, the things visible and the things invisible, no matter whether they are thrones or lordships or governments or authorities" (NWT).

---

[46] *The Divine Name That Will Endure* (Brooklyn: Watchtower Bible and Tract Society, 1997), electronic version.
[47] Brackets are part of the NWT text itself.

In this particular rendering, Jehovah's Witnesses attempt one of the cleverest perversions of the New Testament texts that the author has ever seen. Knowing full well that the word *other* does not occur in this text, or, for that matter, in any of the three verses (16, 17, 19) where it has been added, albeit in brackets, the Witnesses deliberately insert it into the translation in a vain attempt to make Christ a creature and one of the "things" Jehovah is spoken of as having created.

Attempting to justify this unheard-of travesty upon the Greek language and also upon simple honesty, the New World Bible Translation committee enclosed each added "other" in brackets, which are said by them to "enclose words inserted to complete or clarify the sense in the English text."[48] Far from *clarifying* God's Word here, these unwarranted additions serve only to further the erroneous presupposition of the Watchtower that our Lord Jesus Christ is a creature rather than the Eternal Creator.

The entire context of Colossians 1:15–22 is filled with superlatives in its description of the Lord Jesus as the "image of the invisible God, the first begetter [or 'original bringer forth'—Erasmus] of every creature." The apostle Paul lauds the Son of God as *Creator* of all things (v. 16) and describes Him as existing "before all things" and as the one by whom "all things consist" (v. 17). This is in perfect harmony with the entire picture Scripture paints of the eternal Word of God (John 1:1), who was made flesh (John 1:14) and of whom it was written: "All things were made by him; and without him was not any thing made that was made" (John 1:3). The writer of the book of Hebrews also pointed out that God's Son "[upholds] all things by the word of his power" (Hebrews 1:3) and that He is Deity in all its fullness, even as Paul wrote to the Colossians: "For . . . in him should all fullness [of God] dwell" (Colossians 1:19).

The Scriptures, therefore, bear unmistakable testimony to the creative activity of God's Son, distinguishing Him from among the "things" created, as *the* Creator and Sustainer of "all things."

Jehovah's Witnesses, therefore, have no conceivable ground for this dishonest rendering of Colossians 1:16–17 and 19 by the insertion of the word *other,* since they are supported by no grammatical authorities, nor do they dare to dispute their perversions with competent scholars lest they further parade their obvious ignorance of Greek exegesis.

3. *Matthew 27:50.* "Again Jesus cried out with a loud voice, and yielded up his breath" (NWT).

Luke 23:46. "And Jesus called with a loud voice and said: Father, into your hands I entrust my spirit" (NWT).

For many years the Watchtower has been fighting a vain battle to redefine biblical terms to suit their peculiar theological interpretations. They have had some measure of success in this attempt in that they have taught the rank and file a new meaning for tried and true biblical terms, and it is this trait of their deceptive system that we analyze now in connection with the above quoted verses.

The interested student of Scripture will note from Matthew 27:50 and Luke 23:46 that they are parallel passages describing the same event, namely, the crucifixion of Jesus Christ. In Matthew's account, the Witnesses had no difficulty substituting the word *breath* for the Greek *spirit* (*pneuma*), for in their vocabulary

---

[48] *New World Translation,* Foreword, 6.

this word has many meanings, none of them having any bearing upon the general usage of the term; i.e., that of an immaterial, cognizant nature, inherent in man by definition and descriptive of angels through Creation. Jehovah's Witnesses reject this immaterial nature in man and call it "breath," "life," "mental disposition," or "something windlike." In fact, they will call it anything but what God's Word says it is, an invisible nature, eternal by Creation, a spirit, made in the image of God (Genesis 1:27). Sometimes, and in various contexts, spirit (*pneuma*) can mean some of the things the Witnesses hold, but context determines translation, along with grammar, and their translations quite often do not remain true to either.

Having forced the word *breath* into Matthew's account of the crucifixion to make it appear that Jesus only stopped breathing and did not yield up His invisible nature upon dying, the Witnesses plod on to Luke's account, only to be caught in their own trap. Luke, learned scholar and master of Greek that he was, forces the Witnesses to render his account of Christ's words, using the correct term *spirit* (*pneuma*), instead of *breath* as in Matthew 27:50. Thus in one fell swoop the entire Watchtower fabric of manufactured terminology collapses, because Jesus would hardly have said, "Father, into thy hands I commit my *breath*"—yet if the Witnesses are consistent, which they seldom are, why did they not render the identical Greek term (*pneuma*) as "breath" both times, for it is a parallel account of the same scene!

The solution to this question is quite elementary, as all can clearly see. The Witnesses could not render it "breath" in Luke and get away with it, so they used it where they could and hoped nobody would notice either it or the different rendering in Matthew. The very fact that Christ dismissed His spirit proves the survival of the human spirit beyond the grave, or as Solomon so wisely put it: "Then shall the dust return to the earth as it was: and the spirit shall return unto God who gave it" (Ecclesiastes 12:7).

4. *Philippians 1:21–23.* "For in my case to live is Christ, and to die, gain. Now if it be to live on in the flesh, this is a fruitage of my work—and yet which thing to select I do not know. I am under pressure from these two things; but what I do desire is the releasing and the being with Christ, for this, to be sure, is far better" (NWT).

In common with other cults that teach soul-sleep after the death of the body, Jehovah's Witnesses translate texts contradicting this view to suit their own ends, a prime example of which is their rendering of Philippians 1:21–23. To anyone possessing even a cursory knowledge of Greek grammar, the translation "but what I do desire is the releasing" (v. 23) signifies either a woeful ignorance of the rudiments of the language or a deliberate, calculated perversion of terminology for a purpose or purposes most questionable.

It is no coincidence that this text is a great "proof" passage for the expectation of every true Christian who after death goes to be with the Lord (2 Corinthians 5:8). Jehovah's Witnesses realize that if this text goes unchanged or unchallenged it utterly destroys their Russellite teaching that the soul becomes extinct at the death of the body. This being the case, and since they could not challenge the text without exploding the myth of their acceptance of the Bible as the final authority, the Watchtower committee chose to alter the passage in question, give it a new interpretation, and remove this threat to their theology.

The rendering, "but what I do desire is the releasing," particularly the last word, is a gross imposition on the principles of sound Greek exegesis, because the untutored Russellites have rendered the first aorist active infinitive of the verb *analuo* (*analusai*) as substantive, ("the releasing"), which in this context is unscholarly and atrocious Greek. In order to translate it "the releasing," the form would have to be the participle construction (*analusas*), which when used with the word *wish* or *desire* denotes "a great longing" or "purpose" and must be rendered "to depart" or "to unloose." (See Thayer; Liddell and Scott; Strong, Young, and A. T. Robertson.)

Quite frankly, it might appear that I have gone to a great deal of trouble simply to refute the wrong usage of a Greek form, but in truth this "simple" switching of terms is used by the Witnesses in an attempt to teach that Paul meant something entirely different from what he wrote to the Philippians. To see how the Watchtower manages this, I quote from their own appendix to the *New World Translation of the Christian Greek Scriptures* (pp. 780–81):

> The verb *a-na-ly'sai* is used as a verbal noun here. It occurs only once more in the *Christian Greek Scriptures,* and that is at Luke 12:36, where it refers to Christ's return. The related noun (*a-na'-ly-sis*) occurs but once, at 2 Timothy 4:6, where the apostle says: "The due time for my releasing is imminent." . . . But here at Philippians 1:23 we have not rendered the verb as "returning" or "departing," but as "releasing." The reason is, that the word may convey two thoughts, the apostle's own releasing to be with Christ at his return and also the Lord's releasing himself from the heavenly restraints and returning as he promised.
>
> In no way is the apostle here saying that immediately at his death he would be changed into spirit and would be with Christ forever. . . . It is to this return of Christ and the apostle's releasing to be always with the Lord that Paul refers at Philippians 1:23. He says there that two things are immediately possible for him, namely, (1) to live on in the flesh and (2) to die. Because of the circumstances to be considered, he expressed himself as being under pressure from these two things, not knowing which thing to choose as proper. Then he suggests a third thing, and this thing he really desires. There is no question about his desire for this thing as preferable, namely, the releasing, for it means his being with Christ.
>
> The expression *tou a-na-ly'-sai,* or *the releasing* cannot therefore be applied to the apostle's death as a human creature and his departing thus from this life. It must refer to the events at the time of Christ's return and second presence, that is to say, his second coming and the rising of all those dead in Christ to be with him forevermore.

Here, after much grammatical intrigue, we have the key as to why the Witnesses went to so much trouble to render "depart" as "releasing." By slipping in this grammatical error, the Watchtower hoped to "prove" that Paul wasn't really discussing his impending death and subsequent reunion with Christ at all (a fact every major biblical scholar and translator in history has held), but a *third* thing, namely, "the events at the time of Christ's return and second presence." With breathtaking dogmatism, the Witnesses claim that "*the releasing* cannot therefore be applied to the apostle's death. . . . It must refer to the events at the time of Christ's return."

Words fail when confronted with this classic example of unparalleled deceit, which finds no support in any Greek text or exegetical grammatical authority. Contrary to the Watchtower's statement that "the word may convey two thoughts, the apostle's own releasing to be with Christ at his return and also the Lord's releasing himself from the heavenly restraints and returning as he promised," as a matter of plain exegetical fact, Christ's return is not even the subject of discussion—rather it is the apostle's death and his concern for the Philippians that are here portrayed. That Paul never expected to "sleep" in his grave until the resurrection as Jehovah's Witnesses maintain is evident by the twenty-first verse of the chapter, literally: "For me to live is Christ, and to die is gain." There would be no gain in dying if men slept till the resurrection, for "[God] is not the God of the dead, but the God of the living" (Mark 12:27). Clearly, Paul was speaking of but two things: his possible death and subsequent presence with the Lord (2 Corinthians 5:8), and also the possibility of his continuing on in the body, the latter being "more needful" for the Philippian Christians. His choice, in his own words, was between these two (1:23), and Jehovah's Witnesses have gone to great trouble for nothing; the Greek text still records faithfully what the inspired apostle said—not what the Watchtower maintains he said, all their deliberate trickery to the contrary.

Concluding our comments upon these verses in Philippians, we feel constrained to point out a final example of Watchtower dishonesty relative to Greek translation.

On page 781 of the *New World Translation of the Christian Greek Scriptures,* it will be recalled that the committee wrote: "The expression *tou a-na-ly'-sai,* or *the releasing* cannot therefore be applied to the apostle's death as a human creature and his departing thus from this life."

If the interested reader will turn to page 626 of the same Watchtower translation, he will observe that in 2 Timothy 4:6 the Witnesses once more use the term *releasing* (*analuseos*), where all translators are agreed that it refers to Paul's impending death. The *Revised Standard Version,* often appealed to by Jehovah's Witnesses, puts it this way: "For I am already on the point of being sacrificed; the time of my departure has come." (See also *An American Translation* [Goodspeed]; *Authorized Version*; J. N. Darby's Version; James Moffatt's Version; J. B. Rotherham's Version; *Douay Version* [Roman Catholic]; etc.)

Jehovah's Witnesses themselves render the text: "For I am already being poured out like a drink offering, and the due time for my *releasing* is imminent" (2 Timothy 4:6, NWT).

Now, since it is admitted by the Witnesses, under the pressure of every translator's rendering of his text, that this verse refers to Paul's death, and further, since the noun form of the Greek word (*analuseos*) is here used and translated "releasing," why is it that they claim on page 781 that this expression "*the releasing*" (*analusai*—Philippians 1:23) "cannot therefore be applied to the apostle's death as a human creature and his departing thus from this life"? The question becomes more embarrassing when it is realized that Jehovah's Witnesses themselves admit that these two forms (*analusai* and *analuseos*) are "related" (p. 781). Hence, they have no excuse for maintaining in one place (Philippians 1:23) that "the releasing" cannot refer to the apostle's death, and in another place (2 Timothy 4:6) using a form of the same word and allowing that it does refer to his death. This one illustration alone should serve to warn all honest people of the blatant deception employed in the Watchtower's "translations," a term not worthy of application in many, many places.

5. *Matthew 24:3.* "While he was sitting upon the mount of Olives, the disciples approached him privately, saying: 'Tell us, When will these things be, and what will be the sign of your presence and of the conclusion of the system of things?' "(NWT).

Since the days of "Pastor" Russell and Judge Rutherford, one of the favorite dogmas of the Watchtower has been that of the *parousia*, the Second Coming or "presence" of the Lord Jesus Christ. Jehovah's Witnesses, loyal Russellites that they are, have tenaciously clung to the "pastor's" theology in this respect and maintain that in the year A.D. 1914, when the "times of the Gentiles" ended (according to Russell), the "second presence" of Christ began. (See *Make Sure of All Things*, 319.)

From the year 1914 onward, the Witnesses maintain,

> Christ has turned his attention toward earth's affairs and is dividing the peoples and educating the true Christians in preparation for their survival during the great storm of Armageddon, when all unfaithful mankind will be destroyed from the face of the earth. (p. 319)

For Jehovah's Witnesses, then, Christ is not coming; He is already here! (A.D. 1914)—only invisibly—and He is directing His activities through His theocratic organization in Brooklyn, New York. In view of this claim, it might be well to hearken unto the voice of Matthew who wrote,

> Then if any man shall say unto you, Lo, here is Christ, or there; believe it not. For there shall arise false Christs, and false prophets, and shall shew great signs and wonders; insomuch that, if it were possible, they shall deceive the very elect. Behold, I have told you before. Wherefore if they shall say unto you, Behold, he is in the desert; go not forth: behold, he is in the secret chambers; believe it not. For as the lightning cometh out of the east, and shineth even unto the west; so shall also the coming of the Son of man be. (Matthew 24:23–27)

Jehovah's Witnesses, on page 780 of their *New World Translation of the Christian Greek Scriptures*, list the twenty-four occurrences of the Greek word *parousia*, which they translate each time as "presence." They give the following defense found on page 779:

> The tendency of many translators is to render it here "coming" or "arrival." But throughout the 24 occurrences of the Greek word *parousia* . . . we have consistently rendered it "presence." From the comparison of the *parousia* of the Son of man with the days of Noah at Matthew 24:37–39, it is very evident that the meaning of the word is as we have rendered it. And from the contrast that is made between the presence and the absence of the apostle both at 2 Corinthians 10:10–11 and at Philippians 2:12, the meaning of *parousia* is so plain that it is beyond dispute by other translators.

Following this gigantic claim, namely, that their translation of the word *parousia* is "beyond dispute by other translators," the "theocratic authorities" proceed to list the verses in question.

Now, the main issue is not the translation of *parousia* as "presence," because in some contexts it is certainly allowable (see 1 Corinthians 16:17; 2 Corinthians 7:6–7; 10:10; and Philippians 1:26; 2:12). But there are other contexts where it cannot be allowed in the way Jehovah's Witnesses use it, because it not only violates the contextual meaning of the word but the entire meaning of the passages as always held by the Christian church.

Jehovah's Witnesses claim scholarship for this blanket translation of *parousia*, yet not one great scholar in the history of Greek exegesis and translation has ever held this view. Since 1871, when "Pastor" Russell produced this concept, it has been denounced by every competent scholar upon examination.

The reason this Russellite rendering is so dangerous is that it attempts to prove that *parousia* in regard to Christ's second advent really means that His return or "presence" was to be invisible and unknown to all but "the faithful" (Russellites, of course). (See *Make Sure of All Things*, 319–23.)

The *New World* translators, therefore, on the basis of those texts where it is acceptable to render *parousia* "presence," conclude that it must be acceptable in all texts. But while it appears to be acceptable grammatically, no one but Jehovah's Witnesses or their sympathizers accept the *New World Translation's* blanket use of "presence," be the translators Christian or not. It simply is not good grammar, and it will not stand up under comparative exegesis as will be shown. To conclude that "presence" necessarily implies invisibility is also another flaw in the Watchtower's argument, for in numerous places where they render *parousia* "presence," the persons spoken of were hardly invisible. (See again 1 Corinthians 16:17; 2 Corinthians 7:6–7 and 10:10; Philippians 1:26 and 2:12.)

If the Watchtower were to admit for one moment that *parousia* can be translated "coming" or "arrival" in the passages that speak of Christ's return the way all scholarly translators render it, then "Pastor" Russell's "invisible presence" of Christ would explode in their faces. Hence, their determination to deny what all recognized Greek authorities have established.

The late Dr. Joseph H. Thayer, a Unitarian scholar, translator/editor of one of the best lexicons of the Greek New Testament (who, incidentally, denied the visible second coming of Christ), said on page 490 of that work, when speaking of *parousia*: "a return (Philippians 1:26). . . . In the New Testament, especially of the Advent, i.e., the future visible return from heaven of Jesus, the Messiah, to raise the dead, hold the last judgment, and set up formally and gloriously the Kingdom of God." (For further references, see Liddell and Scott, Strong, and any other reputable authority.)

Dr. Thayer, it might be mentioned, was honest enough to say what the New Testament Greek taught, even though he didn't believe it. One could wish that Jehovah's Witnesses were at least that honest, but they are not.

In concluding this discussion of the misuse of *parousia*, we shall discuss the verses Jehovah's Witnesses use to "prove" that Christ's return was to be an invisible "presence" instead of a visible, glorious, verifiable event.

The following references and their headings were taken from the book *Make Sure of All Things*, published by the Watchtower as an official guide to their doctrine.

(1) "Angels Testified at Jesus' Ascension as a Spirit that Christ Would Return in Like Manner, Quiet, Unobserved by the Public" (p. 320).

And after he had said these things while they [only the disciples] were looking on, he was lifted up and a cloud caught him up from their vision. . . . "Men of Galilee, why do you stand looking into the sky? This Jesus who was received up from you into the sky will come thus in the same manner as you have beheld him going into the sky" (Acts 1:9, 11 NWT).

It is quite unnecessary to refute in detail this open perversion of a clear biblical teaching because, as John 20:27 clearly shows, Christ was not a spirit and did not ascend as one. The very text they quote shows that the disciples were "looking on" and saw him "lifted up and a cloud caught him up from their vision" (v. 9). They could hardly have been looking at a spirit, which by definition is incorporeal,[49] not with human eyes at least, and Christ had told them once before, "Behold my hands and my feet, that it is I myself: handle me, and see; for a spirit hath not flesh and bones, as ye see me have" (Luke 24:39).

So it remains for Christ himself to denounce the Russellite error that He "ascended as a spirit." Moreover, since He left the earth visibly from the Mount of Olives, it is certain that He will return visibly even as the Scriptures teach (see Matthew 26:63–64; Daniel 7:13–14; Revelation 1:7–8; Matthew 24:7–8, 30).

(2) "Christ's Return Invisible, as He Testified That Man Would Not See Him Again in Human Form" (p. 321).

A little longer and the world will behold me no more (John 14:19 NWT). For I say to you, You will by no means see me from henceforth until you say, "Blessed is he that comes in Jehovah's name!" (Matthew 23:39 NWT).

These two passages in their respective contexts give no support to the Russellite doctrine of an invisible "presence" of Christ for two very excellent reasons:

(a) John 14:19 refers to Christ's anticipated death and resurrection—the "yet a little while" He made reference to could only have referred to His resurrection and subsequent ascension (Acts 1:9–11), before which time and during the period following His resurrection He appeared only to believers, not the world (or unbelievers), hence the clear meaning of His words. Jesus never said that *no one* would ever "see Him again in human form" as the Watchtower likes to make out. Rather, in the same chapter (John 14, emphasis added) He promised to "*come again*, and receive you unto myself; that where I am, there ye may be also" (v. 3, emphasis added). The Bible also is quite clear in telling us that one day by His grace alone "we shall be like him; for we shall *see* him as he is" (1 John 3:2, emphasis added). So the Watchtower once more is forced into silence by the voice of the Holy Spirit.

(b) This second text, Matthew 23:39, really proves nothing at all for the Watchtower's faltering arguments except that Jerusalem will never see Christ again until it blesses Him in repentance as the Anointed of God. Actually the text hurts the Russellite position, for it teaches that Christ will be visible at His coming, else they could not see Him to bless Him in the name of the Lord. Christ also qualified the statement with the word *until*, a definite reference to His *visible* second advent (Matthew 24:30).

---

[49]Even angels have to take a human form in order to be seen (Genesis 19:1–2).

(3) "Early Christians Expected Christ's Return to Be Invisible. Paul Argued There Was Insufficient Evidence in Their Day" (p. 321).

> However, brothers, respecting the presence of our Lord Jesus Christ and our being gathered together to him, we request of you not to be quickly shaken from your reason nor to be excited either through an inspired expression or through a verbal message or through a letter as though from us, to the effect that the day of Jehovah is here. Let no one seduce you in any manner, because it will not come unless the apostasy comes first and the man of lawlessness gets revealed, the son of destruction (2 Thessalonians 2:1–3 NWT).

This final example from Second Thessalonians most vividly portrays the Witnesses at their crafty best, as they desperately attempt to make Paul teach what in all his writings he most emphatically denied, namely, that Christ would come *invisibly* for His saints.

In his epistle to Titus, Paul stressed the importance of "looking for that blessed hope, and the glorious appearing of the great God and our Savior Jesus Christ" (2:13), something he would not have been looking for if it was to be a secret, invisible *parousia* or "presence."

Paul, contrary to the claims of Jehovah's Witnesses, never believed in an invisible return, nor did any bona fide member of the Christian church up until the fantasies of Charles Taze Russell and his *parousia* nightmare, as a careful look at Paul's first epistle to the Thessalonians plainly reveals. Said the inspired apostle:

> For this we say unto you by the word of the Lord, that we which are alive and remain unto the *coming* of the Lord shall not prevent them which are asleep.
> For the Lord himself shall *descend* from heaven [visible] with a shout [audible], with the voice of the archangel, and with the trump of God: and the dead in Christ shall rise first. (4:15–16)

Here we see that in perfect accord with Matthew 26 and Revelation 1, Christ is pictured as *coming* visibly, and in this context no reputable Greek scholar alive will allow the use of "presence"; it must be "coming." (See also 2 Thessalonians 2:8.)

For further information relative to this subject, consult any standard concordance or Greek lexicon available, and trace Paul's use of the word *coming*. This will convince any fair-minded person that Paul never entertained the Watchtower's fantastic view of Christ's invisible return.

These things being clearly understood, the interested reader should give careful attention to those verses in the New Testament that do not use the word *parousia* but are instead forms of the verb *elthon* and those related to the word *erchomai* (see Thayer, 250ff.) and which refer to the Lord's coming as a visible manifestation. These various texts cannot be twisted to fit the Russellite pattern of "presence," since *erchomai* means "to come," "to appear," "to arrive," etc., in the most definite sense of the term. (For reference, check Matthew 24:30 in conjunction with Matthew 26:64—*erchomenon*; also John 14:3—*echomai*; and Revelation 1:7—*erchetai*.)

Once it is perceived that Jehovah's Witnesses are only interested in what they can make the Scriptures say, and not in what the Holy Spirit has already perfectly revealed, then the careful student will reject entirely Jehovah's Witnesses and their Watchtower "translation." These are as "blind leaders of the blind" (Matthew 15:14), "turning the grace of God into lasciviousness, and denying the only Lord God, and our Lord Jesus Christ" (Jude 4). Further, that they wrest the Scriptures unto their own destruction (2 Peter 3:16), the foregoing evidence has thoroughly revealed for all to judge.

~Recently the Jehovah's Witnesses "reinterpreted" their prophetic scheme to downplay the significance of 1914. As the Watchtower Society approached the new millennium, it had to somehow account for the fact that the Battle of Armageddon had yet to occur, even though, according to the Society's interpretation, it was supposed to happen within the lifetime of those born by 1914.

For decades the *Awake!* masthead contained the statement, "Most important, this magazine builds confidence in the Creator's promise of a peaceful and secure new world *before the generation that saw the events of 1914 passes away.*" However, the November 8, 1995, issue (as well as all subsequent issues) states, "Most important, this magazine builds confidence in the Creator's promise of a peaceful and secure new world *that is about to replace the present wicked lawless system of things*" (emphasis added). This is but the latest in a multitude of reinterpretations by the Watchtower to extend their erroneous end-times scenario into successive decades as their "prophetic" prowess fails. Following is a chart that shows the successive replacement teachings of the Watchtower over the years.

Teaching	Statement	Source
"Beginning of the End" in 1799 (later changed to 1914).	"1799 definitely marks the beginning of 'the time of the end.' . . . 'The time of the end' embraces a period from A.D. 1799, as above indicated, to the time of the complete overthrow of Satan's empire. . . . We have been in 'the time of the end' since 1799."	*The Harp of God* (1928 ed.): 235–36, 239.
Christ's "Invisible Presence" begins in 1874 (later changed to 1914).	"The time of the Lord's second presence dates from 1874. . . . From 1874 forward is the latter part of the period of 'the time of the end.' From 1874 is the time of the Lord's second presence."	*The Harp of God*, 236, 239–40.
The Battle of Armageddon ends in 1914 (later changed to "still future").	"The 'battle of the great day of God Almighty' (Rev. 16:14), which will end in A.D. 1914 with the complete overthrow of earth's present rulership, is already commenced."	Charles Taze Russell, *The Time Is at Hand*, 101.

The Battle of Armageddon will end shortly after 1914.	"In the year 1918, when God destroys the churches wholesale and the church members by millions, it shall be that any that escape shall come to the works of Pastor Russell to learn the meaning of the downfall of 'Christianity.' "	Charles Taze Russell, *The Finished Mystery* (1917 ed.), 485.
The Battle of Armageddon will come around 1925.	"The date 1925 is even more distinctly indicated by the Scriptures because it is fixed by the law God gave to Israel. Viewing the present situation in Europe, one wonders how it will be possible to hold back the explosion much longer; and that even before 1925 the great crisis will be reached and probably passed."	*The Watch Tower* (July 15, 1924): 211.
1914 is the starting date for the last generation before the Battle of Armageddon.	"The thirty-six intervening years since 1914, instead of postponing Armageddon, have only made it nearer than most people think. Do not forget: 'This generation shall not pass, till all these things be fulfilled' " (Matt. 24:34).	*The Watchtower* (November 1, 1950): 419.
People who were present and understood the events of 1914 will live to see the Battle of Armageddon.	"Jesus said, 'This generation will by no means pass away until all these things occur.' Which generation is this, and how long is it? . . . The 'generation' logically would not apply to babies born during World War I. It applies to Christ's followers and others who were able to observe that war and the other things that have occurred in fulfillment of Jesus' composite 'sign.' Some of such persons 'will by no means pass away until' all of what Christ prophesied occurs, including the end of the present wicked system."	*The Watchtower* (October 1, 1978): 31.

Anyone *born* by 1914 will live to see Armageddon.	"If Jesus used 'generation' in that sense and we apply it to 1914, then the babies of that generation are now seventy years old or older. And others alive in 1914 are in their eighties or nineties, a few even having reached one hundred. There are still many millions of that generation alive. Some of them 'will by no means pass away until all things occur' " (Luke 21:32).	*The Watchtower* (May 14, 1984): 5.
Anyone who sees the events signaling the End, regardless of any relationship to 1914, will see the Battle of Armageddon.	"Eager to see the end of this evil system, Jehovah's People have at times speculated about the time when the 'great tribulation' would break out, even tying this to calculations of what is the lifetime of a generation since 1914. However we 'bring a heart of wisdom in' not by speculating about how many years or days make up generation. . . . 'This generation' apparently refers to the peoples of earth who see the sign of Christ's presence but fail to mend their ways."	*The Watchtower* (November 1, 1995): 17–20.

The Watchtower Bible and Tract Society still has not learned to refrain from prophesying falsely. In the January 1, 1997, *Watchtower* (p. 11), it once again raises expectations among its followers that the Battle of Armageddon is just around the corner:

> In the early 1920s, a featured public talk presented by Jehovah's Witnesses was entitled "Millions Now Living Will Never Die." This may have reflected over-optimism at that time. But today that statement can be made with full confidence. Both the increasing light on Bible prophecy and the anarchy of this dying world cry out that the end of Satan's system is very, very near!

And now, as of 2003, the Watchtower refers to the coming end in this way: "Soon, all the distress that Satan and his demons have brought upon earth's inhabitants will end by divine intervention. Then God's promised new world of righteousness will bring about a permanent end to the causes behind hopelessness and suicide."[50]~

---

[50]Official Jehovah's Witnesses Web site, *www.watchtower.org/library/w/2000/9/15/article_02.htm.*

The Deity of Jesus Christ

Throughout the entire content of inspired Scripture, the fact of Christ's identity is clearly taught. He is revealed as Jehovah God in human form (Isaiah 9:6; Micah 5:2; Isaiah 7:14; John 1:14; 8:58; 17:5 [cf. Exodus 3:14]; Hebrews 1:3; Philippians 2:11; Colossians 2:9; and Revelation 1:8, 17–18; etc.). The deity of Jesus Christ is one of the cornerstones of Christianity, and as such has been attacked more vigorously throughout the ages than any other single doctrine of the Christian faith. Adhering to the old Arian heresy of the fourth century A.D., which Athanasius the great church Father refuted in his famous essay "On the Incarnation of the Word," many individuals and all cults steadfastly deny the equality of Jesus Christ with God the Father, and hence, the Triune deity. Jehovah's Witnesses, as has been observed, are no exception to this infamous rule. However, the testimony of the Scriptures stands sure, and the above mentioned references alone put to silence forever this blasphemous heresy, which in the power of Satan himself deceives many with its "deceitful handling of the Word of God."

The deity of Christ, then, is a prime answer to Jehovah's Witnesses, for if the Trinity is a reality, which it is, if Jesus and Jehovah are "One" and the same, then the whole framework of the cult collapses into a heap of shattered, disconnected doctrines incapable of even a semblance of congruity. We will now consider the verses in question and their bearing on the matter.

1. (a) *Isaiah 7:14.* "Therefore the Lord [Jehovah] himself shall give you a sign; Behold, a virgin shall conceive, and bear a son, and shall call his name Immanuel" (literally, "God" or "Jehovah with us," since Jehovah is the only God).

(b) *Isaiah 9:6.* "For unto us a child is born, unto us a son is given: and the government shall be upon his shoulder: and his name shall be called Wonderful, Counsellor, The mighty God, The everlasting Father, The Prince of Peace."

(c) *Micah 5:2.* "But thou, Bethlehem Ephratah, though thou be little among the thousands of Judah, yet out of thee shall he come forth unto me that is to be ruler in Israel; whose goings forth have been from of old, from everlasting."

Within the realm of Old Testament Scripture, Jehovah, the Lord of Hosts, has revealed His plan to appear in human form and has fulfilled the several prophecies concerning this miracle in the person of Jesus Christ. Examination of the above listed texts will more than convince the unbiased student of Scripture that Jehovah has kept His promises and did become man, literally "God with us" (Matthew 1:23; Luke 1:32–33; John 1:14).

The key to Isaiah 7:14 is the divine name "Immanuel," which can only be rightly rendered "God with us"; and since there is no other God but Jehovah by His own declaration (Isaiah 43:10–11), therefore Jesus Christ and Jehovah God are of the same Substance in power and eternity, hence equal. This prophecy was fulfilled in Matthew 1:22–23; thus there can be no doubt that Jesus Christ is the son of the virgin so distinctly portrayed in Isaiah 7:14. Jehovah's Witnesses can present no argument to refute this plain declaration of Scripture, namely that Jehovah and Christ are "One" and the same, since the very term "Immanuel" ("God" or "Jehovah with us") belies any other interpretation.

Isaiah 9:6 in the Hebrew Bible is one of the most powerful verses in the Old

Testament in proving the deity of Christ, for it incontestably declares that Jehovah himself planned to appear in human form. The verse clearly states that all government will rest upon the "child born" and the "son given," whose identity is revealed in the very terms used to describe His attributes. Isaiah, under the inspiration of the Holy Spirit, describes Christ as "Wonderful, Counsellor, The mighty God, The everlasting Father, The Prince of Peace"—all attributes of God alone. The term "mighty God" is in itself indicative of Jehovah, since not only is He the only God (Isaiah 43:10–11), but the term *mighty* is applied to Him alone in relation to His deity. Jehovah's Witnesses dodge this verse by claiming that Christ is *a* mighty god, but not *the* Almighty God (Jehovah). This argument is ridiculous on the face of the matter. However, Jehovah's Witnesses insist that since there is no article in the Hebrew text, "mighty," therefore, does not mean Jehovah. The question arises: Are there two "mighty Gods"? This we know is absurd; yet Jehovah's Witnesses persist in the fallacy, despite Isaiah 10:21, where Isaiah (*without* the article) declares that "Jacob shall return" unto the "mighty God," and we know that Jehovah is by His own word to Moses "the God of Jacob" (Exodus 3:6). In Jeremiah 32:18 (*with* the article) the prophet declares that He (Jehovah) is "the Great, the Mighty God" (two forms of saying the same thing; cf. Isaiah 9:6; 10:21; Jeremiah 32:18). If we are to accept Jehovah's Witnesses' view, there must be two mighty Gods; and that is impossible, for there is only one true and mighty God (Isaiah 45:22).

The prophet Micah, writing in Micah 5:2, recording Jehovah's words, gives not only the birthplace of Christ (which the Jews affirmed as being the City of David, Bethlehem), but he gives a clue as to His identity—namely, God in human form. The term "goings forth" can be rendered "origin,"[51] and we know that the only one who fits this description, whose origin is "from everlasting," must be God himself, since He alone is the eternally existing one (Isaiah 44:6, 8). The overwhelming testimony of these verses alone ascertains beyond reasonable doubt the deity of the Lord Jesus Christ, who became man, identified himself with us in His incarnation, and offered himself "once for all" a ransom for many, the eternal sacrifice who is able to save to the uttermost whoever will appropriate His cleansing power.

2. *John 1:1.* "In the beginning [or "origin," Greek, *arche*] was the Word, [*Logos*] and the Word was with God, [*ton theon*] and the Word was God [*theos*]."

Contrary to the translations of *The Emphatic Diaglott* and the *New World Translation of the Holy Scriptures*, the Greek grammatical construction leaves no doubt whatsoever that this is the only possible rendering of the text. The subject of the sentence is *Word* (*Logos*), the verb *was*. There can be no direct object following "was," since according to grammatical usage intransitive verbs take no objects but take instead predicate nominatives, which refer back to the subject—in this case, *Word* (*Logos*). In fact, the late New Testament Greek scholar Dr. E. C. Colwell formulated a rule that clearly states that a definite predicate nominative (in this case, *theos*—God) never takes an article when it precedes the verb (*was*), as we find in John 1:1. It is therefore easy to see that no article is needed for *theos* (God), and to translate it "a god" is both incorrect grammar and poor Greek, since *theos* is the predicate nominative of *was* in the third sentence-clause of the

---

[51]Brown, Driver, and Briggs, *Hebrew Lexicon of the Old Testament,* 426 [a] Item [2].

verse and must refer back to the subject, *Word* (*Logos*). Christ, if He is the Word "made flesh" (John 1:14), can be no one else except God unless the Greek text and consequently God's Word be denied.

Jehovah's Witnesses, in an appendix in their *New World Translation* (pp. 773–777), attempt to discredit the proper translation on this point, for they realize that if Jesus and Jehovah are "One" in nature, their theology cannot stand, since they deny that unity of nature. The refutation of their arguments on this point is conclusive.

The claim is that since the definite article is used with *theon* in John 1:1b and not with *theos* in John 1:1c, therefore the omission is designed to show a difference; the alleged difference being that in the first case the one true God (Jehovah) is meant, while in the second "a god," other than and inferior to the first, is meant, this latter "god" being Jesus Christ.

On page 776b the claim is made that the rendering "a god" is correct because "all the doctrine of sacred Scriptures bears out the correctness of this rendering." This remark focuses attention on the fact that the whole problem involved goes far beyond this text. Scripture does, in fact, teach the full and equal *deity* of Christ. Why, then, is so much made of this one verse? It is probably because of the surprise effect derived from the show of pseudo-scholarship in the use of a familiar text. Omission of the definite article with *theos* does not mean that "a god" other than the one true God is meant. Let one examine these passages where the definite article is not used with *theos* and see if the rendering "a god" makes sense: Matthew 3:9; 6:24; Luke 1:35, 78; 2:40; John 1:6, 12–13, 18; 3:2, 21; 9:16, 33; Romans 1:7, 17–18; 1 Corinthians 1:30; 15:10; Philippians 2:11–13; Titus 1:1, and many, many more. The "a god" contention proves too weak and is inconsistent. To be consistent in this rendering of "a god," Jehovah's Witnesses would have to translate every instance where the article is absent as "a god" (nominative), "of a god" (genitive), "to" or "for a god" (dative), etc. This they do not do in Matthew 3:9; 6:24; Luke 1:35, 78; John 1:6, 12–13, 18; Romans 1:7, 17, etc. (See the *New World Translation of the Holy Scriptures* and *The Emphatic Diaglott* at above mentioned references.)

You cannot honestly render *theos* "a god" in John 1:1, and then render *theou* "of God" (Jehovah) in Matthew 3:9; Luke 1:35, 78; John 1:6, etc., when *theou* is the genitive case of the *same* noun (second declension), *without* an article and *must* be rendered (following Jehovah's Witnesses' argument) "of *a* god" not "of God" as both *The Emphatic Diaglott* and *New World Translation* put it. We could list at great length, but suggest consultation of the Greek New Testament by either D. Erwin Nestle or Westcott and Hort, in conjunction with *The Elements of Greek* by Francis Kingsley Ball[52] on noun endings, etc. Then if Jehovah's Witnesses must persist in this fallacious "a god" rendition, they can at least be consistent, *which they are not,* and render every instance where the article is absent in the same manner. The truth of the matter is that Jehovah's Witnesses use and remove the articular emphasis *whenever* and *wherever* it suits their fancy, regardless of grammatical laws to the contrary. In a translation as important as God's Word, every law must be observed. Jehovah's Witnesses have not been consistent in their observances of those laws.

---

[52]New York: Macmillan, 1948, 7, 14.

The writers of the claim have exhibited another trait common to Jehovah's Witnesses—that of half-quoting or misquoting a recognized authority to bolster their ungrammatical renditions. On page 776 in an appendix to the *New World Translation of the Christian Greek Scriptures,* when quoting Dr. A. T. Robertson's words, "Among the ancient writers *ho theos* was used of the god of absolute religion in distinction from the mythological gods," they fail to note that in the second sentence following, Dr. Robertson says, "In the New Testament, however, while we have *pros ton theon* (John 1:1–2) it is far more common to find simply *theos,* especially in the Epistles."

In other words, the writers of the New Testament frequently do not use the article with *theos,* and yet the meaning is perfectly clear in the context, namely that the one true God is intended. Let one examine the following references where in successive verses (and even in the same sentence) the article is used with *one* occurrence of *theos* and *not* with another form, and it will be absolutely clear that no such drastic inferences can be drawn from John's usage in John 1:1–2 (Matthew 4:3–4; 12:28; Luke 20:37–38; John 3:2; 13:3; Acts 5:29–30; Romans 1:7–8, 17–19; 2:16–17; 3:5; 4:2–3, etc.).

The doctrine of the article is important in Greek; it is *not* used indiscriminately. But we are *not* qualified to be sure in *all* cases what is intended. Dr. Robertson is careful to note, "It is only of recent years that a really scientific study of the article has been made."[53] The facts are not all known, and no such drastic conclusion, as the writers of the appendix note, should be dogmatically affirmed.

It is nonsense to say that a simple noun can be rendered "divine," and that one *without* the article conveys merely the idea of quality.[54] The authors of this note later render the same noun *theos* as "a god," not as "a quality." This is a self-contradiction in the context.

In conclusion, the position of the writers of this note is made clear in an appendix to the *New World Translation of the Christian Greek Scriptures* (p. 774); according to them it is "unreasonable" that the Word (Christ) should be the God with whom He was (John 1:1). Their own manifestly erring reason is made the criterion for determining scriptural truth. One need only note the obvious misuse in their quotation from Dana and Mantey (pp. 774–75). Mantey clearly means that the "Word was deity" in accord with the overwhelming testimony of Scripture, but the writers have dragged in the interpretation "a god" to suit their own purpose, which purpose is the denial of Christ's deity, and as a result a denial of the Word of God. The late Dr. Mantey publicly stated that he was quoted out of context, and he personally wrote the Watchtower, declaring, "There is no statement in our grammar that was ever meant to imply that 'a god' was a permissible translation in John 1:1" and "It is neither scholarly nor reasonable to translate John 1:1 'The Word was a god.' "[55]

3. *John 8:58.* "Jesus said unto them . . . Before Abraham was [born], *I am.*"[56]

In comparing this with the Septuagint translations of Exodus 3:14 and Isaiah

---

[53]A. T. Robertson, *A Grammar of the Greek New Testament in the Light of Historical Research* (Nashville: Broadman Press, 1934), 755.

[54]Appendix to the *New World Translation of the Christian Greek Scriptures,* 773–74.

[55]Michael Van Buskirk, *The Scholastic Dishonesty of the Watchtower* (Santa Ana, Calif.: CARIS, Inc., 1976), 11.

[56]Author's brackets and emphasis.

43:10–13, we find that the translation is identical. In Exodus 3:14, Jehovah, speaking to Moses, said "I AM," which any intelligent scholar recognizes as synonymous with God. Jesus literally said to the Jews, "I AM Jehovah," and it is clear that they understood Him to mean just that, for they attempted, as the next verse reveals, to stone Him.

Hebrew law on this point states five cases in which stoning was legal—and bear in mind that the Jews were legalists. Those cases were: (1) Familiar spirits, Leviticus 20:27; (2) Cursing (blasphemy), Leviticus 24:10–23; (3) False prophets who lead to idolatry, Deuteronomy 13:5–10; (4) Stubborn and rebellious adult son, Deuteronomy 21:18–21; and (5) Adultery and rape, Deuteronomy 22:21–24 and Leviticus 20:10. Now, any honest biblical student must admit that the only legal ground the Jews had for stoning Christ (*actually* they had none at all) was the second violation—namely, blasphemy. Many zealous Jehovah's Witnesses maintain that the Jews were going to stone Him because He called them children of the devil (John 8:44). But if this were true, why did they not try to stone Him on other occasions (Matthew 23:33, etc.), when He called them sons of vipers? The answer is very simple. They could not stone Christ on that ground because they were bound by the law, which gives only five cases, and would have condemned them on their own grounds had they used "insult" as a basis for stoning. This is not all, however, for in John 10:33, the Jews again attempted to stone Christ and accused Him of making himself God (not *a god*, which subject has already been treated at length).[57] Let us be logical: If the Jews observed the laws of stoning on other occasions when they might have been insulted, why would they violate the law as they would have had to do if Jehovah's Witnesses are right about their interpretation of John 8:58? Little more need be said. The argument is ridiculous in its context; there is only *one* "I AM" in the Scriptures (Isaiah 44:6; 48:12; Revelation 1:8, 17–18), and Jesus laid claim to that identity for which the Jews, misinterpreting the law, set about to stone Him.

Jehovah's Witnesses declare that the Greek rendering of *ego eimi* (I AM) in John 8:58[58] is "properly rendered in the 'perfect indefinite tense'" ("I have been," not "I AM"). To unmask this bold perversion of the Greek text, we shall now examine it grammatically to see if it has any valid grounds for being so translated.

It is difficult to know what the translator means, since he *does not* use standard grammatical terminology, nor is his argument documented from standard grammars. The aorist infinitive as such *does not* form a clause. It is the adverb *prin* that is significant here, so that the construction should be called a *prin* clause. The term "perfect indefinite" is not a standard grammatical term, and its use here has been invented by the authors of the note, so it is impossible to know what is meant.

The real problem in the verse is the verb "*ego eimi.*" Dr. Robertson, who is quoted as authoritative by the NWT translators, states (p. 880) that *eimi* is "absolute." This usage occurs four times (in John 8:24; 8:58; 13:19; 18:5). In these

---

[57] Jehovah's Witnesses point to the *New English Bible*'s rendering of this as "a god" as proof of the validity of their "translation." The fact is, however, that the NEB mistranslated this passage, and no reputable translation would support the Watchtower idea that this passage could mean that Jesus Christ was only claiming to be "a god."

[58] *The New World Translation of the Christian Greek Scriptures*, 312, footnote C.

places the term is the same used by the Septuagint in Deuteronomy 32:39; Isaiah 43:10; 46:4; etc., to render the Hebrew phrase "I (AM) He." The phrase occurs *only* where Jehovah's lordship is pronounced. The phrase, then, is a claim to full and equal deity. The incorrect and rude rendering of the NWT only serves to illustrate the difficulty of evading the meaning of the phrase and the context.

This meaning in the sense of full Deity is especially clear in John 13:19, where Jesus says that He has told them things before they came to pass, that when they do come to pass the disciples may believe that *ego eimi* (I AM). Jehovah is the only One who knows the future as a present fact. Jesus is telling them beforehand that when it does come to pass in the future, they may know that "I AM" (*ego eimi*); i.e., that *He is Jehovah!*

In conclusion, the facts are self-evident and undeniably clear—the Greek allows no such impositions as "I have been." The Watchtower's contention on this point is that the phrase in question is a "historical present" used in reference to Abraham, hence permissible. This is a classic example of Watchtower double-talk. The passage is not a narrative, but a direct quote of Jesus' argument. Standard grammars reserve the use of "historical present" to narratives alone. The term is translated here correctly only as "I AM," and since Jehovah is the only "I AM" (Exodus 3:14; Isaiah 44:6), He and Christ are "One" in nature, truly the fullness of the Deity in the flesh.

The Septuagint translation of Exodus 3:14 from the Hebrew *ehyeh* utilizes *ego eimi* as the equivalent of "I AM" (Jehovah), and Jesus quoted the Septuagint to the Jews frequently, hence their known familiarity with it and their anger at His claim (John 8:59). Additional Old Testament references to Jehovah as "I AM" include Deuteronomy 32:39; Isaiah 43:10; Isaiah 48:12.

4. *Hebrews 1:3.* "He is the reflection of [his] glory and the exact representation of his very being, and he sustains all things by the word of his power" (NWT).

This passage of Scripture, I believe, clarifies beyond doubt the deity of Jesus Christ. It would be illogical and unreasonable to suppose that Christ, who is the image imprinted by Jehovah's *substance,* is *not* of the substance of Jehovah and hence God, or the second person of the triune Deity. No creation is ever declared to be of God's very "substance" or "essence" (Greek, *hupostaseos*); therefore, the eternal Word, who is "the fulness of the Godhead [Deity] bodily" (Colossians 2:9), cannot be a creation or a created being. The writer of the book of Hebrews clearly intended to portray Christ as Jehovah, or he never would have used such explicit language as "the image imprinted by His substance" (Greek interpretation), and as Isaiah 7:14 clearly states, the Messiah was to be Immanuel, literally "God with us." Jehovah's Witnesses attempt the articular fallacy of "a god" instead of God, in reference to Immanuel; but if there has been "before me . . . no God formed, neither shall there be after me" (Jehovah speaking in Isaiah 43:10), then it is impossible on that ground alone, namely, God's declaration, for any other god ("a god" included) to exist. Their argument, based on a grammatical abstraction, fails to stand here, and the deity of the Lord Jesus, as always, remains unscathed.

5. *Philippians 2:11.* "And that every tongue should confess that Jesus Christ is Lord, to the glory of God the Father."

If we compare this verse of Scripture with Colossians 2:9 and Isaiah 45:23, we cannot help but see the full deity of the Lord Jesus in its true light.

Jehovah spoke in Isaiah 45:23: "I have sworn by myself, the word is gone out of my mouth in righteousness, and shall not return, that unto me every knee shall bow, every tongue shall swear." In Colossians 2:9, the apostle Paul, writing under the inspiration of the Holy Spirit, declares, "For in Him [Christ] dwelleth all the fulness of the Godhead bodily." The literal translation of the Greek word *theotetos* (Godhead) is *Deity,* so in Christ all the fullness (*pleroma*) of the Deity resides in the flesh (*somatikos*).

In Thayer's *Greek-English Lexicon of the New Testament,* which is referred to as being "comprehensive" by the Watchtower, a complete analysis of *theotetos* (Godhead, Deity) is given, especially its interpretation in the context of Colossians 2:9. Jehovah's Witnesses will do well to remember that Thayer was a Unitarian (one who denies the deity of Christ), and therefore more prone to accept their interpretations than those of evangelical Christianity. But despite his theological views, Thayer was a Greek scholar whose integrity in the presentation of honest facts, despite their disagreement with his beliefs, is the trait exemplified in all legitimate critics and honest scholars. Thayer states that *theotetos* (Godhead, Deity) is a form of *theos* (Deity), or in his own words: "i.e., the state of Being God, *Godhead*" (p. 288, 1886 ed.). In other words, Christ was the fullness of "the Deity" (Jehovah) in the flesh! *The Emphatic Diaglott* correctly translates *theotetos* "Deity"; but the NWT erroneously renders it "the divine quality," which robs Christ of His Deity. Jehovah's Witnesses arrive at this inaccurate translation by substituting the word *theiotes,* a form of *theiot* (divinity) and thus escaping the condemning evidence of "the Deity" (Jehovah), *tes theotetos.* However, documentary evidence reveals that they cannot rightfully do this, for in Thayer's own words, "*theot* (Deity) *differs* from *theiot* (Divinity) as essence differs from quality or attribute" (p. 288). This fact again exposes the deception employed by Jehovah's Witnesses to lead the unwary Bible student astray into the paths of blasphemy against the Lord Jesus. It is improper; it *cannot* be so translated. The substitution of one word for another in translation is pure scholastic dishonesty, and Jehovah's Witnesses can produce no authority for this bold mistranslation of the Greek text. Jesus Christ, according to the words themselves, is the same *essence* and *substance* as Jehovah, and as the *essence* (Deity) differs from the *quality* (Divinity), so He is God—*tes theotetos* (the Deity)—Jehovah manifest in the flesh.

That Jesus and Jehovah are "One" in nature dare not be questioned from these verses, which so clearly reveal the plan and purpose of God. Paul sustains this argument in his epistle to the Philippians (2:10–11) when he ascribes to the Lord Jesus the identity of Jehovah as revealed in Isaiah 45:23. Paul proclaims boldly, "That at the name of *Jesus* every knee should bow ... and that every tongue should confess that Jesus Christ is Lord, to the glory of God the Father." It is a well-known biblical fact that the highest glory one can give to God is to acknowledge and worship Him in the person of His Son, and as Jesus himself said, "No man cometh unto the Father, but by me" (John 14:6) and "All men should honour the Son, even as they honour the Father" (John 5:23).

It is therefore clear from the context that the wonder of the Godhead is specifically revealed in Jesus Christ to the fullest extent, and it is expedient for all men to realize the consequences to be met if any refuse the injunctions of God's Word and openly deny the deity of His Son, who is "the true God, and eternal life" (1 John 5:20).

6. *Revelation 1:8.* " 'I am the Alpha and the Omega,' says Jehovah God, 'the One who is and who was and who is coming, the Almighty' " (NWT; cf. Revelation 1:7–8, 17–18; 2:8; 22:13; Matthew 24:30; Isaiah 44:6).

In the seventh, eighth, seventeenth, and eighteenth verses of the first chapter of Revelation, a unique and wonderful truth is again affirmed—namely, that Jesus Christ and Jehovah God are of the same *substance,* hence coequal, coexistent, and coeternal. In short, *one nature* (but three persons) in its fullest sense. We shall pursue that line of thought at length in substantiating this doctrine of Scripture.

Comparing Matthew 24:30 with Revelation 1:7, it is inescapably evident that Jesus Christ is the one coming with clouds in both the references mentioned.

> And then shall appear the sign of the Son of man in heaven: and then shall all the tribes of the earth mourn, and they shall *see* the Son of man coming *in the clouds of heaven with power* and great glory. (Matthew 24:30, emphasis added)
>
> Behold, *he cometh with clouds*; and every eye shall see him, and they also which pierced him: and all kindreds of the earth shall wail because of him. Even so, Amen. (Revelation 1:7, emphasis added)

Following this train of thought, we find that Jehovah declares in Isaiah 44:6 that He alone is the first and the last and the *only* God, which eliminates forever any confusion as to their being *two* "firsts and lasts." Since Jehovah is the only God, then how can the *Logos* be "a god," a lesser god than Jehovah, as Jehovah's Witnesses declare in John 1:1? (*The Emphatic Diaglott* and *New World Translation*). Many times Jehovah declares His existence as the "only" God and Savior (Isaiah 41:4; 43:10–13; 44:6; 45:5; 48:12; etc.). This is indeed irrefutable proof, since Christ could not be our Savior and Redeemer if He were not Jehovah, for Jehovah is the only Savior of men's souls (Isaiah 43:11). However, despite the testimony of Scripture that "before me there was no God formed, neither shall there be after me" (Isaiah 43:10), the "a god" fallacy is pursued and taught by Jehovah's Witnesses in direct contradiction to God's Word. In 1 Corinthians 8:4–6, Paul points out that an idol or false god is nothing, and, even though men may worship many things as gods, there is only one true and living God (cf. Acts 5:3–4 and John 1:1 for the other persons of the Trinity).

Revelation 1:17–18 and 2:8 add further weight to the deity of Christ, for they reveal Him as the first and the last, who became dead and lives forever. Now, since Jehovah is the only first and last (cf. Isaiah references), either He and Christ are "One," or, to claim otherwise, Jehovah's Witnesses must deny the authority of Scripture.

In order to be consistent, we must answer the arguments advanced by Jehovah's Witnesses concerning the use of "first" (Greek, *protos*) and "last" (Greek, *eschatos*) in Revelation 1:17 and 2:8.

By suggesting the original use and translation of *prototokos* (firstborn) instead of *protos* (first) in these passages (see the footnotes to the passages in the *New World Translation of the Christian Greek Scriptures* and *The Emphatic Diaglott*), Jehovah's Witnesses attempt to rob Christ of His deity and make Him a created being with "a beginning" (*Let God Be True,* 107). When approached on this point they quickly refer you to Colossians 1:15 and Revelation 3:14, "proving" that the

Logos had "a beginning" (see John 1:1 in both translations). To any informed Bible student, this argument is fallacious. *A Greek Lexicon of the New Testament,* translated and edited by J. H. Thayer (1886), states that the only correct rendering of *protos* is "first," and in Thayer's own words, "*The Eternal One*"—Jehovah (Revelation 1:17). Here again the deity of Christ is vindicated.

Further proof of this synthesis is the fact that the best and most authoritative manuscripts (Sinaiticus, Vaticanus, etc.) have *protos*, "first." The Alexandrinian Manuscript, since it possesses no accent marks, should be translated "Original Bringer Forth"[59] (Erasmus) in keeping with the laws of textual criticism (Colossians 1:15). In short, the whole problem is one of accentuation. Since there are no marks of punctuation or accent in the Alexandrinian Manuscript wording of Revelation 1:17; 2:8; etc., and since all the other manuscripts have *protos*, "first," it is a contradiction to accentuate *prototokos* so as to make Christ a created being instead of the Creator. The correct accentuation of *prototokos* agrees with all the other manuscripts in portraying Christ as "The preeminent one," which is as it should be. These truths, coupled with the fact that all reliable translations and translators bear out the rendering *first* in preference to *firstborn*, expose one more of the many clever attempts to pervert the Word of God by mistranslations and linguistic manipulation.

Jesus said, "I am Alpha and Omega, the beginning and the end, the first and the last" (Revelation 22:13), and not only this, but it is He who is revealing the mysteries to John (Revelation 1:1 and 22:16) and declaring himself to be the "faithful witness" (Revelation 1:5) who testifies "I come quickly" (Revelation 22:20). It is evident that Jesus is the one testifying and the one coming (Revelation 1:2, 7) throughout the book of Revelation, since it is by His command (Revelation 22:16) that John records everything. So in honesty we must acknowledge His sovereignty as the "first" and "last" (Isaiah 48:12; Revelation 1:17; and 22:13), the Lord of all, and the eternal Word of God incarnate (John 1:1).

Revelation 3:14 asserts that Christ is the "beginning of the creation of God," and Colossians 1:15 states that Christ is "the firstborn of every creature." These verses in no sense indicate that Christ was a created being. The Greek word *arche* (Revelation 3:14) can be correctly rendered "origin" and is so translated in John 1:1 of the Jehovah's Witnesses' own 1951 edition of the *New World Translation of the Christian Greek Scriptures.* Revelation 3:14 declares that Christ is the faithful and true witness, the "origin" or "source" of the creation of God. This corroborates Hebrews 1:2 and Colossians 1:16–17 in establishing Christ as the Creator of all things and, therefore, God (Genesis 1:1).

Christ is the firstborn of all creation, since He is the new Creation, conceived without sin (Luke 1:35), the second Adam (1 Corinthians 15:45 and 47), the fulfillment of the divine promise of the God-man (Isaiah 7:14; 9:6; Micah 5:2), and the Redeemer of the world (Colossians 1:14). John 3:13 states that no one has ascended into heaven but Christ who came down; Philippians 2:11 declares that He is Lord (Greek, *kurios*), and as such is "the Lord from heaven" of 1 Corinthians 15:47—God—and not a created being or "a god."

The Lord Jesus is also the "firstborn" from the dead (Revelation 1:5)—that is, the first one to rise in a glorified body (*not* a spirit form—see Luke 24:39–40),

---

[59]Or more literally, "First Begetter" (see Hebrews 1:2).

which type of body Christians will someday possess as in the words of the apostle John: "It doth not yet appear what we shall be: but we know that, when he shall appear, we shall be like [similar to] him; for we shall see him as he is" (1 John 3:2).[60] We know that these promises are sure, "for he is faithful that promised" (Hebrews 10:23), and all who deny the deity of Christ might well take cognizance of His warning and injunction when He said,

> For I testify unto every man that heareth the words of the prophecy of this book, If any man shall add unto these things, God shall add unto him the plagues that are written in this book: And if any man shall take away from the words of the book of this prophecy, God shall take away his part out of the book of life, and out of the holy city, and from the things which are written in this book. (Revelation 22:18–19)

7. *John 17:5.* "And now, O Father, glorify thou me with thine own self with the glory which I had with thee before the world was" (Jesus Christ).

This passage of Scripture, in cross-reference with Isaiah 42:8 and 48:11, proves conclusively the identity of the Lord Jesus and is a fitting testimony to the deity of Christ.

In Isaiah 42:8 Jehovah himself is speaking, and He emphatically declares, "I am the LORD: that is my name: and my glory will I not give to another, neither my praise to graven images." Again in Isaiah 48:11, Jehovah is speaking, and He declares, "For mine own sake, even for mine own sake, will I do it: for how should my name be polluted? And I will not give my glory unto another."

It is plain to see from these references in Isaiah that Jehovah has irrevocably declared that His divinely inherent glory, which is of His own nature, cannot and will not be given to any person other than himself. There is *no* argument Jehovah's Witnesses can erect to combat the truth of God as revealed in these passages of Scripture. The inherent glory of God belongs to God alone, and by His own mouth He has so ordained it to be. God, however, bestowed upon the incarnate Word a certain glory manifested in the presence of the Holy Spirit, through whose power and agency Christ worked while in the flesh, and Jesus in turn bestowed this upon his followers (John 17:22). But it was *not* the glory of God's nature, but instead, the abiding presence of His Spirit. The two quite different types of glory should not be confused. Jesus prayed to receive *back* again the glory He had with the Father "before the world was" (John 17:5). Also, it was *not* the glory given to Him as the Messiah, which glory Christ promised to share with His disciples (v. 22). Nowhere in Scripture are the types of glory equated.

The Lord Jesus Christ, when He prayed in John 17:5, likewise irrevocably revealed that He would be glorified with *the glory of the Father* and that the glory of the Father (Jehovah) was not new to Him, since He affirmed that He possessed it *with* (Greek, *para*) the Father ("the glory which I *had with* thee") even before the world came into existence. Jehovah's Witnesses attempt to answer this by asking that if He were God, where was His glory while He walked the earth?

In answer to this question, the Scriptures list at least four separate instances where Christ manifested His glory and revealed His power and deity. On the Mount of Transfiguration (Matthew 17:2), Christ shone with the inherent glory

---

[60]Author's brackets.

of God, which glory continued undiminished when in John 18:6 the Lord applied
to himself the "I AM" of Jehovahistic identity that radiated glory enough to render His captors powerless at His will. The seventeenth chapter of John, the
twenty-second verse, also confirms the manifestation of Jehovah's glory when
Jesus, looking forward to the cross, prays for His disciples and affirms the origin
of His glory as being the substance of God. The resurrection glory of Christ also
serves to illustrate His deity and reveal it as of God himself.

So it is plain to see that the argument Jehovah's Witnesses advance to the
effect that Christ did not manifest the glory of himself is invalid and finds no
basis in the Scriptures. The truth of the whole matter is that the Lord Jesus did
reveal the true glory of His nature in the very works He performed, and as John
says (1:14), "And the Word was made flesh, and dwelt among us, (and we beheld
his glory, the glory as of the only begotten of the Father,) full of grace and truth."

Paul, in the second chapter of Philippians, removes all doubt on this question when he writes, guided by the Holy Spirit, that Christ never ceased to be
Jehovah even during His earthly incarnation. It is interesting to note that the
Greek term *huparchon*, translated "being" in Philippians 2:6, literally means
"remaining" or "not ceasing to be" (see also 1 Corinthians 11:7); hence, in the
context Christ never ceased to be God, and "remained" in His basic substance;
He was truly "God manifest in the flesh."

A Jehovah's Witness, during an interview, in attempting to escape the obvious declaration of Christ's deity as revealed in this text, reverted to the old Greek
term-switching routine of the Society and asserted that the word *with* (Greek,
para) in John 17:5 really means "through," and therefore the glory that is spoken
of is not proof of Christ's deity, since the glory is Jehovah's and is merely shining
"through" the Son; it is not His own but a manifestation of Jehovah's glory.

Once again we are confronted with the problem of illogical exegesis, the
answer to which must be found in the Greek text itself. If we believe that God
inspired the writers, we must believe the grammar of the Bible is inspired as well;
how else could He have conveyed His thoughts without error? Would God commit His inspired words to the failing grammatical powers of man to record? No!
He could not do this without risking corruption of His message; therefore, as the
wise and prudent Lord that He is, He most certainly inspired the grammar of His
servants that their words might transmit His thoughts without error, immutable
and wholly dependable. With this thought in mind, let us consider the wording
and construction of the verse.

The Greek word *para* (with) is used in the dative case in John 17:5 and is not
translated "through" (Greek *dia*) but is correctly rendered according to Thayer's
Lexicon as "with," and Thayer quotes John 17:5, the very verse in question, as his
example of how *para* (with) should be translated.

Never let it be said that *para* in this context indicates anything less than pos-
sessive equality: "the glory which I had with thee before the world was." The Lord
Jesus Christ clearly meant that He as God the Son was the possessor of divine
glory along with the Father and the Holy Spirit before the world was formed.
Christ also declared that He intended to appropriate that glory in all its divine
power once again, pending the resurrection of His earthly temple, which, by
necessity, since it was finite, veiled as a voluntary act His eternal power and deity
(Philippians 2:5–8). The glory He spoke of did not only shine through the

Father; it was eternally inherent in the Son, and since John, led by the Holy Spirit, deliberately chose *para* (literally, "with") in preference to *dia* (through), the argument that Jehovah's Witnesses advance cannot stand up. The Lord Jesus claimed the same glory of the Father as His own, and since Jehovah has said that He will not give His inherent glory to another (Isaiah 42:8), the unity of substance between Him and Christ is undeniable; they are one in all its wonderful and mysterious implications, which, though we cannot understand them fully, we gladly accept, and in so doing remain faithful to God's Word.

8. *John 20:28.* "Thomas answered and said unto him, My Lord and my God."

No treatment of the deity of Christ would be complete without mentioning the greatest single testimony recorded in the Scriptures. John 20:28 presents that testimony.

Beginning at verse 24, the disciple Thomas is portrayed as being a resolute skeptic in that he refused to believe that Christ had risen and appeared physically in the *same* form that had been crucified on the cross. In verse 25 Thomas stubbornly declares, "Except I shall see in his hands the print of the nails, and put my finger into the print of the nails, and thrust my hand into his side, I will not believe." Following through the sequence of events in verses 26 and 27, we learn that the Lord appeared to Thomas together with the other disciples and presented His body bearing the wounds of Calvary to Thomas for his inspection. This was no spirit or phantom, no "form" assumed for the occasion, as Jehovah's Witnesses maintain. This was the very body of Christ that bore the horrible imprints of excruciating torture and the pangs of an ignominious death. Here displayed before the eyes of the unbelieving disciple was the evidence that compelled him by the sheer power of its existence to adore the One who manifested the essence of Deity. Thomas answered and said unto him, "My Lord and my God." This was the only answer Thomas could honestly give; Christ had proved His identity; He was truly "the Lord God." Let us substantiate this beyond doubt.

Jehovah's Witnesses have vainly striven to elude this text in the Greek (*The Emphatic Diaglott* and the *New World Translation*), but they have unknowingly corroborated its authority beyond refutation, as a brief survey of their sources will reveal.

In *The Emphatic Diaglott* (John 20:28, p. 396) *ho theos mou*, literally "the God of me," or "my God," signifies Jehovahistic identity, and since it is in possession of *the definite article,* to use Jehovah's Witnesses' own argument, it must therefore mean "the only true God" (Jehovah), not "a god." On page 776 in an appendix to the *New World Translation of the Christian Greek Scriptures,* the note states, "So, too, John 1:1–2 uses *ho theos* to distinguish Jehovah God from the Word (Logos) as a god, the only begotten god as John 1:18 calls him." Now let us reflect as sober individuals. If Thomas called the risen Christ Jehovah (definite article *ho kurios mou kai ho theos mou*), and Christ did not deny it but confirmed it by saying (v. 29), "Because thou hast seen me, thou hast believed: blessed are they that have not seen, and yet have believed," then no juggling of the text in context can offset the basic thought—namely, that Jesus Christ is Jehovah God!

The *New World Translation of the Christian Greek Scriptures* carefully evades any explanation of the Greek text on the aforementioned point, but just as carefully it inserts in the margin (p. 350) six references to Christ as "a god," which they attempt to slip by the unwary Bible student. These references, as usual, are used abstractly, and four of them (Isaiah 9:6; John 1:1, 18; and 10:35) have been mentioned already in previous points. The question, then, is this: Is there any other god beside Jehovah that Jehovah's Witnesses affirm to be true by their reference to Christ as "a god" (John 1:1; Isaiah 9:6)? The Scriptures give but one answer: Emphatically *NO!* There is no god but Jehovah. (See Isaiah 37:16, 20; 44:6, 8; 45:21–23; etc.)

To be sure, there are many so-called gods in the Scriptures, but they are not gods by identity and self-existence but by human acclamation and adoration. Satan also falls into this category, since he is the "god of this world," who holds that position only because unregenerate and ungodly men have accorded to him service and worship belonging to God.

The apostle Paul seals this truth with his clear-cut analysis of idolatry and false gods in 1 Corinthians 8:4–6, where he declares that an idol is nothing in itself and that there is no god but Jehovah in heaven or earth, regardless of the inventions of man.

The picture then is clear. Thomas adored Christ as the risen incarnation of the Deity (Jehovah); John declared that Deity from all eternity (John 1:1); and Christ affirmed it irrefutably: "If ye believe not that I am he [Jehovah], ye shall die in your sins" (John 8:24; cf. Exodus 3:14).[61] All of the pseudo-scholastic and elusive tactics ever utilized can never change the plain declarations of God's Word. Jesus Christ is Lord of all; and like it or not, Jehovah's Witnesses will never destroy or remove that truth. Regardless of what is done to God's Word on earth, it remains eternal in the glory, as it is written, "For ever, O LORD, thy word is settled in heaven" (Psalm 119:89).

9. *John 5:18.* "[He] said also that God was his Father, making himself equal with God."

Concluding our discussion on this vital topic, this verse is self-explanatory. The Greek term *equal* (*ison*) cannot be debated; nor is it contextually or grammatically allowable that John is here recording *what the Jews said about Jesus,* as Jehovah's Witnesses lamely argue. The sentence structure clearly shows that *John said it* under the inspiration of the Holy Spirit, and *not* the Jews! Anyone so inclined can diagram the sentence and see this for himself. No serious scholar or commentator has ever questioned it. In the Jewish mind, for Jesus to claim to be God's Son was a claim to equality with God, a fact Jehovah's Witnesses might profitably consider!

We see, then, that our Lord was equal with God the Father and the Holy Spirit in His divine nature, though inferior (as a man), by choice, in His human nature as the last Adam (John 14:28; 1 Corinthians 15:45–47). This text alone is of enormous value and argues powerfully for our Lord's deity.

The Resurrection of Christ

Jehovah's Witnesses, as has been observed, deny the bodily resurrection of the Lord Jesus Christ and claim instead that He was raised a "divine spirit being" or as an "invisible spirit creature." They answer the objection that He appeared in human form by asserting that He simply took human forms as He needed

---

[61]Author's brackets.

them, which enabled Him to be seen, for as the Logos He would have been invisible to the human eye. In short, Jesus did not appear in the *same* form that hung upon the cross, since that body either "dissolved into gases or . . . is preserved somewhere as the grand memorial of God's love."[62] This, in spite of Paul's direct refutation in 1 Timothy 2:5, where he calls "the *man* Christ Jesus" our only mediator—some thirty years after the Resurrection!

The Scriptures, however, tell a completely different story, as will be evident when their testimony is considered. Christ himself prophesied His own bodily resurrection, and John tells us "He spake of the temple of His body" (John 2:21).

In John 20:24–26, the disciple Thomas doubted the literal, physical resurrection of Christ, only to repent (v. 28) after Jesus offered His body (v. 27), the same one that was crucified and still bore the nail prints and spear wound, to Thomas for his examination. No reasonable person will say that the body the Lord Jesus displayed was not His crucifixion body, unless he either ignorantly or willfully denies the Word of God. It was no other body "assumed" for the time by a spiritual Christ; it was the identical form that hung on the tree—the Lord himself; He was alive and undeniably tangible, not a "divine spirit creature." The Lord foresaw the unbelief of men in His bodily resurrection and made an explicit point of saying that He was not a spirit but flesh and bones (Luke 24:39–44), and He even went so far as to eat human food to prove that He was identified with humanity as well as Deity. Christ rebuked the disciples for their unbelief in His physical resurrection (Luke 24:25), and it was the physical resurrection that confirmed His deity, since only God could voluntarily lay down and take up life at will (John 10:18). We must not forget that Christ prophesied not only His resurrection but also the nature of that resurrection, which He said would be bodily (John 2:19–21). He said He would raise up "this temple" in three days (v. 19), and John tells us "He spake of the temple of his *body*" (v. 21).

Jehovah's Witnesses utilize, among other unconnected verses, 1 Peter 3:18 as a defense for their spiritual resurrection doctrine. Peter declares that Christ was "put to death in the flesh, but quickened by the Spirit." Obviously, He was made alive in the Spirit and by the Spirit of God, for the Spirit of God, the Substance of God himself, raised up Jesus from the dead, as it is written, "But if the Spirit of him that raised up Jesus from the dead dwell in you . . ." (Romans 8:11). The meaning of the verse, then, is quite clear. God did not raise Jesus a spirit but raised Him *by* His Spirit, which follows perfectly John 20:27 and Luke 24:39–44 in establishing the physical resurrection of the Lord.

The Watchtower quotes Mark 16:12 and John 20:14–16 as proof that Jesus has "other bodies" after His resurrection. Unfortunately for them, the reference in Mark is a questionable source. A doctrine should not be built around one questionable verse. The reason that Mary (in Mark 16) and also the Emmaus disciples (Luke 24) did not recognize Him is explained in Luke 24:16: "Their eyes were kept from recognizing him" (RSV), but it was "Jesus himself" (v. 15).

Jehovah's Witnesses also try to undermine our Lord's bodily resurrection by pointing out that the doors were shut (John 20:26) when Jesus appeared in the Upper Room. However, Christ had a "spiritual body" (1 Corinthians 15:50, 53) in His glorified state; identical in form to His earthly body, but immortal and thus

---

[62]Charles T. Russell, *Studies in the Scriptures*, Vol. V, 454.

capable of entering either the dimension of earth or of heaven with no violation to the laws of either one.

Paul states in Romans 4:24; 6:4; 1 Corinthians 15:15; etc., that Christ is raised from the dead, and Paul preached the physical resurrection and return of the God-man, not a "divine spirit being" without a tangible form. Paul also warned that if Christ is not risen, then our faith is in vain (1 Corinthians 15:14); to us who believe God's Word there is a Man in the Glory who showed His wounds as a token of His reality and whose question we ask Jehovah's Witnesses: "Has a spirit flesh and bones as you see me have?" (Luke 24:39).

The Atonement of Christ

The infinite atonement of the Lord Jesus Christ is one of the most important doctrines of the Bible, since it is the guarantee of eternal life through the complete forgiveness of sins to whoever appropriates its cleansing power. The Old Testament clearly teaches, "It is the *blood* that maketh an atonement for the soul" (Leviticus 17:11).[63] Hebrews 9:22 corroborates this beyond doubt, for in truth "without shedding of blood is no remission." The Lord Jesus Christ became the one blood sacrifice for sin that ensures everlasting life, as John said upon seeing Jesus: "Behold the Lamb of God, which taketh away the sin of the world" (John 1:29). The apostle John writing in Revelation 13:8 declares that the Lamb (Christ) slain from the foundation of the world is God's own eternal sacrifice that cleanses from all sin and provides redemption for lost souls who trust in its efficacy. The writer of the epistle to the Hebrews goes to great length to show that the sacrifices of the Old Testament were types designed to show forth the coming sacrifices of Christ on Calvary (Hebrews 9 and 10). The Hebrew term *kaphar* (covering) and the Greek term *katallage*, which literally means reconciliation, are used in reference to payment of an obligation or exchange. The picture then portrays Christ as bearing our sins in His own body on the tree (1 Peter 2:24) and giving us peace with God through the *blood* of His cross (Colossians 1:20), which blood is the everlasting covenant that is able to make us perfect, in that God through it empowers us to do His will (Hebrews 13:20–21). The Scriptures give vast testimony to the redeeming power of the Lamb's blood (Romans 3:25; 5:9; Colossians 1:14; Hebrews 9:22; 1 Peter 1:19; 1 John 1:7; Revelation 5:9; 12:11), which *alone* can save and cleanse (Hebrews 9:22).

Charles Taze Russell resigned from a position he once held as assistant editor of a Rochester, New York, newspaper because he disagreed with the editor's view of the Atonement. Whether Russell was right in that disputation or wrong we do not know, but his doctrine of the Atonement and that of the Jehovah's Witnesses we do have knowledge of and know it to be completely unscriptural. Jehovah's Witnesses argue that the Atonement is not wholly of God, despite 2 Corinthians 5:15, 19, but rather half of God and half of man. Jesus, according to their argument, removed the effects of Adam's sin by His sacrifice on Calvary, but the work will not be fully completed until the survivors of Armageddon return to God through free will and become subject to the Theocratic rule of Jehovah. For Jehovah's Witnesses, the full realization of the matter is reconciliation with God, which

---

[63]Author's emphasis.

will be completed in relation to the Millennial Kingdom. This utterly unreasonable and illogical interpretation of Scripture does away with the validity of the "infinite atonement" unconditionally administered by God and through God for man. Russell and Jehovah's Witnesses have detracted from the blood of Christ by allowing it only partial cleansing power.

But the truth still stands; it is either all-sufficient or insufficient; and if the latter were the case, man would be hopelessly lost in an unconnected maze of irrelevant doctrines that postulate a finite sacrifice and, by necessity, a finite god.

The Physical Return of Christ

Jehovah's Witnesses declare that Christ returned to the temple in 1914 and cleansed it by 1918 for judgment upon sinful men and Satan's organizations. They affirm that since He did not rise physically, neither will He return physically.[64]

The first claim is that Jesus said, "The world seeth me no more" (John 14:19); therefore, no mortal eye shall see Him. The second claim is the intimation that *parousia* (Greek for presence, coming, advent, etc.) in Matthew 24:26–28 can only be rendered "exactly" as *presence;* therefore, Christ is now present, not coming.

These arguments are another example of the half-truths used by Jehovah's Witnesses to lead people astray. To begin with, Thayer, who is esteemed reliable in the field of scholarship, clearly states on page 490 of his *Greek-English Lexicon of the New Testament* that *parousia*, especially in the New Testament, refers to the second coming of Christ in *visible* form to raise the dead, hold the last judgment, and set up the kingdom of God. Christ *is* present; His "presence" is always near ("I will never leave thee," Hebrews 13:5; "I am with you always, even unto the end of the world," Matthew 28:20), for as God He is omnipresent—everywhere. But that does not mean He is here physically as the Scriptures attest He will be at the Second Advent. The physical return of Christ is the "blessed hope" of Christendom (Titus 2:13), and the language used to portray its visible certainty is most explicit. In Titus 2:13 the Greek word *epiphaneia* ("appearing") is more correctly translated "manifestation" or "visible" from *phanero*, "to make manifest, or visible, or known"[65] The language is self-explanatory. When the Lord returns with His saints, every eye shall see Him (Matthew 24:30, cf. Revelation 1:7). How then can Jehovah's Witnesses claim that He has already returned but is invisible? The answer is they cannot and still remain honest scripturally. To further establish these great truths, the apostle Paul writing to Timothy in 1 Timothy 6:14 clearly states that the Lord Jesus will appear physically by using *epiphaneia*, another form of *phanero*, which also denotes visibility or manifestations. In 1 Thessalonians 4:16–17, the Lord's return is revealed as being visible and audible, not invisible, as Jehovah's Witnesses affirm contrary to Scripture.

The Old Testament bears out the physical return of the Messiah, also a wonderful testimony to the consistency of God's Word. Comparing Zechariah 12:10; 14:4 with Revelation 1:7; Matthew 24:30; and Acts 1:9–12, it is obvious that the

---

[64] *The Truth Shall Make You Free*, 295.
[65] *Thayer's Greek-English Lexicon of the New Testament*, 648.

Lord's ascension was visible, for the disciples *saw* Him rise, and in like fashion (Greek, *tropos*) the angels declared He would return. Zechariah 12:10 quotes Jehovah (further proof of Christ's deity), "And they shall look upon *me* whom they have pierced."[66] Revelation 1:7 states that Christ is the one pierced and *visible* to human eyes. Zechariah 14:4 reveals Christ as touching the Mount of Olives at His visible return, and the Scriptures teach that this literally corroborates the angelic proclamation of Acts 1:9–12 even to the Lord's return to the exact location of His ascension, the Mount of Olives (v. 12). The doctrine of the physical return of Christ cannot be denied unless a denial of God's Word is also entered.

Jehovah's Witnesses and Human Government

Jehovah's Witnesses refuse to pay homage in any way to the flag of any nation or even to defend their own individual nation from assault by an enemy. Patriotism as displayed in bearing arms is not one of their beliefs, since they claim to be ambassadors of Jehovah and as such deem themselves independent of allegiance to any government other than His. In this age of uncertainty, sincerity is a priceless gem, and no doubt Jehovah's Witnesses believe themselves sincere, but all their arguments avail nothing, because in Romans 13:1–7 Paul clearly outlines the case for human government as instituted by God. Paul goes to great lengths to stress that the "higher powers" (human governmental rules) are allowed and sanctioned by God. As supposed followers of His Word, the Witnesses ought to heed both Christ and Paul and "render therefore to all their dues: tribute to whom tribute is due; custom to whom custom," which in the context of Romans 13:1–7 clearly means subjugation to governmental rule. Paul settles the question decisively, and in conclusion we quote his teaching:

> Let every soul be subject unto the higher powers. For there is no power but of God: the powers that be are ordained of God. Whosoever therefore resisteth the power, resisteth the ordinance of God: and they that resist shall receive to themselves damnation. For rulers are not a terror to good works, but to the evil. Wilt thou then not be afraid of the power? do that which is good, and thou shalt have praise of the same: For he is the minister of God to thee for good. But if thou do that which is evil, be afraid; for he beareth not the sword in vain: for he is the minister of God, a revenger to execute wrath upon him that doeth evil. Wherefore ye must needs be subject, not only for wrath, but also for conscience sake. For this cause pay ye tribute also: for they are God's ministers, attending continually upon this very thing. Render therefore to all their dues: tribute to whom tribute is due; custom to whom custom; fear to whom fear; honour to whom honour. (Romans 13:1–7)

The Existence of Hell and Eternal Punishment

The question of the existence of hell and eternal punishment presents no problem to any biblical student who is willing to practice honest exegesis unhindered by the teachings of any organizations of man. Jehovah's Witnesses use

---

[66]Author's emphasis.

emotionally loaded words such as *hellfire screechers* and *religionists,* etc., to describe the theological views of anyone who disagrees with their philosophy. In order to understand their views, it must first be established that their beliefs are based upon no sound or valid knowledge of the original languages, and it should be remembered that this one factor influences practically every major phase of semantic study. However, we will now consider this problem in its context and contrast it with Jehovah's Witnesses' interpretation, which professes to have solved the problem, though on what grounds it is difficult to ascertain.

1. To begin with, Jehovah's Witnesses use poor reasoning in their construction of grammar, and from the evidence seldom check the original scripts beyond the dictionary and lexicon stage. The following documentation proves the point and reveals this shortcoming. On pages 69 and 70 of *Let God Be True* (1946 ed.), the following statement appears:

> If you were to translate a book from a foreign language into English and there you found the foreign word for bread 65 times, would you translate it 31 times bread, 31 times fish, and 3 times meat? Of course not. Why? Because if you did your translation would not be correct. For what is bread cannot at the same time be fish or meat and vice versa. The same holds true with the word sheol. If sheol is the grave, it is impossible at the same time to be a place of fiery torture and at the same time a pit.

It is most interesting to note in passing that in the Watchtower revision of *Let God Be True* (1951), this paragraph was carefully omitted.

To the average Jehovah's Witness then, hell (*sheol*) is literally "the grave," the place where mortals await the Resurrection. Their chief argument is that a Greek or Hebrew word means one thing and has no contextual connotation. This is a typical Jehovah's Witness approach and again reveals the linguistic failings of the organization. First of all, the very example the author of the chapter uses concerning bread, fish, and meat, etc., is a reality in the text of the Bible, and unless one recognizes the varieties of meanings of words in different contexts, he is unable to understand the plain meaning of Scripture. A little research would have revealed this truth. In the Hebrew text, the word *lechem* is translated "bread" 238 times, one time as "feast," twenty-one times as "food," one time as "fruit," five times as "loaf," eighteen times as "meat," one time as "provision," twice as "victuals," and once as "eat." It is clear that *sheol* has differences of meaning, which must be decided from the context, not by conjectures of misinformed authors.

2. In the second place, Jehovah's Witnesses have conceived of death as being unconsciousness or extinction, which definition cannot be found in the Bible. Death in the biblical sense never means extinction or annihilation, and not one word, Greek or Hebrew, in either Testament will be found to say that it does. Death in the Bible is portrayed as *separation.* "The soul that sinneth . . . it shall be separated" (Ezekiel 18:4) is a better rendition in the sense that the word conveys. When Adam sinned, his soul became *separated* from God in the sense of fellowship—and consequently, as a result of sin, all men die or are separated from God by Adam's as well as their own sins. But God has provided a reconciliation for us in the person of His Son, and we are "born again," regenerated and reconciled to God by the sacrifice of His Son "in whom we have redemption through his blood, even the forgiveness of sins" (Colossians 1:14, cf. John 3:3–7, 15–16;

2 Corinthians 5:17–21). So, then, we see that death in reality is not extinction but conscious existence, as is demonstrated in Matthew 17:1–3, when Moses and Elijah talked with Christ. Moses' body was dead—this no one will deny; his soul was also dead according to Jehovah's Witnesses. Then what or who was talking to Christ? The answer is simple. Moses as a living soul spoke to Christ, and he was alive and conscious! Substantiating all this is Christ's own declaration, "I am the resurrection, and the life; he that believeth in me, though he were dead, yet shall he live: And whosoever liveth and believeth in me shall never die" (John 11:25–26). Therefore, death is only the separation between, not the extinction of, personalities (Isaiah 59:1–2; see also 2 Corinthians 5:8 and Philippians 1:21–23).

3. Jehovah's Witnesses claim in *Let God Be True* (p. 96) that "in all places where hell is translated from the Greek word *gehenna* it means everlasting destruction."

This is indeed a bold-faced misrepresentation of the Greek language and certainly ranks next to the "a god" fallacy of John 1:1 as an outstanding example of complete falsehood. There is no evidence that *gehenna* ever means "annihilation" in the New Testament, but rather, abundant evidence to the contrary. In Matthew 5:22 *gehenna* is portrayed as literally "the hell of fire," and in 10:28 coupled with *apolesai*, "to be delivered up to eternal misery" (see Thayer, 64). It indicates everlasting misery, and in Matthew 18:9 the same words corroborate 5:22, "the hell of fire." If we are to follow through with Jehovah's Witnesses' argument, *gehenna* simply means the smoldering furnaces of Hinnon. But is that fire everlasting? No! For today the valley of Hinnon is not burning, so unless Jesus meant the example for only those living at that time (and this not even Jehovah's Witnesses will affirm), *gehenna* must be what it is, the symbol of eternal separation in conscious torment by a flame that is unquenchable (Isaiah 66:24).

4. It is fruitless to pursue this analysis of the Greek any further, for it must be clear from the contexts that more than the grave or extinction is portrayed in *sheol, hades,* and *gehenna.* Without benefit of any complicated textual exegesis, we shall let God's Word speak its own message and commit to the honest reader the decision as to whether or not eternal punishment, rather than annihilation, is scriptural doctrine. The following verses collectively refer to a place of everlasting conscious torment where Satan and his followers must remain in future eternal wounding or misery, separated from God's presence and "the glory of his power" (2 Thessalonians 1:9; cf. Thayer, 443 on *olethros* and the Latin *vulnus—to wound*).

1. *Matthew 8:11–12.* "And I say unto you, That many shall come from the east and west, and shall sit down with Abraham, and Isaac, and Jacob, in the kingdom of heaven. But the children of the kingdom shall be cast out into outer darkness: there shall be weeping and gnashing of teeth."

2. *Matthew 13:42, 50.* "And shall cast them into the furnace of fire: there shall be wailing and gnashing of teeth."

3. *Matthew 22:13.* "Then said the king to the servants, Bind him hand and foot, and take him away, and cast him into outer darkness; there shall be weeping and gnashing of teeth."

4. *Luke 13:24–28.* "Strive to enter in at the strait gate: for many, I say unto you, will seek to enter in, and shall not be able. When once the master of the house is risen up, and hath shut to the door, and ye begin to stand

without, and to knock at the door, saying, Lord, Lord, open unto us; and he shall answer and say unto you, I know you not whence ye are: Then shall ye begin to say, We have eaten and drunk in thy presence, and thou hast taught in our streets. But he shall say, I tell you, I know you not whence ye are; depart from me, all ye workers of iniquity. There shall be weeping and gnashing of teeth, when ye shall see Abraham, and Isaac, and Jacob, and all the prophets, in the kingdom of God, and you yourselves thrust out."

5. *2 Peter 2:17*. "These are wells without water, clouds that are carried with a tempest; to whom the mist of darkness is reserved for ever."

6. *Jude 13*. "Raging waves of the sea, foaming out their own shame; wandering stars, to whom is reserved the blackness of darkness for ever."

7. *Revelation 14:9–11*. "And the third angel followed them, saying with a loud voice, If any man worship the beast and his image, and receive his mark in his forehead, or in his hand, the same shall drink of the wine of the wrath of God, which is poured out without mixture into the cup of his indignation; and he shall be tormented with fire and brimstone in the presence of the holy angels, and in the presence of the Lamb: And the smoke of their torment ascendeth up for ever and ever: and they have no rest day nor night, who worship the beast and his image, and whosoever receiveth the mark of his name."

8. *Revelation 19:20*. "And the beast was taken, and with him the false prophet that wrought miracles before him, with which he deceived them that had received the mark of the beast, and them that worshiped his image. These both were cast alive into a lake of fire burning with brimstone."

These verses are conclusive proof that everlasting conscious separation from God and real torment exist, and no possible confusion of terminology can change their meaning in context. Revelation 20:10 is perhaps the most descriptive of all the verses in the Greek. John positively states, "The devil that deceived them was cast into the lake of fire and brimstone, where the beast and the false prophet are, and shall be tormented (*basanisthesontai*) day and night for ever (*aionas*) and ever." The Greek word *basanizo* literally means "to torment," "to be harassed," "to torture," or "to vex with grievous pains" (Thayer, 96), and is used throughout the New Testament to denote great pain and conscious misery, not annihilation, cessation of consciousness, or extinction. Further proof of the reality of conscious torment, not annihilation, is found in the following verses where *basanizo* is utilized to exhibit the truth of God's eternal justice.

1. *Matthew 8:6*. The one *tormented* (suffering) with palsy (*basanizomenos*).

2. *Matthew 8:29*. The demons addressing Jesus admit the certainty of future torment (*basanisai*). "Art thou come hither to *torment* us before the time?"

3. *Mark 5:7*. Again the demon cries out, "*Torment* (*basanisas*) me not." He obviously feared conscious pain, not extinction.

4. *Luke 8:28*. A demon once more reveals his knowledge of coming torment (*basanisas*): "*torment* me not" is his supplication to Christ.

5. *Revelation 14:10–11*. "He (the believer in the beast) shall be *tormented* (*basanistheasetai*) with fire and brimstone in the presence of the holy angels, and in the presence of the Lamb. And the smoke of their torment ascendeth up for ever and ever: and they have no rest (*anapausis*, Thayer, 40, also Liddell and Scott) day nor night, who worship the beast and his image, and whosoever receiveth the mark of his name."

The Scriptures, then, clearly teach eternal conscious punishment and torment for those who reject Christ as Lord, and the language of the texts leaves no room for doubt that the apostles intended that confirmation. Jehovah's Witnesses think God a "fiend" because He executes eternal righteous judgment. They make much to-do about God being Love but forget that because He is Love, He is also *Justice* and must require infinite retribution upon anyone who treads underfoot the precious blood of Christ, who is the Lamb slain for lost sinners from the foundation of the world. Death is not extinction, and hell is not an illusion—everlasting conscious punishment is a terrifying reality of God's infinite justice upon the souls of unbelieving men.

The apostle Paul summed up this certainty in Romans 2:8–9, when he declared that God's indignation (*thumos*) and wrath (*orges*) are upon all who work unrighteousness. These two words have identical usage in Revelation 14:10, where John speaks of the eternal torment of those who serve the Beast, "the wine of the wrath [*orges*] of God, which is poured out without mixture into the cup of his indignation [*thumou*]." So then the picture is clear. God is both Love and Justice, and it is not He who condemns man, but man who condemns himself. As it is written: "For by thy words thou shalt be justified, and by thy words thou shalt be condemned" (Matthew 12:37).

5. In *Let God Be True* (p. 93), Jehovah's Witnesses exhibit their lack of knowledge as to what fundamental Christians believe, where, when speaking of the "religious theologians," they declare: "But are not Satan the devil and his demons down in hell keeping the fires and making it hard for those who are in it? This is what is taught by Christendom's clergy." It is nonsense to suppose that the devil and his demons "are in hell keeping the fires," and no responsible clergyman or Christian would make so childish a statement. Jehovah's Witnesses attribute to Christianity the same caliber of reasoning that appeals to their untutored minds, and to claim that "religionists" teach such doctrines is to reveal ignorance of the facts, a symptom not at all healthy in the processes of logical analysis. Further comment is not justified. Further examination is superfluous.

6. Luke 16:19–31 is claimed by Jehovah's Witnesses to be a parable in the text, but nowhere is this substantiated in Luke's account. It is pure conjecture. Jehovah's Witnesses claim that this "parable" portrays a coming event, which was fulfilled in A.D. 1918. The rich man represents the clergy and Lazarus the "faithful body of Christ." The clergy is constantly tormented by the truth proclaimed through the faithful remnant (*Let God Be True*, 98). Comment on this interpretational travesty is senseless, since Jehovah's Witnesses twist the Scriptures to suit their own ends, regardless of the textual background. The Lord Jesus in this account portrayed the condition of a lost soul (the rich man) who rejected God, and a beggar who partook of the Lord's mercy. The rich man went into conscious torment after physical death (Greek, *basanois*), verse 24, and even proclaimed his spiritual conscious anguish (Greek, *odunomai*), "I am being tormented" (see Thayer, 438). There can be no doubt—he was suffering and knew it. Jehovah's Witnesses believe that in order to suffer you must exist physically, but this is naïve, to say the least, since souls suffer, as is demonstrated in this account. It must also be remembered that Christ, in parables, never used personal names, such as

"Lazarus." The language, although literal, is forceful in depicting spiritual suffering.

We must conclude, then, that Luke's account is a record of an actual case, a historical fact in which a soul suffered after death and was conscious of that torment. Regardless of what conjectures are injected at this point, the conclusion is sure: There is conscious punishment after death; and whether it is accepted or not by Jehovah's Witnesses, it still remains a scriptural doctrine substantiated by God's Word.

Satan—the Devil

In Ezekiel 28:16–19, quoted in *Let God Be True* (p. 65), Jehovah's Witnesses maintain Satan's annihilation, but in the light of the Scriptures previously discussed, the area of meanings of the Hebrew words must be considered. The word for "destroy" (*'abad*) does not convey the meaning of annihilation or extinction. The term here used may be rendered validly "to reckon as lost, given up as lost, or cast away" (cf. Ecclesiastes 3:6, and also Gesenius' *Hebrew-English Lexicon*). If Ezekiel 28:19 is as translated in *Let God Be True* (p. 65), "never shalt thou be any more," then the Hebrew word *'ayin* may properly be rendered "to fail" or "to be gone," *not* "to cease to exist" (cf. Isaiah 44:12; 1 Kings 20:40). The use of *'ayin* in Hebrew sentence structure is the standard means employed when negating noun clauses. In 1 Kings 20:40, for example, where the man is spoken of as "gone," the term *'ayin* is utilized to show the man's absence or escape, *not* his extinction. If Jehovah's Witnesses persist in their annihilation doctrine where Satan is concerned, they must also believe that this man was annihilated, and the context rules out that interpretation as absurd. The picture, then, is clear in the light of language interpretation. Satan *must* and *will* endure everlasting torment with his followers, and to this truth God's Word bears irrefutable testimony.

Man the Soul, His Nature and Destiny

Any critical thinker in examining this problem cannot escape the confusion of terms utilized by Jehovah's Witnesses to substantiate their argument that the soul is not an eternal entity. To carry this argument to any great length is foolish, for the Hebrew word (*nephesh*) and the Greek (*psyche*) possess great areas of meaning impossible to fathom without exhaustive exegesis of the original sources. The root of the problem lies in Jehovah's Witnesses' misconception of the soul as merely a principle of life, not an entity. The Bible clearly teaches in numerous places (Genesis 35:18; 1 Kings 17:21–22; Revelation 6:9–11, to state a few) that the soul departs at the death of the body, that it is not destroyed by physical death, and that it can be restored by God at His discretion.

In an exegetical study, it is impossible to overemphasize the importance of defining terms, and in regard to the problem at hand, it is of the utmost importance. Therefore, before we can decide who or what has immortality, we must know what the term *immortality* itself means. Due to the evolution of any language, we must realize that the area of meanings of words changes as time goes on. The English word *immortal* has, among others, a peculiar meaning of "not mortal." However, in most circles and also in theology, the word generally carries the meaning of "exemption from death." The question that will arise, then, is "When the Scriptures use the term *immortal,* is this definition all that is meant?" Contrary to the belief of some, there is *no reference* in Scripture that can be given to show that man, or his soul, is immortal.

To go even one step further, there is nothing in Scripture that states anything or anyone is immortal but God himself. Let us analyze this problem. There are two words in the Greek text that are translated "immortality." The first is *athanasia*—it appears three times and is translated "immortality" each time. The other term is *aphthartos*—it is translated "immortality" twice and "incorruption" four times.

Now let us examine the use of these words. The former word, *athanasian,* is used in 1 Timothy 6:16 and is speaking of God, "Who *only* hath immortality (*athanasian*), dwelling in the light which *no man* can approach unto." In 1 Corinthians 15:53–54, we again have *athanasia* used twice, but in the same verse we have *aphthartos* used twice also. Paul here is speaking of the second coming of Christ, and declares (v. 53), "For this corruptible must put on incorruption [*aphtharsian*] and this mortal must put on immortality [*athanasian*]." And (v. 54), "So when this corruptible *shall have put on* (aorist middle subjunctive of the verb *enduo*) incorruption (*aphtharsian*), and this mortal *shall have put on* immortality (*athanasian*), then shall be brought to pass the saying that is written, *Death* is swallowed up in victory" (emphasis added). We see here that in the two places where *athanasian* is used in reference to man, it is clear that it is an immortality to be given in the future, not one possessed at the present time.

Similarly, when an *aphtharsian* is used here and in Romans 2:7, "seek for," and 1 Peter 1:4, "reserved in heaven for you," it is speaking of the incorruption of man to be given at some future date, not possessed at the present time. Only when immortality or incorruption is used with God, is it in the present tense (1 Timothy 1:17; 6:16; Romans 1:23). Therefore, to say that the saints are immortal (if by immortality we mean *athanasian* or *aphtharsian*), we are not scriptural. We must say the saints *will* be immortal. It is also plain to see in 1 Corinthians 15:53–54 that this immortality (*athanasian*) and this incorruption (*aphtharsian*) will be put on (*endusetai*) as one puts on a garment. Just as Paul exhorts us to put on (*endusasthe*) Christ (Romans 13:14; Galatians 3:27), the armor of light (Romans 13:12), the new man (Ephesians 4:24), and the armor or panoply of God (Ephesians 6:11), we must conclude then that *athanasian* or *aphtharsian* have a larger and broader meaning than to be "everlasting." It must be seen, therefore, that immortality and incorruption, *when given,* will mean a change, not simply the giving and receiving of the attribute—"exemption from death." Jehovah's Witnesses have badly misconstrued the usage of immortality, and that error, coupled with their famous practice of term-switching, has resulted in confusion and poor exegesis.

Now, as to the eternity of the human soul, we must consult the existing language sources. When we use the term *eternal* in association with the soul of man, we mean that the human soul *after* its creating by God will (future) exist somewhere into the eternal, into the everlasting. Since there is only one place where the honest seeker can find pure information on the eternal existence of the soul, and that place is in the revelation that God, who created the soul, has given to man, namely, His Word, let us turn to it and consider therein His revealed will.

First, Revelation does show that God can be known, and second, that man's soul is eternal. In Hebrews 1:1–2 we read, "God, who at sundry times and in divers manners spake in time past unto the fathers by the prophets, hath in these last days spoken unto us by his Son, whom he hath appointed heir of all things, by whom also he made the worlds." All throughout history God has manifested himself to man in different ways, and at no time in history has man been left without a witness of God. In the Old Testament, God manifested himself and His will to man by the prophets, visions, and direct oral contact. However, when the fullness of time was come, God sent forth His Son in the likeness of sinful flesh and completed His progressive revelation. Man, since the time of his creation upon the earth, has always been able to know God and His will, if he so desired, and consequently since the day of Adam, men who know not God are without excuse.

God's revelation is not only a manifestation of God to man, but it is also the answer to the questions: "Where did man come from?" "Is he a spiritual as well as a natural being?" "What is his worth?" and "Where is he going?"

God's revelation shows that man is a creation of God, created in God's spiritual image (Genesis 1:26; 5:1; 1 Corinthians 11:7). He was created to have pre-eminence over other creatures (Genesis 1:28; Psalms 8:6; 82:6; Matthew 6:26; 12:12). He is definitely a spiritual being (Job 32:8; Psalm 51:10; Ecclesiastes 12:7; Acts 7:59; 2 Corinthians 4:13). He is an object of God's love (John 3:16; Revelation 1:5). He sinned and lost God's favor (Genesis 3:1–19). The consequences of Adam's sin passed upon all mankind (Romans 5:12). God sent His Son to redeem man (John 3:16). This redemption is by the vicarious death of Christ (Matthew 26:28; Acts 20:28; Romans 5:9; Colossians 1:20; Hebrews 9:14; 1 Peter 1:18–19; 1 John 1:7; Revelation 1:5; 7:14). This salvation is obtained by a new birth through faith in Jesus Christ (John 3:3–16).

We must conclude that since "God is Spirit" (John 4:24) and as such is incorporeal, He must have imparted to man a spiritual nature created in His own image, or else Genesis 1:26 is not meaningful.

Now the question arises, "If Jesus redeemed those who accept His salvation, what is the difference between those who are redeemed and those who are not?" It is clear that redemption is not simply favor with God here on earth. This brings us to the scriptural teaching of the eternal existence of the soul. First of all, there is much evidence that the soul does exist as a conscious entity after it departs from the body, and there is no scriptural evidence to the contrary. In Luke 20:37–38 the Lord Jesus, there speaking of the revelation God gave to Moses, makes it clear that when God said, "I AM the God of Abraham, Isaac, and Jacob," He *was* not the God of the dead, but *is* the God of the living, for Abraham, Isaac, and Jacob had long since been physically dead. The only reasonable conclusion, then, is that these great Old Testament saints of God possessed spiritual natures that transcended physical death. In Matthew 17 we see Moses and Elijah on the Mount of Transfiguration communing with Christ, yet we know that Moses had been physically dead for centuries, and no record of his resurrection exists in Scripture. Jehovah's Witnesses claim that this was a vision, not a "real" evidence of the soul's existence beyond the grave, and they point to Matthew 17:9, where the English rendition of the Greek (*horama*) is *vision*. However, this Greek term is translated literally in this context as "that which is seen—a spectacle" (see Thayer, 451), not a mere vision.

In Luke 16:19–31, Jesus (remember, this is not a parable) shows the difference between the state of the soul of the redeemed and the state of the soul of the wicked after death. In Revelation 6:9 we see the souls of those who had been martyred for Christ crying out for vengeance. In 2 Corinthians 5:1–9, Paul makes it clear that to be absent from the body is to be consciously "present" or "at home" with the Lord. But the Scriptures go even further, for they speak of a resurrection of the body (Job 19:25; 1 Corinthians 15:35–57; 1 Thessalonians 4:16–17). The answer to this question that the Jehovah Witnesses are laboring under is found in 1 Corinthians 15:35–49 (v. 35): "How are the dead raised up? and with what body do they come?" We notice that in verse 36, Paul addresses one who labors under this question as a "fool."

Now that we have considered the problem of the soul's existence after death and the resurrection of the body, we find Scripture is clear in its teaching that those who reject God's salvation will suffer throughout eternity in outer darkness (Matthew 8:11–12; 13:42–50; 22:13; 2 Peter 2:17; Jude 13; Revelation 14:9–11; 19:20), and those who accept God's salvation will dwell with Christ throughout eternity in joy and peace (John 14:1–3; 17:24; Luke 20:36; 1 Thessalonians 4:17; Revelation 22:5). Here is revealed what we believe is the true meaning of the scriptural terms *immortality* and *incorruption* (*athanasian, aphtharsian*). We must also realize that these words do not apply to God the Father in the same sense that they apply to God the Son. When we come "with" Him from heaven (1 Thessalonians 4:14), we shall be made like Him in the sense that we shall have a soul and body *incapable* of sin, not earthly but heavenly. We shall put on *athanasian* and *aphtharsian* and abide with Christ into the eternal.

As I stated at the beginning of this point, it would be futile to refute all the errors of thought in the Jehovah's Witnesses' theology. Therefore, I have presented what I feel is sufficient evidence to show that man has an eternal soul and will abide somewhere, either in conscious joy or sorrow eternally, and that those who believe and trust in Christ as their personal Savior will "put on" that immortality when Jesus returns.

Regarding the Jehovah's Witnesses, we can only say as Paul said to the Corinthians in 2 Corinthians 4:3–4: "But if our gospel be hid, it is hid to them that are lost: in whom the God of this world hath blinded the minds of them which believe not, lest the light of the glorious gospel of Christ, who is the image of God, should shine unto them," and as he again states in 2 Thessalonians 2:10–11, "because they received not the love of the truth, that they might be saved. And for this cause God shall send them strong delusion, that they should believe a lie."

Honest study of this problem will reveal to any interested Bible student that man does possess an eternal immaterial nature, which was fashioned to occupy an everlasting habitation whether in conscious bliss or torment. This, then, is the nature and certain destiny of man.

Author's Note

The following partial list of references to the soul and spirit of man as drawn from the Old and New Testaments will, we believe, furnish the interested reader

with ample evidence that man is not just a combination of body and breath forming a living soul, as the Jehovah's Witnesses teach, but rather a soul, or spirit,
possessing a corporeal form.

The Hebrew equivalent for soul as used in the Old Testament is *nephesh,* and
for spirit *ruach.* The Greek equivalent for soul is *psyche* and for spirit *pneuma.*

1. It is an entity possessing the attributes of life (Isaiah 55:3). It is also separate from the body (Matthew 10:28; Luke 8:55; 1 Thessalonians 5:23; Hebrews
4:12; Revelation 16:3); i.e., it exists independent of material form.

2. A soul departs at the death of the form (Genesis 35:18).

3. The soul is conscious after death (Matthew 17:3; Revelation 6:9–11).

4. The soul of Samuel was conscious after death (1 Samuel 28:18–19).

5. Stephen had a spirit, which he committed to Christ at his death (Acts
7:59).

6. There is definitely a spirit and soul of man (Isaiah 57:16).

7. The spirit is independent of the body (Zechariah 12:1).

8. The spirit, the soul of man, does that which only a personality can do; it
"wills" (*prothumon*) (Matthew 26:41).

9. We are instructed to worship in the spirit (John 4:23; Philippians 3:3)
because God is a spirit.

10. The spirit of man has the attribute of personality, the ability to testify
(Romans 8:16, 26), and also the faculty of "knowing" (1 Corinthians 2:11).

11. The spirit can be either saved or lost (1 Corinthians 5:5). It belongs to
God, and we are instructed to glorify Him in it (1 Corinthians 6:20).

12. The spirit or soul goes into eternity and is a conscious entity (Galatians
6:8).

13. Christ is with our spirit (2 Timothy 4:22), for the spirit is the life of the
body (James 2:26).

14. We are born of God's Spirit, and as such are spirits ourselves (John
3:5–6).

These references will suffice to show that the immaterial nature of man is far
from the combination of breath and flesh that Jehovah's Witnesses maintain.

The Kingdom of Heaven

The human soul, marred and stained as it is by the burden of personal sin,
seeks constant escape from the reality of that sin and the sure penalty due
because of it. Once the reality of eternal punishment is clouded by idealistic concepts of everlasting bliss without the fear of personal reckoning, the soul can
relax, so to speak, and the sinner, unconscious of the impending doom, which is
God's justice, rests secure in the persuasion that "God is Love." Laboring under
this delusion, it is no wonder that Jehovah's Witnesses can so calmly construct
"The kingdom of heaven," for to them God's infinite justice does not exist, and
eternal retribution is only an invention of "hellfire screechers."

The biblical kingdom of heaven has many aspects, none of which includes
the invented hierarchical construction so vividly outlined in *Let God Be True.* In
Luke 17:20–21, the Lord reveals the kingdom of heaven as within the believer in
one aspect, but clearly states that the heavenly aspect will be visible and observ-
able at His return (vv. 23–26). In Matthew 13, the Lord Jesus portrays the king-

dom of heaven symbolically in parables, yet always it is pictured as reality, not as an invisible phantom government. Jehovah's Witnesses arrive at the year A.D. 1914 as the end of the Gentile times and the beginning of the reign of the invisible heavenly King Christ Jesus. How they arrived at this arbitrary date no one can reasonably or chronologically ascertain, but valuable evidence to the effect that "Pastor" Russell formulated the whole hoax is obtainable from the July 15, 1950, issue of *The Watchtower Announcing Jehovah's Kingdom*, where, on page 216, the following statements are found:

> Away back in 1880 the columns of *The Watchtower* had called notice to Bible chronology marking A.D. 1914 as the year for the 2,520-year period to end and referred to by Jesus as "the times of the Gentiles" in his prophecy on the world's end (Luke 21:24). In harmony with this it was expected that in 1914 the kingdom of God by Christ Jesus in the heavens would be fully established, while this world would be involved in an unprecedented "time of trouble." The religious leaders and the systems of Christendom were all set to laugh at Brother Russell and his fellow witnesses of Jehovah over failure of his announced predictions concerning A.D. 1914. But it was no laughing matter when, at the end of July, World War I broke out and by October it had become global in its scope. Christendom's religious mouths were silenced at this frightening turn of events, but not Brother Russell's. October 1, 1914, on taking his place at the breakfast table in the Brooklyn Bethel dining room, he in a strong voice denoting conviction announced: "The Gentile Times have ended!"
>
> Knowing that the world had now reached the time for its dissolution, he refused to heed the plea of U.S. President Wilson for all clergymen and preachers to join in nationwide prayer for peace.

Thus it was that at the words of one colossally egotistical and unschooled haberdasher, the Times of the Gentiles ended.

To follow through Jehovah's Witnesses' interpretation of the kingdom, it is necessary to understand that only 144,000 faithful servants will rule with King Jesus in the heavenly sphere. They quote Revelation 7:4 and 14:1, 3, but neglect to notice that the 144,000 are of the tribes of Israel (Jews), 12,000 of each tribe, and are in no sense to be construed as anything else. This is not figurative; this is actual, because the tribes are listed by name. To follow out their own argument, Jehovah's Witnesses must believe that only 144,000 Jewish members of their organization will be privileged to reign with Christ Jesus. The argument that they are spiritual Jews is invalid, because even if they were, which they aren't, they would be "children of Abraham," not Israel, and there is a vast difference in interpretation at this point (Galatians 3:29). Ishmael, the father of the Arab race, the ancestor of Muhammad, the founder of Islam, was a son of Abraham (Genesis 16) after the flesh even as Isaac was the father of Jacob, so it can be seen that Abraham's seed differs from the selection of Israel's stock, as it is written, "For in Isaac shall thy seed be called" (Genesis 21:12). The texts are clear that Israel after the flesh is mentioned and not spiritual symbolism; therefore, the 144,000 conjecture pertaining to kingdom rule as advanced by Jehovah's Witnesses crumbles under the light of scriptural truth.

In concluding this point it is imperative to remember that there can be no kingdom without the King, and the Scripture is clear when it states that the true kingdom will be instituted at Christ's visible return.

The Old and New Testaments corroborate each other in establishing the certainty of the visible return and reign of Christ (cf. Zechariah 14:4; Amos 9:8–15; Isaiah 11 and 12; Ezekiel 37:20–28; Luke 17:22ff., and Matthew 24:26–31, to mention only a few). Jehovah's Witnesses unknowingly fulfill the prophecy of Christ in Matthew 24:23ff., where the Lord warns of false Christs and prophets who shall say Christ is here, Christ is there (in the desert, in the secret places, etc.), and shall deceive many with their deceit. Jehovah's Witnesses say He is here now, but the Lord said He would be visible at His return, and that every eye should see Him (Revelation 1:7; cf. Matthew 24:27–30). How, then, can we doubt His testimony when He himself has said,

> And then shall appear the sign of the Son of man in heaven: and then shall all the tribes of the earth mourn, and they shall see the Son of man coming in the clouds of heaven with power and great glory. (Matthew 24:30)

To this we can only say with John: "Even so, come, Lord Jesus" (Revelation 22:20).

In drawing this portion of our study of Jehovah's Witnesses to a close, it is expedient and vitally necessary that a clear picture of what this cult means to all Christians be presented. This organization has mushroomed from a meager beginning in 1881 until now, when it extends to every part of the globe. Because the cult does away with the doctrine of eternal retribution for sin, it appeals greatly to those who believe they have in it an escape from the penalty of personal transgression. Jehovah's Witnesses offer an illusionary "kingdom" to the personalities who desire importance, and most of all an outlet to vent their wrath upon religious leaders and organizations whose doctrines they assail as "of the devil." We do not believe for one moment that the greater body of these people knows the true implications of Charles T. Russell's doctrines; however, let no Jehovah's Witness ever disclaim Russellistic origin. Charles Taze Russell founded, operated, propagated, and gave his life to furthering this cult, and his teachings permeate every major phase of its doctrines, despite the intense aloofness its leaders manifest when his past is mentioned. But now the question arises: "How can so many people be deceived by so obviously fraudulent a type of religion?" To understand this, the teachings and methods of propagation of the cult must be analyzed.

To begin with, no member of the Society is ever allowed to think independently for himself.

All religious leaders and organizations are pictured as false, and anything they say is to be discounted as the "vain philosophies of men." The Scriptures are always made to conform to the Jehovah's Witnesses' beliefs, never Jehovah's Witnesses' beliefs to the Scriptures. Judge Rutherford's legal mind made most of this conjecture and linguistic chicanery reasonable to the minds of the people to whom he addressed it, and his books are masterpieces of illogical and invalid premises and conclusions.

To trace the logic and reasoning processes of Rutherford is the task of a logician, since for Russell or Rutherford a contradictory statement can be a premise that, regardless of the steps, always has a valid conclusion in their system of thinking. Jehovah's Witnesses' doctrine is a mass of half-truths and pseudo-scholastic material, which to the untutored mind appears as "wonderful revelation."

While speaking with an ardent Jehovah's Witness, the following statement fell unashamedly from his lips: "I have never met anyone who knows more about Greek than the Society." In all probability he was right, for had he met someone who did know Greek, he would never have become a member of the cult. The Society, to our knowledge, does not have any Greek scholars of any repute in their ranks, and if they do, I would welcome any opportunity for them to come out from behind their lexicons and explain their renditions of John 1:1, 8:58, and Colossians 2:9, to mention only a few. (Hebrew scholars are also included in this invitation.) ~In recent years there have been a few Jehovah's Witnesses who have taken courses in Greek, and even others who teach Greek. However, their renditions of the Greek New Testament into English, and their *theological interpretations* of those renditions, have no academic or scholastic support.~

Another trait of the Society is its aversion to attributing individual authorship to its publications since the death of Rutherford. All publications now appear anonymously, copyrighted and published by the Society. By not committing persons to their signatures, the Society escapes the unpleasant task of having to answer for their numerous blunders. Their standard answer is, "Many persons worked on the books, not only one particular person," etc. In their predicament, having no recognized scholarship behind them, they have chosen the wisest possible course—silence. The plain truth of the matter is that the "new" books are simply rephrases of Russell's and Rutherford's works and contain no originality other than up-to-date information on world conditions and new approaches to old material.

One of the distinguishing characteristics of an ardent Jehovah's Witness is his or her ability to handle the Scriptures. *The Emphatic Diaglott* and *The Kingdom Interlinear Translation of the Greek Scriptures* with their interlinear readings of the Greek facilitate their progress in this project. Any good Jehovah's Witness, sad to say, can cause the average Christian untold trouble in the Scriptures, though the trouble in most cases has an elementary solution. The Christian is bewildered by the glib manner in which they repeat Scripture verses (usually entirely out of context) and sprinkle their discourses with Greek or Hebrew grammatical terms of which they have no knowledge beyond their *Diaglott* and *Kingdom Interlinear*. The boldness with which they collar the unwary pedestrian, intrude on the quiet of a restful evening, attend their conventions, and propagate their literature is a danger signal that evangelical Christianity would do well to heed and take definite steps to combat. As has been observed, the answer to Jehovah's Witnesses, or "Russellism" if you will, is the deity of Jesus Christ, and in teaching that one cardinal doctrine of the Christian faith all energy ought to be expended to the uttermost. All ministers, Sunday school supervisors, Bible and Tract Societies, and teachers should drill their charges in biblical memorization and doctrinal truths, in order that a united Christian front may be thrown up against this ever-growing menace to sound reasoning in biblical exposition and study. The plan is not difficult, and only procrastination hinders its adoption.

This problem is also the task of Christian colleges, seminaries, and Bible schools, who too long have neglected the institution of strong cult courses in their curricula. The fruit of their neglect is before us today. Must we stand by in silence while the Word of God is defamed, the lordship of Christ blasphemed, and the faith of generations still unborn is threatened by a group of people who will not listen to honest biblical truths, and dare not contest them in scholastic discussion? It is frustrating and exasperating to carry on a discussion with a person or persons who argue in circles and dodge artfully from one refutation to another. These tactics characterize the preaching and argumentation of Jehovah's Witnesses, which must be met by calm dispositions and truthful scriptural exegesis on the part of well-grounded Christians. Information in the form of documentary evidence and cold facts has met and can meet their perversions and emerge triumphant over them. We as Christians must perform this task without delay; we can ill afford to wait any longer.

The end product of this whole cult is the denial of the Lord Jesus Christ as "very God," and despite their protests that they honor Christ, they do indeed dishonor and "crucify Him afresh" since they deny His deity and lordship. Regardless of their biblical names and proficiency in the Scriptures, they constantly reveal their true character in their actions, which are the diametric opposite of scriptural teachings. The following old adage is most appropriate in describing the doctrines of Jehovah's Witnesses: "No matter how you label it or what color bottle you put it in, poison is still poison."

"He that has ears, let him hear." On the cover of *The Watchtower*, Isaiah 35:5 and 43:12 were quoted, and throughout all of their publications they boast themselves as "Jehovah's Witnesses."

There can be no kingdom without the King, however, and His return is visible, with power and glory (Matthew 24:30). Their kingdom has come (A.D. 1914–1918), but with no visible king, power, or glory. Jehovah of the Watchtower is a conjectural myth, a creation of the reactionary theology of Charles Taze Russell, and is conformed to the pattern of Russell's mind and education, which continued through Rutherford, Knorr, Franz, and now Henschel and the Governing Body to the ever-increasing blindness of those misguided souls foolish enough to trust in the Russellite delusion. In comparison to the Scriptures this picture is infinite darkness, for its author is the "Prince of Darkness," and the Word of God clearly and incontestably reveals that "Jehovah of the Watchtower" is not the Jehovah of the Bible, for Jehovah of the Bible is Lord of all—"The great God and our Saviour Jesus Christ" (Titus 2:13).

Selected Terms and Texts Misapplied by Jehovah's Witnesses

To review all the terms and texts that Jehovah's Witnesses have misinterpreted and misapplied to bolster up their fractured system of theology would be impossible in the space here available. Therefore, I have chosen to survey six of their worst perversions of common biblical terms, and various texts that the Watchtower has mauled and mangled almost beyond recognition with little or no regard for hermeneutical principles, contexts, or the laws of sound exegesis.

These examples of Watchtower deceptions are found all neatly cataloged in their handbook of doctrinal subjects, entitled *Make Sure of All Things* (Brooklyn: Watchtower Bible and Tract Society, 1953), upon which this study is principally based, should any care to check further their authenticity, etc.

Misapplied Terms

1. "Only begotten" (Greek, *monogenes*). Jehovah's Witnesses, in their zeal to establish the Christology of Arius of Alexandria, have seized upon this Greek term, translated "only begotten" in the New Testament, and unfortunately they have been most successful in hoodwinking many uninformed persons into believing that "only begotten" really means "only generated." From this erroneous view they, therefore, suggest that since the term is applied to Jesus Christ five times in the New Testament, Christ is but a creature, or as they love to quote Codex Alexandrinus, "The only begotten God" (John 1:18).

It should be noted in this connection, therefore, that the most authoritative lexicons and grammar books, not to mention numerous scholarly works, all render *monogenes* as "only or unique: 'the only member of a kin or kind, hence generally only' " (Liddell and Scott's *Greek-English Lexicon*, 2:1144). Moulton and Milligan, in their *Vocabulary of the Greek New Testament* (416–417), render *monogenes* as "one of a kind, only, unique," facts that establish beyond scholarly doubt the truth of the contention that in both classical and Koine Greek the term *monogenes* carries the meaning of "only," "unique," or "the only member of a particular kind." The Septuagint translation of the Old Testament (LXX) also utilizes the term *monogenes* as the equivalent in translation of the Hebrew adjective *yachid*, translated *solitary* (Psalm 68:6, etc.). This interesting fact reveals that the translators understood *monogenes* to have the meaning of uniqueness attached to it, emphasis obviously being placed on "only" and decidedly not on "genus" or "kind."

In other places in the New Testament, such as Luke 7:11–18; 8:42; 9:38; Hebrews 11:17, etc., the rendering "only begotten" in the sense that Jehovah's Witnesses attempt to employ it in their translations and propaganda is an exegetical impossibility; especially in the instance of Hebrews 11:17, where Isaac is called the "only begotten" son of Abraham. Certainly he was not the eldest child, but rather he was the *sole* or *only* precious son in the sense that Abraham loved him in a unique way.

Dr. Thayer in his *Greek-English Lexicon of the New Testament* (p. 417), referring to *monogenes*, states, "single of its kind, only . . . used of Christ, denotes the only Son of God." Unfortunately, in ancient literature *monogenes* became connected with the Latin term *unigenitus*. However, such a translation is basically incorrect, as any lexicographical study will quickly reveal.

The early church fathers were in essential agreement that Jesus Christ preexisted from all eternity in a unique relationship to God the Father. In the year 325 at the Council of Nicea, it was officially proclaimed that Jesus Christ was of the same substance or nature as the Father, and those who differed from this pronouncement, which the church had always held, were excommunicated. Among them was Arius of Alexandria, a learned presbyter and the Christological father of Jehovah's Witnesses. Arius held that Jesus Christ was a created being, the first and greatest creation of God the Father, that He did not preexist from all eternity and that His only claim to Godhood was the fact that He had been created first and then elevated to the rank of a Deity.

Arius derived many of his ideas from his teacher, Lucian of Antioch, who in turn borrowed them from Origen, who himself had introduced the term "eternal generation," or the concept that God from all eternity generates a second person like himself, ergo the "eternal Son." Arius rejected this as illogical and unreasonable, which it is, and taking the other horn of the dilemma squarely between his teeth, reduced the eternal Word of God to the rank of a creation! It is a significant fact, however, that in the earliest writings of the church fathers, dating from the first century to the year 230, the term "eternal generation" was never used, but it has been this dogma, later adopted by Roman Catholic theology, which has fed the Arian heresy through the centuries and today continues to feed the Christology of Jehovah's Witnesses.

In the year A.D. 328, in his private creed, Arius interestingly enough applies the term *gegennemenon* in reference to Christ, not the terms *monogenes* or *ginomai*. *Gegennemenon* is a derivative of the word *gennao*, which is translated "begotten," and rightly so. Further than this, Eusebius of Caesarea, a follower of Arius (ca. 325), also utilized the term *gegennemenon*, not *monogenes*, a fact that throws a grammatical monkey wrench into the semantic machinations of the Watchtower.

We may see, therefore, that a study of this term *monogenes* reveals that in itself it is understood in both the classical and Koine vocabulary to be a term emphasizing uniqueness, i.e., the only one, the beloved, etc.; and there is no good grammatical ground for insisting, as Jehovah's Witnesses do, that it *must* mean "only generated," i.e., "only created."

Regarding the five times in the New Testament where the term *monogenes* is applied to Jesus Christ (John 1:14, 18; 3:16, 18; 1 John 4:9), it can be easily seen by the interested reader that the proper rendering "only" or "unique," in keeping with the historical usage of the term, in no way disturbs the context but, in fact, makes it clearer Christologically, eliminating the concept fostered by the Arians and carried on by Jehovah's Witnesses that "only begotten" must infer creation, which it most certainly does not!

As we mentioned before, the doctrine of eternal generation relative to the preexistence of the Lord Jesus Christ is one of the great stumbling blocks in any intelligent approach to the Christological problems of the New Testament. This fact being true, the author feels it is wiser to return to the original language of Scripture in its description of the Lord Jesus and His preincarnate existence, where He is never referred to except prophetically in the Bible as the "eternal Son," but as the Word of God (John 1:1) who "was" from all eternity and who "became" flesh (John 1:14), taking upon himself the nature of man, and as such was "begotten" of the Virgin Mary by the power of the Holy Spirit. The "unique," "only" Son of God, then, whose uniqueness stems from the fact that of all men He was the most precious in the Father's sight. He is beloved above all His brethren, so much so that the Father could say of Him when He sent Him into the world, "Thou art my Son, this day have I begotten thee" (Hebrews 1:5). He is not a creature or a demi-god but "God over all, blessed forever. Amen" (Romans 9:5 RSV).

The Bible clearly teaches, then, that Jesus Christ before His incarnation was the eternal Word, Wisdom, or Logos, of God, preexistent from all eternity, co-equal, coexistent, coeternal with the Father, whose intrinsic nature of Deity He shared, and even though clothed in human form He never ceased to be Deity, "God . . . manifest in the flesh" (1 Timothy 3:16), or as Paul put it so directly, "In him dwelleth all the fulness of the Godhead bodily" (Colossians 2:9).

By insisting upon the correct title of the preexistent Christ, orthodox Christianity can successfully undercut the emphasis Jehovah's Witnesses place upon *monogenes*, showing in contrast that "only begotten" is a term of time that can have no meaning outside of the sphere that man knows as recorded experience; and further, that Jesus Christ is not called by Scripture the "eternal Son," the error passed on from Origen under the title "eternal generation," but rather He is the living Word of God (Hebrews 4:12), Creator of the Universe (2 Peter 3:5), Sustainer of all things (2 Peter 3:7), First Begotten from the dead (Acts 13:33), and our "great high priest, that is passed into the heavens, Jesus the Son of God . . . which cannot be touched with the feeling of our infirmities; but was in all points tempted like as we are, yet without sin" (Hebrews 4:15). Let us fix these things in our minds, then:

(a) The doctrine of "eternal generation" or the eternal sonship of Christ, which springs from the Roman Catholic doctrine first conceived by Origen in A.D. 230, is a theory that opened the door theologically to the Arian and Sabellian heresies, which today still plague the Christian church in the realms of Christology.

(b) Scripture nowhere calls Jesus Christ the eternal Son of God, and he is never called Son at all prior to the incarnation, except in prophetic passages in the Old Testament.

(c) The term *Son* itself is a functional term, as is the term *Father,* and has no meaning apart from time. The term *Father,* incidentally, never carries the descriptive adjective "eternal" in Scripture; as a matter of fact, only the Spirit is called eternals[67] ("The eternal Spirit"—Hebrews 9:14 RSV), emphasizing the fact that the words *Father* and *Son* are purely functional, as previously stated.

(d) Many heresies have seized upon the confusion created by the illogical "eternal Sonship" or "eternal generation" theory of Roman Catholicism, unfortunately carried over to some aspects of Protestant theology.

(e) Finally, there cannot be any such thing as eternal Sonship. This would be a logical contradiction of terminology due to the fact that the word *Son* predicates time and the involvement of creativity. Christ, the Scripture tells us, as the Logos, is timeless—the *Word was* in the beginning, *not* the *Son!*

The Lord Jesus Christ, true God and true man, is now and for all eternity Son of God and Son of Man; therefore, in this sense he is the eternal Son. But to be biblical in the true sense of the term, we must be willing to admit that He was known prior to His incarnation as the eternal Word, and knowledge of this fact cuts across the very basic groundwork and foundation of the Arian system of theology espoused by Jehovah's Witnesses. For if "only begotten" means "unique" or "only one of its kind," there cannot be any ground for rendering it "only generated" as Jehovah's Witnesses often attempt to do in a vain attempt to rob Christ of His deity.

If then we relegate the terms *Father* and *Son* to the sphere of time as functional vehicles for the conveyance of the mysterious relationship that existed from all eternity between God and His Word, we will be probing deeper into the truth of the Scripture, which seems to teach us that God calls Christ His Eternal Word, lest we should ever forget that He is intrinsic Deity (for never was there a moment when God had a thought apart from His Logos or Reason). Further than this,

---

[67]The Trinity as such is, however, spoken of as "the everlasting God" (Romans 16:26).

God calls Christ His "Son," lest we should think of the Word as being an impersonal force or attribute instead of a substantive entity existing in a subject-object
relationship, the Eternal God "who is the Savior of all men, especially of those
who believe" (1 Timothy 4:10 RSV).

In summary, since the word *Son* in a temporal sense definitely suggests infe-
riority and derivation, it is absolutely essential that Christ as the Eternal Word be
pointed up as an antidote to the Arian heresy of Jehovah's Witnesses, and in this
light we can understand quite plainly the usages of the term *monogenes*, not in the
Jehovah's Witnesses' sense of creatureliness, but in the true biblical sense of
"uniqueness," i.e., "the unique or only Son of God," generated in the womb of
a woman by the direct agency of the Holy Spirit, "God manifest in the flesh."
"The great God and our Saviour Jesus Christ" (Titus 2:13).

2. "Greater." (Greek: *meizon.*) Another principal term utilized by Jehovah's
Witnesses is the term *greater*, translated from the Greek *meizon*, as it appears in the
gospel of John, chapter 14, verse 28: "Ye have heard how I said unto you, I go
away, and come again unto you. If ye loved me, ye would rejoice, because I said,
I go unto the Father: for my Father is greater [*meizon*] than I." From this particular text, lifted conveniently out of its context by the ever zealous Russellites, the
Watchtower attempts to "prove" that since Jesus in His own words while He was
on earth stated that His Father was "greater" than He was, therefore Christ could
not be equal with God or one of the members of the Trinity, which Jehovah's
Witnesses deny so vehemently.

On the face of the matter, this appears to be a good argument from Christ's
usage of the word *greater*, but a closer examination of the context and of the hermeneutical principles that govern any sound exegetical study of the New Testament quickly reveals that theirs is a shallow case indeed, and, one that rests rather
unsteadily upon one Greek word in a most restricted context.

The refutation of this bit of Watchtower semantic double-talk is found in a
comparison with Hebrews, the first chapter, verse 4: "Being made so much *better*
than the angels, as he hath by inheritance obtained a more excellent name than
they" (emphasis added).

The careful student of Scripture will recognize immediately that in the first
chapter of Hebrews, the verse previously cited, an entirely different word is utilized when comparing Christ and the angels. This word is *kreitton* and is translated
"better" in the *King James Version*. Paralleling these two comparisons, that of Jesus
with His Father in John 14:28 and Jesus with the angels in Hebrews 1:4, one startling fact immediately attracts attention. In the fourteenth chapter of John, as the
Son of Man who had emptied himself of His prerogatives of Deity (Philippians
2:8–11) and taken upon himself the form of a slave, the Lord Jesus Christ could
truthfully say, "My Father is greater than I," *greater* being a *quantitative* term
descriptive of *position*. Certainly in no sense of the context could it be construed
as a comparison of *nature* or *quality*.

In the first chapter of Hebrews, however, the comparison made there
between the Lord Jesus Christ and angels is clearly one of *nature*. The Greek *kreitton* being a term descriptive of quality, *ergo*, Christ was *qualitatively* better than the
angels because He was their Creator (Colossians 1:16–17), and as such He existed
before all things and by Him all things consist (vv. 17–19). Since His intrinsic
nature is that of Deity (John 8:58; cf. Colossians 2:9); therefore, *qualitatively*

speaking He was God manifest in the flesh, while *quantitatively* He was limited as a man and could in all truthfulness state, "My Father is greater than I." When this comparison of *position* in John 14:28 and the comparison of *nature* in Hebrews 1 are clearly understood, the argument Jehovah's Witnesses attempt to raise in order to rob Christ of His deity is reduced to rubble before one of the greatest of all truths revealed in Scripture, i.e., that God who made the world and all things therein so loved us as to appear in our form (John 1:1, 14) that the sons of men might through His measureless grace at length become the sons of God.

We should be quick to recognize, however, that had the Lord Jesus said in John 14:28 that His Father was *better* than He was and had used the proper Greek word denoting this type of comparison, another issue would be involved, but in actuality the comparison between Christ and His Father in that context and verse clearly indicates that Jesus was speaking as a man and not as the second person of the Trinity (John 1:1). Therefore, it is perfectly understandable that He should humble himself before His Father and declare that in the present form in which He found himself, His Father most certainly was "greater," *positionally*, than He. One might be willing to admit that the president of the United States is a *greater* man by virtue of his present *position*, authority, and recognition, etc., but it would be a far different matter to assent to the proposition that the president of the United States is a *better* man than his fellow Americans in the sense of *quality*, because such a comparison then involves a discussion of fundamental natures, attributes, etc. In like manner, Jesus, as the Incarnate Son of God who had by His own voluntary act of will divested himself of His prerogatives of intrinsic Deity, could speak of His Father as being *positionally* greater than He was without in any sense violating His true deity and humanity.

Hebrews 1:4 clearly teaches that Christ is better than the angels *qualitatively* from all eternity and that even while He walked the earth, though He was made lower than the angels *positionally* for the suffering of death in the form of a man, never for an instant did He cease to be the Lord of glory who could say with confident assurance, "Before Abraham was I am" (John 8:58).

Let us constantly be aware of these facts when discussing the nature of Christ with Jehovah's Witnesses, for once the distinction is made between "greater" and "better," their entire argument based upon John 14:28 melts into nothingness, and the deity of our Lord is completely vindicated by the whole testimony of Scripture.

3. "Born again." Many times in their contacts with Christians, Jehovah's Witnesses utilize the evangelical terminology of the gospel of John, chapter 3, where Christ speaking to Nicodemus said, "Except a man be born again, he cannot see the kingdom of God" (v. 3). The Witnesses utilize such terminology because they realize that contemporary evangelical efforts, especially those of Dr. Billy Graham, have popularized this term, and the Watchtower is quick to capitalize on any popularization of a biblical term, especially if it can be twisted to serve its own end. The definition that Jehovah's Witnesses give to the new birth or the act of being "born again" is found in *Make Sure of All Things* (p. 48) and is as follows: "Born again means a birth-like realization of prospects and hopes for spirit life by resurrection to heaven. Such a realization is brought about through the water of God's truth in the Bible and God's holy spirit, his active force."

The interested student can see from this definition that the Witnesses reject flatly the concept of the new birth as taught in the New Testament. The Bible teaches us that when we are born again, it is through repentance, the washing of water by the Word, and the direct agency of the third person of the Trinity, God the Holy Spirit (John 3; Ephesians 5:26; 1 Peter 1:23, etc.). There is not one verse that may be cited in either the Old or New Testament to prove that the new birth means "a birth-like realization of prospects and hopes for spirit life by resurrection to heaven," as Jehovah's Witnesses so brazenly misrepresent it. On the contrary, the new birth guarantees eternal life to *all* believers, entrance into the kingdom of heaven, and a resurrection to immortality in a deathless, incorruptible form similar to that of the Lord Jesus Christ's form when He rose from among the dead.

The theology of Jehovah's Witnesses relevant to the new birth is that there will be only 144,000 "spiritual brothers" who will reign with Christ in heaven for a thousand years; and, further, that only these 144,000 will have a resurrection to heaven and a "spirit life" such as that now allegedly enjoyed by "Pastor" Charles Taze Russell and Judge J. F. Rutherford, who are carrying on the work of the Society "within the veil," according to Watchtower teaching. In direct contrast to this, the Lord Jesus Christ made a universal statement when He said, "Except a man be born again, he cannot see the kingdom of God," and we find no record of either Christ, the disciples, or the apostles ever promulgating the 144,000 "spirit brothers" idea espoused so zealously by the Watchtower. A doctrine of such momentous importance, the author feels, would certainly have been carefully defined in the New Testament; yet it is not, and the only support Jehovah's Witnesses can garner for this weird Russellite interpretation is from the book of Revelation and the mystical number 144,000, which, incidentally, the Bible teaches refers to the twelve tribes of Israel, twelve thousand out of each tribe, and therefore certainly not to members of the Watchtower's "theocracy."

Christians, therefore, should be on guard continually against the Watchtower's perversion of common biblical terms drawn from evangelical sources, for in 90 percent of the cases the author has analyzed, the Witnesses *mean* just the opposite of what they *appear* to say. The new birth, Peter tells us, is a *past* event in the lives of those who have experienced the regenerating power of God's Spirit (from the Greek, "being born again," 1 Peter 1:23); it is not something to be constantly experiencing or to be looking forward to in a type of ethereal spiritual resurrection as the Witnesses would have us believe. Rather, it is a fact to be rejoiced in that we have been born again and are new creations in Christ Jesus (2 Corinthians 5:17), joint heirs in the glory of the kingdom that is yet to be revealed.

The Watchtower Bible and Tract Society most decidedly has its "new birth," but it is not the new birth of Scripture, nor is their theory taught anywhere within the pages of the Bible. It is instead the theological brain-child of Charles Taze Russell, to which the Witnesses cling so tenaciously, and which in the end will be found to have originated with "the god of this world," who has blinded their eyes "lest the light of the glorious gospel of Christ, who is the image of God, should shine unto them" (2 Corinthians 4:4).

4. "Death." In common with other deviant systems of theology, Jehovah's Witnesses espouse a peculiar and definitely unbiblical concept of death in regard

to the physical body and the soul and spirit of man.

According to *Make Sure of All Things* (p. 86), death is defined in the following manner: "Death: loss of life; termination of existence; utter cessation of conscious intellectual or physical activity, celestial, human, or otherwise."

Reverting to their basic trait of text-lifting and term-switching, Jehovah's Witnesses garner a handful of texts from the Old and New Testaments that speak of death as "sleep" or "unconsciousness," and from these out-of-context quotations attempt to prove that at the death of the physical form, man, like the beasts, ceases to exist until the resurrection.

Seizing upon such texts as Ecclesiastes 9:5–6, 10; Psalm 13:3; Daniel 12:2, etc., the Witnesses loudly contend that until the resurrection, the dead remain unconscious and inactive in the grave, thus doing away in one fell swoop with the doctrine of hell and the true biblical teaching regarding the soul of man.

It is impossible in the space allotted here to place all the verses Jehovah's Witnesses lift out of their contexts back into their proper contextual-hermeneutical position, and by so doing to show that their theory is an exegetical nightmare, but the following observation can be made.

Despite the fact that in the Old Testament the term *sleep* is used to denote death, never once is such a term used to describe the immaterial nature of man, which the Scriptures teach was created in the image of God (Genesis 1:26–27). This fact also holds true in the New Testament, as any cursory study of either Strong's or Young's concordances will reveal. The term *sleep* is always applied to the body, since in death the body takes on the appearance of one who is asleep, but the term *soul-sleep* or *the sleep of the soul* is never found in Scripture, and nowhere does it state that the soul ever sleeps or passes into a state of unconsciousness. The only way that Jehovah's Witnesses can infer such a doctrine is by assuming beforehand that death *means* sleep or unconsciousness; hence, every time they are confronted with the term *death* they assign the meaning of the temporary extinction of consciousness to it, and by so doing remove from Scripture the doctrine that they fear and hate the most—that of conscious punishment after death for unregenerate souls, continuing on into the everlasting ages of eternity (Jude 10–13; 2 Peter 2:17).

Since we have already covered the doctrine of hell in a previous section, the simplest refutation of Jehovah's Witnesses' perverted terms such as *death* can be found in the Scriptures themselves, where it easily can be shown that death does not mean "termination of existence" and "utter cessation of conscious intellectual . . . activity" as the Watchtower desperately attempts to establish.

The interested reader is referred to the following references: Ephesians 2:1–5; John 11:26; Philippians 1:21, 23; and Romans 8:10. The usage of "death" in these passages clearly indicates a state of existence solely in opposition to the definition that the Watchtower assigns to the word *death,* and the reader need only substitute the Watchtower's definition in each one of these previously enumerated passages to see how utterly absurd it is to believe that the body has experienced "the loss of life" or "termination of existence" in such a context where Paul writes, "If Christ be in you, the body is dead because of sin" (Romans 8:10). The inspired apostle here obviously refers to a spiritual condition of separation— certainly not to "termination of existence," as the Watchtower's definition states.

We see, therefore, that death is a separation of the soul and spirit *from* the body, resulting in physical inactivity and a general *appearance* of sleep; however, in the spiritual sense death is the separation of soul and spirit from God as the result of sin, and in no sense of the term can it ever be honestly translated "unconsciousness" or "termination of existence" as Jehovah's Witnesses would like to have it.

In his first epistle to the Thessalonians, the fourth chapter, the apostle Paul spoke of the return of the Lord Jesus Christ and most pointedly made use of the term *sleep* as a metaphor for death (1 Thessalonians 4:13–18), and it is interesting to note his concept:

> But I would not have ye to be ignorant, brethren, concerning them which are asleep, that ye sorrow not, even as others which have no hope. For if we believe that Jesus died and rose again, even so them also which sleep in Jesus will God bring *with* him. For this we say unto you by the word of the Lord, that we which are alive and remain unto the coming of the Lord shall not prevent them which are asleep. For the Lord himself shall descend from heaven with a shout, with the voice of the archangel, and with the trump of God: and the dead in Christ shall rise first: Then we which are alive and remain shall be caught up together with them in the clouds, to meet the Lord in the air: and so shall we ever be with the Lord. Wherefore comfort one another with these words.

Verse 14 indicates that Paul, while using the metaphor "sleep" to describe physical death, clearly understood that when Jesus comes again He will bring *with* (in the Greek, *sun*) Him those whose bodies are sleeping. To be more explicit, the souls and spirits of those who are with Christ now in glory (2 Corinthians 5:8; Philippians 1:22–23) will be reunited with their resurrection bodies (1 Corinthians 15); that is, they will be clothed with immortality, incorruptibility, and exemption from physical decay, and they will be coming *with* Jesus. The Greek *sun* indicates in a "side-by-side" position, and the bodies that are sleeping will in that instant be quickened, raised to immortality, and reunited with the perfected spirits of the returning saints. This passage alone would be enough to convince any exegetical scholar that those "sleeping in Jesus" must refer to their *bodies*, since they are in the same verse spoken of as coming *with* Jesus, and by no possible stretch of the imagination could one honestly exegete the passage so as to teach anything to the contrary.

Jehovah's Witnesses are justly afraid of the "everlasting fire" prepared for the devil and his followers (Matthew 25:41), and their entire system of theology is dedicated to a contradiction of this important biblical teaching of God's eternal wrath upon those who perpetrate the infinite transgression of denying His beloved Son. Rightly, then, does the Bible say that "the wrath of God continues to abide upon them" (John 3:36—literal translation; Revelation 20:10; Mark 9:43, 48; Daniel 12:2).

For the Christian, then, physical death involves only the sleep of the body, pending the resurrection to immortality, when our resurrection bodies will be joined to our perfected souls and spirits; but in the intermediate state, should we die before the Lord comes, we have the assurance that we shall be *with Him* and that we shall return *with Him,* or as the apostle Paul stated, "To be absent from the body" is "to be [at home or] present with the Lord" (2 Corinthians 5:8).

5. "Firstborn" (Greek: *prototokos*). The author feels it necessary to include a brief résumé of Jehovah's Witnesses' misuse of the Greek term *prototokos* (Colossians 1:15), which the Watchtower lays much emphasis upon. It is used descriptively of the Lord Jesus Christ, and so in their Arian theology it is construed to teach that Christ is the first creature, since the word *firstborn* implies that of the *first* child.

In Colossians 1, the apostle Paul speaks of the Lord Jesus Christ as the firstborn of every creature or of all creation. And the Witnesses, always eager to reduce Christ to the rank of an angel, have seized upon these passages of Scripture as indicative of His creaturehood. The Watchtower teaches that since Christ is called the "firstborn of all creation," therefore He must be the first one created, and they cross-reference this with Revelation 3:14, which states that the faithful and true witness (Christ) is "the beginning of the creation of God."

On the surface the argument the Watchtower erects appears to be fairly sound, but underneath it is found to be both shallow and fraudulent. The term *firstborn* (*prototokos*) may also rightfully be rendered "first begetter" or "original bringer forth" (*Erasmus*), a term of preeminence, and in Colossians 1 it is a term of comparison between Christ and created *things*. In the first chapter of Colossians, Paul points out that Christ is "before all things" and clearly establishes the fact that the eternal Word of God (John 1:1) existed before all creation (Hebrews 1) and that He is preeminent over all creation, by virtue of the fact that He is Deity; and beyond this, that He is the Creator of all "things," which to any rational person indicates that if He is Creator of all things, He himself is not one of the "things" created! In the eighth chapter of Romans, verse 29, the word *firstborn* is applied to Christ, clearly denoting His preeminence—not the concept that He is "the first creature made by Jehovah God," as the Witnesses would like us to believe—and in Colossians 1:18 we learn that Christ is "firstborn" from the dead, that is, the one with the preeminence, or right to rule, over death. Again the meaning is that of preeminence, not of creation. Revelation 3:14, "the beginning of the creation of God," is easily harmonized with the rest of Scripture, which teaches the absolute deity of the Lord Jesus Christ when we realize that the Greek word *arche*, which is translated "beginning," is translated by the Witnesses themselves as "originally" in John 1:1 of their own *New World Translation of the Christian Greek Scriptures*—and this is a good translation at this point—so applying it to Revelation 3:14, Christ becomes the "origin" or the "source" of the creation of God (*Knox*), and not the very beginning of it himself in the sense that He is the first creation, a fact that Scripture most pointedly contradicts.

Christ is therefore "firstborn," or preeminent, by virtue of the fact that He is Deity, and by virtue of the fact that He is the first one to rise in a *glorified* body. He is, therefore, preeminent over all creation, and through His power all things consist or hold together. He is not one of the "things" (Colossians 1:16–17), but He is the Creator of *all things*, the eternal Word who possesses the very nature of God (Hebrews 1:5).

6. "Soul and spirit" (Greek: *psyche, pneuma*). Jehovah's Witnesses delight in the assertion that man does not possess an immaterial, deathless nature, and they never tire of proclaiming such teaching to be "a lie of the devil" and a dogma derived from pagan religions (Egyptian, Babylonian, Greek, etc.). The literature of Jehovah's Witnesses is filled with condemnations of the doctrine of the

immaterial nature of man. According to the Watchtower, the soul is "a living, breathing, sentient creature, animal or human," and Jehovah's Witnesses also define a spirit as "a life force, or something windlike" (*Make Sure of All Things*, 357).

By so defining these two common biblical terms, the Watchtower seeks to avoid the embarrassing scriptural truth that since man is created in the image of God, and God is Spirit, man must possess a cognizant spiritual entity formed in the image of his Creator (Genesis 1:26–27). To explode this Watchtower mythology is an elementary task when we realize that when the Lord Jesus Christ died upon the cross He said, "Father, into thy hands I commend my spirit" (Luke 23:46), a fact Jehovah's Witnesses are hard put to explain, since if the spirit is nothing but breath or wind, and certainly not a conscious entity as the Bible teaches it is, then it would be fruitless for Christ to commit His breath to the Father—yet He did precisely that! The truth of the matter is that the Lord Jesus Christ committed to His Father His immaterial nature as a man, proving conclusively that the spirit and soul of man go into eternity as a conscious entity (Galatians 6:8).

It will also be remembered that when Stephen was stoned, he fell asleep in death, but not before he said, "Lord Jesus, receive my spirit" (Acts 7:59), and in that particular context it is rather obvious that he was not referring to the exhalation of carbon dioxide from his lungs! However, we may safely say that the meanings Jehovah's Witnesses give to soul and spirit will not stand the test of systematic exegesis in either the Old or New Testaments, and no competent Hebrew or Greek scholar today has ever espoused their cause in open scholastic discussion.

Conclusion

Concluding this synopsis of the misapplications and misinterpretations of Jehovah's Witnesses where biblical terms and texts are concerned, the author feels constrained to state that by no means has he thoroughly covered this vast subject.

Jehovah's Witnesses thrive on the confusion they are able to create, and in their door-to-door canvassing they accentuate this trait by demonstrating extreme reluctance to identify themselves as emissaries of the Watchtower until they have established a favorable contact with the prospective convert. To put it in the terms of the vernacular, until they have "made their pitch" they are careful to conceal their identity. To illustrate this particular point more fully, the *New Yorker* magazine, June 16, 1956, carried a lengthy article by one of its feature writers, Richard Harris, in which Harris recounts his experiences with Jehovah's Witnesses.

In this article, Harris relates that the Witnesses never identified themselves, at first, to prospective converts as Jehovah's Witnesses when Harris accompanied a team of Witnesses on one of their daily canvassing routes in Brooklyn. Harris also pointed out in the article that the Witnesses openly admitted to him that it was necessary for them first to make a successful contact before they fully identified themselves.

In short, Jehovah's Witnesses may be proud to be the only people standing for "Jehovah God," but they are not above neglecting to tell prospective converts their real affiliation if it will help their cause. If evangelical Christianity continues to virtually ignore the activities of Jehovah's Witnesses, it does so at the peril of countless souls. Therefore, let us awaken to their perversions of Scripture and stand fast in the defense of the faith "once delivered unto the saints" (Jude 3).

Author's Note

Nowhere is this point more forcefully demonstrated than in a book written by a former member of the Watchtower Society, W. J. Schnell: *Thirty Years a Watchtower Slave.*[68] In this particular reference, Schnell succinctly stated the Watchtower methodology in the following words:

> The Watchtower leadership sensed that within the midst of Christendom were millions of professing Christians who were not well grounded in "the truths once delivered to the saints," and who would rather easily be pried loose from the churches and led into a new and revitalized Watchtower organization. The Society calculated, and that rightly, that this lack of proper knowledge of God and the widespread acceptance of half-truths in Christendom would yield vast masses of men and women, if the whole matter were wisely attacked, the attack sustained and the results contained, and then reused in an ever-widening circle.

Recommended Resources

1. Apologetics.com: *www.apologetics.com.*
2. Bowman, Robert M. Jr. *Jehovah's Witnesses, Zondervan Guide to Cults and Religious Movements.* Grand Rapids: Zondervan, 1995.
3. *Comments From the Friends. www.cftf.com.*
4. Franz, Raymond. *Crisis of Conscience.* Atlanta: Commentary Press, 2002.
5. Martin, Walter. *Jehovah's Witnesses and the Trinity,* audiotape. Walter Martin Ministries. *www.waltermartin.com.*
6. Reed, David A. *Jehovah's Witnesses Answered Verse by Verse.* Grand Rapids: Baker, 1990.

---

[68] *Thirty Years a Watchtower Slave* (Grand Rapids: Baker Book House, 1956), 19.

Quick Facts About Christian Science

- God is divine principle.

- Jesus is not God. The incarnation and bodily resurrection of Jesus Christ did not occur.

- Scripture is not inerrant.

- Sin, death, and evil do not exist.

- There is no literal, physical existence of the material universe.

Chapter 5

Christian Science

Historical Perspectives

For decades Christian Science was the matriarch of the Mind Science family. With a large and growing membership, secular and religious respect, and great wealth, the Mother Church dominated the Mind Science movement, more important in almost all respects than Unity School of Christianity, Mind Science, Religious Science, Divine Science, and their other siblings. However, during the 1960s a trend became apparent. Christian Science was losing members and income at a steady and significant rate. By the mid-1970s, Christian Science members and even the public media were aware that the decline was long-term and steady. Scandal rocked the Mother Church in 1976 with charges of financial, moral, and spiritual corruption among the top leaders in the church. In the early eighties, the Christian Science cult regrouped its forces. Dissenting membership was eliminated, financial waste reduced, and a calm face presented to the world. ~Since the mid-1980s, it has solidified its public image as a benign Christian denomination of thoughtful, spiritually mature people who enjoy a rather intellectual, quiet faith that gives them peace with God without any of the unappealing aspects of traditional Christianity, such as the existence of hell, the doctrine of the Trinity, or the incarnation, resurrection, and atonement of Jesus Christ.[1]~

The next couple of decades will tell whether Christian Science will be able to survive. Its forces are much diminished from what they once were. Only time will tell if the small core of faithful members will endure and spur growth in excess of attrition. Yet even now the Christian Science cult is a powerful force

---

This chapter updated by Dr. Dan Schlesinger and edited by Jill Martin Rische.

[1]~Cited from Walter Martin, *Kingdom of the Cults* (Minneapolis: Bethany House Publishers, 1997), 245–84.

with which evangelical Christians everywhere must deal. We shall examine its roots, founder, growth, and controversies, and contrast its teachings with the clear word of Scripture.

Mary Ann Morse Baker—better known among the band of faithful Christian Scientists as Mary Baker Eddy—"Mother" and Leader, the "Discoverer and Founder" of Christian Science, was born in Bow, New Hampshire, in 1821 in the humble surroundings of a farmhouse and was reared a strict Congregationalist by her parents, Mark and Abigail Baker. The life of young Mary Baker, until her twenty-second year, was marked with frequent illnesses both emotional and physical in nature,[2] and the then infant science of mesmerism was often applied to her case with some success.

In December 1843, at the age of twenty-two, the future Mrs. Eddy was married to George W. Glover, a neighboring businessman, whose untimely death of yellow fever in Wilmington, South Carolina, some seven months later, reduced his pregnant wife to an emotional and highly unstable invalid, who, throughout the remaining years of her life, relied from time to time upon the drug morphine as a medication.[3]

To be sure, no informed person believes that Mrs. Eddy was a "dope addict," but much evidence from reliable sources is available to show beyond doubt that throughout her life Mrs. Eddy made repeated use of this drug.[4] ~Supporters of Christian Science have continued to deny Eddy's morphine use, but the evidence is incontrovertible. Her biographer, Robert Peel, noted, "In order to lessen the pain of the move the doctor gave her one-eighth of a grain of morphine."[5] Additional documentation of her morphine use, which increased during the last years of her life, is in the works of James Dittemore, Calvin Frye, and unpublished, handwritten material of Eddy's own. Dittemore was the former director of the Mother Church; Frye was Eddy's assistant until her death.~

A decade passed in the life of Mrs. Glover during which she had many trying experiences, and then on June 21, 1853, she married Dr. Daniel M. Patterson, a dentist, who, contrary to the advice of Mrs. Glover's own father, Mark Baker, took the emotionally unstable Mary Glover for his bride. The advice of Mark Baker was indeed ominously accurate, for some years later Mrs. Eddy divorced Dr. Patterson, who, she claimed, had abandoned her, and thus her second attempt at matrimony met with crushing disaster.

The third and last marriage of Mary Baker Glover Patterson was to one Asa G. Eddy when Mrs. Eddy was fifty-six years of age. Asa Eddy's death of a coronary thrombosis prompted Mrs. Eddy to commit a nearly fatal mistake where Christian Science was concerned. She contested the autopsy report, and the physician she chose confirmed her conviction that Asa died of "arsenic poisoning mentally administered."[6] Such a radical report prompted an inquiry into the credentials of Mrs. Eddy's physician, Dr. C. J. Eastman, Dean of the Bellevue Medical College,

[2]Georgine Milmine, *The Life of Mary Baker G. Eddy and the History of Christian Science* (Grand Rapids, Mich.: Baker Book House, 1937), 3–25.
[3]*New York World*, October 30, 1906.
[4]Ernest Sutherland Bates and John V. Dittemore, *Mary Baker Eddy: The Truth and the Tradition* (New York: Knopf, 1932) 41–42, 151, 445.
[5]Robert Peel, *Mary Baker Eddy: The Years of Discovery,* (New York: Holt, Rinehart, and Winson, 1972), 195.
[6]*The Boston Post,* June 5, 1882.

outside Boston. It was found that "Dr." Eastman was running a virtual abortion mill, and had no medical credentials whatever to justify his title. He was sentenced to ten years in prison upon his conviction, and the Bellevue Medical College closed. Mrs. Eddy had contradicted her own advice concerning autopsies.[7] And she would have been far better off to have practiced in this instance what she preached and to have abandoned Asa's remains to the scrap heap of mental malpractice, but the error was virtually unavoidable, since Mrs. Eddy was not to be outdone by any medical doctor. She was an expert healer by her own admissions; the autopsy was therefore inevitable.

Mrs. Eddy's letter to the *Boston Post* dated June 5, 1882, in which she accused some of her former students of mentally poisoning Asa Eddy with malicious mesmerism in the form of arsenic mentally administered is one of the most pathetic examples of Mrs. Eddy's mental state ever recorded and one which the Christian Science Church would like to forget she ever wrote.

The real history of Christian Science, however, cannot be told unless one P. P. Quimby of Portland, Maine, is considered, for history tells us that as Mrs. Eddy was the mother of Christian Science, so Phineas Parkhurst Quimby was undoubtedly its father. "Dr." Quimby in the late 1850s entitled his system of mental healing "The Science of Man," and used the terms "The Science of Christ" and "Christian Science" for some time before Mrs. Eddy gratuitously appropriated the terminology as her own, something she dared not do while the old gentleman was alive and her relationship to him known to all.

Mrs. Eddy's relationship to Dr. Quimby began when she arrived in Portland, Maine, in 1862 and committed herself to his care for treatment of "spinal inflammation." In November of that same year, Mrs. Eddy noised abroad to all that P. P. Quimby had healed her of her infirmity. Said the then adoring disciple of Quimby, "I visited P. P. Quimby, and in less than one week from that time I ascended by a stairway of 182 steps to the dome of the City Hall and am improving ad infinitum."[8]

In later years Mrs. Eddy's recollection of Quimby was somewhat different from her earlier echoes of praise, and she did not hesitate to describe him as a very "unlearned man." Dr. Quimby termed his ideas "Science of Health." Mrs. Eddy entitled her book *Science and Health With Key to the Scriptures,* and published it in 1875, filled with numerous plagiarisms from the manuscripts of P. P. Quimby and by the writings of Francis Lieber, a German-American publisher and authority on the philosophy of Hegel. ~It should be noted here that although Eddy appears to have plagiarized a significant portion of Quimby's material, she did not agree with all of his conclusions. Eddy and Quimby disagreed on the existence of matter, the role of religion, and their perception of God. The basic distinction between the idealism of Eddy differs substantially with the mind-material dualism of Quimby.~ For full documentation on Mrs. Eddy's plagiarism from Quimby, the reader is urged to study the first four chapters of my book *The Christian Science Myth,* which documents exhaustively the entire controversy and proves beyond a shadow of a doubt that Mrs. Eddy plagiarized a great part of her work

---

[7]See *Science and Health With Key to the Scriptures* by Mary Baker Eddy (Boston: Trustees Under the Will of Mary Baker G. Eddy, 1934), 196, and the 1881 edition, Vol. 1, 269.
[8]*Portland Evening Courier,* November 7, 1862.

from Quimby and other sources, and then had it all copiously edited by the Rev. J. H. Wiggin, a retired Unitarian minister. Wiggin revealed his part in her deceptive plan via the posthumus publication of an interview he gave to one Livingstone Wright, later published as a pamphlet entitled *How Reverend Wiggin Rewrote Mrs. Eddy's Book.*

Our authority for exposing this plagiarism on the part of "Mother" Eddy is none other than Mrs. Eddy herself, who wrote, "When needed, tell the truth concerning a lie. The evasion of truth cripples integrity, and casts thee down from the pinnacle. . . . A dishonest position is far from Christianly scientific."[9] In addition, Mrs. Eddy made the following statement on the subject of plagiarism: "There is no warrant in common law and no permission in the gospel for plagiarizing an author's ideas and their words."[10] So it appears that out of her own mouth Mrs. Eddy has condemned plagiarism, a practice from which she seemed to have extreme difficulty abstaining.

Mrs. Eddy's plagiarism of Quimby's writings was well illustrated by *The New York Times,* which published parallel columns of Eddy's and Quimby's writings, proving Quimby to have been at least a partial source of her "revelation" of *Science and Health.*[11]

From Quimby's *Science of Man,* expounded by Eddy in 1868, 1869, and 1870.	From Eddy's *Science and Health,* the textbook of the "Christian Science" she claimed to discover in 1866.
If I understand how disease originates in the mind and fully believe it, why cannot I cure myself?	Disease being a belief, a latent delusion of mortal mind, the sensation would not appear if this error was met and destroyed by truth (1898 edition, 61).
Disease being made by our belief or by our parents' belief or by public opinion there is no formula of argument to be adopted, but every one must fit in their particular case. There it requires great shrewdness or wisdom to get the better of the error.	Science not only reveals the origin of all disease as wholly mental, but it also declares that all disease is cured by mind (62).
I know of no better counsel than Jesus gave to his disciples when he sent them forth to cast out devils and heal the sick, and thus in practice to preach the Truth, "Be ye wise as serpents and harmless as doves." Never get into a passion, but in patience possess ye your soul, and at length you weary out the discord and produce harmony by your Truth destroying error. Then you get the case. Now, if you are not afraid to face the error and argue it down, then you can heal the sick.	When we come to have more faith in the Truth of Being than we have in error, more faith in spirit than in matter, then no material conditions can prevent us from healing the sick, and *destroying error through Truth* (367). We classify disease as error which nothing but Truth or Mind can heal (427). Discord is the nothingness of error. Harmony is the somethingness of Truth (172).

---

[9] *Science and Health.* 448.
[10] Mary Baker Eddy, *Retrospection and Introspection* (Boston: Estate Trustees, 1891), 76.
[11] *The New York Times,* July 10, 1904.

The patient's disease is in his belief.

Error is sickness. Truth is health.

In this science the names are given; thus God is Wisdom. This Wisdom, not an Individuality but a principle, every idea—form, of which the idea, man, is the highest—hence the image of God, or the Principle.

Understanding is God.

All sciences are part of God.

Truth is God.

There is no other Truth but God.

God is Wisdom.

God is Principle.

Wisdom, Love, Truth are the Principle.

Error is matter.

Matter has no intelligence.

To give intelligence to matter is an error which is sickness.

Matter has no intelligence of its own, and to believe intelligence is in matter is the error which produced pain and in harmony of all sorts; to hold ourselves we are a principle outside of matter, we would not be influenced by the opinions of man, but held to the workings only of a principle, Truth, in which there are not in harmonies of sickness, pain or sin.

For matter is an error, there being no substance, which is Truth, in a thing which changes and is only that which belief makes it.

Sickness is part of the error which Truth casts out (478).

God is the principle of man; and the principle of man remaining perfect, its idea or reflection—man remains perfect (466).

Man was and is God's idea (231).

Man is the idea of Divine Principle (471).

What is God? Jehovah is not a person. God is Principle (1881 edition, 169).

Understanding is a quality of God (1898 edition, 449).

All science is of God (513).

Truth is God (183).

Truth, God, is not the father of error (469).

How can I most rapidly advance in the understanding of Christian Science? Study thoroughly the letter and imbibe the spirit. Adhere to its divine Principle, and follow its behests, abiding steadily in Wisdom, Love and Truth (491).

Matter is mortal error (1881 edition, 169).

The fundamental error of mortal man is the belief that matter is intelligent (122).

Laws of matter are nothing more or less than a belief of intelligence and life in matter, which is the procuring cause of all disease; whereas God, Truth, is its positive cure (127).

There is no life, truth, intelligence, or substance in matter (1898 edition, 464).

Another instance of Eddy's plagiarisms is worth documenting. There is no doubt that she copied almost an entire selection from a book by Lindley Murray entitled *The English Reader* (4th ed., Pittsburgh, 1823). This plagiarized material is to be found in Eddy's *Miscellaneous Writings*, (Boston: J. Armstrong, 1897) and is dated in that book September 30, 1895.

From Murray's *The English Reader* (1823), 98

From Eddy's *Miscellaneous Writings* (1895), 147–48

... the man of integrity ... is one who makes it his constant rule to follow the road of duty, according as the word of God and the voice of his conscience point it out to him. He is not guided merely by affections, which may sometimes give the colour of virtue to a loose and unstable character.

The man of integrity is one who makes it his constant rule to follow the road of duty, according as Truth and the voice of his conscience point it out to him. He is not guided merely by affections which may sometime give the color of virtue to a loose and unstable character.

The upright man is guided by a fixed principle of mind, which determines him to esteem nothing but what is honourable; and to abhor whatever is base or unworthy in moral conduct. Hence we find him ever the same; at all times, the trusty friend, the affectionate relation, the conscientious man of business, the pious worshipper, the public-spirited citizen.

The upright man is guided by a fixed Principle, which destines him to do nothing but what is honorable, and to abhor whatever is base or unworthy; hence we find him ever the same—at all times the trusty friend, the affectionate relative, the conscientious man of business, the pious worker, the public-spirited citizen.

He assumes no borrowed appearance. He seeks no mask to cover him, for he acts no studied part; but he is indeed what he appears to be, full of truth, candour, and humanity. In all his pursuits he knows no path but the fair and direct one, and would much rather fail of success than attain it by reproachful means.

He assumes no borrowed appearance. He seeks no mask to cover him, for he acts no studied part; but he is indeed what he appears to be—full of truth, candor, and humanity. In all his pursuits he knows no path but the fair, open, and direct one, and would much rather fail of success than attain it by reproachable means. He never shows us a smiling countenance while he meditates evil against us in his heart. We shall never find one part of his character at variance with another.

He never shows us a smiling countenance while he meditates evil against us in his heart. . . . We shall never find one part of his character at variance with another.

Lovingly yours,
Mary Baker Eddy
Sept. 30, 1895

Finally, the possibility that Mrs. Eddy plagiarized from a third source, a manuscript written by Francis Lieber, should be mentioned. Lieber was a distinguished German-American publisher and scholar. In 1936, a minister named Walter Haushalter published a book entitled *Mrs. Eddy Purloins from Hegel,* in which he made public the contents of a manuscript reportedly written by Lieber on "The Metaphysical Religion of Hegel." This twelve-page document appears to have been plagiarized extensively by Eddy in *Science and Health.*

There is, however, some uncertainty as to the authenticity of the Lieber document. On the one hand, five top scholars examined the manuscript and in 1940 reported that, without a doubt, it was genuinely Lieber's, dated in 1866, and that it had been reproduced in portion without credit by Eddy. These experts included John Calvin French, Ph.D., Johns Hopkins University Librarian; W. Stull Holt, Ph.D., also of Johns Hopkins; Johannes Mattern, Ph.D.; and a top hand-writing and document authority, Arthur P. Myers. Another scholar, Arthur E. Overbury, examined the document personally and declared it authentic. No handwriting experts who have examined the original manuscript have ever declared it to be fraudulent (the study done by experts Osborn and Stein was based on a copy). These would appear to be strong reasons for accepting the Lieber document as genuine.

On the other hand, a great deal of evidence has also been brought to light that raises serious doubts as to its authenticity. A leading expert on Lieber, Frank Friedel, in his 1948 biography of Lieber, gave several reasons why he did not accept the manuscript as genuine, and no recognized authority on Lieber has yet come out in support of the document. According to Friedel, the attitude toward Hegel in "The Metaphysical Religion of Hegel" is the exact opposite of that held by the historical Francis Lieber. Although Lieber was a German scholar, the man-uscript contains a citation of the title of one of Immanuel Kant's books in German, containing the sort of errors in German that one might expect of an English-speaking person whose German was poor. Furthermore, the manuscript appears to have been plagiarized from a book written in the late 1880s by Otto Pfleiderer, which of course it could not have been if it was written in 1866.

In this light, the question of the authenticity of the Lieber document must be considered unsettled. There would appear to be strong reasons both for and against its genuineness. However, it is, at the very least, an example of the con-temporary consensus of opinion in Eddy's day that her writings were not original. On the counts of plagiarism from Murray's *Reader* and from Quimby, the impar-tial observer must find Eddy guilty. Segments illustrating the parallels between Eddy's work and the "Lieber" document are presented below.

From *The Metaphysical Religion of Hegel* by Francis Lieber	From *Eddy's Science and Health With Key to the Scriptures*
For Hegel and his true disciples there is no truth, substance, life, or intelligence in matter; all is Infinite Mind. Thus matter has no reality; it is only the manifestation of spirit. . . . Therefore science is spiritual, for God is Spirit (85).	There is no life, truth, intelligence nor substance in matter. All is Infinite Mind and its infinite manifestation, for God is all in all. . . . Spirit is God, and man is His image and likeness. There-fore man is not material; he is spiritual (468).
Hegel science brings to light truth and its supremacy, universal harmony, God's entirety, and matter's nothing-ness. For him there are but two reali-ties, God and the ideas of God, in other words spirit and what it shadows forth. Properly, there is no physical sci-ence. The Principle of science is God, intelligence, and not matter. Therefore science is spiritual, for God is Spirit and the Principle of the universe is (man).	Christian Science brings to light Truth and its supremacy, universal mind, the entireness of God, good, and the nothingness of evil (293).
	There is no physical science, the principle of science is God, intelli-gence and not matter; therefore, sci-ence is spiritual for God is Spirit and the Principle of the universe and man. We learn from science mind is univer-sal, the first and only cause of all that really is.

We learn from Hegel that Mind is universal, the first and only cause of all that really is. Embryology affords no instance of one species producing another, the serpent germinating a bird, or a lion a lamb. The difference is not as great between the opposite species as between matter and spirit, so utterly unlike in substance and intelligence. That spirit propagates matter or matter spirit, is morally impossible. Hegel repudiates the thought (85–86).

To conclude that Life, Love, and Truth are attributes of personal deity implies there is something in Person superior to Principle. What, then, is the Person of God? Hegel makes clear that He has no personality as we now know personality, for this would imply intelligence and matter.

The body of God is the Idea given of Him, harmonious order of the universe and in man (male and female) formed by Him (82).

Beauty is also eternal. The beauty of matter passes away, fading at length into decay and ugliness. But beauty itself is a thing of Life, exempt from age or decay. To be this must be a thing of spirit (83).

Hegel science brings to light Truth and its supremacy, universal harmony, God's entirety, and man's nothingness" (85).

As music is harmoniously controlled by its Principle, so man governed by his Principle and Being, by Soul and not senses, is harmonious, sinless, and immortal (91).

The first step to understand Hegel is the Idea. He says the world would collapse without intelligence and Idea (74).

These Ideas of God never amalgamate but retain their distinct identities, and are controlled only by the Principle that evokes them. The mineral, vegetable, and animal kingdoms have their distinct identities, wherein one does not create or control the other, but all are created and controlled by God, Spirit (76).

Embryology affords no instance of one specie producing another; of a serpent germinating a bird, or a lion a lamb. The difference is not as great between opposite species as between matter and spirit, so utterly unlike in substance and intelligence. That spirit propagates matter, or matter spirit, is morally impossible; science repudiates the thought (10, 264).

To conclude Life, Love, and Truth are attributes of a personal deity implies there is something in Person superior to Principle.

What is the Person of God? He has no personality, for this would imply Intelligence in matter; the body of God is the idea given of Him in the harmonious universe, and the male and female formed by Him (44, 221–22).

Beauty is eternal; but the beauty of matter passes away, fading at length into decay and ugliness.

But beauty is a thing of Life, exempt from age or decay, and to be this it must be a thing of spirit (212).

Science brings to light Truth, and its supremacy, universal harmony, God's entirety, and matter's nothingness (28).

As music is harmoniously controlled by its Principle, so man governed by his Principle and Being, by Soul and not sense, is harmonious, sinless, and immortal (117).

This world would collapse without Intelligence and its Idea (185).

The ideas of God never amalgamate but retain their distinct identities, and are controlled only by the Principle that evoked them. The mineral, vegetable, and animal kingdoms have their distinct identities, wherein one creates not nor controls the other, all are created and controlled by God (71).

Wrote Eddy in *The First Church of Christ, Scientist, and Miscellany* (Boston: Trustees, 1941, 115) regarding her teachings:

> I should blush to write of *Science and Health with Key to the Scriptures* as I have, were it of human origin, and I, apart from God, were its author. But, as I was only a scribe echoing the harmonies of heaven in divine metaphysics, I cannot be super-modest in my estimate of the Christian Science textbook.

In a letter to a personal friend dated 1877, Eddy stated concerning Christian Science, "The idea given of God this time is higher, clearer, and more permanent than before."[12]

The evidence of Murray's *Reader* and the Quimby manuscripts (and possibly the Lieber document as well) demonstrates Eddy's total lack of ethics in borrowing what was not hers and indicates that the Deity had no part in the authorship of *Science and Health.* One would be foolish indeed to accept her claim at face value in the face of such incontrovertible evidence.

The Figment of Divine Authorship

Let us return, however, to Eddy's explanation of how she "discovered" Christian Science.

According to an authorized statement published by the Christian Science Publishing Society of Boston, Eddy, after a fall on a slippery sidewalk February 1, 1866, was pronounced "incurable" and given three days to live by the attending physician, Dr. Alvin M. Cushing. The third day, allegedly her last on earth, Eddy (the statement makes out) cried for a Bible, read Matthew 9:2, and rose completely healed. Thus the statement claims "she discovered" Christian Science. This is the story maintained by the organization today, as a comment on the First Church of Christ, Scientist Web site states:

> In 1866 [Eddy] was severely injured in a fall, and turned to the Bible as she had been accustomed to doing. All she had pondered in the past came strongly and clearly to her as she read an account of one of Jesus' healings. She was immediately healed. Convinced that God had healed her, she spent the next several years searching the Scriptures to understand the principle behind her healing. She named her discovery Christian Science and explained it in 1875 when she first wrote *Science and Health.*[13]

Corroborating this new story, Eddy in her book *Retrospection and Introspection* (p. 38) declares that in February of 1886 (one month after Quimby's death), she was mortally injured in a sidewalk fall and was not expected to live. She, however, vanquished the angel of death in this skirmish, and on the third day emerged triumphant over her bodily infirmity. These two statements, the interested reader will note, substantiate each other in every detail; it is therefore most unfortunate that they should both be falsehoods. Mrs. Eddy never discovered Christian

---

[12]Georgine Milmine, *The Life of Mary Baker G. Eddy,* 3–25. Based upon *The Life of Mary Baker G. Eddy* originally published in *McClure's* magazine 1907–1908, by Willa Cather & Georgine Milmine.

[13]*www.tfccs.com.*

Science in the manner claimed, never was in danger of losing her life in the manner described, and never "rose the third day healed and free" as she maintained. Two incontrovertible facts establish these truths beyond doubt. They are as follows: (1) Dr. Alvin M. Cushing, the attending physician at this "illness" of Mrs. Eddy, denied under oath in a 1,000-word statement that he ever believed or said that she was in a precarious physical condition.[14] Moreover, Dr. Cushing stated (contrary to the claims of Christian Scientists) that Eddy always enjoyed robust health and that he further attended her in August of the same year four separate times and administered medicine to her for bodily ailments. (2) Julius Dresser (pupil of the late "Dr." Quimby) received a letter from Eddy dated February 15, 1866, two weeks *after* her alleged "recovery" from the fall on an icy sidewalk. In this letter Eddy alludes to the fall and claims Dr. Cushing resigned her to the life of a cripple. Eddy wrote,

> Two weeks ago I fell on the sidewalk and struck my back on the ice, and was taken for dead, came to consciousness amid a storm of vapors from cologne, chloroform, ether, camphor, etc., but to find myself the helpless cripple I was before I saw Dr. Quimby. The physician attending said I had taken the last step I ever should, but in two days I got out of my bed alone and will walk; but yet I confess I am frightened? . . . Now can't you help me? . . . I think I could help another in my condition . . . that yet I am slowly failing. . . .[15]

Barring the obvious medical error of a doctor administering chloroform and ether to an unconscious person, Eddy's account once again demonstrates her ability to think in paradoxes and contradict all reason and logical expression. The accounts are, therefore, spurious and complete fabrications.

Horace T. Wentworth, with whose mother Eddy lived in Stoughton while she was teaching from the *Quimby Manuscripts* (1867–1870), has made the following statement, and no Christian Scientist has ever refuted it:

> As I have seen the amazing spread of this delusion and the way in which men and women are offering up money and the lives of their children to it, I have felt that it is a duty I owe to the public to make it known. I have no hard feelings against Mrs. Eddy, no axe to grind, no interest to serve; I simply feel that it is due the thousands of good people who have made Christian Science the anchorage of their souls and its founder the infallible guide of their daily life, to keep this no longer to myself. I desire only that people who take themselves and their helpless children into Christian Science shall do so with the full knowledge that this is not divine revelation but simply the idea of an old-time Maine healer.

Further than this statement, Wentworth has also recorded as incontestable evidence the very copy of P. P. Quimby's *Manuscripts* from which Eddy taught during the years of 1867 through 1870, which contain corrections in Eddy's own handwriting. Note, please, all this is undeniable fact—yet Eddy maintains that she *alone* "discovered and founded" the Christian Science religion. What a historical perversion the prophetess of Christian Science has attempted to perpetrate. Let

---

[14]Entire statement documented in Milmine, 84–86.
[15]F. W. Peabody, *The Religio-Medical Masquerade*, 80–81.

it also be remembered that Eddy claimed for Quimby's theories, which she expanded, Divine import, owning that she only copied what God Almighty spoke.[16]

Let us return, then, to the personal history of the central figure of this analysis, Mary Baker Eddy—the still-reigning sovereign of Christian Science.

From the home of the Wentworths in Stoughton, Massachusetts, where she taught from the Quimby manuscripts, Eddy went on to Lynn, Massachusetts, where she completed her "writing" of *Science and Health,* which she published in 1875. After leaving Lynn, largely because of the revolt of most of her students, Eddy came to Boston and opened what later became "The Massachusetts Metaphysical College" (571 Columbus Avenue), where she allegedly taught some four thousand students at $300 per student over a period of eight years (1881–1889). One cannot help but wonder what would induce a reasonably intelligent person to spend that amount of money for a course that never lasted the length of a college half-semester and which was taught by a staff hardly qualified intellectually to instruct the ninth grade. Eddy herself knew comparatively nothing of biblical history, theology, philosophy, or the ancient languages. Christian Science sources have attempted for years to prove that Eddy was a scholar in these fields, but the Rev. J. H. Wiggin, her literary adviser for some years, and himself an excellent scholar, has gone on record as saying that she was grossly ignorant of the subjects in question.

When Eddy left the thankless community of Lynn, Massachusetts, she was then sixty-one years old and possessed less than fifty persons she could call "followers." As the calendar neared 1896, however, the indomitable will and perseverance of Mary Baker Eddy began to pay sizable dividends. Her churches and societies numbered well over four hundred, and the membership in them eventually increased from 800 to 900 percent. Considering what she had to work with, Eddy accomplished a financial miracle and a propaganda goal unrivaled for its efficiency and ruthlessness. From her ceaseless efforts for deification and wealth, there flowed continual revisions of *Science and Health,* which the "faithful" were commanded to purchase and sell, or stand in danger of excommunication from the Eddy autocracy. Should the skeptical reader wish proof on this point of history and on Eddy's insatiable greed for the comforts of financial security and power, we quote her announcement to that effect in its entirety:

> Christian Scientists in the United States and Canada are hereby enjoined not to teach a student of Christian Science for one year, commencing on March 14, 1897.
>
> *Miscellaneous Writings* is calculated to prepare the minds of all true thinkers to understand the Christian Science textbook more correctly than a student can.
>
> The Bible, *Science and Health With Key to the Scriptures,* and my other published works are the only proper instructors for this hour. It shall be the *duty* of all Christian Scientists to *circulate* and to *sell* as many of these books as they can.
>
> If a member of the First Church of Christ, Scientist shall fail to *obey* this

---

[16]*Christian Science Journal,* January 1901.

injunction it will render him liable to *lose* his *membership* in this church.—Mary Baker G. Eddy.[17]

Please pay close heed to what Eddy said in the above quote. She did not ask; she *commanded* all Scientists as their duty to her church to "circulate" and "sell" her works and "obey" her "injunction" under penalty of loss of membership. If, perchance, a method of blackmail is ever rendered legal, it could not be stated in more compelling terminology than this encyclical from the Eddy throne.

But let it be observed that her religious pandering was not limited to one edition of *Science and Health*—no, Eddy extended her tactics to other fields as well. For example, in February 1908, she "requested" all Christian Scientists to read the "new" edition of *Science and Health,* which contained on page 442, beginning at line 30, information she affirmed to be of "great importance." Said Eddy,

> *Take Notice*
> I request Christian Scientists universally to read the paragraph beginning at line 30 on page 442 in the edition of *Science and Health,* which will be issued February 29. I consider the information there given to be of *great importance* at this state of the workings of Animal Magnetism, and it will *greatly aid* the students in their individual experiences.—Mary Baker G. Eddy.[18]

One would assume from the tone of the language she used that here was a new revelation imperative to the defense against "Animal Magnetism" (the fiend all Christian Scientists continually ward off mentally), but such was not the case; instead, Eddy merely wrote what she had written a hundred times previously in different language. Said the material of "great importance":

> Christian Scientists, be a law to yourselves, that mental malpractice can harm you neither when asleep nor when awake.

Imagine paying three dollars for a new book in 1908—for *two* sentences. It was the same old volume but with this "new" sage advice. And countless loyal Scientists obliged her wish by dutifully pouring their money into the Eddy treasury. It is no wonder that at her death Eddy's personal fortune exceeded three million dollars. None of this, unfortunately, was left to charity.

Eddy's reign had very little internal opposition and hence went unchallenged during her lifetime, but after her decease a definite scramble for control of her empire ensued. All but the most exacting students of Christian Science history have overlooked this battle for the vacated throne of Christian Science, but it is an important historical conflict and one that deserves consideration. Upon the death of Eddy, the Christian Science board of directors, in good business fashion, assumed control of her thriving empire and consolidated this coup by obtaining from the Massachusetts Supreme Court authority for their self-perpetuating directorate. It was over this issue that a schism appeared in the ranks of Christian Science, and after assuming the title "The Christian Science Parent Church," under the leadership of Annie C. Bill of London, the struggle com-

---

[17]Ibid., March 1897.
[18]Ibid., February 1908.

menced hot and heavy. John V. Dittemore, a member of the Christian Science Board of Directors, left the Boston camp and joined Bill in editing the *Christian Science Watchman* and acclaimed her as Eddy's successor. It was the contention of "The Parent Church" that Eddy intended to have a successor within a half century of her demise and never intended a self-perpetuating board of directors. The directors, no doubt for good financial reasons, stoutly rejected this view and defended their newfound gold mine. On February 6, 1924, Eddy's name was taken off *The Manual's* list of active officers and thus *The Watchman* claimed the board had proven its original intentions by fully occupying the most powerful position in the Christian Science Church, forever eliminating the danger of a successor to Eddy.[19] The claim by Bill and Dittemore that the directors had usurped the authority of Eddy and acted contrary to her expressed wishes went unchallenged for the most part by the Christian Science board of directors, for Dittemore had strong evidence from *The Memoirs of Adam Dickey*, which the board suppressed, and excerpts from the unpublished writings of Eddy's secretary, Calvin A. Frye, that she expected a personal successor within fifty years. Wrote Eddy:

> In answer to oncoming questions I will say: I calculate that about one-half century more will bring to the front the man that God has equipped to lift aloft His standard of Christian Science.[20]

But Eddy never picked her successor, and with the advancing years the Christian Science Parent Church and *The Watchman* faded into obscurity, and the controversy has long since been forgotten.

Continuing further into the Eddy legend, we are once again confronted with the cold, impartial testimony of history where Eddy's boundless "generosity" and "selflessness" are concerned. Shortly after the famous "Woodbury Suit," wherein Eddy was accused of slandering a former disciple, the Christian Science treasury showed a marked decrease in volume, the result of large legal fees due in consideration of services rendered during the case. As a result of this, Eddy perpetrated on the faithful the infamous "Tea Jacket Swindle," calculated to draw from her gullible followers the revenue with which to further strengthen her treasury. In line with this scheme she drafted the following "request" to her church universal, which appeared in the *Christian Science Journal*, December 21, 1899:

> Beloved, I ask this favor of all Christian Scientists. Do not give me on, before, or after the forthcoming holiday aught material except three tea jackets. *All may contribute to these.* One learns to value material things only as one needs them, and the costliest things are the ones that one needs most. Among my present needs material are these—three jackets, two of darkish heavy silk, the shade appropriate to white hair; the third of heavy satin, lighter shade, but sufficiently sombre. Nos. 1 and 2 to be common-sense jackets for Mother to work in, and not overtrimmed by any means. No. 3 for best, such as she can afford for her dressing room.—Mary Baker Eddy

The key to this whole financial angle is to be found in five short words, "*All*

---

[19] *The Christian Science Watchman*, Vol. 4, No. 7, March 1928, 153–54.
[20] Ibid., Vol. 4, No. 5, January 1928.

may contribute to these." Notice Eddy does not request two hundred thousand tea jackets,[21] merely "contributions" toward them. No one was to send them—only send the money to buy them. "Mother" Eddy must have enjoyed this neat trick of replenishing her gold reserve, and none can deny that it was carried off with a finesse that rivals any confidence game ever conceived. All this, mind you, in the name of Jesus Christ and under the banner of Christian Science, allegedly the true religion. Judge Rutherford of Jehovah's Witnesses could not have had Christian Science too far out of mind when he said, "Religion is a racket." Compared to Eddy, "Pastor" Russell and Judge Rutherford of the Watchtower Society were rank amateurs at collecting money. She played for the highest stakes at all times, and with Mary Baker Eddy it was always "winner take all," and she did!

Theological Structure of Christian Science

In outlining this chapter on Christian Science, it is the conviction of the author that a series of primary quotations taken directly from official Christian Science books will prove far more useful to the average reader than any number of statements made by a non-Christian Scientist. Therefore, to enable the reader to have this valuable source material at his fingertips, I have listed sixteen of the major doctrines of historical orthodox Christianity and under each of their respective headings placed contradictory quotations derived from Eddy's writings, which will, I believe, provide more than sufficient documentation should any dispute ever arise concerning the proper classification of Christian Science as an anti-Christian cult.

I. The Inspiration of the Bible
    Referring to Genesis 2:7:

      1. Referring to Genesis 2:7: Is this addition to His creation real or unreal? Is it the truth, or is it a lie concerning man and God? It must be a lie. (*Science and Health*, 524)
      2. ". . . the manifest mistakes in the ancient versions; the thirty thousand different readings in the Old Testament, and the three hundred thousand in the New—these facts show how a mortal and material sense stole into the divine record, with its own hue darkening, to some extent, the inspired pages. (139)

II. The Doctrine of the Trinity and the Deity of Christ

      1. The theory of three persons in one God (that is, a personal Trinity or Triunity) suggests polytheism, rather than the one ever-present I am. (256)
      2. The Christian who believes in the First Commandment is a monotheist. Thus he virtually unites with the Jew's belief in one God and recognizes that Jesus Christ is not God, as Jesus himself declared, but is the Son of God. (361)
      3. The spiritual Christ was infallible; Jesus, as material manhood, was not Christ. (*Miscellaneous Writings*, 84)

---

[21]Estimated Christian Science Church membership in 1899.

III. The Doctrine of God and the Holy Spirit

1. The Jewish tribal Jehovah was a man-projected God, liable to wrath, repentance, and human changeableness. (*S & H*, 140)
2. God. The great I am; the all-knowing, all-seeing, all-acting, all-wise, all-loving, and eternal; Principle; Mind; Soul; Spirit; Life; Truth; Love; all substance; intelligence. (*S & H*, 587)
3. (1) God is All-in-all. (2) God is good. Good is Mind. (3) God, Spirit, being all, nothing is matter.... GOD: Divine Principle, Life, Truth, Love, Soul, Spirit, Mind. (*S & H*, 113, 115)

IV. The Virgin Birth of Christ

1. God is indivisible. A portion of God could not enter man; neither could God's fullness be reflected by a single man, else God would be manifestly finite, lose the deific character, and become less than God. (*S & H*, 336)
2. Jesus, the Galilean Prophet, was born of the Virgin Mary's spiritual thoughts of Life and its manifestation. (*The First Church of Christ Scientist and Miscellany*, 1913, 1941, 261)

V. The Doctrine of Miracles

1. The sick are not healed merely by declaring there is no sickness, but by knowing that there is none. (*S & H*, 447)
2. Sickness is part of the error that Truth casts out. Error will not expel error. Christian Science is the law of Truth, which heals the sick on the basis of the one Mind, or God. It can heal in no other way, since the human, mortal mind so-called is not a healer, but causes the belief in disease. (*S & H*, 482)
3. The so-called miracles contained in Holy Writ are neither supernatural nor preternatural.... Jesus regarded good as the normal state of man, and evil as the abnormal.... The so-called pains and pleasures of matter were alike unreal to Jesus; for he regarded matter as only a vagary of mortal belief and subdued it with this understanding. (*Miscellaneous Writings*, 199–200)

VI. The Atonement of Jesus Christ

1. The material blood of Jesus was no more efficacious to cleanse from sin when it was shed upon "the accursed tree" than when it was flowing in His veins as he went daily about his Father's business. (*S & H*, 25)
2. The real atonement—so infinitely beyond the heathen conception that God requires human blood to propitiate His justice and bring His mercy—needs to be understood. (*No and Yes*, 54)

VII. The Death and Resurrection of Christ

1. Jesus' students, not sufficiently advanced to understand fully their Master's triumph, did not perform many wonderful works until they saw him after his crucifixion and learned that he *had not died*. (*S & H*, 45–46)
2. His disciples believed Jesus to be dead while he was hidden in the

sepulchre, whereas he was alive, demonstrating within the narrow tomb the power of Spirit to overrule mortal, material sense (44).

VIII. The Ascension and Second Coming of Christ

1. Until he himself ascended—or, in other words, rose even higher in the understanding of Spirit, God. . . . Jesus' unchanged physical condition after what seemed to be death was followed by his exaltation above all material conditions; and this exaltation explained his ascension. . . . In his final demonstration, called the ascension, which closed the earthly record of Jesus, he rose above the physical knowledge of his disciples, and the material senses saw him no more. (*S & H*, 46)

IX. Satan and the Existence of Evil

1. Hence, evil is but an illusion, and it has no real basis. Evil is a false belief. God is not its author. The supposititious parent of evil is a lie. (*S & H*, 480)
2. All these vagaries are at variance with my system of metaphysics, which rests on God as One and All, and denies the actual existence of both matter and evil. . . . There was never a moment in which evil was real. (*No and Yes*, 24)

X. The Nature and Existence of Hell

1. The sinner makes his own hell by doing evil, and the saint his own heaven by doing right. (*S & H*, 266)
2. The olden opinion that hell is fire and brimstone has yielded somewhat to the metaphysical fact that suffering is a thing of mortal mind instead of body: so, in place of material flames and odor, mental anguish is generally accepted as the penalty for sin. (*Miscellaneous Writings*, 237)

XI. The Kingdom of Heaven—Its Reality and Significance

1. Definition: HEAVEN. Harmony; the reign of Spirit; government by Principle; spirituality; bliss; the atmosphere of Soul. (*S & H*, 587)
2. Heaven is harmony—infinite, boundless bliss. Heaven is the reign of Divine Science. (*First Church of Christ, Scientist and Miscellany*, 267)

XII. The Doctrine of Eternal Salvation

1. Man as God's idea is already saved with an everlasting salvation. (*Miscellaneous Writings*, 261)
2. One sacrifice, however great, is insufficient to pay the debt of sin. (*S & H*, 25)

XIII. The Doctrine of Prayer

1. Prayer can neither change God, nor bring his designs into mortal modes—I have no objection to audible prayer of the right kind; but inaudible is more effectual. (*No and Yes*, 39–40)
2. If prayer nourishes the belief that sin is cancelled, and that man is

made better by merely praying, prayer is an evil. He grows worse who continues in sin because he fancies himself forgiven. (*S & H*, 4)

XIV. The Creation of Matter and Its Reality

1. There is . . . no intelligent sin, evil mind, or matter: and this is the
only true philosophy and realism. (*No and Yes*, 38)
2. There is no life, truth, intelligence nor substance in matter. All is
infinite Mind and its infinite manifestation, for God is All-in-all. (*S & H*,
468)

XV. Man, the Soul, His True Nature and Destiny

1. Man originated not from dust, materially, but from Spirit, spiritually.
(*Miscellaneous Writings*, 57)
2. Man is God's image and likeness; whatever is possible to God, is possible to man as God's reflection. (183)

XVI. The Existence of Sin, Sickness, and Death

1. DEVIL. Evil; a lie; error; neither corporeality nor mind; the opposite
of Truth; a belief in sin, sickness, and death; animal magnetism or hypno-
tism; the lust of the flesh. (*S & H*, 584)
2. DEATH. An illusion, the lie of life in matter; the unreal and untrue;
the opposite of Life.
Matter has no life, hence it has no real existence. Mind is immortal.
The flesh, warring against the Spirit; that which frets itself free from one
belief only to be fettered by another, until every belief of life where Life is
not yields to eternal Life. Any material evidence of death is false, for it contradicts the spiritual facts of being. (584)

As the preceding quotations indicate, the teachings of Christian Science are
vastly different from those generally understood to comprise the fundamental
teaching of historical Christianity. And it would be a foolish student indeed who
did not take cognizance of these severe deviations from biblical theology and
mark them well as evidence of another gospel, the product of plagiarism, the
amalgamation of sources suitably doctored by a professional literary adviser, and
made palatable to the average mind by the semantic manipulations of Mary Baker
Eddy.

The philosophy of Christian Science is basically syllogistic, embodying all the
logical mazes that the confused and untrained mind of Mrs. Eddy wandered
through. Theoretically, Eddy was an absolute idealist who denied outright the
existence of matter from the tiniest insect to the most gigantic star in the celestial
galaxies. But practically speaking, Eddy was a calculating materialist, an individual
who thoroughly enjoyed all the material comforts derived from denying their
existence. Hundreds of thousands of faithful Christian Scientists supplied their
"leader" with all that money could buy and every material benefit available, yet
Eddy continually affirmed the nonexistence of these material blessings by teaching in effect that they really did not exist to be enjoyed—they were "illusions of
mortal mind," she said. In Eddy's philosophy all that exists is "Mind" (God) and
"It" is "Good"; matter has no "real" existence at all. It should be mentioned

here that Eddy never defined matter to the satisfaction of any qualified logician, so it must be assumed that she meant those elements that were recognizable to the five senses.

However, Eddy's vaunted metaphysical allegiance to this alleged rule crumbles weakly under the relentless hammering of sound logical principles. Let us see if the rule of inversion is always valid by applying it to similar constructions.

All rabbits are quadrupeds—(inverted) all quadrupeds are rabbits. Now, of course, any intelligent person can easily see that this inversion leads to a false conclusion, since dogs, cats, horses, and elephants are all quadrupeds, and it is obvious they have no relation to the rabbit family. No rational person could therefore long entertain such logical absurdity, but it is exactly this kind of reasoning that forms the basis of Eddy's philosophy and the entire foundation of Christian Science practice. Sin, sickness, and death are equally relegated to these peculiar logical dungeons of Christian Science reasoning processes and then represented as "illusions of mortal mind." Regarding this phantom "mortal mind," Eddy wrote,

> At best, matter is only a phenomenon of mortal mind, of which evil is the highest degree; but really there is no such thing as *mortal mind*—though we are compelled to use the phrase in the endeavor to express the underlying thought. (*Unity of Good*, 50)

These are strange words indeed, are they not—giving a name to an illusion that does not exist, representing it as evil, which is equally nonexistent, and then blaming it for all physical woes, which cannot exist, since there is no reality or existence apart from Mind, or God? This type of reasoning is considered sound thinking by Christian Scientists the world over; however, the reader is urged to form his own conclusions dictated by the obvious facts that matter is demonstrably "real" and its decay and death are an ever-present problem.

The syllogism (1) God is all; God is Mind; therefore, Mind is all; and (2) Mind is all; matter is not Mind; therefore, matter has no existence, is only an escape mechanism from the objective world of material reality to the subjective world of idealism, which can never answer the problems of evil, sin, sickness, or material death, since they are negated by the assumption that only Mind exists and it is immaterial, therefore, not included in material categories. By denying even that portion of the mind that recognizes these physical realities and calling it "mortal mind," Eddy has forever isolated herself and Christian Science from the realm of objective reality, since the mind that truly rejects the existence of matter must never allow for the limitations of matter, which constitute physical existence. But in practice, no Christian Scientist holds these tenets as an absolute—they all clothe, feed, and house the "illusion of mortal mind" called their bodies, and many go to dentists and surgeons for the filling of imaginary cavities and the setting of nonexistent bones.

If these facts are not proof positive that the entire philosophy of Christian Science in principle and practice is a huge philosophical hoax, then the author despairs of man's ability to analyze available evidence and arrive at logical conclusions. Even in its basic propositions, the Eddy philosophy is a sorry foundation for faith by all standards and an almost unbelievable imposition upon the principles of sound logic.

Inspiration and Authority of the Bible

Christian Science, as a theology, and all Christian Scientists, for that matter, both affirm that the Bible is God's Word and quote Eddy to "prove" that their whole religion is based upon the teachings of Scripture. Eddy said,

> The Bible has been my only authority. I have had no other guide in "the straight and narrow way" of Truth. (*Science and Health*, 126)

However, Eddy and Christian Science have repudiated and contradicted this affirmation numerous times (see *Miscellaneous Writings*, 169–70, and *Science and Health*, 517, 537, etc.), and in reality have perverted the clear teachings of the Bible to serve their own ends.

In Psalm 119 we read, "For ever, O Lord, thy word is settled in heaven.... Thy word is very pure.... Thy word is true from the beginning." The prophet Isaiah reminds us: "The word of our God shall stand for ever" (Isaiah 40:8), and Christ himself confirmed these great truths when He said: "The scripture cannot be broken.... Heaven and earth shall pass away, but my words shall never pass away" (John 10:35; Matthew 24:35). It will be remembered also that the apostle Paul stamped with divine authority the testimony of the Scriptures when he wrote, "All scripture is given by inspiration of God, and is profitable for doctrine, for reproof, for correction, for instruction in righteousness" (2 Timothy 3:16).

Coupled with these unassailable voices of testimony as to the Bible's authority, it is evident from the words of Jesus himself and the writings of His disciples and apostles that He believed in the authority of the Old Testament most emphatically and even alluded to Old Testament characters and events, thus establishing the authenticity and trustworthiness of the Old Testament.

The Bible declares that *it*, not Eddy and Christian Science, is the supreme authority on the activities of God and His relationship to man. Christian Science employs every art and method of paradoxical reasoning to escape the dilemma with which it is faced. It switches terminology around until the terms in question lose all logical meaning, and it spiritualizes texts until they are milked dry of any divine revelation whatsoever. To the average Christian Scientist, the Bible is a compilation of ancient writings "full of hundreds of thousands of textual errors.... Its divinity is ... uncertain, its inspiration ... questionable.... It is made up of metaphors, allegories, myths, and fables.... It cannot be read and interpreted literally...."[22] Consequently, Christian Scientists believe, owing to the utter and hopeless confusion that the Bible allegedly engenders without a qualified interpreter, that it is necessary to have someone interpret the Bible for them. Eddy is the divinely appointed person to fulfill this task. Through *Science and Health*, she, they affirm, "rediscovered the healing principle of Jesus and His disciples, lost since the early Christian era," and has *blessed the world* with Christian Science—the "Divine Comforter." To all Christian Scientists, then, since they swear allegiance to Eddy, "the material record of the Bible ... is no more important to our well-being than the history of Europe and America" (*Miscellaneous Writings*, 170).

The reader is asked to compare this supposedly "Christian" view with the

---

[22]I. M. Haldeman, *Christian Science in the Light of Holy Scripture*, 377.

foregoing scriptural references and the words of Christ and the apostle Paul, who said and wrote respectively:

> Sanctify them through thy truth: thy *word* is truth. (John 17:17)
> But continue thou in the things which thou hast learned and hast been assured of, knowing of whom thou hast learned them; and that from a child thou hast known the *holy scriptures,* which are able to make thee wise unto salvation through faith which is in Christ Jesus. (2 Timothy 3:14–15)

We are told in the words of Peter:

> Knowing this first, that no prophecy of the scripture is of any private interpretation. For the prophecy came not in old time by the will of man: but holy men of God spake as they were moved by the Holy Ghost. (2 Peter 1:20–21)

By these things, of course, we do not mean that God dictated or mechanically reproduced the Bible, or even that He wrote tangibly, using the hands of men as an adult guides the hand of a child, but that God spoke and caused to be recorded truly and without error those things necessary for our salvation and an understanding of His sovereign purposes and love. The Bible is the inspired Word of God, and is wholly dependable in whatever fields it speaks. This, of course, holds true only for the original manuscripts of the Bible of which we have excellent reproductions. No scholar to our knowledge, however, holds to the infallibility of copies or translations, which sometimes suggest textual difficulties. The Bible, therefore, stands paramount as God's revelation to man, the simple presentation of infinite values and truths clothed in the figures of time and space. Christian Science, by denying many of these truths and the veracity of the Bible itself in favor of Eddy's "interpretations," disobeys directly the injunction of God to "study" and "believe" His Word, which alone is able to make us "wise unto salvation through faith in Christ Jesus."

The Doctrine of the Trinity and the Deity of Christ

One prominent trait of all non-Christian religions and cults is their pointed denial of the scriptural doctrine of the Trinity and the deity of Jesus Christ. Christian Science ranges high in this category on the basis that it unequivocally denies the true deity of our Lord and the triunity of the Godhead (Colossians 2:9). Eddy said, and most decisively so, that "the theory of three persons in one God (that is, a personal Trinity or Triunity) suggests polytheism rather than the one ever-present I AM" (*Science and Health,* 256). Going beyond this declaration Eddy also wrote, "Jesus Christ is not God, as Jesus himself declared, but is the Son of God" (*S & H,* 361), and she crowned this travesty with the astounding "revelation" that "Life, Truth, and Love constitute the triune Person called God" (*S & H,* 331). Thus it was that with one sweep of an unblushing pen, a vindictive, ignorant, untrained, and egocentric old woman banished the God of the Bible from her religion forever. It is hardly necessary to examine at length the doctrine of the Trinity and the deity of Christ to refute Eddy's vague ramblings, but it is profitable, we believe, to review those passages of Scripture that so thoroughly unmask the pronounced shallowness of the Christian Science contentions.

"Let *us* make man in *our* image, after *our* likeness" (Genesis 1:26).

"Let *us* go down, and there confound their language" (Genesis 11:7).

"Who will go for *us?*" (Isaiah 6:8). (Emphasis added.)

Then we could mention Genesis 18, where Abraham addresses God personally as Lord (Jehovah) over ten times; the obvious plurality of the Godhead is strongly implied if not expressly declared by the use of three angels to represent God. The fact that God intended to beget a Son after the flesh and of the line of David by virgin birth (Isaiah 7:14; 9:6; Micah 5:2; Matthew 1:23; Luke 1:35; cf. Psalm 2:7; Hebrews 1:5; 5:5; Acts 13:33), that this Son in the likeness of flesh was His eternal Word (John 1:1, 14, 18), and that He is true deity (Colossians 2:9; Philippians 2:8–11; Revelation 1:8, 17–18; Hebrews 1:1–4, etc.) and a separate person from God the Father are all indicative of the truth that Jesus Christ was truly the God-man of prophecy and the personal Messiah of Israel. It is fruitful to note also that Eddy recognizes the "true" God not as Jehovah but as "I AM" (*S & H,* 256), apparently oblivious of the fact that the word *Jehovah* is itself taken from the Hebrew verb form "to be" (Exodus 3:14), literally "I was, am, I continue to be," or as the Jews render it, "the Eternal" (*YHWH,* the tetragrammaton). Keeping with this vein of thought, it will be easily recognized that Jesus identified himself with the same "I AM" or Jehovah—and, in fact, claimed in no uncertain terms that He was that "I AM," (John 8:58) for which the Jews were ready to stone Him to death on the grounds of blasphemy (John 8:59; 10:30–33).

As to Eddy's argument that Jesus was God's Son, not God, the answer is painfully simple when thoroughly analyzed. The solution is briefly this: Christ was God's Son by nature, not creation, as we are; hence, His intrinsic character was that of Deity—His attributes were Divine—He possessed "all power," etc. (Matthew 28:18). He therefore could not be a true Son unless He were truly divine; therefore, He could not be the Son of God at all without at once being "God the Son," i.e., of the very nature of His Father. The Scriptures declare God's Son is Deity—"The mighty God . . . The Everlasting Father" (Isaiah 9:6), or the image of God (Colossians 1:15) . . . Brightness of his glory . . . express image of his person" (Hebrews 1:3), etc. Innumerable testimonies as to His divinity are given, far too exhaustive to record here, but evidence nonetheless and beyond disputation. To reduce the Trinity so evident at Christ's baptism and the Great Commission ("In the name of the Father and of the Son and of the Holy Spirit" Matthew 28:19) to three of Eddy's choice terms—"Life, Truth, and Love"—and declare all else "suggestive of heathen gods" (*S & H,* 256) is a prime demonstration of crass indifference to biblical terminology and historical theology—an emphatic Christian Science attitude instituted by Eddy.

John tells us that Christ was by His own admission *equal* in deity to God the Father (John 5:18; cf. Philippians 2:8–11; Colossians 2:9; Hebrews 1:3), yet inferior in position and form during His earthly ministry (John 14:28) as a man. The Eternal Word voluntarily humbled himself, became human and subject to our limitations, even to the death of the cross, the Bible tells us, but never for a moment did He cease to be what by nature and inheritance He always was and will be, God the Son, second person of the Trinity, eternal Creator and Savior of the sons of men.

Therefore, let us remember most clearly that Christian Science offers a dual

Christ, a great man inspired by the "Christ idea" as Eddy would have it, one who never really "died" at all for our sins.

The Scriptures hold forth as a ray of inextinguishable light the deity of our Lord and the Trinity of God. We must therefore be ever vigilant in our defense of the personal Jesus who is our personal Savior, lest the impersonal Christ of Christian Science be allowed further opportunity to counterfeit the Christ of the Bible. This counterfeit, so widely taught in Christian Science, is merely another false theory that masquerades under the banner of the Christian religion and attempts to subvert the true Christian faith.

The Personality of God the Father and the Holy Spirit

In Christian Science theology, if it is properly understood, the term *God* is merely a relative one and bears no resemblance whatsoever to the Deity so clearly revealed in the Bible. As has been amply shown, Eddy interchanges the terms *Life, Truth, Love, Principle, Mind, Substance, Intelligence, Spirit, Mother,* etc. with that of *God*; thus, Christian Science contends that God is impersonal, devoid of any personality at all. Biblically speaking, of course, this is a theological and historical absurdity, since the core of Jehovah's uniqueness was His personal nature—I AM—indicative of a reflective and constructive Mind. Jesus repeatedly addressed His Father as a direct object, "I" and "Thou," postulating a logical subject/object relation in communication, and at least twice the Father answered Him (see Matthew 3:17 and Luke 17:5), establishing His independence of person. This would have been impossible if God were circumscribed by Eddy's theology, for only a personality or cognizant ego can think reflectively, carry on conversation, and use the personal pronouns "I" or "He," etc.

The God of the Old Testament and the New is a personal, transcendent Being, not an impersonal spirit or force, and man is created in His image, that of a personal, though finite, being. The higher animals, to whatever degree they "think," are incapable of rationality and, also unlike man, of the faculty of "knowing," as Descartes once put it: "Cogito ergo sum" ("I think, therefore I am").

But far surpassing this elementary distinction between the God of Christianity and that of Christian Science is the inescapable fact that the God of the Bible does what only a personality can do, and these traits forever separate Him from the pantheistic god of Christian Science, which is incapable by definition of performing these things. Briefly, God is described as capable of doing the following things:

1. *God remembers.* "I, even I, am he that blotteth out thy transgressions for mine own sake, and will not remember thy sins" (Isaiah 43:25; also compare Psalm 79:8; Jeremiah 31:20; Hosea 8:13).

2. *God speaks.* "I am the Lord: that is my name: and my glory will I not give to another, neither my praise to graven images" (Isaiah 42:8; see also Genesis 1:26; Isaiah 43:10–13; 44:6; Matthew 17:5; Hebrews 1:1).

3. *God hears, sees, and creates.* "And God saw that the wickedness of man was great in the earth" (Genesis 6:5); "God heard their groaning" (Exodus 2:24); "and when the people complained . . . and . . . the Lord heard it" (Numbers 11:1); "In the beginning God created the heaven and the earth" (Genesis 1:1).

4. *God "knows," i.e., He has a mind.* "The Lord knoweth them that are his" (2 Timothy 2:19); "God is greater than our heart, and knoweth all things" (1 John 3:20); "For I know the thoughts that I think toward you, saith the Lord" (Jeremiah 29:11).

5. *God will judge the world.* "Therefore I will judge you . . . saith the Lord God" (Ezekiel 18:30); "Therefore thus saith the Lord God unto them; Behold, I, even I, will judge" (Ezekiel 34:20); "For we must all appear before the judgment seat of Christ" (2 Corinthians 5:10).

6. *God is a personal Spirit.* "God is a Spirit: and they that worship him must worship him in spirit and in truth" (John 4:24); "I am the Almighty God; walk before me, and be thou perfect" (Genesis 17:1); God's Son is declared to be the "express image of his person" (Hebrews 1:3), therefore God is a person.

7. *God has a will.* "Thy will be done in earth, as it is in heaven" (Matthew 6:10); "Prove what is that good, and acceptable, and perfect, will of God" (Romans 12:2); "He that doeth the will of God abideth for ever" (1 John 2:17); "Lo, I come to do thy will, O God" (Hebrews 10:7, 9).

From this brief résumé of some of God's attributes, the interested reader can doubtless see the vast difference between the God and Father of our Lord Jesus Christ and the "Divine Principle" of Eddy's Christian Science. Psychologically speaking, a principle cannot remember; "Life, Truth, and Love" cannot speak audibly; nor can "Substance, Mind, or Intelligence" hear, see, create, know, judge, or will. The God of the Bible does these things; the god of Christian Science cannot. It is admitted, of course, that a mind or an intelligence can do these things, but Eddy does not recognize the existence of personality in the Deity, and only a personality has a mind or an intelligence. Eddy's god (Principle) cannot create nor can it exert a will because Principle or even a principle, if you desire, does not possess a will by any logical definition. The god of Christian Science is an *it*, neuter in gender—merely a name—incapable of metaphysical definition or understanding outside of the maze that is Christian Science theology. The apostle Paul triumphantly reminds us, "I know whom I have believed, and am persuaded that he is able to keep that which I have committed unto him against that day" (2 Timothy 1:12). The true Christian has a personal relationship with his Lord; he prays through Christ and the power of the Holy Spirit; he asks that it might be given; indeed, personal contact is the very source of the Christian's life and spiritual peace. Christian Scientists have no such contact and consequently no real spiritual life or peace, only the riddles and incoherencies of Eddy and a basic uncertainty about good health.

Concerning the doctrine of the Holy Spirit and the attitude of Christian Science toward it, little need be said, since Eddy's attitude was so obvious, but at the risk of repetition a short review may be profitable. As a matter of course, Eddy denied both the personality and office of the Holy Spirit and for His exalted ministry substituted "Divine Science" (*Science and Health*, 55).

To refute such a decided perversion of Scripture and historical theology one need only recall who the writers of the Bible, and Christ himself, considered the Holy Spirit to be in respect to personality and power. In the sixteenth chapter of John's gospel, Jesus instructed His disciples about their new ministry and duties and promised them a "Comforter" who would strengthen and guide them after His ascension. To quiet their fears, Jesus told them that it was essential to the coming of the Comforter, who issued forth from the Father, that He (Jesus) go away. The Lord said,

> If I go not away, the Comforter will not come unto you; but if I depart, I will send him unto you. And when he is come, he will reprove the world of sin, and of righteousness, and of judgment. (vv. 7–8)

It is useful to observe that the Greek text uses the masculine pronoun "He" and also "Him" for the Holy Spirit and ascribes to Him a will (v. 7) and the power to "reprove" the world of "sin, righteousness, and judgment" (v. 8). "Divine Science" has not, will not, and cannot do any of these things because it denies the reality of sin, hence, excluding the need for righteousness, and teaches in place of judgment the pernicious unbiblical doctrine of man's inherent goodness. The Holy Spirit, therefore, is a person with a will and divine power to regenerate the soul of man (John 3) and glorify Jesus Christ. It should also be remembered that He does what only a person can do—He teaches us (Luke 12:12), He speaks to us (Acts 13:2), He thinks and makes decisions (Acts 15:28), and He moves us to do the will of God as He has moved holy men of God to serve in the past (2 Peter 1:21). Further than this the Holy Spirit can be lied to (Acts 5:5), He can be grieved (Ephesians 4:30), and He is often resisted (Acts 7:51). All these things denote dealings with a personality, not an impersonal force, and certainly not "Divine Science." Beyond these things the Holy Spirit sanctifies and separates us from sin and prays to the Father for us that we might be freed from great temptations (Romans 8:26).

Certainly these points of evidence disprove the meager attempts of Christian Science to reduce the third person of the Trinity to a metaphysical catchword (*Divine Science*), and reveal clearly for all to see the semantic deception Eddy has utilized in attempting to undermine this great scriptural truth.

The Miracles of Christ

The doctrine of the virgin birth of Jesus Christ is indissolubly joined with that of the validity of Old Testament prophecy concerning the Messiah of Israel. Isaiah the prophet tells us that "a virgin shall conceive, and bear a son, and shall call his name Immanuel" (7:14), and that this child was to be miraculous in every sense of the word. Indeed, so unique was this child to be that to Him alone of all the sons of men is the name God applied, "The mighty God" to be specific, "The everlasting Father," and "The Prince of Peace" (9:6). We are told that He shall reign forever (v. 7), and that the zeal of God himself will bring this to pass. Unfolding further the panorama of Old Testament prophecy, we are told that the child in question will be the Son of David (9:7), of royal lineage, and that He will be born in Bethlehem of Judea (Micah 5:2). Even more remarkable than these rays of light from God, the Scriptures further tell us that He was to be crucified for the sins of Israel and the world (Isaiah 53; cf. Daniel 9:26), and that He would rise again to life and come in power to sift the sons of men with eternal judgment (Psalm 22; cf. Zechariah 12:10).

But these facts are all a matter of history, which Jesus of Nazareth fulfilled to the letter, and which only remain to be consummated at His triumphant return as Judge of the world. Both Matthew and Luke declare the human fulfillment of

God's plan in Mary's conception of the Christ child (Matthew 1:18–25; cf. Luke 1:30–38). Thus the physical existence of Jesus Christ is a biologically established fact. Christian Science vehemently denies this fact and teaches instead that Mary conceived the spiritual idea of God and named it Jesus (*Science and Health*, 29). Denying as she did the reality of the physical universe, this was a strangely logical step for Eddy as opposed to her usual contempt for all logical form whatsoever. But be that as it may, all the wanderings of Eddy's mind, be they from Dan to Beersheba, can never change the testimony of Old and New Testament Scripture that a demonstrably "real" child was born to Mary, not an "idea," that this child existed as a concrete physical being apart from His divine nature and is now forever, for our sake, both God and man in Jesus Christ. The Virgin Birth, therefore, is a well-supported biblical doctrine, which contradicts most forcibly the false concept Eddy has incorporated into the Christian Science religion.

Respecting the miracles performed by Christ during His earthly ministry, Christian Scientists, whether they admit it or not, must logically deny that they were miracles in the first place and discount them as merely "illusions of the mortal mind." Eddy states that disease, sin, sickness, and death are all illusions; they are not "real" because only Mind (God) is real and Mind is spiritual, not material. Therefore, following Christian Science theology to its "logical" conclusions, since the "illusion of disease" can exist only in "the illusion called matter," which is itself existent only in the illusion called "mortal mind"—which Eddy denies exists anyway—there were no miracles at all because there was no corporeal body to be diseased, hence no need for a cure. Eddy wrote,

> The sick are not healed merely by declaring there is no sickness, but by knowing there is none. (*Science and Health*, 447)

This reasoning on the part of Christian Science theology presupposes the assumption that there is no evil, since God, or Good, is all that really exists. Unfortunately, it places them in the untenable position of having to account for the origin of the *idea* of evil, for even an illusion must have some basis in experience. Notwithstanding the circularity of this Christian Science argument, the Scriptures send a fresh breath of intellectual honesty into their account of Christ's true attitude toward disease, its reality and cure. The Lord Jesus never told the disintegrating leper, as Mrs. Eddy's practitioner would, "You have no disease, it cannot exist, only God is good and He is all," etc. Rather, He recognized the physical decay and by an act of sovereign grace restored the damaged tissue with one short sentence: "I will, be thou clean." It will be recalled that the leper in question said, "Lord, if thou wilt, thou canst make me clean" (Matthew 8:2–3). Christ's answer included none of Eddy's "Divine Science" or treatments by paid "quacktitioners" as they are sometimes called. He merely restored the form His power had originally created (Colossians 1:16) and destroyed the bacteria responsible for the disease. Jesus never healed by denying the reality of the disease He intended to cure. Rather, He affirmed its reality and glorified God for its cure.

You will remember that at the raising of Lazarus (John 11), Christ waited until his friend was physically dead beyond question (four days) and then restored to the function of life every cell of his decaying body and glorified God for the victory over man's second oldest enemy.[23] We should note in this connection that Jesus did not deny the reality of death, as do Christian Scientists. He did not consider it "an illusion"; rather, He verbally confirmed it: "Lazarus is dead" (John 11:14).

Christian Science finds no support for its denial of the physical miracles of Christ; deny the physical though they may, the facts are established. Should further proof be desired, however, the reader is urged to consult the following biblical references, which prove, we believe, that the miracles of Christ were physical realities, the result of supernatural intervention on the part of God on behalf of His erring creatures:

1. *Matthew 8:14–15.* Jesus heals Peter's mother-in-law.
2. *Matthew 8:26–27.* Christ stills the tempest.
3. *Matthew 9:2, 6–7.* Jesus heals the palsied man.
4. *Matthew 9:27–30.* Christ restores the sight of two blind men.
5. *Mark 1:32–34.* Jesus heals the sick and casts out devils.
6. *John 2:1–11; John 6:10–14.* Christ changes water to wine and miraculously feeds 5,000 people.

Concluding this discussion, it should be noted in reference to John 2:1–11 and 6:10–14 that Christ would hardly have created wine from water or multiplied loaves and fishes to quench the thirst and satisfy the hunger of nonexistent bodies or "illusions of mortal mind," to quote Eddy. The nature of all Christ's miracles was that of a divine/human encounter, comprising empirically verified physical events to meet human needs—whether hunger, thirst, or suffering—not "illusions," as the theology of Christian Science attempts to make the gullible believe.

The Vicarious Atonement of Christ

There is no doctrine found within the pages of the Bible that is better supported or substantiated than that of the substitutionary death of Christ for the sins of the world. As far back in the biblical record as Exodus, Moses wrote of God's symbolic use of blood for purification and sacrifice. It will be recalled that Jehovah delivered the Israelites from Egypt by causing all the firstborn of the nation, including Pharaoh's own son, to fall under the shadow of sudden death (Exodus 12). The Jews were instructed in this instance to sprinkle the blood of the young lamb on the doorposts and lintels of their homes, and God promised, "When I see the blood, I will pass over" (Exodus 12:13). The Lord also instituted the animal sacrifices of the Levitical era and expressly stated, "It is the blood that maketh an atonement [covering] for the soul" (Leviticus 17:11). Following this typology through into the New Testament, we find that Jesus was called "the Lamb of God, which taketh away the sin of the world" (John 1:29), and further, that His blood shed upon the cross is our atonement or "covering" for sin, even for the sins of all mankind (Matthew 26:28; Romans 5:6–8; Ephesians 1:7; Colossians 1:20; etc.).

The believer in Christ, therefore, is saved by grace alone, through faith in His blood and its efficacy for the cleansing of all sin (Romans 3:25). John, the beloved disciple, reminds us in his powerful epistle, "The blood of Jesus Christ

---

[23]Satan occupies the dubious honor of being the first.

his Son cleanseth us from all sin" (1 John 1:7), and Peter no less resoundingly declares, "Ye were not redeemed with corruptible things, as silver and gold . . . but with the precious blood of Christ, as of a lamb without blemish and without spot" (1 Peter 1:18–19). Indeed, like a crimson cord binding the whole Bible into one compact testimony, the trail of blood courses from Genesis to Revelation, testifying from the mouths of unimpeachable witnesses the wondrous story of God's redemptive love. Listen for a moment to the record of Scripture, and the picture comes clearly into focus: God loved us and sent His Son to be our Savior.

"Christ died for the ungodly," Paul triumphantly cries, and "without shedding of blood there is no remission of sins" (Romans 5:6; Hebrews 9:22); He purchased the church with His own blood (Acts 20:28), Luke informs us, and John adds to the witness by declaring that Christ "washed us from our sins in His own blood" (Revelation 1:5). This was not a pagan sacrifice to placate the wrath of a heathen god's justice, as Eddy wrote, but a sacrifice offered "through the eternal Spirit" to free the sons of men from the curse of sin and open the path of salvation by which we can have "boldness to enter into the holiest by the blood of Jesus . . . a new and living way" to the very throne room of God our Father (Hebrews 10:19–20).

Contrasting this picture of concrete biblical theology with the views of Christian Science, no better illustration of Eddy's repudiation of this doctrine can be shown than that which comes from her own pen. In speaking of the Atonement, Eddy said,

> The material blood of Jesus was no more efficacious to cleanse from sin when it was shed upon "the accursed tree," than when it was flowing in his veins. (*Science and Health*, 25)

According to Eddy, Jesus, the disciples and apostles, and the early Christian theologians did not understand the meaning of the vicarious Atonement, but she did! Eddy wrote,

> He atoned for the terrible unreality of a supposed existence apart from God. (*No and Yes*, 55)
> The efficacy of the crucifixion lies in the practical affection and goodness it demonstrated for mankind. (*Science and Health*, 24)

This is, of course, the opposite of anything the Bible teaches. When Jesus said, "This is my flesh which I shall give for the life of the world," and "This is my blood shed for many for the remission of sin," Eddy would have us believe that He anticipated no sacrifice for man's sin at all, but merely martyrdom for "the terrible unreality of a supposed existence apart from God." In light of the obvious denial by Christian Science of this historically accepted biblical doctrine, so strongly supported by the Scriptures of both Old and New Testaments, further comment on the problem is not deemed necessary.

The Death, Resurrection, and Ascension of Christ

In our age of advanced medicine, we read of many miracles ascribed to the labors of medical science; but all these advancements, marvelous though they may be, have only delayed the inevitable decay and death of the body and have yet to guarantee us physical immortality. The Scriptures clearly teach us that "it is appointed unto men once to die, but after this the judgment" (Hebrews 9:27), even as they tell us that our Lord himself physically died at Calvary (Philippians 2:8). In fact, the death of Jesus upon the cross is more thoroughly substantiated from biblical and secular history than is His birth, which makes it even more difficult to believe that rational persons would deny it. However, Eddy and Christian Science do deny it, hence the necessity of refuting their illogical contentions.

Joseph of Arimathaea, it will be remembered, requested the dead body of Jesus from Pontius Pilate (Matthew 27:58) and properly prepared it for burial (vv. 59–60), as was the custom of the Jews. One thing that Joseph knew above anything else in the gathering shadows of the Sabbath that marked the solemn hour rent by bitterness, sorrow, and fear was that the body of the Galilean prophet he buried was physically incapable of life; Jesus of Nazareth was dead. The absolute terror and doubt that gripped the immediate followers of Jesus could have come only from the personal knowledge that He had perished under the unbelieving Judeo-Roman conspiracy, and that their cause was without a visible leader and apparently doomed to failure. The apostle Paul tells us repeatedly, "Christ died" (Romans 5:6); Peter recounts that He "bare our sins in his own body on the tree" (1 Peter 2:24), and John testifies that the soldiers "saw" when they came to Jesus "that he was dead already" (John 19:33). Certainly such intimate accounts cannot be lightly dismissed, yet Eddy and Christian Science boldly assert "His disciples believed Jesus to be dead while he was hidden in the sepulchre, whereas he was alive" (*Science and Health*, 44), and once again Eddy states:

> Jesus' students . . . did not perform many wonderful works until they saw him after his crucifixion and learned that he had not died. (*Science and Health*, 45–46)

The issue, therefore, is a clean-cut one. The Bible says Christ died upon the cross; Eddy and Christian Science say He did not. For those who call themselves Christians, the choice is not a difficult one to make, and for those who are not Christians, we are certain they will accept the words of the Scripture in preference to Eddy, if only on general principles and the testimony of history.

The resurrection of Christ is treated on a similar basis by the Christian Science religion, which affirms that He never rose from the dead physically any more than He died physically, Eddy deliberately perverting numerous texts of Scripture to glean support for her wobbly propositions.

So it is that we learn how Christian Science often attempts to change the obvious meaning of texts. In the twentieth chapter of John's gospel, the resurrected Jesus, to prove to the doubting Thomas that He was not a spirit but genuine "flesh and bones," presented His body bearing the imprint of nails and spear for the disciple's examination. To His disciple at another time Jesus also said, "Handle me . . . for a spirit hath not flesh and bones, as ye see me have" (Luke 24:39). The resurrection of Christ and its startling revelation—namely, that He was who He claimed to be, the Son of God—is the one factor that most probably accounts for the rapid rise of Christianity's power over the lives of men. Here was a genuine opportunity to believe in a Savior who proved His divinity by vanquishing death, and who promised the same victory to those who believe and preach

His Gospel. It is no wonder Satan has so strenuously opposed this doctrine of Scripture, for upon it hangs the verity of our salvation. As Paul puts it, "If Christ be not raised, your faith is vain; ye are yet in your sins" (1 Corinthians 15:17). Eddy and Christian Science may oppose this truth vigorously—as indeed they do—but the Gospel of Christ will not be hindered by mere denials, and their unbelief does not in any sense nullify the truth of God as the Scriptures so powerfully declare it:

> But now is Christ risen from the dead, and become the firstfruits of them that slept. For since by man came death, by man came also the resurrection of the dead. For as in Adam all die, even so in Christ shall all be made alive.[24] (1 Corinthians 15:20–22)

As to the doctrine of the ascension of Christ into heaven, physically, another denial is vouchsafed from the pen of Eddy. By the same method she uses to spiritualize the resurrection of Christ, Eddy also spiritualizes His ascension. She describes it as follows:

> [The disciples'] dear Master would rise again in the spiritual realm of reality, and ascend far above their apprehension. As the reward for his faithfulness, he would disappear to material sense in that change which has since been called the ascension. (*Science and Health,* 34)

Now, to any alert Bible student, the ascension of Christ was a physical one; the disciples saw Him carried into the heavenlies visibly; it was not merely an upward stroke on the "spiritual scale" of existence, as Eddy put it, but a change of position from one sphere to another, visible in part to the human eye. In connection with this, one need only remember the testimony of the angels who escorted their Lord to His throne:

> Ye men of Galilee, why stand ye gazing up into heaven? this same Jesus, which is taken up from you into heaven, shall so come in like manner as ye have seen him go into heaven. (Acts 1:11)

Besides these great declarations of Scripture, the confused writing of Eddy is conspicuously immature and inadequate because, as always, the Bible, which is the supreme Christian authority, confirms the truth as it really happened, not as Christian Science has imagined it happened.

The Existence of Satan, Evil, and Sin

Probably one of the most obvious doctrines of biblical theology is that of the origin, existence, and final disposition of evil. From Genesis to Revelation one can distinguish the powers set in array against God and His people, powers whose ultimate end is spiritual judgment of the most terrible order. We are told in the Scriptures that Satan, or Lucifer, the "god of this world," was once a mighty and perfect angelic son of God whose dazzling and wondrous countenance earned for him the titles "son of the morning" and "cherub that covereth" (Isaiah 14:12;

---

[24]Or to more properly grasp the sense of the Greek, "As in Adam all die, so then through Christ shall all be resurrected."

Ezekiel 28:14). The Scriptures also tell us that this powerful angel secretly cherished the desire to usurp the throne of his Maker (Isaiah 14:13–14), and upon gathering numerous supporters he rebelled against the sovereignty of Jehovah. The outcome of this wicked rebellion was the driving from heaven of Satan and the fallen angels that followed him, and he was subsequently allowed dominion over the celestial universe for reasons best known to God and himself, hence his title "prince of the power of the air" (Ephesians 2:2).

With this rebellion commenced the beginning of all evil or sin, i.e., that which is opposed to the will of God. After his rout in the heavenly encounter, Satan extended his kingdom over the heavenlies and earth, determined to disrupt, if possible, the plans of God. In the Garden of Eden Satan's desires reached fruition, and he succeeded in spiritually corrupting the future parents of the human race, Adam and Eve (Genesis 3). Satan was sentenced to a humiliating defeat by the "Seed" of the very creatures he had so willfully wronged as punishment for this sin against the Lord (Genesis 3:15). This promised Seed who would bruise the head of Satan was to be the Messiah of Israel, who we have already seen is the Lord Jesus Christ. The final judgment of Satan will come after his complete and utter defeat at Armageddon, when he and all his followers from the ancient days of his heavenly citizenship will then be cast into the lake of fire, there to suffer eternally the righteous judgment of God (Revelation 20:10).

Despite this graphic biblical portrayal of Satan available for all to see, Eddy and Christian Science energetically deny his existence referring to him as "another elusive personification" (*Science and Health*, 81). Further establishing her contention that evil is nonexistent, Eddy flatly states,

> Hence, evil is but an illusion, and it has no real basis. Evil is a false belief. God is not its author. The supposititious parent of evil is a lie. (*Science and Health*, 480)
>
> There never was a moment in which evil was real. (*No and Yes*, 24)

Since Christian Science denies the origin of evil or Satan, it is only logical that it should deny evil, and sin as the result of evil. Concerning sin Eddy wrote,

> The only reality of sin, sickness, or death is the awful fact that unrealities seem real to human, erring belief, until God strips off their disguise. They are not true, because they are not of God. (*S & H*, 472)
>
> Sin, sickness, and death are to be classified as effects of error. Christ came to destroy the belief of sin. (*S & H*, 473)

Placing this declaration on a level plane with the biblical definition and development of the doctrine of sin, it is seen to be at complete odds with the biblical record. John reminds us that sin, far from being an "illusion" or a nonexistent force, is in reality a very potent enemy of man. "Sin," writes John, "is the transgression of the law," and further, "All unrighteousness is sin" (1 John 3:4; 1 John 5:17). Paul also admonishes, "For the wages of sin is death" (Romans 6:23). One can hardly be expected to believe that the Christian Science teaching about sin is truthful when both John and Paul, inspired spokesmen of God, so clearly contradict it. The Bible innumerable times declares: "All have sinned, and come short of the glory of God" (Romans 3:23), and, "If we say we have not sinned, we make him [God] a liar, and his word is not in us" (1 John 1:10). As to the personality and power of a personal force of evil (Satan), the Bible equally establishes his existence as opposed to Eddy's denials. Jesus, it will be remembered, spoke with Satan, who tempted Him (Luke 4:5-6). This could hardly have been an illusion, even of the Christian Science variety, and the Lord also announced that He had come to "destroy the works of the devil" (1 John 3:8) whom He described as a liar and a "murderer from the beginning" who "abode not in the truth . . . a liar, and the father of it" (John 8:44). As her literary advisor, the Rev. J. H. Wiggin, so aptly put it, Eddy's devil was Malicious Animal Magnetism, which she invented to explain away the rather obvious fact that evil and sin existed despite her affirmations to the contrary. This doctrine eventually became a mania with Eddy and drove her to irrational behavior and fantastically absurd demonstrations of temper, illness, and rapid excursions to different communities "when she felt the fiend closing in."

The Scriptures, therefore, give more than convincing proof "that God will judge sin" and that it is not an illusion but an ever-present enemy, of which all men, even Christian Scientists, must reap the wages in the end. It is comforting to know from a biblical standpoint that though "the wages of sin is death . . . the gift of God is eternal life through Jesus Christ our Lord" (Romans 6:23).

The Doctrines of Prayer and Eternal Salvation

The doctrines of prayer and salvation are inseparably joined in the Scripture with the decree and plan of God to redeem the fallen race of men. The Bible, in places too numerous to recount, encourages, instructs, and even commands us to "pray without ceasing" (1 Thessalonians 5:17) that God may reward our faith in His righteous judgments. The Lord Jesus often prayed to His Father for strength to meet the physical and spiritual rigors of daily life and finally the cross itself (Matthew 26:36). We remember also at the raising of Lazarus, pictured so vividly in the eleventh chapter of John's gospel, Jesus prayed, "Father, I thank thee that thou hast heard me. And I knew that thou hearest me always" (vv. 41-42), and that He further instructed us to pray to the Father that seeth in secret; and the Father that seeth in secret will reward us openly (see Matthew 6:6). Above and beyond these elementary examples of Christ's attitude toward prayer, it is a well-established biblical fact that prayer by definition is a direct personal request to God for His intervention, whether it is for the purpose of healing the sick, raising the dead, or simply asking for grace and strength to live our individual lives (Philippians 4:6-7). The entire context of John's seventeenth chapter, for example, is devoted to recording the prayer of Christ for all His disciples, present and future, that they might be protected from Satan and the powers of darkness during their ministry of gospel truth. Jesus understood well the need for personal prayer to God in order to maintain close fellowship with our Father, and it is of this that He reminds us when He said: "Men ought always to pray, and not to faint" (Luke 18:1). To Christian Scientists, however, prayer carries none of the meaning that the Bible so clearly portrays, because, as Eddy taught, "Prayer to a personal God hinders spiritual growth."[25]

We have seen, of course, that the God of the Bible is a personal Being, not a

---

[25]Quoted in I. M. Haldeman, *Christian Science in the Light of Holy Scripture*, 268.

mere "Principle," as Christian Science contends; therefore, it is easy to see why the meaning of prayer to a Christian and to a Christian Scientist differs markedly. Eddy also wrote concerning prayer:

> Audible prayer can never do the works of spiritual understanding, which regenerates. . . . (*Science and Health*, 4)
> The danger from prayer is that it may lead us into temptation. (7)
> The mere habit of pleading with the divine Mind, as one pleads with a human being, perpetuates the belief in God as humanly circumscribed—an error which impedes spiritual growth. (2)

It is singularly peculiar, in view of these contradictory claims of Eddy, that Jesus addressed His Father as a personal Being and commanded us to pray a personal prayer, "Our Father which art in heaven, Hallowed be thy name. Thy kingdom come. Thy will be done in earth, as it is in heaven" (Matthew 6:9–10).

If "Give us this day our daily bread, and forgive us our debts, as we forgive our debtors" is not a plea to God, then, perhaps Eddy's followers can tell us what in the name of reason it is. Eddy says, further:

> Prayer cannot change the Science of being, but it tends to bring us into harmony with it. (*Science and Health*, 2)

What is more evident from this bold negation of Scripture than the fact that Christian Scientists cannot even logically claim that they pray in the biblical sense at all, disbelieving as they do the clear definition the Bible gives of what prayer and communication with God really mean? It was written of the Lord Jesus that prayer was His constant habit, His unceasing attitude, and unwearied occupation; it is difficult, therefore, to believe that He would urge us to pray in the sure knowledge that it might "lead us into temptation," as Eddy implied it did. Moreover, the Lord Jesus prayed audibly and commanded His disciples to emulate Him: "Lead us not into temptation." But Eddy says audible prayer itself may lead us into temptation (*Science and Health*, 7). One needs to look no further for evidence of where she obtained her inspiration. It was obviously supplied by the great Counterfeiter (see Genesis 3:4–5). Paul, that noble apostle of personal prayer, instructs us to "let your requests be made known unto God" and to pursue "every thing by prayer and supplication with thanksgiving" (Philippians 4:6). Once again, the inspired apostle flatly contradicts Eddy's unscriptural teachings and those of Christian Science, a fact hardly necessitating further comment upon the subject.

Prayer is the lifeblood of the Christian's spiritual existence, and personal communion with the personal God our ever-present help in trouble, a relationship no Christian Scientist can ever enjoy, since they have never known the God of the Bible or Jesus Christ; both of whom, in the biblical sense, they and Mrs. Eddy, their "leader," unreservedly deny.

The doctrine of eternal salvation is so well-documented in Scripture that I doubt major comment at this stage of study is necessary; however, to clarify the doctrine as opposed to Christian Science's perversion of it, I shall briefly summarize it here.

Eternal life, the Bible reveals to us, is to be found only in the cross of Christ, that supreme symbol of God's immeasurable love toward a lost and dying world.

This life, the Scripture tells us, resides in the person of His Son, Jesus, "the true God" and "eternal life" (John 3:16; 5:24; 6:47; 10:28; 14:6; 17:3; 1 John 5:20, etc.). The Scriptures further testify that God sent His Son to be the "Savior of all men, specially of those that believe" (1 Timothy 4:10). The Lord Jesus Christ by His sacrifice on Calvary has purchased "eternal redemption" for us, promising that if we trust Him fully we shall at length be with Him where He is (John 17:24). God's Word assures us that our Savior is now at the "right hand of the Majesty on high" (Hebrews 1:3), and that someday, by His matchless grace, we too shall leave this vale of tears, forever free of earthly shackles, to "dwell in the house of the Lord for ever" (Psalm 23:6).

> For by grace are ye saved through faith; and that not of yourselves: it is the gift of God: Not of works, lest any man should boast. (Ephesians 2:8–9)

This, then, is the true Christian meaning of salvation; not only freedom from fear, judgment, and the uncertainties of this earthly life, but the knowledge of peace with God "through the blood of His cross" and justification before God by "the power of His resurrection." All these things, according to both John and Peter, are the result of the operation of God's Holy Spirit in the hearts of men, regenerating, renewing, recreating, until eventually, in His redeemed own, the perfect reflection of Christ, God's "express image" (Hebrews 1:3), shall shine forth triumphant over Satan, the flesh, and death itself.

"Ye must be born again," said our Lord to Nicodemus (John 3:3); "being born again ... not of corruptible seed, but of incorruptible," writes Peter (1 Peter 1:23); and Paul adds, "Therefore if any man be in Christ, he is a new creature: old things are passed away; behold, all things are become new" (2 Corinthians 5:17). Thus it is seen that God's salvation is not a reformation of man, but a regeneration; not merely a reorganization of his social habits, but a literal saving of his spiritual life—a complete deliverance of the completely lost.

Christian Science, unfortunately, does not hold this view. It teaches, instead, as Eddy puts it, that salvation is not a personal deliverance from real sin and wickedness, but "boundless freedom and sinless sense," or, as she further stated, "Man as God's idea is already saved with an everlasting salvation" (*Miscellaneous Writings*, 261).

Christian Science does away altogether with the necessity of Christ's death on the cross for sin:

> According to divine law, sin and suffering are not cancelled by repentance or pardon. (*MW*, 261)

These are strange words in contrast to what Christ said, "I am not come to call the righteous, but sinners to repentance" (Matthew 9:13), and to Peter's immortal sentence, "Christ hath also once suffered for sins, the just for the unjust, that he might bring us to God" (1 Peter 3:18). Christian Science offers no eternal life and no salvation for the soul, denying as it does, sin, and hence the necessity of redemption from it. But God's Word stands sure, in powerful opposition to the falsehoods of Eddy and Christian Science: "All have sinned, and come short of the glory of God," and "There is none righteous, no, not one" (Romans 3:23; 3:10); but, "Believe on the Lord Jesus Christ, and thou shalt be saved" (Acts 16:31). This is God's salvation; this is the central message of the Bible; this is eternal life.

Man, His Spiritual and Material Natures

Without fear of contradiction, all rational persons will admit the reality of their physical existence. There are three principal reasons for this admission, which, briefly stated, are these:

1. Man is capable of perceiving his corporeal form.
2. The demands of the body—such as food, clothing, etc., prove that it has a material existence.
3. The human mind is capable of discerning the difference between concrete and abstract ideas, the body being easily discerned as a concrete proposition.

In view of these three facts, it is worthwhile to note that Christian Science denies without reservation all physical existence, as Eddy wrote,

> Man is not matter; he is not made up of brain, blood, bones, and other material elements. . . . Man is spiritual and perfect; and because he is spiritual and perfect, he must be so understood in Christian Science. Man is idea, the image of Love; he is not physique. (*Science and Health*, 475)

Not only did Eddy deny the materially verifiable fact that the body exists, but she even went so far as to correct God in His creative office by asserting that "Man is the offspring and idea of the Supreme Being whose law is perfect and infinite. In obedience to the law, man is forever unfolding the endless beatitudes of Being; for he is the image and likeness of infinite Life, Truth, and Love" (*Miscellaneous Writings*, 82). At this point in her incoherent ramblings and deplorable mental condition, Eddy did the one thing that, by itself, devoid of any theological speculation whatsoever, characterizes her system of reasoning as that of a grossly philosophical perversion. To deny the reality of matter, philosophically speaking, is to predicate the worst type of absurdity, and Eddy was not above such a perpetration.

Genesis 2:7 plainly states, "God formed man of the dust of the ground, and breathed into his nostrils the breath of life; and man became a living soul." Moses further tells us that God created the material Eve, using a part of the material Adam, and David said, "It is he that hath made us, and not we ourselves" (Psalm 100:3). The Scriptures irrefutably declare that God created matter (Genesis 1:1), all forms of living organisms, and finally man himself in the spiritual image and likeness of his immaterial Father. There is, therefore, no conceivable ground, logically speaking, for denying that man exists physically as well as spiritually, and Eddy's repeated attempts to do away with the human body and, for that matter, the material universe itself is only more evidence of her unsound reasoning processes.

In regard to the spiritual nature of man, Christian Science takes a peculiar attitude, but for once an attitude that is logically consistent when followed through. Since man is totally spiritual ("the reflection of God," as Christian Science would have it), and God is perfect and incapable of sin; therefore, man must also be perfect as His reflection and hence incapable of sin. This is exactly what Eddy taught:

> Man's origin and existence being in Him, man is the ultimate of perfection and by no means the medium of imperfection. . . . If God is upright and eternal, man as His likeness is erect in goodness and perpetual in Life, Truth, and Love. . . . The spiritual man is that perfect and unfallen likeness, coexistent and coeternal with God. (*Miscellaneous Writings,* 79)

The logical mind can only deduce from these statements that the biblical account of man's fall from perfection (Genesis 3:6–7) and his definition as a finite being (Psalm 89:48; 1 Corinthians 15:47) are totally in error and that man is God, because if he coexists with an eternal being (*MW,* 79), he himself is eternal. The weakness of this position can easily be demonstrated by the fact that all material things, including the human body, eventually return to the basic elements of existence, and since God is said to have created all that exists, both material and spiritual (John 1:3); therefore, man in both his physical and spiritual forms is a creature, a creation not of a coexistent or inherently eternal character.

In conclusion, it is obvious that the identification of man and God by Christian Science on the basis of a spiritual nature is completely erroneous if the Judeo-Christian viewpoint is to be accepted as to the identity of the true God. Christian Science, it should be noted, claims that it holds the Christian position, and Christian Scientists violently repudiate any attempts to show that their teachings are the opposite of what Jesus taught; yet in every possible sense of the biblical record, all things having been considered, there is not the slightest possibility that the theology of Christian Science resembles even vaguely the revelation of the Bible concerning the teachings of Jesus Christ. The soul of man, it is true, is immaterial and was created in the image of God, but the body of man is purely physical in every sense of the word. To deny its reality, as does Christian Science, and attempt to prove that man is totally spiritual, and spiritually perfect at that, is, to say the least, a flagrant perversion of what biblical theology plainly portrays. The soul of man willfully sinned against God in the person of Adam (Isaiah 43:27; Romans 5); the souls of all men have forever been in rebellion against Almighty God from that day forward. It is only through the Gospel of Jesus Christ that this rebellion is brought into submission and that the sins of man's evil soul are cleansed and the soul regenerated to eternal life. To deny these facts on a biblical basis is dangerous: they are far too obvious. To explain them away, as does Christian Science, is fruitless; for the "word of the Lord endureth for ever," and "this is the word which by the gospel is preached unto you" (1 Peter 1:25).

Christian Science and Healing

The central claim of Eddy and Christian Science is that she has "restored" to Christendom the power of healing "lost" since the days of the early church. It is continually reiterated in the literature of the cult that their "leader" healed as Jesus did and demonstrated, through Divine Science. Not only this, but Eddy herself boldly asserted that she healed all types of diseases including cancer, tuberculosis, and diphtheria. Eddy wrote to the *New York Sun,* December 19, 1898:

I challenge the world to disprove what I hereby declare. After my discovery of Christian Science, I healed consumption in the last stages that the M.D.'s by verdict of a stethoscope and the schools declared incurable, the lungs being mostly consumed. I healed malignant tubercular diphtheria and carious bones that could be dented by the finger, saving them when the surgeon's instruments were lying on the table ready for their amputation. I have healed at one visit a cancer that had so eaten the flesh of the neck as to expose the jugular vein so that it stood out like a cord.

Notice that Mrs. Eddy gives no particulars here; no names of patients, no localities, no dates or witnesses. Indeed, the only persons who ever witnessed her "miraculous" cures were either lackeys of Eddy's without medical training to justify their diagnosis of disease, or Christian Scientists of another era who unfortunately believed as God-breathed truth any claim that either Eddy or her contemporary worshipers conjured up. Eddy's claim of the power to heal presents us with a challenge. Since she denied all of the cardinal doctrines of the Christian faith, we know that her so-called power to heal did not come from God. We are left, then, with two alternatives. Either the so-called healings were not supernatural at all (being actually fraudulent, spontaneous, psychosomatic, etc.) and Eddy stands condemned as a fraud; or they were accomplished by the power of Satan, in the pattern of the magicians of Pharaoh's court in Moses' day (Exodus 7:11, 22). Briefly, then, let us consider this phase of "Mother" Eddy's long career.

To begin with, it should be realized in the process of investigating Eddy's healing claims that she refused outright to treat identical cases of diseases she claimed to have cured. Even when a prominent Cincinnati physician offered her every such opportunity, Eddy remained strangely silent; indeed, she never mentioned the issue again.[26] This is hardly the attitude one would expect from the alleged successor to Jesus Christ. The foregoing is only one fact of a large number that proved beyond doubt that Eddy did not heal as she claimed. During her long life Eddy allowed her own little granddaughter, her beloved brother Samuel's wife, and her close friend Joseph Armstrong all to die painful deaths of cancer, pneumonia, and pleurisy, and never, to any known evidence of the contrary, did she ever lift her "healing" hand to save them.[27] Instead, she recommended "absent treatment" in all three cases, which consisted of reading her book *Science and Health* and concentrating upon mentally repulsing the organic deterioration. Eddy could have at least paid a call on them, and if her claims were true, healed them "at one visit," but she did not because she could not, and no one knew it better than Mary Baker Eddy. There is an overwhelming mass of evidence from sources unchallengeable that this fact is absolute truth, and no better authority can be quoted than the sworn testimony of Alfred Farlow, then chairman of the publications committee of the Christian Science Church and president of the Mother Church in Boston. Farlow's testimony, that of a Christian Scientist in excellent standing with his church and certainly in a position to know the facts about Eddy, clearly stated that he did not know of any healing *ever* having been made by Eddy of any organic disease in her entire life but that of a stiff leg—

---

[26]Dr. Charles A. L. Reed, *New York Sun*, January 1, 1899.

[27]She did, however, send her personal check to defray the cost of her sister-in-law's operation, but by the time the surgeon operated, the time taken in useless Christian Science treatments had taken a fatal toll and she died.

hardly a major illness by any reasonable diagnosis (*The Religio-Medical Masquerade*, F. W. Peabody, n.d., 113).

Much more material could be introduced to further verify this contention of history against the Eddy healing legend, but it is sufficient to say that the issue needs no further support. She who professed to succeed Jesus Christ as the great healer of our age could not heal even her closest emotional contacts; and to conceal this great threat to her system, which was based squarely on her alleged failure to heal, Eddy and her contemporaries have masqueraded to the world and to her gullible followers the legend of her miraculous curative power. This power, so widely trumpeted by Christian Science propaganda, history tells us she never exercised or demonstrated openly, for the obvious reason that it was a complete illusion, a phantom of Christian Science publicity and the delusions of Mary Baker Eddy.

Eddy, however, was not above attaching a price tag to the miraculous healings she claimed for her religion, and so she wrote,

> When teaching imparts the ability to gain and maintain health, to heal and elevate man in every line of life—as this teaching certainly does—is it unreasonable to expect in return something to support one's self and a Cause? If so, our whole system of education, secular and religious, is at fault, and the instructors and philanthropists in our land should expect no compensation. "If we have sown unto you spiritual things, is it a great thing if we shall reap your carnal things?" (*Miscellaneous Writings*, 38)

But that was Eddy, clever to the last and beyond the comprehension and understanding of even her most intimate friends.

It must never be forgotten that Eddy once wrote:

> A patient hears the doctor's verdict as the criminal hears the death-sentence. (*Science and Health*, 198)

Yet she made very rare but real use of doctors for her spasmodic attacks of hysteria, and toward the end of her life even allowed Christian Scientists the right to use anesthetics, surgery, and the services of orthopedists for breaks and fractures, etc. This although she stoutly opposed such practices at the outset of her career!

However, no one can ever accuse Mrs. Eddy of being foolish, since she seemingly made allowance for some situations. But while she provided in a measure for the bodies of her followers, she left their souls poverty-stricken, barren, and destitute, robbed of the true Christ and His Gospel of life.

The chief attraction of Christian Science, then, lies in its seeming power over disease and mental conflict. But to quote psychologist David S. Davis: "What has been induced by suggestion can be cured by suggestion."[28]

Most illnesses "cured" by Christian Scientists are imagined illnesses that lack medical documentation and are seldom thoroughly verified by anyone other than the Scientists or their sympathizers. The physical world to most Christian Scientists is an "illusion of mortal mind," but they are quick to seize every opportunity

---

[28]Prof. David S. Davis, "A Psychologist Views the Cults," from *The Examiner*, Vol. I, January-February, No. 1, 11.

to avail themselves of all the comforts this same "mortal mind" conjures up.[29]

With this philosophy it is easy to see how even sin with all its hideousness is reduced to a state of mind, and death to a flighty "illusion."

Since the central doctrine of almost all cults is the denial of both the deity and Saviorhood of the Lord Jesus, we must exert renewed effort in preaching and teaching these major doctrines of our Christian heritage. We must be quick to expose error and quicker still to extend to all cultists the love of God and the assurance of forgiveness through His Eternal Son, if they will but come to the Christ of Calvary.

Let us not forget, however, that Christian Science can temporarily induce peace of mind, and this cannot be doubted; but, that it is able to cure "diagnosed diseases," give peace of soul, or, most of all, peace with God, is a question to which the Bible emphatically says *No!* The Bible clearly teaches that salvation is effected solely through the grace of God as revealed in Jesus Christ and His substitutionary atonement on the cross. The Christ of Christianity is a Personality— God Incarnate (John 1:1–14)—not the "Divine Idea" of a pantheistic nonentity, as Eddy portrayed Him to be.

It is therefore important to remember that Eddy never believed in a personal God nor does any true Christian Scientist today. Eddy's last words, which she scrawled with a trembling hand on a scrap of paper shortly before her death, "God is my life," might just as well have read, "Principle, Love, Spirit, or Intelligence is my life." To her utterly confused mind, the God of the Bible did not exist; for her, God was not personal in any sense, since her limited theology only permitted an "it," which was "all in all." Aside from adoring this pantheistic, impersonal deity, Eddy, and consequently all Christian Scientist practitioners today, expounds this principle as the master key to resolving all human misery. Paradoxically, however, they deny misery exists in the first place but never tire of trying to convince anyone who will listen, for a handsome fee, that Christian Science can remove this "error of mortal mind" through "prayer." The great byword of Christian Science, incidentally, is "prayer," and they never cease reminding their audience that they always pray to "God" for healing. But is it really prayer? The Scriptures teach that prayer is one's petition to a personal God who sees our needs and answers them (Philippians 4:6–7). Not so in Christian Science. Eddy many times reaffirmed her conviction that prayer to a personal God is a hindrance, not a help. To her and Christian Science, the only true prayer is the affirmation of Principle Allness and the identification of one's self with this pantheistic Principle. From this basic misconception stems the illusion of man's inherent goodness and the denial of the "erroneous" ideas that evil or, for that matter, sin, suffering, disease, or even death is real. With this view of life it is easy to see how Christian Scientists can appear so happy and so oblivious to everyday worries. Whenever they encounter evil they deny its reality; whenever they behold misery, they affirm its nonexistence; and even when death comes to a loved one, they simply assert that it is an "illusion," since Principle (God) is All, and "It" is good.

It would be possible to go on indefinitely with the many strange interpreta-

---

[29]Scripture, however, does cite evidence that Satan can counterfeit the miracles of God (Exodus 7:22ff.), so whatever "cures" Christian Science can present are not the work of our Christ.

tions that Eddy gave to the Scriptures. Suffice it to say, she never believed in them as God's Word or worshiped the Savior within its pages. The Christian's most holy and sacred doctrine of love—Christ crucified for us and His sacrificial blood our atonement with God—Eddy abruptly dismissed as unnecessary. She equally ignored the existence of hell, Satan, or, for that matter, a literal heaven. (For her, it was a "state of mind.") Nowhere in the annals of cultism is there to be found a person who camouflaged so expertly the "broad way of destruction" under a canopy of apparent serenity as did Mary Baker Eddy. Nevertheless, beneath this "serenity" lies a denial of nearly all orthodox Christianity.

In concluding this survey of Mrs. Eddy's religion, it is extremely important that the implications of Christian Science be thoroughly understood by Christians and non-Christians alike. It is important for Christians, because ignorance of Christian Science has been one of the main contributing factors to the success of its rapid early development. For non-Christians, it is important because it is an imitation of the true Gospel and bears no resemblance whatsoever to historical Christian faith.

Christian Science must be understood and its teachings refuted from the Scriptures because they pervert and wrest to the destruction of many misled souls. But Christian Scientists must be loved and evangelized for the cause of the Gospel and because this is God's command to His church. Herein lies the greater challenge by far.

Biblical Texts Helpful in Refuting Christian Science Theology

1. *The Authority of the Bible.* Psalm 119:140; Isaiah 40:8; Matthew 24:35; John 10:35; 17:17; 2 Timothy 3:16.
2. *The Trinity and the Deity of Christ.* Genesis 1:26; 11:7; 18:1–33; Exodus 3:14; Isaiah 6:8; 9:6; John 1:1, 14; 8:58; Colossians 1:15; 2:9; Hebrews 1:3; Revelation 1:7–8, 16.
3. *The Personality of the Holy Spirit.* Luke 12:12; John 16:7–8; Acts 13:2.
4. *The Virgin Birth and Miracles of Jesus.* Isaiah 7:14; 9:6; Micah 5:2; Matthew 1: 18–25; Luke 1:30–38; Matthew 8:14–15, 26–27; 9:2, 6–7, 27–30; Mark 1:32–34; John 2:1–11; 6:10–14.
5. *The Atonement, Death, and Resurrection of Christ.* Exodus 12:13; Leviticus 17:11; Psalm 22; Isaiah 53; Daniel 9:26; Matthew 26:28; 28:5–7; Luke 24:39; John 1:29; 19:33; Romans 5:6–8; Ephesians 1:7; Colossians 1:20.
6. *The Doctrine of Eternal Retribution.* Matthew 13:42, 50; 22:13; Mark 9:44, 46, 48; Luke 3:17; Revelation 20:10.
7. *The Doctrine of Christian Prayer.* Matthew 6:5–15; 7:7–11; Luke 18:1; Philippians 4:6; 1 Thessalonians 5:17; James 5:16.
8. *The Doctrine of Sin.* Romans 3:23; 6:23; 1 John 1:10; 3:4; 5:17.
9. *Jesus Is the Christ (Messiah) of God.* John 4:25, 26; 1 John 2:22.
10. *God Is Not Pantheistic in Any Sense.* Acts 17:24–28; Romans 1:25.
11. *God Is Neither Male nor Female.* Jeremiah 7:18; 1 Corinthians 8:6.
12. *Matter Exists and Is Independent of Spirit.* Matthew 10:28; Luke 24:39.

Commentary

~In the late '80s and early '90s, the Christian Science Church again experienced stormy turmoil due to negative media coverage of lawsuits, financial difficulties, and internal upheaval. Several court battles produced international headlines as members were charged with manslaughter, murder, and child abuse for choosing prayer over medical treatment for illness. In Minnesota, one four-week trial in 1994 levied a $14 million punitive damage award against the Mother Church, which a judge later reduced to $10.4 million.[30] In 1995 the Minnesota Court of Appeals overturned this judgment.[31] This court left intact $1.5 million in compensatory damages against the parents and two Christian Science practitioners.[32] The United States Supreme Court refused to hear the appeal of this case.[33] Now the Mother Church, contrary to its founder's philosophy, has revised its strong prohibition against medical treatment.

Current Christian Science esteem for *Science and Health* is still as great. Today Christian Scientists call the Bible and *Science and Health* their only "pastor," noting, "With the Bible and *Science and Health* as our pastor, Christian Scientists turn to prayer and these two books for counsel and healing."[34] Christian Scientists are promised, "Your dual and impersonal pastor, the Bible and *Science and Health With Key to the Scriptures,* is with you; and the Life these give, the Truth they illustrate, the Love they demonstrate, is the great Shepherd that feedeth my flock, and leadeth them 'beside the still waters.' "[35] Christian Scientists have no problem adding Eddy's book to the Bible as having equal divine authority:

> Humanity had the Bible for close to two millenniums without fully understanding how to use its truths in a scientifically provable way to heal and regenerate people like Christ Jesus did. To arrive at that kind of understanding, humanity needed to comprehend the Bible on a deeper level. They needed to "unlock" the Bible, so to speak. It was the specific mission of *Science and Health* to give the world this "key" to the Scriptures—to open up their treasures and enable everyone to use them.[36]

Though highly regarded by many, the Christian Science Publishing Society's media operations have struggled for years. According to *Forbes* magazine, the influential newspaper *The Christian Science Monitor* won respect not for proselytizing, but for its sober and thoughtful international coverage.[37] Yet it has not turned a profit since 1961, with losses in excess of $250 million.[38]

A television venture that began in 1986 was abandoned in mid-1992 after losing $235 million.[39] To obtain cash with these setbacks, in 1992 more than $40 million was borrowed from the employee pension fund to keep the church solvent.[40]

---

[30]Thomas Johnson, "Healing and Conscience in Christian Science," *The Christian Century* (June 29-July 6, 1994): 640.

[31][No Author Listed], "Court Nixes Wrongful Death Award," *Christianity Today* (May 15, 1995): 53.

[32][No Author Listed], "Christian Science Penalty Overturned," *The Christian Century* (May 3, 1995): 477.

[33][No Author Listed], "Christian Science Hearing Refused," *The Christian Century* (February 28, 1996): 223.

[34]"Questions and Answers: Why Don't You Have Ministers?" on the First Church of Christ, Scientist Web site *www.tfccs.com*, 1997.

[35]Mary Baker Eddy, *Miscellaneous Writings,* 322.

[36]"The Pastor of the Church of Christ, Scientist" TFCCS Web site *www.tfccs.com*, 1997.

[37]Norm Alster, "Netty Douglass's Impossible Task" *Forbes* (September 17, 1990): 188.

[38]Ibid.: 105.

[39][No Author Listed], "Monitor Television Fades to Black," *Time* (April 27, 1992): 21.

[40][No Author Listed], "Television Retreat," *Time* (March 23, 1992): 48.

In 1991 a book rejected by the church over forty years ago, *The Destiny of the Mother Church,* which deified church founder Mary Baker Eddy, was published so that the Mother Church might receive a $97 million bequest from a California church family.[41] According to the April 1, 1992, issue of *The Christian Century,* eight respected church publications editors resigned in protest, as the book violated Eddy's own beliefs.[42] Two other rival beneficiaries, Stanford University and the Los Angeles County Museum of Art, filed suit, arguing that the church had not fulfilled the terms of the will.[43] A 1993 settlement gave the church $53 million, with the remainder split between the other two parties.[44] Also, the church was under investigation by the U.S. Postal Service for violation of nonprofit mailing rates.[45]

It is interesting to note that while groups such as the Mormons, Jehovah's Witnesses, and others are enjoying unprecedented growth in Third World and formerly communist countries, Christian Science continues to maintain the bulk of its membership among North Americans, Northern Europeans, and the better educated, more Westernized people of other countries. In terms of American-based cults, Christian Science ranks financially weak compared to the much larger cults of the Mormons and Jehovah's Witnesses, but is still in competition with other Mind Science–based cults individually, such as Science of Mind and the Church of Religious Science.

Currently the church faces an aging membership. Its resources, however, whether political or financial, appear to be strong. On September 26, 2002, "by unanimous consent, the U.S. Congress passed Resolution H. Con Res. 458 recognizing the new Mary Baker Eddy Library for the Betterment of Humanity as well as the contributions of pioneering nineteenth-century author and thinker Mary Baker Eddy 'for her outstanding achievements and contributions.' " Unfortunately, this honor was bestowed upon Eddy with little fanfare and even less press coverage.[46] That it should go to a woman whose apparent plagiarism is so clearly evident in the historical record is a testimony to the influence of money and connections. Apparently some historians now have assigned Mary Baker Eddy the same prestige as Susan B. Anthony and Elizabeth Stanton Cady, and the U.S. Congress concurs.[47]

It remains to be seen whether Christian Science will continue to be noteworthy or fade into insignificance in the twenty-first century. For the present, however, the Christian Science cult is a powerful force with which evangelical Christians everywhere must deal. *The Christian Science Monitor's* circulation was only 73,000 in 1997; a popular electronic version is available to millions on the Internet. An abundance of other Christian Science theology Web sites exists that espouse the organization's doctrine. Most major university campuses have chapters of Christian Science Organizations (CSOs) consisting of faculty and students

[41]Carolyn Frida, "A Church That Needs Healing," *Newsweek* (March 23, 1992): 60.

[42][No Author Listed], "Christian Science Turmoil," *The Christian Century* (April 1, 1992): 330.

[43]James L. Franklin, "What Ails Christian Science?" *Christianity Today* (April 26, 1993): 54.

[44][No Author Listed], "Accord Reached in Book Lawsuit," *Christianity Today* (November 22, 1993): 42.

[45]James L. Franklin, "What Ails Christian Science?" *Christianity Today* (April 26, 1993): 54.

[46]*www.marybakereddylibrary.org/news/ newsrelease.jhtml?repID=%2Fglobal%2Frepositories%2Fnews%2F2002–09–26-newsreleases.xml.*

[47]114: Ibid.

who put a mainstream face on current issues with Christian Science philosophy. Furthermore, each branch church maintains a Christian Science Reading Room in a prominent neighborhood location or on church property. These rooms contain Christian Science books, newspapers, journals, and Bible lessons that are available for public use, introducing seekers to Christian Science theology by a veneer of scholarship and a hefty coating of compassion. Newcomers are urged to attend a midweek "testimony" meeting, where more experienced Christian Scientists share their testimonies of "spiritual" healing through Christian Science meditation and prayer.[48]

The Christian Science Church is headquartered on the fourteen-acre complex of the First Church of Christ, Scientist in the Back Bay section of Boston, Massachusetts. According to their official Internet homepage, the group had 2,200 branch churches in over sixty countries throughout the world in 1997. But the 2002 statistics have changed significantly, with the official Web site listing only 2,000 churches worldwide.[49] Adherents.com lists 1,885 "units" or congregations worldwide, the majority of which are in the United States. This indicates a staggering drop in membership from the 1997 church numbers.[50] It should be noted, however, that Christian Science does not aggressively recruit new members as other cults do, and members are virtually free to leave the organization without fear of rejection or the stigmatism of guilt.

While the church's by-laws forbid releasing membership statistics, outside sources estimate the number of followers to be somewhere between 150,000 and 400,000. The body is governed by a five-member board of directors. The current president of the Christian Science Church is J. Thomas Black, from Birmingham, Michigan. The organization is run by Black and his board of trustees of Boston's First Church of Christ, Scientist, the "Mother" Church. Unlike many cults in which the founder's successors retain the same status as the founder, in Christian Science all spiritual authority is vested in Mary Baker Eddy, not any other presidents, including Black. Christian Scientists call Eddy their "Leader," explaining, "Christian Scientists refer to Eddy as the Discoverer, Founder, and Leader of Christian Science."[51] It is to her writings and teachings that Christian Scientists refer for guidance: "The truth is in the Bible and *Science and Health*. And the proof is in nearly one hundred twenty-five years of consistent healing based on these books. You have come home. . . . This age is awake with discovery. . . . *Science and Health*, the Church that publishes it, and all of those united with this dynamic movement of thought are at the epicenter of this mental awakening."[52]~

Recommended Resources

1. *Christian Way*. Former Christian Scientists for Jesus Christ. *www.christianway.org*.
2. Fraser, Caroline. *God's Perfect Child: Living and Dying in the Christian Science*

---

[48]See Robert Peel, *Spiritual Healing in a Scientific Age* (San Francisco: Harper & Row, 1987), for further information.

[49]*http://www.tfccs.com/TMCMain.jhtml*.

[50]*http://www.adherents.com/Na_150.html#937*.

[51]"Questions and Answers: Why Do You Call Her Your Leader?" First Church of Christ, Scientist Web site *www.tfccs.com*, 1997.

[52]Annual Meeting, 1997" TFCCS Web site *www.tfccs.com*. Cited from Walter Martin, *The Kingdom of the Cults* (Minneapolis: Bethany House Publishers, 1997), 245–47.

Church. New York: Metropolitan Books, 1999.
3. Institute for Biblical Apologetics. Dr. Dan Schlesinger. *www.ibainfo.org*.
4. Kramer, Linda S. *The Religion That Kills—Christian Science: Abuse, Neglect, and Mind Control*. Los Angeles: Huntington House Publishers, 1999.
5. Martin, Walter. *Christian Science Healing: Devilish or Divine?* Audiotape. Walter Martin Ministries, *www.waltermartin.com*.
6. Martin, Walter, and Norman Klann. *The Christian Science Myth*. Paterson, New Jersey: Biblical Truth Publishing Society, 1954. See also *www.bookfinder.com*.
7. Twain, Mark. *Christian Science*. Harper Brothers, 1907. Text available for viewing at *www.geocities.com/Athens/Olympus/6868/ch00001.html*.

Quick Facts About Church of Jesus Christ of Latter-day Saints (the Mormons)

- The Bible is the Word of God insofar as it is correctly translated. There are three sacred books in addition to the Bible: *The Book of Mormon, Doctrine and Covenants,* and *The Pearl of Great Price.*

- The earth is one of several inhabited planets ruled over by gods and goddesses, who were at one time humans on other planets. Mormonism is polytheistic in its core.

- The Trinity consists of three gods born in different times and places; the Father begot the Son and Holy Ghost through a goddess wife in heaven.

- Humankind is of the same species as God. God begot all humans in heaven as offspring of his wife or wives, who were sent to earth for their potential exaltation to godhood.

- Salvation is resurrection, but exaltation to godhood, for eternal life in the celestial heaven, must be earned through self-meriting works.

Chapter 6

Church of Jesus Christ of Latter-day Saints (the Mormons)

Historical Perspective

The Church of Jesus Christ of Latter-day Saints is distinctive among all the religious cults and sects active in the United States in that it has by far the most fascinating history, and one worthy of consideration by all students of religions originating on the American continent.

The Mormons, as they are most commonly called, are divided into two major groups: The Church of Jesus Christ of Latter-day Saints with headquarters in Salt Lake City, Utah; and the Community of Christ (formerly known before the year 2000 as the Reorganized Church of Jesus Christ of Latter Day Saints) with head-quarters in Independence, Missouri.

One hundred seventy-three years (as of 2003) after the movement's found-ing, the Mormons own considerable stock in the agricultural and industrial wealth of America and circle the earth in missionary activities, energetically rival-ing evangelical Christianity. The former group, which is the main concern of this chapter, claims a membership in excess of ten million (adherents.com. 1999). The Community of Christ (RLDS) has 250,000 members worldwide and has won acceptance in some quarters as a "sect of fundamentalism." The Community of Christ, which rejects the name "Mormon," is briefly reviewed in this chapter, but there can be little doubt that it is composed of a zealous group of dedicated people. They irritate the Utah Mormon Church consistently by pointing out that court decisions have established their claim that they are the true church and Utah the schismatic. From its founding, the Mormon Church has been

---

This chapter revised and updated by Kurt Van Gorden, and edited by Jill Martin Rische.

characterized by thriftiness, zeal, and an admirable missionary spirit, as even before the advent of World War II, it had more than two thousand missionaries active on all the mission fields of the world. Since the close of World War II, however, and in keeping with the acceleration of cult propaganda everywhere, the Mormons had 60,850 active missionaries in 2001.[1]

~The missionary effort of the Mormon Church is seldom matched by any other religious endeavor. The young Mormon children are taught from primary age onward that it is their duty to the church to serve a mission following high school. The entire missionary force is broken down into the following percentages: 75 percent single males, 19 percent single females, and 6 percent married couples.

One interesting fact, however, accounts for this large missionary force, and that is the practice of the Mormon Church encouraging its most promising young people, boys ages nineteen and older and girls ages twenty-one and older, to perform missionary work. Only in recent years did the Mormon Church begin to subsidize the expenses of their American and Canadian missionaries.[2]~

Membership in the Mormon Church now increases each year at an average rate of 300,000 conversions and 75,000 children's baptisms.[3] The Mormons have a birthrate of 28.1 per thousand, in contrast to the average 15.9 birthrate of the United States.[4] According to the teaching of the Mormon Church, Mormons are to preserve their bodies always in the best of health and are cautioned against the use of tobacco and alcohol, and even the drinking of tea, coffee, and other caffeine-bearing drinks, such as Coca-Cola. Strongly insistent upon the Old Testament principle of tithing, the Mormon Church requires all temple Mormons and requests members to meet the biblical one-tenth of their gross income.

~The facts and figures for the wealth of the Mormon Church have been carefully guarded for years. However, in 1991 the *Arizona Republic* newspaper ran a series entitled "Mormon Inc. Finances & Faith," which estimated that the Mormon Church conservatively "collects about $4.3 billion from its members a year plus $400 million from its many enterprises." Stating that "only a few church officials know how the money is spent," the articles maintained that the church's investment portfolio "easily exceeds $5 billion, including $1 billion in stocks and bonds and another $1 billion in real estate.~ The reader should bear in mind that the Mormons put this money to good use in the expansion of their church, a truth borne out by the fact that the church is rapidly expanding its real estate holdings, both for commercial and ecclesiastical purposes. The "Saints" now have 115 temples in operation, with many more either in design or under construction on every continent on the globe. The Mormon university in Utah,

---

[1]Official Web site of the Church of Jesus Christ of Latter Day Saints *www.lds.org/conference/talk/display/0,5232,49-1-266-9,00.html.*

[2]~Cited from Walter Martin, *The Kingdom of the Cults* (Minneapolis: Bethany House Publishers, 1997), 179–243.

[3]Average drawn from Total Church Membership Data—1999, 2000, 2001 LDS Annual Statistical Reports, *www.lds.org.*

[4]The growth of the Mormons since 1900 is an outstanding story: 1900–283,765; 1910–398,478; 1920–525,987; 1930–670,017; 1940–862,664; 1950–1,111,314; 1960–1,693,180; 1970–2,930,810; 1980–4,639,822; 1990–7,761,112; 2000–11,068,861; 2001–11,394,522. *Ensign* magazine, May 2002, *Church Almanac.*

Brigham Young University, boasts more than thirty-seven thousand students on two campuses.

Promulgated as it is by determined, zealous, missionary-minded people who have a practical religion of "good works" and clean living, the Mormons each year spend millions of dollars in the circulation of the writings and teachings of their prophets and apostles, while proselytizing any and all listeners regardless of church affiliation.[5] In addition to their regular tithing fund, the Mormon Church also encourages what it terms "fast offerings." This unusual practice involves the giving up of two meals on the first Sunday of each month, the price of which is turned over to the church as a voluntary contribution to support and feed the poor.

Since education ranks high in Mormon circles, the existence of their "seminary" and "institute" programs for high school and college students with an enrollment of over half a million is what could be expected of such systematic growth. The church also has more than fifty schools outside of the United States, most of which are in Mexico and the South Pacific.

Mormonism, then, is not one of the cults tending to appeal merely to the uneducated, as for the most part Jehovah's Witnesses do, but instead it exalts education, which results in huge amounts of printed propaganda flowing from its presses in the millions of copies annually. The Mormons are also great chapel and temple builders, temples being reserved for the solemnization of "celestial" marriages and sealings, plus proxy baptisms and other ordinances for the dead (nearly 5.5 million sacred endowment rituals performed in 1993 alone). Such temples are forbidden to "Gentiles" (a Mormon term for all non-Mormons) and are truly beautiful buildings, usually extremely costly both in construction and furnishings. Along with their strong emphasis on education, the Mormons believe in sports, hobbies, dramatics, music, homemaking courses for prospective brides, dances, and dramatic festivals. The Mormon organization that sponsors a good deal of this is known as the Mutual Improvement Association, and has sponsored literally thousands and thousands of dances and other programs designed to attract and entertain young people. Each Mormon dance is begun with prayer and closed with the singing of a hymn. Mormonism does all that is humanly possible to make its church organization a home away from home for Mormon children and young people, and its low level of juvenile delinquency is in a marked proportion among Mormons, testifying to the success of the church-centered program.[6]

Emphasizing as they do the importance of missions, the Mormon Tabernacle Choir has become famous and is well known to all radio listeners. The choir contains 350 singers and has a repertoire of hundreds of anthems. The Mormon Tabernacle Choir began network broadcasting in 1929. Those who would tend to write off the Mormons as an influential force in the United States would do well to remember that Mormons have more adherents listed in *Who's Who in America* than any other one religion, and this also holds true for the scientific honor

---

[5]As an example, in April 1978, *Reader's Digest* published an eight-page removable advertisement about church programs, the first of a $12 million series aimed at nearly fifty million *Digest* readers.
[6]However, a review of social statistics in the state of Utah, which is at least 76 percent Mormon, shows that rates of divorce, child abuse, teenage pregnancy, and suicide are above the national average and climbing.

societies of our nation. Mormon leaders have become powerful in almost all branches of American government, headed by former Secretary of Agriculture Ezra Taft Benson, the late thirteenth prophet of the Mormon Church; former Treasury Secretary David M. Kennedy; former Treasurers Angela (Bay) Buchanan and the late Ivy Baker Priest; former Education Secretary Terrel H. Bell; former Michigan governor George Romney; Marriner S. Eccles; numerous U.S. ambassadors; and dozens of U.S. senators and representatives, to name but a few. Far from being an organization of minor influence, the Mormons are, indeed, a potent political and social force to be reckoned with, a fact that few informed persons would doubt.

Church Organization

The organization and general administration of the Mormon Church is directed by its "General Authorities." At the top is the First Presidency (presently composed of ninety-one year-old "prophet" Gordon B. Hinckley and two "counselors"), assisted by a "Council of Twelve" apostles, the "First Quorum of the Seventy," the "Second Quorum of the Seventy," and its Presidency, a "Presiding Bishopric," and the Patriarch of the church. All authority resides in the Mormon "priesthood," established under the titles "Aaronic" (lesser) and "Melchizedek" (higher). Nearly every male Mormon twelve years of age or over belongs to the Aaronic priesthood, and if "worthy" these are ordained to the Melchizedek priesthood at age eighteen. The Mormon Church administration is divided into territories made up of "wards" and "stakes," the former consisting of from five hundred to a thousand people. Each ward is presided over by a bishop and his two counselors. The wards are all consolidated into stakes, each of which is supervised by a stake president and two counselors, aided in turn by twelve high priests known as the "stake high council." At the beginning of 2002, there were approximately 26,084 wards and branches, 2,607 stakes, and 333 missions functioning in the Mormon Church.[7] The various auxiliary groups form a powerful coalition for mutual assistance among Mormons, and it is noteworthy that during the Depression in 1929, the Mormon "Bishop's storehouse" saw to it faithfully that few worthy members were in want of the necessities of life.

In their missionary program the Mormons continue to manifest great zeal and quote the Bible profusely. Thus it is that many true Christians have often been literally quoted into silence by the clever disciples of Joseph Smith and Brigham Young, who flourish a pseudo-mastery of Scripture before the uninformed Christian's dazzled eyes and confuse him, sometimes beyond description.

In common with most cults, Mormonism has had its siege of persecutions and slander, but unlike many of the other cults who prefer to "let sleeping dogs lie," the Mormons have attempted at times to defend their "prophets." This has led them into more than one precarious historical dilemma.[8]

~The young and boastful Joseph Smith went on record with outlandish

---

[7]Official Web site of the Church of Jesus Christ of Latter-day Saints: *http://216.239.51.100/ search?q=cache:0BUZDHsu8QUC:www.lds.org/conference/talk/display/0,5232,49-1-266- 9,00.html+LDS+Statistical+Report+2001&hl=en&ie=UTF-8.*
[8]See Hugh Nibley, *The Myth Makers* (Salt Lake City, Utah: Bookcraft, Inc.), 1958.

statements that later proved to be a trouble source for the Mormon Church. Examination of three examples will suffice. Joseph Smith once said, "No man knows my history," which caused endless suspicion by Mormon historians and non-Mormons who began researching Joseph Smith's background and found dozens of improprieties ranging from occult peep-stone seeking, treasure digging, adultery before the polygamy prophecy, and financial schemes. In another instance, Joseph Smith proclaimed, "The Book of Mormon is the most correct of any book on the earth," which has been amply refuted by both Mormon scholars and Christian apologists. Another regrettable statement made by Smith was, "I have more to boast of than ever any man had. I am the only man that has ever been able to keep a whole church together since the days of Adam. A large majority of the whole have stood by me. Neither Paul, Peter, nor Jesus ever did it. I boast that no man ever did such a work as I. The followers of Jesus ran away from Him; but the Latter-day Saints never ran away from me yet" (*History of the Church*, 6:408–409).

The average active Mormon is usually marked by many sound moral traits. He is generally amiable, almost always hospitable, and extremely devoted to his family and to the teachings of his church. Sad to say, however, the great majority of Mormons are in almost total ignorance of the shady historical and theological sources of their religion. They are openly shocked at times when the unglamorous and definitely unchristian background of the Mormon Church is revealed to them.~ This little known facet of Mormonism is "a side of the coin" that innumerable Mormon historians have for years either hidden from their people or glossed over in an attempt to suppress certain verifiable and damaging historical evidences. Such evidence the author has elected to review in the interest of obtaining a full picture of Joseph Smith's religion.

Early Mormon History

The seeds of what was later to become the Mormon religion were incubated in the mind of one Joseph Smith Jr., "The Prophet," better known to residents of Palmyra, New York, as "Joe Smith."

Born in Sharon, Vermont, December 23, 1805, fourth child of Lucy and Joseph Smith, the future Mormon prophet entered the world with the proverbial "two strikes" against him in the person of his father and his environment.

Joseph Smith Sr. was a mystic, a man who spent much of his time digging for imaginary buried treasure. This fact is, of course, well known to any informed student of Mormonism. ~Former Mormon historian Dr. D. Michael Quinn has thoroughly documented the fact that both Joseph Smith Sr. and Joseph Smith Jr. were avid treasure-seekers. In his book entitled *Early Mormonism and the Magic World View* (1987), Quinn writes, "Joseph Smith, the founding prophet and president of the new church organized on 6 April 1830, had unquestionably participated in treasure seeking and seer stone divination and had apparently also used divining rods, talismans, and implements of ritual magic. His father, one of the Eight Witnesses to the divinity of the Book of Mormon and later the church patriarch, had also participated in divining and the quest for treasure." (*EMMWV*, 194). Quinn states on page 207 that Smith was interested in treasure-seeking even after he became president of the LDS Church and that "occult dimensions of treasure digging was prominent among the first members of the Quorum of the Twelve Apostles, organized in 1835." In the past, Mormon historians have avoided every indication that Joseph Smith owned a peep stone or seer stone. Dr. Quinn's aforementioned book includes photographs of actual seer stones owned by Joseph Smith. It should be noted that D. Michael Quinn was excommunicated from the LDS Church in 1993 after refusing to keep silent about his unflattering research. This newer honesty among Mormon historians is appearing in other books, like the revision of *The Story of the Latter-day Saints* by J. B. Allen and G. M. Leonard, where they discuss Smith's "youthful experiments with treasure-seeking"[9]~

The mother of the future prophet was as much as her husband the product of the era and her environment, given as she was to extreme religious views and belief in the most trivial of superstitions. Lucy Smith later in her life "authored" a book entitled *Biographical Sketches of Joseph Smith and His Progenitors for Many Generations.* When published by the Mormon Church in Liverpool, England, however, it incurred the enduring wrath of Brigham Young, the first successor to Smith, who brought about the suppression of the book on the grounds that it contained "many mistakes" and that "should it ever be deemed best to publish these sketches, it will not be done until after they are carefully corrected."[10]

Mrs. Smith, of course, was totally incapable of writing such a work, the "ghost writing" being done by a Mrs. Martha Jane Knowlton Coray, who faithfully recorded what came to be known as "Mother Smith's History." We will quote from this work as we progress, as we also will the personal history of Joseph Smith Jr. It is merely mentioned now to indicate the contradictory views held by the Mormon Church and by Smith's mother concerning the prophet's homelife, background, and religious habits.

We return now to the central character of our survey, Joseph Smith Jr. The year 1820 proved to be the real beginning of the prophet's call, for in that year he was allegedly the recipient of a marvelous vision in which God the Father and God the Son materialized and spoke to young Smith as he prayed in a neighboring wood. The prophet records the incident in great detail in his book *The Pearl of Great Price* (Joseph Smith—History 1:1–25), wherein he reveals that the two "personages" took a rather dim view of the Christian church and, for that matter, of the world at large, and announced that a restoration of true Christianity was needed, and that he, Joseph Smith Jr., had been chosen to launch the new dispensation.

~The Mormon Church has always held the position that they alone represent true Christianity. Mormon leaders have consistently taught that after the death of the apostles, true Christianity fell into complete apostasy, making it necessary for a "restoration." Mormon Apostle Bruce R. McConkie, on pages 512–513 of his book *Mormon Doctrine* (Salt Lake City: Bookcraft, 1966) writes, "Mormonism is Christianity; Christianity is Mormonism . . . Mormons are true Christians." In 1995 Mormon Apostle Dallin Oaks stated that the differences between "other Christian churches" and the LDS Church "explain why we send

[9]J. B. Allen and G. M. Leonard, *The Story of the Latter-day Saints* (Salt Lake City: Deseret Book Company, 1992), 41.
[10]*Millennial Star,* 17:297–98, personal letter dated January 31, 1885; *Millennial Star,* 27:42 (October 21, 1885).

missionaries to other Christians" (*Ensign*, May 1995, 84).~

It is interesting to observe that Smith could not have been too much moved by the heavenly vision, for he shortly took up once again the habit of digging for treasure along with his father and brother, who were determined to unearth treasure by means of "peep-stones," "divining rods," or just plain digging.[11]

History informs us that the Smith clan never succeeded at these multitudinous attempts at treasure hunting, but innumerable craters in the Vermont and New York countryside testify to their apparent zeal without knowledge.

In later years the "prophet" greatly regretted these superstitious expeditions of his youth and even went on record as denying that he had ever been a money-digger. Said prophet Smith on one such occasion,

> In the month of October, 1825, I hired with an old gentleman by the name of Josiah Stoal, who lived in Chenango County, State of New York. He had heard something of a silver mine having been opened by the Spaniards in Harmony, Susquehanna County, State of Pennsylvania; and had, previous to my hiring to him, been digging in order, if possible, to discover the mine. After I went to live with him, he took me, with the rest of his hands, to dig for the silver mine, at which I continued to work for nearly a month, without success in our undertaking, and finally I prevailed with the old gentleman to cease digging after it. Hence arose the very prevalent story of my having been a money-digger.[12]

This explanation may suffice to explain the prophet's treasure-hunting fiascoes to the faithful and to the historically inept; but to those who have access to the facts, it is at once evident that Smith played recklessly, if not fast and loose, with the truth. In fact, it often appeared to be a perfect stranger to him. The main source for promoting skepticism where the veracity of the prophet's explanation is concerned, however, is from no less an authority than Lucy Smith, his own mother, who, in her account of the very same incident, wrote that Stoal "came for Joseph on account of having heard that he possessed certain means by which he could discern things invisible to the natural eye" (*History of Joseph Smith by His Mother*, 91–92).

Further evidence, in addition to Mrs. Smith's statement (and *prima facie* evidence, at that), proves beyond a reasonable doubt that the prophet was a confirmed peep-stone addict, that he took part in and personally supervised numerous treasure-digging expeditions, and further that he claimed supernatural powers that allegedly aided him in these searches. To remove all doubt the reader may have as to Smith's early treasure-hunting and peep-stone practices, we shall quote two of the best authenticated sources, which we feel will sustain our contention that Smith was regarded as a fraud by those who knew him best. It should also be remembered that Joseph Smith Sr., in an interview later published in *Historical Magazine*, May 1870, clearly stated that the prophet had been a peep-stone enthusiast and treasure digger in his youth, and, further, that he had also told fortunes and located lost objects by means of a peep stone and alleged

---

[11]Peep stones, peek stones, or seer stones: supposedly magical rocks, which, when placed in a hat and partially darkened, allegedly reveal lost items and buried treasure. Divining rods were sticks that were supposed to lead to treasure or water, etc.

[12]Joseph Smith, *History*, 1:56.

supernatural powers therein. Substantiating Joseph's father's account of his rather odd activities is the testimony of the Reverend Dr. John A. Clark after "exhaustive research" in the Smith family's own neighborhood.

> Long before the idea of a Golden Bible entered their minds, in their excursions for money digging . . . Joe used to be usually their guide, putting into a hat a peculiar stone he had, through which he looked to decide where they should begin to dig. (*Gleanings by the Way*, by J. A. Clark, [Philadelphia: W. J. and J. K. Simon, 1842], 225)

The proceedings of a court hearing dated March 20, 1826—*New York* vs. *Joseph Smith*—revealed that Joseph Smith "had a certain stone which he had occasionally looked at to determine where hidden treasures in bowels of the earth were . . . and had looked for Mr. Stoal several times."[13] The hearing ruled the defendant guilty of money digging.

~Peep-stone gazing was one of several occult practices deemed illegal in the 1820s. That Joseph Smith's peep-stone gazing episodes met their challenge with the law is irrefutably documented. The original court bill of 1826, charging Smith with "glass looking," was discovered by Rev. Wesley P. Walters, in 1971, at the Chenango County Jail, Norwich, New York. The trial for the misdemeanor crime cost two dollars and sixty-eight cents, which Smith apparently paid. A copy of the original court bill is reproduced in Walter Martin's *The Maze of Mormonism* (Santa Ana: Vision House, 1978, 37).~

In 1820 Joseph Smith Jr. claimed a heavenly vision that he said singled him out as the Lord's anointed prophet for this dispensation, though it was not until 1823, with the appearance of the angel Moroni at the quaking Smith's bedside, that Joe began his relationship to the fabulous "golden plates," or what was to become The *Book of Mormon*.

According to Smith's account of this extraordinary revelation, which is recorded in *The Pearl of Great Price* (Joseph Smith—History, 1:29–54), the angel Moroni, the glorified son of one Mormon, the man for whom the famous book of the same name is entitled, appeared beside Joseph's bedside and thrice repeated his commission to the allegedly awestruck treasure hunter. Smith did not write this account down until some years later, but even that fails to excuse the blunder he made in transmitting the angelic proclamation. This confusion appears in the 1851 edition of *The Pearl of Great Price*, wherein Joseph Smith identifies the messenger as Nephi, an entirely different character found in The *Book of Mormon*. This unfortunate crossing up of the divine communication system was later remedied by thoughtful Mormon scribes who have exercised great care to ferret out all the historical and factual blunders not readily explainable in the writings of Smith, Young, and other early Mormon writers. In current editions, Moroni is identified as the nighttime visitor. However, whether Nephi or Moroni carried the message to Smith apparently makes little difference to the faithful.

~The nightmarish blunder of crediting the revelation of The *Book of Mormon* to Nephi instead of Moroni has never ceased to be a proverbial thorn in the side of Mormon historians. Try as they will, it is impossible to erase it from the handwritten manuscripts of the Mormon Church history, which were supervised by

---

[13]*Frazers Magazine* (New Series, February 1873): 7:229.

Joseph Smith during his life.[14] Later, in 1842, these manuscripts formed the basis of the published history of Mormonism, again, overseen by Smith before his death, where Nephi appears as the revelatory angel (*Times and Seasons*, Vol. 3 [Nauvoo, Ill.: Times and Seasons], 753). The first edition of *The Pearl of Great Price* (1851), with the subtitle "Choice selections of revelations, translations, and narrations of Joseph Smith," contained the name Nephi because the unchallenged history of Mormonism had set such a foundation.~

In 1827 Smith claimed to receive the golden plates upon which *The Book of Mormon* is alleged to have been written. Shortly after this historic find, unearthed in the hill Cumorah, near Palmyra, New York, Smith began to "translate" the "reformed Egyptian"[15] hieroglyphics, inscribed thereupon by means of the "Urim and Thummim," a type of miraculous spectacles, which the angel Moroni had the foresight to provide for the budding seer. The account of how Smith went about "translating" the plates and of the attendant difficulties with one Martin Harris, his wife, and Professor Charles Anthon, a noted scholar, will be dealt with more fully later in this chapter. However, the plot is obvious to anyone who is even basically informed concerning the real character of Joseph Smith; so we will continue with the prophet's history.

During the period when Joseph was translating the plates (1827–1829), one Oliver Cowdery, an itinerant schoolteacher, visited Smith at the home of his father-in-law (who after some months, for the sake of his daughter, had received Joseph into his home), where he was duly "converted" to the prophet's religion and soon after became one of several "scribes" who faithfully wrote down what Joseph said the plates read, in spite of the fact that he and Smith were separated by a curtain during the "translation." In the course of time, Smith and Cowdery became fast friends, and the progression of the "translation" and spiritual zeal allegedly attained such heights that on May 15, 1829, John the Baptist, in person, was speedily dispatched by Peter, James, and John to the humble state of Pennsylvania with orders to confer the "Aaronic Priesthood" on Joe and Oliver.

This amazing event is recorded in *The Pearl of Great Price* (Joseph Smith—History, 1:68–73), following which Oliver baptized Joe and vice versa; and they spent time blessing each other and prophesying future events "which should shortly come to pass." Smith was careful not to be too specific in recording these prophecies, because of the fact that more often than not Mormon prophecies did not come in on schedule, which no doubt accounted for Smith's hesitancy in alluding to details.

From the now hallowed state of Pennsylvania, immortalized by Smith's initiation into the priesthood of Aaron by John the Baptist, Joseph returned shortly to the home of Peter Whitmer in Fayette, New York, where he remained until the "translation" from the plates was completed and *The Book of Mormon* published and copyrighted in the year 1830. On April 6 of the same year, the prophet, in company with his brothers Hyrum and Samuel, Oliver Cowdery, and David and Peter Whitmer Jr., officially founded a "new religious society" entitled "The

---

[14]A reproduction of the manuscript may be found in Jerald and Sandra Tanner's *Mormonism—Shadow or Reality* (Salt Lake City: Utah Lighthouse Ministry, 1987, fifth edition), 136.

[15]Reformed Egyptian is an undocumented language never seen by any leading Egyptologist or philologist who has ever been consulted on the problem. However, the Mormons still maintain their claim with the full knowledge that these are the facts.

Church of Christ" (later to be named the Church of the Latter-day Saints [1834], and finally as the Church of Jesus Christ of Latter-day Saints in 1838). Thus it was that one of the more virulent strains of American cults came into existence— Mormonism had begun in earnest.

Following this "momentous" occasion, a conference consisting of thirty men was called by the "prophet" on June 9, 1830. A few months later missionary efforts were decided upon and some of the newly ordained elders were set aside to become missionaries to the Indians. In September 1830, a zealous preacher, Parley P. Pratt, was "converted" to Mormonism, and allegedly in November, Sidney Rigdon, a powerful Campbellite preacher from Ohio, "saw the light" and "converted" more than one hundred of his congregation to Smith's religion, which had begun to take root outside of New York State and Pennsylvania.

Sidney Rigdon and Parley P. Pratt, it should be noted, were almost from the day of their "conversions" slated for greatness in the Mormon hierarchy, as was Orson Pratt; and it is their writings, along with those of Young, Charles Penrose, and James Talmage, which best argue in favor of the Mormon cause, even to this very day. The role Sidney Rigdon played in the Mormon saga will be discussed later, but it must be remembered that Rigdon would eventually be accused of apostasy and excommunicated from the Mormon Church in 1844. Rigdon soared to the heights of inflammatory rhetoric against the citizens of Jackson County, Missouri, when, on Independence Day, 1838, he virtually challenged the whole state to do pitched battle with the "Saints," who were subsequently terribly persecuted and expelled in November 1838.

Shortly after the original conference meeting in Fayette, on April 6, 1830, the nucleus of the Mormon Church moved to Kirtland, Ohio, where in a period of six years they increased to over sixteen thousand souls. It was from Kirtland that Smith and Rigdon made their initial thrust into Jackson County, Missouri. Joseph and Sidney were no strangers to persecution and suffered the indignity of an old-fashioned tar and feathering, accompanied by a trip out of town on the proverbial rail. While in Missouri, Smith purchased sixty-three acres, which he deemed "holy ground," and there marked the exact spot on which he declared that the temple of Zion, the earthly headquarters of the kingdom of Jesus Christ, was eventually to be built. It is an interesting fact of history that one small branch of Mormonism (the Church of Christ, Temple Lot) today owns that temple site and claims that it once refused five million dollars from the Utah church for the "hallowed ground."

~Some of the more prominent divisions of the work of Joseph Smith have survived, though barely, to this day. In the 1990 edition of his book, *Divergent Paths of the Restoration* (Los Angeles, Calif.: Restoration Research), author Steven L. Shields lists well over one hundred "restoration" churches that claim Joseph Smith, his first vision, and *The Book of Mormon* as their foundation. Most of their differences concern his work and revelations following *The Book of Mormon*. To the far left are those who reject all or nearly all revelations since the early 1830s. These are the Community of Christ (RLDS) (Independence, Missouri), The Church of Christ, Temple Lot (Independence, Missouri), The Church of Christ (Bickerton, Pennsylvania), and other factions. To the far right are the fundamentalist Mormon groups that sustain every revelation of Smith and subsequent prophets through 1890. These often practice polygamy and are mostly located in the western United States, Canada, and Mexico. Some prominent groups are the Church of the Firstborn, the Order of Enoch, and the communal clans of Johnson, Allred, Barlow, and Musser.~

In Kirtland, also, the First Stake of Zion was established and a quorum of twelve apostles was chosen, presided over by a First Presidency of three, supervised by the president, Joseph Smith, the Seer. It appears that the chief reason for the Mormons moving to Kirtland, Ohio, however, was the extreme unpopularity of Smith and his revelations among the people who knew him best and who regarded his new religion as a sham and a hoax, thus hardly recommending them as prospective converts. Smith, of course, had a revelation from God as authorization for the move. In fact, between the years 1831 and 1844, the "prophet" allegedly received well over one hundred thirty-five direct revelations from God, revelations that helped build Kirtland and, later, the Mormon metropolis of Nauvoo, Illinois. Smith's infamous practice of polygamy was instituted at Kirtland and later confirmed by "divine revelation." Some misinformed persons have declared that Smith was not a polygamist, but one needs only to search the famous Berrian collection in the New York Public Library for volumes of primary information to the contrary, written by Mormon men and women who lived through many of these experiences and testified to the outright immorality of Smith and the leaders of the Mormon Church. Gradually, of course, polygamy filtered down through the Mormon Church, so that it was necessary for the United States government to threaten complete dissolution as well as to confiscate all Mormon property in order to stamp out the accepted practice.

~The "fundamentalist" or polygamist Mormon groups claim no revelation was ever given from God for the disbanding of polygamy. They wholeheartedly reject the 1890 "Manifesto" of Wilford Woodruff, claiming this fourth Mormon prophet apostatized from the revelations of Smith, Young, and Taylor. Fundamentalist Mormons delight in publishing revelations of John Taylor (third prophet) and Mormon apostles of that period who despised the United States government for the sake of polygamy. Most fundamentalist Mormons adhere to obscure teachings abandoned by the Mormon Church, such as the Adam-god and the restoration of Zion in Jackson County, Missouri. It is a matter of historical record that leaders of the Mormon Church were tried and convicted of unlawful cohabitation with plural wives after the 1890 Manifesto. For instance, Heber J. Grant, who would later become Mormonism's seventh prophet, was fined $100 after pleading guilty to unlawful cohabitation in September 1899. In 1906 sixth LDS President Joseph F. Smith was found guilty of the same and fined $300. Following his plea, Smith stated, "When I accepted the manifesto issued by President Wilford Woodruff, I did not understand that I would be expected to abandon and discard my wives" (*Deseret Evening News*, November 28, 1906).~

In 1890 President Wilford Woodruff officially abolished polygamy as a practice of the Mormon Church, one concrete instance, at least, of the fact that the religious convictions of the Mormons were sacrificed for their political and economic survival. The facts still remain that in Kirtland, Nauvoo, Jackson County, etc., the Mormons had a chance to win converts to Smith's religion because they were strangers and the character of the prophet was unknown in those areas. But in New York, Smith was known by the most uncomplimentary terms, some of which have a direct bearing upon a proper understanding of his character.

Pomeroy Tucker, in his classic work *The Origin, Rise, and Progress of Mormonism* (New York, 1861), collected a number of duly sworn statements by neighbors of the Smith family and by acquaintances of Joseph Smith Jr. particularly. According to the unanimous consensus of those who testified at the time, Joseph Smith Jr. was known for "his habits of exaggeration and untruthfulness . . . by reason of his extravagances of statement, his word was received with the least confidence by those who knew him best. He could utter the most palpable exaggeration or marvelous absurdity with the utmost apparent gravity"(16).

E. D. Howe, a contemporary of Smith who did tremendous research during Joseph's lifetime, obtained one of the most interesting statements concerning the early life of Joseph Jr. and of the Smith family. Smith himself never dared to answer Howe's charges, though they were well known to him, so great was the weight of contemporary evidence.

Mr. Howe obtained a statement signed by sixty-two residents of Palmyra, New York, one that cannot be ignored by any serious student of Mormonism:

> We, the undersigned, have been acquainted with the Smith family for a number of years while they resided near this place, and we have no hesitation in saying that we consider them destitute of that moral character which ought to entitle them to the confidence of any community. They were particularly famous for visionary projects, spent much of their time in diggings for money, which they pretended was hid in the earth; and to this day, large excavations may be seen in the earth, not far from their residence, where they used to spend their time in digging for hidden treasures. Joseph Smith Sr., and his son Joseph, were in particular considered entirely destitute of *moral character* and *addicted to vicious habits*. (*Mormonism Unveiled* [Painsville, Ohio, 1834], 261)

~Mormons attempt to dissuade members from Howe's research by pretending that his publication resulted from the revengeful vendetta of one Dr. Philastus Hurlbut (sometimes spelled Hurlbert), a Mormon excommunicated in 1833. The fact that Howe published stories that were publicly circulated previous to Hurlbut's excommunication is incontestable, despite Hurlbut's assistance in research.~

Some persons reading this may feel that it is unfair to quote only one side of the story; what about those who are favorable to the Mormons, they will ask. In answer to this, the amazing fact is that *there exist no contemporary pro-Mormon statements from reliable and informed sources who knew the Smith family and Joseph intimately*. It has only been the overwise Mormon historians, utilizing hindsight over a hundred-year period, who have been able to even seriously challenge the evidence of the neighbors, Joseph's father-in-law, and many ex-Mormons who knew what was going on and went on record with the evidence that not even Mormon historians have bothered to dispute.

As the Mormons grew and prospered in Nauvoo, Illinois, and as the practice of polygamy began to be known by the wider Mormon community and outsiders as well, increasing distrust of prophet Smith multiplied, especially after one of his former assistants, John C. Bennett, boldly exposed the practice of polygamy in Nauvoo. When the prophet (or "general," as he liked to be known in this phase of his career) could tolerate this mounting criticism no more and ordered the destruction of its most threatening mouthpiece, an anti-Mormon publication entitled *The Nauvoo Expositor,* the State of Illinois intervened. The "prophet" and his brother, Hyrum, were placed in a jail in Carthage, Illinois, to await trial for their part in the wrecking of the *Expositor.* However, on June 27, 1844, a mob comprised of some two hundred persons[16] stormed the Carthage jail and brutally murdered Smith and his brother, Hyrum, thus forcing upon the vigorously unwilling prophet's head the unwanted crown of early martyrdom, insuring his perpetual enshrinement in Mormon history as a "true seer."

With the assassination of Joseph Smith, the large majority of Mormons accepted the leadership of Brigham Young, then forty-three years of age, and the man who had previously led the Mormons to safety from the wrath of the Missouri citizenry.

In 1846 Young announced that the Saints would abandon Nauvoo. In 1847, after a brutal trek through the wilderness of the Great Plains and the Rocky Mountains, Young brought the first band of Mormons to the valley of the Great Salt Lake and is credited with the exclamation, "This is the place!" The destiny of the Saints was sealed—they were in what was to become the state of Utah.

For thirty years Brigham Young ruled the Mormon Church, and as is still the case, he inherited the divinely appointed prophetic mantle of the first prophet. So it is that each succeeding president of the Mormon Church claims the same authority as Joseph Smith and Brigham Young—an infallible prophetic succession.

The "spiritual deed" that the Mormons felt entitled them to possession of the valley of the Great Salt Lake was "granted" in June 1848, when the first Mormon crops were largely saved from a plague of locusts by a vast armada of sea gulls; thus, according to Mormon teaching, God gave visible evidence of His blessing upon the Latter-day Saints Church.

We cannot, of course, discuss the history of the Mormons under Brigham Young in great detail because that would easily necessitate a full volume by itself, but suffice it to say that Smith gave the movement its initial thrust and Brigham Young supplied the momentum necessary to establish it as a bona fide religion. Young himself was a character of many facets, and one cannot understand the theology of Mormonism without understanding the tremendous influence exercised upon it by the person of "prophet" Young and his teachings. Smith and Young, in company with the pronouncements of the succeeding presidents, have made Mormon theology what it is, and apart from Brigham Young, Mormonism cannot be thoroughly understood.

Young was a man of indomitable courage, possessed of a canny nature, but given to fits of ruthlessness now conveniently forgotten by Mormon historians. One such evidence of his determination to control Utah was the order that he gave to those involved in the massacre of around one hundred twenty non-Mormon immigrants to remain quiet about what has now become known as the

---

[16]Numbering the mob at about two hundred seems to be a fairly good average in light of the many conflicting sources available. For instance, Willard Richards, who was in the jail cell when the mob attacked, estimated the mob at around one hundred to two hundred men (*History of the Church,* 7:110). *The Encyclopedia of Mormonism* claims the mob consisted of about one hundred fifty men. D. Michael Quinn quotes the Chicago Historical Society and estimates the mob was "about two hundred fifty strong" (*The Mormon Hierarchy—Origins of Power,* 1994), 374.

infamous Mountain Meadows Massacre. In September 1857, John D. Lee and a group of LDS cohorts devised a plan to mercilessly annihilate a wagon train of virtually helpless immigrants. Twenty years later he was imprisoned, tried, convicted, and executed by the government of the United States for this vicious action.

~The Mountain Meadows Massacre has definitely become a lamentable part of Mormon history. Whereas Mormons often like to point to persecutions brought on them from outside sources, this is one area of history where there is no doubt that the Mormons were guilty of the most heinous of crimes. According to *The Comprehensive History of the Church* (4:177), when Brigham Young was told of the deed, he said, "As soon as we can get a court of justice we will ferret this thing out, but till then, don't say anything about it." In her book entitled *The Mountain Meadows Massacre,* the late LDS historian Juanita Brooks admits that the secrecy surrounding the tragedy has prevented the whole truth from ever being known. It would take nearly two decades before John D. Lee would be made the lone scapegoat. On March 23, 1877, he was executed by firing squad while sitting on the edge of his coffin. Brooks writes on pages 219–220, "The Church leaders decided to sacrifice Lee only when they could see that it would be impossible to acquit him without assuming a part of the responsibility themselves." She also states on page 219 that while Brigham Young and other church authorities "did not specifically order the massacre, they did preach sermons and set up social conditions that made it possible." Before Lee would be executed, he would face excommunication from the LDS Church. This decision, however, was overturned, when on April 20, 1961, the First Presidency and Council of the Twelve reinstated John D. Lee's membership and former blessings.~

In his memorable book *The Confessions of John D. Lee,* a consistent sore spot in the Mormon scheme of historical "reconstruction," Lee confessed to his part in the infamous doings, but he swore that he believed he acted upon the approval of Brigham Young. As we further study Mormon theology, it will become apparent that this was not at all beyond the limits of Young's character. He *was* the law in Utah, and as it has been so wisely observed, "Power corrupts and absolute power corrupts absolutely."

Mormonism today, then, is a far cry from quite a number of the principles and practices of its early founders. To be sure, it remains faithful to their basic tenets, but, as in the case of polygamy, when those tenets come in conflict with government statutes or political influence, the Latter-day Saints have wisely chosen to ignore (the word commonly used is *reinterpret*) the counsels of their two chief prophets. The history of the Mormons is a vast and complex subject; it is a veritable labyrinth of books, testimonies, affidavits, photographs, hearsay, and opinions, and it is only after the most careful analysis of the contemporary evidence that a picture emerges consistent with verifiable facts. For the average faithful Mormon, one can but have sympathy and regard. He is, by and large, honest, industrious, thrifty, and zealous in both the proclamation and promulgation of his beliefs. One only regrets that he has accepted at face value a carefully edited version of the origin and doctrinal development of his religion instead of examining the excellent sources that not only contradict but irrefutably prove the falsity of what is most certainly a magnificent reconstructed history. It is to be hoped that as we further study the unfolding drama of Mormon doctrine and the basis of such doctrine, the reader will come to appreciate the evolution of Mormonism and the pitfalls which most certainly exist in taking at face value the gospel according to Joseph Smith and Brigham Young. The verdict of history, then, is overwhelmingly against the Mormon version, particularly where Smith and Young are concerned. There is a vast amount of documentation all but a few Mormons seem content to ignore, but the facts themselves remain too well verified to be ignored.

A New Revelation—the "Mormon Bible"

Aside from the King James Version of the Bible, which the Mormons accept as part of the Word of God "as far as it is translated correctly" (*Eighth Article of Faith*), they have added *Doctrine and Covenants, The Pearl of Great Price,* and the initial volume, *The Book of Mormon,* to the canon of what they would call authorized Scripture—the "Four Standard Works." The last mentioned is a subject of this chapter, since it occupies a pivotal place in Mormon theology and history and therefore must be carefully examined. A great deal of research on the part of a number of able scholars and organizations has already been published concerning *The Book of Mormon,* and we have drawn heavily upon whatever documented and verifiable information was available. The task of validating the material was enormous, and so we have selected that information that has been verified beyond refutation and is available today in some of our leading institutions of learning (Stanford University, Union Theological Seminary, the Research Departments of the Library of Congress, the New York Public Library, and others).

It is a difficult task to evaluate the complex structure of *The Book of Mormon,* and the reader is urged to consider the bibliography at the end of this volume if he should desire further and more exhaustive studies.

The Story of the Ancient People

The Book of Mormon purports to be a history of two ancient civilizations, which were located on the American continent. According to the Mormon version, the first of these great civilizations, named the Jaredites, left the tower of Babel (about 2,250 B.C., by Mormon reckoning) and emigrated to the Western hemisphere. The Jaredites were destroyed as a result of "corruption" and were punished for their apostasy, their civilization undergoing total destruction.

The second group allegedly left Jerusalem somewhere in the neighborhood of 600 B.C., before the destruction of the city and the Babylonian captivity of Israel. According to traditional Mormon thinking, that group crossed the Pacific Ocean, landing on the west coast of South America. *The Book of Mormon* is supposedly a condensation of the high points of these civilizations. The author of the abridged book was a prophet named Mormon. The book is "the translation of the abridgment of the record of these civilizations" and "includes a brief outline of the history of the earlier Jaredite people, an abridgment made by Moroni, son of Mormon, taken from the Jaredite record found during the period of the second civilization."

The second group, who came to America about 600 B.C., were righteous

Jews, led by Lehi and later his son Nephi. This group eventually met a fate similar to the Jaredites and was divided into two warring camps, the Nephites and the Lamanites (Indians). The Lamanites received a curse because of their evil deeds, and the curse took the form of dark skin.

~Racism is a charge that has been leveled at the Mormon Church throughout its history by a number of civil rights groups. Naturally, Mormons reject such claims by pointing to a small number of African-American and Native-American members. The fact remains, however, that the god of Mormonism elevates "white" races as supreme and has demeaned African-Americans and Native Americans as "unrighteous." *The Book of Mormon* describes the Native-American curse as "They were white, and exceeding fair and delightsome; that they might not be enticing unto my people the Lord God did cause a skin of blackness to come upon them" (2 Nephi 5:21). Post-1981 editions of *The Book of Mormon* have deleted the strength of the racist overtones by changing the word *white,* in the original 1830 *Book of Mormon,* to *pure,* (cf. 2 Nephi 30:6).[17] The racism concerning African-Americans surfaces in *The Pearl of Great Price, Book of Moses* (7:8–12) and *Book of Abraham* (1:24), but is greatly amplified by Brigham Young's degrading comments found in the *Journal of Discourses* (7:290; 10:110). The *Journal of Discourses* is a twenty-six-volume collection of sermons of early Mormon authorities, still published today by the Church's Deseret Publishing Company. The preface to various volumes written by Brigham Young (1:v), Orson Pratt (3:iii), George Q. Cannon (8:iii), Brigham Young Jr. (11:iii), and Joseph F. Smith (18:iii) harmoniously agree that these volumes are authoritative for Latter-day Saints.~

The Mormon's record claims that Christ visited the American continent, revealed himself to the Nephites, preached to them the gospel, and instituted both baptism and Communion—or "the sacrament" as Latter-day Saints call it.

The Nephites, unfortunately, proved to be no match for the Lamanites, and they were defeated by them and annihilated in a great battle near the hill Cumorah, approximately A.D. 421. ~The traditional view held by the LDS Church is that the hill called Cumorah in *The Book of Mormon* is the same hill where Joseph Smith dug up the gold plates. This would place the final battle between the Nephites and Lamanites near Palmyra, New York, or near the Smith farm. This view has been vehemently challenged by various Mormon scholars who hold to the view that the hill Cumorah of *The Book of Mormon* fame was located rather in

---

[17]One Mormon scholar comments upon how the textual change took place. BYU professor Robert J. Matthew wrote, "Instead of 'white and delightsome,' as in most earlier editions, the 1981 edition uses 'pure and delightsome,' in reference to future Lamanite generations. The printer's copy says 'white.' Unfortunately, the remaining portion of the original dictated manuscript does not include this scripture. The 1830 and 1837 editions of *The Book of Mormon,* based on the printer's copy, also say 'white.' However, the 1840 edition, which was 'carefully' revised by the Prophet Joseph Smith, uses 'pure' in place of 'white.' All subsequent editions have reverted to 'white,' probably because the 1852 edition (the next after the 1840) was based on the 1837 edition rather than on the 1840. In the process of arranging the 1981 edition, the committee presented all of the textual corrections along with the reason for each proposed correction to the First Presidency and the Twelve for approval. The decision to use 'pure' in this passage was made not on the basis of the original manuscripts (as were most other cases), but on the 1840 revision by the Prophet Joseph Smith and the judgment of living prophets. This correction does not negate the concept that future generations of Lamanites will become white, but it removes the concept that one has to be white to be delightsome to the Lord." (Robert J. Matthew, *BYU Studies,* vol. 22, no. 4, 398). From CD-ROM *Brigham Young University Studies,* edited by Clinton F. Larson, et al., 33 vols. (Provo, Utah: Brigham Young University Press, 1959–1996. [51 issues added, vols. 21–33]).

Central America. Both theories have serious flaws and because of this, it is doubtful that a general consensus is forthcoming.~

Some fourteen hundred years later, the Mormons claim, Joseph Smith Jr. unearthed Mormon's abridgment, which was written in "reformed Egyptian" hieroglyphics upon plates of gold, and with the aid of Urim and Thummim (supernatural spectacles) translated the reformed Egyptian into English. It thus became *The Book of Mormon*, which was published in 1830, bearing the name of Joseph Smith Jr. as "Author and Proprietor."

Lest there be any confusion, there are four classes of record plates, which were allegedly revealed to Smith: (1) the plates of Nephi; (2) the plates of Mormon; (3) the plates of Ether; and (4) a set of plates mentioned throughout *The Book of Mormon* as the "plates of brass" or brass plates of Laban.

The plates of Nephi recorded mostly the secular history, although the smaller plates of Nephi allegedly recorded sacred events. The second group is an abridgment from the plates of Nephi, which was made by Mormon and which included his commentaries and additional historical notes by his son, Moroni. The third set of plates recorded the history of the Jaredites, also abridged by Moroni, who added his own comments. It is now known as the *Book of Ether.*

The fourth set of plates is alleged to have come from Jerusalem and appear in the form of extracts in Nephite records. They are given over to quotations from the Hebrew Scriptures and genealogies. Joseph Smith is alleged to have received the plates from the hand of Moroni, "a resurrected personage," in the year 1827.

~The conflicting methods Smith used for translating *The Book of Mormon* leaves little doubt that the story changed often through its progressive history. Mormon missionaries will only discuss the official version of the church: that Joseph Smith received the golden plates with the Urim and Thummim and viewed the plates through the clear stones to translate the reformed Egyptian hieroglyphics into Elizabethan English. The other version, offered by those who saw Smith conducting his work, claims that he often didn't even look at the golden plates. Instead, he placed a seer stone into a hat and covered his face with the hat to see wonderful visions in the stone concerning the hieroglyphics and English translation (cf. David Whitmer, *An Address to All Believers in Christ* [Richmond, Mo.: 1887], 12; *Deseret News, Church Section*, [Salt Lake City: September 20, 1969], 32; Emma Smith, *The Saint's Herald* [Independence, Mo.: May 19, 1888], 310).~

Purpose of *The Book of Mormon*

The purpose of *The Book of Mormon* and its mission generally eludes Christian theologians, archaeologists, and students of anthropology because of the many difficulties that the book introduces in the light of already established facts. But the following explanation of the purpose of the book ought to be considered.

> It is a principle of divine and civil law that, "In the mouth of two or three witnesses every word shall be established" (2 Corinthians 13:1). The Bible, its history of the dealings and providences of God with man upon the Eastern continent, is one witness for the truth. *The Book of Mormon* is another

witness to the same effect. It recites the providences of God in the basic and vastly important matter of redemption, as also in general in the laws of nature, and indicates that such provisions were not limited, not confined to the Eastern world, "God so loved the *world*" (John 3:16), not a mere portion of it, that he likewise ministered in behalf of the race in the great Western continent. Being the seat of mighty civilizations, it was entitled to and partook of the ministrations of the Father of the race.

The stated purpose of the *Book of Mormon* (in its introduction) is universal: to witness to the world the truth and divinity of Jesus Christ, and his mission of salvation through the gospel He taught. Its witness is for Jew and Gentile. The house of Israel rejected its Messiah, and in consequence was rejected, scattered, and the government overthrown. The gospel refused by them was then preached to the Gentiles. Israel has ever since remained in unbelief in Christ and without the ministration of inspired men. Bible prophecy frequently declares its restoration in the latter days to divine favor, the gathering of Israel, and their permanent establishment in their ancient homeland of Palistine. The sealed book, the *Book of Mormon,* is predicted by Bible prophecy and by its own declarations to be a confirming, additional revelation from God of the Messiahship of Jesus Christ and of the covenants made with their fathers. It repeatedly predicts regathering, restoration, and other manifold blessings to Israel. The God of Israel is to make a "new covenant" with that people—not the old Mosaic covenant, but another and later one, by which they are to be reinstated as a nation in their holy land. (See also Jeremiah 31:34; Ezekiel 20:33–38, etc., Bible predictions to the same effect.) *The Book of Mormon* interprets Old Testament prophecy to that effect, as it recites predictions of its inspired men. It claims to be part of the new covenant to Israel.

It claims to be the sealed book of Isaiah, chapter 29, which it quotes and interprets. It recites that as a result of its revealment, Israel would come to an understanding of the Christ message of salvation; that they would no longer fear but be secured and greatly blessed by divine favor; that the coming forth of its record would be followed by physical blessing upon Palestine to its redemption from sterility to fertility, and thus made capable of maintaining that nation as in ancient times. It is a fact that since the appearance of the book that land has been favored. It produces abundantly. The Jews are now permitted to return and establish cities and industrial and agricultural units. Many Jews, according to predictions of the book, are beginning to believe in Christ. Proponents of the book state that with such predictions fulfilled it is now too late for any similar fulfillment by another record.

The book declares also that the remnants of the former inhabitants of ancient America, scattered throughout North, Central, and South America—the Indian populations—will by means of the coming to light of the record of their fathers be converted to the faith and share in the covenants made with their progenitors. It indicates their emergence from primitive conditions to enlightenment. It declares that the Gentile nations occupying their lands would favor their emancipation from degenerate conditions. This is part of the purpose of the book.

The Gospel of Saint John 10:16 contains a statement of Jesus Christ quoted by believers in the divinity of the *Book of Mormon.* It reads, "And other sheep I have, which are not of this fold: them also I must bring, and they shall hear my voice; and there shall be one fold, and one shepherd." Citing also that Christ declared these words: "I am not sent but unto the lost sheep of the house of Israel" (Matthew 15:24), they believe that since Jesus Christ, according to the record, never appeared to the Gentiles, and "salvation is of the Jews," or Israel (John 4:22), the promise concerning "other sheep" was realized by the appearance of Christ to the Nephites.[18]

For the Mormons, then, the Bible predicts *The Book of Mormon; The Book of Mormon* interprets Old Testament prophecy, and it claims to be part of the new covenant to Israel. It is also supposed to be "another witness" to the truth of the Christian gospel. It is unfortunate for the Mormons that this witness is so often found in conflict with the biblical revelation, as we shall see. It is at the very least a gross assumption, unjustified by any of the internal evidence of the book or the testimony of science and history, that *The Book of Mormon* should be considered "part of the new covenant" in any sense.

Scientific Evidence Against *The Book of Mormon*

In an attempt to validate and justify the claims of *The Book of Mormon*, the highest authority in Mormonism, Joseph Smith Jr., the Mormon prophet, related an event which, if true, would add significant weight to some of the Mormon claims for their sacred book. Fortunately, it is a fact on which a good deal of evidence can be brought to bear.

Smith put forth his claim in the book *The Pearl of Great Price* (Joseph Smith— History, 1:62–64, 1982 edition), and it is worthwhile to examine it:

> I commenced copying the characters off the plates. I copied a considerable number of them, and by means of the Urim and Thummim I translated some of them. . . . Mr. Martin Harris came to our place, got the characters which I had drawn off the plates, and started with them to the city of New York. For what took place relative to him and the characters, I refer to his own account of the circumstances, as he related them to me after his return, which was as follows: "I went to the city of New York, and presented the characters that had been translated, with the translation thereof, to Professor Charles Anthon, a gentleman celebrated for his literary attainments. Professor Anthon stated that the translation was correct, more so than any he had before seen translated from the Egyptian. I then showed him those which were not yet translated, and he said that they were Egyptian, Chaldaic, Assyriac, and Arabic; and he said they were true characters."

According to Joseph Smith, then, Martin Harris, his colleague, obtained from the learned Professor Charles Anthon of Columbia University a validation of Smith's translation of the reformed Egyptian hieroglyphic characters found on the plates that Moroni made available to him. The difficulty with Smith's statement is that Professor Anthon never said any such thing, and fortunately he went on record in a lengthy letter to Mr. E. D. Howe, a contemporary of Joseph Smith who did one of the most thorough jobs of research on the Mormon prophet and the origins of Mormonism extant.

Upon learning of Smith's claim concerning Professor Anthon, Mr. Howe wrote him at Columbia. Professor Anthon's letter reproduced here from Howe's

---

[18]R. K. Salyards Sr., *The Book of Mormon* (Independence, Mo.: Herald House, n.d.), 13–16.

own collection is a classic piece of evidence the Mormons would like very much to see forgotten.

New York, N.Y.
Feb. 17, 1834
Mr. E. D. Howe
Painsville, Ohio
Dear Sir:

I received this morning your favor of the 9th instant, and lose no time in making a reply. The whole story about my having pronounced the Mormonite inscription to be "reformed Egyptian hieroglyphics" *is perfectly false.*[19] Some years ago, a plain and apparently simplehearted farmer called upon me with a note from Dr. Mitchell of our city, now deceased, requesting me to decipher, if possible, a paper, which the farmer would hand me, and which Dr. Mitchell confessed he had been unable to understand. Upon examining the paper in question, I soon came to the conclusion that *it was all a trick, perhaps a* [only the word hoax is italicized in the original sentence] *hoax.* When I asked the person who brought it how he obtained the writing he gave me, as far as I can now recollect, [he gave] the following account: A "gold book," consisting of a number of plates of gold, fastened together in the shape of a book by wires of the same metal, had been dug up in the northern part of the state of New York, and along with the book an enormous pair of "gold spectacles [italicized]"! These spectacles were so large that if a person attempted to look through them, his two eyes would have to be turned toward one of the glasses merely, the spectacles in question being altogether too large for the breadth of the human face. Whoever examined the plates through the spectacles, was enabled not only to read [italicized] them, but fully to understand [italicized] their meaning. All this knowledge, however, was confined at the time to a young man, who had the trunk containing the book and spectacles in his sole possession. This young man was placed behind a curtain, in the garret of a farm house, and, being thus concealed from view, put on the spectacles occasionally, or rather, looked through one of the glasses, deciphered the characters in the book, and, having committed some of them to paper, handed copies from behind the curtain to those who stood on the outside. Not a word, however, was said about the plates having been deciphered "by the gift of God." Everything, in this way, was effected by the large pair of spectacles. The farmer added that he had been requested to contribute a sum of money toward the publication of the "golden book," the contents of which would, as he had been assured, produce an entire change in the world and save it from ruin. So urgent had been these solicitations, that he intended selling his farm and handing over the amount received to those who wished to publish the plates. As a last precautionary step, however, he had resolved to come to New York and obtain the opinion of the learned about the meaning of the paper which he brought with him, and which had been given him as a part of the contents of the book, although no translation had been furnished at the time by the young man with the spectacles. *On hearing this odd story, I changed my opinion about the paper, and, instead of viewing it any longer as a hoax upon the learned, I began to regard it as a part of a scheme to cheat the farmer of his money, and I communicated my suspicions to him, warning him to beware of rogues.* [Not itali-

---

[19]Italics are E. D. Howe's for emphasis.

cized in original.] He requested an opinion from me in writing, which of course I declined giving, and he then took his leave carrying the paper with him. *This paper was in fact a singular scrawl. It consisted of all kinds of crooked characters disposed in columns, and had evidently been prepared by some person who had before him at the time a book containing various alphabets. Greek and Hebrew letters, crosses and nourishes, Roman letters inverted or placed sideways, were arranged in perpendicular columns, and the whole ended in a rude delineation of a circle, divided into various compartments, decked with various strange marks, and evidently copied after the Mexican Calendar given by Humboldt, but copied in such a way as not to betray the source whence it was derived.* [Not italicized in original.] I am thus particular as to the contents of the paper, inasmuch as I have frequently conversed with my friends on the subject, since the Mormonite excitement began, and well remember that *the paper contained anything else but "Egyptian Hieroglyphics."* Some time after, the same farmer paid me a second visit. He brought with him the golden book in print, and offered it to me for sale. I declined purchasing. He then asked permission to leave the book with me for examination. I declined receiving it, although his manner was strangely urgent. I adverted once more to the roguery which had been in my opinion practiced upon him, and asked him what had become of the gold plates. He informed me that they were in a trunk with the large pair of spectacles. I advised him to go to a magistrate and have the trunk examined. He said the "curse of God" would come upon him should he do this. On my pressing him, however, to pursue the course which I had recommended, he told me that he would open the trunk, if I would take the "curse of God" upon myself. I replied that I would do so with the greatest willingness, and would incur every risk of that nature, provided I could only extricate him from the grasp of the rogues. He then left me.

I have thus given you a full statement of all that I know respecting the origin of Mormonism, and must beg you, as a personal favor, to publish this letter immediately, should you find my name mentioned again by these wretched fanatics.

Yours respectfully,

Charles Anthon[20]

Professor Anthon's letter is both revealing and devastating where Smith's and Harris' veracity are concerned. We might also raise the question as to how Professor Anthon could say that the characters shown to him by Martin Harris and authorized by Joseph Smith as part of the material copied from the revelation of *The Book of Mormon* were "Egyptian, Chaldaic, Assyriac, and Arabic" when *The Book of Mormon* itself declares that the characters were "reformed Egyptian," the language of the Nephites. Since the language of *The Book of Mormon* was known to "none other people," how would it be conceivably possible for Professor Anthon to have testified as to the accuracy of Smith's translation? To this date, no one has ever been able to find even the slightest trace of the language known as "reformed Egyptian"; and all reputable linguists who have examined the evidence put forth by the Mormons have rejected them as mythical.

---

[20]E. D. Howe, *Mormonism Unveiled* (Painsville, Ohio: n.p., 1834), 270–72.

Archaeological Evidence

The Book of Mormon purports to portray the rise and development of two great civilizations. As to just how great these civilizations were, some excerpts from the book itself adequately illustrate.

"The whole face of the land had become covered with buildings, and the people were as numerous almost, as it were the sand of the sea" (Mormon 1:7).

". . . fine workmanship of wood, in buildings, and in machinery, and also in iron and copper, and brass and steel, making all manners of tools" (Jarom 1:8; 2 Nephi 5:15).

". . . grain . . . silks . . . cattle . . . oxen . . . cows . . . sheep . . . swine . . . goats . . . horses . . . asses . . . elephants . . ." (see Ether 9:17–19).

". . . did multiply and spread . . . began to cover the face of the whole earth, from the sea south to the sea north, from the sea west to the sea east" (Helaman 3:8).

". . . had been slain . . . nearly two million [Jaredites]" (see Ether 15:2).

". . . their shipping and their building of ships, and their building of temples, and of synagogues and their sanctuaries" (Helaman 3:14. See also 2 Nephi 5: 15–16; Alma 16:13).

". . . there were ten more who did fall . . . with their ten thousand each" (see Mormon 6:10–15).

". . . swords . . . cimeters . . . breastplates . . . arm-shields . . . shields . . . head-plates . . . armor" (see Alma 43:18–19; 3:5; Ether 15:15).

". . . multiplied exceedingly, and spread upon the face of the land, and became exceeding rich" (Jarom 1:8).

See 3 Nephi 8:9–10, 14; 9:4–6, 8: where cities and inhabitants were sunk in the depths of the sea and earth.

In addition to the foregoing statements from *The Book of Mormon,* which indicate the tremendous spread of the cultures of these races, there are numerous cities catalogued in *The Book of Mormon,* evidence that these were indeed mighty civilizations, which should, by all the laws of archaeological research into the culture of antiquity, have left vast amounts of "finds" to be evaluated. But such is not the case as we shall show. The Mormons have yet to explain the fact that leading archaeological researchers not only have repudiated the claims of *The Book of Mormon* as to the existence of these civilizations, but have adduced considerable evidence to show the impossibility of the accounts given in the Mormon Bible.

The following letter was addressed to the Rev. R. Odell Brown, pastor of the Hillcrest Methodist Church, Fredericksburg, Virginia, an ardent student of Mormonism and its claims. Dr. Brown, in the course of his research, wrote to the Department of Anthropology at Columbia University in New York City. The answer he received is of great importance in establishing the fact that *The Book of Mormon* is neither accurate nor truthful where the sciences of archaeology and anthropology are concerned.

> Dear Sir:
> Pardon my delay in answering your letter of January 14, 1957. The question which you ask concerning the *Book of Mormon* is one that comes up quite frequently. . . . However, . . . I may say that I do not believe that there

is a single thing of value concerning the prehistory of the American Indian in the *Book of Mormon* and I believe that the great majority of American archaeologists would agree with me. The book is untrue biblically, historically, and scientifically.

Concerning Dr. Charles Anthon of Columbia University, I do not know who he is and would certainly differ with his viewpoint, as the Latter Day Saints (Mormons) tell it. What possible bearing Egyptian hieroglyphics would have on either the *Book of Mormon* or the prehistory of the American Indian I do not know. . . . I am,

Very sincerely yours,
Wm. Duncan Strong [Signed]

The Smithsonian Institution in Washington has also added its voice against the archaeological claims of *The Book of Mormon*. Such a highly regarded scientific source the Mormons can ill afford to ignore.

1. The Smithsonian Institution has never used the *Book of Mormon* in any way as a scientific guide. Smithsonian archaeologists see no direct connection between the archaeology of the New World and the subject matter of the book.

2. The physical type of the Native American is basically Mongoloid, being most closely related to that of the peoples of eastern, central, and northeastern Asia. Archaeological evidence indicates that the ancestors of the present Native Americans came into the New World—probably over a land bridge known to have existed in the Bering Strait region during the last Ice Age—in a continuing series of small migrations beginning from about 25,000 to 30,000 years ago.

3. Present evidence indicates that the first people to reach this continent from the East were the Norsemen who briefly visited the northeastern part of North America around A.D. 1000 and then settled in Greenland. There is nothing to show that they reached Mexico or Central America.

4. One of the main lines of evidence supporting the scientific finding that contacts with Old World civilizations, if indeed they occurred at all, were of very little significance for the development of Native American civilizations is the fact that none of the principal Old World domesticated food plants or animals (except the dog) occurred in the New World in Pre-Columbian times. Native Americans had no wheat, barley, oats, millet, rice, cattle, pigs, chickens, horses, donkeys, or camels before 1492. (Camels and horses were in the Americas, along with the bison, mammoth, and mastodon, but all these animals became extinct around 10,000 B.C. at the time the early big game hunters spread across the Americas.)

5. Iron, steel, glass, and silk were not used in the New World before 1492 (except for occasional use of unsmelted meteoric iron). Native copper was used in various locations in pre-Columbian times, but true metallurgy was limited to southern Mexico and the Andean region, where its occurrence in late prehistoric times involved gold, silver, copper, and their alloys, but not iron.

6. There is a possibility that the spread of cultural traits across the Pacific to Mesoamerica and the northwestern coast of South America began several hundred years before the Christian era. However, any such interhemispheric contacts appear to have been the result of accidental voyages originating in eastern and southern Asia. It is by no means certain that such

contacts occurred; certainly there were no contacts with the ancient Egyptians, Hebrews, or other peoples of Western Asia and the Near East.

7. No reputable Egyptologist or other specialist on Old World archaeology and no expert on New World prehistory has discovered or confirmed any relationship between archaeological remains in Mexico and archaeological remains in Egypt.

8. Reports of findings of ancient Egyptian, Hebrew, and other Old World writings in the New World in pre-Columbian contexts have frequently appeared in newspapers, magazines, and sensational books. None of these claims has stood up to examination by reputable scholars. No inscriptions using Old World forms of writing have been shown to have occurred in any part of the Americas before 1492, except for a few Norse rune stones which have been found in Greenland. (Revised, May 1980)

From this evidence, it is clear that the cities mentioned in *The Book of Mormon* are imaginary, that elephants never existed on this continent, and that the metals described in *The Book of Mormon* have never been found in any of the areas of contemporary civilizations of the New World. This is not a theologian attempting to discredit the Mormons on the basis of their theology, but recognized archaeological experts challenging *The Book of Mormon* on the basis of the fact that its accounts are not in keeping with the findings of science. Mormon missionaries are generally reluctant to discuss these areas when the evidence is well known, but it *is* evidence, and from the most authoritative sources.

~One of the most damaging claims against the archaeology of *The Book of Mormon* was the publication of former Brigham Young University professor Thomas Stuart Ferguson's paper written in 1975. Ferguson's leadership in two nonprofit foundations was purposed to discover archeological evidence for *The Book of Mormon*. Both organizations, the New World Archaeological Foundation and the Society for Early Historic Archaeology, the latter located at BYU, received direct funding from the Mormon Church, but produced nothing recognized by scholars as evidence. After twenty-five years of dedicated archaeological research, Ferguson found nothing to back up the flora, fauna, topography, geography, peoples, coins, or settlements of the book and, in fact, he called the geography of *The Book of Mormon* "fictional." In *Ferguson's Manuscript Unveiled* (Salt Lake City: Utah Lighthouse Ministry, 1988), the reader is treated to a wealth of insights into the sheer nonexistence of *Book of Mormon* antiquities.~

The Mongoloid Factor

It is one of the main contentions of Mormon theology that Native Americans are the descendants of the Lamanites and that they were of the Semitic race; in fact, of Jewish origin. As we have seen, this claim is extensive in Mormon literature, and if evidence could be adduced to show that the Native American could not possibly be of Semitic extraction, the entire story of Nephi and his trip to America in 600 B.C. would be proven false.

It is, therefore, of considerable value to learn that in the findings compiled both by anthropologists and those who specialize in genetics that the various physical factors of the Mediterranean races from which the Jewish or Semitic race spring bear little or no resemblance to those of the Native American. Genotypically, there is, therefore, little if any correlation, and phenotypically speaking, Native Americans are considered to be Mongoloid in extraction, not Mediterranean Caucasoids, as confirmed in the previously quoted Smithsonian Institution letter.

Now, if the Lamanites, as *The Book of Mormon* claims, were the descendants of Nephi, who was a Jew of the Mediterranean Caucasoid type, then their descendants, Native Americans, would by necessity have the same blood factor genotypically, and phenotypic or apparent characteristics would be the same. But this is not at all the case. Instead, the Native American, so say anthropologists, is not of Semitic extraction and has the definite phenotypical characteristic of a Mongoloid. A thorough study of anthropology and such writers as W. C. Boyd (*The Contributions of Genetics to Anthropology*) and Bentley Glass, the gifted geneticist of Johns Hopkins University, reveals that Mormon findings based upon *The Book of Mormon* are out of harmony with the findings of geneticists and anthropologists. There simply is no foundation for the postulation that the Native American (Lamanites, according to the Mormons) is in any way related to the race to which Nephi (a Semite) allegedly belonged.

Corrections, Contradictions, and Errors

There is a great wealth of information concerning the material contained in *The Book of Mormon* and the various plagiarisms, anachronisms, false prophecies, and other unfortunate practices connected with it. At best we can give but a condensation of that which has been most thoroughly documented.

Since the publication of *The Book of Mormon* in 1830, the first edition has undergone extensive "correction" in order to present it in its current form. Some of these "corrections" should be noted.

~The former major revision of *The Book of Mormon* was in 1920. That standard edition is still found in many public libraries and in millions of homes. In the latest revision, 1981, a subtitle was added to the cover: "Another Testament of Jesus Christ," and no less than one hundred verses were changed without consulting the missing golden plates. A note closing the introduction to the 1981 edition says, "Some minor errors in the text have been perpetuated in past editions of *The Book of Mormon*. This edition contains corrections that seem appropriate to bring the material into conformity with prepublication manuscripts and early editions edited by the prophet Joseph Smith." Without blushing, the Mormon Church boldly asserts the unfounded claim that the prepublication manuscripts agree with their most recent changes. Our access to the handwritten copies of the original *Book of Mormon* deny such a claim and proves once again that the Mormon Church will sacrifice truth for the sake of public relations.~

1. In Mosiah 21:28, it is declared that "King Mosiah had a gift from God"; but in the original edition of the book, the name of the king was Benjamin—an oversight that thoughtful Mormon scribes corrected. This is not, of course, a typographical error, as there is little resemblance between the names Benjamin and Mosiah; rather, it appears that either God made a mistake when He inspired the record, or Joseph made a mistake when he translated it. But the Mormons will admit to neither, so they are stuck, so to speak, with the contradiction.

2. When compared with the 1830 edition, 1 Nephi 19:16–20 reveals more

than twenty changes in the "inspired *Book of Mormon,*" words having been dropped, spelling corrected, and words and phraseology added and turned about. This is a strange way to treat an inspired revelation from God.

3. In Alma 28:14–29:11, more than eighteen changes may be counted from the original edition. On page 303 the phrase, "Yea, decree unto them that decrees which are unalterable," was dropped in later editions, but strangely reappeared in 1981. (See Alma 29:4.)

4. On page 25 of the 1830 edition, *The Book of Mormon* declares:

"And the angel said unto me, behold the Lamb of God, yea, even the Eternal Father."

Yet in 1 Nephi 11:21, the later editions of the book read:

"And the angel said unto me: Behold the Lamb of God, yea even the son of the eternal Father."

5. The Roman Catholic Church should be delighted with page 25 of the original edition of *The Book of Mormon,* which confirms one of their dogmas, namely, that Mary is the mother of God.

"Behold, the virgin which thou seest, is the mother of God."

Noting this unfortunate lapse into Romanistic theology, Joseph Smith and his considerate editors changed 1 Nephi 11:18 (as well as 1 Nephi 11:21, 32; 13:40), so that it now reads:

"Behold, the virgin whom thou seest, is the mother of the Son of God."

From the above, which are only a handful of examples from the approximately four thousand word changes to be found in *The Book of Mormon,* the reader can readily see that it in no sense can be accepted as the Word of God. The Scripture says, "The word of the Lord endureth for ever" (1 Peter 1:25); and our Savior declared, "Sanctify them through thy truth: thy word is truth" (John 17:17).

The record of the Scriptures rings true. *The Book of Mormon,* on the other hand, is patently false in far too many instances to be considered coincidence.

Added to the evidence of various revisions, *The Book of Mormon* also contains plagiarisms from the King James Bible, anachronisms, false prophecies, and errors of fact that cannot be dismissed. Some of these bear repetition, though they are well known to students of Mormonism.

The testimony of the three witnesses, which appears at the front of *The Book of Mormon* (Oliver Cowdery, David Whitmer, and Martin Harris) declares that "An angel of God came down from heaven, and he brought and laid before our eyes, that we beheld and saw the plates, and the engraving thereon."

It is quite noteworthy that Martin Harris denied that he had actually seen the plates with his "naked eyes." In fact, when pressed, he stated, "No, I saw them with a spiritual eye" (Recollections of John H. Gilbert, 1892, Typescript, BYU, 5–6).

The Mormons are loath to admit that all three of these witnesses later apostatized from the Mormon faith and were described in most unflattering terms ("counterfeiters, thieves, [and] liars") by their Mormon contemporaries (cf. *Senate Document 189,* February 15, 1841, 6–9).

A careful check of early Mormon literature also reveals that Joseph Smith wrote prophecies and articles against the character of the witnesses of *The Book of Mormon,* which in itself renders their testimony suspect (cf. *Doctrine and Covenants,*

3:12; 10:7; *History of the Church*; 3:228, 3:232).

~Mormons try to cover this historical predicament by saying that two of the three witnesses, Oliver Cowdery and Martin Harris, were rebaptized into Mormonism. What they fail to reveal is more significant: The *Times and Seasons* (2:482) published that Oliver Cowdery denied his *Book of Mormon* testimony. He spent several years as a baptized Methodist before his rebaptism into Mormonism. Martin Harris, likewise, has suspicious circumstances surrounding his rebaptism. He denied the teachings of Brigham Young after rebaptism and was banned from preaching by Young because of their differences. David Whitmer changed the details of his testimony concerning the angel with the golden plates to say that it was a vision and not an actual visitation by an angelic person (*An Address to All Believers in Christ*, 32). Certainly testimony from such unstable personalities is dubious at best.~

Plagiarisms—The King James Version

A careful examination of *The Book of Mormon* reveals that it contains thousands of words from the King James Bible. In fact, verbatim quotations, some of considerable length, have caused the Mormons no end of embarrassment for many years.

The comparisons of Moroni 10 with 1 Corinthians 12:1–11; 2 Nephi 14 with Isaiah 4; and 2 Nephi 12 with Isaiah 2 reveal that Joseph Smith made free use of his Bible to supplement the alleged revelation of the golden plates. The book of Mosiah, chapter 14, in *The Book of Mormon*, is a reproduction of the fifty-third chapter of Isaiah the prophet, and 3 Nephi 13 copies Matthew 6 almost word-for-word.

There are other instances of plagiarisms from the King James Bible, including paraphrases of certain verses. One of these verses (1 John 5:7) is reproduced in 3 Nephi 11:27. The only difficulty with the paraphrase here is that the text is considered by scholars to be an interpolation missing from all the major manuscripts of the New Testament, but present in the King James Bible, from which Smith paraphrased it not knowing the difference.

Another example of this type of error is found in 3 Nephi 11:33–34, and is almost a direct quotation from Mark 16:16, a passage regarded by many New Testament Greek scholars as one of three possible endings to that gospel. But Joseph Smith was not aware of this, so he even copied in translational variations, another proof that neither he nor the alleged golden plates were inspired of God.

Two further instances of plagiarisms from the King James Bible that have backfired on the Mormons are worth noting.

In the third chapter of the book of Acts, Peter's classic sermon at Pentecost paraphrases Deuteronomy 18:15–19. While in the process of writing 3 Nephi, Joseph Smith puts Peter's paraphrase in the mouth of Christ when the Savior was allegedly preaching to the Nephites. The prophet overlooked the fact that at the time that Christ was allegedly preaching His sermon, the sermon itself had not yet been preached by Peter.

In addition to this, 3 Nephi makes Christ out to be a liar, when in 20:23 Christ attributes Peter's words to Moses as a direct quotation, when, as we have pointed out, Peter paraphrased the quotation from Moses (Acts 3:22–23); and the wording is quite different. But Joseph did not check far enough, hence this glaring error.

Secondly, *The Book of Mormon* follows the error of the King James translation that renders Isaiah 4:5, "For upon all the glory shall be a defense" (see 2 Nephi 14:5).

Modern translations of Isaiah point out that it should read "For over all the glory there will be a canopy," not a defense. The Hebrew word *chuppah* does not mean defense, but a protective curtain or canopy. Smith, of course, did not know this, nor did the King James translators from whose work he copied.

There are quite a number of other places where such errors appear, including Smith's insistence in Abraham 1:20 that "Pharaoh signifies king by royal blood," when in reality the dictionary defines the meaning of the term Pharaoh as "a great house or palace."

The *Revised Standard Version* of the Bible renders Isaiah 5:25, "And their corpses were as refuse in the midst of the streets," correctly rendering the Hebrew *suchah* as "refuse," not as "torn." The King James Bible renders the passage "And their carcasses were torn in the midst of the streets." *The Book of Mormon* (2 Nephi 15:25) repeats the King James' text word-for-word, including the error of mistranslating *suchah*, removing any claim that *The Book of Mormon* is to be taken seriously as reliable material.

Anachronisms and Contradictions

Not only does *The Book of Mormon* plagiarize heavily from the King James Bible, but it betrays a great lack of information and background on the subject of world history and the history of the Jewish people. The Jaredites apparently enjoyed glass windows in the miraculous barges in which they crossed the ocean, and "steel" and a "compass" were known to Nephi despite the fact that neither had been invented. ~Although the Book of Mormon does not use the word *glass* in Ether 2:23, it does say, "Ye cannot have windows, for they will be dashed in pieces," clearly emphasizing the fragile nature of the window material. Three verses later, the word *glass* is actually used: "molten rock . . . white and clear, even as transparent as glass," so the context plainly speaks of glass as we know it today—the implication being that Jared was familiar enough with glass to make a comparison with it.~ This demonstrates once again that Joseph Smith was a poor student of history and of Hebrew customs.

Laban, mentioned as one of the characters of *The Book of Mormon* (1 Nephi 4:9), makes use of a steel sword; and Nephi himself claims to have had a steel bow. The ancient Jaredites also had steel swords (Ether 7:9). The Mormons justify this by quoting Psalm 18:34 as a footnote to 1 Nephi 16:18 in *The Book of Mormon*, but modern translations of the Scriptures indicate that the word translated *steel* in the Old Testament (since steel was nonexistent) is more properly rendered *bronze*. Nahum 2:3, NASB, uses "steel," but it is taken from the Hebrew word *paladah*, probably meaning iron.

~William Hamblin, in his preliminary report entitled *Handheld Weapons in the Book of Mormon* (1985), published by the Foundation for Ancient Research and Mormon Studies (F.A.R.M.S.), uses the bronze argument as a possible justification for the rendering of steel in *The Book of Mormon*. He writes, "Another possibility is to equate this Jaredite steel with the 'steel' of the King James translation of the Old Testament, which actually refers to the Hebrew word for bronze." The problem with using this explanation to protect *The Book of Mormon* is that it defies Mormon history. Numerous contemporaries of Joseph Smith have claimed that Smith could not continue "translating" the gold plates unless the scribe read each word back to him *correctly*. If the word *steel* in *The Book of Mormon* should really have been bronze, it undermines the LDS claim that the book was translated by the gift and power of God, since it shows that errors crept into Joseph Smith's translation.~

Mormons sometimes attempt to defend Nephi's possession of a *not yet invented* compass (known in *The Book of Mormon* as a Liahona) by the fact that Acts 28:13 states, "And from thence we fetched a compass." Modern translations of the Scripture, however, refute this subterfuge by correctly rendering the passage: "And from there we made a circle."

Added to the preceding anachronisms is the fact that *The Book of Mormon* not only contradicts the Bible, but contradicts other revelations purporting to come from the same God who inspired *The Book of Mormon*. The Bible declares that the Messiah of Israel was to be born in Bethlehem (Micah 5:2), and the gospel of Matthew (chapter 2, v. 1) records the fulfillment of this prophecy. But *The Book of Mormon* (Alma 7:9, 10) states,

". . . the son of God cometh upon the face of the earth. And behold, he shall be born of Mary, at Jerusalem, which is the land of our forefathers. . . ."

The Book of Mormon describes Jerusalem as a city (1 Nephi 1:4), as was Bethlehem described as a separate town in the Bible. The contradiction is irreconcilable.

~Another area of contradiction between the Bible and *The Book of Mormon* concerns sin and Mormon baptism at eight years of age. Moroni 8:8 states the doctrine that "little children are whole, for they are not capable of committing sin; wherefore the curse of Adam is taken from them in me." Anyone who thinks that children under age eight cannot sin has not visited the classrooms of today's schools. The Mormon concept directly contradicts Psalm 51:5, which places sin at the point of conception. The book of Romans leaves no exemption to the sin and guilt that Adam passed on to all; no exceptions are made (Romans 5:12–15). Furthermore, it clearly states that "there is none righteous, no, not one" (Romans 3:10–12).~

There are also a number of instances in Mormon scripture where God did not agree with himself, if indeed He inspired *The Book of Mormon, The Pearl of Great Price, Doctrine and Covenants,* or the other recorded utterances of Joseph Smith.

In *The Book of Mormon,* for instance (3 Nephi 12:2; Moroni 8:11), the remission of sins is the accomplishment of baptism:

"Yea, blessed are they who shall . . . be baptized, for they shall . . . receive a remission of their sin. . . . Behold baptism is unto repentance to the fulfilling the commandments unto the remission of sin."

But in *Doctrine and Covenants* (20:37), the direct opposite is stated:

"All those who humble themselves . . . and truly manifest by their works that they have received of the Spirit of Christ unto the remission of their sins, shall be received by baptism into his church."

Mormon theologians conspicuously omit any serious discussion of the contradiction.

Joseph Smith did not limit his contradictions to baptism; indeed, polygamy is a classic example of some of his maneuvering.

"Go ye, therefore, and do the works of Abraham; enter ye into my law and ye shall be saved. God commanded Abraham, and Sarah gave Hagar to Abraham to wife. And why did she do it? Because this was the law; and from Hagar sprang many people" (*Doctrine and Covenants*, 132:34, 32).

The Book of Mormon, on the other hand, categorically states:

"Wherefore, I the Lord God will not suffer that this people shall do like unto them of old . . . for there shall not any man among you have save it be one wife; and concubines he shall have none; for I, the Lord God, delight in the chastity of woman" (Jacob 2:26–28).

It appears that Smith could manufacture revelations at will, depending upon his desires. In the last instance, his reputation and subsequent actions indicate that sex was the motivating factor.

A final example of the confusion generated between *The Book of Mormon* and other "inspired" revelations is found in this conflict between two works in *The Pearl of Great Price:* The *Book of Moses* and The *Book of Abraham.*

"I am the Beginning and the End, the Almighty God; by mine Only Begotten I created these things; yea, in the beginning I created the heaven, and the earth upon which thou standest" (Moses 2:1).

The *Book of Abraham,* on the other hand, repudiates this monotheistic view and states, "And then the Lord said: Let us go down. And they went down at the beginning, and they, that is the Gods, organized and formed the heavens and the earth" (Abraham 4:1).

Just how it is possible to reconcile these two allegedly equal pronouncements from Mormon revelation escapes this author, and the Mormons themselves appear reluctant to furnish any concrete explanation.

The question of false prophecies in Mormonism has been handled adequately in a number of excellent volumes, but it should be pointed out that Joseph Smith drew heavily upon published articles both in newspapers and magazines. In fact, one of his famous prophecies concerning the Civil War is drawn chiefly from material already published at the time.

~In the *History of the Church,* Volume 1, page 301, Joseph Smith states,

> Appearances of troubles among the nations became more visible this season than they had previously been since the Church began her journey out of the wilderness. . . . The people of South Carolina, in convention assembled (in November), passed ordinances, declaring their state a free and independent nation.

From this we know that Smith could have been aware of South Carolina's succession as early as November 1832. If not in November, then the *Boston Daily Advertiser & Patriot,* December 10, 1832, could be his resource. Fifteen days before Smith's prophecy, the Mormon Apostle Orson Hyde was in Boston while that paper was published. Five days before Smith's prophecy, Mr. Hyde arrived at Smith's house in Ohio.~

Smith declared in *Doctrine and Covenants,* Section 87:

At the rebellion of South Carolina . . . the Southern States will call on other nations, even the nation of Great Britain . . . and then war shall be poured out upon all nations. And . . . slaves shall rise up against their masters . . . and that the remnants . . . shall vex the Gentiles with a sore vexation.

Though the Civil War did break out some years after Smith's death in 1844, England did not become involved in any war against the United States. "All nations" were not involved in war as was prophesied. The slaves did not rise up against "their masters," and the "remnants" who were Native Americans were themselves vexed by the Gentiles, being defeated in war and confined to reservations.

Prophet Smith was an extremely ineffective prophet here, as well as in *Doctrine and Covenants* 124:22–23, 59, when he prophesied that he would possess the house he built at Nauvoo "for ever and ever."

The fact of the matter is that neither Joseph nor his seed "after him" lived from "generation to generation" in the Nauvoo house. ~According to *The Comprehensive History of the Church* 1:160,

The Nauvoo House was never completed; and after its unfinished walls had stood unprotected for a number of years and were crumbling to decay, they were taken down; the foundations were torn up and the excellent building stone of which they were constructed sold for use in other buildings in and about Nauvoo.

However, the LDS church has rebuilt the house in "Nauvoo" and offers it as a tourist attraction.~

These and other instances indicate that Smith was not only a poor scribe but a false prophet, and his prophecy concerning the restoration of Israel to Palestine clearly reveals that he anticipated the millennium in his own lifetime, whereas in reality the prophecy of Ezekiel 37 began to be fulfilled in 1948, more than a century after Smith's death.

The question quite naturally arises in summing up the background of *The Book of Mormon*: Where did the book come from, since it obviously did not come from God? The answer to this has been propounded at great length by numerous students of Mormonism, particularly E. D. Howe, Pomeroy Tucker, and William A. Linn.

All the aforementioned concur that *The Book of Mormon* is probably an expansion upon the writings of Solomon Spaulding, a retired minister who was known to have written a number of "romances" with biblical backgrounds similar to those of *The Book of Mormon*. The Mormons delight to point out that one of Spaulding's manuscripts, entitled "Manuscript Story," was discovered in Hawaii more than one hundred years ago, and it differed in many respects from *The Book of Mormon*.

But in his excellent volume *The Book of Mormon*, Dr. James D. Bales makes the following observation, which is of great importance and agrees in every detail with my research:

It has long been contended that there is a connection between *The Book of Mormon* and one of Solomon Spaulding's historical romances. The Latter-day Saints, of course, deny such a connection.

What if the Latter-day Saints are right and there is no relationship between *The Book of Mormon* and Spaulding's writings? It simply means that those who so contend are wrong, but it proves nothing with reference to the question as to whether or not *The Book of Mormon* is of divine origin.

One could be wrong as to what man, or men, wrote *The Book of Mormon,* and still know that it was not written by men inspired of God. One can easily prove that *The Book of Mormon* is of human origin. And, after all, this is the main issue. The fundamental issue is not *what* man or men wrote it, but whether it was written by men who were guided by God. We know that men wrote it, and that these men, whoever they were, did not have God's guidance.

This may be illustrated by *Science and Health With Key to the Scriptures*— the textbook of Christian Science churches. Mrs. Eddy claims to have been its author, under God's direction. There are others who claim she reworked and enlarged a manuscript of Mr. Quimby and the evidence seems to prove that such is the case. But what if those who so maintained failed to prove their case?

Would that prove that it was inspired of God? Not at all. It would prove only that Quimby's manuscript had nothing to do with it. But it would not prove that some other uninspired being did not write it. Regardless of what human being or beings wrote *Science and Health,* it is of human, not divine origin. Just so *The Book of Mormon* is of human origin and uninspired, even though it were impossible to prove what particular man wrote it.

It has not been maintained that all *The Book of Mormon* was written by Spaulding. Thus, it has not been claimed that the theological portions were put in by him. Those portions bear the imprint of Smith, Cowdery, and Sidney Rigdon (see the proof offered in Shook's *The True Origin of the Book of Mormon,* 126ff.). It is maintained, however, that some things, including a great deal of Scripture, were added to one of Spaulding's manuscripts and that his work was thus transferred into *The Book of Mormon* (see the testimony of John Spaulding, Solomon's brother; Martha Spaulding, John's wife): They maintained that the historical portion was Spaulding's. (E. D. Howe, *Mormonism Unveiled,* 1834, 278ff.; Shook, *The True Origin of the Book of Mormon,* 94ff).

The Mormons contend that the discovery of one of Spaulding's manuscripts demonstrates that it was not the basis of The Book of Mormon.

"I will here state that the Spaulding manuscript was discovered in 1884, and is at present in the library of Oberlin College, Ohio. On examination it was found to bear no resemblance whatever to *The Book of Mormon.* The theory that Solomon Spaulding was the author of *The Book of Mormon* should never be mentioned again—outside a museum." (William A. Morton, op. cit., 6.)

There are three errors in the above paragraph: viz., that Spaulding wrote but one manuscript; that the manuscript discovered in 1884 is the one that non-Mormons have claimed constituted the basis of *The Book of Mormon;* that the manuscript in Oberlin bears no resemblance whatever to *The Book of Mormon.*

(a) *Spaulding wrote more than one manuscript.* This was maintained by D. P. Harlburt [Hurlbut] and Clark Braden before the Honolulu manuscript was found (Charles A. Shook, *op. cit.,* 77). Spaulding's daughter also testified that her father had written "other romances." (Elder George Reynolds, *The*

Myth of the "Manuscript Found," Utah, 1833, 104). The present manuscript story looks like a rough, unfinished, first draft.

(b) *The manuscript found in Honolulu was called a "Manuscript Story" and not the "Manuscript Found."* This Honolulu manuscript, *The Manuscript Story,* was in the hands of anti-Mormons in 1854. However, they did not claim that it was the manuscript which was the basis of *The Book of Mormon.* It was claimed that another manuscript of Spaulding was the basis of *The Book of Mormon,* (Charles A. Shook, op. cit., 77, 15, 185. The *"Manuscript Found or Manuscript Stop"* of the late Rev. Solomon Spaulding, Lamoni, Iowa: Printed and Published by the Reorganized Church of Jesus Christ of Latter Day Saints, 1885, 10).

(c) Although the *Manuscript Story* has not been regarded as the *Manuscript Found,* which constituted the basis of *The Book of Mormon,* there is a great deal of resemblance between the *Manuscript* and *The Book of Mormon.* These points of similarity can be accounted for on the basis that the *Manuscript Story* was the first, and rough draft of one of Spaulding's works, which he reworked into the *Manuscript Found.*

"Howe, in 1854, published a fair synopsis of the Oberlin manuscript now at Oberlin (Howe's *Mormonism Unveiled,* 288) and submitted the original to the witnesses who testified to the many points of identity between Spaulding's *Manuscript Found* and *The Book of Mormon.* These witnesses then (in 1834) recognized the manuscript secured by Harlburt and now at Oberlin as being one of Spaulding's, but not the one that they asserted was similar to *The Book of Mormon.* They further said that Spaulding had told them that he had altered his original plan of writing by going farther back with his dates and writing in the old scripture style, in order that his story might appear more ancient" (Howe's *Mormonism Unveiled,* 288; Theodore Schroeder, *The Origin of the Book of Mormon, Re-Examined in Its Relation to Spaulding's "Manuscript Found,"* 5).

This testimony is borne out by the fact that there are many points of similarity between the manuscript in Oberlin College and *The Book of Mormon.*[21]

It is fairly well established historically, then, that the Mormons have attempted to use a manuscript that is admittedly *not* the one from which Smith later copied and amplified the text of what is now known as *The Book of Mormon* as the basis for denying what eye witnesses have affirmed: that it was another Spaulding manuscript (*Manuscript Found*) that Smith drew upon to fabricate *The Book of Mormon.*

Dr. Bales is right when he states:

There are too many points of similarity for them to be without significance. Thus, the internal evidence, combined with the testimony of witnesses, as presented in Howe's book and reproduced in Shook's, shows that Spaulding revised the *Manuscript Story.* The revision was known as the *Manuscript Found,* and it became the basis of *The Book of Mormon* in at least its historical parts. Also its religious references furnished in part the germs of the religious portions of *The Book of Mormon.*

However, in ordinary conversation, and in public debate on *The Book of Mormon,* it is unnecessary to go into the question of who wrote *The Book of*

---

[21]James D. Bales, Ph.D., *The Book of Mormon?* (Fort Worth: The Manney Company), 138–42.

Mormon. The really important issue is whether or not *The Book of Mormon* is of divine origin. There are some Mormons who seem to think that if they can prove that Spaulding's manuscript had nothing to do with *The Book of Mormon,* they have made great progress toward proving its divine origin. Such, however, is not the case. And one should show, from an appeal to the Bible and to *The Book of Mormon* itself, that *The Book of Mormon* is not of divine origin.[22]

Let us not forget that the *Manuscript Story* itself contains at least seventy-five similarities to what is now *The Book of Mormon,* and this is not to be easily explained away.

Finally, students of Mormonism must, in the last analysis, measure its content by that of Scripture, and when this is done it will be found that it does not "speak according to the law and the testimony" (Isaiah 8:20), and it is to be rejected as a counterfeit revelation doubly condemned by God himself (Galatians 1:8–9).

Joseph Smith, the author of this "revelation," was perfectly described (as was his reward) in the Word of God almost thirty-three hundred years before he appeared. It would pay the Mormons to remember this message:

If there arise among you a prophet, or a dreamer of dreams, and giveth thee a sign or a wonder, and the sign or the wonder come to pass, whereof he spake unto thee, saying, "Let us go after other gods," which thou hast not known, "and let us serve them;" thou shalt not hearken unto the words of that prophet, or that dreamer of dreams: for the Lord your God proveth you, to know whether ye love the Lord your God with all your heart and with all your soul.

Ye shall walk after the Lord your God, and fear him, and keep his commandments, and obey his voice, and ye shall serve him, and cleave unto him.

And that prophet, or that dreamer of dreams, shall be put to death; because he hath spoken to turn you away from the Lord your God, which brought you out of the land of Egypt, and redeemed you out of the house of bondage, to thrust thee out of the way which the Lord thy God commanded thee to walk in. So shalt thou put the evil away from the midst of thee.

If thy brother, the son of thy mother, or thy son, or thy daughter, or the wife of thy bosom, or thy friend, which is as thine own soul, entice thee secretly, saying, "Let us go and serve other gods," which thou has not known, thou, nor thy fathers; namely, of the gods of the people which are round about you, nigh unto thee, or far off from thee, from the one end of the earth even unto the other end of the earth:

Thou shalt not consent unto him, nor hearken unto him; neither shall thine eye pity him, neither shalt thou spare, neither shalt thou conceal him:

But thou shalt surely kill him; thine hand shall be first upon him to put him to death, and afterwards the hand of all the people.

And thou shalt stone him with stones, that he die; because he hath sought to thrust thee away from the Lord thy God, which brought thee out of the land of Egypt, from the house of bondage. (Deuteronomy 13:1–10)

The Book of Mormon stands as a challenge to the Bible because it adds to the

[22]Bales, 146–47.

Word of God and to His one revelation, and the penalty for such action is as sobering as it is awesome:

> For I testify unto every man that heareth the words of the prophecy of this book, If any man shall add unto these things, God shall add unto him the plagues that are written in this book:
>
> And if any man shall take away from the words of the book of this prophecy, God shall take away his part out of the book of life, and out of the holy city, and from the things which are written in this book.
>
> He which testifieth these things saith, Surely I come quickly. Amen. Even so, come, Lord Jesus. (Revelation 22:18–20)

~It does no good for the Mormon to argue that Revelation 22:18–20 only pertains to the book of Revelation, since this serves only to prove our point. In the 1981 edition of the King James Version of the Bible, published by the Mormon Church, they have no less than forty-five verses footnoted in the book of Revelation where Joseph Smith added and took away from the "words of the book." These footnotes are conveniently noted as JST (Joseph Smith Translation), beginning at Revelation 1:1 and ending at 19:21. He truly did what the apostle John warned against. Smith both added to and took away from the book of Revelation.~

We need not make this a personal issue with the Mormons, but a historical and theological issue, which, for all the politeness and tact demonstrably possible, cannot conceal the depth of our disagreement. Even the famous "witnesses" to the veracity of *The Book of Mormon* are impugned by their own history. This does not speak well for the characters of those concerned or for their reliability as witnesses.

It was Joseph Smith who declared theological war on Christianity when he ascribed to God the statement that branded all Christian sects as "all wrong," their creeds as "abominations," and all Christians as "corrupt . . . having a form of godliness, but they deny the power thereof" (Joseph Smith—History 1:19).

The onus of hostility rests upon the Mormons, and their history of persecution (largely the result of their mouthing of Smith's abusive accusations and their practice of polygamy) may be properly laid at their own doorstep. They were the initial antagonists, *not* the Christian church. We do not excuse those who persecuted the early Mormons, but in a great many instances those who were involved were provoked to action by Mormon excesses. (Note: An example of this would be the Mormon expulsion from Jackson County, Missouri.)

We may safely leave *The Book of Mormon* to the judgment of history and Mormon theology to the pronouncements of God's immutable Word. But we must speak the truth about these things and keep foremost in our minds the fact that the sincerity of the Mormons in their faith is no justification for withholding just criticism of that faith or of its refuted source, *The Book of Mormon* and the "revelations" of Joseph Smith. The truth must be spoken in love, but it must be spoken.

The Theology of Mormonism

The Mormon church almost from its inception has claimed what no other church today claims to possess: the priesthoods of Aaron and Melchizedek.

The Mormons maintain that Joseph Smith and Oliver Cowdery received the Aaronic priesthood from the hand of John the Baptist on May 15, 1829, and that "the Melchizedek Priesthood was conferred upon Joseph Smith and Oliver Cowdery through the ministration of Peter, James, and John, shortly after the conferring of the Aaronic order."[23]

In the theology of Mormonism, both the Melchizedek and Aaronic orders are considered to be but one priesthood "without beginning of days or end of years" (*Doctrine and Covenants*, 84:17), and through the authority of this priesthood alone, they maintain, men speak and act in the name of the Lord for the salvation of humanity. In order that this may be clearly understood, the following quotation from the leading Mormon volume on the subject of the priesthood must be considered:

> This authoritative Priesthood is designed to assist men in all of life's endeavors, both temporal and spiritual. Consequently, there are divisions or offices of the Priesthood, each charged with a definite duty, fitting a special human need.
>
> The prophet Joseph Smith once said that all Priesthood is Melchizedek. That is to say that the Melchizedek Priesthood embraces all offices and authorities in the Priesthood. This is clearly stated in the *Doctrine and Covenants*, Section 107, Verse 5: "All other authorities or offices in the church are appendages to this (i.e., Melchizedek) Priesthood. . . ."
>
> There are two Priesthoods spoken of in the Scriptures, viz., the Melchizedek and the Aaronic or Levitical. Although there are two Priesthoods, yet the Melchizedek Priesthood comprehends the Aaronic or Levitical Priesthood; and is the grand head, and holds the highest authority that pertains to the Priesthood, and the keys of the kingdom of God in all ages of the world to the latest posterity on the earth; and is the channel through which all knowledge, doctrine, the plan of salvation, and every important matter is revealed from heaven.[24]

The Mormon concept of the priesthood holds that God has placed in that church presidents, apostles, high priests, seventies, and elders; and that the various offices all share specific authorities.

The president of the church, they maintain,

> may hold and dispense the powers of the administrative responsibilities of that office, the power of the Priesthood is decentralized: first, according to offices and the jurisdictions of those respective offices; second, according to individual Priesthood-bearers. This means that while the church as a whole is delicately responsive to central authority for church-wide purposes, the central-local relationships in the organization do not restrict the full initiative and free development of either territorial divisions of the Church, individual quorums, groups of quorums, or the member as an individual. . . .
> The Priesthood provides a "functional" instrumentality for church government that is at once efficient and responsible in centralization, but flexible and decentralized in actual administration.[25]

---

[23]John A. Widtsoe, *The Priesthood and Church Government* (Salt Lake City: Deseret Book Company, 1939), 107.
[24]Ibid., 102–103.
[25]Ibid., 103.

It is therefore apparent that in Mormon theology the priesthood occupies a position of great importance and comprehends nearly every male member of the church above the age of twelve in one capacity or another; and therefore by necessity the refutation of the Mormon claims to its possession undercuts the very foundations of Mormonism.[26]

With the foregoing in mind, let us examine the Scriptures that most thoroughly refute the Mormon contentions. The Scripture, indeed, provides a wealth of information.

In the seventh chapter of the epistle to the Hebrews, Melchizedek, who was the king of Salem and priest of the Most High God, is mentioned briefly in connection with Abraham. The author of Hebrews points out that the priesthood of Melchizedek is superior to the Aaronic priesthood and the administrations of the Levites because Abraham, who was the father of the sons of Levi, paid tithe to Melchizedek. This establishes the fact that Melchizedek was superior to Abraham. The writer of Hebrews puts it this way: "And without all contradiction the less is blessed of the better. And here men that die receive tithes; but there he receiveth them, of whom it is witnessed that he liveth. And as I may so say, Levi also, who receiveth tithes, paid tithes in Abraham. For he was yet in the loins of his father, when Melchizedek met him" (7:7–10).

The establishment of the fact that the Melchizedek priesthood is superior to the Aaronic would be virtually meaningless if the writer of Hebrews had not gone on to say:

> If therefore perfection were by the Levitical priesthood (for under it the people received the law), what further need was there that another priest should rise after the order of Melchizedek, and not be called after the order of Aaron? For the priesthood being *changed*, there is made of necessity a change also of the law. (vv. 11–12, emphasis added)

The whole point of the seventh chapter of Hebrews, as any careful exegesis will reveal, is the fact that Jesus Christ, who is "a priest forever after the order of Melchizedek" (v. 17), has by virtue of His sacrifice upon the cross changed the priesthood of Aaron (v. 12), instituting in its place His own priesthood of the Melchizedek order.

Christ was not of the tribe of Levi and not of the priesthood of Aaron; He was of the tribe of Judah, yet His priesthood is infinitely superior to that of Aaron. It is quite evident that the Levitical priesthood could not evolve into the Melchizedek priesthood, but that it passed away as symbolized by the tearing of the veil leading to the Holy of Holies at the crucifixion (Matthew 27:51).

The writer of Hebrews further states that Christ is our great High Priest and that He has "passed through the heavenlies" to "appear in the presence of God for us." In addition to this, it is declared, "Christ is not entered into the holy places made with hands, which are the figures of the true; but into heaven itself. . . . Nor yet that he should offer himself often, as the high priest entereth into the holy place every year with blood of others; for then must he often have

---

[26]Until June 1978, men of African descent were denied the priesthood because of a teaching that they were under a curse for their lack of valiance in their premortal existence. Under this ban they were unable to attain the status of "exaltation" (godhood).

suffered since the foundation of the world: but now once in the end of the world hath he appeared to put away sin by the sacrifice of himself" (Hebrews 9:24–26).

The previous reference is clearly to the truth that the old priesthood, which enabled the priests to enter into the temple apartment once every year on the Day of Atonement, had come to a close because Christ has once offered an eternal atonement for the sins of the whole world (1 John 2:2).

How significant indeed are these facts when placed beside the Mormon claim to possession of the Aaronic priesthood, which God's Word says has been "changed" and completely consummated in the Priest whose order is after Melchizedek, Jesus Christ himself.

Our Lord's priesthood is not dependent upon its continuation from father to son as the Aaronic was through the Levitical order, something necessitated by virtue of the fact that all men die; hence its transference. But the writer of Hebrews tells us that the Lord Jesus Christ "arose after the similitude of Melchizedek." He is "another priest, Who is made, not after the law of carnal commandment [which is temporary by nature], but after the power of an endless life" (Hebrews 7:15–16). The Greek word *akatalutos* is rightly translated "imperishable, indestructible, and indissoluble"; and in this context it refers to His life. He was not consecrated a priest as were the Levites from father to son, but His priesthood is after the order of endless Being. His is an infinite priesthood because He is eternal.

All this background is of vital importance in refuting the Mormon claims to the perpetuity of the Aaronic priesthood, but even more so in refuting their concept of the Melchizedek priesthood, which they also claim to have received.

In the same chapter of Hebrews, a second Mormon claim is tersely dispensed with by the Holy Spirit in an emphatic and irrevocable manner.

> By so much was Jesus made a surety of a better testament. And they truly were many priests, because they were not suffered to continue by reason of death: But this man, because he continueth ever, hath an unchangeable priesthood. Wherefore he is able to save them to the uttermost that come unto God by him, seeing he ever liveth to make intercession for them. For such an high priest became us, who is holy, harmless, undefiled, separate from sinners, and made higher than the heavens; who needeth not daily, as those high priests, to offer up sacrifice, first for his own sins, and then for the people's: for this he did once, when he offered up himself. For the law maketh men high priests which have infirmity; but the word of the oath, which was since the law, maketh the Son, who is consecrated for evermore. (vv. 22–28)

Particular attention should be paid to verse 24, which, in the Greek, is devastating to the Mormon claim. Verse 24, in Greek, literally reads, "But he continues forever, so his priesthood is untransferable"[27] (GOODSPEED).

The Greek word *aparabatos* literally rendered as *untransferable*, carries the note of finality. Thayer's *Greek-English Lexicon* puts it this way:

---

[27]The Mormon claim that Melchizedek conferred his priesthood on Abraham when the latter paid tithe to him (Genesis 18) finds no support in Scripture (John A. Widtsoe, *Priesthood and Church Government*, 109). Mormons should be pressed at this juncture for the biblical evidence, the absence of which affords further opportunity to undercut their already weakened position.

"Priesthood unchangeable and therefore not liable to pass to a successor," Hebrews 7:24 (54).

Since the word appears but once in New Testament Greek, there is not even the appeal to possible contextual renderings. Here is one instance where no amount of semantic juggling can escape the force of the context and grammar.

The writer of Hebrews, under the inspiration of the Holy Spirit, declares that the priesthood of Melchizedek is the peculiar possession of Jesus Christ, not only by virtue of the fact that He is God and possessed of imperishable life, but because it cannot be transferred to another. It consummated the Aaronic priesthood; it terminated the Levitical order; it resides in the Son of God; and by the will of His Father, it cannot be transferred. There is no escape from the force of these revelations of Scripture, and no exegetical theologian or commentator has ever held otherwise. It is all well and good for the Mormons to claim the priesthoods of Aaron and Melchizedek, but it should be pointed out that they do so by contradicting the expressed teaching of the Word of God that they claim to respect.

In his interesting and informative booklet *Gods, Sex, and the Saints* (Rock Island: Augusta Press, 1957), Dr. George Arbaugh makes the following observation:

> The Mormons are advised that the harvest is ripe and that the sickle should be thrust into the Christian churches. The bold proselytizing usually includes certain stereotyped challenges, questions, and arguments. (39)

Dr. Arbaugh then goes on to point out that the priesthood is one of the areas the Mormons emphasize. They never tire of stating to any and all who will listen, particularly to those who are likely proselytes, "You do not have the priesthood!"

To answer this, the alert Christian should point out that the Mormons themselves do not have any priesthood, but that the church of Jesus Christ has always had a priesthood, a priesthood very clearly taught in the New Testament. This priesthood was emphasized by the great Reformation theologian Martin Luther, who described it as "the priesthood of all believers."

Dr. Arbaugh rightly observes,

> There are many millions more priests in the Lutheran Church than in the Latter-day Saint organization, for this reason: that every believer is a priest. There is a universal priesthood of believers. This means that each believer can come to God in prayer, in his own right, and that he can speak about his Lord to his fellowmen. He need not wait for some priest to do the essential Christian things for him. For that matter, how could any priest do the essential Christian thing for you, namely, to love God and your fellowman also?
>
> In the original Mormon Church the only officers were elders, but subsequently many additional offices were established. For this reason *Doctrine and Covenants*, Section 20, verses 65 through 67, was "corrected" from the original form in *The Book of Commandments*. Mormonism even stoops to falsifying its scriptures in order to pretend that there have been the same priestly offices in all ages. (Ibid., 44)

The True Priesthood

In the opening sentences of the book of the Revelation, John the apostle makes an astounding statement when he declares:

> Blessing and peace to you from him who is, and was, and is coming, and from the seven spirits before his throne and from Jesus Christ, the trustworthy witness, the first born of the dead, the sovereign of the kings of the earth. To him who loves us and has released us from our sins by his own blood—he has made us a kingdom of priests for his God and Father—to him be glory and power forever" (1:4–6, GOODSPEED).

How incisive is this plain declaration by apostolic authority. Jesus Christ who is the sovereign of the kings of the earth, the One who continues to love us and who has released us from our sins through His own blood, has also made us "a kingdom of priests for His God and Father." Here is the true priesthood indeed.

The Christian does not need temples, secret services, rituals, and mysteries. His priesthood knows no special offices or power to communicate with the dead—things that the Mormon priesthood most definitely claims. The Christian priesthood embraces all those who have been loosed from their sins by the blood of Jesus Christ, and who enjoy the perpetual love of the Lamb of God, who takes away the sins of the world.

~Communication with the dead is a possibility that many Mormons look forward to. In 1877 Wilford Woodruff expounded on the importance of temple work on behalf of those who are deceased and said, "The dead will be after you, they will seek after you as they have after us in St. George" (*Journal of Discourses,* 19:229). In his book *Life Everlasting* (Salt Lake City: Bookcraft, 967), Mormon author Duane S. Crowther compiled scores of sightings of the dead by Mormon leaders. Joseph Heinerman, in a smaller book, *Temple Manifestations* (Salt Lake City: Magazine Printing and Publishing, 1979), gives numerous examples of visitations from the dead in Mormon temples.~

The authentic Christian priesthood is further developed in the writings of Peter, who affirms,

> You are the chosen race, the *royal priesthood,* the consecrated nation, his own people, so that you may declare the virtues of him who has called you out of darkness into his wonderful light; you who were once no people, but are now God's people; once unpitied, but now pitied indeed. (1 Peter 2: 9–10, GOODSPEED)

In this context, the words of the apostle establish that long before there were any mythological Mormon priesthoods, there was a priesthood embracing all the redeemed, a "royal priesthood," neither of Aaron nor of Melchizedek. This priesthood is composed of all consecrated "ambassadors for Christ," to quote the apostle Paul, whose task it is to exhort men to be "reconciled to God . . . knowing the terror of the Lord" (see 2 Corinthians 5:20, 11).

As has been observed, Mormonism places great stress upon the priesthood. But as we have also seen, it is not the priesthood described in the Scriptures. Instead, they have substituted the revelation of "prophet" Smith concerning a priesthood. Scripture reveals that the Aaronic priesthood has been changed

(Hebrews 7:12), and the Melchizedek priesthood by its nature is "untransferable" (7:24). The resulting dilemma is that Mormons have no priesthood at all, since their denial of the true deity of Jesus Christ and the nature of God rules out the possibility that they could share in the priesthood of all believers. In order for one to be one of the "kings and priests unto God and His Father" (Revelation 1:4–6) and a member of the "royal priesthood" (1 Peter 2:9–10), one must first have undergone personal regeneration in a saving encounter or experience with the God-Man of Scripture—Jesus Christ. Mormon theology with its pantheon of gods, its perverted view of the Virgin Birth, and its outright condemnation of all churches as an "abomination" (Joseph Smith—History 1:19), removes itself from serious consideration as a form of Christianity. There is more to Christianity than the application of the Christian ethic. There is a great deal more to the gospel than the similarity of terms, albeit redefined. Christianity is not merely a system of doctrinal pronouncements (though they are of vast importance). It is a living, vital experience with the God of the Bible as He was incarnate in the man from Nazareth. Mormonism, with its many doctrinal vagaries and outright denials of historic Christian teachings, disqualifies itself. And its priesthood, on which it places so much emphasis, is shown to be the antithesis of the divine revelation.

It is to be earnestly hoped that more Christians will acquaint themselves with the biblical evidence concerning the true priesthood in which we all participate. It is only when a thorough understanding of the fundamentals of Christian theology is obtained that it is possible to successfully encounter and refute the Mormon doctrine of the priesthood.

The Mormon Doctrine of God

It will be conceded by most informed students of Christianity that one cannot deny the existence of the one true God of Scripture and at the same time lay claim to being a Christian. The New Testament writers, as well as our Lord himself, taught that there was but one God, and all church theologians from the earliest days of church history have affirmed that Christianity is monotheistic in the strictest sense of the term. Indeed it was this fact that so radically differentiated it and the parental Judaism from the pagan, polytheistic societies of Rome and Greece. The Bible is particularly adamant in its declaration that God recognizes the existence of no other "deities." In fact, on a number of occasions the Lord summed up His uniqueness in the following revelation:

> Ye are my witnesses, saith the Lord, and my servant whom I have chosen: that ye may know and believe me, and understand that I am he: before me there was no God formed, neither shall there be after me. I, even I, am the Lord; and beside me there is no saviour. . . . Thus saith the Lord the King of Israel, and his redeemer the Lord of hosts; I am the first, and I am the last; and *beside me there is no God.* . . . Ye are even my witnesses. Is there a God beside me? *yea, there is no God; I know not any.* . . . *I* am the Lord, and there is none else, *there is no God beside me:* I girded thee, though thou hast not known me. . . . *There is no God else beside me,* a just God and a Saviour; *there is none beside me.* Look unto me, and be ye saved, all the ends of the earth: *for I am God, and there is none else.* (Isaiah 43:10–11; 44:6, 8; 45:5, 21–22, emphasis added)

Throughout the Old Testament, God is known by many titles. He is Elohim, Jehovah, Adonai, El Gebor, and He is also spoken of by combinations of names, such as Jehovah-Elohim, Jehovah-Sabaoth, etc. If the Hebrew Old Testament tells us anything, it is the fact that there is but one God: "Hear, O Israel: The Lord our God is one Lord" (Deuteronomy 6:4). And Jewish monotheism, as all know, at length gave birth to Christian monotheism, the one developing from the other by progressive revelation from God the Holy Spirit. It is not necessary to belabor the point; it is common knowledge that the facts as they have been stated are true. But as we approach our study of the Mormon concept of God, a subtle yet radical change takes place in the usage of the vocabulary of Scripture as we shall see.

It must also be admitted at the outset that the Bible does designate certain individuals as "gods," such as Satan who is described by Christ as "the prince of this world" and elsewhere in Scripture as "the god of this world." It must be clearly understood, however, that whenever this term is assigned to individuals, to spirit personalities, and the like, metaphorical and contextual usage must be carefully analyzed so that a clear picture emerges. For instance, the Lord declared to Moses: "See, I have made thee a god to Pharaoh: and Aaron thy brother shall be thy prophet" (Exodus 7:1). The Hebrew indicates here, when cross-referenced with Exodus 4:16 ("And he shall be thy spokesman unto the people: and he shall be, even he shall be to thee instead of a mouth, and thou shalt be to him instead of God."), that a definite relationship was involved. The context also reveals that Moses, by virtue of the power invested in him by God, became in the eyes of Pharaoh "a god." Aaron, in turn, became a prophet of the "god" (Moses) that Pharaoh beheld because he was the spokesman for Moses. So metaphorical usage is obviously intended, from the very usage of the language and its contextual analysis. On this point all Old Testament scholars are agreed. But this should never cloud the issue that there is only one true and living God as the previous quotations readily attest.

Another instance of similar usage is the application of the term *Elohim*, the plural usage of the term often translated *God* in the Old Testament. In some contexts the judges of Israel are referred to as "gods," not that they themselves possessed the intrinsic nature of Deity, but that they became in the eyes of the people as gods, or more literally, "mighty ones" (Psalm 82; cf. John 10:34), representing as they did the Lord of Hosts. In the New Testament usage, the apostle Paul is quite explicit when he declares that in the world, i.e., as far as the world is concerned, "(there be gods many, and lords many,) but to us there is but one God, the Father . . . and one Lord Jesus Christ" (1 Corinthians 8:5–6), a statement emphasized by our Lord when He stated, "I am the first and the last: I am He that liveth, and was dead; and, behold, I am alive for evermore" (Revelation 1:17–18). We conclude, then, that polytheism is totally foreign to the Judeo-Christian tradition of theology. In fact, it is the antithesis of the extreme mono-theism portrayed in Judaism and Christianity. The God of the Old Testament and the God and Father of our Lord Jesus Christ are one and the same Person; this the Christian church has always held. In addition to this, God's nature has always been declared to be that of pure spirit. Our Lord declared, "God is spirit, and they that worship Him must worship Him in spirit and in truth" (John 4:24—as correctly translated from the original Greek text). In numerous other places within the pages of the inspired Word of God, the Holy Spirit has been pleased to reveal God's spiritual nature and "oneness." The apostle Paul reminds us that "a mediator is not a mediator of one, but God is one" (Galatians 3:20). The psalmist reminds us of His unchangeable nature, "From everlasting to everlasting, thou art God" (Psalm 90:2); and Moses records in the initial act of creation that "the spirit of God moved upon the face of the waters" (Genesis 1:2). The "gods" mentioned in Scripture, then, are never gods by either identity or nature; they are "gods" by human creation or acclamation as we have seen. This, then, is a far cry from comparison with the one true and living God described by the writer of the epistle to the Hebrews as "the Father of spirits" (Hebrews 12:9; see also Galatians 4:8–9).

~The Mormons misuse John 10:34, "Ye are gods," falsely implying that Jesus endorsed godhood for man. This cannot be true for several reasons. It does not fit the context of John 10:24–36, where Jesus shows His equality with the Father and deservedly is called God. In contrast, the judges (so-called gods) in Psalm 82:6 were so called because of their lofty position over the people, but God rebuked them for their sins, and they were proven to be not gods after all but fallen, sinful men.

How this passage is to support the Mormon position is baffling, because Mormons say they are gods in embryo and they have not yet reached godhood. Whatever they wish John 10:34 to say, it does not support their position. The Mormon can only say he hopes to become a god. Psalm 82 and John 10:34 are in the present tense, a distinction apart from their position.

In fact, upon a reading of Psalm 82, it is a wonder that Mormons would want to identify with the Psalm at all. It says nothing good about these men. But if that is the position they desire, only the judgment of God follows.

Furthermore, the Mormon should be made aware that LDS Apostle James Talmage correctly identified the "gods" of Psalm 82 and John 10:34 as merely judges when he wrote,

> Divinely Appointed Judges Called "gods." In Psalm 82:6, judges invested by divine appointment are called "gods." To this Scripture the Savior referred in His reply to the Jews in Solomon's Porch. Judges so authorized officiated as the representatives of God and are honored by the exalted title "gods" (*Jesus the Christ*, [Salt Lake City: Deseret Book Co., 1948], 501).~

The Truth About the God of the Mormons

In sharp contrast to the revelations of Scripture are the "revelations" of Joseph Smith, Brigham Young, and the succeeding Mormon "prophets." So that the reader will have no difficulty understanding what the true Mormon position is concerning the nature of God, the following quotations derived from popular Mormon sources will convey what the Mormons mean when they speak of "God."

1. "In the beginning, the head of the Gods called a council of the Gods; and they came together and concocted a plan to create the world and people it" (*Teachings of the Prophet Joseph Smith*, 349).

2. "God himself was once as we are now, and is an exalted man" (*Teachings of the Prophet Joseph Smith*, 345).

3. "The Father has a body of flesh and bones as tangible as man's: the Son also; but the Holy Ghost has not a body of flesh and bones, *but is* a personage of Spirit" (*Doctrine and Covenants*, 130:22).

4. "Gods exist, and we had better strive to be prepared to be one with them" (Brigham Young, *Journal of Discourses*, 7:238).

5. "As man is, God once was: as God is, man may become" (Prophet Lorenzo Snow, quoted in Milton R. Hunter, *The Gospel Through the Ages*, 105–106).

6. "Each of these Gods, including Jesus Christ and His Father, being in possession of not merely an organized spirit, but a glorious immortal body of flesh and bones" (Parley P. Pratt, *Key to the Science of Theology*, ed. 1978, 23).

7. "And then the Lord said: Let us go down. And they went down at the beginning, and they, that is the Gods, organized and formed the heavens and the earth" (Abraham 4:1).

8. "Remember that God, our heavenly Father, was perhaps once a child, and mortal like we ourselves, and rose step by step in the scale of progress, in the school of advancement; has moved forward and overcome, until He has arrived at the point where He now is" (Apostle Orson Hyde, *Journal of Discourses*, 1:123).

9. "Mormon prophets have continuously taught the sublime truth that God the Eternal Father was once a mortal man who passed through a school of earth life similar to that through which we are now passing. He became God—an exalted being—through obedience to the same eternal Gospel truths that we are given opportunity today to obey" (Hunter, op. cit., 104).

10. "Christ was the God, the Father of all things. . . . Behold, I am Jesus Christ. I am the Father and the Son" (Mosiah 7:27 and Ether 3:14, *Book of Mormon*).

11. "When our father Adam came into the garden of Eden, he came into it with a celestial body, and brought Eve, one of his wives, with him. He helped to make and organized this world. He is MICHAEL, the Archangel, the ANCIENT OF DAYS! about whom holy men have written and spoken—HE is our FATHER and our GOD, and the only God with whom we have to do"[28] (Brigham Young, in the *Journal of Discourses*, 1:50).

12. Historically this doctrine of Adam-God was hard for even faithful Mormons to believe. As a result, on June 8, 1873, Brigham Young stated, "How much unbelief exists in the minds of the Latter-day Saints in regard to one particular doctrine, which I revealed to them, and which God revealed to me—namely that Adam is our father and God.

> "Well," says one, "Why was Adam called Adam?" He was the first man on the earth, and its framer and maker. He with the help of his brethren brought it into existence. Then he said, "I want my children who are in the spirit world to come and live here. I once dwelt upon an earth something like this, in a mortal state. I was faithful, I received my crown and exaltation" (*Deseret News*, June 18, 1873, 308).

It would be quite possible to continue quoting sources from many volumes and other official Mormon publications, but the fact is well established.

---

[28]It is important to note that Brigham Young taught that he had "never yet preached a sermon and sent it out to the children of men, that they may not call Scripture" (*Journal of Discourses*, 13:95). That includes the Adam-God Doctrine.

The Community of Christ (RLDS), which disagrees with the Utah church on the subject of polytheism, steadfastly maintains that Joseph Smith Jr. never taught or practiced either polygamy or polytheism, but the following direct quotation from Smith, relative to the plurality of gods and the doctrine that Mormon males may attain to godhood, vexes the Community of Christ (RLDS) no end. But, it is fact, nonetheless.

The following quotations are excerpted from a sermon published in the Mormon newspaper *Times and Seasons* (August 15, 1844, 5:613–614) four months after Smith delivered it at the funeral of Elder King Follett, and only two months after Smith's assassination in Carthage, Illinois.

~Tenth LDS President Joseph Fielding Smith notes that the King Follett sermon was given at the April conference of the Church in 1844 and was heard by around twenty thousand people. The argument that Smith was misquoted is discounted by the fact that it was recorded by four scribes: Willard Richards, Wilford Woodruff, William Clayton, and Thomas Bullock. BYU Professor George W. Pace wrote in *The Encyclopedia of Mormonism* that Smith's two-hour-and-fifteen-minute message "may be one of the Prophet's greatest sermons because of its doctrinal teachings" (Daniel H. Ludlow, ed., *The Encyclopedia of Mormonism* [Millan Publishing Co., 1992], 772).~

It is significant that the split in Mormonism did not take place for more than three and a half years. Apparently, their ancestors did not disagree with Smith's theology, as they themselves do today. Nor did they deny that Smith preached the sermon and taught polytheism, as does the Community of Christ (RLDS) today. But the facts must speak for themselves. Here are the abovementioned quotes:

> I want you all to know God, to be familiar with him. . . . What sort of a being was God in the beginning?
>
> First, God himself, who sits enthroned in yonder heavens, is a man like unto one of yourselves . . . if you were to see him today, you would see him in all the person, image and very form as a man. . . .
>
> I am going to tell you how God came to be God. We have imagined that God was God from all eternity. These are incomprehensible ideas to some, but they are the simple and first principles of the gospel, to know for a certainty the character of God, that we may converse with him as one man with another, and that God himself; the Father of us all dwelt on an earth the same as Jesus Christ himself did . . . what did Jesus say? (mark it elder Rigdon) Jesus said, as the Father hath power in himself, even so hath the Son power; to do what? Why what the Father did, that answer is obvious. . . . Here then is eternal life, to know the only wise and true God. You have got to learn how to be Gods yourselves; to be kings and priests to God, the same as all Gods have done before you—namely, by going from a small degree to another, from grace to grace, from exaltation to exaltation, until you are able to sit in glory as doth those who sit enthroned in everlasting power. (Joseph Smith, *Journal of Discourses*, 6:3–4)

Mormon theology is polytheistic, teaching, in effect, that the universe is inhabited by different gods who procreate spirit children, which are in turn clothed with bodies on different planets, "Elohim" being the god of this planet (Brigham's teaching that Adam is our heavenly Father is now officially denied by Mormon authorities, but they hold firm to the belief that their God is a resurrected, glorified man). In addition to this, the "inspired" utterances of Joseph Smith reveal that he began as a Unitarian, progressed to tritheism, and graduated into full-fledged polytheism, in direct contradiction to the revelations of the Old and New Testaments as we have observed. The Mormon doctrine of the trinity is a gross misrepresentation of the biblical position, though they attempt to veil their evil doctrine in semi-orthodox terminology. We have already dealt with this problem, but it bears constant repetition lest the Mormon terminology go unchallenged.

On the surface, they appear to be orthodox, but in the light of unimpeachable Mormon sources, Mormons are clearly evading the issue. The truth of the matter is that Mormonism has never historically accepted the Christian doctrine of the Trinity; in fact, they deny it by completely perverting the meaning of the term. The Mormon doctrine that God the Father is a mere man is the root of their polytheism, and forces Mormons to deny not only the Trinity of God as revealed in Scripture, but the immaterial nature of God as pure spirit. Mormons have gone on record and stated that they accept the doctrine of the Trinity, but, as we have seen, it is *not* the Christian Trinity. God the Father does not have a body of flesh and bones, a fact clearly taught by our Lord (John 4:24; cf. Luke 24:39). Mormon Apostle James Talmage describes the church's teaching, as follows, in his book *The Articles of Faith*:

> The Church of Jesus Christ of Latter-day Saints proclaims against the incomprehensible God, devoid of "body, parts, or passions," as a thing impossible of existence, and asserts its belief in and allegiance to the true and living God of scripture and revelation. . . . Jesus Christ is the Son of Elohim both as spiritual and bodily offspring; that is to say, Elohim is literally the Father of the spirit of Jesus Christ and also of the body in which Jesus Christ performed His mission in the flesh. . . . Jehovah, who is Jesus Christ the Son of Elohim, is called "the Father" . . . that Jesus Christ, whom we also know as Jehovah, was the executive of the Father, Elohim, in the work of creation as set forth in the book *Jesus the Christ*, chapter IV. ([Salt Lake City: The Church of Jesus Christ of Latter-day Saints, 1952], 48, 466–67)

In these revealing statements, Talmage lapses into the error of making Elohim and Jehovah two separate gods, apparently in complete ignorance of the fact that Elohim, "the greater god," and Jehovah—Jesus the lesser god, begotten by Elohim—are compounded in the Hebrew as "Jehovah the Mighty One," or simply "Jehovah God," as any concordance of Hebrew usage in the Old Testament readily reveals (LORD—Yahweh; God—Elohim). This error is akin to that of Mary Baker Eddy, who, in her glossary to *Science and Health With Key to the Scriptures*, made exactly the same error, she too being in complete ignorance of the Hebrew language. In this grammatical error, Christian Science and the Mormons are in unique agreement.

Talmage's argument—"to deny the materiality of God's person is to deny God; for a thing without parts has no whole and an immaterial body cannot exist"—is both logically and theologically an absurdity. To illustrate this, one needs only to point to the angels, whom the Scriptures describe as "ministering spirits" (Hebrews 1:7), beings who have immaterial "bodies" of spiritual substances and yet exist. The Mormons involve themselves further in a hopeless contradition when, in their doctrine of the preexistence of the soul, they are forced to redefine the meaning of soul as used in both the Old and the New Testaments to teach that the soul is not immaterial, while the Bible clearly teaches that it is. Our Lord, on the cross, spoke the words, "Father, into thy hands I commend my spirit" (Luke 23:46). Certainly this was immaterial. And Paul, preparing to depart from this world for the celestial realms, indicated that his real spiritual self (certainly immaterial, since his body died) was yearning to depart and to be with Christ, which is far better (Philippians 1:21–23). The martyr Stephen also committed his spirit (or immaterial nature) into the hands of the Father, crying, "Lord Jesus, receive my spirit" (Acts 7:59). And there are numerous passages in both the Old and New Testaments that indicate an "immaterial nature" can exist, provided that form is of a spiritual substance as is God the Father and the Holy Spirit, and as was Jesus Christ as the preincarnate Logos (John 1:1; cf. John 1:14). Far from asserting their "belief and allegiance to the true and living God of Scripture and revelation," as Talmage represents Mormonism, Mormons indeed have sworn allegiance to a polytheistic pantheon of gods, which they are striving to join, there to enjoy a polygamous eternity of progression toward godhood.

One can search the corridors of pagan mythology and never equal the complex structure that the Mormons have erected and masked under the terminology of orthodox Christianity. That the Mormons reject the historic Christian doctrine of the Trinity no student of the movement can deny, for after quoting the Nicene Creed and early church theology on the Trinity, Talmage, in *The Articles of Faith*, declares,

> It would be difficult to conceive of a greater number of inconsistencies and contradictions expressed in words as here. . . . The immateriality of God as asserted in these declarations of sectarian faith is entirely at variance with the scriptures, and absolutely contradicted by the revelations of God's person and attributes. (p. 48)

After carefully perusing hundreds of volumes on Mormon theology and scores of pamphlets dealing with this subject, the author can quite candidly state that never has he seen such misappropriation of terminology, disregard of context, and utter abandon of scholastic principles demonstrated on the part of non-Christian cultists than is evidenced in the attempts of Mormon theologians to appear orthodox and at the same time undermine the foundations of historic Christianity. The intricacies of their complex system of polytheism cause the careful researcher to ponder again and again the ethical standard that these Mormon writers practice and the blatant attempts to rewrite history, biblical theology, and the laws of scriptural interpretation that they might support the theologies of Joseph Smith and Brigham Young. Without fear of contradiction, I am certain that Mormonism cannot stand investigation and wants no part of it unless the results can be controlled under the guise of "broad-mindedness" and "tolerance."

On one occasion, when the Mormon doctrine of God was under discussion with a young woman leaning in the direction of Mormon conversion, I offered in the presence of witnesses to retract this chapter and one previous effort (*Mormonism*, Zondervan Publishing House, 1958) if the Mormon elders advising this young lady would put in writing that they and their church rejected polytheism for monotheism in the tradition of the Judeo-Christian religion. It was a bona fide offer; the same offer has been made from hundreds of platforms to tens of thousands of people over a twenty-year period. The Church of Jesus Christ of Latter-day Saints is well aware of the offer. To the unwary, however, they imply that they are monotheists, to the informed they defend their polytheism, and like the veritable chameleon, they change color to accommodate the surface upon which they find themselves.

G. B. Arbaugh, in his classic volume *Revelation in Mormonism* (Chicago: University of Chicago, 1932), has documented in exhaustive detail the progress of Mormon theology from Unitarianism to polytheism. His research has been invaluable and available to interested scholars for over sixty years, with the full knowledge of the Mormon Church. In fact, the Mormons are significantly on the defensive where the peculiar origins of the "sacred writings" are involved or when verifiable evidence exists that reveals their polytheistic perversions of the Gospel of Jesus Christ. It is extremely difficult to write kindly of Mormon theology when they are so obviously deceptive in their presentation of data, so adamant in their condemnation of all religions in favor of the "restored gospel" allegedly vouchsafed to the prophet Joseph Smith. We must not, however, confuse the theology with the person, as is too often the case, for while hostility toward the former is scriptural, it is never so with the latter.

Continuing with our study, Apostle Orson Pratt, writing in a Mormon periodical, *The Seer,* declared, "In the Heaven where our spirits were born, there are many Gods, each one of whom has his own wife or wives, which were given to him previous to his redemption, while yet in his mortal state" (37). In this terse sentence, Pratt summed up the whole hierarchy of Mormon polytheism, and quotations previously adduced from a reputable Mormon source support Pratt's summation beyond reasonable doubt. The Mormon teaching that God was seen "face to face" in the Old Testament (Exodus 33:9, 11, 23; Exodus 24:9–11; Isaiah 6:1, 5; Genesis 5:24, etc.) is refuted on two counts, that of language and the science of comparative textual analysis (hermeneutics).

From the standpoint of linguistics, all the references cited by the Mormons to prove "that God has a physical body that could be observed" melt away in the light of God's expressed declaration, "Thou canst not see my face: for there shall no man see me, and live" (Exodus 33:20).

"Face to face" in Exodus 33:11 is rendered "intimate" in the Hebrew, and in no sense is it opposed to verse 20. Similar expressions are utilized in Deuteronomy 5:4, while in Genesis 32:30 it is the Angel of the Lord who speaks, *not* Jehovah himself. The Old Testament is filled with theophanies (literally, God-appearances), instances where God spoke or revealed himself in angelic manifestations, and it is accepted by all Old Testament scholars almost without qualification that anthropomorphisms (ascribing human characteristics to God) are the logical explanation of many of the encounters of God with man. To argue, as the Mormons do, that such occurrences indicate that God has a body of flesh and bone, as "prophet" Smith taught, is on the face of the matter untenable and another strenuous attempt to force polytheism on a rigidly monotheistic religion. Progressing beyond this, another cardinal Mormon point of argument is the fact that because expressions such as "the arm of the Lord," "the eye of the Lord," "the hand of the Lord," "nostrils," "mouth," etc., are used, all tend to show that God possesses a physical form. However, they have overlooked one important factor. This factor is that of literary metaphor, extremely common in Old Testament usage. If the Mormons are to be consistent in their interpretation, they should find great difficulty in the Psalm where God is spoken of as "covering with his feathers," and man "trusting under his wings." If God has eyes, ears, arms, hands, nostrils, mouth, etc., why then does He not have feathers and wings? The Mormons have never given a satisfactory answer to this, because it is obvious that the anthropomorphic and metaphorical usage of terms relative to God are literary devices to convey His concern for and association with man. In like manner, metaphors such as feathers and wings indicate His tender concern for the protection of those who "dwell in the secret place of the Most High and abide under the shadow of the Almighty." The Mormons would do well to comb the Old Testament and the New Testament for the numerous metaphorical usages readily available for observation. In doing so, they would have to admit, if they are at all logically consistent, that Jesus was not a door (John 10:9), a shepherd (John 10:11), a vine (John 15:1), a roadway (John 14:6), a loaf of bread (John 6:51), and other metaphorical expressions any more than "our God is a consuming fire" means that Jehovah should be construed as a blast furnace or a volcanic cone.

The Mormons themselves are apparently unsure of the intricacies of their own polytheistic structure, as revealed in the previously cited references from Joseph Smith, who made Christ both the Father and the Son in one instance, and further on indicated that there was a mystery connected with it and that only the Son could reveal how He was both the Father and the Son. Later, to compound the difficulty, Smith separated them completely into "separate personages," eventually populating the entire universe with his polytheistic and polygamous deities. If one peruses carefully the books of Abraham and Moses as contained in *The Pearl of Great Price* (allegedly "translated" by Smith), as well as sections of Ether in *The Book of Mormon, Doctrine and Covenants,* and *Discourses of Brigham Young,* the entire Mormon dogma of the preexistence of the soul, the polygamous nature of the gods, the brotherhood of Jesus and Lucifer, and the hierarchy of heaven (telestial, terrestrial, and celestial—corresponding to the basement, fiftieth floor, and observation tower of the Empire State Building, respectively), and the doctrines of universal salvation, millennium, resurrection, judgment, and final punishment, will unfold in a panorama climaxing in a polygamous paradise of eternal duration. Such is the Mormon doctrine of God, or, more properly, of the gods, which rivals anything pagan mythology ever produced.

The Holy Spirit in Mormonism

Having discussed the nature and attributes of God in contrast to Mormon mythology and its pantheon of polygamous deities, it remains for us to understand what the Mormon teaching concerning the third person of the Christian Trinity is, since they deign to describe Him as "a personage of spirit."

It is interesting to observe that in their desire to emulate orthodoxy where possible, the Mormons describe the Holy Ghost in the following terms:

> The term Holy Ghost and its common synonyms, Spirit of God, Spirit of the Lord, or simply Spirit, Comforter, and Spirit of Truth occur in the Scriptures with plainly different meanings, referring in some cases to the

person of God the Holy Ghost, and in other instances to the power and authority of this great personage, or to the agency through which He ministers. . . . The Holy Ghost undoubtedly possesses personal powers and affections; these attributes exist in Him in perfection. Thus, He teaches and guides, testifies of the Father and the Son, reproves for sin, speaks, commands, and commissions. . . . These are not figurative expressions but plain statements of the attributes and characteristics of the Holy Ghost. (Talmage, *The Articles of Faith,* 115)

It is interesting to recall that according to Talmage,

It has been said, therefore, that God is everywhere present; but this does not mean that the actual person of any one member of the Godhead can be *physically* present in more than one place at one time. . . . Admitting the personality of God, we are compelled to accept the fact of His materiality; indeed, an "immaterial" being, under which meaningless name some have sought to designate the condition of God, cannot exist, for the very expression is a contradiction in terms. If God possesses a form, that form is of necessity of definite proportions and therefore of limited extension in space. It is impossible for Him to occupy at one time more than one space of such limits. . . . (Ibid., 42–43)

Here exists a contradiction in Mormon theology if ever there was one. Talmage declares that the Holy Spirit is a personage of spirit, obviously "an immaterial being" and obviously God (cf. *Doctrine and Covenants,* 20:28), and yet not possessing a form of material nature; hence, not limited to extension and space, and therefore rendering it possible for Him to occupy at one time more than one space of such limits, in direct contradiction to Talmage's earlier statements in the same volume. For the Mormon, "a thing without parts has no whole and an immaterial body cannot exist" (*Articles of Faith,* 48), and yet the Holy Spirit is a "personage of Spirit," one of the Mormon gods, according to *Doctrine and Covenants.* To cap it all, "He is an immaterial being possessed of a spiritual form and definite proportions"! Mormon theology here appears to have really become confused at the roots, so to speak; but Talmage does not agree with Talmage, nor does *The Doctrine and Covenants;* they are forced into the illogical position of affirming the materiality of God in one instance, and denying that materiality in the next instance where the Holy Spirit is concerned.

Parley P. Pratt, the eminent Mormon theologian, further complicated the doctrine of the Holy Spirit in Mormon theology when he wrote,

This leads to the investigation of that substance called the Holy Spirit or Light of Christ. . . . There is a divine substance, fluid or essence, called Spirit, widely diffused among these eternal elements. . . . This divine element, or Spirit, is immediate, active or controlling agent in all holy miraculous powers. . . . The purest, most refined and subtle of all these substances and the one least understood or even recognized by the less informed among mankind is that substance called the Holy Spirit. (*Key to the Science of Theology,* Liverpool: F. D. Richards, 1855, ed. 1978, 24–25, 64)[29]

---

[29]Some Mormons, quoting early Mormon writers, have attempted to differentiate between the Holy Spirit and the Holy Ghost! (See Widtsoe, *Evidences and Reconciliations* [Bookcraft, 1987 edition], 76). This is linguistically impossible in New Testament Greek, as any Greek lexicon reveals. Both Spirit and Ghost are translated from the same Greek word, *pneuma.*

In the thinking of Pratt, then, the Holy Spirit is a substance, a fluid, and a person, but this is not the teaching of Scripture, which consistently portrays God the Holy Spirit, third person of the Trinity, as an eternal, omnipotent, omnipresent, omniscient Being, sharing all the attributes of Deity, and one with the Father and the Son in unity of substance. Mormons are, to say the least, divided in their theology on the issue, although Talmage bravely attempts to synthesize the mass of conflicting information and "revelations" found within the writings of Smith and Young and the other early Mormon writers. Try as he will, however, Talmage cannot explain the Mormon confusion on the subject, as evidenced by the following facts.

In *Doctrine and Covenants* 20:37, the following statement appears: "All those who humble themselves . . . and truly manifest by their works that they have received of the Spirit of Christ unto the remission of their sins, shall be received by baptism into his church."

Joseph Smith the prophet was the recipient of this alleged revelation, and he is to be believed at all costs; yet the same Joseph Smith translated *The Book of Mormon*, which unreservedly declared: "Yea, blessed are they who shall . . . be baptized, for they shall . . . receive a remission of their sins. . . . Behold, baptism is unto repentance to the fulfilling of the commandments unto the remission of sins" (3 Nephi 12:2; Moroni 8:11).

In one instance, Smith taught that baptism follows the initial act—remission of sins—and in the second instance, the initial act—remission of sins—reverses its position and follows baptism. According to Talmage,

> God grants the gift of the Holy Ghost unto the obedient; and the bestowal of this gift follows faith, repentance, and baptism by water. . . . The apostles of old promised the ministration of the Holy Ghost unto those only who had received baptism by water for the remission of sins. (*The Articles of Faith,* 163)

The question naturally arises: When, then, is the Holy Spirit bestowed? Or indeed, can He be bestowed in Mormon theology when it is not determined whether the remission of sins precedes baptism or follows it? Here again, confusion on the doctrine of the Holy Spirit is evidenced in Mormon thinking.

It would be possible to explore further the Mormon doctrine of the Holy Spirit, especially the interesting chapter in President Charles Penrose's book *Mormon Doctrine Plain and Simple or Leaves From the Tree* (Salt Lake City: G. Q. Canon, 1897), in which he refers to the Holy Spirit as "it" more than twenty times—devoid of personality, although, in the usual polytheistic Mormon scheme, endowed with Deity. Penrose closes his comment by stating,

> As baptism is the birth of water, so confirmation is the birth or baptism of the Spirit. Both are necessary to entrance into the Kingdom of God. . . . The possessor of the Holy Ghost is infinitely rich; those who receive it can lose it, and are of all men the poorest. But there are various degrees of its possession. Many who obtain it walk but measurably in its light. But there are few who live by its whisperings, and approach by its mediumship into close communion with heavenly beings of the highest order. To them its light grows brighter every day. (18–19)

Mormonism, then, for all its complexities and want of conformity to the revelation of God's Word, indeed contradicts the Word of God repeatedly, teaching in place of the God of pure spiritual substance (John 4:24) a flesh-and-bone Deity and a pantheon of gods in infinite stages of progression. For Mormons, God is restricted to a narrow, rationalistic, and materialistic mold. He cannot be incomprehensible, though Scripture indicates that in many ways He most certainly is. "My thoughts are not your thoughts, neither are your ways my ways, saith the Lord. For as the heavens are higher than the earth, so are my ways higher than your ways, and my thoughts than your thoughts" (Isaiah 55:8–9). Mormon theology complicates and confounds the simple declarations of Scripture in order to support the polytheistic pantheon of Joseph Smith and Brigham Young. It is obvious, therefore, that the God of the Bible and the "god" of the Mormons, the "Adam-god" of Brigham Young and the flesh-and-bone deity of Joseph Smith, are not one and the same; by their nature all monotheistic and theistic religions stand in opposition to Mormon polytheism. Christianity in particular repudiates as false and deceptive the multiplicity of Mormon efforts to masquerade as "ministers of righteousness" (2 Corinthians 11:15).

The Virgin Birth of Christ

One of the great doctrines of the Bible, which is uniquely related to the supreme earthly manifestation of the Eternal God, is the doctrine of the Virgin Birth of Jesus Christ. In one very real sense, this doctrine is indissolubly linked with that of the Incarnation, being, so to speak, the agency or instrument whereby God chose to manifest himself. Time and again the Bible reminds us that Deity was clothed with humanity in the manger of Bethlehem, and Christians of all generations have revered the mystery prefigured by the cryptic words of Isaiah the prophet:

> Behold, a virgin shall conceive, and bear a son, and shall call his name Immanuel. . . . For unto us a child is born, unto us a son is given: and the government shall be upon his shoulder: and his name shall be called Wonderful, Counselor, The mighty God, The everlasting Father, The Prince of Peace. (Isaiah 7:14; 9:6)

The apostle Paul refers numerous times to the deity of our Lord, declaring that "In Him dwelleth all the fullness of the Godhead bodily" (Colossians 2:9).

Attempts to minimize the Virgin Birth of Christ or to do away with it altogether, as some liberal theologians have energetically tried to do, have consistently met with disaster. This is true because the simple narratives of this momentous event recorded in Matthew and Luke refuse to surrender to the hindsight reconstruction theories of second-guessing critics.

Some persons have, on the other hand, decided upon a middle course where this doctrine is concerned. They affirm its biological necessity. In a word, Matthew and Luke, who had access to eyewitness testimonies (Mary, Joseph, Elizabeth, etc.), never really believed the teaching as recorded; rather it was a pious attempt to endow Christ with a supernatural conception in order to add glory to His personality. Regardless of how distasteful the unbiblical concepts of liberal and so-called neoorthodox theologians may be concerning the Virgin Birth of our Savior, no group has framed a concept of the Virgin Birth doctrine in the terms employed by the Mormon prophet Brigham Young. ~Mormon doctrine concerning the Virgin Birth of Christ was first delivered in the pronouncements of Brigham Young and has been consistently found in the teachings of all General Authorities throughout their history. It has never been contradicted and consequently represents the doctrine of the Mormon Church.~

Relative to the doctrine of the Virgin Birth of Christ, Brigham Young has unequivocally stated,

> When the Virgin Mary conceived the child Jesus, the Father had begotten him in his own likeness. He was *not* begotten by the Holy Ghost. And who was the Father? He is the first of the human family; and when he took a tabernacle [body], it was begotten by his Father in heaven, after the same manner as the tabernacles of Cain, Abel, and the rest of the sons and daughters of Adam and Eve; from the fruits of the earth, the first earthly tabernacles were originated by the Father, and so on in succession. . . . Jesus, our elder brother, was begotten in the flesh by the same character that was in the garden of Eden, and who is our Father in Heaven. (*Journal of Discourses*, 1:50–51)

Now, in order to understand what "prophet" Young was saying, another of his pronouncements found in the same context should be considered:

> When our father Adam came into the garden of Eden, he came into it with a celestial body, and brought Eve, *one of his wives*, with him. . . . He *is our* FATHER *and our* GOD, *and the only God with whom* WE *have to do.* (Ibid.)

As we have seen in the Mormon doctrine of "God," Mormon theology teaches that polytheism is the divine order. Belief in many gods is the cornerstone of their theology, and polygamous gods they are. Parley P. Pratt, a leading Mormon writer whose books are recommended by Mormon publishing houses as representing their theological views, also writes concerning this doctrine:

> Each of these Gods, including Jesus Christ and his Father, being in possession of not merely an organized spirit but also a glorious immortal body of flesh and bones. . . . (*Key to the Science of Theology*, ed. 1978, 23)

Added to this polytheistic picture are other official Mormon sources, many of whom confirm the sexual conception of Jesus enunciated by Young and many others. Wrote Apostle James Talmage in *The Articles of Faith*:

> His [Christ's] unique status in the flesh as the offspring of a mortal mother [Mary] and of an immortal, or resurrected and glorified, Father [Elohim]. (ed. 1974, 473)

Brigham Young, therefore, taught this unbiblical doctrine of which he spoke openly more than once as the following shows:

> When the time came that His first-born, the Saviour, should come into the world and take a tabernacle (body), the Father came Himself and favoured that spirit with a tabernacle instead of letting any other man do it. (*Journal of Discourses*, 4:218)
>
> The birth of the Saviour was as natural as are the births of our children; it was the result of natural action. He partook of flesh and blood—was begotten of his Father, as we are of our fathers. (*Journal of Discourses*, 8:115)

The base polytheism of Mormonism was never more clearly dissembled than in the foregoing statements, and Young's classification of the Father as a glorified, resurrected "man" cannot be misunderstood. The phrase "any *other* man" rules out the efforts of Mormon apologists to defend Young and unmasks the entire anti-Christian teaching.

We see, then, the Mormon teaching concerning our Lord's birth is a revolting distortion of the biblical revelation and one that is in keeping with the Mormon dogma of a flesh-and-bone god. In Mormon thinking, as reflected in the authoritative declarations of one of their prophets, our Savior was produced, not by a direct act of the Holy Spirit, but by actual sexual relations between "an immortal or resurrected and glorified Father" and Mary—a blasphemous view, which takes its place beside the infamous mythology of Greece, wherein the gods fathered human sons through physical union with certain chosen women.

Brigham Young further declared: "He [Christ] was *not* begotten by the Holy Ghost. . . . Jesus, our elder brother, was begotten in the flesh by the same character that was in the garden of Eden, and who is our Father in Heaven" (*Journal of Discourses*, 1:50–51). There can be no mistaking the fact that the Adam-God doctrine is meant here, no matter how vehemently the Mormon apologists of today may deny that it was ever taught. The language is too clear, the cross-reference easily demonstrable, and the denial of His conception by the Holy Spirit evident for all to see.

Mormon leaders, however, while accepting the doctrine as Young declared it, are extremely careful not to allow "the Gentiles" (all non-Mormons) to understand the full impact of the teaching until they have come under extremely favorable Mormon influences. This is understood by the fact that in Leo Rosten's *A Guide to the Religions of America* (New York: Simon & Schuster, 1963, 131–41), the Mormons employed the subterfuge of semantics to escape declaring this position to the general public.

In Rosten's book, the question was asked, "Do Mormons believe in the Virgin Birth?" (p. 134). To which the Mormon spokesman, a high-ranking member of the Mormon hierarchy, replied, "Yes. The Latter-day Saint accepts the miraculous conception of Jesus the Christ."

Now, it is obvious that if LDS Apostle Richard L. Evans, the Mormon spokesman, had set forth the doctrine of Brigham Young, a doctrine that has been taught by his church and which appears in authoritative publications, even nominal Christians would have been shocked and goaded to some comments, and the one thing the Mormon Church does not desire is adverse publicity. Indeed, they maintain a public relations staff in order to avoid such embarrassments. Mr. Evans resorted to semantic vagaries in an attempt to make his religion appear "orthodox," which it is not.

According to the revelation of the Virgin Birth as recorded within the Scripture, our Lord was conceived by a direct act of God the Holy Spirit, wholly apart from human agency. The Scripture is explicit in declaring that this conception took place while Mary was "espoused to Joseph, *before* they came together." Matthew, therefore, flatly contradicts Brigham Young in no uncertain terms, declaring, "She was found with child by the Holy Spirit" (Matthew 1:18). And the angel Gabriel, who appeared to Joseph to reassure him concerning the divine origin of Christ's conception, reiterated this fact by declaring, "That which is conceived in her is *of* the Holy Ghost" (v. 20). (Emphasis added.)

Luke, the beloved physician, in his narrative of the Virgin Birth, describes the revelation of our Lord's conception in unmistakable terms: "The Holy Ghost shall come upon thee, and the power of the Highest shall overshadow thee: therefore also that holy thing which shall be born of thee shall be called the Son of God" (Luke 1:35).

Some Mormon apologists have attempted to prove from this verse, however, that the phrase "the power of the Highest shall overshadow thee" in fact refers to the Mormon god's impregnation of Mary, thus proving "the truthfulness" of Brigham Young's assertion. But as we shall see from Matthew's account, this is an impossible contention and is unworthy of further refutation.

It is true that many debates have been instigated over the nature of the Virgin Birth of Christ, but the Christian position has always been based upon a literal acceptance of the event as recorded in the first chapters of Matthew and Luke. It might be noted that even liberal and neoorthodox scholars have repudiated the grossly polytheistic and pagan concept enunciated by Brigham Young and handed down through Mormon theology.

We would do well to remember "prophet" Young's denials, "He [Jesus] was not begotten by the Holy Ghost. . . . Jesus, our elder brother, was begotten in the flesh by the same character that was in the garden of Eden, and who is our Father in Heaven," and contrast them with the reliable testimony of the Word of God:

> When as his mother Mary was espoused to Joseph, before they came together, she was found with child of the Holy Ghost. . . . The angel of the Lord appeared unto him in a dream, saying, Joseph, thou son of David, fear not to take unto thee Mary thy wife: for that which is conceived in her is of the Holy Ghost. (Matthew 1:18–20)

The Mormon Church today finds itself, no doubt, in a very difficult position where this errant teaching concerning our Lord's conception is concerned. Some Mormons with whom the author has spoken repudiate vehemently Brigham Young's doctrine of the Virgin Birth, maintaining that he never really taught such a thing; but upon being faced with statements from Young's *Journal of Discourses* and quotations from Mormon periodicals and magazines between the years 1854 and 1878, particularly, they are forced to admit that such was the teaching of their church under Brigham Young. Then, not wanting to appear as though they lack loyalty to President Young, they lapse into silence or reluctantly affirm it.

One Mormon writer and historian, B. H. Roberts, writing in the *Deseret News* (July 23, 1921, Section 4:7), went so far as to deny that the Mormon Church taught the Adam-God doctrine or the doctrine of the Virgin Birth as pronounced by Young. Mr. Roberts wrote, in answer to the charge of the Presbyterian Church, "The Mormon church teaches that Adam is God . . . and that Jesus is his son by natural generation":

> As a matter of fact, the "Mormon" church does not teach that doctrine. A few men in the "Mormon" church have held such views: and several of them quite prominent in the councils of the church. . . . Brigham Young and others *may* have taught that doctrine but *it has never been accepted by the church as her doctrine.*

The unfortunate thing about Mr. Roberts' statement is that (1) he was not empowered to speak for the church, and (2) he is in direct conflict with the teachings of his church on the subject of prophetic authority, not to mention Talmage's *Articles of Faith* previously cited. He also used a carefully qualified term when he said that "Brigham Young and others *may* have taught that doctrine." As we have seen, Brigham Young *did* teach that doctrine; and according to the Mormon faith, Brigham Young was a prophet of God as was Joseph Smith, in the same category as Jeremiah, Ezekiel, or Daniel. So the fact that Brigham taught it—and no General Authority has ever contradicted it—demonstrates that it is the doctrine of the Mormon Church, despite any claims to the contrary. That the Mormon Church accepts as her doctrine the teachings of Joseph Smith and Brigham Young must, we feel, be documented beyond reasonable doubt so that the reader will become familiar with the unfortunate Mormon habit of redefining terms and qualifying statements to elude detection of their true teachings.

The following quotation is taken from *The Latter-day Saints Biographical Encyclopedia,* an official publication of the Mormon Church, and clearly reveals the authority of Brigham Young and his high position in the church. In the light of this statement and numerous others, it is hard to see how his doctrines can be denied by the Mormons.

> In a revelation given through the prophet Joseph Smith, Jan. 19, 1841, the Lord says: "I give unto you my servant, Brigham Young, to be a President over the Twelve traveling council, which Twelve hold the keys to open up the authority of my kingdom upon the four corners of the earth, and after that to send my word to every creature."
>
> The Quorum of the Twelve stands next in authority to the Presidency of the Church, and in the case of the decease of the Prophet, the Twelve preside over the church with their president at the head, and thus was brought to the front Brigham Young, the man whom God designed should succeed the prophet Joseph Smith. . . . When the Twelve were sustained as the presiding authority of the Church, Brigham Young arose to speak, and in the presence of the multitude was transfigured by the spirit and power of God, so that his form, size, countenance and voice appeared as those of the martyred Prophet. Even non-members were struck with amazement and expected to see and hear the departed Seer.
>
> From that moment doubt and uncertainty were banished from the hearts of the faithful and they were fully assured that the mantle of Joseph Smith had fallen upon Brigham Young. After the martyrdom of Joseph and Hyrum, persecution did not cease; the Prophets were slain but truth did not die. The man who stood at the earthly head was taken away, but the authority which he held had been conferred upon others. . . . During his administration of thirty years as President of the church, he made frequent tours, accompanied by his associates in the Priesthood. . . . Though he did not utter so many distinct prophecies, he builded faithfully upon the foundation laid through the Prophet Joseph Smith, and all his movements and counsels were prophetic, as fully demonstrated by subsequent events. He was a Prophet, statesman, pioneer, and colonizer. (Andrew Jenson, ed., *Latter-day Saints Biographical Encyclopedia* [Salt Lake City: A. Jenson, 1936,] 1:8)

Supplementing this detailed account of Brigham Young's authority and position as a source of doctrinal reliability, the reader will find innumerable statements concerning the government of the Mormon Church in their circulated literature, all of which indicate that every succeeding first president of the church wears the "prophetic mantle" of Joseph Smith and Brigham Young; they too are considered prophets of God as were Joseph and Brigham.

When all the facts are considered, two things emerge from the mass of evidence available, which no Mormon writer has yet attempted to explain away—that is, the fact that the Mormon Church teaches the absolute authority of its prophetic office and that Brigham Young is regarded as *second* greatest in lineage. When one reads, therefore, Young's statements concerning the nature of God and the Virgin Birth of our Lord in particular, and duly notes the circuitous tactics of the Mormons and their pointed lack of official denial where the teachings of Young and other prominent Mormons are involved, there is very little left to the imagination as to their true teachings. The Christian who reverences the revelation God has given concerning the nature of His Son's birth cannot find fellowship with the Mormons who subscribe to the teachings of their prophet. Henceforth, when Mormons speak of "the miraculous conception of Jesus the Christ," let it be well remembered what they mean by these terms, for in no way can it be equated with the teaching of the New Testament wherein God has so effectively spoken: "That which is conceived in her is of the Holy Ghost" (Matthew 1:20).

~The blasphemous Mormon concept of Jesus' entrance into this world through a sexual union between Father God (an exalted man) and the Virgin Mary is reduced to sireship like that of the lower animal kingdom. Apostle James Talmage referred to the act as "celestial sireship" (*Jesus the Christ*, 81), and prophet Ezra Taft Benson said, "The Church of Jesus Christ of Latter-day Saints proclaims that Jesus Christ is the Son of God in the most literal sense. The body in which He performed His mission in the flesh was sired by that same Holy Being we worship as God, our Eternal Father" (*Teachings of Ezra Taft Benson,* [Salt Lake City: Bookcraft, 1988], 7).~

Salvation and Judgment in Mormonism

Personal salvation in Mormonism is one of the doctrines most heavily emphasized, and since Christianity is the Gospel or "Good News" of God's redemption in Christ, it is inevitable that the two should come into conflict.

The Mormon doctrine of salvation involves not only faith in Christ, but baptism by immersion, obedience to the teaching of the Mormon Church, good works, and "keeping the commandments of God (which) will cleanse away the stain of sin" (*Journal of Discourses,* 2:4). Apparently Young was ignorant of the biblical pronouncement that "without shedding of blood there is no remission [of sin]" (Hebrews 9:22).

The Mormon teaching concerning salvation is, therefore, quite the opposite of the New Testament revelation of justification by faith and redemption solely by grace through faith in Christ (Ephesians 2:8–10).

Brigham Young, an authoritative Mormon source by any standard, was quite opposed to the Christian doctrine of salvation, which teaches that a person may at any time sincerely repent of his sins, even at the eleventh hour, and receive forgiveness and eternal life. Wrote Young:

> Some of our old traditions teach us that a man guilty of atrocious and

murderous acts may savingly repent on the scaffold; and upon his execution will hear the expression "Bless God! he has gone to heaven, to be crowned in glory, through the all-redeeming merits of Christ the Lord!" This is all nonsense. Such a character will never see heaven. (*Journal of Discourses*, 8:61)

However, Jesus addressed the thief on the cross who had repented of his sins at the last moment, so to speak, crying, "Lord, remember me when thou comest into thy kingdom" (Luke 23:42). The answer of our Savior was unequivocal: "Today shalt thou be with me in paradise" (Luke 23:43).

~Mormon teaching skirts these verses by claiming that "paradise" is the spirit prison where the dead go to hear the Mormon "gospel" preached. On page 309 of *Teachings of the Prophet Joseph Smith*, Joseph Smith claimed Luke 23:43 should read, "This day thou shalt be with me in the world of spirits." It should be noted, however, that Smith does not give this rendering in his *Joseph Smith Translation* of the Bible (JST). In the JST it reads the same as the King James Version (in the JST it is verse 44, not 43).

The parable of the laborer (Matthew 20:1–16) presents Christ's teaching that God agrees to give to all who will serve Him the same inheritance, i.e., eternal life.~ Brigham Young would most likely have been numbered among the voices that "murmured against the goodman of the house, saying, 'These last have wrought but one hour, and thou hast made them equal unto us, which have borne the burden and the heat of the day' " (vv. 11–12).

The answer of the Lord is, however, crystal clear: "Friend, I do thee no wrong: didst not thou agree with me for a penny? Take that thine is, and go thy way: I will give unto this last, even as unto thee. Is it not lawful for me to do what I will with mine own? Is thine eye evil, because I am good?" (vv. 13–15).

Our Lord was obviously teaching, to use a modern illustration, that the "base pay" given to all laborers in the kingdom is the same; namely, eternal redemption. But the rewards are different for length and content of the services rendered, so whoever comes to Christ for salvation receives it, whether at the first hour or the eleventh hour. The "gift of God," the Scripture tells us, is "eternal life," and although rewards for services may be earned as the believer surrenders himself to the power of the Holy Spirit and bears fruit for the Lord, God is no respecter of persons. His salvation is equally dispensed without favor to all who will come.

According to the Mormon scheme of salvation, the gods who created this earth actually planned that Adam, who was to become ruler of this domain, and his wife, Eve, were foreordained to sin so that the race of man that now inhabits this earth might come into being and eventually reach godhood. The fall in the Garden of Eden was necessary for procreation to take place. According to 2 Nephi 2:25 in *The Book of Mormon*, "Adam fell that men might be; and men are, that they might have joy."

Since Mormons believe in the preexistence of the human soul, it is part of their theology that these preexistent souls must take human forms, since it is necessary, in order to enjoy both power and joy, that bodies be provided. This was the early Mormon justification for polygamy, which accelerated the creation of bodies for these preexistent offspring of Joseph Smith's galaxy of gods. A careful reading of *The Book of Abraham* will reveal that life on this earth was designed by the gods to discipline their spirit children and at the same time provide them with the opportunities to reproduce and eventually inherit godhood and individual kingdoms of their personal possessions.

According to Mormon revelation, the site for the conception of these plans was near the great star Kolob, and it will come as no surprise to students of Mormonism to learn that Lucifer, who was a spirit brother of Jesus prior to His incarnation, fell from heaven because of his jealousy of Christ. Christ was appointed by the gods to become the Redeemer of the race that would fall as a result of Adam's sin, and it was this office to which Lucifer aspired, hence his antipathy (*Journal of Discourses*, 13:282).

Lucifer is even quoted as saying, "Behold, here am I, send me, I will be thy son, and I will redeem all mankind, that one soul shall not be lost, and surely I will do it; wherefore give me thine honor"[30]

The *Book of Moses* also records the fact that Cain, the first murderer, was the progenitor of the Negro race, his black skin being the result of a curse by God. On this basis the Mormons avoided and ignored blacks for years in their missionary work, believing that preexistent souls that were considered less than valiant in the "war in heaven" between Christ and Satan were punished by being assigned to black bodies during their mortality. Until 1978 they were denied all of the "blessings" and "privileges" of the priesthood, but a revelation of convenience gave them full access to these glories and neatly removed the last major obstacle to the Mormon "evangelization" of Africa and the rest of the free world.

The Indians, who are supposedly the descendants of *The Book of Mormon's* wicked Lamanites, have allegedly been cursed by the Mormon deity with dark skin as a punishment for the misdeeds of their forefathers. Mormonism, then, is clearly a religion with a shameful history of white supremacist doctrines and practices.

These and many other interesting factors comprise the background of the Mormon doctrine of salvation, but it is also important to understand the Mormons' teaching concerning their redeemer, one of the main areas of their controversy with historic Christianity.

The Mormon Savior

The record of the Bible concerning the Savior of the world, the Lord Jesus Christ, is well known to students of the Scriptures. In Christian theology, there is but one God (Deuteronomy 6:4; 1 Corinthians 8:4–6), and Jesus Christ is His eternal Word made flesh (John 1:1; 1:14). It was the function of the second person of the Trinity, upon His reception by the sons of men, to empower them to be the sons of God (John 1:12); and this, the Scripture teaches, came about as a result of God's unmerited favor and His great love toward a lost race.

The Lord Jesus offered one eternal sacrifice for all sins, and His salvation comes not by the works of the law or any human works whatever, but solely by grace through faith (Galatians 2:16; Ephesians 2:8–9). The Savior of the New Testament revelation existed eternally as God; lived a holy, harmless, and undefiled life, separate from sinners; and "knew no sin." He was "a man of sorrows,

---

[30]Chapter 4 of The *Book of Moses*, found in *The Pearl of Great Price*, catalogs all of these events, including the fall of Satan and the establishment of the Garden of Eden, chapter 6, which Joseph Smith elsewhere "revealed" was actually located in Missouri and not the Mesopotamian area.

and acquainted with grief" (Isaiah 53:3), "the Lamb of God, which taketh away the sin of the world" (John 1:29).

The Savior of Mormonism, however, is an entirely different person, as their official publications clearly reveal. The Mormon "Savior" is not the second person of the Christian Trinity, since, as we have previously seen, Mormons reject the Christian doctrine of the Trinity, and he is not even a careful replica of the New Testament Redeemer. In Mormon theology, Christ as a preexistent spirit was not only the spirit brother of the devil (as alluded to in *The Pearl of Great Price*, Moses 4:1–4, and later reaffirmed by Brigham Young in the *Journal of Discourses*, 13:282), but celebrated his own marriage to "Mary and Martha, and the other Mary," at Cana of Galilee, "whereby he could see his seed, before he was crucified" (Apostle Orson Hyde, *Journal of Discourses*, 4:259; 2:82). As we have seen previously, the Mormon concept of the Virgin Birth alone distinguishes their "Christ" from the Christ of the Bible.

In addition to this revolting concept, Brigham Young categorically stated that the sacrifice made upon the cross by Jesus Christ in the form of His own blood was ineffective for the cleansing of *some* sins. Brigham went on to teach the now suppressed but never officially repudiated doctrine of "blood atonement."

To better understand Young's limitation of the cleansing power of Christ's blood, we refer to his own words:

> Suppose you found your brother in bed with your wife, and you put a javelin through both of them, you would be justified, and they would atone for their sins, and be received into the kingdom of God. I would at once do so in such a case; and under such circumstances, I have no wife whom I love so well that I would not put a javelin through her heart, and I would do it with clean hands.
>
> There is not a man or woman, who violates the covenants made with their God, that will not be required to pay the debt. The blood of Christ will never wipe that out, your own blood must atone for it; and the judgments of the Almighty will come, sooner or later, and every man and woman will have to atone for breaking their covenants. . . . All mankind love themselves, and let these principles be known by an individual, and he would be glad to have his blood shed. . . . I could refer you to plenty of instances where men have been righteously slain, in order to atone for their sins. . . . This is loving our neighbor as ourselves; if he needs help, help him; and if he wants salvation and it is necessary to spill his blood on the earth in order that he may be saved, spill it. (*Journal of Discourses*, 3:247; 4:219–220)

So clear-cut was Brigham's denial of the all-sufficiency and efficiency of the atoning sacrifice of Christ in the foregoing quotation that Mormons have had to develop an argument "to explain" what the prophet really meant. It is their contention that a criminal is "executed to atone for his crimes and this is all Brigham Young meant."

However, they completely omit any discussion of the fact that Young's statement is not dealing with this subject at all. Young's statement declared that what Christ's blood could *not* cleanse, a man's own blood atonement could. This teaches that in some instances human sacrifice, which Brigham states took place and which he sanctioned, was efficacious where Christ's blood was not.

The Mormons want no part of the biblical doctrine of the all-sufficiency of

Christ's atonement, in the words of John: "The blood of Jesus Christ his Son cleanses us from *all* sin" (1 John 1:7, emphasis added). This both contradicts Young and reveals the true biblical teaching.

There can be no doubt from the biblical record that it is in Jesus Christ that we have redemption and that His blood is the means of the cleansing of the conscience (Hebrews 9:14) and of the loosening from sin (Revelation 1:5). It is the very basis of our justification (Romans 5:9).

The Christ of the Mormons cannot save, for He is, as the apostle Paul describes him, "another Jesus," the subject of "another gospel," and the originator of a "different spirit," whose forerunner (the angelic messenger Moroni) was anticipated by the apostle (Galatians 1:8–9), and who along with the entire revelation is to be considered "anathema" or, more literally from the Greek, "cursed" by God.

It may be difficult for some to grasp what is, in fact, an incredible concept, but Mormonism fits perfectly into the descriptions given by the Word of God. The greatest of the apostles, in his second letter to the Corinthian church, after mentioning a counterfeit Jesus, gospel, and spirit, goes on to state that such occurrences should not come as a surprise to the Christian church.

"For such are false apostles, deceitful workmen, transforming themselves into apostles of Christ, and it is not surprising, for Satan himself transforms himself into an angel of light. It is therefore no great marvel if his servants also transform themselves as servants of righteousness whose end will be according to their works" (2 Corinthians 11:13–15, from the Greek).

This is harsh language, indeed, but it is the language of God's choosing and it cannot be ignored by anyone who takes seriously the revelations of Scripture and apostolic authority.

Mormonism, with its apostles, priesthood, temples, secret signs, symbols, handshakes, and mysteries, claims to be "the church of the restoration"; but at its heart, in its doctrine of the Messiah, it is found to be contrary to every major biblical pronouncement.

Salvation by Grace?

It is common to find in Mormon literature the statement: "All men are saved by grace alone without any act on their part." Although this appears to be perfectly orthodox, it is necessary to study *all* the Mormon statements relative to this doctrine in order to know precisely what is meant.

In one such official Mormon publication (*What the Mormons Think of Christ*, Bruce R. McConkie, [Salt Lake City: Bookcraft,] 1973), the Mormons give their own interpretation:

> Grace is simply the mercy, the love and the condescension God has for his children, as a result of which he has ordained the plan of salvation so that they may have power to progress and become like him. . . . All men are saved by grace alone without any act on their part, meaning that they are resurrected and become immortal because of the atoning sacrifice of Christ. . . . In addition to this redemption from death, all men, by the grace of God, have the power to gain eternal life. This is called salvation by grace coupled with obedience to the laws and ordinances of the gospel. Hence

Nephi was led to write: "We labor diligently to write, to persuade our children, and also our brethren, to believe in Christ, and to be reconciled to God; for we know that it is by grace that we are saved *after all we can do.*"

Christians speak often of the blood of Christ and its cleansing power. Much that is believed and taught on this subject, however, is such utter nonsense and so palpably false that to believe it is to lose one's salvation. Many go so far, for instance, as to pretend and, at least, to believe that if we confess Christ with our lips and avow that we accept Him as our personal Saviour, we are thereby saved. His blood, without other act than mere belief, they say, makes us clean. . . . Finally in our day, he has said plainly: "My blood shall not cleanse them if they hear me not." Salvation in the kingdom of God is available because of the atoning blood of Christ. But it is received only on condition of faith, repentance, baptism, and *enduring to the end in keeping the commandments of God.* (27–33, emphasis added)

The above quote is a typical example of what might be termed theological double-talk, which in one breath affirms grace as a saving principle and in the next declares that it is "coupled with obedience to the laws and ordinances of the gospel," and ends by declaring that confession of Christ and acceptance of Him as "personal Saviour" is "utter nonsense" and "palpably false." McConkie decries the fact that Christ's blood "without other act than mere belief . . . makes us clean" (Ibid., 31).

The biblical position is, however, quite clear in this area; we are saved by grace alone, as previously mentioned, but it in no way enables us to "have power to progress and become like him." As we have seen, in the Mormon sense such a progression refers to becoming a god, not to the Christian doctrine of sanctification, or of the life of the believer being brought into conformity to the Holy Spirit as clearly enunciated in the epistle to the Romans (chapters 8 and 12).

Mr. McConkie's assertion—that "salvation by grace" must be "coupled with obedience to the laws and ordinances of the gospel" in order for a person to be saved—introduces immediately the whole Mormon collection of legalistic observances and requirements. In the end, salvation is not by grace at all, but it is in reality connected with human efforts: "baptism, and enduring to the end in keeping the commandments of God" (33).

This is not the Christian doctrine of redemption that the apostle Peter described graphically when he wrote:

> Forasmuch as ye know that ye were not redeemed with corruptible things, as silver and gold, from your vain conversation received by tradition from your fathers; but with the precious blood of Christ, as of a lamb without blemish and without spot. . . . Being born again, not of corruptible seed, but of incorruptible, by the word of God, which liveth and abideth for ever (1 Peter 1:18–19, 23).

In diametric opposition to the Mormon concept, the confession of Christ with the lips and the acceptance of Him as "our personal Savior" is indeed the very means of personal salvation. It is the biblical record, which states that "with the heart man believeth unto righteousness; and with the mouth confession is made unto salvation" (Romans 10:10). The gospel's command is "believe on the Lord Jesus Christ, and thou shalt be saved" (Acts 16:31). This is, of course, totally foreign to what the Mormons would have us believe. Jesus Christ did not die merely to ensure our resurrection, as Mr. McConkie declares (p. 27), but He died to reconcile us to God, to save us by grace, to redeem us by His blood, and to sanctify us by His Spirit. But such biblical doctrines the Mormons most decidedly reject. It appears that they cannot conceive of a God who could save apart from human effort, and Nephi's statement betrays this: "For we know it is by grace that we are saved *after all we can do*" (28).

In Mormonism, it is the individual who must strive for perfection, sanctification, and godhood. Grace is merely incidental.

It was no less an authority than Brigham Young who taught concerning salvation: "But as many as received Him, to them gave he power to *continue* to be the sons of God" (*Journal of Discourses,* 12:100–101).

In Brigham's theology, "instead of receiving the gospel to become the sons of God, my language would be—to receive the gospel that we may continue to be the sons of God. Are we not all sons of God when we are born into this world? Old Pharaoh, King of Egypt, was just as much a son of God as Moses and Aaron were His sons, with this difference—he rejected the word of the Lord, the true light, and they received it."

In agreement with their doctrine of the preexistence of souls, the Mormons believe that they are already the sons of God and that the acceptance of God merely enables them to "continue to be the sons of God," a direct contradiction of the biblical record, which states:

"But as many as received him, to them gave he power to become the sons of God, even to them that believe on his name" (John 1:12).

The apostle Paul points out, with devastating force, the fact that "they which are the children of the flesh, these are *not* the children of God: but the children of the promise are counted for the seed" (Romans 9:8, emphasis added).

The apostle, with equal certainty, affirms that only those who are led by God's Spirit can be called the sons of God (Romans 8:14). It is difficult to see how in any sense of the term, "Old Pharaoh, King of Egypt, was just as much a son of God as Moses and Aaron were His sons," as Brigham Young declared.

The biblical teaching is that "ye are all the children of God *by faith* in Christ Jesus" (Galatians 3:26, emphasis added), a fact Young obviously overlooked.

It is one of the great truths of the Word of God that salvation is not of him that wills or of him that strives, but of God who shows mercy (Romans 9:16), and that Jesus Christ has redeemed us from the curse of the law, having become a curse for us (Galatians 3:13).

It was the teaching of our Lord that "all that the Father giveth me shall come to me; and him that cometh to me I will in no wise cast out" (John 6:37), and the salvation that He still offers to lost men is "not by works of righteousness which we have done, but according to his mercy he saved us" (Titus 3:5).

In the Mormon religion, they boldly teach universal salvation, for as Mr. Evans, the Mormon apostle and spokesman, put it: "Mormons believe in universal salvation that all men will be saved, but each one in his own order" (*Rosten,* 136).

It is the teaching of the Scriptures, however, that not all men will be saved, and that at the end of the ages some shall "go away into everlasting punishment: but the righteous into life eternal" (Matthew 25:46).

The somber warnings of the apostle John stand arrayed against the Mormon doctrine of universal salvation:

> And I saw the beast, and the kings of the earth, and their armies, gathered together to make war against him that sat on the horse, and against his army. And the beast was taken, and with him the false prophet that wrought miracles before him, with which he deceived them that had received the mark of the beast, and them that worshipped his image. These both were cast alive into a lake of fire burning with brimstone. . . . And the devil that deceived them was cast into the lake of fire and brimstone, where the beast and the false prophet are, and shall be tormented day and night for ever and ever. . . . And whosoever was not found written in the book of life was cast into the lake of fire. . . . But the fearful, and unbelieving, and the abominable, and murderers, and whoremongers, and sorcerers, and idolaters, and all liars, shall have their part in the lake which burneth with fire and brimstone: which is the second death. . . . The same shall drink of the wine of the wrath of God, which is poured out without mixture into the cup of his indignation; and he shall be tormented with fire and brimstone in the presence of the holy angels, and in the presence of the Lamb: And the smoke of their torment ascendeth up for ever and ever: and they have no rest day nor night, who worship the beast and his image, and whosoever receiveth the mark of his name. (Revelation 19:19–20; 20:10, 15; 21:8; 14:10–11)

By no conceivable stretch of the imagination is universal salvation to be found in these passages where the Greek words in their strongest form indicate torment, judgment, and eternal fire that defy human chemical analysis.

The Mormon doctrine of "celestial marriage" derived from their original concept of polygamy and substituted for it in 1890, when they were forced to abandon this immoral conduct lest Utah not be given statehood, is tied to their doctrine of salvation. The Mormons believe that the family unit will endure unto the eternal ages, hence their insistence upon the sealing of Mormon men to many women, and the sealing of their families. It was for this reason that there are many special rites and ceremonies instituted on behalf of the dead (particularly relatives); hence, their practice of baptism for the dead and laying on of hands (for the bestowing of the gift of the Holy Ghost), all by proxy.

Mormon Eschatology

Believing as they do in the literal second advent of Christ, the Mormons teach that at His return the Jews will have been gathered to Palestine, the Mormons will be miraculously gathered together in Missouri, and the judgment of the Lord will be poured out upon the earth everywhere except on old and new Jerusalem. (See *Doctrine and Covenants*, 29:9–11.)

The Mormons also have something in common with the cult of Anglo-Israel, believing as well in the restoration of the ten lost tribes. The difference is that the Anglo-Israelites believe that the ten lost tribes are the English people, whereas the Mormons believe the ten lost tribes are somewhere in what Mormons call the "north country." ~In the words of Mormon Apostle Bruce McConkie, "In due course the one who holds the keys shall direct the return of the ten tribes from the land of the north. With 'their rich treasures' they shall come to their American Zion to 'be crowned with glory' by 'the children of Ephraim,' who already have assembled at the Lord's house in the tops of the mountain" (*Doctrinal New Testament Commentary,* 2:26). *Doctrine and Covenants,* 110:11, states that Joseph Smith and Oliver Cowdery were given those keys by which to lead them.~

Mormons also believe in the bodily resurrection of all men and in salvation in a threefold heaven. In Mormon theology, there are three heavens: the telestial, the terrestrial, and the celestial. ~McConkie states that "most adults" will go to the telestial kingdom and that it is composed of "the endless hosts of people of all ages who have lived after the manner of the world; who have been carnal, sensual, and devilish; who have chosen the vain philosophies of the world rather than accept the testimony of Jesus; who have been liars and thieves, sorcerers and adulterers, blasphemers and murders" (*Mormon Doctrine,* 1966, 778).~ The second kingdom (the terrestrial) will be inhabited by Christians who did not accept the Mormon message, Mormons who did not live up to their church's requirements, and men of good will of other religions who rejected the revelations of the Latter-day Saints (*Mormon Doctrine,* 1966, 784). The highest, or celestial, heaven is itself divided into three levels. Only in this highest level is godhood or the possession of a kingdom for one's self and one's family to be gained. This particular estate has as its prerequisite the candidate's having been sealed by celestial marriage in a Mormon temple while upon the earth. Even in the celestial kingdom godhood is by slow progression, and in the end each who becomes a god will, with his family, rule and populate a separate planet of his own.

It is almost superfluous to comment that this entire scheme of the consummation of Mormon salvation is the antithesis of the biblical revelation, which knows nothing of godhood, either constituted or progressive, and which teaches instead that in heaven the destiny of the redeemed will be the special providence of God himself, which "eye hath not seen, nor ear heard," and which "neither have entered into the mind of men" for these are "the things which God hath prepared for them that love Him" (1 Corinthians 2:9). God has revealed many of these things to us by His Spirit; but as Paul so eloquently puts it, we "see through a glass, darkly; but *then* face to face" (1 Corinthians 13:12, emphasis added).

Let us understand clearly, then, that salvation, in the biblical sense, comes as the free gift of God by grace alone through faith in the vicarious sacrifice of Christ upon the cross. The Lord Jesus Christ said, "He that hears my word and believes Him that sent me *has* eternal life, and shall never come into judgment; but has passed out of death into life" (John 5:24, emphasis mine, from the Greek).

The command of the Gospel to all men everywhere is to repent. "Because [God] hath appointed a day, in which he will judge the world in righteousness by that man whom he hath ordained; whereof he hath given assurance unto all men, in that he hath raised him from the dead" (Acts 17:31).

The Scriptures disagree with the Mormons in their insistence upon good works as a *means* of salvation. The book of James clearly teaches (chapter 2) that good works are the *outgrowth* of salvation and justify us before men, proving that we have the faith that justifies us before God (Romans 4 and 5).

No Mormon can today claim that he *has* eternal life in Christ. This is the very power of the gospel, which is entrusted to Christ's church (Romans 1:16–17). Let us, therefore, use it in an attempt to bring them to redemptive knowledge of the true Christ of Scripture and the costly salvation He purchased for us with His own blood.

John, the beloved apostle, has summed it up:

> If we receive the witness of men, the witness of God is greater: for this is the witness of God which he hath testified of his Son. He that believeth on the Son of God hath the witness in himself: he that believeth not God hath made him a liar; because he believeth not the record that God gave of his Son. And this is the record, that God hath given to us eternal life, and this life is in his Son. He that hath the Son hath life; and he that hath not the Son of God hath not life. These things have I written unto you that believe on the name of the Son of God; that ye may know that ye have eternal life, and that ye may believe on the name of the Son of God. And this is the confidence that we have in him, that, if we ask any thing according to his will, he heareth us: And if we know that he hear us, whatsoever we ask, we know that we have the petitions that we desired of him. . . . And we know that we are of God, and the whole world lieth in wickedness. And we know that the Son of God is come, and hath given us an understanding, that we may know him that is true, and we are in him that is true, even in his Son Jesus Christ. This is the true God, and eternal life. (1 John 5:9–15, 19–20)

Let us follow in His train, "for the hour is coming in which no one can work," and the Mormons, too, are souls for whom Christ died.

We have seen in the preceding pages how the Mormon religion utilizes biblical terms and phrases and even adopts Christian doctrines in order to claim allegiance to the Christian faith. Mormons have also come to lay much stress upon public relations and take pains to make certain that they do not use language that might reveal the true nature of their theological deviations. We have also seen that the Mormon Church considers itself alone the true church of Christ in our age, and further that they consider all other groups to be Gentiles and apostates from the true Christian religion.

We further read the words of Joseph Smith himself, whom all Mormons are bound to recognize as the prophet of God, equal if not superior to any of the Old Testament prophets.

Wrote "prophet" Smith concerning an alleged interview with the deity:

> My object in going to inquire of the Lord which of all the sects was right, that I might know which to join. No sooner, therefore, did I get possession of myself, so as to be able to speak, than I asked the Personages who stood above me in the light, which of all the sects was right and which I should join.
>
> I was answered that I must join none of them, for they were all wrong, and the Personage who addressed me said that all their creeds were an abomination in His sight; that those professors were all corrupt; that: "they draw near to me with their lips, but their hearts are far from me, they teach for doctrines the commandments of men, having a form of godliness, but they deny the power thereof."
>
> He again forbade me to join any of them; and many other things did he say unto me, which I cannot write at this time."[31]

---

[31]Joseph Smith, *History*, 1:18–20.

In addition to this statement of Smith's, Twelfth Mormon Prophet Spencer W. Kimball gave the following comment:

> Latter-day Saints are true Christians. We cannot understand how anyone could question our being Christians. . . . We are the true followers of Jesus Christ; and we hope the world will finally come to the conclusion that we are Christians, if there are any in the world" (*Teachings of Spencer W. Kimball* [Salt Lake City: Bookcraft, 1982], 434).

From these facts it is evident for all to see that Mormonism strives with great effort to masquerade as the Christian church complete with an exclusive message, infallible prophets, and higher revelations for a new dispensation that the Mormons would have us believe began with Joseph Smith Jr.

But it is the verdict of both history and biblical theology that Joseph Smith's religion is a polytheistic nightmare of garbled doctrines draped with the garment of Christian terminology. This fact, if nothing else, brands it as a non-Christian cult system.

Those who would consider Mormonism would be greatly profited by a thoughtful consideration of the facts and evidence previously discussed, lest they be misled into the spiritual maze that is Mormonism.

Recommended Resources

1. Berean Christian Ministries. *www.bcmmin.org.*
2. Christian Ministries International. *www.jude3.com.*
3. Martin, Walter. *Martin Under Fire.* Audiotapes. *Walter Martin Ministries. www.waltermartin.com.*
4. McKeever, Bill, and Eric Johnson. *Mormonism 101: Examining the Religion of the Latter-day Saints.* Grand Rapids, Mich.: Baker Book House, 2000. See also *www.mrm.org.*
5. Reed, David, and John Farkas. *Mormons Answered Verse by Verse.* Grand Rapids, Mich.: Baker Book House, 1992.
6. *Saints Alive in Jesus. www.saintsalive.com.*
7. Tanner, Jerald, and Sandra Tanner. *The Changing World of Mormonism.* Chicago: Moody Press, 1980. See also *www.utlm.org.*
8. Van Gorden, Kurt. *Mormonism.* Grand Rapids, Mich.: Zondervan, 1995.
9. White, James R. *Is the Mormon My Brother?* (Minneapolis: Bethany House Publishers, 1997). See also Alpha & Omega Ministries, *www.aomin.org.*

Quick Facts About Spiritism

- Spiritism teaches: the fatherhood of God and the brotherhood of man

- Continuous existence and a path of endless progression

- Communion of spirits and ministry of angels

- Personal responsibility

- Compensation and retribution in the hereafter for good and evil done on Earth.

Chapter 7

Spiritism — The Cult of Antiquity

By far the oldest form of religious cult extant today, and certainly one of the deadliest where the certainty of divine judgment is concerned, is that of Spiritism, often erroneously referred to as "Spiritualism." However, in speaking of this cult, it is sometimes necessary to use that term in order to communicate in the vernacular of our day.

In 1949 Dr. Charles Braden wrote that in America, spiritist leaders "estimate [there are] from 500,000 to 700,000 spiritualists in the United States; and ... 1,500,000 to 2,000,000 in the world" (*These Also Believe*, New York: Macmillan Company, 1960, 356).

This estimate today, as far as the United States is concerned, is difficult to substantiate. In 1976 the International General Assembly of Spiritualists, the Nationalist Spiritualist Alliance of the United States of America, and the National Spiritualist Association of Churches reported more than two hundred churches, with a total membership of over ten thousand, and more than two hundred clergy. ~As of 2002 the National Spiritualist Association of Churches lists only eighty-nine churches on its Web site and does not put forward total membership numbers.[1] This is a noteworthy reduction in total church numbers since the 1976 figures, but its impact on actual membership is open to discussion. Adherents.com, a respected Web site on worldwide religion statistics, notes that Spiritism membership can be reasonably estimated at twenty million worldwide.~ This includes statistics for other countries of the world where the movement is much stronger than in the States. South American spiritist numbers could even exceed the fifty million mark if specific religious categories are taken into account. In Brazil alone there are more than 15 million professed spiritists.[2] Spiritism is

---

This chapter updated and edited by Kevin Rische and Jill Martin Rische.
[1] *www.nsac.org/*churches/index.htm
[2] *www.adherents.com/*Religions_By_Adherents.html#Spiritism

finding new life, even in what is referred to as the scientific age of physics and quantum mechanics!

Dr. Marcus Bach, the noted liberal scholar who has examined a great deal of spiritistic phenomena, states that, in his opinion, "The *raison d'etre* of Spiritualism is . . . demonstration and proof of the continuity of life, coupled with the comforting assurance that the life is good."

Dr. Bach went on in the same context to explain that in a seance, he saw the apparent reunion of a family, "a son telling his mother that life over there was just a continuation of life on earth. There were not two worlds at all; there was but one interblended, interrelated world, closely interwoven by memory and the love of life. Consciousness could not die. Personality could not be destroyed. The spirit of man was indeed eternal."

Dr. Bach concluded his observation with the statement:

> I left the room overpowered by a strange onrush of comfort about life and death: If this is all true, I thought, it will be difficult to speak of it without emotion. I have always believed in life after death. The traditional church has believed it too. Spiritism went a step further. It asked us to believe that the spirits were interested and active in human affairs; that they could be reached, seen and communicated with. The sense of assurance and comfort lingered. The feeling of genuineness persisted. I walked past the Chesterfield grotto. Someone was praying within the shrine. For those who believe, Spiritualism leads to God.[3]

We cannot agree with Dr. Bach that "for those who believe, Spiritualism leads to God," for it is the direct testimony of Holy Scripture that Spiritualism is the masquerade of demonic forces, who pretend to be departed spirits with the intent of deceiving through the power of Satan those foolish enough to believe the testimony of demons in preference to the authority of the Word of God himself. One need only to read 1 Samuel 28 to learn that King Saul's encounter with the medium of Endor brought divine condemnation and Saul's death; for God interrupted the seance, shocked the medium (v. 12) who was expecting the usual counterfeiting of personalities by her own familiar spirit, and allowed Samuel to speak to Saul of God's displeasure and coming wrath.

Spiritists repeatedly attempt to prove that the Bible endorses Spiritism; in fact, they cite any number of references in an attempt to prove that many biblical characters, not excepting the apostles and our Lord himself, were indeed mediums, and encouraged such practices.

Spiritism does, indeed, have a tremendous appeal to the minds of many persons, because, as Dr. Bach points out, it confirms for them life after death and reunion with their loved ones, something that the Scriptures also teach, and further declares that it is not necessary to confirm such truth through Satanic channels, unless one wishes to court the judgment of God.

Spiritism—Yesterday and Today

Since the First World War the religious horizons of the globe have seen the rapid rise of various forms of Spiritism, a religion unique in that it offers contact

---

[3]Marcus Bach, *They Have Found a Faith* (New York: Bobbs-Merrill, 1946), 116, 121.

with and information from beings beyond the grave. Much of contemporary Spiritism has been exposed by competent professionals as fraudulent. The classic exposé was by Houdini and Dunninger (*Magic and Mystery,* New York: Weathervane Books, 1967). Other exposés include that by former "psychic" M. Lamar Keene (*The Psychic Mafia,* New York: St. Martin's Press, 1976) and a joint investigation by a Christian physician, Paul Meier, and a Christian magician, Danny Korem (*The Fakers,* Grand Rapids: Baker Book House, 1980).

However, not all psychic or spiritistic phenomena can be exposed as fraudulent. There is a spiritual dimension that cannot be ignored. Authentic spiritists draw their power from the one the Bible calls "a roaring lion" who seeks "whom he may devour" (1 Peter 5:8), who is Satan. Spiritism, as we shall see, directly contradicts the Bible, God's Word. As well as constituting something akin to consumer fraud, Spiritism also constitutes biblical heresy.

In contemporary American life, so acute and complete is the recognition of supernatural sensitivity of communication and spirit manifestations that Duke University set up a special division for the study of extrasensory perception (ESP, as it commonly is referred to in discussion). There are other such centers for psychic research and the studies of perception that transcend the normal senses, but all are calibrated to achieve the same end—confirmation of what God has forbidden—the exploration of the psychic dimension.

The greatest of all source books on the subject of Spiritism is, of course, the Bible, which gives a historical outline of Spiritism in a most concise and dependable form.

Beginning graphically in Exodus, Scripture reveals that the ancient Egyptians were practitioners of cultism of magic sorcery and necromancy, which were utilized by the priests of the demon gods of Egypt to duplicate the miracles of Moses when he appeared before Pharaoh with the divine command (Exodus 7:11, 22; 8:18).

The attitude of God toward those who practice the forbidden sin is also clearly outlined in Scripture. The Lord ordered the death penalty for all sorcerers as recorded in Exodus 22:18 and Leviticus 20:27, to cite two specific instances. The Old Testament also named as those cursed by God, persons consorting with "familiar spirits" and "wizards" (Leviticus 19:31 and 20:6), in our language, demons and mediums.

In company with these violators of divine command, Daniel the prophet often speaks of the magicians, sorcerers, soothsayers, and astrologers (Daniel 1:20; 2:2, 27; 4:7; and 5:7), who specialized along with the Chaldeans in the art of interpreting dreams and visions. The prophet Isaiah also speaks of ancient spiritists as casting sorceries upon Israel (Isaiah 8:19; 19:3; 47:9), and King Saul, before his apostasy, under God's command drove such practitioners from Israel (1 Samuel 28:3, 9) as did the righteous King Josiah after him (2 Kings 23:24-25).

The Scriptures likewise bear record that Manassah's downfall came about as the result of his delving into Spiritism (2 Kings 21:6; 2 Chronicles 33:6) and his ensuing practice of idolatry in defiance of the command of God. The Bible then presents a devastating résumé of man's forbidden desire to uncover the hidden spiritual mysteries of the universe, even if witchcraft, divination, or enchantments must be employed to further his unholy quest. Egyptians, Babylonians, Chaldeans, and the Canaanites, the Scriptures tell us, all practiced Spiritism, which practice, in one form or another, continued through the ages. In 1848 Spiritism received its modern rebirth at Hydesville, New York, in the persons of Kate and Margaret Fox, two of the best-known of the nineteenth century promulgators of Spiritism. (For further biblical references to the practices of Spiritism, see such verses as Exodus 8:18; Leviticus 19:31; 1 Samuel 15:23; 2 Kings 9:22; 2 Chronicles 33:6; Daniel 2:2; Micah 5:12; and Nahum 3:4.)

The Revival of Modern Spiritism

Modern Spiritism had its birth, as far as most church historians are concerned, on March 31, 1848. On that date Mrs. John Fox, of Hydesville, New York, heard peculiar noises in the upstairs rooms and cellar of her home. Margaret and Kate Fox seemed to be peculiarly sensitive to these noises, and through this sensitivity they developed into mediums, and their communications became known as "The Rochester Rappings."

Some time afterward, the Fox sisters allegedly stated that the noises originated from their cracking the joints of their toes, but modern-day spiritists scorn this explanation, and today in Lilydale, New York, the Fox sisters' cottage has become a spiritualistic shrine, with a large marker, "There Is No Death," reaffirming the ancient practices of those whom God condemned as practitioners of abominations (Deuteronomy 18:9–12).

The roster of those interested in Spiritism is not inconsiderable. Dr. Bach lists a number of "great names" interested in psychic phenomena and research, names such as James Fenimore Cooper; William Cullen Bryant; Robert Dale Owen; Daniel Webster; Harriet Beecher Stowe; Elizabeth Barrett Browning; Horace Greeley; Elisha Cane; Sir Oliver Lodge, English physicist and author; E. Lee Howard, former pastor of the historic Congregational Church at Painesville, Ohio; Sherwood Eddy, world traveler and writer; Arthur Conan Doyle and Sir William Crooks, the last of whom was honored with degrees from at least five English universities and was inventor of the Crooks tube and discoverer of thallium. According to Bach, "Crooks reported 'that he had seen manifestations of levitation, and heard accordions play without being touched by human hands; had seen a luminous hand write upon the wall, and a medium handle live coals with bare hands.' All of this he had subjected to scientific tests to prove there were forces at work which could not be explained by any known physical law."

While some of these names might be readily challenged, we are concerned only with the judgments of the Bible, in which we are admonished to "prove [test] all things; hold fast that which is good" (1 Thessalonians 5:21).

It is interesting to note that Spiritism has made its strongest appeal to those who have suffered great loss, and after each great war, Spiritism always seems to be on the upgrade following the death of loved ones.

One of the great early prophets of modern-day Spiritualism was Andrew Jackson Davis, a poorly educated but extremely earnest disciple of spirit communication.

In 1847 Davis published his *Principles of Nature, Her Divine Revelations and a Voice to Mankind,* which is reputed to have gone through over fifty editions in the United States. To this day Davis is revered by modern spiritualists as one of the great prophets of the movement. In 1852 Spiritualism was introduced in England,

and in Germany in 1856 there were exhibitions or so-called "Spiritistic or Automatic Writings."

Other famous mediums were Daniel Douglas Home, William Stainton Moses, and Leonora Piper. Chiefly through the works of these people, the famous British scientist Sir William Crooks accepted Spiritualism as genuine, and his testimony in no small way influenced Dr. William James, the noted philosopher and psychologist at Harvard.

The American Mercury carried in detail one of James' exhaustive verifications of spiritistic phenomena, which stands today as a scientific confirmation of supernatural activity and empirical evidence of an existence that transcends the death of the body. Extensive quoting from that article follows.

From the Housewife Who Confounded Two Countries

In the city of Boston in 1885, Mrs. Leonora E. Piper, wife of a Boston merchant, and possessed of but limited education, began what was to be a forty-year career as a spiritistic medium, a career which was to confound the best minds in psychical research in both the United States and Europe with scientifically validated evidence which has never been refuted. Mrs. Piper became interested in Spiritism after visiting a clairvoyant for the relief of severe pain after the birth of her first child. It was during sessions with him that she lapsed into trances during which period she could answer with amazing accuracy questions concerning persons who had died.

For some 26 years she continued under the various "spirit controls" that possessed her during her trances as a medium and stopped only in 1911 when "the spirits" suggested that her health would not bear the strain of their manifestation.

In 1924 Mrs. Piper conducted a special series of seances and the records of these seances run more than 3,000 pages in length with a fantastic score for accuracy. (n.d.)

Mrs. Piper gave some eighty-eight sittings, for example, carefully observed at all times by members of the British Society for Psychical Research. Professor Oliver Lodge, later Sir Oliver Lodge, one of England's most brilliant scientists and a careful psychic investigator, compiled a checklist of some forty-one specific incidents wherein Mrs. Piper stated facts and general information concerning those who attended her seances, facts that were unknown to those persons at the very time the seances were in session! This was carefully verified and is beyond refutation.

Mrs. Piper also had the amazing capacity to find lost objects and to relate incidents that were taking place many hundreds of miles away from where she was in a trance. Professor William James testified to this when Mrs. Piper informed him that his aunt living over two hundred miles away in New York had died early that very morning. According to James:

"On reaching home an hour later I found a telegram reading as follows: 'Aunt Kate passed away a few minutes after midnight.' "

Dr. James, undaunted by Mrs. Piper's capabilities, went so far as to bring visiting professors from foreign universities with whom Mrs. Piper was not acquainted, only to have her give the correct names of the professors, some of their parents, and the illnesses from which they died. James once wrote of her:

"I now believe her to be in possession of a power as yet unexplained." The British Society for Psychical Research enlisted the aid of detectives and investigators, who observed Mrs. Piper under all conditions while she was in England, and Dr. Richard Hodgson, who had dedicated his life to exposing "psychic wonders," threw up his hands in complete capitulation when without any previous encounter with him, she informed him of his real name, members of his family that were still living, and two who had died.

Hodgson brought her to England only to have her sit under the control of a spirit named Dr. Phinuit who communicated through her to Dr. Hodgson during the course of three months of exhaustive investigation. During the course of that investigation, she told him the exact movements of persons in distant cities, and at another time, under the control of a spirit who identified himself as "George Pellew," Mrs. Piper informed Dr. Hodgson of events and facts that were subsequently verified by more than thirty of Pellew's friends. Pellew correctly rejected more than a hundred persons claiming to have known him in life and showed only those whom he had known!

Under the control of Pellew, Mrs. Piper translated perfectly a Greek phrase composed on the spur of the moment by a classical Greek scholar. Mrs. Piper knew no Greek whatever, but George Pellew did. She also reported under Pellew's control, with complete accuracy, what Pellew's father, who lived in another city, was doing at that moment.

Professor James Hyslop, of Columbia University, was totally bewildered by Mrs. Piper when with the cooperation of Dr. Hodgson, he interviewed Mrs. Piper in Sion seventeen times, only to be told by her his correct name and perfect answers to the questions he addressed to her, though she could not possibly have had access to the answers. Dr. Hyslop ended up believing that through Mrs. Piper he had actually communicated with the spirit of his departed father!

> Mrs. Piper herself believed that the powers which she possessed were not supernatural. In fact, she stated:
> "I never heard of anything being said by myself during the trance which might not have been latent in my own mind or in the mind of the sitters or in the mind of some absent person alive somewhere else in the world. The theory of telepathy strongly appeals to me as the most plausible solution of the problem."

Despite this modest statement, Mrs. Piper convinced Sir Oliver Lodge, Sir William Crooks, Dr. William James, Dr. Hodgson, and Dr. Hyslop (after more than $150,000 was spent on "the most prolonged investigation in the history of psychical research") that she was indeed possessed of supernatural capacities.

Evidence such as this cannot be dismissed, but must indeed be studied carefully, and will, I believe, demonstrate beyond a question of a doubt not only the existence of a spiritual dimension of reality but of the capacity of some to penetrate this dimension. In the terms of Scripture such a penetration can only culminate in a liaison with the forces of darkness of whom, in the light of Scripture, Mrs. Piper was the vehicle of communication.

~Over the last decade of the 1990s through the present year 2003, the media has greatly contributed to the growth of Spiritism by making available such TV shows as *Crossing Over*, hosted by medium Jonathan Edwards—an hour-long program on the Science Fiction Channel—and the Animal Planet show *Pet Psychic* with animal "communicator" Sonya Fitzpatrick. Fitzpatrick talks directly to the animals featured on the show, and her commentary could easily be dismissed as absurd except for the detailed knowledge she appears to possess about the animals' likes, dislikes, happy times, and traumatic experiences. This information is specific enough to warrant a second look at Fitzpatrick and to question her "sources" of information; whether natural or supernatural. Edwards' commentary also contains many disturbing details—enough to pique the interest of millions of viewers. He appears frequently as a popular guest on *Larry King Live* and numerous other celebrity talk shows.~

It would be negligent to give the reader the impression that all so-called psychic phenomena are always genuine, albeit demonic. By far the majority of such activity is fraudulent. There is abundant testimony (see Bibliography) to the consistently fraudulent world of Spiritism. Christian authors Danny Korem and Paul Meier reflect some of the balance that a Christian should have in his assessment of psychic phenomena: "The reader, because of my perspective may assume that I have ruled out the possibility of the intervening of supernatural agents in the flow of day-to-day existence. I do believe such intervention can and does take place. . . . The goal of this treatise is not only to debunk much of what is considered supernatural phenomena, but also to come full circle and identify those supernatural powers that do exist and their origins" (Korem and Meier, 32).

It is important to reiterate that much psychic activity is in reality fraud, deception, or simply misplaced sincerity. This pseudo-spiritism is, in one way, as dangerous and non-Christian as actual demonic communication. As Houdini and Dunninger stated in their classic exposé of fraudulent mediums: "The fact remains that a great number of self-styled mediums have played upon the credulity and sufferings of a public anxious to believe anything—anything which seems to assure continued life to those who have been loved, and who have passed the barrier of this life" (Houdini and Dunninger, 17).

The history of Spiritism literally spans the ages, but throughout it all, two things remain constant. The first is that Spiritism is to be found everywhere, posing as a universal, common denominator for all religious groups, not excepting Judaism and Christianity. It teaches the continuity of life and the eternal progression of man toward perfection in the spirit realm. Second, the Eternal God has condemned its practice in the sternest possible terms, maintaining that the interpretation of the supernatural realms belongs solely to Him (Genesis 40:8), and that those who practice intrusion into these realms are worthy of death (Exodus 22:18).

We are repeatedly warned in the strongest terms not to seek after mediums and not to dabble in the realms of divine dominion (Leviticus 19:31). Only the deluded prefer the doctrines of demons to faith in the Word of God, and, as we shall see, the doctrines of Spiritism are precisely of such a nature.

Verified Instances of Spiritistic Phenomena

Following are two instances of spiritistic phenomena that I accept as indicative of true occultic/demonic involvement as described by the Bible. Both I feel have sound evidence attesting to their validity. There are many Christians, unfortunately, who suffer from the illusion that all Spiritism, or spiritistic evidence, is fraudulent, and prefer to rest in the falsely secure belief that Spiritism can never be demonically empowered.

I do believe that much spiritistic evidence is manufactured and comes from overactive imaginations or outright deception on the part of the "performer." Spiritism, legitimate or fraudulent, is big business. The lure of easy money is more than enough to draw many unsuspecting would-be mediums into occultic and/ or deceptive spiritistic practices. Ex-psychic M. Lamar Keene said of the largest Spiritist camp, in Chesterfield, Indiana, that it was "spiritualism's answer to Disneyland. That first season of mine, more than 65,000 pilgrims crowded onto the grounds from here, there, and everywhere. They spent more than a million dollars to commune with their beloved dead."[4]

Case I

The first of these instances was reported by Dr. Marcus Bach, the well-known religious observer and writer whose unbiased approach to Spiritism led him to visit the Spiritist camp in Chesterfield and to attend seances that his investigation convinced him were authentic.

> On August 26 I drove into Chesterfield, Indiana, and proceeded immediately to the spiritualist camp adjoining the town. It is called a city of peace, a New Jerusalem, a Great Mecca. Expecting a morbid cloister for communication with the dead, I found to my surprise a bucolic vacationland. Two large hotels and twenty cottages look out upon a grass-carpeted amphitheater and a grotto in a "garden of prayer."
>
> Symbolizing the unbroken tradition of spiritualism, there is a "Trail of Religions." Spiritualists say there is nothing like it in the world. Life-sized busts of Abraham, Buddha, Zoroaster, Mohammed, Lao-tse, Confucius, Vardhamana, Zeus, Osiris, and Jesus suggest that spiritualism is universal in appeal and application. Overlooking the scene, an Indian stands with face uplifted to the invisible heavens of the spirit world. (Bach, op. cit., 99)

After arriving at this Mecca of modern American Spiritism, Dr. Bach visited two seances. He records this for us as a skeptic who became a believer in the phenomena of Spiritism:

> The moments passed. My eyes became accustomed to the dark and I could make out the vague outline of Pressing next to me. He leaned over and whispered somberly, "Well, when's something going to happen?"
>
> Before I could answer
>
> "How do you do, Dr. Bach! How do you do, Mr. Pressing!" came to us out of the darkness. It was a tantalizing, childish voice with a slightly roguish touch. It might have been a winsome little prodigy stepping out in the debut. It might have been a tiny actress in a puppet show.
>
> "Good afternoon," responded Mr. Pressing.
>
> "Who are you?" I asked.
>
> With a friendly lilt the answer came, "I'm Sylvia. . . . We are glad you

---

[4]*The Psychic Mafia* (New York: St. Martin's Press, 1976), 43.

are here, Dr. Bach," she said with a neat curtsy in her voice. "This is going to be a good seance. There are good vibrations. Look!"

The small trumpet was slowly rising from the floor. It stopped slightly above the larger one and hovered uncertainly. . . .

"But who are you?" I insisted.

"Sylvia!" said the voice emphatically. "Didn't I tell you I am Sylvia? . . . I can get other spirits for you, if you want me to."

"How?" I demanded. "With millions of spirits in the spirit world, how do you get them? Call Bob Whitehand for me."

"Bob Whitehand?" The voice seemed to drift from us for a moment. "Bob Whitehand?" it returned reflectively. "I'll try. It is done by vibrations. . . . I'll try to get Bob Whitehand afterwhile. But look at the trumpet now, Dr. Bach!"

It had risen to five or six feet above the floor and was slowly floating in space. . . .

"Where would you like the trumpet to go?" asked Sylvia.

"Bring it close to me," I told her.

Outlined by the luminous bands, the trumpet floated toward me. It stopped close to my right ear.

"Put it in my hands, Sylvia," I said.

"Hold them out!"

I extended my hands and the trumpet came to rest in them. Now, I thought, here's my chance to find those strings. Balancing the feather-light tube in my left hand, I passed my right hand completely around it. No strings.

"Put your hands on each end of the trumpet," Sylvia directed.

I did, holding the trumpet about elbow's length from my body. "Now I'll talk to you from inside the trumpet."

A whispered voice—Sylvia's—came from within the trumpet. I put it to my right ear—the voice was there; to my left ear—Sylvia speaking.

"Well," I admitted, "that's interesting." Then I withdrew both hands quickly. Unaided, the trumpet remained fixed in space.

A conversation between Sylvia and Pressing was lost in the amazement upon seeing the other trumpet begin a slow take-off. Without stopping, it ascended to a point near the ceiling. It hung there, then started a slow swinging motion, round and round, like the retarded movement of a helicopter.[5]

Dr. Bach continued the discussion of the seance to point out that Dr. William James then addressed him for perhaps fifteen or twenty minutes. The trumpet continued its levitating motion, and after Dr. James stopped speaking, Sylvia, the capricious spirit creature, took the trumpet that seemed suspended from the air, and caused it to crash with a bang against the wall behind Dr. Bach. Dr. Bach records Mr. Pressing asking, "What the devil was that?"

Sylvia's impish laugh was the answer. "I wanted to show you how poltergeists work! Well, that's the way!" The room was quiet for a few moments. Nothing could be seen save the luminous bands of the small trumpet. Then Sylvia's voice said, "I think I have Bob Whitehand for you."

"Good!" I said in a tone of cooperation. "Bob? Bob? Can you hear me?"

5Ibid., 104–106.

A luminous head appeared levitated about four feet from the floor. It was not materialized in the way that materialization is usually described. It simply appeared out of nothingness. It was like a blurred flashlight reflected on a human face. I made out the unmistakable features of my friend who had been killed in France. This apparition hovered in the room for only a few seconds and then blacked out. How should I explain it? If it were actually a human face illuminated by a flashlight, it must have been shrouded in a curtain in the center of the room. But I knew there had been no curtain. Besides, why would the flashlight diffuse over no other single part of the room, curtain or apparatus—if apparatus were used? And if it were someone impersonating Bob Whitehand, how could he make up such a marked resemblance of Bob, inasmuch as no one knew that I would request Bob's appearance? It was an inexplicable happening and remained the most vivid of the afternoon's demonstration.

Sylvia was now bidding us good-bye. The little trumpet returned to its original position.[6]

Dr. Bach records one more confrontation in the seance that certainly bears close study and analysis, because it was of a closely personal nature. He described it this way:

> I was making minute mental notations of all that was happening—the hovering, swaying motion of the "spirits," the rhythm of life, like the rise and fall of a tide, as many as four speaking simultaneously in whispered voices, excited, hurried persuasive. Suddenly the galaxy of spirits melted away. For a long still moment nothing happened. Then the swirling ectoplasmic effluvia glowed from the floor and quickly took on the form of a girl. Before the figure was complete, it spoke.
>
> "Marc, dear—Marc, dear—Marc, dear."
>
> Those who know me well call me Marc; those who know me better call me Marc, dear, so I knew this must be a "familiar spirit!" I got up and walked over until there was a space of less than four feet between us. "Yes?" I said. "Who are you?"
>
> The answer was fraught with disappointment. "Don't you know me?"
>
> I did not. I had no idea who this might be. I had really been too absorbed to think very much about personal contact with the spirits. . . . Nor did I propose to offer any hint of whom I thought she *might represent*. No leads, I determined.
>
> "I do not know you. Who are you?"
>
> "Paula," came the answer.
>
> The name and soft manner in which it was uttered brought the sudden unfolding of a forgotten drama. Twenty years ago my sister Paula had died at the age of twenty-three. Her child Janette had died shortly before. These deaths had been among the deep sorrows of our family, but time and travel reduce the past into forgetfulness. No medium or spirit had plucked this name out of my mind because I wasn't thinking of Paula. I had not thought of her even once during the seance.
>
> I looked at the presence before me closely.
>
> "How do I look?" she asked.
>
> "You look fine," I replied.
>
> "The right height?" she whispered. "Do you think I should be taller?"

6Ibid., 108-109.

"No. You are about the height I remember."

"I wanted to do a good job," she told me earnestly. "Do I look all right?"

"Yes," I assured her, recalling that one theory of materialization is that the spirit "takes" the ectoplasm and fashions according to its memory the human form which clothed it on earth.

. . . Did this form and these features resemble Paula? I must admit they did. Very much. The outline of the figure was recognizable and convincing. It was like a "false front," a flat, two-dimensional body with the semblance of arms clothed in a shadowy gray-white film. The face, though typically mask-like, was strikingly reminiscent. There was an illusion of long blond hair. I cannot say whether the voice was Paula's or not. After twenty years I would not remember. Just now, however, it was Paula returned.

But why shouldn't it be? I asked myself as I stood there. The spiritualists at Chesterfield knew I was coming. If, as some people say, they have a well-laid system of espionage they could easily have traced my family and got Paula's description. If this was someone "dressed up," play-acting, if this was a marionette using the voice of a ventriloquist, naturally it would be con-structed as to represent Paula. This thought haunted me more than the presence. I wished I could convince myself some way. The impulse to reach out and touch the figure became stronger. I moved closer. I moved slightly to one side so that the red light would strike the spirit's face more directly. We were about three feet apart now. Paula was talking about life in the spirit world. I was asking hasty questions: Have you seen Jesus? What is heaven like? What about the element of time? Can you be everywhere at once? Are terms like Methodist, Reformed, Presbyterian, Catholic ever used where you are?

Her voice seemed to laugh. She answered, "No, no," to all questions save the one about heaven. It was like speaking to a living person secretly, clandestinely, knowing that time was running out. Her features seemed to become clearer. Perhaps it was my mind playing tricks.

And then a thought came to me. "Paula," I said, "do you remember the catechism we learned at home?"

"Of course!"

"Paula, do you remember the first question in that catechism?"

"I remember."

"What was it?" I asked almost fearfully.

The answer came at once. " 'What is your chief comfort in life and in death?' "

"Go on," I urged.

" 'That I, with body and soul, both in life and in death am not my own—' " She interrupted herself. "Here where we are the words have a greater meaning!"

Then quickly, breathlessly, she told me that serving God means per-sonal development. Life on the spirit plane is an evolvement. Like the break-ing of a chrysalis. Like the ascent in a spiral. Like the growth of moral affec-tion to higher and higher "heavens." Several times she interrupted herself with "Do you understand? Is that clear?" as if she felt her message was vital, all-absorbing. Death, she insisted, was not a violent result of sin. It had no sting. It was neither friend nor enemy. It was part of the divine purpose, a purpose without beginning or end.

The whispering grew fainter. "I can stay no longer. I must go now."

"Paula, one more thing. Can you put your arms around me?"

"I'll give you a kiss," she said. "Come closer."

"You come close to me." I wanted her to come nearer the red light. She did. There was now scarcely a foot between us. Her face was luminous, seemingly transparent, and without depth.

I leaned forward and lowered my head. The weblike texture of ecto-plasmic arms encircled my neck. Something soft and flaxen brushed my forehead. Then Paula vanished—into the floor, it seemed.

I walked back to my chair and sat down. . . . The seance was ended.[7]

Camp Chesterfield has not always enjoyed such favorable inspection as it received from Dr. Bach. In 1960 a Spiritist advertising project blew up in the spiritists' faces, exposing some of the fraudulent activities occurring there. M. Lamar Keene, ex-psychic and ex-Chesterfield staff member, recounts:

Two sympathetic researchers, Tom O'Neill and Dr. Andrija Puharich, had tried to get the first motion pictures ever of the materialization of a spirit. O'Neill was a believing spiritualist, editor of the monthly newspaper *Psychic Observer,* an ordained minister of the Indiana Association of Spiritualists . . . and a close friend of . . . other stalwarts at the camp. Puharich was a physician and psychical researcher whom O'Neill had recruited to give the project scientific credibility. . . .

The experiment was a disaster for the spiritualists. Peering through the snooperscope in the dark, Puharich saw that what were supposed to be spirit forms of shimmering ectoplasm materializing out of thin air, were actually figures wrapped in chiffon entering the seance room through a hidden door from an adjacent apartment.

The infrared motion picture confirmed Puharich's observations. There, etched unmistakably on the film, were the familiar faces of camp mediums, dressed up in gauze, impersonating departed spirits. (Keene, op. cit., 41–42)

Case II

An example of spiritistic demonstration is recorded by J. Arthur Hill in his book *Spiritualism: Its History, Phenomena, and Doctrine* (New York: George Doran, 1919, 74–75), wherein Mr. Hill cites the case of Daniel Douglas Home, medium extraordinary, who practiced communication and levitation:

In 1885, Daniel D. Home, a young man of Scottish-American descent, arrived in the British Isles, and it is in the case of Home and his claims of spiritistic mediumship, that the objective observer finds evidence of super-natural manifestations that has been challenged by no one who has thoroughly investigated the life of Mr. Home.

There are many instances recorded of Home's ability to communicate with forces beyond this earth, but the physical phenomena or manifestations of spirit influence which reveal themselves in Home's fantastic ability, are the best testimonies to his possession by supernatural powers.

Sir Wm. Crooks, famed British scientist and acknowledged authority on the phenomena of spiritualism, testified that beyond a shadow of a doubt in

[7]Ibid., 117–21.

the case of Mr. Home, there was "definitely the operation of some agency unknown to science."

In the presence of Sir William and Home, "an accordion placed under the table and untouched by the medium, played tunes, and could manage a few notes, though no tune, when it was held by Mr. Crooks himself. A lath of wood on a table, three feet from Home, rose 10 inches and floated about in the air for more than a minute, moving gently up and down as if it were on rippling water, the medium's hands, meanwhile, being held by Mrs. Walter Crooks and Mrs. William Crooks. A pencil on the table stood up on its point and tried to write, but fell down: the lath then slid across to it and buttressed the pencil, while it tried again. Tables slid about, untouched. Luminous clouds were seen and materialized hands, which carried flowers about. And Home himself was lifted into the air, thus paralleling the levitations of many saints. All this in a fair light, usually one gas burner.

The most famous of the levitations, however, occurred in 1868, at 5, Buckingham Gate, London, in the presence of Lords Lindsay and Adare, and Captain Wynne. Home floated or appeared to float out of one window and in at another. The windows were 76 inches apart, 85 feet above the ground, and there was no ledge or foothold between them. . . . It is difficult to believe that the whole of Home's phenomena were due to fraud or hallucination. As we so often have to say, certainty concerning matters of history, which are vouched for only by a few people, most or all of whom are now dead, is not attainable, and when the alleged events are of a kind to which our own experience supplies no parallel, it is easiest to suppose that the things were done fraudulently somehow. But we must admit that this conclusion is due to prejudice, for in any other matter we should unhesitatingly accept as final the word of so distinguished a man of science as Sir William Crooks, especially when supported by such massive testimony.

It must be noted that not every investigator of psychic phenomena accepts the validity of this particular event. Houdini and Dunninger remained unconvinced, as have some others (*Magic and Mystery*, New York: Weathervane Books, 1967, 97).

There are many other instances that we could cite to demonstrate the claims of Spiritists, that they do indeed make contact with powers beyond this earth, and such claims are doubtless quite valid. The question is, are such contacts approved of in the Word of God, and if not, then is not the practice of such contacts disobedience to the expressed will of God and harmful to the soul of man?

As we have noted, the Bible speaks emphatically on this very point, and as we move on to discuss doctrinal content and contrasts of spiritistic teachings with those of Christianity, we shall be better able to understand the divine viewpoint where Spiritism and the practices of Spiritists are concerned. In this connection, let us note at least two specific things in the account given us by Dr. Bach and Mr. Hill. In the case of Dr. Bach, it will be remembered that the apparition that purported to be his departed sister, Paula, completely contradicted the New Testament, particularly the fifteenth chapter of 1 Corinthians, where death is described as an enemy (v. 26). Death does, indeed, have a sting for mankind that can only be removed by faith in the resurrection of Jesus Christ, which makes possible the resurrection of those who believe in Him (vv. 55–57).

It might also be profitably recalled that in his epistle to the Romans, the apostle Paul spoke quite markedly of the reality of sin, evil, and spiritual death or separation from fellowship with God. Chapters five and six particularly point out that Christ alone restores man to fellowship, and this He did by ruining Satan's power. (See Hebrews 2:14.) In the revelation of the New Testament, death is indeed the result of sin. (See also Genesis, chapter three.) It is a part of the divine purpose that God has permitted to take place and has provided a solution for: i.e., its eventual destruction by resurrection, in Christ. Although it is a part of the divine purpose, it is not neutral; it is, indeed, the "last enemy" to be destroyed (1 Corinthians 15:26).

Though we may also find ourselves in agreement with the statement of Mr. Hill concerning Daniel Home and his supernatural powers, we ought not to forget that Home was a true spiritist-medium who denied the deity of Jesus Christ, the Atonement, and the bodily resurrection of our Lord. The powers that controlled him (spiritists are wrong when they claim to control the spirits) were not powers from God. On the contrary, they were the demonic spirits spoken of and condemned in the Bible. The Father of Spirits, God Almighty, will be the eventual judge of him who is known as "the prince of the powers of the air," Satan.

The Theology of Spiritism

Its "Seven Principles" have been set forth as follows:
I.   The Fatherhood of God
II.   The Brotherhood of Man
III. Continuous Existence
IV.   Communion of Spirits and Ministry of Angels
V.   Personal Responsibility
VI.   Compensation and Retribution Hereafter for Good and Evil Done on Earth
VII. A Path of Endless Progression

> *Secretary of the Spiritualists' National Union,*
> *The Seven Principles of Spiritualism, 2–3*

1. Spiritualism is the Science, Philosophy and Religion of continuous life, based upon the demonstrated fact of communication, by means of mediumship, with those who live in the Spirit world.
2. A Spiritualist is one who believes, as the basis of his or her religion, in the communication between this and the spirit world by means of mediumship, and who endeavors to mold his or her character and conduct in accordance with the highest teachings derived from such communion.

> National Spiritualist Association,
> *Definitions,* 1914, 1919

Infinite Intelligence pervades and controls the universe, is without shape or form and is impersonal, omnipresent and omnipotent.

It teaches that the spark of divinity dwells in all.

Every soul will progress through the ages to heights, sublime and glorious, where God is Love and Love is God.

> "What Spiritualism Is and Does,"
> *Spiritualist Manual,* 1940

Man is a spiritual being, evolved from the lower forms of life, up through the period of consciousness, to the state of the higher moral and spiritual faculties, which survive, unaffected, the decomposition of the physical body.

Good deeds, springing from a good heart, have a creative force in building pleasant abodes in spirit life, and conversely the sinful create their own unhappy habitations. The wicked must compensate for their evil deeds, here or hereafter, and attain a state of justice before they are prepared to enter upon the path which leads to spiritual happiness and progression.

"Philosophy of Spiritualism,"
Spiritualist Manual, 1940

Spiritualism is an outpouring of the spirit upon humanity, a divine revelation from the spheres of light. It is the highest message of truth which we have, as yet, grown to grasp; and one whose depth, beauty and mighty significance we still imperfectly realize.

Spiritualism is the broad educator, the great redeemer, the emancipator which releases human souls from the bondage of superstition and ignorance, lifts the clouds or error that have so long enshrouded the world, and illumines the darkness of the world's materiality.

"What is Spiritualism?"
Spiritualist Manual, 1940

The Spiritualistic Hymnal indicates changes made on well-known hymns and we have listed one to demonstrate their theological position in so doing.

Just As I Am

Just as I am, without one plea,
But that, O God, Thou madest me,
And that my life is found in Thee
O God of Love, I come, I come.
Just as I am, nor poor, nor blind,
Nor bound by chains in soul or mind;
For all of Thee within I find
O God of Love, I come, I come.
Just as I am, Thou wilt receive,
Tho' dogmas I may ne'er believe,
Nor heights of holiness achieve
O God of Love, I come, I come.

It is an absurd idea that Jesus was any more divine than any other man. —*Weisse*

Tom Paine is the seventh sphere, one above our Lord, though he was so many centuries behind him in entering into the spirit life. —*Weisse*

The miraculous conception of Christ is merely a fabulous tale. —*Haweis*

Advanced spirits do not teach the atonement of Christ—nothing of the kind. —*Nocholas*

Your doctrine of the atonement is the very climax of a deranged imagination, and one that is of the unrighteous and immoral tendency. —*Hall*

We regret and condemn the practice of Spiritualists sending their children to be instructed in the teaching of a vicarious atonement, or salvation by faith and not of works. —*A resolution passed at the Spiritualistic Convention in Bradford, England*

All advanced Spiritualists—though few have the courage to confess it—repudiate marriage in its legal sense, and believe in the doctrine of affinities.
—*The Founder of the Free Love Society, a spiritualist, in a letter to the New York World in 1856*

The writings of noted spiritualists as recorded in William Edward Biederwolf's *Spiritualism* (Grand Rapids, Mich.: Eerdmans, 1952, 32)

I am here tonight as one of the founders of Spiritualism to denounce it as an absolute falsehood from beginning to end, as the flimsiest of superstitions, the most wicked blasphemy known to the world.
—R. B. Davenport, *The Deathblow to Spiritualism*, 1888, 76 (cf. *The New York Daily Tribune*, Oct. 22. See also *New York World*, Oct. 21, 1888)

LeRoy Edwin Froom, *Spiritualism Today* (Washington, D.C.: *Review and Herald*, 1963, 6)

Lord Dowding, a strong advocate of Spiritualism, says in his book *Many Mansions* (107): "The first thing which the orthodox Christian has to face is that the doctrine of the Trinity seems to have no adherents in advanced circles of the spirit world. The Divinity of Christ as a co-equal partner with the Father is universally denied. Jesus Christ was indeed the Son of God, as also are we sons of God. . . . We (i.e., orthodox Christians) are taught to believe in the remission of sins to the penitent, through the virtue of Christ's sacrifice and atonement. This doctrine Imperator (the pseudonym of one of these advanced spirits) vigorously combats in a score of passages."

Quoted in J. Stafford Wright's *Spiritualism* (London: The Church Book Room Press, 1959, 11)

Sir Arthur Conan Doyle: "Spiritualism is the greatest revelation the world has ever known. . . . I have seen spirits walk around the room and join in the talk of the company. . . . We are continually conscious of protection around us. . . . General experience shows that a facile acceptance of these claims of spirit is very rare among earnest thinkers and that there is hardly any prominent Spiritualist whose course of study and reflection has not involved a novitiate of many years."

"The History of Spiritualism," *Spiritualist Manual*, 1940, 131

Every Human Soul born into life is a child of GOD and the opportunity for development will at some time be realized and taken advantage of by each one.

Spiritualism proclaims "THE DOORWAY TO REFORMATION IS NEVER CLOSED AGAINST ANY SOUL HERE OR HEREAFTER."

Spiritualist Manual, 181

We no not believe in "fairies," "demons," "elementals," "astral shells," nor any such imaginary beings, whose existence cannot be proven. We know no reason why such creatures should exist. Such beliefs are neither scientific, nor do they follow the Laws of Nature, as these are disclosed by our science and philosophy or by the other natural sciences. We impress upon you once more that our belief contains nothing but what is in accord with Natural Law and which can be concretely proven.

Spiritualist Manual, 181

We believe in intelligent and ignorant spirits. No being is naturally "bad"; evil always originates in ignorance. Merely leaving the physical body does not change the condition of the spirit, which is the actual personality. It must learn to desire, and to progress to higher and better conditions, just as we do on earth.

"Miracle" means something done in defiance of Natural Law, therefore there are no Miracles. The demonstrations you speak of can be manifested today by our Sensitives (often called mediums) by the application of perfectly natural forces, when necessary conditions for such manifestations are provided.

Spiritualist Manual, 182

We do not believe in such places as Purgatory and Hell. Communicating spirits have merely graduated from this form of life into another. That life can be heaven or hell-like, just as each spirit chooses to make it; the same applies to our life here.

Spiritualist Manual, 183

Even the most degraded personality can in time attain to the greatest heights. It is easier, however, to begin progression in earth life.... Each must work out his own salvation; each has an equal opportunity to do this when he shall have atoned for the wrongs and overcome the temptations and allurements to the sense gratifications of earth life.

Spiritualist Manual, 184

The Verdict of the Holy Spirit

The previously cited quotations show most clearly some of the basic teachings of Spiritism. Such quotations from their representative literature, when contrasted with familiar Christian truths, reveal that Spiritism cannot in any sense qualify as Christianity. In fact, it is a particularly virile form of cultism, opposed in almost every specific to the historic doctrines of the Christian faith. It is hardly necessary therefore to refute Spiritism, since its own statements are of such an anti-Christian nature as to be self-convicting.

Perhaps the most striking example in the New Testament of the immutable attitude of God toward Spiritism and mediums is recorded in the thirteenth chapter of the book of Acts and merits careful scrutiny:

Now there were in the church that was at Antioch certain prophets and teachers; as Barnabas, and Simeon that was called Niger, and Lucius of Cyrene, and Manaen, which had been brought up with Herod the tetrarch, and Saul. As they ministered to the Lord, and fasted, the Holy Ghost said, Separate me Barnabas and Saul for the work whereunto I have called them. And when they had fasted and prayed, and laid their hands on them, they sent them away. So they, being sent forth by the Holy Ghost, departed unto Seleucia; and from thence they sailed to Cyprus. . . . And when they had gone through the isle unto Paphos, they found a certain sorcerer, a false prophet, a Jew, whose name was Bar Jesus; which was with the deputy of the country, Sergius Paulus, a prudent man; who called for Barnabas and Saul, and desired to hear the word of God.

But Elymas the sorcerer (for so is his name by interpretation) withstood them, seeking to turn away the deputy from the faith. Then Saul, (who also is called Paul) filled with the Holy Ghost, set his eyes on him, And said, O full of all subtilty and all mischief, thou child of the devil, thou enemy of all righteousness, wilt thou not cease to pervert the right ways of the Lord? And now, behold, the hand of the Lord is upon thee, and thou shalt be blind, not seeing the sun for a season. And immediately there fell on him a mist and a darkness; and he went about seeking some to lead him by the hand. (Acts 13:1–4, 6–11)

The context of this chapter indicates that Paul and Barnabas were set apart specifically by the Holy Spirit (vv. 2, 4) to preach the Word of God as the Spirit directed.

In the course of discharging the duties assigned to them by the Holy Spirit, they found a certain magician or medium, a false prophet, a Jew, whose name was Bar-jesus (v. 6).

We learn from the account that this man deliberately obstructed the preaching of the Gospel to the deputy of the country, Sergius Paulus, a man of integrity who desired to hear the Word of God (v. 7). The judgment of God fell upon this man (v. 11). But it is not significant until it is noted that in verses 9 and 10 the judgment was preceded by the announcement that Paul was "filled with the Holy Ghost," when he set his eyes upon him. Paul's scathing denunciation of the medium identifies him as a destructive, mischievous son of Satan, the enemy of all divine righteousness, and the perverter of twister or the right pathway of the Lord.

The Scripture reminds us that we are the temple of the Holy Spirit (1 Corinthians 6:19). The Spirit of God dwells within each Christian, and Scripture assures us that "greater is he that is in you, than he that is in the world" (1 John 4:4). The Christian, then, can never be possessed by demonic forces; he is constantly shielded and protected by the power of the indwelling Spirit. There is no demonic force that can withstand the presence and power of the Holy Spirit. This is why in the thirteenth chapter of Acts, the Scripture reminds us that Paul dealt with forces of darkness in his capacity as a believer filled with the Holy Spirit, and with complete assurance and confidence that God's power, grace, and all-pervading presence would give him the victory over any medium, false prophet, or "child of the devil" (as the Holy Spirit, through Paul, so graphically describes Bar-jesus).

As we close our study of Spiritism, three important factors can be gleaned from the comparison of Spiritism historically and theologically with the Gospel of Jesus Christ.

First, Spiritism as a cult has been from its beginning in opposition to the Judeo-Christian religions. In order for one to embrace its teachings, every major doctrine of the Christian faith must be rejected, including the inspiration and final authority of the Bible, the doctrines of the Trinity, the deity of Christ, the Virgin Birth, Vicarious Atonement, and the bodily resurrection of our Lord from the grave. The biblical doctrine of salvation by grace alone, through faith in Christ, apart from the works of the Law, is anathema to spiritist theology, which relies on progressive evolution, or growth in the "spirit world," to attain final perfection.

No informed student of Spiritism for a moment denies these things, and the previously noted quotations taken from bona fide spiritist publications more than substantiate the validity of this contention.

Second, it cannot be forgotten that amid the vast majority of spiritistic phenomena, which are fraudulent, there are truly supernatural manifestations. Authorities have given credence to a number of those that do not readily admit to natural or trick explanations. True Spiritism, then, can produce supernatural manifestations, which the Bible describes as originating in demonic forces, and thus under the judgment of God (Deuteronomy 18:9–11; Leviticus 19:31; 20:6; 1 Samuel 28:3–9; 2 Kings 21:6; 2 Chronicles 33:6; and Isaiah 47:9).

Third, Christians must realize that Spiritism is practiced by persons who willfully ignore the God of the Bible and His declared means of making men holy, i.e., the sending of His Son into the world that the world through Him might be saved (John 3:16, 36).

In the spirit of Christian love, we are committed to bear witness to Spiritists, refute their teachings, and confront them with the Christ of Calvary, who alone can take "away the sin of the world" (John 1:29). Spiritism properly understood is indeed a cult of antiquity, but its motivating force comes from Satan, who said long ago, in pristine Eden, "Ye shall not surely die," and of whom Jesus Christ said, "He is a liar" and "a murderer from the beginning, and abode not in the truth" (John 8:44).

Recommended Resources

1. Koch, Kurt E. *Occult Bondage and Deliverance.* Kregel Publications, December 1972.
2. Martin, Walter. *Spiritism.* Audiotape. *Walter Martin Ministries.* *www.waltermartin.com.*
3. ———. *Tools of the Occult,* audiotape. *Walter Martin Ministries.*
4. Montenegro, Marcia. *Christian Answers for the New Age. http://cana.userworld.com.*
5. Watchman Fellowship. *www.watchman.org.*

Quick Facts About the Theosophical Society

- Theosophy teaches a pantheistic, impersonal Supreme Being.

- Jesus Christ is not unique: Jesus is a reincarnated being separate from "christ." All men become christs.

- Mahatmas or Masters communicate esoteric truths through reincarnated emissaries, of whom Madame Blavatsky and Annie Besant are among the few.

- Theosophy draws its authoritative teachings from Hindu, Buddhistic, and early Gnostic sources. The Bible is used minimally to proof-text preconceived Theosophical notions.

- Reincarnation is the way of salvation.

Chapter 8

The Theosophical Society (Gnosticism)

Theosophy as a cult system derives its name from the Greek term *theosophia,* meaning literally, divine wisdom. And, in the words of J. H. Russell, its teachings are:

> At the same time religious, philosophic, and scientific . . . [postulating] one eternal, immutable, all-pervading principle, the root of all manifestation. From that one existence comes forth periodically the whole universe, manifesting the two aspects of spirit and matter, life and form, positive and negative, "the two poles of nature between which the universe is woven." Those two aspects are inseparably united; therefore all matter is ensouled by life while all life seeks expression through forms. All life being fundamentally one with the life of the Supreme Existence, it contains in germ all the characteristics of its source, and evolution is only the unfolding of those divine potentialities brought about by the conditions afforded in the various kingdoms of nature. The visible universe is only a small part of this field of evolution.[1]

Theosophy may be recognized at the outset as a pantheistic form of ancient Gnosticism, which attempts to embrace religious, philosophical, and scientific truth as it is found in all religio-philosophical sources. ~The Pasadena, California, office of the Society explains:

> A primary idea is the *essential oneness* of all beings. Life is everywhere throughout the cosmos because all originates from the same unknowable

This chapter revised and updated by Kurt Van Gorden and edited by Jill Martin Rische.
[1]J. H. Russell, "Theosophy," *The New Shaff-Herzog Encyclopedia of Religious Knowledge* (Grand Rapids, Mich.: Baker Book House, 1977), reprint, 11:407.

divine source. Consequently, everything from the subatomic to plants, animals, humans, planets, stars, and galaxies is alive and evolving. Each is divine at its root and expresses itself through spiritual, intellectual, psychological, ethereal, and material ranges of consciousness and substance.[2]~

According to the views of Theosophists, their Society "is a growing system of thought, the result of careful study and research," and further, "it is nothing less than the bedrock upon which all phases of the world's thought and activity are founded."[3] The "Three Declared Objects" of the Theosophical Society include:

1. To form a nucleus of the universal brotherhood of humanity without distinction of race, creed, sex, caste, or color.
2. To encourage the comparative study of religion, philosophy, and science.
3. To investigate unexplained laws of nature and the powers latent in humanity.[4]

This noble ideal dreams of a brotherhood of all faiths, or, if we may use the term, a type of homogenized religion, in which all men will agree to the cardinal tenets of Theosophy in one degree or another. In this respect, it is related to Spiritism, Rosicrucianism, Baha'ism, and the Great I AM cults.

In theory, of course, and quite apart from the Christian Scriptures, this idea is most appealing. But even a cursory perusal of man's demonstrably depraved nature as revealed in history and in the Bible renders this Utopian concept an absurd theological farce.

Theosophy as a religion is opposed to virtually every cardinal doctrine of the Christian faith, and finds no support from Judaism, little from Islam, and certainly none from the majority of world religions, with the exceptions of Buddhism and Hinduism. Christianity, Judaism, and Islam all confess a personal God and all believe in a resurrection of the body and in the authority of the Old Testament. Theosophy, on the other hand, rejects *all* these doctrines. Yet it continues to claim qualification for the role as a "unifier and peacemaker in religion." ~In fact, Theosophy claims that it is wrong to make any objective religious truth claim: We must only experience religious truth for ourselves in a subjective way.

> As beings rooted in divinity, we each have the ability to discover reality for ourselves. To do this we must learn to judge what is true and false, real and illusory; not blindly follow the dictates of authority, however high. . . . By following our own spiritual instincts and intuitions, we awaken our latent potentials. Trying to force others to adopt what we believe to be the "proper" avenue of thought may be harmful. Everyone follows his or her own unique path of unfoldment.[5]~

---

[2]"Some Basic Concepts of Theosophy," Pasadena, California, *www.theosophical.org*: Theosophical Society Web site, 1997 1.
[3]Irving S. Cooper, *Theosophy Simplified* (Wheaton, Ill.: The Theosophical Press, 1964), 7th ed., 22–23.
[4]"What Is the Theosophical Society?" *www.theosophical.org*: Theosophical Society Web site, 1997.
[5]"Some Basic Concepts," 2.

It is an interesting fact that Theosophy speaks in glowing terms of the ancient cult of Gnosticism, which thrived in the first three centuries of the Christian era, and which almost succeeded in doing irreparable damage to historic Christian faith. Paul's epistle to the Colossians and the epistle of 1 John are recognized by all biblical scholars to be direct apologetic thrusts against the teachings that spawned this cult: spiritualizing the Old Testament, redefining contemporary Christian terminology, substituting an impersonal god for the God of revelation, and reducing Jesus Christ to a demigod, or a pantheistic emanation from the unknowable divine essence. The well-known theosophical writer L. W. Rogers, however, disdains the counsel of the Holy Spirit, not to mention the warnings of the apostles Paul and John when he states,

> The antagonism between scientific and religious thought was the cause of great controversy that occurred in the intellectual world in the late nineteenth century. If the early teaching of the Christian Church had not been lost, the conflict could not have arisen. The Gnostic philosophers who were the intellect and heart of the Church had a knowledge of nature so true that it could not possibly come into collision with any fact of science; but unfortunately, they were enormously outnumbered by the ignorant, and the authority passed wholly into the hands of the latter. It was inevitable that misunderstanding followed.[6]

Theosophists are great admirers of the Gnostics, and this is not at all surprising, since they have adopted much of the terminology and vocabulary of ancient Gnosticism, which looked with disdain upon the material properties of both the world and man, depersonalized God, and created various planes of spiritual progression, culminating in universal salvation and reconciliation through reincarnation and the wheel concept of progression borrowed unblushingly from Buddhism.

Theosophy does not hesitate to declare that

> God and man are the two phases of the one eternal life and consciousness that constitutes our universe! The idea of the immanence of God is that He is the universe; although he is also more than it is; that the solar system is an emanation of the Supreme Being as clouds are an emanation of the sea. This conception makes man a part of God, having potentially within him all the attributes and powers of the Supreme Being. It is the idea that nothing exists except God, and that humanity is one portion of him—one phase of his Being.[7]

In the theology of Theosophy there are seven distinct planes in the universe. The Physical is the most dense of these planes; that which is next in the order is called the Astral Plane, and above it, the Mental. There are four higher spiritual planes, but to all except initiates and adepts they are as yet "mere names." Man, of course, has a physical body, a mental body, and an astral body. But at this

---

[6]L. W. Rogers, *Elementary Theosophy* (Wheaton, Ill.: The Theosophical Press, 1956), 22.
[7]Ibid., 23.

particular stage of cosmic evolution, with but few exceptions, the so-called higher spiritual bodies are still awaiting organization.[8]

A little further on in the chapter, we shall see what relationship this has to the basic doctrines of Christianity. But there can be little doubt that such hypothetical fancies, saturated with Gnostic terminology and concepts, cannot help but generate conflict where biblical theology is concerned.

Historical Sources

It is one of the strange historical peculiarities of the saga of cultism that some cults were either started by women or were influenced in a major way by the allegedly weaker sex: Christian Science, Mary Baker Eddy; the Unity School of Christianity, Myrtle Fillmore; Spiritism, the Fox sisters; Jehovah's Witnesses, Marie Russell; Theosophy, Helena Blavatsky and Annie Besant; the Peace Mission Movement (Father Divine), Sister Penny and Faithful Mary (Viola Wilson).

A woman founded this modern form of Hindu and Buddhism philosophy, popularized in our age as the Theosophical Society.

The term *theosophy* was introduced, to the best knowledge of reputable scholars, in the third century by a noted philosopher, Ammonius Saccas, the teacher of Plotinus, the great Roman philosopher. Theosophy, however, has a long history traceable directly to the Orient, particularly India, where the Upanishads and Vedas, or Hindu Scriptures, form the basis for no small part of the doctrines. The writings of Gautama Buddha and the early Christian Gnostics also heavily influenced the formulation of theosophical doctrines.

Theosophy claims to be a universal world religion of a distinct nature. But any careful study of its eclectic background readily reveals that much of its "original theology" is borrowed from easily recognizable sources. The modern American history of Theosophy began with the activities of the young and mystically inclined Russian Madame Helena Blavatsky, in the year 1875, in New York City. Helena Petrovna was born in Ekaterinoslav, Russia, in 1831, the daughter of Peter Hahn, the son of the noble Von Hahn family of Germany. At the age of seventeen, Helena married the Czarist general Blavatsky, a cultured gentleman many years her senior, whom she promptly left after only three months of marriage. It is a known fact that Madame was notoriously short of patience and had a violent temper. It is asserted by at least one of her biographers that she married General Blavatsky merely to spite her acid-tongued governess, who, in a moment of sarcasm, declared that even the noble old gentleman would not marry a shrew like Helena. To her credit, Madame Blavatsky repented quite hastily of her revenge upon the governess, but she had already beguiled the general and was forced into a position of compliance with matrimony.[9]

Shortly after her separation from General Blavatsky, Helena embarked upon a long career of travel that eventually led her into the field of mystical religion, which she studied from Tibet, India, and Egypt to Texas, Louisiana, Cuba, and Canada, settling eventually in New York long enough to found, in the year 1875, the Theosophical Society, in conjunction with Colonel H. S. Olcott and W. Q. Judge, two ardent devotees.

---

[8]H. P. Blavatsky, *Theosophical Glossary* (Los Angeles: The Theosophy Company, 1892, 1973).
[9]Baseden G. Butt, *Madame Blavatsky* (London: Marchand Bros., 1926), 13.

In 1879 Madame Blavatsky left the United States for India, and later died in London, England, in 1891. W. Q. Judge split the Society in 1895, and then saw his organization also divided into the "Universal Brotherhood and Theosophical Society" and "The Theosophical Society in America."

Madame Blavatsky held Judge in the highest esteem, and Judge wore her mantle of leadership to all intents and purposes as head of the Aryan Theosophical Society of which he was president until 1896, when he died. Madame Blavatsky also founded the Esoteric School of Theosophy in London in 1888, and during her travels in India and England, influenced profoundly Annie Wood Besant, who took over leadership of the school after the deaths of Madame Blavatsky, Judge, and his successor, Catherine Tingley.

~When Catherine Tingley died in 1929, G. D. Purucker assumed the presidency of the British Society, taking charge of the administrative and policy-making aspects of the Theosophists. Additionally, he developed and explained the more esoteric of Blavatsky's teachings for his students. He died in 1942. The Society was governed by its Cabinet until Colonel Arthur L. Conger was recognized as president in 1945. James A. Long succeeded Conger after the latter's death in 1951. The present leader, Grace F. Knoche, assumed office as president of the American Society at the time of Long's death in 1971.~

Helena Blavatsky was a woman of tremendous physical proportions with piercing, almost hypnotic eyes, and she ruled the Theosophists during her life and in many areas, even after her death, through her literary works—principally *The Secret Doctrine,* which is still regarded as divinely inspired interpretations or oracular instructions by most loyal Theosophists.

Annie Besant (1847–1933) was the most prominent of all the British Theosophical luminaries, and one destined to become a bright star in the political fortunes of India. Among her many accomplishments, Besant founded the Central Hindu College at Benares, India, in 1898, and also the Indian Home Rule League in 1916. In the year 1917 she was elected president of the Indian National Congress, and was almost always regarded as a powerful figure in Indian politics.

In 1889 Mrs. Besant, a native of London, became enthralled by the personality and teachings of Madame Blavatsky and forthwith became a devout pupil and disciple. Mrs. Besant believed firmly in the teachings of Madame Blavatsky; her writings best represent the true doctrines of the cult and are always laudatory of the departed Russian seer.

Mrs. Besant herself had not a few idiosyncrasies, and she was highly mystical in her approach to both life and religion, as evidenced in 1925, when she claimed for her adopted son Krishnamurti, an Indian mystic, the title of "Messianic Leader and Reincarnation of the World Teacher."

Such grandeur, however, was renounced by the new Messiah on November 20, 1931, at Krotana, California, then headquarters of the American branch of Theosophy. Mrs. Besant died in 1933, after which time George Arundale and C. Jinara Jodosa succeeded to the presidency of the American Society.[10]

---

[10]See Horton Davies, *The Challenge of the Sects* (Philadelphia, Pa.: Westminster Press, 1961); Charles Ferguson, *Nehru Books of Revelation* (Garden City, N.Y.: Doubleday, 1929); and J. K. Van Baalen, *The Chaos of the Cults* (Grand Rapids, Mich.: William B. Eerdmans Publishing Company, 1962).

It should be remembered that the apostle Paul enjoined the Christian church to forbid women to usurp authority over the male head, and leadership roles should more properly be filled by men where available to meet this need:

> Let the woman learn in silence with all subjection. But I suffer not a woman to teach, nor to usurp authority over the man, but to be in silence. For Adam was first formed, then Eve. And Adam was not deceived, but the woman being deceived was in the transgression. (1 Timothy 2:11–14)

It can be clearly seen from the study of non-Christian cults, ancient and modern, that the female teaching ministry has graphically fulfilled what Paul anticipated in his day by divine revelation, and brought in its wake, as history tells us, confusion, division, and strife. This is true from Johanna Southcutt to Mary Baker Eddy to Helena Blavatsky and the Fox sisters, all of whom were living proof of the validity of our Lord's declaration that "if the blind lead the blind, both shall fall into the ditch" (Matthew 15:14b).

Theosophy and Christian Theology

According to the literature of the theosophical cult as represented chiefly by Helena Blavatsky, Annie Besant, I. C. Cooper, A. P. Sinnett, L. W. Rogers, and C. W. Leadbeater, there is a great fraternity of "Mahatmas" or "Masters," who are highly evolved examples of advanced reincarnations whose dwelling place is somewhere in the far reaches of remote Tibet.[11] These divine beings possessed Madam Blavatsky and utilized her services to reach the generations now living upon the earth with the restored truths of the great religions of the world, which have been perverted by mankind. In this highly imaginative picture, the Theosophists add seven planes of progression, previously noted, through which the souls of men must progress on their way to the Theosophists' "heaven" or Devachan.

In keeping with the Theosophists' concept of heaven, in the final analysis, is the *nirvana* of Buddhism, where the absorption of the personality or the soul into a type of world soul eventually extinguishes personal cognizance—the Theosophists also have their "hell," which, oddly enough, resembles the Roman Catholic purgatory, with indescribable tortures and degrees of degradation. The name for this intermediate state of existence where the departed souls suffer for their past sins while awaiting reincarnation, or the chance to start living in a new body, is Kamaloka, where the atmosphere is "gloomy, heavy, dreary, depressing to an inconceivable extent . . . the man who is full of evil passions *looks* the whole of them; bestial appetites shape the astral body into bestial forms, and repulsively human animal shapes are the appropriate clothing of brutalized human souls. No man can be a hypocrite in the astral world and cloak foul thoughts with a veil of virtuous seeming; whatever a man is that he appears to be in outward form and semblance, radiant in beauty if his mind be noble, repulsive in hideousness if his nature be foul."[12]

---

[11]See Blavatsky's *Glossary*.

[12]Annie Besant, *The Ancient Wisdom: An Outline of Theosophical Teachings* (London: Theosophical Publishing Society, 1897), 92–93.

Contrary to the Christian doctrines of redemption and punishment, Theosophy offers no forgiveness for sin except through myriads of reincarnations ever progressing toward Devachan, and no eternal retribution for man's rebellion or sin, only the evolutionary terrors of Kamaloka.

With regard to the "The Three Declared Objects" mentioned previously, assent to the first is required for membership, the remaining two being optional. " 'The Society has no dogmas or creed, is entirely nonsectarian, and includes in its membership adherents of all faiths and of none, exacting only from each member their tolerance for the beliefs of others that he would wish them to exhibit toward his own.' "[13]

Theosophy makes no demands of absolute allegiance to any religion or religious leader, and it is resolutely opposed to any form of dogmatism, particularly that type manifested by the Son of God, who said, "I am the way, the truth, and the life: no man cometh unto the Father, but by me" (John 14:6).

God and Man in Theosophy

In common with Christian Science, Unity, and other pantheistic theologies, Theosophy conceives of God in strictly impersonal terms, while asserting that man is, in a spiritual sense, part of God. L. W. Rogers put it this way, when he wrote,

> In divine essence, latent power and potential spirituality, man is an image of God, because he is part of Him. The same idea is more directly put in the Psalms, with the assertion "ye are gods." If the idea of the immanence of God is sound, then man is a literal fragment of the consciousness of the Supreme Being, is an embryo-god, being destined to ultimately evolve his latent powers into perfect expression. The oneness of life was explicitly asserted by Jesus. . . . It is an unqualified assertion that humanity is a part of God as leaves are part of the tree, not something a tree has created, in the sense that a man creates a machine, but something that is an emanation of the tree and is a living part of it. Thus only has God made man. Humanity is a growth, a development, an emanation, an evolutionary expression of the Supreme Being. . . . It is simplicity itself when we think of the solar system as simply an emanation of the Supreme Being, as something generated from a central life, an expression of that life which gives rise to the poles within it that we know as consciousness and matter. The human soul is an individualized fragment of that divine life . . . is literally a spark of the divine fire, and latent within it are the characteristics of that central light from which it originated. The theosophical conception of the soul is that it is literally an emanation from God, and since it is therefore of its own essence, it becomes clear why Theosophists assert that man is a god in the making.[14]

---

[13]Russell, *Schaff-Herzog*, 408–409.
[14]Rogers, *Elementary*, 22–25; 19–20.

In keeping with this position, Mrs. Besant once declared, "Man is spiritual intelligence, a fragment of divinity clothed in matter."[15] Mrs. Besant's adopted son, Krishnamurti, once declared that all of us are a part of God and must dig down within ourselves to find the God within us.

These pantheistic views of the Deity are drawn from the deadly trinity of Hinduism, Buddhism, and Gnosticism. And one wonders why Theosophy even attempts to use Christian terms at all, except when it is realized that it is easier to reach the Western mind in terms of the Christian religion than in the language of Hinduism, Buddhism, and Gnosticism. So this is the obvious reason for the utilization of redefined Christian terminology by Theosophists.

Concerning the deity of Jesus Christ and His unique place as *the* Savior of the world, Theosophy declares that all men are innately divine, "so that in time all men become Christs."[16]

The clearest position on this subject, however, is declared by Rogers, who summed up the views of Theosophy where our Lord and His mission are concerned when he wrote,

> Most readers will probably agree that a world teacher known as the Christ did come, and that he founded a religion nearly 2,000 years ago. Why do they think so? They reply that God so loved the world that he sent his son the Christ to bring it light and life. If that is true, how can we avoid the conclusion that he or his predecessors, must have come many times before. The belief that he came but once is consistent only with the erroneous notion that Genesis is history, instead of allegory . . . when a new era in human evolution begins, a world teacher comes in a voluntary incarnation and founds a religion that is suited to the requirements of the new age. Humanity is never left to grope along alone. All that it can comprehend and utilize is taught in the various religions. World teachers, the christs and saviours of the age, have been appearing at propitious times since humanity began existence. . . . In the face of such facts, what becomes of the assertion that God so loved the world that he sent his son to help ignorant humanity about 2,000 years ago—but never before? What about the hundreds of millions of human beings who lived and died before that time? Did he care nothing for them? Did he give his attention to humanity for a period of only 2,000 years and neglect it for millions of years? Has anybody believed that God in his great compassion sent just *one* world teacher for that brief period. . . . If God so loved the world that he sent his son 2,000 years ago, he sent him, or some predecessor very many times before.
>
> Supermen are not myths or figments of the imagination. They are as natural and comprehensive as human beings. In the regular order of evolution, we shall ourselves reach their level and join their ranks, while younger humanity shall attain our present state. As they rose, we too shall rise. Our past has been evolution's night. Our present is its dawn. Our future shall be

[15]Annie Besant, *Man's Life in Three Worlds* (London: Theosophical Publishing Society, 1899), 3.
[16]Annie Besant, *Is Theosophy Anti-Christian?* (London: Theosophical Publishing Society, 1901), 16.

its perfect day. . . . That is the magnificent future the Theosophist sees for the human race.[17]

The refutation of these non-Christian concepts concerning God and the Lord Jesus Christ are clearly found in various places in the Bible. The personality of God and the deity of Christ are forcefully set forth along with many of the other things that Theosophists deny. The God of the Bible created man and is separate and distinct from him (Genesis 1:27). He is a cognizant ego or personality (Exodus 3:14; Isaiah 48:12; John 8:58), and He is triune—three separate persons—Father, Son, and Holy Spirit, yet one in essence or nature (Deuteronomy 6:4; Galatians 3:20). The God of the Bible cannot be equated with the God of Theosophy, nor can Jesus Christ be redefined so that Christ becomes innately divine, "so that in time all men become Christs."[18] Neither the laws of language, logic, nor biblical theology can permit such extravagances as the Theosophists must insist upon to arrive at such inconceivable equations.

The Theosophist, in his depersonalization of God, however, fails to recognize that man is a cognizant, reflective ego, and that he is a creation of God, in the divine spiritual image, debased though he may be by sin. How is it possible to claim for the creation what is not possessed by the Creator, namely, personality? Are we to assume that the creation, even though part of the divine, is greater in that part, i.e., the possession of ego and personality, than the divine itself? To use the analogy of Rogers, is the spark greater than the flame, the ray greater than the source from which it emanated? Of course not! So, then, neither is man greater than God. If man possesses personality and ego, and the Theosophists grant this, then God, by definition, must be personality and ego—a disconcerting fact, but a fact nonetheless!

The Bible gives much evidence to this effect by underscoring the personality of God in terms of attributes that only a personality can manifest. These traits forever separate Him from the pantheistic God of Theosophy, which is incapable, by definition, of performing these things.

1. *God remembers.* "I, even I, am he that blotteth out thy transgressions for mine own sake, and will not remember thy sins" (Isaiah 43:25).

2. *God creates.* "In the beginning God created the heaven and the earth" (Genesis 1:1).

3. *God knows, i.e., He has a mind.* "The Lord knoweth them that are his" (2 Timothy 2:19). "For I know the thoughts that I think toward you, saith the Lord" (Jeremiah 29:11).

4. *God is a personal Spirit.* "I am the Almighty God; walk before me, and be thou perfect" (Genesis 17:1).

5. *God has will.* "Lo, I come to do thy will, O God" (Hebrews 10:9).

From this brief résumé of some of God's attributes, the interested reader can doubtless see the vast difference between the God and Father of our Lord Jesus Christ and the impersonal God of Theosophy. Theosophy's God is not a personal being. He cannot remember, He cannot create, He cannot will, He cannot know,

---

[17]Rogers, *Elementary Theosophy*, 260–63.
[18]Besant, *Is Theosophy Anti-Christian*, 16.

because He is not a personality, but an impersonal "it," an abstract, pantheistic principle, not the God of divine revelation.

Theosophy makes the grave error of all Gnostic cults: it divides Jesus and Christ, making Jesus only the outer man and Christ a divine consciousness immanent within Him and within all men, to a greater or lesser degree. For Theosophists, Jesus is not *the* Christ of divine revelation, as distinct from the Christ who is immanent within all men. They do not understand that the word *Christ* (*Christos* in the Greek) is a title corresponding to the Hebrew *Messiah*. It is not a force, essence, or divine spark, as any careful reading of a good Greek lexicon will speedily reveal. In the sixteenth chapter of Matthew's gospel, the apostle Peter affirmed this truth by pointing out in his confession of faith, "Thou art the Christ, the Son of the living God" (Matthew 16:16). And John reminds us, "Who is a liar but he that denieth that Jesus is the Christ? He is antichrist, that denieth the Father and the Son" (1 John 2:22).

It is unnecessary to pursue this point any further, since Christian theology has always maintained that Jesus of Nazareth was the Christ, the anointed Redeemer of God, very God himself (Isaiah 9:6; Micah 5:2; John 1:1, 14, 18; Colossians 2:9; Revelation 1:16–17; Isaiah 44:6; etc.). He is the second person of the Trinity, not the theosophical emanation from the impersonal essence they acknowledge as God. And this is why Theosophy is not Christian and is, indeed, the very antithesis of historic Christian theology.

In regard to the lengthy statement previously quoted from Rogers, the argument that God must have sent other "world teachers" to meet the requirements for humanity's redemption prior to Christ is the purest speculation and directly contradicts the statement of our Lord who affirmed,

> Verily, verily, I say unto you, He that entereth not by the door into the sheepfold, but climbeth up some other way, the same is a thief and a robber. But he that entereth in by the door is the shepherd of the sheep. To him the porter openeth; and the sheep hear his voice: and he calleth his own sheep by name, and leadeth them out. . . . All that ever came before me are thieves and robbers: but the sheep did not hear them. . . . The thief cometh not, but for to steal, and to kill, and to destroy: I am come that they might have life, and that they might have it more abundantly. (John 10:1–3, 8, 10)

The epistle to the Romans points out that God has revealed himself to the hundreds of millions of human beings about whom Rogers is concerned, and that in the face of His revelation, "professing themselves to be wise, they became fools, and changed the glory of the incorruptible God into an image made like to corruptible man, and to birds, and fourfooted beasts, and creeping things. Wherefore God also gave them up to uncleanness through the lusts of their own hearts, to dishonour their own bodies between themselves: who changed the truth of God into a lie, and worshipped and served the creature more than the Creator, who is blessed for ever" (Romans 1:22–25). And as a direct result of this, the apostle Paul informs us, God abandoned them to themselves so that "when they knew God, they glorified him not as God . . . but became vain in their imaginations, and their foolish heart was darkened" (Romans 1:21).

So it is apparent that mankind has never been without a witness of God's grace and love, but that every time it has been manifested in His law, His prophets, and finally, in His Son, men have responded with violence, evil, and sin of every proportionate degree, so that they are without excuse and *deserving* of eternal condemnation.

Quite to the contrary, the idea is not preposterous, as Rogers suggests, but consistent with the character of God and His judgment upon depraved human nature (Romans 3:23). It is a fact that Theosophists refuse to face despite the atrocities frequent in even modern society, the horrible Nazi concentration camps, the selective incarceration, torture, and even murder by modern communistic regimes, and the other testimonies to the fallen nature of mankind. They apparently think that when Adam sinned (an allegory) the race fell spiritually upward, a condition controverted by all the facts of history!

It is true that God so loved the world that He gave His only begotten Son, but it is not true that He has many sons, that they came many times, and that Christ was only one among them. This He himself denied, and on far better authority than any Rogers or Theosophist can muster (John 12:44–50).

The Vicarious Atonement

Theosophy is opposed to not only the true biblical teaching of God's personality and nature, as well as the deity of His Son, but it also vigorously denies Christ's substitutionary sacrifice for all sin (1 John 2:2).

One of the most concise statements concerning the views of Theosophy in this area comes from the pen of L. W. Rogers, who wrote,

> Back of the ancient doctrine of the vicarious atonement is a profound and beautiful truth, but it has been degraded into a teaching that is as selfish as it is false. That natural truth is the sacrifice of the Solar Logos, the Deity of our system. Sacrifice consists of limiting himself in the manner of manifested worlds, and it is reflected in the sacrifice of the Christ and other great teachers. Not the sacrifice of life, but a voluntary returning to live in the confinement of material body. Nobody more than the Theosophist pays to the Christ the tribute of the most reverent gratitude; we also hold with St. Paul that each must work out his own salvation. Were it not for such sacrifice, the race would be very, very far below its present evolutionary level. The help that such great spiritual beings have given mankind is incalculable, and is undoubtedly altogether beyond what we were able to comprehend. But to assume that such sacrifice has relieved man from the necessity of developing his spiritual nature, or in any degree nullify his personal responsibility for any evil he has done, is false and dangerous doctrine. . . . And true, too, we know that any belief that is not in harmony with the facts of life is a wrong belief . . . the vital point against this plan of salvation is that it ignores the soul's personal responsibility, and teaches that whatever the offenses against God and man have been, they may be canceled by the simple process of believing that another suffered and died in order that those sins might be forgiven. It is the pernicious doctrine that wrongdoing by one

can be set right by the sacrifice of another. It is simply astounding that such a belief could have survived the middle ages and should continue to find millions who accept it in these days of clearer thinking.

The man who is willing to purchase bliss by the agony of another is unfit for heaven, and could not recognize it if he were there.

A heaven that is populated with those who see in the vicarious atonement the happy arrangement letting them in pleasantly and easily, would not be worth having. It would be a realm of selfishness, and that would be no heaven at all. . . . The hypothesis of reincarnation shows our inherent divinity, and the method by which the latent becomes the actual. Instead of the ignoble belief that we can fling our sins upon another, it makes personal responsibility the keynote of life. It is the ethics of self-help. It is the moral code of self-reliance. It is the religion of self-respect.[19]

The inconsistency of Theosophists is eclipsed only by their apparent lack of concern for the validity of established terms in both philosophy and theology. Here is a classic example of what we mean: Rogers wants Christians to believe that "nobody more than the Theosophist pays to the Christ the tribute of the most reverent gratitude." But he denies categorically the expressions of that very Christ and the prophecies concerning Him, which state that He came for the express purpose of paying the penalty for all sin.

The Theosophist wants no part of the vicarious sacrifice of Jesus; in fact, it is personally repugnant to him. By his own admission, he considers it "an ignoble belief" that we can fling our sins upon another. But this is exactly what we are called upon to do in the New Testament.

The Scriptures bear incontrovertible witness to the truth that "Christ died for the ungodly" (Romans 5:6), and that "The blood of Jesus Christ . . . cleanseth us from all sin" (1 John 1:7). There is no doctrine found within the pages of the Bible that is better supported or substantiated than that of the substitutionary death of Christ for the sins of the world. As far back in the biblical record as Exodus, Moses wrote of God's symbolic use of blood for purification and sacrifice. It will be recalled that Jehovah delivered the Israelites from Egypt by causing all the firstborn of the nation, including Pharaoh's own son, to fall under the shadow of sudden death (Exodus 12). The Jews were instructed in this instance to sprinkle the blood of the young lamb on the doorpost and lintels of their homes, and God promised, "When I see the blood, I will pass over you" (Exodus 12:13). The Lord also instituted the animal sacrifices of the Levitical era and expressly stated, "It is the blood that maketh an atonement for the soul" (Leviticus 17:11).

Following this typology through into the New Testament, we find that Jesus was called the Lamb of God, who takes away the sin of the world (John 1:29), and further, that His blood, shed upon the cross, is our atonement or covering for sin, even for the sins of all mankind (Matthew 26:28; Romans 5:6–8; Ephesians 1:7; Colossians 1:20).

The believer in Christ, therefore, is saved by grace alone through faith in His blood, and its efficacy for the cleansing of all sin (Romans 3:25). John, the

---

[19]Rogers, *Elementary Theosophy*, 201–206.

beloved disciple, reminds us in his powerful epistle of this fact (1 John 1:7), and Peter declares, "[We] were not redeemed with corruptible things, as silver and gold ... but with the precious blood of Christ, as a lamb without blemish and without spot" (1 Peter 1:18–19).

The pages of the New Testament bear incontrovertible testimony that Jesus Christ on Calvary purchased the church with his own blood (Acts 20:28), and in the great message of Christ to John recorded in the book of Revelation, we are told that He "washed us from our sins in his own blood" (Revelation 1:5). This was not a pagan sacrifice to placate the wrath of a heathen god's justice. The sacrifice was offered through the Eternal Spirit, to free the sons of men from the curse of sin and to open the path to salvation, through which we now can have boldness to enter into the holiest by the blood of Jesus—a new and living way to the very throne of God our Father (Hebrews 10:19–20).

Contrasting this picture of concrete biblical theology with the views of Theosophy, the facts speak for themselves, and they cannot honestly be ignored.

Theosophy, on the other hand, refuses to accept the vicarious atonement of Jesus Christ for the forgiveness of all sin. Instead, Theosophy teaches the inexorable law of Karma (the accumulated weight of one's bad actions that can only be "atoned for" through personal and individual good actions during a succession of lives [reincarnation] and which is sometimes called "the Law of Cause and Effect"). Annie Besant described it as the "law of causation ... bidding man ... surrender all the fallacious ideas of forgiveness, vicarious atonement, divine mercy and the rest of the opiates that superstition offers to the sinner."[20]

Consequently, through the application of the law of Karma, the biblical doctrine of the Atonement is neatly supplanted and the authority of Scripture circumvented or negated. Mrs. Besant once wrote that "The atonement wrought by Christ lies not in the substitution of one individual for another."[21]

As the daughter of an Anglican clergyman and the former wife of another, Mrs. Besant must have known better, but despite this, she never satisfactorily explained what the biblical doctrine of the Atonement *does* mean, if it does not mean what the Christian church has always maintained.

For Theosophists the redemptive love of a personal God as revealed in the substitutionary sacrifice of His most precious possession, His Son, Jesus Christ, is totally unnecessary and is not the way of salvation. This fact alone would remove Theosophy from any serious consideration of compatibility with Christianity, and we can be grateful that the cult, as of 1984, was so insignificant in number that it does not even appear in the *Yearbook of American and Canadian Churches 1975* (Constant H. Jacquet Jr., ed., New York: Abingdon Press, 1975), although its "chapters" or centers can be found in many major cities of the United States and throughout the world. Its rate of growth seems considerably slower than it was in the 1920s, and we can hope that the very fact of its complexity and the involved vocabulary utilized to describe its mazelike theology may yet render it more ineffective in an age in which precision of definition is at last coming into its own.

---

[20]Annie Besant, *Karma* (London: The Theosophical Publishing Society, 1904), 23.
[21]Besant, *Is Theosophy Anti-Christian*, 11.

What at first appeared to be a decline has changed to a rise in popularity at the close of the twentieth century (1997), largely through attracting many followers who were first introduced to Eastern religious ideas through the New Age movement. The American "section" headquarters for the Theosophical Society is in Wheaton, Illinois, on a beautiful estate named the Olcott Estate, after the first Theosophical president, Colonel Henry Steel Olcott. The international headquarters is in Adyar, Madras, India. The educational program of the society is in Illinois, engaged in publications, seminars, lectures, correspondence, and classes (both at the Olcott center and in satellite locations).

In order to be Christian, one must conform to the Scriptures. Theosophy fails to meet this requirement and must be considered anti-Christian.

Sin, Salvation, and Prayer

The Christian concepts of sin, salvation, and prayer need but passing mention relative to the reinterpretation they receive at the hands of theosophical writers. The teaching of Theosophy on these principal Christian doctrines is very definite and important and should be understood.

The Bible plainly states that all men have come under the divine indictment of sin (Romans 3:23). The divine remedy for sin, as we have seen, is the redemptive work of Jesus Christ who died, "the just for the unjust that he might bring us to God" (1 Peter 3:18). So hideous and degrading was human sin in the eyes of a Holy God that it required the God-man's death to satisfy the righteous judgment of His Father. Salvation from sin is full and complete by faith in Jesus Christ "once for all" (Hebrews 10:10). "For the wages of sin is death" (Romans 6:23). Since the Theosophist wants no part of the redeeming sacrifice of the Cross, and since he denies that personal sin must be atoned for by a power outside himself, like Petra of old, he is deceived by the pride of his heart (Obadiah 3). There can be little doubt that Theosophists, like Unitarians, consider salvation gained by character and progression. Theirs must be a God of love who allows the penalty of sin to be worked out on the wheel of reincarnation and by infinite progression. He does not judge; He cannot, for the spectacle of an impersonal principle judging the actions of a personal being is too much for any serious student of the philosophy of religion, and Theosophists are no exception.

The biblical doctrine of prayer also suffers at the hand of Theosophy. In the biblical vocabulary, prayer is personal communion with a personal God, not an abstract force or a cosmic consciousness. Jesus Christ himself encouraged us to pray many times (see Matthew 5:44; 6:6–7, 9; 9:38). He repeatedly emphasized its virtues and benefits. For the Christian, then, prayer is the link with the Eternal by which man can come to "the throne of grace" in the power of the Holy Spirit and find "grace to help in time of need" (Hebrews 4:16).

Salvation for the Christian is by grace and true faith in God's only method for making men holy and through the only "name under heaven given among men, whereby we must be saved" (Acts 4:12). Human sin makes it necessary for this grand redemption, and since Theosophy denies it, it follows of necessity that redemption would also be negated. Since Theosophy rejects the God of the Bible or any concept of a personal God, prayer in the biblical sense becomes impossible, and the sinner's most desperate need, which is to "call upon the name of the Lord" that he might be saved (Romans 10:13), not from a wheel of incarnations, but from eternal, spiritual, and conscious separation from the life and fellowship of God himself, is ignored or denied.

Contrasted to this biblical picture of sin, salvation, and prayer, Theosophy equates God the Father with the pagan gods Buddha and Vishnu,[22] and defines prayer not as personal supplication for divine mercy and grace (Philippians 4:6–7), but as "concentrated thought."[23] Theosophists also believe that personal sin is removed only by suffering in Kamaloka, "the semi-material plane, to us subjective and invisible, where the disembodied 'personalities,' the astral forms . . . remain. . . . It is the Hades of the ancient Greeks and the Amenti of the Egyptians, the land of Silent Shadows."[24] Personal salvation is obtained through various reincarnations, ending in absorption of the individual ego. These cannot be viewed as pleasant alternatives to biblical revelation, but they are all that Theosophy offers.

Resurrection Versus Reincarnation

In bringing to a conclusion this chapter on Theosophy, it is necessary for the Christian to understand the one great doctrine that forever removes any possibility of realizing fellowship with Theosophists.

The apostle Paul, in his great and grand chapter on the resurrection of the body (1 Corinthians 15), cites the resurrection of Christ and its subsequent effect upon the bodies of all mankind as *the* proof that God exists, that Christ is His Son, and that the redemption of all believers is assured by His personal triumph over the grave.

Paul goes to great lengths in this chapter to show that "if Christ be not raised, your faith is vain; ye are yet in your sins" (v. 17). For the great apostle, our hope for physical immortality lies alone in the triumphant physical resurrection of Christ (v. 14), who visibly and tangibly presented himself alive "by many infallible proofs" (Acts 1:3) to over five hundred persons who knew that it was, indeed, Jesus who had conquered the grave on their behalf.

Our risen Lord also promised that one day we should be physically and morally as He is, and that God the Father, through Him, would raise the believing dead and clothe them with immortality at His second advent (1 Thessalonians 4).

The condition of the Christian in death, however, is not one of suffering or repeated reincarnations while atoning for sin, as Theosophy would have it, but one of cognizant personal joy, literally the state of being "at home with the Lord" (2 Corinthians 5:8 NIV).

The resurrection of Jesus Christ and, for that matter, the resurrection of all mankind leave no room for the Theosophical dogma of concurrent reincarnations. We indeed concur with the apostle Paul: "If in this life only we have hope in Christ, we are of all men most miserable" (1 Corinthians 15:19). The souls of the dead do not pass through various reincarnations as Theosophy contends;

---

[22]Annie Besant, *The Seven Principles of Man* (London: The Theosophical Publishing Society, 1902), 58.
[23]Annie Besant, *The Changing World* (London: The Theosophical Publishing Society, 1901), 68.
[24]Blavatsky, *Glossary,* 171–72.

rather, these souls are either experiencing happiness in Christ's presence (Philippians 1:21), in which case, to die is gain; or they are suffering conscious separation from His presence (Luke 16:19–31). In any case, Scripture clearly shows that reincarnation is not man's destiny, nor is it God's revealed plan for perfecting the souls of men. The Bible tells us that Christ died to fully redeem (Romans 5:6; Hebrews 9:26; 10:12).

Out of the Labyrinth, Into the Light

To wend our way completely out of the mazelike labyrinth of Theosophy and its anti-Christian doctrines into the light of biblical reality would probably take many volumes of exacting systematic analysis of this cult. But suffice it to note that Theosophy offers to the sinner no hope of full redemption from sin, only seemingly endless reincarnations; it guarantees no relationship with a loving, personal heavenly Father, and it ignores completely the true nature, person, and work of the Lord Jesus Christ.

The entire system is Eastern in its origin; it is Hinduistic and Buddhistic in its theology, Gnostic in its vocabulary, and Christian only in its key terminology, which is specifically designed to imitate the true content of the Gospel.

The Theosophist proudly rejects the Atonement on the cross, preferring to trust in his own righteousness (and the working out of the law of Karma), and is willing to brave the terrors of Kamaloka itself rather than to bow the knee to Jesus Christ (Philippians 2:10–11).

Let us not, then, be deceived by the veneer of the intellectual and metaphysical jargon the Theosophist has mastered, nor retreat before his attempt to belittle the preaching of the Cross as "foolishness." We need not defer to his alleged "deeper revelation," to his claims that Theosophy is a higher form of revelation for our age. We are informed in Scripture repeatedly that "the preaching of the cross is to them that perish foolishness; but unto us which are saved it is the power of God" (1 Corinthians 1:18). Theosophy is just another attempt to supplant the authority of Christ and Scripture with the "philosophy and empty deceit" of the world (Colossians 2:8 RSV).

Theosophy, in common with the other non-Christian religions of the world, offers no living redeemer, no freedom from the power of sin, and in the end no hope for the world to come. Jesus Christ, on the other hand, offers promises by the mouths of prophets and the God who cannot lie that those who trust in and serve Him shall "receive [for their faith] an hundredfold, and shall inherit everlasting life" (Matthew 19:29).

We must seek to win Theosophists to a saving knowledge of the Gospel, but we must not forget that their theology has many labyrinths, for "there is a way which seemeth right unto a man," in the words of Solomon, "but the end thereof are the ways of death" (Proverbs 14:12).

Recommended Resources

1. Ankerberg, John, and John Weldon. *Encyclopedia of Cults and New Religions.* Eugene, Ore.: Harvest House, 1999.

2. Mather, George A., and Larry A. Nichols. *Dictionary of Cults, Sects, Religions and the Occult.* Grand Rapids: Zondervan Publishers, 1993.
3. McDowell, Josh, and Don Stewart. *A Handbook on Today's Religions.* Nashville: Thomas Nelson, 1993.

Quick Facts About Buddhism

- Siddhartha Gautama followed the paths of previous "buddhas," or enlightened ones, until he discovered the Middle Path, the Four Noble Truths, and the Eightfold Path, and achieved enlightenment.

- Buddhism shows a heavy influence of Brahmanism, gods, and goddesses in Buddha's history and teachings; its description of a universal cosmic consciousness is that of a nonpersonal essence, sometimes called the Void.

- The Pali *Tripitaka* text is considered by many to be the most reliable teachings of Buddha, although Mahayana Buddhism and other sects add to it.

- Man suffers because his desires are fixated on the illusion of self, which confines him to nonpermanence within the laws of Karma and reincarnation.

- Self-salvation is achieved by following the Middle Path, the Four Noble Truths, and the Eightfold Path. The ultimate goal is to reach the state of Nirvana, where the self becomes extinguished in the Void.

Chapter 9

Buddhism—
Classical, Zen,
and Nichiren Shoshu

Preface

~Although Classical Buddhism is one of the four major world religions and not a "cult" as defined in chapter 1 of this volume, it still birthed a cultic brood that was repackaged in many ways, including Scientology, Est, Forum, Lifespring, and its older forms of Zen and Nichiren Shoshu.[1]~

As of 2000, the worldwide estimate for followers of the Buddha stood at more than three hundred fifty million.[2] ~Buddhism—once a religion of the East—has become a popular faith in the West. American converts to Buddhism number in the thousands and include many notable celebrities, among them: Joan Baez, Tina Turner, Richard Gere, Larry Hagman, and Harrison Ford.[3]~ People from all walks of life are interested in various aspects of Buddhism's religious philosophy, and as we approach this study, it is important to understand why there has been such a penetration of Asian philosophy on American college campuses: People are pursuing Eastern religions in the United States because their message has been dressed up to meet our cultural needs—they are responding to it because there is a deep awareness of a need for spiritual reality.[4] A great many

This chapter researched and compiled by Kurt Van Gorden, and edited by Paul Copan and Jill Martin Rische.
[1]~Kurt Van Gorden commentary (first paragraph).
[2]Statistics taken from *www.adherents.com/largecom/com_buddhist.html.*
[3]~Second paragraph cited from Walter Martin, *Kingdom of the Cults* (Minneapolis: Bethany House Publishers, 1997), 302.
[4]Walter Martin, *Zen Buddhism, Hare Krishna, and Meher Baba* (Santa Ana, Calif.: One Way Libraries, 1976), cassette tape, side 1.

Christian churches are not presenting Jesus Christ's Gospel with a compelling relevancy. They are not attempting to come to grips with today's problems and issues. People are quite literally leaving the church in droves because they have not truly heard the Gospel, and those with no background whatsoever in historic Christianity go after Eastern religions en masse because they cloak their Eastern philosophy or religion in Western terminology.

Classical Buddhism

~To understand the core of Buddhism and its far-reaching impact on India and the world, one must first become a student of history. Twenty-five hundred years ago Hinduism reigned supreme in India, and the people were subject to and enslaved by it.[5]

J. Isamu Yamamoto explains the Indian history:

> Over three thousand years ago the Aryans (a powerful group of Indo-European-speaking people) . . . [conquered] the Indus valley, the Aryans instituted Brahmanism (today it has developed into Hinduism) and the caste system in the Indian culture, which enabled the invaders to maintain the purity of the Aryan race and establish themselves as spiritual and social masters over the native Indians.[6]

The enslaving caste system played an important part for Indian reformers, like Buddha, who sought liberation from Hinduism.

> Another important aspect of modern Hindu life, the caste system, began to emerge during the Vedic period. The system of classifying individuals into castes is vocational and related to skin color. The Rig-Veda speaks of five social castes:
>
> (1) the Brahmins—the priestly scholarly caste;
> (2) the Kshatriyas—the warrior-soldier caste;
> (3) the Vaishyas—the agricultural and merchant caste;
> (4) the Sudras—the peasant and servant caste;
> (5) the Harijan—the outcasts or "untouchables."
>
> Over time these castes underwent thousands of subdivisions. The top of the social scale remains the Brahmins, while the very bottom is comprised of what became known as "untouchables."[7]

Under Hinduism, the lot of the masses was poverty and despair, and the wheel of reincarnation or *samsara* loomed constantly before them like a never-ending nightmare of suffering and death. Discontent grew among the people, and many searched for something to break the relentless hold of Hinduism:

---

[5]Martin, 1974, cassette tape, side 1.
[6]J. Isamu Yamamoto, "The Buddha," *Christian Research Journal* (Spring/Summer 1994): 11.
[7]George A. Mather and Larry A. Nichols, "Hinduism History" in *Dictionary of Cults, Sects, Religions and the Occult* (Grand Rapids: Zondervan, 1993), 117.

As the vast majority of the people were illiterate and indescribably poor, the gap widened between the few literates and the host of illiterates, between the few princes and rulers and their millions of subjects, between the few privileged of high caste and the great underprivileged population that belonged to the lower castes and outcastes. This gap grew wider and wider. And from the hopelessness among the many arose despair.[8]

There seemed no escape from the fate of having to endure an endless succession of painful lives before one could be freed to merge for eternity with the "World-Soul"—a state known as *Nirvana*.[9] Into this religion of strict castes and oppression was born the son of a minor *Raja* or King sometime between 490 and 410 B.C.[10] His philosophy of life would impact the world for centuries to come.~

Gautama Buddha, founder of the Buddhist religion, was the son of Suddhodana, a chieftain reigning over a district near the Himalayas in what is known today as the country of Nepal. At an early age, Siddhartha Gautama,[11] his true name, observed the many contradictions and problems of life; he abandoned his wife and son when he felt he could no longer endure the life of a rich nobleman, and became a wandering ascetic in search of the truth about life. Buddhist historians tell us that after almost seven years of wandering, inquiring, meditating and searching, he found "the true path," and "great enlightenment," under the legendary Bo[12] tree (tree of wisdom), and thus attained Nirvana. Classical Buddhism maintains that cycles of rebirths are necessary in order to attain Nirvana.[13] The teachings of the Buddha are concerned with the ramifications of the "Four Noble Truths" and the "Eightfold Path": (1) Suffering; (2) Its cause; (3) Its cessation; and (4) The Way which leads to this cessation:

In its shortest form Buddha's teaching may be summarized as follows: Birth is sorrow, age is sorrow, sickness is sorrow, death is sorrow, clinging to earthly things is sorrow. Birth and rebirth, the chain of reincarnation, result from the thirst of life together with passion and desire. The only escape from this thirst is to follow the Eightfold Path: Right belief, right resolve, right word, right act, right life, right effort, right thinking, right meditation. The goal of Buddhism is Nirvana. A definition of this term is almost impossible for the simple reason that Buddha himself gave no clear idea, and in all probability possessed none, of this state. He was indeed asked by more than one of his disciples whether Nirvana was postmundane or postcelestial existence, or whether it was annihilation. To all these questions, however, he refused an answer, for it was characteristic of his teachings that they were

---

[8]Joseph Gaer, *What Great Religions Believe* (Signet, The New American Library: New York, 1963), 40.
[9]Ibid., 30.
[10]*www.buddhanet.net/e-learning/history/b_chron.htm*. This date is approximate, as there are no written historical records from the time of the Buddha.
[11]Siddhartha Gautama Buddha. Buddha is not his name, although today he is addressed as such; it is a title of enlightenment. The family name is Gautama (excellent cow or best cow), and his given name was Siddhartha (one who achieved his goal). Buddha is also known as *Sakyamuni* "Sage of the Sakyas" (his tribal ethnicity, where his family dwelt in northern India near Nepal).
[12]Also spelled Bodhi Tree (Wisdom Tree), which is a fig tree located at Uruvela (State of Bihar, India), under which Siddhartha Gautama meditated for forty-nine days until he attained enlightenment, or Nirvana.
[13]Walter Martin, *Kingdom of the Cults* (Minneapolis: Bethany House Publishers, 1985), 261.

practically confined to the present life, and concerned themselves but little either with problems of merely academic philosophy or with the unknowable. . . . the *summum bonum* is release from karma and reincarnation, a goal which is to be attained by knowledge, and which consists in absorption into or reunion with the Over-Soul. This involves the annihilation of individuality, and in this sense Nirvana is nihilism, so that with the tacit ignoring of any real conception of the divine in the teachings of Buddha, Nirvana seems to imply the annihilation of the soul rather than its absorption.[14]

Dr. Wing-Tsit Chan, professor of Chinese Culture (Dartmouth College, Hanover, N.H.), provides valuable insight:

Buddha taught the Four Noble Truths. The first of the Noble Truths is the Truth of Suffering. . . . Existence is pain . . . because it is irrevocably bound to the cycle of births and deaths. In this connection, suffering is an undeniable fact of existence.

The second Noble Truth is the Truth of the Cause of Suffering. The cause is craving [desire], which is in turn due to ignorance. . . . The Buddha was not interested in the deduction of categories; he was wholly concerned with the practical problem of removing the cause of suffering. To this end he put forth the doctrines of impermanence and non-ego. . . . This does not mean . . . a denial of the empirical self, but a refutation of the permanent, abiding personal identity. . . .

The third Noble Truth is the Truth of the Cessation of Suffering. When suffering is destroyed, Nirvana, negatively the extinction of passions and positively the state of bliss, is attained. One then becomes an Arhat or Worthy One, either in this life or after death.

The fourth Noble Truth is the Truth of the Way to remove Suffering. This involves a comprehensive system of moral cultivation, but the fundamental way is the Noble Eightfold Path: right views (of the Four Noble Truths), right intention (to renounce sensual pleasure, to bear no malice, to do no harm, etc.), right speech, right action (such as love, joy, abstinence from immorality), right livelihood, right effort (to avoid evil state and produce good state of mind through the practice of Morality, Meditation, and Wisdom), right mindfulness (to be alert with regard to sensations, ideas, etc.), and right concentration. These form the standard of our threefold karma (action energy) or conduct, speech, and thought. . . . The most important element of these teachings is the middle path, between two extremes of passions and asceticism. . . . Throughout the entire history of Buddhism, the middle path has remained the central concept, although its interpretation varies with the different schools. To the Buddha it was a way of life, a sensible, moderate, comprehensive, practical system of ethics. He called the troughs noble, because he regarded nobility as a moral and not a racial quality. His order established on moral principles, a brotherhood without distinction of castes.[15]

---

[14]Samuel Macauley Jackson, ed., *The New Schaff-Herzog Encyclopedia of Religious Knowledge* (Grand Rapids, Mich.: Baker Book House, 1977 reprint, volume 2), 293, as quoted in Martin (1985), 262.

[15]Wing-Tist Chan, "Buddhahood," Vergilius Ferm, ed., *An Encyclopedia of Religion* (New York: Philosophical Library, 1945), 95.

It is important to remember that there is a common denominator to Zen, Buddhism, I Ching, and all Eastern religious or philosophical backgrounds— none of them believes in the existence of a personal God. None of them believes that we can address Him as "Father." All of these, however, are trying to establish a quest for truth or establish an identification with this unknowable essence. They cannot define God, since God is the great unknowable. They claim unity with some kind of unknowable nature. They use Hindu philosophical terms, because Buddhism was derived from Hinduism.[16]

> While frequently regarded as a new religion, it is, strictly speaking, only a reformation of Brahmanism [Hinduism], and can not be understood without some knowledge of the conditions preceding it. The religious system of India as outlined in its oldest religious books, the Vedas, had reached in the Brahmanas and Sutras a degree of ritualism such as, perhaps, never existed elsewhere. This formalism produced a revolt, and from time to time arose various teachers, philosophers, and reformers, of whom the most influential was . . . Buddha.[17]

We become lost in a maze of terminology when God is reduced to an unknowable essence. What do we mean when we talk about God? Can we talk about God as subject and object relationship? Do we talk about God as "I and Thou"?

No. These religions do not talk about God in this way. They do not talk about God as a person. They sometimes use personal terms, but God is not a person. They behold God when they behold themselves, because all creation shares in their understanding of God. Reality, to them, is grounded in us, as human beings. It is not grounded in God and certainly not grounded in His divine Revelation, the Bible.

If you go to Japan, you can hear a song that sounds familiar to most Christians' ears. It sounds like "Jesus loves me, this I know, for the Bible tells me so." But if you know anything about Japanese Buddhism, then it is "the Buddha" whom we know.

In Luke 21:8 Christ said, "Take heed that ye be not deceived: for many shall come in my name, saying, 'I am Christ, and the time draweth near.' Go ye not therefore after them." That is a very important verse. A cult is a group of people gathering around somebody's interpretation of religious truth, which inevitably claims to be in accord with historic Christianity. But it always ends up denying the centrality of the message that Jesus Christ is incarnate deity.[18]

> Jesus sought to save the world, not himself. Buddha began by saving himself and then taught the world. The aim of Jesus is faith and individual existence in heaven in the presence of God; the *Summum Bonum* of Buddha is knowledge and the annihilation of self in Nirvana. In the face of such essential divergencies, the parallels alleged to exist between Buddha and Jesus seem to be cases of accidental coincidence, and it is almost certain

---

[16]Martin, 1976, cassette tape, side 1.
[17]Jackson, 1977, 292.
[18]Martin, 1976, cassette tape, side 1.

that, despite the travel between Palestine and India, which may have influenced to some degree the apocryphal Gospels on the one hand and late Northern Buddhism on the other, Christianity and Buddhism developed to all intents and purposes independently.[19]

If we really want to deal with the problems of the East, we ought to go there and see what these religions have produced.[20] If you really want to understand Buddhism, if you really want to understand Hinduism, if you really want to understand Zen, if you really want to understand all of these sects and cults that have been imported into the United States, then go and look at what they have created over their thousands of years of existence: enslaved and impoverished peoples. It is through their imitation of Christianity and our pioneering within the context of the parable of the Good Samaritan that they have begun to reach out to the needs of others. There is an imitation of the methodology of Christianity; not the content, but the methodology. Pragmatically, something in Christianity works. The religions of the world and the cultic structures of the world recognize that. They are taking Christian terminology and pouring their theology into the mold of our terminology. Then it is sold to the Western world quite successfully. Zen Buddhism, for example, is engineered and designed to be an appeal to the Western mind.

Nirvana, what every Buddhist is seeking, is reaching a state of enlightenment of the soul or spirit until you are at last absorbed totally in the cosmic consciousness. The Buddha supposedly attained this. This is the most desirable of all states. Buddhists say that this is something in the future for the individual, whereas Zen teachers make it available now.

However, in your quest for spiritual reality, you can sit cross-legged on the floor and contemplate stones, pools of water, or even a spider's web, but you will never truly understand what is wrong with you until you recognize that man fell from his state of fellowship with God in Eden (Genesis 3). That fall, or separation from God, is not remedied by looking inside yourself. That fall is remedied by looking outside of yourself to God, who, in Jesus Christ on the cross, reconciled the world to himself.

In these Eastern cultic structures, everyone is looking within. In Christianity, God would have us look out to the cross of Jesus Christ and to His resurrection.[21] That is our deliverance, through faith in Jesus Christ.

The Many Facets of Buddhism

There are fragmentations of these Eastern world religions that have produced cultic structures, but they essentially say the same thing.[22]

Professor Chan comments:

---

[19]Jackson, 1977, 294.

[20]Walter Martin traveled India and the Orient in the 1950s, observing Eastern religions in some of their strongest settings.

[21]In his teachings, Walter Martin frequently contrasted the difference between the bodily resurrection of Jesus Christ with the decaying remains of Gautama Buddha, who died and was buried after eating spoiled food at the age of eighty.

[22]Martin, 1977, cassette tape, side 2.

1. Mahayana and Hinayana Buddhism

It was but natural that divergent opinions should arise within the faith itself. These remained comparatively unimportant, however, until the schism [A.D. 100] into the Mahayana and Hinayana [Theravada], or the "Great Vehicle" and "Little Vehicle." The latter still adhered strictly in the main to the original tenets of Buddhism. . . . The Mahayanists, on the contrary, who form by far the larger sect, devoted themselves to all manner of speculation, being influenced not only by Hinduism but at a later period by Shamanism as well. The Mahayana postulates the existence of a thousand Buddhas with a supreme god. . . .

Buddhism was introduced into Tibet about the seventh century A.D. . . . Here is evolved the . . . celestial types of the Buddhas which appear on earth as men . . . who are represented on earth by the Dalai-Lama at Lhassa, and is the type of the Bodhisatva Maitreya, the future earthly Buddha and the savior of the world.

Buddhism was introduced into China in its Mahayanistic form by the emperor Mingti in A.D. 61, and . . . was carried to Japan, where numerous sects have arisen, although the results have been little more than a further departure from the original faith.[23]

2. Zen

The second oldest of all the cult systems considered in this book is a form of Buddhism with a following of many millions.

"Zen," as it is known in America, is derived from the Japanese branch of the "meditation" school of Buddhist philosophy. Today, Zen claims more than eight million followers worldwide.[24] Zen cannot be taken lightly, especially when it receives favorable attention from magazines of the standing of *Time, Newsweek, Life, U.S. News and World Report,* and *Reader's Digest,* to name a few.

Zealous followers of Zen trace their origin to Buddha, who, they claim, imparted to one of his disciples, Mahakasyapa (or Kasyapa), what has become known as "the doctrine of the Buddha mind." Buddha, as the legend goes, merely picked the flower in silence, and thus communicated the mystical fragment of his mind, hence the emphasis upon the "Buddha mind" in Zen.

The Theological Implications of Zen

When we come to the Zen variety of Buddhism, we find a strong emphasis on the present and on practical meditation. The late Alan Watts, American proponent of Zen, described it this way:

Perhaps the special flavor of Zen is best described as a certain directness. In other schools of Buddhism, awakening or *bodhi* seems remote and almost superhuman, something to be reached only after many lives of patient effort. But in Zen there is always the feeling that awakening is

[23]Chan, op. cit., 96.
[24]See adherents.com *www.adherents.com/Na_653.html.*

something quite natural, something startlingly obvious, which may occur at any moment. If it involves a difficulty, it is just that it is much too simple. Zen is also direct in its way of teaching, for it points directly and openly to the truth, and does not trifle with symbolism.[25]

Zen is hence revolutionary, holding that enlightenment comes with clarification and simplification through acting out of old values of time and experience, and depending upon only the supreme experience, "now." One state of consciousness and the next cannot be measured by hours or miles, as the Master tries to say, in a *koan* . . . the standard advice of Zen, using one of the 1,700 traditional questions to highlight it. The snap of a finger can be a lesson . . . indicating that this very moment is the immediate experience of reality, past time and embracing all dimensions.

> Zen is brusque in its teachings, aimed at the roots of inconsistency. It demands action of a curious sort. This can only be achieved when it is simple, natural and totally correct. It finds truth through shrinking away from error, not discovering a way to truth.
> Such a mystic philosophy, oddly enough, bears a kinship to primitive Christianity. Like the ardent fundamentalist awaiting the second coming which will bring heaven to earth, the Zen ideal is to achieve a Nirvanic state and a saintly condition on this earth. . . . The *koan,* which goes back to the twelfth century, when it was devised to test the students' understanding of the Zen spirit and shake his mind from conventional thinking, leaves most professed Zen followers in Japan uninterested today. And, of course, one can never achieve *satori*—the nonrational, clear and intuitive understanding of reality—until he understands the exercises of *koan* . . . .
> Zen is a paradox within a paradox, a mystical doctrine which laughs at all doctrines and dogma, and becomes a doctrine and dogma in the doing.[26]

With a philosophy such as this, it is easy to understand how Zenists can sit cross-legged (*zazen* Japanese), meditating upon a flower petal or a rock thrown haphazardly over a floor or on a garden path. For them, reality is not objective correlative truth, but subjective, egocentric reflection, which becomes reality if they deign to participate in its manifestation. The following quotations deal with the theology of Zen Buddhism in a general way, for if ever a system was devoid of a theology, except by implication and interpretation, it is Zen.

Zen Teachings

1. *Revelation*

> Zen is at once the knower and the known. It is also the factor which unites the two in one. It is a way to Truth and not facts about Truth. As Dr. Suzuki puts it, "When we think we know something, there is something we

---

[25]Alan W. Watts, *The Way of Zen* (New York: The New American Library, 1957), 83.
[26]Richard Mathison, *Faith, Cults and Sects of America* (New York: The Bobbs-Merrill Company, Inc., 1960), 365, 367–68.

do not know." For there is still an antithesis, the known and the knower, and Zen seeks that which lies beyond antitheses, however subtle.

Strictly speaking, however, Zen is incommunicable. Even as "The Tao that can be expressed is not the Eternal Tao," so Zen translated into the terms and apparatus of the intellect is not true Zen. There is therefore an inevitable distinction between Zen and the forms of Zen, between expressions of Zen, and facts *about* Zen. . . .[27]

2. *Authority*

Zen has nothing to teach us in the way of intellectual analysis; nor has it any set doctrines which are imposed on its followers for acceptance. In this respect Zen is quite chaotic if you choose to say so. Probably Zen followers may have sets of doctrines, but they have them on their own account, and for their own benefit; they do not owe the fact to Zen. Therefore, there are in Zen no sacred books or dogmatic tenets, nor are there any symbolic formula through which an access might be gained into the signification of Zen. If I am asked, then, what Zen teaches, I would answer, Zen teaches nothing. Whatever teachings there are in Zen, they come out of one's own mind. We teach ourselves; Zen merely points the way. Unless this pointing is teaching, there is certainly nothing in Zen purposely set up as its cardinal doctrines or as its fundamental philosophy.[28]

3. *The Nature of God (Pantheism) and Morality*

I see much common ground in Zen and the mysticism of Meister Eckhart, as he wrote: The eye by which I see God is the same as the eye by which God sees me. My eye and God's eye are one and the same—one in seeing, one in knowing, and one in loving. . . . When I have shut the doors of my five senses, earnestly desiring God, I find him in my soul as clearly and as joyful as he is in eternity. . . .[29]

Zen consciousness is a mind made one with life, and even at its lowest produces a sense of oneness with all humanity. Who, having this, needs rules of morality?[30]

Is Zen a religion? It is not a religion in the sense that the term is popularly understood; for Zen has no God to worship, no ceremonial rites to observe, no future abode to which the dead are destined, and last of all, Zen has no soul whose welfare is to be looked after by somebody else and whose immortality is a matter of intense concern with some people. Zen is free from all these dogmatic and "religious" encumbrances.

When I say there is no God in Zen, the pious reader may be shocked, but this does not mean that Zen denies the existence of God; neither denial nor affirmation concerns Zen. When a thing is denied, the very denial involves

---

[27]Christmas Humphreys, *Zen Buddhism* (London: George Allen and Unwin, Ltd., 1957), 2.
[28]Daisetz Teitaro Suzuki, *An Introduction to Zen Buddhism* (London: Rider and Company/The Buddhist Society, n.d.), 38.
[29]Sohaku Ogata, *Zen for the West* (Westport, Conn.: Greenwood Press, Publishers, 1959), 17–18.
[30]Humphreys, *Zen*, op. cit., 178.

something not denied. The same can be said of affirmation. This is inevitable in logic. Zen wants to rise above logic; Zen wants to find a higher affirmation, where there are no antitheses. Therefore, in Zen, God is neither denied nor insisted upon; only in Zen there is no such God as has been conceived by Jewish and Christian minds. For the same reason Zen is not a philosophy; Zen is not a religion.[31]

4. Self-Salvation

... for it is not the life of the soul that lives in perfect freedom and in perfect unity? There is no freedom or unity in exclusion or in limitation. Zen is well aware of this. In accordance with the demands of our inner life, therefore, Zen takes us to an absolute realm wherein there are no antitheses of any sort.

Therefore, Zen does not mean a mere escape from intellectual imprisonment, which sometimes ends in sheer wantonness. There is something in Zen that frees us from conditions and at the same time gives us a certain firm foothold, which, however, is not a foothold in a relative sense. The Zen master endeavours to take away all footholds from the disciple which he has ever had since his first appearance on earth, and then to supply him with one that is really no foothold.[32]

In Zen there are no miracles, supernatural interventions, ways nor refuges. We bear the whole responsibility for our actions and no Sage whomsoever he be has the right to encroach on our free will.

We are at the same time responsible for our slavery and our freedom; the chains of our enslavement have been forged by ourselves, and only we can break them. . . .[33]

5. Sin and Evil

The opposites (dvandva) of light and darkness, good and evil, pleasure and pain, are the essential elements of the game, for although the Godhead is identified with Truth (sat), Consciousness (chit), and Bliss (ananda), the dark side of life has its integral part in the game just as every drama must have its villain, to disrupt the status quo, and as the cards must be shuffled, thrown into chaos, in order that there may be a significant development of the play. For Hindu thought there is no Problem of Evil. The conventional, relative world is necessarily a world of opposites. Light is inconceivable apart from darkness; order is meaningless without disorder; and likewise, up without down, sound without silence, pleasure without pain.[34]

For this reason, the masters talk about Zen as little as possible, and throw its concrete reality straight at us. This reality is the "suchness" (tathata) of our natural, nonverbal world. If we see this just as it is, there is nothing good, nothing bad, nothing inherently long or short, nothing subjective and nothing objective. There is no symbolic self to be forgotten, and no need for any idea of a concrete reality to be remembered.[35]

---

[31]Suzuki, op. cit., 39.
[32]Ibid., 67–68.
[33]Robert Linssen, *Living Zen* (London: George Allen and Unwin, Ltd., 1958), 74.
[34]Watts, op. cit., 45–46.
[35]Ibid., 127.

From the foregoing, the deep-seated philosophical mysticism of the Zen school of meditation of Buddhism is accurately reflected, revealing Zen to be a philosophy that negates a personal God. Second, it denies the reality of sin due to the absence of an absolute standard of revealed law and holiness. Third, it rejects the necessity of personal redemption from the penalty of sin revealed in the Person of Jesus Christ, who *is* the Way.

Zenists have no antidote for the piercing analytical pronouncements of Scripture: "All have sinned, and come short of the glory of God. . . . There is none righteous, no, not one" (Romans 3:23; 3:10). And the reality of divine judgment can be brought to bear upon them through proper use of the Scriptures and logic. As we have mentioned previously, one trip through the gas ovens of Dauchau, Belsen, Auschwitz, and Buchenwald is worth a thousand theological propositions, and Zenists ought to be reminded of the fact that those crimes were crimes against an absolute standard that is not subjective, but objective and universal, i.e., "You shall not murder" (Exodus 20:13 NIV).

The Zenist is a stranger to social responsibility also, which leaves little to justify his existence.

The finest work from a Christian standpoint on the subject of Zen Buddhism was written by Lit-Sen-Chang, a Christian convert from Zen, the former president of Kiang-nan University, and special lecturer in missions at Gordon Divinity School (now Gordon-Conwell Theological Seminary) in Massachusetts. Mr. Chang has performed a real service for evangelical Christianity by analyzing Zen from the inside, so to speak, in his illuminating book *Zen-Existentialism: The Spiritual Decline of the West.*

Excerpts below illustrate some of the foundational defects and inadequacies of Zen:

> Thus, while Zen is seemingly commendable in some features, with its plausible teachings, it is nevertheless objectionable by reason of its serious inadequacy and sheer futility. . . .
>
> 1. It supersedes the doctrine of a real Creator. In the first place, Zen is a very peculiar and subtle form of Atheism. It denies the infinity and transcendence of a living personal God by identifying Him with nature. All visible objects thus become subjective modifications of self-existence, unconscious and impersonal essence, which may be called God, Nature, the Absolute, Oneness, Suchness, or Tathata, etc. It robs God of His sovereignty by denuding Him of His power of self-determination in relation to the world. God is reduced to the hidden ground. . . .
>
> 2. It engenders a spirit of mysticism. Secondly, it has a strong tendency to engender (although they deny it) a spirit of mysticism by taking refuge in its doctrines of radical intuition, i.e., "No dependence upon words and letters"; "Special transmission of the Mind"; . . . Satori is almost entirely lacking in intellectual content and yet filled with intense emotion of conviction and the mystic returns from it with a sense of great illumination. "The source phenomenon is common among Christian mystics who frequently after ecstasy assert that they have had tremendous revelation, yet are unable to state explicitly any of them."
>
> Furthermore, mysticism without divine revelation is dangerous and will lead men to destruction. . . .

3. It disregards the holiness of God. Thirdly, Zen is a very radical form of iconoclasm. According to Prajnaparamita-hrdaya Sutra, "The void nature of all dharmas is not arising or extinction, not pure or impure, not increasing nor decreasing. . . . If one understands that reality is neither pure nor impure, he finds the Buddha in the dung as well as in Heaven. ". . . In the conception of Zenists, sin against God does not exist. . . ."

4. It denies the need of a Savior. Fourthly, Zen is a most radical form of auto-soterism. The principle of heathenism, as Herman Bavinck remarks, is negatively the denial of the true God and the gift of His grace; and positively, the notion that salvation can be secured by man's own power and wisdom.

III. THE UTTER FAILURE OF ZEN

1. In "seeing into one's own nature." Certain of the philosophers have called man a microcosm, as being a rare specimen of divine power, wisdom and goodness and containing within himself wonders sufficient to occupy our minds. This is not altogether improper. For Paul, after reminding the Athenians that they "might feel after God and find him," immediately adds that "He is not far from everyone of us"; every man having within himself undoubted evidence of the heavenly grace by which "he lives and moves and has his being!" . . .

2. In the attainment of Enlightenment. In 1 Corinthians 2:5, Paul well said that: "Your faith should not stand in the wisdom of man, but in the power of God." . . .

Zen asserts that without "Satori" (Enlightenment), "Zen is a sealed book." But the problem is that without special revelation, "Satori" can never be real. This is not our prejudice against Zen, even a psychologist as sympathetic to Zen as Dr. Carl G. Jung shares the same opinion. He says, "We can never decide definitely whether a person is really enlightened, or whether he merely imagines it, we have no criterion of this." . . .

3. In the way of salvation. Can Zen offer the way of salvation? . . . Satori always requires a certain amount of subconscious incubation. It is said that a merely chance occurrence—a sight, a sound—may bring it about. Often it is accompanied by intense emotional phenomena such as a trembling, a rash of tears or a cold sweat. . . .

IV. [ZEN] CONCLUSION

From the foregoing discussions, it is evident that Zen attracts people by its specious arguments, but offers no truth. It is the delusion of "blind guides," but is not the true way. It casts some dim light, but does not give the true light, nor the life, "the life (that) was the light of man." The whole creation groans and travails in pain, searches and probes in darkness. Yet man comprehended not the light which is come into the world and shines in darkness; they loved the darkness rather than the light and thus became easy preys of the false prophets.

Zen is objectionable not only because it is inadequate in its teachings but also futile in its effects. Zen is inadequate, because (1) it denies the infinity and transcendence of a living and personal God by identifying Him with nature. It is in fact a very subtle form of Atheism, disguised by the language of theism, and embellished with seductive eloquence. (2) It engenders a spirit of mysticism by taking refuge in its doctrine of radical intuition by looking into one's own nature. But to look "within" for an authoritative guide without divine revelation will surely fall into the delusion of Satan. . . .

(3) It denies the need of external rules of morality. This will inevitably plunge mankind into pure anarchic relativism. (4) It rejects the grace of God and the need of a Savior by exalting and deifying man. This will surely lead the world to eternal perdition because "the whole godless world lies in the power of the evil one." Indeed, it is "a way which seems right unto a man, but the end thereof are the ways of death!" . . .

In a word, Zen is not only Biblically and theologically untenable, but also psychologically and socially detrimental. As we pointed out in another chapter, Zen is a technique by which to achieve "a mental breakdown." . . .

Now many Westerners, weary of their conventional religion and philosophy, find some charm in Zen and have become prey to its plausible teachings. If unchecked, the consequences will be surely disastrous to our culture.[36]

The Core of Zen

Zen Buddhism is one of the more philosophic and orientally flavored imports of cultism, peculiarly adapted to the Western mind in that it decidedly shuns outright supernaturalism, but encourages a "Satori" (enlightenment) experience, "an awakening of our original inseparability with the universe." The ultimate goal of Zen Buddhism is "the freeing of the will," so that "all things bubble along in one interrelated continual." Those who would be disciples of Zen must allow their ego to be detached until "one's real self calmly floats over the world's confusion" like a ping-pong ball skimming over the turbulent rapids of life. In a world faced with deprivation, hunger, disease, death, and the ever-present shadow of nuclear warfare, the denial of such reality borders on the criminal. Zen Buddhism, in our opinion, is the most self-centered, selfish system of philosophy that the depraved soul of man can embrace, for it negates the two basic principles upon which all spiritual reality exists: "Thou shalt love the Lord thy God with all thy heart, and with all thy soul, and with all thy mind . . .[and[thy neighbour as thyself" (Matthew 22:37, 39).

For Zenists, it is love of self first, last, and always. This is the core of Zen, which releases one from spiritual responsibility and substitutes intellectual enlightenment for conversion, and the absence of concern for one's fellowman for peace with God. Historically, Buddhism has produced nothing but indescribable conditions under which its subjects live. For in almost every area of the world where Buddhism of any form holds sway, there stalks the specter of disease, hunger, and moral and spiritual decay. The peoples of the Orient are the slaves of their religions, and Buddhism, with its egocentricity and inherently selfish concept of life and of responsibility to society, is by all odds one of the greatest offenders. Let those who consider Zen as a superior form of religious philosophy look well at its history and its fruit, for "by their fruits ye shall know them" (Matthew 7:20).

---

[36]Lit-sen Chang, *Zen-Existentialism: The Spiritual Decline of the West* (Nutley, N.J.: Presbyterian and Reformed Publishing Company, 1969), 128–47.

3. Nichiren Shoshu Buddhism[37]

While claiming to be compatible with Christianity, Nichiren Shoshu Buddhism (NSB) proclaims doctrines and practices antithetical to biblical Christianity. One cannot follow both NSB and Jesus at the same time.

History

Nichiren Shoshu is the religious group founded after the teachings of the Japanese reformer Nichiren Daishonin (A.D. 1222–82). He denounced all other Buddhist sects. During his lifetime he wrote 430 volumes, called collectively Gosho. He believed himself to be the fulfillment of a prophecy in the Lotus Sutra about the coming of a second Buddha. After Nichiren's death in 1282, his immediate successor, Nikko Shonin, founded the religious system of Nichiren Shoshu.

Nichiren Shoshu boasts of a 700-year unbroken tradition and lineage of priests who have kept their teachings inviolate since the time of Nichiren Daishonin.[38] Their daily ritual is called *Gongyo*, and consists of three separate activities. First the devotee kneels before the Gohonzon, and then he recites passages from the Lotus Sutra. While rubbing rosary-type beads, he chants, and then the ceremony is concluded in silent prayer. The Lotus Sutra passages are recited eight times during the day—five times in the morning and three times at night. Chanting of the Daimoku continues "until one feels satisfied" (sometimes four hours).

The goal of personal worship by NSB members is oneness with the essence of Buddha—the underlying essence of the universe. As with other Eastern religious systems,[39] NSB is pantheistic. God is all and all is God. All existence is one. All creation is in some way a reflection of the divine, impersonal Source.

> [The Buddha's] entity is neither being nor non-being: Neither cause nor effect; neither itself nor another ... neither this nor that, past or future. . . .[40]

In one place the state of Buddhahood is described as being the only place of "absolute, indestructible happiness," "the state of immutable, permanent happiness," etc. Inconsistently, NSB also asserts that "even in the Buddhahood realm there may exist the possibility of retrogression to one of the other realms."[41]

From the above two quotes we see that not only does NSB assert some sort of objective truth, but it also claims to be superior to Christianity—a claim shared by almost all cults. NSB's misunderstanding of Christianity is part of the reason for its rejection of Christianity.

---

[37]Adapted from Walter Martin, *The New Cults* (Santa Ana, Calif.: Vision House Publishers, 1980), 321–50. Researched by John Weldon.

[38]This is contrary to the traditional teachings of Buddha, who was said to declare, "Do not accept . . . tradition, do not accept a statement because it is found in our books, nor because it is in accord with your belief, nor because it is the saying of your teacher" (Huston Smith, *Religions of Man*, 105).

[39]See chapter 3 for further information on Eastern thought.

[40]*NSB Quarterly*, op. cit., Spring 1974, 68–69; Fall 1973, 54.

[41]Ikeda, *Buddhism: The Living Philosophy*, op. cit., 39–40, 56.

It seems that the impulse arising from a sort of hatred and hostility because of worshipping the crucifix is more dominant [among Christians] than the concept of love explained in the Bible. These dark emotions have not yet lost their devilish influence upon Westerners or humanity as a whole.[42]

To our eyes, the Christian doctrine of love is much inferior and much shallower than the Buddhist teaching of Jiki [mercy]. This is the very reason why Christians, though fully aware of the evil of war, have not yet succeeded in completely eliminating war among themselves. . . . Christians pay only lip service to absolute peace. They will never be able to fulfill that ideal.[43]

By attacking Christianity as inferior, Nichiren Shoshu Buddhism has challenged Christians everywhere to assert the truthfulness of Christianity. We must examine the doctrines of NSB and compare them to the doctrines of the Bible, which has been declared to be the Word of God by the One who rose from the dead to prove objectively His identity as the God of the universe (Luke 24:39; John 20:28; 1 Corinthians 15:14–20; Romans 1:3,4).

Nichiren Shoshu Buddhism's Doctrines

God

The monistic worldview of Nichiren Shoshu Buddhism precludes its belief in a God separate from His creation. According to conflicting NSB writings, the God of NSB is pantheistic, polytheistic, and henotheistic.

The Dai Gohonzon (and its representations in the individual Gohonzons) is like the supreme God of NSB. It is the visible manifestation of the pantheistic NSB God. The attributes we ascribe to the God of the Bible are in NSB ascribed to the Gohonzon, of which it is said:

1. It is the savior of mankind.
2. It is the source of all divine help.
3. The believer has faith in the Gohonzon.
4. It is the only source of eternal good fortune.
5. One must render it full devotion.
6. It is the source of happiness.
7. It is the ultimate source of the universe.
8. It purifies believers.
9. It forgives sin and answers prayer.
10. It is omnipotent.
11. The Dai Gohonzon is said to anxiously await the world's worship, and holds the key to world peace and happiness.[44]

Mankind and Salvation

The Nichiren Shoshu doctrine about mankind comes from a monistic worldview. Since NSB believes that all is God and God is all, it teaches that man is one with all existence and is, in fact, divine.

---

[42]*NSB Quarterly*, Fall 1973, 127.

[43]*Seikyo Times*, Nov. 1972, 45.

[44]Ibid., March 1973, 23–24, 49, 50–51, 53–54, 58; October 1971, 55; *NSB Quarterly*, Spring 1974, 43; Spring 1973, 87.

Nichiren Shoshu Buddhism also believes that man's existence is unalterably bound to the cyclical flux that comprises the world. When a soul passes from realm one through realm ten, he has passed through seemingly endless cycles of life and death to reach oneness with the life principles of the universe. Man is said to be locked into an eternal cycle, and yet at the same time NSB says that the cycles will end for souls that reach the tenth realm. The goal is to be able to control the condition of your life by chanting.[45]

> Those who chant Daimoku to the Gohonzon are able to display the purest and most powerful life in their daily activities, controlling the other nine conditions from *Jigoku* [hell] to *Bosatsu* [Bodhisattva].[46]

In the Nichiren view, death is only a return to a latent and different form of life. Life and death are one. This belief in the essential unity of all things, even life and death.

Salvation according to Nichiren Shoshu Buddhism is not the salvation described in the Bible. Salvation in NSB is twofold, including one's ability to recognize his own divinity and one's own efforts to remove the penalty of his own bad Karma through penance, chanting, and even reincarnation.

As with other cults that claim exclusivity, deliverance is possible only through NSB:

> In the light of the Daishonin's doctrine of Ichinen Sanzen, the most Christians can do is reach to the state of Rapture. . . . I state with the utmost certainty that as long as a life, whether of an individual or of a nation, is confined to the world of Rapture, it will inevitably fall into darkness sooner or later. . . .
>
> Salvation as promised by Christianity is limited in the sense that the most its followers can do it, as I have pointed out, is to enter the world of Rapture. Very few, if any, reach the state of Bodhisittva.[47]

The biblical doctrine of salvation is very different from the salvation of NSB. Biblical salvation is the hand of God reaching out to man, the one created in His image, who willfully sinned and cannot now save himself. Salvation is offered freely to anyone who comes to God on God's terms. There is no organization that can save. The living God, who cannot be contained in anything material, is not like the god of the Gohonzon. The living God has himself paid the punishment for sin because of His great love for sinful mankind. The result of salvation, according to the Bible, is peace with God and self and the promise of an eternity in the presence of God. Man is cleansed from the guilt of sin and will ultimately achieve the created perfection that God intended him to have. Christian salvation is completely by grace and has nothing to do with one's own works. Finally, Christian salvation does not depend on anything other than the grace and love of God, the Lord of the universe.

---

[45]*Buddhism: The Living Philosophy*, op. cit., 34–36.
[46]*Seikyo Times*, March 1973, 57.
[47]Ibid., Nov. 1972, 45.

Man cannot save himself. Even the best of man's works are considered as filthy rags in God's perfect sight (Isaiah 64:6). The only "work" God approves is the one promoted by Jesus in John 6:29: "The work of God is this: to believe in the one he has sent" (NIV).

The salvation of Nichiren Shoshu Buddhism is empty self-effort. It cannot produce genuine peace with God and the eternal life of personal fellowship with God so freely offered through the sacrifice of God's Son (Acts 20:28).

Conclusion

Nichiren Shoshu Buddhism attracts many followers because it is self-centered and sometimes produces material benefits through chanting to the Gohonzon. However, the offerings of NSB are transient and insignificant compared to the eternal riches offered—and delivered—by the God of the Bible. The Bible tells us to seek the things of God before we seek material benefits. By coming to God first, we can be assured that He will take care of our material needs (Matthew 6:33–34) and will give us true spiritual joy for all eternity (Philippians 1:6).

Answering the Buddhistic Doctrine of Rebirth

The Scriptures teach that man is not eternal. He is a direct creation of God (Psalm 139:13; Genesis 1:26–27). He is not incarnated successively, forced to physically atone for his sins of a previous life that he does not remember. Hebrews 9:26–27 categorically denies such ideas and instead asserts the justice of God: "And as it is appointed unto men once to die, but after this the judgment."

Rebirth, like other cults, teaches salvation by works. This self-salvation (autosoterism) is accomplished through the inexorable law of Karma. Karma, an Eastern term, refers to the principle that one must atone for his own sins throughout successive rebirths. This is the backbone of the teaching of samsara (the cycle of rebirths). Since the weight of sin is so heavy on each individual, the samsarist reasons that no one life is long enough to work one's way out of the depths of such sin. Therefore, reasons the samsarist, man has many lives. He is reincarnated.

The doctrine of Karma is not found in the Bible. God is just, but He is also loving and merciful. Man's sin must be atoned for; in this one respect the samsarists are right. However, God is the One who has the right to decree the method of payment. After all, He is the one against whom we sin! God has not decreed the "inexorable law of Karma." He has decreed that our sins can be atoned for only in the Person of His Son on the cross: "After he had provided purification for sins, he sat down at the right hand of the Majesty in heaven" (Hebrews 1:3 NIV). The Samsarist is right in saying that man cannot atone for all of his sins in one lifetime. The Bible implies that man could not atone for his own sins if he had a thousand lifetimes (Romans 3:10–12).[48]

---

[48]This section adapted from Walter Martin, *The New Cults* (Santa Ana, Calif.: Vision House Publishers, 1980), 371-74. Researched by Cal Beisner.

Refutation[49]

Rebirth can easily be refuted from the Bible by at least ten Old and New Testament doctrines, but for the sake of brevity we have elected to list only four, all of which those believing in rebirth deny automatically. These biblical doctrines are:

(A) The personality of God; (B) The atonement of Christ; (C) The physical resurrection; and (D) divine retribution.

(A) *The personality of God,* for some unknown reason, is rejected by all samsarists. They reject the fact that He is a personal cognizant Spirit, a Divine Ego (Exodus 3:14), capable of a subject-object relationship with man and within the Godhead.

All samsarists, then, are committed to a pantheistic concept of the Deity—God is conceived of as being the fountain of all existence from the tiniest atom to the most gigantic forms of matter, and further, these things are all *part* of His Substance, which permeates every particle *of* existence.

This position that God is all, and all is God, or a manifestation of Him, is thoroughly refuted by the following verses of Scripture, which teach incontrovertibly that God is a personal Spirit possessed of attributes only a personality has, imminent in creation but apart from it as Creator: transcendent in that He does not share His spiritual substance (John 4:24; Hebrews 1:3) with the products of His creative will.

1. God "remembers"—Isaiah 43:25; Jeremiah 31:20; Hosea 8:13.

2. God "speaks" (Subject/object relationship)—Exodus 3:12; Matthew 3:17; Luke 17:5.

3. God "hears," "sees," and "creates"—Genesis 6:5; Exodus 2:24; Genesis 1:1.

4. God "knows" (He has a mind)—Jeremiah 21:11; 2 Timothy 2:19; 1 John 3:20.

5. God is a personal Spirit—John 4:24; Hebrews 1:3.

6. God has a will—Matthew 6:10; Hebrews 10:7, 9; 1 John 2:17.

7. God will judge—Ezekiel 18:30; 34:20; 2 Corinthians 5:10.

(B) *The atonement of Jesus Christ* refutes most decisively rebirth, since the doctrine of the atonement teaches that God, through Christ's sacrifice on the cross, "purges" believers from all their sins (Hebrews 1:3) and counts them righteous for the sake of His Son (2 Corinthians 5:21). Samsarists, on the other hand, claim that successive "rebirths" are the instrument of cleansing for the soul, and thereby do away with not only the efficacy of the Atonement but the very necessity itself of Christ's dying at all for the sins of the world.

The Bible, however, clearly teaches that "without shedding of blood is no remission" (Hebrews 9:22) of sin, and Christ purchased the church with His own blood, which is not corruptible as silver or gold are (1 Peter 1:18–19), but which is "precious," and the price of the soul's redemption "for it is the blood that makes atonement, by reason of the life" (see Leviticus 17:11 RSV).

For the adherent of the rebirth theory, then, almost endless cycles of rebirth are necessary to cleanse the soul from sin, but for the Christian, "the blood of

---

[49]Adapted from Walter Martin, *The Christian and the Cults* (Grand Rapids, Mich.: Zondervan, 1956), 123–27.

Jesus Christ, his Son cleanseth us from all sin" (1 John 1:7). This is the message of the Bible from Genesis to Revelation, redemption by blood through the sacrifice of "him that loved us, and washed us from our sins in his own blood" (Revelation 1:5). (For further Scripture references, see Matthew 26:28; Romans 5: 6–8; Ephesians 1:7; Colossians 1:20.)

(C) *The physical resurrection of Jesus Christ* (and all men, for that matter) is the foundation stone upon which the validity of Christianity stands, for in the words of the apostle Paul: "If Christ be not raised your faith is vain, ye are yet in your sins" (1 Corinthians 15:17). The Bible plainly states that Jesus rose from the grave in a physical form (John 20:27), that He was not raised a spirit (Luke 24:39–44), and that Christ himself, after He had risen, rebuked His disciples for their unbelief in His physical resurrection (Mark 16:14). It is evident, therefore, that though Jesus Christ was raised physically He had what the Bible terms a "spiritual body" (1 Corinthians 15:44–49), not a spirit form but an immortal, incorruptible physical body possessed of spiritual characteristics forever exempt from death (Romans 6:9), a body the likes of which all believers shall one day possess at His glorious return and our resurrection (Philippians 3:4; 1 Corinthians 15:52–54).

Samsarists, however, do away altogether with physical resurrection and even claim that Christ rose spiritually, not physically, pointing to the facts that Mary Magdalene (John 2:14–15) and the Emmaus disciples did not recognize their risen Lord until He revealed himself (Luke 24:16, 31), whereas if He had risen in His former body, it is claimed they would have known Him immediately. Further than this, such persons often refer to 1 Peter 3:18, where it states that Christ was "made alive by the Spirit" (NIV), the inference being that His was a spiritual resurrection. These objections, though apparently valid, crumble under the relentless pressure of sound exegesis, for in no way does Christ's veiling His identity from some persons after His Resurrection "prove" that He was not physically raised, as any cursory study of the Greek at the respective texts clearly indicates. The key to understanding these veiled appearances is found in Luke 24:16 and 31, two texts samsarists religiously avoid commenting upon for the obvious reason that a correct exegesis of them *decimates* their spiritual resurrection claims.

Luke 24:16, in the Greek, states simply that the eyes of the disciples "were kept from recognizing Him," (Greek—*ekratounto*) which proves conclusively that Christ willed that they should behold His features yet be incapable of knowing that it was He, not because His form had changed, but because His will had dictated otherwise!

The other text, Luke 24:31, fully substantiates the Greek of 24:16 by showing that although the disciples had been conversing with Christ, *the eyes of their understanding were closed* by His will so that they could not comprehend until He chose to reveal it, that the risen Christ was their companion (Greek—*dienoichthesan—*opened).

In regard to 1 Peter 3:18, a word study of the Greek completely corroborates the testimony of Scripture that Christ was raised in a physical form by God the Father, but *through* the agency of the Holy Spirit (Romans 8:11). Thus when Peter says "put to death in the flesh," he quickly announces the triumph of God the Father who raised His Son Jesus from the dead (Acts 17:31) "by the Spirit" (1 Peter 3:18). Going beyond this, we further see that Jesus Christ was not raised a Spirit (John 20:28) and that in the Bible a spiritual resurrection is never taught at all, for His body did not know corruption (Acts 2:31; 13:37), and on the third day His Spirit and soul returned to that *same* body and brought it to life (Matthew 28:9). Henceforth, it was a glorified body (Philippians 3:21), model of all the bodies of the saints (1 John 3:2). It could pass through walls (John 20:19), but it could be handled and felt (Luke 24:36–39). It could ascend into heaven (Acts 1:9), but before it did so it could eat fish and honey (Luke 24:41–43). What is unmistakably asserted, then, is that while Christ died on Calvary, He was "made alive" in a spiritual body; thus we see that the eternal Word made flesh for the suffering of death ceased living a mortal, fleshly existence and began to live a resurrection life in a spiritual body. As Luther so succinctly stated:

> ... Christ by His suffering was taken from the life which is flesh and blood ... and is now placed in another life and made alive according to the Spirit ... He has now passed into a spiritual and supernatural life.

The great doctrine of the physical resurrection of all men, saved and unsaved (John 5:28-29), therefore, eliminates the necessity of concurrent rebirths and proves once more the fallacy of the entire system of rebirth.

(D) *Divine retribution for sin,* a doctrine inseparably connected with the nature of man and the state of the dead, further refutes rebirth.

The Bible unmistakably teaches that at the death of the physical form, the soul leaves the body (Genesis 35:18), and if saved, is instantly transported to the presence of God (2 Corinthians 5:8; Philippians 1:21–23). Those who have rejected Jesus Christ, on the other hand, go instantaneously to hell, a place of conscious separation from God and spiritual torment of a terrible nature (Luke 16:19–31). In addition to this, the Bible further warns that at the last judgment (Matthew 25:31–46) the unsaved dead will be cast into "outer darkness," there to wander *forever* in conscious separation and the indescribable retribution of eternal fire, for the endless ages of eternity (Matthew 8:12; 25:41, 46; 2 Peter 2:17; Jude 13; Revelation 20:15).

Such is the divine will, Scripture tells us, for those who have committed the infinite transgression of rejecting God's love as expressed in Jesus Christ (John 3:16, 36). To this eternal pronouncement, samsarists can offer no refutation, only a denial, and the pretended mysticism that dictates cycles of reincarnations in a clever attempt to accomplish what the Lord in His Word has already ordained, perfect justice at the hands of God's Son, the perfect righteous Judge (John 5:22).

Christians do not look forward to rebirth; we look forward to *resurrection,* when Christ will return and clothe us with glorified bodies so that we may eternally serve and worship God (1 Corinthians 15:5). Our glorification is not accomplished by our own efforts, but by the "victory though our Lord Jesus Christ" (1 Corinthians 15:57). Christians have the assurance from God's Word through the Holy Spirit that "He who raised Christ from the dead will also give life to your mortal bodies through his Spirit, who lives in you (Romans 8:11 NIV).[50]

---

[50] *The New Cults,* 374-75.

Recommended Resources

1. Anderson, Norman J., editor. *The World's Religions*. Grand Rapids, Mich.: William B. Eerdmans Publishing Company, 1975.
2. Halverson, Dean C., general editor. *The Compact Guide to World Religions*. Minneapolis, Minn.: Bethany House Publishers, 1996.
3. Mather, George A., and Larry A. Nichols. "Hinduism History" in *Dictionary of Cults, Sects, Religions, and the Occult*. Grand Rapids, Mich.: Zondervan, 1993, 117.
4. Yamamoto, J. Isamu. *Beyond Buddhism*. Downers Grove, Ill.: InterVarsity Press, 1982.
5. ———. *Buddhism, Taoism, and Other Far Eastern Movements*. Grand Rapids, Mich.: Zondervan, 1998.
6. Zacharias, Ravi. *The Lotus and the Cross: Jesus Talks With Buddha*. Sisters, Ore.: Multnomah, 2001. See also, Ravi Zacharias International Ministries, *www.rzim.org*.

Quick Facts About the Baha'i Faith

- The Bible is only one of the many sacred texts in the world, but the final authority is the writings of Bahá'u'lláh.

- Bahá'u'lláh fulfilled a worldwide messianic calling, which equated him with other world religion leaders (i.e., Christ, Buddha, Mohammed).

- God is one person. The doctrine of the Trinity is denied.

- Jesus Christ was only one of nine manifestations of the messiah: He was not virgin born, not God incarnate, and did not rise bodily from the grave.

- Salvation is based upon man's good works coupled with God's mercy. The blood of Jesus Christ is not efficacious to cleanse anyone of sin.

Chapter 10

The Baha'i Faith

A Brief History

The Baha'i Faith is a non-Christian cult of distinctly foreign origin that began in Iran in the nineteenth century with a young religious Iranian businessman known as Mírzá' Ali Muhammad, who came to believe himself to be a divine manifestation projected into the world of time and space as a "Bab" (Gate) leading to a new era for mankind.

As Christianity, almost since its inception, has had heretics and heresies within its fold, so Islam was destined to experience the same fragmenting forces. Mírzá' Ali Muhammad, alias the "Bab," thus became one of the sorest thorns in the flesh of Islamic orthodoxy; so much so that he was murdered by Islamic fanatics in 1850 at the age of thirty-one. He had derived much of his early encouragement and support from a small Islamic sect in Iran, and he was a prominent teacher among them for six years prior to his death. Though Christians have not been known historically for putting to death those who disagreed with them (notable exceptions are the Reformation and Counter-Reformation, the Inquisition, and certain phases of the Crusades), violence may generally be said to follow in the wake of "new" revelations in most other religions, and, unfortunately, in the case of Mírzá' the pattern held true.

So then, the history of the Baha'i Faith began with the stupendous claims of a young Iranian to the effect that "the religious leaders of the world had forgotten their common origin. . . . Moses, Jesus, and Mohammed were equal prophets, mirroring God's glory, messengers bearing the imprint of the Great Creator."[1]

Today, this still remains the basic tenet of the Baha'i Faith, albeit with the

---

This chapter updated by Kurt Van Gorden and edited by Jill Martin Rische.
[1]Richard Mathison, *Faith, Cults, and Sects in America* (New York: Scribners, 1952), 105.

addition of Zoroaster, Buddha, Confucius, Krishna, Lao, and Bahá'u'lláh, the last great manifestation of the Divine Being, whose name literally means "the glory of God." The focus of Baha'ism is often popularized as "The Oneness of God, the Oneness of Religion, and the Oneness of Humanity."

As Baha'i history records it, the Bab was sentenced to death and was executed July 8, 1850, at Tabriz. In the view of thousands, as the Baha'is tell it, 750 Armenian soldiers raised their rifles and fired at the figure of the prophet. When the smoke cleared, the Bab had not only emerged unscathed from the fusillade of bullets, but the bullets had burned through the ropes that held him, and he stood unfettered.

The story goes on to relate that he then disappeared from their vision, but upon returning to his cell, the guards found him lecturing his disciples. After he had finished speaking with them, he is reported to have said, "I have finished my conversation. Now you may fulfill your intention."

He was then led out before the same firing squad, and this time they did not miss.

All of these events were accompanied by the cries of "Miracle! Miracle!" from the assembled populace, who, though they outnumbered the luckless Armenian soldiers, failed to rescue the Bab from his appointment with the Dark Angel.

The Baha'i history of the event also records that a fierce black whirlwind swept the city immediately after the execution of the Bab, somewhat reminiscent of the earthquake and darkness that fell over the earth upon the death of Jesus Christ on Golgotha, eighteen centuries before.

The death of the Bab, however, did not dim the rising star of the new faith. Instead, he had, according to his followers, prophesied that "the oneness of all mankind" was an inevitability, and that in time there would come "a Promised One" who would unify all the followers and would himself be a manifestation of the only true and living God.

Modern Baha'ism considers that the Bab's great prophecy has been fulfilled by Mirza Husayn' Ali, better known to the initiated as "Bahá'u'lláh," who succeeded the messianic throne of Baha'ism upon the death of his unfortunate predecessor, the Bab.

In the year 1863 this same Bahá'u'lláh declared himself as that one prophesied by the Bab thirteen years previously, the One who was "chosen of God, and the promised one of all the prophets."[2]

Apparently Bahá'u'lláh's conviction that he was to play Christ to the Bab's John the Baptist convinced the majority of "Babis," as they were then known. However, his brother, Mirza Yahya, apparently did not receive the message clearly, for he forthwith renounced Bahá'u'lláh and allied himself with the enemies of the newfound religion, the Ski-ihs.

His nefarious plot, however, miserably failed, and the Baha'i movement gradually evolved into what is known today as the Baha'i Faith, a worldwide religious organization that continues to teach in the tradition of Bahá'u'lláh, who, despite his claims to immortality, was rather unceremoniously deprived of his earthly existence by the Angel of Death who overtook him in 1892 in Bahji in Palestine. He was seventy-five at the time.

---

[2]J. E. Esslemont, *Bahá'u'lláh and the New Era* (Wilmette, Ill.: Baha'i Publishing Committee, 1951), 38.

The Baha'is have had their share of persecution, and more than nine thousand were killed between 1850 and 1860. But in their emigration to America in the person of 'Abdu'l Bahá, son of Bahá'u'lláh, who arrived in the United States in 1912, Baha'ism truly received "a new birth of freedom." Today they carry on their work in more than two hundred thirty-five countries and territories worldwide, representing more than twenty-one hundred ethnic, racial, and tribal groups, and with more than five million practitioners.[3]

They have gained some notable converts in the past, and no less a figure than Count Leo Tolstoy spoke warmly of their "spirit of brotherhood," and Woodrow Wilson's daughter became one of the first converts to Baha'ism through the work of Bahá'u'lláh in the United States. Some members of the rock music group Crosby, Stills, Nash, and Young shared their new faith in Baha'ism during public concerts and network television talk shows.

The world headquarters of the Baha'i Faith is in Haifa, Israel, from whence are circulated the writings of Bahá'u'lláh and 'Abdu'l Bahá. Bahá'u'lláh reputedly left behind him two hundred books and tablets, which, along with the writings of his son, constitute the final authority for religious faith and conduct where members of the cult are concerned.

This author had the opportunity to visit the famous nonagon (nine-sided) structure or Temple, as it is known, in Wilmette, Illinois; a building that utilizes the symbolic number nine, sacred to Baha'is. Its architecture is a combination of synagogue, mosque, and cathedral, in which there are nine concrete piers, nine pillars representing the nine living world religions, and nine arches. The building is beautifully centered in a park having nine sides, nine avenues, and nine gateways, and containing nine fountains. The worship service consists of readings from Bahá'u'lláh, 'Abdu'l Bahá, and whatever sources from the major religions are thought to be meaningful for the worshipers that day. Around the central dome of the building are various quotations both inside and out, all of which emphasize the unity of all the great religions of the world.

The Baha'i Faith utilizes the calendar for observances designed by the Bab, which consists of nineteen months, each having nineteen days. New Year's Day falls on March 21. There are no ministers and no ecclesiastical machinery or organization. The Baha'is employ only teachers who conduct discussion groups in homes or Baha'i centers, and who are willing to discuss with anyone the unity of all religion under Bahá'u'lláh.

The Baha'i cult also maintains schools for study in Colorado Springs, Colorado; Geyserville, California; Eliot, Maine; and Davison, Michigan.

~The Baha'i Faith today is not directed by an individual representative of God, such as the Bab or the Guardian Shoghi Effendi, but by a council. A British Baha'i center representative explains,

> The Universal House of Justice is the supreme governing body of the Baha'i Faith to which all Baha'is may turn. Its nine members are elected by National Spiritual Assemblies from all over the world.
>
> The Universal House of Justice consults on all issues and guides the entire Baha'i world within the light and framework of the teachings of Bahá'u'lláh.

---

[3] Official Baha'i Web site, *www.bahai.org.*

To continue the work of the Hands of the Cause, the Universal House of Justice appointed an International Teaching Centre.

The National Spiritual Assembly in each country is elected every year by delegates at a National Convention. The nine members consult and decide about the affairs of the Faith in that country.

Every city, town, and village that has enough adult believers elects a Local Spiritual Assembly to consult on the affairs of the Faith within their community.

All Baha'i Assemblies work within the same framework based on Bahá'u'lláh's teachings, and their decisions should be obeyed by Baha'is. In Baha'i consultation all parties are considered equal.

Individuals are also appointed at various levels to aid in the spread of the Faith and to protect the spiritual health of the Baha'is. They are called Counselors, Auxiliary Board Members, or Assistants to the Auxiliary Board and work closely with the Local and National Spiritual Assembles.[4]

Baha'ism seeks to bring together all faiths in a common world brotherhood, in effect giving men a right to agree to disagree on what the Baha'is consider peripheral issues—the main goal being unity on all the great central truths of the world religions, with Bahá'u'lláh as the messiah for our age. 'Abdu'l Bahá did his work well, and when he died at the age of seventy-seven in Palestine (in 1921), he bequeathed a budding missionary arm of his father's faith to Shoghi Effendi (Guardian of the Faith), whose influence continues in and through the teaching hierarchy of the contemporary Baha'i movement in America.

Basic Baha'i Beliefs

Baha'i teaching is often difficult to identify and evaluate because it usually expresses itself in the terminology and images of various religions. However, it does have a set of basic principles, laws, and other teachings to which Baha'is worldwide subscribe, no matter what terminology they might use to express these ideas.

The basic principles of the Baha'i Faith include the oneness of the world of humanity; the foundation of all religions as one; religion must be the cause of unity; religion must be in accord with science and reason; one must pursue independent investigation of truth; equality between men and women; the abolition of all forms of prejudice; universal peace; universal education; a universal language; the spiritual solution of economic problems; and an international tribunal.

The laws and obligations of the Baha'i Faith include to pray and read the Holy Writings (from various religions) daily; to observe the Baha'i Fast from sunrise to sunset on the Baha'i "New Year," March 20–21; to teach the cause of God; to contribute to the Baha'i financial fund; to observe Baha'i Holy Days, including the Nineteen Day Feast (every nineteen days from New Year's Day, or March 20–21); to consider work as worship; to avoid alcohol and other drug abuse; to observe sexual chastity; to obey the government of the land; and to avoid gossip.

The qualifications for becoming a Baha'i differ from country to country, and it is primarily a matter of individual, private faith. However, when one "catches the spark of Faith," understands the identities of Bahá'u'lláh, the Bab, and

---

[4] *www.bahai.org/article-1-3-6-1.html.*

'Abdu'l Bahá, respects the Baha'i leadership, and learns and adopts the teachings and laws of Baha'ism, then one generally makes a public declaration of faith and is welcomed into his or her local Baha'i community.[5]~

An Interview With a Baha'i Teacher

In the course of researching the history and theology of Baha'ism, I conducted numerous interviews with authoritative spokespersons for the Baha'i movement. The following is a transcription of relevant portions of an interview conducted with a well-prepared and candid Baha'i teacher.

Question: Do you in Baha'ism believe in the Holy Trinity?

Answer: If by the Trinity you mean the Christian concept that the three persons—Father, Son, and Holy Spirit—are all the one God, the answer is no.

We believe that God is one person in agreement with Judaism and Islam. We cannot accept the idea that God is both three and one and find this foreign to the Bible, which Christianity claims as its source. Not a few Jewish scholars are in complete agreement with us on this point, as is the Koran.

Question: Is Jesus Christ the only manifestation of Deity, that is, is He to be believed when He said, "I am the way, the truth, and the life: no man cometh unto the Father, but by me" (John 14:6)?

Answer: No, we believe that Jesus was only one of nine manifestations of the divine being and appeared in His era of time to illumine those who lived at that time. Today, Bahá'u'lláh is the source of revelation.

Jesus was the way, the truth, and the life for His time but certainly not for all time.

'Abdu'l Bahá points out that we are to honor all the major prophetic voices, not just one of them. He said,

> Christ was the prophet of the Christians, Moses of the Jews—why should not the followers of each prophet recognize and honor the other prophets?[6]

'Abdu'l Bahá also occupied an exalted place in the thinking of Baha'is. It was he who said:

> The revelation of Jesus was for His own dispensation, that of the Son, and now it is no longer the point of guidance to the world. Baha'is must be severed from all and everything that is past—things both good and bad— everything. . . . Now all is changed. All the teachings of the past are past.[7]

Question: Since you believe that Jesus spoke to His own dispensation, how do you account for the fact that in numerous places in the New Testament both He and His apostles and disciples asserted that He was the same "yesterday, and to day, and for ever" (Hebrews 13:8), and that His words were binding and would never pass away?

---

[5]See *www.bahai.org/article-1-7-0-1.html* for more information. Marked sections in this chapter are editorial commentary, cited from Walter Martin, *Kingdom of the Cults* (Minneapolis: Bethany House Publishers, 1997), 321–31.

[6]*The Wisdom of Baha'u'lláh* (Wilmette, Ill.: Baha'i Publishing Committee, n.d.), 43.

[7]*Star of the West* (Wilmette, Ill.: Baha'i Publishing Committee, December 31, 1913), brochure.

Answer: You must realize that many of the things written in the New Testament were written long after Jesus died, hence it is impossible to have absolute accuracy in everything. It would be natural for His followers to assert such things, but the revelation of Bahá'u'lláh supersedes such claims.

Question: The resurrection of Jesus Christ from the dead is the true foundation of Christian experience. Does Baha'ism accept His bodily resurrection and ascension into heaven, and do you believe that He is indeed a high priest after Melchizedek order as intercessor before the throne of God for all men?

Answer: The alleged resurrection of Jesus and His ascension into heaven may or may not be true depending upon your point of view. As I said before, we are concerned with Bahá'u'lláh and the new era or age, and while we reverence Jesus as we do the great prophets of other religions, we do not believe that it is necessarily important that the Baha'i Faith recognize every tenet of a specific religion. We believe that Jesus conquered death, that He triumphed over the grave, but these are things that are in the realm of the spirit and must receive spiritual interpretation.

Question: Then you do not actually believe in the bodily resurrection of Christ?

Answer: Personally, no. But we do believe that resurrection is the destiny of all flesh.

Question: In Jewish theology and Christian theology, much stress is laid upon sacrificial atonement for sin. The theology of Christianity in particular emphasizes that Jesus Christ is the Lamb of God who takes away the sin of the world. It was John the Baptist who so identified Him, and the New Testament gives ample testimony to His substitutionary atonement for the sins of the world. If, as Christianity maintains, "He is the propitiation for our sins: and not for ours only, but also for the sins of the whole world" (1 John 2:2), why, then, is 'Abdu'l Bahá, or, for that matter, Bahá'u'lláh, important? If God has revealed himself finally and fully as the New Testament teaches in Jesus Christ (Colossians 2:9), why should further manifestation be necessary?

Answer: But, you see, that is precisely our position. God has not finally and fully revealed himself in any of the great manifestations, but through all of them, culminating in Bahá'u'lláh. A Christian may find spiritual peace in believing in a substitutionary atonement. In Baha'ism this is unnecessary. That age is past. The new age of spiritual maturity has dawned through Bahá'u'lláh, and we are to listen to his words.

Question: If, as you say, Moses, Buddha, Zoroaster, Confucius, Christ, Mohammed, Krishna, Lowe, and Bahá'u'lláh are all equal manifestations of the divine mind, how do you account for the fact that they contradict each other, for we know that God is not the author of confusion, or is He?

Answer: While it is true that there are discrepancies between the teachings of the great prophets, all held to basic moral and spiritual values. So we would expect unity here, and in the light of man's perverse nature, variety of expression in the writings and teachings of their disciples.

Question: Do you accept all of the sacred books of the world religions, that is, do you consider them all to be of equal authority with the writings of Bahá'u'lláh?

Answer: The writings of Bahá'u'lláh, since they are the last manifestation, are to be considered the final authority in matters of religion so far as the Baha'i faith is concerned.

Question: Jesus Christ taught that salvation from sin could be effected only by acceptance of Him as the sin-bearer mentioned so prominently in the fifty-third chapter of the prophet Isaiah. Just how in Baha'ism do you deal with the problem of your own personal sin?

Answer: We accept the fact that no one is perfect, but by the practice of principles laid down by Bahá'u'lláh and by making every effort through prayer and personal sacrifice to live in accord with the character of the divine being revealed in him, we can arrive at eventual salvation as you like to term it.

Question: What you mean, then, is that you, yourself, are cooperating with God in working for your salvation?

Answer: Yes, in a sense I suppose you could say this is true, though God in the end must be merciful to us or no one would be fit to escape the divine judgment.

Question: Then, you do believe in final judgment and the existence of paradise and hell?

Answer: Yes, the Baha'i Faith recognizes divine judgment, though not in the graphic terms that Christians portray it. We know nothing of eternal flames where sinners will be confined forever without respite. We do believe in the paradise of God, which will be the abode of the righteous and in the resurrection and the final righting of all things.

Question: Putting this on a personal basis, without meaning to be offensive, might I ask you if you personally this moment believe that you are a good practicing disciple of Bahá'u'lláh; and, this being true, do you at this moment know with certainty that your sins have all been forgiven you, and that if you were to be called tonight before the throne of God, you would be judged fit and worthy to enter His kingdom?

Answer: I don't believe any person can make that statement, for no one is perfect or holy enough to merit the paradise of God, and those who so claim to have attained this exalted position are in the eyes of the Baha'i Faith presumptuous, to say the very least. I could not at the moment say this for myself, but I hope that this will be the case when I die.

Question: Does the Baha'i Faith recognize the personality and deity of the Holy Spirit of God as revealed in the New Testament?

Answer: I believe it is in your gospel of John that Jesus promised another Comforter who would abide always. We understand this to be the coming of Bahá'u'lláh, a direct fulfillment of the words of Jesus.

Question: Is it not true that a great deal of your theology is borrowed from Islam and that Muslims have made the same claim for Mohammed where Christ's prophecy in John 14 is recorded as you have for Bahá'u'lláh?

Answer: There is no doubt that we reverence the Koran as one of the divine manifestations of illumination and Mohammed as one of the nine revelators, but Islam historically has persecuted us; in fact, it was followers of Islam who killed the Bab and persecuted Bahá'u'lláh.

With reference to the Islamic claim in John 14, I believe it is true they also make this claim.

The above excerpt has much more impact than my analysis alone would have. From an authoritative Baha'i spokesperson, it most clearly expresses what separates Baha'ism from historic Christianity. No true follower of Bahá'u'lláh, by his own admission, can claim this momentous peace with God and the joy of sins forgiven, an experience that belongs only to those who have put their faith and trust in the grace and sacrifice of the Son of God (John 5:26; 6:47; Ephesians 2:8–10).

The fact that the major prophets of Baha'ism contradict one another is paradoxically overlooked by Baha'ism, which in its quest for an ecumenical syncretism prefers to avoid rather than explain the great contradictions between the major faiths.

As do most cults, the Baha'i Faith will pick and choose out of the Bible that which will best benefit the advancement of their own theology, irrespective of context or theological authority. The author was impressed during this interview with the fact that the Baha'i teacher who granted it had been a disciple for more than fifty years and was certainly in a position to understand the historic views of Baha'ism. Throughout the course of the interview, which was held at a Baha'i meeting in her home, we had the opportunity time and time again to present the claims of Jesus Christ, and it became apparent that her "god" was Bahá'u'lláh. The Baha'i plan of salvation is faith in him plus their own good works. Their concept of hell is largely remedial, not punitive. Their eschatology, a combination of Islam, Judaism, and Christianity; and their authority, the writings of Bahá'u'lláh and 'Abdu'l Bahá.

All of the some thirty persons present took extreme pride in the fact that they had arrived at a faith that they felt was progressively superior to all other religions, and each was magnanimously willing to embrace the truth that was in every one of them to bring about the new era of which their leader had prophesied.

There was no virgin-born Son, there was only an Iranian student; there was no miraculous ministry, there was only the loneliness of exile; there was no power over demons, there were only demons of Islam; there was no redeeming Savior, there was only a dying old man; there was no risen Savior, there was only 'Abdu'l Bahá; there was no Holy Spirit, there was only the memory of the prophet; there was no ascended High Priest, there were only the works of the flesh; and there was no coming King, there was only the promise of a new era. In that room the words of the Lord of hosts were fulfilled with frightening accuracy:

> These people honor me with their lips, but their hearts are far from me. They worship me in vain; their teachings are but rules taught by men (Matthew 15:8–9 NIV).

All the Baha'i temples in the world and all the quotations from sacred books cannot alter the fact that the heart of man is deceitful above everything and desperately wicked. Who can understand it? Bahá'u'lláh could not, but could his disciples today? Penned in the words of our Lord:

> If ye were blind, ye should have no sin: but now ye say, We see; therefore, your sin remaineth. . . . Ye are from beneath; I am from above: ye are of this world; I am not of this world. I said therefore unto you, that ye shall die in your sins: for if ye believe not that I am he, ye shall die in your sins. . . . When ye have lifted up the Son of man, then shall ye know that I am he, and that I do nothing of myself; but as my Father hath taught me, I speak these things. . . . He that believeth on me, believeth not on me, but on him that sent me. . . . And if any man hear my words, and believe not, I judge him not: for I came not to judge the world, but to save the world. He that rejecteth me, and receiveth not my words, hath one that judgeth him: the word that I have spoken, the same shall judge him in the last day. For I have

not spoken of myself; but the Father which sent me, he gave me a commandment, what I should say, and what I should speak. And I know that his commandment is life everlasting: whatsoever I speak therefore, even as the Father said unto me, so I speak. (John 9:41; 8:23–24, 28; 12:44, 47–50)

A Response to the Interview

~After the appearance of the above dialogue in an earlier edition of *Kingdom of the Cults*, Baha'i apologist Udo Schaefer responded to this devastating exposé in a book, *The Light Shineth in Darkness*. None of Schaefer's defenses adequately answered the criticisms. A few of his disclaimers are presented here as examples of the lengths to which Baha'is will go to convince people that they can embrace all religions, including Christianity, at the same time. Udo Schaefer declares that all Christian critics of Baha'i are biased and unable to be objective or truthful because they fear changing their beliefs:

> The Baha'i Faith gives a particular challenge to orthodox Christians who cannot see its existence as other than a threat to their long-held and cherished beliefs. Many, unable to examine the claim of Bahá'u'lláh objectively because they are not sufficiently unbiased and detached from their old-fashioned traditional doctrines, nevertheless pass judgment on the Cause of God. (55:2)

He goes further, declaring that anyone who attempts to defend an objective, unchanging doctrinal standard in Christianity is spiritually blind and incapable of reformation:

> Someone who is accustomed to think only in the hidebound categories of a dogmatic system that demands exclusiveness, someone who throughout his life has inveighed even against other Christian denominations, directly they deviate from his creedal dogmas, can certainly be expected to give a rigid "no" when challenged from outside. Churchmen just cannot see the rival great religions as other than "lies" or at best issues of truth, half-truth, error, superstition, illusion and charlatanry. . . . This blindness is a fact which has to be accepted. (56:1)

Schaefer agrees that the centrality of the Cross in Christian theology is considered heresy by the "enlightened" Baha'i:

> [The theologian] accused the Baha'is of "helplessness in face of the message of the Cross." In this charge the proverbial 'usperbia theologorum'—the pride of the theologians—is manifested: anyone who deviates from Protestant dogma, who contradicts the central teachings of Christian theology, is "helpless," i.e. intellectually inadequate, or—to put it quite clearly—just too stupid to understand these teachings. This favorite trick of Christian apologists, protecting themselves from undesirable criticism by charging the critic with not knowing what Christian faith is and fighting against a caricature, shows an infuriating arrogance: because the critic is not taken seriously, he is made out to be incapable of passing judgment. (76:3)

Regarding the development of Christianity and the subsequent Reformation,

Schaefer asserts that the apostle Paul changed Christianity from what Jesus had taught, and the Reformation therefore embraced a heretical imitation of Christianity:

> First then, there was the work of a usurper [Paul] and the split he caused at the time of Christianity's origin; second, Luther's fatal mistake (and the mistake of his Christian successors) in finding the truth where in reality there was error. (80:3)

Schaefer quite clearly rejects the central biblical teaching of salvation by grace alone through faith by repeating his false assertion that Paul had corrupted and changed the simple teachings of Jesus himself:

> The most essential and effective alteration of Jesus' message carried out by Paul was in his denying the Law's power of salvation and replacing the idea of the Covenant . . . with faith in Christ and in the atoning power of his sacrificial death; [replacing] the concrete Mosaic law with a mystical doctrine of salvation. (82:1)
>
> The "message of Jesus" with which conservative theologians confront the Baha'is is not the teaching of Jesus but the message of Paul, "the preaching of the Cross," as he called his Gospel (1 Corinthians 1:18; 2:2). And if they say that the basic questions of our existence are only grasped in their true depth in "the preaching of the Cross," I reply with Steinheim who said, "It may be a good philosophical idea, a thoughtful myth, a comfortable emotional religion—that I can accept. Only don't let it be called the teaching and revelation of Christ, but a decline from it" (85:3).

In one bold statement Schaefer dismisses all of Christian orthodoxy regarding justification, original sin, the Trinity, and salvation as a mere invention, foreign to the teachings of Jesus. The teachings of Jesus, he asserts without any evidence, harmonize with the teachings of Baha'ism:

> Measured by the standard of Bahá'u'lláh's revelation, the Pauline doctrine of Justification, the doctrine of Original Sin, the doctrine of the Holy Trinity, the sacramentalization of the Christian religion, the whole Church plan of salvation . . . these are a deformation of Jesus' teaching. (87:1)

Today, the Baha'i Faith still stands diametrically opposed to the Christian faith. There can be no harmony of all world religions, not the least any harmony between Baha'ism and Christianity.

Conclusion

Looking back over our survey of Baha'ism, we can learn a number of things about this strange cult. First, we can discern that, although it is Islamic in its origin, Baha'ism has carefully cloaked itself in Western terminology and has imitated Christianity in forms and ceremonies wherever possible in order to become appealing to the Western mind.

Second, Baha'ism is eager not to come into conflict with the basic principles of the Gospel, and so, Baha'is are perfectly willing that the Christians should maintain their faith in a nominal sense, just so long as they acknowledge Bahá'u'lláh and the general principles of the Baha'i Faith.

Third, Baha'ism deliberately undercuts the foundational doctrines of the Christian faith by either denying them outright or by carefully manipulating terminology so as to "tone down" the doctrinal dogmatism that characterizes orthodox Christianity.

Baha'ism has few of the credentials necessary to authenticate its claims to religious supremacy. An honest Baha'i will freely admit that in not a few respects their system was patterned after many of the practices of Islam and Christianity.

Baha'is will quickly draw upon the scriptures of any religion of their sacred nine to defend the teachings of Bahá'u'lláh and 'Abdu'l Bahá. In this they have a distinct advantage because not a few of them are well informed concerning the scriptures of the religions of the world, particularly the Old and New Testaments and the Koran.

Thus, it is possible for a well-trained Baha'i cultist literally to run the gamut of the theological quotations in an eclectic mosaic design to establish his basic thesis, i.e., that all men are part of a great brotherhood revealed in this new era by the manifestation of Bahá'u'lláh.

The cardinal doctrines of the Christian faith, including the absolute authority of the Bible, the doctrines of the Trinity, the deity of Jesus Christ, His Virgin Birth, vicarious atonement, bodily resurrection, and Second Coming are all categorically rejected by Baha'ism. They maintain that Christ was *a* manifestation of God, but not the *only* manifestation of the Divine Being.

There is very little indeed that a true Christian can have in common with the faith of Baha'i. There is simply no common ground on which to meet or to talk once the affirmations have been made on both sides of Jesus Christ, as opposed to Bahá'u'lláh. Of course, there is the common ground of Scripture upon which we can meet all men to proclaim to them the indescribable gift of God in the person of Christ, but there can be no ground for fellowship with the Baha'i Faith, which is, at its very core, anti-Christian theology.

Finally, as is always the case with non-Christian cults, the refutation of Baha'ism must come from a sound knowledge of doctrinal theology as it appears in the Scriptures. No Christian can refute the perversions of the Baha'i Faith unless he is first aware of their existence and of their conflict with the doctrines of the Bible. We must, therefore, be prepared to understand the scope of the teachings of the Baha'is, their basic conflict with the Gospel, and the means by which we may refute them as we witness for Christ.

Recommended Resources

1. Ankerberg, John, and John Weldon. *Encyclopedia of Cults and New Religions.* Eugene, Ore.: Harvest House, 1999.
2. House, H. Wayne. *Charts of Cults, Sects, and Religious Movements.* Grand Rapids, Mich.: Zondervan Publishers, 2000.
3. Martin, Walter. *Bahai.* Audiotape. Walter Martin Ministries. *www.waltermartin.com.*
4. Mather, George A., and Larry A. Nichols. *Dictionary of Cults, Sects, Religions and the Occult.* Grand Rapids, Mich.: Zondervan Publishers, 1993.
5. Miller, William McElwee. *What Is the Baha'i Faith?* Grand Rapids, Mich.: Wm. B. Eerdmans Publishing Co., 1977.

Quick Facts About Unitarian Universalism

- The Unitarian Universalist Association (UUA) espouses religious pluralism and "tolerance" of all faith positions as a great virtue.

- The Bible and other sacred books are not to be regarded as absolute or infallible.

- Many UUs do not believe in God at all, and among those who do a wide variety of views may be found. All UUs reject the Triune God of Scripture.

- Christ's miracles, virgin birth, and bodily resurrection are rejected. Christ is not divine. Some UUs regard Jesus Christ to have been a great moral teacher while others dispute even this.

- UUs do not accept the biblical teaching on salvation from sin. People are basically good; they do not need a "savior" to deliver them from sin. They can "save" themselves through their own moral character.

Chapter II

Unitarian Universalism[1]

Come, return to your place in the pews,
and hear our heretical views:
You were not born in sin so lift up your chin,
you have only your dogmas to lose.
—Leonard Mason, Unitarian Universalist minister[2]

In the past thirty years, Christian apologists have virtually ignored the Unitarian Universalist Association (UUA), leaving it to spend its force in what they perceived to be random doctrinal chaos. Perhaps apologists felt this was a safe course, since the UUA was in steady decline and was therefore seen as less threatening than more virulent groups—such as the Jehovah's Witnesses and the Mormons—who were aggressively proselytizing and reaping a harvest of souls.[3] Though larger than some notorious and well-publicized cults, such as the Worldwide Church of God and The Way, International, the perceived threat was less because the UUA was not evangelistic, keeping largely to itself.

Much has changed, however, and Christian apologists can no longer ignore the UUA. Two factors support this conviction: (1) the UUA has moved further away from even its unorthodox "Christian" roots and into arguably more serious

---

This chapter written by Dr. Alan Gomes and edited by Kevin Rische and Jill Martin Rische.

[1]Dr. Alan W. Gomes adapted this material from his article "Unitarian Universalists and the Second Law of Thermodynamics: The Rise of Militant Pluralism," *Trinity Journal* 17NS (1996): 147–66. Used by permission.

[2]John Sias, from interviews with Rev. Steve Edington, *One Hundred Questions That Non-Members Ask About Unitarian Universalism* (n.p.: Transition Publishing, 1994), 1.

[3]A review of the classic works on cult apologetics readily bears out the fact that the UUA was at best relegated to a footnote or an appendix. For example, the previous edition of *The Kingdom of the Cults* by Walter Martin devoted a scant six-page appendix to them. Other major works on cults (e.g., Ruth Tucker, *Another Gospel*) ignore them altogether. While that approach may have been reasonable at one time, I believe it is no longer so.

forms of theological error;[4] and (2) the UUA has shed its passivity and is now spreading its "saving message" with a vengeance—quite literally—in its attempt to blunt the so-called "religious right."[5]

Apologists need to put this latest strain of Unitarianism under the microscope and formulate ways to inoculate against it. To do so, apologists must: (1) gauge accurately the importance and influence of the UUA, from a demographic and statistical standpoint; (2) have a basic understanding of the group's doctrinal roots; (3) assess its present doctrinal trajectories, both in continuity and discontinuity with its historical manifestations; and (4) pay due attention to current UUA efforts at spreading its influence. Only then can evangelical apologists formulate a reasoned course of action. Such are the limited goals of this chapter, which is largely descriptive. A thorough refutation of UU theological views is also needed but lies beyond our present scope. However, such a refutation is provided in the book *Unitarian Universalism,* of the fifteen-volume *Zondervan Guide to Cults and Religious Movements,* which is recommended the interested reader consult.[6]

Importance of the Unitarian Universalist Association: Vital Statistics and Demographics

For a religious group so largely ignored, the UUA is surprisingly influential, far beyond what its official membership figures might suggest. Russell Chandler notes that the Unitarian Universalist Association has "exerted influence far greater than its numerical strength."[7]

Yet, according to recent surveys, 60 percent of Americans know "little or nothing" about the UUA,[8] often confusing it with the "Unification Church" or "Unity School of Christianity."[9] According to the official membership rolls, there are presently 221,687 members of the UUA worldwide in 1,055 congregations.[10]

The UUA is almost entirely an American phenomenon: officially, 213,812

---

[4]In speaking of Unitarianism's "Christian" roots, I do not wish to be misunderstood as implying that this group was ever genuinely Christian. Historic Unitarianism regarded itself as Christian and arose out of a historically Christian context. In most instances I have placed the word "Christian" in quotation marks or have provided other qualifiers to avoid confusion, unless the context makes it plain enough that the attribution is one of self-description.

[5]Neil Chethik, "The Saving Message: The New UU Evangelists," *The World,* 9:3 (May/June 1995): 14–18; Russell Chandler, "Unitarians: Oneness in Diversity," *Los Angeles Times* (May 27, 1986): Part I, 1, 20–21; Diane Winston, "Unitarian 'Boomer' Following Growing," *Denver Post* (May 9, 1991): 2-A; Gayle White, "Tide Turns for Unitarians As Scope Widens, Membership Grows," *Atlanta Journal and Constitution* (January 13, 1990): B–9; David B. Parke, "Theological Directions of Unitarian Universalism for the Next Twenty-Five Years," *Unitarian Universalist Christian,* 44; 3–4 (1989): 5–20; Jack Mendelsohn, *Meet the Unitarian Universalists* (Boston: Unitarian Universalist Association, 1993); Scott W. Alexander, ed., *Salted With Fire: Unitarian Universalist Strategies for Sharing Faith and Growing Congregations* (Boston: Skinner House, 1995); Lawrence X. Peers, *The Congregational Handbook: How to Develop and Sustain Your Unitarian Universalist Congregation* (Boston: Unitarian Universalist Association, 1995).

[6]Alan W. Gomes, *Unitarian Universalism* (Grand Rapids, Mich.: Zondervan Publishing Company, 1998).

[7]Chandler, "Unitarians: Oneness in Diversity," 1.

[8]Ibid. See also Winston, "Unitarian 'Boomer' Following Growing," 2-A; Tony A. Larsen, "Evangelizing Our Children," chapter in *Salted With Fire,* 124.

[9]Chethik, "The Saving Message," 16, quoting Rev. Al Boyce.

[10]*Unitarian Universalist Association 2002–2003 Directory* (Boston: Unitarian Universalist Association, 2002), 54.

Unitarians reside in the United States, with 6,514 in Canada. Massachusetts, the Unitarian stronghold, boasts the largest concentration of UUs, with a total of 35,291 registered Unitarians in 141 congregations.[11]

In the mid-1960s, official UUA membership stood at around 250,000, and steadily declined for seventeen years to a low of 166,000 in 1980. Since 1981 the trend has reversed and membership has grown to its present level.[12]

Official figures notwithstanding, the total number of Americans who consider themselves UUs far outstrips the number who have bothered to sign the membership roster. In 1990 Barry A. Kosmin and Seymour P. Lachman, researchers at the City University of New York, surveyed 113,000 people across the continental United States on matters of religious self-identification, correlating these responses with a variety of demographic measures. This computer-generated survey represents "the largest and most comprehensive poll ever on religious loyalties, and the most accurate and detailed as to geographical distribution."[13]

This fascinating and well-crafted study turned up some surprising facts about Unitarian Universalists. According to this survey, there are actually about 502,000 Americans who regard themselves as Unitarian Universalists—over twice the number published by the UUA.[14]

Interestingly, this means that there are nearly as many UUs as Muslims in the United States (527,000) and significantly more than Buddhists (401,000)[15]— groups that arguably generate more attention from missiologists and apologists than the UUA.[16]

Also noteworthy is the social status and prestige of Unitarian Universalists. Kosmin and Lachman's study shows that UUs sit on top of the sociological heap. They calculated an aggregate score of four important social indicators: pattern of employment, extent of home ownership, level of education, and median family income. The Unitarian Universalists hold first place, with second through fifth places going to Disciples of Christ, agnostics, Congregationalists, and Episcopalians respectively. (Jehovah's Witnesses bring up the rear in thirtieth place.)[17]

For example, fully 49.5 percent of UUs are college graduates (higher than Jews at 46.7 percent, Roman Catholics at 20 percent, Mormons at 19.2 percent, and Baptists at 10.4 percent);[18] and their median annual household income is

---

[11]*Unitarian Universalist Association 2002–2003 Directory,* 55. Note that Unitarians not part of the Unitarian Universalist Association are found in other parts of the world, particularly in Romania (80,000) and in Great Britain (10,000), where historical Unitarianism made significant inroads in the sixteenth and seventeenth centuries. Though organizationally distinct, these foreign groups do maintain some contacts with the UUA.

[12]Chandler, "Unitarians: Oneness in Diversity," 20.

[13]Barry A. Kosmin and Seymour P. Lachman, *One Nation Under God* (New York: Harmony Books, 1993), 2.

[14]Ibid., Table 1–2, p. 16. Interestingly, Kosmin and Lachman (p. 2) point out that Catholics, Baptists, Methodists, Episcopalians, Lutherans, and Presbyterians have similarly underreported membership figures, while the actual number of religious Jews, Muslims, and Eastern Orthodox Christians is actually less than shown on the official records. Of particular interest to cult apologists is the fact that Mormons are among the groups with significantly overreported membership figures (p. 289).

[15]Kosmin and Lachman, *One Nation Under God,* Table 1–2, p. 16.

[16]It is important to note that this study measured religious *self-identification:* respondents were asked simply to state their religious affiliation, and their responses were recorded. No predefined categories were imposed from without; the classifications were determined after the fact.

[17]See note 16.

[18]See note 16; "Educational Ranking by Religious Group," Table 7-IA, p. 258.

$34,800 (second only to Jews, at $36,700).[19]

Unitarians also have been disproportionately influential in our country's highest institutions. There has been a "marked overrepresentation" of Unitarian U.S. Supreme Court justices appointed since 1790 (i.e., eight),[20] and in more recent times, the UU presence in the 101st Congress (1989–1991) was disproportionately high.[21] A total of five United States presidents professed Unitarianism.[22]

Thus, Unitarian Universalists have often been the movers and shakers in society, even though this is not widely known.

The Doctrinal Direction of Unitarian Universalism

As noted elsewhere, heterodox religious movements observe a kind of "second law of theological thermodynamics."[23]

Unorthodox theological systems generally slide further away from orthodoxy over time, devolving into a kind of "doctrinal entropy." Few groups illustrate this principle as clearly as the UUA. When compared to its "Christian" roots, the extent of the UUA defection from even the most liberal brand of Christian faith becomes striking.

"Christian" Roots.[24] The UUA traces its roots to the radical wing of the Reformation, which considered itself the true heirs of New Testament Christianity.[25] Though never viewed as genuinely Christian by its orthodox foes, it has until this century seen itself as such. Earl Morse Wilbur, in his monumental *History of Unitarianism,* points out that the flow of Unitarianism was from Poland and Transylvania through Germany and Holland to England and America.[26] Throughout this migration, the various manifestations of Unitarianism all claimed Christian allegiance.

It is neither possible in the space available nor necessary to give a detailed

---

[19]Ibid., "Income Ranking by Religious Group," Table 7-1C, p. 260. Note that although Jewish respondents slightly edged out the Unitarians on this particular measure, the Unitarians still received the top *aggregate* score for social prestige.

[20]Ibid., 252–53.

[21]Ibid., 253.

[22]They are John Adams, John Quincy Adams, Thomas Jefferson, Millard Fillmore, and William Howard Taft. Although some would classify Jefferson as a deist rather than a Unitarian, the categories are by no means mutually exclusive. Also, "In 1825 Thomas Jefferson wrote to Dr. Benjamin Waterhouse, 'The population of my neighborhood is too slender and is too much divided into other sects to maintain any one preacher well. I must therefore be contented to be a Unitarian by myself.'" See William F. Schulz, "About the Church of the Larger Fellowship," in *The Unitarian Universalist Pocket Guide,* second edition (Boston: Beacon, 1993), 97; Chandler, "Unitarians: Oneness in Diversity," 21. Jefferson also stated, "I confidently expect that the present generation will see Unitarianism become the general religion of the United States." (George N. Marshall, *Challenge of a Liberal Faith,* revised, updated, and enlarged [New Canaan, Conn.: Keats Publishing, 1980], 29.)

[23]Alan W. Gomes, "Winds of Change in the Worldwide Church of God: With Special Emphasis on the Doctrine of the Trinity," *Presbyterion* 20:2 (1994): 91.

[24]See note 4 for an explanation of the sense in which I consider Unitarianism's roots to be "Christian."

[25]For a fine, general treatment of the radical reformation written by a scholar sympathetic to it, see George H. Williams, *The Radical Reformation* (Philadelphia: Westminster, 1962).

[26]Earl Morse Wilbur, *History of Unitarianism,* 2 vols. (Boston: Beacon Press, 1945), 1:4. See also, Lloyd F. Dean, "The Withering of Unitarianism," *Gordon Review* 5:1 (Spring 1959): 15. Though sometimes the connections are loose, the movements are related nonetheless.

treatment of Unitarian history. Several fine works are available to be consulted on this subject.[27]

In this context it will be sufficient to consider but three representative luminaries of classic Unitarianism: one each from the Continent, England, and America. This is not to gloss over individual differences between thinkers or to suggest that they were all cut from the same cloth. The point is simply to show the representative attitude toward the Christian faith of classic Unitarianism that is classically held.

Faustus Socinus (1539–1604): The Beginnings of Unitarianism

The beginnings of Unitarianism as a movement may be traced almost immediately to the radical anti-Trinitarians of the sixteenth century, who were active on the Continent. Servetus, an anti-Trinitarian who was burned at the stake in 1553, is often seen as the direct forerunner or even founder of the movement.[28] However, the anti-Trinitarian party actually grew and was organized under Faustus Socinus (1539–1604), an Italian who migrated to Poland.[29] Socinus became the de facto leader of the so-called "Polish Brethren," known officially as the Minor Reformed Church.[30] He championed their cause in writing and in oral debate,

---

[27]The best work on Socinianism/Unitarianism in Europe and America is Earl Morse Wilbur's two-volume *History of Unitarianism*. Though Wilbur, himself a Unitarian, gives a generally favorable treatment of the movement, his work nonetheless represents one of the classic works on Unitarian history that anyone interested in the background of the movement must consult. See also Henry H. Cheetham, *Unitarianism and Universalism: An Illustrated History* (Boston: Beacon Press, 1962); Sydney E. Ahlstrom and Jonathan S. Carey, *An American Reformation: A Documentary History of Unitarian Christianity* (Middletown, Conn.: Wesleyan University Press, 1985); J. H. Allen, *An Historical Sketch of the Unitarian Movement Since the Reformation* (New York: Christian Literature Co., 1894); Earl Morse Wilbur, *Our Unitarian Heritage* (Boston: Beacon, 1925); and Conrad Wright, *The Beginnings of Unitarianism in America* (Starr King Press; distributed by Beacon Press [Boston], n.d.).

[28]George N. Marshall, *Challenge of a Liberal Faith*, 15.

[29]The best comprehensive, general history of Socinianism, including the lives and backgrounds of both Laelius and Faustus Socinus, is Earl Morse Wilbur's two-volume *History of Unitarianism*, cited earlier. Another thorough but much older work is Otto Fock's classic *Der Sozinianismus nach seiner Stellung in der Gesamtentwicklung des christlichen Geistes, nach seinem historischen Verlauf und nach seinem Lehrbegriff* (Keil: C. Schröder, 1847). For compact treatments of Socinus, see Alexander Gordon, "The Sozzini and Their School," *Theological Review*, 65 (1879): 293–22; Earl Morse Wilbur, "Faustus Socinus, Pioneer," *Hibbert Journal*, 33 (1935): 538–48 (hereafter cited as "Pioneer"); David Cory, *Faustus Socinus* (Boston: Beacon Press, 1932); and H. J. McLachlan, *Socinianism in Seventeenth-Century England* (Oxford: Oxford University Press, 1951), 3–24.

More recent discussions of Socinian history include Delio Cantimori, Eretici *Italiani del Cinquecento* (Florence: G. C. Sansoni, 1967); Zbigniew Ogonowski, "Faustus Socinus," in *Shapers of the Religious Traditions in Germany, Switzerland, and Poland, 1560–1600*, ed. Jill Raitt (New Haven: Yale University Press, 1981), 195–97; George H. Williams, *The Radical Reformation*, 518 ff.; Giampaolo Zucchini, "Unpublished Letters Added to the Letters of Fausto Sozzini, 1561–1568," *Socinianism and its Role in the Culture of the Sixteenth to Eighteenth Centuries* (Warsaw: Polish Academy of Sciences, 1983), 17–24; Ralph Lazzaro, "Four Letters from the Socinus-Calvin Correspondence (1549)," *Italian Reformation Studies in Honor of Laelius Socinus*, ed. John A. Tedeschi (Florence: Felice Le Monnier, 1965), 215–30; and David Willis, "The Influence of Laelius Socinus on Calvin's Doctrines of the Merits of Christ and the Assurance of Faith," *Italian Reformation Studies*, 231–41.

[30]Wilbur, *History of Unitarianism*, 1:328. Note that Poland was the most religiously tolerant country of the day. Indeed, King Sigismund (1540–1571), himself a Unitarian, issued the first public decree of religious toleration. See F. Forrester Church, "Deeds Not Creeds," *Our Chosen Faith: An Introduction to Unitarian Universalism*, by John Buehrens and F. Forrester Church (Boston: Beacon, 1989), 58.

disputing with the orthodox on such key issues as the Trinity, the deity of Christ, and the doctrine of satisfaction.[31]

The overtly biblical character of Socinus' theology is especially relevant. The Unitarians saw themselves as true followers of Christ who "showed to us the way of salvation, which we may obtain by imitating him."[32] They believed that their faith embodied the most accurate representation of biblical teaching. One can hardly peruse the works of Socinus without observing that he sought biblical support for his positions at every turn. Speaking of the Unitarianism of this period, Arthur Cushman McGiffert notes, "Christianity became in their hands more completely than ever before a book religion."[33] Indeed, Socinus himself wrote one of the first works of modern biblical apologetics, arguing for the veracity of the biblical miracles and the general reliability of the Bible.[34] Some have called Socinus a "rationalist" because he attacked orthodoxy on rational grounds,[35] but this classification is inaccurate. Socinus made it clear that the Bible, rightly understood, does not contradict sound reason. Any interpretation of Scripture that contradicts right reason cannot be a correct exegesis of the text; Socinus would "seek another interpretation" that would "produce an interpretation of those passages

---

[31]For example, see his *Explicatio primae partis primi capitis euangelistae [Exposition of the First Part of the First Chapter of the Gospel (of John)]*; *Tractatus de Deo, Christo, & Spiritu Sancto [A Discussion Concerning God, Christ, and the Holy Spirit]*; *De Jesu Christi filii Dei natura sive essentia, nec non de peccatorum per ipsum expiatione disputatio, adversus Andream Volanum [A Disputation Concerning the Nature or Essence of Jesus Christ the Son of God, and Also Concerning the Expiation of Sins through Him]*; and especially his *De Jesu Christo Servatore, hoc est, cur & qua ratione Jesus Christus noster servator sit, Fausti Socini Senensis disputatio [A Disputation Concerning Jesus Christ the Savior, i.e., Why and How Jesus Christ Is Our Savior]*. The collected works of Socinus represent the first two volumes of the *Bibliotheca Fratrum Polonorum quos Unitarios Vocant [The Books of the Polish Brethren, Whom They Call "Unitarians"]*, ed. Andreas Wissowatius (Irenopoli [Amsterdam], 1668) (hereafter cited as BFP). Many of the main Socinian writings are in this collection with the noteworthy omission of the *Racovian Catechism*, the main Socinian statement of faith.

For modern treatments of Socinus' Christology and soteriology, see John C. Godbey, "A Study of Faustus Socinus' *De Jesu Christo Servatore*" (Ph.D. diss., University of Chicago, 1968); Godbey, "Fausto Sozzini and Justification," *Continuity and Discontinuity in Church History*, eds. F. F. Church and T. George; *Studies in the History of Christian Thought*, 10 (Leiden: E. J. Brill, 1979); Alan W. Gomes, "*De Jesu Christo Servatore*, Part III: Historical Introduction, Translation, and Critical Notes" (Ph.D. diss., Fuller Theological Seminary, 1990); and Alan W. Gomes, "De Jesu Christo Servatore: Faustus Socinus on the Satisfaction of Christ," *Westminster Theological Journal*, 55 (1993): 209–31. On the continent his doctrine was known as "Socinianism" and his followers "Socinians." In Transylvania, England, and eventually America, the movement was commonly called "Unitarianism."

[32]"*De Jesu Christo Servatore*," 1:1–2.

[33]Arthur Cushman McGiffert, *Protestant Thought Before Kant* (New York: Charles Scribner's Sons, 1924), 115.

[34]"*De Sacrae Scripturae Autoritate [Concerning the Authority of Holy Scripture]*," BFP, Tomus [Tome] 1.264.

[35]See, for example, *An Encyclopedia of Religions*, 1921 ed., s.v. "Socinians" by Maurice A. Cauney; and Bengt Hagglund, *History of Theology* (St. Louis: Concordia, 1968), 322. For a recent work of the same persuasion, see Martin I. Klauber and Glenn S. Sunshine, "Jean-Alphonse Turrettini on Biblical Accommodation: Calvinist or Socinian?" *Calvin Theological Journal*, 25 (1990): 13. Others have tempered this conclusion by classifying Socinianism as a hybrid of rationalism and supernaturalism. See McLachlan, *Socinianism*, 12; Philip Schaff and J. Herzog, *A Religious Encyclopedia or Dictionary of Biblical, Historical, Doctrinal, and Practical Theology* (New York: Funk and Wagnalls, 1891), SN. "Socinianism"; Clow, s.v. "Socinianism"; and Adolph Harnack, *History of Dogma*, 7 vols. (New York Russell and Russell, 1958), 7:159.

which is both internally consistent and which agrees with the general tenor of Scripture."[36]

Don't misunderstand the statement that Socinus based his interpretations on Scripture. Socinus was wrong to reject orthodoxy; his effort was flawed. The point here is simply to highlight the effort as such, which reveals much about early Unitarian attitudes toward the Christian faith in general and toward Scripture in particular.

John Biddle (1615–1662), the Father of English Unitarianism

John Biddle, known as the Father of English Unitarianism, had not read Socinus before he formed his judgments on the Trinity. Biddle arrived at his initial convictions quite apart from Socinus, though he eventually did come into possession of Socinus' writings. Biddle's *Twelve Arguments Drawn Out of Holy Scripture*, which attempted to refute the orthodox doctrine of the Godhead, rested "at every step solely on statements of Scripture."[37] Likewise, his *A Confession of Faith Touching the Holy Trinity According to the Scripture* attempted to prove both from reason and from Scripture that the doctrine of the Trinity is illogical and unbiblical.[38] In 1654 Biddle published his *Twofold Catechism*,[39] in which "the answers are exclusively in the language of Scripture."[40] Wilbur pointed out that in Biddle's preface to the work, he lamented that other catechisms foist human constructs on the biblical text rather than taking Scripture at its literal word.[41]

Again, the point here is not to endorse Biddle's conclusions or to suggest that they are in any sense orthodox or to intimate that they are legitimately biblical. In fact, Biddle's overly literalistic interpretations of Scripture were considered bizarre in his own day and are largely considered so even today.[42]

But even these obviously heterodox views ought not to obscure the point at issue, namely, that Biddle considered Scripture to be the authoritative rule of Christian faith and sought to base his views on it.

William Ellery Channing (1780–1842), the Apostle of American Unitarianism

Dr. William Ellery Channing, arguably the greatest light of American Unitarianism, was the most robust and articulate Unitarian advocate of his day. It was under his influence that the American Unitarian Association was founded in May of 1825.[43] Channing's so-called "Baltimore sermon," preached at the ordination of Jared Sparks in 1819, marked a watershed in the debate. This sermon stands

---

[36]"*De Jesu Christo Servatore*," 3.6.282. Socinus is here speaking in the context of the doctrine of satisfaction. His point is that even if certain passages appear to teach Christ's satisfaction, they cannot really do so, and he would seek an alternative interpretation in order to harmonize such passages with the overall tenor of Scripture.

[37]Wilbur, *History of Unitarianism*, 2:194.

[38]Ibid., 195.

[39]The full title is *A Twofold Catechism: The One Simply Called a Scripture-Catechism: The Other, a Brief Scripture-Catechism for Children* (1654).

[40]Ibid., 202.

[41]Ibid., 203.

[42]For example, Biddle ascribed bodily parts to God, restricted him to a particular spatial locale, and affirmed God's "openness" by limiting his knowledge. See ibid.

[43]Mendelsohn, *Meet the Unitarian Universalists*, 14.

as one of the most pungent apologetics for the Unitarian approach to the Christian faith. As F. Forrester Church observes, "Channing's sermon was published and reprinted seven times, and became the most popular pamphlet in America since Thomas Paine's *Common Sense*."[44]

In this clarion call to Unitarianism, Channing gathered a chain of biblical citations to prove the exegetical soundness of Unitarian theology and Christology. He made his commitment to Holy Writ explicit: "We regard the Scriptures as the records of God's successive revelation to mankind, and particularly of the last and most perfect revelation of his will by Jesus Christ. Whatever doctrines seem to us to be clearly taught in the Scriptures, we receive without reserve or exception."[45] Further, he declared that there can be no real contradiction in Scripture; seeming contradictions are only apparent, not genuine, for "God never contradicts in one part of Scripture what He teaches in another."[46]

Thus whether one considers Socinus in the sixteenth century, Biddle in the seventeenth, or Channing in the nineteenth, classic Unitarians affirmed Scripture's authority, whatever one may think of their conclusions.

The Slide Away From Unitarian "Christianity"

Just as space does not permit a detailed examination of Unitarianism in its "biblical" phase, neither is it possible to trace all of the steps in the dissolution of that phase. Only the briefest summary must here suffice.

Nineteenth-Century Transcendentalism

Lloyd F. Dean, in an older but still pertinent article, identified the key steps in Unitarianism's abandonment of theism generally and of Christian theism in particular.[47] Dean considered early nineteenth-century Transcendentalism as pivotal: "At this point," Dean states, "Unitarianism passed from the status of a heresy to that of a clearly non-Christian philosophy."[48] Dean cited Ralph Waldo Emerson in particular. "Following intuition as a guide, Emerson and the Transcendentalists considered nature the Oversoul of which man was a part."[49] Thus intuition replaced Scripture; "immanent divinity in man himself both makes this possible and guarantees the accuracy of the conclusions reached."[50] Unitarian Duke T. Gray pinpoints in Emerson a philosophical shift from the authority of Jesus Christ to "the sovereignty of the self." That shift having taken place, further developments in Unitarian theology were, in Gray's opinion, "merely footnotes" to this.[51]

---

[44]Church, "Neighborhood," *Our Chosen Faith*, 121.

[45]William Ellery Channing, "Unitarian Christianity," *Three Prophets of Religious Liberalism: Channing, Emerson, Parker*, edited and with an introduction by Conrad Wright (Boston: Beacon, 1961), 48.

[46]Ibid., 52.

[47]L. F. Dean, "The Withering of Unitarianism," 13–29.

[48]Ibid., 16–17.

[49]Ibid., 21.

[50]Ibid., 21–22.

[51]Duke T. Gray, "Letter to the Christians," *The Unitarian Universalist Christian*, 47, nos. 3–4 (Fall/Winter 1992): 43. Gray observes, "in the Emersonian epistemology, each individual person is invited to tailor-make a designer religion out of one's own experience, needs, and taste. As one seminary faculty friend and U.U. Christian colleague expressed it, 'You read Emerson, and then go out and destroy the Church.'"

Channing was aghast at the seemingly pantheistic doctrines Emerson espoused. The situation was so grim for the "conservative" Unitarian wing that in one rather ironic instance, Andrews Norton of Harvard (a prominent Unitarian theologian and ally of Channing) was so desperate to stem the tide that he republished a critique of Emerson appearing in the Calvinistic *Princeton Review*![52]

The Erosion of Christian Uniqueness

Another element leading to the dissolution of Christian consensus among both Unitarians and Universalists was an increasingly global and pluralistic approach toward world religions. Emerson also demonstrates this shift, as his writings were at times a conduit of Hindu and Eastern mystical beliefs. As George N. Marshall observes, "By the 1850s, Emerson had fully launched the emerging Unitarian movement upon the quest for its larger inclusiveness in the family of world religions."[53] This pluralistic impulse would achieve its terminal velocity by mid-twentieth century.

On the Universalist side, the 1948 Massachusetts Universalist Convention radically redefined what it meant by the term *Universalist*. Whereas the term historically referred to those who affirmed universal salvation, the label was "refashioned to mean a 'universal world religion,' " a syncretistic blend of various global faith positions.[54] The Unitarians likewise embodied this "global impulse" in their "shift away from explicitly Christian symbols, rites, and thought forms toward other faiths, peoples, and struggles."[55] The activities of minister John Haynes Holmes of New York illustrate this clearly.[56] "In the years following the Armistice [he] reconstituted the Unitarian Church of the Messiah as the Community Church of New York, proclaimed Gandhi the greatest man in the world, and in a bold act of syncretism assimilated the festivals of the world's major religions into the church's liturgical year."[57]

Twentieth-Century Humanism

Humanism stands as another major way station on the road to Unitarian doctrinal diversity. The humanist-theist controversy rocked Unitarianism, particularly between 1918 and 1937.[58] As Edd Doerr of *The Humanist* journal observes, "Half of the signers of the 1933 *Humanist Manifesto I* were Unitarian Universalist ministers, as were the first four presidents of the American Humanist Association, the AHA's first executive director, and this journal's first editor. The two surviving *Manifesto* signers, Lester Mondale and Edwin H. Wilson, are both Unitarian ministers."[59] The humanists affirmed the doctrine of evolution rather than of special

---

[52]Dean, "The Withering of Unitarianism," 21.

[53]Marshall, *Challenge of a Liberal Faith,* 87–88.

[54]Gray, "Letter to the Christians," 44.

[55]Parke, "Theological Directions of Unitarian Universalism for the Next Twenty-Five Years," 10.

[56]Holmes was co-founder of the American Civil Liberties Union and the National Association for the Advancement of Colored People.

[57]Parke, 10.

[58]Mason Olds, "Religious Humanism and Unitarianism," *Religious Humanism,* 12, no. 1 (1978): 15.

[59]Edd Doerr, Book Reviews: "The Quality of Religious Life in Unitarian Universalist Congregations: A Survey by the Commission on Appraisal and Our Chosen Faith: An Introduction to Unitarian Universalism," *The Humanist* (May/June 1990): 45.

creation, gave science and reason the place of supremacy, and sought to found ethical values on a human rather than a divine basis.[60] Thus "the highest value is the complete realization of human personality and the quest for the good life here and now."[61] Some within the Unitarian movement vigorously opposed this antitheistic philosophy but to no avail; humanism carried the day.[62]

In 1989 a UUA survey of its membership showed that fully three-fourths of all members considered themselves to be some flavor of humanist.[63] (Some options included "humanist-existentialist," "feminist-humanist," and even "Christian-humanist."[64]) However, it appears that the UUA is departing from its rationalistic and humanistic stance toward a more "spiritual" position. This has caused disquiet among some humanists within the movement to the point where even some of the staunchest have left in protest.[65]

The Current State of Unitarian Universalist Pluralism

The Move From Humanism to Alternative Spiritualities

The leaven of tolerance and pluralism has bred new doctrinal ferment in the UUA. It appears that humanism, which once held sway, is loosening its grip. Humanists Paul Kurtz and Vern Bullough observe, "While humanism is influential in the UUA, it is not the dominant voice." They conclude, "There seems to be some basis for the interpretation that, although humanism is a strong strand of the UUA, there are many other strands, and humanism seems to be diminishing in influence as a spiritualistic concern begins to be felt more strongly."[66]

This departure from humanism has not escaped notice both within and without the movement.[67] Schulz conceded that the skeptical stance that has characterized the UUA "has been in transposition for at least the past decade." Schulz affirmed that UUs are now recognizing "that there are some angles from which

---

[60]Paul Kurtz and Vern L. Bullough, "The Unitarian Universalist Association: Humanism or Theism?" *Free Inquiry* 11, no. 2 (Spring 1991): 12–13.

[61]Ibid. Kurtz and Bullough mention the distinction between religious and secular humanists, which is worth observing. They point out that while all humanists "eschew any belief in a supernatural deity or salvation of the soul," there is disagreement as to whether "the terms *God, religion,* and *religious* should be used in describing humanism. Many humanists felt that these terms could be redefined in a naturalistic sense. Ever since, the humanist movement has been divided in this linguistic debate, with some feeling that use of such language clouds the issue, is inappropriate, and apt to confuse; others hold that religious language is perfectly legitimate and that the strategy to advance the cause of humanism is to enter and influence liberal churches."

[62]A good, concise historical summary of this controversy appears in Olds, "Religious Humanism and Unitarianism."

[63]Doerr, Book Reviews, 45.

[64]In this context the term "Christian-humanism" refers to a syncretistic blend of twentieth-century humanism and radically liberal Christianity, not to the Renaissance humanism of Erasmus and other sixteenth-century literati.

[65]Kurtz and Bullough, "The Unitarian Universalist Association: Humanism or Theism?" 13: "Where does the UUA stand today in regards to humanism? Many feel that it is de-emphasizing its humanistic roots and putting more attention on religious values and spiritual concerns. We should point out that both authors of this article had been members of the UUA for many decades, but resigned because we felt that the UUA was becoming increasingly theistic and Christian in its message."

[66]Ibid., 13–14.

[67]See, for example, Winston, "Unitarian 'Boomer' Following Growing"; Parke, "Theological Directions of Unitarian Universalism for the Next Twenty-Five Years"; and Alexander, *Salted With Fire* *(passim)*.

the Spirit cannot be glimpsed by even the sharpest empirical eye."[68]

Gustav Neibuhr, in his article entitled "With a New Spiritualism, Unitarians Welcome People of All Beliefs," points out that many UU pulpits have abandoned their "cool, cerebral sermons on the greatness of human reason" and now preach a more "spiritual" message instead.[69] Neibuhr correlates earlier declines in membership (e.g., in the '60s and '70s) with the abandonment of God-talk in Unitarian churches. Neibuhr quotes Scott Alexander, minister of the Unitarian Church of the Larger Fellowship, who speaks of the influx of spiritual seekers now making the UUA their homes. "They don't come to church anymore to hear some dry humanist tell about the United Nations and world federalist thinking."[70] David Parke, in charting the theological direction of Unitarianism for the next quarter century, observes that "increasing numbers of men and women have come to our congregations not from orthodoxy but from secularism." These people often seek "a robust, textured, life-giving religious faith."[71]

Many link this renewed spiritual interest with an influx of "baby boomers" who are seeking a spiritual home. Of this group, Arvid Straube notes, "The word 'God' is much less problematic to the boomer seekers in our churches than it may have been to previous generations of potential Unitarian Universalists. . . . They are thirsty for spirit from whatever source."[72]

Where are the popular spiritual watering holes in today's UUA?

The New Age and Unitarian Universalist Spirituality

For some UUs, New Age spirituality seems to fit the bill. Unitarian Ann Fields speaks of "our collective consciousness, which, in every instant of time, grows richer and more vibrant, as the universe becomes aware of itself." This process she calls God, "the spiritual evolution of the cosmos—creation flowing free."[73] Schulz likewise affirms that "Everything is . . . dependent and connected in an elaborate web of creation. A holistic view of creation is becoming more and more central to a sophisticated understanding of what being is all about." He cites approvingly Capra's monistic worldview, embracing a "deep ecology" of "the divine One."[74]

Some connect the New Age emphasis with the UUA's traditional stress on social activism: "We have to realize that these [ministries toward the homeless, the environment, etc.] are all part of a whole. . . . When we can establish harmony of earth, mind, and spirit, we'll have what we need to save ourselves and save the world."[75] The UUA's seventh principle in its *Statement of Principles and Purposes* also embodies the New Age thrust when it speaks of the UUA's "respect for the interdependent web of all existence."[76]

---

[68]William F. Schulz, Foreword, *Our Chosen Faith*, xiv.

[69]Gustav Neibuhr, "With a New Spiritualism, Unitarians Welcome People of All Beliefs," *Washington Post* (July 6, 1993): A-3.

[70]Ibid.

[71]Parke, "Theological Directions of Unitarian Universalism for the Next Twenty-Five Years," 18.

[72]Arvid Straube, "Spirituality and Church Growth," *Salted With Fire*, 173.

[73]Ann Fields, "Continuous Creation," *Unitarian Universalist Views of God*, ed. Doris Hunter (Boston: Unitarian Universalist Association, n.d.), 3.

[74]Chandler, "Unitarians: Oneness in Diversity," 21.

[75]White, "Tide Turns for Unitarians As Scope Widens, Membership Grows," B–9.

[76]The UUA adopted the "Principles and Purposes" as bylaws at the 1984 and 1985 General Assemblies. They are reproduced in numerous UUA publications. See, for example, the *Unitarian Universalist Association 2002–2003 Directory*, 5. They are also listed on the official UUA Web site, at *www.uua.org/aboutuua/principles.htm*.

Neo-Pagan Spirituality in the Unitarian Universalist Association

Neo-pagans have also made significant inroads in the UUA. In 1985 Neo-pagans formed the Covenant of Unitarian Universalist Pagans at the UUA General Assembly in Atlanta. Among the group's stated goals are "the study and practice of contemporary pagan and Earth and nature-centered spirituality," "networking among pagan UUs," and working "for the healing of the Earth."[77] According to Lattin, as of 1991 the affiliate had grown to sixty chapters nationwide.[78]

Some, though not all, of the interest in Neo-paganism is connected to radical feminism. As Kosmin and Lachman observe, goddess religions, which revere matriarchy and regard the Earth as a goddess, have become increasingly important in some feminist circles. The UUA has warmly embraced the Neo-pagan fringe. "Wicca priestesses have been accepted into Unitarian seminaries and gained academic credibility as a result."[79] Past president William F. Schultz affirms that paganism "fits very neatly with our tradition. . . . For us, a religion grounded in nature is part and parcel of our heritage. . . . We have gone too far on this side of rationalism."[80]

Accordingly, one is not surprised to find a "popular Unitarian course" entitled "Cakes for the Queen of Heaven," which teaches women about worshiping the goddess.[81] One also finds Neo-pagan hymns in the lately revised hymnbook *Singing the Living Tradition*.[82] Included in this eclectic menagerie are feminist and Neo-pagan hymns and readings, such as the song "We are Dancing Sarah's Circle" by feminist theologian Nelle Morton; a reading entitled "The Womb of the Stars" by Joy Atkinson ("written to acknowledge and celebrate the 'interdependent web' of existence, using maternal imagery to speak about the cosmos-source of our being"); a reading entitled "I who am the beauty of the green earth" from Starhawk's *Spiral Dance*; and Starhawk's prayer entitled "Earth mother, star mother."[83]

Evangelism and Church Growth Among Unitarian Universalists

From the foregoing it should now be clear that Unitarian Universalism has continued its slide ever further away from its once Christian framework. Indeed, as Gray observes, "The UUA is unique in the annals of Church History—it being perhaps the only branch of the Body of Christ ever to vote itself out of Christendom and declare itself no longer a Christian denomination, but an interfaith Association."[84]

At this juncture, an evangelical might well ask whether these developments are really cause for concern. After all, one might argue as follows: (1) The group never was truly orthodox. Therefore, why should evangelicals regard this "doctri-

---

[77]*Unitarian Universalist Association 2002–2003 Directory*, 434.

[78]Don Lattin, "Pagans to Light Up the Year's Longest Night," *San Francisco Chronicle* (December 21, 1991): A-19.

[79]Kosmin and Lachman, *One Nation Under God*, 154.

[80]Ibid., citing William F. Schulz.

[81]Christina Robb, "In Goddesses They Trust," *Boston Globe* (July 9, 1990): sec. 32:2. The article also mentions that goddess religion is a "hot" topic at some theology schools, such as Episcopal and Harvard Divinity in Cambridge. This is due to the emphasis in those schools on women's issues.

[82]Unitarian Universalist Association, *Singing the Living Tradition* (Boston: Beacon Press, 1993).

[83]Jacqui James, ed., *Between the Lines: Sources for Singing the Living Tradition* (Boston: Unitarian Universalist Association, 1995), 59, 103, 116–17.

[84]Gray, "Letter to the Christians," 41. This took place at the 1985 UUA General Assembly.

nal slide" with alarm? The Unitarians have just exchanged one flavor of doctrinal error for another. (2) The UUA has always kept to itself anyway. Therefore, whatever its views and however great its doctrinal shift, would not the most prudent course be simply to ignore it rather than call attention to it?

Both questions merit serious consideration, but space does not permit a detailed explication of both. As to the first, a Unitarianism that has scuttled even a liberal Christian framework arguably poses a greater *societal* danger than a Unitarianism within the Judeo-Christian orbit. The spread of humanism, Neo-paganism, multicultural religious pluralism, and New Age spiritism only speeds the erosion of our country's precipitously weakened "Christian" moral base. Also, from an apologetic standpoint, this lack of common ground makes the task of evangelism that much more difficult, since such "givens" as biblical authority (however watered down) and the importance (if not uniqueness) of Jesus Christ must now be proven and not automatically assumed.

Even granting that Unitarianism's present doctrinal pluralism is no worse than its earlier heterodox "Christian" stance, it is certainly no more salutary; their doctrinal positions are, from an orthodox perspective, as objectionable as ever, even if no worse. Thus, the second question is the one of the greatest concern. From the vantage point of an evangelical Christian apologist, is the best course to ignore the UUA, or is there reason to think that its increasingly heterodox views will spread if left unchecked?

Embracing the "E" Word

For years the UUA refrained from any mention of "evangelism" except in a derisive context. By their own admission, the words *evangelism* and *evangelist* were virtual Unitarian expletives, for evangelism by nature was seen as hostile to the twin ideals of tolerance and pluralism. Unitarians were careful to avoid "proselytizing" or seeking "converts" in the traditional sense.[85] However, this "laid-back" approach has given way to systematic efforts at outreach and growth, which have now become fashionable among a newer and more aggressive breed of UUs.[86] "UUA officials have even begun using . . . 'the dreaded e-word.' The association's new training course, *Sharing the Unitarian Universalist Faith,* includes 'evangelism' in its subtitle."[87] And whereas old-guard Unitarians explicitly disavowed that Unitarianism was a "salvation religion,"[88] the "new UU evangelists" proudly tout their "saving message."[89]

Leading the charge is the Rev. Scott Alexander, senior minister of the 2,000-member Church of the Larger Fellowship in Boston, the largest congregation in the denomination.[90] Alexander published *Salted With Fire in 1995,* a strategy guide

[85]George N. Marshall, "Unitarian Universalism," *Encounters With Eternity: Religious Views of Death and Life After Death,* Christopher Jay Johnson and Marsha G. McGee, eds. (New York: The Philosophical Library, 1986), 300. See also Marshall, *Challenge of a Liberal Faith,* 237.

[86]Larsen, "Evangelizing Our Children," *Salted With Fire,* 124.

[87]Chethik, "The Saving Message," 18. On the traditional reluctance of Unitarians even to use the word *evangelism* in polite company, see also Scott W. Alexander, Introduction, *Salted With Fire,* 1.

[88]Marshall, "Unitarian Universalism," *Encounters With Eternity,* 302.

[89]Chethik, "The Saving Message," 14–18.

[90]For a biographical sketch of Rev. Alexander, see Craig Wilson, "Minister Preaches Gay Acceptance." *USA Today* (August 20, 1991): sec. D, 4:2.

that presents a militant program for expansion through evangelism. Though not all UUs embrace Alexander's approach, it does appear to have high-level support. Alexander's book sports contributions from leading denominational officials, including a foreword by past president William F. Schulz and a chapter by then president John A. Buehrens.[91] Indeed, the spirit of the volume seems well in keeping with Schulz's own preelection campaign promise, in which he vowed to make Unitarian Universalism "a household word."[92] Even if resisted by traditionalists within the movement, the new evangelistic thrust appears to be here to stay, if the demand for Alexander's seminars and printed materials is any indication. Since 1993, Alexander has visited nearly half of the denomination's twenty-three districts and reports that he simply cannot keep up with the clamor for his workshops.[93]

Fueling this new interest in outreach is a desire to counteract the so-called "religious right." Alarmed by what they perceive to be an increasingly conservative shift in the political climate, these UU evangelists feel they must blunt the religious right's attack by presenting the Unitarian alternative. Alexander states, "The religious right has shown us how endangered our values are, how high are the stakes. We're realizing that if we don't stand up in the public square and proclaim our beliefs, our message will never be heard."[94] He directly credits the activism of the religious right with instilling "a renewed sense amongst Unitarian Universalists . . . that we have a unique and valuable religious vision to offer others!"[95] Alexander says that the Unitarians have a "saving message," a message that he wants to broadcast as never before.

Just what is the "saving message"—this Unitarian version of the "good news"? According to Harvey M. Joyner Jr., "The 'good news' of Unitarian Universalism is that it gives us a 'safe house' in which to wage our own heresy, whatever tradition we might have come from."[96] In short, the saving Unitarian message is *pluralism*—"a theology centered on tolerance, interdependence, and compassion."[97]

Church Growth, Unitarian Style

Pragmatically, the new UU evangelists are systematically applying well-calculated techniques to grow their churches. One approach is to make greater use of mass media. Always supportive of left-wing social causes, the UUs are seeking greater media coverage for their social agenda. For example, in August 1992 the First Unitarian Church in Portland, Oregon, decided to protest an Oregon ballot initiative designed to keep homosexuals from receiving special rights. They tied a red ribbon around the entire block occupied by the church, declaring it a

---

[91]Alexander, in his introductory essay, describes the book as "comprised of twenty-two essays written by a group of unashamedly evangelistic Unitarian Universalist leaders from all over the continent" (p. 5).

[92]Chandler, "Unitarians: Oneness in Diversity," 1, 20.

[93]Chethik, "The Saving Message," 14–15.

[94]Ibid., 14.

[95]Ibid., 15, citing Scott Alexander's book, *Salted With Fire*.

[96]Harvey M. Joyner Jr., "The Bold Witness," *Salted With Fire*, 76. Likewise, the Rev. Al Boyce did a 50,000-piece mailing in the Miami area, outlining the main Unitarian beliefs. In it he assures readers that "heretics are welcome" (Chethik, "The Saving Message," 17).

[97]Scott Alexander, quoted in Chethik, "The Saving Message," 15.

"hate-free zone."[98] They also put signs up at various points along the ribbon, proclaiming, "Hate is not a family value," "Hate-Free Zone," and other such sentiments. The media came out in force: three TV stations, two radio stations, and a newspaper covered the event.[99] Apparently the publicity paid off: the congregation grew by 41 percent in the year following the coverage.[100]

The UU evangelists are also taking some lessons from the evangelical church growth movement. They are finding that they can apply evangelical church growth techniques with little or no adaptation. The UUs have no difficulty separating form from content: "Religious liberals can learn from and employ these evangelical methods," Alexander states, "without in any way adopting, mimicking, or supporting their orthodox message." Alexander goes on to state that many UUs "have enthusiastically adopted (and adapted) the evangelical techniques of religious conservatives to trumpet and spread our *liberal* 'good news.' "[101] For example, the growth-oriented Unitarians are courting the baby boomers, tailoring services to meet their felt needs. Taking a page from the church growth playbook, the Rev. Suzanne Meyer (minister of the First UU Church of New Orleans) declares that "if the new evangelism is going to succeed, Sunday services must appeal to a new generation of churchgoers looking primarily for spiritual and emotional nourishment. . . . That means, among other things, more inspiring music, richer liturgy, and less intellectualism from the pulpit."[102] In her chapter "Courting the Baby Boomers," she strikes the same chord. She notes that "boomers are seeking spiritual nurture and direction. Their tastes are wide-ranging and eclectic and embrace both traditional religious symbols as well as New Age philosophies."[103] Thus, the new "spiritual" direction of the UUA (cited earlier) is the perfect prescription for growing a boomer church.[104] Likewise, the UUA's "openness to different family forms, deep antiauthoritarianism [and] egalitarian sex roles" fits the boomer ethos well.[105] Not surprisingly, a 1990 *Newsweek* article dubbed the UUA the "quintessential boomer church."[106]

Some Modest Suggestions

How should Christians respond—especially professional Christian apologists? The first and most important step is informational and educational. Christians must be made aware of today's UUA and what a serious challenge it poses. Most Christians see the UUA (if they've heard of it at all) as a group of dormant, non-proselytizing humanists, declining in membership and talking primarily to themselves. Unfortunately, this perspective appears to be as common among "cult watchers" as it is among the general Christian public. This view is twenty years out of date and has led to a serious and possibly even dangerous disregard of this

---

[98] Marilyn Sewell, "Slaying Dragons of Hate With Ribbons of Love," *Salted With Fire*, 250.
[99] Ibid., 250–51.
[100] Chethik, "The Saving Message," 17.
[101] Alexander, Introduction, *Salted With Fire*, 2–3 (emphasis in the original).
[102] Chethik, "The Saving Message," 18.
[103] Suzanne P. Meyer, "Courting the Baby Boomers," *Salted With Fire*, 94.
[104] See the discussion of Unitarian spirituality in this essay.
[105] Winston, "Unitarian 'Boomer' Following Growing," 2-A.
[106] See Kenneth L. Woodward, et al., "And the Children Shall Lead Them: Young Americans Return to God," *Newsweek* (December 17, 1990): 50–56.

group. This chapter represents a practical step toward sounding the alarm among thoughtful Christians to take the UUA seriously. A further and more detailed critique is now available in the book *Unitarian Universalism*.[107] It is the only large scale evangelical critique of the UUA produced in recent years. Hopefully, it will spur other researchers to devote renewed attention to this group and to develop even more resources for dealing with it.

Second, apologists must map out a strategy for countering and evangelizing the UUA. Doing so will not be simple: Because of the departure from its Christian base, much "pre-evangelism" is required. Apologists need to focus special energy on certain key pressure points of UUA theology. The watershed issues are the reliability and authority of Scripture, the uniqueness of Jesus Christ, and the necessity of faith in Him. However diverse the UUA may be, there is considerable unanimity in their rejection of historic Christian orthodoxy on these foundational doctrinal topics. A robust and relevant apologetic in these areas will be crucial if any progress is to be made. This will not be an easy sell to a group whose trinity is pluralism, tolerance, and freedom.

Finally, given the diverse doctrinal positions within the UUA, evangelism may best be done collaboratively; apologists with specialized expertise may need to pool resources to accomplish the task. For example, one cannot speak of a UU *doctrine* of God but must deal rather with the UU *doctrines* of God. Therefore, apologists particularly versed in countering, say, a pantheistic view of Deity (e.g., an expert on the New Age movement) ought to help craft strategies that would work well against pantheistic forms of UU belief. Viewed from another angle, as apologists work in their specialty areas, they should cast a weather eye for connections between their research interests and the UUA: the UUA remains a safe haven for such groups as Neo-pagans and radical feminist theologians. As apologists work to counteract, for example, Neo-pagans generally, they need to note the linkage with the UUA and adapt their polemic to take this linkage into account.

Concluding Thoughts

"There is a Men's Support Group, a Friday Morning Meditation Group, a Hatha Yoga group, the Wednesday Night Minister's Class, a Parenting Class, a Spiritual Autobiography Class, a New Physics Class, a Neo-Pagan group, and several Women's Spirituality groups. In addition, there are Saturday workshops, such as Living With Awareness and Compassion, Spirituality in the Workplace, and Chinese Medicine."[108]

Yes, the Unitarian Universalists have something for everybody. The denomination is a one-stop spiritual supermarket. Through its adoption of church growth principles, it seeks to maximize its tremendous market potential, tapping into legions of savvy baby boomer consumers.

The following is a brief summary of the Unitarian Universalist beliefs:

1. *Freedom, Tolerance, and Pluralism*: The Unitarian Universalist Association (UUA) espouses religious pluralism and touts "tolerance" of all faith positions as

---

[107]Alan W. Gomes, *Unitarian Universalism* (Grand Rapids, Mich.: Zondervan Publishers, 1998). Part of the fifteen-volume *Zondervan Guide to Cults and Religious Movements* series.

[108]Arvid Straube, "Spirituality and Church Growth," *Salted With Fire*, 169–70.

a great virtue. Conversely, Unitarian Universalists (UUs) eschew all religious "exclusivism," including the claim that the Christian faith is exclusively true. As UU Philip Hewett states, the UU position "excludes all exclusiveness."

2. *Revelation*: Some UUs find inspiration in the Bible or other sacred books, while other UUs do not. Regardless, such books are not to be regarded as absolute or infallible. In particular, the Bible is a human book and therefore contains moral, scientific, and historical errors. Reason, conscience, and experience are the final test of all religious truth claims.

3. *God*: Many UUs do not believe in God at all, and among those who do, a wide variety of views may be found. Some view God as a "higher power" or divine spark within themselves. Others believe that *God* is just a word for an ordering principle in nature. Still others take a Neo-pagan view of God (or the Goddess). Regardless, all UUs reject the Triune God of Scripture.

4. *Christ*: Some UUs regard Jesus Christ to have been a great moral teacher, while other UUs dispute even this. Regardless, Christ's miracles, virgin birth, and bodily resurrection are rejected. Christ is not divine in the way that orthodox Christians believe, and, in fact, others have attained or can attain to the same level of spirituality that he did.

5. *Man and Sin*: All human beings have inherent dignity and worth. At the same time, human beings came about through evolution. UUs deny the biblical doctrine of "original sin," namely, that people are born with sinful dispositions and that they are condemned for Adam's sin. Rather, UUs emphasize the natural human ability to do good.

6. *Salvation*: UUs do not accept the biblical teaching on salvation from sin. Because people are basically good, they do not need a "savior" to deliver them from sin. Rather, they can "save" themselves through their own moral character. When UUs speak of "salvation," they mean making this present world a better place.

7. *Heaven, Hell, and the Afterlife*: Probably most (though not all) UUs deny any afterlife at all. UUs tend to focus their efforts on the here and now in an attempt to create "heaven on earth," often through political activism or various social programs. UUs reject the bodily resurrection as unscientific and impossible. They also reject the doctrine of hell or a time of future judgment. People experience "hell" right here on earth as the natural consequence of the bad deeds that they choose to do.

Unfortunately, what the Unitarians cannot provide a generation of hungry seekers is the one food that will satisfy: the Lord Jesus Christ, the Living Bread from heaven. Christians must take this mission field seriously, holding forth the Bread of Life to a group that prides itself on knowledge, but which never comes to a knowledge of the truth. May God cause many in the UUA to buy that food without price, which only the Triune God of Scripture can supply.

Recommended Resources

1. Alexander, Scott W., ed. *Salted With Fire: Unitarian Universalist Strategies for Sharing Faith and Growing Congregations*. Boston: Skinner House, 1995.
2. Gomes, Alan W. *Unitarian Universalism*. Grand Rapids, Mich., Zondervan Publishing Company, 1998.
3. Wilbur, Earl Morse. *History of Unitarianism*, 2 vols. Boston: Beacon Press, 1945.

Quick Facts About Scientology

- Scientology teaches that the Bible is a byproduct of Hindu scriptures.

- God or gods may exist, but the individual must decide for himself.

- Christ is a legend that preexisted earth-life on other planets and was implanted into humans on earth. Jesus was just a shade above "clear" and was no greater than Buddha or Moses.

- Reincarnation sufficiently explains man's existence, but Scientology is the freedom from reincarnation.

- Man is basically good and in his evolution, he will finally become a godlike being known as "homo novis."

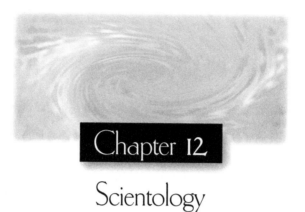

Chapter 12

Scientology

Historical Perspective

The Church of Scientology[1] is the most litigious religion in the history of churches founded in the United States. They have been the plaintiffs in an enormous number of lawsuits compared with most churches and/or religions. A few of their court battles have benefited others' rights. In that regard, Scientology's legal claims have helped stay the erosion of religious liberty. On the other hand, critics of Scientology claim that they intended many of their lawsuits as malicious vendettas against ex-members and perceived enemies of the church. These actions by Scientology have soured many people toward their church. Every Christian should cherish his religious freedom as a gift from God. In juggling the freedom of speech and freedom of religion, a Christian can allow freedom of religion for every Scientologist while exercising free speech in labeling Scientology a false religion according to the biblical teachings embraced by the historical orthodox Christian church over nearly two thousand years.

Several articles, both pro and con, have been written about Scientology's religious nature. In our observation, it has all the marks of a religion. It has its own set of scripture, it holds a worldview, and it seeks spiritual enlightenment. By biblical standards we justifiably call it a false religion. We define any religion as false whenever and wherever it departs from the biblical God and His plan of salvation as understood and proclaimed by the historical orthodox Christian church. So yes, Scientology is a religion, but a false religion by biblical standards. Jesus sharply rebuked false teachers of His day without denying their freedom of belief.

This chapter written and edited by Kurt Van Gorden.
[1]Scientology, Dianetics, Hubbard, and E-Meter are trademarks and service marks of the Religious Technology Center.

Consider His "woes" to the Pharisees as an example (Matthew 23:13–30). Religions that deny Christ's deity, atonement, resurrection, and grace lead to an eternal hell and separation from God (John 10:1, 8; Matthew 5:29–30; 10:28; 18:9). Like Jesus, we can freely speak against false religion without denying one's rights to hold such. We must categorically separate denial of rights from proper examination by Scripture. We intend to do the latter only.

This chapter focuses on the theological aspects of Scientology. We will also examine its history to see how it came about. If the founder and the Church of Scientology have a questionable background, then that background warrants examination by Scripture. In 1 Thessalonians 5:22, we are warned to abstain from all appearance of evil. Ephesians 5:11 counsels us, "Have no fellowship with the unfruitful works of darkness, but rather reprove them." We do not find any clandestine or questionable background in the person of Jesus Christ. For centuries people everywhere have investigated the life of Jesus Christ by the same standards that we will apply to L. Ron Hubbard and Scientology. Jesus, being sinless and God incarnate, has no equal, nor can He be superseded by any other (John 1:1; 8:46; 18:20).

The Dianetics movement was once seen as a 1950s fad, which some erroneously thought would fade away as many fads do.[2] Others had a different perspective of Dianetics, calling it a cult from the beginning.[3] Within our theological definition of cultism, we describe the Church of Scientology as a non-Christian cult. In particular, Scientology's magazine *Advance!* speaks of its Buddhistic root, that L. Ron Hubbard is a second Buddha, the Meitreya. It says, "In Buddhist lands Mettaya [also spelled, Meitreya] became a great favorite [second Buddha]. Various cults devoted to him arose."[4] Scientologists acknowledge the religious validity of Buddhistic cults centered on Meitreya in past centuries. What they fail to realize is the same Meitreya-cult syndrome exists in their church, with L. Ron Hubbard as the figure.

What is this movement called Scientology? It claims to be a "church" and an "applied religious philosophy." How do its teachings compare with the teachings of the Bible? What background and qualifications does founder L. Ron Hubbard have for developing a system that claims to be "the most vital movement on Earth today"?[5] In this analysis of a complex religious and philosophical system, we will explore some answers to these questions. We will provide a survey of Scientology and, by contrast, show the major points at which statements in Scientology materials contradict biblical teaching.

L. Ron Hubbard

The founder of Scientology, Lafayette Ronald Hubbard (L. Ron Hubbard, affectionately called "Ron" by Scientologists), was born on March 13, 1911, in

---

[2]See Martin Gardner, *Fads and Fallacies in the Name of Science* (New York: Dover Publishing, 1957), 263, and Paul Sann, *Fads, Fallacies, and Delusions* (New York: Crown Publishing, 1967), 113ff.

[3]*Time* (July 24, 1950): 64; *Newsweek* (October 16, 1950): 59; *American Mercury* (August 1951): 76; and *Time* (September 3, 1951).

[4]*Advance!* (December 1974): 27:5.

[5]L. Ron Hubbard, "The Aims of Scientology" (Hollywood: The Church of Scientology Celebrity Center, 1974, 1977), one-page flyer.

Tilden, Nebraska. Hubbard, a popular science fiction writer of the 1930s and 1940s, changed venues midstream by allegedly announcing at a New Jersey science fiction convention, "Writing for a penny a word is ridiculous. If a man really wanted to make a million dollars, the best way would be to start his own religion."[6] The following year, in May 1950, Hubbard released *Dianetics: A Modern Science of Mental Health*,[7] which has become entry-level reading for converts to Scientology. Hubbard's overnight success with *Dianetics* virtually gave him a new career in writing self-help and religious books. His first book on Scientology was published in 1951, and the Church of Scientology of California was incorporated on February 18, 1954.

Building a global religion of six million adherents (perhaps 200,000 active) in a few decades was no small victory for Mr. Hubbard, whose abilities should not be underestimated. His claim to fame as a writer includes fifteen million published words in science fiction, essays, and articles. He supersedes this with twenty-five million published words for Scientology. Mr. Hubbard's publishing achievements are notable, but his background upholds very few biblical Christian values, as we will see.

He was raised on a small ranch near Helena, Montana, a town with four hometown churches, but his later cynicism of Christianity betrays his virtually faithless upbringing. His father served a career in the U.S. Navy, which allegedly afforded L. Ron Hubbard frequent travel abroad. He was also one of the youngest Eagle Scouts in the history of the Boy Scouts of America.

His books often carry a short biographical sketch of his accomplishments, also described in the Scientology *Dictionary*:

> [He traveled] extensively in Asia as a young man. . . . He studied science and mathematics at George Washington University, graduating from Columbian College. He attended Princeton University and Sequoia University. . . . Crippled and blind at the end of the war [World War II], he resumed his studies of philosophy and by his discoveries recovered so fully that he was reclassified in 1949 for full combat duty. It was a matter of medical record that he has been twice pronounced dead and that in 1950 he was given a perfect score on mental and physical fitness reports.[8]

Several competent writers have gathered contradictory evidence of Hubbard's exaggerated vita and have challenged his claims. None are so thoroughly damaging to his credentials than Russell Miller's *Bare-Faced Messiah: The True Story of L. Ron Hubbard*[9] and former Scientologist Bent Corydon's *L. Ron Hubbard, Messiah or Madman?*[10] Miller showed that Hubbard attended high school in America while he was claiming to have been traveling Asia. His medical records showed that he was never crippled, blinded, or wounded in World War II, let alone being pronounced dead twice. Bent Corydon, formerly head of one of the most

---

[6]*Time* (April 5, 1976): 57.
[7]Unless otherwise noted, all quotations are from the 1986 edition: L. Ron Hubbard, *Dianetics: The Modern Science of Mental Health* (Los Angeles: Bridge Publications, Inc., 1986).
[8]L. Ron Hubbard, *Scientology Abridged Dictionary* (Los Angeles: American Saint Hill Organization [ASHO], 1970), 36–37.
[9]Russell Miller, *Bare-Faced Messiah: The True Story of L. Ron Hubbard* (London: Michael Joseph/Penguin Books, Ltd., 1987).
[10]Bent Corydon, *L. Ron Hubbard, Messiah or Madman?* (Fort Lee, N.J.: Barricade Books, 1992).

successful Scientology missions (Riverside, California), has countless court transcripts, affidavits, and firsthand testimonies that lay many of L. Ron Hubbard's claims to rest.[11]

Hubbard's academic degrees have come under question, since Sequoia University was discovered to be an unrecognized diploma mill located in a two-story house in Los Angeles. It was closed down in 1958 by an act of the California Legislature.

It is true that he attended George Washington University for two years. He was placed on academic probation, as he said, for "some very poor grade sheets."[12] Although there are times he calls himself a "nuclear physicist," he failed his only class on molecular and atomic physics. He also spent three months in a military course at the Princeton School of Military Government. Nothing has yet surfaced to confirm his alleged degree from Columbian College.

The success of Hubbard's writing skills cannot be argued. The manuscript for *Dianetics* (180,000 words) was supposedly completed in three weeks' time. Those who knew him said that he could type ninety words per minute with the old two-finger method. He had an altered typewriter with special keys for often used words, such as "and," "the," and "but."

His personal qualifications as a religious leader were everything but saintly. His first two marriages were disastrous. His second wife, Sara Northrup Hubbard, sued him for divorce on April 23, 1951, in Los Angeles County Superior Court. The microfilm copy of that case mysteriously vanished from the court records. However, an industrious *St. Petersburg Times* newspaper reporter found the original in storage at the courthouse. It was a twenty-eight-page complaint to dissolve their Chestertown, Maryland, marriage of August 10, 1946. This was a bigamous marriage for Mr. Hubbard. He pretended to be a bachelor to Miss Northrup, yet he had not divorced his first wife, Margaret Grubb Hubbard. His first marriage was not legally dissolved until over one year after his second marriage.

His second wife's 1951 divorce allegations contained more than bigamy charges. She claimed sleep deprivation, beatings, strangulation, kidnapping of their child and fleeing to Cuba, and Ron counseling her to commit suicide, "if she really loved him."[13] The kidnapping was reported in several newspapers in 1951.

Sara Northrup had first met Hubbard through a Pasadena-based occult group led by Jack Parsons, a disciple of the late Alister Crowley, whose alias was "The Beast 666." Crowley was a leading Satanist, sorcerer, and black magician. He founded the Ordo Templi Orientis (OTO), which promoted sexual magick.[14] At its New York headquarters, the group's historical records include letters between Parsons and Crowley that mention Hubbard several times. Northrup was Parsons' girlfriend when they both met L. Ron Hubbard. As Parsons' partner, she

---

[11]The prudent Christian reader should exercise discretion in reading these two books. Both contain offensive, vulgar, and obscene quotations attributed to Hubbard and others. Even Scientologists have expressed surprise at the filthy language of their leader. One Scientologist asked, "You mean the leader of the church speaks like *that?*" Another Scientologist responded, "Oh yes, he doesn't believe in keeping anything back" (Miller, *Bare-Faced,* 354).

[12]Miller, *Bare-Faced,* 50.

[13]Corydon reproduced nearly the entire document (Corydon, *Madman,* 302ff.).

[14]"Magick" instead of "magic" was used by Crowley and other occultists to distinguish their rituals and spells from the sleight of hand entertainment provided by stage magicians.

represented the Babylonian woman in Revelation, chapter 17. Before she could fulfill Parsons' plan, Hubbard swept her away in an out-of-state bigamous marriage (representing himself as a bachelor the entire time). In Parsons' letters, he blamed Hubbard for taking her from him.

Scientology defends Hubbard's connection to the Parsons black magick cult by stating that he went undercover to infiltrate it on orders of the Naval Intelligence. Supposedly, several prominent scientists were visiting Parsons' OTO temple, and Ron's job was to shut it down. Jack (John Whiteside) Parsons was a noted rocket scientist, but the explanation presented by Hubbard seems far-fetched. It lacks rationalization for why an undercover agent would soil the operation with a bigamous marriage. No record has ever been produced to prove that Naval Intelligence hired Hubbard for such an operation.[15]

Hubbard's working knowledge of black magic and the occult satisfied Parsons. In one letter he wrote to Crowley, he speaks highly of Ron's knowledge of the rituals.[16] The Bible, however, condemns occult practices as abominable, and God says that He will cut off the participants from His presence (Deuteronomy 18:9–12).

The resources claimed by Hubbard for Dianetics include, "the medicine man of the Goldi people of Manchuria, the shamans of North Borneo, Sioux medicine men, the cults of Los Angeles, and modern psychology. Among the people questioned about its existence were a magician whose ancestors served in the court of Kublai Khan and a Hindu who could hypnotize cats. Dabbles had been made in mysticism, data had been studied from mythology to spiritualism."[17]

Hubbard's third marriage, to Mary Sue Whipp, lasted the rest of his lifetime. She captivated worldwide attention in 1977 as the mastermind behind a sinister covert operation against various levels of the United States government that could rival a spy novel. Hubbard was living in California at the time, but his impenetrable shield prevented direct connection with the illegal activities.

Hubbard spent his final years in seclusion from the public eye. Top Scientologists isolated him from most family and church members until his death in Creston, California (a small town north of San Luis Obispo). According to a copy of his death certificate, he succumbed to a cerebral vascular accident (stroke) on January 24, 1986. In their refusal to believe that such a great "science of the mind" master could die a horrific death, the word "dead" or "died" was never used at his eulogy. Scientologists announced that L. Ron Hubbard decisively "discarded the body" to move on to the next level of research, outside his body.[18] How this new research would become available to planet earth is left unsaid.

Hubbard himself apparently encouraged an examination of his belief system, such as that undertaken in this volume. The seventh article of the Creed of Scientology states, "All men have the inalienable rights to think freely, to talk freely, to

[15]Scientologists also defend Hubbard by producing a document signed by Sara Northrup Hubbard declaring false everything she had stated in the divorce papers. Corydon made contact with Sara for his book. She reconfirmed her divorce statements and added that she had signed the disclaimer for protection (Corydon, *Madman,* 305).

[16]Corydon, *Madman,* 275.

[17]L. Ron Hubbard, "Dianetics, the Evolution of a Science," *Astounding Science Fiction* (May 1950): 48.

[18]Corydon, *Madman,* 17.

write freely on their own opinions and to counter or utter or write upon the opinion of others." If they hold faithful to their creed, they should expect counter writings. With this, we counter the opinions of L. Ron Hubbard.

The Dianetics Movement

As an accomplished science fiction writer, Hubbard had no difficulty coining new terms. This talent became the bedrock for new terminology in Dianetics and Scientology. Church publications often contain glossaries for the new terms. They also publish a technical dictionary with three thousand new terms and definitions. It is interesting, however, that the word *Scientology* was originally used in 1934 by a German social psychologist, Dr. A. Nordenholz.[19] A French physiologist, Richard Semon, coined "engram" in 1904.[20] *Engram* is one of the most commonly used words in Dianetics and Scientology.

Dianetics means "through thought" or "through the soul." Hubbard promoted Dianetics by publishing three lengthy excerpts of his theory in the periodical *Astounding Science Fiction*, May 1950, October 1950, and January 1951. According to *Publisher's Weekly, Dianetics* sold 55,000 copies in the first two months and more than 750 Dianetics groups started nationwide.[21] They advertised its readership a year later as 150,000 people with 2.5 million followers. Dianetics swept college campuses and blazed through middle-class America with a faddish appeal that evolved into a cultic structure.

The glowing benefits of Dianetics seem virtually unlimited as Hubbard promotes his new "science of the mind."[22] Mankind, according to Hubbard, "is basically good."[23] The basic instinct for all people is survival.[24] Man's environmental conditions and painful experiences result in failure. So if a man changes his circumstances and eliminates pain, then his condition improves. Two important factors for man's survival, then, are avoiding pain and gaining pleasure.[25]

The structure of man's mind is simplified by dividing the mind into three main categories: the analytical mind, reactive mind, and somatic mind.[26] The analytical mind works like a "perfect computer, it never makes a mistake."[27] It is also the "I" of a person.[28] The reactive mind works on a "totally stimulus/response basis."[29] The reactive mind holds mental picture images of past experiences called "engrams," which are apparently the "single source of aberrations and psychosomatic ills."[30] Some liken the reactive mind to the subconscious mind. The analytical and reactive minds direct the somatic mind and "place solutions

[19]George Malko, *Scientology: The Now Religion* (New York: Dell Publishing, 1970), 64. Malko parallels Hubbard's and Nordenholz's models, which reveals some scant hypothetical resemblance (116–19).
[20]Daniel L. Schacter, *Stranger Behind the Engram* (Hillsdale, N.J.: Lawrence Erlbaum Associates, Publishers, 1982), 186.
[21]*Publisher's Weekly* (September 16, 1950): 1124.
[22]Hubbard, *Dianetics*, 7.
[23]Ibid., 26.
[24]Ibid., 29.
[25]Ibid., 44.
[26]Ibid., 61.
[27]Ibid., 62.
[28]Ibid., 61.
[29]Ibid., 577.
[30]Ibid.

into effect on the physical level."[31] This mind keeps the body regulated and functioning.

The problem of humanity is that the reactive mind frequently interrupts the analytical mind. The analytical mind, which essentially "*is* the person,"[32] could flawlessly run a person's life (being a perfect computer) except for the interference from the reactive mind.[33]

It appears that this villain of the analytical mind causes it to shut off. Scientology calls this a moment of unconsciousness, though often the body is awake and animated. Hubbard explains, "When the individual is 'unconscious' in full or in part, the reactive mind is cut in, in full or in part. When he is fully conscious, his analytical mind is fully in command of the organism."[34] During these unconscious moments, the reactive mind takes in a detailed recording from the sensory organs. This recording is not a "memory," but an image, like a motion picture, called an "engram."[35] Everything said, seen, touched, or sensed is recorded by the reactive mind as the "engram." The reactive mind stores this engram, which works to stimulate the person to react to the stimulus.

The example is given: "Suppose as an example of an engram and its effects on the Spirit, Mr. A has a tonsillectomy under anesthetic. During the operation, the surgeon, who wears glasses, comments angrily to a clumsy nurse, 'You don't know what you are doing.' Mr. A recovers. A few months later, Mr. A, a bit tired during a hard day at the office, has an argument with his employer (who happens to also wear glasses), who says, 'You don't know what you are doing.' Mr. A suddenly feels dizzy, stupid, and gets a pain in his throat. There is installed a kind of conditioned semantic response that affects the Thetan (a cyclical reincarnated entity 'discovered' by L. Ron Hubbard)."[36] These engrams make man react insanely in society; in fact, they make man "mad, inefficient, and ill."[37]

The solution to the reactive mind interrupting the analytical mind is to rid the reactive mind of all engrams. Once this is accomplished, the person is called "clear." The clear person has no reaction to the same situation because no engram stimulates it. The goal of Dianetics is to clear the individual of all engrams of his past.[38] At first, Dianetics only dealt with engrams in this lifetime. After more probing, Scientologists claim that they carry engrams from past lives (reincarnation) that also need to be cleared.

The "clear" person is on the evolutionary journey to the next stage of man, a godlike being called *homo novis*. Hubbard informs us that a clear individual

> . . . can be tested for all psychoses, neuroses, compulsions, and repressions (all aberrations) and can be examined for any autogenetic (self-generated) diseases referred to as psychosomatic ills. These tests confirm the clear to be entirely without such ills or aberrations. Additional tests of his

[31]Ibid., 56.
[32]Ibid., 61.
[33]Ibid., 66.
[34]Ibid., 82.
[35]Ibid., 83.
[36]Staff of Scientology, *Scientology: A World Religion Emerges in the Space Age* (Los Angeles: Church of Scientology Information Service, 1974), 28.
[37]Hubbard, *Dianetics*, 84.
[38]Ibid., 14.

intelligence indicate it to be high above the current norm.[39]

Hubbard continues the potential expectation for the clear. It improves eyesight, stops ear-ringing, increases the IQ, cures the common cold, speeds thinking computations 120 times faster than normal, and saves marriages.[40]

The application of Hubbard's hypothesis is to vanquish the engrams through "Dianetic therapy." This is accomplished by an "auditor" who "audits" the engram through a form of counseling. After *Dianetics* was published, Hubbard introduced an electronic galvanometer, the E-meter, to help in auditing. The "pre-clear" (the person not yet clear) holds two tin cans connected by wires to the E-meter, while the auditor sits opposite him watching the needle on the E-meter. As the auditor gives "commands" to the pre-clear, the needle's fluctuation determines if they have detected a possible engram. By tracking the engram through questioning the pre-clear, they can erase the engram. That may only be the beginning of problems for the pre-clear, though. They may detect other engrams in connection with the first, producing a chain of engrams. It may take years of auditing for a person to become finally clear.

Hubbard claims that his results are scientifically valid and are based upon clinical study. Critics, however, renounced it from the start. *Publisher's Weekly*[41] reported that the American Psychological Association initiated the "first concerted action against" Dianetics at their September 1950 meeting. A resolution, adopted unanimously by the organization's eight thousand members, said that Hubbard's claims for Dianetics "are not supported by empirical evidence of the sort required for the establishment of scientific generalizations."

Dr. Morris Fishbeck, former editor of the *Journal of the American Medical Association*, went on record warning people about "mind-healing cults . . . like Dianetics."[42] Psychologist Eric Fromm aimed his comments at Hubbard's techniques. "Dianetics," he said, "has no respect for and no understanding of the complexities of personality." Dr. Fromm revealed that Hubbard had saturated Dianetics in "oversimplified truths, half-truths, and plain absurdities."[43]

One other problem that seemed to face Hubbard was that no "clears" could be found until February 1966, when John McMaster was called the world's first clear. It troubled critics that Hubbard never claimed to be clear himself until some years after *Dianetics* was published. Still, a little known story of an earlier clear is found in several newspapers of 1950.

On August 10, 1950, Hubbard rented the Shrine Auditorium in Los Angeles. An estimated crowd of four thousand came to see the world's first clear, Miss Sonya Bianca, a physics student from Boston. Fitting with the Dianetic theory, Hubbard announced that she had perfect recall and could remember every moment of her life. When members of the audience questioned her, she could not remember basic physics formulas nor the color of Hubbard's necktie, which she had seen moments before. People began leaving the auditorium as they threw more taunting questions at Bianca. Hubbard quickly explained that he had acci-

---

[39]Ibid.
[40]Ibid., 17–18, 122, 125, 228, 411.
[41](September 16, 1950): 1124.
[42]*Newsweek* (October 16, 1950): 59.
[43]Sann, *Delusions*, 114.

dentally placed her in the "now" by calling her to "come out now." Therefore, Hubbard reasoned, she could only remember the present "now" and nothing past. No reporters seemed convinced of his explanation, and on that note the Bianca debacle ended.

Although most Scientologists still claim that the world's first clear came in 1966, this is apparently not true according to Hubbard. In *The Journal of Scientology* (January 15, 1954), Hubbard wrote of how he had cleared fifty people. He added that auditors had cleared many times that number.

The Church of Scientology

The first nonprofit organization Hubbard set up was the Hubbard Dianetic Research Foundation. By November 1950 they had developed three courses in Dianetics. In 1954 the Church of Scientology was founded as a nonprofit corporation. The meaning of Scientology, Hubbard says, is "knowing about knowing, or science of knowledge."[44] The Church of Scientology uses a cross similar to the historical cross of Christianity, with the exception that it has four short sunburst points protruding from the center. The *Technical Dictionary* states that Hubbard borrowed the cross from Christianity. It says, "The model of the cross came from a very ancient Spanish mission in Arizona, a sand casting, which was dug up by Ron."[45] Ministers of Scientology often dress in black clergy garments and a white collar with a three-inch cross hanging from the neck. Since they also use the title "Reverend," they could easily be mistaken for Christian ministers, but their theology tells a different story.

Hubbard's discovery of the "Thetan" contributed to the religious nature of Scientology. They liken the Thetan to man's spirit. In Scientology, the Thetan is a timeless entity, which reincarnates in interplanetary life-forms. Once reaching earth as man, its goal is freedom from the cycle of birth and rebirth, which is where Scientology enters the scheme.

Most people who join the church do so after reading *Dianetics*. They follow this with advanced levels and the hope of obtaining "clear" in one lifetime. Additional courses are offered for survival through the eight dynamics of life: self, sex, group, mankind, other life-forms, MEST, spirits, and a Supreme Being. The cleared Thetan must learn to gain control over his environment and become an "Operating Thetan" (OT). Matter, energy, space, and time (MEST) are the physical universe. Everything but the Thetan is MEST. A Thetan can potentially control MEST by operating independently of his body.[46] Since the OT no longer needs his body, he can leave it at will through the act of "exteriorization," similar to astral projection.[47] OTs climb fifteen levels, but the highest courses are obtainable by only a few members.

On the practical level, they often remind Scientologists that "Scientology works." However, Scientologists, whose goal is to make the world a better place, were caught deep in criminal activity that seems contrary to their religion and

---

[44]Hubbard, *Dianetics*, 369.
[45]Ibid., 371.
[46]Hubbard, *Technical Dictionary*, 279.
[47]Hubbard, *Dianetics*, 115.

philosophy. More than five thousand Scientologists were involved in one of the most clandestine covert spying operations ever aimed at the United States government. Evidently, none of those involved felt any religious or moral obligation to expose the crimes. Quite accidentally, two Scientologists working undercover, using a phony IRS badge to gain entrance to the Assistant U.S. Attorney's office, made a grave mistake and the cover was blown. The three-year operation came to a screeching halt.

These illegal activities were publicized when eleven top Scientologists were indicted in 1977. They named Mary Sue Hubbard, wife of the founder and director of the operation, among those charged with crimes. Court evidence, numbering approximately 33,000 documents, connected Scientologists to infiltrating the government, burglarizing, bugging, wiretapping, and stealing classified information. The operation targeted "the Federal Trade and Atomic Energy Commissions; the National Security Defense Intelligence Agencies; the Departments of Labor, Army, and Navy; the U.S. Customs Service; Interpol, and numerous U.S. police departments."[48] All eleven charged Scientologists originally pleaded innocent to the twenty-eight-count grand jury indictment. After much plea bargaining and examining mounting evidence against them, they pleaded guilty to one charge instead of a trial and a heavier sentence. Nine Scientologists (two of the eleven were in England) were sentenced on October 26, 1979. L. Ron Hubbard and twenty-four other Scientologists were named coconspirators, but not indicted.[49] Mary Sue Hubbard and four top Scientologists were given five-year prison terms and fined $10,000 each.

The Church of Scientology argues that it has long been oppressed by the American government. If this were true, then criminal activity is not the correct solution. The religious benefits of Scientology waned at this junction, because a "clear" person, especially an OT, should not be committing crimes. In these cases, Scientology did not work. This is a dark shadow for Operating Thetans, who are supposedly "cleared of all wrong answers or useless answers that keep them from living or thinking."[50]

The world headquarters for the Church of Scientology is in Clearwater, Florida. For several years, L. Ron Hubbard conducted business out of governmental reach aboard a floating headquarters, the *Apollo,* in international waters. Today's leadership may be imitating its founder with a new floating office, the *Freewinds.* Wealthy Scientologists pay up to $15,000 for a week-long Caribbean cruise aboard the *Freewinds,* while it duplicates as a high-level decision-making office for top Scientologists.[51] Another recent development has been the multimillion-dollar construction of a nuclear-proof vault tunneled into Walker Mountain, near Eureka, California, to store L. Ron Hubbard's writings.

The arm of Scientology reaches into several areas of life. People often point to the success stories of Scientology's anti-drug program. It apparently has a successful drug-rehabilitation program, Narcanon. It has a criminal rehabilitation program, Criminon. And it has a "non-religious" moral education program, The Way to Happiness. (Contrary to their claim, we see the "religion" of L. Ron Hub-

---

[48]*People's Weekly* (August 14, 1978): 23. See also *Christianity Today* (December 7, 1979).
[49]*Reader's Digest* (May 1980): 91.
[50]Hubbard, *Technical Dictionary,* 75.
[51]*The Cult Observer,* 9:4 (1992): 9.

bard sprinkled throughout the text.) Scientology's Celebrity Center caters to renowned figures, often using their endorsements for programs. Those lending their notoriety to Scientology programs include actresses Karen Black, Priscilla Presley, and Kirstie Alley; singers Lou Rawls and Isaac Hayes; actors John Travolta and Tom Cruise; and jazz musicians Chick Corea and Stanley Clarke. These programs often become stepping-stones to lead the unaware person into the biblically false teachings of the church, although Scientologists will point out many who have been helped without joining. The testimony of rehabilitation is not to be confused with biblical salvation. We can rejoice when anybody leaves an addictive past, but they are destitute of salvation without Jesus Christ. Many non-Christian groups have used rehabilitative skills, but that says nothing about their doctrines. Scientology's false theology will lead people into an eternal hell without Christ. Recovered alcoholics and drug addicts still need to find a genuine and personal relationship with the Lord Jesus Christ, who alone regenerates man through the working of the Holy Spirit (Acts 4:12; Hebrews 1:2; Titus 3:5).

Scientology Scripture

The source of authority in any religion quickly tells the reader his or her worldview. Much of Scientology's literature never mentions God, Jesus Christ, the Holy Spirit, the Bible, salvation, or other theological terms associated with Christianity. All of L. Ron Hubbard's Scientology writings since *Dianetics* are considered "scripture" by the church. If his writings are scripture, then we must compare them with the genuine Scripture of God, the Bible. Jesus reminds us that we do not gather grapes of thorns nor figs of thistle plants (Matthew 7:16). The fruit of Scientology can be measured by its scripture, the writings of L. Ron Hubbard. We will also draw from their 1954 California Articles of Incorporation, which have a systematic outline of their tenets not found in other writings.

They described their "Holy Book" in their California Articles of Incorporation (2.i.14) as "a collection of the works of and about the Great Teachers, including the work, St. Luke." Yet, strangely, references to Luke's gospel in Scientology writings are virtually nonexistent. Hubbard revealed his sources for his church in his *Phoenix Lectures* (1954). He said, "The [Hindu] Veda . . . is best read in a literal translation from the Sanskrit. . . . A great deal of our material in Scientology is discovered right back there. Tao means knowingness," he said. "In other words, it's an ancestor to Scientology, the study of 'knowing how to know.' " Further, he said, "The Veda, the Tao, the Dharma, all mean knowingness. . . . We first find this Buddha called actually *Bodhi*. . . . This probably would be a Dianetic Release. . . . Another level has been mentioned to me—Arhat, with which I am not particularly familiar, said to be more comparable to our idea of Theta Clear." And, "Dhyana . . . could be literally translated as 'Indian for Scientology,' if you wished to do that."[52] From this we see the eclectic nature of Hubbard's theological authorities. He seemed to favor Buddhistic prophetic interpretation and believed it applied to his life. "The truth of the matter is," he wrote, "that you are studying an extension of the work of Gautama Siddhartha, begun about 2,500

[52]L. Ron Hubbard, *The Phoenix Lectures* (Los Angeles: The Church of Scientology of California Publications Organization United States, 1969), 12, 16, 18–19.

years ago. . . . Buddha predicted that in 2,500 years the entire job would be finished in the West. . . . Well, we finished it!"[53]

Scientology claims its church "does not conflict with other religions or religious practices, as it clarifies them and brings understanding of the spiritual nature of Man."[54] But Hubbard questioned the origin of the Bible, saying, "It is no wonder why we look into the Christian bible and find ourselves reading the Egyptian *Book of the Dead*." And, "The parables that are discovered today in the New Testament were earlier discovered, the same parables, elsewhere in many places. One of these was the Egyptian *Book of the Dead*, which predates the New Testament considerably."[55] Typical of Hubbard's writings, no evidence or source is provided in support of his claim.

There are important contradictions between the Bible and the sources of Scientology. Jesus, as the unique Son of God, gave no credence to other scriptures or distorted views of God. One example of Jesus distinguishing between truth and error is the account of the Samaritan woman (John 4). The Samaritans are closely related to Judaism, yet He told the Samaritan woman—in John 4:22—that Samaritans do not know whom they worship. If Jesus differentiated between the Samaritan god and the Jewish God, then we should also distinguish between Mr. Hubbard's synthesizing of religions and Christianity. Jesus also challenged world teachers in John 10:8, "All that ever came before me are thieves and robbers." Since the Vedas, Confucius, Lao-tzu (Taoism), the Buddha, and the Egyptian *Book of the Dead* all came before Christ, He openly renounces them as "thieves and robbers." Rather than attempting homogenization, as Hubbard did, Jesus isolated His teachings from all others. Jesus singled himself out as man's only hope (Matthew 7:22–23; John 8:24; 14:6).

Truth for the individual in Scientology is often subjective and existential. To quote Hubbard, "Know thyself . . . and the truth shall set you free." In contrast, Jesus said, "If ye continue in my word, then are ye my disciples indeed; and ye shall know the truth, and the truth shall make you free" (John 8:31–32). Jesus gave an objective standard for truth: himself (John 14:6) and the Word of God (John 17:17). Never is man called "truth" in the Bible, nor is man's inner self. God is called truth (Deuteronomy 32:4; Isaiah 65:16), as are Jesus (John 14:6), the Holy Spirit (1 John 5:6), the Word of God (John 17:17), and the Gospel (Galatians 2:5, 14). Never is man or knowledge of "thyself" called truth. The subjective nature of truth in Scientology allows variation on some items. Hubbard wrote, "What is true for you is what you have observed yourself."[56] What one person perceives as truth may not be what another person perceives. So, what by normative standards would be called a contradiction outside of Scientology can be synthesized within the organization. An example found in Hubbard's book *Axioms and Logics*, Axiom 31, states, "Goodness and badness, beautifulness and ugliness are alike considerations and have no other basis than opinion."[57] We would biblically challenge the first proposition on the basis that goodness and

---

[53]*Advance!* (December 1974): 5, as quoted from L. Ron Hubbard's 1966 taped lecture, Scientology, Definitions III.

[54]L. Ron Hubbard, *Volunteer Minister's Handbook* (Los Angeles: Church of Scientology, 1976), xiv.

[55]Hubbard, *Phoenix Lectures*, 9, 27.

[56]L. Ron Hubbard, *Technical Bulletin* (Los Angeles: Scientology Publications, 1976), 4:203.

[57]L. Ron Hubbard, *Axioms and Logics* (Los Angeles: American St. Hill Organization, 1973), 5.

badness are moral terms, not merely synthesized opinions. By biblical standards, the absolutes of God's moral law provide a basis for determining the value of human conduct. In our following study, Hubbard can apparently state two contradictory and opposing propositions without determining which is true. Hubbard at times can speak of one God (monotheism) and at other times of many gods (polytheism), without denial of either and while affirming truth in both statements. Hubbard also taught that "Truth is relative to environments, experience, and truth."[58] If truth is relative, in Hubbard's thinking, then he can apparently justify holding two opposing propositions without contradiction. Therefore, there can be one God and many gods simultaneously.

Scientology's Theology

Scientology describes deity in three ways: Supreme Being, God, and gods. Members are free to choose their concept of God. In *The Scientology Catechism* (as found in *What Is Scientology*) states, "What is the Scientology concept of God? We have no dogma in Scientology and each person's concept is different. . . . Each person attains his own certainty as to who God is and exactly what God means to him. The author of the universe exists. How this is symbolized is dictated by your early training and conscience."[59] The most organized statement of Scientology's catechism is found on pages 197–220 of *What Is Scientology?*[60] They further teach, "Although the existence of the Supreme Being is affirmed in Scientology, His precise nature is not delineated, since the Church holds that each person must seek and know the Divine Nature in and for himself."[61] They address God in the monotheistic sense in many places, yet Hubbard also speaks of the activity of gods elsewhere. In their Articles of Incorporation (California, 1954, section 2.h), we find "Believing that Man's best evidence of God is the God he finds within himself . . . the Church of Scientology is formed to espouse such evidence of the Supreme Being and Spirit as may be knowable to Men."

Hubbard, then, finds no contradiction in promulgating polytheism. In his *Phoenix Lectures,* he indiscriminately allowed for monotheism or polytheism: "Let us take up what amounts to probably ten thousand years of study on the part of Man, on the identity of God or gods."[62] He also exposes false gods commingled with true gods. "There are gods above all other gods," he wrote. "There is not argument here against the existence of a Supreme Being or any devaluation intended. It is that amongst the gods, there are many false gods elected to power and position. . . . There are gods above other gods, and gods beyond the gods of the universes."[63] Furthermore, he wrote a hymn stating, "There can be love for Gods." And, "Behave[,] Obey[,] Be Courteous[,] To gods[,] Lord Buddha[,] And myself[,] And to your leaders."[64]

[58]Ibid., 12.

[59]Staff of Scientology, "The Scientology Catechism," *What Is Scientology?* (Los Angeles: Church of Scientology of California, 1979), 200.

[60]Ibid., 197–20.

[61]Staff of Scientology, *Scientology: A World Religion Emerges in the Space Age* (Los Angeles: Church of Scientology Information Service, 1974), 17.

[62]Hubbard, *Phoenix Lectures,* 3.

[63]L. Ron Hubbard, *Scientology,* 8–8008 (Los Angeles: ASHO, 1967), 73.

[64]L. Ron Hubbard, *Hymn of Asia* (Los Angeles: Church of Scientology of California Publications Organization, 1974), 227, 241.

Their book on world religion leaves little doubt that the Hindu Brahman is closely paralleled with Scientology's understanding of the Supreme Being. Here God is spoken of in terms of Hinduism.[65]

Though Hubbard provides no strict definition of the Supreme Being, his descriptive characteristics are enough for the Christian reader to see its unbiblical nature. Hubbard rejects the Christian doctrine of the Trinity. His *Phoenix Lectures* state, "The Christian god is actually much better characterized in the Vedic Hymns [Hinduism] than in any subsequent publication, including the Old Testament."[66] Again, he said, "The god the Christians worshiped is certainly not the Hebrew god. He looks *much* more like the one talked about in the Veda."[67] What he mistakenly assumed is that the Hindu "triad" is the basis for the Christian "Trinity." This is not historical or biblical. The Trinity is based solely upon the revelation of God's Word, as noted in chapter 4, pages 83–84. Hubbard also wrote, "For a long while, some people have been cross with me for my lack of cooperation in believing in a Christian Heaven, God, and Christ. I have never said I didn't disbelieve in a Big Thetan but there was certainly something very corny about Heaven *et al.*"[68]

Scientologists are taught by Hubbard that man is part God and can attain a "godlike" nature. He wrote, "A pre-clear is a precise thing, part animal, part pictures, and part God."[69] In Hubbard's evolutionary development of Homo sapiens, he teaches that man will evolve into "*homo novis,*" described as "very high and godlike."[70]

Scripture denies the possibility of other gods besides the true God. There is but one God (Deuteronomy 4:39; 6:4; Isaiah 43:10; 44:8; Mark 12:32; Ephesians 4:6; 1 Timothy 2:5; and James 2:19).

The Bible always presents a sharp distinction between God and man. Scripture reminds us in Numbers 23:19, "God is not a man, that he should lie." Hosea 11:9 says, "I am God, and not man, the Holy One in the midst of thee." A study of God's omnipotence, omnipresence, and omniscience truncates the words of Hubbard (1 Samuel 2:3; 1 Kings 8:27; Job 42:2; Jeremiah 23:24; 32:17; Romans 11:33).

Scientology's Jesus

When L. Ron Hubbard mentions Jesus Christ, it is rarely in reverence and mostly with disparagement. A few lines previously, we saw that Mr. Hubbard refused to believe in the Christian Christ. Implants are false concepts forced upon a Thetan, and Scientology chalks up "Christ" as an implant more than a million years ago. He wrote, "You will find . . . the Christ legend as an implant in pre-clears a million years ago."[71]

[65]Staff, *A World Religion*, 5.
[66]Hubbard, *Phoenix Lectures*, 31.
[67]Ibid., 27.
[68]L. Ron Hubbard, "Heaven," *Hubbard Communication Office Bulletin* (hereafter *HCOB*) (May 11, 1963), one page, as quoted by Kevin Anderson, *Report of the Board of Inquiry into Scientology* (Melbourne: Australia Parliament Government Printer, 1965), 150.
[69]L. Ron Hubbard, *Scientology Clear Procedure, Issue One* (Los Angeles: ASHO, 1969), 21.
[70]L. Ron Hubbard, *History of Man* (Los Angeles: ASHO, 1968), 38.
[71]L. Ron Hubbard, *Professional Auditor's Bulletin 31*, quoted by Anderson, *Report*, 150.

Mr. Hubbard casts doubt upon the uniqueness of Jesus as the Messiah. His *Phoenix Lectures* state, "Now the Hebrew definition of Messiah is one Who Brings Wisdom—a Teacher. Messiah is from 'messenger'. . . . Now here we have a great teacher in Moses. We have other Messiahs, and we then arrive with Christ, and the words of Christ were a lesson in compassion and they set a very fine example to the Western world."[72] It does not take a great deal of biblical knowledge to refute Hubbard here, for many young students in Christian churches are aware that the Hebrew definition for Messiah is "anointed." It does not come from "messenger," but from "to rub" or "anoint." Hubbard proves his ignorance of Hebrew and Christian terminology. Had Mr. Hubbard fairly investigated and understood the biblical claims about Jesus, then perhaps he would not have so carelessly criticized Christ as an implanted legend.

The Church of Scientology teaches that Jesus Christ may have believed in reincarnation: "There is much speculation on the part of religious historians as to the early education of Jesus of Nazareth. It is believed by many authorities that Jesus was a member of the cult of the Essenes, who believed in reincarnation."[73] Hubbard attributes Hindu teachings to Jesus. "Christ," he wrote, "was a bringer of information. He never announced his sources. He spoke of them as coming from God. But they might just as well have come from the god talked about in the Hymn to the Dawn Child . . . the Veda."[74] Hubbard looks down upon Jesus from his OT VIII position, claiming, "Neither Lord Buddha nor Jesus Christ were OT, according to the evidence. They were just a shade above clear."[75]

Let us remember that the apostle Peter dealt with Hubbardian theories long ago. Peter, denying any mythology or legend to Christ, said, "We have not followed cunningly devised fables, when we made known unto you the power and coming of our Lord Jesus Christ, but were eyewitnesses of his majesty" (2 Peter 1:16). Jesus also denied anyone could be the Messiah other than himself (Matthew 24:3–5, 11). He unashamedly said, "No man cometh unto the Father, but by me" (John 14:6). Luke settles the idea of multiple ways of salvation in Acts 4:12, "For there is none other name under heaven given among men, whereby we must be saved."

Jesus was not a man looking for salvation with the rest of humanity. He was sinless (John 8:46; 1 Peter 2:22) and had no need to be "a shade above clear." He fully announced His sources (Luke 24:44), which have nothing to do with the Essenes nor the Vedas. In the Bible He is seen as an eternal, active person (Micah 5:2) who is one with the Father (John 10:30) and the second person of the Trinity (Matthew 28:19).

Scientology's View of Man

Beginning with *Dianetics,* Hubbard taught, "Man is basically good." Scientology carries this theme throughout Hubbardian writings. In contrast, biblical Christianity observes that man's nature is basically evil: "There is none righteous,

---

[72]Hubbard, *Phoenix Lectures,* 27–28.
[73]Staff, *A World Religion,* 15.
[74]Hubbard, *Phoenix Lectures,* 27.
[75]L. Ron Hubbard, *Certainty Magazine,* 5:10, as quoted by Anderson, *Report,* 150.

no, not one" (Romans 3:10). Hubbard also borrows the Oriental philosophy that "I am not this body." In contrast, again, the Bible observes both parts of man's nature, the body and the spirit. We have one nature, human, with two parts, physical and spiritual. Biblically, then, man is both physical and spiritual (Ecclesiastes 12:7; Genesis 2:7). The separation of the two is death, for the body without the spirit is dead (James 2:26).

The Thetan (spirit) has some amazing characteristics, according to Hubbard. It is more than eighty trillion years old and dwells somewhere within the skull of an individual.[76] When the individual organism dies, the Thetan reports to an implant station (one is on Mars) before being shot down to earth. This is the "between lives area. Here he 'reports in,' is given a strong forgetter implant, and is then shot down to a body just before it is born."[77] Thetans have been known to fight other Thetans over inhabiting a body. They communicate by telepathy, move objects by kinetics, and travel at high rates of speed. Thetans can be packed in ice and frozen, or they may be dumped into the ocean from a flying saucer. This, Hubbard assures us, "is quite authentic."[78]

Hubbard also taught a Darwinian form of evolution for man. Hubbard has laid out various life-forms in his book *Scientology: A History of Man*. Hubbard often roots the problem for today's Scientologist in engrams collected from past lives. Many common activities also result from past lives. Hubbard tells us that man began his journey some 60 trillion years ago. The first stage of life is the Photon Converter, which converted light into energy as its main function. The Photon Converter had nothing to do at night, therefore our need for sleep.

Following later came the jellyfish, but the jellyfish got tired of being pressed against stones. It compensated by forming a shell and becoming the clam. The clam had two hinges that would fight over which one would be opened or closed. This caused engrams. Later, in man's evolution, these hinges became man's jaws. Small barnacle-like spores attached to the outer edge of the clam shell later became the pattern for man's teeth.

Another shellfish was the Weeper, sometimes called the "Grim Weeper or Boohoo." Its main function was to adapt to the seashore. It had two small tubes for pumping salt water in and out of its shell. These two holes later became man's eyes. The name Boohoo, or Weeper, was coined because some Scientologists would cry during Scientological auditing due to recalling that sand being caught in the pumping tubes.

Hubbard suggests in *History of Man* that many of our problems may be traced to former lives. Smoking tobacco results from smokers dramatizing volcanoes they saw in previous lives. Psoriasis is an engram received from when an animal ate you; the psoriasis resembles the digestive fluids of the animal that ate you. Vegetarians got tired of being eaten by animals in former lives. Fear of falling can be traced to being a sloth and falling out of trees.[79]

Hubbard's *History of Man* also teaches that Piltdown Man was part of the evolutionary chain for man. He called it man's first real manhood. Hubbard had

---

[76]L. Ron Hubbard, *Scientology: The Fundamentals of Thought* (Los Angeles: Church of Scientology Publications Organization, 1972), 55.

[77]Hubbard, *History of Man*, 53.

[78]Ibid., 20, 43, 64–66.

[79]Ibid., 5–6, 27–34, 38.

already published his Piltdown Man statements prior to the Piltdown skull having been declared a hoax in 1953. Rather than retract the statements for this new religion, since *History of Man* forms a part of its scripture, Hubbard simply ignored it and never spoke of the evolution of Piltdown Man again. Our concern is that this Scientological scripture conflicts with the creation account in the Bible. Eventually Hubbard arrives at Homo sapiens in his evolutionary story. Hubbard developed a future step in man's evolution, called *homo novis*. Man at this point becomes a "godlike" being.[80]

The biblical view of man's origin does not include evolution, where great difficulties arise due to the lack of transitional fossils, spontaneous generation, and cross-breeding species. Each life-form has its origin in God's creative works outlined in Genesis, chapter one. Specifically, man and woman were created to reflect God's image and likeness (Genesis 1:26–27), which separates man from beasts. Due to man's fall from his righteous state, in Genesis, chapter three, all humanity has inherited a sinful nature like Adam's (Romans 5:12). This has resulted in the evil of the world around us.

Hubbard disagreed with the Bible at this point. "It is despicable and utterly beneath contempt to tell a man he must repent, that he is evil."[81] Yet Jesus did just that. He told men to repent and said that they were evil (Matthew 4:17; 7:11).

Scientology's Salvation

Scientologists prefer to use the term *rebirth* instead of "reincarnation," although the term *reincarnation* is found in their writings. Hubbard emphasized that salvation is to be free from the endless cycle of birth and rebirth. The way to salvation is to erase engrams through auditing. In some auditing situations, Scientologists may experience accompanying signs when engrams are released. "When one releases an engram," Hubbard wrote, "the erasure is accompanied by yawns." At other times tears, sweat, odor, panting, urine, flatulence, vomiting and excreta may indicate a released engram, although it is not universally experienced.[82]

Scientology's view of reincarnation includes extraterrestrial life, evolution on other planets, evolution on earth, implant stations, forgetter implants, and engrams that keep people trapped in reincarnation. The OT III, section three, material was entered into court cases, from which we find Hubbard's journey of the Thetan. He claims this discovery was in December 1967:

> The head of the Galactic Confederation (76 planets ... 95,000,000 years ago) solved overpopulation (250 billion or so per planet) by mass implanting. He caused people to be brought to Teegeeack (Earth) and put an H-bomb on the principal volcanoes ... and then the Pacific area ones were taken in boxes to Hawaii and the Atlantic ones to Las Palmas and there "packaged." His name was Xenu.
>
> [The result of Hubbard's investigation into this formerly undiscovered data was that] one's body is a mass of individual Thetans stuck to oneself or

---

[80]Ibid.
[81]Hubbard, *Auditor's Bulletin*, 31.
[82]L. Ron Hubbard, *Science of Survival* (Los Angeles: AHOS, 1973), 2:255.

to the body.... Thetans believed they were one. This is the primary error . . . by [a] BODY THETAN is meant a Thetan who is stuck to another Thetan or body but is not in control. . . . A CLUSTER is a group of body Thetans crushed or held together by some mutual bad experience.[83]

Scientologists thought they only needed to clear their Thetan, but now Hubbard tells them they have body Thetans and clusters to be rid of. This keeps them bound to the church for longer periods trying to achieve salvation.

Hubbard tells them that some of these body Thetans have been asleep on their Thetan for seventy-five million years. Ridding it makes the body Thetan as sort of a cleared being. Hubbard also believes he went back four quadrillion years ago (give or take a few years).

These incarnations and reincarnations are the supposed dilemma of the Scientologist. Reincarnation is answered in Hebrews 9:27: "It is appointed unto men once to die, but after this the judgment." Biblically, we live and die once. We have no preexistence in other bodies, and we did not come from outer space. Jesus denied preexistent souls for people. "Ye are from beneath; I am from above: ye are of this world; I am not of this world" (John 8:23). We find that reincarnation does not fit into God's plan of salvation. Jesus' death upon the cross would be unnecessary if reincarnation were true. Nevertheless, we find that Jesus was foreordained as the "Lamb slain from the foundation of the world" (Revelation 13:8). Jesus' sermons on heaven and hell would be a lie if reincarnation were true. But we find that Jesus always spoke the truth (Hebrews 4:15). Jesus' bodily resurrection from the tomb refutes reincarnation, since He resurrected to the same body (John 20:27). "He showed himself alive after his passion by many infallible proofs, being seen of them forty days, and speaking of the things pertaining to the kingdom of God" (Acts 1:3; see also 1 Corinthians 15:1–8). The resurrection of Jesus is proof that His grace will save us who place our trust in Him for our salvation. Every Christian has what every Scientologist is looking for—that is, salvation.

Conclusion

Scientology is undoubtedly a religion, and deserving of the same freedom of belief and expression as any other religion in the United States, including biblical Christianity. It is also open to the same kind of critical evaluation by the Bible that responsible Christians put their own teachings to on a regular basis (Acts 17:11). When the teachings of Scientology are compared to biblical truth, Scientology is illuminated as the empty façade of biblical imitation it truly is.

Recommended Resources

1. Atack, Jon. *A Piece of Blue Sky: Scientology, Dianetics, and L. Ron Hubbard Exposed.* New York: Carol Publishing Company, 1990.
2. Corydon, Bent. *L. Ron Hubbard: Messiah or Madman?* Fort Lee, N.J.: Barricade Books, 1992.

---

[83]Church of Scientology International v. Steven Fishman and Uwe Geertz, United States District Court, Central District of California, case 91–6426HLH(Tx), pp. 76–100.

3. Gruss, Edmund C. *Cults and the Occult.* Nutley, N.J.: Presbyterian and Reformed Publishing, 2002.

4. McDowell, Josh, and Don Stewart. *The Deceivers.* Nashville, Tenn.: Thomas Nelson Publishers, 1992.

5. Miller, Russell. *Bare-Faced Messiah: The True Story of L. Ron Hubbard.* London: Michael Joseph/Penguin Books Ltd., 1987.

6. Miller, Stephen M. *Misguiding Lights?* Kansas City, Mo.: Beacon Hill Press of Kansas City, 1991.

Quick Facts About the Unification Church

- The Unification Church believes that the Bible is untrustworthy in its reliability.

- God is dualistic in His nature, like the Yin and yang of Taoism.

- The crucifixion of Jesus was an alternative plan, and it only saved mankind halfway. Sun Myung Moon is the Messiah, and true salvation comes by being a member of the Unification Church.

- The Trinity was an invention of Jesus, and there have been many "trinities" through the ages, including a satanic trinity.

- The Holy Spirit is a female spirit—the female aspect of God's nature.

Chapter 13

The Unification Church

The Unification Church, founded and led by Korean-born Rev. Sun Myung Moon, demonstrates the growing trend toward New Age beliefs worldwide.[1] The distinctive features of this kind of cult include (1) its special appeal to educated young people from the middle class; (2) its habit of conducting business, especially recruiting, under multiple pseudonyms or anonymously; (3) its Westernization of Eastern religious ideas; and (4) its misinterpretations of Scripture to persuade outsiders that its Eastern religious orientation is compatible with and, indeed, is the fulfillment of biblical Christianity. Such groups as the Unification Church are further characterized by what appears to be obvious, widespread, and forceful psychological pressure on members to conform and remain loyal to the group at all costs. This psychological pressure is present in all the cults, as we noted in the opening chapters of this book. It is perhaps more obvious with groups newly arrived in America whose converts are mainly young people whose families have had little or no previous exposure to the group.

The Hare Krishnas, Transcendental Meditation, the followers of the late guru Rajneesh, the Church Universal and Triumphant, and other such groups share the same features, although in their own unique expressions. ~The Unification Church is one of the best cults at disguising its unusual, nontraditional beliefs from the unsuspecting secular world. This was not always the case, as history testifies regarding the "brainwashing" scare that seemed to follow Unification proselytizing efforts everywhere during the late 1970s and early 1980s. Much like the Mormons in the century before them, however, the Unification leadership rose above the turmoil and began to project a public persona that intrigued many secularists as well as unsuspecting religious leaders—even evangelical Christian leaders. Today, just as the Mormons are more well known for their

This chapter revised, expanded, and updated by Kurt Van Gorden and edited by Jill Martin Rische.
[1]Frederick Sontag, *Sun Myung Moon and the Unification Church* (Nashville: Abingdon, 1977), 133. See also chapter entitled "The New Age Cults" for further information on the New Age movement.

social welfare programs, family values, and wholesome lifestyles than for their belief in eventually becoming gods and ruling their own planets, so the Unification members ("Moonies") are better known for their support of conservative values and right-wing politics than for their belief that Moon is the new Messiah sent to propagate the perfect family on earth. The reputation of the Unification-owned *Washington Times* is reaching the caliber of the *Christian Science Monitor* as a publication of pivotal value in the public square. The Unification Church is a fascinating study of how a religious movement can move from everybody's bogeyman to a respected public voice of conservatism in two short decades. Beneath the public veneer, however, Unification is no more biblical or Christian than Mormonism or Christian Science.~ In this review of Unification theology and practice, we will touch on some of the teachings that cause it to be classified as a non-Christian cult both by theology and practice.

History

On January 6, 1920, Yong Myung Moon (Shining Dragon Moon) was born of Confucian parents, humble farmers, in the town of Dok A, Jung-Juin, the providence of Pyongyang Buk-do, in North Korea. The family converted to the Presbyterian Church in 1930, but the youthful Yong Myung Moon retained ancestral veneration common to Confucianism. According to Unification writer Kwang-Yol Yoo, Moon experimented in contacting ancestors in the spirit world during his early teen years, and his spiritual quest was likened to that of Buddha.[2]

~The climax of Moon's spiritual search was a vision he reportedly received of Jesus Christ on April 17, 1936, at age sixteen. The year of Moon's vision varies, with some Unification authorities placing him at age seventeen (eighteen by Korean reckoning).[3] Yoo places Moon at age fifteen (sixteen by Korean reckoning), but the majority of writers place him at age sixteen (seventeen by Korean reckoning). The dubious year and age for which Moon claimed his vision is reminiscent of the first vision of Joseph Smith, the American Mormon prophet, who also had difficulty giving consistent details about his vision of Jesus Christ. If Moon did not see Jesus, then the entire system of Moon's foundation crumbles. Devastating to the credibility of Moon's supposed vision is that every Unification writing gives the date as "April 17, 1936, Easter morning." *The gravest error in Unification history occurs here.* Our calculations prove beyond a doubt that Moon's vision could not have occurred on Easter morning, because April 17, 1936, was a *Friday*, not a Sunday. Just how this vision of Jesus unfolded is also questionable. One of the most astounding confessions by Moon himself was under oath in 1982, during a Unification suit against a deprogrammer. Moon, in a New York Federal Court testimony, on May 27 and 28, stated that he had met Jesus, whom he had recognized from "holy cards." He also testified that he had met Moses and Buddha.[4] To imagine that the test for identifying Jesus Christ is to match His image with "holy cards" is the height of absurdity. In Yoo's history, Moon was told to

---

[2]Kwang-Yol Yoo (in a five-part series), "Unification Church History From the Early Days," *New Hope News*, Washington, D.C.: The Unification Church, 1:9–10, 12–13; 2:1.

[3]Dr. Young Oon Kim, *Divine Principle* (San Francisco: The Holy Spirit Association for the Unification of World Christianity, 1960, third ed. 1963), ix. Kim was the first Unification missionary to the U.S. She was also a well-read theologian for the Unification Church.

[4]Richard A. Blake, "The Attraction of the Moonies," *America Magazine* (June 12, 1982): 452.

complete Jesus' unfinished mission. Strangely, though, Moon claims he already knew that he was to complete Jesus' mission before he had the vision announcing the same.[5]

Foundational to any church or religion is the manner in which the founder claims revelation or a calling from God. Sun Myung Moon claimed consistently throughout his messianic career that his calling came through a vision of Jesus on Sunday, Easter morning, April 17, 1936. If we find that Easter did not occur on April 17, 1936, then Mr. Moon could not have seen the purported vision of Jesus that began his messianic role, and he would be marked as a deceiver and false prophet. Such is the case.

Moon's reckoning that April 17, 1936, was a Sunday (let alone Easter Sunday) is falsified by simply appealing to the 1936 calendar. Easter in 1936 fell on April 12. *April 17 was a Friday.* In the 1930s Easter fell just twice on April 17; in 1932 and 1938. It did not reoccur until 1949. The impossibility of Moon seeing Jesus on Easter Sunday, April 17, 1936, obliterates his vision of Jesus. It is a false date given by a false prophet.

In light of this irrefutable calculation, Moonies will have to scramble for answers to cover their prophet's falsified date. Their rescue efforts cannot change history or the fact that Moon consistently claimed this date as his messianic calling. Hence, his messiahship is falsified as well. If the date is false, then nothing says that anything else is accurate. No matter how good a politician or humanitarian Moon is, he is a false prophet and false messiah who falsified a vision of Jesus to lure unsuspecting people into his cult.~

It is stated in their history that Moon struggled for nine years (the original *Divine Principles* says seven) to discover the truth of *Divine Principle. The Divine Principle* is authoritative scripture in the Unification Church and is considered superior to the Bible. ~Through *Divine Principle,* in its latest version, Moon's followers understand and interpret the Bible. As is true with all cults, the Unification Church members cannot understand the Bible as it is. It must be *explained* by the organization and God's prophet for today: Rev. Sun Myung Moon.~ The varied accounts of its coming forth shade its history equally with that of his vision. It seems that some Unification writers believe *Divine Principle* came by revelation, while others say it was "discovered."

Astute investigators point to Moon's former teacher, Elder Baik Moon Kim, of Sup Lee, Kyung Gi, North Korea—who founded a church called the Monastery of Israel—at least as its inspiration. Elder Kim had taught similar "principles" to Moon in 1946. Moon's *Divine Principle* was not written until six years later, in 1952. It was also in 1946, while being taught by Elder Kim, that he changed his name to Sun Myung Moon (Shining Sun and Moon). Although he goes by the title "Reverend," there is no history of his ordination by any bona fide denomination in Korea or America. In fact, many of the earliest Unification writings from the 1960s consistently call him "Mr. Moon." It was not until his reemergence in America in the early 1970s that he was quite suddenly known as "Reverend" Sun Myung Moon. The Unification Church ordains no ministers, so Rev. Sun Myung Moon is in a class by himself. One becomes a church member upon completion of a twenty-one-day training course. Members affectionately call Sun Myung Moon their Father.

---

[5]Yoo, *Early Days,* 5.

Shortly following the Second World War, Moon drifted from one "Pentecostal" group to another. From Yoo's history, it is no hidden fact that most of these groups had blended seances, spiritism, ancestral spirit guidance, and a host of occult practices with their untrained "Pentecostal Christian" faith. What one ends up with is spiritism practiced in the name of Christianity, something exercised by many cults and abhorred by all genuine Christians.

It was through these spiritistic endeavors that Moon claimed to discover the nine levels of the spirit world, each of which he subjugated by questioning the spirits he faced. His supposed proof of authenticity is that Jesus, Confucius, Mohammed, and Buddha all appeared and agreed with his conclusions. Finally, Moon faced off with Satan himself and questioned Satan about the fall of Adam and Eve until he found the real cause of the Fall. He claims to have conquered Satan and accomplished what no other man before him has done, including Jesus. According to Moon, the fall of Adam and Eve, which we will discuss in detail later, was first Eve's sexual intercourse with Satan, and second her passing on sin through sexual intercourse with Adam before he had matured to perfection.[6] Like many other cult leaders before him, Moon has brought sexuality to center stage, cloaked in religiosity.

Moon may have been too preoccupied with the subject of sex during the formation of his church. There are several reports bearing examination concerning Moon's marriages, bigamy, and promiscuous sexual affairs, called "blood cleansing," with the female members of his church. Even the noted philosopher Dr. Frederick Sontag, who wrote favorably of Moon and had the very rare occasion of interviewing him, could not avoid the rumored escapades of Moon. "There are unconfirmed reports of other marriages," he wrote, "but at least it is clear that his first wife could not accept the religious role thrust on her."[7]

According to a well-documented report by Dr. Shin Sa Han, Dean of Religion at Seoul University, Seoul, Korea, Moon's first wife, Choi Sun Kil, married him in 1945 and immediately bore him a son. Dr. Shin reports that Sun Myung Moon was arrested for irresponsible sexual activity at Bo An Police Department, Dae Village, North Korea, on August 10, 1948. He was excommunicated from the Presbyterian Church that same year. Adding more trouble to his history, Moon evidently married Kim X, February 22, 1949, without divorcing his first wife. He was reportedly sentenced to five years in Hung Nan prison, North Korea, for bigamy. Kim X was convicted with him and was sentenced to ten months. During the Korean War, the United Nations Forces bombed Hung Nam and freed the prisoners on October 14, 1950, of whom Moon was one. He made his way southward along a torturous six-hundred-mile journey with two friends and established himself in Pusan, South Korea.

Moon wrote *Divine Principle* in 1951–1952 under postwar hardships in Pusan, but, strong-willed, he trekked onward and established the Unification Church on May 1, 1954, in Seoul, South Korea. Again, he was arrested on July 4, 1955, for irresponsible sexual activity that caused a scandal at Ewha Women's (Methodist) University in Seoul. Several Korean newspapers covered the story. Moon was

[6]Yoo, *Early Days*, 7.
[7]Frederick Sontag, *Sun Myung Moon and the Unification Church* (Nashville: Abingdon, 1977), 80. See also, J. Isamu Yamamoto, *The Puppet Master* (Downers Grove, Ill.: InterVarsity Press, 1977), 21. Yamamoto points out that there may have been four marriages.

released October 4, 1955, because the eighty women involved in the incident exercised their right of silence in court. It was also reported by the Church of the Nazarene Korea Mission that Moon's church was involved in an unusual sexual "blood cleansing" rite where a woman was to have sexual intercourse with Sun Myung Moon to cleanse her blood from Satan's lineage. The "cleansed" woman could then cleanse her husband through sexual union with him. This ritual was based upon the Unification doctrine that Eve fell by having intercourse with Satan; therefore, a woman having intercourse with Moon, who is Lord of the Second Advent, would be cleansed. Just as Eve passed Satan's tainted blood lineage on to Adam, likewise the cleansed Unification member passes purification of blood on to her spouse.[8]

Obviously, as Moon's church grew larger, it complicated the doctrine, and his haunting arrest records required abandonment of the rite. There is no evidence it is practiced today.

Sun Myung Moon married his current wife, Hak Ja Han, in March 1960, when he was forty and she was seventeen. She has since borne him thirteen "sinless" children, and is referred to as Mother by Unification members. Together, Rev. and Mrs. Moon, Father and Mother, are known as True Parents. Their wedding is viewed as a fulfillment of the "marriage of the Lamb" in Revelation 21:9. To Unification members, this monumental event ushers in the "New Age, the Cosmic Era."[9] Moon and his wife are the first True Parents and have the power to bless other marriages with pureness and "sinless" offspring. Incidentally, this is why the Unification Church conducts massive weddings, with up to three hundred thousand couples at a time. These blessed couples supposedly are sinless families on earth.

Rev. Moon, steeped in reliance upon spirit guides, sought the spiritist-medium Arthur Ford on May 13, 1964, for insight on his mission. "Mr. Fletcher," the disincarnate spirit that spoke through Ford, evidently discussed pleasing confirmations to Moon, for the Unification Church widely published the seance sitting.[10] Upon realizing that evangelical Christians disdain such practices as abominable before God, the Ford seance, and the often used terms New Age, medium, clairvoyant, and clairaudient are suppressed in current Unification writings. Nevertheless, the true foundation for Moon's revelations, from age sixteen to the present, is rooted in contact with disincarnate spirits in the spirit world.

Moon claimed God appeared to him: "I came to America primarily to declare the New Age and new truth. . . . This is why God appeared to me and told me to go to America to speak the truth."[11]

In obedience to his vision, in 1972, he began touring major cities in the United States for his "Day of Hope" crusade. When the infamous Watergate

---

[8]The major points of this ritual were confirmed by a Korean government cable, February 1963, and sent to the United States Central Intelligence Agency. See James Coates, "Moon Church Traced From Sex Cult," *Chicago Tribune* (March 27, 1978).

[9]Dr. Young Oon Kim, *Divine Principle* (San Francisco: The Holy Spirit Association for the Unification of World Christianity, 1960, third edition, 1963), iii. The original title of this work was *Divine Principles*. However, since it is much more widely known by its later title, *Divine Principle*, this text uniformly refers to it as such. If the original edition is referred to, that is indicated in the text or footnote.

[10]*Sun Myung Moon* (Washington, D.C.: The Holy Spirit Association for the Unification of World Christianity [HSAUWC], 1969), ii, iii.

[11]Sontag, *Moon and Unification*, 133.

scandal broke out in the White House years of President Nixon, Rev. Moon wasted no time in pouring thousands of dollars into a self-promoting "God loves Nixon" crusade. Moon's opportunism succeeded with instant notoriety throughout the United States. Then came the opposition from parents' groups who claimed that Moon stole their children's minds and future. Moon has fought an uphill battle since then to gain acceptance, even though most critics claim that his celebrity-status supporters are mere dupes, often rewarded in monetary benefits.

Moon divided his twenty-one-year campaign for the restoration of Christianity into three seven-year segments, beginning with his marriage in 1960. The year 1976 was pivotal in Moon's third segment. He poured millions of dollars into two rallies, one at New York's Yankee Stadium and the other at the Washington Monument. His predicted success was dampened at the Yankee Stadium event when it rained relentlessly for three hours. With the stadium less than half full, Moon went on with the show. Moon, who incessantly compares himself with Jesus, spiritualized the Yankee Stadium event, claiming that he and the church had endured their crucifixion, death, and resurrection.

The Washington Monument rally brought better success, drawing some two hundred to three hundred thousand people. Moon then claimed that his work had broken down all the walls of the spirit world, and spirits were descending rapidly upon the earth.[12] He predicted the next rally would be held in Moscow.

Rev. Moon's work was to be accomplished by 1981, but to his dismay, he found himself under the scrutiny of a House subcommittee and the Internal Revenue Service in the late 1970s. The latter investigation ended up in charges, and Moon went to trial in 1983, later being convicted of tax evasion. Moon spent thirteen months of an eighteen-month sentence at the federal prison in Danbury, Connecticut. The remaining five months of his sentence was served at a halfway house.

The Unification Church spent 4.5 million dollars to clear Moon's name with a mass-mailing campaign to three hundred thousand pastors in the United States. The unsolicited mailing contained three video tapes, two books, and introductory letters from Dr. Mose Durst, president of the Unification Church in America. Their main message was couched in fear and hysteria—if Rev. Moon could be sent to prison, then every American pastor faces the same future. In addition, the Unification Church campaigned in the media declaring Moon's innocence and changed the ordeal into governmental racial and religious persecution. Upon entering prison, Moon stated, "I am here today only because my skin is yellow and my religion is Unification Church."[13] Apparently, some Christian leaders took the bait and brushed aside Moon's tax evasion in lieu of ecumenical brotherhood, because "friends of the court" briefs were filed on Moon's behalf by the National Council of Churches, the National Association of Evangelicals, the United Presbyterian Church, the American Baptist Churches, the American Methodist Episcopal Church, the Unitarian Universalist Association, the National Black Catholic Clergy Caucus, and the American Jewish Congress.[14] Moon's campaign worked well. Upon his release from prison, August 20, 1985, he was cele-

---

[12]"Buses, Buses, and More Buses," *New Hope News* (October 21, 1976): 5.

[13]"Moon Pleads Not Guilty in Tax Case, Cites Discrimination," *Christianity Today* (November 20, 1981): 7.

[14]John McCaughry, "The Uneasy Case Against Reverend Moon," *National Review* (December 23, 1983): 1612; Kenneth L. Woodward and Patrice Johnson, "Rev. Moon's New Friends," *Newsweek* (May 3, 1982): 88.

brated at a banquet by seventeen hundred clergy with Baptist evangelist Rev. Jerry Falwell as the main speaker, who unsuccessfully called upon President Reagan to pardon Moon.[15]

What these well-meaning, but perhaps misled, clergy seem to confuse as illegal activities is not justified by a First Amendment religious cloak. Clearly Moon was convicted of evading taxes on $112,000 in personal income derived from interest on $1.6 million he had deposited for the church. He also received another $50,000 in unreported stocks for the taxable years 1973–1976.[16] Rev. Moon's accountant, Takeru Kamiyama, was sentenced for conspiracy to file false tax returns, lying before a grand jury, and obstructing justice.[17] In contrast to Moon's claim that it was the church's funds, the testimony showed he personally purchased fifteen-hundred-dollar gold watches and stock, and that he paid tuition for his children's education from the accounts. Rev. Moon was not persecuted by the IRS: he and his accountant evaded personal taxes and lied to the grand jury, which places them under the same laws as any other American citizen. It is noteworthy that Moon could have received a fourteen-year sentence, so his eighteen-month sentence shows the mercy of the jurors, not persecution.

The Unification Church is not much larger today than it was in the mid–1970s. They still claim about three million people worldwide.[18] It is probable that they have fewer followers in the United States than before. They once had thirty-seven thousand members in America, but sources close to the church project less than ten thousand today.[19] There are over nine hundred worship centers in Korea and fifty-five in the United States. The largest following Moon has is in Japan. The followers are usually called Moonies, and Moon apparently takes no great offense at this, since he often uses it in his speeches. He predicted that there will be a day when they will be called Sunnies, and in the spirit world, Kingies.[20]

Two Distinguishing Features

There are two features that distinguish the Moonies from all other cults: their fund-raising tactics and their mass weddings. Much has been written in magazines and newspapers about the deceptive tactics used in fund-raising, called "heavenly deception." This is the practice of justified lying, which is permissible because it is for good. During one of Moon's training sessions, a student asked, "What about white lies?" Rev. Moon answered, "If you tell a lie to make a person better, then that is not a sin." He further adds, "Even God tells lies very often; you can see this throughout history."[21]

Moonies have been found raising funds from wheelchairs while in perfectly good health. They have even been spotted carrying the wheelchair back to their automobile! Most often they give names of false charities to gain sympathy. On

[15]James H. White, "Unification Church's Anti-Communist Drive," *Christian Century* (August 28–September 4, 1985): 772.

[16]"Of Moon and Mammon," *Time* (October 26, 1981): 24.

[17]Jane O'Hara, "Taxing Times for the Reverend," *McCleans Magazine* (April 5, 1982): 32.

[18]Statistics derived from Adherents.com, *www.adherents.com/Na_619.html#3977*

[19]John B. Judis, "Rev. Moon's Rising Political Influence," *U.S. News and World Report* (March 27, 1989): 29.

[20]Sun Myung Moon, *Master Speaks* (March 19, 1978): 6.

[21]Ibid. (March 16, 1972): 11.

one occasion, as former Moonie Chris Elkins relates, they were heavily repri-
manded in Atlanta, Georgia, for selling leftover Girl Scout cookies under false
pretenses.[22]

Rev. Moon gloats about how he rakes in huge profits from the unsuspecting
public on flowers that cost him eighty cents and sell for a five-dollar donation.[23]
At one point he told his followers that he would train them to make thirty million
dollars monthly, and then he could purchase the Empire State Building.[24] In all,
Moon receives annually approximately one hundred million dollars from Japan,
thirty-five million from the United States, and twenty million from Europe in
charitable donations.[25] The Mobilized Fund-Raising Teams (MFT) often work
fourteen or more hours daily with little sleep and sparse food. This has attributed
to a number of vehicular accidents in which several MFT workers have been
killed. Rev. Moon admitted that eighty-two accidents occurred in one month.[26]

The business holdings and spending power of the Unification Church are
unparalleled for any other group its size. They have at least three hundred thirty-
five businesses worldwide, and another two hundred eighty in the United States.
Their business conglomeration rivals any international corporation. They produce weapons, soft drinks, ginseng products, computers, automobile parts, heavy
machinery, and clothing; they also own convenience stores, real estate, fishing
fleets, daily newspapers, magazines, and journals. One estimate is that the Unification Church controls ten billion dollars worth of businesses.[27]

Moon is known to sink hundreds of millions of nonrefundable dollars into
floating the Unification-owned *Washington Times* newspaper and another ten million dollars annually on an intellectual journal. He spent forty-eight million dollars to produce a film, *Inchon*, which flopped at the box office. Over thirty million
dollars were allocated to lure scholars and clergy from around the world to conferences at exotic resorts. Foreign students are offered Unification Church schol-
arships at his universities. And he pledged to build a one-billion-dollar automobile plant in China, called Panda Motors. However, after sinking hundreds of
millions into the plant, the Unification Church abruptly closed it in 1991. This
vacant building shell stands as a monument to the whimsical decisions Moon
makes concerning his shifting financial empire.

The massive weddings that have drawn international attention to Rev. and
Mrs. Moon result from their concept of the fall of man. Everything in Unification
theology is interpreted through the Taoist philosophy of dualism, Yang and Yin
(positive and negative, male and female). When Adam and Eve fell from perfection, they fell two ways, physically and spiritually. Through the Fall, mankind's
blood became tainted through Eve's union with Satan.

When Jesus came to earth, His mission was to save man physically and spiritually by getting married. The Jews, John the Baptist, and His disciples failed to form
a family unit with Him and find Him a suitable bride. Realizing their failure, He
chose to die on the cross and save mankind spiritually. Instead of saving man two

---

[22]Chris Elkins, *What Do You Say to a Moonie?* (Wheaton, Ill.: Tyndale House Publishers, 1981), 55.
    See also Chris Elkins, *Heavenly Deception* (Wheaton, Ill.: Tyndale House Publishers, 1980).
[23]Sun Myung Moon, *Master Speaks* (February 8, 1975): 14.
[24]Ibid. (September 20, 1974).
[25]T. Harvey Holt, "A View of the Moonrise," *Conservative Digest* (Jan/Feb 1989): 40.
[26]Moon, *Master Speaks* (October 3, 1976): 16.
[27]Christopher Byron, "Seems Like Old Times," *New York Magazine* (September 27, 1993): 22.

ways, corresponding to the fall of man, Jesus saved man spiritually, only halfway.

Therefore, it was necessary for another messiah to come to finish Jesus' incomplete work by finding the perfect bride, marrying, and establishing a God-centered family through which sinless children could be born. In this way sin would be eradicated from the world and man saved both physically and spiritually. Rev. Moon and his wife are these supposed True Parents of mankind. All weddings they bless are cleansed, and sinless children are hence born. This is their reasoning for massive wedding ceremonies.

The largest mass wedding was held by satellite television in 160 countries and conducted by Sun Myung Moon. On August 6, 1995, 300,000 couples exchanged their vows. Every couple spends the following forty days in celibacy, and then consummates the marriage for three days, only to practice three additional years of celibacy.

Lord of the Second Advent

It was not until Moon was released from prison in Danbury that he publicly called himself "Lord of the Second Advent." In his unedited speech, he said, "I am now in the position of Lord of the Second Advent to the world. . . . But with my emergence as the victorious Lord of the Second Advent for the world, a new order has come into being."[28]

In Sun Myung Moon's sermons, he leaves little doubt that he proclaims himself as the new messiah. It is not difficult for any reasonable person to draw the only conclusion he allows. If the messiah is the Lord of the Second Advent, and the Lord of the Second Advent includes the True Parents, then Moon is claiming all titles for himself by claiming to be the True Parent. Under direct questioning, Unification leaders often skirt the issue by claiming that Moon has never called himself the messiah. But decades of official literature, written by top leaders and published at church expense, openly declare Moon's messiahship. One example is Dr. Kim Sudo's *120-Day Training Manual*, which states, "Then they can understand that Rev. Moon is Messiah, Lord of the Second Advent."[29] And, "if only they can understand the fall of man they can understand that Father is the Messiah."[30] Again he writes, "Unless people can understand Father is Messiah, then they cannot move in."[31]

Rev. Moon's oldest son, Heung Jin Nim Moon, died in 1984, at age seventeen, in an automobile accident. Heung was groomed by Rev. Moon for future leadership of his organization, but his sudden death left Moon depressed. His belief in contact with the spirit world became his relief. His son supposedly became king in the spirit world through a proxy marriage ceremony. Then a strange turn of events occurred in 1987. An unnamed Zimbabwean member claimed that Heung began speaking through him as a medium. The Zimbabwean began giving spiritistic utterances from Heung at the Unification Seminary in Barrytown, New York.[32] Moon evidently accepts the utterances as authentic. He

---

[28]Sun Myung Moon, *CAUSA Seminar Speech* (August 29, 1985): 7–8. Other subsequent published versions have edited these lines out.
[29]Dr. Kim Sudo, *120-Day Training Manual* (HSAWU, n.d.): 160.
[30]Ibid. (HSAWU, n.d.): 222.
[31]Ibid. (HSAWU, n.d.): 400.
[32]Nancy Cooper and Mark Miller, "Rev. Moon's Rising Son," *Newsweek* (April 11, 1988): 39.

has elevated the Zimbabwean to a paid position in the organization. Meanwhile, the theory is that Heung is king in the spirit world, and the twelve remaining children of Rev. and Mrs. Moon represent the twelve tribes of Israel or the twelve disciples of Christ on earth.

Unification Theology Versus the Bible

Unification theology is a homogenization of dualism, using Taoist philosophy and the Bible. The church publishes a number of books to explain this concept, but the most authoritative is *Divine Principle.*

All spiritual and physical entities are described in dualistic terms in Unification theology. Moon believes that God has a "key," called "new truth," which will unlock "all these difficult biblical mysteries."[33] That key is later revealed as the Taoist *Book of Changes (I Ching),* through which Moon interprets the Bible and history.[34] Nothing is exempt in essence or relationship from dualism. "God," Moon revealed, "consists of dual characteristics."[35]

Although the Bible is considered a scripture, it is essentially replaced by Moon's *Divine Principle.* There is no question that Moon distrusts the text of God's Word. He taught, "The Bible, however, is not the truth itself, but contains the truth."[36] To say that the Bible is not truth, but only contains truth, is to cast doubt upon its authority. This argument is quickly laid to rest by the words of Jesus, who said, "Thy word is truth" (John 17:17). We are also reminded of Psalm 119:151, which says, "Thou art near, O Lord; and all thy commandments are truth."

Moon holds the opinion that the Bible is outdated by our scientific age. He counts it "impossible" in this "modern scientific civilization" to use "the same method of expressing the truth" as found in the New Testament.[37] Therefore, a "new truth must appear."[38] And, like other cult leaders before him, Moon is proclaimed as the sole source for this new truth. The introduction of *Divine Principle* summarizes the matter: "This truth must appear as a revelation from God himself. This new truth has already appeared! God has sent His messenger. . . . His name is Sun Myung Moon."[39]

We have already seen that Moon's revelations are utterly dependent upon spiritism. Moon indicates that spiritism is a replacement, or substitute, for the Holy Spirit. He taught, "Spirit men pour out spiritual fire. . . . They enable earthly men to see many facts in the spirit world in a state of trance, give them the gift of prophecy, and inspire them spiritually. Through such activities, substituting for the Holy Spirit, they cooperate with earthly men to fulfill the will of God."[40]

It is no wonder, then, that Moon's "new truth" disagrees with the Bible, since he admits that his insight comes from spirits other than the Holy Spirit. The Holy Spirit inspires the true Word of God (2 Peter 1:21). Jesus tells us that the Holy Spirit brings His words to the remembrance of the disciples (John 14:26) as the

---

[33]Kim, *Principle,* 15.
[34]Ibid., 26.
[35]Ibid., 26.
[36]Ibid., 9.
[37]Ibid., 131.
[38]Ibid., 131.
[39]Ibid., 16.
[40]Ibid., 182.

divine protector from error in Scripture. He also speaks only what is truth (John 16:13), which prevents any distortion in God's message. There cannot be any substitution for the Holy Spirit; such is the warning of Paul (2 Corinthians 11:4).

Contact with departed spirits becomes the test for authenticity in *Divine Principle.* It says, "Any Christian who, in spiritual communication, can see John the Baptist directly in the spirit world will be able to understand the authenticity of all these things."[41] The idea that proof for revelation is grounded in spiritism is in direct violation of God's Word. Anyone who reads Deuteronomy 18:10–12 or Isaiah 8:19–20 will quickly see that God counts all such activity as abominable.

Revelation for Moon carries an unusual dispensational motif. He believes in three "testaments": the Old Testament, the New Testament, and the Complete Testament. The Complete Testament is *Divine Principle.* Even though the Complete Testament was given by Moon, he indicates that further revelation is yet to come. The "Complete" Testament evidently lacks completeness. A quarter of a century ago Moon promised an additional revelation called "Book Two,"[42] which is yet to surface. Its content, according to Moon, will irresistibly turn the heart of the most stubborn toward him. A book with such powerful influence seemingly should have been released by Moon some years ago, since his church is not much larger today than it was at that time.

God in Unification Theology

God is described in dualistic characteristics by Moon. God's internal essence is both male and female, positive and negative (yang and yin). God's external relationship is subject and object, male and female (yang and yin). Our discussion begins with the essence of God—what is His nature in Unification theology?

Much of the normative terminology found in standard Christian theology is adopted by Unification teachers. When the definitions are examined, however, the semantic changes, however slight, alter the true meaning. Such words as *trinity, omnipresent, omnipotent, omniscient,* and *immutable* have lost value in Unification thinking. The god presented by Moon is not the Trinity: he changes, and he has needs, without which he would cease to exist.

Beginning with God's essence, Moon teaches that God "exists with His dual characteristics of positivity and negativity."[43] The standard symbol representing Taoism is a circle with an "s" curve through the middle. The left side is white and the right side black. Each side contains its opposite color represented by a small circle. This symbol also underlies the Unification thesis for God. God is white and black simultaneously. He is positive and negative, male and female, subject and object, yang and yin. The god of Unification theology is dualistic.[44]

In expressing his view of God, Moon teaches, "The *Book of Changes (I Ching)* . . . emphasizes that the foundation of the universe is Taeguk (ultimacy) and from this comes Yang and Yin." He adds, "Taeguk . . . represents God, the subject who contains dual essentialities."[45] The original *Divine Principle,* translated

---

[41]Kim, *Principle,* 163.
[42]Moon, *Master Speaks,* HSAUWC (March 16, 1972): 4.
[43]Kim, *Principle,* 24.
[44]Anonymous, *Outline of the Principle: Level 4* (New York: HSA-UWC, 1980): 4–6.
[45]Kim, *Principle,* 25–26.

by Dr. Young Oon Kim, explains the relationship, "though there are dual characteristics in God's nature, namely, true fatherhood and motherhood, He appears as a masculine character [subject] to His creation [object]."[46] Moon expounds upon this dual nature, "A man can be divided into two identical halves. Because God is like that He made man the same so He could interact with him. God created everything to resemble himself, especially man."[47]

Rev. Moon apparently has no understanding of the eternal, undivided essence of God. As often stated in creedal form, we do not confuse the persons of the Trinity (Father, Son, and Holy Spirit), nor do we divide the substance (one eternal, omnipotent, omniscient God). In the case of the second person of the Trinity, the Son, the creeds additionally summarize the scriptural teaching that he was one divine *person* who, from the incarnation on, possesses two *natures*, his eternal divine nature and his human nature, which came to be at his conception by the power of the Holy Spirit "overshadowing" the Virgin Mary. The personal unity of Christ is indisputable throughout Scripture as Christ said, for example, "Before Abraham was, *I* am" (John 8:58); and Paul affirmed, "There is *one* Lord, Jesus Christ" (1 Corinthians 8:6). The apostle John declares "The Word was God" (John 1:1) and "The Word became flesh" (John 1:14), so that we "beheld *his* glory" (John 1:14). Moon's illustration that God is divisible, the same as man, fails. God does not even divide His attributes with another: "I am the Lord: that is my name; and my glory will I not give to another" (Isaiah 42:8). Had the dualism of Moon been true, the Bible would be false, and we would have to deny the clear statement of Scripture: "Thus saith the Lord the King of Israel . . . I am the first, and I am the last; and beside me there is no God" (Isaiah 44:6). Rev. Moon wishes to correct the Holy Spirit here and say that God is dualistic, but the Holy Spirit's record of truthfulness, unlike Moon's, is spotless.

The Unification Church denies the historical Christian doctrine of the Trinity. Although they use the term *trinity* at times, they have redefined it into any group of three beings. The word *Trinity* is used to summarize what we see of God's nature in the Bible. Therein we find one God and no others (Isaiah 43:10). God is personal as the Father (Matthew 6:9). God is personal as the Son (Matthew 3:17). God is personal as the Holy Spirit (Acts 5:3). And together the three persons are uniquely one God in Scripture (Isaiah 48:16; Matthew 28:19; see also chapter 4, pages 83–84).

Dr. Kim apparently misunderstood this biblical doctrine, because she erroneously attaches polytheism to its definition. She said, "Many Christians seem to worship three Gods: Father, Son, and Holy Spirit. . . . We believe the doctrine of the Trinity is mistaken, if it means the Father, Son, and Holy Spirit are three personal Gods."[48] Is it any surprise, then, that Moonies reject the Trinity, when one of their best theologians defines it neither correctly nor historically? Moon also redefines the Trinity: "Jesus and the Holy Spirit become one body centered on God; this is called 'Trinity.' "[49] Even more clearly, in the original *Divine Principle*, Moon teaches, "By uniting with the Holy Spirit, Jesus established the Holy

---

[46]Kim, *Principle*, 3.
[47]Moon, *Master Speaks*, HSAUWC (March 19, 1978): 10.
[48]Young Oon Kim, *Speeches on Unification Teaching* (Barrytown: Unification Theological Seminary, 1986), 4–7.
[49]Kim, *Principle*, 217.

Trinity for the first time—but spiritually."[50] Now Rev. Moon informs us that the Trinity had a beginning! Only after Jesus united with the Holy Spirit the first time did the Trinity begin. It is impossible, by any biblical standard, to arrive at Moon's conclusion without forsaking every Scripture that speaks of God's nature. The Bible speaks from cover to cover of the tri-personal nature of God. Beginning in Genesis 1:26–27; 3:22; 11:7–8, to Isaiah 6:8, we find God speaking of himself as "us" and "our." Throughout the Old Testament we find God speaking of another person who shares His nature, showing more than one person (Isaiah 48:16; Jeremiah 50:40; Zechariah 2:8–11; 10:12). In the New Testament the relationship and equality of the persons of God is well established (Matthew 28:19; 2 Corinthians 13:14; and John 15:26).

The word *trinity* for Moon was God's ideal family of Adam and Eve, centered (foundationally) upon God. These three were to become the original trinity, but the fall of man truncated this hope. What occurred in Eden was a satanic trinity, which Moon believes was passed on to humans everywhere. He teaches, "Due to the Fall, Adam and Eve . . . centered on Satan, thus resulting in a trinity centered on Satan. Therefore, their descendants have also formed trinities centered on Satan."[51]

All created entities are in a subject/object relationship with God, according to Moon. Creation is actually God's "second self, the visible God."[52] Moon describes God's nature, "We cannot see God because God exists as a spiritual force."[53] God is "the center," the "internal character" of the physical universe.[54] The universe "is the substantial manifestation of the invisible God."[55] The original *Divine Principle* says, "God is energy itself."[56]

Unification theology is immediately recognized as panentheism; that is, God is said to be invisibly "in" everything, but He is distinguished from the material atoms themselves. Panentheism is superbly dealt with and refuted by Dr. Norman L. Geisler in *Christian Apologetics*.[57] Biblically, if God existed before creation (and Moonies will admit this), then for creation to become his "visible second self," it requires a change in His nature. This is refuted by any number of verses that demonstrate God is unchangeable, such as Psalm 102:26–27 or Malachi 3:6.

One other interesting aspect of Creation in Unification theology is that apparently Lucifer and angels assisted God in creating all things. Moon says, "The archangel [Lucifer] had worked with God to create all the things in the universe; he knew everything."[58] Moon also explains, "God created the angels as servants who were to assist in the creation of the universe."[59] Yet one can search the Bible in vain to find a single line that tells of Lucifer or angels assisting in Creation. Instead, we find that Jesus Christ is revealed as Creator in His preexistence (John 1:3, 10; 1 Corinthians 8:6; Colossians 1:16–17; and Hebrews 1:2, 10). The biblical fact is that Jesus created all things, not Lucifer.

---

[50]Kim, *Principle*, 68.

[51]Ibid., 217.

[52]Sun Myung Moon, *God's Warning to the World* (New York: HSAUWC, 1985), 18.

[53]Moon, *Master Speaks*, HSAUWC (March 16, 1972): 1.

[54]Kim, *Principle*, 25.

[55]Ibid., 40.

[56]Ibid., 4.

[57]Norman L. Geisler, *Christian Apologetics* (Grand Rapids, Mich.: Baker Book House, 1976), 193–213.

[58]Moon, *Master Speaks*, HSAUWC (March 16, 1972): 8.

[59]Kim, *Principle*, 76.

The god whom Moon portrays is weak, needful, and without all power. Moon speaks of God as one who is destructible. He says, "Since God must live in everything that is created, God himself must have these two separate elements [Sung Sang and Hyung Sang]. God must have the same nature as the rest of His creation, for without having such characteristics, He would eventually be destroyed by trying to exist in such a world."[60] Again, he says, "If man did not exist then God would vanish."[61] Even *Divine Principle* carries this theme, "In order for God to exist externally, God has dual essentialities."[62] It is utterly inconceivable that God would be dependent upon creation for His existence. Biblical verses that speak of His eternality, from everlasting to everlasting, show that He exists independent of creation (1 Chronicles 16:36; Job 36:26; Psalm 41:13; 90:1–4; 93:2; 102:24–27; Isaiah 40:28). God speaks in exacting terms: "God is not a man" (Numbers 23:19); "I am God, and not man" (Hosea 11:9), which forever lay to rest the idea of His dependency upon man.

Jesus in Unification Theology

Sun Myung Moon openly states that "[John 8:58] does not signify that Jesus was God himself. Jesus, on earth, was a man no different from us except for the fact that he was without original sin."[63] In further elaboration, Moon insists, "After his crucifixion, Christianity made Jesus into God."[64] Moon makes all men equal in "divinity" to Jesus, thereby striking a blow at the uniqueness of Christ.[65] In hopes of gaining converts, Moon attributes demigod status to Jesus, saying, "Jesus, being one body with God, may be called a second God."[66] But, far from correct, this statement breeds polytheism, which is rejected throughout the Bible.

Unification theology denies the Virgin Birth of Jesus Christ. Dr. Kim wrote, "If Joseph was not the Father, who was? The New Testament is silent on such matters. . . . As the son of Zechariah, Jesus would become a half-brother to John the Baptist, producing in effect another Abel-Cain relationship at the very beginning of God's new dispensation. This explanation of Jesus' paternity would also serve to illustrate the traditional Christian comparison between Mary and Eve."[67]

Matthew 1:18–25 and Luke 1:26–2:20 give such detail of the virginal conception and birth of Jesus that no serious Bible student could miss it. Just how Rev. Moon and Dr. Kim missed the biblical account indicates the depth of their study. In addition, to suggest that Jesus was born of an incestuous and adulterous relationship between Zechariah and Mary (his sister-in-law) is unspeakable. We see here, as often seen in other cults, how new revelation leads people astray from God's Word.

The vicarious atonement, crucifixion, and resurrection of Jesus were all an unplanned mistake, according to Moon. God's real purpose in sending Jesus was

---

[60]Moon, *Master Speaks*, HSAUWC (March 19, 1978): 9.

[61]Moon, *Master Speaks* (May 22, 1977): 6.

[62]Kim, *Principle*, 40.

[63]Ibid., 212.

[64]Sun Myung Moon, *Christianity in Crisis* (New Hope, Washington, D.C.: HSAUWC, 1974), 12.

[65]cf. *Principle*, 209.

[66]Kim, *Principle*, 211.

[67]Young Oon Kim, *Unification Theology and Christian Thought* (New York: Golden Gate Publishing Co., 1975), 116. See also, Kim, *Unification Theology* (New York: HSAUWC, 1987), 171–72.

to find a bride, marry, and produce sinless children. The original *Divine Principle* said, "The crucifixion of Jesus was a universal tragedy! The suffering of Jesus on the cross was not the Will of God, nor was it an event predestined by God."[68] It adds, "The crucifixion of Jesus was a secondary choice . . . after it became obvious that he would not be able to fulfill his mission."[69] The current *Divine Principle* agrees, saying, "redemption by the cross has been unable to remove our original sin."[70] Furthermore, "We, therefore, must realize that Jesus did not come to die on the cross."[71] Moon explains that Jesus' marriage was God's primary will, for "there had to be a bride, a Mother—another Eve. So God intended for this perfected Adam—Jesus Christ—to restore his bride, the perfected Eve."[72]

The original *Divine Principle* states the reason for Jesus' demise. "Satan used the condition made by John the Baptist, the disbelieving Jews, and Judas Iscariot to cause Jesus' downfall."[73] The best Jesus could provide for man's dual fall (spiritual and physical) is halfway salvation, spiritual only. Moon teaches, "Because Jewish people disbelieved Jesus and delivered him up for crucifixion, his body was invaded by Satan, and he was killed. . . . Therefore, all the saints since the resurrection of Jesus . . . enjoyed the benefit of the providence of spiritual salvation only."[74] At times Moon shows contempt for the blood of Jesus, "Today the Christian gospel preaches salvation by the blood of Jesus. How ridiculous that is in the sight of God!"[75]

What Rev. Moon fails to realize is that the crucifixion of Jesus was, indeed, the foreordained plan of God in redeeming lost sinners. Revelation 13:8 declares Him "the Lamb slain from the foundation of the world." Far from being ridiculous, and quite opposite of Moon, the apostle Peter calls the blood of Jesus "precious" (1 Peter 1:19–20). Jesus, in His Last Supper, spoke unforgettable words: "For this is my blood of the new testament, which is shed for many for the remission of sins" (Matthew 26:28). Paul encapsulates this truth: "In whom we have redemption through his blood, the forgiveness of sins, according to the riches of his grace" (Ephesians 1:7). Many other verses could be cited to refute Moon's denial of Christ's atoning blood, with which every student of God's Word should be familiar.

It is taught in the Unification Church that there are three main categories of the spirit world, subdivided into nine levels. Each world religion has their compartment, and they graduate from one level to another by assisting people on earth. Jesus, according to Moon, was not bodily resurrected, as plainly taught in Scripture. He was stuck for the past two thousand years in a particular level of paradise, awaiting liberation by Moon in the twentieth century.

On Jesus' resurrection, Moon says, "Many Christians today truly misunderstand. They preach resurrection, but resurrection does not mean that dead bodies will rise again."[76] He informs us that "God was not happy at all to see the

---

[68]Kim, *Principle*, 52.
[69]Ibid., 60–61.
[70]Ibid., 142.
[71]Ibid., 144.
[72]Sun Myung Moon, *The New Future of Christianity* (Washington, D.C.: The Unification Church, 1974), 124.
[73]Kim, *Principle*, 172.
[74]Ibid., 148.
[75]Moon, *Master Speaks* (April 8, 1978): 12.
[76]Moon, *Warning*, 136.

resurrected Jesus."[77] All Unification denials of Jesus' resurrection are answered in the Bible. Luke 24:39 and John 20:27 leave no doubt that Jesus rose in His physical body. He predicted it in John 2:19–21 and John 10:17–18. Its fulfillment is in every gospel, and Acts 1:3 reminds us that it was with "many infallible proofs." The apostle Paul gives a wonderful serial account of many, up to five hundred people at once, who witnessed the physical resurrection (1 Corinthians 15:1–11).

The Holy Spirit in Unification Theology

Even though the Unification Church has as its official name, the Holy Spirit Association for the Unification of World Christianity (HSAUWC), its followers know little of the third person of the Trinity. As quoted earlier, Moon teaches that disincarnate spirits are a valid substitute for the Holy Spirit, which is abominable doctrine and not short of blasphemy. In furtherance of their mystical labyrinth, Moon informs us that the Holy Spirit is the female aspect of God, and became the spiritual bride of Jesus—his spiritual wife! Moon begins, "The Holy Spirit is a female spirit, this is because she came as the True Mother, that is, the second Eve."[78] He elaborates, "In Christianity we have only spiritual parents. The Holy Spirit is the mother spirit; and with Jesus Christ and the Holy Spirit working together we cleanse our sins and are given rebirth on the spiritual level."[79] Green auras, according to Moon, represent the Holy Spirit.[80] And Dr. Kim adds, "Unification Theology portrays the Holy Spirit not as an individual person, but rather as divine energy. . . . Like God himself, the Spirit is invisible and incorporeal—a bright light or a field of magnetic energy, so to speak."[81]

The biblical understanding of the genuine person and deity of the Holy Spirit is evident in many places (2 Samuel 23:2–3; John 14:26; 15:26; 16:5–15; Acts 5:3–4; and 1 Corinthians 6:19–20). From all of the above Unification theology, one need not go much further than 2 Corinthians 11:4 for refutation. It says, "For if he that cometh preacheth another Jesus, whom we have not preached, or if ye receive another spirit, which ye have not received, or another gospel, which ye have not accepted, ye might well bear with him." Failure in any single point disqualifies one from fellowship, but Moon has succeeded in violation of all three.

Salvation in Unification Theology

Finally, let us examine salvation in Unification theology.

"We must realize that through the crucifixion on the cross, God and Jesus lost everything. . . . At that moment of crucifixion, nothing was there—nothing—no nation of Israel, no Jewish faith, no disciples, no salvation; and there was no beginning of Christianity. There was not redemption; there was not salvation; and there was no beginning of Christianity. So there on the cross, salvation was not given."[82]

~As in other areas, Rev. Moon utilizes Christian terms such as *grace*, but

---

[77]Moon, *Master Speaks* (April 3, 1973): 2.
[78]Kim, *Principle*, 215.
[79]Moon, *Master Speaks*, HSAUWC (September 22, 1974).
[80]Ibid. (March 16, 1972): 7.
[81]Kim, *Speeches*, 5.
[82]Sun Myung Moon, *The Way of the World* (Washington, D.C.: HAS-UWC, 1973), 13.

alters the meaning. It is taught that God did ninety-five percent of the work, and left only five percent for man. But even five percent of works still desecrates what God has said concerning grace (Ephesians 2:8–9; Titus 3:5).

Sun Myung Moon believes that as the Lord of the second advent, the second messiah, he must set the foundation for physical salvation, which he claims Jesus failed to accomplish. By uniting with the perfect bride, Rev. and Mrs. Moon became True Parents, the Third Adam and Third Eve. They also form a new "trinity" of God, Moon, and Mrs. Moon.[83] Rather than closing prayer in the name of Jesus, Moonies close prayer in the name of the True Parents.[84] Moon and his wife appear in spirit form to members in 120 countries of the world.[85] Moonies believe their works will save them, but more so, spirit ancestors descend upon them and work with them, therefore the spirit gains another level in the spirit world by assisting Moonies on earth.[86] Their goal is to become divine, like God, for this is Moon's promise for the highest level of heaven.[87]~

Conclusion

It is hardly necessary to make any extended comment upon the Moon doctrine of salvation, since it is totally eclipsed by the cross. Multiple passages of Scripture teach us that at Calvary redemption was fully accomplished, that the old covenant was fulfilled, and that Christ "by himself purged our sins" and became "the propitiation for our sins, and not for ours only: but also for the sins of the whole world" (Hebrews 1:3 and 1 John 2:2). In Unification theology salvation is not by grace through the all-sufficient sacrifice of the Lord Jesus, but must be augmented by human works and by the teachings, revelations, and requirements of Mr. Moon.

The warning of the Lord Jesus Christ against false Christs and false prophets is most apropos where Moon is concerned, for he can make no genuine claim to messianic office being Korean, for as Christ said, "Salvation is from the Jews" (John 4:22 NIV).

Recommended Resources

1. Bjornstad, James. *Sun Myung Moon and the Unification Church.* Minneapolis: Bethany House, 1984.
2. Elkins, Chris. *Heavenly Deception.* Wheaton: Tyndale House, 1981.
3. Hong, Nansook. *In the Shadow of the Moons: My Life in the Reverend Sun Myung Moon's Family.* New York: Little, Brown & Company, 1998.
4. Martin, Walter. *Unification,* audiotape. Walter Martin Ministries. *www.waltermartin.com.*
5. McDowell, Josh, and Don Stewart. *The Deceivers.* Nashville, Tenn.: Thomas Nelson Publishers, 1992.
6. Yamamoto, J. Isamu. *Unification Church.* Grand Rapids: Zondervan Publishing House, 1995.

---

[83] *Outline of The Principle: Level 4,* 146.
[84] Moon, *Master Speaks* (April 1965): 32.
[85] Ibid. (January 1, 1977): 5.
[86] Kim, *Speeches,* 14–15.
[87] Moon, *New Future,* 72; and Kim, *Theology,* 164.

Quick Facts About Eastern Religions

- There is no single Hindu idea of God.

- All souls are eternal and accountable for their own actions.

- Karma is the debt of one's bad actions for which one must atone.

- Hinduism denies the Trinity, the deity of Christ, the Atonement, sin, and salvation by grace through the sacrifice of Jesus Christ.

- Hinduism replaces resurrection with reincarnation, and both grace and faith with human works.

Chapter 14

Eastern Religions

Rajneeshism, ISKCON, and Transcendental Meditation

This book has undertaken to survey some of the major cults that exist and are active in the United States today. During my ministry of more than thirty years in this field of apologetics, I have seen hundreds of smaller cults come and go. During this time, I have observed trends in cultic structures. Often the fads of society are reflected in the fads of cults or cultic belief. Nowhere is this more evident than in the general American culture's strange preoccupation with anything Eastern or Asian. This "fad" traces its roots to the appearance of a Hindu guru at the Chicago World's Fair at the turn of the century, although popular interest in Eastern things did not explode in American society until the 1960s and 1970s. From Nehru jackets in the 1960s to Tao and the new physics in the 1980s, Eastern influence has pervaded Western society.

The last few decades have seen the explosive growth of New Age (or occultic) religious cults with their roots in classic Hindu thought. ~As America enters the new millennium, this fascination with Eastern religions shows no signs of abating. While many Eastern influences have been seamlessly incorporated into New Age cults, three more purely Eastern religions still have a strong presence in America and are discussed in this chapter. The founders of two of the groups have died, but their followers continue to exert a strong religious influence on segments of American society. The third, Transcendental Meditation, is still led by its founder, Maharishi Mahesh Yogi. It too is a strong but subtle influence in American religious practice.[1]~

This chapter updated and edited by Kevin Rische and Jill Martin Rische.

[1]Marked sections in this chapter are editorial commentary, cited from Walter Martin, *Kingdom of the Cults* (Minneapolis: Bethany House Publishers) 1997, 387–402, unless otherwise noted.

Today there are literally hundreds of large and small cults in America with Eastern ideas and practices. In this short summary, we will survey the Hindu roots of these cults and then present a quick look at three of the most well-known imports: Rajneeshism, the International Society for Krishna Consciousness (ISKCON, or Hare Krishnas), and Transcendental Meditation (TM). What follows is a brief history and description of Hinduism and a brief introduction to and doctrinal summary of Rajneeshism, ISKCON, and TM.

Hinduism

Hinduism today is not the same as Hinduism five thousand years ago. The Hindu religion has evolved over the past five millennia of Indian religious history. Hinduism seeks to be a synthesis of the various religious ideas and influences from throughout the Indian subcontinent, representing hundreds of separate cultural, social, and tribal groups. The term *Hindu* itself is not indigenous to India. It comes from the Persian designation of the Indus River. Yogi Ramacharaka notes,

> The different Hindu sects, while practically appearing as different religions, in reality regard themselves as but different sects and divisions of the One Eternal Religion of India, of which each, of course, considers itself the best and most favored channel of expression and interpretation.[2]

Scripture

The Hindu scriptures were collected over hundreds of years, beginning with the writing of the oral traditions around the last half of the second millennium B.C. These scriptures are known as the *Vedas* ("wisdom" or "knowledge"). The concluding portions of the Vedas are called the *Upanishads,* which are a synthesis of Vedic teachings. The general assumptions of the Upanishads include a belief in pantheism, karmic retribution, and reincarnation. Perhaps the most well-known section of the Vedas is the Hindu epic called the *Bhagavad-Gita,* which tells the story of the warrior-prince Arjuna and his charioteer, Krishna, who is actually the disguised incarnation of the Hindu god Vishnu. The Gita was written down and subsequently modified between 200 B.C. and A.D. 200.

An illustration of the pluralism or contradictory nature of Hinduism is found by comparing the god of the Gita with the god of earlier Vedic literature. God, as described by the Gita, is personal and often sounds even monotheistic (only one God who is personal and not a part of creation exists). However, when one reads earlier Vedic scripture, God is presented as being definitely pantheistic (all of existence is, in some way, divine) and perhaps even monistic (all of existence is one, whether any divinity exists at all). The monotheistic characteristics of the Gita were appropriated by the founder of ISKCON, and consequently ISKCON teaches a more monotheistic rather than pantheistic idea of God today.

---

[2]Yogi Ramacharaka, *The Philosophies and Religions of India* (Chicago, Ill.: The Yogi Publication Society, 1930), 271–72.

Contemporary Hinduism

There are three basic classifications into which the hundreds of Hindu sects can be divided: (1) the abstract monists, who stress the philosophical oneness of the universe instead of religious or theistic ideas; (2) the Vishnuites, who are devoted to the worship (in many different manners) of the god Vishnu (in many different manifestations) as the supreme form of divinity; and (3) the Shivaites, who are devoted to the worship of the god Shiva as the highest manifestation of divinity. TM, with its philosophical concentration, relates to the monistic classification, while ISKCON believes that Krishna, the supreme God, is also known as Vishnu and so they are identified with the Vishnuites. Rajneesh differed from them both in that he was philosophically agnostic and pragmatically Hindu. He had no inhibitions about subjecting Hinduism to any interpretation that fit his presuppositions, particularly in the realm of morality.

World religion expert Professor Ninan Smart notes the problems of the varieties of contemporary Hindu systems:

> It might be asked, by way of conclusion, What is the essence of Hinduism? A hard question. There are orthodox Hindus who deny the existence of God. There are others who while not denying God, relegate him to a second place, as a secondary or illusory phase of the Absolute. Amid such a variety of theological views, what remains as necessary to Hindu belief? Certainly the doctrines of rebirth and that of an eternal soul. The picture of the world as a place where the immortal spirit within man is virtually endlessly implicated in the round of reincarnation has dominated the Indian imagination for about three millennia. In addition, a complex social system has given shape to the actual religion of the subcontinent over a long period.[3]

Hindu Beliefs

God. There is no single Hindu idea of God. Hindu concepts of deity can include any of the following: monism (all existence is one substance); pantheism (all existence is divine); panentheism (God is in creation as a soul is in a body); animism (God or gods live in nonhuman objects such as trees, rocks, animals, etc.); polytheism (there are many gods); henotheism (there is one god we worship among the many that exist); and monotheism (there is only one God).

Karma and Samsara. Fundamental to Hindu thought is the idea that all souls are eternal and accountable for their own actions throughout time. Karma refers to the debt of one's bad actions, which must be atoned for (through various Hindu systems) in order for one to escape the wheel of *samsara*, or reincarnation (the soul inhabits successive human bodies), or transmigration (the soul inhabits successive bodies—human, animal, or even plants or inanimate objects).

Salvation. The three major paths to Hindu "salvation" include *karma marga* (method), the way of disinterested action; *bhakti marga*, the way of devotion; and *jnana marga*, the path of knowledge or mystical insight. Jnana marga achieves self-realization through intuitive awareness and mystical insight. Bhakti marga achieves self-realization through ritualistic sacrifice and discipline.

[3]Ninan H. Smart, *The Religious Experience of Mankind* (New York: Charles Scribner's Sons, 1976), 155–56.

Bhagwan Shree Rajneesh (Rajneeshism)

In terms of media attention and exposure, Bhagwan Shree (Sir God) Rajneesh (born 1931) gradually achieved greater notoriety than any recent cult leader—with the possible exception of Sun Myung Moon. He was indisputably the preeminent Eastern guru of the 1980s.

In an interview in *Forward* magazine,[4] Eckart Flother, a former follower of Rajneesh, gave an excellent thumbnail sketch of the cult leader's background:

> Rajneesh Chandra Mohan was born on the 11th of December, 1931, in a village in central India, the eldest in a family of five sisters and seven brothers. His childhood was overshadowed by the fact that his father, an unsuccessful businessman, was often on the road. The "father figure" in Rajneesh's life was instead occupied by his grandfather, to whom he became very attached. His grandfather died when he was seven years old. This was a very traumatic experience for young Rajneesh. From then on he felt strangely attracted to the subject of death. In his 1979 diary (which is made public), it is reported that he followed after funerals as other children would follow circuses.
>
> Rajneesh pursued his education and in 1957 obtained a Master of Arts in Philosophy. He proceeded to teach philosophy in two universities between 1957 and 1966. In 1966, Rajneesh resigned from his service as a teacher in order to, as he puts it, concentrate on the wish of God. He felt called to work for the spiritual regeneration of humanity, which he feels is necessary in order to survive the holocaust which he is predicting and fearing.
>
> Rajneesh then became a "master" and called himself "Acharya"[5] Rajneesh, and he walked and rode a donkey around India in various states in order to teach people that they have to change their lives and turn around in order to survive.
>
> His mission wasn't very successful, and in 1970 he was a tired and poor man who nevertheless recognized that he possessed charisma and power. In Bombay, he decided to gather people around him to whom he could teach his message. As more and more disciples flocked around him, the apartment where he lived was unable to accommodate them. Thus, in 1974 he moved to Poona, 120 miles south of Bombay, rented several houses, and founded his ashram.[6] There he changed his name from Acharya to Bhagwan (which means God), designed orange robes and a wooden bead necklace for his disciples, and started the movement we are dealing with today.

Rajneesh, bald, bearded, and photogenic, first attained major media exposure in the United States in early 1978 when *Time* magazine featured an article on the guru entitled " 'God Sir' at Esalen East." *Time* magazine reported that the charismatic guru had come into vogue among certain celebrities and prominent apostles of the Human Potential Movement who were joining thousands of other spiritual seekers in making the pilgrimage to Rajneesh's ashram in Poona, India. Rajneesh's appeal stemmed partly from his use of "tantric yoga" (involving nudity and free sex) and partly from his incorporation of a wide variety of popu-

---

[4]Forerunner of *The Christian Research Journal.*
[5]"Acharya" means teacher.
[6]Religious community/monastery.

lar "psychospiritual" therapies and techniques.

In the late 1970s and early 1980s, Rajneesh's acclaim continued to spread within the New Age Movement in America, Great Britain, Germany, and nearly every free-world, industrialized nation. With as many as six thousand Westerners in Poona at a time, the ashram population rose to ten thousand, while five hundred Rajneesh centers were established in twenty-two nations by orange-and-red garbed *sannyasins*[7] (now more commonly called *Rajneeshees*), returning from Poona to their homelands. As of 1984, Rajneesh had gathered some 359,000 followers, whose average age was thirty-four.

Rajneesh's discourses, which are delivered daily, have been transcribed into over three hundred fifty books and diaries, which average in price between $15 and $22. Videotapes of each discourse range in price between $50 and $170, while audiotapes cost almost $10 each. These are all disseminated by Rajneesh Foundation International, a multimillion-dollar corporation. As a follower stated in the film *Ashram*, a documentary on the Rajneesh cult, "The organization understood long ago what powerful energy money is." Rajneesh, whose evergrowing fleet of Rolls-Royces numbered more than seventy at the time of this writing, believes that "spirituality is the luxury and privilege of the rich."[8]

Rajneesh is a self-proclaimed spiritual rebel who thrives on the controversy that he has created, first in India, and now in America. Tal Brooke, a former devotee of the popular Indian guru Sathya Sai Baba, after visiting Poona, effectively summed up the scene there:

> An object of media fascination and horror, Rajneesh is known for his bizarre revelations on sex. He has constructed a vision of the New Man that repudiates all prior norms and traditions. Man, by Rajneesh's thinking, is the hedonist-god, fully autonomous (barring the inner voice of Rajneesh), and free to carve out the cosmos in his own image. He is the sovereign pleasure seeker, self-transcender, who owes nobody anything. The family is anathema, children extra trash. And so long as the Neo-sannyasin has the money the fun ride continues. Afterward, however, he or she is usually a nonfunctional casualty. Homicides, rapes, mysterious disappearances, threats, fires, explosions, abandoned ashram children now begging in Poona's streets, drug busts—all done by those amazing hybrids in red who believe they are pioneering new and daring redefinitions of the word "love." Christians working in a Poona asylum confirm such accounts, adding the breakdown rate is so high the ashram has wielded political power to suppress reports.[9]

Rajneesh has often openly expressed hostility toward established religions: "This is a revolution . . . I am burning scriptures here, uprooting traditions . . . unless I am shot I'll not be proved right."[10]

By early 1981, threats on Rajneesh's life were reported. The ashram was heavily guarded, and no one was allowed to enter without first being searched for weapons. Then an ashram warehouse was set on fire, and an explosion was set off

---

[7] Initiated disciples. Males take on the title "Swami," and females go by the appellation "Ma."

[8] Russell Chandler and Tyler Marshall, "Guru Brings His Ashram to Oregon," *Los Angeles Times* (August 13, 1981): 1:14.

[9] "Pied Piper of Poona," *Eternity* (September 1981): 14.

[10] *This Is a Revolution*, Bhagwan Shree Rajneesh, videocassette 18C236 (December 28, 1980).

near the cult's health center. According to the cult's own account, when an actual attempt on the guru's life was made in February, ashram officials hastened a process (which had already been initiated) of looking for a new headquarters.

According to the reputable magazine *India Today*, however, "Both police and . . . officials in [Poona] are unanimous in their charge that the incidents were rigged by Rajneesh followers."[11] Why? The Indian periodical explains that "Disclosures in [Poona] last fortnight revealed that the Rajneesh Foundation was up to its neck in income tax arrears, defalcation with the charities commissioner, a major insurance fraud, and a string of cases for criminal offenses, which were still being investigated when they left."[12]

The U.S. Consulate in Bombay issued Rajneesh a visa, and on June 1, 1981, he secretly flew to New York with seventeen of his closest disciples.

Since Rajneesh left Poona, his followers spread throughout the West. "In Europe the present strategy is to establish 'Sacred Cities.' The European Newsletter, issue 8, 1981, says, 'A sannyasin city is to be set up in each major European country. Bhagwan has suggested that the cities should be self-supporting, alternative societies, which will be models of sannyas.' "[13]

In America, efforts were undertaken to create the ultimate "sacred city," one fit for the "master" himself. On July 10, 1981, the Chidvilas Rajneesh Meditation Center of Montclair, New Jersey, purchased the Big Muddy Ranch (where the John Wayne movie *Big Muddy* was filmed) for $6 million ($1.5 million of it in cash) from an investment company in Amarillo, Texas. The land, near Madras, Oregon, covers more than one hundred square miles. The Center also managed to lease 14,889 acres in the same area from the U.S. Bureau of Land Management.

Two hundred Rajneeshees from sixteen Western countries soon flocked to the Big Muddy, and in September they jubilantly welcomed their master to his new home.

Not long after the ranch was purchased, plans were announced to build "America's first enlightened city," which was to be called *Rajneeshpuram* (expression or city of Rajneesh). On November 4, 1981, the Wasco County Commission voted two-to-one to allow an election to be held the following May to determine if the Big Muddy property should be incorporated as a city. Since the only ones allowed to vote in such an election are those who *live* on the site (in this case, the Rajneeshees), the outcome was predictable: 154 votes in favor of the incorporation of Rajneeshpuram, none opposed. Rajneesh, his followers, and their "enlightened city" have been making headlines ever since.

Working twelve hours a day, seven days a week for no wages (their basic necessities are provided for), the 2,000 members of the Rajneesh Neo-Sannyas International Commune have been appropriately tagged the "red ants" because of their impressive industry and accomplishments. "The Rajneeshees have taken 81,000 acres of rocky, steep, dry, and useless land . . . and are building a self-sufficient city complete with dam, substation, parks, housing developments,

[11]Chander Uday Singh, "Sins of Bhagwan," *India Today* (June 15, 1982).
[12]Ibid.
[13]Jens Johansen, "The Master Will Not Speak Again," *New Religious Movements Update* 5:5/4 (December 1981): 81.

roads, fields, greenhouses, and airport."[14]

From the beginning, the cult's efforts to carve a paradise out of the Oregon desert have been heatedly opposed. The legal status of the city has been challenged on two grounds: (1) that it violates the constitutional separation of church and state, and (2) that the Wasco County Commission's decision to allow an incorporation election violated state land-use zoning laws. At the time of this writing, neither issue had been resolved. A final ruling against the city on either count could result in the dismantling of most of its buildings.

As a security measure, in case Rajneeshpuram is disincorporated (to make sure the cult has access to municipal powers and services), the Rajneeshees have politically taken over a nearby town, changing its name from Antelope to Rajneesh. Most of Antelope's original forty residents (mostly elderly), after being subjected to constant observation by the sannyasin-manned police force, having their taxes tripled to support cult interests, and watching the Rajneesh-dominated city council designate an area within a local park for nude sunbathing, have quit fighting and moved away.

The town has been growing, nonetheless, as Rajneeshees buy existing homes and build new ones.

In the meantime, the Immigration and Naturalization Service (INS) has been "conducting an ongoing investigation into suspected violations of immigration laws and related criminal statutes by the Rajneesh Foundation International and related organizations and/or their members," said Carl Houseman, Portland's INS District Director.[15] Twenty-five to thirty Rajneeshees (including top leaders) are suspected of engaging in "marriages of convenience" between U.S. citizens and foreign nationals. The permanent resident status of Rajneesh himself is also in jeopardy if the INS can prove that his original travel visa was granted on the basis of an exaggerated illness.

It was the takeover of Antelope, in particular, that fed the surrounding communities' worst fears about the cult's political ambitions. The Rajneesh Humanity Trust's "share a home" experiment in the fall of 1984, which imported thirty-five hundred street people to the ranch, was interpreted by most observers as a bold (though abortive) attempt to establish a large enough voting bloc to gain political mastery over Wasco County.

The Rajneeshees eclipsed even the national elections in the Oregon media that November, and "rumor controls" had to be started to quiet runaway fears, such as a concern that the cult was threatening to take over the entire state.

Visions of a Jonestown-like confrontation between the Rajneeshees and governmental authorities, entertained ever since the cult purchased the Big Muddy, have been fueled by Sheela Silverman, Rajneesh's personal secretary and president of Rajneesh Foundation International. The pugnacious Indian disciple, whose word is final in earthly matters, has persistently taken an inflammatory stance.

> In an interview on KGW-TV aired June 29 [1984] . . . Sheela . . . told
> how she would deal with any attempt to dismantle buildings at

---

[14]Bill Dietrich, "Conflict Over Rajneeshpuram," Seattle *Times* (September 9, 1984): A2.
[15]Win McCormack and Bill Driver, "Rajneeshpuram: Valley of Death?" *Oregon Magazine* (September 1984): 26.

Rajneeshpuram. "I *will* be dead," she said. "I *will* paint the bulldozers with my blood." Then, in a July 5 article in the *San Francisco Chronicle,* quotations from Sheela implied that she would block any attempt to arrest people at Rajneeshpuram for immigration or other legal violations. "I mean business," Silverman said through (according to the *Chronicle* account) lips trembling with anger. "You will find out what *will* happen to you if you come here to harm me or Bhagwan or any of my people . . . I'll take things as they come. We are willing to die for human freedom. I have 100 percent support from my people."[16]

While it is uncertain at this time how seriously Sheela's threats are to be taken, there is no doubt that Rajneesh has been inculcating a catastrophic mindset in his followers. In 1983 the guru published his vision of a worldwide crisis:

> The period of this crisis *will* be between *1984* and *1999.* During this period there *will* be every kind of destruction on earth including natural catastrophes and man manufactured auto-suicidal efforts. In other words there will be floods which have never been known since the time of Noah, along with earthquakes, volcanic eruptions and everything else that is possible through nature. . . . There *will* be wars which are bound to end in nuclear explosions, hence no ordinary Noah's arks are going to save humanity. Rajneeshism is creating a Noah's ark of consciousness, remaining centered exactly in the middle of the cyclone.
>
> I say to you that except this [i.e., Rajneeshism] there is no other way.
>
> Tokyo, New York, San Francisco, Los Angeles, Bombay, etc.—all these cities are going to disappear and the holocaust is not going to be confined to certain places. It is going to be global so no escape will be possible. You can only escape within and that's what I teach.[17]

In early 1984 Rajneesh further expounded his vision of impending disaster by specifying that, in supposed fulfillment of a prediction made by Nostradamus, Acquired Immune Deficiency Syndrome (AIDS) will kill two-thirds of the world's population.

As the quote above indicates, Rajneesh perceives himself as a Savior, comparable (indeed, even superior) to Jesus. The key to understanding his sense of mission is discovered in these anticipated global catastrophes. He is hurriedly attempting to build his "Noah's ark of consciousness" in his followers, before mankind destroys itself. He teaches that "A revolution in human consciousness is no more a luxury, it has become an absolute need as there are only two alternatives—suicide or a quantum leap in consciousness, which Nietzsche called Superman."[18]

When asked if Rajneeshees would survive the predicted nuclear holocaust, Rajneesh replied:

> . . . monkeys took a jump and became human beings, but not all monkeys did. The remaining ones are still monkeys. . . .
>
> I will not say that Rajneeshees will survive the holocaust, but I can say

[16]Ibid., 30–31.
[17]Bhagwan Shree Rajneesh, *Rajneeshism: An Introduction to Bhagwan Shree Rajneesh and his Religion* (Rajneeshpuram, Oregon: Rajneesh Foundation International, 1983), 56–57.
[18]Ibid., 60.

with an absolute guarantee that those who will survive will be the Rajneeshees and the remaining will be monkeys [i.e., humans who did not evolve
into "Superman"] or commit suicide. In fact, *the remaining don't matter*
[author's emphasis].[19]

Since Rajneesh believes he is the only "Awakened One" on the face of the
earth, he also believes he is the only one capable of orchestrating this "quantum
leap in consciousness" to save the race. Therefore, all of "Bhagwan's work is
directed toward creating the circumstances for this change of consciousness to
take place."[20]

Rajneeshpuram, then, can be viewed as a colossal human experiment: the
"enlightened Master" trying to create the conditions and spiritual energy (*Bud-
dhafield*, as Rajneesh calls it) necessary to give birth to a super race. Those who
cannot or will not fit in with this group "don't matter." All that really matters is
that the spiritual aspirations of Bhagwan Shree Rajneesh for mankind be fulfilled.

And what is the spirituality upon which these aspirations are based? Even the
briefest exposure to Rajneesh's teachings makes it explicitly clear that "Rajneeshism" is in every respect hostile to the Christian faith. Consider the following sam-
plings from his discourses:

> You can be a Christ: Why be a Christian?[21]
>
> Let *me* be your death and resurrection.[22]
>
> Nobody is a sinner. Even while you are in the darkest hole of your life,
> you are still divine; you cannot lose your divinity. I tell you, there is no need
> for salvation, it is within you.[23]
>
> . . . disobedience is not a sin, but a part of growth.[24]
>
> God is neither a he nor a she . . . if you say he is a she, I will say he is a
> he and if you say he is a he, I will say he is a she . . . *whatsoever your belief is,
> I'm going to destroy it . . .*[25] [emphasis ours].
>
> If Jesus had a little intelligence and rationality he would not have gone
> [to Jerusalem and the cross]. But then, there was no need [for Him] to
> declare [that He was] the Messiah and Son of God. . . . Those messiahs are
> basically insane. He believed totally that crucifixion is going to prove him
> right, that's why I believe there was a hidden current of suicidal intent. . . .
> If anyone is responsible for the crucifixion, he himself is responsible. He
> asked for it. And no Jewish source or contemporary source says there was
> resurrection. Only the New Testament. It is fictitious. There was no resurrec-
> tion.[26]
>
> The argument the devil gave Eve was that God wants you to remain
> ignorant. . . . He is jealous. And it makes sense, because the Jewish God is
> very jealous. He doesn't want them to become equal. This is not a loving

[19]Ibid., 61.

[20]Ibid., 15.

[21]Videocassette 18C144 (September 2, 1980).

[22]*Discourses on the Sufi Way,* quoted in the *Victor Valley Daily Press* (September 18, 1981): B3.

[23]*Sannyas* (April, 1978): 18.

[24]*Jesus, Buddha: Their Days Are Finished,* videocassettes 18C321 and 18C322 (March 7, 1981).

[25]*He or She? On Beliefs—The Book of the Books VI,* videocassettes 18S133 (April 22, 1980).

[26]Bhagwan Shree Rajneesh in a discourse given to thirty disciples at Rajneeshpuram (November 12,
1984).

father. . . . Knowledge is not a sin . . . I counsel you to eat of the tree of knowledge. . . .[27]

To anyone who takes biblical teaching seriously, the above quotes unmask once and for all the true spirit underlying and driving Rajneesh and his "religion" (1 Timothy 4:1–6; Matthew 24:2, 4–5, 23–24; 7:15).

> . . . every spirit that does not confess Jesus is not from God; and this is the spirit of antichrist, of which you have heard that it is coming, and now it is already in the world (1 John 4:3 NRSV).

It would seem evident that the same spiritual power that spoke through the serpent in the Garden of Eden speaks through Rajneesh freely. He appears to be unreservedly given over to it. The danger that this fact portends for the thousands of sincere seekers of truth who now adoringly sing to Rajneesh, "I place my heart, my heart, in your hand"[28] is a matter demanding serious prayer from the concerned Christian.

The ultimate significance that Rajneesh and his followers attached to their experiment at Rajneeshpuram could potentially have led to a violent confrontation if the government had stepped in to dismantle their dream. And, far from being "centered exactly in the middle of the cyclone," Rajneesh's "ark of consciousness" was fated to capsize in the storm of God's judgment against man's idolatry (e.g., Revelation 16:17–21). Those who naïvely fled to him for refuge instead found themselves swept up in the consequences of his own extreme rebellion and blasphemy.

Sannyasins, and especially those more reachable seekers who are considering but have not yet made a commitment to Rajneesh, need to be alerted to the true antihuman, antichrist nature of his teachings, and be pointed instead to the biblical Jesus, who is as different from Rajneesh as light is from darkness.

Eckart Flother is the only person known to date who, after his conversion to Christ, confronted Rajneesh. His own words are, to say the least, compelling:

> In July, right as I was getting more deeply involved with the ashram, I had a very extraordinary experience. On one of those hot, humid Indian nights filled with mosquitoes, I was sitting in my hotel room and reading Rabi Maharaj's book, *Death of a Guru.* Suddenly I saw a brilliantly shining being standing in the hotel room, and He said to me with a mighty voice, "I want you to become my disciple." I immediately understood that Jesus had called me, yet I really didn't know what to do with it.
>
> I went to Rajneesh and told him what had happened to me. As I was talking to him about this experience, I could feel a kind of very warm energy or light radiating from me and I saw that Rajneesh was very irritated, and even startled as he looked at me. He was unable to speak. At that moment I could see that he was not a master like Jesus Christ, as he claims. It was at this time I decided to become a disciple of Jesus.[29]

Flother left Rajneeshism and today devotes considerable time to helping people escape from the system that imprisoned him both spiritually and mentally.

---

[27]Ibid.
[28]Dietrich, "Conflict Over Rajneeshpuram," B3.
[29]Vol. 5, No. 1, Spring 1982, *Forward* magazine.

How to Reach the Sannyasins for Christ

Editor: *In seeking to communicate with sannyasins from the Christian standpoint, there is the obvious difficulty of their not wanting to use their minds, not wanting to think objectively about what they are experiencing. The more they have progressed within the movement, the more difficult this becomes. Are there any means of approaching them in which one can get them to think critically about what they are experiencing and to look objectively at what Rajneesh is doing to them and to others?*

Eckart Flother: I found by working with people who wanted to get out that any logical or rational argument does not help at first.

The approach that I have found useful is to create an emotional situation, such as helping them to recall a childhood event in the family, or a particular time or place where they felt they needed privacy (which they don't have in the ashram), or an incidence in which they helped others. I have advised parents and friends to re-create a situation where they showed charity to others. Reliving this normally creates an emotional outburst, a flashback of a previous experience, which is called "snapping back."

After this I have found that I can talk to them on a rational level again, and most of them shake their heads as if to say, "I must have been in a long, long dream."

So one has to first create a situation where they can feel something very deeply that they felt before joining the movement, in order to help them to go back and become whole again. Then let them ask questions, because normally they say, "Where am I? What was happening?" and they have many questions. Then one can come with a message.

The best approach is not to criticize at first what Rajneesh is doing, but to go through the differences between his teaching and that of Jesus Christ, point by point, and show the ways in which the teachings of both cope with reality. In this way one can help people make up their minds by themselves, and not impose a certain belief system on them.

Editor: *So you find criticizing Rajneesh or coming against his philosophy in a direct manner is not effective?*

Eckart Flother: Not in the first attempt, because one has to realize that Rajneesh is, in effect, the foundation of their lives, and his belief system is their structure of reference. So if one starts stripping his foundation out from under them, it could be considered dangerous, and no sannyasin would be likely to go for it.

To criticize Rajneesh and his system can be left to the man or woman who comes out, because he or she will find out sooner or later what has happened. If this critical attitude is not appearing two or three weeks after the person has left the movement, it will be important to initiate criticism, but not at first.

Editor: *What are the needs of an individual coming out of involvement with this cult?*

Eckart Flother: It is very important that the family and friends create a very strong and loving support system. It is important that somebody who has been with Rajneesh not only feels supported, loved, and wanted by family and friends, but feels *needed* as well. They need to feel that they have not only been missing something, but that *they* have been missed.

A second important point I've found is that one of the reasons people leave their families and join Rajneesh is because their parents and friends very often pretended that everything was all right, and nobody had a problem. So parents, family members, and friends must share their problems in dealing with life, and their struggles in coping with reality, to show that they are human too. It is important that somebody who comes out realizes that to be human means to be imperfect. It means to have problems and not always know how to resolve them.

Above all, not only the sannyasins, but also their families and friends, must realize that our problems can only be ultimately resolved through a personal relationship with Jesus Christ. He has the answers that we so often lack.

ISKCON (Hare Krishnas)

The second major Hindu sect is the International Society for Krishna Consciousness, or ISKCON, a modern school of Vishnu Hinduism that developed from the fifteenth-century teachings of a man named Chaitanya, who instituted worship of Vishnu as God, against the prevailing local worship of Shiva. Chaitanya taught that Krishna was the supreme personality of the Godhead.

ISKCON itself began in the 1960s in New York City, founded by the Vishnu yogi His Divine Grace Abhay Charan De Bhaktivedanta Swami Prabhupada, born in Calcutta, India, in 1896. ~It was officially incorporated in July 1966. Shortly afterward, Prabhupada traveled to San Francisco and found a ready audience of enthusiastic followers among the hippies of Haight-Ashbury.~ Hare Krishnas, the followers of ISKCON, are well known today in America for their fund-raising activities through public solicitation, their public *sankirtanas*, or spiritual chanting, their community vegetarian "feasts," and their often public ceremonies honoring their idols. ~One of the most well-known such ceremonies takes place annually on the beach west of Los Angeles and involves elaborate feasting, a parade as the devotees take their idols to the ocean for "spiritual" bathing, and a mini-festival to which thousands of Southern Californians flock as though it were a country carnival.~

Prabhupada received his "calling" to preach the gospel of Krishna to English-speaking people in 1922, from his spiritual master, Srila Bhaktisiddhanta Sarasvati Thakur. However, it was not until 1936, on the death of his master, that he finally assumed the responsibility. As his following grew, he was elevated to a higher spiritual position; in 1950 he took the order of *sannyasa*, which includes the full renunciation of material life.

The ISKCON magazine, *Back to Godhead,* began publication in 1944, and continues today as the best-known publication of the ISKCON publishing company, the Bhaktivedanta Book Trust.

Prabhupada died in 1977. At the time of his death, there were 108 ISKCON centers worldwide, fifty-one volumes of literature published in English, and more than five thousand full-time communal members, or disciples. His most well-known book is *Bhagavad-Gita As It Is.*

After the death of Prabhupada, inner turmoil and public suspicions threatened to dismantle the international organization. ISKCON went through a series of leadership changes, resulting from inner power struggles, competing claims of succession to Prabhupada, the resignation and/or defection of numerous leaders, the indictment and eventual conviction of various leaders for crimes ranging from tax evasion through drug dealing to murder, and charges by family members of false recruitment and deliberate concealment of underage converts from their parents and authorities.

Once the dust settled, the current leadership structure was instituted. ISKCON is led by a Governing Body Commission, which consists of thirty top leaders worldwide. Day to day operations are handled by the various GBC members in their respective areas of authority, and general policy changes are decided upon during the annual GBC meeting, in Mayapur.

ISKCON places of worship (called temples), preaching centers, housing complexes, and other operations work independently of one another, but under the direction of the area GBC member. A Temple President runs each temple, assisted by a Treasurer, Secretary, and Temple Commander. In areas where there are not sufficient numbers of full-time practicing initiated devotees for a temple, there might be a preaching center or a *nama-hatta* center servicing the interested but not-yet-initiated community. "All temples, preaching centers, *nama-hatta* centers, restaurants, shops, and so on, must be recognized by ISKCON before they may use the trademarked names of ISKCON, such as 'ISKCON,' 'The Hare Krishna Movement,' 'Govinda's,' and so on."

ISKCON Beliefs

God. Although the bulk of Hindu scripture is pantheistic (everything is a part of God), portions of the Hindu scripture, notably the Bhagavad-Gita, are basically monotheistic presentations of Hinduism. Hinduism, in seeking to be a synthesis of a variety of Indian thought and belief, contains within its vast scriptural tradition a variety of beliefs about God, even though those beliefs may contradict one another. Since the Bhagavad-Gita, which implies a form of monotheism, is the most sacred scripture to ISKCON, we find that the ISKCON belief in God is essentially monotheistic, and Krishna is said to be the supreme personality of the Godhead. Any incarnation of the one God is an incarnation of Krishna: "ALL the lists of the incarnations of Godhead are either plenary expansions or parts of the plenary expansions of the Lord, but Lord Sri Krsna is the original Personality of Godhead Himself."[30]

Christ. To ISKCON, Jesus Christ is Krishna's Son, but in a position no more unique to God than any other man could strive to attain. To the Hare Krishna, then, Jesus Christ is not the unique Son of God, God manifest in the flesh. He is not an incarnation of Krishna.

Salvation. Salvation in ISKCON is obtained by removing one's karmic debt through devotion to Krishna and right actions through multiple incarnations: "All these performers who know the meaning of sacrifice become cleansed of sinful reactions, and, having tasted the nectar of the remnants of such sacrifices, they go to the supreme eternal atmosphere."[31] ISKCON also says, "From the body of any person who claps and dances before the Deity, showing manifestations of

---

[30]Siddha Swarup Ananda Goswam, *Jesus Loves KRSNA* (Los Angeles: Vedic Christian Committee and Life Force, Krsan Yoga Viewpoint, 1975): 14.
[31]A. C. Bhaktivedanta Swami Prabhupada, *Bhagavad-Gita As It Is* (New York: The Bhaktivedanta Book Trust, 1968), 81.

ecstasy, all the birds of sinful activities fly away upwards."[32] ~ISKCON salvation comes to those initiates who "follow the four regulative principles, chant sixteen rounds of the Hare Krishna *mantra* on beads every day, and follow all the regulated temple programs."[33]~

TM (Transcendental Meditation)

TM is a spiritual practice, or yoga, which was first introduced to the Western world by its founder, Maharishi Mahesh Yogi, as a religious exercise or philosophy. Encountering skepticism from nonreligious Westerners, Maharishi revamped his TM program. In the 1970s he promoted the movement as a scientifically sound, nonreligious psychological exercise designed to relieve stress, to bring peace to the inner man, thereby having a positive effect on society, and to enable the advanced practitioner to participate in astral projection (his soul leaving his body) and levitation.

TM still wears its secular label in its own promotions today, and most Westerners are unaware of its religious presuppositions and nature.

TM Beliefs

God. TM concentrates on those Hindu scriptures that present a pantheistic view of God. Therefore, God in TM is pantheistic, and one's goal is to lose his own personality in the oneness of God. This also, of course, takes away from the unique and separate personality of God: "Being is the living presence of God, the reality of life. It is eternal truth. It is the absolute in eternal freedom."[34]

Jesus Christ. TM ignores Jesus Christ almost entirely, although Maharishi teaches that anyone can become as enlightened as Jesus Christ through the application of TM techniques. It is clear from his neglect of Jesus Christ and from his worldview that he does not consider Jesus Christ to be the unique Son of God, God manifest in the flesh.[35]

Salvation. Salvation in TM is accomplished by realizing that one is in union with the Creative Intelligence: "The answer to every problem is that there is no problem. Let a man perceive this truth and then he is without problems."[36] This realization comes through practicing the meditations of TM: "A huge mountain of sins extending for miles is destroyed by Union brought about through transcendental meditation, without which there is no way out."[37] Salvation is almost a misnomer, since one is not truly a sinner, but just forgetful of his oneness with the divine.

---

[32]A. C. Bhaktivedanta Swami Prabhupada, *The Nectar of Devotion* (New York: The Bhaktivedanta Book Trust, 1970), 75.

[33]Anon., The Structure, 1.

[34]Maharishi Mahesh Yogi, *The Science of Being and the Art of Living* (New York: The New American Library, 1968), 22.

[35]See, for example, Maharishi Mahesh Yogi, *Meditation of Maharishi Mahesh Yogi*, 123–24.

[36]Maharishi Mahesh Yogi, *Maharishi Mahesh Yogi on the Bhagavad-Gita* (New York: Penguin Books, 1967), 257.

[37]Ibid., 299.

Conclusion

There are hundreds of other Eastern groups. Rajneeshism, ISKCON, and TM have served as just three examples of Eastern thought. For further information on Eastern groups and Hinduism in general, the reader is directed to the bibliography.

In conclusion, Hinduism, for all of its diversity and contradictions, is not compatible with Christianity. In all its forms, Hinduism denies the biblical Trinity, the deity of Christ, and the doctrines of the Atonement, sin, and salvation by grace through the sacrifice of Jesus Christ. It replaces resurrection with reincarnation, and both grace and faith with human works. One cannot, then, achieve peace with God through Hinduism or any of its sects. C. S. Lewis wisely observed that at the end of all religious quests one must choose between Hinduism and Christianity; the former absorbs all others and the latter excludes them. Peace with God is not achieved by looking inside oneself but by looking up to Him of whom Moses and the prophets did write—Jesus of Nazareth, the Christ and Son of God.

Commentary

~After Rajneesh was expelled from the United States by the Immigration and Naturalization Service (INS) in 1985, he returned to his religious community in India and continued to rule his followers in the United States through his representatives. Shortly before his death (on January 19, 1990), he repudiated the title "Bhagwan," which means "the embodiment of God," saying it was a "joke." And "the joke is over." Instead, he declared, he was the reincarnation of Buddha and should be addressed as "Rajneesh Gautaman the Buddha." Finally he took the title "Osho Rajneesh," to which he is still referred by his followers, and which is a Buddhist term meaning "on whom the heavens shower flowers." After he "left his body" or died (which his followers attributed to poison from the United States government, but others attributed to AIDS), his financial empire in the United States and his closely controlled communities of American believers largely disintegrated. However, his books, tapes, videos, and teachings are still immensely popular, and many who explore alternative belief systems and practices are still attracted to the chaotic practices of Rajneeshism.~

Recommended Resources

1. Bjornstad, James. *The Transcendental Mirage*. Minneapolis: Bethany House Publishers, 1976.
2. Carlson, Ron, and Ed Decker. *Fast Facts on False Teachings*. Eugene, Ore.: Harvest House, 1994.
3. Copan, Paul. *True for You But Not for Me*. Minneapolis: Bethany House Publishers, 1998.
4. Martin, Walter. *Transcendental Meditation*, audiotape. Walter Martin Ministries. *www.waltermartin.com*.
5. Zacharias, Ravi. *Jesus Among Other Gods*. Nashville: Word, 2000. See also Ravi Zacharias International Ministries. *www.rzim.org*.

Quick Facts About the New Age Cult

- Man is inherently divine. All things are divine.

- All is one and all is God. God is an impersonal consciousness and power.

- Jesus was an enlightened teacher.

- Salvation is accomplished by good works and reincarnation.

- There is no absolute truth. All beliefs are valid.

Chapter 15

The New Age¹ Cult

This is a very difficult section to write, not because the subject is unimportant—it is terribly important—but because so many people, Christian and non-Christian alike, know so little about the evils of New Age thinking.

It is also difficult because almost *thirty-five* years ago I warned of the New Age movement and correctly predicted the growth of the occult. I wish I had been wrong! I wrote articles and chapters in books on the cults of Theosophy, the Unity School of Christianity, Christian Science, Spiritism, Baha'ism, and Rosicrucianism, all of which were spearheads of current New Age teachings.

As founder and director of Zondervan Publishing House's division of Cult Apologetics from 1955 to 1965, and founder and director of Christian Research Institute since 1960,² I urged Christian publishers to commission and distribute books, booklets, pamphlets, and tracts on these cults and the occult, which were even then a growing threat to the church. I have delivered thousands of lectures, crisscrossing America and the world for over *thirty-eight* years trying to get the message across. Sometimes I felt like a frustrated Paul Revere calling out *"The cults are coming, the cults are coming!"* which I'm sure sounded to many like a litany of impending disaster. But so it has proved to be.

Today some 35 to 50 million people are involved in some form of cultic organization throughout America and on foreign mission fields. Almost 60 million dabble in some New Age practice or occultic thinking.³ Over the last 40 years, national magazines, newspapers, and radio and television programs have proclaimed and trumpeted the New Age cult.

This chapter updated and edited by Kevin Rische and Jill Martin Rische.
¹Material for this chapter was excerpted from Walter Martin, *The New Age Cults,* (Minneapolis: Bethany House Publishers, 1989). Marked sections in this chapter include editorial commentary, cited from Walter Martin, *The Kingdom of the Cults* (Minneapolis: Bethany House Publishers, 1997), 333-
²Walter Martin passed away in 1989.
³Adherents.com, *www.adherents.com/Na_456.html#2782.*

Time magazine has featured the New Age movement (or the world of the occult) in at least two cover stories, one showing Shirley MacLaine and the other, a masked high priest of the church of Satan.

The dusty old occult bookstores and virtually unknown publishers have given way to well advertised sections in B. Dalton's, Waldenbooks, Doubleday, and other major bookstores. Obscure names and titles such as Alice Bailey, Madame Helena Blavatsky, Annie Besant, Moses Hull, the Secret Doctrine, The Plan, Anthroposophy, and the Lucis Trust are familiar in the mass media, even admired in some cases and revered by New Age adherents.

During the late 1950s and into the mid-1960s, the New Age movement—or *cult,* as it is properly designated—was like a great iceberg, nine-tenths below the surface. However, in the 1960s it began to grow bold, surfacing in full force by the 1980s. The church, by and large, did not respond to it until the iceberg had surfaced, and even then we only halfheartedly attacked the problem. But there can be little doubt now that in the wake of the New Age holocaust, we *must* act and we must be prepared to "give an answer to every man that asketh you a reason of the hope that is in you" (1 Peter 3:15).

We have had *enough* of "Just be positive and preach the gospel" or "Don't offend people by defending your Christian faith or criticizing false teachings; God will protect the church." Throughout history, every time the church has failed to defend the faith and expose what is wrong, false doctrines and heretical teachings have plagued us. Only the church militant can become the church triumphant. The challenge is here; the time is now! By divine grace, we still have time to confront and evangelize those in the New Age Cult, for this is the world of occultic darkness and spiritual danger beyond belief.

The World of the Occult and the New Age

The turbulent '60s provided the perfect atmosphere for the rebirth of what we now recognize as the New Age movement or the New Age Cult. ~The word *occult* (derived from the Latin) basically means "hidden/secret" things. The term is used to describe practices such as astrology, numerology, witchcraft, crystal gazing, necromancy (communication with the dead), magic, and palm reading, which, according to the Bible, are forbidden to man and cursed by God (Leviticus 20:6; Deuteronomy 18:9–11; Acts 19:19). These satanically energized methods of obtaining otherwise unobtainable knowledge comprise the very heart and soul of the New Age movement, because they are the primary means through which New Age teachings are proclaimed. They may have modern-sounding names (e.g., astral projection, psychometry, radiance therapy, channeling), but they are the same practices the church of Jesus Christ has been standing against for more than nineteen centuries.~ The neoorthodox theologian Nels Ferre correctly predicted the influx of Eastern and Indian philosophy and theology that characterized the '60s, and concluded that the imported ideas would be a major challenge to historic Christianity.

The great English apologist and writer C. S. Lewis saw the battle lines clearly drawn. He noted that in the final conflict between religions, Hinduism and Christianity would offer the only viable options, because Hinduism absorbs all religious systems, and Christianity excludes all others, maintaining the supremacy of the claims of Jesus Christ.

New Age Roots

To understand the New Age movement, it is necessary that we recognize its ancient roots in the occult. The Bible forbids occultic practices, stating that they draw on satanic power. It describes several different dimensions or realms of reality, such as heaven, hell, and the visible universe. And there is still another dimension that commands our attention. In Ephesians 2 and 6, the apostle Paul speaks of this dimension as the realm of "the prince of the power of the air, the spirit that now worketh in the children of disobedience" (Ephesians 2:2). He declares that the Christian is engaged in spiritual combat against the forces that dominate that realm. In Paul's words, "Our struggle is not against flesh and blood, but against the rulers, against the authorities, against the powers of this dark world and against the spiritual forces of evil in the heavenly realms" (Ephesians 6:12 NIV). The apostle goes to great lengths in his writings to warn us against "the devil's schemes" (Ephesians 6:11 NIV), echoing the words of Moses to the Israelites in the Old Testament. Moses communicated God's extreme displeasure with the inhabitants of the land of Canaan, who practiced abominable things and were, in effect, Satan worshipers:

> When you enter the land the Lord your God is giving you, do not learn to imitate the detestable ways of the nations there. Let no one be found among you who sacrifices his son or daughter in the fire, who practices divination or sorcery, interprets omens, engages in witchcraft, or casts spells, or who is a medium or spiritist or who consults the dead. Anyone who does these things is detestable to the Lord, and because of these detestable practices the Lord your God will drive out those nations before you. You must be blameless before the Lord your God. The nations you will dispossess listen to those who practice sorcery or divination. But as for you, the Lord your God has not permitted you to do so. (Deuteronomy 18:9–14 NIV)

This veritable glossary of the occult warned Israel of impending wrath if they followed in the footsteps of the inhabitants of the land that God had chosen to give them.

The occult might be called a substitute faith that is found throughout the history of world religions—including the Hebrews themselves, as seen in their esoteric and occultic book *The Kabala*. The Bible speaks repeatedly against all occultic practices, giving special attention to astrologers (Isaiah 47) and those who were called "sorcerers" or "magicians," as recorded in the book of Daniel.

There can be little doubt after reading 2 Kings 21 that God's judgment did come upon Israel for her failure to obey His commands concerning the occult. King Manassah violated all the prohibitions against the occult, bringing about the exile of the Jews, which eventually led to their repentance and restoration.

The New Age Cult is a revival of this ancient occultism. It holds historical ties to Sumerian, Indian, Egyptian, Chaldean, Babylonian, and Persian religious practices.

The terms "New Age movement" or "New Age Cult" are fresh titles, but, as

Time magazine pointed out, the occult is nothing new: "So here we are in the New Age, a combination of spirituality and superstition, fad and farce, about which the only thing certain is that it is not new."[4]

The Theosophical Connection

For all practical purposes, the New Age Cult can be equated with the transplantation of Hindu philosophy through the Theosophical Society founded by Helena Blavatsky in the latter part of the nineteenth century in the United States. Madame Blavatsky, as she was known, promoted spiritism, seances, and basic Hindu philosophy while manifesting a distinct antagonism toward biblical Christianity.

Marilyn Ferguson, in her book *The Aquarian Conspiracy,* notes that the "Age of Aquarius" occupies a center seat in the arena of New Age thinking, and when coupled with the emphasis of such cults as Christian Science, New Thought, Unitarian Universalism, Rosicrucianism, and Science of Mind, or Religious Science, it becomes a formidable vehicle for New Age thinking.

The theology of the New Age movement assumes an evolutionary process. The world is waiting for more revealers of truth (*avatars*), such as Buddha, Mohammed, Confucius, Zoroaster, Moses, Krishna, and ultimately one designated as the Lord Maitreya, an incarnation of the Buddha, the Enlightened One. The Lord Jesus Christ is relegated to the role of a demi-god or "one of many equally good ways." He's most surely not *the* way, *the* truth, and *the* life, as He taught in John 14:6.

A tremendously significant figure in the history of the development of the New Age thinking is Alice Bailey, who was involved with Madame Blavatsky in the Theosophical Society. She wrote more than twenty books, allegedly influenced by a spirit guide who communicated with her telepathically. Elliot Miller, writing in the Summer 1987 *Christian Research Journal,* made this observation: "In Bailey's *The Externalization of the Hierarchy,* the same book in which the year 1975 is given significance in the Hierarchy's plan, we are also told that 'in 2025, the date in all probability will be set for the first stage of the externalization [bodily appearances] of the Hierarchy' (*EH,* 530). Later on we are told that after these first masters appear, "If these steps prove successful, other and more important re-appearances will be possible, beginning with the return of Christ" (*EH,* 559).

Miller correctly points out that if Bailey's disciples are following her plan, and if Bailey is right about the significance of the year 1975, then the "christ" cannot appear until some time after 2025. In context, 1975 represents only a beginning, a stepping up of preparatory activity for a fifty-year period.

In *Problems of Humanity,* by Alice Bailey, we also find another interesting observation relative to the event that is called "the festival of humanity":

"[The festival of humanity] will be preeminently [the day] on which the divine nature of man will be recognized and his power to express goodwill and establish human rights relations [because of his divinity] will be stressed. On this festival we are told Christ has for nearly 2,000 years represented humanity and has stood before the Hierarchy as the god-man, the leader of his people and the

---

[4]*Time* magazine (Dec. 7, 1987): 62.

eldest in the great family of brothers" (*PH*, 164).

Important as Alice Bailey's writings are, they obviously cannot be held as an infallible guide for New Age evolution. But the Theosophical Society did fuel the emerging New Age movement, and through the activities of Madame Blavatsky and Annie Besant, the society planned for the Lord Maitreya to appear in the person of Mrs. Besant's protégé, Krishna murti. However, Krishna murti declined the honor of Mrs. Besant's anointing due largely to the death of his brother and his subsequent disillusionment with the claims of Theosophy. And so the search and the anticipation continued.

The Christ of the New Age

In 1982 newspapers across the country displayed full-page advertisements, boldly stating, "The world has had enough ... of hunger, injustice, and war. There is an answer to our call for help, a world teacher for all humanity. THE CHRIST IS NOW HERE."

This was sponsored by the Tara Foundation under the leadership of Benjamin Creme, and asked such interesting questions as *Who Is the Christ? What Is He Saying?* and *When Will We See Him?* The ad ended in a call for peace: "Without sharing there can be no justice, without justice there can be no peace, without peace there can be no future."

Three other New Age groups joined the Tara Foundation, but the nebulous ad inevitably failed to attract the kind of attention Creme had anticipated. The "christ" of whom the Tara Foundation was speaking was not the Christ of biblical revelation, but an Indian guru who had flown to England (thus fulfilling Revelation 1:7), and now lives in London. Mr. Creme stated that this christ would meet the press, but the press conference was later postponed.

Mr. Creme, in his book *The Reappearance of the Christ*, ran true to New Age thought when describing the relationship of Jesus Christ to the New Age:

> The christ is not God, he is not coming as God. He is an embodiment of an aspect of God, the love aspect of God. He is the embodied soul of all creation. He embodies the energy which is a consciousness aspect of the Being we call God. . . . He would rather that you didn't pray to him, but to God within you, which is also within him. . . . He said it himself. "The kingdom of God is within you" (*RC*, 135).

Such statements from New Age leaders characterize the movement as pointedly anti-Christian and particularly hostile to the unique claim of deity by the Lord Jesus Christ and confirmed by apostolic witness. In a fact sheet released by the Christian Research Institute dealing with the New Age movement, a report with which I concur, the New Age movement has been described as:

"The most common name used to portray the growing penetration of Eastern and occultic mysticism into Western culture. The words *New Age* refer to the Aquarian Age, which occultists believe to be dawning, bringing with it an era of enlightenment and peace. Encompassed within the New Age movement are various cults that emphasize a mystic experience (including Transcendental Meditation, the Rajneesh cult, Eckankar, the Church Universal and Triumphant, and many others). The followers of various gurus, such as the late swami Muktananda,

Sai Baba, Baba Ram Dass, and Mahareeshi Mahesh Yoga personify the essence of modern New Age leadership. Other groups, such as the "Human Potential Movement" exemplified in Est (now incorporated into Landmark Forum), Lifespring, Silva Mind Control, Summit Workshops, etc., and many (though not all) of the advocates of the various approaches to holistic health, accurately represent the spirit of the New Age."

Though the beliefs and emphases of the various groups and individuals who make up the New Age movement can vary widely, they share a common religious experience and philosophical base. The theological similarity in the midst of diversity is much like the many traditions within historic Christianity that differ on peripheral doctrines and yet share a common experience with the Holy Spirit, resulting from a common faith in Jesus Christ. Members of the New Age movement share a common belief that "all is one," that is, everything that exists together composes one essential reality or substance. This ultimate reality is identified as God, usually seen as an impersonal consciousness and power.

The Divinity of All Mankind

The New Age derives its belief in the inherent divinity of man from this belief in the divinity of all things. Thus the separation of the human race from God, which is obvious to the Christian church, is treated differently by the New Age movement. Whereas historic Christianity believes that man was separated from God by his transgression of God's law, the New Age movement believes that man is separated from God *only* in his own consciousness. He is the victim of a false sense of separate identity that blinds him to his essential unity with God.

Thus the New Age movement advocates various methods of altering the consciousness (Yoga, meditation, chanting, ecstatic dancing, drugs, etc.) as the means of salvation. These enable man to consciously experience his supposed union with God, an experience defined as "enlightenment."

The New Age Cult also heavily emphasizes the ancient Hindu doctrines of *reincarnation* and *Karma*. The law of Karma teaches that whatever a person does, good or bad, will return to him in *exact* proportion in another existence. Since most people are not able to pay off in one lifetime all of the bad Karma that they have accumulated for their bad deeds, they are compelled to return in new incarnations until all of their bad Karma has been balanced by the good Karma they achieve.

The New Age Conspiracy

We can state that the Aquarian Conspiracy, which the New Age writer Marilyn Ferguson describes in her book by that title, actually exists. Many people within the overall New Age movement believe that they can hasten the coming of the age of peace by working together to influence developments in Western culture's political, economic, educational, and religious life.

Among some of these people there are definite efforts underway to promote the development of a united worldwide society. However, we have not found anything to substantiate claims that everyone involved in the New Age movement is a part of this conspiracy. (Many of the New Age cults are exclusive, so it is difficult to imagine their working to enthrone any world ruler besides their own particular leaders.) Nor have we yet found evidence that any specific individual has been selected to occupy the place of world ruler. We have not seen evidence to show that the conspiracy is so highly developed and influential that it is presently in a position to accomplish its goal of a one-world culture.

However, the New Age movement could certainly play a part in the great deception of the tribulation described in various biblical prophecies, and we should definitely keep it under observation. But it would be counterproductive for the body of Christ to respond to this movement with hysteria over a public declaration that the New Age movement is involved in conscious conspiratorial activities that cannot be factually substantiated.

The New Age movement's efforts to infiltrate our society with Eastern mysticism must be resisted, and their activities must be monitored, but it must be done in a sane, biblical manner, in a spirit of "peaceful sobriety."

The rise of the New Age Cult over the last quarter of a century should be a sobering reminder to the Christian church that we cannot rest upon the laurels of past evangelism and pioneer missionary activities. The old maxim is true: "The price of liberty is eternal vigilance."

The Importance of the New Age Movement

The New Age movement is not only important because it has a multibillion-dollar balance sheet, but because it reaches out to multiple millions who are dazzled by celebrities such as Shirley MacLaine, Merv Griffin, Linda Evans, Phylicia Rashad, and Sharon Gless, who all say their concept of reality and religious truth works.

Shirley MacLaine is a prime example of this. In her book *Out on a Limb*, she promotes New Age thinking. She sponsored seminars that have raised millions of dollars to build the New Age showcase center in Baca, Colorado, between 1989 and 1990. It is virtually impossible to turn on talk shows—radio or TV—that do not feature some New Age psychic, astrologer, or guru with the latest word on "spiritual reality." Headlines told us that even Nancy Reagan, wife of the former president of the United States, consulted an astrologer, especially after the assassination attempt on her husband confirmed an astrologer's warning of imminent danger.

The New Age movement is penetrating our educational system as well as some of our state legislatures. It threatens not only the foundation of the Judeo-Christian religion, but challenges fundamental belief in the existence of objective truth. In New Age thinking, truth is perceived *individually,* and it is not uncommon for the New Age believer to say, "That's your truth; this is mine," as if truth like beauty exists only in the eye of the beholder. The threat of the New Age movement cannot be underestimated in our public schools, where children are taught *mantras*, meditation words, and meditation techniques. They are subjected to "values clarification," in which moral, ethical, and spiritual values become purely subjective in nature and not subject to any meanings apart from those assigned by the child. In this jumbled scenario, reality becomes lost in a shuffle of conflicting vocabulary, and the law of the semantic jungle declares pragmatism: "If it works, use it—if it feels good, do it."

It is no wonder that *Time* magazine, quoting several Christian writers, noted:

> Humans are essentially religious creatures and they don't rest until they
> have some sort of answers to the fundamental questions. Rationalism and
> secularism don't answer those questions. But you can see the rise of the New
> Age is a barometer of the disintegration of American culture. Dostoyevsky
> said [that] anything is permissible if there is no God. But anything is also
> permissible if everything is God. There is no way to make any distinction
> between good and evil . . . once you've deified yourself, which is what the
> New Age is all about, there is no higher moral absolute. It's a recipe for
> ethical anarchy . . . it's both messianic and millennial.[5]

Sacrificing Biblical Revelation

The deification of man by the New Age Cult requires the abandonment of
absolute truth, worship at the altar of relativism, and obsession with reincarnation. The movement is a growing threat to Christians and to those who take seriously biblical admonitions, such as

> I have made the earth . . . even my hands have stretched out the heav-
> ens. . . . Thou shalt love the Lord thy God with all thy heart, and with all thy
> soul, and with all thy mind. . . . Thou shalt love thy neighbor as thyself. On
> these two commandments hang all the law and the prophets. (Isaiah 45:12;
> Matthew 22:37–40)

The New Age movement embraces what has been termed "monistic pantheism," all is one and all is God. Since the movement believes man is divine, as
Satan once promised he would be in Eden (Genesis 3:5), the next great event is
the dawn of the millennial kingdom. In the Aquarian era, peace, prosperity, love,
and satisfaction are all within the grasp of those who are willing to exchange
biblical revelation for Hindu speculation and the Prince of Life for the Prince of
Darkness.

There can be little doubt that the Aquarian Conspiracy, the rise of the New
Age Cult, and the Bible have one common denominator: The Bible prophesies
that at the end of the ages, false prophets, christs, and teachers will proliferate,
proclaiming, "Look, here is the Christ!" or "There he is!" (Matthew 24:23 NIV).
In the words of the living Christ, "Today this scripture is fulfilled in your hearing"
(Luke 4:21 NIV).

Ten Key Doctrines of the New Age Movement

We often find ourselves reading someone's interpretation of what the leaders
of the New Age movement say. In this section we will look at ten key doctrines
and present, without interpretation, what New Age writers have said.

God

The late Jane Roberts used to channel a disembodied entity named Seth.
This is a thumbnail sketch of Seth's concept of God:

_____

[5]Ibid., 72.

He is not one individual, but an energy gestalt . . . a psychic pyramid of interrelated, ever-expanding consciousness that creates, simultaneously and instantaneously, universes and individuals that are given—through the gift of personal perspective—duration, psychic comprehension, intelligence, and eternal validity. This absolute, ever-expanding, instantaneous psychic gestalt, which you may call God if you prefer, is so secure in its existence that it can constantly break itself down and rebuild itself. Its energy is so unbelievable that it does indeed form all universes; and because its energy is within and behind all universes, systems, and fields, it is indeed aware of each sparrow that falls, for it is each sparrow that falls.[6]

"In a sense there is no such thing as God, God does not exist. And in another sense, there is nothing else but God—only God exists. . . . All is God. And because all is God, there is no God."[7]

The Trinity

"Eternal Thought is one; in essence it is two—Intelligence and Force; and when they breathe, a child is born; this child is Love.

"And thus the Triune God stands forth, whom men call Father-Mother-Child."[8]

Jesus Christ

People have been led to leave the churches in large numbers because the churches have presented a picture of the Christ impossible for the majority of thinking people today to accept—as the one and only Son of God, sacrificed by His Loving Father to save Humanity from the results of its sins; as a Blood Sacrifice straight out of the old and outworn Jewish Dispensation; as the unique revealer of God's nature, once and forever, never to be enlarged and expanded as man himself grows in awareness and ability to receive other revelations of that Divine nature; and as waiting in some mythical and unattractive Heaven until the end of the world, when He will return in a cloud of glory to the sound of Angels' trumpets, and descending from these clouds, inherit His Kingdom. The majority of thinking people today have rejected this view. . . .[9]

What is the Christ? Within all life there exists a quality, an energy, which has as its basic characteristic irresistible growth, irresistible and inevitable expression of divinity. It is a quality which says that whatever form I am enclosed in, I will not be held a prisoner by that form, but I will transform it into a greater form. I will use all life, all experiences as stepping stones to greater revelations of divinity. The Christ is the basic evolutionary force within creation.[10]

The true birth of the Christ was not the birth of Jesus. Jesus was an individual who himself had to recapitulate certain stages. He built upon the pattern the Buddha had established. . . . He himself had to become

[6]Jane Roberts, *The Seth Material* (Englewood Cliffs, N.J.: Prentice-Hall, 1970), 237–38.
[7]Benjamin Creme, *The Reappearance of the Christ and the Masters of Wisdom* (London: The Tara Press, 1980), 110.
[8]Levi, *The Aquarian Gospel of Jesus the Christ* (Santa Monica, Calif.: DeVorss & Co., 1907), 100.
[9]Creme, *The Reappearance of Christ*, 25.
[10]David Spangler, *Reflections on the Christ* (Moray, Scotland: Findhorn Publications, 1978), 13.

awakened. He had to, in his consciousness, touch this Christ pattern.[11]

Jesus was an ideal Jew, born in Bethlehem of Judea. His mother was a beautiful Jewish girl named Mary. As a child Jesus differed but little from other children only that in past lives he had overcome carnal propensities to such an extent that he could be tempted like others and not yield. . . .

In many respects Jesus was a remarkable child, for by ages of strenuous preparation he was qualified to be an avatar, a saviour of the world, and from childhood he was endowed with superior wisdom and was conscious of the fact that he was competent to lead the raid into the higher ways of spiritual living. . . .

Edward was not always king, and Lincoln was not always president, and Jesus was not always Christ. Jesus won his Christship by a strenuous life.[12]

Jesus: "Men call me Christ, and God has recognized the name; but Christ is not a man. The Christ is universal Love and Love is King. . . .

"This Jesus is but man who has been fitted by temptations overcome, by trials multiform, to be the temple through which the Christ can manifest to men. . . .

"Then hear, you men of Israel, hear! Look not upon the flesh (i.e., the person of Jesus); it is not king. Look to the Christ within who shall be formed in every one of you, as he is formed in me."[13]

Jesus: "You know that all my life was one great drama for the sons of men; a pattern for the sons of men. I live to show the possibilities of man.

"What I have done all men can do, and what I am, all men shall be."[14]

Jesus (claimed to be communicating through the late trance-channel Helen Schucman): "Equals should not be in awe of one another because awe implies inequality. It is therefore an inappropriate reaction to me. . . . There is nothing about me that you cannot attain. I have nothing that does not come from God. The difference between us now is that I have nothing else. This leaves me in a state which is only potential in you.

"No man cometh unto the Father but by me" does not mean that I am in any way separate or different from you except in time, and time does not exist.[15]

The Atonement

Jesus: "In milder forms a parent says, 'This hurts me more than it hurts you,' and feels exonerated in beating a child. Can you believe your Father really thinks this way? It is so essential that all such things be dispelled that we must be sure that nothing of this kind remains in your mind. I was not 'punished' because you were bad. . . .

"God does not believe in retribution. His Mind does not create that way. He does not hold your 'evil' deeds against you. Is it likely that He would hold them against me? . . .

"Sacrifice is a notion totally unknown to God. It arises solely from fear, and frightened people can be vicious. Sacrificing in any way is a violation of

[11]Spangler, *Reflections*, 6.
[12]Levi, *The Aquarian Gospel*, 13–14.
[13]Ibid., 14.
[14]Ibid., 265.
[15]*A Course in Miracles* (Foundation for Inner Peace, 1975), vol. 1, 5.

my injunction that you should be merciful even as your Father in Heaven is merciful."[16]

Jesus: "The crucifixion is nothing more than an extreme example. Its value, like the value of any teaching device, lies solely in the kind of learning it facilitates. . . .

"The message the crucifixion was intended to teach was that it is not necessary to perceive any form of assault in persecution, because you cannot *be* persecuted (i.e., because you are 'God's Son,' and therefore indestructible). If you respond with anger, you must be equating yourself with the destructible, and are therefore regarding yourself insanely."[17]

This is really the true crucifixion. It was not so much hanging Jesus on the physical cross, but it was the entry of the cosmic Christ in the physical, etheric, mental, and emotional energy patterns of the planetary body itself.

From that point onward, the Christ was no longer an educative force standing outside the planet, beckoning evolution forward. It had become a very powerful force operative within the very structure of the planet itself.[18]

Salvation

Jesus: "The real world is achieved when you perceive the basis of forgiveness is quite real and fully justified [i.e., that as 'God's Son' you are really sinless and thus *deserve* forgiveness]. While you regard it as a gift unwarranted, it must uphold the guilt you would 'forgive.' Unjustified forgiveness is attack [i.e., it 'attacks' you by telling you that you are a sinner in spite of your forgiveness]. And this is all the world can ever give. It pardons 'sinners' sometimes, but remains aware that they have sinned. And so they do not merit the forgiveness that it gives.

"This is the false forgiveness which the world employs to keep the sense of sin alive. And recognizing God is just, it seems impossible His pardon could be real. Thus we have a fear of God, the sure result of seeing pardon as unmerited. No one who sees himself as guilty can avoid the fear of God."[19]

Jesus: "How simple is salvation! All it says is what was never true (i.e., sin and its punishment) is not true now, and never will be. The impossible has not occurred, and can have no effects. And that is all."[20]

Today the motive shifts from the concept of personal salvation (which is assumed or taken for granted), and the preparation required is that of working with strength and understanding to bring about right human relations—a broader objective. There we have a motive which is not self-centered but which ranges each individual worker and humanitarian on the side of the spiritual Hierarchy, putting him in touch with all men of goodwill.[21]

---

[16]Ibid., 32–33.
[17]Ibid., 84–85.
[18]Spangler, *Reflections,* 7.
[19]*Course in Miracles,* 594.
[20]Ibid., 600.
[21]Alice A. Bailey, *The Reappearance of the Christ* (New York: Lucis Publishing Company, 1948), 171.

Heaven and Hell and the Last Judgment

Christianity has emphasized immortality but has made eternal happiness dependent upon the acceptance of a theological dogma: Be a true professing Christian and live in a somewhat fatuous heaven or refuse to be an accepting Christian, or a negative professional Christian, and go to an impossible hell—a hell growing out of the theology of the Old Testament and its presentation of a God full of hate and jealousy. Both concepts are today repudiated by all sane, sincere, thinking people. No one of any true reasoning power or with any true belief in a God of love accepts the heaven of the churchmen or has any desire to go there. Still less do they accept the "lake which burneth with fire and brimstone" (Revelation 21:8) or the everlasting torture to which a God of love is supposed to condemn all who do not believe in the theological interpretations of the Middle Ages, of the modern fundamentalists, or of the unreasoning churchmen who seek through doctrine, fear, and threat to keep people in line with the obsolete old teaching.[22]

Jesus: "My brother, man, your thoughts are wrong; your heaven is not far away; and it is not a place of metes and bounds, is not a country to be reached; it is a state of mind.

God never made a heaven for man; he never made a hell; we are creators and we make our own.

"Now, cease to seek for heaven in the sky; just open up the windows of your heart, and, like a flood of light, a heaven will come and bring a boundless joy; then toil will be no cruel task."[23]

Those who believe in a hell and assign themselves to it through their belief can indeed experience one, but certainly in nothing like eternal terms.[24]

Jesus: "The Last Judgment is one of the most threatening ideas in your thinking. This is because you do not understand it. Judgment is not an attribute of God. It was brought into being only after the separation (i.e., man's fall into delusion), when it became one of the many learning devices to be built into the overall plan. . . .

"The Last judgment is generally thought of as a procedure undertaken by God. Actually it will be undertaken by my brothers with my help. It is a final healing rather than a meting out of punishment, however much you may think that punishment is deserved. Punishment is a concept totally opposed to right-mindedness, and the aim of the Last Judgment is to restore right-mindedness to you. The Last judgment might be called a process of right evaluation. It simply means that everyone will finally come to understand what is worthy and what is not. After this, the ability to choose can be directed rationally."[25]

Demonic Powers

It is important to see that Lucifer, as I am using this term, describes an angel, a being, a great and mighty planetary consciousness. It does not

---

[22]Ibid., 146–47.
[23]Levi, *The Aquarian Gospel,* 71.
[24]Jane Roberts, *Seth Speaks* (Englewood Cliffs, N.J.: Prentice-Hall, 1972), 282–83.
[25]*Course in Miracles,* 29–30.

describe that popular thought-form of Satan who seeks to lead man down a path of sin and wrongdoing. That is a human creation, and yet it is a creation that has some validity but represents the collective thought-form of all those negative energies which man has built up and created.

Man is his own Satan just as man is his own salvation. But since the energies of Lucifer go to build up this thought-form, Lucifer, or shall I say a shadow Lucifer, can be identified with this thought-form and in this there is confusion. If one can approach this collective thought-form with love, without fear, then one can go beyond this shadow and see the true angel of light that is there seeking to bring light to man's inner world.[26]

Of course, yes, the forces of evil are part of God. They are not separate from God. Everything is God.[27]

The Second Coming of Christ

In a very real sense, Findhorn (a New Age community in Scotland) represents the Second Coming. Any individual, any center, who so embodies the new that it becomes a magnetic source to draw the new out of the rest of the world, embodies the Second Coming.[28]

In the esoteric tradition, the Christ is not the name of an individual but of an Office in the Hierarchy. The present holder of that office, the Lord Maitreya, has held it for 2,600 years, and manifested in Palestine through His Disciple, Jesus, by the occult method of overshadowing, the most frequent form used for the manifestation of avatars. He has never left the work, but for 2,000 years has waited and planned for the immediate future time, training His disciples, and preparing himself for the awesome task which awaits Him. He has made it known that this time, He himself will come.[29]

Reincarnation

If the goal of right human relations will be taught universally by the Christ, the emphasis of His teaching *must* be laid upon the Law of Rebirth. This is inevitably so, because in the recognition of this law will be found the solution of all the problems of humanity, and the answer to much of human questioning.

This doctrine will be one of the keynotes of the new world religion, as well as the clarifying agent for a better understanding of world affairs. When Christ was here, in person, before ... He told them to "Be ye therefore perfect even as your Father which is in Heaven is perfect" (Matthew 5:48).

This time, He will teach men the method whereby this possibility can become accomplished fact—through the constant return of the incarnating soul to the school of life on Earth, there to undergo the perfection process of which He was the outstanding example. That is the meaning and teaching of reincarnation.[30]

---

[26]Spangler, *Reflections*, 39.
[27]Creme, *The Reappearance of Christ*, 103.
[28]Spangler, *Reflections*, 10.
[29]Creme, *The Reappearance of Christ*, 30.
[30]Bailey, *The Reappearance*, 116–17.

"Whatsoever a man soweth, that shall he also reap" (Galatians 6:7) is a truth which needs reemphasizing. In these words, St. Paul phrases for us the ancient and true teaching of the Law of Cause and Effect, called in the Orient the law of karma.

The immorality of the human soul, and the innate ability of the spiritual, inner man to work out his own salvation under the Law of Rebirth, in response to the Law of Cause and Effect, are the underlying factors governing all human conduct and all human aspiration. These two laws no man can evade. They condition him at all times until he has achieved the desire and the designed perfection and can manifest on earth as a rightly functioning son of God.[31]

The New Age

The Aquarian Age is preeminently a spiritual age, and the spiritual side of the great lessons that Jesus gave to the world may now be comprehended by multitudes of people, for the many are now coming into an advanced stage of spiritual consciousness. . . .[32]

As we enter into the New Age, what we are entering into is a cycle, a period of time, a period of unfoldment when truly humanity is the world initiate, the world saviour, and ultimately it is upon the shoulders of humanity that the future and the translation for the entry into light of this planet rest.

Its meaning as a new age is that for the first time in human history we have a chance to take up a conscious creative recognition of this fact and can begin acting upon it. Up to this time we have moved with evolution. Now comes the time to become the servants of evolution and through our own consciousness to release the light, the love, and the wisdom that will bring our renunciation of spiritual estate (i.e., an attitude of self-sacrifice, to "give up the good in order to get the best") to its fruition in the occult redemption of the world.[33]

Biblical Answers to New Age Teachings

There are many different answers that have been given to New Age teachings, for the church has been on the front lines resisting the occult for almost 2,000 years. It is fair to say that most modern errors are only ancient heresies and doctrines in a different guise, tailor-fitted for the age in which we live.

Therefore, it should not surprise us that the old answers from the accumulated wisdom and theological expertise of the apostles, church fathers, and reformers are the best means of fighting ancient occultism in its modern forms. It is difficult, if not impossible, to improve on what the historic scholarship of the Christian church has to say about the revival of occultism in the New Age Cult.

---

[31]Ibid., 147.
[32]Levi, *The Aquarian Gospel*, 10–11.
[33]Spangler, *Reflections*, 11.

The Personal, Triune God

In New Age theology, the triune God of the Bible cannot be properly described in personal terms. "He is not one individual, but an energy gestalt."[34] God is seen as an impersonal energy field whose only real personal structure is the sum of *its* parts. Both Judaism and Christianity abominate this essentially Hindu concept, affirming an unshakable monotheism—a personal, benevolent, and loving Deity, who is immanent within His creation, and yet transcends it by infinity because He is its Creator.

The greatest authorities on the nature and identity of God are His Son and His Word. Jesus Christ is the living Word of God, and the Bible is the written Word of God. Both testify that the highest of all truths is the unity of Deity. The great commandment is this: "Hear, O Israel: The Lord our God, the Lord is one" (Deuteronomy 6:4; Mark 12:29 NIV).

Christian scholars down through the centuries have recognized the fact that if Jesus Christ does not know God's nature, and someone else claims that he does, it is readily apparent that the challenger has placed himself above Christ. New Age gurus and avatars make this claim. The Christian must respond by reviewing the superiority of the life and influence of Jesus Christ upon this world, a world whose very calendar is dated by His birth.

That the God of the Bible is a personal Being, that He designates himself as Creator of the universe, and that the biblical view of Creation is scientifically preferable to all versions cited by New Age leaders, is clear evidence. The view of the world held by pagan sources upon which the New Age must draw fails all scientific criteria.

The characters and the attributes of the Creator are detailed in the Old and the New Testaments, and they bear repeating.

In the third chapter of Exodus, Moses encountered God in the burning bush experience, and God identified himself as a personal being, saying, "I am the God of thy father, the God of Abraham, the God of Isaac, and the God of Jacob. . . . I AM THAT I AM" (Exodus 3:6, 14).

When Moses persisted in asking questions such as "When I return to the land of Egypt, whom shall I say has sent me?" God responded by saying, "Thus shalt thou say unto the children of Israel, I AM hath sent me unto you" (Exodus 3:14).

Jewish scholars have properly translated this as "the Eternal," since God affirmed, "This is my name for ever, and this is my memorial to all generations" (Exodus 3:15).

Contrary to what the New Age Cult declares, God is a personal spirit (John 4:24). He has told us, "I am the Almighty God; walk before me, and be thou perfect" (Genesis 17:1).

This eternal God revealed himself in the Bible as the Father, the Son, and the Holy Spirit (Matthew 28:19).

The God of creation has reflective memory: "For I know the thoughts that I think toward you, saith the Lord. . . ." (Jeremiah 29:11).

He affirms His uniqueness: "I am the Lord: that is my name: and my glory will I not give to another" (Isaiah 42:8).

---

[34]Roberts, *The Seth Material*, 237.

The knowledge possessed by this all-powerful being is declared to be without limitation: "God . . . knoweth all things" (1 John 3:20).

He possesses a will (Romans 12:2) to which even His Son is subject: "Lo, I come . . . to do thy will, O God" (Hebrews 10:7).

Far from the triune God being "Father-Mother-Child" as the New Age movement maintains, the personal living God proclaims, "I am the first, and I am the last; and beside me there is no God" (Isaiah 44:6).

God the Creator loves us; God the Creator remembers us and will tolerate no interference with His decrees. As the Lord Jesus said, "Thy kingdom come, Thy will be done in earth, as it is in heaven" (Matthew 6:10).

The God of the Bible is also the judge of the universe. Ezekiel writes, "Therefore thus saith the Lord God unto them; Behold, I, even I, will judge . . ." (Ezekiel 34:20; Acts 17:31).

The apostle Paul draws our attention to the fact that we must all appear before the judgment seat of Christ (2 Corinthians 5:10), and that all kingdoms will come under the absolute control of His kingdom, and His reign will be everlasting (Revelation 11:15).

These are just some of the descriptions given in Scripture, but they are more than adequate to reveal the sharp contrast that exists between gods fashioned in the image of men or Satan, and "the living God, who is the Savior of all men, especially of those that believe" (1 Timothy 4:10).

Often New Age cultists will say that they reject the biblical concept of God and even the authority of the Scriptures, but their inconsistency surfaces because they persist in quoting Scriptures to buttress their own position. Why quote for proof what you say is untrustworthy? The truth is they find it impossible to function without some foundational reference to the eternal God, and we should not hesitate to cite examples of their use of the Bible as proof of inconsistency and lack of spiritual and scholastic integrity.

Jesus Christ

New Age teaching concerning Jesus Christ, though varied, has basic areas of agreement. No New Age cultist will accept Jesus Christ "as the one and only Son of God sacrificed by His loving Father to save humanity from the results of its sins."[35]

The New Age Cult's attack upon the person of Jesus Christ—and attack is surely what it is—concentrates on Christ's unique claim to deity. The Lord Jesus is indeed proclaimed in the New Testament as "the one and only Son of God" by virtue of the Greek term *monogeneses* (cf. John 1:1, 14, 18; 3:16). The second person of the Trinity does not share His throne with Krishna, Buddha, Mohammed, Zoroaster, or any of the endless assortment of gurus and gods. As the Savior of the world, He bore our sins in His own body upon the cross (1 Peter 2:24), and His miraculous powers have never been duplicated; He is, indeed, unique among the sons of men.

In answer to those who challenged His identity and authority during His earthly ministry, the Lord Jesus stated, "Even though you do not believe me, believe the miracles" (John 10:38 NIV).

---

[35]Creme, *The Reappearance of the Christ,* 25.

He let the facts speak for themselves. To a questioning John the Baptist in prison, Christ recited the miraculous works He had done. To dispel John's doubt, He said, "Go back and report to John what you hear and see: The blind receive sight, the lame walk, those who have leprosy are cured, the deaf hear, the dead are raised, and the good news is preached to the poor" (Matthew 11:4–5 NIV).

Even today, the verified miracles of Jesus of Nazareth proclaim Him as the Word of God made flesh. New Agers will search in vain for any guru in their history who fed five thousand people with five loaves and two fishes, who in front of countless witnesses healed the sick, cleansed lepers, raised the dead, opened the eyes of the blind and the ears of the deaf, cast out demons, and demonstrated the love of God for the poor in so many wonderful ways. And how many of them have ever walked on water?

There is good reason for the great antipathy toward the historic Christ and biblical revelation in the New Age. Jesus simply defies all their categories and humbles all their works. This He does precisely because He is the unique Son of God. The New Testament record testifies that He received the worship of men (John 20:28), that He is our great God and Savior (Titus 2:13), that He conquered death itself (Matthew 28:1), and with the coming of His Spirit at Pentecost illumined the world as a flaming torch. That flame has spread to the ends of the earth and burns brightly, even now.

The man from Nazareth was not just an extraordinarily good person, prophet, or sage indwelt by the Christ or Cosmic Consciousness, as the New Age proclaims. He is the King of Kings and the Lord of Lords, Creator of all ages (Hebrews 1:1–3), and He remains the Way, the Truth, and the Life. No one comes to the Father but by Him (John 14:6).

The Fallenness of Mankind

It is a cardinal New Age teaching that man is born into this world both good and divine in his nature. Salvation depends upon his looking inward at his spiritual nature and recognizing that he is a god. One New Age writer declares:

> Man as the image of God is already saved with an everlasting salvation. . . . Man is God's image and likeness; whatever is possible to God, is possible to man as God's reflection.[36]

The biblical record constantly reflects the fact that man is a sinner, that he has transgressed the law of God. Jesus Christ recognized this and said, "I am not come to call the righteous, but sinners to repentance" (Matthew 9:13).

The apostle Peter informs us that Christ died for our sins with the purpose of reconciling us, the unjust, to God (1 Peter 3:18). Paul agrees, writing, "All have sinned, and come short of the glory of God. . . . There is none righteous, no, not one" (Romans 3:23, 10).

Sin, a transgression of the law, is described as "all unrighteousness" (1 John 5:17), and Isaiah tells us that it was for our transgressions that Jesus the Messiah suffered and died (Isaiah 53).

The New Age movement denies the biblical doctrine of sin and substitutes reincarnation as the means of atonement, evading the significance of the cross.

---

[36]Mary Baker Eddy, *Miscellaneous Writings*, 183, 261.

But as one New Age writer said, "No one who sees himself as guilty can avoid the fear of God."[37]

It is not that the New Age movement is ignorant of what the Christian church has been talking about and what Jesus Christ did; it is rather that they refuse to "fear God and keep his commandments" (Ecclesiastes 12:13), and have chosen not to "work the works of God" as God prescribed it should be done (John 6).

The doctrine of personal redemption or salvation from sin is the core of Judaism and Christianity, the oldest monotheistic religions. It is no wonder that such conflict is inevitable, given the New Age movement's definition of salvation. The apostle John spoke the final word on this when he wrote, "If we confess our sins, he is faithful and just to forgive us our sins, and to cleanse us from all unrighteousness. If we say that we have not sinned, we make him a liar, and his word is not in us" (1 John 1:9-10).

Judgment, Heaven, and Hell

The problem of evil, judgment for wrongdoing, and reward for righteousness are all dealt with in the New Age movement essentially under the concept of reincarnation. According to the law of Karma, stated in Christian terms, "Whatsoever a man sows, that shall he also reap." New Age teaching eliminates heaven and substitutes Nirvana, the Buddhist idea that all human souls will eventually be absorbed into the great "world soul." Hell is what we reap here in the form of "bad Karma" or punishment for errors committed in our past lives. This is as close as the New Age movement gets to the concept of divine judgment.

The Bible describes the judgment when the Lord Jesus Christ will preside and separate the sheep from the goats, the believers from unbelievers. The believers will enter the kingdom of God with heaven as their home, and the others will enter that realm that Jesus said was "prepared for the devil and his angels since the foundation of the ages." Christ also clearly said, "These shall go away into everlasting punishment: but the righteous into life eternal" (Matthew 25:46).

The Problem of Evil

When discussing the problem of why evil exists and why God allows Satan and demonic powers to have any control in this world, the New Age movement takes a very definite stand:

> It is important to see that Lucifer, as I am using this term, described an angel, a being, a great mighty planetary consciousness. It does not describe the popular thought form of satan who leads man down the path of sin and wrongdoing. . . . Man is his own satan just as man is his own salvation.[38]

In recognizing Lucifer as a "planetary consciousness," New Age writers acknowledge the biblical story of the origin of evil and, probably quite unconsciously, adopt biblical descriptions of Satan.

In New Age theology, Satan becomes the "other dark side of the Force," to put it in the vernacular of George Lucas's *Star Wars*. This "Force" fills the entire universe and sustains it by virtue of the fact that it is one with the universe. Ben-

---

[37] *A Course in Miracles*, vol. 1, 594.
[38] Spangler, *Reflections on the Christ*, 39.

jamin Creme can thus write quite blithely:

> Of course, yes, the forces of evil are part of God. They are not separate from God. Everything is God.[39]

However, the Bible paints quite a different picture of the "Force." The Bible emphatically describes Satan as "the god of this age" (2 Corinthians 4:4 NIV), or in the words of Jesus, "the prince of this world" (John 12:31). He is labeled "a murderer from the beginning" (John 8:44). His titles "son of the morning" (Isaiah 14:12) and "covering cherub" (Ezekiel 28:14) tell us that he fell from a place of great glory and power. After his ejection from heaven, he assumed the title "prince of the power of the air" (Ephesians 2:2), and 2 Corinthians 11:14 says, "Satan himself is transformed into an angel of light."

With his great power and alleged benevolence, he entered the Garden of Eden and, but for divine grace, would have destroyed the creation that God had designed in His own image and likeness.

Because of his evil acts, he will inevitably be defeated by the last Adam, the "Lord from heaven" (1 Corinthians 15:47–49), who is the manifest "seed of the woman" (Genesis 3:15). The New Testament proclaims the Lord Jesus Christ to be this seed who will finally defeat Satan and cast him into the lake of fire (Revelation 20:10).

The New Testament fairly bristles with the activities of a personal Satan, not the empty creation of New Age thinking. It was this personal entity who both tempted the Lord Jesus Christ and resisted Him during His years of earthly ministry (Luke 4).

The Lord Jesus has given the church power over these demons in His name (Luke 9:1). Paul urges us to arm ourselves for spiritual warfare against the prince of darkness. Satan arrays himself as an angel of light so that, if it were possible, he would deceive even the chosen of God. The apostle Paul describes his final deception as the "man of sin . . . who opposeth and exalteth himself above all that is called God . . . so that he as God sitteth in the temple of God, showing himself that he is God" (2 Thessalonians 2:3–4). The thirteenth chapter of the book of Revelation catalogs his persecution of the church during the first part of the tribulation that will test the whole earth, and John shows him broken and defeated eternally with all his followers (Revelation 20).

The New Age movement fails to recognize that the so-called "higher beings" masquerading as divine avatars (messengers), or even as the spirits of the dead, are in reality fallen angels directly controlled by Satan and his avowed enemies of the church of Jesus Christ.

Mahareeshi Mahesh Yoga, in his meditations, speaks of studying the Hindu scriptures and Transcendental Meditation for the purpose of getting in contact with "higher beings or gods" on other planes of spiritual reality.

The words of the Bible return with awesome force: "The things which the Gentiles sacrifice, they sacrifice to devils" (1 Corinthians 10:20) and "For though there be that are *called* gods, whether in heaven or in earth . . . to us there is but one God, the Father, of whom are all things, and we in him; and one Lord Jesus Christ" (1 Corinthians 8:5–6, emphasis added).

---

[39]Creme, *The Reappearance of Christ*, 103.

New Agers employ the tools of the occult (tarot cards, crystals, Ouija boards, mediums or channelers, astrologers, and fortune-tellers) and are in reality seeking after the powers of "the god of this age." We need to remember the old proverb: "He that would sup with Satan had best have a long spoon." Practices such as astral projection—leaving your physical body during sleep to travel to other realms of reality, as taught by some New Age groups (Eckankar, for example)—place the soul in jeopardy and enter that dimension of spiritual darkness ruled by Satan, the enemy of all righteousness (cf. Ephesians 6:11–12).

The occultic prophet Nostradamus predicted that in 1999 a great and powerful world leader would arise, subduing all things to himself. It may well be that the Antichrist will be a figure like Maitreya, who will succeed in consolidating all authority and then reveal himself with "all power and signs and lying wonders" (2 Thessalonians 2:9), deluding the world with his evil charisma.

No matter how all these things may occur, they will come to pass, and behind it all will be those described by the apostle Paul as "false apostles, deceitful workers, transforming themselves into the apostles of Christ. And no marvel; for Satan himself is transformed into an angel of light. Therefore it is no great thing if *his* ministers also be transformed as the ministers of righteousness; whose end shall be according to their works" (2 Corinthians 11:13–15). The New Age Cult fits that description, and only time will reveal the extent of its power.

The Second Coming of Christ

Down through the ages, the doctrine of the resurrection of Jesus Christ has plagued the enemies of Christianity. It has been attacked vigorously in every era, because it is both the cornerstone and capstone of the Christian faith. This doctrine is inextricably bound up with the doctrine of our Lord's second coming to deliver His church from persecution and to punish with flaming fire and everlasting ruination those who "obey not the gospel of our Lord Jesus Christ" (2 Thessalonians 1:6–10).

New Age theology attempts to blunt this cosmic event by either spiritualizing it, connecting it with the appearance of "divine messengers" such as Maitreya, or attempting to point to a specific event as its fulfillment. David Spangler, a respected New Age writer, put it another way: "In a very real sense, Findhorn represents the second coming."[40]

This is perfectly acceptable from the perspective of the New Age worldview, which ignores the historic person of Jesus Christ and the fact that He personally promised, "I will come again, and receive you unto myself; that where I am, there ye may be also" (John 14:3).

The picture of Christ descending from the clouds of heaven as John records in Revelation 1, and Paul in 1 Thessalonians 4, is directly dependent upon the doctrine of the resurrection of Christ. Repeatedly in the New Testament, Christ prophesied His bodily resurrection from the dead, not His reincarnation! (Matthew 20:19; Mark 8:3; 9:31; 10:34).

One of the most powerful passages on this subject, and the only one that describes the nature of the Resurrection, is found in the second chapter of John's gospel. After Christ had cleansed the temple in Jerusalem and the Jews sought a

---

[40]Spangler, *Reflections*, 10.

sign from Him to justify His authority in performing that act, He answered them, " 'Destroy this temple, and I will raise it again in three days.' The Jews replied, 'It has taken forty-six years to build this temple, and you are going to raise it in three days?' But the temple he had spoken of was his *body*" (John 2:19–21 NIV).

Since we may assume that the disciples and apostles of Christ were men like ourselves—capable of rational, logical thought—we can assume that if Jesus did not come back from the dead in His own body in three days, He would have been considered a false prophet by Old Testament standards and worthy of rejection by His followers. It is significant that John 2:22 reminds us that the apostles remembered this statement about raising the temple when Christ rose from the dead and appeared to them with "infallible proofs" (Acts 1:3).

New Agers tend to think that if the Resurrection took place at all, it was a spirit resurrection portending the future reincarnation of the Christ or Cosmic Consciousness. They are in no way prepared to confess Christ's bodily resurrection.

Since New Age writers talk about the spiritual survival of the Christ after the death of His body, the only records that they can turn to are the accounts of His appearances after that event. Considering Luke 24, we must note that Christ said concerning himself that a spirit does not have flesh and bones as He had—and this came in response to the disciples perceiving Him as only a spirit. A rational person must reject the New Age redefinition of the Resurrection on the basis of what the Scriptures show us.

The gospel of John records that Christ appeared to His disciples and the apostles, even presenting *His body* for examination to Thomas the doubter (John 20:24–28), thus confirming the prophecy of John 2 with unimpeachable verification. In a word, Christ refuted all arguments about the nature of His resurrection and the fact of His resurrection by just being there! The apostle Paul tells us in 1 Corinthians 15 that Christ was raised from the dead and "he appeared to more than five hundred of the brothers at the same time, most of whom are still living" (1 Corinthians 15:6 NIV). It is no wonder that Satan and those who are under his captive control (2 Timothy 2:26) fear the resurrection of Jesus Christ. It is the seal of the church's redemption and of Satan's own judgment.

The Age of Aquarius fears above all else the preaching of the gospel of Jesus Christ and the fact of His resurrection. Hindu philosophy and Christian revelation stand face-to-face today on the spiritual battleground of time and eternity; but the battle is the Lord's (1 Samuel 17:47), God's kingdom will come, and His will be done on earth as it is in heaven.

Let us prepare "to give reason for the hope that lies within us"; let us study the Scriptures, our constant source of strength, under the guidance of the Spirit that inspired them, and resist the devil, and he will flee from us. In the words of a great hymn of the church:

> Crown Him the Lord of life,
> who triumphed o'er the grave;
> Who rose victorious to the strife
> for those He came to save.
> His glories now we sing
> who died and rose on high;

Who died eternal life to bring
and lives that death may die.[41]

Christian Confrontation With New Agers

The practical side of learning about New Age occultic and cultic theology
and those who have become its victims is to encounter them with the stark contrast between historic Christian theology and New Age beliefs. But in order to do
this effectively, there are certain steps that must be taken and methods that must
be applied to insure maximum exposure and penetration of Christian evangelism
and apologetics.

The Christian will learn almost immediately that after he witnesses to the
truthfulness of the gospel message, he will have to introduce Christian apologetics, a reasoned defense of the validity of Christian truth.

Though some disagree with the need for the two-pronged approach, I have
been successfully walking the line between evangelism and apologetics for over
thirty-eight years. It is by no means an easy task, but from my own experience and
study, I include the following suggestions. They can be extremely helpful, allowing you to get beyond the basics without the error of becoming a master of the
obvious.

The Preparation of Prayer
The apostle John reminds us, "If we ask any thing according to his will, he
heareth us: and if we know that he hear us, whatsoever we ask, we know that we
have the petitions that we desired of him" (1 John 5:14–15). Since we know this
to be true and that His will is that everyone be saved (2 Peter 3:9), we must pray
before we encounter the person we have been led to confront, continue to pray
while we are speaking with them, and pray more after the confrontation. It must
be specific prayer, calling to mind the promises that God has made, and asking
Him to open the eyes and ears of the soul and mind of that person. We want the
glorious light of the gospel of Christ, who is the image of God, to penetrate what
is most assuredly spiritual and mental darkness. The apostle Paul said,

> But if our gospel be hid, it is hid to them that are lost: in whom the god
> of this world hath blinded the minds of them which believe not, lest the
> light of the glorious gospel of Christ, who is the image of God, should shine
> unto them. (2 Corinthians 4:3–4)

This should not surprise us, because the Scriptures are clear in stating, "The
natural man receiveth not the things of the Spirit of God: for they are foolishness
unto him: neither can he know them, because they are spiritually discerned"
(1 Corinthians 2:14).

We know, then, that if we are praying for God to open the eyes and ears of
their minds and of their spiritual natures, our prayers are in accordance with His
will. We are to plant the seed of scriptural truth just as the proverbial sower did,
ever watering it with prayer, confident that "He which hath begun a good work
in you will perform it until the day of Jesus Christ" (Philippians 1:6).

---

[41]Matthew Bridges, Godfrey Thring, and George J. Elvey, "Crown Him With Many Crowns."

Repeat and Reword

We must cultivate with consistency the spiritual fruit of patience, and learn to state our position at least three times in different words (a dictionary of synonyms is very helpful here). People frequently simply do not "hear" the first time, but need the reinforcement of repetition. Should you find yourself losing patience, simply remember how difficult it was for you to accept the truth of the gospel when you were in the same condition as the person you are talking with. Pray that the Lord would multiply this fruit during your time of encounter.

Communicate Your Love

Whenever possible, communicate your spiritual concern for the person, citing Leviticus 19:18 as your motive, and go beyond the desire to make a statistic out of the person for some local congregation. New Agers are particularly sensitive to sincere love and concern for their well-being. Love demonstrates that concern. Medieval theologians had a saying: "The love of God conquers all things." Remember, the Lord would never have commanded us to love our neighbor as ourself if we did not have the capacity to do so. If you pray for this, it will manifest itself to that person.

Seek Common Ground

Find a common ground from which you can approach the controversial issues—perhaps from his religious background, his family, or certain goals or practices that you have in common with him. You might discuss abortion, ecology, or patriotism. Whatever helps establish an amicable relationship facilitates communication, particularly if it is in the realm of spiritual values.

Define Terminology

Define your terminology in an inoffensive way, and when he is talking about God, love, Jesus Christ, salvation, or reincarnation, ask him to explain what he means. Try to arrive at a dictionary definition rather than a subjective judgment. There is a formidable difference between a dictionary definition and an encyclopedia of subjective comments. We can *communicate* with properly defined words in a context of objective truth, but a "feeling" about what a term means says nothing.

Be sure that you yourself are familiar with definitions, particularly when you get to the special terminology redefined by the cults and occult. These red-flag words can be easily defused with a dictionary reference. This is particularly true when it comes to such subjects as the nature of man, human sin, the problem of evil, and divine judgment or justice. Take care to keep the definitions simple.

Dr. Donald Grey Barnhouse once compared the communication of the gospel to feeding cows. He said, "Get the hay down out of the loft onto the barn floor where the cows can get at it." Keep it as simple as possible. You are not there to impress the person with how much you know or how articulate you can be. You are there to be a representative of the Holy Spirit, whose task it is to "reprove the world of sin, and of righteousness, and of judgment" (John 16:8).

God has not called us to convert the world; God has called us to plant the seeds of the gospel and water them with prayer. It is the task of the Spirit to bring those seeds to life, and He has promised that if we are faithful, He will.

Question, Don't Teach

Do not try to teach a New Ager or cultist, for the moment you don the teacher's garment, he will "tune out" just as he has been programmed to do. When the Lord Jesus Christ was teaching during His earthly ministry, He reasoned with people and consistently asked questions. When they could not answer what He had to say, then He began to teach them. His dialogue was more successful than if He had begun teaching.

People are threatened by others who intimidate them with a professorial attitude that communicates an air of superiority, whether it is real or imagined. However, because our manner may be interpreted as haughtiness, the watchword is caution.

Jesus questioned the Pharisees, the Sadducees, the scribes, the Herodians, and even common men on subjects for which they had no real answers of enduring value. If incarnate Truth was that tactful, we could use a little sanctified tact ourselves. Jesus' encounter with the woman at the well (John 4) was a good illustration of our Lord's techniques, and the Holy Spirit thought it important enough to record so that we might profit from the Lord's knowledge of human nature.

Read the Word

Wherever possible, use your Bible and ask the New Ager to read the specific passages under discussion. I call this technique "falling on the sword." Since the Bible is called the sword of the Spirit (Ephesians 6), we need only position the sword properly as they read, and it will penetrate, even where all of our arguments and reasoning have failed.

The Bible reminds us again and again, "The word of God is not bound" (2 Timothy 2:9), but it is "quick, and powerful, and sharper than any two-edged sword, piercing even to the dividing asunder of soul and spirit, and of the joints and marrow, and is a discerner of the thoughts and intents of the heart" (Hebrews 4:12). You must consistently bring the New Ager back to the authority of what God has said, particularly in regard to the consciousness of personal sin.

Do not attack the New Ager with the sword of the Spirit, but rather permit the Spirit to use *His* instrument to cut through the scar tissue that sin has created on the minds and spirits of unregenerate men. The Spirit is the master teacher and the greatest of all surgeons; let Him do the work. You must simply prepare the patient for surgery.

Avoid Criticism

Avoid attacking New Age cult leaders or founders of specific groups, for even if the New Ager knows that you are correct, he remains true to human nature and defends against what he considers to be unloving criticism. The New Ager is unaware that revealing truth is the most loving thing a person can do, but that truth must be spoken in love, and then only after much work has been done on your part to show that you speak not out of bitterness or an accusatory spirit, but simply from the perspective of historical fact.

Commend

Praise the zeal, dedication, and (wherever possible) the goals of the New Age movement, because its basic nature is both messianic and millennial. The New

Age Cult is seeking the right things, but with the wrong methods and with wrong reasons, sometimes merely because their vision is impaired by sin. Remind them that their quest for an end to poverty, disease, suffering, racial discrimination, inequalities, and economic and political tyranny are things with which Christianity has been concerned for almost two millennia.

Many New Agers are genuinely seeking millennial conditions on the earth. But there will be no kingdom without the King, no love without justice, and no power without control. Point out to them from the Scriptures that those who follow Jesus Christ will inherit all these things as *a gift* from God and that the kingdoms of this world, when they become the kingdoms of our Lord and of His Christ, will reflect many of the values they now profess to hold sacred.

Take time to laud them for their efforts in the area of conservation and concern for the well-being of the planet as well as the creatures that live on it. Impress upon them your concern in these same areas, but use the opportunity to point out that no matter how hard we work, we still live in a world that is suffering from irremediable conditions caused by man's rebellion against his Creator.

Cite a few of the imperfections that demonstrate that fact: war, the oppression of minorities, and the abuse of human rights. These are all reminders of the fact that "all have sinned, and come short of the glory of God" (Romans 3:23).

New Agers are sometimes disarmed by commendations because they have been incorrectly taught to believe that Christianity is so heavenly minded that it is of no earthly good, and that the God of the Bible doesn't care about His creation. Let them see that you understand and that you care. Show that you care because God has shown us His concern in His Word.

Study the New Age

When dealing with New Age thinking, be sure that you can accurately quote New Age leaders, writings, and terms. ~New Agers employ a mixed bag of an almost infinite number of occult practices. There are, however, words and phrases that may serve as warning signs that a particular belief, practice, or group is involved with the New Age movement and incompatible with the Christian faith. These include: Monism, Pantheism, Reincarnation, Karma, Evolution, Personal Transformation, Unlimited Human Potential, Reality Creating, Energy Alignment, Energy Healing, Energy Focusing, Attunement, At-one-ment, Enlightenment, Inner Power, Goddess Within, Mother Earth, Sensory Deprivation, Intuitive Abilities, Near-Death Experiences, Chakras, Gurus, Tarot, Kabbalah, Pyramids, Crystal, Power, Auras, Color Balancing, Psychic Centering, Extraterrestrials, Brotherhood of Light, Higher Consciousness, Cosmic Consciousness, The Christ, Ascended Masters, Spirit Guides, Meditation, Yoga, Guided Imagery, Visualization, Astral Projection, Silver Cord, Inner Light, Out-of-Body Experiences, Mystics, Metaphysical, Holistic Healing, Therapeutic Touch, Biofeedback, Transpersonal Psychology, Hypnotherapy, Paranormal, Parapsychology, Higher Self, Personal Transformation, and Values Clarification.~

If you do not understand or have not read what your opponent is talking about, make it a point to check it out before you check back with him. This will show him that you are consistent and interested in his well-being, and truth as a whole. Be prepared to say, "Well, I haven't seen or read that, but I certainly would like to look into it." Then do so.

Define "Jesus"

Ask the New Age believer if he can explain the difference between the Jesus found in the Bible and the Jesus who appears in New Age literature. Take him to 2 Corinthians 11 and pay particular attention to verses three and four:

> But I am afraid that just as Eve was deceived by the serpent's cunning, .
> your minds may somehow be led astray from your sincere and pure devotion
> to Christ. For if someone comes to you and preaches a Jesus other than the
> Jesus we preached, or if you receive a different spirit from the one you
> received, or a different gospel from the one you accepted, you put up with
> it easily enough. (NIV)

Let him see that the name "Jesus" means nothing unless it is defined within the context of New Testament revelation.

We can say anything we choose about Jesus, but an accurate portrayal of Him requires facts from the source documents, not from someone attempting to "restore" the "historical Jesus" hundreds or almost two thousand years later when, in fact, the only historical Jesus is the Jesus of the New Testament.

It is always helpful to show that the word *Jesus* is defined by the New Age completely differently than the context of history demands. Use the opportunity to exalt the Lord Jesus Christ, not as one of many messengers sent for a specific period in time for a specific set of needs, but rather as the Lord of the ages, *the* way to God, the embodiment of truth, and the incarnation of life itself.

Let the New Ager understand that his view of Christ as merely an avatar, a messenger of God, is inconsistent with what Jesus said of himself and what the church has believed. (At this juncture, John 3:16–17 can be very helpful if you can read it with them.)

Reveal the Weakness of Moral Relativism

By asking questions, show the New Ager how logically flawed it is to allow subjectivism and moral relativism to lead him. Help him understand that he cannot live consistently with these principles. For instance, ask, "If your truth is your truth and my truth is my truth, how can we be certain about anything? Let us say that my truth happens to be that Einstein was wrong in the theory of relativity and the unified field theories, whereas you and objective truth in both mathematics and physics confirm that he was right. Does it make any difference whether the truth is based on facts or subjective feelings? Was Einstein wrong because I think he was wrong?" Relativism produces no truth.

A good method at this juncture is to point out what the great philosopher Mortimer J. Adler of the University of Chicago said concerning subjective "truth." Dr. Adler wisely observed that the Nazis' argument for killing Jews was a position that could not be refuted in a world of relative morality and ethics. Who could condemn Hitler for murdering six million Jews if their extinction was "his truth." To argue that he was wrong, if you are a relativist, is fallacious because your own definition of truth entitles Hitler as much right to his view as you to yours.

But right and wrong are not determined by voice vote or social criteria; they are founded in abiding standards recognized universally as true—rightly designated as "moral absolutes." You can point out to the New Ager that speeding down Broadway in New York City at ninety miles an hour and failing to be influenced by red, yellow, or green traffic lights merely because he believes them to be irrelevant to the goal of reaching his destination on time will allow him to confront the objective truth that his action constitutes reckless driving when the police arrest him.

Show the Bible to Be Reliable

It is important to set forth the historic reliability of the Bible when discussing the concept of absolute truth with New Agers. The Bible must be seen as a guide to truth superior to those with no credentials whatsoever. We can benefit from a study of biblical history and archeology to add credibility to our position. There are many excellent books on these subjects designed for the pastor and the layman.[42]

Reveal the Inconsistency of the New Age Worldview

Point out the underlying differences between Christian and New Age worldviews and show that the Christian worldview is radically more consistent with the world and mankind as we find them.

The worldview of the New Age movement is a monistic pantheistic concept. Monistic pantheism, as noted previously, teaches that all is one and all is divine. It makes no division between God and His creation. This is inconsistent with logic and experience, since billions of people can speak the personal pronoun "I" from the context of their own experience and lives. Each person is different from all the rest of his fellowmen. Mankind cannot even collectively account for the earth, life, or the problem of evil apart from divine revelation.

I was once talking to a New Age talk show host who, when I quoted Descartes' famous proof "I think, therefore I am," said, "Descartes was obviously mistaken. What he should have said is 'I think I think, therefore I think I am.' "

I replied, "It sounds good, but I can refute that in thirty seconds if you don't interrupt me."

He promised, "I won't interrupt you, but you're not gonna *hit* me to prove that I'm here, are you?"

We both laughed, and I assured him that no violence would ensue.

He looked at his wristwatch and said, "Go for it."

"I have been carrying on a conversation with you for about fifteen minutes, have I not?" He looked at me in silence. "If you say that I have not been carrying on a conversation with you, and you have not been carrying on a conversation with me, then one of us is insane and people who talk to people that aren't there are not here very long."

He thought for a moment, then said, "That's a good point, but truth is really as each of us perceives it."

I couldn't resist the argument Dr. Adler had made, so I said, "I'm glad to see that you agree with Adolf Hitler in his destruction of the Jews."

He recoiled in horror, but under the pressure of Dr. Adler's argument admitted vigorously that Hitler was wrong, that his perception was wrong. Yet the host,

---

[42]See particularly *Evidence That Demands a Verdict* by Josh McDowell.

remaining consistent with his philosophy, could find no way to condemn Hitler. He concluded, "I've become illogical in the framework of my own views and must abhor as evil what Hitler did."

The New Age worldview simply doesn't work in the hard, nitty-gritty world of everyday experience. It requires ideal conditions to find a place in the mind of the individual and in the events surrounding his life from day to day. Without this, it disintegrates under the hammer blows of sin and circumstances.

We must never allow ourselves to forget that God has planted three things in the minds of all men according to Romans 1. He has made us conscious of His existence as Creator, and it makes us uncomfortable. We are imbued with a conscience that constantly reveals the choices before us as good or evil. And He has made our spirits aware that since there is not perfect justice in this world, judgment must surely come from another one. Descartes called these "innate ideas," but they are actually imparted spiritual concepts that are part of our creation in the image and likeness of God (Genesis 1:26-27). The words of St. Augustine ring ever true: "Thou hast made us, O Lord, and we are thine, and our souls are restless until they rest in Thee."

Provide Books or Tapes

Refer the New Ager to some good Christian books, tapes, videocassettes, audiocassettes, booklets, or tracts addressing New Age thinking (or you might give him one). If it is possible, find one that you think communicates effectively and fairly, and tell him that you hope he will seriously consider another point of view and pray about it, because God has promised, "You will seek me and find me when you seek me with all your heart" (Jeremiah 29:13 NIV).

A Note of Warning

As we think about encountering or confronting people in the New Age Cult, we ought to remember that Christians sometimes can be influenced and even led astray by New Age thinking. John Weldon and John Ankerberg have written:

> Christians are being influenced by the New Age Movement (NAM) principally because of ignorance of biblical teachings and lack of doctrinal knowledge. Because of America's emphasis on materialism, commitment to Christ as Lord in every area of life is sadly lacking. This brings disastrous results. Unfortunately there are Christians who love "the praise of men more than the praise of God" (John 12:43), who integrate the world's ways with their Christian faith (James 1:27; 1 John 2:15; 4:4), or who are ignorant of the extent of spiritual warfare (Acts 20:28–34; 2 Cor. 4:4; Eph. 6:11–23; 2 Pet. 2:1; 1 John 4:1–3).
>
> These sins of American Christianity open us to false philosophy such as the NAM. There are always some Christians who will actively embrace their culture. Whether they attempt to learn from it intellectually or borrow from it spiritually, or relish the enjoyment of worldly pleasures and pastimes, or attempt some kind of social reform along nominal Christian lines, the result is that their Christian faith becomes diluted or absorbed by an initially appealing but alien culture. This means that to the extent America turns to

the New Age, to some degree there will be Christians who will adopt New Age practices or beliefs.[43]

In dealing with the New Age Cult, we are in reality dealing with spiritual warfare against the forces of darkness, and we are told by God to put on the whole armor of heaven so that we will be able to withstand the forces of Satan (Ephesians 6:11).

There is no substitute in this conflict for knowledge of the Word of God and the proper use of the sword of the Spirit and the shield of faith to deflect all the flaming arrows of the Evil One. The forces arrayed against us are great, and the stakes are high: the souls of millions of people. But the promise of God stands sure; we can "overcome them: because greater is he that is in you, than he that is in the world" (1 John 4:4).

Prepare yourself for spiritual combat, study and show yourself approved by God, a workman who won't need to blush with embarrassment, rightly interpreting the word of truth. And above all, lift the shield of faith declaring, "Jesus Christ is Lord to the glory of God the Father." The Christian church looks to that glorious moment when "the Sun of righteousness [will] arise with healing in his wings" (Malachi 4:2), and the former things of the cursed earth will pass away and God will make all things new.

This is our blessed hope, the appearing of the glory of the great God and of our Savior Jesus Christ—this is the hope of the church. This is the hope of the ages.

Recommended Resources

1. Ankerberg Theological Research Institute. *www.ankerberg.org.*
2. Copan, Paul. *That's Just Your Interpretation: Responding to Skeptics Who Challenge Your Faith.* Grand Rapids, Mich.: Baker Book House, 2001.
3. Martin, Walter. *The World of the Occult,* audiotape. Walter Martin Ministries. *www.waltermartin.com.*
4. Montenegro, Marcia. Christian Answers for the New Age (*CANA*). *www.cana.userworld.com/cana_house.html.*
5. Zacharias, Ravi. *Deliver Us from Evil: Restoring the Soul in a Disintegrating Culture.* Nashville: Word Publishing, 1996.

---

[43]John Ankerberg and John Weldon, *The Facts on the New Age Movement,* 22.

Quick Facts About Islam

- The sovereignty of Allah is paramount: He is the one, true God. Mohammed is his chief prophet.

- There is no original sin. Humans are not predisposed toward sin, but they commit sins.

- Jesus was not the Son of God. He is revered as a spiritual guide.

- Salvation is by the will of God through human obedience to God's law.

- The Qur'an is the perfect Word of Allah.

Chapter 16

Islam—The Message of Muhammad

Preface

~Islam is the second largest religion in the world, next to Christianity. Although Islam is a world religion and not technically a "cult" as defined in this book, it is included in this volume because of its growing presence in the United States and its influence in American religious life. Since September 11, 2001, there has been an unprecedented interest in Islam and worldwide debate about its essence. Islam in America is growing rapidly despite concerns created by the infamous attacks on the World Trade Center and the Pentagon. Unfortunately, most Christians understand very little about Islamic teaching and need to learn more in order to witness effectively to their Muslim neighbors.[1]~

"There is no God but Allah, and Muhammad is the prophet (or messenger) of Allah" states the great *Shahada*, or "confession," which faithful Muslims around the world declare daily. This declaration of faith effectively distinguishes Muslims from every other world religion, including Christianity and Judaism. More than 1,800,000,000 people worldwide claim Allah as their God and Muhammad as their prophet.[2] In this short survey of Islam, we will review its history, discuss its most prominent sects, define the most important terms of this religion, and compare its basic teaching to biblical Christianity. We will also give practical advice for sharing the gospel with a Muslim.

Millions of people embrace the Islamic faith. Entire countries are ruled and dominated by Islamic teachings, practices, and laws. Much of the Western world

---

This chapter revised and updated by Dr. James Beverley, and edited by Kevin Rische and Jill Martin Rische.
[1]Marked sections in this chapter include editorial commentary, cited from Walter Martin, *The Kingdom of the Cults* (Minneapolis: Bethany House Publishers, 1997), 609–31, unless otherwise noted.
[2]Statistics taken from Adherents.com, *www.adherents.com/adh_i.html, 2003.*

is dependent on Islamic nations for a major portion of its petroleum needs. Western towns, universities, and businesses are seeing a larger influx of Muslims now than has ever been seen before. Islam is a religious, social, and political force, and every Christian should be aware of it. Western Christians, especially, need to equip themselves to give an active defense of the biblical faith against the claims of Islam, and to share the Gospel of Jesus Christ, in love, with the followers of Muhammad. Aware of this challenge, let us begin our survey of Islam.

Definitions

Islam, like many religions, has its own vocabulary to describe its beliefs. A quick look at some of the most important religious terms in Islam will provide a basis for further discussion of Islamic history and belief.

Islam,[3] the Arabic term for "submission," is the name of the religion that came out of the revelations and teachings of Muhammad. Jane I. Smith argues,

> In the broadest terms, I believe that . . . while *Islam* originally meant at once the personal relationship between man and God *and* the community of those acknowledging this relationship, it often has come to be used as one *or* the other, with a greatly increased emphasis on the objectified systemization of religious beliefs and practices.[4]

Muslim[5] is the name given to one who adheres to the religion of Islam. *Muslim* is a cognate of *Islam*, and means "one who submits." The Muslim submits to the will of Allah as revealed by Muhammad.

Allah is the Arabic term for God and cannot be translated easily into English. One Muslim writer defined it thus: "The word means the unique God who possesses all the attributes of perfection and beauty in their infinitude. Muslims feel strongly that the English word *God* does not convey the real meaning of the word *Allah*."[6]

Muhammad was an Arab born in the city of Mecca in A.D. 570 (died A.D. 632). He claimed that he was the prophet to restore true religion and the praise of Allah throughout the world, just as Jesus Christ was a prophet in His time for His people. Muhammad means "the one who is praised."

Qur'an (Koran is the older spelling) is Arabic for "the recitation," and refers to the collection of revelations supposedly given by Allah through his archangel to Muhammad and preserved as the Islamic scripture. Muslims believe in the Law of Moses, the Psalms of David, and the Injil, or Gospel of Jesus Christ. However, they believe that those Scriptures were superseded by the scripture given through Muhammad, and that the Bible used by Christians and Jews is a distorted version of those other scriptures. Wherever the

---

[3]Since there is no standardized method of transliterating Arabic script into Roman script, Islamic terms are often spelled in a variety of ways (e.g., Muhammad, Mohammed; Moslem, Muslim, etc.). We have chosen to use the spelling most popular with Muslims who write in English.

[4]Jane I. Smith, *An Historical and Semitic Study of the Term "Islam" as Seen in a Sequence of Qur'an Commentaries* [Harvard Dissertations in Religion] (Missoula, Mont.: Scholars Press for Harvard Theological Review, 1975): 2.

[5]It is incorrect to refer to a Muslim as a "Mohammadan." Muslims have a strong aversion to anything resembling idol worship. If a Muslim would accept the appellation "Mohammadan," he would think that he could be accused of worshiping Mohammed.

[6]Badru D. Kateregga, with David W. Shenk, *Islam and Christianity* (Grand Rapids, Mich.: William B. Eerdmans Publishing Company, 1980), 1.

Bible contradicts Islam, the Muslim says the Bible is incorrect. *Sura* refers to the divisions within the Qur'an, much like the "chapters" in the Bible. The Qur'an contains 114 revelations, each composing one sura or chapter. Apart from the famous first chapter of the Qur'an, the shortest revelations appear first, the longest ones last. The *Hadith,* Arabic for the "collected traditions," is also important in Islamic literature. These are the supposed words and deeds of Muhammad and are used to provide the basis of every aspect of Islamic law and practice.

Caliph is Arabic for "deputy" and refers to the main leaders of Islam, especially the immediate successors of Muhammad.

Ayatollah refers to a spiritual master or leader in Shi'ite Islam.

"Schools"[7] of Islam

Out of the more than one billion Muslims worldwide, by far the greatest number are the members of the Sunnite school. They accept the first four caliphs in direct succession from Muhammad and no others. Ninety percent of the Muslims in the Middle East and most parts of the Muslim world are Sunnis.

The second largest school of Islam is the Shi'ite school. The name Shi'ite refers to those early Muslims who chose to follow Ali, the son-in-law of the prophet, as the prophet's heir to the leadership of Islam. For the Twelver Shi'ites, there followed a line of twelve *Imams,* or spiritual heads,[8] who claimed Ali as an ancestor. Most of them were killed, and the twelfth and final Imam, Muhammad, disappeared as a child in A.D. 878. It is believed that eventually he will miraculously return to his people (as the *Mahdi*) in a manner not altogether unlike the Judeo-Christian Messiah. He is the hidden *Imam* who will bring about a golden age before the end of the world. Although much smaller than the Sunnite school, the Shi'ites gained incredible international attention when the Ayatollah Khomeini, the radical Shia leader, took control of Iran in 1979. Ninety-five percent of Iran's Muslims are Shi'ites, and today Iran is a Shi'ite Islamic republic. Azerbaijan, Bahrain, Iraq, and Yemen also have large numbers of Shi'ites. Shi'ites are especially strong in Iran, Iraq, Afghanistan, and Pakistan.

A third school of Islam is known as the Ishmailites, or Sevener Shi'ites, who hold that Ismail was the final Imam. The billionaire Aga Khan is the current leader of the Ishmailites.[9]

Another Muslim school of note is the Ahmdiyan school, which was founded in the 1800s by Mirza Ghulam Ahmad (1839–1908) of Punjab, India. He claimed to be the Messiah and the very image of Muhammad. He taught that Christ fainted and was revived by medication (an ointment called Marham Esau, "Jesus salve") and traveled to India, where he died in Kashmir. This small group has produced the bulk of Islamic apologetics against Christianity and Judaism over the last forty years. The Ahmdiyans are highly visible on American campuses and practice strong proselytizing techniques on American students.

---

[7]"School" as used here means "school of thought"—comparable to denominations in Christianity.
[8]In Sunni Islam, "imam" refers only to the leader of a congregation.
[9]Caesar E. Farah, *Islam* (New York: Barron's Educational Services, 1994), 185.

The Sufi "school" is the mystical branch of Islam.[10] Sufis have often been rejected by both Sunni and Shiite Islam and declared to be heretical. Some Sufi writings seem to reject the strict unitarian monotheism of traditional Islam for a form of Immanent Pantheism. Rumi is the most famous Sufi poet and was the founder of the Sufi movement famous for the mystic dance of the Whirling Dervish.

A Brief History

~According to Scripture, the ancestors of modern Arabs can be traced back to Shem and are properly known as Semites. Shem's descendant Eber gave rise to two lines: Peleg's line, from which Abraham is descended, and Joktan's line, which contains the names of many Arab groups. However, many Arab tribes trace their ancestry to Ishmael, the firstborn son of Abraham.[11] The word *Arab* refers to nomads or bedouins and may be connected with the word for desert or wilderness.[12] The original meaning expanded to refer to Arabic speakers and those living in Arabia. "Arabness" seems to be inherited through the male, since intermarriage with non-Arab women was common and is still permitted by the Qur'an. The Spanish Umayyad Caliph Abd-er Rahman III (ruled 929–961), who was proud of his ancestry from the former ruling clan of Mecca before Muhammad, was actually only 0.93 percent Arab.[13]

The first recorded extrabiblical mention of Arabs was during the reign of Assyrian king Shalmaneser III (859–824 B.C.). Early Arabian kingdoms include Magan and Hadramaut. Their deities included *'Athtar* the male Venus star, *Ilmuqah* (also known as Hawbas, 'Amm, Anbay, Wadd, Sin, or Mawl) the moon god, and a sun goddess, *Dhāt Ba 'adān* or *Dhāt Himyan*.[14] Among nomadic groups, the

---

[10]Other schools include Wahhabism (a literal, puritanical form of Sunni Islam held by the Saudi rulers), Ibadites (who believe that the Qur'an is created, and are spiritual descendants of the Kharijite "Seceders," who broke away from the main group after Ali compromised with the Caliphate, and thrive in Oman and a few African countries), Qarmatians (a communal, property- and wife-sharing group found mostly in Yemen), and the Khojas or Mawlas of India, Oman, northern Syria, and Zanzibar, who are derived from the infamous, hashish-smoking Assassins. Islam also has its sects, such as the esoteric Druze who are not considered Muslims by orthodox Sunnis and believe in ten Imams, similar to the Shi'ites. They live primarily in Israel and Lebanon. Like the Druze, the Alawites are esoteric and considered outside of Islam by orthodoxy. They claim to be followers of Ali (hence the name) and they believe in reincarnation, that women do not have souls, and that God presented himself as divine emanations through Salman, Muhammad, and Ali. They have a separate holy book (the *Kitab al-Majmu*) and also have Gnostic and even Masonic religious elements. President Hafez Assad of Syria is an Alawite, and they are most populous in Syria, although still a minority. Another group getting some notoriety is the Muslim Brotherhood, or *Ikhwan*, a xenophobic Egyptian fundamentalist group that strongly believes that Islamic civil law, *sharia*, should be the law of the state. Members of this group are known for their terrorist activities, and a member's offshoot was responsible for the death of Egyptian president Anwar El-Sadat (Thomas W. Lippman, *Understanding Islam: An Introduction to the Muslim World* [New York: Mentor Books, 1990], 157–65). Other contemporary groups include the Hezbollah (Party of God) and Hamas, both devoted to the destruction of Israel. (For more, see Farah, 170–87, and John Esposito, *The Islamic Threat* [New York: Oxford University Press, 1993]).

[11]For more information, see Louis Bahjat Hamada, *Understanding the Arab World* (Nashville: Thomas Nelson, 1990), 40–59.

[12]A. K. Irvine, "The Arabs and Ethiopians," in D. J. Wiseman, ed., *Peoples of Old Testament Times* (Oxford University Press, 1973), 289–90.

[13]Cited in Peter Mansfield, *The Arabs* (New York: Penguin Books, 1978), 46.

[14]Irvine, "The Arabs and Ethiopians," 303.

basic ruling unit consisted of an elected leader, or *sheikh*, who had no authoritative powers and was only considered "first among equals," and was usually selected from a powerful "sheikhly" family that was governed by custom or tradition (*sunnah*).[15] Their religion was polytheistic and was related to the paganism of the ancient Semites. The beings it adored were the inhabitants and patrons of single places, living in trees, fountains, and especially in sacred stones. There were some gods in the true sense, transcending in their authority the boundaries of purely tribal cults. The three most important were *Manāt*, *'Uzzā*, and *Allāt*. These three were themselves subordinate to a higher deity, usually called *Allah*.

The religion of the tribes had no real priesthood; the migratory nomads carried their gods with them in a red tent forming a kind of ark of the covenant, which accompanied them to battle. Their religion was not personal but communal. The tribal faith centered around the tribal god, symbolized usually by a stone, sometimes by some other object. It was guarded by the "sheikhly house," which thus gained some religious prestige. God and cult were the badges of tribal identity and the sole ideological expressions of the sense of unity and cohesion of the tribe. Conformity to the tribal cult expressed political loyalty. Apostasy was the equivalent of treason.[16]

The Qur'an mentions these pagan deities in Sura 53:19–20: "Have ye seen *Lat*, and *'Uzzā*, and another, the third (goddess), *Manāt?*"[17] This is followed by an assertion (vv. 21–23) that these goddesses, the daughters of *Allah*, the moon god, according to pre-Islamic Arab theology,[18] are mere human creations that divide God into parts. These deities were popular at Mecca at the time of Muhammad's birth. *Lat*, or *al-Lat* ("the goddess"), was the sun god; *'Uzza*, or *al-'Uzzā* ("the mighty one"), the planet Venus; and *Man'amat*, the god of good fortune. Other gods mentioned in the Qur'an include *Wadd* (another Moon god, mentioned above), *Suw'a*, *Yaghuth*, and *Nasr* (Sura 71:23). Of these gods, al-'Uzza appears to be the supreme deity in Mecca.

It is believed by some scholars that Allah, or al-Ilah ("the god"), can be traced to *Ilāh*, the South Arabian moon god. Henotheism, or the worship of only one god while not denying the existence of other gods, may have existed in pre-Islamic society. The Qur'an speaks of *hanifs*, pre-Islamic Arab monotheists who were neither Christian nor Jewish. Extant evidence shows that *Allah* meant "the (one) God" for the many Christians, Jews, monophysites, and Nestorians who lived throughout the Arabian peninsula.[19] *Monophysitism* is the belief that Christ has a single divine nature that inhabits a fleshly body, which has a different nature from other human bodies, or that the human and divine natures were mixed. It may be traced to Apollinaris (c. 310–390) and Eutychius (c. 378–454) and presently continues in some Armenian, Coptic, Ethiopian, and Syrian Jacobite churches. *Nestorianism* is a heresy that was falsely attributed to Nestorius (d. c. 451), Patriarch of Constantinople; namely, that Christ had two persons and two

[15]Bernard Lewis, *The Arabs in History* (New York: Harper & Row, 1966), 29–30.
[16]Ibid., 30. "Cult" in this sense refers to ritualized worship of supernatural beings and includes ancestor worship, nature worship, and worship of gods or God.
[17]From the translation of A. Yusuf Ali, *The Holy Qur'an: Translation and Commentary* (Brentwood, Md.: Amana Corp., 1983 [1934]), 1445.
[18]See Alfred Guillaume, *Islam* (London: Penguin Books, 1954), 6.
[19]Ibid., 7.

natures. He actually taught that Mary was the *Christotokos* ("Christ-bearer"). Christ possessed a common *prosopoôn* (literally "face," but used here metaphorically for "person," especially for one's innermost being). See Peter Toon, "Nestorianism; Nestorius" in J. D. Douglas, ed., *The New Dictionary of the Christian Church* (Grand Rapids, Mich.: Zondervan, 1978), 699–700.

Muhammad was born in Mecca, near the Middle Western coastal region of Arabia, about A.D. 570, to Abdullah (or Abd Allah), who died two months after he was born, and Aminah, his mother, who died when he was six. Mecca was a large commercial city known for the Ka'aba ("cube"), a building famous for its 360 idols containing images of the moon god *Hubal, al-Lāt, al- 'Uzza* and *Manāt*, and the Black Stone. Muhammad's family was of the relatively poor Hashemite clan of the Quraysh tribe, and it is the patriarch of that tribe, Fihr (known as *qirsh*, or "shark") of the *Kinñah* tribe, who Muslims claim to be a descendant of Ishmael and an inheritor of God's promise to Hagar in Genesis 21:18.[20] After the death of his mother, he was sent to live with his grandfather, Abd-al-Muttalib, who provided a Bedouin foster mother for him, Halimah, and was raised in the desert. After the death of his grandfather when Muhammad was eight, he returned to Mecca to live with his uncle, Abu Talib. At twenty-five, Muhammad married a wealthy forty-year-old widow, Khadijah, after she proposed to him. Muhammad remained with Khadijah for twenty-five years and had two sons, who died in infancy, and four daughters. After Khadijah died in 619 or 620, Muhammad married widow of a disciple and a six-year-old (who moved in with him when she was nine), Ayisha. His seventh wife was his ex-daughter-in-law; by the time of his death he had twelve wives and two concubines (including Maryam, an Egyptian Coptic slave).[21] Interestingly, Sura 4:3 limits the number of wives to four, and in Sura 4:31, marriage to one's daughter-in-law was prohibited. But in Sura 33: 36–40, Muhammad was conveniently given a new revelation from God that ordered Zaid, Muhammad's adopted son, to divorce his wife so Muhammad could marry her by God's command. This is called abrogation, to be discussed later.

According to extra Qur'anic sources, Muhammad's first mystical experience was allegedly being attacked by two men who cut his belly open in search of something. His foster mother thought he was demon-possessed after finding him

---

[20]A divine promise is given regarding Ishmael's descendants in verse 16:10 (also 17:20; 21:13, 18): they are to make a great nation. According to 16:11–12, Ishmael will be "a wild ass of a man," which may mean "unrestrained," but can also mean "lawless," since he will be constantly fighting with all men while "he shall dwell in (or preferably *against* [see Derek Kidner, *Genesis: An Interpretation and Commentary*, Tyndale Old Testament Commentaries (Downer's Grove, Ill.: InterVarsity Press, 1967), 127], or *in defiance of*, Victor P. Hamilton, *The Book of Genesis, Chapters 1–17*, The New International Commentary on the New Testament [Grand Rapids, Mich.: Eerdmans, 1990], 454–545) the presence of his brethren" (v. 12). Ishmael and his mother, Hagar the Egyptian (Genesis 16; 21:9), left Abraham after Sarah found Ishmael to be mocking during or after the feast given for the weaning of Isaac (Genesis 21:9–12). They wandered to Beersheba in southern Canaan (v. 14) and later to Paran in the southern Sinai region (v. 21). His twelve children ruled as princes from Havilah (central or northern Arabia) to Shur (northern Sinai) according to Genesis 25:12–18. Muhammad, according to Muslim historians, is descended from either Nebajoth, Ishmael's firstborn, or Kedar, his second son. Many authorities, however, are dubious of an Ishmaelite ancestry for Muhammad, noting that the issue was first brought up only after Meccan Jews refused to convert to Islam.

[21]Ali Dashti believes that he had sixteen wives, two concubines, and four "lovers" (see *Twenty-Three Years: A Study of the Prophetic Career of Mohammed* [London: George Allen & Unwin, 1985], 120–38).

standing and not having appeared to be the victim of any violence. He later claimed his nonexistent attackers to be angels who cleansed his heart. In A.D. 610 he claimed to have received his first of a series of revelations of the Qur'an from God through the angel Gabriel. His first disciple was his wife, then his cousin Ali, then his slave, and then his friend Abu Bakr. His wife and his uncle, who was his protector, both died in 619 or 620. The following year he was offered protection from powerful families in Yathrib, north of Mecca.

After his uncle Abu Talib died, the leaders of the various Meccan tribes and clans vowed to assassinate him. The angel Gabriel warned him of this, and he and his friend Abu Bakr fled to Yathrib, renamed Medina. This migration is known as the *hijra* and marks the beginning of the Islamic calendar. Yathrib was a town dominated by Jewish groups but was at that time without a stable government, primarily consisting of feuding Arab factions and mediating Jewish tribes. Muhammad soon established the *umma*, a theocracy (or dictatorship) under his authority, and held complete control of the town.

Badr was conquered in 626, and in 627 a Meccan army, ten-thousand-strong, arrived to attack Medina, but Muhammad and his three thousand men had prepared by digging a trench around the city. The Meccans later gave up and turned back. The Medinans retaliated by attacking a Jewish tribe, the Banu Qurayza, for allegedly conspiring with the Meccans, and Muhammad ordered the death of hundreds of Jewish males by beheading them. The women and children of the tribe were sold into slavery. Two other Medinan Jewish tribes, the Banu Qaynuqa and the Banu Nadr, were driven from their homes and had all of their property confiscated. In 628 they conquered another group of Jews at Khaybar, and paid the *jizya*[22] to be left alone. Finally, in 630, Muhammad and his army conquered Mecca. On June 8, 632, Muhammad died.

His successors soon wrested Palestine and Syria away from the Byzantines (629–641), conquered Iraq and Persia (633–643), Egypt (639), Tripoli (644), Toledo in Spain and western India (712), Crete (825), and Sicily (899). In West Africa, Muslims under Almoravid rulers pillaged the capital of Ghana (1076). Nubia, in East Africa, survived, as did a few small Christian nations until the 1500s.

Arab domination of conquered lands did not last forever, and soon many Muslim states declared their independence. In the early 1000s, the Seljuk Turks, who had only recently embraced Islam, began taking over territory previously held by Arab Muslims. By 1055 Tughrul Beg, leader of the Seljuk Turks, took control of Baghdad. Eventually under the Ottoman Turks, who supplanted the Seljuks, Muslims went far into Europe, conquering Serbia (1459), Greece (1461), Bosnia (1463), Herzegovina (1483), Montenegro (1499), parts of Hungary (1526–1547), and Poland (1676). Although there were wars with European countries in the interim, many countries did not regain independence until the 1800s. Many Middle Eastern areas held by the Turks were lost under Napoleon Bonaparte, and later held by the British and French.

Several modern Middle Eastern countries did not come into existence as we know them until the early twentieth century. Iraq became independent in 1921,

---

[22]A special poll tax non-Muslim "People of the Book" paid in order to have legal rights and protection. They were also to be excluded from military service.

Egypt in 1937, Lebanon in 1945, Syria in 1946, Jordan in 1946, and Kuwait in 1961.

Muslim and Non-Muslim Relations

When Muhammad started his new movement, he encouraged nonbelievers to freely consider Islam: Sura 2:256 says, "Let there be no compulsion in religion." Later, however, he seemed to have developed a much harsher attitude, probably in reaction to the rejection of his message. The Qur'an states in Sura 9:5: "Fight and slay the idolaters wherever you find them, and seize them, and besiege them, and lie in wait for them." What may be considered crimes against the state and crimes against God are dealt with in Sura 5:33: "The punishment of those who wage war against God and His Apostle, and strive with might and main for mischief through the land is: execution, or crucifixion, or the cutting off of hands and feet from opposite sides, or exile from the land." Jews and Christians are "People of the Book" (Sura 5:5; 5:19), but that does not mean that Muhammad always had the highest regard for them; in Sura 5:41 Jews are called people "who will listen to any lie" and Christians are enemies (Sura 5:14), and Muslims were not to have Christians and Jews as friends (Sura 5:51).

The Pact of Omar, originally written around 637 by Christians under Caliph Omar I, was essentially rewritten, and most of the religious rights given to Muslims. Christians and Jews agreed not to repair damaged churches or erect new ones, agreed to provide shelter to any Muslim traveler, agreed not to display crosses on churches, agreed not to preach too loudly when a Muslim happened to be present, agreed not to bear arms, and agreed not to adopt any aspect of Muslim culture, among other conditions, in order to receive Muslim protection. Any failure to follow these provisions meant loss of protection and possible persecution. Despite such restrictions, many Christians and Jews became intellectual leaders in Islamic nations, and many held high political positions. However, penalties for not following the strict demands could be quite severe. In 1796 the early American statesman Joel Barlow described conditions in Turkish-controlled Algeria: "The number of mosques . . . is infinite in Algiers. One can look in while passing before the door, but it is forbidden for an Infidel to enter. The penalty for this crime is to become a Muhammadan, to be hanged, or burned alive, depending on whether one is a Christian or a Jew. If it happens to me, through intoxication or some other accident to fall into this death, I shall become a Muhammadan immediately, for I have not enough religion of any kind to make me a martyr."[23]

Christians and Jews under Islamic rule usually fared well, in many cases much better than in Roman Catholic Western Europe. Eastern Christians, such as Theophanes (writing in the early 800s), regarded Islam as a heresy and challenged it as they had challenged Arianism, monophysitism, and monothelitism. The earliest Western Christian contacts with Islam were when the Muslims conquered Spain. By the ninth century, Christians and Jews worked as tax collectors, political ministers, bodyguards, and soldiers. Except for a brief revolt in Toledo

---

[23]Charles Burr Todd, *Life and Letters of Joel Barlow* (New York: Da Capo Press, 1970), 127 (letter dated March 14, 1796).

in 837 by some Christians and Jews, most Spanish Christians regarded Muslims as fellow monotheists who held the Bible in high regard; one priest complained about the large numbers of Spaniards who preferred to study Arabic literature to Scripture. Things changed in the 850s, when Eulogius (d. 859) denounced Islam as a heresy and called Muhammad "the Antichrist" and a false prophet. In Córdova during this time, about fifty Spaniards denounced Islam and were put to death.[24] Although as late as the fourteenth century Islam continued to be seen as a Christian heresy, dialogue and debate were almost nonexistent.[25] Except for Francis of Assisi (1181 or 1182–1226) and Raymond Lull (1235–1315),[26] there were no significant evangelistic missions to Muslims until Henry Martyn spread the gospel in Muslim India in the early 1800s.

From the historical example of the Medinan Jews, to the more recent examples of the 50,000 Greeks and Armenians massacred in 1822, the 10,000 Armenians and Nestorians murdered in 1850, 11,000 Maronites and Syrians in 1860, 15,000 Bulgarians in 1876, 10,000 Armenians in 1894, 325,000 Armenians from 1895 to 1908, 30,000 Armenians in 1909, and 80 percent of the Armenian population (1.5 million) wiped out in 1915 to 1918, religious persecution has been a frequent occurrence under Islam. In the 1980s and '90s, Muslims in North Sudan were either starving or selling into slavery Black Christians and animists in the South. Oppression against non-Muslims in general, but Christians in particular, has also occurred in Saudi Arabia, Pakistan, Libya, Mauritania, Nigeria, and Tanzania. In 1990 it was believed that Mauritania had at least 400,000 slaves. In 1994 Iran began a campaign of persecution against Christians, especially the Assemblies of God.

~Christians have every right to be critical of Islam for the persecution of the church. However, Islam cannot be dismissed simply because of its "dark" moments any more than the Gospel should be denied because of tragic moments in church history, such as the Crusades and the Inquisition. The theology of any religion must be judged separately from the behavior of its participants. Furthermore, it must be admitted that many Christians and *so-called* Christians have committed their share of atrocities: the Crusades, witch burnings, and the Inquisition being prime examples.~

Islamic Beliefs

At first glance, Islamic belief appears to be almost compatible with Christianity and/or Judaism. Often people claim that the Muslims believe in the same God as Christians: "They just don't accept Jesus Christ." However, as we shall see, the Muslim God is not like the Christian God. Islam rejects the biblical doctrines of the Trinity and the deity of Christ.

---

[24]Kenneth Baxter Wolf, "The Earliest Spanish Christian Views of Islam," *Church History*, 55:3 (September 1986).

[25]Dante in his *Divine Comedy*, 28:31–36, refers to Muhammad as a heretic and a "sower of scandal and schism."

[26]Lull was a Spanish missionary and philosopher who sought to win over Jews and Muslims by rational argumentation. He began his missionary work at age forty, and was stoned to death in North Africa on June 30, 1315, after preaching before a crowd in an open market.

God

For the Muslim, Allah is the only true God. There is no such blasphemous thing as the "Trinity." The Muslim God is unapproachable by sinful man, and the Muslim's desire is to submit to the point where he can hold back the judging arm of Allah and inherit eternal life in a heavenly paradise, often pictured in terms of food, wine, and sexual pleasure.

~But Allah is not only a harsh, wrathful god, although the overwhelming impression given by the Qur'an is that he is sovereign, distant, and angry. Muslims also believe he is loving and merciful, as Sura 11:90 says, "Ask forgiveness of your Lord, then repent to him; surely my Lord is All-compassionate, All-loving," and 85:14 says, "He is the All-forgiving, the All-loving." The Qur'an is clear that Allah is compassionate and merciful. But unlike Christians, Muslims do not emphasize a *personal* relationship with God. Scripture tells us that those who trust in Christ and do the Father's will have been redeemed and have been adopted as sons (Romans 8:14–15; Galatians 3:26). We are heirs of God (Galatians 4:7), and the Father deals with us as His children (Matthew 12:47; Mark 3:35; Hebrews 12:5, 7). We can even be called His friends (John 15:13–15; James 2:23). On the other hand, those who deny the Son have the devil for their father (John 8:44).

To Muslims, God has no likeness (Sura 42:11), is transcendent (Sura 4:171), is unknowable (apart from revelation), and is wholly other and totally different. He is neither physical nor spirit. The Bible, contradicting the Qur'an, tells us that we have been created in God's image and likeness (Genesis 1:26–27), and that we have knowledge of God in our hearts (Romans 1:19–20). Moreover, Scripture tells us that God is spirit (John 4:24).

Currently, there are two schools of thought in Islam that offer varying interpretations of who God is. According to the orthodox school, God is said to have a "face, hand, and soul, but it is not legitimate to inquire how, for these belong to his qualities; God has no body."[27] Guillaume adds that in the *Fiqh Akbar*, a creed compiled around the year 1000 and representative of orthodoxy, "Allah is absolute in his decrees of good and evil. He does not resemble his creatures in any respect. He has existed from eternity with his qualities, those belonging to his essence and those pertaining to his activity."[28] The Qur'an is the eternal speech of God, the angel Gabriel to Muhammad. The Qur'an contains terms that attribute qualities to God, and the orthodox Muslim believes that God has attributes, but is not sure what they mean.

Nevertheless, many Muslims believe that God is neither physical nor spirit. God is a totally unique being that has no similarity in any sense to any other being. This view is based on the assumption that to believe otherwise would mean that God somehow shares his attributes and by implication leads to the grave sin of assigning partners to God (called *shirk*) (Sura 4:116; 5:72; 9:31).

The other school consists of "Muslim scholars, many of them thoroughly established in Western centers of learning, who reject the minutiae of traditional Qur'anic commentary, plead for the 'major themes' of the book, and aim to invoke them by intelligent translation of their meaning in the seventh century

---

[27]Guillaume, 135.
[28]Ibid.

A.D. to their relevance today."[29] One example is Fazlur Rahman, who in *Major Themes of the Qur'an* tells us that "the Qur'an is no treatise about God and his nature: His existence, for the Qur'an, is strictly functional."[30] Yet Rahman does find that within the Qur'an it can be shown that God is an organic unity, transcendent, merciful, purposeful, good, and omnipotent. He also allows for metaphors in the Qur'an,[31] something orthodox Islam seems to have historically avoided. To do otherwise might lead to contradiction, such as where one day can equal one thousand years (Sura 32:5) or fifty thousand years (Sura 70:4). He also argues that the laws of nature, including moral laws, can be created and uncreated at will by Allah.[32] This seems to indicate *voluntarism*, that is, it is from the deeds and acts of God that standards are derived. This is opposed to *essentialism*, where standards would be derived from God's nature.

One of the prerogatives of the Qur'an is *abrogation*, a legal term referring to the "destruction or annulling of a former law by an act of the legislative power, by constitutional authority, or by usage."[33] This is taught in three separate places in the Qur'an. Sura 2:100/106 says, "And for whatever verse we abrogate or cast into oblivion, we bring one better or like it"; Sura 13:39 has, "Every term has a Book. God blots out, and he establishes whatsoever he will; and with him is the Mother of all Books"; and Sura 16:101 (A. J. Arberry's translation) says, "And when we exchange a verse in the place of another verse—and God knows very well what He is sending down—they say, 'Thou art a mere forger!' Nay, but the most of them have no knowledge. Say, 'The Holy Spirit [in Islam the angel Gabriel is the Holy Spirit] sent it down from the Lord in truth, and to confirm those who believe, and to be a guidance and good tidings to those who surrender.'"[34] On pages 89 and 90 Rahman argues that abrogation in the Qur'an does not have the legal meaning, but should be understood as "substitution" necessary for progressive revelation. Since substitution means replacing one thing for another for some purpose, why is it necessary if the Qur'an is the eternal speech of God? This seems to indicate that God can change his mind, something vastly different from the biblical God who is unchangeable in his character and essence. If God is the All-knowing, on what basis is there a need to substitute? Jesus said He did not come to destroy the Law, but to fulfill it (Matthew 5:17) and that heaven and earth would pass away before even the smallest jot or tittle would pass away (5:18). Scripture is never abrogated, because God does not change (Malachi 3:6). So despite all arguments to the contrary, if the Qur'an is abrogated, we run into a multitude of theological problems. Here are six:

1. The Qur'an cannot be trusted because it contains "divinely inspired" contradictions. If God has a history of abrogating his own revelation, the "eternal speech of God," how can one be certain that he will not abrogate it again in the future?

2. It may be argued that it cannot be abrogated again in the future, since

---

[29] *The Call of the Minaret* (Maryknoll, N.Y.: Orbis Books, 1985), 22.
[30] *Major Themes of the Qur'an* (Minneapolis: Bibliotheca Islamica, 1980), 1.
[31] Ibid., 66.
[32] Ibid., 13, 78–79.
[33] *Black's Law Dictionary*, abridged 5th ed. (St. Paul, Minn.: West Publishing Co., 1983), 3.
[34] *The Koran Interpreted* (London: George Allen & Unwin, 1955).

Muhammad was "the last prophet." But how do we know that God will not abrogate that and send us more prophets?

3. If God can abrogate his eternal speech, how can we trust him with our eternal soul? Shall we depend on his mercy and compassion? How do we know that he will continue to be as merciful in the future as he has been in the past? How do we even know that he has been merciful in the past since the mercy sections of the Qur'an may themselves actually be substitutions?

4. If God has done any abrogating, as the Qur'an indicates, it does not indicate progressive revelation, which is additive. It indicates a *contradiction* and *annulment,* which subtracts from revelation, since at least some portion of past revelation has been canceled. This would mean that God either did not know how future contingent events would turn out, or that he did but purposefully changed his mind. So the God of Islam is either not All-knowing or is a liar. A third possibility would be that God can *have* the attribute of omniscience and *not have* it at the same time (thereby actualizing a contradiction) by not having a physical or spiritual nature—or any kind of nature![35] Obviously this is absurd, but it does seem to follow from the Qur'anic view of God.

5. If God can abrogate past divine revelation, it seems to indicate intellectual weakness at the very least. It not only causes problems for omniscience, since he did not have sufficient foreknowledge to avoid the need for abrogation, but also for omnipotence (because if he did have sufficient foreknowledge he apparently did not have the power to carry out effective preventive measures), as well as other attributes.

6. If the Muslim God is not consistent, then his creatures have no foundation for morality and ethics. Morality and ethics must either be absolute, invariant, and universal or not absolute, invariant, and universal. There is no third option. If God is not invariant, then the moral/ethical system derived from him would necessarily be inconsistent, and we would essentially be on our own. We would be autonomous (a law unto ourselves), because we lacked that divine absolute standard that exists only in Christianity. If each person had their own moral standard, there could be no legal basis for a society of any kind. This would seem to conflict with the Muslim concept of *sharia.* This would make it not only inherently contradictory, but impossible.~

Jesus Christ

To the Muslim, Jesus Christ is merely one of the many prophets of Allah (Sura 4:171; 5:74). According to Islam, the prophet Muhammad supersedes Jesus Christ. Jesus Christ is not the Son of God or a part of any Trinity (Sura 5:17; 5:116; 19:35).[36] We are told that He was nothing but a slave on whom God showed favor (Sura 43:59); yet elsewhere we are told the Messiah is not a slave (Sura 4:172).

---

[35]For more on this concept, see Alvin Plantinga, *Does God Have a Nature?* (Milwaukee, Wis.: Marquette University Press, 1980), especially 91.

[36]It is possible, as Geoffrey Parrinder argues, that Muhammad was not refuting Christianity but early pseudo-Christian cults. The Islamic "trinity" referred to may be related to the Collyridian heresy previously mentioned. The Nestorians would have agreed that to say "God is Christ" would be misleading, since to them it would imply that *all* of God is Christ. This is the reason they objected to the term *theotokos* ("God bearer"), preferring instead *Christotokos,* or if *theotokos* were to be used, it would be in combination with *anthrotokos* ("man bearer"). It is known that there were many Nestorian missions to Arabia in Muhammad's day.

Jesus Christ did not atone for anyone's sins, although he was himself sinless (Sura 3:46) and is one of those who are near to God (Sura 3:45). Positively, the Qur'an says that Jesus Christ performed miracles (Sura 3:49; 5:110) and was the Messiah (Sura 3:45; 4:157, 171). But Jesus Christ did not die on the cross. Various Muslim traditions say that he either miraculously substituted Judas Iscariot for himself on the cross, or that God miraculously delivered him from the hands of the Romans and Jews before He could be crucified. Most Muslims believe that Jesus Christ was taken bodily into heaven without having died (Sura 4:157). However, Sura 199:33 says He died and would be resurrected.

~It is interesting to compare Jesus and Muhammad according to the Qur'an:

Jesus did miracles (Sura 3:49; 5:110), but Muhammad did not (Sura 13:8: "thou art a warner [of coming divine judgment] only"; also 6:37; 6:109; 17:59 and 17:90–93).

Jesus was sinless (Sura 3:46), but Muhammad sinned and needed forgiveness (Sura 40:55: "Ask forgiveness of thy sin"; 42:5: "Ask forgiveness for those on the Earth"; 47:19: Ask forgiveness for thy sin"; 48:2: "that Allah may forgive thee of thy sin").

Jesus was called "the Messiah" and was even born of a virgin (Sura 3:45–57)! Yet Muhammad is supposed to be the greatest of the prophets.~

Sin and Salvation

The Qur'an teaches that all have sinned: "If God were to take mankind to task for their wrongdoing, he would not leave here one living creature" (Sura 16:61a; see also 42:5), and all were created weak (Sura 4:28). We are even told that Muhammad sinned (Sura 40:55; 47:19; 48:2). Every Muslim who hopes to escape the judgment of Allah must fulfill the works of the Five Pillars of the Faith (Sura 10:109):

1. Recitation of the *Shahada* ("There is no God but Allah, and Muhammad is the prophet of Allah");

2. Five daily prescribed prayers (*Salat* or *Namaz*) in Arabic. These prayers include genuflection and prostration in the direction of the holy city, Mecca;

3. Almsgiving (*Zakat*), which involves the duty to give a certain percentage of one's total income to help others. This is not considered charity but an obligation arising out of the realities of a world where there is poverty, inequality, injustice, and suffering. Generally, performing *zakat* is to be done privately, unless there is a pressing reason for the giving to be made known publicly.

4. Fasting (*Saum* or *Ruzeh*) during the entire month of Ramadan, when Muslims are supposed to fast from all food and drink from sunrise to sunset in atonement for their own sins over the previous year. Muslims are allowed to eat and drink after sunset and some get up before sunrise to eat before the fast begins again.

5. A pilgrimage (*Hajj*) to Mecca, the holy city, at least once in a Muslim's lifetime. The *hajj* takes place after Ramadan. The Muslim pilgrims engage in elaborate rituals both at the famous mosque in Mecca that holds the Kaba and in areas surrounding their most sacred city.

~*Jihad* is sometimes referred to as a sixth pillar of Islam. Since September 11, 2001, there has been constant debate about the meaning of the term. Many

Muslims, and some secular experts on Islam, have tried to say that *jihad* **only** refers to personal spiritual struggle. *Jihad* can and often does mean one's individual efforts to be righteous, but it is often used by Muslims both past and present to refer to actual military struggle or "holy war." Saying that *jihad* is simply spiritual struggle ignores Islamic history and the actions of contemporary Muslims, including militants like Osama bin Laden, who use it to refer to acts of killing in the name of Allah.~

Sharing the Gospel With a Muslim

The three key topics of discussion between a Christian and a Muslim should be the nature of God, the identity and deity of Jesus Christ, and salvation by grace alone apart from works. Christians can share with Muslims that the Christian God transcends man's finitude and sinfulness because He cares about people individually, and He loves individuals. Divine love is a concept often missing from Islam, and yet it is essential to human peace and happiness with God. A powerful witness of Scripture to God's love is John 3;16: "For God so loved the world, that he gave his only begotten Son, that whosoever believeth in him should not perish, but have everlasting life." When told about Jesus, many Muslims will refuse to listen, claiming that our Scriptures are distorted and untrustworthy. The Christian can refer the interested Muslim to the many fine volumes available showing the inerrancy and inspiration of the Bible, both Old and New Testaments. This can provide a foundation for the Christian to present the New Testament teaching that Jesus Christ is truly God and is the only way to salvation (see chapter 4 on Jehovah's Witnesses for a thorough discussion of the deity of Christ).

~A second approach would be to show how the Muslim view of a God who can change the scriptures of Judaism, Christianity, and Islam prevents any system of morality and ethics from ever existing. Such a God is self-contradictory and prevents us from ever knowing anything for certain, especially our salvation. The Christian can also share how the Qur'an holds to a high view of Scripture (Sura 4:47; 4:54), and that believers should check the Qur'an against the Bible (Sura 5:44–49; 10:95). The Muslim may charge that Jews and Christians have mistranslated the Bible, but the Qur'an says that they only *misinterpret* and *disbelieve* it (Sura 3:70–71). According to the Qur'an, only Jews have mistranslated Scripture (Sura 2:75–79; 4:46). Textually, all variations of the Qur'an were destroyed by Caliph Uthman (ruled 646–656), and his version is the only version in existence.

The Old Testament has several extant versions that were around many years before Muhammad was even born, such as the Septuagint, the Syrian Peshitta, and the Targums. The New Testament has at least 9,000 manuscript copies existing before Muhammad, as well as over 36,000 quotations in the writings of the early church Fathers. The Qur'an cites its elegance as evidence for its inspiration (Sura 17:88), but many eloquent books have been written throughout history, from the *Iliad* and the *Odyssey* to *Paradise Lost* and *Moby Dick*. Does their eloquence also make them divine revelation? Obviously eloquence, even if true (and it is debatable that the Qur'an is stylistically elegant), is totally irrelevant.

The evidence clearly shows that the Bible we have is very close to the original and that it has not been tampered with. Moreover, there are multiple discrepancies in the Qur'an as well as many places where it contradicts Scripture. Sura

11:42–43 contradicts Genesis 6–7 by saying that Noah had a son who died in the Flood, and Sura 3:41 contradicts Luke when it says that Zechariah was speechless for three days (Luke 1:18–20). Sura 61:6 claims that Muhammad fulfills prophecy both in the Torah and in the Gospels.

The Qur'an claims to fulfill prophecies in Deuteronomy 18:15–18 and John 14:16. Deuteronomy 18:15–18 is a portion of a speech given by Moses to the Israelites, beginning at Deuteronomy 5:1, in which Moses prophesied that God would raise up a prophet like him from their midst. The meaning of this prophecy is partially explained in verse 34:10: "And there arose not a prophet since in Israel like unto Moses, *whom the Lord knew face to face*" (italics added). Yet the Qur'an was revealed to Muhammad by the angel Gabriel, not directly by God, and Muhammad never claimed to be a descendant of Israel, but of Ishmael. If the Qur'an is to fulfill the Torah and the Gospels as it claims, the Muslim should read Acts 3:22–23, in which Peter speaks of Jesus as the prophet spoken of by Moses.

John 14:16 reports that Jesus said that the Father will give the Helper to His disciples and that He would abide with them forever. Verse 17 adds that He would dwell with them and be in them. The Greek word for "Helper," or more properly "Advocate," *paracletos*, is claimed by Muslim apologists to be *periclutos*, "renowned." Somehow this word, which is not found anywhere in the New Testament, is understood by Muslims to mean "praised one," since the Sura claims that Jesus prophesied that he was sending the "good tidings of the Messenger who comes after me, whose name shall be Ahmad ['Praised One']." To add to their claim, Muslim apologists argue that the verse has been tampered with by Christians (contradicting Sura 2:73–79). But there is not a single manuscript copy that has *periclutos*, nor is there any contextual sense where Muhammad could somehow be fitted into the verse. Muhammad, being human, could not abide with Christ's disciples forever, dwell with them over five hundred years before he was born, nor live in them. If he could, he would be a much greater prophet than he claimed! On the other hand, there is ample evidence to suggest that Sura 61:6 was interpolated after Muhammad's death. W. Montgomery Watt cogently shows, "*It is impossible to prove that any Muslim child was called Ahmad after the Prophet before about the year 125.*"[37]

At any rate, John 14:26 specifically identifies the *paracletos* with the Holy Spirit.[38]

Sometimes the Muslim will argue that the rapid spread of Islam shows the truth of the religion (Sura 41:53), but several empires have spread faster than Islam, such as the empires under Alexander the Great and Genghis Khan. One could also counter that the rapid spread of communism was evidence of its truthfulness. Their argument is simply an appeal to irrelevancy.～

It is important to share the good news that salvation and peace with God do

---

[37] *Early Islam: Collected Articles* (Edinburgh: Edinburgh University Press, 1990), 43–50. Italics his. The year 125 means 125 years after the Hijra, according to the Muslim dating system (ca. A.D. 755. For additional evidence that this is a later insertion, see Parrinder, *Jesus*, 96–100.

[38] For more on the meaning of *paracletos*, see Leon Morris, *The Gospel According to John*, The New International Commentary on the New Testament (Grand Rapids, Mich.: Eerdmans, 1971), 662–66. For more contradictions between the Bible and the Qur'an, see Gleason L. Archer Jr., *A Survey of Old Testament Introduction* (Chicago: Moody Press, 1964), 498–500, as well as the previously mentioned works by Parrinder and Dashti.

not depend on one's own insufficient efforts, but on the grace of God displayed through the atonement of Jesus Christ on the cross. No one can work his way to heaven (or Muslim paradise). The Muslim will agree that Allah could justly choose to bar all men from paradise, since no man is perfect as Allah is perfect. However, *biblical* salvation does not depend on man's imperfections. Biblical salvation depends on the work and love of God. "For by grace are ye saved through faith; and that not of yourselves: it is the gift of God: not of works, lest any man should boast" (Ephesians 2:8–9).

Finally, the Christian should love the Muslim. Muslims have a definite zeal for God. They desire to follow God and express their worship of God through their lives. The Christian should respect the Muslims' sincere intentions and share with them the life-changing Gospel of Jesus Christ. The Christian should also share the fact that he believes God is great. When a Christian can demonstrate the power of the Word of God through the Holy Spirit and use his own life as an example of the joy and peace possible to those who love Jesus Christ, he becomes an effective example to the Muslim of the opportunity to know and worship the true God rather than Muhammad's distorted concepts about God.

The Nation of Islam

~With an estimated one hundred thousand members in the United States,[39] the Nation of Islam is a force to be reckoned with. Spike Lee's 1992 film *Malcolm X* and the many well-publicized speeches of Rev. Louis Farrakhan and Khallid Abdul Muhammad have helped to keep the Nation of Islam in the national spotlight for years. It is influential among African-Americans of all generations, but especially the young. Rappers and rap groups such as Public Enemy and Ice Cube and numerous African-American college and university student publications actively promote many of the beliefs and ideas held by the Nation of Islam.

The Nation [of Islam] derives from a group called the Moorish-American Science Temple in Newark, New Jersey, established in 1913 by B. Timothy Drew (1866–1929). Drew (who changed his name to Noble Drew Ali), a black North Carolinian, claimed to have received a commission from the king of Morocco to spread Islam in the United States, but his version of Islam avoided African ancestral teachings and instead taught that all non-whites are Asians. Christianity is the white Europeans' religion, and Islam is for the Asian, or more specifically, the Moor (black Asians). After Drew died, he was succeeded by John Givens El in Chicago and Wallace D. Fard (or Farad) in Detroit, each claiming to be the reincarnation of Drew. El's followers are known as Moorish Americans and Fard's as Black Muslims of the Nation.

Fard, who changed his name to Wallace Fard Muhammad, claimed to have been born in Mecca in 1877 and to have been trained as a diplomat for the Arabian Kingdom of Hejaz. However, he seems to have worked as a street vendor and amateur magician before becoming a minister of the Nation who promoted black

---

[39]See Adherents.com for more information; also Frank S. Mead and Samuel S. Hill, *Handbook of Denominations in the United States* (Nashville: Abingdon Press, 1990), 61. Others report much lower figures, such as ten to thirty thousand. Members often refuse pollsters' questions and defer to their leaders.

separatism and himself as a Christ figure. He taught that Asians, blacks in particular, were inherently good, and whites were inherently evil. Using the Bible, the
Qur'an, and his own books, he also taught that eventually Asians and whites
would fight it out in the battle of Armageddon.[40]

In the late 1950s and early 1960s the FBI had a misinformation campaign,
which claimed Fard was actually a Caucasian. His real name was Wallace Dodd
Ford, and he was born in Hawaii on February 25, 1891. His parents were the
British Zared Ford and Maori Beatrice Ford of New Zealand. He also had been
released from San Quentin on May 27, 1929, for selling heroin before moving to
the predominantly black section of Chicago and then to Detroit.[41]

Fard left the Nation after being arrested in 1933 and was succeeded by Elijah
Muhammad (Elijah Poole, 1898–1975) in Chicago. Under Fard's leadership the
Nation had grown to receive at least eight thousand members, and under Elijah
Muhammad's leadership the movement went national. With Malcolm X (Malcolm Little, 1929–1965) as Elijah Muhammad's prized speaker for the Nation,
members grew to perhaps 300,000. Membership began to decline after Malcolm
left the Nation, altered his beliefs, became El-hajj Malik El Shabazz, and was
finally murdered. But Elijah Muhammad remained steadfast in his beliefs. Before
and during World War II, he fostered political friendship with the Japanese as a
means to destroy white America before and during World War II. Later in the
1980s, under his successor, the Nation had an alliance with Libya, another country that was considered a political enemy of the United States.

Elijah Muhammad was followed by his son, Warith (Wallace Deen) Muhammad, who changed the group to a form of Islamic orthodoxy. The Nation became
the World Community of Al-Islam in the West (later the American Muslim Mission), and has forsaken the racial separatism, racism, and belief in the divinity of
Wallace Fard. Ministers became imams, and temples became mosques. The belief
that blacks are descendants of the Asian tribe of Shabazz was converted to a belief
that they are Bilalians, that is, they have a spiritual bond with the first Ethiopian
who became Muslim (Bilal). Accordingly, the newspaper of the Nation, *Muhammad Speaks*, became the *Bilalian News* and later the *Muslim Journal.* Voting is now
encouraged, and strict dress codes relaxed.[42] To account for his father's teachings, Warith Muhammad says they need to be understood metaphorically.

In 1977 the Honorable Louis Abdul Farrakhan (b.1933) broke away from the
movement to retain the original name and beliefs of the Nation as it was under
Elijah Muhammad. Farrakhan is a charismatic speaker who has appeared on television numerous times, is a sought-after speaker by African-American university
student groups, and publishes his beliefs and opinions in *The Final Call.* He is also
well known for his hatred of whites and Jews, and was accused by Malcolm X's
widow of involvement in the assassination of her late husband.[43] In 1984 he
denounced Judaism as "a gutter religion" and referred to Adolf Hitler as a

[40]Clifton E. Marsh, *From Black Muslims to Muslims* (Metuchen, N.J., and London: The Scarecrow
Press, 1984), 41–50. Other sources for Fard include Jehovah's Witnesses literature.
[41]Karl Evanzz, *The Judas Factor: The Plot to Kill Malcolm X* (New York: Thunder's Mouth Press, 1992),
131–46. The fact that Fard had a white father is not significant, since it is recognized by Black
Muslims that most American blacks have at least one white ancestor. Malcolm X, who had a white
grandfather, was aware of Fard's white father.
[42]Marsh, *From Black*, 94–95.
[43]"Malcolm X's Widow Accuses Farrakhan," *Orange County Register* (March 13, 1994): News-33.

"wickedly great man."[44] In 1993 he tried to sell the public a softer image of himself by reaching out to politically mainstream and "progressive" African-Americans and being involved in a national summit of black political leaders, including many from the Black Congressional Caucus. He even had dinner with a rabbi.[45]

Despite his attempts to reach out, he agreed with the "truths" spoken by his then spokesman, Khallid Abdul Muhammad, at Kean College, New Jersey, on November 29, 1993. In the speech, Muhammad called the Pope a "cracker" and referred to Jews as "bloodsuckers," who are in a conspiracy to control the finances of the world. They even control the presidency of the United States regardless of who is in office.[46] Farrakhan followed up Muhammad's speech with rhetoric of his own, condemning whites and Jews.[47] Despite all this, a 1994 poll showed that 63 percent of African-Americans believe Farrakhan speaks the truth,[48] and a New York Times survey reports that more than one-third of African-Americans polled "express a favorable view" of him.[49] The most recent publicity event, the "Million Man March" on Washington, D.C., although it did not draw the number of participants anticipated, did demonstrate Farrakhan's ability to convince many Christian leaders (especially African-American leaders) that he is a peace-loving man.

The historical beliefs of the Nation include a type of quasi-pantheistic dualism that teaches that all members of the Nation are God, but that Allah is incarnate only in Wallace Fard Muhammad, who is also the Mahdi and the Messiah.[50] Nation members believe that God was at one time a scientist who wanted to create a single language on the earth, but was unable to do so. After failing to do this, he decided to destroy the earth, only succeeding in causing the moon to separate from the earth sixty-six trillion years ago.[51] This is something clearly condemned by the Qur'an, which in innumerable places teaches that God is One. But like orthodox Islam, they reject the Christian concept of God as a Spirit, or to use their word, a "spook."

However, if "all Black Muslims are Allah, and Allah is incarnate as Wallace Fard Muhammad" is their doctrine, why have Asians—especially blacks (according to them)—made mistakes like anyone else? Is Allah "all-knowing" or not? If Black Muslims are Allah, how could they be deceived by the devil? If Allah can be deceived, why trust him? Why trust the writings of Wallace Fard Muhammad, Elijah Muhammad, Louis Farrakhan, the Qur'an, or the Bible when they might be full of errors as well? If I am Allah, how can I trust myself? Ultimately, we are left with a radical form of agnosticism and skepticism.

[44] *Time* (February 28, 1994): 25–26.

[45] *Newsweek* (June 28, 1993): 30.

[46] *New York Times* (January 16, 1994): A-11.

[47] "Farrakhan Attacks Jews and Whites," *Orange County Register* (February 28, 1994): News-3.

[48] *Time* (February 28, 1994): 22.

[49] *Orange County Register* (March 3, 1993): News-27.

[50] C. Eric Lincoln, *The Black Muslims in America*, 3rd ed. (Grand Rapids, Mich. and Trenton, N.J.: Eerdmans and Africa World Press, 1994), 68–69. See also paragraph 12 of *Muhammad Speaks* (July 13, 1973), quoted in C. Eric Lincoln, *The Black Church Since Frazier* (New York: Schocken Books, 1974), 199; and Malcolm X, Alex Haley, and Betty Shabazz, *The Autobiography of Malcolm X* (New York: Ballantine Books, 1965), 158, 61.

[51] Elijah Muhammad, *Message to the Blackman in America* (Newport News, Va.: United Brothers Communications, 1992 [1965]), 31.

Another historical belief of the Nation is that the earth and the original Black Man were created by Allah, and that all living blacks are descendants of the tribe of Shabazz. Fifty thousand years ago, the members of the tribe suffered the misfortune of having their hair turned kinky by another mad scientist who wanted to make life hard for them.[52]

Many years later, a 600-year-old scientist, Yakub, who was exiled to the island of Patmos, began experimenting with genetics and created the brown man. Two hundred years later, he created the red man, then the yellow in another two hundred years, and finally, in another two hundred years he created the white man. This was about sixty-six hundred years ago, in 4004 B.C.[53] This Yakub is the same Jacob of the book of Genesis, allegedly distorted by the writers of the King James Version of the Bible (which, according to them, included William Shakespeare and Francis Bacon).[54] The white man is the devil and was given 6,000 years to rule the earth, a period that ended in 1914.[55] Therefore, it should be no surprise that the white man has invented nuclear weapons, concentration camps, or even the virus causing AIDS. The Qur'an, however, says that Allah created mankind in different colors as a sign of his glory (Sura 30:22).

Christianity is the white man's religion, and only a true Asian can be a Muslim, but it is the Jew who is the "brains" of the white-dominated world. If German Nazis happen to kill Jews, that is simply one group of whites killing another, or one problem among many for the devil. Farrakhan frequently says he is not anti-Semitic because he does not wish the extermination of the Jewish people. Here he equivocates, since that is not what "anti-Semitic" means, although it may include that meaning. The definition of anti-Semitic is: "hostile expressions toward, or negative behavior against, individuals or groups because of their Jewish faith or heritage."[56] In American usage, "anti-Semitic" refers specifically to Jews,

---

[52]Elijah Muhammad, *Message to the Blackman in America* (Newport News, Va.: United Brothers Communications, 1992 [1965]), 31.

[53]The version of the Bible apparently used by Fard and Elijah Muhammad was the *King James Version* with marginal notes by Bishop Ussher. On pages 94–95, Elijah Muhammad wrote, "When was the beginning? There in the Genesis the writer tells us that this is [*sic*] was 4004 B.C." James Ussher (1581–1656) was the archbishop of Almagh and was famous for, among other things, his bizarre chronology, in which he came up with a figure for Creation that was totally original: Saturday, October 22, 4004 B.C. This was published in the marginal notes of the 1701 edition of the *King James Version*, and remained popular for over 200 years. Somehow it was concluded by Fard and Elijah Muhammad that this was part of the text.

[54]This is similar to the orthodox Muslim claim of intentional Christian mistranslation. While the translating committee for the *King James Version* did not include the forenamed historical celebrities, even if it did and they *had* intentionally mistranslated the KJV, it would be irrelevant, because the Roman Catholic Spaniards (who must be included in this claim for the "400 years of slavery and oppression" argument to be true) used a Bible based on the *Latin Vulgate*; the Puritans used the *Geneva Bible*; and the many varied versions in existence today are based on older Greek manuscripts and are therefore much more accurate than the text behind the KJV. Incidentally, both Bacon and Shakespeare had non-Christian beliefs, Bacon being an empiricist philosopher and Shakespeare an Elizabethan "free-thinker." Neither was known for being a Greek or Hebrew scholar or devoutly Christian in any sense. The KJV was translated and written by a group of fifty-four scholars from Cambridge, Oxford, and Westminster, and we have forty-seven names available to us today (Charles C. Butterworth, *The Literary Lineage of the King James Bible, 1340–1611* (New York: Octagon Books, 1971 [1941]), 208). Neither Bacon nor Shakespeare are on that list, and both were very famous during their lifetimes.

[55]Elijah Muhammad, *Message*, 110–18; and Malcolm X, et al., *Autobiography*, 159–67. This is a distortion of the Watchtower (Jehovah's Witness) teaching that the Christ returned invisibly in 1914.

[56]Leonard Dinnerstein, *Antisemitism in America* (New York: Oxford University Press, 1994), ix.

although Arabs are also Semites. Farrakhan also holds that modern Jews are all descendants of the Khazars, a Turkish tribe that lived in the Caucasus Mountains from about 700–1100. Their book *The Secret Relationship Between Blacks and Jews* claims that modern Jews, as descendants of the Khazars, are the people primarily responsible for African slavery.[57]

The Nation is known for promoting pseudo-scholarship in many other areas in order to justify their erroneous beliefs. They are taught that blacks have endured 400 years of slavery under white Christian America, but while acknowledging the horrible record of white Christians who did not follow biblical teachings in oppressing their fellow human beings created in God's image, it must also be acknowledged that orthodox Islam was involved in the African slave trade much earlier than white Europeans, and it continues to be practiced in some Muslim countries today.[58] As David Brion Davis noted, "Although black captives had appeared in Egyptian iconography in the third millennium B.C. . . . through Hellenistic and Roman times, the Arabs and their Muslim allies were the first people to develop a specialized, long-distance slave trade from sub-Saharan Africa. They were also the first people to view blacks as suited by nature for the lowest and most degrading forms of bondage."[59]

Theologically, the Nation of Islam is not very sophisticated. It is rejected by all orthodox Muslim religious leaders, and clearly contradicts the unitarian concept of God that Islam holds to. Moreover, it is guilty of *shirk* (Sura 4:116; 5:72; 9:31), or associating things with God. Not all translations of the Qur'an are accepted by the Nation. Only Muslim translations, such as A. Yusuf Ali's *The Holy Qur'an: Translation and Commentary*, and the translation by Maulvi Muhammad Ali are accepted; translations by Christians are poisonous.[60] The Nation also holds to the Ahmdiyan Islam belief that Jesus Christ was not actually crucified, but later died in Kashmir. The Qur'an teaches Jesus was taken into heaven and gives no indication that he died in India (Sura 4:157; 199:33). Moreover, they differ with both Christianity and Islam by denying a physical resurrection and instead affirming a mental resurrection.

Sharing the Gospel

Racism and apartheid existed in America until the 1960s and 1970s civil rights legislation. Ideally, if Christian churches had stayed true to the Gospel of Jesus Christ while exemplifying a strong sense of community, they would possess a formidable witness today. But unfortunately, many Black Muslims have experi-

---

[57]Published in Chicago by Third World Press, 1992. This conspiratorial theory has been soundly refuted by Harold Brackman, *Farrakhan's Reign of Historical Error: The Truth Behind the Secret Relationship Between Blacks and Jews* (Los Angeles: Simon Wiesenthal Center, 1992).

[58]The enslavement of others was practiced by Muhammad and was extended to Africa shortly after his death. The first West Africans enslaved by Europeans were brought to Portugal in 1441, and African slaves were first brought to the English-speaking portion of what is now the United States in 1619.

[59]*Slavery and Human Progress* (New York: Oxford University Press, 1984), 8. See also, Bernard Lewis, *Race and Slavery in the Middle East: An Historical Inquiry* (New York: Oxford University Press, 1990), and Orlando Patterson, *Slavery and Social Death: A Comparative Study* (Cambridge, Mass.: Harvard University Press, 1982).

[60]Elijah Muhammad, *Message*, 21.

enced the lack of love and the hypocrisy and politics that mark many so-called Christian churches.

Recognizing the racism that existed during this time, it is important to understand and convey the difficult truth that Black Muslims are simply replacing one form of oppression with another; embracing slavery to a cult that binds them to a bigoted ideology and a heretical view of God.

Many Black Muslims need to hear what Christianity really is—the love of God for all mankind represented by the sacrifice of His only Son, Jesus Christ. The powerful truth of John 3:16 must be presented in a rational, logical manner. Black Muslims have heard that Christians believe contradictory things that must be accepted on faith alone: they have experienced a barrage of false beliefs presented in a systematic manner that appear to fit in with their experiences or the experiences of their ancestors. The Christian needs to understand and share the fact that his faith is logical—clearly showing that, despite the racism that has existed among many professed Christians, the New Testament strongly condemns it (Acts 8:26–40; Galatians 2:11–21; 3:28). The Bible teaches that if we hate our brother we are walking in spiritual darkness (1 John 2:11), and that he who does not love does not love God (1 John 4:8).

Finally, the Nation, like Islam, is a works-oriented religion. They have some positive entrepreneurial enterprises, but a large return is expected by the Nation not only for alms, but for Nation-owned businesses as well. Raboteau writes that they demand "the federal government set aside separate land for Afro-Americans in reparation for slavery. Black Muslims refused to vote [this has been lifted under Farrakhan], to participate in armed services, or to salute the flag. The separate identity of members of the Nation of Islam was reinforced by a strict ethical code. Alcohol, drugs, tobacco, sports, movies, and cosmetics were forbidden, along with pork and other foods identified as unclean or unhealthy."[61] They are even encouraged to eat no more than one meal a day. Violation of their codes may result in strong penalties. Since the Nation is so works-oriented, exposure to the Christian doctrine of grace can be a very effective witness. To the Muslim especially, salvation by grace should be "good news." ~

Recommended Resources

1. Answering Islam: *www.answering-islam.org.uk.*
2. Beverley, James A. *Understanding Islam.* Thomas Nelson, 2001.
3. Braswell, George W. Jr. *Islam.* Broadman & Holman, 1996.
4. Warraq, Ibn. *Why I Am Not a Muslim.* Prometheus, 1995.
5. *The World of Islam.* Global Mapping International, 2001. *www.gmi.org.*

---

[61]Albert J. Raboteau, "Afro-American Religions: Muslim Movements," Mircea Eliade, ed., *The Encyclopedia of Religion*, vol. 1 (New York: Macmillan Publishing Company, 1987), 101–102.

Quick Facts About the Cults on the World Mission Field

- The cults do not generally identify themselves by their popular names.

- The literature of many cult systems is unmarked and their public meetings are seldom identified with the official name of the sponsoring group.

- All major cult systems use the Bible.

- Most cultists utilize terminology of historical Christianity.

- Missionaries of the cults deny the historic doctrines of the Trinity, the deity of Jesus Christ, and salvation by grace alone.

Chapter 17

The Cults on the World Mission Field

We have observed in our study of the various cults that they are particularly effective among those in whom the early seeds of Christianity have been planted. It is much easier for cultists to promulgate their doctrines among young Christians, nominal Christians, and those who have only a passing acquaintance with the Scriptures. Throughout the United States, the various non-Christian cults are in evidence everywhere; they boldly advertise themselves and eagerly covet the one great prize that all of them desperately seek—prestige and recognition as "Christians." This, however, is not always the case, especially on the foreign mission field, and it is with this area that we shall now briefly concern ourselves.

In the summer of 1958 it was the privilege of the author to be a part of the Pastor's Conference Team of World Vision Incorporated, led by Dr. Bob Pierce. These conferences were specifically designed to meet the needs of pastors, missionaries, and Christian workers on the various foreign mission fields of Asia and Africa. In the course of this tour of some twenty-five thousand miles, I had the opportunity to meet and speak to over five thousand dedicated Christian workers and students on the problem of non-Christian cults on those mission fields. Beginning in Japan, with the largest pastors' conference in Japanese church history (1,560 persons), we journeyed through Formosa (now Taiwan), Hong Kong, Singapore, Thailand, Burma, India, and Ghana, Africa. At the conclusion of the African meetings, I had the opportunity to travel throughout Europe, meeting and interviewing Christian workers there, so it was possible for me to get a fairly well-rounded picture of what the various cults were doing in these specific locales. I returned to Europe in 1961 to lecture on the cults, and then interviewed missionaries whose work ranged from Scandinavia through Germany, Switzerland, Italy, Belgium, Holland, and France. I traveled in most of these countries and

---

This chapter updated by Kevin Rische and edited by Jill Martin Rische.

gathered firsthand impressions, which gave me the theological pulse of cultism in Europe.

A few things emerged very clearly from this unprecedented opportunity, which Dr. Pierce made possible, as well as from my subsequent European trip. I say unprecedented because never before in the history of Christian missions has any researcher in the field of cults been able to visit so many mission fields in so short a time (two and one-half months), delivering lectures and gathering information on a subject about which very little is known. In the course of my travels, I learned much about cult methodology on the mission fields, and in contrast to our previous statements concerning their activities in the United States, the cults generally are happy to remain virtually anonymous until they have established a bridgehead. This is important in an area where a work has already begun or has been functioning for many years.

One missionary explained to me how young converts, in particular, were the prey of such cults as the Jehovah's Witnesses' Watchtower organization and the Mormons' Church of Jesus Christ of Latter-day Saints, two of the most virulent strains of non-Christian cults, and both of which are found in practically every major mission area throughout all of the continents of the world. In addition to their evangelical endeavors, the cults specialize in reaching people in their own language, and it is here that the printing establishments of Jehovah's Witnesses, the Mormons, and the Unity School of Christianity are revealed at their effective best. The average missionary who encounters a Jehovah's Witness in Japan, for instance, can expect to find copies of *The Watchtower* and *Awake* magazines translated into the language of the people and dutifully mailed from cult headquarters in Brooklyn, New York. There is also the very real problem of literature to combat these movements; literature that itself must, by the very nature of cult propaganda, also be in the language of the country in question, and such literature today is virtually unobtainable. At the Japanese conference many hours were consumed, both in the lecture period and in private counseling sessions with missionaries and native pastors, explaining the vulnerable areas of cult theology and, in turn, gleaning much valuable information on the tactics of cults abroad.

We learned that Jehovah's Witnesses were making an attempt to convince people that their own translation of the Bible (*The New World Translation*) is "the latest American translation" and should be accepted in questionable areas of theology as "the best and most recent rendering of the original languages."

The informed person, of course, knows that the Watchtower's translation is accepted as sound *only* by the Watchtower and those who have not carefully checked its many perverted renderings. But when one is at least 15,000 miles from home, laboring among people of a foreign tongue, and generally beset by the pressing problems of hostile indigenous religions (Buddhism, Islam, Shintoism, Taoism, Confucianism, Hinduism, etc.), it is difficult to check these things. And the Watchtower eagerly supplies *their* Bible to all interested persons, converts and pagans alike—something the Christian church has found difficult to accomplish, even in the twentieth century.

The startling growth of Jehovah's Witnesses, and the astronomical figures in publishing and distribution that the Watchtower accomplishes yearly, can only be appreciated when one sees a mission field literally inundated by tracts, pamphlets, Bibles, books, and magazines, all stamped Brooklyn, New York, U.S.A.! The world today is hungry to read, and the underdeveloped countries of Asia and Africa will read anything, even Watchtower propaganda, which appears as a torrent in comparison with the trickle of Christian literature currently in circulation.

It also became apparent, while questioning missionaries, that many of them are disturbed by the fact that Watchtower people always seemingly have enough literature to proselytize Christian converts, but the missionary has little, if any, literature that will answer such cultists, much less evangelize them or their converts.

A chart of growth for Jehovah's Witnesses over four years illustrates the growing danger of the major cults. This information has been compiled from the Watchtower's own publications, and one cannot but be astounded at their steady growth and the dedication of their members, of whom those who contributed extraordinary amounts of volunteer door-to-door "missionary" time are called "Kingdom Publishers."

Growth Comparisons for Jehovah's Witnesses Publishers and Baptisms

Year	Average number publishers	Change from previous year	Baptisms	Change from previous year
1978	513,673	−3.15%	20,469	−26.9%
1979	521,370	+1.50%	26,958	+31.7%
1980	543,457	+4.24%	27,811	+3.16%
1981	563,453	+3.68%	28,496	+2.46%

~As of the year 2001, the Watchtower claims 6,117,666 "Peak Witnesses" (Kingdom Publishers) worldwide.[1] Their official Web site maintains, "The Watch Tower Society publishes in 354 languages and calls on the volunteer services of more than 1,000 translators worldwide. . . ."[2]~

From these statistics, Christian missions can draw little comfort, and Christian Bible colleges, institutes, and seminaries would do well to consider the ramifications of such rapid growth, since very little, if anything, is being done to prepare missionaries and ministers to meet these problems, either at home or on the field of world missions.

When we remember that about 15 percent of the membership of Jehovah's Witnesses resides in the United States and *85 percent* on the mission field, the gravity of the problem that confronts the Christian church is apparent to all but the most adamantly obtuse.[3]

The Witnesses in 2001, at their worldwide communion service, known as their Memorial, numbered 15,374,986 persons, compared to 12,921,933 persons

---

[1] *www.watchtower.org/statistics/worldwide_report.htm.*
[2] *www.jw-media.org/people/statistics.htm.*
[3] *www.watchtower.org/statistics/worldwide_report.htm.*

in 1996, a total increase of 2,453,053 people! These statistics should be the cause of significant alarm.[4]

During 2001, Jehovah's Witnesses worldwide spent over 1,169,082,225 hours in "preaching."[5] New members baptized in 2001 were 263,431. Hundreds of millions of pieces of literature were distributed. In 2001 the circulation of their feature publication, *The Watchtower* magazine, reached more than 24,000,000 and was published in more than 144 languages. In addition to this, *Awake!* is published in 87 languages with an average printing of 21 million.[6]

It is no wonder that many missionaries are discouraged, and that in the United States an increasing number of pastors are beginning to share that discouragement. This stems from the fact that a cult so obviously non-Christian as Jehovah's Witnesses is becoming increasingly successful in its missionary outreach, particularly in the field of literature, when both clergy and missionary representing the historic Gospel of Jesus Christ find little or no support in this vital area of literary mass evangelism.

The Watchtower Society has not restricted itself, however, merely to the publication of literature on the mission field. Their two-by-two doorstep evangelism has become the plague of the British Commonwealth and most of the countries of Europe, Asia, and Africa.

2001 Report of Jehovah's Witnesses Worldwide[7]

Witnesses	6,117,666
Baptisms	263,431
Congregations	93,154
Preaching Hours	1,169,082,225
Bible Studies	4,921,702
Memorial Attendance	15,374,986

Watchtower missionaries have made it extremely difficult for truly orthodox Christian efforts throughout the various trouble spots of the world, such as East Germany, Africa, Japan, Indonesia, Vietnam, and Cuba, by emphasizing the organization's rigid anti-government stand, based upon their theological presupposition that all governments are under the direct supervision of Satan and are opposed to the theocratic rule of Jehovah. Since they identify themselves as Christian and utilize the Bible and vocabulary of Christianity, those hostile to the Christian message—seeking the opportunity to persecute it and restrict its activities—seize upon Watchtower Organization statements that appear to incite disloyalty to governmental authority as well as a militant pacifism and allegiance to a theocracy in place of the individual nation.

The Watchtower Society seems totally oblivious to the thirteenth chapter of Romans and its demand that "every soul be subject unto the higher powers. For . . . the powers that be are ordained of God." And for the average Jehovah's

---

[4]Ibid.
[5]Ibid.
[6]*www.jw-media.org/people/statistics.htm.*
[7]*www.watchtower.org/statistics/worldwide_report.htm.*

Witness, all governments and all forms of supposed Christianity, except his own, are enemies to be harassed, vilified, and condemned as tools of Satan. This hardly makes for good public relations, and in the fervent spirit of emerging nationalism, particularly in the so-called underdeveloped countries of the world, those in authority have taken a rather dim view of the Watchtower's activities, resulting in the persecution of *true* disciples of the cross, who suffer because of the Watchtower's mistaken identification with biblical Christianity.

~The Jehovah's Witnesses have taken full advantage of the political openness, social and political unrest, and technological advances of the last two decades of the twentieth century. They have focused intense evangelism campaigns on former Soviet-controlled countries, countries with continuing civil unrest, and countries emerging into technological sophistication. There are now Watchtower evangelistic efforts in 235 countries, and over one hundred branch offices worldwide.[8]~

All in all, Jehovah's Witnesses are a growing concern everywhere and a challenge to evangelical Christianity, which desires to win them to a redemptive knowledge of Jesus Christ and, in the process, to give every man an answer: "a reason of the hope that is in you . . . Christ in you, the hope of glory" (1 Peter 3:15; Colossians 1:27).

Mormon Missionary Efforts

Even surpassing the Jehovah's Witnesses is the rapidly burgeoning missionary effort of the Church of Jesus Christ of Latter-day Saints (Mormons).

Boasting a missionary force approaching 60,850 full-time workers, and bolstered by a church with an estimated gross income in 1997 of 5.9 billion dollars, the Mormon cult is moving at a rapid pace, particularly in its new mission fields of South America and Africa.[9]

The following charts demonstrate the growth of Mormon missions over recent years and should suffice to remind us that Jehovah's Witnesses are not the only cult that competes with Christianity on a large scale on most of the large mission fields.

Growth of the Mormon Church

1900	268,331	1960	1,693,180
1910	393,437	1962	1,965,786
1920	526,032	1975	3,700,000
1930	672,488	1982	5,000,000+
1940	862,664	2001	11,394,522[10]
1950	1,111,314		

---

[8]*www.watchtower.org/library/rq/article_14.htm.*
[9]*www.lds-mormon.com/time.shtml* and *www.lds.org/news/article/0.5422.116-10235.00.html.*
[10]*www.lds.org/news/article/0.5422.116-10235.00.html*

Convert Baptisms Since 1983[11]

1983	189,419	1990	330,877
1984	192,983	1991	297,770
1985	197,640	1992	274,477
1986	216,214	1993	304,808
1987	227,284	1994	300,730
1988	256,515	1995	304,330
1989	318,938	2001	292,612[12]

Latter-day Saints 2001 Statistics[13]

World Membership	11,394,522
United States Membership	5,208,827[14]
Non-U.S. Membership	6,185,695 (approximate)
Female	53% (1997)
Male	47% (1997)
Wards and Branches	26,084
Temples, Worldwide	107 since 1836;18 announced or under construction; 2 no longer operating/owned by LDS (1997)
Literature Languages	145 (1997)
The *Book of Mormon*	78 million since 1830, 4.5 million (1995), 90 languages
Missions	333
Missionaries	60,850; 75% young males; 18% young females; 7% older couples[15]
Service Missionaries (health services, agriculture, etc.)	7,000
Missionary Training Centers	15

Mormon missionary work far surpasses that of the Jehovah's Witnesses, and together the missionary efforts of the two cults present a real and present danger to the spread of the true Gospel throughout the world today.

The methodology of Mormon missionaries is similar in many respects to that of Jehovah's Witnesses. They, too, are door-to-door canvassers and tireless, round-the-clock "back-callers" on contacts previously made either by themselves or by those missionaries who preceded them. Mormon missionaries, unlike those of the

[11] *www.lds.org (Global Media Guide,* March 1997.) See also *www.lds.org/news/article/0.5422.116-10235.00.html.*
[12] Ibid.
[13] Ibid. See also *www.adherents.com/Na_211.html.*
[14] 2001 Yearbook of American and Canadian Churches cited on *www.adherents.com/rel USA.html.*
[15] *www.lds.org/newsroom/page/0,15606,3899-1_6-168,00.html.*

Jehovah's Witnesses, come fully equipped with slick multimedia presentations and free copies of *The Book of Mormon, Doctrine and Covenants,* and *The Pearl of Great Price,* the sacred books they believe "properly interpret" the Bible. Whereas the Jehovah's Witnesses will emphasize the absolute authority of the Scriptures as a supreme criterion for truth, the Mormons will hedge at this juncture, maintaining that the Bible is the Word of God insofar as it is "correctly translated." They will insist gently, but firmly, that the *Book of Mormon* and the other two sacred books throw light upon the Bible, and explain the Bible in the light of restored Christianity and the ministry of the prophet Joseph Smith. In England, where the Latter-day Saints once doubled their membership, they are particularly proud to point out that Brigham Young came from an English background and did missionary work in England himself prior to the assassination of Joseph Smith in 1844. Young returned from England to assume the leadership of the Mormon Church, and some of his wives were English girls whom Brigham Young recruited on his missionary journey. It is not unusual to find second-generation Mormons returning to the same country where their parents did missionary work, to carry on the family tradition.

Another aspect of Mormon missionary activity is their preoccupation with the anthropological background of the *Book of Mormon,* which leads them to declare that the Native American and the Central and South American Indian races have similar origins and are mentioned in the *Book of Mormon.* They do not hesitate to suggest the linkage of the Inca civilization, the Aztec civilization, and other such archaeologically verified Indian groups as giving credence to the teachings of the *Book of Mormon.* The fact that no reputable archaeologist has ever verified their hypothetical and unsupported propositions (in fact, others have gone on record as repudiating them outright [see chapter on Mormonism]) apparently does not hinder the zeal of Mormon missionaries one whit.

Such archaeological and anthropological razzle-dazzle, however, does have quite an effect on the untutored and uninformed mind outside the United States, where verifications or contradictions of the Mormon claims would be difficult, if not impossible, to obtain. Thus we see that in Mexico and South America particularly, Mormon missionaries appealing to the nationalistic pride of both Indians and Latins are telling them that they are the heirs of great civilizations that the *Book of Mormon* reveals are connected with the origins of Christianity and its nineteenth-century "restoration" through the establishment of the Mormon Church. By utilizing the *Book of Mormon* as a prophetic volume and "new light on the Bible," the Mormons have succeeded to an amazing degree in Mexico and in South America, to the great dismay of many mission agencies and a large company of missionaries. As we previously observed, however, the Mormons are careful not to point out their previous discrimination against the black race, for it simply would not do for the "Restored Church of Jesus Christ" to be on the one hand busily engaged in promoting the archaeological myth of the *Book of Mormon* and the races of the Americas, while virtually ignoring the black race purely on the ground of their skin color and imagined curse! Wherever possible, it is good for Christian missionaries to point out this glaring inconsistency, which is well known in Africa, where the Mormons in force have been, until recently, conspicuously absent. For almost all of its controversial history, Mormon missionary efforts were confined to those races that qualified in the theology of Joseph Smith and Brigham Young, but one could hardly seriously consider, on the basis of such racial discrimination, the claims of the Mormons to being the restored church of Christ.

The Mormon missionary approach also differs from that of other cults, particularly Jehovah's Witnesses, in that it emphasizes the need for education, preferring to reach a higher strata of intellect, generally speaking, than the Jehovah's Witnesses have been able to attain. From a standpoint of educational background, social graces, and personal habits, which include a quiet, tolerant regard for evangelical Christianity (something lacking most pointedly in the methods of Jehovah's Witnesses), the Mormons make a good impression on prospective converts, and many ex-members of Christian denominations are now the disciples of Joseph Smith and Brigham Young because of this distinctive Mormon emphasis.

A typical Mormon missionary approach is oriented around three prime factors:

1. *The Mormon Church alone has the marks of true Christianity.* It is called the Church of Jesus Christ; it has apostles and prophets; it has a priesthood (Melchizedek and Aaronic) as well as elders and other New Testament practices.

The Mormons claim the unique ability to baptize for the dead (1 Corinthians 15:29), and have sacred extra-biblical literature that interprets the Bible.

2. *The Mormons maintain that Christianity is an open apostasy,* as evidenced by the rise of Roman Catholicism during the Dark Ages and the various and multiple divisions in Christendom since the Reformation.

3. *The outward success of the Mormon Church,* its enormous prosperity and growth since 1830 in the face of persecutions and ostracism (due in part to their own immoral practices of polygamy, one should note), proves conclusively, say the Mormon missionaries, that the Church of Jesus Christ of Latter-day Saints is the restoration of true biblical Christianity, and should be embraced as such.

Since the average person knows very little of church history, and even less of the backgrounds of Joseph Smith, Brigham Young, and the early "Mormon saints," some of these things will go unchallenged. But if even a general knowledge of the massive contradictions and historical myth-making about the origins of Mormonism is known to a prospective convert, not to mention the Mormons' polytheistic theology, which by definition is not Christian, the "saints" have a difficult time, indeed, defending the maze that is their history and theology. Usually when this occurs, they will depart and never return.

The Reverend Gordon Fraser, who has spent some fifty years working as a missionary among the Navaho Indians in Arizona and New Mexico, has had numerous encounters with Mormon missionaries, and his judgment in this realm is most relevant.

> The Mormons have striven for years to gain recognition as a Christian body. Until within a decade or so, their claim has been denied by even the most liberal groups of professing Christians. Lately, however, with the general lowering of Christian standards of thought and with the remarkable buildup in the public press and on the radio, the Mormons have achieved

their goal in the thinking of the general public. But are the Mormons Christians? If the term covers all who use the name of Christ in their titles or in their teaching, we would have to allow the Mormons their claim, but we would have to include with them the Jehovah's Witnesses, Christian Scientists, and most of the other metaphysical cults, as well as Unitarians, Universalists, Baha'is, and a host of so-called liberal adherents to the various Christian denominations, which were originally completely orthodox.

All of these refer freely to Jesus Christ and use quotations from the Bible to support their views, but these, along with Mormons, deny what we consider to be the indispensable tenets of true . . . Christianity.

The Mormons are well trained in their methods, and nominal Christians are an easy prey to their arguments. We have yet to see, however, an intelligent and regenerate person who knows the Bible and its doctrines, succumb to Mormonism.

The Mormon missionaries who come to your door will be well-mannered, attractive young people. They will introduce themselves as "Christian missionaries," or will use some other innocuous term.

One team, recently returned from Honduras, announced themselves as members of the Central American Mission. Another team encountered recently merely asked, "Could we step in and have a Christian word with you?"

They will avoid identifying themselves as Mormons or Latter-day Saints until they have gained an audience.

These young missionaries are given very careful training, both in the fine points of good sales approach and in the best methods of appealing to the members of the various churches. It is part of their training to attend services of the various churches, so as to be informed on matters of phraseology and doctrine.

We should insist that such visitors identify themselves.

What Mr. Fraser says is, of course, a sound evaluation of Mormon practices, and we are forced to his conclusion when he says,

Many Christians, uninformed as to the true nature of the Mormon teachings, will defend their Mormon neighbors as good, clean-living, pious and honest folks. They will point to the wonderful relief practices of the Mormon Church. They will extol the thrift and industry of the Mormons as a whole. All these things we recognize and appreciate as valuable contributions to society. We cannot criticize these things. These virtues do not make one a Christian. Satan is delighted when his followers put up a good appearance. We insist that these virtues have nothing to do with one's acceptance before God, if one has never yielded to God's claims concerning His Son, Jesus Christ. When Christians fail to demonstrate the above virtues, they are coming short of God's purpose, but these are the by-products of the Christian life.[16]

---

[16]Gordon R. Fraser, *Is Mormonism Christian?* (Chicago, Ill.: Moody Press, 1977), 7–8, 117.

We must look beyond the appearances of Mormonism and its missionaries; we must consider the fruit of its tree: not only its social benefits and moral reform, but its doctrine, which, as has been noted, is as much fruit from the tree of religion as is the practice of that religion.

In the case of the Mormons, their doctrinal fruit is corrupt, denying as they do the Christian doctrine of the Trinity, the deity of our Lord, and salvation by grace through justifying faith in Jesus Christ (Ephesians 2:8–10). The Jehovah's Witnesses and the Mormons share one thing in common—both are dedicated opponents of historical Christianity. Although they utilize the name of Christ and the methods of Christianity where witnessing and evangelism are concerned, the content of Christianity, which by necessity revolves about the person of Jesus Christ, is either ignored or redefined by them. In the end, it is the gospel of "another Jesus, another spirit" and the product of that supreme architect of religious deviltry, who delights in arraying himself and his ministers as angels of light. Of him Jesus Christ said, "He was a murderer from the beginning, and . . . a liar"—Satan, the god of this age (John 8:44).

There is scarcely a mission field of the world that has not felt the impact of these two major cult systems, and we would be foolish, indeed, in discussing the problem of missionary activities of the cults, to ignore their methodology and their already fantastic accomplishments in a relatively short amount of time.

Much more could be written on this subject, but everything that needs to be said could hardly be included in a chapter of this length. It might be observed, however, that the cults do share some traits in common when it comes to missionary methodology, and the primary ones are worth noting.

1. *The cults do not generally identify themselves by their popular names* (Jehovah's Witnesses, Mormons, Swedenborgians, etc.). They prefer such titles as Latter-day Saints or the Church of the New Jerusalem, and they generally reveal themselves in their historical connections only when the prospect is on the way to indoctrination.

2. *The literature of many cult systems is unmarked,* so it is difficult to identify them because of the similarity of terminology employed in the setting forth of their teachings.

3. *Most cultists utilize terminology of historical Christianity* and are masters of evangelical clichés, as Fraser has pointed out.

4. *Their public meetings are seldom identified with the official name of the sponsoring group.* But the fact that many are reluctant to identify themselves underscores some of their divisive methods of proselytizing, which though regretted by some quarters of leadership, still continue on many mission fields around the world.

5. *All major cult systems will use the Bible,* quoting profusely from it, mostly out of context. In the case of Jehovah's Witnesses, they will even offer copies of their own translation (the Mormons have an "inspired version" also) to "aid a deeper understanding of the Scriptures."

6. *Missionaries of the cults will also, when pressed, deny the historic doctrines* of the Trinity, the deity of Jesus Christ, and salvation by grace alone.

7. *Cult missionaries will follow up major evangelistic campaigns,* such as Billy Graham, as they did in England and elsewhere. Mormons and Jehovah's Wit-

nesses specialize in this, and have even been found in counseling rooms after altar calls, attempting to proselytize the young converts.

These are some of the marks of the methods and content of some of the major cults on the world mission fields. There can be no doubt that they are effective and that the church must rise to meet this challenge while there is yet time.

Quick Facts About the Jesus of the Cults

■ Understand the nature of the "other Jesus."

■ Give biblical reasons *why* Christians must identify him as counterfeit and refute his "other gospel."

■ Remember that the message of the Cross itself is offensive and controversial by nature.

■ Defend the faith and evangelize because Christ commanded it.

Chapter 18

The Jesus of the Cults

Since the earliest days of Christianity, both apostle and disciple alike have been confronted with the perversion of the revelation God has given us in the person of Jesus Christ. Historically, this perversion has extended not only to the teaching of our Lord, but, more important, to the person of Christ; for it is axiomatic that if the doctrine of Christ himself, i.e., His person, nature, and work are perverted so that the identity of the life-giver is altered, then the life that He came to give is correspondingly negated. And it is at precisely this juncture that in this day and age we come face-to-face with the phenomenon that the apostle Paul described in Second Corinthians, chapter eleven, as "another Jesus."

The problem is twofold, in that we must understand the nature of the "other Jesus" and then give the biblical reasons why it is the obligation of Christians to identify him as a counterfeit and refute his other gospel.

There can be little doubt that the Christian of today can expect to encounter the very same or, at least, similar errors and perversions of the gospel message that his ancestors before him did. He should not be discouraged when they appear to have more success in twisting the truth of God than the Christian has in presenting it.

The epistle to the Galatians reminds us that there are those who would "pervert the Gospel of Christ," and who represent "any other gospel," which in reality is not another gospel but a counterfeit of the original, designed by the master craftsman of all evils, our adversary, the devil.

It may seem like oversimplification and naïveté to some people to suggest that Satan is the prime mover and architect of the major cult systems, but a careful consideration of the biblical evidence will allow no other conclusion.

In his Second Corinthian epistle, Paul penned one of the most solemn warnings recorded anywhere in the Bible, to which we have made previous reference.

This chapter updated by Kevin Rische and edited by Jill Martin Rische.

He addressed this warning to Christians who were in great danger of having their minds (not their soul's salvation) corrupted from the simplicity that is in Christ Jesus. He was afraid, he said, that if someone should come to Corinth preaching "another Jesus . . . another spirit . . ., or another gospel," the Corinthians might well be swept along with it to the sterilization of their Christian life and witness for Christ. Paul went on to underscore this point by drawing a deadly parallel between true Christianity and pseudo-Christianity that he likened to a carefully designed copy of the original revelation of God in Christ.

After revealing the existence of a counterfeit Jesus, Holy Spirit, and gospel, Paul completed the parallel by showing that there are also counterfeit "apostles" and counterfeit "disciples" (workers) who transform themselves in appearance and demeanor to appear as ministers of Christ, but in reality, Paul states, they are representatives of Satan (2 Corinthians 11:13–15). He further informs us that this is not to be considered fantastic, unbelievable, and incredible, for Satan himself is often manifested as "an angel of light." So we are not to be surprised when his ministers emulate their master and disguise themselves as ministers of righteousness (2 Corinthians 11:14–15).

Now, of course, Paul was speaking of those who could be readily identified as spiritual wolves in sheep's clothing the moment their teachings were compared with the true Gospel (Galatians 1:8–9), not just anyone with whom we have a disagreement in the realm of theology.

Simply because Christians disagree on certain peripheral issues cannot be taken as a valid reason for asserting that such are dissenters and ministers of Satan, unless that dissent involves the person and work of our Lord, in which case their unbelief would automatically invoke the apostolic judgment.

The Nature of the Other Jesus

The person and work of Christ is indeed the very foundation of Christian faith. And if it is redefined and interpreted out of context, and therefore contrary to its biblical content, the whole message of the Gospel is radically altered and its value correspondingly diminished. The early apostles clearly saw this, including John and Jude; hence, their repeated emphasis upon maintaining the identity and ministry of the historical Jesus over against the counterfeits of that Person already beginning to arise in their own era.

The "other Jesus" of the false cults of that day (Gnosticism and Galatianism, or Legalism) threatened the churches at Colosse, Ephesus, and Crete, and invoked powerful apostolic condemnation and warning in the epistles of First John, Galatians, and Colossians.

In order that we may better understand precisely how these Scriptures may be applied in our own day, we need only cite some contemporary illustrations of the "other Jesus" the Bible so graphically warns against, and the entire issue will come into clear perspective.

1. The Jesus of Christian Science

In the theological structure of the Christian Science religion, as we have already seen, Gnosticism was revived, and Mrs. Eddy became its twentieth-century exponent. Mrs. Eddy declared concerning *her* Jesus:

The Christian who believes in the First Commandment is a monotheist. Thus he virtually unites with the Jew's belief in one God and recognizes that Jesus Christ is not God as Jesus Christ himself declared, but is the Son of God. (*Science and Health,* 152)

Mrs. Eddy spelled out her view so that no one could possibly misinterpret her when she wrote:

The spiritual Christ was infallible; Jesus, as material manhood, was not Christ. (*Misc. Writings,* 84)

Now, a careful study of Matthew, chapter sixteen, will reveal that Jesus Christ acknowledged the confession of Peter to the effect that He was Jesus the Christ, the Son of the living God. And it would be foolish to maintain that Jesus was not material manhood in the light of the New Testament record that He was born of a woman, subject to the limitations of our nature apart from sin, and physically expired upon the cross in our place. The Jesus of Mrs. Eddy is a divine ideal or principle, inherent within every man, and Jesus was its supreme manifestation. Since Mrs. Eddy denied the existence of the physical universe, she also denied the reality of human flesh and blood, maintaining that it was an illusion of mortal mind. Hence, neither Christ, nor any man, for that matter, possesses a real body of flesh and bones and, for her, Jesus Christ has not come in the flesh.

It seems almost unnecessary to refer to the fact that our Lord acknowledged the reality of flesh and blood when He declared to Peter: "Blessed art thou, Simon Barjona: for flesh and blood hath not revealed it unto thee, but my Father which is in heaven" (Matthew 16:17).

At this particular juncture, the words of the apostle John take on new meaning when he declares:

Every spirit that confesseth not that Jesus Christ is come in the flesh is not of God: and this is that spirit of antichrist, whereof ye have heard that it should come; and even now already is it in the world. (1 John 4:3)

John's previous words then apply with great force to the Jesus of Christian Science and its "prophetess," Mrs. Eddy:

Who is a liar but he that denieth that Jesus is the Christ? He is antichrist, that denieth the Father and the Son. (1 John 2:22)

We need not emphasize the point, for it is quite evident that the "other" Jesus of Christian Science is a Gnostic Jesus, an idea, a principle—but not God incarnate (John 1:14). Because of this, although Mrs. Eddy, her literature, and Christian Scientists utilize the name of Jesus, theirs is not the Christ of the Scriptures, but an extremely clever counterfeit about whom the Holy Spirit graciously saw fit to warn the church.

2. The Jesus of Jehovah's Witnesses

The next example is quite different from the Jesus of Christian Science, but another Jesus, nonetheless. According to the theology of the Watchtower,

The true Scriptures speak of God's Son, the Word, as "a god." He is a "mighty god," but not the Almighty God who is Jehovah. (*The Truth Shall Make You Free*, 47)

In other words, he was the first and direct creation of Jehovah God. (*The Kingdom Is at Hand*, 46–47, 49)

The founder of Jehovah's Witnesses, Charles Taze Russell, described this Jesus as having been Michael the archangel prior to his divesting himself of his angelic nature and appearing in the world as a perfect man (*Studies in the Scriptures*, 5:84). For Jehovah's Witnesses, their Jesus is an angel who became a man; he is a god, but he is not God the Son, second person of the Holy Trinity.

As the chapter on Jehovah's Witnesses amply demonstrates, the Scriptures refute this and flatly controvert the Watchtower's theology by teaching that Jesus Christ is the Word, God the only begotten one (John 1:18, from the Greek), and no less than the great "I am" of Exodus 3:14 (compare John 8:58) and the First and the Last of the apocalyptic-Isaiah contrast, well known to any informed student of the Scriptures (compare Revelation 1:16–17 with Isaiah 44:6).

Just as Mrs. Eddy's Christ is an abstract idea, the Christ of Jehovah's Witnesses is a second god with an angelic background. He, too, qualifies as "another Jesus" in the context of the Pauline prophecy.

3. The Jesus of the Mormons

The teachings of the Mormon religion, which differ from both Christian Science and Jehovah's Witnesses, claim that their god is one among many gods, as evidenced by their own literature:

> Each of these gods, including Jesus Christ and his Father, being in possession of not merely an organized spirit, but a glorious body of flesh and bones. (Parley P. Pratt, *Key to the Science of Theology* [1973 ed.], 44; see also, *Doctrine and Covenants*, 130:22)

Theologian Pratt held no unique view where Mormonism was concerned; in fact, the Mormons have a full pantheon of gods. Jesus, who before his incarnation was the spirit-brother of Lucifer, was also a polygamist, the husband of the Marys and Martha, who was rewarded for his faithfulness by becoming the ruler of this earth (see chapter 6, on Mormonism).

The apostle Paul reminds us in his epistle to the Galatians that "God is one" (Galatians 3:20). Numerous passages from the Old Testament, previously cited in the chapter on Mormonism, demonstrate the absolute falsity of the idea that there are a multiplicity of gods and an exaltation to godhood to which men can aspire. As for the concept of Jesus as a polygamist and a brother of Lucifer, this need not be dignified by further comment.

The Jesus of the Mormons is quite obviously "another Jesus" with whom truly redeemed men have nothing in common, even though he be arrayed as an angel of light and with all the credentials of the angel Moroni's angelic proclamation to Joseph Smith, the prophet of the restored Christian religion!

It would be possible to go on listing the other cult systems, but it is apparent that further comment would be superfluous; the evidence is overpowering.

The Jesus of the Christian Scientists, the Mormons, the Jehovah's Witnesses, and of all the cult systems is but a subtle caricature of the Christ of divine revelation. In cult theology, He becomes an abstraction (Christian Science, Unity, Metaphysics, New Thought), a second god (Jehovah's Witnesses, Mormonism, Theosophy, Rosacrucianism, Baha'ism), a pantheistic manifestation of deity (Spiritism, the Great I Am), but he is still incontrovertibly "another Jesus," who represents another gospel and imparts another spirit, which by no conceivable stretch of the imagination could be called holy.

Herein lies the problem that Christians must face and come to grips with, and there are excellent reasons why it is not only our responsibility, but our duty to do so.

To Every Man an Answer

In the course of delivering numerous lectures on the subject of non-Christian cults and their relationship to the Christian church, one of the most frequently asked questions has been, "Why should Christians oppose and criticize the beliefs of others whether they be cults or other world religions?"

To answer this question we must first recognize that to oppose and criticize is neither unethical, bigoted, nor unchristian; rather, it is the epitome of proper Christian conduct where a very vital part of the Christian witness is concerned. There are some good people who feel that it is beneath their dignity to engage in the criticism of the beliefs of others, and the society in which we live has done much to foster this belief. "Live and let live" is the motto of our civilization; don't buck the tide of uncritical tolerance or, as the saying goes, "Bend with the wind or be broken." In addition to this type of reasoning, there also has been promulgated a distinctly noncontroversial spirit mirrored in the fact that leading newspapers and periodicals, not to mention the mass media of communication, radio and TV, refuse to carry advertisements for debates on religious issues for fear of being thought un-American, since it is now fashionable to equate criticism of another's religion with an un-American spirit!

We must remember, however, that controversy in itself has always been a stimulus to thought and in our own great country has provoked many needed reforms in numerous instances. We might also observe that there is the easily verifiable fact that the criticism of another's religious beliefs does not necessarily postulate personal antagonism toward those who entertain such beliefs. Hence it is possible for a Protestant to criticize Roman Catholicism or Judaism, for example, without being in the least antagonistic to members of either faith. Let us not forget that honest criticism, debate, and the exploration of controversial issues involves the basic right of freedom of speech within constitutional limits; and the New Testament itself, the very cradle of Christianity, reflects in a startling way the fact that the faith of Jesus Christ was built and nourished upon the controversy that it provoked. It was said of the early Christians that they "turned the world upside down" (Acts 17:6); indeed, the message of the Cross itself is offensive and controversial by nature. Robert Ingersoll, the late great agnostic and renowned antagonist of Christianity, was wise enough to recognize this fact and stated in his famous lectures, "If this religion is true, then there is only one Savior, only one narrow path to life. Christianity cannot live in peace with any other religion."

There are many reasons why books and chapters like this should be written, but we shall turn to the Bible itself for the basic reasons—believing that in God's

Word, the source of our faith, will be found the evidence that its defense is very much His will.

Let us begin by noting the historical fact that Jesus Christ and His apostles warned repeatedly of false prophets and teachers.

Throughout His entire ministry, our Lord was constantly on guard against those who attempted to ensnare Him with trick questions and supposed contradictions between what He taught and the teachings of Moses and the prophets. Added to this, these professional interrogators masqueraded as religious, pious, and even tolerant zealots and professed that they were the descendants of Abraham, heirs to the covenant, and the servants of God. To these people our Lord addressed His most scathing denunciations, calling them, among other things, "whited sepulchres," "children of the devil," "dishonorers of God," "liars," "murderers," and "wolves." Since our Lord was both God and man, He alone could gaze through the centuries and see those who would arise following in the train of His contemporary antagonists, and at least two very graphic prophecies of their characters and objectives are to be found in His discourses.

In the seventh chapter of the gospel according to Matthew, Christ enunciated a very definite warning:

> Beware of false prophets, which come to you in sheep's clothing, but inwardly they are ravening wolves. Ye shall know them by their fruits. Do men gather grapes of thorns, or figs of thistles? Even so, every good tree bringeth forth good fruit; but a corrupt tree bringeth forth evil fruit. A good tree cannot bring forth evil fruit, neither can a corrupt tree bring forth good fruit. Every tree that bringeth not forth good fruit is hewn down, and cast into the fire. Wherefore by their fruits ye shall know them. Not every one that saith unto me, Lord, Lord, shall enter into the kingdom of heaven; but he that doeth the will of my Father which is in heaven. Many will say to me in that day, Lord, Lord, have we not prophesied in thy name? and in thy name have cast out devils? and in thy name done many wonderful works? And then will I profess unto them, I never knew you: depart from me, ye that work iniquity. (Matthew 7:15–23)

From this discourse we learn some very important things. We learn that there shall be false prophets, that they shall appear in sheep's clothing, and that their inward or spiritual nature is that of wolves (v. 15). We are further told that we shall be able to recognize them by their fruits. We are informed that they will prophesy in His name; in His name cast out devils, and in His name perform miracles (vv. 16, 22). With the full knowledge that they would do these things, our Lord then adds, "I will profess unto them; I never knew you . . . ye that work iniquity" (v. 23). There can be little doubt that He intended this as a warning, for He prefaces His statements with a very strong Greek term: *beware*; literally, "Be wary of or take care, because of" false prophets. The designation "wolves in sheep's clothing," then, is not that of some misguided or overzealous Christian apologist, but one that finds its authority in the words of God the Son, and this is the reason why Christians are to listen to it.

Our Lord supplemented His discussion of these individuals when in the twenty-fourth chapter of Matthew, while speaking of the circumstances surrounding His second advent, Christ declared, "For there shall arise false Christs, and false prophets, and shall show great signs and wonders; insomuch that, if it were possible, they shall deceive the very elect" (v. 24).

Further comment on this point is not necessary; He designated them "false Christs" and "false prophets"; it was He who prophesied that they would show great signs and wonders, and it was He who warned that if it were possible, the subtlety of their evil would deceive the very elect, or the church. Apparently, our Savior thought it important enough to repeat, for in verse twenty-five He says, "Behold, I have told you before."

The apostle Paul, utilizing the identical language of the Lord Jesus Christ, succinctly phrases a divine warning concerning these same people.

> For I have not shunned to declare unto you all the counsel of God. Take heed therefore unto yourselves, and to all the flock, over which the Holy Spirit hath made you overseers, to feed the church of God, which he hath purchased with his own blood. For I know this, that after my departing shall grievous wolves enter in among you, not sparing the flock. Also of your own selves shall men arise, speaking perverse things, to draw away disciples after them. Therefore watch, and remember, that by the space of three years I ceased not to warn every one night and day with tears. (Acts 20:27–31)

It appears from this very pointed statement that Paul was not afraid "to declare unto you all the counsel of God." Indeed, the greatest of the apostles warns us to "take heed," and this is to involve not only ourselves, but all Christians; and though it is addressed principally to pastors, it underlines the existence of "grievous wolves" about whom Paul says, "I ceased not to warn every one night and day with tears." Should not that which was important to him be as important to us for whom he intended it? It is of no small interest and importance that this charge of Paul to the Ephesian elders was taken very seriously by them, for in Revelation, chapter two, Christ commends the church at Ephesus for heeding Paul, in that he "tried them which say they are apostles, and are not, and hast found them liars" (v. 2).

Paul, of course, made much mention of such persons elsewhere, describing them as "enemies of the cross of Christ" (Philippians 3:18) and "false apostles, deceitful workers, transforming themselves into the apostles of Christ" (2 Corinthians 11:13). He does not even hesitate to describe them as "Satan's ministers" (2 Corinthians 11:14–15). The first and second epistles to Timothy, also of Pauline authorship, reflect the same attitude: "Now the Spirit speaketh expressly, that in the latter times some shall depart from the faith, giving heed to seducing spirits, and doctrines of devils; speaking lies in hypocrisy; having their conscience seared with a hot iron" (1 Timothy 4:1–2).

The express speaking of the Spirit, of course, underscores the importance of the counsel given, and it is significant to observe that it is to take place in the "latter times," when men shall "depart from the faith," listen to "seducing spirits," and become captives of "the doctrines of demons." This is tremendously strong language in the original Greek and is followed by his counsel in the second epistle to "preach the Word" and to "reprove, rebuke, and exhort with all longsuffering and doctrine" those who in the time to come "will not endure sound doctrine; but after their own lusts shall heap to themselves teachers who shall tickle their ears; and the truth shall be turned into fables" (2 Timothy 4:3–4, from the Greek).

It is more than a casual coincidence that the apostle Peter acknowledges the authority of Christ and Paul by utilizing their very language: "But there were false prophets also among the people, even as there shall be false teachers among you, who privily shall bring in damnable heresies, even denying the Lord that bought them, and bring upon themselves swift destruction" (2 Peter 2:1).

For Peter, it appears "false prophets" were a distinct reality, "false teachers" not figments of overwrought fundamentalist imaginations, and "destructive heresies," which denied "the Lord that bought them," vivid dangers to be guarded against. As we approach the end of the New Testament, we find John, always noted for his doctrine of love, balancing that doctrine magnificently with the teaching of divine judgment upon those whom he describes as "false prophets . . . gone out into the world" (1 John 4:1) and "deceivers . . . entered into the world, who confess not that Jesus Christ is come in the flesh. This is a deceiver and an antichrist" (2 John 7).

The next to the last book in the Bible, the comparatively small epistle of Jude, is likewise in full agreement with the verdict of our Lord and the other apostles:

> Certain men crept in unawares, who were before of old ordained to this condemnation, ungodly men, turning the grace of our God into lasciviousness, and denying the only Lord God, and our Lord Jesus Christ. . . . These are spots in your feasts of charity . . . clouds they are without water, carried about of winds; trees whose fruit withereth, without fruit, twice dead, plucked up by the roots; raging waves of the sea, foaming out their own shame; wandering stars, to whom is reserved the blackness of darkness for ever. (vv. 4, 12–13)

As we have noted, all of the quotations are in context, refer to the same individuals, and characterize them in an identical manner. The description is not pleasant, but it is a biblical one, originating with God the Holy Spirit, not with the so-called interpretational fancies or bigoted intolerances of uninformed extremists. God used these terms for people He describes in His Word; God warns the church of Christ about their existence, their methods, their teachings, their subtleties, and their final judgment. The church neglects, at her peril, such divine counsel.

There are naturally some who will not agree with this position; they will quote the advice of Gamaliel, which he addressed to the Jews in the book of Acts (5:38–39). They too will say, "Let them alone: for if this counsel or this work be of men, it will come to nought: But if it be of God, ye cannot overthrow it; lest haply ye be found even to fight against God." The only difficulty, as we have noted earlier, is that the context clearly indicates the advice was given by Gamaliel to the Jews, and Gamaliel was not an inspired writer, an apostle, or even a Christian. If his advice is to be followed and his criterion to be recognized, then the thriving growth of the various non-Christian cults, all of which deny the fundamentals of the Christian faith, must be acknowledged as the work of God! No consistent thinker of Christian orientation could long entertain such a warped conclusion without doing violence to a great portion of the New Testament.

There are also others who, in their attempt to excuse themselves from meeting the challenge of the Jesus of the cults, will refer to the ninth verse of Jude, where Michael the archangel, when contending with the devil, refused to argue with him, but rather referred him to the Lord for rebuke. Once again, however, the context reveals that Michael did not keep silence by choice, but by necessity, because as the Greek so clearly reveals, "He did not dare bring against Satan a blasphemous judgment," for the simple reason that Satan was his superior in authority. The Greek word translated *durst* in our King James Bible carries the meaning of not doing something for fear of retaliation by a superior power (Greek: *etolmese*), so this line of reasoning also fails.

The reasons why we must answer as well as be prepared to evangelize such people are quite clear. The church must do it because Christ and the apostles commanded her to do so, unpopular though it may be, and to this all true Christians should be unequivocally committed, for no other reason than out of respect for our Lord. Certainly if our mothers, wives, children, or country were attacked and misrepresented, our love for them would *compel us* to defend them. How much more, then, should love for our Redeemer so motivate us in the defense of Him and His Gospel.

The Jesus of the cults is a poor substitute for the incarnate God of the New Testament. Along with the equally important imperative of cult evangelism stands the very real need to give to everyone that asks of us "a reason of the hope that is in you" (1 Peter 3:15). That hope is the Jesus of biblical theology and of history, and once we understand the true nature of the Jesus of the cults, we can discharge our duty faithfully and by contrast unmask him and his creator for all to see. We may sum this up with the thought-provoking words of our Lord when with absolute finality He declared, "Behold, I have told you before" (Matthew 24:25).

Quick Facts About Cult Evangelism: Mission Field on Your Doorstep

■ Remember that cultists are precious souls for whom Jesus Christ offered himself; they are human beings who have homes, families, and friends.

■ Distinguish between the *theology* of Christianity, which is the real source of the antagonism, and the *personality* of the individual Christian.

■ Find a common ground of understanding— preferably the inspiration and authority of the Scriptures or the nature and attributes of God.

■ Use the Word of God and prayer—the most powerful motivating force in the universe—to implant seed thoughts about the Gospel of Christ.

■ Recognize that regardless of what a cultist says or does, he is doing it out of spiritual blindness.

■ Persevere.

Chapter 19

Cult Evangelism—Mission Field on Your Doorstep

The last one hundred years of American history have seen the evangelization of large segments of the American populace to a degree never imagined by any evangelist in the history of Christianity.

Beginning with the evangelical emphasis of Charles G. Finney, through the massive impact of D. L. Moody, Gypsy Smith, Billy Sunday, culminating in Billy Graham, and now the enormous "Harvest" crusades, American Christianity has enjoyed great spiritual privileges withheld from the world since the days of the Reformation and the Knox, Wesley, and Whitefield revivals so dear to the memory of church historians.

Yet there are many people today, in both the clergy and the ranks of the laity, who are seriously reevaluating the meaning of evangelism and its importance, if not to the church, at least to themselves. More and more, Christians are beginning to think in terms of *personal* evangelism as opposed to mass evangelism, primarily because all *successful* evangelism of enduring worth—since the earliest days of Christianity—has been of a personal nature. While it is true that great evangelists draw crowds and preach to multitudes of people, they too are dependent upon the so-called "personal touch," as evidenced by the fact that Billy Graham has more than once attempted to remove the "tag line" from his *Hour of Decision* radio program, "The Lord bless you real good," only to have such attempts reversed by the constituency that, despite its size, still desires the feeling of a personal relationship.

The follow-up work of every major evangelical crusade must be on a personal basis to be effective. A stamped envelope and a short memory course are no substitute for the personal workers, whose on-the-spot faithfulness, patience, and

This chapter reviewed by John Morehead and Everett Shropshire and edited by Jill Martin Rische.

perseverance build up and edify young converts after the first warm glow of the conversion experience has begun to abate.

This, of course, brings us to a consideration of the all-important question: What is evangelism? Is it merely mass rallies, where so-called "wholesale" decisions for Christ are made? Is it, on the other hand, only the task of the local church to shoulder the responsibility of having a week or two of meetings for revival and evangelistic purposes each year? By evangelism, do we mean massive emphasis upon radio and television to communicate the Good News of redemption? Or is evangelism somehow or other bound up with *all* of these forms of expression, and yet, in essence, none of them? Is it perhaps possible that evangelism was intended, in its primary purpose, to be personal and individualistic to the degree that each Christian feels the responsibility to evangelize his neighbor, and that this is really the root of the whole matter from which the tree of church evangelism and mass evangelism, both in crusades and the mass media, are to draw their strength and spiritual stamina? To answer these questions, and to place evangelism in its proper perspective where the challenge of non-Christian cults is concerned, we must consider carefully the pattern laid out for us in the New Testament.

Holding Forth the Word of Life

If anything proceeds from the pages of the New Testament, it is the message that the early Christian church labored under the magnificent obsession of the divine paradox. They were separate as individuals in each congregation, whether it was Ephesus, Corinth, Crete, or Philippi. But in some mysterious sense, they were "one body" in Christ (Ephesians 4:4). Through acceptance of the divine Redeemer, God had shattered and broken down the walls of race, color, and social status. They were no longer "Barbarian, Scythian, bond nor free: but Christ is all, and in all" (Colossians 3:11).

Each of these New Testament Christians was admonished by the Holy Spirit to be an ambassador or representative for his Savior (2 Corinthians 5:20). The apostle Paul set the supreme example of this in the New Testament church by declaring that the primary responsibility of the Christian was to preach the Gospel (1 Corinthians 15:1–4), and it is precisely at this juncture that, if we are willing, we can understand the meaning of New Testament evangelism.

The Greek word translated *gospel* literally means "good news," as most Christians well know. But what many do not know is that the word translated *preach* comes from the Greek *evangelizomai*, which means "to publish" the Gospel or declare it abroad for all the world to hear.

The early Christians considered themselves evangelists in that sense (1 Corinthians 1:17), and in the writings of Paul, Peter, John, and others, this great unalterable truth shines through. Christianity was not something entrusted only to clergymen, pastors, teachers, or professional evangelists. It was a personal message entrusted to those who had experienced the power of its transforming properties in their own lives, and who went literally from house to house and turned the world upside down, because they were not ashamed to proclaim it. The early Christians went forth two by two. They went forth in the power of the resurrected Christ. They went forth with a message—a message based upon experience shared by all and an experience that strengthened and comforted all. These were not people who were preoccupied with the things of the world, with contemporary political intrigues or the reigns of the Caesars, with the showplaces of Ephesus and the coliseums of Rome. These were people who were possessed by a Spirit totally removed from the spirit of the age in which they lived—a Spirit who commanded them to convict the world of sin, because though they had been its victims, they had now become its conquerors because of the Redeemer.

The incredible zeal with which they proclaimed this message of the living Christ, the Gospel of the Resurrection, the certainty of sins forgiven, the present possession of peace with God, exerted an awesome influence and power over the minds of those with whom they came in contact, almost without exception. The Philippian jailer abused Paul and Silas, until he experienced the presence of their Master. Then he, too, with his whole house, believed the incredible. Sergius Paulus, beset though he was by a demonic medium who sought to pervert the Gospel and turn him away from the faith of Christ, was stunned by the authority of a man filled with the Holy Spirit: Saul, who was also called Paul, and whose amazement turned to faith and life eternal. Even those who resisted the magnificence of New Testament evangelism were frightened by its clarity and power and felt even as Festus, who raved at the apostle, "Paul, thou art beside thyself; much learning doth make thee mad" (Acts 26:24). Agrippa the king could not be dissuaded even by the remarks of Festus, but withdrew from the presence of the Holy Spirit with the trembling admission, "Almost thou persuadest me to be a Christian" (Acts 26:28).

All of these evangelists had three things in common. First, they had experienced the person of the risen Christ and had passed out of death into life. Second, they were dominated by the Holy Spirit, alien to this world because the world does not know Him and cannot receive Him, because the world is evil and He is God. Third, they obeyed the injunction of the apostles, and as ambassadors for Christ fearlessly published the Good News that Light had come into the world, and that God had, indeed, appointed a day in which He would judge the world in righteousness by the man whom He had ordained and given assurance to all men by raising Him from among the dead.

It is not difficult to see why the Christians of the first century were able to spread Christianity throughout the earth without the aid of radio, television, traveling caravan, precision crusades, or yearly evangelistic and revival meetings. Every day was an evangelistic campaign for them; every service a revival meeting; every road a path to someone who needed Christ; every house a dwelling place for those for whom He died. These were people who were evangelists in the full meaning of the term as God had intended and commanded it. They rose to the challenge with a supreme confidence and conviction born of experience and faith, which, despite their limitations and human frailties, made them worthy of the name "saints." They could do all this because they had truly found Him "of whom Moses in the law, and the prophets, did write, Jesus of Nazareth" (John 1:45), and they had believed Him that "where two or three are gathered together in my name, there am I in the midst of them" (Matthew 18:20).

If we want to have evangelism in the true biblical sense of the term, we must return to the *content* of the evangel and to the *methods* of the New Testament church. We must utilize every modern method possible, but we must not allow them to overshadow or interfere with the great personal responsibility that rests upon every Christian. For in that very real and personal sense, it is true of us as it was of the apostle Paul, "For Christ sent me not to baptize, but to preach the gospel" (1 Corinthians 1:17).

The Philippian Christians were admonished by the apostle Paul to "shine as lights in the world; holding forth the word of life" (2:15–16). This they could do only by being willing to shine in contrast to the darkness that surrounded them and by being willing to stand in the defense of the Gospel as they held forth the Word of Life.

We are told in the simplest terms that the Gospel is God's power unto salvation (Romans 1:16), but what *is* that Gospel?

The apostle Paul states it for us in what might be called a capsule version. When writing to the Corinthians he said,

> For I delivered unto you first of all that which I received, how that Christ died for our sins according to the scriptures; and that he was buried, and that he rose again the third day according to the scriptures. (1 Corinthians 15:3–4)

The very usage of the word *Christ* in the Pauline theology identifies the office of the Anointed One with that of the second person of the Trinity, He who is God "over all, God blessed for ever. Amen" (Romans 9:5, from the Greek).

Paul does not, however, stop at this, but goes on to point out that Christ died for our sins, that is, *in place of our sins,* a clear statement of the substitutionary atonement of the Cross. Then he concludes with "He rose again the third day," which in the context of 1 Corinthians 15 can *only* refer to a bodily resurrection (Luke 24:39ff.).

We can see then that the content of the Gospel is, at its very minimum, the deity of Christ, the substitutionary atonement of the Cross, and His bodily resurrection from the grave. This Good News, when enunciated and published fearlessly by believers, has the effect of convicting men of their sins and leading them to true repentance toward God and faith in the Lord Jesus Christ. J. I. Packer, in his stimulating book *Evangelism and the Sovereignty of God,* has put it this way:

> What was this Good News Paul preached? It was the news about Jesus of Nazareth. It was the news of the incarnation, the atonement, the kingdom, the cradle, the cross and the crown of the Son of God. It was the news of how God glorified His Servant, Jesus, by making Him Christ, the world's long-awaited Prince and Saviour. It was the news of how God made His Son man, and how as man, God made Him Priest and Prophet and King, and how as Priest, God also made Him a sacrifice for sins, and how as a Prophet, God also made Him a law-giver to His people, and how as King, God has also made Him judge of all the world, and given Him prerogatives which in the Old Testament are exclusively Jehovah's own—namely to reign until every knee bows before Him, and to save all who call on His Name. In short, the good news was just this, that God has executed His eternal intention of glorifying His Son by exalting Him as the great Saviour for great sinners. Such was the Gospel which Paul was sent to preach; it was a message of some complexity, needing to be learned before it could be lived by, understood before it could be applied and needed therefore to be taught. Hence Paul as a preacher of it, had to become a teacher. He saw this as part of his call-

ing; he speaks of "the Gospel whereunto I am appointed a preacher . . . and a teacher" (2 Timothy 1:11ff.).[1]

Evangelism, then, has content as well as zeal, courage, and an attitude of constant prayer—distinct methods of propagation.

Techniques of Cult Evangelism

It is the testimony of the Word of God that He has raised up the Gentile nations and made available to them the Gospel of the kingdom and its Messianic King, which Israel rejected because of unbelief. The Scriptures declare that the purpose of God in doing this is to "provoke them to jealousy" (Romans 11:11) that they may perceive what they have lost and repent, that the natural olive branch may be grafted in again, whereas now only the wild branch (Gentiles) shares the blessing of Messiah's covenant and coming kingdom.

In the kingdom of the cults today, we are witnessing something akin to this and yet, despite its corrupt purposes, the cults are progressing at an alarming rate of speed. We see the various cult systems, specifically Jehovah's Witnesses, Mormonism, Unity, and others, utilizing the methods of Christianity and of New Testament propagation of the Christian message, wooing converts from professing Christian fellowships—Protestant as well as Roman Catholic! This bewildering proselytizing has caused consternation in many congregations and parishes across America and abroad, and it is accelerating, not slowing down.

We see the strange, but just, judgment of God upon the Christian church because of her *lethargy* in that He is allowing the forces of darkness to succeed with the methods of light while denying the *source* of light and life, the Gospel of Jesus Christ. In order that we may offset the ever-widening circle of cultic influence, Christians must, first of all, face the fact that we have been woefully delinquent in the exercise of our responsibility of personal evangelism. Second, many Christians have taken for granted the great doctrines of the Bible they learned and accepted at their conversion, and have not studied to show themselves "approved unto God, a workman that needeth not to be ashamed, rightly dividing the word of truth" (2 Timothy 2:15). Third, the average Christian knows *what* he believes, but is unable to articulate *why* he believes, insofar as being able to document the *why* of his belief from the Scriptures, which he frequently finds a frustrating and exasperating task. The clergy is largely at fault in this respect because they do not always emphasize the teaching ministry of the pulpit, but rather settle for an evangelistic emphasis with very little doctrinal depth.

A survey was taken in the department of Biblical Studies at King's College. Of some three hundred students polled, less than ten had heard a sermon in the last four years in their respective churches on the doctrines of the Trinity, the deity and humanity of Jesus Christ, or the relationship of grace and faith to works. Similar surveys have been conducted in colleges, seminaries, and Bible institutes in many major cities throughout the country. The result has been almost identical. There *must* be something fundamentally wrong when important areas of doctrine such as these are neglected or glossed over lightly.

---

[1] J. I. Packer, *Evangelism and the Sovereignty of God* (Downers Grove, Ill.: InterVarsity Press, 1975), 47.

The various cult systems, particularly Jehovah's Witnesses and the Mormons, capitalize on conditions such as these. Many an embarrassed Christian rushes to the telephone when he has a Jehovah's Witness "minister" or Mormon "elder" in his living room to get answers from a generally overworked pastor, when a little consistent study of the Scriptures would have given him a tremendous sense of security and, more important, provided him an opportunity to preach Christ in the true sense of personal evangelism to the cultist.

Throughout the world today, Christian missionaries are faced with proclaiming the unsearchable riches of the Gospel. And due to the tremendous amount of funds made available for world missions in the last one hundred years in the United States, a good many Christians have become lethargic and apathetic as to their own personal responsibility toward proclaiming the Gospel of Christ here at home. Ministers are constantly discovering that their congregations are dwindling at prayer meetings, that even their Sunday evening services have been winnowed considerably by television and other extracurricular social activities. ~Yet many don't see evangelism in the United States as a *pressing* need. Given the postmodern spirituality of American culture—openly hostile to Christianity—the growth of a variety of new religions, and a resurgence of Paganism, the time has come for mission strategists and denominations to view the United States as a fertile mission field in desperate need of trained missionaries, finances, and resources.~ Here then, lies part of the problem.

As we have shown in the preceding chapters, the non-Christian cult systems in America have grown tremendously in the last one hundred years. By a subtle utilization of a redefined terminology coupled with a surface knowledge of the Bible, and encouraged by the fact that a great many Christians are unable to answer their perversions (a fact that serves to confirm them even more definitely in those deviations), the zeal and missionary activities of the cults have tremendously increased. The only way to offset this is by a return to positive Christian evangelism on the fiercely personal basis of door-to-door and neighbor-to-neighbor effort whenever the opportunity presents itself. But over and beyond this, it is time that the church of Jesus Christ begins to consider the cults themselves as a mission field—a mission field on the doorstep of the church wherever she exists in the world, both at home and abroad.

This is by no means an impossible task. The last thirty years of the writer's life have been spent largely in this field and have confirmed his opinion that cultists too can be reached with the Gospel. They are part of the world that God so loved that He sent His only begotten Son to redeem.

Precisely how we may implement the evangelization of cultists is an important and vital subject about which nothing has been written, comparatively speaking, in the last century, and which today presents an ever-expanding challenge to the Christian. We too must obey, as did the apostle Paul, the command to publish the Good News and to pick up our credentials as ambassadors for Christ and present them to those who would evangelize *us* with a gospel other than that which the New Testament proclaims.

The following techniques and observations would be useful in any genuine Christian effort to evangelize cultists, when they are offered not as a panacea to the problem but as a tested means toward the end of bringing cultists to personal faith in Jesus Christ. This is the object of all true evangelism in any century.

1. The Human Element

One of the first things that confronts a Christian as he attempts to evangelize a cultist is the *psychological barrier* that exists in the minds of a great many persons, to the effect that cultists must be a special breed of individuals impervious to standard techniques of evangelism and generally well enough versed in the Bible to confuse, if not convince, the average Christian.

While there is an element of truth in both of these statements, it is generally traceable to experiences the Christian has had personally, either directly or indirectly, with cultists, or to those encounters with cultists in which the Christians did not fare too well. In fact, in not a few instances, they have been routed, frustrated, and embarrassed. This generally brings a tendency toward reticence, lest there be a repeat performance.

The second explanation for this phenomenon is the seemingly implanted fear that cultists should not be permitted to enter the Christian's home, in the light of 2 John 10:

> If there come any unto you, and bring not this doctrine, receive him not into your house, neither bid him God speed.

Now in context, this passage is a sentence in a letter to the Elect Lady, in whose home a Christian church quite obviously met, as the early church was prone to do, there being no cathedrals or modern churches such as we know them today. In this connection, a very common one (see Philemon 2), John warns her not to allow anyone to preach in church meetings or teach doctrines that do not honor Christ in every aspect of His person, nature, and work. It is clear that he is referring to false teachers being given a voice in the church, not to a cultist sitting in your living room! That the passage cannot be taken literally in that connection is quite evident, because if a twenty-first-century Christian's plumbing froze when the weather was twenty degrees below zero, and his cellar was rapidly flooding with water, he would not dream of asking the plumber who came over at two in the morning to fix the pipes whether or not he believed and brought the doctrine of Christ with him. Such a question would not enter his mind. Yet the plumber might be a Unitarian, Mormon, or a Jehovah's Witness! Doubtless, Christians have had them in their homes, fixing their plumbing, electricity, or furnaces and never once inquired of their views concerning the doctrine of Christ. Yet some Christians who utilize 2 John 10 as an excuse for not evangelizing cultists would never dream of using it if the cultist were a plumber!

Many pastors have instructed their flocks on the basis of this passage and other out-of-context quotations to close the doors in the faces of cultists rather than to invite them in and, in the tradition of Christian evangelism, confront them with the claims of Christ. There is no authority in the Word of God for neglecting one's responsibility as an ambassador of Christ, and the cults do not constitute a special category of evangelism.

The Christian is probably right in assuming that the average cultist does have a working knowledge of the Bible. Most of them are quite diligent in their study, both of their own literature and that of the Scriptures. And it may be true that the well-trained cultist may appear to be impervious to the proclamation of the Gospel and its defense (when necessary). But that he is some special species of unbeliever in whose presence the Christian must remain mute, and the Holy

Spirit impotent, is a gross misconception and should be abandoned by all thinking Christians.

We *must* strive to keep foremost in our minds that cultists are precious souls for whom Jesus Christ offered himself, and that they are human beings who have homes, families, friends, emotions, needs, ambitions, fears, and frustrations, which all men have in common. The cultist is special in only one sense, that he is already "deeply religious," and, therefore, probably one of the most difficult persons in the world to reach with the Gospel of Christ. He has rejected historical Christianity, and in most cases entertains hostility, if not active antagonism, toward its message. The cultist, therefore, considers evangelical Christians his greatest potential, if not actual, adversaries. Hence, an attitude of tolerance and love should always be manifested by the Christian in order to relieve, where possible, this tension and the hostile feelings of the cult adherent.

The technique of "setting the cultist at ease" does, indeed, take a great deal of patience, for the individual cultist firmly believes that he has found "the truth," and, as such, often considers the Christian message to be inferior to his own revelation. This fact is generally reflected in his attitude of superiority and even genuine resentment when the Gospel is presented. This resentment may take many forms, but it always conforms to the general thrust that since he has found the truth, how can the Christian dare to attempt to convert *him*? Cultists believe they already have progressed far beyond the evangelical Christian stage or station on the "religious railroad track" through their special revelations and superior experiences with God.

According to one psychologist, cultists also transfer their antagonism for the theology of historical Christianity to those who propagate its message, thus identifying the belief with the individual and personalizing the controversy. If the Christian who is interested in evangelizing cultists would realize this fact at the outset of his conversation with a cult adherent, he could then make a careful distinction between the theology of Christianity, which is the real source of the antagonism, and the personality of the individual Christian, thereby allowing the cultist to see the Christian as a redeemed personality, independent of his theological structure. This would make possible a form of objective discussion of biblical truth, subject to the categories of analysis, logical consistency, context, and exegesis.

While this may not necessarily undercut any portion of the cultist's theological system, it will break down or assist in breaking down the psychological conditioning of the cultist to the attitude that any person who disagrees with *his* interpretation of Christianity is automatically an object of antagonism.

In approaching the problem of cult evangelism, it must be remembered that cultists, in their respective systems of theology, are almost always by nature dependent upon forms, ceremonies, rituals, good works, right living, or self-sacrifice as a means of pleasing God and obtaining justification. Fundamentally then, cultism is a form of *self-salvation*, emphasizing deliverance from sin through human effort or merit in cooperation with their concept of the personality of the Deity.

The Christian must, therefore, in the light of this fact, point out from Scripture (since most cults recognize it as authoritative or at least partially binding), the folly of self-justification, righteousness, or human effort as a means of obtaining redemption. We should always remember that repentance, atonement, regeneration, resurrection, and retribution in the biblical sense are seldom part of the cultist's vocabulary, and *never* of his personal experience. The Christian must *define, apply,* and *defend* the historical meanings of these term before it is possible to effectively proclaim the Gospel. In a word, one must begin at the beginning, repeat, emphasize, and repeat. This is the sowing of seed that one day, by God's grace alone, will bear fruit to eternal life.

Adherents of the cults are constituted, psychologically speaking, so that they are, almost always, victims of what might be termed a mass delusion of grandeur coupled with a dogged sense of personal pride. The Scripture records that Satan fell from his first estate through measureless pride (Isaiah 14:12–14); so also today he uses the same weaknesses of the human character as a tool in shaping cult adherents to his own ends. This pride is evident in most cultists, and contributes to the delusion that they are the possessors of the true faith that saves, guardians and defenders of that which is alone holy, and administrators of divine revelation to the mass of mankind who are enmeshed in a Christianity that all cultists agree has been perverted by theologians and philosophers, thus necessitating the true restoration of the gospel through their efforts.

It has been the writer's experience that almost all cultists suffer from the concept that his or her group will at last emerge victorious over all its adversaries, inherit an eternal kingdom, and have the pleasure of viewing its adversaries being either tormented or destroyed. Such cultists cling to an illusion of impending and imminent majesty or greatness, which, when linked with their intrinsic concepts of human ability and supposed merit before God, leads to mass delusion and spiritual darkness of the most terrible nature imaginable.

The task of the Christian evangelist, then, is to reveal tactfully the true nature of man as Scripture portrays him. And, in a spirit of deep concern together with the practice of earnest prayer, reveal to the cultist God's view of fallen man and the certain destiny of those who follow in the pride-filled footsteps of Lucifer, "the god of this world" (2 Corinthians 4:4).

The nature of cultists is to be on the defensive, for they are acutely aware of the lack of unity and brotherly love clearly evidenced in many reputedly evangelical movements. They know that evangelicals are united, insofar as the cultist is concerned, only in their opposition to *him.* They, therefore, lay much stress upon the various divisions in orthodox circles, not to mention the lack of clarity where the cardinal doctrines of the Christian faith are concerned. They apparently never tire of stating, "At least we are united; you are divided, even in your own groups." It is this type of accusation that cuts the true Christian deeply. He must answer this charge by admitting differences of opinion on minor issues, but emphasizing solidarity on the fundamentals of the Gospel, which all cultists deny in one form or another.

The Christian must never forget that a well-trained cultist can be a powerful opponent, adept at text-lifting, term-switching, and surprise interpretations of "proof-texts." He should be on guard constantly lest he be deceived into admitting something that will later be utilized against him and to the detriment of both the Gospel and his personal witness.

2. Common Ground

Before attempting to evangelize a cultist, the Christian should, whenever possible, find a common ground of understanding (preferably the inspiration and authority of the Scriptures or the personality of God), and work from that point onward. Christian workers must, in effect, become all things to all men that we might by all means save some (1 Corinthians 9:22). The Christian cannot afford to have a superiority complex or reflect the idea that he is redeemed and the cultist is lost. Redemption of the soul is a priceless gift from God and should be coveted in all humility, not superiority, as just that—a gift—unearned and unmerited, and solely the result of sovereign grace.

The necessity of a common ground cannot be overemphasized for any sane approach to the problem of cult evangelism. Unless some place of agreement, some starting point, be mutually accepted by both parties, the discussion can only lead to argument, charges, counter-charges, rank bitterness, and, in the end, the loss of opportunity for further witness; and the soul of the cultist could be forfeited! Friendliness, then—open and free manifestation of Christian love and a willingness to talk over the points of diversions—will go a long way toward allaying the suspicion of the average cultist and opening further vistas for profitable and effective witnessing.

Throughout all of this, the Christian should be governed by increased activity in his prayer life, praying wherever possible in the presence of, and with, cultists, so that through the prayers that are uttered, the cultist may sense the relationship of the Christian to Him who is the Father of spirits, and our Father by faith in Jesus Christ.

3. Subliminal Seeding

The advertising industry of America has pioneered in motivational research and has taught us that ideas may be implanted in our minds beneath the level of consciousness or conscious awareness, and that they are dutifully recorded, and do in no small measure influence our thinking and actions. Jingles sung on the radio and on television quite often motivate people to purchase the product about which the jingle chants.

Christians who wish to evangelize cultists can profit from the findings of such motivational research into subliminal suggestion to an amazing degree.

It is the conviction of this writer that the Word of God and prayer, addressed to Him through the Holy Spirit, is the most powerful motivating force in the universe, and can be subliminally utilized in cult evangelism by the implantation of seed thoughts about the Gospel of Christ, as well as the Gospel itself.

How this may be done is best illustrated by examples drawn from the writer's own experiences.

Jehovah's Witnesses are probably the most active and zealous of all the missionaries of cultism in America today. When called upon by Jehovah's Witnesses, the writer for many years employed the following approach with great success.

I would invite the Watchtower adherent or adherents into the living room, but before they had opportunity to speak concerning their literature, I would state that I never discussed religion or the Bible unless such a discussion was preceded by prayer, to which all present agreed. I would then quickly bow my head and address the Lord as Jehovah God. One must be particularly careful in dealing with Jehovah's Witnesses, to always address the Deity by the name Jehovah, or else the Witnesses may not pray or bow their heads. Instead, they will admire the bric-a-brac, thumb through their Bibles, reach for their briefcases, and generally keep occupied until you have completed your prayer. Should the reader be interested in knowing how I learned this, I must confess that on occasion—I peeked!

When the name *Jehovah* is being used, the average Watchtower adherent will immediately bow his head, and after you have finished praying and *before* they can pray, begin the conversation by saying, "Now, what was it that you wanted to discuss?"

Always keep in mind in dealing with Jehovah's Witnesses that they come equipped with a portable arsenal in the form of a briefcase, which contains the major publications of the Watchtower Society for their handy reference. At the outset you must insist that they use nothing but the Scriptures and that it must be a recognized translation (King James, *Revised Standard Version, New International, New American Standard,* etc.). You must further insist upon a discussion of cardinal doctrines, particularly concerning the person, nature, and work of Jesus Christ. Thus deprived of his Watchtower material and his Watchtower translations, and circumscribed to the person of Christ in discussion, even the best trained Jehovah's Witness is at a distinct disadvantage. On the other hand, the Christian who is indwelt by the Holy Spirit then has a definite advantage.

After the discussion has gone on for some time, and I have listened to as much of "Pastor" Russell's theology as I can tolerate for one evening, I would remind the Witnesses of the lateness of the hour and ask if we could close with a word of prayer. I would then immediately bow my head and begin praying again.

Now what I have mentioned is, by itself, only an outline of how to conduct oneself in the presence of Jehovah's Witnesses, with one important exception. During my opening and closing prayers, I would totally preach the Gospel, emphasizing the deity of Christ, His death for our sins, the certainty of knowing that we have eternal life *now,* by faith in Him, and that salvation comes by grace alone, independent of human works. I would profusely quote the Scriptures, and in actuality be preaching a three-minute sermonette, subliminally implanting the true Gospel of Jesus Christ and, I might add, blissfully uninterrupted. For no one, not even the most zealous disciple of "Pastor" Russell, Joseph Smith, or Brigham Young, can interrupt a prayer. I have seen such a methodology or technique of evangelism make a tremendous impact upon Jehovah's Witnesses and other cultists, because, for six minutes of the evening at least, the Christian has the opportunity to present the true Gospel of Christ without interruption.

We must believe that God's Word will not return unto Him void, but will accomplish what He pleases and prosper in the thing whereto He has sent it (Isaiah 55:11).

4. The Vocabulary of Redemption

Non-Christian cultists of all varieties are prone to one psychological and spiritual insecurity: They are all aware of the fact that they do not *now* possess eternal life or peace with God. In fact, it is toward this end that they are vigorously pursuing the theology and practices of their respective systems.

There can never be a substitute, therefore, for an individual Christian's personal witness to what Christ has done for him. A word of caution, however, must be inserted at this juncture. As we know, cultists have their own vocabulary, so it will be necessary for the Christian to define carefully his terms when he speaks of conversion—its means and its effect upon his spirit, mind, and life. The only really unanswerable argument is the argument of a transformed life, properly grounded in the authority of the Scriptures and motivated by love for God and for one's fellow man. Key terms that must be carefully defined are: new birth or "born again"; justification; atonement; deity and resurrection of Christ; resurrection; forgiveness; grace; and faith. It is inevitable that eternal retribution be discussed, because this is the very thing from which Christ died to save us.

The Scriptures admonish us to be "His witnesses," and in order to do this we must be willing to endure all things and be governed by patience, temperance, grace, and love. Then regardless of how the truth of God is assailed, perverted, or distorted, and no matter how much our own character and motives are attacked, Christ will be honored by our conduct.

The vocabulary of redemption involves personal involvement, testimony to the effect of Christ's power both to redeem the soul and to transform the individual, his morals, his ethics, his life. And most of all, it involves the power to impart to him the peace of God that passes all understanding, the peace that Christ said would come only to those who make peace with God (Philippians 4:7).

5. The Secret of Perseverance

One of the most important techniques of cult evangelism is that of perseverance with the cultists. Anyone who has ever worked extensively in the field of cults will readily testify that this takes a great deal of grace and understanding on the part of the Christian. Many times cultists (particularly Jehovah's Witnesses and the Mormons) will deliberately "bait" Christians in an attempt to provoke the Christian into losing his patience, thus justifying their own teachings. In order to avoid such pitfalls and to be able to endure the many forms of abuse and persecution, which will come about when a Christian penetrates the theology of the cultist with the sword of the Spirit, one must discover a secret that, when prayerfully understood and applied, can make the endurance of *anything*, for the sake of Christ, possible.

We are forever in debt to the apostle Paul, who pointed out in his second letter to the Corinthians that those who are outside of Christ have indeed been spiritually blinded by the god of this age. Satan has caused a cloak of *delusion* to descend over their minds and understanding, so that Christ's Gospel, which is the light of the world, cannot penetrate it. The secret of perseverance is to know and to understand, regardless of what a cultist says or does, that he is doing it out of spiritual blindness. Since our warfare as Christians is not against flesh and blood (the cultist), but against the spiritual forces of darkness that rule this world (Satan and his emissaries), it is possible to love the cultist, endure his abuses, perversions, and recriminations, while at the same time faithfully bearing witness for Christ.

This technique of cult evangelism should never be minimized. And once it is properly appreciated, it can become a great asset to the Christian.

There are doubtless many, many more things that could be mentioned in connection with cult evangelism, such as the important fact that when dealing with the Gnostic cults (Christian Science, Unity, New Thought, etc.), distinct emphasis must be placed upon personal sin, which they all negate or deny; also the certainty of retribution as taught by the Lord Jesus Christ should be emphasized. We might also profitably note that in dealing with religions that have had their origin outside the United States (Baha'ism, Theosophy, Zen, etc.), the Christian ought to have a working knowledge of what the doctrines of these cults are in relation to the historical Christian revelation. It is foolish to attempt to discuss Christian doctrines with those who do not accept the authority of the Scriptures, which is most certainly the case in regard to the three cults just mentioned.

Finally, evangelism, particularly cult evangelism, must never fail to emphasize that Christ and the disciples taught certain irrevocable doctrines as well as consistent ethics and morality.

It has been the experience of the author, based upon numerous personal contacts with cultists of all varieties, that there has yet to be born a cultist who can confuse, confound or in any way refute a Christian who has made doctrinal theology an integral part of his study of the Scriptures. Cults thrive upon ignorance and confusion where the doctrines of the Scriptures are concerned, but are powerless to shake Christians in their faith or effectively proselytize them when the Christian is well grounded in the basic teachings of the Bible and given over to a study of the great doctrinal truths of the Word of God. These mighty buttresses of Christian theology must no longer be taken for granted by Christian believers, nor should pastors and teachers assume that the average Christian has sound knowledge concerning them. The rise of cultism to its present proportions indicates a great dearth of knowledge where doctrine is involved, and is a decided weakness in the battlements of orthodox theology, which the church ignores at the risk of innumerable souls.

Accepting, then, the fact that the poison of cultism can be effectively combated only by the antidote of sound doctrine, the next problem is the immunization of Christians against the teachings of the cults. The answer to this problem lies within the pages of God's Word; it involves study (2 Timothy 2:15) on the part of Christians, instruction on the part of the pastor and teacher (1 Timothy 4:1–6), coupled with a willingness to start at the beginning, where sound doctrine is concerned, even as the risen Christ did with the doubting disciples, and to reexamine the reason *why* Christians believe what they believe. Particularly recommended for intensive study are the doctrines of biblical inspiration, the Trinity, the deity of Christ, the personality and work of the Holy Spirit, the Atonement, justification by faith, works, the bodily resurrection of Christ, and the resurrection of all mankind.

The great and true Trinitarian doctrine of God and the deity of Jesus Christ should be inculcated ceaselessly in Christian minds so that the Lord's people may never forget that Jesus Christ is the core of God's plan for the ages. The fact that He vicariously died and bodily arose, thus vindicating His claim to deity through obedience to the righteous character of both His Father's will and law, both of which He perfectly fulfilled at Calvary, must be perpetually emphasized.

It is a well-known fact that no antidote for poison is effective unless it is administered in time and in the proper dosage prescribed by a competent physician. In like manner, Christian doctrine should not be taught in a dry, matter-of-fact way, as it so often is, but should be given in small doses over a long period. The treatment should begin at once, from the Sunday school level right through college and seminary, where the need is urgent.

Christians must realize while the opportunity is yet ours that the teaching of sound doctrine does not predicate a dead orthodoxy. When properly understood, a living acceptance of and familiarity with doctrine form the giant pillars of truth upon which our faith rests, a familiarity that has always produced great leaders and effective workers for the proclamation of the Gospel of grace.

The evangelization of cultists is the task of the Christian church, of which each Christian is a member, a part of the body of Christ. Until this is recognized, and Christians are urged and encouraged by their pastors and leaders to forsake the portals of Hollywood and the domain of the great gods, television, etc., for door-to-door publishing of the Good News of God's love in Jesus Christ for a lost world, the evangelization of cultists will continue to be one of the great tragedies of the Christian church in our day. It is excellent that we support foreign missions and send the light of God's Gospel around the globe, but it is quite another thing for us to begin here, where the demand is personal, challenging, and equally rewarding. This challenge is cult evangelism, the mission field on *your* doorstep.

Commentary

~The explosion of technology and information systems at the end of the twentieth century has rendered cult evangelism and recruitment more prolific than anyone could have imagined. The birth and exponential growth of the Internet has made thousands of alternative belief systems as accessible as one's desktop computer and telephone. The simplicity of personal computer operation combined with its amazingly sophisticated capabilities has turned the publishing world upside down, providing the cults with a new and powerful means of publishing and communicating their false gospels. As alarming as this development is, it also brings us a fresh hope for effective, widespread communication of the Gospel. The same advances that enable the cults to evangelize so effectively can and should be used by Christians to proclaim the *truth* of the Gospel as evidenced by Jesus Christ and His resurrection from the dead (1 Corinthians 15:1–4).

It has never been truer that the claims of Christ are the defining issues of salvation and eternal life. These claims are the heart and soul of the Christian faith, and the central reasons for the antagonism believers encounter. The command to defend the faith, "once for all delivered, the saints" (Jude 3 RSV) is intrinsically tied to these claims. Our responsibility, then, is twofold: to *preach* the message of Christ, and to *defend* that message against those who would *alter* it to accomplish their own purposes.

To this end, it is vital that all Christians be educated in the basic doctrines and vocabulary of the biblical faith; it is *imperative* for all Christians to be trained to share their faith simply, clearly, and persuasively—with all non-Christians, including cultists. And, above all, it is essential that the love of Christ be demonstrated daily through relationships that communicate the Gospel and meet the needs of people.[2]~

---

[2]Marked sections in this chapter are editorial commentary, cited from Walter Martin, *Kingdom of the Cults*, (Minneapolis: Bethany House Publishers, 1997), 443–57.

Recommended Resources

1. Clegg, Tom, and Warren Bird. *Lost in America: How You and Your Church Can Impact the World Next Door.* Loveland, Co.: Group Publishing, 2001.
2. Clifford, Ross, and Philip Johnson. *Jesus and the Gods of the New Age.* Oxford, England: Lion Publishing, 2001.
3. Copan, Paul. *True for You but Not for Me: Deflating the Slogans That Leave Christians Speechless.* Minneapolis: Bethany House Publishers, 1998.
4. Hesselgrave, David J. *Communicating Christ Cross-Culturally.* Grand Rapids, Mich.: Zondervan, 1991, 2nd edition.
5. Martin, Walter. *Spiritual Warfare.* Audiotape. Walter Martin Ministries. *www.waltermartin.com.*
6. Watchman Fellowship. *www.watchman.org.*

Chapter 20

The Road to Recovery

In the preceding chapters of this volume, we have studied and evaluated in the light of the Word of God the major non-Christian cults or sects that have consistently challenged the missionary outreach of the church of Jesus Christ. All the groups that were discussed are admitted rivals of historic Christianity. The question, then, quite logically arises, "What action can the church take, in both the ecumenical and independent wings of Christendom, to meet the challenge of contemporary American cults?" It is the purpose of this chapter to outline both a methodology and a plan whereby we may not only bring the inroads of the cults under control, but, what is more important, to actually take positive steps to evangelize cultists, which of course is the primary task of the Christian church. By traveling what might be called "the road to recovery," the church may once again see the day when, by speaking the truth in love and with clarity, much of the ground lost to cults in the last century may be regained. It should never be forgotten that whatever a specific cult offers to attract individuals is infinitesimal compared with what Jesus Christ offers to the soul who will cast all his care upon Him. The church has nothing to fear from the cults as long as she is faithful to her mission of both proclaiming and vigorously contending for the faith that was once for all delivered unto the saints (Jude 3).

It is the feeling of the writer that if the following suggestions were put into immediate practice, both in the United States and on the foreign mission fields, a constructive approach to the mounting problem of cults would emerge.

Project One—Research

In order to provide information of any type for the pastor, teacher, missionary, student, or layman, it is vitally important that there be careful research into the background and theology of the major cult systems. There already exists a

This chapter updated and edited by Kevin Rische and Jill Martin Rische.

considerable amount of data that could be utilized, once it has been validated, codified, and carefully weighed by mission agencies and field representatives of the major denominations and independent Christian groups. The average cultist is willing to listen to facts, particularly if he is at variance with what he has been taught, but only if those facts, once he checks them, are shown to be accurate and reliable. We have seen more than a few Jehovah's Witnesses and Mormons, for instance, carefully reevaluate their religion as a result of careful research on the part of interested Christians.

Second, a statistical breakdown of the growth and development of the major cult systems at home and abroad must be worked out so that those areas where they have grown most rapidly may be plotted and the factors contributing to that growth analyzed in contrast to their lack of growth in other areas.

Third, questionnaires must be sent out to key personnel in all Christian movements, seeking their reaction to the challenge of the cults in those areas under their jurisdiction. In this way, a broad perspective of cult methodology will be obtained.

Clipping services must also be utilized, for major population centers through the world are generally the targets of the major sects, and it is always helpful to know the coming and going of cult missionaries, as well as their planned area meetings (international conventions, missionary report sessions, special lectures, etc.).[1]

Of course, a research center dealing with cults is not a new proposal. The Christian Research Institute, of which I am the founder and director, was incorporated in 1960 to meet this need. It is our aim to collate and disseminate information to all Christian groups, ecumenical as well as independent, helping them to win those in the cults to Christ. Walter Martin Ministries (*www.waltermartin.com*) continues this work.

Walter Martin Ministries, as a bureau of information on comparative religions, provides Christian leaders, missionaries, and workers throughout the world with ready access to information that is currently important. But the project is far too involved to be merely an independent effort. There must be cooperation and the free interchange of information between all concerned Christian groups, followed by financial support, in order that any research project of such scope and magnitude succeed in its objective.

Project Two—Computer Retrieval System

One of the newest ways for combating the forces of the cults is through the use of computers. Christian Research Institute is proposing a plan, which, if adopted, could revolutionize the field of apologetics. I propose that a computer information retrieval system be developed that can provide answers on the cults to practically anyone with access to a university or college library. This would be called the Christian Research Lending Library (SENT/EAST).

For example, many of the arguments that Jehovah's Witnesses bring forth against orthodoxy are mangled attempts to force the Greek text of the New Testament into their theological framework. What recourse does the average Christian have against such mistranslation if he does not have any knowledge of New

---

[1]*www.clippingservice.com/*

Testament Greek? Through our projected computer network, individuals would be able to tap our resources via computer terminals. This person would be able to type his question at a terminal and receive an almost instantaneous reply complete with documentation.

There are more than nine million Americans involved in cults and the occult in the United States today, and this is one way that they can be reached with very little struggle.[2] This computer network will hopefully be used even in other countries. We will be able to take all of our research and information that we have been gathering for the last thirty years and make it available to anyone who needs it.

Of course, there are many things that are necessary to a viable program like this. We need the cooperation of all of the other organizations in this field in the United States and abroad. We need to share the information that is available in so many different locations.

A program like this is also very expensive, and although we visualize that participants in the program will contribute a share of the costs, donations and volunteers are needed to offset the enormous expense.

With the prayers and help of dedicated Christian laymen and leaders all over the country, a program such as SENT/EAST will energize the missionary forces as they seek to bring the Gospel to those in the cults.

Project Three—Specialized Literature

Just as the function of Project One would be the collecting, sorting, and condensing of usable facts and information, so Project Three would be its logical outgrowth, the publication and distribution and also the translation of such material on an international scale. The value of tracts, pamphlets, and books printed and disseminated at cost, both in the United States and on those mission fields where specific cults are rapidly growing, is incalculable, as any foreign missionary will readily testify.

Through the facilities of Walter Martin Ministries, Ravi Zacharias International Ministries, Jude 3 Ministries, Institute for Biblical Apologetics, Christian Research Institute, and numerous other interested groups, practically all missionaries would have information available for distribution to indigenous churches and to Christian workers on their respective fields, so that no longer would it be possible for such organizations as Jehovah's Witnesses and the Mormons to capitalize on the absence of literature accurately describing their faith and refuting their claims.

In South America alone, where the Mormons and the Jehovah's Witnesses, not to mention the indigenous animistic and spiritistic cults, exist in growing numbers and force of influence, preliminary surveys indicate that almost 90 percent of those questioned not only desire but earnestly request literature that will assist them in both refuting and evangelizing cults.

In the United States and Canada—where much headway is being made by cult systems—universities, colleges, seminaries, Bible institutes, and local churches have consistently requested reliable literature from recognized denominational and independent sources. But since funding and support services are

---

[2]*www.adherents.com/rel_USA.html* and *www.gc.cuny.edu/studies/key_findings.htm*

so unequal to the task, those organizations working tirelessly to provide such information are deluged with more requests than can be handled. Special commissions should therefore be appointed similar to that already sponsored by the World Council of Churches, so that Christian individuals, organizations, churches, and denominations may pool their information and erect a systematic defense against cult proselytizing. Though conservatives and liberals may disagree theologically, they suffer from the inroads of the cults individually, and yearly the ranks of American cultism are swelled by former Methodists, Episcopalians, Lutherans, Baptists, Congregationalists, etc., who attended both liberal and conservative churches until they were converted by the cults.

That there is a desperate need for literature and that it must be doctrinally oriented, no serious scholar in the field of cults will deny. But that such literature can be made available without the cooperation of interested church members, educators, and lay readers is quite dubious if not impossible. The cults have capitalized on the fact that the Christian church has not made any really significant effort to halt their proselytizing techniques and to answer the propaganda directed against all forms of Christianity. This has been, in no small measure, a contributing factor to their success. It is true that research will produce and has already produced considerable amounts of useful information, but its printing and distribution is a fundamental concern if we are to deal effectively with the issues that face us.

Project Four—Educational Reevaluation

Samuel Johnson, the great educator, once wrote, "The foundation of every state is the education of its youth," and we would do well to paraphrase this in the context of Christianity: "The future of the church is in the education of its leaders."

As a college professor, the writer has been deeply interested in the courses offered in Bible institutes, colleges, universities, and seminaries, as well as pre-theological schools, dealing with the subject of comparative religions and particularly with non-Christian cults or sects. In this area a very real problem exists, and it will do no good to let the matter rest with this observation. Rather, the facts, appalling as they may be, should be aired.

Since the advent of Christian missionary activities on an organized scale some two hundred years ago, the proclamation of the Gospel message has faced many problems. Obstacles of language, culture, race, militant nationalism, and the competition between missionaries of different doctrinal persuasions have contributed to a stormy atmosphere in world missions.

In addition to these difficulties, major non-Christian religions, such as Islam, Buddhism, Hinduism, Taoism, Shintoism, etc., have actively opposed Christian missionaries, so that progress has been slow in many areas and in some instances hardly recognizable.

Beyond this aspect, however, looms, as we have mentioned, the formidable obstacle of non-Christian American cults, many of which are now worldwide. Some of these movements have proselytized new converts on already established fields with startling success. Utilizing the methods reminiscent of early Christianity, the cults cater to the culture patterns of those they proselytize, provide literature in the language of the people, and one way or another, keep a certain emphasis on the Bible in the forefront of their work. In many instances, they preach a militant "separation" from tobacco, alcohol, and other practices classified as worldly and unspiritual. All these activities are bolstered by their so-called revelations (all of nineteenth-century vintage), with an appeal to which they wage unceasing warfare against all religions, but against Christian denominations in particular. It is significant that they first approach known Christians. Seldom do they attempt to reach unbelievers, which should be the first step in any genuine missionary program.

We are not to suggest that the activities of these movements be curtailed by law or that they should become the target of an evangelical barrage of abuse. Full freedom of worship and the right to promulgate one's convictions are historical planks in the platform of Protestant evangelism. Even such terms as "sect" or "cult" seem more appropriate in lands with a state church than in open religious situations. But Christianity will need to preserve the distinction between truth and heresy if it is to have a future. Some groups, particularly Jehovah's Witnesses, by their demonstrated hostility to governmental authorities, have frequently jeopardized the reputation and efforts of others of genuine Christian persuasion. As a result, there has been great friction between their workers and Christian missionaries. It is difficult, indeed, for Christian missionaries to compete successfully with such divisive forces in a positive way and to evangelize missionaries of such zealous groups as the Mormons, Jehovah's Witnesses, and other virulent indigenous groups.

Now we might ask at this juncture, "What is being done to train Christian missionaries abroad (and, for that matter, pastors, teachers, and leaders in the United States) to deal with this growing problem? On the educational level, are Christian institutions taking seriously the needs at home and on the mission fields? Are there mandatory courses for future Christian leaders to aid them in both evangelizing and refuting cultists?"

The cults continually emphasize the Bible, but despite the prominence given the Scriptures, without exception they place themselves in the roles of infallible interpreters of the Word of God, their dogmatism rivaled only by Jesuit scholars. Instead of being the infallible rule of faith and practice, the Bible is relegated to a secondary position. This is accomplished almost subliminally, so that the convert is unaware that his primary authority is not really grounded in Scripture, but rather in the interpretation of Scripture put forth by the respective cult.

Though this fact is well known among missionaries and Christian workers, it apparently has not filtered back to seminaries, Bible colleges, and Bible institutes. It is a fact that at present less than 5 percent of all such institutions in the United States require as a prerequisite of graduation that a student take a course on comparative religions or non-Christian American cults, a fact that staggers the imagination when one can see the obvious inroads the cults have made both at home and abroad.

In a classic periodical article, Professor Gilbert Peterson, Chairman of the Department of Religious Education at the Philadelphia College of the Bible, made the following observations concerning the educational curricula of American Bible colleges, institutes, and seminaries:

Preparation is a word which is found to headline some newspapers, on the lips of statesmen, military leaders and educators as well as church leaders and mission board directors. It has taken on a significant meaning in our times as the threats of world leaders, nations and the varied ideologies of men vie for prominence in the world around us. Christian educators need to stop from time to time, and evaluate the preparation men and women are receiving in the various Christian schools of higher learning. . . .

It is with a sense of great urgency that the graduates of Bible colleges, along with Christian young people from other educational backgrounds, face the task of living and witnessing to the truth of the Gospel in these troubled times. Each spring a new group of young people receives its diplomas or degrees to serve God as missionaries, both at home and on the foreign field.

In a recent survey conducted by the author, of over twenty-three Bible colleges in the United States and Canada, representing a total number of graduates in excess of fifteen thousand, it was found that approximately 12 ½ percent of this number, or about nineteen hundred individuals, are presently serving on the foreign mission fields of the world. Our concern at present is not with the percentage of Bible college graduates going to the mission field, but rather the preparation they receive in the area of formal cult apologetics before going to the mission field.

In the past ten years the outreach of cults and isms through the mediums of radio, the printed page, and missionary endeavors, has reached enormous proportions. The rapidity of their growth is traceable in large measure to the dearth of information among Christians in regard to what is being promulgated by the various cults on the one hand, and a failure to act upon the scriptural command to resist them on the other. In the survey, questionnaires were sent to over fifty Bible colleges. In the twenty-three schools replying, there was great diversity of requirements in the section of the curriculum dealing with apologetics, cults, and unchristian religions. The course most often required of all graduates was "Cults and Isms." The course usually entailed the study of the history and development of several cults, their doctrinal position, and a refutation of their position from the Scriptures. Apologetics was next in order of numbers of requirements. This course covers a systematic presentation of the reasons and evidences of the Christian faith. The course offered most often was Comparative Religions, with nine schools offering it as an elective, three requiring it for all mission majors, and four schools requiring it of all graduates. This course covers a comparative study of the major living religions of the world.

In order to meet the challenge of our day in preparing our young people to face the present religious world situation, we need to realize what is being offered to the students in our Bible colleges, institutes, and seminaries by way of preparing them to serve Christ in the midst of the rise of cultism. The following is offered as a suggestion as to how we might structure this one area of the curriculum. This is, of course, not a final pronouncement, but rather a recommendation for exploration of this difficult field.

There is no substitute for a thorough knowledge of the Word of God and the truth of God that it reveals. Courses in direct Bible study and doctrine provide one with the necessary foundation. In addition to this, a three-hour course in Apologetics is needed where the needs of men, the Christian answer to these needs, and the reasons for the uniqueness and truth of Christianity are presented.

It is not enough that one know only his own beliefs when faced by the average non-Christian and cultist, and, therefore, following Apologetics there should be a three-hour course in Cults and Isms. This course, as previously suggested, would examine the historical and doctrinal development of such non-Christian groups as Jehovah's Witnesses, Christian Science, Mormonism, Unity, and the like. The course would include the Christian answer to these systems and an evaluation of their terminologies, and an accurate, consistent method of approaching them with evangelism as the goal.

A course such as comparative religions could be offered on an elective basis to give the student a broader view of non-Christian religions. When a student goes to the mission field, a far more detailed study of the religion of that particular field must be made by the missionary candidate, and can be made in comparative religions. Therefore, specialized courses should be offered in these fields. Also the training received in apologetics and cults along the lines of definitive terminology and doctrinal evaluation will prove extremely valuable.

At present, of the twenty-three Bible colleges reporting, ten offer a course in Apologetics, with six requiring it of all students; eleven schools offer a course in Cults, with seven requiring it of all students; sixteen schools offer a course in Comparative Religions, with three requiring it of all mission majors and four requiring it of all students.

This means that a little more than one-fourth of the Bible colleges replying already follow the suggested curriculum outlined, or one very similar to it, and a little less than one-half of the reporting schools offer all three courses (Apologetics, Cults, and Comparative Religions) in their present curriculums.[3]

Mr. Peterson's remarks are very much to the point, for when it is remembered that only eleven schools out of twenty-three offered courses on Cult Apologetics, and only seven out of those eleven required it for graduation, the situation is seen to be acute.

In the case of seminaries and Bible institutes in the United States, a detailed study now in preparation indicates even at this early date that the problem of non-Christian cults is not taken seriously by the majority.

Such information will not paint an encouraging picture to be sure, especially in the light of accelerated cult growth on our major mission fields.

Mission fields have the added problem of dealing with certain indigenous cults with strong nationalistic overtones, particularly in Africa and Asia. These groups amalgamate some of the teachings of Christianity with the older pagan religions, particularly Animism and Spiritism, and come equipped complete with their own special revelations and messiahs. The situation is particularly true in the Philippine Islands, Japan, and Africa, where Christianity is caricatured as a "white man's religion," a Western import superimposed on native cultural and religious patterns. Such an approach by the cults has been disastrously successful, particularly in South America, where in Brazil we have seen a resurgence of Spiritism on an unprecedented scale. *Time* magazine even devoted its religious section once to comments by a Roman Catholic missionary deploring the inroads of the spiritists into the Roman Catholic Church. Unfortunately, the same can be said also in respect to some Protestant agencies; so the problem is universal. In

---

[3]Gilbert Peterson, *Religious Research Digest* (December 1961): 8–11.

passing, it might be noted that the Roman Catholic Church has recently begun detailed research in the area of non-Christian cults and sects, so effective have been the methods of both American-based and indigenous cults in proselytizing Roman Catholic converts.

On the basis of past performance, it is safe to prognosticate that within the next decade, all things remaining constant, the cults will intensify their propaganda activities to three or four times their present rate. The question is, will the church of Jesus Christ rise to the occasion while time remains? The church must be prepared to defend the claims of Scripture interpreted by the Holy Spirit that it alone is "given by inspiration of God, and is profitable for doctrine, for reproof, for correction, and for instruction in righteousness" (2 Timothy 3:16).

The Christian church must also be ready to remind indigenous nationalistic sects that Christianity is an Eastern religion, that Christ was born, died, and was resurrected in Asia, and ascended from the Mount of Olives; so it is anything but "a foreign religion." But if the cults are to be effectively dealt with at home and on the foreign mission fields of the world, then missionaries, pastors, and particularly educators, who mold the curricula of Christian institutions, must press for strong curricula in those institutions. Christians must be taught not only what they believe but why they believe it, that they may be able, as the Scripture admonishes us, to "be ready always to give an answer to every man that asketh you a reason of the hope that is in you with meekness and fear" (1 Peter 3:15).

The teachings of the major sects must be codified and indexed and a running commentary provided for all interested parties in the form of the publication of literature and perhaps a semi-annual journal. It will then be possible to understand the methodology of the cults at home and abroad, to note the areas of their doctrinal emphasis and growth, and their use and abuse of Christian terminology. The Church of Jesus Christ, as we have noted, has nothing to fear from the zeal and competition of the cults, but she has much to fear from her own apathy and lethargy in this vital area of missionary concern. The means to evangelize and combat adherents of the cults can be made readily available to all interested parties. It remains for Christians of both ecumenical and independent persuasion to agree to cooperate in the dissemination of pertinent literature on this ever-growing field of mutual concern.

On every front the church is faced with unrelenting and mounting pressures from anti-Christian forces. Our Lord has warned us, "The night cometh, when no man can work" (John 9:4), but the publication of literature may yet give us some time to work in the twilight that precedes the sunset.

It will do us little good, however, to sponsor research and to publish and distribute literature if at the fountainhead of all Christian work, the educational preparation of Christian leadership, we do not revise the curricula of numerous Bible institutes, universities, and seminaries to meet these needs, both in the United States and on the mission field. So it appears that education, as always, is of vital significance.

Project Five—Conferences on Cults

A final suggestion to help implement support for a unified approach to the challenge of the cults is the sponsoring of specialized conferences or lectures on the local church level, at Bible conferences and in schools and seminaries, by competent students of the major cult systems. I have used such conferences for years, and other cult-watching organizations have followed the same successful pattern. These conferences continually stimulate a great deal of interest, showing as they would by contrast the differences between the teachings of the cults and historical Christianity. If conducted in a dignified, scholarly, and yet popular manner, with question and answer periods following each lecture, such conferences would serve a dual purpose. They would both explain the divergent doctrines of the cults and, at the same time, strengthen the faith of Christians in the great fundamental teachings of Christianity. The author has been engaged in such a ministry for some years with considerable success, but much more yet remains to be done. For as the Scripture reminds us, "Lift up your eyes and look on the fields; for they are white already to harvest. . . . The harvest truly is plenteous, but the labourers are few. Pray ye therefore the Lord of the harvest, that he will send forth labourers" (John 4:35; Matthew 9:37–38). Speakers are available from Walter Martin Ministries in these areas, and there are many other organizations and individuals throughout the country that provide similar services. However, the need is much greater than the supply, and it must be met quickly.

If the preceding suggestions were adopted and put into operation, it is the conviction of this writer that the major cult systems would soon feel the impact and receive the benefit of the unified Christian witness to the veracity of the faith that they have chosen to reject.

Through the use of good research material, properly disseminated and translated where possible into the language of the fields where the cults are most active, and aided by clipping services, which would keep the research center informed of major cult efforts around the world, Christians of all denominations, as well as pastors, educators, and missionaries, would be kept abreast of the activities of the larger cult systems.

Concluding our observation, then, the road to recovery will not be an easy one to travel, and will be fraught with problems and conflicts; but if we will begin to travel it, we will find at the end of it and along the way those who have been delivered from the cults, those who have been dissuaded from joining them, and those who have been both evangelized and strengthened by a determined effort of the Christian church not only to proclaim the message of redeeming grace but also to defend the claims and the Gospel of her Savior. We can go a long way toward recovering the ground we have lost, but we must begin now.

Commentary[4]

~Dr. Walter Martin first proposed the following projects in 1960, upon the founding of the Christian Research Institute. His foresight almost forty years ago gives these recommendations a poignancy and urgency that are remarkable.

Of particular note is Dr. Martin's vision, in project number two, for the use of a computer-based research program. He saw the gigantic, building-sized mainframe computers of major universities as the satellite repositories of apologetics research by which individuals could access needed information by subscription

---

[4]Marked sections in this chapter include editorial commentary, cited and updated from Walter Martin, *Kingdom of the Cults,* (Minneapolis: Bethany House Publishers, 1997), 462.

and return mail. At the time of the original announcement of his plans, most people rejected it as a Jules Verne fantasy that would never see fruition.

The primary source of research at that time was by means of old-fashioned legwork, painstaking firsthand interviews of cult leaders, accumulation of cultic literature by on-site visits to cult meetings and headquarters, and careful perusal of dusty records, files, and books in specialized archives. The few Christians who had committed their lives to researching, writing about, and evangelizing the cults worked in relative isolation, not only from one another but from most other full-time Christian workers, pastors, educators, and missionaries. Records were carefully typed with carbon copies and kept in banks of filing cabinets.

Four decades later the entire face of Christian cult apologetics has changed. Nowhere is this more evident than in the once unimaginable realm of the World Wide Web computer information system. The electronic explosion, beginning in the 1980s and continuing on into the new millennium, has transformed research, evaluation, publication, and evangelism in the field of cult apologetics. Contemporary electronic developments have enabled cults to publish their heresies in unprecedented quantity, but these advances also have enabled cult apologetics researchers to track and research those same cultic movements.

When the relatively obscure and very small UFO cult Heaven's Gate ended its more than twenty-year existence by the suicide of its leader and thirty-eight members in March 1997, those few researchers who had seen cult apologetics develop over the decades participated in a remarkable fusion of the old methods and the new technology. Within a few short hours of the discovery of the tragedy, Christian cult apologetics organizations were able to access voluminous information from the Internet on the Heaven's Gate cult, their commercial computer software business, their theology, their fascination with the Hale-Bopp Comet and extra-terrestrials, the identity and claims of their leader, Marshall Applewhite, and their fatal destiny. At the same time, those who had worked in the field for decades hunted through memories and dusty filing cabinets for the yellowed newspaper clippings, faded flyers, and handwritten notes from our earlier research and evangelism encounters with the group in the mid-1970s.

At the end of the century, what had been mocked as delusion is now a reality through the Apologetics Index (*www.apologeticsindex.com*) and many other excellent Christian research sites. Anyone with a personal computer and a telephone can access the resources of Walter Martin Ministries with a few keystrokes. The *Essential Christianity* radio broadcast is heard daily nationwide, and is also available through the Internet to anyone with a computer connection. Through the resources of the Walter Martin Ministries and other cult apologetics organizations easily contacted via the Internet, answers to the cults have never been so readily available to Christians everywhere. Whether a Christian is evangelizing a Mormon, protesting a public school antireligious policy, testing the doctrines of a new church, or researching a world religion, the answers are available through computers as small and almost as light as a notebook, right in one's own home.

It is unfortunate, however, that the same five projects Dr. Martin outlined so long ago still need further development and implementation. If his admonitions had been taken seriously by American Christian leadership in 1960, the focus of this chapter at the close of the century would have been a review of the overwhelming resurgence of biblical faith and of the devastation of cultic strongholds.

Instead, his plea seems even more urgent today. Cultic doctrine has permeated every religious forum in America, Christian as well as non-Christian. While Walter Martin's ministry was focused primarily on cultic heresies outside the church, the cults have now come into the church itself. Liberal denominations welcome Paganism, Shamanism, and Eastern Pantheism into their worship services, hymnals, and statements of faith: while some in the so-called "Christian" media continue to spread the plague of heresy.

Christianity in America suffers because many Christians still have not taken their scriptural responsibility to heart, to "contend for the faith" (Jude 3), "give an answer" (1 Peter 3:15), "test everything" (1 Thessalonians 5:21–22 NIV), and "search the scriptures" (Acts 17:11). Without a solid commitment to education in the defense of the faith, especially against the heresies of the kingdom of the cults, the church becomes a helpless flock of believers with little knowledge of critical doctrine and church history.

It is not too late to make a difference. The new millennium can be a time of new commitment to the truth of the Gospel, the propagation of the true faith, and the evangelization of those lost in false belief and unbelief. With assistance from Walter Martin Ministries, Ravi Zacharias International Ministries, and other apologetic organizations, the cooperation of local churches, and the assistance of pastors and Christian educators, cult evangelism will take a firm stand against cult heresies wherever they may be found—inside the church or outside, in the United States or abroad. Capturing and supporting Walter Martin's original vision can make a measurable difference in the strength of the church.~

Quick Facts About the Worldwide Church of God—From Cult to Christianity

- Armstrongism teaches that the Bible is God's Word, but it is best interpreted by Herbert W. Armstrong—God's Apostle.

- Jesus and the Father are two gods of the "God Family."

- The resurrection of Jesus was spiritual, not physical.

- Salvation is a result of good works and Christ's sacrifice.

- Mankind becomes a God Being and part of the God Family after salvation.

Appendix A

The Worldwide Church of God— From Cult to Christianity

~Doctrinal heresy is a sin against God (Galatians 5:20). An ideal world would be free from doctrinal heresy and the other results of sin, but this ideal world we must await in Christ Jesus who will grant such perfect existence in His future kingdom (Revelation 7:17; 21:4). Until that time we must contend with heresies and cults that dot church history, leaving their mark of remembrance. Cults come and go, but rare indeed is the repentance of cult leadership that results in heresy being replaced with biblical Christianity. Such is the story of the Worldwide Church of God. Once known far and wide as the cult of Armstrongism, it now, through repentance, joins hands with conservative Christians in heralding the Gospel. Its official organ, *The Plain Truth* magazine, embraces the very doctrines its past issues condemned. It interviews contemporary Christian leaders it once derided. It accepts advertising from various Christian publishers it once shunned.

The Worldwide Church of God, originally founded by Herbert W. Armstrong (1892–1986), was led through this remarkable change by his successor, Joseph W. Tkach (1927–1995). He reversed Armstrong's most damnable doctrines in full acceptance of the Trinity, Christ's divinity and humanity, the person and deity of the Holy Spirit, the bodily resurrection of Jesus, and salvation by grace through faith alone. Gone is Anglo-Israelism. Gone is the bondage of legalism as a test for fellowship. Gone is the God Family of divine humans. Gone is the elitism and cultism.

Not all followers of Armstrong, whose teaching we term "Armstrongism," accepted this welcomed change. Joseph W. Tkach and the administrators made earnest attempts to hold the church together during their doctrinal reexamination

---

This appendix updated, expanded, and revised by Kurt Van Gorden and edited by Jill Martin Rische.

period. But those dedicated to Armstrong's cultism grew impatient, forming about fifty splinter groups from 1985 to 1995. These groups are disassociated from the Worldwide Church of God, and each claims succession from Armstrong.

Preceding them, another fifty splinter groups separated from Herbert W. Armstrong during his lifetime. Armstrong's teaching bred a hundred factions, of which ninety presently remain. The founder's son, Garner Ted Armstrong, leads quite a successful movement with the Church of God, International. Garner Ted Armstrong was once viewed by millions on television as the flamboyant commentator of *The World Tomorrow* program. Amid charges of sexual misconduct, his forced departure from his father's domain landed him in Tyler, Texas, with thousands of television followers. His playboy lifestyle followed him into the 1990s with new charges of sexual misconduct, again forcing a temporary step-down from his new church (*Los Angeles Times*, Nov. 23, 1995). Nevertheless, faithful Church of God, International members reinstated him as their iconic representative on 315 cable stations in North America. His espoused doctrines follow those of his father, namely, denial of the Trinity, denial of the bodily resurrection, and denial of biblical salvation.

Among those that broke away during the reformation of the Worldwide Church of God, the largest is led by another self-proclaimed successor to Armstrong, Gerald Flurry. The Philadelphia Church of God, located in Edmond, Oklahoma, has a television log of sixty stations in five countries. Their program, *The Key of David*, echoes Armstrong's prophetic speculation. *The Philadelphia Trumpet*, their official magazine, is a constant reminder of Herbert W. Armstrong's old doctrines in the face of the reborn Worldwide Church of God. Gerald Flurry minces no words in prodding and jostling the Worldwide Church of God for its baptism into historical Christianity.

Most of the splinter cults of Armstrongism retain the name "Church of God" somewhere in their title. They mix legalism, including strict Sabbatarianism, with a variety of Armstrong's leading doctrines. Two other noteworthy groups among these are the Global Church of God, located in San Diego, California, and the United Church of God in Arcadia, California. The former has a television following on two superstations covering much of the United States, while the latter publishes *The Good News* magazine and covers thirty television stations with programming.

Joseph Tkach Jr., son of Joseph W. Tkach, currently heads the Worldwide Church of God. Leading this church through the exodus of error was costly, which is seen in the loss of many thousands of members. *The Plain Truth* magazine now circulates approximately 130,000, down considerably from their high of eight million. Much better, though, is the loss of size than the compromise of truth. *The World Tomorrow* television program has ceased, and actual church membership has dropped to half of its normative, or 40,000 constituents. Their Pasadena, California, campus is shrinking, and the church-supported Ambassador College in Big Sandy, Texas, has closed its doors.

On the positive side, the Worldwide Church of God has a remnant of 300 pastors committed to preaching an uncompromised gospel. Their message is that you must be born again by grace through faith in the shed blood of Jesus Christ. *The Plain Truth* magazine is greeted as a refreshing Christian voice. Prominent denominations and Christian leaders have extended the right hand of fellowship to its church leaders. The church now holds membership in the National Association of Evangelicals, while the magazine is a member of the Evangelical Press Association and the Evangelical Christian Publishers Association.

As for the present changes in the Worldwide Church of God, they wrote, in an interview with this writer, "The Worldwide Church of God has abandoned unbiblical doctrines of Herbert W. Armstrong." This abandonment may be viewed as parallel to one of Armstrong's toughest decisions, which was to excommunicate his son, Garner Ted Armstrong, from his church. He said, "Perhaps another evidence of the Worldwide Church of God being the one original Church of God is that its apostle did remove his son, who was secularizing God's Church and college, besides other sins."[1] Again, he wrote, "Finally, four leaders . . . came to God's apostle, saying, 'We have to report to you that your son has systematically destroyed all that Christ has built through His apostle and is building something for himself. Like a spoiled child, he wants his own way.' God's apostle, to be not guilty of Eli's sin, removed his son from all authority and disfellowshipped him from the church."[2] In a similar way, those in the Worldwide Church of God have abandoned the false teachings of their founder, Herbert W. Armstrong. It was emotionally painful, for many of them had known Armstrong for decades. But to stand for biblical truth and accuracy one must hurtle all barriers.

The changes did not occur overnight. Their progressive change is reflected in their newest statement of beliefs, which says, "This Statement of Beliefs does not constitute a closed creed. The Church constantly renews its commitment to truth and deeper understanding and responds to God's guidance in its beliefs and practices."[3] Since they have left an open book on their creeds, we write this chapter based upon current publications offered to the public. Accordingly, newer information may demand further analysis.

In the remainder of this chapter, we will sketch Herbert W. Armstrong's background and examine his teachings with Scripture. We must be careful to distinguish the doctrines of Armstrongism and today's Worldwide Church of God. The cults that follow Mr. Armstrong's teachings are cults indeed, denying the major tenets of the Christian faith. Based upon the published changes, the Worldwide Church of God is not a cult, however, because it has shown repentance and abandonment of Armstrong's false doctrines and demonstrates adherence to biblical truth. Therefore, we will make known the changes in the Worldwide Church of God that separate it from the cults of Armstrongism. The ninety cults of Armstrongism believe that Mr. Armstrong spoke with the authority of "Elijah." We cannot list all ninety groups on every subject, so we will generalize their teachings as that of "Armstrongism," while comparing it to the Worldwide Church of God or the Bible.~

The Rise of Herbert W. Armstrong

Herbert Armstrong, born July 31, 1892, in Des Moines, Iowa, was raised in a Christian home in the Midwestern farmlands. He speaks fondly of his Christian

[1] Herbert W. Armstrong, "Seven Proofs of God's True Church," *The Plain Truth* (April 1979): 3:40.
[2] Ibid., 3.
[3] *Statement of Beliefs of the Worldwide Church of God* (Pasadena: Worldwide Church of God, 1995), 1.

background: "Both my father and mother were of solid Quaker stock. My ancestors came to America with William Penn, a hundred years before the United States became a nation. Indeed, I have the genealogy of my ancestors back to Edward I of England, and through British Royal genealogy back to King Herremon of Ireland, who married Queen Tea Tephia, daughter of Zedekiah, King of Judah."[4] Armstrong also claimed to be a descendant of the biblical King David on his mother's side.[5] These credentials, coupled with his appellation of "apostle" and the second "Elijah," produced his unquestioned authority among his followers.

Armstrong temporarily succeeded in the advertising business, which he claims was special training for his future mission. He wrote, "All this advertising instruction was the most valuable possible training for the real mission in life to which I was later to be called—God's worldwide ministry. It was a training such as one could never receive in any university or theological seminary."[6]

Armstrong's spiritual odyssey was launched primarily through his wife's discovery that "obedience to God's spiritual laws summed up in the Ten Commandments is necessary for salvation. Not that our *works*[7] of keeping the Commandments save us—but rather that sin is the transgression of God's spiritual law (1 John 3:4) and Christ does not save us *in* our sins, but *from* our sins. We must *repent* of sin—*repent* of transgressing God's law, which means *turning from* disobedience, as a prior condition to receiving God's free gift."[8]

"[His] Sunday school days had taught him that there are no works to salvation. . . . God's law was done away with. To him religion had not been a way of life, but a mere belief, an acceptance of the fact of God's existence, Christ's virgin birth, the efficacy of Christ's shed blood. Controversy arose between Mr. and Mrs. Armstrong. She refused to give up the truths she had found. He was angered into his first real study of the Bible, undertaken for the avowed purpose of proving to his wife that 'all these churches can't be wrong.' "[9]

Armstrong's long solitary study of the Scriptures led him to the same conclusions he had fought so bitterly against with his wife. Ambassador Press publications indicate that Armstrong's struggle to change from "traditional" Christian belief to this newfound "legalism" caused within him "a furious inner struggle."[10]

After the study of his Bible and much prayer, we are informed, Mr. Armstrong began writing and doing evangelical work. It was in June of 1931 that Arm-

---

[4]Herbert W. Armstrong, *The Autobiography of Herbert W. Armstrong* (Pasadena: Ambassador Press, 1967), 1:26.

[5]Herbert W. Armstrong, "How the Seven Mysteries Were Revealed," *The Plain Truth* (September 1985): 16.

[6]Armstrong, *Autobiography*, 75.

[7]Armstrong continuously used typographical symbols to emphasize his writings, including small capitals, exclamation points, italics, bold face, etc. Quotations in this text are always accurate word-for-word, and usually his unique typesetting is followed, unless it detracts from clear communication.

[8]Roderick Meredith, *The Inside Story of the World Tomorrow Broadcast* (Pasadena: Ambassador Press), 47.

[9]Ibid.

[10]Ibid., 48.

strong conducted an evangelistic campaign in Eugene, Oregon, and at that time was ordained as a minister of Jesus Christ.

His tremendous zeal, tireless energy, writing, speaking, and promotional ability stood Armstrong in good stead through the years and culminated in the founding of the Ambassador College, *The Plain Truth* magazine, which was started in February 1934, and *The World Tomorrow* program, which originated in Eugene, Oregon, January 1934.

Herbert Armstrong made it a career to become a senior statesman of diplomacy for his church, and visited the various leaders of established and emerging nations, attracting their attention by his expensive gifts and direct aid programs in areas where the individual country may have had a need.

An example of Armstrong's diplomacy was his high standing with the Israeli government, for whom he had sponsored archeological digs, not the least of which was his much-publicized excavations around and underneath the site of the second temple in Jerusalem. The Armstrong religion is strong in England, throughout the United Kingdom, and on the European continent, as well as in the United States.

The Eclecticism of Herbert W. Armstrong

Unsuccessful attempts have been made to unite Armstrong with groups of similar views, such as Seventh-Day Adventists, Jehovah's Witnesses, and Mormons. In rebuttal, Armstrong's biographer, Roderick Meredith, goes to great pains to point out that "there was *never* any association in any way with Jehovah's Witnesses, Seventh-Day Adventists, Mormons, or any such sects, as some accusers have falsely claimed."[11] In his *Autobiography,* Armstrong denies having attended any Seventh-Day Adventist church services, although he admits becoming familiar with their literature.[12] We will discover, though, that he was a member of a sect produced from the multiple factions of the Adventist movement.

1. Seventh-Day Adventism, the Church of God (Adventist), and Herbert W. Armstrong
Although past writers, such as George Burnside for the *Bulletin of the Ministerial Association of Seventh-Day Adventist Ministers,* concluded that Mr. Armstrong belonged to offshoots of Seventh-Day Adventism, this claim has been difficult to substantiate. However, Mr. Armstrong's previous denial of connection with "any such sects" should not go unchallenged. It seems that the Seventh-Day Adventists and Church of God (Adventist) arose simultaneously from the Adventist remnants of the post–1844 great disappointment. That Mr. Armstrong was connected with the Church of God Seventh-Day is no question. The fact that this church is a divergent sect of non-Trinitarian Adventism settles many questions as to Mr. Armstrong's apparent source for legalistic teaching and Adventist theology.

This Church of God (Adventist) was strengthened in 1884 by consolidating independent congregations into the General Conference of the Church of God (Adventist). In 1923 the name was changed to the Church of God Seventh-Day,

---

[11]Meredith, *Story,* 48–49.
[12]Armstrong, *Autobiography,* 302, 338.

which later ordained Mr. Armstrong in Oregon. He worshiped with the Oregon congregation and was baptized by a Baptist minister in 1927. The Oregon state conference formed in 1931 and ordained him that same year. According to information from the Worldwide Church of God, the other connection with Seventh-Day Adventism is only incidental. He read Seventh-Day Adventist literature and counseled with one of their ministers.

Governmental splits in the conference provided the exit for Mr. Armstrong and his Eugene, Oregon, congregation. In 1934 he had begun radio broadcasting and published the first issue of *The Plain Truth*. He continued loose ties with them until 1947.

The Church of God Seventh-Day's view of God was largely Arian. This Unitarian theology promoted anti-Trinitarian sentiments, which provided ammunition for Mr. Armstrong against Trinitarians without any Jehovah's Witness alliance. Although Mr. Armstrong rejected Arianism in favor of his "Family of God" doctrine, he maintained staunch anti-Trinitarianism and a number of peripheral doctrines in agreement with the Church of God Seventh-Day.

2. Anglo-Israelism

Anglo-Israelism (sometimes called British-Israelism) is, properly speaking, neither a sect nor a cult, since it transcends denominational and sectarian lines and because it does not set up an ecclesiastical organization. It has existed for more than a century in the United States, having come to this hemisphere from England. Apparently it originated there shortly after the close of the Elizabethan era, its "first apostle" being Richard Brothers (1757–1824).

The most vocal proponents of the Anglo-Israelite system of biblical interpretation in North America were James Lovell of Fort Worth, Texas, and Howard Rand of Destiny Publishers.

The teachings of these men and their followers are comparatively innocuous and free from serious doctrinal error. The chief harm results from the appeal to nationalism with its accompanying vanity and the two-fold way of salvation, which some advocates have implied.

Herbert Armstrong and Anglo-Israelism

~Few organized religions teach Anglo-Israelism as does Armstrongism. The Worldwide Church of God brought Anglo-Israelism under biblical review in 1990 and concluded that Armstrong was incorrect. Hence they ceased publication and dissemination of Armstrong's major works on Anglo-Israelism. Most of the splinter cults of Armstrongism, however, readily promote it in their publications and broadcasts. One such group claims a divine calling for keeping Armstrong's teachings in print. The Philadelphia Church of God wrote, "We derive our authority to print the works of Mr. Armstrong from God, and from Mr. Armstrong's own wishes."[13] We see, then, that Armstrong's Anglo-Israelism did not cease with the repentance of the Worldwide Church of God, but has multiplied through the splinter groups.~

---

[13]Gerald Flurry and Dennis Leap, "The Key of David Vision," *The Philadelphia Trumpet* (March 1997): 24.

To sum up the theories of the Anglo-Israel cult in a concise manner is not difficult, and to refute them from the Scriptures as noted scholars and biblical expositors have done many times is essentially an elementary task. But with the advent of Herbert Armstrong's version of the old error and his utilization of it as a cloak for his own confusion on biblical theology, the problem is no longer elementary; in fact, it is quite complex and deserves the careful consideration of responsible Christian ministers and laymen. For it is certain that they will be affected, sooner or later, by the plausible propaganda that flows from the Armstrong presses and out over the airwaves.

We shall deal with Anglo-Israelism, then, only as a prelude to dealing with the theology of Herbert Armstrong, with which it has now become identified in the minds of most people—in England, Canada, and the United States.

The basic premise of the Anglo-Israelite theory is that ten tribes were lost (Israelites) when the Jews were captured by the Assyrians under King Sargon, and that these so-called "lost" tribes[14] are in reality, the Saxae, or Scythians, who surged westward through Northern Europe and eventually became the ancestors of the Saxons, who later invaded England. The theory maintains that the Anglo-Saxons are the "lost" ten tribes of Israel and are substituted, in Anglo-Israel interpretation and exegesis, for the Israel of the Bible.[15]

In the heyday of the British Empire, when their colonies spanned the globe under Victoria, Anglo-Israelites were in their glory, maintaining that since the British were the lost tribes and, therefore, inheritors of the covenants and blessings of God, it was obvious that God was honoring His promises and exalting His children in the latter days.

In light of recent history, however, and the loss by Britain of virtually all her colonial possessions, Anglo-Israelites are content to transfer the blessings of the covenant to the United States, maintaining as they do that Ephraim is Great Britain and Manasseh, the United States. The fact that Ephraim is called "the exalted one" in Scripture and that Manasseh is designated as the inferior of the two creates both historical and exegetical problems for the Anglo-Israelites. This is particularly true because the United States, the inferior (Manasseh), has now far surpassed the allegedly superior Ephraim, a minor problem that will not long forestall the cogitations and prophetic conjectures of the Anglo-Israelites' school of biblical interpretation.

Relative to the relationship of Israel to Judah in Scripture, Anglo-Israelism maintains that Judah represents the Jews who are still under the divine curse and are not to be identified with Israel at all. In this line of reasoning, all the promises recorded in the Scripture are applied not to a nation (Israel), which, as we have seen, is, in their system of thought, to be identified with Great Britain and the United States!

---

[14]J. H. Allen, *Judah's Scepter and Joseph's Birthright* (Boston: A. A. Beauchamp, 1918, 6th ed.), 124–45.

[15]Rev. Commander L. G. A. Roberts, *Commentary on the Book of the Prophet Isaiah* (London: The Covenant Publishing Company, 1951), 159.

Herbert Armstrong, in dealing with this subject, enunciates the basic idea of Anglo-Israelism, that Israel is to be distinguished from the Jews[16] (Judah) in these words:

> We want to impress here that Israel and Judah are not two names for the same nation.[17] They were and still are, and shall be until the Second Coming of Christ, two separate nations. The House of Judah always means Jew.
>
> This distinction is vital if we are to understand prophecy. Because most so-called Bible students are ignorant of this basic distinction; they are unable rightly to understand prophecy!
>
> The next place where the term "Jew" is mentioned in the Bible, the House of Israel had been driven out in captivity, lost from view, and the term only applies to those of the House of Judah. There are no exceptions in the Bible.[18]

It is further maintained by Anglo-Israelites that in their migration of the Mediterranean area across Europe to the British Isles, the "lost" tribes left behind landmarks, bearing names of the tribes. Thus the Danube River and Danzig are clear indications to them of the Tribe of Dan.[19] The term Saxon is obviously derived from the Hebrew and means Isaac-son, or "the son of Isaac!"[20]

Another Anglo-Israel exercise in semantics is their insistence that the Hebrew terms for "covenant" (*berith*), and for "man" (*ish*) are to be interpreted as meaning "the man of the covenant,"[21] a fact that would be amusing if it were not for the unpleasant truth that the Hebrew and Anglo-Saxon tongues have as much in common as do Chinese and pig Latin!

It is sufficient to point out at this stage that the Hebrew words *berith* and *ish* literally mean "covenant" and "man," not, "men of the covenant," as Armstrong and Anglo-Israelites maintain. When to this is added the unbiased and impeccably researched conclusions of the venerable *Oxford English Dictionary* and every other major English work on etymology, there is absolutely no evidence or support for the Anglo-Israelite contention that there is a connection between the Anglo-Saxon tongue and the Hebrew language, and the paucity of their claims becomes all too apparent.[22]

---

[16]"There is not a particle of evidence to support that the Jews of today are other than the house of Judah, or that they represent the lost Twelve Tribes. The evidence is clear that Israel did not rejoin the Jews" (J. Llewellyn Thomas, *God and My Birthright,* London: The Covenant Publishing Company, Ltd., n.d., 21). It should be noted that the Covenant Publishing Company is in no way associated with Herbert Armstrong or his teaching, does not subscribe to his beliefs, does not believe he has the correct interpretations of prophecy, and does not think he has rightly drawn conclusions concerning modern Israel in the latter days.

[17]Thomas (Ibid., 5) states: "All Jews and Levites were Israelites, but all Israelites were not Jews or Levites."

[18]Herbert W. Armstrong, *Where Are the Ten Lost Tribes?* (Pasadena, Calif.: Ambassador Press, n.d.), 8.

[19]Adam Rutherford, *Israel-Britain or Anglo-Saxon Israel* (London: Self-published, 3rd ed., 1936), 36.

[20]Anonymous, *The Roadbuilder: God's Commonwealths, British and American* (Toronto: Commonwealth Publishers, Ltd., 1930), 161ff. See also Rutherford, *Israel-Britain,* 9.

[21]Rutherford, *Israel-Britain,* 30.

[22]Ibid., 306–309.

Moreover, it should be noted that the Anglo-Israelite theory and the World-wide Church of God both maintain that the throne of England is the throne of David. In the June 1953 issue of *The Plain Truth* appears the statement:

> Herbert L. Hoeh now reveals the astonishing fact that Elizabeth II actually sits on the throne of King David of ISRAEL—that she is a direct descendant, continuing David's dynasty. . . .[23]

Following other Anglo-Israelites, Mr. Armstrong believed that the biblical throne of David became the throne of England. The 1953 *Plain Truth* writer Herman Hoeh makes this revelation plain, "that Elizabeth II actually sits on the throne of King David of Israel—that she is a direct descendant, continuing David's dynasty—the very throne on which Christ shall sit after his return."[24] Armstrong also wrote, "Many kings in the history of Ireland, Scotland, and England have been coronated sitting over this stone—including the present queen. The stone rests today in Westminster Abby in London, and the coronation chair is built over and around it. A sign beside it labels it 'Jacob's pillar-stone.' "[25]

The disturbing scientific fact is that the Stone of Scone has been examined and analyzed, and found to be "calcareous, a sandstone of reddish or purplish colour and (containing) heterogeneous pebbles" and undoubtedly of Scottish origin. This fact has been reconfirmed by many reputable geologists.[26]

~The notable feature of Anglo-Israelite writings is their disregard for scholarly support. They often form superficial conclusions on word associations and unfounded parallelism. Armstrong, in line with other writers, falls into these trappings. For example, he stated,

> The house of Israel is the covenant people. The Hebrew word for "covenant" is *beriyth,* or *berith.* . . . The Hebrew for "man" is *iysh,* or *ish.* . . . In the original Hebrew language vowels were never given in the spelling. So, omitting the vowel "e" from *berith,* but retaining the "I" in its anglicized form to preserve the "y" sound, we have the anglicized Hebrew for covenant, *brith.*
>
> The Hebrews, however, never pronounced their "h's". . . . So the Hebrew word for "covenant" would be pronounced in its anglicized form as *brit.*

---

[23]Dr. Henry Hedyt, of the American Board of Mission to the Jews, has a letter from the Office of the Lord Chamberlain, which states that no known reason exists why any assertion should be made that Her Majesty Queen Elizabeth was crowned Queen of Israel. It goes on to say that she is demonstrably not the Queen of Israel and cites a portion of the Coronation Service in which the Queen took the oath. He also has a letter from Brigadier Wieler, the Resident Governor of the Tower of London, which states clearly that in the Tower of London and in the Public Records Office no ancestral chart is known which substantiates the claim, "Yes, on the throne of England reigns a daughter of David. . . . a dynasty that has ruled Ireland, Scotland and England for over 2,500 years!" Hoeh, "The Coronation Stone," *The Plain Truth* (June 1953): 640.

[24]Herman L. Hoeh, "The Coronation Stone," *The Plain Truth* (June 1953): 64.

[25]Herbert W. Armstrong, *The United States and Britain in Prophecy* (Pasadena: Ambassador College Press, 1980), 100.

[26]Quoted in Harry W. Loe, *Radio Church of God* (Mountain View, Calif.: Pacific Press Publishing Association, 1970), 78.

And the word for "covenant man," or "covenant people," would there-fore be simply "*Brit-Ish.*" And so, is it mere coincidence that the true cove-nant people *are called* the "*British*"? And they reside in the "*British Isles.*"

They were descended from Isaac, and therefore are Isaac's sons. Drop the "I" from "Isaac" (vowels are not used in Hebrew spelling), and we have the modern name "Saac's Sons," or, as we spell it in shorter manner, "*Sax-ons*"![27]

One could belabor the point with an arsenal of Armstrong quotations from his fifty years of writing. Problematic to his thesis are his spelling gymnastics and twisted words. His confidence in espousing his view is found in supposed land-marks of the lost ten tribes. Regarding the tribe of Dan, he tracks their trail through Europe. "Remember," he wrote, "in the Hebrew, vowels were not writ-ten. . . . Thus, the word 'Dan' in its English equivalent could be spelled, simply, 'Dn.' It might be pronounced as 'Dan,' or 'Den,' or 'Din,' or 'Don,' or 'Dun'—and still could be the same original Hebrew name. . . . Then, in either ancient or later geography, we find these waymarks: "*Dan*-au, the *Dan*-inn, the *Dan*-aster, the *Dan*-dari, the *Dan*-ez, the *Don*, the *Dan*, and the U-d*on*; the Eri-*don*, down to the *Danes.* 'Denmark' means 'Dan's Mark.' "[28] The old adage that one could prove nearly anything with extrapolated Bible verses has found its home in Armstrong's works.~

The Biblical Answer to Anglo-Israelism

There are two principal areas in which the Anglo-Israel theory must either stand or fall. They are, first, the question whether any tribes *were* lost, and there-fore later reappeared as the British and American nations; second, there is the question of whether or not it is possible, in either the Old or New Testaments, to teach that:

> Israel and Judah are not two names for the same nation. They were and still are, and shall be until the Second Coming of Christ, two separate nations. The House of Judah always means Jew. . . . the term applies only to those of the House of Judah. There are no exceptions in the Bible.[29]

The final blow to Armstrong's teaching on Anglo-Israelism came after his death by those in leadership at the Worldwide Church of God. In their effort to promote only the truly biblical message, they reexamined and rejected much of Armstrong's message. In particular, they aptly point out the historical and scien-tific weaknesses that devastate the theory.

In a published paper, they state:

> When reading Anglo-Israelite literature, one notices that it generally depends on folklore, legends, quasi-historical genealogies, and dubious ety-

---

[27]Armstrong, *United States,* 95–96.
[28]Ibid., 97–99.
[29]Armstrong, *Where Are the Lost Ten Tribes,* 8.

mologies. None of these sources prove an Israelite origin for the peoples of northwestern Europe. Rarely, if ever, are the disciplines of archaeology, sociology, anthropology, linguistics, or historiography applied to Anglo-Israelism. Anglo-Israelism operates outside of the sciences. Even the principles of sound biblical exegesis are seldom used, for . . . whole passages of Scripture that undermine the entire system are generally ignored.

Why this unscientific approach? This approach must be taken because to do otherwise is to destroy Anglo-Israelism's foundation. Those who apply scientific disciplines and the principles of sound historiography to this subject eventually come away disbelieving the theory. . . . Even lay students of the Bible can find serious flaws in the idea.

No firsthand account exists that traces the lost ten tribes in northwestern Europe. No eyewitnesses to European tribal migrations ever claimed an Israelite origin for any of them. No medieval or ancient genealogies ever linked the royal families of the British Isles with the Israelites. Not until the nineteenth century (long after the supposed migration) did anyone attempt to prove such an idea.[30]

There are a number of Old Testament verses that historically account for the lost ten tribes. Apparently the writers of the Old Testament had no difficulty acknowledging the so-called lost tribes as the house of Israel. The book of Ezra (2:70; 6:17; 8:25; and 10:5) irrefutably demonstrates the accountability of the twelve tribes. One could also reference Nehemiah 7:73 and 12:47 to find an accounting of all the house of Israel. Both historically and, most important, scripturally, we find no support for the wanton theories of Anglo-Israelism.

The second barrier is that of the identification of Israel and Judah as separate nations, as seen by Mr. Armstrong's previously quoted statement. This matter can be summarily dismissed by careful consideration of the following facts.

First, after the Babylonian captivity, from which the Jews returned, Ezra records that the remnant were called by the name "Jews" (eight times) and by the name "Israel" forty times. Nehemiah records eleven times that they were Jews, and proceeds to describe them as Israel twenty-two times. The book of Esther records their partial restoration, calling them Jews forty-five times, but never Israel. Are we to conclude that only Judah (the Jews), and not Israel, was restored under Zerubbabel and Josiah? History, archaeology, and a study of Hebrew refute this possibility completely.

The sixth chapter of Ezra describes the sin offering, mentioning specifically that "twelve male goats, one for each of the tribes of Israel" were offered for all Israel (v. 17 NIV), a fact attested to by Ezra 8:35.

While it is true that in the post-exilic period we no longer have two kingdoms, but one nation, the prophet Zechariah describes them in comprehensive terms as "Judah," "Israel," and "Jerusalem" (Zechariah 1:19), literally, "the House of Judah," and "the House of Joseph" (Zechariah 10:6). Zechariah 8:13 identifies Judah and the House of Israel as one nation, and Malachi called the Jews "Israel" or "Jacob," in contrast to "Esau."

---

[30]Anonymous, *United States and Britain in Prophecy: Study Paper* (Pasadena: Worldwide Church of God), November 1995, 3.

The *coup de grace* to Anglo-Israelism's fragmented exegesis is given by the prophet Amos of Judah, a man specifically set apart by God to prophesy to the ten-tribed kingdom of the North (Amos, dwelling in Bethel, prophesied against Israel's restoration as a separate kingdom [Amos 9:8–10]). We learn from this prophecy that as a kingdom, the ten tribes were to suffer destruction, and their restoration would never be realized. How, then, is it possible for them to be "lost" for almost three millenniums, and then reappear as the British Kingdom when the kingdom was never to be restored? . . . Second, and finally, the New Testament speaks on the subject of the equation of Israel and Judah as one nation, described alternately and interchangeably as "the Jews" and "Israel."

Peter, at Pentecost, proclaims the message of redemption to "all the house of Israel." Paul in Acts 26:6–7 apparently took Zechariah's statement:

"As you have been an object of cursing among the nations, O Judah and Israel, so will I save you, and you will be a blessing. Do not be afraid, but let your hands be strong" (Zechariah 8:13 NIV).

In this context, Israel shall indeed be scattered among the nations, and so will Judah, and they shall be redeemed again together to bring forth a blessing in the person of the Messiah, whose gospel is to the Jew first (not only to the house of Israel, but as a separate nation), and also to the Gentile (Romans 1:16 NIV).

A cursory reading of the tenth chapter of Matthew indicates that Jesus Christ himself considered "the lost sheep of the house of Israel," to include the Jews, since the missionary journeys of the twelve were limited to the environs of Palestine.

It should be recalled also that Pauline theology, especially in the book of Romans (chapters 9–11), deals specifically with Israel, not as a nation in the sense of geography, but in the sense of spiritual transgression. He refers to them as God's people who have not been cast away.

If Israel and Judah are separate nations, why then does the apostle Paul describe the Jews as his "brethren" and as "kinsmen according to the flesh," and then identify them as "Israelites," heirs to the promise of God, as those promises are provided for in the coming Messiah?

The apostle Paul made this clear by declaring, "I am . . . a Jew. . . . I also am an Israelite. . . . Are they Israelites? so am I" (Acts 21:39; 22:3; Romans 11:1; 2 Corinthians 11:22; Philippians 3:5).

Jesus Christ sprang from Judah as "a Jew," in Anglo-Israelite reckoning, and the apostle Paul declares in Romans that it was in Israel that "Christ came, who is God over all, blessed for ever" (9:5, from the Greek).

Let it not be forgotten that Anna the prophetess was "of the tribe of Asher" (Israel), but she is called "a Jewess" of Jerusalem, facts that forever decimate the concept of Armstrong and British-Israelites that England is the throne of David and is Ephraim, while America is Manasseh.

The words of Jeremiah the prophet conclude our observations, where he states:

" 'The days are coming', declares the LORD, 'when I will bring my people Israel and Judah back from captivity and restore them to the land I gave their forefathers to possess' " (30:3 NIV).

This is proof positive that both the house of Israel and the house of Judah would return from the Captivity, and that as the New Testament amply demonstrates, it would be considered as one nation, no longer a kingdom in the historical meaning of that term.

Anglo-Israelism stands refuted by the facts of Scripture and history, and it would be unworthy of scholarly attention if it were not being utilized as a tool by the Armstrong cult (Armstrongism), which opens a Pandora's box of multiple and destructive heresies, some of which we shall consider.

The Theology of the Worldwide Church of God

I. The Divine Origin of the Worldwide Church of God

~Our greatest concern between the Worldwide Church of God and the cults of Armstrongism is in their theology. The Worldwide Church of God has moved into biblical Christianity through interaction in the 1990s with evangelical theologians and ministers of various Protestant backgrounds. The Worldwide Church of God gives us insight on the thousands who broke away: "They have placed Mr. Armstrong ahead of the Bible in their own minds."[31]

This admirable step for the Worldwide Church of God is the very stumbling-block of the factions. Gerald Flurry, of the Philadelphia Church of God, remarks, "The only hope for today's Laodicean is to get back to what Christ revealed to Mr. Armstrong. . . . The Laodiceans will have to admit that Mr. Armstrong was Christ's messenger. And they will have to believe the message in the same manner Mr. Armstrong did."[32]

The Armstrong cults believe that Armstrong was God's sole channel of divine truth. Armstrong believed that biblical truth had been lost from the first century until rediscovered by him in 1927. He wrote about himself as the "Elijah" who would preach before the second advent of Jesus Christ. He also taught that he was unique in the human race as Christ's new "apostle" and that he had "restored" essential truths to Christianity. He championed his work in gloating terms, as when he introduced the *Mystery of the Ages* in 1985, saying, "I candidly feel it may be the most important book since the Bible!"[33]

Such self-glorifying sentiments are not uncommon to Armstrong. He had previously announced in January 1979 that his book *The Incredible Human Potential* had Jesus Christ as the author and Mr. Armstrong as the stenographer! "Actually," he wrote, "I feel with deep conviction that I myself did not author this book—that the living Jesus Christ is its real author. I was merely like a stenographer writing it down. And with that understanding, I feel I may say that this is the most important—the most tremendously revealing—book since the Bible!"[34]

Two of Armstrong's books mediate between humanity and the Bible. He claimed his writings were more than mere interpretation or commentary by ruling out all others as equal, second only to the Bible. "I am not writing foolishly,"

---

[31]Joseph W. Tkach, "Personal From Joseph W. Tkach," *The Worldwide News* (May 21, 1990): 5.

[32]Flurry & Leap, *Key,* 21.

[33]As quoted by Gerald Flurry, "Personal," *The Philadelphia Trumpet* (February 1997): 1.

[34]Herbert W. Armstrong, "Personal From . . ." *The Plain Truth* (January 1979): 45.

he boldly stated, "but very soberly, on *authority* of the *living Christ!*"[35] These stupendous claims either need to be upheld or exposed as fraudulent. Under the spotlight of God's Word, we will discover the indeed fraudulent nature of Armstrong's twisted biblical texts.~

Of his mission, Armstrong said,

> I know of no other who has ever become founder of a religion, or a religious leader of any kind, who ever came into the truth in the way God brought me into it. . . . God brought me through a process that erased former misknowledge—and, as it were, gave me a clear start from "scratch." I wonder if you realize that every truth of God, accepted as truth doctrine and belief in the Worldwide Church of God, came from Christ through me, or was finally approved and made official through me. . . . I was appointed by Jesus Christ, the head of the Church.[36]

Others had less of the Holy Spirit than he did, he affirmed:

> The Holy Spirit is given to us by degrees. . . . I firmly believe that God by His grace granted me a much fuller portion of His Spirit at the very beginning than is the average experience.[37]

Uniquely he is Christ's apostle, "His one apostle for this twentieth century."[38] He revealed that he was the "Elijah" type who precedes the return of Jesus Christ.[39] He claims special privileges during the millennial reign of Christ. According to Armstrong, he will also run the "Headquarters Church" himself under Jesus Christ for the entire planet earth.

~His parallels for Elijah, John the Baptist, and himself break down because the Bible speaks of one messenger like Elijah, not two messengers. Both Isaiah 40:3 and Malachi 3:1–5 speak singularly of one messenger, which ample New Testament evidence reveals to be John the Baptist (Luke 1:17). Armstrong hangs his premise upon Matthew 17:11; that John the Baptist did not "restore all things."[40] However, the verses following this (Matthew 17:12–13) make it clear from the mouth of Jesus Christ that John, indeed, fulfilled Malachi's prophecy. Simply because Armstrong does not know how John fulfilled the prophecy gives no justification for claiming that he did not do so, nor that there should be another futuristic "Elijah" type. Anyone who believes in Jesus can rest assured that Jesus knew more on the subject than Armstrong. Furthermore, Matthew 17:13 (NIV) finalizes the subject in saying, "Then the disciples understood that he was talking to them about John the Baptist." Notice the missing element for Armstrong's theory. It is not John the Baptist and some future figure in the twentieth century, but John the Baptist alone.

---

[35]Herbert W. Armstrong, "End Vietnam War Now!" *The Plain Truth* (February 1967): 47.

[36]Herbert W. Armstrong, "Personal From . . ." *The Plain Truth* (February 1977): 17.

[37]Herbert W. Armstrong, "The True Facts of My Own Conversion," *The Plain Truth* (June 1977): 9.

[38]*The Plain Truth* (July 1977): 1; and (February 1978): 43.

[39]Herbert W. Armstrong, *Mystery of the Ages* (Pasadena: Worldwide Church of God, 1985), 8:284–286.

[40]Ibid., 285.

In 1958 Mr. Armstrong wrote a letter to Robert Sumner, a writer on cults and false religions. "First," he wrote, "let me say—this may sound incredible, but it's true—*Jesus Christ foretold this very work—it is, itself the fulfillment of his prophecy* (Matthew 24:14 and Mark 13:10). . . . Astounding as it may seem, there is no other work on earth proclaiming to the whole world this very *same gospel* that Jesus taught and proclaimed!"[41]

Throughout the years Armstrong continually maintained that his organization alone truly represented Christianity, while all others were false. Since 1933, he credited himself with restoring "at least eighteen basic essential truths . . . to the true Church."[42] In order to combat the obvious representation of Christianity during the last two millennia, Armstrong referred to the true church as an "underground" remnant called the "little flock." Armstrong's lofty pedestal crashes to the ground in the face of Jesus' words in Matthew 16:18, where He said that the gates of hell shall not prevail against His church. This demonstration of the church of Christ as a perpetually visible entity destroys Armstrong's notion. What went out in the first century was never lost and continuously grew. The undeniable fact is that the church of Jesus Christ has always been visible and remains so until His return, as Paul said, "throughout all generations" (Ephesians 3:21 NIV). The church is built upon the foundation of the apostles and prophets with Jesus Christ as the chief cornerstone (Ephesians 2:20).

In specific reference to the "little flock" statement of Jesus in Luke 12:32, it was never intended as a description of the church for two millennia. It was spoken to the twelve before Christ's crucifixion. The conversion of three thousand souls in Acts, chapter two, began the rapid church expansion and dispels such folly. Armstrong was not the first to appeal to the "little flock" quotation in support of his small following, but to claim this represents the entire story of the church through nineteen centuries makes the commission of Christ (Matthew 28:19 and Mark 16:15) positively absurd. Christ commissioned his followers to go into the entire world not for a "little flock," but that "a great multitude that no one could count, from every nation, tribe, people and language" (Revelation 7:9 NIV) could be reached.

Herbert W. Armstrong's View of Scripture

The Bible, according to Mr. Armstrong, was not properly understood since the first century because it was a coded jigsaw puzzle. He claimed special anointing to decode it and put the puzzle together. The story went that God purposefully hid the biblical message from the world until the second Elijah (Armstrong) preached in the final days preceding Christ's return.

On the Bible, Armstrong said, "It is like a jigsaw puzzle which must be assembled piece by biblical piece . . . and since before A.D. 70, it has been entirely *suppressed*."[43] Further, he wrote, "The Bible was a coded book, not intended to be understood until our day in this latter half of the twentieth century. . . . I learned

---

[41]Personal letter to Robert Sumner, November 27, 1958.
[42]Armstrong, *Mystery,* 207.
[43]Herbert W. Armstrong, "How Far Can You Get From Being 'A Prophet of Doom'?" *The Plain Truth* (Oct./Nov. 1977): 3.

that the Bible is like a jigsaw puzzle—thousands of pieces that need putting together."[44]

Imagine that God hid His Word for 1,900 years, awaiting the arrival of Armstrong! In blatant contrast, Jesus told us, "Thy word is truth" (John 17:17), thus expressing God's intention for all mankind to find plainly stated, uncoded, unsuppressed truth upon examination. It would have been easier for Armstrong if Jesus had said, "Thy word is a coded jigsaw puzzle," but no such thought exists. The most damaging blow to Armstrong's theory is found in 1 John 2:27 (NIV), where it states, "You do not need anyone to teach you." Here, the apostle John clearly tells the church that the Holy Spirit teaches us beyond dependency upon Armstrong (or anyone else). So much does God expect the common Christian, led by His Spirit, to understand what they read that the Bible is replete with such references (Psalm 119:4, 104; Luke 11:28; Revelation 1:3).

Armstrong's New Revelations

The introduction to *Mystery of the Ages* states, "The final crystal-clear reason that impelled me to write this book did not fully reveal itself to my mind until December of 1984. It was a mind-boggling realization—a pivotal truth."[45] Again, "All these mysteries were . . . a coded message not allowed to be revealed and decoded until our time."[46] At times Armstrong claimed his writings are "a last warning from the *Eternal God!*"[47] New revelation outside of Scripture is a mark of all of the cults.

1. New Revelations That Breed False Predictions

When one stands parallel with biblical prophets, it becomes a short step to predicting future events. Armstrong wrote, "God dealt with me in no uncertain terms, even as he had dealt with Moses, Isaiah, Jeremiah, Jonah, Andrew, Peter and the apostle Paul."[48] The mark of God's prophets is that they never erred (Deuteronomy 13:1–5; 18:20–22; Isaiah 8:19–20). In contrast, even a false prophet may have a sign come to pass (Deuteronomy 13:2), but eventually he will miss the mark, which undoubtedly proves he is not from God.

One may quickly protest that Armstrong claimed he was not a prophet.[49] But when one prognosticates and even adds the biblical "Thus saith the Lord" to his predictions, he is acting in all respects as a prophet. Jeremiah speaks clearly about those who prophesy in God's name when he did not give them the word (Jeremiah 23:25–32). Even if one claims that Armstrong only observed the times, we find biblical injunctions against that as well. A person who falsely predicts the "signs" stands equally as condemned as the false prophet who says, "Thus saith the Lord." Armstrong did both. The Bible specifically addresses those who are "observers of times" (Leviticus 19:26; Deuteronomy 18:10, 14; 2 Kings 21:6; and

---

[44]Armstrong, *Mystery*, xii.
[45]Ibid., x.
[46]Ibid., xiii.
[47]Armstrong, *Vietnam*, 47.
[48]Armstrong, *Mystery*, 14.
[49]Herbert W. Armstrong, *Tomorrow's World* (February 1972): 1ff.

2 Chronicles 33:6), which is not restricted to divination. May the reader keep in mind Armstrong's self-proclamations of inspiration from God and Christ as we chronologically review a number of false predictions.

1934—As nearly as we can calculate from the dates of ancient history, the year 1936 will see the *end* of the Times of the Gentiles. Those "Times" have not been completely fulfilled until that year.

And for Great Pyramid students, a point in this connection will be of interest. The present depression, or tribulation, is there symbolized as occupying the entire low passage continuing from May 29, 1928, when the tribulation struck Europe, until September, 1936.

The present world-chaos Tribulation, [is] to be followed, by or quickly after 1936, but the heavenly signs, which shall be followed by the "Day of the Lord" . . . to the time-sequences fixed by these prophecies, the Revelation story-flow agrees exactly.[50]

1938—But then what will Mussolini and these ten dictators do? Notice the prophecy—absolutely *sure* to happen—in Revelation 17:16–17. . . . Thus shall the Catholic Church come to her final *end. Thus saith the Lord!*

Mussolini and the Pope will hatch up an idea between [them] of setting up a world headquarters at *Jerusalem*—and so Mussolini's armies will enter into *Palestine* (Daniel 11:14), and eventually will capture just half of the city of Jerusalem!

Then, at last, Stalin will decide he is ready. . . . Finally, *all* nations shall be gathered for the final great and mighty battle. . . . It will be at the time of the last of the seven plagues of the great *day of the Lord!* And then shall the *Lord* go forth—the *second coming of Christ!*[51]

1939—Once world war is resumed it must continue on through the great Tribulation, the heavenly signs, the plagues of the Day of the Lord, and to the Second Coming of Christ, at the last battle, at Armageddon! . . . This you *may know!* This war will be ended by *Christ's Return!* And war may be started within six weeks! We are just *that near* Christ's coming! That should make every reader stop to *think!*[52]

1941—*Plain Truth* readers know world events, *before they occur!* . . . Hitler is the "*Beast*" of Revelation. . . . There, Bible prophecy does indicate that Hitler *must be the victor* in his present Russian invasion![53]

1943—But Hitler (or his successor, if there is one), and the False Prophet shall *fight* against Christ! They shall fight desperately to retain their foul system. And the *battle* that ensues in this struggle to see whether Hitler's New Order or Christ's Kingdom shall rule this earth for the next *Thousand Years,* is the *battle* of the *great day of God Almighty!* . . . Note it! "And I saw the beast (Hitler) and the kings of the earth (his junior partners), and their armies" (Revelation 19:19). . . . It is *Christ* and the Angels that Hitler will fight! . . . *That is to be Hitler's end!*[54]

---

[50]Herbert W. Armstrong, *The Plain Truth* (June/July 1934): 5.
[51]Ibid., (March 1938): 8.
[52]Ibid., (August 1939): 6.
[53]Ibid., (October 1941): 7.
[54]Ibid., (March/April 1943): 6.

1956—*1975 in Prophecy* . . . Mysteries of God, never before understood, now become crystal-clear. God's own time for this revealing has come. . . . Yes, millions of lukewarm, inactive professing Christians will suffer *martyrdom*—and that *before* the anticipated push-button leisure-year of 1975 dawns upon us![55]

1957—God prophesies that finally, within the next fifteen years [by 1972], fully one third of our whole population will die of disease and famine![56]

1962—It's time we face the hard, cold, realistic *fact*: humanity has two alternatives: either there is an Almighty, all-powerful God who is about to step in and set up *the kingdom of God* to rule all nations . . . or else there will not be a human being alive on this earth twenty years [by 1982] from now! . . . It's about time you come to know *who* are the false prophets, and *who* is speaking the true Word of God faithfully![57]

1967—The *"Day of the Eternal"*—a time foretold in more than thirty prophecies—is going to strike between five and ten years [by 1977] from now! You will *know*, then, how *real* it is. . . . I am not writing foolishly, but very soberly, *on authority* of the living *Christ!*[58]

It appears that by 1972 Mr. Armstrong realized that date-setting for future events was futile. He wrote, "It is utterly unsafe to try to *set dates* in regard to future prophesied events."[59] In looking over this list we find one failed prediction after another. The Lord did not destroy the Catholic Church through Mussolini in 1936. Jesus did not return at the end of World War II. Hitler was not the beast and did not fight Jesus Christ at Armageddon. One third of the world was not wiped out in 1972. Millions of lukewarm Christians went unmartyred in 1975. And the human race was not extinct by 1982. It would do the ninety factions of Armstrongism well to thoroughly examine their founder's false predictions. It is inescapable that some were credited as from the mouth of God, Christ, or the Lord, which makes them false prophecies readily condemned by the Bible.

2. New Revelations Outside of God's Word

A synopsis of Armstrong's cosmology divulges that he goes far beyond interpreting the Bible by adding to God's revelation:

In the very beginning—before this physical universe was created—there existed *only* the two Superbeings—God and the "Word". . . . These two Superpersonages in space *first* created angels, composed solely of spirit, *before* any physical matter was ever produced. . . . When the angels rebelled against the government of God, the preservation of the physical earth and all of its original beauty and glory ceased—and physical destruction to the

[55]Herbert W. Armstrong, *1975 in Prophecy* (Pasadena: Radio Church of God, 1956), 1, 20.
[56]Armstrong, *The Plain Truth* (December 1957): 23.
[57]Herbert W. Armstrong, *Just What Do You Mean . . . Kingdom of God?* (Pasadena: Ambassador College, 1962), 19.
[58]Armstrong, *The Plain Truth* (February 1967): 47.
[59]Armstrong, *Tomorrow's World* (February 1972): 1.

surface of the earth resulted.... The rebellion of Lucifer and his angels brought this extreme cataclysm to the earth. And in all probability *it did more!*... It is apparent, therefore, based upon what is revealed in the Bible, that a similar cataclysm of destruction happened to the surface of our moon and the other planets of our solar system—perhaps extending to all of the astral bodies in the universe. And all of this was caused by the rebellion of Lucifer and his angels.

Satan and his angels were then *disqualified* to administer God's government over the earth. But it is a principle of God that a government must never be without a head. Consequently Satan was to be left here on earth until his successor, who has already been qualified to rule, *is inducted into office.*

In the six days of renewing the face of the earth and lavishly decorating it with flora and fauna, God made it beautiful—gloriously beautiful!... The only possible assurance of accomplishing His great purpose of finishing the creation—populating and beautifying the entire universe—was for Him to reproduce himself.... God needs millions or billions of perfect and righteous beings, governed by His divine government, *to complete* the creation of ... not only the other planets of our solar system (now in utter waste and decay), but also our galaxy, and countless other galaxies of the limitless, vast universe.[60]

The story continues:

Then, in His greatest Master Plan of all, God undertook the actual reproduction of himself, through *man.* God created man in His image— form and shape—for a special relationship with God. But Satan got to Adam through Eve, his wife. Adam followed Satan in rejecting the government of God.... On Adam's fateful decision and rebellion, Adam's world, descended from him, was sentenced to being *cut off* from God for 6,000 years, after which God decreed Christ should come to *restore* the *government of God* on earth, establishing the *Kingdom of God* with worldwide rule.[61]

In summary, Armstrong argues:

God's *PURPOSE* is to reproduce himself through man—reproduce the *God Family* from the human family.... The Messiah, Jesus Christ, would restore the government of God to the planet earth.... Since God's *purpose* is to reproduce himself—expand the God *Family*—and since it shall be the world-ruling family, then the *kingdom of God* is the born family of God ruling the entire world.[62]

In this scheme of things, man has a spirit and body, but is incomplete; therefore, he needs another spirit, the Holy Spirit from God. This Holy Spirit comes to impregnate man as a "begotten child of God," but not yet

---

[60]Herbert W. Armstrong, "Why Humans Were Put on the Earth," *The Plain Truth* (Oct./Nov. 1978): 3, 45.

[61]Herbert W. Armstrong, "Supernatural Forces on a Collision Course!" *The Plain Truth* (January 1979): 4–5.

[62]Herbert W. Armstrong, "A World Held Captive," *The Plain Truth* (June 1984): 6, 39.

"born again" until birth occurs as a spirit-body in the resurrection. Once born at the resurrection, he becomes a God Being and joins the persons of God as part of the God Family.

All of those who died before Christ's first advent will then be revived in mortal flesh to hear the message and accept Jesus as their savior. The ones who accept Jesus will receive the immortal resurrection of a spirit-body. Hence, they become God Beings and finish creating the many planets in the universe.[63]

This story spun by Armstrong is everything but biblical. More than filling gaps in his jigsaw puzzle, he invented a soteriology that expels his followers from genuine salvation.~

II. The Trinity of God and the Divinity of Man

Armstrong was an outspoken anti-Trinitarian, as revealed in these quotations:

But the theologians and "Higher Critics" have blindly accepted the heretical and false doctrine introduced by *pagan* false prophets who crept in, that the *Holy Spirit* is a *third person*—the heresy of the "*Trinity*." This limits God to "Three Persons."[64]

The false Trinity teaching does limit God to three persons. But God is not limited. As God repeatedly reveals, his purpose is to reproduce himself into what well may become billions of God persons. It is the false Trinity teaching that limits God, denies God's purpose and has palpably deceived the whole Christian world.[65]

Armstrong's denial of the Trinity was superseded by his "binitarian" (two persons in the Godhead) view. He held to the deity of Jesus, correctly calling Him Jehovah from the Old Testament. His denial of the deity of the Holy Spirit left him with two persons as God (binitarian), instead of three persons (Trinitarian). Within this scope, however, he diverges into "ditheism" (two god Beings). We have seen in a previous quotation his address of "two Superbeings" and "Superpersonages." He speaks elsewhere: "In the very beginning, before all else, there existed two living Beings composed of Spirit. . . . One was named the Word. . . . The other was named God. . . ."[66] When Armstrong calls the Father and Son two beings, then it is difficult to maintain monotheism, since two beings requires ditheism, a form of polytheism.

The nature of God is spirit, according to Armstrong, but His shape, form, and stature are those of a man! In their correspondence course, he asks, "Does the Father therefore appear like a man? Comment: Christ clearly indicated that

[63]Armstrong, *The Plain Truth* (Oct./Nov. 1977): 3ff.

[64]Herbert W. Armstrong, *Just What Do You Mean: Born Again?* (Pasadena: Radio Church of God, 1962), 19.

[65]Armstrong, *Mystery*, 37.

[66]Herbert W. Armstrong, "World Peace Just around the Corner," *The Plain Truth* (Nov./Dec. 1984): 4.

the Father has the general form and stature of a mortal man!"[67] *The Plain Truth* reveals, "We are made of material flesh, but in the form and shape of God. . . ."[68] And, "Now notice once again Genesis 1:26: 'God (*Elohim*) said, Let us make man in our image, after our likeness (form and shape). . . .' God is described in the Bible as having eyes, ears, nose, mouth, hair, arms, legs, fingers, toes."[69] Still, "Man was made in the form and shape of God. For example, notice the human hand. God has hands (2 Chronicles 6:4)."[70] Finally, in *Mystery of the Ages*, he reveals,

> Perhaps it will make God more real to you when you realize he is in the same form and shape as a human being. . . . God is invisible to human eyes. . . . But even though God is composed of spirit and not visible matter, God nonetheless does have form and shape. . . . In various parts of the Bible, it is revealed that God has a face, eyes, a nose, mouth and ears. He has hair on his head. It is revealed God has arms and legs. And God has hands and fingers. . . . God has feet and toes and a body. . . . If you know what a man looks like, you know what is the form and shape of God, for he made man in his image, after his very likeness.[71]

In this section we cannot sidestep his "God Family" doctrine. He taught that "God" was a family name for two beings, the Father and Son. The God Family will soon become billions of God Beings comprised of those "born again." The quotations are numerous because he equivocated the terms "immortal," "resurrection," "saved," "born again," "Church of God," "God Family," and "Kingdom of God."[72]

His God Family doctrine projects a future divine human race. He expressed the future divinity of mankind: "God's purpose is to make us immortal like God, until we become God as he is God."[73] Elsewhere he wrote, "That is, once born again, one is born not of a human father in mortal physical human flesh, but of god, impregnated by God's Spirit, in immortal *spirit composition,* as a God Being! *Born of God!* . . . But he is *born again* only in the immortal spirit life to come—at the time of the resurrection. When born again, he will be spirit—no longer mortal flesh and blood."[74] Once again, "You and I potentially may *become God*! For *God* is a collective *Family*—the *Divine Family*—into which *the Church* is to be born!"[75] And, "By a resurrection, we become *born* God personages—personages

---

[67]Herbert W. Armstrong, ed., *Ambassador College Bible Correspondence Course (Lesson 9)* (Pasadena: Ambassador College, 1966): 8.

[68]Armstrong, "Just What Do You Mean: Born Again?" *The Plain Truth* (February 1977): 28.

[69]Armstrong, *The Plain Truth* (February 1979): 42.

[70]Armstrong, "Never Before Understood," *The Plain Truth* (September 1981): 26.

[71]Armstrong, "Never Understood," *Mystery of the Ages*, 26.

[72]Armstrong, *Mystery*, 37–39.

[73]Herbert W. Armstrong, "Why Must Man Suffer?" *The Plain Truth* (October 1983): 21.

[74]Herbert W. Armstrong, "This Is the Worldwide Church of God," *The Plain Truth* (January 1979): 3.

[75]Herbert W. Armstrong, "A Voice Cries Out Amid Religious Confusion," *The Plain Truth* (December 1980): 40.

just as are God the Father and Christ the Son! We shall have the entire *universe* put under our feet (Hebrews 2:8)."[76]

In agreement with the current Worldwide Church of God, Christians need to repudiate such blasphemous doctrines. Their current *Statement of Beliefs* nicely describes, in Trinitarian terms, a refutation to the above heresies of Armstrong. They state, "God, by the testimony of Scripture, is one divine Being in three eternal, coessential, yet distinct Persons—Father, Son, and Holy Spirit."[77] We add to this the scriptural support that there can exist but one God (Deuteronomy 4:39; 6:4; Isaiah 44:6–8; 45:21–22; and Mark 12:32). Yet the Bible also shows us the three distinct Persons within God's nature (Father, Romans 1:7; Son, John 20:28; and Holy Spirit, Acts 5:3–4). All three persons are coequal in the nature of God (Matthew 28:19; Isaiah 48:16). For the avid student of God's Word, we recommend a more thorough study of the Trinity found in a number of reliable Bible encyclopedias. (See also Index: Trinity.)

Isaiah 43:10 plays an important role in refutation of Armstrong, for God unequivocally states that "Before me no god was formed, nor will there be one after me." The "God family," "Born Gods," "God personages," and "God Beings" are dealt a deathblow in the face of Isaiah 43:10. None preceded Him, and absolutely none will follow. Armstrong's idea of two God Beings coexisting in eternity is answered well by Isaiah 44:8, where God tells us He knows of no others beside himself. No other beings existed with Him.

Isaiah succinctly deals with Armstrong's concept that God the Father is in the form, stature, and shape of man. Rhetorically, he asks, "To whom then will you liken God? Or what likeness will you compare to Him?" (Isaiah 40:18 NKJV). Here, Isaiah tells us nothing is likened to God, but Armstrong believes God had parts in comparison to man's likeness. Any number of biblical passages on the omnipresence of God destroys this view. When the Bible states, "Heaven and the heaven of heavens cannot contain You" (1 Kings 8:27 NKJV), then how does Armstrong purpose that he is limited to the form, shape, and stature of man? Scripture answers this well (2 Chronicles 2:6; 6:18; Jeremiah 23:24).

III. The Nature of Christ

Armstrongism taught that Jesus was Jehovah, but not the Son, before His birth through Mary. We must understand that his view of the incarnate Christ destroys the very foundation of God's eternal nature! For example, God cannot lie (Hebrews 6:18), because it is against the nature of One who is pure holiness and truth. Armstrong made the immutable, eternal, immortal God contradict His essence by giving up His immortality while on earth and converting His spirit-essence into flesh. He made Jehovah divest himself totally of immortal spirit, convert into flesh, then reconvert His mortal flesh back to immortal spirit at His resurrection, making Him the first "born again" saved person. He stopped being "very God" and then became "very God" again. While He was dead, the other God Being, the Father, ran the universe, since the immortality of Jesus was temporarily dysfunctional. Then, when Jesus rose from the dead, He rose in a spirit-body, but not the physical body that had died.

---

[76]Armstrong, *The Plain Truth* (September 1980): 30.
[77]*Statement*, 2.

Armstrong wrote:

Jesus did not become the Son of God until about 4 B.C., when born in human flesh of the virgin Mary.[78]

Christ was converted into flesh . . . he who had existed from eternity . . . he who was *God*—he *was made flesh*—converted *into* flesh, until he *became* flesh; and then he *was* flesh! . . . He divested himself of inherent immortality for the time being. He gave up immortality for us—that he might *die* for us . . . that he, even as we, might be resurrected from the *dead,* and given by the Father immortal life—that is, converted back into spiritual immortality so that he by the resurrection once again *became* divine Spirit—or very *God!*

Jesus was also *God*—he was both human and divine. But he was not *God* inside of, yet separate from, the body of flesh—he, God, *was made flesh,* until he, still *God*—God *with us*—became God *in* (*not* inside of) the human flesh—God manifest *in the flesh* (1 Timothy 3:16). . . . Jesus *died!* Jesus *was dead!* . . . If there were no other Person in the Godhead, then the Giver of all life was dead and all hope was at an end! . . . But the Father still reigned in high heaven!

Not Resurrected in Same Body. . . . Now notice carefully, God the Father did not cause Jesus Christ to get back into the body that had died. . . . And the resurrected body was no longer human—it was the Christ resurrected *immortal,* once again *changed!* As he had been changed, converted *into* mortal human flesh and blood, subject to death, and for the *purpose of dying for our sins,* now by a *resurrection from the dead, he was again changed, converted into immortality.*[79]

Because they knew what Jesus had looked like—and in his born-again, resurrected body he looked the same, except he now was composed of spirit instead of matter! . . . He was born in a spirit body, which was manifested to his apostles in the same apparent size and shape as when he died.[80]

The Worldwide Church of God, in contrast to Armstrong's wayward Christology, states, "When the Word came in the flesh, though he was fully human and fully divine, he voluntarily set aside the prerogatives of divinity."[81] They also state that he was "two natures in one Person" and "raised bodily from the dead."[82] These statements, written in agreement with historic creeds of Christianity, stand in biblical opposition to Armstrong's fallacy. Add to that these supportive verses on Christ's immutability: "Jesus Christ the same yesterday, and to day, and for ever" (Hebrews 13:8). And, "Before Abraham was, I am" (John 8:58). Jesus, the eternal I AM, could not stop being who He is and then regain an unchangeable nature. That would be a contradiction of terms. Philippians 2:6–8 answers the contrived story of Armstrongism. Jesus had two natures, that of eternal God, and

---

[78]Armstrong, *The Plain Truth* (February 1979): 41.
[79]Armstrong, "Why Christ Died and Rose Again," *The Plain Truth,* abbreviated version (April 1982): 20.
[80]Armstrong, "Personal From . . ." *The Plain Truth* (January 1978): 44.
[81]Anonymous, *God Is . . .* (Pasadena: Worldwide Church of God, 1992), 30.
[82]Ibid.

that of a servant, man. Neither nature (*morphe* in Greek) was altered during the incarnation. His deity was not altered by His humanity, and His humanity was unaltered by His being God. This shows that His deity was distinct from His humanity. One did not merge or convert into the other.

According to Colossians 2:9, all the fullness of Deity dwells in Him bodily, which means nothing was lacking in his deity; it was the fullness. Had He given up immortality, then He would not have the fullness of Deity, but Colossians corrects Armstrongism here. See also John 1:1; 1:18; 5:18; 20:28; Acts 20:28; and Revelation 1:8.

Was Jesus referred to as the Son previous to His incarnation? We find an affirmative answer in the Psalms: "Kiss the Son, lest he be angry" (Psalm 2:12). Also, in Proverbs 30:4 (NKJV), the question is asked, "Who has established all the ends of the earth? What is His name, and what is His Son's name?" We must also remember that Jesus was the Son sent into the world (John 3:16), which agrees with these Old Testament passages that He was the Son before His incarnation.

The physical resurrection of the same body that Jesus had died with on the cross is central to Christianity. It cannot be some nonmaterial spirit-body that only looked similar to the one that died. Paul reminds us that if the Resurrection did not happen, our faith is in vain (1 Corinthians 15:14).

When Jesus made His post-resurrection appearances, He offered the print of the nails in His hands (John 20:27) as proof that it was the same crucified body. Otherwise, Jesus would have been deceiving His disciples with imitation prints. He offered His hands and feet as evidence (Luke 24:39). Of utmost importance, He denied that He was other than "flesh and bones, as ye see me have" (Luke 24:39). He proved His physical body by eating with His disciples (Luke 24:42; John 21:12–13). This is how Luke can assuredly tell us that He showed himself alive with many infallible proofs (Acts 1:3).

IV. The Personality of the Holy Spirit

The teaching of Armstrong on the Holy Spirit is twofold. First, he believed that the Holy Spirit was not God, nor a person within the nature of God. Second, he believed the Holy Spirit impregnates the believer (begotten) in Jesus as a down payment for salvation. In this his purpose was to name the Holy Spirit a "divine sperm" and "sperm" impregnating the believer. Once the Holy Spirit leads a person through a faithful life, then the "begotten" person is finally "born again" at the resurrection to become a member of the God Family.

Armstrong specifically focused upon the person and deity of the Holy Spirit. He wrote, "He [Simon the sorcerer] taught, and his false church later (A.D. 321) made official, the 'Trinity' doctrine, saying the Holy Spirit of God is a *ghost*—a third spirit *person*—thereby doing away with the fact that we can be begotten by God's Spirit."[83] Further, he says, "The theologians . . . have blindly accepted the false doctrine introduced by *pagan* false prophets who crept in, that the Holy Spirit is a third person."[84]

---

[83]Armstrong, "Foundation, History, Authority, and Doctrine of the Worldwide Church of God," *The Plain Truth* (February 1978): 41.
[84]Armstrong, *Born Again*, 19.

About the Holy Spirit impregnating the repentant person, he said, "The Holy Spirit also is the divine 'spiritual sperm' that impregnates with immortal God-life!"[85] And, "If 'fertilized' by the male divine sperm of God (his Holy Spirit—actually God-life), he would have been begotten, but not yet born as God."[86]

~The Christian doctrine of the Holy Spirit is guarded as precious in the sight of believers. Therefore, denial of His person is an assault upon the very nature of God. The Bible shows us that the Holy Spirit acts only as a person can act or respond (John 14–16; Matthew 12:31; Romans 8:26–27; Ephesians 4:30; and Hebrews 10:29). The Holy Spirit has the attributes that belong only to God (Luke 1:35–37; Isaiah 40:13; Hebrews 9:14). The Holy Spirit is also called God (2 Samuel 23:2–3; Acts 5:1–4; 1 Corinthians 6:19–20).

V. Salvation

Armstrong summarized his plan of salvation:

> Salvation, then, *is a process!* . . . But how the "god of this world" (2 Corinthians 4:4) would blind your eyes to that! He tries to deceive you into thinking all there is to it is just "accepting Christ"—with "no works,"—and presto chango, you're pronounced saved![87]
>
> People have been taught, falsely, that "Christ *completed* the Plan of Salvation on the Cross"—when actually it was only *begun* there. The popular denominations have taught, "*Just believe*—that's all there is to it; believe the Lord Jesus Christ, and you are that instant *saved!*". . . . The *blood* of Christ does not finally save any man. The death of Christ did pay the penalty of sin in our stead—it wipes the slate clean of past sins—it saves us merely from the *death penalty*—it removes that which separated us from God and reconciles us to God. . . . It is only those who, during this Christian Spirit-begotten life, have grown in knowledge and grace, have overcome, have developed spiritually, done works of Christ, and endured unto the end, who shall finally be given immortality—finally changed from mortal to immortal at the time of the second coming of Christ."[87]

Salvation, as outlined in *Mystery of the Ages,* needs to be carefully considered because of the redefinition of terms foisted by Armstrong. Begotten, for example, is the state of the believer on earth after accepting Christ's forgiveness and becoming impregnated by the Holy Spirit. Impregnation by the Holy Spirit is when the Holy Spirit commingles with the human spirit, giving it a gestation period until "birth" in the resurrection. Even so, it needs to be remembered that the Holy Spirit is not God to him, but only the "power" or emanation of the Father and Son. The resurrection is defined as the birth of the person, becoming "born again" into a spirit-body, but not a human body. The kingdom of God is the destiny of those "born again" in the resurrection. They will receive rewards for their works on earth.

---

[85]Armstrong, "Confusion," 6.
[86]Armstrong, "Captive," 42.
[87]Armstrong, *Born Again*, 21.

The dead who died from Adam to Christ will revive into mortal human bodies to receive a chance to hear the Gospel during the millennium and accept the message. This is where Armstrongism holds the similitude of soul-sleep. Those who are awakened to a mortal resurrection, and believe, will be changed to spirit-bodies at the final resurrection. He attempts to steer clear of accusations of "second chance" salvation by saying that this only presents each person with a first chance. Those before Christ, he says, had no first chance.

The faithful resurrected persons will become God Beings in the God Family and rule over cities on this planet or finish God's creation on other planets. Those who rejected the message of Christ will suffer hellfire, albeit temporarily. Armstrong's niche is that the soul of the unrepentant is mortal, so the suffering by hellfire will last only until the soul is destroyed. That is the second death. Much of this was evidenced from quotations in our earlier section on Armstrong's cosmology. Tucked neatly within his doctrine of the mortality of the soul is his doctrine of soul-sleep. He appealed to all of the standard arguments advanced by the Seventh-Day Adventists and Jehovah's Witnesses. These, however, are quickly refuted by a number of verses in both the Old and New Testaments that show conscious existence after death: Isaiah 14:9–11; Matthew 17:1–9; 22:32; Mark 9:38–48; Luke 16:19–31; Romans 8:38; 2 Corinthians 5:6–8; Philippians 1:23; and Revelation 6:9.

One stands perplexed after reading *Mystery of the Ages*, wondering where to begin unraveling a soteriology that is so far from Scripture it ranks with science fiction. (Small wonder, then, that the Worldwide Church of God abandoned the book!) But despite Armstrong's bewildering dogma, the truth of the genuine gospel message remains strong:~

In his epistle to the Ephesians, the apostle Paul is adamant in his declaration that "by grace you have been saved through faith; and this is not your own doing, it is the gift of God—not because of works, lest any one should boast" (Ephesians 2:8, from the Greek). Here is the usage of the past tense in reference to Christians, an instance that is amply supplemented throughout the New Testament by such passages as John 5:24; 3:36; 6:47; Romans 8:1; 1 Peter 1:18; and 1 John 5:1, 11–13, 20.

It is wholly unnecessary to pursue this thought further, since Armstrong has no scholarly precedent for subdividing the new birth and attempting to attach it to the resurrection of the body, something that the Scripture nowhere does. His is a lame attempt to distort the basic meaning of *gennao*, which he admits is listed in the lexicon as "to be born, to bring forth, to be delivered of." It is only one more indication of the limitations of his resources.

When Jesus Christ addressed Nicodemus (John 3) and spoke of the new birth, He connected this birth to the person of the Holy Spirit, whom the disciples received in the Upper Room (John 20), and whose power and presence were manifested at Pentecost (Acts 2). This has always been accepted in Christian theology for just what the Bible says it is, an instantaneous experience of spiritual cleansing and re-creation synonymous with the exercise of saving faith in the person of Jesus Christ and through the agency of the grace of God (Acts 16:31; 2:8–10; Colossians 1:13–14; Galatians 2:20; 1 Corinthians 6:11, 19; 2 Corinthians 5:17).

The apostle Paul instructs us that our salvation has been accomplished not by any efforts on our part, but by "the kindness and love of God our Saviour" (Titus 3:4–7). It is not something we must wait for until the resurrection; it is our present possession in Christ totally separate from the immortality of the body, which is to be bestowed at the return of Christ and the resurrection of the body (1 Corinthians 15:49–54; 1 John 3:2; Romans 6:5).

~There are many other errors in Armstrong's theology that could easily fill a small volume. Let it be said, however, that the theology of Armstrongism contains just enough truth to make it attractive to the listener who is unaware of the multiple sources of heretical doctrine he has drawn upon for the balance of his theological system.

Armstrongism is dangerous, as it makes profuse use of the Bible and professes to swear allegiance to only "the plain truth of the Scripture," while, in reality, its allegiance is to the interpretations of the Scripture propagated by Herbert W. Armstrong, whom one author has aptly described as "Mr. Confusion."

Since "God is not the author of confusion" (1 Corinthians 14:33), there is one sure remedy to the problem of the spread of Armstrongism. Turn off the television and radio wherever it is promoted and open your Bible, for within its pages God is always broadcasting the eternal message of the Gospel of grace impregnated by the Spirit of God in every essential necessary to the redemption of the soul and re-creation and living of the Christian life. When this is supplemented by attendance in a truly Christian church where that Gospel is preached, there is no need to listen to the Herbert Armstrongs of our day, for as the psalmist so beautifully described it, "The entrance of thy words giveth light."~

Recommended Resources

1. Chambers, Roger R. *The Plain Truth About Armstrongism.* Grand Rapids, Mich.: Baker Books, 1988.
2. Feazell, J. Michael. *Liberation of the Worldwide Church of God.* Grand Rapids, Mich.: Zondervan, 2001.
3. Nicoles, Larry, and George Mather. *Discovering the Plain Truth: How the Worldwide Church of God Encountered the Gospel of Grace.* Downers Grove, Ill.: InterVarsity Press, 1999.
4. Tkach, Joseph. *Transformed by Truth.* Sisters, Ore.: Multnomah Publishers, 1997.

Quick Facts About the Puzzle of Seventh-day Adventism

- SDA believe in the Spirit of Prophecy, which was the anointing upon their founder, Ellen G. White, as the proper interpretation of Scripture. But the Bible is inerrant and superior to White's writings.

- The doctrine on the Trinitarian Godhead is orthodox.

- The doctrine of hell and eternal torment of the wicked is exchanged for soul-sleep. There is a heaven for true believers.

- SDA teach an aberrational doctrine concerning the completion of Christ's atonement, who the "sin-bearer" is in Scripture, and Christ's present work in heaven.

- Salvation requires personal works combined with God's grace.

Appendix B

The Puzzle of Seventh-day Adventism

Preface

In a volume such as this, dealing with the problem of non-Christian cults, the question might logically be asked, "Why include Seventh-day Adventism, especially since the writer has classified them in a full-length volume as a Christian denomination?"

The answer to this is that for over a century Adventism has borne a stigma of being called a non-Christian cult system. Whether or not this was justified in the early development of Adventism has already been discussed at length in an earlier book,[1] but it should be carefully remembered that the Adventism of today is different in not a few places from the Adventism of 1844, and with that change the necessity of new evaluation comes naturally.

Together with the Evangelical Foundation (founded by the late Dr. Donald Grey Barnhouse and publishers of the now-defunct *Eternity* magazine), we conducted a thorough new evaluation of the Seventh-day Adventists several years ago. The results of that new evaluation were presented comprehensively in the book *The Truth About Seventh-day Adventism* and then later in the previous editions of this volume.

It is my conviction that one cannot be a true Jehovah's Witness, Mormon, Christian Scientist, etc., and be a Christian in the biblical sense of the term; but it is perfectly possible to be a Seventh-day Adventist and be a true follower of Jesus Christ despite certain heterodox concepts, which will be discussed.

Such Christian leaders as Louis T. Talbot, M. R. DeHaan, John R. Rice,

---

This appendix updated, expanded, and revised by Kurt Van Gorden and edited by Jill Martin Rische.
[1]Walter Martin, *The Truth About Seventh-day Adventism* (Grand Rapids: Zondervan Publishing House, 1960).

Anthony A. Hoekema, J. K. Van Baalen, Herbert Bird, and John R. Gerstner have taken the position that Adventism is, in fact, a cult system; whereas, the late Donald Grey Barnhouse, E. Schuyler English, Josh McDowell (*Understanding the Cults: A Handbook on Today's Religions* and *The Deceivers*), and quite a few others, including myself, have concluded the opposite.

Since the opposing view has had wide circulation over a long period of time, I felt it was necessary to include here Seventh-day Adventism as a proper counterbalance—presenting the other side of Adventism and representing the theology of Adventism as the Adventists themselves believe it and not as many critics have caricatured it.

This, of course, is not to be construed in any sense of the term as an endorsement of the entire theological structure of Seventh-day Adventism, a portion of which is definitely out of the mainstream of historical Christian theology, and which I have taken pains to refute. But I believe it is only fair and ethical to consider both sides of an extremely difficult and provocative controversy, which shows very little sign of abating in our day.

In fact, since the early 1970s the Seventh-day Adventist denomination has seen turbulence, both administratively and doctrinally, that is more extensive than any turmoil in the organization's history. Administratively, there have been a number of Adventist leaders and pastors who have been removed from their positions because of supposed or proven improper financial activities, including misappropriation of funds. On the United States federal government level, the IRS, SEC, FBI, and Justice Department have all initiated investigations, and some Seventh-day Adventist conference administrators may even face trial for fraud. Doctrinally, the church has developed a large rift between those members and leaders who are solidly within the evangelical Christian camp, and those members and leaders who, because of their emphasis on works-righteousness, legalism, and the prophetic status accorded to founder Ellen G. White, may well move the denomination over time outside of the evangelical camp and perhaps even into actual cultism.

~There is a third growing faction within Seventh-day Adventism that is much more theologically liberal than either the traditionalists or the evangelicals, and the future may even bring *three* Adventist groups, one aligning itself roughly with mainstream, theologically liberal Protestantism, one with sectarian or cultic groups, and one with mainstream evangelicalism. Writing in *Christianity Today* in 1990,[2] author Kenneth Samples provided a conclusion with which we can still agree:

> In the late 1970s, Seventh-day Adventism was at the crossroads: Would it become thoroughly evangelical? Or would it return to sectarian traditionalism? Denominational discipline in the 1980s against certain evangelical advocates gave a strong indication that there is a powerful traditionalist segment that desires to retain Adventism's 1844 "remnant" identity. As well, the liberal perspective, with its emphasis on pluralism, appeals to many Adventists. While Evangelical Adventism has lost ground in the 1980s, its supporters remain, though they are not nearly as prominent today.[3]~

---

[2]This article postdates Dr. Martin.
[3]Kenneth R. Samples, "The Recent Truth About Seventh-day Adventism," *Christianity Today* (February 5, 1990): 21.

Since I have always stressed the importance of doctrinal integrity in my evaluations of religious movements, the doctrinal upheaval in Adventism is of special concern. Consequently, on February 16, 1983, I wrote the General Conference of Seventh-Day Adventists (Washington, D.C.), calling for the Conference's public and official statement reaffirming or denying the authority of the Adventist book *Questions on Doctrine*,[4] which was the representative Adventist publication on which I based my earlier evaluation and book. ~The current standard doctrinal exposition book is called *Seventh-day Adventists Believe: A Biblical Exposition of Seventeen Fundamental Doctrines* and was published by the General Conference in 1988. In almost all cases, this newer volume agrees in substance with *Questions on Doctrine*.~ On April 29, 1983, W. Richard Lesher, vice-president of the General Conference, responded in a personal letter. His reply read, in part:

> You ask first if Seventh-day Adventists still stand behind the answers given to your questions in *Questions on Doctrine* as they did in 1957. The answer is yes. You have noted in your letter that some opposed the answers given then, and, to some extent, the same situation exists today. But certainly the great majority of Seventh-day Adventists are in harmony with the views expressed in *Questions on Doctrine*.
>
> Secondly, you addressed the question of the interpretation of Scripture in relation to the writings of Ellen White. As an attested agent of the prophetic gift we believe communication based on Ellen White's revelatory experience to be trustworthy and dependable. However, we do not believe that the writings of Ellen White exhaust the meaning of Scripture. We still hold with the statements on Ellen White included in *Questions on Doctrine*.

On the basis of the above letter, dialogue with several Adventist leaders, and the continuing state of flux within Adventism itself, I must, for the time being, stand behind my original evaluation of Seventh-day Adventism as presented comprehensively in my first book on the subject and later in this volume. Only events not yet unfolded, but within the knowledge of the Lord himself, will determine whether my evaluation will need to be revised in the future. It is my prayer that the aberrational currents within contemporary Adventism will not prevail and that Adventism will continue to be an evangelical, albeit unique, Christian denomination.

It was Dr. Donald Grey Barnhouse who said that simply because a person is a member of a specific denomination, there is no reason to suppose that the entire denomination is represented by that person's theology, nor is it proper to assume that because there are heretical Baptists, Presbyterians, Methodists, Episcopalians, etc., that all such denominations are therefore heretical.

To expand upon this we might say that simply because a denomination is Christian in its profession does not guarantee that all members of that denomination are Christian by their confession and experience. Hence, it is our position that Seventh-day Adventism as a denomination is essentially Christian in a sense that all denominations and groups professing Christianity are Christian if they conform to the classical mission of Christianity as given in the Bible and the creeds and counsels of the Christian church. But this does not mean that all

[4] *Questions on Doctrine* (Washington, D.C.: Review and Herald Publishing Association, 1957).

Baptists, all Methodists, all Episcopalians, all Lutherans, or all Adventists are necessarily Christians. This is a matter between the individual and God and is to be viewed in the light of the revelation of Scripture and the testimony of the Holy Spirit.

This section on Seventh-day Adventism is an attempt to present for consideration facts that are little known in many areas and often distorted in others. It is an effort to examine, commend, and criticize where necessary the theological structure of the Adventist denomination, and is submitted with a prayerful hope that honest investigation, even if it does not agree with our preconceived notions, is to be encouraged and profited from, under the guidance of the Spirit of God.

The Historical Background of Seventh-day Adventism

Seventh-day Adventism sprang from the "Great Second Advent Awakening," which shook the religious world just before the middle of the nineteenth century, when a reemphasis on the second advent of Jesus Christ was rampant in Britain and on the continent of Europe. Before long, many of the Old World views of prophetic interpretation crossed the Atlantic and penetrated American theological circles.

Based largely upon the apocalyptic books of Daniel and Revelation, the theology of the Advent Movement was discussed in the newspapers as well as in theological journals. New Testament eschatology competed with stock market quotations for front-page space, and the "seventy weeks," "twenty-three hundred days," and "the abomination of desolation" (Daniel 8–9) were common subjects of conversation.

Following the chronology of Archbishop Ussher, and interpreting the 2,300 days of Daniel as 2,300 years, many Bible students of various denominations concluded that Christ would come back about the year 1843. Of this studious number was one William Miller, a Baptist minister and resident of Lower Hampton, New York. The Great Second Advent Awakening, which swept the United States in the 1840s, stemmed largely from the activities of this William Miller, who confidently taught in the year 1818 that in "about" twenty-five years, i.e., 1843, Jesus Christ would come again. As Miller himself put it, "I was thus brought in 1818, at the close of my two-year study of the Scriptures, to the solemn conclusion that in about twenty-five years from that time all the affairs of our present state would be wound up."[5]

Miller further wrote:

> I believe the time can be known by all who desire to understand and to be ready for his coming. And I am fully convinced that some time between March 21st, 1843 and March 21st, 1844, according to the Jewish method of computation of time, Christ will come and bring all his saints with him; and that then he will reward every man as his work shall be.[6]

At length his associates set October 22, 1844, as the final date when Jesus Christ would return for His saints, visit judgment upon sin, and establish the kingdom of God upon earth.

---

[5]Francis D. Nichol, *The Midnight Cry* (Washington, D.C.: Review and Herald, 1944), 35.
[6]William Miller, *Signs of the Times* (January 25, 1843).

One need only read the words of the Lord Jesus Christ to realize that Miller was teaching in contradiction to the Word of God. Jesus said, "But of that day and hour knoweth no man, no, not the angels of heaven, but my Father only" (Matthew 24:36; also 24:42, 44; 25:13).

The gospel of Mark also shows that dates cannot be set, for in verse 35 of chapter 13 our Lord stated, "Watch ye therefore: for ye know not when the master of the house cometh." And almost His last words to His disciples are a rebuke to those who set dates: "It is not for you to know the times or the seasons, which the Father hath put in his own power" (Acts 1:7). Certainly this should have been deterrent enough for William Miller and his associates, but, sad to say, it was not.

Compare the two positions, Miller versus the Scriptures: God declared that no man would know the time; Miller stated that he did know the time. God said the times and seasons were within His own power; the Millerites declared that they had the prophetic key given to them. Jesus Christ stated, "No man knows the day or the hour," but the Millerites set the exact day (October 22, 1844). And history bears a bitter record of their terrible disappointment.

Lest anyone reading the various accounts of the rise of "Millerism" in the United States come to the conclusion that Miller and his followers were "crackpots" or "uneducated tools of Satan," the following facts should be known:[7] The Great Advent Awakening movement that spanned the Atlantic from Europe was bolstered by a tremendous wave of contemporary biblical scholarship. Although Miller himself lacked academic theological training, actually scores of prophetic scholars in Europe and the United States had espoused Miller's views before he himself announced them. In reality, his was only one more voice proclaiming the 1843/1844 fulfillment of Daniel 8:14, or the 2,300-day period allegedly dating from 457 B.C. and ending in A.D. 1843–1844.

William Miller was born in Pittsfield, Massachusetts, on February 15, 1782, and while he was still a young child his family moved to Lower Hampton, New York, close to the Vermont State border. Miller was raised by a deeply religious mother, but despite her zeal for his conversion, Miller became a deist. Only after a soul-searching experience that culminated in his conversion did he begin his preparation for ministry in the Baptist church. A great many books have been written about William Miller and the Millerite movement, but to this writer's knowledge none of them proved Miller to be dishonest or deceptive in his prophetic interpretation of Scripture. Indeed, he enjoyed the reputation, among all who knew him, of being an honest, forthright Christian. One does not have to endorse the errors of Millerism, therefore, to respect the historical figure of William Miller. Regardless of his shortcomings, Miller was a deeply religious Christian who, had he had a more extensive understanding of the Scriptures, most probably would never have embarked upon his disastrous date-setting career.

Clearly it may be seen that although Miller popularized the 1843/1844 concept of Christ's coming again, he was by no means alone. If we condemn him, we must also condemn a large number of internationally known scholars who were

---

[7]The various charges to the effect that the Millerites were fanatics who waited on rooftops attired in white "ascension robes" anticipating the return of Christ; and further, that insanity swept the Millerite ranks in 1843 and 1844 in the wake of the "Great Disappointment" are purely mythological in character and have little basis in verifiable facts (see *The Midnight Cry,* 321–98).

among the most highly educated men of their day. Yet they, too, had a blind spot in prophetic interpretation and endorsed this fallacious system of date-setting. Regardless of the number of scholars who confirmed his errors, however, the fact remains that Miller and the Millerite movement operated contrary to the express injunctions of Scripture. Both Miller and his followers lived to reap the reward of their foolhardy quest and to suffer crushing humiliation, ridicule, and abject despair.

William Miller set the time for the return of the Lord between March 21, 1843, and March 21, 1844, reckoning according to the Jewish calendar.[8] As the first-named date approached, religious frenzy shook the Millerite world—the Lord was coming back!

Though the followers of Miller were zealous and sincere, stark disappointment awaited them as the Jewish year 1843 faded from time, and the Lord did not come. When the dream closest to their hearts failed to materialize, they eagerly sought enlightenment from William Miller, who replied with characteristic honesty. Wrote Miller, in the very shadow of spiritual anguish:

> Were I to live my life over again, with the same evidence that I then had, to be honest with God and man I should have to do as I have done. Although opposers said it would not come, they produced no weighty arguments. It was evidently guess-work with them; and I then thought, and do now, that their denial was based more on an unwillingness for the Lord to come than on any arguments leading to such conclusion. I confess my error, and acknowledge my disappointment; yet I still believe that the Day of the Lord is near, even at the door; and I exhort you, my brethren, to be watchful and not let that day come upon you unawares.[9]

In the wake of this stunning declaration, the Millerites strove vainly to reconcile their interpretations of the prophetic Scriptures with the stark truth that Christ had not returned. With one last gasp, so to speak, Miller reluctantly endorsed "The Seventh-Month Movement," or the belief that Christ would come on October 22, 1844, the tenth day of the seventh month according to the Karaite reckoning of the Jewish Sacred Calendar.[10] Once again the Millerites' hopes were lifted, and October 22, 1844, became the watchword for the return of the Lord Jesus Christ. The outcome can best be summed up in the words of Dr. Josiah Litch, a Millerite leader in Philadelphia who wrote on October 24: "It is a cloudy and dark day here—the sheep are scattered—the Lord has not come yet."[11]

From Litch's statement, it is easy to piece together the psychological framework of the Millerites in the wake of these two disappointments. They were a shattered and disillusioned people—Christ had not come to cleanse the "sanctuary" (the earth), to usher in judgment, and to bring the world into subjugation to the "everlasting gospel." Instead, the sky was cloudy and dark, and the historical horizons were black with the failure of the Millerite movement. There was, of course, terrible confusion, of which God, Scripture tells us, is not the author (1 Corinthians 14:33).

---

[8]*The Midnight Cry*, 169.
[9]Sylvester Bliss, *Memoirs of William Miller* (Boston, Mass.: n.p., 1855), 256.
[10]*The Midnight Cry*, 243.
[11]Ibid., 256.

The final phase of the movement closed with the "Great Disappointment of 1844," but as the Millerites disbanded, there emerged other groups, such as the First-day Adventists. However, in our study we are concerned primarily with three segments that later fused to produce the Seventh-day Adventist denomination. William Miller, it should be noted, was *never* a Seventh-day Adventist, and stated that he had "no confidence" in the "new theories" that emerged from the shambles of the Millerite movement. Dr. LeRoy Froom, professor of prophetic interpretation at the Seventh-day Adventist Theological Seminary, Takoma Park, Washington, D.C., in the fourth volume of his masterful series *The Prophetic Faith of Our Fathers*, succinctly states what Miller's position was:

> Miller was outspokenly opposed to the various new theories that had developed following October 22, 1844, in an endeavor to explain the disappointment. He deplored the call that had been given to come out to the churches, and he never accepted the distinctive positions of the Sabbatarians. The doctrine of the unconscious sleep of the dead and the final destruction of the wicked was not, he maintained, part of the original Millerite position, but was introduced personally by George Storrs and Charles Fitch. He even came to deny the application of the parable in *The Midnight Cry* to the Seventh-month Movement and eventually went so far as to declare unequivocally that the movement was not "a fulfillment of prophecy in any sense."[12]

Aside from chronological speculation, therefore, the theology of William Miller differed from Seventh-day Adventist theology on three distinct points: He denied the Seventh-day Sabbath; the doctrine of the sleep of the soul; and the final, utter destruction of the wicked—all doctrines held by the Seventh-day Adventist denomination. Also, he never embraced the "sanctuary" and "investigative judgment" theories developed by Seventh-day Adventists. For William Miller, the era of chronological speculation was over, and he died shortly after the fiasco, a broken and disillusioned man, who was, nevertheless, honest and forthright when in error or when repudiating error. I believe he now enjoys the presence of the Lord whose appearing he so anxiously awaited.

In order to understand the background of Seventh-day Adventist history and theology, let us look at the three segments of Millerism, which eventually united to form the Seventh-day Adventist denomination. Each of these groups held a distinctive doctrine. The group headed by Hiram Edson, in western New York, proclaimed the doctrine of the sanctuary "as embracing a special or final ministry of Christ in the Holy of Holies in the *heavenly* sanctuary," thus giving new meaning to the message "The Hour of God's Judgment Has Come." The second group, headed by Joseph Bates, whose main following was in Massachusetts and New Hampshire, advocated the observance of the Seventh-day Sabbath "as involved in the keeping of the commandments of God." The third group, in Maine, emphasized the "Spirit of prophecy" or "the testimony of Jesus," which they believed was to be made manifest in the "remnant" (Revelation 14:6–12; also Revelation 12:17; 19:10) or "the last segment of God's church of the

---

[12] *The Prophetic Faith of Our Fathers* (Takoma Park, Washington, D.C.: Review and Herald Publishing Association, 1950), 828–29.

centuries." Between the years 1844 and 1847, the thinking of these groups crystallized and was actively declared and promulgated in the writings of their respective leaders: Hiram Edson, O. R. L. Crosier, Joseph Bates, James White, and Ellen G. White.

At this point in our historical analysis of Seventh-day Adventism, we believe it will be profitable to briefly review "The Great Disappointment of 1844" and its relationship to the Seventh-day Adventist doctrines of the heavenly sanctuary and the investigative judgment. The entire superstructure of the Millerites' prophetic interpretation was based upon their view of the book of Daniel, chapters 8 and 9, with particular emphasis upon Daniel 8:14 and 9:24–27. The Millerites believed that the prophecy of the seventy weeks of Daniel 9 must date from the year 457 B.C., which, as recent archaeological evidence confirms,[13] was the exact date of the decree of King Artaxerxes to rebuild Jerusalem (Daniel 9:25). Tracing the seventy weeks of Daniel on the theory that, as the Hebrew indicated, it should be rendered "seventy weeks of years" or 490 years, the Millerites arrived at the date A.D. 33; that is, from 457 B.C. to A.D. 33. Since this date generally corresponds with Christ's crucifixion, Millerites then linked it to Daniel 8:14—"Unto two thousand and three hundred days; then shall the sanctuary be cleansed"—with the seventy weeks of years prophecy, and the 2,300 days became 2,300 years. Thus, if you subtract 490 years (adding, of course, A.D. 1 to 33), the figure arrived at is 1843. Many biblical scholars have historically shown that in Scripture a day frequently symbolizes a year; further, that the seventy weeks and 2,300 days of Daniel could have begun on the same date. And that date, according to the Millerites, was 457 B.C. In *The Prophetic Faith of Our Fathers*,[14] Dr. LeRoy Froom shows that many expositors had embraced the same method of interpretation, which is no argument for accepting it, but a strong argument for the *right* of the Millerites to do so.

As we have seen, when the Millerite calculations failed, all appeared to be lost; but a singular event took place, only three days later, in a cornfield near Port Gibson, New York, which changed the face of Adventist history and brought about a reinterpretation of the eighth and ninth chapters of the book of Daniel, an interpretation that is a keystone in the arch of the Seventh-day Adventist view of prophecy.

On October 25, 1844, following the "Great Disappointment," Hiram Edson, a devout Adventist and follower of William Miller, was wending his way homeward with his friend O. R. L. Crosier. In order to avoid the mocking gazes and taunts of their neighbors, they cut across a cornfield.

As they walked through the cornfield in deep silence and meditation, Hiram Edson stopped, became more deeply immersed in meditation, and then with upturned face indicative of a heartfelt prayer for spiritual light, he suddenly received a great spiritual "revelation." In the words of Dr. Froom,

> Suddenly there burst upon his mind the thought that there were *two* phases to Christ's ministry in the heaven of heavens, just as in the earthly sanctuary of old. In his own words, an overwhelming conviction came over

---

[13]Siegfried H. Horn and Lynn H. Wood, *The Chronology of Ezra 7* (Washington, D.C.: Review and Herald Publishing Association, 1959).
[14]*The Prophetic Faith of Our Fathers*, vols. 1–4.

him "that instead of our high priest *coming out of* the most holy of the heavenly sanctuary to come to this earth on the tenth day of the seventh month at the end of the 2,300 days, he for the first time entered on that day the second apartment of that sanctuary, and that he had a work to perform in the Most Holy before coming to this earth."[15]

In that instant, according to Seventh-day Adventist history, Hiram Edson found the reason why the Millerites had been disappointed. They had expected Christ to come to earth to cleanse the sanctuary, but the sanctuary was not the earth. It was located in heaven! Instead of coming to earth, therefore, Christ had passed from one "apartment" of the sanctuary into the other "apartment" to perform a closing work now known as the "investigative judgment." In the year 1846 this new interpretation of Daniel was convincingly put forth by O. R. L. Crosier,[16] who outlined and defended Hiram Edson's concept in a lengthy article in a special number of *The Day Star,* a Millerite publication in Cincinnati, Ohio. F. D. Nichol in *The Midnight Cry* refers to "a fragment," which Edson wrote about his experience in the cornfield. But as Dr. Froom has pointed out, Edson himself really believed that Christ had passed from the "holy place" to the "most holy" place in the heavenly sanctuary. The Old Testament tabernacle was divided by a veil into two apartments, the holy place and the most holy place. In the most holy place was the Ark of the Covenant. Into this apartment the high priest went once a year to sprinkle blood upon the mercy seat to make atonement for the sins of the people. In Christian theology, this blood symbolized prophetically the death of the Lord Jesus Christ, the Lamb of God, for the sins of all the world.

Transferring this Old Testament ceremonial concept to the New Testament, and making an extremely literalistic interpretation of the book of Hebrews, Edson and Crosier formulated the doctrines of "the heavenly sanctuary" and "investigative judgment." These concepts are now understood to mean that in 1844 Christ entered the "second phase" of His ministry in the heavenly sanctuary, and ever since He has been reviewing the cases of believers to determine their worthiness for eternal life. Further, He will come forth from the "second apartment," or finish the "second phase" of His ministry in the sanctuary, to usher in judgment upon the world at His Great Second Advent. This, in essence, was the interpretation that shaped the later concepts of the "heavenly sanctuary" and the "investigative judgment" in Seventh-day Adventist theology. Thus, good Millerite-Adventists were justified in endorsing the work of William Miller. They even maintained that God had allowed Miller to make mistakes for the greater blessing of the "little flock." In her *Early Writings,* Ellen G. White made this assertion:

I have seen that the 1843 chart was directed by the hand of the Lord, and that it should not be altered; that the figures were as He wanted them;

---

[15] *The Prophetic Faith of Our Fathers,* IV:881. An extremely literalistic concept, which is refuted by Hebrews 9:12, 24 and Acts 1, and shows that at His ascension Christ entered into the "holy places," not the "second apartment" of the heavenly sanctuary in 1844. Seventh-day Adventists have redefined their teaching in terms of "phases."

[16] Crosier later rejected this concept, though it was endorsed by Ellen G. White and other prominent Adventist leaders. (See D. M. Canright, *Life of Mrs. E. G. White,* 107.)

that His hand was over and hid a mistake in some of the figures, so that none could see it, until His hand was removed.[17]

In this context, White was distinctly referring to Fitch's prophetic chart, utilized by the Millerites, which led them to the year 1843 instead of the date that she considered to be correct—October 22, 1844.

F. D. Nichol, in *Ellen G. White and Her Critics*,[18] attempts to explain White's statement in the light of Acts 24, Mark 16, Exodus 8:15, and Exodus 10. Of course, any are at liberty to accept his interpretation of the problem, which I do not. The fact remains, however, that the Millerites erred in their prophetic, chronological interpretation of the book of Daniel, and only the concept of Hiram Edson in the cornfield and the explanatory writings of O. R. L. Crosier, buttressed by the "revelations" of Ellen G. White, saved the day.

Although I do not accept White's explanation or the interpretations of Edson, Crosier, Froom, or Nichol, I would be at a loss to account for the growth and development of Seventh-day Adventism apart from the psychological framework of the "Great Disappointment of 1844." Therefore, I have carefully reviewed the doctrines that evolved from the Edson-Crosier-White pronouncements. The psychological factor is very important in Seventh-day Adventist history.

The second of the three Millerite-Adventist groups mentioned is also of great historical import. In Fairhaven, Massachusetts, following the "Great Disappointment of 1844," one Joseph Bates, a retired sea captain, issued a forty-eight-page pamphlet entitled *The Seventh-day Sabbath, A Perpetual Sign* (self-published, 1846). In it he argued for the Sabbath as a divine institution ordained in Eden, prefigured in Creation, and buttressed at Mt. Sinai. Some three years later Bates wrote a second pamphlet entitled *A Seal of the Living God* (self-published, 1849), based largely upon Revelation 14:9–12. Bates' Sabbatarianism exerted a great influence upon what later became the Seventh-day Adventist denomination.

In Volume 4 of *The Prophetic Faith of Our Fathers* (957–58), Dr. Froom sums it up:

> This became henceforth a characteristic and separating feature of Sabbatarian Adventist preaching. Bates here held that the message of Revelation 14 is the foundation of the full Advent message "Fear God, and give glory to him; for the hour of His judgment is come." This, he maintained, began to be fulfilled in the preaching of the Millerite movement. And the second angel's message on the fall of Babylon, with its climax in the call, "Come out of her, my people," was likewise initially sounded in 1844–1848. . . . They must not stop with the first two messages. There is a third, inseparable in the series, to be received and obeyed—namely, full obedience to God's holy commandments, including the observance of the Seventh day as a Sabbath. But that obedience is by faith. The Sabbath was next set forth as the "seal of God" as based on the sealing work of Revelation 7. In January 8, 1849, Bates issued his tract *A Seal of the Living God*. From the fact of John's

[17]*Early Writings* (Washington, D.C.: Review and Herald Publishing Association, n.d.), 74.
[18]*Ellen G. White and Her Critics* (Washington, D.C.: Review and Herald Publishing Association, n.d.), 332–34.

declaration that the number of sealed was 144,000, Bates drew the conclusion that the "remnant" who keep the commandments of God and have the testimony of Jesus Christ would number 144,000. So to the concept of Christ's entering the most holy place of the heavenly sanctuary on October 22, 1844, for the final work of judgment and the receiving of His kingdom, was added the Sabbath, as involved in the third of this commissioned series of special "latter-day" messages. This concept of the "seal" was likewise built into the message of the Sabbath, as an added prophetic element. And this thought was similarly attested by Ellen White, who wrote, "This seal is the Sabbath," and described the "most holy place" in which was the ark (Revelation 11:19), containing the Ten Commandments, with a halo of light surrounding the fourth. Thus the Sabbath and the sanctuary became inseparably tied together.

The third group, which fused with the other two to form the Seventh-day Adventist Church, emphasized "the Spirit of prophecy" (Revelation 19:10). This body of former Millerites accepted the interpretations of one Ellen G. Harmon of Portland, Maine. Ellen Harmon, later Mrs. James White, was recognized by this group as the possessor of the "Spirit of prophecy," a restoration of the spiritual gift of prophecy (1 Corinthians 12:10) or counsel to the Seventh-day Adventist Church. White had numerous visions that confirmed many Adventist doctrines. When the Edson, Crosier, Bates, and White adherents joined forces, the Seventh-day Adventist denomination was launched.

~Today the Seventh-day Adventist church seems to downplay White's role as a "prophet," describing her as "a gifted author, speaker, and administrator, who . . . enjoyed God's special guidance."[19] In any case, the church today clearly affirms that any post-biblical prophet's words must be tested by the Bible: "The Scriptures retain authority even over the gifts that come from the Holy Spirit, including guidance through the gift of prophecy or speaking in tongues."[20]~

Although the name "Seventh-day Adventist" for the denomination was not officially assumed until 1860 at a conference held in Battle Creek, Michigan, nevertheless, Seventh-day Adventism had been launched. In 1855 Adventist headquarters were established in Battle Creek and remained there until 1905, when they were transferred to Takoma Park, a Maryland suburb of Washington, D.C.

The three distinctive doctrines of Seventh-day Adventism—the Sabbath, the Sanctuary, and the "Spirit of prophecy"—will be discussed later. The Adventists had a definite theological platform, which for many years remained almost constant. In recent years, however, there has been a definite movement toward a more explicit declaration of belief in the principles of the Christian faith and the tenets of Christian theology. In short, "clarification" and "redefinition" have characterized recent Seventh-day Adventist theological activities.

~The Seventh-day Adventist church today claims around twelve million members worldwide in more than two hundred countries. It is growing especially rapidly in Third World countries. "During the last five years [1997—2001] 96 percent of the 4,659,785 baptisms and professions of faith occurred outside

---

[19]Seventh-day Adventist official Web site, *www.adventist.org.*
[20]*Seventh-day Adventists Believe: A Biblical Exposition of Twenty-Seven Fundamental Doctrines* (Washington, D.C.: Ministerial Association, General Conference of Seventh-day Adventists, 1988), 13.

North America."[21] Seventh-day Adventists are headquartered in Silver Spring, Maryland, but also operate twelve international administrative offices and thirteen Agencies of the General Conference in the United States and the Philippines. "The Seventh-day Adventist Church now ranks as the eighth largest *international* religious body on this planet."[22]

> Seventh-day Adventists have one of the broadest centralized Protestant educational systems in the world (5,530 schools, colleges, and universities) and have one of the most comprehensive networks of health-care providers (635 hospitals, clinics, medical launches and medivac planes, orphanages, and homes for the elderly). Adventists speak in at least 717 languages and another thousand dialects, leading to the establishment of fifty-six Church-owned printing plants and editorial offices including the newest in Russia and Bulgaria.[23]~

We cannot hope to cover the entire scope of Seventh-day Adventism's historical development in this brief résumé; but we see that from meager beginnings in the wake of the "Great Disappointment of 1844" and the collapse of the Millerite movement, the Seventh-day Adventist denomination has pressed forward and expanded until today it constitutes an important, albeit controversial, segment of American Protestantism.

Although this is but a background sketch, the reader can readily see that in Seventh-day Adventism, religious historians have an interesting subject for study, a subject from which many unusual theological speculations have emerged and continue to emerge.

Psychological Factors

One of the principal problems in understanding the Seventh-day Adventist movement is discovering the psychological motivation and basis of this thriving denomination of zealots.

I. Early Handicaps

From the beginning, the Adventists were regarded with grave suspicion by the great majority of evangelical Christians, principally because the Seventh-day Adventists were pre-millennial in their theology. That is, they believed that Christ would come before the millennium and saw themselves squarely in opposition to the predominant post-millennial and a-millennial schools of thought of that era. The "Great Disappointment of 1844" and the collapse of the Millerite movement naturally brought pre-millennialism into disrepute. Certain authors of the time considered pre-millenarians "peculiar," even to the point of condemning pre-millennialism outright, and dubbed as "Adventist" all who held that view of eschatology. This is especially interesting when we consider that pre-millennialism is an accepted school of thought in eschatology today and that those who hold

---

[21]Seventh-day Adventist official Web site, *www.adventist.org*, 2001 Statistical Report.
[22]Detailed statistical information available at the Seventh-day Adventist official Web site, *www.adventist.org*.
[23]From the Seventh-day Adventist Official Web site *http://statistics.gc.adventist.org/ast/stats/*.

post-millennial and a-millennial views are considered by the pre-millenarians to be peculiar.

Thus the Adventists started out with two great psychological handicaps: They had incurred disapproval of the group or the mainstream of Christianity, and the Millerites from which they sprang had been publicly humiliated by the failure of their chronological calculations. These two factors and the constant jeering by opposing schools of eschatology united the Seventh-day Adventists into a closely knit group, habitually on the defensive and suspicious of the motives and intentions of other Christians.

Moreover, the Adventists were drawn together by the "special truths" of the Advent message. They were convinced that they had a proclamation for the world—a great "last-day message." Later we shall describe how this attitude widened the chasm between Adventists and Christians of other denominations. It is sufficient here to note that the Adventists considered themselves a special "remnant people" ordained by God to revive certain neglected truths of the Christian message. Filled with burning zeal to fulfill this mission, they laid themselves open to serious misunderstanding by Christians of other denominations who did not agree with them about the proper day of worship, the state of the dead, and investigative judgment.

Engaged in open conflict with Christians of virtually all denominations, the Adventists retreated into an "exclusivistic shell," despising what they termed "certain antinomian tendencies in contemporary Christian theology." They laid strong emphasis upon man's responsibility to the moral law of God, which eventually brought upon them the label "Galatianists" or "legalists." Now, as we shall see, there can be little doubt that there was and still is legalism in Adventism, as in some other Christian churches; but when we consider these early psychological factors, certain of which still pertain today, their reactions are understandable, though hardly defensible.

Of course, the aforementioned "neglected" truths made few friends for the Adventists with Christians of other denominations, mainly because these truths were frequently presented in such manner as to arouse opposition instead of inviting investigation. Seventh-day Adventism has woefully demonstrated many times the old but true adage, "Not what we say but how we say it makes or breaks a case."

II. Identity Concealed

In his book *Answers to Objections*, F. D. Nichol demonstrates how the psychological defense that Adventists erected in their early days has carried over into modern times. Nichol quotes the charge:

> When Seventh-day Adventist ministers go into a community to hold a series of lectures, they conceal, at first, their denominational connection. They thus hope to draw into their audience people who would never have come if they knew that Seventh-day Adventists were conducting the meetings. This is a form of deception. There is something the matter with a religious body that is afraid to identify itself as soon as it begins to carry on any activity in a community.[24]

---

[24]F. D. Nichol, *Answers to Objections* (Washington, D.C.: Review and Herald Publishing Association, 1952), 420–22.

Nichol answers:

Now, it is a fact that during most of the history of the Seventh-day Adventist church, the very word "Adventist" has conveyed to the minds of most people a picture of a deluded band of fanatics sitting on housetops in ascension robes, awaiting the opening of the heavens. This story of ascension robes has become a part of American folklore and has been embalmed in impressive encyclopedias. And the ascension robe story is only part of the fanciful picture that has come into the minds of many when they have heard the word "Adventist."

The ascension robes story is a myth, and 99 percent of related stories are likewise myths—as has now been proved—but that has not prevented people from believing them. The net result has been that many people have seen Seventh-day Adventists only through the distorting mists of slanderous myths. This is nothing new in religious history; witness, for example, the early history of the Quakers and the Baptists.

It should not be difficult, therefore, for any reasonable person to see why Adventist ministers through the past years have sought first to cause people to see them simply as Christian preachers before announcing their Adventist connection. After all, we seek to be first, and before all else, Christian preachers of righteousness. Then we hope to build on the timely messages from Bible prophecy that may be described in the words of the apostle Peter as "present truth" for these last days of earth's history.

It has undoubtedly been true in years past that Adventists could not have gotten a crowd out to hear them, in certain cities at least, if they had revealed their identity at the outset. But we think that proves, not the weakness of the Adventist case, but the strength of distorted ideas founded on fanciful myths. The other side of the picture is that many people, after they have attended Adventist meetings for a time, frankly admit that they have changed their ideas about us and are glad that they first came to the meetings not knowing who was conducting them.

In more recent years our activities have become so much better known that in many places the former distorted picture has been largely corrected. Accordingly, we are increasingly following the plan of announcing at the outset the Adventist sponsorship of the public meetings. That is what we like to do, and what we hope erelong to be able to do everywhere. We are not ashamed of our Adventism, far from it. . . . No, we don't want to boast, we simply want to proclaim to the world a message that we earnestly believe should be given at this time. And if, in order to secure an initial hearing, we must at first conceal the name, we do so for a brief period only with a view to a clear-cut announcement of our Adventist connections a little later in the meetings. Then those who have been coming may decline to come further, if they desire. They generally decide to stay!

Unhappily, as the literature of many objectors to Adventism reveals, it is *they* who have often been most active in spreading the distorting myths regarding us. And then they are wont to add, as though to prove conclusively their case against us, that we sometimes fail to reveal our Adventist connection at the outset of a series of evangelistic lectures! If they will help us to clear away completely the slanderous myths that folklore has often thrown around the name "Adventist," we will be most happy to preface every one of our public meetings with the announcement of its Adventist sponsorship! In the meantime we shall, in such instances and areas as the situation necessitates, follow the precedent set by our Lord's instruction to His disciples as regards the time of disclosing our name.[25]

Thus we see that some Adventist leaders, at least, maintain the premise that everyone's prejudice against them is based on myths and folklore, and on the fact that they deliberately disguise themselves until they can obtain a hearing and demonstrate that they are Christians. These practices have given rise to the charge of proselytizing, and it is not without foundation. In general, however, Nichol makes some very good points, though inadvertently he reveals only too clearly that he and many Adventists have been reared in this unhealthy climate of distrust, prejudice, and suspicion.

The only difficulty with Nichol's statement about identifying themselves is that the burden of proof lies not upon the other denominations, but upon the Adventists themselves. By openly saying who they are, they can refute these charges of deception and proselytizing.

On page 420 Nichol makes the mistake of using passages in the gospel of Matthew (8:4; 9:30; 16:20), where Christ enjoined secrecy, to prove that Adventists are only following Him when they conceal their identity, and he unfortunately tries to establish that such a behavior pattern on the part of Adventists is "honorable." Says Nichol,

> We have yet to hear any devout Christian expressing misgivings and doubts about the ministry of Christ or declaring that He was ashamed or afraid because He concealed His identity for a time. Evidently, then, this much at least may be established at the outset as being proved by these texts: Concealing one's identity is not an insult or proof that one is either ashamed or afraid. There may be honorable and altogether reasonable grounds for such concealment.[26]

Although Nichol's argument appears plausible, the cases are not parallel, for over and against the incidents that he cites, the Lord Jesus did many miracles in public and taught openly in the temple as He himself declared before Caiaphas (John 18:20). To compare the motives of Adventists with the motives of the Lord Jesus Christ is just a bit more than I am willing to concede.

True, there is much misinformation about Adventist history and theology, but not infrequently it can be traced to unfortunate statements in their own official publications. Although other denominations are likewise guilty, Adventists have largely been outside the mainstream of Christian fellowship and so are in an unenviable position. They must go the "second mile" in this respect.

It is evident, then, that because of the opposition and abuse suffered in their early days, and also because of the "special truths" of the Advent message and emphasis upon certain areas of theology, the Adventists have been at a distinct psychological disadvantage and so have tended to band together against other churches. Other denominations, of course, have encouraged this recluselike behavior by endless repetition of some of the Millerite myths. These factors, therefore, must be soberly evaluated if we are to understand Seventh-day Adventism.

---

[25]Ibid.
[26]Ibid., 420.

Adventist Theology and Classical Orthodoxy

For many years Seventh-day Adventists have been handicapped by the lack of a comprehensive volume that adequately defines their doctrinal position. Many publications clearly set forth certain aspects of Adventism, particularly the writings of F. D. Nichol, LeRoy Froom, and Ellen G. White, whose role is that of inspired commentator and "messenger" to the Adventist denomination.

Except for the brief statement of fundamentals in the Seventh-day Adventist Yearbook, the average Adventist has been somewhat at a loss to explain conflicting theological opinions within his denomination, and even expressions in the writings of Ellen G. White were in certain contexts so ambiguous as to frustrate even the most devout believer. As a result of this, in 1957, the General Conference of Seventh-day Adventists released the first definitive and comprehensive explanation of their faith, an authoritative volume entitled *Questions on Doctrine*.

This book truthfully presents the theology and doctrine that the leaders of Seventh-day Adventism affirm they have always held. Members of other denominations will find it a reliable source to consult when seeking to understand what the Adventists themselves describe as "the position of our denomination in the area of church doctrine and prophetic interpretation."[27]

There can be no doubt of the fact that there are conflicting statements in Adventist publications and diverse opinions about certain areas of Adventist theology and interpretation, some of which is quite the opposite of classical orthodox Christianity; but this situation is not peculiar to the Adventist, since all Christian denominations have various "wings," in most instances quite vocal, which are a source of constant embarrassment, because they represent their own particular interpretations of the denomination's theology as the viewpoint of the denomination itself.

It is, therefore, unfair to quote any one Adventist writer or a group of writers as representing "the position of our denomination in the area of church doctrine and prophetic interpretation," even though the writings of such persons may in a large area qualify as Adventist theology. One must consult in good faith what the denomination itself represents as its theology and assume that the Seventh-day Adventist theologians know better than non-Adventists the implications and conclusions that they are willing to admit as representative of their church's theology.

This section is divided into several parts, each of which contains statements of the official Adventist position of particular aspects of theology, and is thoroughly documented from the primary source material provided in *Questions on Doctrine*. It is hoped that the reader will weigh carefully the declarations of the Seventh-day Adventist Church as represented by its General Conference, which alone is empowered to speak for the denomination. They have asserted initially, and reaffirmed currently, the authoritative force of *Questions on Doctrine* as accurately representative of Adventist doctrine. Until such time as there is clear, unequivocal, and equally authoritative evidence to the contrary, we must let the doctrine revealed in this book stand as Adventist doctrine. These doctrinal points we shall present and biblically evaluate below.

---

[27] *Questions on Doctrine*, 8.

It is unnecessary to document at great length the fact that Seventh-day Adventism adheres tenaciously to the foundational doctrines of Christian theology as these have been held by the Christian church throughout the centuries. Dr. Anthony Hoekema, who believes that Seventh-day Adventism is a non-Christian cult, makes this interesting admission, and since Dr. Hoekema is no friend of Adventism, his testimony on this point could hardly be called prejudiced:

> I am of the conviction that Seventh-day Adventism is a cult and not an evangelical denomination. . . . It is recognized with gratitude that there are certain soundly scriptural emphases in the teaching of Seventh-day Adventism. We are thankful for the Adventists' affirmation of the infallibility of the Bible, of the Trinity, and of the full deity of Jesus Christ. We gratefully acknowledge their teachings on creation and providence, on the incarnation and resurrection of Christ, on the absolute necessity for regeneration, on sanctification by the Holy Spirit, and on Christ's literal return.[28]

It is puzzling to me, as a student of non-Christian cult systems, how any group can hold the above doctrines in their proper biblical context, which Dr. Hoekema admits the Adventists do, and still be a non-Christian cult. However, we shall deal with this aspect of the critics of Adventism at the end of the chapter; therefore, suffice it to say that the Adventists do have a clean bill of health where the major doctrines of Christian theology are involved.

Lest there be any doubt on the subject, the following quotations taken from *Questions on Doctrine* are still upheld by the Seventh-day Adventist hierarchy as authoritative, and forthrightly declare the Seventh-day Adventist position in relation to historical Christianity as well as those areas where Adventism differs from the orthodox Christian position.

I. Inspiration and Authority of the Scriptures

1. Seventh-day Adventists believe that "all Scripture," both Old and New Testaments, from Genesis to Revelation, was "given by inspiration of God" (2 Timothy 3:16), and constitutes the very Word of God—the truth that "liveth and abideth for ever" (1 Peter 1:23). We recognize the Bible as the ultimate and final authority on what is truth (26).

2. Seventh-day Adventists hold the Protestant position that the Bible and the Bible only is the sole rule of faith and practice for Christians. We believe that all theological beliefs must be measured by the living Word, judged by its truth, and whatsoever is unable to pass this test, or is found to be out of harmony with its message, is to be rejected (28).

3. We believe in the authority, veracity, reliability, and truth of the Holy Scriptures. The same union of the divine and the human that is manifested in Christ, exists in the Bible. Its truths, revealed, are "given by inspiration of God" (2 Timothy 3:16), yet are couched in the words of men (27–28).

II. The Nature of Christ

1. Jesus Christ is very God, and He has existed with the Father from all eternity (22).

---

[28]Anthony Hoekema, *The Four Major Cults* (Grand Rapids, Mich.: William B. Eerdmans Publishing Company, 1963), 389, 403.

2. Christ, the Word of God, became incarnate through the miraculous conception and the Virgin Birth; and He lived an absolutely sinless life here on earth (22).

3. Christ is called the Second Adam. In purity and holiness, connected with God and beloved by God. *He began where the first Adam began. Willingly He passed over the ground where Adam fell, and redeemed Adam's failure* (650).

4. In taking upon himself man's nature in its fallen condition, *Christ did not in the least participate in its sin. He was subject to the infirmities and weaknesses* by which man is encompassed. . . . He was touched with the feeling of our infirmities, and was in all points tempted like as we are. And yet He *"knew no sin."* He was the Lamb *"without blemish and without spot."* . . . *We should have no misgivings* in regard to the *perfect sinlessness of the human nature of Christ* (651).

5. *In His human nature He maintained the purity of His divine character. . . .* He was *unsullied by corruption, a stranger to sin. . . .* He was a mighty petitioner, *not possessing the passions of our human, fallen natures,* but compassed with like infirmities, tempted in all points like as we are (658–659).

6. *He was perfect, and undefiled by sin. He was without spot or blemish. . . . Jesus, coming to dwell in humanity, received no pollution* (660).

III. The Atonement

1. Those who teach that a completed atonement was made on the cross view the term in its popular theological sense, but really what is meant by them is that on Calvary, the all-sufficient atoning sacrifice of Christ was offered for our salvation. With this concept all true Christians readily and heartily agree. "We are sanctified through the offering of the body of Jesus Christ, once for all" (Hebrews 10:10). Those who view this aspect of the work of Christ as a completed atonement, apply this term only to what Christ accomplished on the cross. They do not include in their definition the application of the benefits of the atonement made on the cross, to the individual sinner (342).

2. Seventh-day Adventists do not believe that Christ made but partial or incomplete sacrificial atonement on the cross (349).

3. Most decidedly the all-sufficient atoning sacrifice of Jesus our Lord was offered and completed on the cross of Calvary. This was done for all mankind, for "he is the propitiation . . . for the sins of the whole world" (1 John 2:2). . . . This sacrificial work will actually benefit human hearts only as we surrender our lives to God and experience the miracle of the new birth. In this experience, Jesus, our high priest *applies to us the benefits* of His atoning sacrifice. Our sins are forgiven, we become the children of God by faith in Christ Jesus, and the peace of God dwells in our hearts (350).

4. When, therefore, one hears an Adventist say, or reads in Adventist literature—even in the writings of Ellen G. White—that Christ is making atonement now, it should be understood that we mean simply that Christ is now *making application of the benefits of the sacrificial atonement He made on the cross;* that He is making it efficacious for us individually, according to our needs and requests. Mrs. White herself, as far back as 1857, clearly explained what she meant when she wrote of Christ's making atonement for us in His ministry:

The great Sacrifice had been offered and had been accepted, and the Holy Spirit which descended on the day of Pentecost carried the minds of the disciples from the earthly sanctuary to the heavenly, where Jesus had entered by His own blood, to shed upon His disciples the benefits of His atonement (354–355).

5. When the Father beheld the sacrifice of His Son, He bowed before it in recognition of its perfection. "It is enough," He said, "the *Atonement is complete*" (663).

IV. The Resurrection

1. Jesus Christ arose literally and bodily from the grave. "He ascended literally and bodily into heaven." He now serves as our advocate in priestly ministry and mediation before the Father (22).

2. There shall be a resurrection both of the just and the unjust. The resurrection of the just will take place at the second coming of Christ; the resurrection of the unjust will take place a thousand years later, at the close of the millennium (John 5:28–29; 1 Thessalonians 4:13–18; Revelation 20:5–10) (14).

V. The Second Coming

1. [Jesus Christ] will return in a premillennial, personal, imminent second advent (22).

2. As our denominational name indicates, the second coming of Christ is one of the cardinal doctrines of the Adventist faith. We give it such prominence in our beliefs because it occupies a pivotal place in Holy Scripture, not only in the New Testament, but also in the Old (449).

3. JESUS WILL ASSUREDLY COME THE SECOND TIME ... [His] SECOND ADVENT WILL BE VISIBLE, AUDIBLE, AND PERSONAL ... Seventh-day Adventists believe on the evidence of Scripture that there will be one visible, personal, glorious second coming of Christ (451–452, 459).

VI. The Plan of Salvation

1. The vicarious, atoning death of Jesus Christ, once for all, is all-sufficient for the redemption of a lost race.... Man was created sinless, but by his subsequent fall entered a state of alienation and depravity.... Salvation through Christ is by grace alone, and through faith in His blood.... Entrance upon the new life in Christ is by regeneration, or the new birth.... Man is justified by faith ... sanctified by the indwelling Christ through the Holy Spirit (22–23).

2. Every person in order to obtain salvation must experience the new birth. That this comprises an entire transformation of life and character by the recreative power of God through faith in the Lord Jesus Christ (John 3:16; Matthew 18:3; Acts 2:37–39) (12).

3. The law of the Ten Commandments points out sin, the penalty of which is death. The law cannot save the transgressor from his sin, nor impart power to keep him from sinning. In infinite love and mercy, God provides a way whereby this may be done. He furnishes a substitute, even Christ the Righteous One, to die in man's stead, making "him to be sin for us, who knew no sin; that we might be made the righteousness of God in him" (2 Corinthians 5:21). That one is justified, not by obedience to the law, but by the grace that is in Christ Jesus. By accepting Christ, man is reconciled to God, justified by His blood for the sins of the past, and saved from the power of sin by His indwelling life (12–13).

4. One who truly understands and accepts the teachings of the Seventh-day Adventist Church can assuredly know that he is born again, and that he is fully accepted by the Lord. He has in his soul the assurance of present salvation, and need be in no uncertainty whatsoever. In fact, he may know

this so fully that he can truly "rejoice in the Lord" (Philippians 4:4), and in "the God of his salvation" (Psalm 24:5) (105).

5. NOTHING WE CAN EVER DO WILL MERIT THE FAVOR OF GOD—SALVATION is of grace. It is grace that "bringeth salvation" (Titus 2:11). It is "through the grace of the Lord Jesus Christ we shall be saved" (Acts 15:11). We are not saved by "works" (Romans 4:6; Ephesians 2:9; 2 Timothy 1:9), even though they be good works. . . . Neither can we be saved by "law" (Romans 8:3), nor by the "deeds" or the "works" of the law (Romans 3:28; Galatians 3:2, 5, 10). . . . The law of God was never designed to save men. It is a looking glass, in which, when we gaze, we see our sinfulness. That is as far as the law of God can go with a sinful man. It can reveal his sin, but is powerless to remove it or to save him from its guilt and penalty and power (108–109).

VII. The Spiritual Nature of Man

1. Some have maintained that man was created mortal, so far as his body was concerned, but that he possessed an immortal entity called either a "soul" or a "spirit." Others have felt equally certain that man was not in any sense created immortal. They have been convinced that man was not in possession of an ethereal soul, or spirit, which survived death as a conscious entity, apart from the body. . . . We as Adventists believe that, in general, the Scriptures teach that the soul of man represents the whole man, and not a particular part independent of the other component parts of man's nature; and further, that the soul cannot exist apart from the body, for a man is a unit (511, 515).

2. We, as Adventists, have reached the definite conclusion that man rests in the tomb until the resurrection morning. Then, at the first resurrection (Revelation 20:4–5), the resurrection of the just (Acts 24:15), the righteous come forth immortalized, at the call of Christ the Life-giver. And they then enter into life everlasting, in their eternal home in the kingdom of glory. Such is our understanding (520).

VIII. Punishment of the Wicked

1. In the expression "eternal punishment," just as in "eternal redemption" and "eternal judgment," the Bible is referring to all eternity—not as of *process*, but as of result. It is not an endless process of punishment, "but an effectual punishment, which will be final and forever" (540).

2. We reject the doctrine of eternal torment for the following major reasons: (1) Because everlasting life is a gift of God (Romans 6:23). The wicked do not possess this—they "shall not see life" (John 3:36); "no murderer hath eternal life abiding in him" (1 John 3:15). (2) Because eternal torment would perpetuate and immortalize sin, suffering, and woe, and contradict, we believe, divine revelation, which envisions the time when these things shall be no more (Revelation 21:4). (3) Because it seems to us to provide a plague spot in the universe of God throughout eternity, and would seem to indicate that it is impossible for God himself ever to abolish it. (4) Because in our thinking, it would detract from the attribute of love as seen in the character of God, and postulates the concept of a wrath which is never appeased. (5) Because the Scriptures teach that the atoning work of Christ is to "put away sin" (Hebrews 9:26)—first from the individual, and ultimately from the universe. The full fruition of Christ's sacrificial, atoning work will be seen not only in a redeemed people but in a restored heaven and earth (Ephesians 1:13–14) (543).

IX. The Sanctuary and the Investigative Judgment

1. *Does your teaching of the sanctuary service mean that the work of Christ on Calvary was not an all-sufficient, complete, once-for-all sacrifice—a sacrifice that obtains for us eternal redemption? Or was something subsequently necessary to make the sacrificial work of Christ effective for the salvation of man?*

To the first part of the question our answer is an unequivocal *No.* The death of Christ on Calvary's cross provides the only sacrifice by which man can be saved. . . . This "one sacrifice" (Hebrews 10:12) or "one offering" of Christ was "forever" (verse 14), and wrought "eternal redemption" (Hebrews 9:12) for man. The sacrifice was completely efficacious. It provided complete atonement for all mankind, and will never be repeated, for it was all-sufficient and covered the needs of every soul (356–357).

2. The expression "once" or "once for all," in connection with the sacrifice of Christ, is deeply significant. . . . "He died to sin, *once for all*" (Romans 6:10); "offering of the body of Jesus Christ *once for all*" (Hebrews 10:10). He did this not by "the blood of goats and calves" but by "his own blood" he entered *once for all* into the holy place (or "holies"), "thus securing an eternal redemption" for us (Hebrews 9:12, RSV).

The Greek word here translated "holy place" is *hagia*, and is in the plural form. A correct translation would be "the holies," or "holy places," as in Hebrews 9:24. This entrance, Scripture teaches, occurred at His ascension to glory (Acts 1), having already finished His sacrificial work on the cross. The word translated "obtained," in the Greek is from *heurisko*, and is rendered "found," "procured," "gained," or in the RSV, "secured" (380–381).

3. Jesus our surety entered the "holy places," and appeared in the presence of God for us. But it was not with the hope of obtaining something for us at that time, or at some future time. No! *He had already obtained it for us on the cross.* And now as our high priest He ministers the virtue of His atoning sacrifice to us (381).

4. The time of the cleansing of the sanctuary, synchronizing with the period of the proclamation of the message of Revelation 14, is a time of investigative judgment; first, with reference to the dead, and second, with reference to the living. This investigative judgment determines who of the myriad sleeping in the dust of the earth are worthy of a part in the first resurrection, and who of its living multitudes are worthy of translation (1 Peter 4:17–18; Daniel 7:9–10; Revelation 14:6–7; Luke 20:35) (15).

5. The great judgment scene of heaven will clearly reveal those who have been growing in grace and developing Christlike characters. Some who have professed to be God's people, but who have disregarded His counsel, will in amazement say to the Lord, "Have we not prophesied in thy name? and in thy name have cast out devils? and in thy name done many wonderful works?" His reply to such will be brief but emphatic: "I never knew you: depart from me, ye that work iniquity" (Matthew 7:22–23) (417).

6. In view of the principles here set forth, it seems to us abundantly clear that the acceptance of Christ at conversion does not seal a person's destiny. His life record after conversion is also important. A man may go back on his repentance, or by careless inattention let slip the very life he has espoused. Nor can it be said that a man's record is closed when he comes to the end of his days. He is responsible for his influence during life, and is just as surely responsible for his evil influence after he is dead (420).

7. It is our understanding that Christ, as High Priest, concludes His intercessory ministry in heaven in a work of judgment. He begins His great work of judgment in the investigative phase. At the conclusion of the investigation, the sentence of judgment is pronounced. Then as judge, Christ descends to *execute* or carry into effect that sentence. . . . When God's final sentence of judgment is consummated, the redeemed will be singing the song of Moses and the Lamb (422).

8. The blotting of names out of the book of life is, we believe, a work of the investigative judgment. A complete and thorough check of all the candidates for eternal life will need to be completed before Christ comes in the clouds of heaven, for when He appears, the decisions for life and death are already made. The dead in Christ are called to life, and the living followers of Christ are translated (1 Thessalonians 4:15–17)—the entire citizenry of the everlasting kingdom. There's no time subsequent to the second advent for such decisions (438–439).

X. The Scapegoat Teaching

1. Two goats were obviously required, and used, on the Day of Atonement, because there is a twofold responsibility for sin—first, my responsibility as the perpetrator, agent, or medium; and second, Satan's responsibility as the instigator, or tempter, in whose heart sin was first conceived.

Now, concerning my sin, Christ died for my sins (Romans 5:8). . . . He assumed my responsibilities, and His blood alone cleanses me from all sin. (I John 1:7) The atonement for my sin is made solely by the shed blood of Christ.

And concerning Satan's sin and his responsibility as instigator and tempter, no salvation is provided for him. He must be punished for his responsibility. There is no savior, or substitute, to bear his punishment. He must himself "atone" for his sin in causing men to transgress, in the same way that a master criminal suffers on the gallows or in the electric chair for his responsibility in the crimes that he has caused others to commit. It is in this sense only that we can understand the words of Leviticus 16:10 concerning the scapegoat, "To make an atonement with him."

Under criminal law, the instigator, or mastermind, may be punished more severely than his agents. . . . Satan is the responsible mastermind in the great crime of sin, and his responsibility will return upon his own head. The crushing weight of his responsibility in the sins of the whole world—of the wicked as well as the righteous—must be rolled back upon him. Simple justice demands that while Christ suffers for my guilt, Satan must also be punished as the instigator of sin (397–399).

2. Satan makes no atonement for our sins. But Satan will ultimately have to bear the retributive punishment for his responsibility in the sins of all men, both righteous and wicked . . . Seventh-day Adventists, therefore, repudiate *en toto* any idea, suggestions, or implication that Satan is in any sense or degree our sin bearer. The thought is abhorrent to us, and appallingly sacrilegious. Such a concept is a dreadful disparagement of the efficacy of Christ and His salvation, and vitiates the whole glorious provision of salvation solely through our Savior.

Satan's death, a thousand times over could never make him a savior in any sense whatsoever. He is the archsinner of the universe, the author and instigator of sin. . . . Only Christ, the Creator, the one and only God-man, could make a substitutionary atonement for men's transgressions. And this

Christ did completely, perfectly, and once for all, on Golgotha (400).

XI. The Sabbath and the Mark of the Beast
1. We believe that the Sabbath was instituted in Eden before sin entered, that it was honored of God, set apart by divine appointment, and given to mankind as a perpetual memorial of a finished creation. It was based upon the fact that God himself had rested from His work of creation, had blessed His Sabbath, or rest day, and had sanctified it, or set it apart for man (Genesis 2:1–3; Mark 2:27) (149).

2. We believe that the restoration of the Sabbath is indicated in the Bible prophecy of Revelation 14:9–12. Sincerely believing this, we regard the observance of the Sabbath as a test of our loyalty to Christ as Creator and Redeemer.

Seventh-day Adventists do not rely upon their Sabbath-keeping as a *means* of salvation or of winning merit before God. We are saved by grace alone. Hence our Sabbath observance, as also our loyalty to every other command of God, is an expression of our love for our Creator and Redeemer.

We are saved through the righteousness of Jesus Christ received as a gift of grace, and grace alone. Our Lord's sacrifice on Calvary is mankind's only hope. But having been saved, we rejoice that the righteous requirements of the law are fulfilled in the experience of the Christian "who walks not after the flesh but after the spirit," and who by the grace of God lives in harmony with the revealed will of God (153, 190).

3. *Do Seventh-day Adventists teach in their authorized literature that those who worship on Sunday and repudiate in its entirety the Seventh-day Adventist teaching as a consequence have the mark of apostasy, or "the mark of the beast"? Does not Mrs. White teach that those who now keep Sunday already have the mark of the beast?*

Our doctrinal positions are based upon the Bible, and not upon Mrs. White's writings. But since her name has been introduced into the question, an explicit statement from her pen should set the record straight. The following was penned by her in 1899: "No one has yet received the mark of the beast. Testing time has not yet come. There are true Christians in every church, not excepting the Roman Catholic communion. *None are condemned until they have had the light and seen the obligation of the fourth commandment.* But when the decree shall go forth enforcing the counterfeit Sabbath, and the loud cry of the third angel shall warn men against the worship of the beast and his image, the line will be clearly drawn between the false and the true. Then those who still continue in transgression will receive the mark of the beast" (183).

4. To your inquiry, then, as to whether Mrs. White maintained that all those who do not see and observe the seventh day as the Sabbath now have the "mark of apostasy," the answer is definitely No (184).

5. We hold the firm conviction that millions of devout Christians of all faiths throughout all past centuries, as well as those today who are sincerely trusting in Christ their Savior for salvation and are following Him according to their best light, are unquestionably saved (184).

XII. The Question of Unclean Foods
1. It is true we refrain from eating certain articles . . . but *not because* the law of Moses had any binding claims upon us. Far from it, we stand fast in the liberty with which God has set us free (623).

2. Our health teaching is not a matter of religious taboos; in fact, it is much more than careful selection in diet. It is, to us, the following of a well-balanced health program. We feel it to be our Christian duty to preserve our bodies in the best of health for the service and glory of God. We believe that our bodies are the temples of the Holy Spirit (1 Corinthians 3:16; 2 Corinthians 6:16), and that whether therefore we eat, or drink, or whatsoever we do we should "do all to the glory of God" (1 Corinthians 10:31) (624).

XIII. The "Remnant Church"

1. *It is alleged that Seventh-day Adventists teach that they alone constitute the finally completed "remnant church" mentioned in the book of Revelation. . . . Do Adventists maintain that they alone are the only true witnesses of the living God in our age?*
The answer to this threefold question will depend quite largely on the definition given to the word "remnant." If, as is implied in the second part, "remnant" is taken to mean the church invisible, our answer to the first part is an unqualified No. Seventh-day Adventists have never sought to equate their church with the church invisible—"Those in every denomination who remain faithful to the Scriptures" (186).

2. It is in a spirit of deep humility that we apply this Scripture to the Advent Movement and its work, for we recognize the tremendous implications of such an interpretation. While we believe that Revelation 12:17 points to us as a people of prophecy, it is in no spirit of pride that we thus apply the Scripture. To us it is the logical conclusion of our system of prophetic interpretation (191).

3. But the fact that we thus apply this Scripture does not imply in any way that we believe we are the only true Christians in the world, or that we are the only ones who will be saved (191–192).

4. Seventh-day Adventists firmly believe that God has a precious remnant, a multitude of earnest, sincere believers, in every church (192).

5. We believe the majority of God's children are still scattered in this way throughout the world. And of course, the majority of these in Christian churches still conscientiously observe Sunday. We ourselves cannot do so, for we believe that God is calling for a reformation in this matter. But we respect and love those of our fellow Christians who do not interpret God's Word just as we do (192–193).

6. We fully recognize the heartening fact that the host of the true followers of Christ are scattered all through the various churches of Christendom, including the Roman Catholic communion. These God clearly recognizes as His own. Such do not form a part of the "Babylon" portrayed in the Apocalypse (197).

Author's Notes

1. The Concept of Christ's Sinful Human Nature

Since almost all critics of Seventh-day Adventism contend that Seventh-day Adventists believe Christ possessed a sinful human nature during the Incarnation, a word should be said to clarify this point. These charges are often based on an article in *Signs of the Times,* March 1927, and a statement in *Bible Readings for the Home Circle,* edition of 1944. Regarding the first reference, a critical article states:

My . . . quotation is from L. A. Wilcox, for many years an editor of *The Signs of the Times,* which according to the latest figures given by the Adventists has been published by them for eighty-two years. Certainly a statement by an editor of that publication may be considered official. I'm sure that anything that Mr. Wilcox wrote did not just happen to get in. In March 1927 he wrote, "In His [Christ's] veins was the incubus of a tainted heredity like a caged lion ever seeking to break forth and destroy. Temptation attacked Him where by heredity He was weakest, attacked Him in unexpected times and ways. In spite of bad blood and an inherited meanness, He 'conquered.' "

And again, in the December 1928 issue of *Signs of the Times,* this editor Mr. Wilcox stated: "Jesus took humanity with all its liabilities, with all its dreadful risks of yielding to temptation."[29]

First, L. A. Wilcox was never on the editorial staff of *Signs of the Times.* Moreover, Mr. L. A. Wilcox, who wrote the article, in a letter dated April 26, 1957, stated:

> The writer of the *Signs* article was a very young man in 1927, and not by any means always felicitous in his phraseology. I know, for I was the writer. The first sentence quoted is crude and shocking and theologically inaccurate, and I was properly spanked for it by Adventist officials, which proves that this article cannot be truly represented as "official" or "authoritative."
>
> It is no more than fair to point out that no man has taught more earnestly or fervently than I, as an Adventist minister, the deity of the Lord Jesus Christ, the sinlessness of Christ, salvation by grace, righteousness by faith, the finished work of Calvary, a Christ-centered religion, than I—with the "Amen" of Seventh-day Adventist leadership.

Virtually every critic of Seventh-day Adventism, including the author quoted above, also uses a statement quoted from *Bible Readings for the Home Circle* (1944 edition, 174)—even though in 1945 the statement was expunged by Adventists because it was not in line with official Adventist theology.

A further quotation often seized upon is taken from the book *Desire of the Ages* by Ellen G. White. On page 117 she says, "Our Savior took humanity, with all its liabilities. He took the nature of man, with the possibility of yielding to temptation." White also speaks of "fallen nature." Understandably, not having read all she has written on the subject, these critics conclude that she means that Christ possessed a sinful, carnal, or degenerate human nature. However, White's writings clearly indicate that when she speaks of the fallen nature of Christ, she means the physical properties of the race, which degenerated since the time of Adam, who was created perfect without the ravages of sin upon either his physical or spiritual being. Adam did not age before the Fall, but Christ was born into the world a true man and with the curse of sin operative upon the physical properties of the human race. For over thirty years He endured the aging process. He could not have reached this point in life without organic changes taking place in His body, and were He not subject to the physical decline of the race, he would not have been a true man, "made under the law" (Galatians 4:4). White's position

---

[29] *The King's Business,* April 1957.

has been held by many eminent scholars who have never been accused of being either heretics or non-Christians. Why, then, should she and the Adventists be condemned for holding this view? For centuries Christians have argued about the human nature of Christ. Some have believed that He could have sinned, but did not. Others, including this writer, that He could not have sinned. However, it is a theological issue not likely to be resolved by trite phrases and dogmatic pronouncements.

It is true that various Adventist publications, in the past and present, sometimes have contradicted one another. However, at its release and up through this year (see, for example, the quote presented earlier from the April 29, 1983, Adventist letter to me), *Questions on Doctrine* presents the official position of the Adventist denomination regarding Christ's sinless nature. It is to that position that I can say "Amen."

Dr. Anthony Hoekema, in his volume *The Four Major Cults,* falls into the same error as E. B. Jones, Louis Talbot, and other critics of Seventh-day Adventism and ignores totally the fact that Wilcox publicly and in print (1957) repudiated his position. This fact they all know but seem determined to ignore, since Wilcox's statement suits so well their assumption that despite official Adventist statements on doctrine, they, the critics, know more than the Adventists do about their own faith!

2. The Concept of Incomplete Atonement

It is also often charged that inherent in Adventist theology is the unbiblical teaching that "the atonement was not finished on the cross of Calvary." Certain Seventh-day Adventist sources are cited to bolster these charges. For instance, Uriah Smith, a prominent Adventist of the past, stated in his book *Looking Unto Jesus,* "Christ did not make the atonement when He shed His blood upon the cross." Other earlier writers, such as J. H. Waggoner, have expressed the same thought. He said, "There is a clear distinction between the death of Christ and the atonement."[30] Even some later writers, such as C. H. Watson, have been influenced by these early exponents of Adventism.

However, a little investigation of these writings would show that Smith and Waggoner wrote it eighty years ago. As demonstrated elsewhere in this book, this concept has been repudiated by the Seventh-day Adventist denomination. The current position of the Seventh-day Adventist denomination—not the opinions of a few scattered writers over a hundred-year period—should be considered in judging this charge of an "incomplete atonement."

Current Adventist writings teach that the atonement was completed on the cross, and no less an Adventist than Ellen G. White, writing in the *Review and Herald,* September 21, 1901, stated, "Christ planted the cross between heaven and earth and when the Father beheld the sacrifice of His Son, He bowed before it in recognition of His perfection. 'It is enough,' He said. 'The atonement is completed.' " In the same periodical, under the date of August 16, 1899, White stated, "No language could convey the rejoicing of heaven or God's expression of satisfaction and delight in His only begotten Son when He saw the completion of the atonement."

---

[30] *The Atonement in the Light of Nature and Revelation,* n.p., n.d., 181.

Many more quotations could be cited, but critics usually overlook the greater number of statements relative to the completeness of the atonement that are readily available in past and present Seventh-day Adventist literature.

Nothing could be clearer than the Adventist declaration:

> When ... one hears an Adventist say or reads in Adventist literature—even in the writings of Ellen G. White—that Christ is making atonement now, it should be understood that we mean simply that Christ is now making application of the benefits of the sacrificial atonement He made on the cross; that He is making it efficacious for us individually, according to our needs and requests. Mrs. White herself, as far back as 1857, clearly explained what she means when she writes of Christ's making atonement for us in His ministry:
>
> The great Sacrifice had been offered and had been accepted, and the Holy Spirit which descended on the day of Pentecost carried the minds of the disciples from the earthly sanctuary to the heavenly, where Jesus entered by His own blood, to shed upon His disciples the *benefits* of His atonement. (*Questions on Doctrine*, 354–55)

Is Seventh-day Adventism a Non-Christian Cult?

We earlier mentioned Dr. Anthony Hoekema's book *The Four Major Cults*, in which he classifies Seventh-day Adventism as a non-Christian cult system. It is necessary for me to take exception with Dr. Hoekema in this area because, in my opinion, the reasons that Dr. Hoekema gives cannot be justified by the Word of God, historical theology, or present-day practices in denominational Christianity as a whole. To illustrate this point, Dr. Hoekema stated, "I am of the conviction that Seventh-day Adventism is a cult and not an evangelical denomination. In support of this evaluation I propose to show that the traits that we have found to be distinctive of the cults do apply to this movement" (389).

Dr. Hoekema then proceeds to list his reasons:

1. An Extra-Scriptural Source of Authority (Ellen G. White).
2. The Denial of Justification by Grace Alone.
   a. The Investigative Judgment.
   b. The Keeping of the Sabbath.
3. The Devaluation of Christ.
4. The Group as the Exclusive Community of the Saved.

It is Dr. Hoekema's contention that Ellen White is an extrabiblical authority in that her counsels are taken to be manifestations of the gift of prophecy (1 Corinthians 12). But granting that the Adventists are entitled to believe that this gift was manifested in White as evidence of the *charismata* (a fact Dr. Hoekema could hardly honestly challenge, since the gifts of the Spirit have been and are still manifested in the Christian church), why does he not take into consideration the repeated emphasis of Adventist writers concerning their official pronouncement—*Questions on Doctrine*—to the effect that they do not consider White to be an extrabiblical authority, but that her writings are only authoritative in those areas where they are in agreement with the Word of God, which is the final standard for judging all the gifts of the Spirit?

If the Adventists put White's writings on a par with Holy Scripture; if they interpreted the Bible in the light of her writings, and not the reverse; if they willingly admitted this and owned it as their position, his criticism would be justified, but they do not do so. Dr. Hoekema has apparently ignored what the Adventists say they believe concerning White in favor of what he thinks they mean as a result of his deduction from certain of their publications. It is far safer to accept at face value the published statements of a denomination representing its theology, particularly if, as in the case of *Questions on Doctrine,* they are answering direct questions bearing on the subject, than it is to rely upon one's own preconceived interpretations, as Dr. Hoekema has apparently done in this instance.

It is a serious charge to maintain that any professing Christian group denies justification by grace alone as the basis of eternal salvation; and, if the Adventists were guilty of this, surely there would be ground for considering them as a cultic system. However, literally scores of times in their book *Questions on Doctrine,* and in various other publications, the Adventists affirm that salvation comes only by the grace of God through faith in Jesus Christ's sacrifice upon the cross.

Why it is necessary again for Dr. Hoekema to question the sincerity of the Adventists in this area and yet accept at face value their other statements concerning their faith in the Scriptures, the Trinity, the full deity of Jesus Christ, Creation, Providence, Incarnation, the resurrection of Jesus Christ, the absolute necessity for regeneration, sanctification by the Holy Spirit, and Christ's literal return, is a puzzling inconsistency in his presentation. (See *The Four Major Cults,* 403.)

Dr. Hoekema insists that the investigative judgment and the keeping of the seventh-day Sabbath are part of the reasons why he classifies Seventh-day Adventists as cultists, but, in doing this, he makes his Calvinistic interpretation of theology the criterion, while ignoring the claims of the Arminian school and of semi-Arminian and semi-Calvinistic theologians, many of whom take strong exception to Dr. Hoekema's pronounced Calvinism. On the basis that Dr. Hoekema would call the Adventists a cult, the same charge could be leveled against all devoted Calvinists who consider the *Institutes of the Christian Religion* and Calvin's *Commentaries* every bit as much illumination and guides in the study of the Scriptures as the Adventists do where White's writings are concerned. In addition to this, the Seventh-day Baptists are Arminian in their theology and keep the seventh-day Sabbath. Are they too a non-Christian cult? They certainly meet some of Dr. Hoekema's qualifications.

Underscoring his Calvinistic oppositions, Dr. Hoekema writes:

> Adventists further teach that it is possible for a person through subsequent sinful deeds and attitudes to lose the justification he once received. This teaching implies that one can only be sure of retaining his justification if he continues to do the right kind of deeds and to maintain the right attitudes throughout the rest of his life (390).

This point on the investigative judgment is clear evidence of Arminianism in which Dr. Hoekema finds sufficient ground to justify the cult label being applied to Adventists. But why only to Adventists? Why not to Pentecostals, Methodists, Anglicans, Episcopalians, Lutherans, and others who accept the same Arminian premises, though they have not carried them out to the literalism that the Adventists have in the investigative judgment?

Relative to Sabbatarianism, the fourteenth chapter of Romans justifies the keeping of the seventh-day Sabbath or any other day by any Christian who believes he is keeping it unto the Lord. It can become legalistic as Sunday can become legalistic, but merely because the seventh day is honored instead of the first day is no ground for the description of "cult."

Dr. Hoekema, on page 394 of his volume, affirms:

> Seventh-day Adventists do not . . . deny the full deity of Jesus Christ or the doctrine of the Trinity. . . . Seventh-day Adventists today affirm Christ's complete equality with the Father, and the preexistence of the Son from eternity. . . . Adventists also accept the doctrine of the Trinity, and that of the personality and full deity of the Holy Spirit.
>
> As far as the work of Christ is concerned, Seventh-day Adventists teach the vicarious, substitutionary atonement of Christ. . . . Yet there remains some ambiguity in their teachings on the question of whether the atonement has been finished on the cross, since Mrs. White says on more than one occasion that Christ is making atonement for us today and frequently refers to a "final atonement" after the one completed on the cross.

Dr. Hoekema follows this up by listing five reasons for his feeling that the Adventists "devalue" Christ. Three of these points involve Arminianism, concerning which Dr. Hoekema has an admitted prejudice; the fourth concerns the Sabbath, which is a matter of Christian liberty, unless one presupposes Calvin's interpretation; and the fifth reiterates the old accusation that the Seventh-day Adventists believe that "the sins of all men will be laid on Satan just before Christ returns, and that only in this way will sin finally be 'eradicated' or 'blotted out' of the universe" (395–96).

Once again Dr. Hoekema defeats his own case by admitting that the Adventists are soundly orthodox in their Christology, hardly a devaluation of Christ!

The implications and deductions that he draws from their Arminianism cannot be considered as evidence against the Adventists, since not only they but the entire Arminian school of theological interpretation could argue vigorously for the principles that the Adventists lay down.

Finally, the Adventists themselves have repeatedly affirmed that Christ alone vicariously bears the sins of the world and that Satan only bears "his responsibility" for tempting the world to sin.

A careful reading of the book *Questions on Doctrine,* which Dr. Hoekema lists in his bibliography in *The Four Major Cults,* would have answered his question regarding White's usage of the terms "making atonement now" and "final atonement."

The Adventists declare forthrightly that whenever terms of this nature are used, they understand them to refer to the benefits of the atonement of Christ being shed abroad through the ministry of the Holy Spirit, and disown completely any implication or suggestion that the atonement of Christ was not completed on the cross.

Dr. Hoekema, in company with other critics of Adventism, has not hesitated to draw upon repudiated sources to underscore the claim that the Adventists devalue Christ. On page 114 of *The Four Major Cults,* Dr. Hoekema states,

One of the best known is the statement by L. A. Wilcox, to the effect that Christ conquered sin "in spite of bad blood and an inherited meanness." Though the discussion of this matter in *Questions on Doctrine* implies that the denomination would now repudiate this statement, nowhere in the book are we definitely told that this has been done.

In my book *The Truth About Seventh-day Adventism,* conclusive proof was introduced of the total repudiation of that statement by Wilcox himself. Dr. Hoekema lists the book in his bibliography, but unfortunately omits reference to Wilcox's repudiation in order to utilize Wilcox's statement. This is not a fair representation of what the Adventist denomination has taught or teaches in this area.

These are a few of the problems that face the interested student of the puzzle of Seventh-day Adventism, and they must be fairly considered before hastily classifying Adventism as a non-Christian cult.

Ellen G. White and the Spirit of Prophecy

In most religious movements, one extraordinary and gifted personality dominates the scene, and so it was with Seventh-day Adventism. This dominant personality was and is today, through her writings, Ellen G. White. She was one of the most fascinating and controversial individuals ever to appear upon the horizon of religious history. Her memory and work have been praised by Adventists and damned by many of their enemies since the early years of the movement. Born Ellen Gould Harmon at Gorham, Maine, in 1827, and reared a devout Methodist in the city of Portland, White was early recognized as an unusual person, for she bore witness to certain "revelations," which she believed she had received from heaven.

When Ellen was thirteen, the Harmon family came under the influence of the Millerite movement. William Miller delivered a series of addresses in the Casco Street Christian Church in Portland in 1841 and 1842. At the age of seventeen, Ellen embraced the Adventist faith of the Millerites.[31] Although deeply stirred by Miller's sincerity and his chronological calculations, the Harmon family remained in fellowship with the Chestnut Street Methodist Church of Portland, which in 1845 disfellowshipped them because they believed in the premillennial second advent of Jesus Christ.

Despite her youth, Ellen Harmon passed through trying times, emotionally, physically, and spiritually, between 1837 and 1843. In the words of Dr. Froom, "She rebelled against the dismal prospects resulting from an early accident, and its attendant invalidism."[32] In 1840, at a Methodist camp meeting at Buxton, Maine, Ellen Harmon found wonderful deliverance and "her burden rolled from her shoulders," for she experienced great joy in learning that she was truly a child of God, which she publicly confessed afterward by requesting baptism by immersion. Many points still perplexed her, among them the doctrine of the eternal punishment of the wicked, which in subsequent years she surrendered to as well as the concept of conditional immortality and the sleep of the soul while

---

[31]Ellen G. White, *Life Sketches* (Washington, D.C.: Review and Herald Publishing Association, n.d.), 64–68.

[32]*The Prophetic Faith,* 4:978.

awaiting the resurrection. In December 1844, after "The Great Disappointment," while visiting a friend in Portland, Ellen Harmon experienced what she termed her first vision that portrayed the "vindication" of the Adventist faith. In that vision she claimed to see the Adventists triumphant over their critics—pressing upward to heaven in the face of insuperable obstacles.

For many years controversy has raged about White and her "revelations," and there are conflicting opinions within and without Adventism regarding both the extent and nature of her "revelations" and "inspiration." The position of Ellen White in Adventist teaching, then, is most significant and must be understood if we are to get a proper picture of this people. The writings and counsels of Ellen Harmon (later Ellen G. White by her marriage to James White, a prominent Adventist leader) are termed the "Spirit of prophecy," an expression taken from Revelation 19:10. Adventists believe that in the last days special counsels from God are to be revealed, which neither add to nor contradict Scripture, and that these counsels are primarily for the Seventh-day Adventist denomination. And, while following these counsels, they claim they always test them by the Word of God. Finally, they believe that the visions of Mrs. White and her counsels to their denomination are the "Spirit of prophecy" for their church.

There is a circular reasoning involved in defending White. Adventists say that the writers of the Bible did the same thing in quoting (without credit) pagan sources as did White. If they are permitted to do so, then she should be permitted to do so. That only holds, however, if one assumes that White is to be considered as one of the writers of the Bible. That is giving her a rank official Adventist representatives won't give her!

Through the years, some overzealous Adventist writers have given the impression that everything White said or wrote, even in private letters, was inspired and infallible. This is decidedly not the official position. The Adventist denomination readily admits that not everything White said or wrote was either inspired or infallible, although some individual Adventists still cling to that idea. Until the Adventists officially repudiate the doctrinal statements of *Questions on Doctrine* and officially espouse the errant doctrinal statements of some Adventists and Adventist factions, we can use *Questions on Doctrine* as representative of the denomination's official views. This we have done below.

I. Seventh-day Adventist Statements—Life and Ministry of Ellen G. White[33]

    1. We do not regard the writings of Ellen G. White as an addition to the sacred canon of Scripture. We do not think of them as of universal application, as is the Bible, but particularly for the Seventh-day Adventist Church. We do not regard them in the same sense as the Holy Scriptures, which stand alone and unique as the standard by which all other writings must be judged (89).

    2. Seventh-day Adventists uniformly believe that the canon of Scripture closed with the Book of Revelation. We hold that all other writings and teachings, from whatever source, are to be judged by and are subject to the Bible, which is the spring and norm of the Christian faith (89–90).

---

[33]Page numbers are in *Questions on Doctrine,* unless otherwise indicated.

3. I recommend to you, dear reader, the Word of God as the rule of your faith and practice. By that Word we are to be judged (90).

4. The Spirit was not given—nor can it ever be bestowed—to supersede the Bible; for the Scriptures explicitly state that the Word of God is the standard by which all teaching and experience must be tested (90).

5. We have never considered Ellen G. White to be in the same category as the writers of the canon of Scripture (90).

6. It is in . . . the category of messengers [other than the biblical writers] that we consider Ellen G. White to be. Among Seventh-day Adventists, she was recognized as one who possessed the gift of the Spirit of prophecy, though she herself never assumed the title of prophetess (91).

7. Seventh-day Adventists regard her writings as containing inspired counsel and instruction concerning personal religion and the conduct of our denominational work. . . . That portion of her writings, however, that might be classified as predictions, actually forms but a small segment. And even when she deals with what is coming on the earth, her statements are only amplifications of clear Bible prophecy (92).

8. In His Word, God has committed to men the knowledge necessary for salvation. The Holy Scriptures are to be accepted as an authoritative, infallible revelation of His will. They are the standard of character, the revealer of doctrines, and the test of experience (92–93, quoting Ellen G. White).

9. While Adventists hold the writings of Ellen G. White in highest esteem, these are not the source of our expositions. We base our teachings on the Scripture, the only foundation of all true Christian doctrine. However, it is our belief that the Holy Spirit opened to her mind important events and called her to give certain instructions for these last days. And inasmuch as these instructions, in our understanding, are in harmony with the Word of God, which Word alone is able to make us wise unto salvation, we as a denomination accept them as inspired counsels from the Lord. But we have never equated them with Scripture as some falsely charge. Mrs. White herself stated explicitly the relation of her writings to the Bible: "Little heed is given to the Bible, and the Lord has given a lesser light to lead men and women to the greater light" (*Review and Herald,* January 20, 1903; *Questions on Doctrine,* 93).

10. While Seventh-day Adventists recognize the Scripture canon closed nearly two thousand years ago and that there have been no additions to this compilation of sacred books, yet we believe that the Spirit of God, who inspired the Divine Word known to us as the Bible, has pledged to reveal himself to the church and through the various gifts of the Spirit. . . . It is not our understanding that these gifts of the Spirit take the place of the Word of God, nor does their acceptance make unnecessary the Scripture of truth. On the contrary, the acceptance of God's Word will lead God's people to a recognition and acceptance of the manifestation of the Spirit. Such manifestations will, of course, be in harmony with the Word of God. We know that some earnest Christians have the impression that these gifts ceased with the apostolic church. But Adventists believe that the closing of the Scripture canon did not terminate heaven's communication with men through the gifts of the Spirit, but rather that Christ by the ministry of His Spirit guides His people, edifying and strengthening them, and especially so in these last challenging days of human history (93–95).

11. The Spirit of prophecy is intimately related to the gift of prophecy, the one being the Spirit that indicted the prophecy, the other the evidence of the gift bestowed. They go together, each inseparably connected with the other. The gift is the manifestation of that which the Spirit of God bestows upon him whom, according to His own good purpose and plan, He selects as the one through whom such spiritual guidance is to come. Briefly then, this is the Adventist understanding of Ellen G. White's writings. They have been for a hundred years, to use her own expression, "a lesser light" leading sincere men and women to "the greater light" (96).

12. Concerning the matter of church fellowship, we would say that while we revere the writings of Ellen G. White ... we do not make acceptance of her writings as a matter for church discipline. She herself was explicit on this point. Speaking of those who did not fully understand the gift, she said: "Such should not be deprived of the benefits and privileges of the church, if their Christian course is otherwise correct and they have formed a good Christian character" (*Testimonies,* vol. 1, 328; *Questions on Doctrine,* 96–97).

13. We therefore do not test the world in any manner by these gifts. Nor do we in our intercourse with other religious bodies who are striving to walk in the fear of God, in any way make these a test of Christian character (J. N. Andrews in *Review and Herald,* February 15, 1870; *Questions on Doctrine,* 97).

14. James White, thrice General Conference president, speaking of the work of Ellen G. White, expressly declares that Adventists believe that God called her "to do a special work at this time, among this people. They do not, however, make a belief in this work a test of Christian fellowship" (*Review and Herald,* June 13, 1871; *Questions on Doctrine,* 97).

15. In the practice of the church it has not been customary to disfellowship one because he did not recognize the doctrine of spiritual gifts.... A member of the church should not be excluded from membership because of his inability to recognize clearly the doctrine of spiritual gifts and its application to the second advent movement (98).

It may be seen from these quotations that Seventh-day Adventists hold to the restoration of the "gift of prophecy" in the last days of the Christian church, and that they believe this restoration occurred in the life and ministry of Ellen G. White. The Adventists differ from other churches in that while they hold the Bible to be the unique, complete, infallible, and inerrant Word of God, they maintain that in specific contexts Ellen White's writings are to be accepted by Adventists as "testimonies" from the Spirit of God to guide their denominational activities.

Dr. Wilbur M. Smith has summed up the objections of most evangelicals where Seventh-day Adventism's emphasis upon White and the Spirit of prophecy is involved when he recently observed White's place in the new Seventh-day Adventist Bible Commentary.

I do not know any other denomination in all of Christendom today that has given such recognition, so slavishly and exclusively, to its founder or principal theologian as has this commentary to the writings of Ellen White. At the conclusion of every chapter in this work is a section headed, "Ellen G. White Comments." For example, on Genesis 28, the blessing conferred upon Jacob, there are less than three pages of comment, but at the end, forty references to the various works of Ellen White. In addition, at the end of the first volume of this commentary is a section again headed, "Ellen G. White Comments," containing eighty columns of material quoted from her writings. There is no section devoted to anyone else—Calvin, Luther, Wesley, or anyone else.

The Preface to this commentary contains the statement: "At the close of each chapter is a cross reference or index to those passages in Ellen G. White's writings that comment on the various texts in that chapter." And the second sentence following reads: "The Advent movement has grown strong through the study of the Bible; and it can be said with equal truth that the movement has been safely guided in that study by the light shining from the Spirit of prophecy." I would say that the writers of this commentary believe that "the Spirit of prophecy" has rested conclusively upon Ellen G. White, for no one else is so classified in this work.[34]

Dr. Smith is correct in his evaluation of the place of Ellen G. White's writings in the denomination. Seventh-day Adventists are of necessity committed to her visions and counsel because they believe that the Spirit of prophecy rested upon her and upon no other person of their group.

This writer rejects this concept of inspiration, but one should carefully note that, for Adventists, "inspiration" in connection with White's writings has a rather different meaning from the inspiration of the Bible. Adventists freely admit that the Bible is objectively the Word of God, the final authority in all matters of faith and morals. But the writings of White cannot be so regarded, and they are the first to say so. Apparently, they have adopted a qualified view of inspiration as related to her writings—"a lesser light to lead men and women to the greater light"—which emphasizes subjective interpretation as the criterion for determining specifically where in White's writings the "Spirit of prophecy" has decisively spoken. There is no doubt in my mind that the Adventists are defending a situation which is at best paradoxical and at times contradictory. But this position, as a matter of religious liberty, they are entitled to hold so long as they do not make faith in White's writings a test of fellowship between themselves and other denominations, and do not attempt to compel other Christians to accept the "testimonies" of White as indispensable to a deeper, richer experience of Christian consecration and living.

If Seventh-day Adventists did indeed claim for White inspiration in every area of her writings, then we might well be cautious about having fellowship with them. However, this they do not do, as I have amply demonstrated from official denominational sources. Since they do not consider White's teachings the source of their expositions of faith, the claim that one has only to refute Ellen G. White and her writings in order to refute Seventh-day Adventism falls by its own weight.

II. Mrs. White and Her Critics

Through the years a great deal of literature has appeared, criticizing the life and works of Ellen G. White. These criticisms have ranged from the mild judg-

---

[34]Excerpt from a letter to the author.

ment that White was a sincere but emotionally disturbed mystic to the charge that she was a "false prophetess" who sought material gain and deliberately plagiarized much of her writing. In the interest of honest investigation and truth, and since it is impossible in a book of this size to analyze all the conflicting data, we shall present some highlights of the controversy and let the reader determine the validity of these charges.

The inspiration for 90 percent of the destructive personal criticisms leveled against White is found in the writings of Dudley M. Canright, an ex-Adventist leader of great ability, and a one-time personal friend of Ellen G. White and her husband, James, as well as a great number of prominent Adventist leaders. Canright, one of the most able of the Seventh-day Adventist writers and debaters of his day, left the movement because he lost faith in the inspiration of White and in many doctrines then held by the Adventist Church. While it is true that Canright thrice ceased to preach, his credentials as a minister were never revoked. He finally resigned from the Seventh-day Adventist ministry in 1887 to become a Baptist minister. By Canright's own admission, his personality conflicts with Ellen G. White and her advisers were largely responsible for his turning away from the active ministry at the times mentioned. He, however, apparently maintained close personal relations with James White, Mrs. White's husband, and other prominent Seventh-day Adventist leaders, as is evident from the correspondence quoted below. Canright rebelled violently against Arianism (the denial of the deity of Christ) and extreme legalism, which existed among some of the early Seventh-day Adventists; and his convictions led him later to write two volumes (*Seventh-day Adventism Renounced* and *Life of Mrs. E. G. White*), which systematically and scathingly denounced Seventh-day Adventism theologically and impugned the personal motives and integrity of White.

In these two volumes D. M. Canright laid the foundation for all future destructive criticism of Seventh-day Adventism, and careful research has confirmed the impression that nearly all subsequent similar publications are little more than repetitions of the destructive areas of Canright's writing, buttressed by standard theological arguments. This is especially true of the writings of a former Seventh-day Adventist missionary printer, E. B. Jones, editor of a small news sheet, *Guardians of the Faith,* who has issued a number of vitriolic pamphlets against Seventh-day Adventism, all of which are drawn almost exclusively from Canright and other critics, and are for the most part outdated and in some cases both scholastically and ethically unreliable. It can be seen, therefore, that what D. M. Canright has written about Ellen G. White is of prime importance as firsthand evidence, and no Seventh-day Adventist apologist, regardless of the scope of his knowledge of Adventism or the breadth of his scholastic learning, can gainsay all that Canright has written.

In the March 22, 1887, issue of the *Review and Herald,* his former brethren wrote of Elder Canright:

> We have felt exceedingly sad to part in our religious connection with one whom we have long esteemed as a dear brother. . . . In leaving us he has taken a much more manly and commendable course than most of those who have withdrawn from us, coming voluntarily to our leading brethren and frankly stating the condition of mind he was in. He did this before his own

church in our presence and so far as we know has taken no unfair under-handed means to injure us in any way. He goes from our midst with no immoral stain upon his character. He chooses associations more pleasant to himself. This is every man's personal privilege if he chooses to take it.

Writing to Canright on May 22, 1881, from Battle Creek, Michigan, James White, Ellen's husband, stated, "It is time there was a change in the offices of the General Conference. I trust that if we are true and faithful, the Lord will be pleased that we should constitute two of that Board." In another letter to Can-right, dated July 13, 1881, James White said, "Brother Canright, I feel more inter-est in you than in any other man because I know your worth when the Lord is with you as a laborer." It is apparent, therefore, that Canright was in good stand-ing with the Adventists, despite his later renunciation of White's testimonies and the "special truths" of the Adventist message.

In 1951 a carefully documented volume of almost seven hundred pages was issued by the Review and Herald Publishing Association of Washington, D.C. The author was Francis D. Nichol, leading apologist of the Seventh-day Adventist denomination. This volume, entitled *Ellen G. White and Her Critics,* attempts a point-for-point refutation of many of the charges made by D. M. Canright in his *Life of Mrs. E. G. White.* Nichol has dug deep into early Adventist history—even beyond Canright's day. In addition, after reading both Nichol and Canright, I have concluded that there is much to be said on both sides. But Canright, we believe, has the edge because he can say, "I was there" or "White said," and contradictory contemporary statements are not to be found where many of Can-right's charges are concerned.

My own conclusion is that in some areas (particularly theology) Canright's statements are irrefutable, especially with regard to his personal relationships with White and the leading members of the Adventist denomination. It is also significant to note that many charges that are based on personal experiences and have been well documented have never been refuted.

By this I do not mean that all of Canright's writing is to be trusted, for many of his criticisms of White's activities have been neatly undercut by contemporary evidence unearthed by F. D. Nichol and others. Where Nichol is concerned, "methinks he doth protest too much," and he often goes to extremes to defend White. This, in my judgment, has hurt his case and has proved nothing except that he is a devoted disciple of White and therefore strongly biased. Nonetheless, Nichol is the most able Adventist apologist.

III. The Verdict of the Evidence

After considering all the evidence obtainable, of which the foregoing is only a part, this writer is convinced that Ellen G. White was a highly impressionable woman, strongly influenced by her associates. That she sincerely believed the Lord spoke to her, none can fairly question, but the evidence set forth in this book gives good reason, we believe, to doubt the inspiration of her counsels, whether Seventh-day Adventists will concede this or not.

My personal evaluation of the visions of Ellen G. White is best summed up in the following statement from a friendly critic. In 1847, at the outset of her work, one of White's cousins stated,

> I cannot endorse Sister Ellen's visions as of Divine inspiration, as you and she think them to be; yet I do not suspect the least shade of dishonesty in either of you in this matter. I may, perhaps, express to you my belief in the latter without harm—it will, doubtless, result either in your good or mine. At the same time I admit the possibility of my being mistaken. I think that what she and you regard as visions from the Lord are only religious reveries in which her imagination runs without control upon themes in which she is most deeply interested. While so absorbed in these reveries she is lost to everything around her. Reveries are of two kinds: sinful and religious. In either case, the sentiments in the main are obtained from previous teaching or study. I do not by any means think that her visions are from the Devil.[35]

If Seventh-day Adventists are to defend their claim for White's inspiration, they must explain a number of contradictions in her writings. They would do better to admit, we believe, that she was very human, capable of errors in judgment, and subject to lapses of memory.

It is my considered opinion that Ellen G. White had an extremely complex personality, and that she plagiarized materials because she believed the Lord had shown her that what the sources said was the truth. She simply appropriated material and gave it out. Her actions cannot be excused, but they can be understood as the actions of a Christian who made mistakes. She was both mortal and a sinner like anyone else. I think those around her aided and abetted her in her "cover-up." Also, I think the White estate continued the cover-up for many years after her death. No objective person, in possession of all the facts, can doubt this.

The difference between her and, for example, the Jehovah's Witnesses, is not the crime itself. What she did was wrong. The difference is in the nature of the person we are talking about. Was Jehovah's Witness founder Charles Taze Russell a Christian? Did he hold to the foundations of the Gospel? Did he promulgate the things of Christianity and stand in their defense? No. Did Ellen White? Yes. Therefore, although she committed the same crime he did, she cannot be judged on the same basis as Charles Russell. She was a Christian who committed a sin. Christians can and do commit sins.

A biblical false prophet was not a believer. A biblical false prophet was a servant of the devil attempting to lead people away from the truth. White, in my opinion, made false statements. She misused what she claimed was the prophetic gift she had. But one cannot say that she was like a biblical false prophet. Of course, technically, all would agree that the person who prophesies in the name of God and turns out to be wrong has prophesied falsely. But White was not as a biblical false prophet because she was a true Christian, even though what she did was sinful.

White was definitely influenced in some of her writings by time and circumstances, and also by the powerful personalities who surrounded her. Some Adventists maintain that this would in no way prevent her conveying messages from the Lord. However, as I see it, anyone who attempts to prove she was divinely inspired or infallible (no informed Adventist holds the latter) must first dispose of the evidence here presented, as well as other evidence that space does not

---

[35]Reproduced in Elder James White, *A Word to the Little Flock* (n.p., 1847), 29.

admit to include. F. D. Nichol, in *Ellen G. White and Her Critics,* makes a masterful attempt to answer some of these problems, but not all of them can be answered with a good conscience or an airtight defense of White and her actions. It does not detract from her stature as a sincere Christian or from the quality of her contribution to insist upon an honest and systematic evaluation of her statements by thinking Adventists, or to ascertain to what degree Adventists may rightfully maintain that the Lord "spoke" through White. Non-Adventists, of course, reject the claims made for White and her writings and hope that Adventists will some day amend their questionable view of "Ellen G. White and the Spirit of prophecy."

After reading the publications of the Seventh-day Adventist denomination and almost all the writings of Ellen G. White, including her *Testimonies,* the writer believes White was truly a regenerate Christian woman who loved the Lord Jesus Christ and dedicated herself unstintingly to the task of bearing witness for Him as she felt led. It should be clearly understood that some tenets of Christian theology, as historically understood, and White's interpretations of them do not agree; indeed, they are at loggerheads. Nevertheless, Ellen G. White was true to the cardinal doctrines of the Christian faith regarding the salvation of the soul and the believer's life in Christ. We must disagree with White's interpretation of the sanctuary, the investigative judgment, and the scapegoat; we challenge her stress upon the Sabbath, health reform, the unconscious state of the dead, and the final destruction of the wicked, etc. But no one can dispute the fact that her writings conform to the basic principles of the historical Gospel, for they most certainly do. However, we must not assume as many Adventists do that White's writings are free from theological and exegetical error, for they are not. Although I believe that the influence of White's counsels on the Adventist denomination parallels the influence of J. N. Darby of the Plymouth Brethren and A. B. Simpson of the Christian and Missionary Alliance, the claim that she possessed a "gift of prophecy" akin to that described in 1 Corinthians 14, as believed by the Seventh-day Adventist Church, I cannot accept.

Contemporary Adventists affirm that White was not infallible, did borrow (unfortunately, usually without attribution) from other sources, and taught from within a nineteenth-century theological context. Adventist professor Gary Land notes, "The research of the 1970s established three points: Ellen White borrowed much material from others; she was a part of late-nineteenth-century culture; and she was not inerrant. From the furor of opposition to Ronald Number's study in the mid-1970s, the denomination—though obviously uncomfortable with public discussion of the issue—had by the end of the decade moved toward accepting the general points that the entire body of research had established."[36]

Many critics of Seventh-day Adventism have assumed, mostly from the writings of professional detractors, that White was a fearsome ogre who devoured all who opposed her, and they have never ceased to make the false claim that Seventh-day Adventists believe that White was infallible, despite the often-published authoritative statement to the contrary. Although Seventh-day Adventists do hold White and her writings in great esteem, they maintain that the Bible is their only

---

[36]Gary Land, ed., *Adventism in America* (Grand Rapids, Mich.: William B. Eerdmans Publishing Company, 1986), 223.

"rule of faith and practice." Christians of all denominations may heatedly disagree with the Seventh-day Adventist attitude toward White, but all that she wrote on such subjects as salvation or Christian living characterizes her as a Christian in every sense of the term.

Farther on in this discussion, we shall look at White's relations with the Adventist denomination, particularly in the field of theology. Enough has been presented here, however, to show that she was a most interesting personality, far different from the "Sister White" idealized beyond reality in certain Seventh-day Adventist publications.

Dudley M. Canright, the chief critic of Seventh-day Adventism, has, I feel, rendered good service in this respect. He has presented the human side of White from the standpoint of a firsthand friendship that lasted through the formative years of the Seventh-day Adventist denomination. Despite his criticisms of Seventh-day Adventism and of White, Canright himself never ceased to believe that despite what he believed to be her errors in theology and her mistaken concept of visions, she was a regenerate Christian. With his brother, Canright attended the funeral of White in 1915. His brother describes the occasion thus: "We joined the passing throng, and again stood by the bier. My brother rested his hand upon the side of the casket, and with tears rolling down his cheeks, he said brokenly, 'There is a noble Christian woman gone!' "[37]

The controversy between Seventh-day Adventist historians and the personal recollections of D. M. Canright will probably never be settled this side of heaven, but beyond question, Canright has left an indelible mark upon the history of both the denomination and Ellen G. White, a woman of great moral fortitude and indomitable conviction. Her influence will doubtless affect the religious world through the Seventh-day Adventist denomination for many years to come.

The Sleep of the Soul and the Destruction of the Wicked

The doctrine of conditional immortality, commonly called "soul-sleep" outside Adventist circles, and its necessary corollary, annihilation, have been cardinal teachings from the beginning of the Seventh-day Adventist Church. They must be dealt with from an exegetical standpoint if the theology underlying the basic premise is to be understood. These positions, incidentally, are held today by the Advent Christian Church, an affiliate of the National Association of Evangelicals, and by outstanding Bible scholars in not a few denominations.

The purpose here is essentially to review the historical position of the Christian church from the days of the apostles to the present, and to examine the teaching of the Scriptures on these subjects. Many noted Christians of the past believed in conditional immortality, among them Martin Luther, William Tyndale, and John Wycliffe, all of whom were competent Greek scholars. Luther even stated that he could not support the doctrine of immortality of the soul, which he called one of the "endless monstrosities in the Roman dunghill of decretals."[38] Tyndale declared:

---

[37]W. A. Spicer, *Our Day in the Light of Prophecy* (Washington, D.C.: Review and Herald Publishing Association, n.d.), 127.
[38]Weimar edition of Luther's *Works,* VII:131–132.

In putting them [the souls of the departed dead] in heaven, hell, and purgatory [you] destroy the arguments wherewith Christ and Paul prove the resurrection. . . . And again, if the souls be in heaven, tell me why they be not in as good case as the angels be? And then what cause is there for the resurrection?[39]

However, in his *Commentary on Genesis*, Luther later categorically stated, "In the interim [between death and resurrection], the soul does not sleep but is awake and enjoys the vision of angels and of God, and has converse with them."[40]

In any case, neither preponderance of one opinion nor the opinions of a few great thinkers can validate theological speculation or interpretation. The Christian church does not base its belief in the conscious bliss of departed saints on the opinions of individuals, no matter how prominent or learned, but upon the historical, biblical foundation of the Christian faith.

I. Textual Analysis

The Seventh-day Adventist doctrine of the sleep of the soul is best expressed in their own words: "We as Adventists believe that, in general, the Scriptures teach that the soul of man represents the whole man, and not a particular part independent of the other component parts of man's nature; and further, that the soul cannot exist apart from the body, for man is a unit. . . . We, as Adventists, have reached the definite conclusion that man rests in the tomb until the resurrection morning. Then, at the first resurrection (Revelation 20:4–5), the resurrection of the just (Acts 24:15), the righteous come forth immortalized at the call of Christ, the Lifegiver. And they then enter into life everlasting in their eternal home in the kingdom of glory. Such is our understanding."[41]

In the 1988 explanation of Adventist doctrine, *Seventh-day Adventists Believe*, the grave is described: "The grave is not a place of consciousness. Since death is a sleep, the dead will remain in a state of unconsciousness in the grave until the resurrection, when the grave (*Hades*) gives up its dead."[42]

The key to the preceding statements, of course, is the last phrase of the former quote: "They then enter into life everlasting in their eternal home in the kingdom of glory." Now, the majority of Christians through the centuries have held that this proposition contradicts the teaching of the Word of God contained in the following passages:

1. *1 John 5:11–13:* "And this is the record, that God hath given to us eternal life, and this life is in his Son. He that hath the Son hath life; and he that hath not the Son of God hath not life. These things have I written unto you that believe on the name of the Son of God; that ye may know that ye have eternal life, and that ye may believe on the name of the Son of God." In the grammar and context of this passage, eternal life (*eionion zoes*) is the present possession of every believer in the Lord Jesus Christ, and if the term eternal life does not include conscious fellowship, then the whole New Testament meaning is destroyed. The Holy Spirit used the present indicative active of the verb *echo*,

---

[39] *An Answer to Sir Thomas More's Dialogue*, Parker's 1850 reprint, book 4, chap. iv, 180–81.
[40] *Works*, 25:321.
[41] *Questions on Doctrine*, 515, 520.
[42] *Seventh-day Adventists Believe*, 353.

expressing present, continuous action. Thus we see that the believer, having been regenerated by the Holy Spirit, already possesses never-ending life as a continuing quality of conscious existence.

2. *John 11:25–26:* "Jesus said unto her, I am the resurrection, and the life: he that believeth in me, though he were dead, yet shall he live: And whosoever liveth and believeth in me shall never die. Believest thou this?" The context here indicates that the Lord Jesus Christ was consoling Martha upon the death of her brother Lazarus. Therefore, the words *life* and *dead* must refer to that particular occasion. To attempt to wrest the meanings of these terms from their expressed context, and to teach that the end of the age is primarily in view or somehow close, is a violation of the grammar and context.

All thorough students of the Word of God, including the Adventists, recognize that in any study of the doctrines of eternal life and immortality, it is vitally essential to apply the hermeneutic principle (comparing all texts on a given subject) of interpretation, and the application of this principle, we believe, leads to the following facts. The root meanings for the words *death* and *life* in the New Testament usage ("death" *thanatos*, in its verb form *apothnesko*, and "life" *zoe*, or its verb form *zac*) are respectively "separation or to separate" from communion or fellowship. The Scriptures describe two types of death, physical and spiritual, the former being the separation of the body from the soul, and the latter being the separation of the soul from God as the result of sin. Also, two kinds of life are spoken of in the New Testament: physical life (*bios*), which is the union or communion of body and soul; and spiritual life (*zoe*), which is the communion or fellowship of the soul with God. These terms we equate with the Greek of the New Testament, and they are essential to an understanding of Christ's words to Martha.

He was assuring her that despite the physical evidence of death, Jesus, the eternal Word of God made flesh, was himself the source of life. And as such, He was able to give life, even though death had actually occurred. Let us, therefore, take His words literally.

Christ's primary purpose was to comfort Martha. And what better comfort could He give than the knowledge that her family's limited concept of life as dependent upon the resurrection was depriving her of the joyous knowledge that the Prince of Life gives to the believer eternal life, unaffected by physical death.

Now let us look carefully at this context with no violation to hermeneutics or grammar, and this great truth becomes clear. John 11:20 tells us that as soon as Martha heard that Jesus was coming to Bethany, she went out to meet Him. In verse 21 she greets Him thus: "Lord, if thou hadst been here, my brother had not died." In answer to her obvious affliction and grief, Jesus, with divine compassion, stated, "Thy brother shall rise again." Verse 24 indicates, however, that Martha thought He was referring to the resurrection of the dead that will take place at "the last day."

To dispel her confused and grief-instilling concept of life (spiritual life), Jesus gives comfort beyond measure: "I am the resurrection, and the life," He declares; "he that believeth in me, though he were dead, yet shall he live: and whosoever liveth and believeth in me shall never die."

Now it is apparent from the context of verse 25 that Jesus was referring to Martha's brother Lazarus, one who believed in Him and had physically died.

Christ's promise is, "Yet shall he live." But going beyond this, Jesus lifts the veil and reveals that, in the realm of the physically alive, whoever believes in Him shall never experience the greatest of all terrors: spiritual death.

The Greek is extremely powerful in verse 26, for our Lord deliberately used the double negative, a construction which intensifies with great emphasis that to which it is applied. Jesus could not grammatically have been more emphatic in stating that the believer, who is alive both physically and spiritually, can never experience loss of communion or fellowship as a spiritual entity, though his body may "become" dead.

We see, further, that Seventh-day Adventists have no warrant for the idea that death is a state of unconsciousness. The New Testament frequently indicates that the unregenerate man is already "dead," but not even the Adventists would say that he was extinct or unconscious! Some instances of this are: Matthew 8:22, "Let the dead bury their dead"; John 5:25, "The hour is coming, and now is, when the dead shall hear the voice of the Son of God: and they that hear shall live"; and Ephesians 2:1, "You hath he quickened, who were dead in trespasses and sins."

Admittedly, in the New Testament death is compared with sleep, but this is recognized by Bible scholars generally as a grammatical metaphor. One does not develop a doctrine from a figure of speech, as conditional immortalists apparently have done, but upon the sound principles of biblical hermeneutics, contextual analysis, and linguistic exegesis. The application of these principles leads to the one conclusion that the Scripture unreservedly teaches, that eternal life is vastly different from "immortality"; although immortality will be bestowed upon the believer at the resurrection, in this life he already possesses "eternal life," a spiritual quality of existence that will at length be united with the physical quality of incorruptibility, which the Bible speaks of as immortality, and "we shall be like him; for we shall see him as he is" (1 Corinthians 13:12; 1 John 3:2). A study of these words in any Greek lexicon, and of their use in the New Testament, will show that immortality and eternal life are neither identical nor synonymous. For certain Adventist writers, therefore, to treat these terms as interchangeable is clearly a linguistic impossibility.

3. *2 Timothy 1:10:* The apostle Paul writes that God's eternal purpose "is now made manifest by the appearing of our Saviour Jesus Christ, who hath abolished death, and hath brought life and immortality to light through the gospel." In this verse "life" (*zoe*) and "immortality" (*aphtharsian*) are clearly distinguished. Life has been bestowed upon the believer at the moment of regeneration by faith in Jesus Christ (1 John 5:11–12); immortality is a future gift, to be bestowed upon the believer's body at the second advent of our Lord, or as Paul expressed it, "This corruptible must put on incorruption [*aphtharsian*], and this mortal must put on immortality" (*athanasian*, 1 Corinthians 15:53).

Again, in Romans 2:7, the apostle clearly distinguishes between "eternal life" as a conscious quality of spiritual existence bestowed upon the believer as a gift; and "immortality," which, in this connection in the New Testament, refers to the resurrection bodies of the saints or to the nature of God himself. Thus, God's Word clearly indicates the difference between "life" as spiritual existence and "immortality" as incorruptibility in a body like that of our risen Lord.

4. *Philippians 1:21–24:* "For to me to live is Christ and to die is gain. But if I live in the flesh, this is the fruit of my labour: yet what I shall choose I [know] not. For I am in a strait betwixt two, having a desire to depart, and to be with Christ; which is far better: Nevertheless to abide in the flesh is more needful for you."

Seventh-day Adventists say here:

> Of course it will be better to be with Christ. But why, it must be asked, should we conclude [from this remark] that the apostle expects, immediately upon death, to go at once into the presence of Christ? The Bible does not say so. It merely states his desire to depart, and be with Christ. One might reason that the implication is to the effect that being with Christ would be immediately on his departure. But it must be admitted that such is not a necessary implication, and it certainly is not a definite statement of the text. In this particular passage, Paul does not tell us when he will be with his Lord. In other places he uses an expression similar to one in this passage. For instance, he says, "The time of my departure is at hand" (2 Timothy 4:6). The Greek word used in these two texts, *analuo,* is not used very often in the Greek New Testament, but the word has the meaning "to be loosened like an anchor." It is a metaphor drawn from the loosened moorings preparatory to setting sail.[43]

Now, of all the texts in the New Testament on the state of the believer after the death of his body, this one alone gives us Paul's mind on the subject, so we need to pay strict attention to what he says. In the main, Seventh-day Adventists support their arguments with Old Testament passages, most of which, I maintain, are taken out of context while ignoring metaphorical usages, implications, and deductions. To treat literally such words as *sleep, death,* and *destroy* is, I feel, unwarranted. However, in the New Testament, when faced with a positive statement like this one by the apostle Paul, it seems that they refuse to be literal and insist upon metaphors, deductions, and implications. They seem unwilling to accept the apostle's statement at face value. The noted Adventist author F. D. Nichol, in his book *Answers to Objections,* states that if Philippians 1:21–24 were the only passage about the condition of man in death, he would be forced to acknowledge the accepted orthodox position. Nichol then attempts to strengthen his argument by taking texts out of context to "prove" that Paul does not mean what he most decidedly says. With this thought in mind, let us examine the context and grammar of the apostle's statement, for it answers the Seventh-day Adventist contention.

In verse 21 Paul states that to continue to live is Christ and to die "is gain." Since Paul was ordained to preach the Word of God to the Gentiles while enjoying fellowship with the living Christ, what would he gain by death or unconsciousness? According to the Adventist idea, fellowship with Christ would end, and Paul would merely go to sleep until the resurrection. This argument violates both context and grammar.

Verse 23 is grammatically uncomplicated. It is a series of coordinate statements tied together by the conjunctions *kai* and *de.* The phrase "to depart, and

---

[43] *Questions on Doctrine,* 527–28.

to be with Christ; to which is far better" (*eis to analusai kai sun christo einai*) is grammatically devastating to the Seventh-day Adventist position. The preposition *eis* plus the definite article *to* shows "true purpose or end in view"—the strong desire that causes Paul's dilemma. Both infinitives (*analusai* and *einai*) have one construction—they are used with one definite article—and so are one thought, one grammatical expression: literally, "My desire is to the 'to depart and to be with Christ.' " In simple English, Paul's one desire has a twofold object: departure and being with Christ! If departure did not mean his immediately being with Christ, another construction would have been employed. It, therefore, seems impossible that soul-sleep was in the mind of the apostle, since he desired to depart from his body and to spiritually enjoy the presence of his Lord. The Second Advent could not have been in view in this passage, for the context indicates that Paul expected death—and instantaneous reunion with Christ—*then*, not at the resurrection. There would have been no need of his staying to instruct the Philippians (v. 24) if he were speaking of the Second Advent, for they would all be glorified together and no longer in need of His presence to strengthen them. Most translators and recognized Greek authorities contend that Philippians 1: 21–24 teaches the historical position of the Christian church, i.e., the conscious presence of the believer with Christ at the death of the body.

As quoted above, the Adventists, in common with all conditional immortalists, say, "Why . . . should we conclude [from this remark] that the apostle expects immediately upon death to go at once into the presence of Christ? The Bible does not say so. It merely states his desire to depart and [to] be with Christ." We answer that the context of the chapter, the grammatical construction of the verse, and every grammar book on New Testament Greek usage teaches that from the construction utilized, the apostle expected to go at once into the presence of his Lord. Nevertheless, the Adventists insist, "The Bible does not say so. It merely states his desire to depart and [to] be with Christ." This statement is not accurate, it is not exegetically sound, and it will not stand the test of contextual criticism. It is only an attempt, I believe, to justify a doctrine that is not supported by the Word of God.

In reply to the Adventist statement, "In this particular passage, Paul does not tell us when he will be with his Lord," we point out that the apostle categorically states that his desire is "to depart." If this departure did not mean immediate presence with Christ, he would have used a different grammatical construction, as previously noted; but as it stands, it can have no other meaning. In the face of these facts, Seventh-day Adventists disregard the preponderance of historical scholarship in favor of the doctrine of "soul-sleep."

5. *1 Thessalonians 4:13–18:* "I would not have you to be ignorant, brethren, concerning them which are asleep, that ye sorrow not, even as others which have no hope. For if we believe that Jesus died and rose again, even so them also which sleep in Jesus will God bring with him. For this we say unto you by the word of the Lord, that we which are alive and remain unto the coming of the Lord shall not prevent them which are asleep. For the Lord himself shall descend from heaven with a shout, with the voice of the archangel, and with the trump of God: and the dead in Christ shall rise first: Then we which are alive and remain shall be caught up together with them in the clouds, to meet the Lord in the air: and

so shall we ever be with the Lord. Wherefore comfort one another with these words."

This final passage, I believe, refutes the Adventist teaching on the intermediate state of the dead. It is marked by explicit emphasis of construction in the Greek and cannot be ignored by any serious student of the language.

The key is the preposition *sun*, which carries the primary meaning of "together with." In verse 14 the Holy Spirit tells us that God intends to bring with Him (*sun auto*), that is, with Jesus at His second advent, believing Christians who have experienced physical death. The physical state of their bodies is described as "sleep," a common metaphor in the New Testament. In every instance where the word *sleep* is used to describe death, it always refers to the body and cannot be applied to the soul, especially since "sleep" is never used with reference to the soul. This fact Seventh-day Adventists seem to overlook.

The second use of *sun* is in verse 17, which tells us that believers who survive to the coming of the Lord will be caught up together with them (*sun autois*), that is, with the dead in Christ (*oi nekroi en Christo*) to meet the Lord in the air. Here again, *sun* has no meaning other than "together with," a fact most difficult for Seventh-day Adventists to explain.

The last use of the preposition *sun* is also in verse 17: "And so shall we ever be with the Lord" (*sun kurio*). It is quite obvious, therefore, that at the second advent of Christ, those who at death departed to be spiritually with the Lord (Philippians 1:21–24) *return* with Him or "together with" Him to claim their resurrected, immortal bodies. Simultaneously, their corrupting bodies in the graves, spoken of as "asleep," are instantly metamorphosed or changed and reunited with the returning personalities. This fact is consistently emphasized by continual use of the preposition *sun*, "together with." Since the preposition *sun* means "together with" both times in verse 17, grammatically it cannot mean something altogether different in the same context and parallel usage of verse 14. Therefore, if at Christ's advent our bodies are to go with Him physically (v. 16), it is obvious that the saints who preceded us in death have been with Him from the moment of death, since they accompany Him in His return (v. 14).

A final grammatical point is the Holy Spirit's use of *nekroi*, which throughout the New Testament refers primarily to the physical body of man, and only metaphorically to the soul. We see, then, that the corpses (*nekroi*) of the physically dead saints are to be raised and united with their returning souls (verse 14). Not once does the context or grammar indicate that the souls of departed believers are "asleep." Instead, it categorically states that they are "with Jesus" or returning "together with" Jesus.

The great hope of the believer is the joy of personal union with the Lord, and this union, the apostle Paul tells us, takes place at the death of the body. That this has been the position of the large majority of the Christian church since the times of the apostles, the Adventists have never denied. In 1 Thessalonians 4, the apostle Paul was giving comfort to people who were mourning for departed loved ones; and his words carry the undeniable conclusion that they are not "dead" in the usual pagan sense. Although physically dead, they are spiritually alive and with Christ, awaiting the day when they will return "together with him" (verse 14) to claim their inheritance of completion, physical immortality, or incorruptibility.

II. "Soul" and "Spirit"

For a fuller treatment of Adventist teaching on soul-sleep, we must discuss briefly the Bible's use of "soul" and "spirit." In the Old Testament the words *soul* and *spirit* are the Hebrew *nephesh* and *ruach.* In the New Testament they are the Greek *psuche* and *pneuma.* Although in the Old Testament *nephesh* and *ruach* frequently refer only to the principle of life in both men and animals, in many other places they mean the intellectual and spiritual nature of man. Such verses as Isaiah 57:16; Zechariah 12:1; Isaiah 55:3; and Genesis 35:18[44] belie the Adventists' criterion for determining the spiritual nature of man. On page 522 of *Questions on Doctrine,* the Adventists list eight Scripture passages about death to show that at the death of the body, the intellect, will, and spirit of man (*nephesh* and *ruach*) lapse into unconsciousness pending the resurrection. However, seven of these are from the Old Testament and each refers to the body. Adventists lean strongly on the book of Ecclesiastes, especially 9:5–6, to substantiate their doctrine. But Ecclesiastes 12:7 tells us that upon the death of the body, "the spirit [*ruach*] shall return unto God." Unlike the mere principle of life in the animals, man possesses a cognizant, immaterial nature created in God's image.[45]

It is a basic Christian principle, with which Adventists agree, that the Old Testament must be interpreted by the New Testament, and not the reverse. However, where conditional immortality is involved, Adventists do not follow this principle. The New Testament teaches that the immaterial nature of man (soul and spirit) is separate from the body (Matthew 10:28; Luke 8:55; 1 Thessalonians 5:23; Hebrews 4:12; Revelation 16:3),[46] and also that it is independent of man's material form and departs from that form at death to go either into the presence of the Lord (Philippians 1:23) or into a place of punishment (Luke 16). In Acts 7:59, Stephen committed his spirit (*pneuma*) into the hands of the Lord Jesus Christ. This establishes the fact that the immaterial nature of man is independent of his body. At the same time, the Scripture tells us, "He [Stephen] fell asleep" in death; that is, his physical body took on the appearance of "sleep." But he as a unit did not die; he merely experienced separation of the soul from the body, and he went to be with the Lord, into whose hands he had committed his spiritual nature.

---

[44]"For I will not contend for ever, neither will I be always wroth: for the spirit should fail before me, and the souls which I have made" (Isaiah 57:16); "The burden of the word of the Lord for Israel, saith the Lord, which stretcheth forth the heavens, and layeth the foundation of the earth, and formeth the spirit of man within him" (Zechariah 12:1); "Incline your ear, and come unto me: hear, and your soul shall live; and I will make an everlasting covenant with you, even the sure mercies of David" (Isaiah 55:3); "And it came to pass, as her soul was in departing, (for she died) that she called his name Benoni: but his father called him Benjamin" (Genesis 35:18).

[45]It is almost universally agreed among biblical scholars that Ecclesiastes portrays Solomon's apostasy and is therefore questionable for determining doctrine. It sketches man's life "under the sun" and reveals the hopelessness of the soul apart from God.

[46]"And fear not them which kill the body, but are not able to kill the soul: but rather fear him which is able to destroy both soul and body in hell" (Matthew 10:28); "And her spirit came again, and she rose straightway: and he commanded to give her meat" (Luke 8:55); "And the very God of peace sanctify you wholly; and I pray God your whole spirit and soul and body be preserved blameless unto the coming of our Lord Jesus Christ" (1 Thessalonians 5:23); "For the word of God is quick, and powerful, and sharper than any twoedged sword, piercing even to the dividing asunder of soul and spirit, and of the joints and marrow, and is a discerner of the thoughts and intents of the heart" (Hebrews 4:12); "And the second angel poured out his vial upon the sea; and it became as the blood of a dead man: and every living soul died in the sea" (Revelation 16:3).

In Luke 23:46 the Lord Jesus Christ said, "Father, into thy hands I commend my spirit." This verse would be meaningless if it applied only to the "breath of Jesus." The classic example of the penitent thief, who in his last moments believed on the Lord Jesus Christ, is proof that eternal life is a quality including conscious existence. It does not terminate with the death of the physical but continues in never-ending personal fellowship with our Lord. "Today shalt thou be with me in paradise" (v. 43) is the guarantee of the Son of God that those who trust Him will never be separated from His presence and fellowship. Seventh-day Adventists, in company with other conditional immortalists, attempt to explain this by reading the text with different punctuation: "Verily, I say unto thee today, shalt thou be with me in paradise." The reason is that Christ's statement calls into serious question their doctrine of soul-sleep. Moreover, Adventists seem to overlook the important fact that whenever Jesus used the words, "Verily I say unto you," He never qualified them because qualification was unnecessary. It would have been redundant for Jesus to say, "Verily I say unto you, that is, today I am saying unto you." By this type of interpretation, the Adventists violate the plain sense of one of Christ's common expressions of emphasis.

In Matthew 17:3 we see Moses and Elijah with Christ on the Mount of Transfiguration. We know that Moses died (Deuteronomy 34:5), and Elijah was translated (2 Kings 2:11). However, it *was* Moses who was communing with our Lord. Since the Scripture nowhere states that Moses had been raised from the dead for this occasion (Adventists attempt to teach this from the book of Jude, where such an assertion is not made), it is evident that the soul of Moses appeared to our Lord. Thus, conscious existence is a necessary predicate of the intermediate state.

It is the strong conviction of mine, based upon Scripture, that the doctrine of soul-sleep cannot stand in the light of God's revelation. Perhaps the reader will think that there has been too much space given to the meanings of words and the grammar of the Greek New Testament. However, this is most essential because the crux of Adventist argument, it seems to me, is a denial of the meaning of terms in their context. For example, they say:

> There is nothing in the word *psyche* [soul] itself that even remotely implies a conscious entity that is able to survive the death of the body. And there is nothing in the Bible use of the word indicating that the Bible writers held any such belief.... There is nothing inherent in the word *pneuma* [spirit] by which it may be taken to mean some supposed conscious entity of man capable of existing apart from the body, nor does the usage of the word with respect to man in the New Testament in any way imply such a concept.... A careful study of all the adjectives used in Scripture to qualify the word "spirit" as applied to man, indicates that not one even remotely approaches the idea of immortality as one of the qualities of the human "spirit."[47]

As demonstrated in Matthew 10:28, Jesus Christ apparently believed and taught that the soul was more than "body and breath," which Seventh-day Adventism teaches, for He said, "Fear not them which kill the body, but are not able to kill the soul."

---

[47] *Questions on Doctrine*, 514, 517–18.

Seventh-day Adventist writers charge that orthodox theologians have been overly dogmatic about the nature of man, while Adventists have maintained a guarded reserve. But Adventists have been equally dogmatic in denouncing the orthodox position. To be dogmatic one should have a sound, scholarly basis for his dogmatism, and such a basis exegetically speaking is conspicuously absent from the historical position of conditional immortalists. As mentioned above, Adventists generally confuse "immortality" with "eternal life." We quite agree that "a careful study of all the adjectives used in Scripture to qualify the word *spirit*, as applied to man, indicates that not one even remotely approaches the idea of immortality," as our Adventist brethren have stated. But as we have shown, "immortality" refers only to the resurrection body of the saints and to the nature of God himself. Therefore, since the saints are to be clothed with their resurrection bodies at the Second Advent, they do not now possess "immortality." For Adventists to confuse "immortality" with "eternal life" and then to argue that "immortality" means "eternal life" and is never applied to the spirit is logical and theological error.

The question of soul-sleep, however, should cause no serious division between Christians, since it does not affect the foundational doctrines of the Christian faith or the salvation of the soul. It is merely an area of theological debate and has no direct bearing upon any of the great doctrines of the Bible. The ground of fellowship is not the condition of man in death but faith in the Lord Jesus Christ and the love He commanded us to have one for another (John 13:34–35). Seventh-day Adventists are welcome to hold this doctrine, but when one is faced with such concrete Old Testament instances as Samuel's appearance to Saul (1 Samuel 28:18–19) and such New Testament accounts as those given by the apostle Paul (2 Corinthians 5:8), "to be absent from the body, and to be present with the Lord," or (Philippians 1:23) "to depart, and to be with Christ; which is far better," it is difficult to see how our Adventist brethren can sufficiently substantiate their claim for the "sleep of the soul."

III. Hell and Punishment As Taught in New Testament Greek

The grammar of the Greek New Testament teaches unquestionably the doctrine of hell and eternal punishment. Nowhere is this more pointedly brought out than in the following passages:

1. *Matthew 5:22 and 10:28:* "Whosoever shall say, Thou fool, shall be in danger of hell fire," and "Fear him which is able to destroy both soul and body in hell."

In both passages the Greek word *gehenna* portrays a place of punishment for the unsaved. *Gehenna* originally meant the Valley of Hinnom, a garbage dump that smoldered perpetually outside Jerusalem. The rabbis believed that punishment after death could be likened to *gehenna* and often threatened their people with punishment after death. The Lord Jesus Christ, however, pointed out to the unbelieving Jews that those who rejected Him could look forward to everlasting *gehenna.* In Matthew 10:28 He coupled *gehenna* with *apolesai,* which Thayer's Greek lexicon defines as "to be delivered up to eternal misery." Gehenna, then, symbolizes eternal separation and conscious punishment for the spiritual nature of the unregenerate man. This eternity of punishment is also taught in the Old

Testament; e.g., "Their worm shall not die, neither shall their fire be quenched" (Isaiah 66:24).

2. *2 Thessalonians 1:8–9:* "In flaming fire taking vengeance on them that know not God, and that obey not the gospel of our Lord Jesus Christ: Who shall be punished with everlasting destruction from the presence of the Lord and from the glory of his power."

From the context, "everlasting destruction" is to be that of "flaming fire," visited upon those who "obey not the gospel of our Lord Jesus Christ." The heart of the problem here is the meaning of the word *destruction,* which the Adventists claim is reduction to a state of nonexistence (*Questions on Doctrine,* 14). As a matter of fact, the Greek word *olethros* used here has the clear meaning of "ruining." (For this and the following lexical studies, any standard New Testament Greek lexicon or grammar bears out the meanings presented here.) We see, then, that everlasting destruction or "ruination" is the lot of those who know not God. Many people who are not well versed in Greek try to make "destruction" synonymous with "annihilation." This does violence to New Testament Greek, which supports no such concept. A common illustration will show the fallacy of this idea.

In the course of her work, a housewife may change a light bulb. What happens if it drops to the floor and breaks? It is, of course, "destroyed," but no one would say that it had been annihilated, for there is a difference between the function of an object and its nature. The function of the bulb is to give light. When broken, its function is destroyed, but the glass remains, although in fragments, and so does the metal base. Although the bulb has been "ruined" or "destroyed," it certainly has not been "reduced to nothing."

The Bible teaches that unregenerate mankind will suffer the eternal wrath of God and must undergo destruction and ruin of their original function, which was "to glorify God and to enjoy Him forever." But the human spirit, created in the image of God (Genesis 1:26–27), remains intact, a spiritual entity of eternal existence, capable of enduring eternally the righteous and just Judge.

3. *Revelation 20:10:* "The devil who deceived them was cast into the lake of fire and brimstone where the beast and the false prophet are, and they will be tormented day and night into the everlasting of the everlasting" (literal translation).

The root meaning of the Greek word *basanizo* is "to torment, to be harassed, to torture or to vex with grievous pain," and is used throughout the New Testament to denote great conscious pain and misery, never annihilation or cessation of consciousness. The reader who wishes to pursue this point may look up the following verses where this word is used: Matthew 8:6, 29; Mark 5:7; Luke 8:28; Revelation 14:10–11. In each place, *basanizo* means conscious "torment." In Revelation 14:10–11, speaking of the followers of the Beast, unmistakably it means torment or punishment, everlasting or never-ceasing.

In Revelation 20:10, Satan, the beast, and the false prophet are described as tormented (*basanis thesontai*) "day and night into the everlasting of the everlasting." So if language means anything at all, in these contexts alone the theory of annihilation, or, as the Adventists say, the final destruction of the wicked, is itself annihilated.

4. *John 3:36:* "He that believeth on the Son hath everlasting life: and he that believeth not the Son shall not see life; but the wrath of God abideth on him."

Our fourth and final grammatical point relative to the doctrine of annihilation is made by coupling Romans 2:8–9 and Revelation 14:10 with John 3:36. Jesus tells us that the one who believes in the Lord Jesus Christ already has everlasting life (present tense); and then, of one who "believeth not the Son," he states that he "shall not see life, but the wrath of God abideth on him." The Greek word *menei*, here translated *abide*, appears several times in the New Testament. It carries the idea of continuous action (see John 1:33; 2:12; 8:31; 15:9). Thus, in John 3:36 the Holy Spirit says that the wrath of God continually abides on the one who "believeth not the Son." Comparing this with Romans 2:8–9, we see that those who do not obey the truth but do evil are the objects of God's wrath, which Revelation 14:10–11 describes as eternal. "The same shall drink of the wine of the wrath of God . . . and the smoke of their torment ascendeth up for ever and ever: and they have no rest day nor night."

Orges, translated "wrath," appears in each of the verses cited, so there can be no doubt that the same subject is being discussed. It is apparent then that, far from the comparatively blissful prospect of total annihilation, those who "believeth not the Son shall not see life,"[48] and "the wrath of God abideth on him."[49] God's wrath even now hangs like the sword of Damocles over the heads of those who deny Jesus Christ. It will strike when the rebellious soul goes into eternity and appears before the bar of God's eternal justice.

Seventh-day Adventists should not be ostracized because they cling to this doctrine, since they believe that an undetermined period of punishment will elapse before the actual ultimate destruction of the wicked with Satan and his host.

Dr. Francis Pieper, the great Lutheran scholar and author of the monumental *Christian Dogmatics,* states my views in essence when he says:

> Holy Scripture teaches the truth of an eternal damnation so clearly and emphatically that one cannot deny it without, at the same time, rejecting the authority of Scripture. Scripture parallels the eternal salvation of the believers and the eternal damnation of the unbelievers. Whoever therefore denies the one must, to be consistent, deny the other (Matthew 25:46). We find the same juxtaposition and antithesis in other passages of Scripture. This parallelism proves that the term eternity in the sense of limited duration as sometimes used in Holy Writ, is inapplicable here. We must take the predicate eternal in its proper or strict sense, a sense of *sine fine* in all Scripture texts that use it to describe the duration and the penalties of the wicked in yonder life (see 2 Thessalonians 1:9; Matthew 18:8; Mark 3:29). . . . The objections raised in all ages to the endlessness of the infernal punishment are understandable; for the thought of a never-ending agony of rational beings fully realizing their distressing plight is so appalling that it exceeds comprehension. But all objections are based on the false principle that it is proper and reasonable to make our human sentiments and judgments the measure of God's essence and activity.

---

[48]i.e., personal communion or fellowship with Christ. Spiritual death is the opposite of eternal life in that the soul is deprived of such communion or fellowship and is conscious of it.

[49]Death (spiritual), far from being unconsciousness, is eternal conscious endurance of God's just wrath.

This is the case in particular with those who contend that an everlasting punishment of a part of mankind does not agree with the unity of God's world plan, or that it is compatible neither with divine love nor with divine justice, who accordingly substitute for eternal damnation eventual salvation by gradual improvement in the next life, or an immediate or later annihilation of the wicked. Against such views we must maintain the general principle that God's essence, attributes, and actions exceed our comprehension, that we can therefore not know *a priori* but only from God's revelation in His Word what agrees or conflicts with God's essence and attributes. The nature of eternal damnation consists in eternal banishment from the sight of God or, in other words, in being forever excluded from communion with God. . . . To illustrate the terrible agony setting in with this banishment from the sight of God, the dogmatician points to the agony of the fish removed from its element. But there is this difference; the fish that is removed from its element soon dies, whereas the man who is banished from communion with God must by God's judgment live on, "is guilty of eternal judgment" (Mark 3:29).[50]

Seventh-day Adventists would do well to heed Dr. Pieper's observation as well as the testimony of the Christian church generally for the last two thousand years. But most important, they should heed the teaching of the Word of God that the soul of man, whether regenerate or unregenerate, exists after the death of the body. The justice of God makes everlasting punishment for the unregenerate and everlasting life for the saved to be two sides of one coin—God's justice and God's love. We believe the Bible clearly teaches that there is neither authority nor warrant for the doctrines of conditional immortality and annihilation. God grant in the fullness of His wisdom that none of His children will persist in setting up their standards as the criterion to determine His perfect righteousness. It is my opinion that Seventh-day Adventists have done just this; first by predicating that a God of love would not eternally punish a conscious being, and second by attempting to force the Scriptures into their frame of thought while seeming to ignore context, hermeneutics, and exegesis. Their fellow Christians can only pray that they may soon be led to embrace the historical position of the church, which is the antithesis of the sleep of the soul and the annihilation of the wicked.

The Sabbath, the Lord's Day, and the Mark of the Beast

Certainly the most distinctive doctrine promulgated by the Seventh-day Adventist denomination, and one of the two from which they derive their name, is the Seventh-day Sabbath. How Adventists came to hold the Sabbath as the true day of worship, and why they continue to champion it and jealously urge it upon all who worship on Sunday, provides the key to understanding their psychological and theological motivations.

I. The Sabbath or the Lord's Day

Seventh-day Adventists from the beginning have always attempted to equate the Sabbath with the Lord's Day. Their principal method for accomplishing this

---

[50]Francis Pieper, *Christian Dogmatics* (Grand Rapids, Mich.: Zondervan Publishing House, n.d. (reprint), 3:544–55.

is to link Mark 2:28 with Revelation 1:10, and thus to undercut one of the strongest arguments against their position, i.e., the Lord's Day as opposed to Sabbath observance.

They reason that since "the Son of Man is Lord also of the sabbath" (Mark 2:27–28), when John says he "was in the Spirit on the Lord's day" (Revelation 1:10), the Sabbath and the Lord's Day must be the same! The weakness of their position is that they base their argument on an English translation instead of on the Greek original. When one reads the second chapter of Mark and the first chapter of Revelation in Greek, he sees that there is no such interpretation inherent in the grammatical structure. The Greek of Mark 2:28 clearly indicates that Christ did not mean that the Sabbath was His possession (which the Adventists would like to establish); rather, He was saying that as Lord of all, He could do as He pleased on the Sabbath. The Greek is most explicit here.

Nothing could be clearer from both the context and the grammar. In Revelation 1:10 the Greek is not the genitive of possession, which it would have to be in order to make *te-kuriake* (the Lord's) agree with *hemera* (day). John did not mean that the Lord's Day was the Lord's possession, but rather that it was the day dedicated to Him by the early church, not in accordance with Mosaic law, but in obedience to our Lord's commandment of love.

We may certainly assume that if the Sabbath had meant so much to the writers of the New Testament, and if, as Adventists insist, it was so widely observed during the early centuries of the Christian church, John and the other writers of Scripture would have equated it with the Lord's Day, the first day of the week. Scripture and history testify that they did not, and Adventists have, therefore, little scriptural justification for their Sabbatarianism.

A. Testimony of the Fathers[51]

The church fathers provide a mass of evidence that the first day of the week, not the seventh, is the Lord's Day. Some of this evidence is here submitted for the reader's consideration. In company with the overwhelming majority of historians and scholars, we believe that not only the New Testament but the following citations refute Sabbatarianism. We have yet to see any systematic answer to what the Christian church has always believed.

1. *Ignatius, Bishop of Antioch,* in the year A.D. 110, wrote, "If, then, those who walk in the ancient practices attain to newness of hope, no longer observing the Sabbath, but fashioning their lives after the Lord's Day on which our life also arose through Him, that we may be found disciples of Jesus Christ, our only teacher."

2. *Justin Martyr* (100–165): "And on the day called Sunday, all who live in cities or in the country gather together in one place and memoirs of the apostles or the writings of the prophets are read, as long as time permits. . . . Sunday is the day on which we all hold our common assembly because it is the first day on which God, having wrought a change in the darkness in matter, made the world; and Jesus Christ our Saviour on the same day rose from the dead."

3. *The Epistle of Barnabas* (between 120 and 150): " 'Your new moons and your Sabbaths I cannot endure' (Isaiah 1:13). You perceive how He speaks: Your pres-

[51]Early Church Fathers, *www.ccel.org/fathers2/*.

ent Sabbaths are not acceptable to me but that which I had made in giving rest to all things, I shall make a beginning of the eighth day, that is a beginning of another world. Wherefore also, we keep the eighth day with joyfulness, a day also in which Jesus rose from the dead."

4. *Irenaeus, Bishop of Lyons* (about 178): "The mystery of the Lord's resurrection may not be celebrated on any other day than the Lord's Day."

5. *Bardaisan* (born 154): "Wherever we be, all of us are called by the one name of the Messiah, namely Christians and upon one day, which is the first day of the week, we assemble ourselves together and on the appointed days we abstain from food."

6. *Cyprian, Bishop of Carthage* (200–258): "The Lord's Day is both the first and the eighth day."

7. *Eusebius* (about 315): "The churches throughout the rest of the world observe the practice that has prevailed from the apostolic tradition until the present time so that it would not be proper to terminate our fast on any other day but the resurrection day of our Saviour. Hence, there were synods and convocations of our bishops on this question and they unanimously drew up an ecclesiastical decree which they communicated to churches in all places—that the mystery of the Lord's resurrection should be celebrated on no other than the Lord's day."

8. *Peter, Bishop of Alexandria* (about 300): "We keep the Lord's Day as a day of joy because of Him who arose thereon."

9. *Didache of the Apostles* (about 70–75): "On the Lord's own day, gather yourselves together and break bread and give thanks."

10. *The Epistle of Pliny* (about 112, addressed to the Emperor Trajan): "They [the Christians] affirmed . . . that the whole of their crime or error was that they had been wont to meet together on a fixed day before daylight and to repeat among themselves in turn a hymn to Christ as to a god and to bind themselves by an oath (*sacramentum*). . . . These things duly done, it had been their custom to disperse and to meet again to take food—of an ordinary and harmless kind. Even this they had ceased to do after my edict, by which, in accordance with your instructions, I had forbidden the existence of societies."

Thus it appears that from apostolic and patristic times, the Christian church observed the Lord's Day or the first day of the week; further, the Jewish Sabbath, in the words of Clement of Alexandria (about 194) was "nothing more than a working day."

In their zeal to establish the authority of the Sabbath, Adventists either reject contrary evidence as unauthentic (and so they conflict with the preponderance of scholastic opinion), or they ignore the testimony of the early church. Although they seem unaffected by the evidence, the fact remains that the Christian church has both apostolic and historical support for observing the Lord's Day in place of the Sabbath.

B. "Authoritative Quotations"

Recently the Adventist radio program *Voice of Prophecy* circulated a thirty-one-page pamphlet entitled *Authoritative Quotations on the Sabbath and Sunday*. In it they quoted "leading" Protestant sources to "prove" that Sunday usurped the Sabbath and is a pagan institution imposed by Constantine in A.D. 321.

However, many of the sources quoted actually establish what the Adventists flatly deny; i.e., that the Seventh-day Sabbath is not the Lord's Day or the first day of the week, but is, in fact, the seventh day, as its name indicates.

Since the Adventists are willing to quote these authorities to buttress their position in one area, surely they will give consideration to contradictory statements by these same authorities in another:

1. "The Lord's Day did not succeed in the place of the Sabbath. . . . The Lord's Day was merely an ecclesiastical institution. . . . The primitive Christians did all manner of work upon the Lord's Day" (Bishop Jeremy Taylor, *Ductor Dubitantium*, Part 1, Book 2, Chapter 2, Rule 6, Sections 51, 59).

2. "The observance of the Lord's Day [Sunday] is founded not on any command of God, but on the authority of the church" (*Augsburg Confession of Faith*, quoted in *Catholic Sabbath Manual*, Part 2, Chapter 1, Section 10).

3. "But they err in teaching that Sunday has taken the place of the Old Testament Sabbath and therefore must be kept as the seventh day had to be kept by the children of Israel" (J. T. Mueller, *Sabbath or Sunday*, 15–16).

4. "They [the Catholics] allege the Sabbath changed into Sunday, the Lord's Day, contrary to the Decalogue as it appears; neither is there any example more boasted than the changing of the Sabbath Day" (Martin Luther, *Augsburg Confession of Faith*, Article 28, Paragraph 9).

5. "Although it [Sunday] was in primitive times and differently called the Lord's Day or Sunday, yet it was never denominated the Sabbath, a name constantly appropriate to Saturday, or the seventh day both by sacred and ecclesiastical writers" (Charles Buck, *A Theological Dictionary*, 1850, 537).

6. "The notion of a formal substitution by apostolic authority of the Lord's Day [meaning Sunday] for the Jewish Sabbath (or the first for the seventh day). . . . The transference to it, perhaps in a spiritualized form of the Sabbath obligation established by promulgation of the fourth commandment, has no basis whatever either in Holy Scripture or in Christian antiquity" (Sir William Smith and Samuel Cheetham, *A Dictionary of Christian Antiquities*, Volume 2, 182, article on the Sabbath).

7. "The view that the Christian's Lord's Day or Sunday is but the Christian Sabbath deliberately transferred from the seventh to the first day of the week does not indeed find categorical expression till a much later period. . . . The Council of Laodicea (A.D. 364) . . . forbids Christians from Judaizing and resting on the Sabbath Day, preferring the Lord's Day and so far as possible resting as Christians" (*Encyclopedia Britannica*, 1899 ed., Volume 23, 654).

Thus the Adventists have, in effect, destroyed their argument by appealing to authorities who state unequivocally that the first day of the week is the Lord's Day and that it was observed by the early Christian church from the time of the apostles.

It should also be carefully noted that in their *Authoritative Quotations*, the Adventists overlook the fact that nearly all the authorities argue forcefully for the Lord's Day as the first day of the week, and state that legal observance of the Sabbath terminated at the cross (Colossians 2:16–17). The Adventists also, in their compilation of quotations, appeal even to the Church of Jesus Christ of Latter-day Saints (Mormon), and to Fulton Ousler, a Roman Catholic laywriter.

The Mormons are a non-Christian cult, a fact that the Adventists admit; and Ousler, a layman, hardly represents the position of Rome.

On page thirteen of this same pamphlet, the Adventists make misleading use of the ellipsis. The following is a direct quotation as it appears:

> Sunday (*dies-solis*, of the Roman calendar, day of the sun, because dedicated to the sun), was adopted by the early Christians as a day of worship. The sun of Latin adoration they interpreted as the "sun of righteousness." . . . No regulations for its observance are laid down in the New Testament, nor, indeed, is its observance even enjoined. (Schaff-Herzog, *Encyclopedia of Religious Knowledge*, 1891 ed., Volume 4, Article on Sunday)

Now here is the paragraph as it appears in the *Encyclopedia*:

> Sunday (*dies-solis*, of the Roman Calendar, day of the sun, because dedicated to the sun), was adopted by the early Christians as a day of worship. The sun of Latin adoration they interpreted as "the sun of righteousness." SUNDAY WAS EMPHATICALLY THE WEEKLY FEAST OF THE RESURRECTION OF CHRIST, AS THE JEWISH SABBATH WAS THE FEAST OF THE CREATION. IT WAS CALLED THE "LORD'S DAY," AND UPON IT THE PRIMITIVE CHURCH ASSEMBLED TO BREAK BREAD (Acts 20:7; 1 Corinthians 16:2). No regulations for its observance are laid down in the New Testament, nor, indeed, is its observance even enjoined; YET CHRISTIAN FEELING LED TO THE UNIVERSAL ADOPTION OF THE DAY, IN IMITATION OF APOSTOLIC PRECEDENCE. IN THE SECOND CENTURY ITS OBSERVANCE WAS UNIVERSAL. (Sentences in capital letters were omitted by the writer of the Adventist pamphlet on page 22. This mutilation of authoritative sources first occurs in *The Present Truth*, Volume 1, Number 9, published in the 1880s. So our Adventist brethren apparently failed to check the quotation's validity.)

Such use of the ellipsis is not uncommon in certain Seventh-day Adventists' writings in connection with the Sabbath, the Lord's Day, etc., and we regret that they resort to it in order to substantiate their position.

In this pamphlet they quote Martin Luther, despite the well-known fact that Luther violently opposed Sabbatarianism. His refutation of his Sabbatarian colleague, Dr. Carlstadt, is a monument to his apologetic genius. Thus, to quote Luther in order to support the doctrine of the Seventh-day Sabbath suggests that Adventists are not familiar with Luther's theology.

We admire the boldness of our Adventist brethren in their claims for the Sabbath, but their boldness is misplaced and leads to a distorted concept of the value of the law of God, for when a person believes and teaches that "the fourth commandment is the greatest commandment in the Decalogue," it is apparent that he has no understanding of the spirit of the law. Volume 4 of the *International Standard Bible Encyclopedia* represents the reasons why the Christian church observes the Lord's Day in preference to the Sabbath, and also clearly states (2629–2634) the Seventh-day Adventist position.[52] On page 2633 the Adventists

---

[52]Bible Question Column in *Signs of the Times* (January 8, 1952).

contend: "According to church history the seventh-day Sabbath was observed by the early church, and no other day was observed as a Sabbath during the first two or three centuries."

This sentence epitomizes the Adventist propensity for overstating their case; i.e., attempting to read "Sabbath" into "Lord's Day," which all leading authorities confute as we have seen.

II. Primary Anti-Sabbatarian Texts

In more than one place, the New Testament comments unfavorably upon the practice of any type of legalistic day-keeping. In fact, from the ascension of Christ on, the New Testament or early church observed the first day of the week or the Lord's Day (Revelation 1:10), as we have endeavored to show. Besides the passages that contrast the Lord's Day with the Sabbath, the apostle Paul—Hebrew of the Hebrews and Pharisee of the Pharisees, apart from our Lord, the outstanding New Testament authority—on the Law of Moses declared that the Sabbath as "the law" was fulfilled at the cross and was not binding upon the Christian (Colossians 2:16–17). Since the subject is so vast in scope, the reader is referred to the bibliography, especially to Dr. Louis Sperry Chafer's *Grace,* and Norman C. Deck's *The Lord's Day or the Sabbath, Which?* These contain excellent refutations of Sabbatarianism. D. M. Canright in *Seventh-day Adventism Renounced* also dealt exhaustively and ably with the Sabbath subject.

To narrow the issue down to simple analysis, we shall review the major New Testament texts that in context and in the light of syntactical analysis refute the Sabbatarian concept, and substantiate the historical position of the Christian church since the days of the apostles and the Fathers.

A. Colossians 2:13–17

Of all of the statements in the New Testament, these verses most strongly refute the Sabbatarian claim for observance of the Jewish Sabbath. Let us listen to the inspired counsel of Paul, not only the greatest of the apostles, but once a Pharisee whose passion for fulfilling the law outperformed that of the most zealous Seventh-day Adventist:

> And you, who were dead in trespasses and the uncircumcision of your flesh, God made alive together with him, having forgiven us all our trespasses, having canceled the bond which stood against us with its legal demands; this he set aside, nailing it to the cross. He disarmed the principalities and powers and made a public example of them, triumphing over them in him. Therefore let no one pass judgment on you in questions of food and drink or with regard to a festival or a new moon or a sabbath. These are only a shadow of what is to come; but the substance belongs to Christ. (Colossians 2:13–17 RSV)

This translation, one of the best from the Greek text today, contains tremendously important teaching.

First, we who were dead have been made alive in Christ and have been forgiven all trespasses and sins. We are free from the condemnation of the law in all its aspects, because Christ took our condemnation on the cross. As already observed, there are not two laws, moral and ceremonial, but one law containing many commandments, all perfectly fulfilled by the life and death of the Lord Jesus Christ.

"Therefore," the apostle Paul boldly declares, "let no one pass judgment on you in questions of food and drink or with regard to a festival or a new moon or a sabbath. These are only a shadow of what is to come; but the substance belongs to Christ."

In the face of this clear teaching, Sabbatarians revert to their dual-law theory and argue that Paul is referring only to observance of the Jewish ceremonial law, not to the Sabbath, which, they insist, is a moral precept because it is one of the Ten Commandments. We have seen, however, that the Ten Commandments are but a fragment of the moral law encompassed by the commandment "Thou shalt love thy neighbor as thyself" (Leviticus 19:18; Romans 13:9).

Sabbatarians overlook the mass of contradictory evidence and appeal to certain commentators who do not analyze the uses of the word *Sabbath,* or exegete the New Testament passages where the word occurs. Such commentators are Albert Barnes, *Notes on the New Testament;* Jamieson, Fausset, and Brown, *Critical and Explanatory Commentary;* and Adam Clarke in his *Commentary.* If a commentator's opinion is not in accord with sound exegesis, it is *only an opinion,* and the commentators named above make no grammatical or textual analysis of the second chapter of Colossians!

Many New Testament commentators try to retain the moral force of the Sabbath (although all of these transfer it to the first day of the week) because it is the subject of the fourth commandment. For this serious theological error, there is no warrant in the New Testament. Sabbatarians fail to mention that all the commentators whom they cite repudiate the Sabbath, and most of them teach that the true Sabbath was the Lord's Day (Revelation 1:10), carried over by the early church from apostolic tradition as a memorial to redemption or the re-creation of mankind through the regenerative power of the Holy Spirit. Adventists are, therefore, without historical or exegetical support when they make the Lord's Day the same as the Sabbath.

With regard to this passage, Adventists maintain that since the word in Colossians 2:16 (*sabbaton*) is in the plural, it means the ceremonial Sabbaths, not the weekly Sabbath, which they contend is still in effect. However, their argument seems to be that Colossians 2:16–17 refers to Sabbaths and feast days that were shadows of things to come, and thus part of ceremonial laws; but that the Seventh-day Sabbath is not a shadow of redemption, but a memorial of Creation and part of the moral law. The leading modern translations, following the best New Testament scholars, render Colossians 2:16 as "a Sabbath" or "a Sabbath day," not "sabbath days" as in the King James Version. Their reason for doing this is well stated by W. E. Vine:

> *Sabbaton* or *sabbata,* the latter the plural form, was transliterated from the Aramaic word, which was mistaken for a plural: hence the singular *sabbaton* was formed from it. . . . In the epistles the only direct mentions are in Colossians 2:16 "a Sabbath day" (RV), which rightly has the singular . . . where it is listed among things that were "a shadow of things to come"; i.e., of the age introduced at Pentecost, and in Hebrews 4:4–11 where the

perpetual *sabbatismos* is appointed for believers. . . . For the first three centuries of the Christian era the first day of the week was never confounded with the Sabbath; the confusion of the Jewish and Christian institutions was due to declension from apostolic teaching.[53]

Supplementing Dr. Vine's statement is the comment of M. R. Vincent:

Sabbath days (*sabbaton*), the weekly festivals revised correctly as day, the plural being used for the singular. See Luke 4:31 and Acts 20:7. The plural is only once used in the New Testament of more than a single day (Acts 17:2). In the Old Testament, the same enumeration of sacred seasons occurs in 1 Chronicles 23:31; 2 Chronicles 2:4; 2 Chronicles 31:3; Ezekiel 45:17; Hosea 2:11.[54]

As Dr. Vincent points out, the revisers' rendering of *sabbaton* in the singular accords with the use of the word throughout the New Testament. It is significant that in fifty-nine of sixty occurrences in the New Testament, Adventists affirm that they refer to the *weekly* Sabbath; but in the sixtieth occurrence they maintain it does not, although all grammatical authorities contradict them.

With regard to Albert Barnes, whom the Adventists delight to quote because he agrees with their interpretation of Colossians 2, his comments are demolished by Dean Henry Alford, a truly great biblical exegete whom the Adventists also frequently quote. Wrote Dean Alford concerning Colossians 2:

Let no one therefore judge you (pronounce judgment of right or wrong over you, sit in judgment on you) . . . in respect of feasts or new moon, or Sabbaths (i.e., yearly, monthly, or weekly celebrations). (The relative may refer either to the aggregate of the observances mentioned, or to the last mentioned, i.e., the Sabbath. Or it may refer to all.)[55]

After making significant comments on the grammar, Dean Alford went even further in his insistence that in verse seventeen, grammatically speaking, the apostle Paul contrasts all the Jewish laws with their fulfillment in Christ, the former being a shadow, pointing forward to the real substance (*soma*), which was Christ. Alford summed up his comments thus:

The blessings of the Christian covenant: These are the substance, and the Jewish ordinances the mere type of resemblance, as the shadow is of the living man. . . . We may observe that if the ordinance of the Sabbath had been in any form of lasting obligation on the Christian church, it would have been quite impossible for the apostle to have spoken thus. The fact of an obligatory rest of one day, whether the seventh or the first, would have been directly in the teeth of his assertion here: The holding of such would have been still to retain the shadow, while we possess the substance. And no

[53]W. E. Vine, *An Expository Dictionary of New Testament Words* (Old Tappan, N.J.: Fleming H. Revell Company, 1940), 311–13.

[54]M. R. Vincent, *Word Studies in the New Testament* (MacDill AFB, Fl.: MacDonald Publishing Company, n.d.), 2:494.

[55]D. H. Alford, *The New Testament for English Readers* (Grand Rapids, Mich.: William B. Eerdmans Publishing Company, n.d.), 1299–300.

answer can be given to this by the transparent special-pleading, that he is speaking only of that which was Jewish in such observances: the whole argument being general, and the axiom of verse seventeen universally applicable.[56]

We see that, from a grammatical standpoint, if the Adventists insist that Colossians 2:16 refers only to ceremonial Sabbaths, they run against the use of the word for weekly Sabbaths in the entire New Testament; and, as Alford points out, if "Sabbaths" be allowed, it must include all Sabbaths, weekly, monthly, or yearly. On the other hand, if Adventists admit to the correction of the revisers and render Colossians 2:16 "a Sabbath day," its use in the New Testament still refers almost exclusively (see Acts 17:2) to the weekly Sabbath, which Adventists maintain is permanent, although Paul deliberately classes it with the penalty for violating the ordinances that Christ by His death nailed to the cross! (Colossians 2:14).

Dr. J. B. Lightfoot, an acknowledged authority on New Testament Greek, makes this interesting observation:

> The word *sabbata* is derived from the Aramaic *shabbatha* (as distinguished from the Hebrew), and accordingly preserves the Aramaic termination of "a." Hence it was naturally declined as a plural noun, *sabbata, sabbaton.* The New Testament *sabbata* is only once used distinctively as more than a single day, and there the plurality of meaning is brought out by the attached numeral (Acts 17:2).[57]

It is apparent, therefore, that the use of "Sabbath" in the New Testament refutes the Adventist contention that in Colossians 2 it means Sabbaths other than the weekly Sabbath of the Decalogue. Since it is impossible to retain the "shadow" while possessing the "substance" (Colossians 2:17), the Jewish Sabbath and the handwriting of ordinances "which was contrary to us" found their complete fulfillment in the person and work of the Lord Jesus Christ.

Seventh-day Adventists are also deprived of the support of Albert Barnes, because he admits that if Paul had "used the word in the singular number, 'the Sabbath,' it would then of course have been clear that he meant to teach that that commandment had ceased to be binding and that a Sabbath was no longer to be observed.[58]

Since Barnes makes this admission, and since modern conservative scholarship establishes the singular rendering of "Sabbath" in the New Testament (see RSV, et al.), Adventists find even less support for their position.

We conclude our comments on this passage of Scripture by observing that in Numbers 28 and 29, which list the very "ordinances" referred to in Colossians 2:16–17, the Sabbath is grouped with burnt offerings and new moons (Numbers 28:1–15). Since these offerings and feasts have passed away as the shadow (*skia*), fulfilled in the substance (*soma*) of the cross of Christ, how can the Seventh-day Sabbath be retained? In light of this Scripture alone, I contend that the argument

---

[56]Ibid., 1300.

[57]D. H, Alford, *Commentary on Colossians* (Grand Rapids, Mich.: William B. Eerdmans Publishing Company, n.d.), 225.

[58]Alford, *The New Testament for English Readers,* 229.

for Sabbath observance collapses, and the Christian stands under "the perfect law of liberty," which enables him to fulfill "the righteousness of the law" by the imperative of love.

B. Galatians 4:9–11

> But now that you have come to know God, or rather to be known by God, how can you turn back again to the weak and beggarly elemental spirits, whose slaves you want to be once more? You observe days, and months, and seasons, and years! I am afraid I have labored over you in vain. (RSV)

Paul's epistle to the Galatians was primarily a massive theological effort to bolster the young church against the Judaizers who added to the gospel of grace "another gospel" (1:6), and sought to "pervert the gospel of Christ" (1:7).

Though steeped in Jewish lore and the law of Moses, Paul steadfastly opposed the Judaizers. The entire epistle to the Galatians is an apologetic against those who would seek to bring the Christian "under the law." After mentioning the errors into which the Galatian church had fallen, Paul, evidently with great disgust, remarks, "You observe days, and months, and seasons, and years! I am afraid I have labored over you in vain." In the Greek, the expression "days, and months, and seasons, and years," matches both the Septuagint (Greek) translation of the ordinances in Numbers 28 and 29, of which all Sabbaths are a principal part, and the ordinances mentioned in Colossians 2. Paul was familiar with the Septuagint and quoted it, and the law, including the weekly Sabbaths, was so cherished by the Judaizers of his day that its legalistic observance called forth his strong words. Adventists insist that Paul meant ceremonial feasts and yearly Sabbaths, not the weekly Sabbath; but Paul's language and the Septuagint translation of Numbers 28 and 29 refute their objections. It is one thing to interpret your way out of a verse when your interpretation is feasible; it is another to ignore grammar, context, and comparative textual analysis (hermeneutics) as our Adventist friends and others appear to do. To substantiate their interpretation of Paul's statements, they do not practice exegesis (taking out of), but eisegesis (reading into) the texts.

After studying Seventh-day Adventist literature, it is my opinion that the overwhelming majority of Seventh-day Adventists do not actually consider themselves "under the law." I believe they fail to realize that by trying to enjoin Sabbath observance upon other members of the body of Christ, they are in serious danger of transgressing the Gospel of grace. To them Paul says,

> Tell me, you who desire to be under the law, do you not hear the law? . . . Now before faith came, we were confined under the law, kept under restraint until faith should be revealed. So that the law was our custodian until Christ came, that we might be justified by faith. But now that faith has come, we are no longer under a custodian; for in Christ Jesus you are all sons of God, through faith. (Galatians 4:21; 3:23–26 RSV)

Bearing in mind that "the law" in its larger connotation includes the entire Pentateuch, it is apparent from Paul's language that one is "under the law" when he attempts to observe any part of it, because the Christian has been freed from the law. Seventh-day Adventists are doubtless Christians, saved by grace, but we do not find scriptural warrant for their attempt to enjoin the Sabbath upon their fellow believers.

C. Romans 13:8–10

> Owe no one anything, except to love one another; for he who loves his neighbor has fulfilled the law. The commandments, "You shall not commit adultery, You shall not kill, You shall not steal, You shall not covet," and any other commandment, are summed up in this sentence, "You shall love your neighbor as yourself." Love does no wrong to a neighbor; therefore love is the fulfilling of the law. (RSV)

It is really unnecessary to comment extensively upon the foregoing verses, because they speak plainly for themselves.

The Greek word *pleroma*, translated respectively "fulfilled" and "fulfilling" in Romans 13:8–10 (RSV) appears ninety times in the New Testament and has the same basic meaning. The apostle Paul surely understood this term; since the Adventists confess the divine inspiration of the Scriptures, they must concede that the Holy Spirit guided his pen. Quoting from the Decalogue upon which the Adventists rely for perpetual Sabbath-keeping, Paul declares, "The commandments . . . are summed up in this sentence, 'You shall love your neighbor as yourself.' Love does no wrong to a neighbor; therefore love is the fulfilling of the law." In verse eight the apostle declares, "He who loves his neighbor has fulfilled the law"; and since he quotes from the Decalogue as part of the law, the fourth commandment is also fulfilled, not by rigid observance of a given day, but by loving one's neighbor as oneself! Since it is impossible in the Christian context to love one's neighbor at all apart from loving God as the prerequisite, the issue is clear. The false teaching that love of one's neighbor does not fulfill all the law of God comes from a failure to realize that our love for God and neighbor stems from God's initiating act of love in Christ. This law of love is first enunciated in Leviticus 19:18, which our Lord coupled with the commandment to "love the Lord thy God" (Deuteronomy 6:4–5), and stated that observance of those two commandments fulfilled "all the law and the prophets."

While our Adventist brethren may seek to escape the implications of Colossians 2:14–17 and to explain away Galatians 4:9–11, in the present passage, the Holy Spirit twice declares that love fulfills the law. They cannot exempt the Sabbath from this context without destroying the unity of the "Eternal Ten," hence their dilemma.

In Galatians Paul also declares, "The whole law is fulfilled in one word, 'You shall love your neighbor as yourself'" (5:14 RSV). So we see that Paul's theology rested upon the imperative of love. Therefore, it is my conviction that the Holy Spirit, not the Christian church, is the authority for the nullification of all Sabbath-keeping. How any student of New Testament Greek could read the unmistakable language of the apostle and then exclude the Sabbath commandment from his argument passes my understanding.

D. Romans 14:4–6, 10, 12–13

Who are you to pass judgment on the servant of another? It is before
his own master that he stands or falls. And he will be upheld, for the Master
is able to make him stand. One man esteems one day as better than another,
while another man esteems all days alike. Let every one be fully convinced
in his own mind. He who observes the day, observes it in honor of the Lord.
He also who eats, eats in honor of the Lord, since he gives thanks to God;
while he who abstains, abstains in honor of the Lord and gives thanks to
God. . . . Why do you pass judgment on your brother? Or you, why do you
despise your brother? For we shall all stand before the judgment seat of
God. . . . So each of us shall give account of himself to God. Then let us no
more pass judgment on one another, but rather decide never to put a stumbling-block or hindrance in the way of a brother (RSV).

In this writer's opinion, and according to Romans 14, the Seventh-day
Adventist is entitled to observe the seventh-day Sabbath if he feels that this is what
God desires. Further than this, the Holy Spirit adjures us not to "pass judgment"
on our fellow Christians regarding such matters as observance of days and diet. I
believe that Seventh-day Adventists, Seventh-day Baptists, and Sabbatarians of
other religious groups have the right to worship on the seventh day in the liberty
wherein Christ has made us free. It is wrong and unchristian to discriminate
against Sabbatarians merely because they "esteem" the Sabbath above the first
day of the week, or the Lord's Day. I suggest it is no more legalistic for them to
observe the seventh day out of conviction than it is for the Christian church to
observe the first day. It is a matter of liberty and conscience.

If Seventh-day Adventists, however, would follow the biblical teaching of
Romans 14 with regard to those who wish to observe Sunday, we would not have
the conflict that has been generated by their dogmatic insistence that all should
worship on the Sabbath. The sad fact is, however, that all Sabbatarians transgress
the very counsels given by the apostle Paul in the above cited passage.

Of course, Seventh-day Adventists feel that they are called upon to perpetuate or promulgate certain truths that they believe are found in the Word of God,
and which they believe are to be emphasized in "these last days." Furthermore,
they believe that the counsels of Ellen G. White emphasize the importance of
these truths. Granting their basic premise that God has indeed spoken to them
concerning Sabbath observance, it is easy to see the source of their zeal. But I
feel that there is good evidence that the "Spirit of prophecy" is not what they
claim; and their "special truths" have, to say the least, questionable theological
origins. Non-Adventists reject the claims that they make for White, and merely
because Adventists accept her counsel is no reason for other Christians to feel
bound to do so. We repeat—the faith the Adventists place in "the Spirit of prophecy," which has endorsed their "special truths," sincere though they may be, does
not entitle them to contradict the counsel of the Holy Spirit as revealed in the
Word of God. This I believe they have done. I could cite scores of references from
contemporary Adventist writers who do, indeed, pass judgment upon their Christian brethren and upon the Christian church at large, because the latter do not
observe the Seventh-day Sabbath. It is my opinion in these cases that they neglect
the counsel of the Holy Spirit: "One man esteems one day as better than another,

while another man esteems all days alike. Let everyone be fully convinced in his own mind. He who observes the day, observes it in honor of the Lord. . . . Happy is he who has no reason to judge himself for what he approves . . . for whatever does not proceed from faith is sin" (Romans 14:5–6, 22–23 RSV).

By contending that other members of the body of Christ should recognize "the Spirit of prophecy," Seventh-day Adventists appear to juxtapose the "Spirit of prophecy" with the Holy Spirit, who says, "Then let us no more pass judgment on one another, but rather decide never to put a stumbling block or hindrance in the way of a brother" (v. 13).

There can be little doubt that the great majority of Christians who worship on Sunday would never have discriminated against the Seventh-day Adventists, had the latter not insisted upon "passing judgment" on first-day observance as opposed to Sabbath-keeping. Although motivated by the best intentions and sincere in faith, Adventists have, nevertheless, put a stumbling block or hindrance in the way of fellow Christians by their rigid Sabbatarianism. It is, indeed, unfortunate that such a source of strife exists among Christians.

The fourteenth chapter of Romans is a masterpiece on the subject of Christian liberty, not only in diet but in worship, and in the context of all Paul's writings on the subject it appears that Adventists ignore the plain teaching of Scripture about the observance of days. We ask, should they not be more charitable in the light of 1 Corinthians 13? They would thus avoid opposition from their fellow Christians.

These four passages from the writings of Paul reflect the position of the historical Christian church from the times of the Fathers and the Reformers to the leading exegetical commentators of our day. The reader should remember that Adventist arguments, although buttressed by selected Bible passages (sometimes cited out of context), must be studied in the clear light of these four passages, which contain the comprehensive New Testament teaching on Sabbatarianism. The early Christian church met on the first day of the week (1 Corinthians 16:2). The disciples received the Holy Spirit on the first day of the week; collections were taken for the saints on the first day of the week; and historical evidence establishes that the first day of the week was the Lord's Day, the memorial of the new creation in Christ Jesus that completely fulfilled the law in Christ.

No amount of argument by Adventists can alter these facts, and if we believe the apostle Paul was inspired by the Holy Spirit, it is apparent that we must reject Sabbatarianism. We do not judge Seventh-day Adventists for their Sabbath observance, and they in turn should extend the same charity to their fellow Christians. Only in the recognition of the principles of Romans 14 can true unity in the body of Christ be realized. There can be no legislation of moral choice on the basis of "special revelation." This we believe is the case in Seventh-day Adventism, for it was Ellen G. White's "vision" confirming Joseph Bates' "Seal of the Living God" concept as set forth in his pamphlet on the Sabbath that established Sabbatarianism in Seventh-day Adventism. The Bible must be the supreme court of appeal and authority, and the verdict of this court, it appears to me, invalidates the contentions of our Adventist friends.[59]

---

[59]For further study on the issue, see D. A. Carson, General Editor, *From Sabbath Day to Lord's Day* (Grand Rapids, Mich.: Zondervan Publishing House).

III. Author's Note on "The Mark of the Beast"

The subjects of the Seventh-day Sabbath and the mark of the beast already have been covered in sufficient detail. However, it is often charged that Adventists teach that salvation depends upon observance of the seventh day as Sabbath, and that the mark of the beast (Revelation 13:16–17) rests upon all Sunday-keepers. For this reason, the record should be examined.

One ex-Adventist layman writes that there are "characteristic false doctrines of the sect . . . [notably] the obligation of seventh-day Sabbath observance on the part of all professing Christians, the 'mark of the beast' for Sunday-keepers." Now if this charge were correct, we too would doubt the possibility of fellowship with Adventists. But such is not the case. Ellen G. White on a number of occasions pointedly denied what is claimed to be the position of the Adventist denomination on this point. Wrote White:

> No one has yet received the mark of the beast. Testing time is not yet come. There are true Christians in every church, not excepting the Roman Catholic communion. *None are condemned until they have had the light and have seen the obligation of the fourth commandment.* . . . Sunday-keeping is not yet the mark of the beast, and will not be until the decree goes forth causing men to worship this idol Sabbath.[60]

In addition to this quotation, the Adventists have stated,

> When Sunday observance shall be enforced by law, and the world shall be enlightened concerning the obligation of the true Sabbath, then whoever shall transgress the command of God, to obey a precept which has no higher authority than that of Rome, will thereby honor popery above God.[61]

To sum up, the Adventists declare,

> God surely does not hold men accountable for truth that has not yet come to their knowledge and understanding. . . . We hold the firm conviction that millions of devout Christians of all faiths throughout all past centuries, as well as those today who are sincerely trusting in Christ their Saviour for salvation and are following Him according to their best light, are unquestionably saved. Thousands of such went to the stake as martyrs for Christ and for their faith. Moreover, untold numbers of godly Roman Catholics will surely be included. God reads the heart and deals with the intent and understanding. . . . Seventh-day Adventists interpret the prophecies relating to the beast, and the reception of his work, as something that will come into sharp focus just before the return of our Lord in glory. It is our understanding that this issue will then become a worldwide test.[62]

The statement, then, that Seventh-day Adventists believe that anyone who is a Sunday-keeper has the mark of the beast or the mark of apostasy is made without regard to the facts. Why do these critics attempt to make it appear that Adventists believe that their fellow Christians are lost? The authoritative state-

---

[60] *Questions on Doctrine*, 183–84.
[61] Ibid., 178.
[62] Ibid., 178, 184–85.

ments of this denomination are available for all to read. Doubtless some Seventh-day Adventist writers have gone contrary to the teaching of the denomination, but to indict the entire denomination for the excesses of a few is neither ethical nor Christian.

The Sanctuary, the Investigative Judgment, and the Scapegoat

The foundation of Seventh-day Adventism is its view of prophecy, which is of the historicist school of interpretation, a school that maintains that prophecy is to be understood in the light of consecutive fulfillment in history. The exaggeration of this idea led William Miller and his followers to teach that the 2,300 days of Daniel 8:14 were actually 2,300 years. Figuring from 457 B.C., the now verified time of the decree to rebuild Jerusalem (Daniel 9:25), the Millerites thought that A.D. 1843 would be the date of the second advent of Jesus Christ. Miller and his followers, among whom were James and Ellen G. White and other prominent Seventh-day Adventists, understood "the sanctuary" of Daniel 8:14 to be the earth that would be cleansed by Christ at the "great and terrible Day of the Lord," which they interpreted as the second advent of Christ. We have seen, however, that the Millerites were bitterly disappointed; and when Christ did not appear, Miller himself renounced the system and all resultant movements, including Seventh-day Adventism. But the early Seventh-day Adventists, relying upon the "vision" of Elder Hiram Edson, transferred the location of the sanctuary from the earth to heaven, and taught that in 1844 Christ went instead into the second apartment of the sanctuary in heaven (which contemporary Seventh-day Adventists term the second phase of His ministry), there to review the cases of those deemed to be worthy of eternal life. This phase of our Lord's ministry the Seventh-day Adventists call the "investigative judgment." This unique theory is intended, I believe, to discipline Christians by the threat of impending judgment and condemnation upon those whose cases are decided upon unfavorably by our Lord. When concluded, the investigative judgment will usher in the second advent of Jesus Christ, according to the Seventh-day Adventist theology, and the devil, prefigured by the second or scapegoat of Leviticus 16 (*Azazel*), will bear away unto eternal destruction or annihilation his responsibility for causing sin to enter the universe.

James White, a stalwart Seventh-day Adventist leader, when first confronted with the doctrine of the investigative judgment, opposed it *en toto*, giving in substance the very arguments put forth by all subsequent ex-Seventh-day Adventists. And it was only after considerable time that James White finally acceded to the doctrine of the investigative judgment. There are many critics of Seventh-day Adventism who, when approaching the sanctuary, investigative judgment, and scapegoat concepts, deride and mock the early Adventists and their descendants for accepting such unsupported, extrabiblical theories, but derision is not the answer, and it should be remembered that Adventists hold these doctrines in sincerity. Therefore, if they are ever to be persuaded of the mistaken nature of their faith, in these areas at least, only the facts of Scripture and the guidance of the Holy Spirit will bring it about.

The view of Hiram Edson is, so far as this writer is concerned, an attempt to escape the terrible calamity that befell the Millerite movement and the disappointment and embarrassment that must have followed the failure of the Millerite prophecies and their interpretations of the book of Daniel. We shall confine ourselves in this short analysis to the salient points of the theological issues raised by these special teachings or doctrines of the Advent message. In the matter of prophetic interpretation, this writer is convinced that the Holy Spirit has wisely veiled from the prying eyes and intellect of man many great truths that will doubtless be revealed toward the end of the age. It is not for us to judge whether the preterist, historicist, or futurist schools of interpretation are correct, and we ought not to overly concern ourselves with when Christ is coming, whether before, during, or after the Great Tribulation. Rather, we ought to be concerned that He *is* coming, because His coming is indeed "the blessed hope" of the Christian church (Titus 2:13), which hope Adventists and non-Adventists alike who share the Christian message and faith anticipate with joy.

~The heavenly sanctuary and investigative judgment teaching is still an integral part of foundational Adventist doctrine. It is described in point twenty-three of the "Fundamental Beliefs of Seventh-day Adventists" in the following words:

> There is a sanctuary in heaven, the true tabernacle, which the Lord set up and not man. In it Christ ministers on our behalf, making available to believers the benefits of His atoning sacrifice offered once for all on the cross. He was inaugurated as our great high priest and began His intercessory ministry at the time of His ascension. In 1844, at the end of the prophetic period of 2300 days, He entered the second and last phase of His atoning ministry. It is a work of investigative judgment, which is part of the ultimate disposition of all sin, typified by the cleansing of the ancient Hebrew sanctuary on the Day of Atonement. In that typical service the sanctuary was cleansed with the blood of animal sacrifices, but the heavenly things are purified with the perfect sacrifice of the blood of Jesus. The investigative judgment reveals to heavenly intelligences who among the dead are asleep in Christ and therefore, in Him, are deemed worthy to have a part in the first resurrection. It also makes manifest who among the living are abiding in Christ, keeping the commandments of God and the faith of Jesus, and in Him, therefore, are ready for translation into His everlasting kingdom. This judgment vindicates the justice of God in saving those who believe in Jesus. It declares that those who have remained loyal to God shall receive the kingdom. The completion of this ministry of Christ will mark the close of human probation before the Second Advent.[63]~

I. The Sanctuary

Since the Seventh-day Adventists believe that the sanctuary to be cleansed is in heaven (Daniel 8:14), which the Millerites identified as the earth (a regrettable early mistake), we might ask, What is the purpose of the heavenly sanctuary and its cleansing? What are the Adventists really teaching?

The book of Hebrews definitely sets forth a "heavenly sanctuary" of which Christ is the minister (Hebrews 8:1–2), and the writer of the epistle repeatedly

---

[63] *Seventh-day Adventists Believe: A Biblical Exposition of Twenty-Seven Fundamental Doctrines* (Washington, D.C.: Ministerial Association, General Conference of Seventh-day Adventists, 1988), 312. (These twenty-seven doctrines were published earlier in a special edition of the *Adventist Review*, 1981).

contrasts the Lord Jesus Christ, our risen high priest, with the Aaronic priesthood. He shows that as a priest after the order of Melchizedek, Christ derives His authority from the power of "an endless life" (Hebrews 7:16), and that He was both high priest and an offering on Calvary.[64] And this Adventists also emphasize.

It is futile, therefore, to argue that the word *sanctuary* does not apply to heaven or something of a heavenly nature, since the Scriptures teach that it does. But the Adventists' error is that they draw from the Scriptures' interpretations that cannot be substantiated by exegesis, but rest largely upon inference and deduction and are taken from theological applications of their own design.

In their sanctuary teaching, the Adventists do indeed declare, in the words of Ellen G. White:

> As anciently the sins of the people were by faith placed upon the sin offering and through its blood transferred, in figure, to the earthly sanctuary, so in the new covenant the sins of the repentant are by faith placed upon Christ and transferred, in fact, to the heavenly sanctuary. And as the typical cleansing of the earthly was accomplished by the removal of the sins by which it had been polluted, so the actual cleansing of the heavenly is to be accomplished by the removal, or blotting out, of the sins which are there recorded.[65]

Here we have the very heart of Seventh-day Adventist teaching relative to the expiation of sin, which is that the sins of believers have been transferred, deposited, or recorded in the heavenly sanctuary, and are now being dealt with in the investigative judgment.

Let us again listen to White:

> In the sin offerings presented during the year, a substitute had been accepted in the sinner's stead; but the blood of the victim had not made full atonement for the sin. It had only provided a means by which the sin was transferred to the sanctuary. By the offering of the blood, the sinner acknowledged the authority of the law, confessed the guilt of his transgression, and expressed his faith in Him who was to take away the sin of the world; but he was not entirely released from the condemnation of the law. On the Day of Atonement the high priest, having taken an offering for the congregation went into the most holy place with the blood and sprinkled it upon the mercy seat, above the table of the law. Thus the claims of the law, which demanded the life of the sinner, were satisfied. Then in his character of mediator the priest took the sins upon himself, and, leaving the sanctuary, he bore with him the burden of Israel's guilt. At the door of the tabernacle he laid his hands upon the head of the scapegoat, confessed over him "all the iniquities of the children of Israel, and all their transgressions and all their sins, putting them upon the head of the goat." And as the goat bearing these sins was sent away, they were, with him, regarded as forever separated from the people.[66]

---

[64]Hebrews 7:2, 4–7, 14, 16, 22, 25–26; 8:1–2, 6–8, 10; 9:2–12, 14, 23–24, 26–28; 10:1–10, 12, 19–21.

[65]*The Great Controversy,* 421–22.

[66]Ibid.

White further stated, "Not until the goat had been thus sent away did the people regard themselves as freed from the burden of their sins.[67]

The Adventist teaching is that Christ as our high priest transferred the sins of believers (i.e., the record of sins, in Adventist thinking) to the heavenly sanctuary, which will be finally cleansed at the conclusion of the great Day of Atonement, the investigative judgment having been concluded. Then the cases of all the righteous having been decided, their sins will be blotted out, followed by the return of the Lord Jesus Christ in glory. White made it clear that the sin transferred to the sanctuary in heaven would remain there until the conclusion of the investigative judgment and the subsequent cleansing of the sanctuary.

> The blood of Christ, while it was to release the repentant sinner from the condemnation of the law, was not to cancel the sin; it would stand on record in the sanctuary until the final atonement; so then the type, the blood of the sin offering removed the sin from the penitent but it rested in the sanctuary until the Day of Atonement.[68]

To substantiate this particular position, Adventists quote Acts 3:19 in the King James Version: "Repent ye therefore, and be converted, that your sins may be blotted out, when the times of refreshing shall come from the presence of the Lord."

The chief difficulty with the Adventist contention is that the Greek of Acts 3:19 does not substantiate their teaching that the blotting out of sins will take place as a separate event from the forgiveness of sins. Modern translations read closer to "Repent therefore, and turn again, that your sins may be blotted out, that times of refreshing may come from the presence of the Lord"(RSV). Peter was urging his listeners to repent, to turn from their sins, in order to receive the forgiveness that comes only from the presence of the Lord. This text gives our Adventist brethren no support for their "heavenly sanctuary" and "investigative judgment" teachings.

II. The Investigative Judgment

The Bible explicitly declares that when one accepts Christ as Lord, God freely forgives all his sins and ushers him from spiritual death to spiritual life solely on the merits of the perfect life and death of the Lord Jesus Christ. To this Adventists fully agree, and this makes their teaching on investigative judgment inconsistent. In John 5:24 the Greek deals a devastating blow to the Seventh-day Adventist concept of investigative judgment: "He that hears my word and believes him that sent me has everlasting life and shall not come under judgment but is passed from death to life" (literal translation).

Christians, therefore, need not anticipate any investigative judgment for their sins. True, we shall all appear before the judgment seat of Christ to receive the things done in the body (2 Corinthians 5:10), but this has nothing to do with any investigative judgment. It is a judgment for rewards. Several judgments are

---

[67]Ellen G. White, *Patriarchs and Prophets* (Washington, D.C.: Review and Herald Publishing Association, n.d.), 355–56.
[68]Ibid., 357.

mentioned in the Bible, but it is my opinion that not one passage substantiates the "investigative judgment" theory—for theory it truly is, relying upon out-of-context quotations and supported by the "Spirit of prophecy." They are welcome to this dogma, but faithfulness to New Testament teaching forbids the idea that "the blood of Christ, while it was to release the repentant sinner from the condemnation of the law, was not to cancel the sin; it would stand on record in the sanctuary until the final atonement" or "until blotting out of all sins." The Scriptures clearly teach, "If we confess our sins, he is faithful and just to forgive us our sins, and to cleanse us from all unrighteousness" (1 John 1:9). Further evidence of the completeness of the forgiveness of God and the cleansing power of the blood of Christ is found in the first chapter of the book of Hebrews, where the Holy Spirit informs us that Christ as "the express image of his person [upholds] all things by the word of his power" and that on Calvary "he . . . by himself purged our sins" (1:3).

For the word translated "purged" or "purification," the Holy Spirit chose the Greek word *katharismon,* from which we derive cathartic. Hence, it is said of the Lord Jesus and His sacrifice that He alone, "by himself," gave to our sinful spiritual natures the complete catharsis of forgiveness and purification on the cross. Christians may now rejoice that the Lord Jesus Christ is not engaged in weighing our frailties and failures, for "He knoweth our frame; he remembereth that we are dust" (Psalm 103:14). We cannot, therefore, accept the Adventist teaching on the investigative judgment, since we are convinced that it has no warrant in Scripture. We must reject what we believe to be their unbiblical concept that the sins of believers remain in the sanctuary until the day of blotting out of sins.

Our Adventist brethren, in teaching this doctrine, are overlooking the fact that "the Lord knoweth them that are his" (2 Timothy 2:19), and it was no less an authority than the Lord Jesus Christ who declared, "I . . . know my sheep" (John 10:14). The apostle Paul declares that "Christ died for the ungodly . . . while we were yet sinners, Christ died for us . . . we were reconciled to God by the death of his Son" (Romans 5:6, 8, 10). This does not balance with the Seventh-day Adventist teachings of the heavenly sanctuary, the transfer of sins, and the investigative judgment. In his epistle to the Colossians, the apostle Paul further declared, "Having made peace through the blood of his cross . . . you, that were sometime alienated and enemies in your mind by wicked works, yet now hath he reconciled in the body of his flesh through death, to present you holy and unblameable and unreproveable in his sight" (1:20–22). Once again the Holy Spirit declares that we are now reconciled through the death of Christ, having been forgiven all our trespasses through the blood of the cross (Colossians 2:13–14).

Seventh-day Adventists, relying upon Daniel 7:9–10; 8:14; and Revelation 14:7; 11:18, which refer to "judgment" and "books," attempt to "prove" that the investigative judgment is meant, but examination of each of these texts in context reveals the paucity of the claim. None of these texts has anything to do with any judgment going on now. Neither the grammar nor context supports such a contention. One can only base this interpretation by acknowledging the Adventist premise that the historicist school of prophetic interpretation is the only accurate one, and by accepting the Adventist definition of the sanctuary and judgment. It is significant that non-Adventist biblical scholars have never allowed these so-called "investigative judgment" interpretations, because there is no scriptural warrant for them apart from implication and inference.

As mentioned previously, James White at first categorically denied the teaching of the investigative judgment and gave good reasons for his rejection. Although he later embraced this doctrine, his objections are still valid:

> The event that will introduce the judgment day will be the coming of the Son of Man to raise the sleeping saints and to change those that are alive at that time. . . . It is not necessary that the final sentence should be given before the first resurrection as some have taught; for the names of the saints are written in heaven and Jesus and the angels will certainly know who to raise and gather to the New Jerusalem.[69]

Relative to the time for the beginning of the great judgment, James White quoted, "I charge thee therefore before God, and the Lord Jesus Christ, who shall judge the quick and the dead at [not before] his appearing in his kingdom" (2 Timothy 4:1).[70]

Asked when he expected the judgment of Daniel 7 to take place, James White stated,

> Daniel in the night vision saw that judgment was given to the saints of the most high, but not to mortal saints. Not until the ancient of days comes will the little horn cease prevailing, which will not be until he is destroyed by the brightness of Christ's coming.[71]

We see by this that James White at the beginning rejected the investigative judgment with good reasons. But two more of his statements are quite revealing:

> The advent angel, Revelation 14:6–7, saying with a loud voice, "Fear God, and give glory to him; for the hour of his judgment is come" does not prove that the day of judgment came in 1840 or in 1844, nor that it will come prior to the Second Advent. . . . Some have contended that the day of judgment was prior to the Second Advent. This view is certainly without foundation in the Word of God.[72]

At that time James White was on good biblical ground, but he later forsook this position for the theories and prophetic speculation promulgated by his wife and other influential Adventist leaders. The Lord Jesus Christ himself placed the judgment after His second advent when He said, "When the Son of man shall come in his glory, and all the holy angels with him, then shall he sit upon the throne of his glory: and before him shall be gathered all nations" (Matthew 25:31–32). One need only read the following passages to see that the judgments of God upon believers and unbelievers are future events. Notice the language employed:

---

[69]*A Word to the Little Flock* (1847), 24.
[70]James White in the *Advent Review* (August 1850); the brackets are his.
[71]Ibid.
[72]Ibid.

1. "The quick and the dead at his appearing and his kingdom" (Acts 10:42; 1 Peter 4:5; 2 Timothy 4:1).
2. "When the Son of Man shall come in his glory . . . he shall set the sheep on his right hand, but the goats on the left" (Matthew 25:31–33).
3. The wheat and the tares: "The harvest is the end of the world" (Matthew 13:24–30, 36–43).
4. "For we must all appear before the judgment seat of Christ; that every one may receive the things done in his body . . . whether it be good or bad" (2 Corinthians 5:10).
5. "So then every one of us shall give account of himself to God" (Romans 14:10–12).
6. "Every man's work shall be made manifest: for the day shall declare it" (1 Corinthians 3:13).

In addition to these verses, which unmistakably indicate future judgment, the writer to the Hebrews declares, "As it is appointed unto men once to die, but after this the judgment" (Hebrews 9:27). This, to any non-Adventist, is conclusive evidence that there is no investigative judgment now going on for believers to fear.

Hebrews 4:13 also exposes the faulty concept of investigative judgment: "Neither is there any creature that is not manifest in his sight: but all things are naked and opened unto the eyes of him with whom we have to do." Since our Lord knows the disposition of "cases" allegedly being reviewed in heaven, what need is there for "investigative judgment"? We believe the Scriptures decidedly do not warrant such a doctrine.

Concluding our comments on the investigative judgment, note that rewards for believers will be meted out after the second coming of our Lord, or at "the resurrection of the just," for the resurrection of life (John 5:29; Luke 14:14). Even the Adventists concur in believing that the judgment of the wicked will not take place until the end of the millennial age (Revelation 20:11–12; Matthew 25:31–46). Once again the investigative judgment theory conflicts with the biblical teaching on judgment regarding both believer and unbeliever. To this writer's mind, the great error of the sanctuary and investigative judgment teachings is the premise that sins confessed by Christians are not fully dealt with until the conclusion of the investigative judgment, a position Scripture will not allow.

Adventists, in the opinion of conservative biblical scholars, not to mention the liberal wing of Protestantism, are only speculating with their sanctuary and investigative judgment theories. Actually, most are agreed that they have created doctrines to compensate for errors in prophetic interpretation. But the very doctrines intended to solve their theological problems have, in turn, only increased their dilemma—a dilemma that they have yet to solve! Romans 8:1 declares, "There is therefore now no condemnation [i.e., judgment] to them which are in Christ Jesus" (bracketed added); and here every Christian's case must rest. We can never be indicted again for our sins or convicted for them, because Christ has fully paid the penalty. For those who believe in Jesus Christ, there is no judgment for the penalty of sin, i.e., eternal separation from God. However, as 2 Corinthians 5:10 teaches, we shall be judged for how we live as Christians. Seventh-day Adventists, we believe, needlessly subscribe to a doctrine that neither solves their difficulties nor engenders peace of mind. Holding as they do to the doctrine of the investigative judgment, it is extremely difficult for us to understand how they can experience the joy of salvation and the knowledge of sins forgiven. Of course, this is true of so-called Arminian theology on the whole, which teaches that eternal life, given by God to the believer, is conditioned by the sustained faith of the believer in the grace of God.

There is, however, clarification and summary of the doctrine of investigative judgment in *Questions on Doctrine.*

> It is our understanding that Christ, a high priest, concludes His intercessory ministry in heaven in a work of judgment. He begins His great work of judgment in the investigative phase. At the conclusion of the investigation, the sentence of judgment is pronounced. Then as judge, Christ descends to execute, or carry into effect, that sentence. For sublime grandeur, nothing in the prophetic word can compare with the description of our Lord as He descends the skies, not as a priest, but as King of kings and Lord of lords. And with Him are all the angels of heaven. He commands the dead, and that great unnumbered host of those that are asleep in Christ spring forth into immortality. At the same time those among the living who are truly God's children are caught up together with the redeemed of all ages to meet their Saviour in the air, and to be forever with the Lord.
>
> As we have suggested, . . . Seventh-day Adventists believe that at the second coming of Christ the eternal destiny of all men will have been irrevocably fixed by the decisions of a court of judgment. Such a judgment obviously would take place while men are still living on the earth. Man might be quite unaware of what is going on in heaven. It is hardly to be supposed that God would fail to warn men of such an impending judgment and its results. Seventh-day Adventists believe prophecy does foretell such a judgment, and indeed point out the very time at which it is to begin.
>
> When the high priest in the typical service had concluded his work in the earthly sanctuary on the Day of Atonement, he came to the door of the sanctuary. Then the final act with the second goat, Azazel, took place. In like manner, when our Lord completes His ministry in the heavenly sanctuary, He, too, will come forth. When He does this, the day of salvation will have closed forever. Every soul will have made his decision for or against the divine Son of God. Then upon Satan, the instigator of sin, is rolled back his responsibility for having initiated and introduced iniquity into the universe. But he [Satan] in no sense vicariously atones for the sins of God's people. All this Christ fully bore, and vicariously atoned for, on Calvary's cross.[73]

It is apparent, then, that for Adventists, the investigative judgment is something very real, and they believe that the final blotting out of their sins depends upon the results of that judgment, culminating in the final destruction (annihilation) of the wicked and of Satan, typified by the scapegoat of Leviticus 16.

III. The Scapegoat

Perhaps no doctrine of Seventh-day Adventism has been more misunderstood than the teaching concerning the scapegoat (Leviticus 16). Because of certain unfortunate choices of words by a few Adventist writers, the impression has

---

[73] *Questions on Doctrine,* 422–23, 444.

been given that Adventists regard Satan as a partial sin bearer for the people of God. This may be accounted for by the fact that in the early days of Adventism they built much of their theology on the typology of the Mosaic sanctuary, using almost exclusively the phraseology of the King James Version. Hence, they got into difficulty when dealing with such involved Old Testament concepts as the scapegoat. Not a few scholars, however, support the Seventh-day Adventist concept that Azazel represents Satan. Be that as it may, the important thing is the place of the scapegoat with regard to the atonement of Christ. Do Seventh-day Adventists believe that Satan eventually becomes their vicarious sin bearer? Not at all! This writer is convinced that the Adventist concept of the scapegoat in connection with the Day of Atonement, the sanctuary, and the investigative judgment is a bizarre combination of prophetic interpretation and typology; but it is by no means the soul-destroying doctrine that many people think it is. Let the Adventists speak for themselves:

> We take our stand without qualification on the gospel platform that the death of Jesus Christ provides the sole propitiation for our sins (1 John 2:2; 4:10); that there is salvation through no other means or medium, and no other name by which we may be saved (Acts 4:12); and that the shed blood of Jesus Christ alone brings remission for our sins (Matthew 26:28). That is foundational.
>
> When Satan tempted our first parents to take and eat of the forbidden fruit, he as well as they had inescapable responsibility in that act—he the instigator, and they the perpetrators. And similarly, through the ages—in all sin, Satan is involved in responsibility, as the originator and instigator, or tempter (John 8:44; Romans 6:16; 1 John 3:8).
>
> Now concerning my sin, Christ died for my sins (Romans 5:8). He was wounded for my transgressions and for my iniquities (Isaiah 53). He assumed my responsibilities, and His blood alone cleanses me from all sin (1 John 1:7). The atonement for my sin is made solely by the shed blood of Christ....
>
> Concerning Satan's sin, and his responsibility as instigator and tempter, no salvation is provided for him. He must be punished for his responsibility.... He must himself "atone" for his sin in causing men to transgress, in the same way that a master criminal suffers on the gallows or in the electric chair for his responsibility in the crimes that he has caused others to commit. It is in this sense only that we can understand the words of Leviticus 16:10 concerning the scapegoat, "to make atonement with him"...
>
> Satan is the responsible mastermind in the great crime of sin, and his responsibility will return upon his own head. The crushing weight of his responsibility in the sins of the whole world—of the wicked as well as of the righteous—must be rolled back upon him. Simple justice demands that while Christ suffers for my guilt, Satan must also be punished as the instigator of sin....
>
> Satan makes no atonement for our sins. But Satan will ultimately have to bear the retributive punishment for his responsibility in the sins of all men, both righteous and wicked.
>
> Seventh-day Adventists therefore repudiate *en toto* any idea, suggestion, or implication that Satan is in any sense or degree our sin bearer. The thought is abhorrent to us, and appallingly sacrilegious....

Only Christ, the Creator, the one and only God-man, could make a substitutionary atonement for men's transgressions. And this Christ did completely, perfectly, and once for all, on Golgotha.[74]

To be sure, the Seventh-day Adventists have a unique concept of the scapegoat, but in the light of their clearly worded explanation, no critic could any longer with honesty indict them for heresy where the atonement of our Lord is concerned. The Adventists have stated unequivocally that Jesus Christ is their sole propitiation for sin and that Satan has no part whatsoever in the expiation of sin. This writer agrees that Satan is the master criminal of the universe and that it is axiomatic, therefore, that he should suffer as the instigator of angelic and human rebellion. There are, of course, many interpretations of Leviticus 16 set forth by learned scholars, the great majority of whom are most certainly not Adventists; so at best the question is quite open. The *Abingdon Bible Commentary* (Methodist), relative to Leviticus 16 and the scapegoats states,

On the goats lots are to be cast, one for Jehovah and the other for Azazel. The translation "Dismissal" in the Revised Version margin here (cf. removal in ASV margin) is inadmissible being based on a false etymology. What the word meant is unknown but it should be retained as a proper name of a wilderness demon.

To this statement could be added the opinions of Samuel Zwemer, E. W. Hengstenberg, J. B. Rotherham, and J. Russell Howden, the last of whom wrote in the *Sunday School Times* of January 15, 1927:

The goat for Azazel as it is sometimes misleadingly translated, typifies God's challenge to Satan. Of the two goats, one was for Jehovah signifying God's acceptance of the sin offering; the other was for Azazel. This is probably to be understood as a person being parallel with Jehovah in the preceding clause. So Azazel is probably a synonym for Satan.

Although Seventh-day Adventists have no exegetical support for their sanctuary and investigative judgment theories, one thing is certain: They have more than substantial scholastic support for assigning the title "Satan" to Azazel in Leviticus 16 concerning the scapegoat. Nevertheless, where the Scripture does not speak specifically, it is far wiser to withhold comment. Many critics, in their zeal to shred Seventh-day Adventism and classify it as "a dangerous non-Christian cult," lay much stress upon the scapegoat teaching. In the light of current Adventist statements concerning their concept of the scapegoat, the misunderstandings of the past have at last been brought out into the open, clarified, and presented in a plausible manner.

Much, much more could be written concerning the Seventh-day Adventist concepts of the sanctuary, investigative judgment, and the scapegoat, since they are inseparably linked together. But such writers as W. W. Fletcher (*The Reasons for My Faith*), and other ex-Seventh-day Adventists, have exhaustively refuted the position of their former affiliation. The reader is urged to consider the bibliog-

---

[74]*Questions on Doctrine*, 396, 398–400.

raphy for additional information on this subject. The saving grace of the entire situation is that the Adventists fortunately deny the logical conclusions to which their doctrine must lead them; i.e., a negation of the full validity of the atonement of Christ, the validity of which they absolutely affirm and embrace with considerable fervor—a paradoxical situation at best!

IV. Author's Note on "The Scapegoat"

We could wish that some of the earlier nonrepresentative Seventh-day Adventist statements on the scapegoat teaching had not been made or, better yet, that they were not still circulated in some quarters. However, to ignore their honest current declarations is, I believe, fundamentally unfair. It appears to me to be little more than blind prejudice. One review of the book *Questions on Doctrine* contains an error frequently found in critical writings. Imputing to their account a position the Adventists do not hold, the review then proceeds to destroy it as if, in the final analysis, it had both exposed and refuted a pernicious error. While it is true that the Seventh-day Adventists do believe that Azazel, in Leviticus 16, does represent Satan, their interpretation of it is far removed from this reviewer's straw man. After quoting the Seventh-day Adventist statement: "Seventh-day Adventists repudiate *en toto* any idea . . . that Satan is in any sense our sin bearer," this review states, "But then two entire chapters are devoted to proving that Satan did bear our sin." It goes on to describe the Adventist position as "repulsive blasphemy" and "unholy twisting of the Scripture. If the Seventh-day Adventists were sound in everything but this and still held this one gross error, we would still have to consider them as an unscriptural cult."[75]

Now, with some other portions of this review we are in agreement. But many of the statements show a marked predisposition toward removing various statements from context and placing them together to prove contradiction without respect to their setting. It ignores all the Seventh-day Adventist statements that contradict these out-of-context criticisms. The very chapter alluded to clearly shows that Adventists repudiate the meaning the reviewer has attached to the scapegoat concept. As we have noted, it is regrettable that this teaching has been so stated in some Adventist writings as to give the impression that the scapegoat represents Satan in the vicarious role of sin bearer, but the Adventists have clarified this beyond reasonable doubt in the large majority of their publications.

Questions on Doctrine clarifies the concept of the scapegoat in Seventh-day Adventist theology. For Adventists, when the Lord Jesus Christ returns, He will place upon Satan the full responsibility for his role of instigator and tempter to sin. Since Satan caused angels and man to rebel against their Creator, Adventists reason that Azazel, the scapegoat of Leviticus 16, is a type of Satan receiving the punishment due him. However, as we have seen, Adventists repudiate the idea that Satan is their vicarious sin bearer in any sense. They point out, and rightly so, that in Leviticus 16 only the first goat was slain as the vicarious offering. The second goat was not killed, but was sent into the wilderness to die. Satan similarly bears the weight of guilt and final punishment culminating in annihilation as the master criminal, who has promulgated sin during the period of God's grace toward lost men. To quote the Adventists again:

---

[75] *The King's Business* (March 1958): 22–23.

Satan's death, a thousand times over could never make him a savior in any sense whatsoever. He is the archsinner of the universe, the author and instigator of sin. . . . Only Christ, the Creator, the one and only God-man, could make a substitutionary atonement for men's transgressions. And this Christ did completely, perfectly, and once for all on Golgotha.[76]

Law, Grace, and Salvation

In order to understand the Adventist view of law and grace, especially in relation to eternal salvation, we must consider the Adventist antipathy toward antinomianism.

The very word *antinomian* (*anti*, against, and *nomos*, law) describes the conflict between those who believe that not only were the Ten Commandments abrogated at Calvary, but even the principles underlying them were "abolished" so that the Christian is bound neither by them nor by those who believe that the Decalogue is as binding today as when it was given at Sinai.

From the beginning of church history, the great majority of evangelical Christians have been as strongly opposed to antinomianism as are the Adventists. Unfortunately, however, the latter have tended to label antinomian anyone who disagrees with their definition of "the law of God." Consequently, this has created a great problem in semantics, which has disrupted the lines of communication, so to speak, between Adventists and other Christians. Although we believe in obeying the laws of God and in good works as the evidence of saving faith, we strenuously object to "commandment-keeping" to the extent of supposed spiritual superiority. A principal cause of their legalistic tendencies is the Adventists' abhorrence of antinomianism.

By virtue of the fact that they obey the Fourth Commandment as well as the other nine, Adventists maintain that they alone are God's commandment-keeping church. To be sure, theologians have differed over the nature and extent of the moral law of God, and doubtless the controversy will continue until our Lord comes again. Any group, however, that feels they are the only ones that keep God's commands is likely to foment schism in the body of Christ.

From their beginning, Adventists have concentrated upon "the law of God," and in *Questions on Doctrine* they devote thirty-four pages to the exposition of this subject. Although the Adventists repudiate legalism, that is, the doctrine that keeping the law merits salvation, a legalistic spirit does exist in some of their teaching. For example, although denying that the ceremonial law is binding upon Christians, they quote from it to defend their classifying certain foods as "unclean." Although Adventists reject antinomianism, in their desire to avoid the abuses of grace they actually abuse grace by magnifying the letter of the law. How Adventists arrived at this position has been well explained by D. M. Canright (*Seventh-day Adventism Renounced*, chapter 17). In one place, Canright sets forth a series of propositions that, in some areas, are exegetically irrefutable, and with which I am in full agreement.

Now let us examine the Adventist claim that the law is binding upon the Christian, as stated in their Fundamental Beliefs, *Questions on Doctrine*, and wherever their writings touch on this subject.

---

[76] *Questions on Doctrine*, 400.

I. *The Principle of Law*

To begin with, we agree to the proposition that the principle underlying the moral laws of God is, indeed, eternal and consistent with His character. However, we must distinguish between the principle of the law of God and the expression of that principle in specific statutes such as those in the Pentateuch. Because Adventists do not seem to make this distinction, it appears to this writer that they relate law to grace, which is an unhealthy practice. They claim that "the Law" was in effect in Eden and during all the centuries thence to Sinai. Wherever the Bible speaks of "commandments" or "law," most Adventists apparently assume that it means the Decalogue. We must, however, clearly differentiate between the principle of the law of God and the function of the law of God as revealed in the Pentateuch. Not only the Adventists but many historical Protestant groups have failed to make this distinction, and therefore have been guilty of carrying over into the New Covenant some of the legalistic Jewish functions of the law.

A. The Dual-Law Theory

In *Questions on Doctrine,* the Adventists distinguish between "the moral law of God—the Decalogue—and the ceremonial law," setting forth the distinctions in two columns.[77] In column one is the Decalogue, which was spoken by God, written by Him on tables of stone, given to Moses, and deposited in the Ark. It dealt with moral precepts, revealed sin, and is in effect today. They insist that Christians must "keep the whole law" (James 2:10), and that we shall be judged by this law (James 2:12). They believe that the Decalogue is established in the life of a Christian by faith in Christ (Romans 3:31), and that Christ magnified the law (Isaiah 42:21), which Paul described as "spiritual" (Romans 7:14).

In column two, Adventists analyze the law of ceremonial ordinances, which were abolished at the cross. They contrast this with "the moral law of God—the Decalogue," stating that the latter was not abolished because it was separate from the ceremonial law. Concerning the ceremonial law, Adventists teach that it was spoken and written by Moses and given to the Levites, who deposited it by the side of the Ark, and that it governed ceremony and ritual. This law prescribed offerings for sins, but the apostles gave no commandment to keep it, and the Christian is not bound by it, nor can he be blessed by it. Indeed, they say, "The Christian who keeps this law loses his liberty"; it "was abolished by Christ," and was "the law of a carnal commandment" containing nothing of a moral nature, the Decalogue being "the moral law of God."

Now, although there are both moral and ceremonial aspects of the law in the Pentateuch, as well as civil and judicial, nowhere does the Bible state that there is any such juxtaposition of ceremonial with moral law. In fact, the whole Bible teaches that "the law was given through Moses" (John 1:17) and that it is essentially a unit, a fact that the Adventists have overlooked. We make this observation after comparing the application of the term *law* in the Old and New Testaments.

To illustrate: As noted above, the Adventists claim that the Law of Moses and the Decalogue are separate, the one being ceremonial, the other "the moral law of God." Therefore, although the ceremonial law was abolished at the cross, the moral law remains in effect; and so they insist in "commandment-keeping," not

---

[77] *Questions on Doctrine,* 130–31.

to earn salvation, but, as it works out in the practice of many, to retain salvation. If, however, the ceremonial law and the Decalogue are inextricably bound together, and if both are referred to as "the law," the distinction that the Adventists and others make between them is fictitious. To prove this is to nullify their interpretation concerning "the moral law." Let us examine the Scriptures to see whether such a distinction as they propose can be sustained.

The highest authority on this subject is the Lord Jesus Christ. When speaking of "the law," He alluded to both moral and ceremonial precepts; e.g., Mark 10:19 (moral) and Luke 5:12–14 (ceremonial). The Gospels abound with similar references to "the law" without distinguishing between the moral and the ceremonial, and certainly not teaching that they are separate codes.

We do not mean that the law has no moral and ceremonial aspects, for it has, but they are only aspects, not separate codes or units. They are parts of the one law, which "was our schoolmaster to bring us unto Christ, that we might be justified by faith" (Galatians 3:24). The apostle Paul, certainly an authority on "the law," dogmatically affirms that the role of the schoolmaster has ceased and that the Christian is "dead to the law." Note, also, that the word *schoolmaster* is in the singular, which destroys the Adventist notion that there is more than one law. If the moral law were separate from the ceremonial law, instead of both being aspects of one law, Paul would have had to write that the laws were our schoolmasters to bring us to Christ, and that now "we are no longer under schoolmasters." But he knew and taught that the law was a unit and that it was perfectly fulfilled as such in the life of our Lord and on the cross of Calvary.

By His perfect life, the Lord Jesus met all the requirements of the moral aspect of the law. By His death, He fulfilled all the ceremonial ordinances that prefigured His incarnation and sacrifice. He himself said,

> Think not that I am come to destroy the law, or the prophets: I am come not to destroy, but to fulfill. For verily I say unto you, till heaven and earth pass, one jot or one tittle shall in no wise pass from the law, till all be fulfilled. (Matthew 5:17–18)

Which law did Christ fulfill? If He fulfilled only the ceremonial law as the dual-law theory states, the moral law is yet to be satisfied. But "Christ is the end of the law for righteousness to every one that believeth" (Romans 10:4); and as we have shown, there are no distinct codes such as moral as contrasted with ceremonial law. The distinction is arbitrary and contradicts the declaration of Scripture that the believer lives by a higher principle: "The law of the Spirit of life in Christ Jesus hath made me free from the law of sin and death" (Romans 8:2).

In order to maintain the dual-law theory against the biblical declaration that the one law has divisions or aspects, Adventists must explain why this is true in relation to at least twenty passages in the New Testament, a dozen of them in the words of Jesus Christ. The Holy Spirit teaches that there are not two laws, but one; that this law is not only in the five books of Moses, but in the Prophets and the Psalms as well. Christ looked upon moral, ceremonial, and prophetic precepts as parts of the one law, which pointed to His life, ministry, death, and resurrection. As He said to His disciples that first Easter Day, "These are the words which I spake unto you, while I was yet with you, that all things must be fulfilled, which were written in the law of Moses, and in the prophets, and in the psalms concerning me" (Luke 24:44).

A study of the relevant biblical passages (including John 8:17, cf. Deuteronomy 19:15; John 10:34, cf. Psalm 82:6; John 12:34, cf. Psalm 72:17; John 15:25, cf. Psalm 35:19; and John 19:7, cf. Leviticus 24:16) should convince any objective reader that the law is a single gigantic structure comprised of several aspects: moral, ceremonial, civil, judicial, and prophetic. This whole structure was referred to by Christ and the apostles under the heading of "the law," and which structure was completely fulfilled in the life and death of the Lord Jesus Christ, who instituted the universal principle of divine love as the fulfillment of every aspect and function of the law. Our Lord said:

> Therefore all things whatsoever ye would that men should do to you, do ye even so to them: for this is the law and the prophets. . . . Thou shalt love the Lord thy God with all thy heart, and with all thy soul, and with all thy mind. This is the first and great commandment. And the second is like unto it, Thou shalt love thy neighbor as thyself. On these two commandments hang all the law and the prophets. (Matthew 7:12; 22:37–40)

Instead of the Adventist belief that the law must be "kept" as a sign of obedience to God, Christ here teaches that the Christian obeys God when he obeys the supreme commandment of love. This teaching is reiterated by the greatest of the apostles, who wrote to the Galatians, "All the law is fulfilled in one word, even in this; Thou shalt love thy neighbour as thyself" (Galatians 5:14). Obviously, if we love our neighbors as ourselves, we do so because we love God with all our heart, soul, and mind. If we do not so love God, we cannot love our neighbors as ourselves. Thus on this "great commandment" rests the law in all its aspects.

Note the language of these passages, for they indicate the strong emphasis given by our Lord. In Matthew 22:40 Christ uses the Greek word *holos*, translated sixty-five times in the New Testament as "all," forty-three times as "whole," twice as "every whit," once "altogether," and once "throughout." With these renditions all lexicons agree, so there can be no linguistic doubt that the all-inclusive principle that binds and seals all aspects of the law into a unit to be fulfilled in the life of a believer, because it has been fulfilled by the Savior, is once again declared to be "love."

The apostle Paul uses an entirely different word to sum up the unifying principle of the law and the only principle that the Scriptures say fulfills it. This is the Greek word *pas*.

In the New Testament *pas* is translated 748 times as "all," 170 times as "all things," 117 times as "every," 41 times as "all men," 31 times as "whosoever," 28 times as "everyone," 12 times as "whole," and 11 times as "every man." We see, then, how the Holy Spirit rendered linguistically impossible any escape from the clear declaration that the principle of love indeed fulfills all the precepts of the law in their entirety, since the two terms used most frequently in the New Testament to describe inclusiveness were utilized by both Christ and Paul to enunciate this vital issue.

Finally, notice Paul's powerful admonition to the believers at Rome:

> Owe no man any thing, but to love one another: for he that loveth
> another hath fulfilled the law. For this, Thou shalt not commit adultery,
> Thou shalt not kill, Thou shalt not steal, Thou shalt not bear false witness,
> Thou shalt not covet; and if there be any other commandment, it is briefly
> comprehended in this saying, namely, Thou shalt love thy neighbour as thy-
> self. Love worketh no ill to his neighbour: therefore love is the fulfilling of
> the law. (Romans 13:8–10)

In this context the greatest authority on the law in the New Testament, next
to Jesus Christ, used the very emphatic Greek word *etera*, which is translated forty-
two times in the New Testament as "other." Unquestionably, the apostle Paul not
only considered the law a unit of which the Decalogue is only a part (quoting five
of the Ten Commandments), but he indicated the rest of the law—ceremonial,
civil, and judicial—by the word *other*. Thus, if one is to be a true "commandment-
keeper," he has only to obey the divine principle of love, and God looks upon
this as fulfillment of "the law." The Holy Spirit does not specify the moral, ceremonial, or civil law. He emphatically states that love is the fulfillment of "the
law"—a tremendously important statement, to say the least!

It is significant that in the thirteenth chapter of Romans, after quoting five
of the Ten Commandments, that the Adventists steadfastly affirm constitute "the
moral law," the apostle conspicuously omits what the Adventists maintain is God's
great "seal"—the Sabbath. In fact, the words "any other commandment" must
include even the Sabbath in the law of love. Nowhere is this more decidedly
emphasized than in the usage of a peculiar term that appears but twice in the
New Testament; here in Romans 13:9, and again in Ephesians 1:10. The term in
question is the Greek *anakephalaioutai*, which in both instances means "to sum
up, to repeat summarily, and so to condense into a summary . . . to bring
together."

We see that the apostle Paul, under the inspiration of the Holy Spirit, taught
in both Romans 13:9 and Ephesians 1:10 that as God in the fullness of time
intended to "gather together" (KJV) or "sum up" (RSV) those whom He had
chosen in Christ, in like manner He has forever condensed or summed up, comprehended or gathered together, the law in all its aspects and divisions under the
all-embracing principle of love. By not adhering strictly to the established laws of
sound biblical interpretation, Seventh-day Adventists seem to have overlooked
this fact in the New Testament. In the course of our study of Seventh-day Adventist literature, we have been impressed by the fact that some Adventists will cite
texts largely out of their context and grammatical structure in what appears to be
an attempt to enforce an arbitrary theory of two laws (moral and ceremonial)
upon the believer in the age of grace. In so doing, they violate that principle
which the apostle Paul states "sums up" or "condenses" all of the commandments of the entire law, perfectly fulfilling them under the one heading, "the
great commandment," upon which, our Lord declared, "hang all the law and the
prophets," the imperative of love.

On page 131 of *Questions on Doctrine*, it is stated that the ceremonial law is
now "abolished" (Ephesians 2:15); and, "the Christian who keeps this law is not
blessed" (Galatians 5:1–6), but "loses his liberty" (Galatians 5:1, 3). Nevertheless,
Adventists religiously observe some ceremonial laws, especially with regard to

"unclean food." Now, although they deny that their rejection of "unclean" food is based on Mosaic prohibitions, all their literature on the subject appeals to the very law that they insist has been "abolished." Under the covenant of law, nowhere but in the Mosaic ceremonial aspects of the law are people forbidden to eat oysters, clams, lobsters, crabs, reptiles, rabbits, and swine's flesh, but the Adventists still claim the validity of such prohibition. We wish that they would be consistent in following their dual-law theory and abandon their "unclean foods" restriction, which binds them to what even they admit is an abolished ceremonial teaching; a teaching that they also declare can cause the Christian to "lose his liberty" and miss the blessings of God. Writing on this subject of unclean foods with apostolic authority and the power of the Holy Spirit, the apostle Paul unequivocally declared, "Therefore let no one pass judgment on you in questions of food and drink" (Colossians 2:16 RSV). And he warns Timothy that in the latter days some persons will "enjoin abstinence from foods which God created to be received with thanksgiving by those who believe and know the truth. For everything created by God is good, and nothing is to be rejected if it is received with thanksgiving; for then it is consecrated by the word of God and prayer." Finally, he sums it up thus:

> I know, and am persuaded in the Lord Jesus, that there is nothing unclean of itself: but to him that esteemeth any thing to be unclean, to him it is unclean. . . . For the kingdom of God is not meat and drink; but righteousness, and peace, and joy in the Holy Ghost. For he that in these things serveth Christ is acceptable to God, and approved of men. (Romans 14:14, 17–18)

From these texts it is apparent that Adventists limit their own liberty in Christ by voluntary bondage to ceremonial precepts, and it is the dual-law theory that has largely caused their confusion and the consequent error of law-keeping.

For this teaching, which lapses so easily into legalism, we find no biblical authority, since it is demonstrably true that the Law of Moses and the Decalogue are a unit described throughout Scripture as "the law." The fact that the Decalogue was written on stones (Exodus 31:18) and the Law of Moses written in a book (Exodus 24:4, 7; Deuteronomy 31:24) in no way proves that one is moral and the other ceremonial. As we have seen, the law of Moses, written in a book and deposited by the Levites by the side of the Ark, deals not only with ceremonial ritual matter but also with those moral precepts contained in the Decalogue itself. One could not be fulfilled, as Christ prophesied and accomplished, and the other left unfulfilled, for then God's sacrificial plan would not have been consummated at Calvary.

B. "Law" in the New Testament

When New Testament writers spoke of "the law," they usually meant all five books of Moses, which contain moral, ceremonial, and civil ordinances. It was national and applied only to Israel and to anyone who became an Israelite. Nowhere in Scripture is it applied to anyone else. Although the Gentiles, as Paul says, "have not the law," its great moral principle applied to them, so that the

Gentiles "do by nature that which is contained in the law," but they did not come under law as given to Israel.

Acts 15:23–32 describes how the leaders of the Christian church at Jerusalem, all Jews, were very careful not to impose the demands of the law upon the Gentiles. For them, the complete "law"—moral, ceremonial, and civil—had been fulfilled, and the one law to observe now was to love God and your neighbor. St. Augustine remarked, "Love God, and do as you please," for if we truly love God with heart, soul, mind, and strength, we do only those things that please Him. This is "the law" of the New Testament, the only guide for the Christian. We are "no longer under the law, but under grace," and the function of the "schoolmaster" (Galatians 3:24) has forever and irrevocably ceased.

Let us see how these first Christian leaders solved the problem of "the law":

> And they wrote letters by them after this manner; The apostles and elders and brethren send greetings unto the brethren which are of the Gentiles in Antioch and Syria and Cilicia. Forasmuch as we have heard, that certain which went out from us have troubled you with words, subverting your souls, saying, Ye must be circumcised, and keep the law: to whom we gave no such commandment: It seemed good unto us, being assembled with one accord, to send chosen men unto you. . . . We have sent therefore Judas and Silas. . . . For it seemed good to the Holy Ghost, and to us, to lay upon you no greater burden than these necessary things; that ye abstain from meats offered to idols, and from blood, and from things strangled, and from fornication: from which if ye keep yourselves, ye shall do well. Fare ye well. (Acts 15:23–25, 27–29)

Since "the law" includes the precepts of the Pentateuch and certain sections of the Psalms and Prophets, this message to the Gentiles contradicts all dual-law teachers who insist that we must for any purpose "keep the law." We know from a comparison of the New Testament with the Old that the Decalogue of itself is not the entire moral law of God, as our Adventist brethren often insist, for there are many other commandments that are neither inferred from, implied, nor contained in the Decalogue, but which are just as moral as anything appearing in Exodus 20. Although nine of the Ten Commandments are enunciated in the New Testament, we have seen that they are "comprehended, summed up, or condensed" in the words of Paul in the great commandment of love (Romans 13:8; Galatians 5:14). So the Adventists have no argument against the total fulfillment of all the law by the life and death of our Savior.

In Acts 15:24 the leaders of the church in Jerusalem reiterate this principle in their letter to the Gentiles in Antioch, Syria, and Cilicia: "Certain which went out from us have troubled you with words, subverting your souls, saying, Ye must be circumcised, and keep the law: to whom we gave no such commandment."

Now, although Seventh-day Adventists affirm that law-keeping cannot merit salvation, nevertheless they teach that by breaking the law one forfeits salvation. They invoke a principle that was fulfilled in the life and death of Christ, and in so doing they place themselves in direct opposition to the great law of love enunciated by Christ and the apostles, and are in effect putting "a yoke upon the neck of the disciples, which neither our fathers nor we were able to bear" (Acts 15:10). To those who invoke the law as the criterion of obedience in the Christian life, the Word of God replies, "We gave no such commandment" (Acts 15:24).

Paul's phrase "any other commandment" in Romans 13:9, of course, includes abstinence from meats offered to idols, blood, things strangled, and fornication, for love of God would enjoin discernment and obedience in all these things.

To support their argument that a Christian must obey the commandments, Adventists and other Christian bodies cite such passages as the following:

> If ye love me, keep my commandments. He that hath my commandments, and keepeth them, he it is that loveth me . . . And hereby we do know that we know him, if we keep his commandments. He that saith, I know him, and keepeth not his commandments, is a liar, and the truth is not in him. . . . And whatsoever we ask, we receive of him, because we keep his commandments, and do those things that are pleasing in his sight. . . . He that keepeth his commandments dwelleth in him, and he in him. And hereby we know that he abideth in us, by the Spirit which he hath given us. . . . By this we know that we love the children of God, when we love God, and keep his commandments. For this is the love of God, that we keep his commandments: and his commandments are not grievous. (John 14:15, 21; 1 John 2:3–4; 3:22, 24; 5:2–3)

We, too, yield to the authority of those verses; but the fallacy of the position lies in the concept that the word *commandments* always refers to the Ten Commandments, which Adventists maintain are "the moral law of God." This claim cannot be substantiated from Scripture; in fact, it is contradicted by the Bible. Let us see how the Lord Jesus and the apostle John applied the words *commandments* and *law*. First, consider the conversation of our Lord with the lawyer in Luke 10:25–28:

> And, behold, a certain lawyer stood up, and tempted him, saying, Master, what shall I do to inherit eternal life?
> He said unto him, What is written in the law? how readest thou?
> And he answering said, Thou shalt love the Lord thy God with all thy heart, and with all thy soul, and with all thy strength, and with all thy mind; and thy neighbour as thyself.
> And he said unto him, Thou hast answered right: this do, and thou shalt live.

Clearly, the Lord Jesus did not subscribe to the Seventh-day Adventist view that "commandment-keeping means keeping all of the Ten Commandments," none of which He mentions in this passage. Christ did not say, "Keep the Ten Commandments, especially the fourth one, and thou shalt live." He said, in effect, "Obey the law of love upon which all the law and the prophets rest, and thou shalt live." This refutes the Adventist claim that when Jesus spoke of commandments He meant only the Decalogue.

Among those who listened to our Lord's discourse in the Upper Room was the apostle John, who records the "new commandment . . . that ye love one another; as I have loved you" (John 13:34). To this commandment John refers in the passages quoted from his first epistle. Nowhere does he mention the Decalogue or any part of the moral law of God. Instead, he writes,

> This is his commandment, That we should believe on the name of his Son Jesus Christ, and love one another, as he gave us commandment. . . . And this commandment have we from him, That he who loveth God love his brother also. (1 John 3:23; 4:21)

And in his second epistle he says,

> I beseech thee, lady, not as though I wrote a new commandment unto thee, but that which we had from the beginning, that we love one another. And this is love, that we walk after his commandments. This is the commandment, That, as ye have heard from the beginning, ye should walk in it. (2 John 5–6)

From this it is clear what John means when he speaks of "commandment" or "commandments." How different from ironclad obedience to what many, including Adventists, sometimes call "The Eternal Ten." By "the righteousness of the law" and fulfillment of the law, Christ and all the New Testament writers mean not the Ten Commandments but the eternal law of love. The motivating power of the universe—love—is to motivate obedience to God. By loving Him and one another, we fulfill all moral law. The chief function of the law was to reveal sin and to "slay" the soul that righteousness might come by faith, and it was given for the unregenerate, not the redeemed: "Knowing this, that the law is not made for a righteous man, but for the lawless and disobedient, for the ungodly and for sinners, for unholy and profane, for murderers of fathers and murderers of mothers, for manslayers" (1 Timothy 1:9).

C. The Charge of Pharisaism

By believing they are God's commandment-keeping church, Adventists have exposed themselves to the charge of Pharisaism. Because they monopolize such passages as the following, they give the impression of claiming to be the only people on earth: (1) "Which keep the commandments of God"[78]; (2) "They that keep the commandments of God, and the faith of Jesus"; and (3) "Blessed are they that do his commandments, that they may have right to the tree of life, and may enter in through the gates into the city" (Revelation 12:17; 14:12; 22:14).

We admire the desire of our Adventist brethren to obey the commandments of God; but, we ask, what commandments? If they answer, "The Decalogue," we reject their effort to bring us under bondage, for we "are not under the law, but under grace" (Romans 6:14). If some fail to recognize that "the law" of the New Testament is love for God and for one another, and that it fulfills and supersedes

---

[78]All the oldest and best Greek manuscripts of Revelation 22:14 read, "They that wash their robes," so the verse gives no support whatever for "commandment-keeping." This fact well-informed Adventists recognize, but a large segment still attempt to utilize certain faulty and incorrect English translations to "prove" their position.

all previous embodiments of divine principle, then the issue is clear. Such people speak like "a noisy gong or a clanging cymbal," because they do not give supremacy to the "new" and "great commandment."

Concluding this section on the principle of law, we may sum up our position briefly:

The Adventist insistence that there are two separate codes of laws, the moral and the ceremonial, and that the former is in effect today and the latter was abolished at the cross, finds, we believe, no exegetical or theological basis in Scripture. We have also shown that they select numerous texts out of context and juxtapose them in order to validate their contention. We have seen that the greatest of all commandments is not included in the Decalogue or "moral law." And yet upon this great commandment, love for the Lord and for one's neighbor, "hang all the law and the prophets." The nineteenth chapter of Leviticus alone is sufficient to refute the dual-law theory, for it contains moral, ceremonial, and civil laws sometimes all appearing in the same verse, and yet Leviticus is called by Christ "the law," as are the other four books of Moses.

The Adventist contention that since the Ten Commandments were spoken by God, inscribed on stone, and placed within the Ark, they are superior to the law written by Moses in a book and placed by the side of the Ark is fallacious. This is true because the book placed by the side of the Ark actually contains more moral law than does the Decalogue itself. It is, therefore, superior to the Decalogue, at least in scope.

The Bible refutes the Adventist contention that the law was in force in Eden and that it was known to Adam, Noah, Abraham, and the patriarchs. Not one verse of Scripture can be cited free from inference, deduction, and implication that teaches such a doctrine. The Word of God states,

> The law was given by Moses. . . . Did not Moses give you the law? . . . If therefore perfection were by the Levitical priesthood (for under it the people received the law). . . . The covenant, that was confirmed before of God in Christ, the law, which was four hundred and thirty years after, cannot disannul. . . . The Lord our God made a covenant with us in Horeb. The Lord made not this covenant with our fathers, but with us. (John 1:17; 7:19; Hebrews 7:11; Galatians 3:17; Deuteronomy 5:2–3)

The Adventists' contentions, therefore, concerning the eternal nature of the Decalogue and the time of its application to man are mere conjecture. Although we admit that the principle of the law was, in effect, written upon the hearts of men by the Holy Spirit, so that they were judged by it (Romans 2), there is a vast difference between the principle of the law and the embodiment of that principle in a given code (Sinaitic-Mosaic), which the Adventists fail to recognize.

Finally, the Old Testament Scriptures all teach the unity of the law. Christ endorsed it, and the apostles pointed out that its chief purpose was to condemn man and show him his need of redemption that he might come to Christ, the author and fulfiller of all the law. We who are "led of the Spirit . . . are not under the law" (Galatians 5:18), for "love is the fulfilling of the law" (Romans 13:10). This love energizes us to "walk not after the flesh, but after the Spirit" that in us "the righteousness of the law might be fulfilled" (Romans 8:4). In Jeremiah 31:31–34, the prophet states that under the new covenant, God would write His law "in their inward parts, and write it in their hearts." In 2 Corinthians 3:3 the apostle Paul declares that Christians are "the epistle of Christ . . . written not with ink, but with the Spirit of the living God; not in tables of stone, but in fleshy tables of the heart." The motive for obedience to this law is the imperative of love: "We love him, because he first loved us" (1 John 4:19).

The great foundational moral law of the universe is therefore declared to be unchanging love. This is vastly different from the national or Mosaic law given only to Israel. That law was designed to be fulfilled, even though it was based upon the eternal principles of the moral character of God (Colossians 2:14–17). And when its fulfillment did take place and the character of God was imputed to the believer and imparted to his life by the power of the indwelling Spirit, the entire Mosaic system passed away; but the eternal principle, the law's foundation, remained, and is operative today as the law of love, the supreme "commandment" and the only "law" under which the Christian is to live.

The concept of law in Seventh-day Adventism, then, leads them to the unbiblical and at times legalistic position that although they are "under grace," by failing to "keep the commandments" they are in danger of coming "under law" again.

The Word of God, however, describes the Christian under grace as "dead to the law" that he might "live unto God" (Galatians 2:19), and nowhere is it taught that one can "come alive" again so that the function of the law is resumed.

II. The Relationship of Grace to Salvation

Although Adventists lay great stress on "commandment-keeping" and "obedience to the moral law of God as contained in the Ten Commandments," they devote a large portion of their writings to the New Testament doctrine of grace. As we saw earlier, Seventh-day Adventists believe in salvation by grace alone, and vehemently deny that "law" plays any part as a basis for redemption. In their own words,

> Salvation is not now, and never has been, by law or by works; salvation is only by the grace of Christ. Moreover, there never was a time in the plan of God when salvation was by human works or effort. Nothing men can do, or have done, can in any way merit salvation.
>
> While works are not a means of salvation, good works are the inevitable result of salvation. However, these good works are possible only for the child of God whose life is inwrought by the Spirit of God. . . . One thing is certain, man cannot be saved by any effort of his own. We profoundly believe that no works of the law, no deeds of the law, no effort however commendable, and no good works—whether they be many or few, sacrificial or not—can in any way justify the sinner (Titus 3:5; Romans 3:20). Salvation is wholly of grace; it is the gift of God (Romans 4:4–5; Ephesians 2:8).[79]

These and many similar clear-cut statements in current authoritative Seventh-day Adventist literature reveal that, despite the "dual-law theory" and the

---

[79] *Questions on Doctrine*, 141–42.

peculiar concept that the law is still operative in the life of the believer, Adventists confess the basis of their salvation to be grace, and grace alone, the only basis upon which God deigns to save the fallen children of Adam.

In chapter 14 of *Questions on Doctrine*, Adventists spell out their allegiance to divine grace as the only channel of salvation: "According to Seventh-day Adventist belief, there is, and can be, no salvation through the law, or by human works of the law, but only through the saving grace of God."[80]

Christians who are familiar with historical theology know that the Adventists' position on law, though tinged with legalism, has its roots in the basic Arminian position that one receives salvation as a free gift of God; but, once he has received this gift, the believer is responsible for its maintenance and duration, and the chief means of accomplishing this is "commandment-keeping" or "obedience to all the laws of God."

Since Adventists are basically Arminian, we may logically deduce that, in a sense, their salvation rests upon legal grounds. But the saving factor in the dilemma is that by life and by worldwide witness, Adventists, like other so-called Arminians, give true evidence that they have experienced the "new birth," which is by grace alone, through faith in our Lord and His sacrifice upon the cross. One would be callous and uncharitable, indeed, not to accept their profession of dependence upon Christ alone for redemption, even though there is inconsistency in their theological system.

Some Christians make a great issue of the teaching of "eternal security," and perhaps rightly so because it is an important truth. However, no matter how strongly we may feel about it, our conviction does not entitle us to judge the motives and spiritual condition of other believers in this respect. This is our principal reason for taking the position that Seventh-day Adventists are Christians who believe the historical Gospel message. They cannot rightly be called non-Christian cultists or "Judaizers," since they are sound on the great New Testament doctrines, including grace and redemption through the vicarious offering of Jesus Christ "once for all" (Hebrews 10:10) and give evidence of "life in Christ."

For many centuries there has been much controversy over the juxtaposition of the principles of law and grace in the Scriptures. If evangelicals today were asked, "Do you believe that grace and law are in direct opposition?" the answer in most cases would be a strong affirmative. Through the years confusion has been caused by the abuse of both principles by two groups of equally sincere Christians. One group believes that all law has ceased; the other that the Ten Commandments are still God's standard of righteousness and must be obeyed or salvation is forfeited. What both groups have failed to grasp is that the great conflict is not between law and grace as such; rather it centers around a proper understanding of their relationship and respective functions.

We have established that love is the ground and source of the doctrine of grace, but the law was necessary to expose the sinfulness of sin and the depth of man's moral depravity. When law becomes the ground of salvation or of restraining the Christian from practicing sin, it intrudes upon the province of grace. When a Christian is not controlled by love, grace is abused and its purpose is

---

[80]Ibid., 135.

nullified. All law is fulfilled by love, as our Savior and the apostles taught, but the Christian can never please God if he obeys for fear of the law. Life under law binds the soul, for the tendency is for man to obey not because he wants to please God but because he fears God's judgment. Under grace, love works upon the regenerate heart, and what was legalistic duty under law becomes gracious obedience under grace. Actually, grace and love demand more than the law, which to the Pharisees required only outward obedience. Grace commands us to do "the will of God from the heart" (Ephesians 6:6). Seventh-day Adventists declare that they obey the law not out of fear but out of love for God. However, it is to be regretted that in a large proportion of their literature on the subject, they declare that the keeping of the law is necessary to maintain salvation, and thus they introduce the motive of fear instead of the biblical imperative of love.

The apostle John defined the issue when he wrote, "The law was given by Moses, but grace and truth came by Jesus Christ" (John 1:17). As a governing principle, a measure of righteousness, a schoolmaster, and an instrument of death, the law was supplanted by grace—the unmerited favor of God. All believers in the Lord Jesus Christ, having passed from death to life through the sacrifice of the Son of God, possess the divine nature and righteousness. Because He first loved us, we are compelled and impelled to love and serve Him. In obedience to the great law of love, the Christian fulfills the righteousness of the law (not the law itself; this Christ alone did); and by the transforming power of the indwelling Holy Spirit, he will "walk not after the flesh, but after the Spirit" (Romans 8:4).

Seventh-day Adventists believe, we repeat, that they are saved by grace. However, they are often prone to believe that their remaining saved depends on "commandment-keeping."

More recently, an Adventist professor summed up the church's present understanding of this issue as a generally unified but still tension-filled affirmation of salvation by grace alone through faith—evidenced by obedience. Dr. Gary Land, Andrews University in Berrien Spring, Michigan, explained,

> The committee issued a statement on "the dynamics of salvation." Because humanity is desperately in need of salvation, it said, God has taken the initiative to provide it. When the individual human being, with the Holy Spirit's help, decides to accept reconciliation with God, he receives a new status in Christ, encompassed by such terms as justification, reconciliation, forgiveness, adoption, and sanctification. This new status involves a new life in Christ characterized by new birth, restoration, growth, grace and faith, assurance, and praise. Consummation is achieved with Christ's Second Coming, which will restore the universe to a "perfect, sinless state."
>
> In essence, the statement addressed the righteousness by faith debate by analyzing the theological terms involved, attempting to bring together all elements of the subject, and placing the whole within an Adventist eschatological context. Although it included an emphasis on sanctification, that concept was now one of several elements. By offering an enlarged understanding of salvation, the statement appeared to provide room for both sides of the debate.
>
> It appears on the surface that the righteousness by faith debate pivoted on the technical issue of a definition. But the fact that so many people could

get so disturbed over the question indicates that it hit a raw nerve within Adventism. The justification by grace through faith position seems to have appealed to a large number of Adventists because it offered an assurance of salvation that they felt the traditional emphasis on sanctification had not allowed. On the other hand, many of those who opposed the new teaching feared that it might open the door to an antinomianism that would undermine the Adventist concern with God's law.

In the view of most denominational theologians, Seventh-day Adventists had the unique problem and unique opportunity of understanding the relationship of justification and sanctification, or law and gospel, in a way that did justice to both.[81]

That current Adventist teaching regarding sanctification is based on grace, not works, is clear from the Adventists' doctrinal discussion in *Seventh-day Adventists Believe*, which states,

> True repentance and justification lead to sanctification. Justification and sanctification are closely related, distinct but never separate. They designate two phases of salvation: Justification is what God does *for* us, while sanctification is what God does *in* us.
>
> Neither justification nor sanctification is the result of meritorious works. Both are solely due to Christ's grace and righteousness. . . . The three phases of sanctification the Bible presents are: (1) an accomplished act in the believer's past; (2) a process in the believer's present experience; (3) and the final result that the believer experiences at Christ's return.[82]

III. The Author of Salvation

Because He took our sins upon himself, in obedience to His Father's will, the Lord Jesus "became the author of eternal salvation unto all them that obey him" (Hebrews 5:8–10). This truth Seventh-day Adventists believe. They strongly assert their belief in the deity of the Lord Jesus Christ, His equality with the Father, and His perfect, sinless human nature, and expound these truths in detail. However, they teach that before His incarnation the Lord Jesus Christ bore the title of Michael the archangel. This interpretation differs greatly from that of Jehovah's Witnesses, who believe that Christ was a created being and that "He was a god, but not the Almighty God who is Jehovah."[83] The Adventists make this very clear:

> We emphatically reject the idea . . . and the position held by the Jehovah's Witnesses. We do not believe that Christ is a created being. We as a people have not considered the identification of "Michael" of sufficient prominence to dwell upon it at length either in our literature or in our preaching. . . . We believe that the term Michael is but one of the many titles applied to the Son of God, the second person of the Godhead. But such a view does not in any way conflict with our belief in His full deity and eternal preexistence, nor does it in the least disparage His person and work.[84]

---

[81]Gary Land, ed., *Adventism in America* (Grand Rapids, Mich.: William B. Eerdmans Publishing Company, 1986), 218–19.
[82]*Seventh-day Adventists Believe,* 123.
[83]*Let God Be True* (Brooklyn, N.Y.: Watchtower Bible and Tract Society, 1952), 100.
[84]*Questions on Doctrine,* 71.

Although a number of authoritative commentators support the Adventist view, the New Testament, I believe, does not warrant this conclusion. Most of the evidence that the Adventists submit is from the book of Daniel, the rest from the Apocalypse. By comparing such designations as "angel of Jehovah," "angel of the Lord," "Prince," and "Michael," the Adventists conclude that Michael is another title for the Lord Jesus Christ. But Seventh-day Adventists maintain that although he is called "the archangel" (*archangelos* or "first messenger"), he is not a created being, since, in the Old Testament, "angel of Jehovah" is a term of Deity. In the light of this, we do not judge them because of their view of Michael, but call the reader's attention to the ninth verse of the book of Jude, which says, "Yet Michael the archangel, when contending with the devil he disputed about the body of Moses, durst not bring against him a railing accusation, but said, The Lord rebuke thee."

The word translated "durst" in the King James Bible is the archaic past tense of "dare"; so Michael "did not dare" bring against Satan a railing or blasphemous (*blasphemos*) judgment. The Greek word for "dare" is *tolmao* and appears sixteen times in the New Testament, and in the negative always means "not daring through fear of retaliation." Thus if Michael was Christ, according to the Seventh-day Adventists, "He did not dare" to rebuke Satan for fear of retaliation.

Adventists agree that fifteen times in the New Testament *tolmao* carries the meaning indicated. But since its use in Jude 9 refutes their notion that Michael is a title of Christ, they reverse its meaning here! As the Adventists know, none of the commentators to whom they appeal has grammatically analyzed or diagrammed the passage in the Greek or for that matter commented upon exclusive usage of *tolmao* in the Scripture of the New Testament. The agreement of such commentation, therefore, gives no validity whatever to the Adventists' misuse of *tolmao*. The preincarnate Christ, the *Logos*, having the nature of God (John 1:1), certainly would not refer the creature Satan to God the Father for rebuke. While He was on earth, Christ the Creator rebuked Satan many times. Would He then fear him during His preincarnate life? Scripture contradicts this.

The Adventist explanation is:

> The devil, the prince of evil, could rightly be said to deserve a railing accusation, but to such a thing Michael would not stoop. To say that Michael could not, in the sense that He did not have the power or the authority to do so, would not be true. It is not that Michael could not, in the sense of being restricted, but rather that He would not take such an attitude.[85]

This statement appears to be an attempt to escape the fact that the word "dare" (*tolmao*) in the New Testament always connotes fear, including its use in Jude 9. The text teaches that because Michael did not have the authority to rebuke Satan, "he did not dare" to do so through fear of superior retaliation. There is no implication that Michael's position was so high that he "would not stoop." The context, grammar, and root meaning of *tolmao* contradict the Adventists' attempt to make this text support their view of Michael. All authorities on

[85] *Questions on Doctrine*, 80.

Greek grammar agree that the Adventist interpretation violates the classic and New Testament usage of *tolmao*.

Thus the Adventist statement about Michael is neither linguistically nor scripturally accurate. Although they repudiate the Jehovah's Witnesses' position, they wrest this passage from its true meaning and read into it their own theory concerning Michael as Christ.

In conclusion, I am convinced of the sincerity of the Adventists' claim to regeneration and allegiance to the New Testament principle of saving grace. I appreciate their high regard for the law of God and their desire to obey it. I cannot agree, however, with their insistence upon linking "commandment-keeping" to observance of the ceremonial law, especially with regard to "unclean" foods. I feel, moreover, that they err in saying that Michael is a title of Christ, and I believe that I have shown that they violate the linguistic and scriptural meaning of Jude 9.

Author's Note

One of the chief critics of Seventh-day Adventism is a vocal ex-Adventist printer of Minneapolis, a man who has written much against his former church. Writing in *The Sword of the Lord,* August 2, 1957, he bitterly assailed Seventh-day Adventists as willful deceivers. Since his writings are repeatedly quoted by most of the other critics, we shall discuss his charge, but in the interest of brevity we shall confine ourselves to one of his chief areas of criticism—law and salvation in Seventh-day Adventist theology.

This critic quotes the book *Steps to Christ,* by Ellen G. White, in the following manner: "The condition of eternal life is now just what it has always been . . . perfect obedience to the law of God."

He then maintains that Seventh-day Adventism teaches this, and on the surface it appears that he has proved his point; namely that to Adventists, salvation is a combination of grace, faith in Christ, plus the keeping of the law. A closer look at the statement in the context from which the critic removed it, however, serves to refute this position. Wrote White in the very same context:

> We do not earn salvation by our obedience, for salvation is the free gift of God to receive by faith. But obedience is the fruit of faith . . . here is the true test. If we abide in Christ and the love of God dwells in us, our feelings, our thoughts, our actions will be in harmony with the will of God as expressed in the precepts of His Holy law. . . . Righteousness is defined by the standard of God's holy law as expressed in the ten precepts given on Sinai. That so-called faith in Christ that professes to release men from the obligation of obedience to God is not faith but presumption. "By grace are ye saved through faith." But "faith, if it has hath not works is dead." Jesus said of himself before He came to earth, "I delight to do thy will, O my God: yea, Thy law is within my heart." And just before He ascended again to heaven, He declared, "I have kept my Father's commandments and abide in His love." The Scripture says, "Hereby we do know that we know him, if we keep his commandments. . . . He that saith he abideth in Him ought himself also to so walk even as he walked," because "Christ also suffered for us, leaving us an example, that ye should follow His steps."

The condition of eternal life is now just what it always has been—just what it was in Paradise before the fall of our first parents—perfect obedience to the law of God, perfect righteousness.... Since we are sinful, unholy, we cannot perfectly obey a holy law. We have no righteousness of our own with which to meet the claims of the law of God. But Christ has made a way of escape for us. He lived on earth amid trials and temptations such as we have to meet. He lived a sinless life. He died for us, and now He offers to take our sins and give us His righteousness. If you give yourself to Him and accept Him as your Saviour, then, sinful as your life may have been, for His sake you are counted righteous. Christ's character stands in place of your character, and you are accepted before God just as if you had not sinned....

So we have nothing in ourselves of which to boast. We have no ground for self exaltation. Our only ground of hope is in the righteousness of Christ imputed to us and in that wrought by His Spirit working in and through us.[86]

In the light of White's complete statement on this subject, we see that our critic omitted her principal thesis—that we are saved by grace. There are not a few instances of similar carelessness on the part of the writer of this article. The result is that his work is largely discredited and discounted by those who know the proper methods of research.

Seventh-day Adventists are well aware of the law and grace problem, and in *Questions on Doctrine* they state,

There has been regrettable misunderstanding as to our teaching on grace, law, and works, and their interrelationships. According to Seventh-day Adventist belief, there is, and can be, no salvation through the law or by human works of the law, but only through the saving grace of God. This principle, to us, is basic.[87]

Further the Adventists state,

Salvation is not now, and never has been, by law or works; salvation is only by the grace of Christ. Moreover, there never was a time in the plan of God when salvation was by human works or effort. Nothing men can do, or have done, can in any way merit salvation.

While works are not a means of salvation, good works are the inevitable result of salvation.... One thing is certain, man cannot be saved by any effort of his own. We profoundly believe that no works of the law, no deeds of the law, no effort however commendable, and no good works—whether they be many or few, sacrificial or not—can in any way justify the sinner (Titus 3:5; Romans 3:20). Salvation is wholly of grace; it is the gift of God (Romans 4:4–5; Ephesians 2:8). (*Questions on Doctrine*, 141–42)

Ellen G. White, certainly an authoritative voice in Adventism, summarized it thus:

---

[86]Ellen G. White, *Steps to Christ* (Washington, D.C.: Review and Herald Publishing Association, 1945), 36–49.
[87]*Questions on Doctrine*, 135.

Christ is pleading for the church in the heavenly courts above, pleading for those for whom He paid the redemption price of His own lifeblood. Centuries, ages, can never diminish the efficacy of this atoning sacrifice. The message of the gospel of His grace was to be given to the church in clear and distinct lines, that the world should no longer say that Seventh-day Adventists talk the law, but do not teach or believe Christ.[88]

Recommended Resources

1. Martin, Walter. *Seventh-day Adventism,* audiotape. Walter Martin Ministries. *www.waltermartin.com.*
2. ———. *The Truth About Seventh-day Adventism.* Grand Rapids: Zondervan Publishing House, 1960.
3. McDowell, Josh, and Don Stewart. *A Handbook on Today's Religions.* Nashville: Thomas Nelson, 1993.
4. Paxton, Geoffrey J. *The Shaking of Adventism.* Grand Rapids, Mich.: Baker Book House, 1977.
5. Rea, Walter T. *The White Lie.* Turlock, Calif.: M & R Publications.

---

[88]Ellen G. White, *Testimonies to Ministers* (Mountain View, Calif.: Pacific Press, n.d.), 92.

Quick Facts About Swedenborgianism

- God is not three distinct persons but three "essentials" of one God (modalism). The Trinity is a false belief.

- Some Scripture—as interpreted by Emmanuel Swedenborg—is the word of God.

- Salvation is a continuing process of overcoming evil and serving God.

- The devil does not exist. Man chooses heaven or hell based on his earthly relationships. In heaven, man becomes an angel; in hell, man becomes an evil spirit.

- Final judgment is not evaluation by a supreme being; it is facing the truth about your real self.[1]

---

[1]See official Web site of Watchman Fellowship, *www.watchman.org/profile/swedenborgpro.htm*; see also official Web site of the Swedenborg Church, *www.swedenborg.org/tenets.cfm;* and the official Web site of Christian Apologetics & Research Ministry, *www.carm.org/list/swedenborg.htm.*

Appendix C

Swedenborgianism

Historical Perspectives

It is virtually impossible to study the field of cult systems without coming to grips with the theology of the Church of the New Jerusalem, which, although small in number in America (around fourteen thousand members in three different conferences), wields a considerable influence in intellectual church circles. This is true both in the United States and abroad. In foreign countries, particularly in England and in the Scandinavian nations, this particular cult has declined in growth over the last few years, with a worldwide membership that is difficult to pinpoint because of the various organizations active in over thirty countries.[1]

Whereas most if not all of the major cult systems are the products of individuals who could scarcely be called intellectuals, the Church of the New Jerusalem had as its founder one of the most gifted and respected intellectuals of any age—Emanuel Swedenborg.

Swedenborg was born in Stockholm, Sweden, on January 29, 1688. He died in London on March 29, 1772, in his eighty-fifth year. The son of the Reverend Jasper Swedenborg, noted Lutheran minister and court chaplain to the king of Sweden, he was later to become a professor and dean of the University of Upsala. Swedenborg, indeed, sprang from noble roots, and at an early age distinguished himself as a mathematician, mining expert, engineer, and inventor. So enormous were his contributions to his homeland, particularly in the area of high finance and in mining, that in 1808, thirty-six years after his death, his remains were removed from their crypt in the Lutheran church in Princes Square, Radcliffe Highway, London, and transported by the Swedish navy to their final resting place in a cathedral

---

This appendix updated and edited by Kevin Rische and Jill Martin Rische.
[1] *www.watchman.org/profile/swedenborgpro.htm.*

in Upsala. Some two years after this, the king of Sweden and his family, in the presence of numerous dignitaries and churchmen, dedicated a memorial to him, which action had been unanimously voted by the Swedish parliament.

Swedenborg received his education at Upsala and then traveled for the next four years in Germany, Holland, England, and France. He occupied his spare time between studies with various inventions.

William White, in his life story of Swedenborg, stated that, as a result of his inventive genius, Swedenborg produced "a new stove, a magazine air gun, methods of salt manufacture . . . and drew plans for a flying machine and the construction of docks" (p. 29, also see *Transactions of the International Swedenborg Congress,* 1910, p. 5).

To add to his achievements during this particular period of inventive genius, Swedenborg was working on what he called a sort of ship in which a man can go below the surface of the sea and do great damage to the fleet of an enemy.

At the close of his journeys abroad, Swedenborg wrote various books and attracted the attention of his sovereign, King Charles XII, who recognized his genius and appointed him a professor in the Swedish College of Mines. Following the death of the king in 1718, Swedenborg became a member of the *Swedish Diet.* In his capacity as *Royal Assessor of Mines,* he traveled extensively throughout Europe, broadening his background and already tremendous grasp of philosophy, art, theology, and metaphysics. This he dutifully recorded in his *Diary of Travel,* a type of John Gunther approach to the Europe of the eighteenth century.

Swedenborg was the associate of kings, princes, scholars, mathematicians, engineers, astronomers, and theologians. Few men have ever attained the degree of acceptance and prominence that he enjoyed during his long life, a recognition that extended to multiple fields of interest, and was a lasting tribute to his intellectual breadth and brilliance.

The year 1745 marks the turning point in Swedenborg's career as a world figure in many fields of endeavor, for it was then that he maintained that he received a divine summons to become both a seer and a revelator of the things of the spiritual world, and simultaneously of the spiritual truth and doctrine that underlies the literal and symbolic sense of the sacred Scriptures. Between the years 1743 and 1749, Swedenborg maintained that he experienced heavenly visions and periods of great temptation, which culminated in a prodigious writing program, producing such works as *Arcane Coelestia; The Earths in the Universe; The White Horse of the Apocalypse; The Apocalypse Explained; The Last Judgment; The New Jerusalem and Its Heavenly Doctrines;* and *The Apocalypse Revealed.*

Swedenborg went on to publish *The Angelic Wisdom Respecting the Divine Love and Wisdom,* 1763; *The Angelic Wisdom Respecting the Divine Providence,* 1764; *The Delights of Wisdom Concerning Conjugal Love,* 1768; *A Re-fixed Position Concerning the Doctrine of the New Church, Signified by the New Jerusalem in Revelation,* 1769; and his final work, *The True Christian Religion Containing the Universal Theology of the New Church, or Universal Theology and the New Church,* 1771. This was, quite literally, a compendium of his entire theological structure. One authority on Swedenborg also points out:

> He wrote books on algebra, giving the first account in Swedish of the
> differential in integral calculus; on a mode of finding the longitude at sea

by the moon; on decimal money and measures; on the motion and position of the earth and planets; on the depth of the sea and the greater force of the tides in the ancient world; on docks, sluices and salt works; on chemistry and on atomic geometry.... After some philosophical writing, dissatisfied with his results, he studied anatomy and physiology and wrote books thereon.... At the age of fifty-four, Swedenborg was probably one of the most learned men alive, taking learning as meaning acquaintance with the universe as then known. One small indication of this is the fact that the then president of our royal society, Sir Hans Sloan, invited him to become a corresponding member.

Then a curious thing happened. In 1743 he had spiritual illumination, with tremblings, voices, lights, etc. and began to have access to the spiritual world, or to think that he had. During the years 1749 to 1756 he published in London his *Arcana Coelestia,* in four volumes quarto, and later, other works containing the exposition of his doctrines, which were mainly concerned with the spiritual interpretation of the Scriptures, and particularly, of Genesis and Exodus. Much of this seems fanciful, but the thought is always systematic, and no one can reasonably say that Swedenborg was insane. Moreover, he was shrewd in worldly affairs, affable in society, and discussed politics and finance in the Swedish Diet like a man of the world. For a score of years after, he began to write and publish his theological works, which number about forty volumes.

But this exposition of Scripture, received, as he believed, direct from the Lord, and considered by him to be the important part of his work, is less interesting to us than his spiritual experiences, which are mostly described in his spiritual diary, from whence he copied extracts occasionally into his theological works. These experiences were admittedly of such a character, that in an ordinary man they would have sufficed to qualify him for an asylum. Swedenborg talked, or thought he talked, with Luther, Calvin, St. Augustine, St. Paul—arguing theological questions with them and disagreeing violently with the last-named, and many others including "one who, it was given me to understand, was Cicero."

All this, although probably not hallucinatory, is at least perilous stuff, and the Swedenborgians have done wisely not to base much on it. He wrote automatically, heard clairaudiently, and saw writings and the very words of the writings, even with the eyes shut. But there are a few incidents on record which are evidential, and these may reasonably give us pause before deciding for a subjective explanation of this seer's experiences.[2]

I shall allude in a few moments to this passage. But enough has been shown to establish beyond reasonable doubt that Swedenborg was a unique individual whose mind and influence reached into many quarters in the age in which he lived. Frank Sewall best summed it up when he wrote:

> Like many leaders of the world's thought, Swedenborg has required the vistas of the years by which to be seen in his real significance. Immanuel Kant concealed his indebtedness to him under the persiflage of the "Dreams of the Spirit-Seer"; Goethe is more outspoken in his gratitude and his *Faust* is full of the Swedenborg world-view. Swedenborg's trinal monism,

---

[2]J. Arthur Hill, *Spiritualism: Its History, Phenomena, and Doctrine* (New York: George Doran, 1919), 42–44.

the doctrine that the one embraces in itself the three essential degrees, end, cause, effect: the grand man, or the human form of society; the spiritual, as being the real, world; the spiritual meaning as the true and essential meaning of the Scriptures; God as divine Man, visible and adorable in the glorified humanity of Jesus Christ; the doctrine of the world as a vast system of tremulations set in motion by its center, the infinite divine love, and transmitted through successive spiritual and natural spheres and atmospheres; of the kingdom of heaven as a kingdom of uses—these ideas are permeating all the newer developments of philosophic and religious thought. Early theological prejudice is giving way to profound respect; the time seems near when Swedenborg's own prophecy, from the words of Seneca, will be realized: "There will come those who will judge without offense or favor."[3]

I cannot agree with Mr. Sewall relative to any idea of accepting Swedenborg's basic theological system, which I shall review shortly. But that his place in the intellectual hall of man is secure, no objective person can deny. Swedenborg's theological position, however, in the realms of non-Christian cultism, constitutes quite another area of concern. For genius though he was, his concept of the Bible, the writings of the apostle Paul and numerous other books of the Old and New Testaments, places him well outside the pale of Christian theology. This is true not only concerning the Canon, but concerning such doctrines as the nature of God, the holy Trinity, the atonement of Jesus Christ, and the doctrines of salvation and resurrection. We cannot ignore the person of Emanuel Swedenborg; in fact, as the years pass, through the church that he inspired and the reputation that he earned, he is becoming a growing influence to be reckoned with and carefully examined in the light of historic Christianity. No less an authority than the noted scholar, Conrad J. Bergendoff, writing in the *Encyclopedia of Religion*, edited by Virgilius Ferm, declared of Swedenborg's theology and background:

> Swedenborg's student days included impressions from Rudbeck at Upsala, Newton, Boyle, Halley, Locke in England, Polhem in Sweden, the Cartesian philosophy and the Cambridge Neo-Platonists.
>
> The *Principia (1734)* explained the universe in mechanistic terms. A mystical view pervaded the *Oeconomia regni animalis (1736)*; the world was now less a machine, more an organism. The *anima* receives illumination from the central source of life and light when the *mens* controls man's physical nature. Between the physical and spiritual world there is a close correspondence, each natural phenomena shadowing a spiritual reality ... this idea was extended to the mystical correspondence between words and their inner meaning—a basis for his later spiritual interpretation of Scripture, which was a means whereby the divine was communicated to the mind of man.
>
> In Amsterdam, *1736*, Swedenborg had an experience of photism; in Amsterdam, *1744*, and in London, *1745*, he experienced visions, which he interpreted as revelations of the Creator-Redeemer. Henceforth he proclaimed the truth received by direct vision, though the biblical imagery of *De Cultu Amore Dei (1745)* concealed much the same cosmology and psychology as the earlier works. Even his visions were more confirmation than a source of his speculations.

---

[3]Frank Sewall in *The New Schaff-Herzog Encyclopedia of Religious Knowledge*, Samuel M. Jackson, ed. (Grand Rapids, Mich.: Baker Book House, 1977) reprint, vol. 11, 188.

The theology of Swedenborg is systematically presented in *The True Christian Religion (1771)*. The orthodox doctrines of the Trinity and the Atonement were repudiated. Redemption consists of the Incarnate God overcoming the increasing powers of hell. Man's freedom enables him to choose and follow the good. On death he enters the realm of the spirits, when he either ascends to the heavenly sphere, becoming an angel, or descends to hell, becoming an evil spirit. Following a spiritual mode of interpreting Scripture which he held to be inspired, Swedenborg considered the Judgment to have come in *1757* and Christ's Second Coming as a victory over rebellious spirits. The heavenly world corresponds to the human, and even marriage finds transcendent meaning in heavenly marriage of kindred souls. . . . The orthodox churches must give way to the New Church (which dates from the completion of *The True Christian Religion, 1771*) when men will be correctly instructed in the truth of God.[4]

The organization of The Church of the New Jerusalem took place in London in 1788, although it is generally traced back by its membership to the Second Coming of Christ, which, according to Swedenborg, took place when he received "the key to the interpretation of Scripture." There can be little doubt that Swedenborg's revelation of what he termed the spiritual meaning of Scripture did indeed become the doctrinal basis of the church formed in his honor.

The first general conference of the church met in 1789. It was organized in 1821, the "General Conference of the Ministers and Other Members of the New Church Signified by the New Jerusalem in the Apocalypse, or Revelation of John." This particularly British convention in 1926 numbered seventy societies, with more than 7,000 members.

The Swedenborg Society since the year 1810 has published a voluminous amount of literature, specializing in translations of Swedenborg's works. Branches of the church are today to be found in Africa, South America, Russia, Italy, Sweden, and many other countries.

In the United States, the church was organized in Baltimore, Maryland, in 1792. Its name is "The General Convention of the New Jerusalem in the United States," the name taken in 1817. The churches are essentially autonomous, but are bound together in a cooperative type of association governed by a general convention, which meets annually. Under the powers of the convention, the education and ordination of pastors for the establishment of missions, orders of worship, and church government, etc., are carried out.

The Church of the New Jerusalem has had its internal controversies, however, particularly in 1890 when the Pennsylvania association, which might be termed "fundamentalist Swedenborgians," insisted upon the virtual canonization of Swedenborg's writings, and withdrew when they could not force this upon the convention. In 1897 this group became known as "The General Church of the New Jerusalem," which has a presiding bishop, a cathedral, and an educational institution, located in Bryn Athyn, Pennsylvania. ~ *The New Church*, as it is called today, claims a worldwide membership of about 30,000.[5] Their official Web site states, "In Swedenborg's 35 volumes of theology, which we call the "Writings,"

---

[4]Conrad Bergendoff in *Encyclopedia of Religion*, Vergilius Ferm, ed. (New York: Philosophical Library, 1945), 752.

[5]Statistics as of early 2003 on the Official Web site of The New Church, *www.newchurch.org/*.

what is set forth is the Lord's plan for a rebirth of Christianity . . ." indicating a "scriptural" quality to Swedenborg's writings.[6]

The Church of the New Jerusalem, known today as the *Swedenborgian Church,* claims a worldwide membership of 50,000, with a total membership in the United States of 2,600. The Swedenborgian Church operates Urbana University in Urbana, Ohio, and a "seminary" known as the University House of Studies, affiliated with Pacific School of Religion in Berkeley, California.[7] Their official Web site states, "The Swedenborgian church bases its teachings on the Bible as illuminated by the works of Emanuel Swedenborg. . . ."[8]~

These organizations, therefore, are inextricably bound to the teachings of Swedenborg and his interpretations of the Bible. Women may join the church at the age of eighteen, and men at the age of twenty-one, but only after studying the writings of Swedenborg for some six months. The Christian sacraments of baptism and communion are copied in the church, as are the marriage and burial services. The official liturgy (resembling in practically every detail the Anglican *Book of Prayer*) and the church government are Episcopal, with but minor alterations.

Such is the background of Swedenborgianism, seen in the perspective of history. In the realm of theology, however, a somewhat different picture emerges.

The Occult Theology of Swedenborg

As has been noted in the preceding history, Swedenborg considered himself, from 1745 until his death, the seer of a new revelation from God that superseded the interpretational powers of the apostles, church fathers, and the reformers. This is a singular fact, which emphasizes that modesty was not one of his strong points. Mr. Hill has already mentioned a point that can be easily documented, namely Swedenborg's preoccupation with dreams, visions, and alleged messages and conversations with spirits and the spirit world. It is of no small significance that Sir Arthur Conan Doyle, the great advocate of Spiritism, and every spiritist, historian, and theologian of note, claim Swedenborg as a medium who practiced clairvoyance and other phenomena associated with Spiritism. Swedenborg never denied such practices, and, therefore, whether his followers wish to concede it or not, he was most certainly, in a large area of his theological and metaphysical practices and thought, a thoroughgoing spiritist. One instance of Swedenborg's clairvoyance should be noted in order to underscore this fact:

In September 1759 Swedenborg was one of a party of sixteen guests at the home of Mr. William Castel at Gottenburg, three hundred miles from Stockholm. He had arrived from England at four o'clock in the afternoon.

About six o'clock Swedenborg went out and returned to the company, quite pale and alarmed. He said a dangerous fire had just broken out in Stockholm at the Sodermalm (Gottenburg is about fifty German miles from Stockholm), and that it was spreading very fast. He said that the house of one of his friends, whom he named, was already in ashes, and that his own was in danger. At eight o'clock,

---

[6]*www.newchurch.org/.*
[7]There are about forty-five churches in the United States. See *www.swedenborg.org/chtoday.cfm.*
[8]Official Web site of the Swedenborgian Church *www.swedenborg.org/beliefs.cfm.* Statistical and doctrinal information are not publicly posted by the third organization of Swedenborgianism, the General Conference of the New Church in Great Britain. *http://newchurch.newearth.org/gcncgb.php.*

after he had been out again, he joyfully exclaimed, "Thank God! The fire is extinguished the third door from my house!" This news occasioned great commotion throughout the whole city. It was announced to the governor that same evening. Sunday morning, Swedenborg was summoned to the governor, who questioned him concerning the disaster. Swedenborg described the fire precisely, how it had begun and in what manner it ceased, and how long it had continued. On the same day the news spread throughout the city, and as the governor thought it worthy of attention, the consternation was considerably increased; because many were troubled because of their friends and property. On Monday evening a messenger arrived at Gottenburg, who was dispatched by the Board of Trade during the term of the fire. In the letters brought by him the fire was described in precisely the manner stated by Swedenborg. On Tuesday morning a royal courier arrived at the governor's with a melancholy intelligence of the fire, of the losses it had occasioned, and of the houses that had been damaged and ruined, not in the least differing from that which Swedenborg had given at the very time when it happened; for the fire was extinguished at eight o'clock.[9]

This remarkable piece of clairvoyance is in company with Swedenborg's actual communication with a deceased Dutch ambassador. This "ghost" had informed Swedenborg that his wife should not pay for a silver service as demanded by a goldsmith, for he declared he had paid the smith several months earlier. The receipt of the transaction was in a bureau in a room upstairs in the house, which the widow then occupied. The lady insisted that the bureau had been thoroughly searched, but Swedenborg informed her that her husband had a secret drawer behind the left drawer of the bureau where the receipt would be found. Upon complying with Swedenborg's instructions, the widow found the receipt precisely as he had described it. Jung Stilling in his *Theory of Pneumotology*, (p. 92), recounts this, as does Kant in *Dreams of a Spirit Seer* (appendix, pp. 157–58). The gentleman who "received the proof from Swedenborg" was an intimate friend of Stilling.

Such evidence of Swedenborg's communication with the spirit world in direct violation of the express commands of Scripture (Leviticus 19:31; 20:6) would be sufficient to make any thoughtful Christian suspicious of his theological system, even before examining it thoroughly. But happily, an exhaustive analysis of his voluminous works is not necessary to reveal the fact that Swedenborg was far from being a Christian, and certainly was not a Christian theologian.

The following quotations drawn from his basic writings reveal his thinking in certain key areas of Christian theology and are reproduced for the purpose of contrast with the teachings of Scripture.

Doctrines

I. *The Holy Scriptures—the Word of God*
    Which are the books of the Word? That the books of the Word are all those which have the internal sense; but that those books which have not

---

[9]See Borowsky's *Darstellung Des Lebens und Charakters,* Immanuel Kant, Konigsberg 1804, 211–25. Trans. in *Dreams of a Spirit Seer,* 158–59, appen. Letter from Kant to Charlotte Von Knobloch. See also Tafels, *Documents Concerning Swedenborg*, Vol. II, Part One, 628.

the internal sense are not the Word. The books of the Word in the Old Testament are: The five books of Moses, the book of Joshua, the book of the Judges, the two books of Samuel, the two books of the Kings, the Psalms of David, the prophets Isaiah and Jeremiah, Ezekiel, Daniel, Hosea, Joel, Amos, Obadiah, Jonah, Micah, Nahum, Habakkuk, Zephaniah, Haggai, Zechariah and Malachi. In the New Testament, the four evangelists, Matthew, Mark, Luke and John and The Apocalypse. The rest have not the internal sense. . . . The book of Job is an ancient book, which indeed contains internal sense, but not in series. . . . (Emanuel Swedenborg, *Miscellaneous Theological Works* [New York: Philosophical Library, 1916], 312)

II. *The Trinity of God*

1. That many of the false tenets . . . as likewise concerning the person of Christ, together with all the heresy from the first ages down to the present day, have flowed from no other source than from a doctrine founded upon the idea of three Gods. We have not room to demonstrate within the limits of this epitomy, but that assertion shall be shown and proved at large in the work itself. (C. O. Sigstedt, *The Swedenborg Epic* [New York: Twayne, 1952], 177)

2. From the Nicene Trinity and the Athanasian Trinity together a faith arose by which the whole Christian Church has been perverted. That both the Nicene and Athanasian trinities are a Trinity of Gods can be seen from the creeds. (Ibid.)

3. After this they proceeded to deliberate about the Holy Spirit; and previous thereto they laid open the idea generally received concerning God the Father, the Son and the Holy Spirit which is, that God the Father is seated on high with the Son at His right hand, that by them is sent forth the Holy Spirit to enlighten and instruct mankind. But instantly a voice was heard from heaven saying, "We cannot endure an idea formed on such a conception. . . . There is not a mediating God distinct from Him (Jehovah); much less is there a third God distinct from two others, as one person is distinct from two others, as one person is distinct from another person; wherefore, let the former idea which is vexing and frivolous be removed, and let this which is just and right be received, then you will see clearly. . . . One God cannot come forth and proceed from another, by another, but what is divine may come forth and proceed from one God? Is not the Divine Essence one and indivisible, and inasmuch as the Divine Essence is God, is not God therefore one indivisible?" On hearing these words, they that sat on the seats unanimously agreed in this conclusion, that the Holy Spirit is not a distinct person of Himself, consequently not a distinct God of Himself; but that by the Holy Spirit is meant the divine sanctity, coming forth and proceeding from the one and only omnipresent God, who is the Lord. (*Miscellaneous Theological Works*, op. cit., 249–50)

III. *Vicarious Atonement*

1. "Who does not know that God is essential compassion and mercy . . . and who does not hereby see that it is a contradiction to assert that mercy itself or goodness itself can heal man from anger, become his enemy, turn himself away from him and determine on his damnation, and still continue to be the same divine being or God? Such things can scarcely be attributed to a good man, but only to a wicked man, thus not to an angel of heaven, but only to an angel of hell; wherefore, it is abominable to ascribe them to God. That they have been ascribed to Him appears evident from the declaration of many fathers, churches and councils from the first ages unto the

present day; also from the inferences which have necessarily followed from first principles and to their derivatives, or from causes and to their effects, as from a head into the members; such as, that He required to be reconciled; that He is reconciled through the love He bears toward the Son, and by His intercession and mediation; that He required to be appeased by the view of the extreme sufferings of His Son; so to be brought back to mercy and constrained as it were, to show it, and thus from an enemy to be made a friend, and to adopt those who were the children of wrath, as the children of grace. That the notion that God can impute the righteousness and merits of His Son to an unrighteous man, who supplicates it from faith alone, is also a mere human invention, as will be seen in the last analysis of this work" (Ibid., 202–203).

2. "This I can affirm, that whenever the angels hear anyone say, that God determined in anger on the damnation of the human race, and as an enemy was reconciled by His Son, as by another God begotten from Himself, they are affected in a manner similar to those who from an uneasiness in their bowels and stomach are excited to vomiting; on which occasion they say, What can be more insane than to affirm such things to God?" (Ibid.).

3. "That no other salvation is believed this day than such as is instantaneous, from an immediate act of mercy is evident from hence . . . for if the cooperation is taken away which is effective through the exercise of charity by man as of himself, the spontaneous cooperation which is said to follow faith of itself, becomes passive action, which is nonsense, and a contradiction of terms; for supposing this to be the case, what need would there be of anything more than such momentary and immediate prayer as this: 'Save me, O God, for the sake of the sufferings of Thy Son, who has washed me from my sins in His own blood, and presents me pure, righteous and holy before thy throne?' . . . And this ejaculation of the mouth might avail even at the hour of death, if not sooner, as a seed of justification. But nevertheless, instantaneous salvation, by an immediate act of mercy, is to this day a fiery, flying serpent in the church, and that thereby religion is abolished, security introduced and damnation imputed to the Lord, may be seen . . . in the work concerning Divine Providence, published at Amsterdam in the year 1764" (Ibid., 204–205).

4. "Hence may be seen the import of the Lord's words in Mark, 'He that believeth and is baptized shall be saved, but he that believeth not shall be damned' " (Mark 16:16).

"Here, to believe, signifies to acknowledge the Lord and to receive divine truths from him by means of the Word, and to be baptized, is to be regenerated by the Lord by means of those truths . . . hence it is evident what is signified by these words of the Lord, 'Except a man be gotten of water and of the spirit, he cannot enter into the kingdom of God'; namely, that unless man is regenerated by the truths of faith, and by a life according to them, he cannot be saved . . . that all regeneration is effected by the truths of faith and by a life according to them. . . . Let those therefore who are baptized remember that baptism itself confers upon its subjects neither faith nor salvation, but testifies that they will receive faith and that they will be saved if they are regenerated" (Ibid., 110–11).[10]

---

[10]It is generally recognized as poor biblical scholarship to *base* any doctrine upon a passage of questionable authenticity such as Mark 16:16. The testimony of some of the best and most ancient New Testament manuscripts *is* that the last portion of Mark was interpolated *after* the original composition of the gospel. Swedenborg and his "ghosts" should have stayed with biblical texts of undisputed veracity!

IV. *The Destiny of Man*

1. "Man is so created that, as to his internal, he cannot die . . . this internal exists in every man who is born: his external is that by which he brings into effect the things which belong to his faith and love. The internal of man is the spirit, and the external is the body. The external, or the body, is suited to the performance of uses in the natural world, and is rejected or put off, at death, but the internal, which is called the spirit, and which is suited to the performance of uses in the spiritual world, never dies. After death, this internal exists as a good spirit and an angel, if the man has been good during his abode in this world, but if during that time he has lived in evil, he is, after death, an evil spirit. . . . The spirit of man after the dissolution of the body appears in the spiritual world in a human form in every respect, as in the natural world . . . except that he is not encompassed with the gross body which he had in the world. This he leaves when he dies, nor does he ever resume it. This continuation of life is meant by the resurrection. The reason why men believe that they shall not rise again before the Last Judgment, when, as they suppose, the whole creation will be destroyed, is that they do not understand the Word, and because sensual men place all their life in the body and imagine that unless the body be re-animated, the man be no more" (Ibid., 117–18).

Some Answers to Swedenborg

Swedenborg is consistently and energetically refuted by the epistles of Paul, particularly, the book of Romans, chapters 5 through 8, which Swedenborg detested with abject horror. By attempting to circumscribe the New Testament revelation of Christianity to the Gospels and the book of Revelation, Swedenborg revealed the essential weakness of his theological system. He was apparently well aware of the fact that Pauline theology, if accepted at face value, would vitiate almost *in toto* his own. So he began with the basic assumption that *he* was right, and that the apostle Paul was wrong! In some of his visions and dreams, he stated that he actually argued with Paul, Luther, Calvin, and others. And, as ego triumphed, these great thinkers all retreated before Swedenborg's new revelations.

However, one factor must never be forgotten, and that is the statement that the New Testament is the criterion for measuring all subsequent revelations, and whatever is found to be contrary to it, must be and always has been, rejected by the Christian church.

Swedenborg would have done well to remember that the interpretations of dreams and visions, and the things of the dimension of the spirit "belong to God" (Genesis 40:8), and that we are constantly admonished to accept no other gospel, even if it be revealed by an "angel from heaven" (Galatians 1:8–9)—two points he apparently overlooked. The apostle Peter, ever consistent with Paul, urges the Christian church to always remember that "prophecy came not in old time by the will of man, but holy men of God spoke as they were moved by the Holy Ghost" (2 Peter 1:21). But since Swedenborg did not believe in the person of the Holy Spirit, it is easy to understand how he could reject such divine counsel.

True to the pattern of most non-Christian cults and cult leaders, Swedenborg vigorously attacked the Christian doctrine of the Trinity. Apparently he was unaware of the fact that he was involved in contradiction when he asserted that Jesus Christ was Jehovah, while at the same time he denied the triunity of Jehovah, so clearly taught in both the Old and New Testaments (see Genesis 1:26; Isaiah 6:8; Zechariah 12:10; Luke 1:35; Matthew 3:16, 17; Matthew 28:19, etc.).

Dr. Charles Hodge, the great Princeton theologian, recognized the dangers of Swedenborg's theology and summed them up in his own terse manner when he wrote:

> Concerning God, he taught that He was not only essence but form, and that that form was human. He called God "the eternal God-Man." There are two kinds of bodies, material and spiritual. Every man, besides his external material body has another, which is internal and spiritual. The latter has all the organs of the former, so that it can see, hear, and feel. At death the outer body is laid aside, and the soul thereafter acts through the ethereal or spiritual vestment. This is the only resurrection which Swedenborg admitted. There is no rising again of the bodies laid in the grave. As however the spiritual corresponds to the material, those who know each other in this world will enjoy mutual recognition in the world to come. This feature of his anthropology is connected with his doctrine concerning God. For as the soul from its nature forms for itself a body for action . . . so the essence of God forms for itself a spiritual body for external manifestation.
>
> As there is but one divine essence, Swedenborg maintained that there can be but one divine person. The Church doctrine of the Trinity he regarded as tritheistic. He admitted a Trinity of principle, but not of person. As soul and body in man are one person, and from them proceeds the activity that operates without, so in God the divine and human are the Father and the Son, as one person, and the Holy Spirit is their efficiency or sanctifying influence.
>
> Concerning man, Swedenborg taught that he was created in the image of God, and was a creature of a very exalted nature. The scriptural account of the fall he understood allegorically of the apostasy of the church. Men, however, he admits, are sinful, and are even born with a bias to evil, but they have not lost their ability to do good. They consequently need redemption. They are susceptible to being delivered from evil not only because they retain their moral liberty but also because in virtue of the inward spiritual body they are capable of intercourse with spiritual beings. . . . Swedenborg reports many instances in which he conversed with God and angels, good and bad. By angels, he meant men who had departed this life. He did not admit the existence of any created intelligence other than man.
>
> Christ he held to be Jehovah, the only living and true God, the creator, preserver, and ruler of the world. As this divine person was God and man from eternity, his incarnation, or manifestation in the flesh, consisted in his assuming a material body with its physical life in the womb of the Virgin Mary. This was the body which grew, suffered, and died. In the case of ordinary men, the material body is left forever in the grave, but in the case of Christ, the outward body was gradually refined and glorified, until it was lost in that which is spiritual and eternal. This idea of a twofold body in Christ is not by any means peculiar to Swedenborg. . . .
>
> Christ's redemptive work does not consist in his bearing our sins upon the tree, or in making satisfaction to the justice of God for our offenses. All idea of such satisfaction Swedenborg rejects. The work of salvation is entirely subjective. Justification is pardon granted on repentance. The people of God are made inwardly righteous, and being thus holy are admitted to the presence of God and holy spirits in heaven. (Charles Hodge, *Systematic*

Theology (Grand Rapids, Mich.: William B. Eerdmans Publishing Company, 1977), reprint, vol. 2, 421–23)

Dr. Hodge's evaluation is, of course, accurate, and Swedenborg's denial of the person of the Holy Spirit, as previously mentioned, places him and his followers not only outside historic Christian theology, but in diametric opposition to the express declaration of the Word of God.

The apostle Peter, in dealing with the sin of Ananias and Sapphira, most explicitly declared that the Holy Spirit was a person to whom men could lie, as did they, and that in perpetrating this sin, its magnitude could only be realized when it was understood that "thou hast not lied unto men, but unto God" (Acts 5:4-5).

Numerous other incidents in the New Testament can be used to document the person of the Holy Spirit, and Swedenborg's denial of the vicarious nature of the atonement needs no serious refutation in the light of such passages as Isaiah 53; Matthew 20:28; Mark 10:45; and 1 Peter 2:24.

In his epistle to the Romans, chapter 5, the apostle Paul underscores the role of our Lord as the "second Adam," who died for us when we were "yet sinners," and his entire fifteenth chapter of his first epistle to the Corinthians is devoted to proving the resurrection of the body, citing Christ as the archetype of that resurrection (see also Colossians 1:15–18; 1 Thessalonians 4:13–17; 2 Thessalonians 1). Far from Swedenborg's concept that Christ's body was not raised in mortal flesh and bones, and that man will not participate in this resurrection, the redeemed to immortality and the unregenerate to eternal judgment, the Bible is replete with references to just such a historical and still future event. The Book of Revelation, of which he was so fond, refutes his position entirely by teaching the very thing Swedenborg denied, namely, that there will be a resurrection of both the just and the unjust (Revelation 20:1–14), an event declared to be in conjunction with the "appearing of the glory of the great God and our Saviour Jesus Christ" (Titus 2:13).

Quite to the contrary, then, where Swedenborg's theology is involved, Jesus Christ's second coming did not take place in the eighteenth century.

The New Jerusalem has not descended out of heaven from God. Our resurrection has not taken place, and judgment has neither begun nor is consummated. Swedenborg, despite his acknowledged brilliance and abilities, is found in far too many places to be in opposition to the teachings of the Word of God, and demonstrates in a most unique way an analysis of this type of mind. Oddly enough, this type was described by the apostle Paul, whom Swedenborg could not abide:

> For Christ sent me not to baptize, but to preach the gospel: not with wisdom of words, lest the cross of Christ should be made of none effect. For the preaching of the cross is to them that perish foolishness; but unto us which are saved, it is the power of God. For it is written, I will destroy the wisdom of the wise, and will bring to nothing the understanding of the prudent. Where is the wise? where is the scribe? where is the disputer of this world? Hath not God made foolish the wisdom of this world? For after that in the wisdom of God the world by wisdom knew not God, it pleased God by the foolishness of preaching to save them that believe. For the Jews require a sign, and the Greeks seek after wisdom: But we preach Christ crucified, unto the Jews a stumbling block, and unto the Greeks foolishness; But unto them which are called, both Jews and Greeks, Christ the power of God, and the wisdom of

God. Because the foolishness of God is wiser than men; and the weakness of God is stronger than men. For ye see your calling, brethren, how that not many wise men after the flesh, not many mighty, not many noble, are called: But God hath chosen the foolish things of the world to confound the wise; and God hath chosen the weak things of the world to confound the things which are mighty; And base things of the world, and things which are despised, hath God chosen, yea, and things which are not, to bring to nought things that are: That no flesh should glory in his presence. But of him are ye in Christ Jesus, who of God is made unto us wisdom, and righteousness, and sanctification, and redemption: That, according as it is written, He that glorieth, let him glory in the Lord. (1 Corinthians 1:17–31)

It would be possible to go on at some length in a refutation of Swedenborg's theology, but the issues, we believe, are clearly discernible, as is the verdict of Scripture. Swedenborg was a rationalist, and paradoxically, a mystic. He was one who absorbed the introspective and subjective philosophy of Rene Descartes, and the empiricism of John Locke, which he combined with the transcendentalism of Immanuel Kant, thus forming a mold into which Christian theology was poured, and what would not go into the mold (selected Old Testament works, the Pauline epistles, Acts, James, Peter, Jude, etc.), he simply discarded. What emerged was a deeply speculative philosophical system of theology, couched in a redefined Christian terminology, and buttressed with mystical visions, trances, and dreams. These, when apparently confirmed by clairvoyant experiences, such as the Stockholm fire episode previously narrated, gave some credence to his claims and still continue to deceive many so-called intelligent persons today.

In his counsel to the church at Colosse, the apostle Paul uttered a warning that the followers of Swedenborg in particular might well take cognizance of:

> Beware lest any man spoil you through philosophy and vain deceit, after the tradition of men, after the rudiments of the world, and not after Christ. For in him dwelleth all the fulness of the Godhead bodily. (Colossians 2:8–9)

The great tragedy of Emanuel Swedenborg is that he would not submit himself and his great mind to the discipline of the Holy Spirit and the Scriptures. Because of this, and because of his deliberated preoccupation with spiritism and the occult, in direct disobedience to the express teachings of God, he was despoiled, even as Paul had warned. He was deceived by dreams and visions and the machinations of him whom the Scriptures describe as the "spirit that now worketh in the children of disobedience" (Ephesians 2:2b).

Recommended Resources

1. Christian Apologetics & Research Ministry. *Leaving Swedenborgianism: A Testimony by David Weaver*. *www.carm.org/testimonies/david_weaver.htm*.
2. Jackson, Samuel Macauley, ed. *The New Schaff-Herzog Encyclopedia of Religious Knowledge*. Grand Rapids, Mich.: Baker Book House, 1977), reprint. See also *www.bookfinder.com*.
3. Judah, J. Stillson. *The History and Philosophy of the Metaphysical Movements in America*. Philadelphia: The Westminster Press, 1967.
4. Walter Martin Ministries. *www.waltermartin.com*.
5. Watchman Fellowship. *www.watchman.org*.

Quick Facts About Rosicrucianism

- God is an impersonal being composed of seven spirits. God is all: all of reality is a part of or an expression of the essence/nature of God (Pantheism).

- Jesus Christ was not the Son of God. He was a spirit belonging to human evolution.

- There is no vicarious atonement.

- Resurrection is replaced by reincarnation.

- Man is evolving into a divine being.

Appendix D

Rosicrucianism

"May the roses bloom upon your cross," intones the mystical and authoritative voice of the leader, and the echoed response, "And on yours also," from the disciples, probationers, and students making up a typical Rosicrucian Fellowship Center, signals the beginning of another excursion into the metaphysical labyrinths of the 600-year-old cultic movement, which today, with its several factions, is known collectively as the Rosicrucian Fellowship.

Of all the cult systems under discussion in this book, the Rosicrucians most certainly qualify, along with the spiritists, Theosophists, and Swedenborgians, as the most mystically inclined. More than any of the others, they are also devoted to a detailed system of doctrine composed of so many strains of other cult viruses, as to be almost beyond the point of comprehension, much less analysis.

Rosicrucianism is not only an eclectic theological system that mixes pagan mythology with Judaism, and Christianity with traces of Hinduism and Buddhism throughout, but it is a system of thinking that seeks to synthesize the basic truths of all religions and absorb them into a master system.

In the literature of Rosicrucianism, one will find enormous deposits of symbolism, anthropology, transmigration, and even some Spiritism.

There is a great similarity in some areas to the vocabulary of Theosophy and to the concept that man progresses through many reincarnations, each of which purges him of his preceding sins.

In Rosicrucian theology, there exist seven worlds with seven sections or divisions presided over on the highest level by a "universal spirit." All nature, for that matter all creation, is unified and bears a direct relationship to the cross, which represents man's evolutionary past as well as his future destiny. In Rosicrucian theology, the cross loses what the Bible describes as its "reproach," and no

---

This appendix updated and edited by Kevin Rische and Jill Martin Rische.

Rosicrucian stands ready to "go forth therefore unto him without the camp, bearing his reproach" (Hebrews 13:13).

The cross in Rosicrucianism is the mystical symbol of man's evolutionary development—past, present, and future—and has no true significance as the symbol of what it cost God to redeem the sons of men (Revelation 1:5).

Prominent still, though it has been redefined, the cross stands at the center of Rosicrucianism, circled with roses. This creates the concept of the rosy cross.

Man progresses by the mystical number seven, for at seven, he possesses a vital body; at fourteen, a desire body; at twenty-one, a full formation of the mind; though the so-called "dense body" is present at birth.

The mission of the Lord Jesus Christ in Rosicrucian theology was to manifest himself for the aid of mankind in the evolutionary struggle. Rosicrucian theology relegates Him to the highest manifestation or initiate of the Son. And He, along with Buddha and other great leaders, was revealed to facilitate human progress. Sovereign over all the manifestations is the highest initiate from Saturn. This is designated the Father. The Holy Spirit is known as the highest initiate of the moon. However, neither the Holy Spirit nor the Son has any activity in vicarious atonement or spiritual regeneration, which consummates in personal redemption apart from psychic reincarnation.

As one travels through the mazes of Rosicrucian terminology and theology, one encounters the fabulous three heavens, which are attained through suffering, silence, thought, and eventually the reincarnation wheel. A silver chord allegedly connects the physical or dense body with the spiritual body, and at death the chord is broken, releasing the higher nature from the physical. We are told in Rosicrucian literature that Plato was a believer in Rosicrucianism, due to his emphasis upon the world soul, and that countless others were secret initiates of Rosicrucian truths. Even the lost continent of Atlantis and the mysterious Lemuran race are included in Rosicrucian speculation. In fact, there is very little that Rosicrucianism does not seek to enfold within its mythological-magical lore, yet everything Christian that it touches suffers violence at its hands.

By the time the average reader of Rosicrucian literature extricates himself or herself from the various Periods (Sun, Moon, Saturn, etc.), ethers, bodies, and multiple hypotheses of Rosicrucian philosophy, he or she is pretty generally impressed with the enormous amount of data the Rosicrucians have amassed as a substitute for the revelations of the Bible. Most always, he is confused by the fact that Rosicrucian terminology and concepts do have a distinct Christian flavor and sound. But somehow or other, the taste is distinctly different!

The Rosicrucians have a pantheistic worldview. By this they believe that in some way, all of reality is a part of or an expression of the essence or nature of God. God is all. This pantheism colors every aspect of Rosicrucian belief. Because of this, it has much in common with other pantheistic cults, such as Christian Science and Theosophy.

It is not our intention in this appendix to occupy ourselves at great length with the theology of Rosicrucianism, which will generate, in the minds of most Christians, a great deal of heat, and very little, if any, light. But since the cult is effective in the southwestern and western parts of the United States and is penetrating the eastern seaboard and the Midwest with steady effectiveness, as evidenced by the establishment of Rosicrucian Fellowship Centers in key cities throughout the Midwest and the East, some mention should be made of its history and its theological structure as it affects the Christian doctrine of God, the person, nature, and work of Jesus Christ, and the destiny of mankind.

Historical Perspectives

The founder of present-day Rosicrucianism was Christianus Rosenkreutz (1378–1484), a German scholar who roundly opposed Roman Catholicism and claimed to be the revealer of the mysteries of the rose cross.[1] From its inception, Rosicrucianism put emphasis upon the occult and the mystical relationship of Christianity to all the great religions of the world. It was by admission a secret society. It flourished in a day when secret societies were in vogue, and "a century after its origin, Rosicrucianism underwent a recrudescence in connection with Free Masonry, which not only deemed Rosicrucianism genuine but even borrowed usages and customs from the writings of those who had satirized the fraternity" (Samuel Macauley Jackson, ed., *The New Schaff-Herzog Encyclopedia of Religious Knowledge* [Grand Rapids, Mich.: Baker Book House, 1977], reprint, vol. 10, 97).

In a world that was trying to analyze the meaning of comets, alchemy, and Eastern occultism, Rosicrucianism proved to be an attractive alternative to orthodoxy. It was careful to utilize an orthodox Christian vocabulary, however, and to speak out vehemently against Roman Catholicism, alchemy, and dogmatic theology of any type, although it zealously promoted some of the principles of the Protestant Reformation, the theology of which, it might be noted, is the antithesis of Rosicrucian teaching!

Today there are Rosicrucian centers in over one hundred countries throughout the world, and the headquarters of the largest faction of the movement, the Rosicrucian Order (AMORC) to all intents and purposes, is in San Jose, California.[2] The writer visited the headquarters in 1961 in San Jose, California, and obtained valuable information about the methods of the Rosicrucians in propagating their beliefs, as well as additional data about some of the more "spiritual" teachings.

Of all the modern Rosicrucian writers, the best known is the late Max Heindel.

In this age of ecumenicity, the Rosicrucians play heavily upon the notes of "universal brotherhood," publish millions of copies of their magazines, *The Rosicrucian Digest* and *Rosicrucian Forum,* and maintain the "supreme temple of North and South America," which is located in San Jose, California, in Rosicrucian Park.

This group of Rosicrucians, identified by the letters AMORC, deny being either a religion or a church. They identify themselves as a brotherhood or organization that is attempting to help mankind to master its destiny. AMORC, the largest Rosicrucian faction, has a membership of around 250,000, represented by about fifteen hundred "Affiliated Bodies," and accounts for over 90 percent of worldwide Rosicrucian membership,[3] but due to a heavy advertising campaign, the zealous propagation of their brotherhood and destiny publications, Rosicrucianism

---

[1]The Ancient and Mystical Order of the Rosae Crucis (AMORC) was founded by H. Spencer Lewis in 1915.

[2]Official Web site of the Rosicrucian Order *www.rosicrucian.org*. See also *www.amorc.org*.

[3]See Adherents.com, *http://216.239.33.100/search?q=cache:7qyN2uDoLoOC:www.adherents.com/Na_24.html+Statistics+for+AMORC&hl=en&ie=UTF-8. Added note:* The Rosicrucian Fellowship with International Headquarters in Oceanside, California, lists only 5,527 active members.

is, in our time, a successful non-Christian cult, which uses the terminology of Christianity whenever possible (and profitable) to lead the untutored mind into the mazes of a philosophical religion so complex that those who know it best are content to admit readily the limitations of their own understanding.

Rosicrucianism and Christianity

1. *The Nature of God.*

It is a historic affirmation of Rosicrucianism that God is an impersonal being, composed of seven spirits, which manifest themselves as a "triune godhead," or Father, Son, and Holy Spirit. Lest there be any doubt on the subject, Heindel, in one of his many books, declares,

> ... The seven spirits before the throne ... collectively, they are God, and make *up* the triune godhead ... the Father is the highest initiate among the humanity of the Saturn. ... The Son is the highest initiate of the Sun ... the Holy Spirit (Jehovah) is the highest initiate of the Moon. ...[4]

In such a semantic jungle, the nature of God, the holy Trinity, or Triune Deity of biblical revelation undergoes total, if not complete, mutilation. It becomes a type of occult pantheism, culminating in an impersonal spirit-being, who is "collectively" God.

The Rosicrucians believe that the Trinity portrays aspects of God:

> ... the only begotten, the Word of whom John speaks, is the second aspect of the Supreme Being. This word, and it alone, is begotten of His Father, first aspect before all worlds. ... Therefore, the Only Begotten is the exalted Being which ranks above all else in the universe, save only the Power aspect, which created it.[5]

For the Rosicrucians, the Holy Spirit is Jehovah, the third aspect of the triune Godhead. But in the sense of Christian theology, these definitions are meaningless, since the Bible declares unequivocally that God is the Father, the Son, and the Holy Spirit, three divine Persons, all sharing the same nature and attributes, coexistent, coequal and coeternal, and, above all else, personal. The Lord himself declared,

> I AM THAT I AM. ... Thus shalt thou say to the children of Israel, I AM hath sent me unto you. (Exodus 3:14)

The Christian doctrine of the Trinity, then, cannot be equated with the Rosicrucian caricature of it, although it is significant that the Rosicrucians do usually bend over backward, as it were, in an attempt to make their pantheistic theology sound Christian, thus identifying it with the predominant form of religion in the United States, which is the Christian religion. They are equally at home among the Buddhists, Hindus, or Mohammedans, and can adapt their theology, much like chameleons adapt the color of their skins, to the protective coloration of the theological climate in which they find themselves. Such passages as Matthew 28:19; John 14:16, 26; Luke 1:35; John 1:1, 14; Colossians 2:9; and Acts 5:3–4,

---

[4]*The Rosicrucian Cosmo-Conception* (San Jose, Calif.: AMORC, n.d.), 376, 252.
[5]Ibid., 374.

etc., demonstrate the Christian doctrine of the Trinity beyond reasonable doubt.

2. *The Nature and Work of Jesus Christ.*

As Rosicrucianism stands opposed to the historic Christian doctrine of the Trinity, so also it opposes the true divinity of the Lord Jesus. Rosicrucianism teaches that Jesus Christ was neither Jesus nor the only begotten Son of God. Instead, Jesus was a man, the highest luminary possible. The Christ-spirit was a manifestation of the cosmic Christ and the only begotten is "an exalted being which ranks above all else in the universe, save only the power aspect which created it."[6]

It is obvious, then, that as Christian Science divides Jesus and Christ, into Jesus, an apparent manifestation of manhood indwelled by a Christ-consciousness or idea, so Rosicrucianism employs the same type of spiritual schizophrenia and ends, as does Christian Science and all the Gnostic cults, with a divided Messiah.

In the philosophy of Rosicrucianism, "the Christ-spirit which entered the body of Jesus when Jesus Himself vacated it, was a ray from the cosmic Christ. We may follow Jesus back in His previous incarnations and can trace His growth to the present day."[7]

Jesus Christ, in the theology of the Rosicrucians, "was a spirit belonging to our human evolution, and so was Gautama Buddha," a theology that makes no allowance for the incarnation of the only God in the person of the man from Nazareth (John 1:1, 14, 18).

Christianity and Rosicrucianism can never be reconciled, because the former declares the absolute and unique deity of the central figure of all history, and the latter relegates Him to a pantheon of incarnate deities or spirits. Our Lord vigorously denied such inferences when He stated, concerning His own mission: "All that ever came before me are thieves and robbers: but the sheep did not hear them" (John 10:8).

The Christ of Holy Scripture cannot be divided and subdivided into pantheistic and Gnostic segments. He refuses to be considered one of many equally good ways, or a mere aspect of the truth. Instead, it is His declaration that He is the Life itself, and as such, the only Way and the Truth. It is folly of the highest order to attempt to equate the Christ of revelation with the Christ of Rosicrucianism. For Heindel's Christ, and the Christ of the "brotherhood," is in reality, "another Jesus" (2 Corinthians 11:4), the creation of a fertile imagination and a broad intellect (Heindel) projected into the twentieth century, infused with occult and mystical teachings, and lightly coated with Biblical terminology. He is a clever counterfeit, but nevertheless, he is a counterfeit!

It is unnecessary to point out the Rosicrucian concept of the atonement, since for them it is not vicarious, in the sense that Christ paid the penalty for all sin. The primary reason is that they do not believe that Jesus was *the* Christ.

It is the teaching of Holy Scripture that there is but one God (Deuteronomy 6:4; Galatians 3:20), and that to know Him and Jesus Christ whom He has sent, is to possess life eternal (John 17). The Rosicrucian Fellowship does not know Him; it does not accept His vicarious sacrifice for all sin (Isaiah 53), and substitutes reincarnation for resurrection, teaching that man passes through stages of

---

[6]Ibid., 374.

[7]Max Heindel, *The Rosicrucian Philosophy*, 181.

incarnations, through various spheres of progressive perfection, all a product of cosmic evolution.

The History and Destiny of Mankind

We conclude this brief survey of the Rosicrucian Fellowship by noting that its concept of mankind is also unbiblical. In the thinking of Rosicrucians, there have been various epics or stages of the development of man upon the earth. For instance, blacks were known as the Lemurian, or the third of these epics. He was followed by the red race, the yellow race, and the white race. The white race, according to the Rosicrucians, was originally Semetic and was the fifth of the Atlantean race.

Along with this type of occult anthropology, the Rosicrucians would have us believe that Atlantis, a mythical lost continent, brought forth this race, which was composed of the ancestors of those destined to become the fathers of the Aryan race of our day.

For Rosicrucianism, man is evolving into a divine being, and, in fact, he is a divine being of sorts, a type of demigod, in the grand cosmic evolutionary scale.

With such a view of man, the Rosicrucians can indeed forge ahead to build an international world brotherhood, because, in their theology, cosmic evolution and the law of progression point ever onward and upward to the eventual salvation of all mankind.

The reader might take into consideration in this connection the words of the apostle Paul, who dimmed the Rosicrucian illumination of occult anthropology when he declared, "The first man [was] Adam" (1 Corinthians 15:45).

This is a terse judgment of the concept of progressive races, some of which, according to Rosicrucianism, antedate Adam. Under the inspiration of the Holy Spirit, the apostle declares that there was only *one* human race, and the father of it is Adam, and that in this man Adam, all have died (Romans 5:12; 1 Corinthians 15:22) because of sin, Rosicrucians not excepted. All the occult mumbo jumbo, secret symbols, and rosy crosses in creation, therefore, cannot put "Humpty" Adam together again. There has been only one remedy for sin in all of history, and that is divine grace, expressed prophetically before the cross, and experientially after the cross. There can be no substitute for the commands of God, and the Rosicrucian Fellowship would do well to hearken to the words of Him who left as His heritage to mankind a blood-spattered cross, not one shrouded with roses. It was His promise to His followers: "Because I live, you will live also." This is the Christ of historic Christianity, and it is His word, not ours, that will be the judge of all men, including the Rosicrucians "in that day" (2 Timothy 1:12, 18).

Recommended Resources

1. Heindel, Max. *The Rosicrucian-Cosmo Conception.* Oceanside, Calif.: The Rosicrucian Fellowship, 1922. See also *bookfinder.com.*
2. Spencer, Lewis H. *Rosicrucian Questions and Answers With Complete History of the Rosicrucian Order.* San Jose, Calif.: Supreme Grand Lodge of AMORC, 1981. 15th ed.
3. Van Baalen, Jan Carol. *The Chaos of the Cults.* Grand Rapids, Mich.: W. B. Eerdmans Publishing Co., 1962. 4th ed., rev.
4. Walter Martin Ministries. *www.waltermartin.com.*

Bibliography

General References

Adair, James R., and Ted Miller, eds. *Escape From Darkness.* Wheaton, Ill.: Victor Books, 1982.

Alnor, William M., and Ronald Enroth. "Ethical Problems in Exit Counseling," *Christian Research Journal,* 14:3:1992.

Anderson, Susan M., and Philip G. Zimbardo. "Resisting Mind Control," *USA Today,* November 1990.

Ankerberg, John, and John Weldon. *Encyclopedia of Cults and New Religions.* Eugene, Ore.: Harvest House, 1999.

Anthony, Dick, and Thomas Robbins. "Law, Social Science, and the 'Brainwashing' Exception to the First Amendment," *Behavioral Sciences and the Law,* 10:1:1992.

Apologetics.com. *www.apologetics.com,* 2003.

Atkins, G. *Modern Religious Cults and Movements.* New York: Fleming H. Revell Co., 1923.

Bach, Marcus. *Strange Sects and Curious Cults.* New York: Barnes and Noble Books, 1961.

———. *They Have Found a Faith.* New York: Bobbs-Merrill, 1946.

Barker, Eileen. *New Religious Movements: A Practical Introduction.* London: Her Majesty's Stationery Office, 1989.

Bjornstad, James. *Counterfeits at Your Door.* Ventura, Calif.: Gospel Light Publications, 1979.

———. "Cultic and Christian Conversion: Is There a Difference?" *Update,* 6:1:1982.

Boa, Kenneth. *Cults, World Religions, and You.* Wheaton, Ill.: Victor Books, 1977.

Braden, Charles S. *These Also Believe.* New York: Macmillan, 1951.

Bromley, David G., and Edward F. Breschel. "General Population and Institutional Elite Support for Social Control of New Religious Movements: Evidence From National Survey Data," *Behavioral Sciences and the Law,* 10:1:1992.

Bromley, David G., and Anson D. Shupe. *Strange Gods.* Boston: Beacon Press, 1981.

———. "Public Reaction Against New Religious Movements," *Cults and New Religious Movements.* Marc Galanter, ed. Washington, D.C.: American Psychiatric Association, 1989.

Budansky, Stephen, Erica E. Goode, and Ted Gest, "The Cold War Experiments," *Newsweek*, January 24, 1994.

Clark, Elmer T. *The Small Sects in America*. Rev. ed. Nashville: Abingdon Press, 1949.

Clegg, Tom, and Warren Bird. *Lost in America: How You and Your Church Can Impact the World Next Door*. Loveland, Colo.: Group Publishing, 2001.

Clifford, Ross, and Philip Johnson. *Jesus and the Gods of the New Age*. Oxford: Lion, 2001.

Collins, Gary. *Search for Reality*. Santa Ana, Calif.: Vision House Publishers, 1969.

Conway, Flo, and Jim Siegelman. "Deprogramming Deprogrammed," *Cornerstone*, 6:36.

———.*Snapping: America's Epidemic of Sudden Personality Change*. New York: Dell Publishing Company, Inc., 1979.

Dart, John. "Doubt Cast on 'Brainwashing' by Cults," *The Los Angeles Times*, November 19, 1983.

Davies, Horton. *The Challenge of the Sects*. Philadelphia: Westminster Press, 1961.

Davis, Deborah (Linda Berg), with Bill Davis. *The Children of God: The Inside Story*. Grand Rapids, Mich.: Zondervan, 1984.

Davis, Deborah, with Bill Davis. "Cults, Brainwashing, and Personal Responsibility," *Forward*, Summer 1985.

Duncan, R., and M. Weston-Smith, compilers. *Lying Truths*. New York: Pergamon Press, 1979.

Enroth, Ronald. "Cult/Countercult," *Eternity*, November 1977.

Enroth, Ronald, et al. *A Guide to Cults and New Religions*. Downers Grove, Ill.: InterVarsity Press, 1983.

———.*Youth, Brainwashing, and the Extremist Cults*. Grand Rapids: Zondervan Publishing House, 1977.

Ferguson, Charles. *New Books of Revelation*. Garden City, N.J.: Doubleday-Doran, 1929; first published as *Confusion of Tongues* in 1928.

Ferm, Vergilius. *Religion in the Twentieth Century*. New York: Philosophical Library, 1948.

Freyd, Pamela, ed. *Newsletter*. Philadelphia: False Memory Syndrome Foundation, various issues.

Galanter, Marc. *Cults: Faith, Healing, and Coercion*. New York: Oxford University Press, 1989.

Galanter, Marc, ed. *Cults and New Religious Movements: A Report of the American Psychiatric Association*. Washington, D.C.: American Psychiatric Association, 1989.

Gerstner, John H. *The Theology of the Major Sects*. Grand Rapids, Mich.: Baker Book House, 1960.

Griffin, Em. *The Mind Changers*. Wheaton: Tyndale House, 1976.

Gruss, Edmond C. *Cults and the Occult*. Grand Rapids, Mich.: Baker Book House, 1982.

Hassan, Steven. *Combatting Cult Mind Control*. Rochester, Vt.: Park Street Press, 1990.

Hesselgrave, David J., ed.*Communicating Christ Cross-Culturally*. Grand Rapids: Zondervan, 1991.

———. *Dynamic Religious Movements*. Grand Rapids, Mich.: Baker Book House, 1978.

Hoekema, Anthony A. *The Four Major Cults*. Grand Rapids, Mich.: Eerdmans Publishing Company, 1963.

Langone, Michael D. "Treatment of Individuals and Families Troubled by Cult Involvement," *Update*, 7:1:1983.

Langone, Michael D., and Paul R. Martin. "Deprogramming, Exit Counseling, and Ethics: Clarifying the Confusion," *Christian Research Journal*, 15:3:1993.

Lewis, Gordon R. *Confronting the Cults*. Grand Rapids, Mich.: Baker Book House, 1966.

MacHovec, Frank. "Cults: Forensic and Therapeutic Aspects," *Behavioral Sciences and the Law*, 10:1:1992.

Martin, Paul R. *Cult Proofing Your Kids*. Grand Rapids, Mich.: Zondervan, 1993.

———. "Dispelling the Myths: The Psychological Consequences of Cultic Involvement," *Christian Research Journal*, Winter/Spring 1989.

Martin, Walter R. *The Christian and the Cults.* Grand Rapids, Mich.: Zondervan, 1956, republished as *The Rise of the Cults.* Ventura: Gospel Light Publications, 1984.

———. *Spiritual Warfare.* Audiotape. Walter Martin Ministries. *www.waltermartin.com.*

———. *Walter Martin's Cults Reference Bible.* Santa Ana, Calif.: Vision House Publishers, 1981.

Mathison, Richard R. *Faiths, Cults, and Sects of America.* Indianapolis, Ind.: Bobbs-Merrill, 1960.

Mayer, F. E. *Religious Bodies of America.* St. Louis, Mo.: Concordia, 1954.

Mead, Frank S. *Handbook of Denominations in the United States.* Rev. ed. Nashville: Abingdon, 1956.

Melton, J. Gordon. *The Encyclopedia of American Religions.* 2 vols. Wilmington, N.C.: McGrath Publishing Company, 1978.

Neve, J. L. *Churches and Sects in Christendom.* Minneapolis, Minn.: Augsburg, 1952.

Ogloff, James R. P., and Jeffrey Pfeifer. "Cults and the Law: A Discussion of the Legality of Alleged Cult Activities," *Behavioral Sciences and the Law,* 10:1:1992.

Petersen, William J. *Those Curious New Cults.* New Canaan, Conn.: Keats Publishers, Inc., 1973.

Peterson, Gilbert. *Religious Research Digest,* December 1961.

Pfeifer, Jeffrey, and James R. P. Ogloff. "New Religious Movements and the Law: Past Interactions and New Directions," *Behavioral Sciences and the Law,* 10:1:1992.

Robbins, Thomas, and Dick Anthony, eds. *In Gods We Trust: New Patterns of Religious Pluralism in America.* New Brunswick: Transaction Books, 1981.

Rosten, Leo, ed. *Religions in America.* New York: Simon & Schuster, 1962, 1963.

Sanders, J. Oswald, and J. Stafford Wright. *Some Modern Religions.* London: Tyndale Press, 1956.

Sargant, William. *Battle for the Mind.* London: Pan Books, 1957.

Schaff, Philip, and Johann Herzog. *The New Schaff-Herzog Encyclopedia of Religious Knowledge.* 15 vols. Grand Rapids, Mich.: Baker Book House, n.d.

Shupe, Anson, and David G. Bromley. "The Modern American Anti-Cult Movement: A Twenty-Year Retrospective," *Association for the Sociology of Religion,* August 1991.

———. *The New Vigilantes: Deprogrammers, Anti-Cultists, and the New Religions.* Beverly Hills: Sage Library of Social Research, 1980.

Singer, Margaret Thaler. "Coming Out of the Cults," *Psychology Today,* January 1979.

Sire, James W. *Scripture Twisting.* Downers Grove, Ill.: InterVarsity Press, 1980.

Sparks, Jack. *The Mind Benders.* Nashville: Thomas Nelson Publishers, 1977.

Spittler, Russell P. *Cults and Isms.* Grand Rapids, Mich.: Baker Book House, 1962.

Strong, James. *Strong's Exhaustive Concordance of the Bible.* New York: Abingdon-Cokesbury Press, n.d.

Tucker, Ruth. *Another Gospel.* Grand Rapids, Mich.: Zondervan, 1989.

Van Baalen, Jan Karel. *Chaos of the Cults.* 4th rev. ed. Grand Rapids, Mich.: Eerdmans Publishing Company, 1962.

Watters, Ethan. "Doors of Memory," *Mother Jones,* January/February, 1993.

Wyrick, Herbert M. *Seven Religious Isms.* Grand Rapids, Mich.: Zondervan, 1940.

Young, John L., and Ezra E. H. Griffith. "A Critical Evaluation of Coercive Persuasion as Used in the Assessment of Cults," *Behavioral Sciences and the Law,* 10:1:1992.

Authority of the Scriptures

Allis, Oswald T. *The Old Testament: Its Claims and Its Critics.* Nutley, N.J.: Presbyterian and Reformed Publishing Company, 1972.

Archer, Gleason L. *Encyclopedia of Bible Difficulties.* Grand Rapids, Mich.: Zondervan, 1982.

Bruce, F. F. *The Books and the Parchments: Some Chapters on the Transmission of the Bible.* Rev. ed. Westwood, N.J.: Fleming H. Revell Company, 1953.

————. *The New Testament Documents: Are They Reliable?* Grand Rapids, Mich.: Eerdmans Publishing Company, 1953.

Geisler, Norman L. *Christian Apologetics.* Grand Rapids, Mich.: Baker Book House, 1976.

————. *Decide for Yourself: How History Views the Bible.* Grand Rapids, Mich.: Zondervan, 1982.

Geisler, Norman L., and William E. Nix. *From God to Us.* Chicago: Moody Press, 1974.

————. *A General Introduction to the Bible.* Chicago: Moody Press, 1968.

Laird, R. *Inspiration and Canonicity of the Bible.* Grand Rapids, Mich.: Zondervan, 1966.

Lewis, C. S. *The Case for Christianity.* New York: Macmillan, 1956.

Lewis, Gordon R. *Testing Christianity's Truth Claims: Approaches to Christian Apologetics.* Chicago: Moody Press, 1976.

McDowell, Josh. *Evidence That Demands a Verdict: Historical Evidence for the Christian Faith.* Arrowhead Springs, Calif.: Campus Crusade for Christ, 1972.

————. *More Evidence That Demands a Verdict: Historical Evidence for the Christian Scriptures.* Arrowhead Springs, Calif.: Campus Crusade for Christ, 1975.

————. *More Than a Carpenter.* Wheaton, Ill.: Tyndale House, 1980.

Montgomery, John W. *History and Christianity.* Downers Grove, Ill.: InterVarsity Press, 1965.

Unger, Merrill Frederick. *Archaeology and the New Testament.* Grand Rapids, Mich.: Zondervan, 1962.

————. *Archaeology and the Old Testament.* Grand Rapids, Mich.: Zondervan, 1966.

Jehovah's Witnesses

Ball, Francis K. *The Elements of Greek.* New York: Macmillan, 1950.

Bergman, Jerry. *Jehovah's Witnesses and Blood Transfusions.* Costa Mesa, Calif.: CARIS, 1979.

————. *Jehovah's Witnesses and Mental Illness.* Costa Mesa: CARIS, 1983.

Bowman, Robert M., Jr. *Jehovah's Witnesses.* Zondervan Guide to Cults and Religious Movements. Grand Rapids, Mich.: Zondervan, 1995.

Bowser, Arthur. *What Every Jehovah's Witness Should Know.* Denver: B/P Publications, 1975.

Breese, Dave. *Know the Marks of the Cults.* Wheaton, Ill.: Victor Books, n.d.

Bullions, Peter. *Principles of Greek Grammar.* New York: Farmer, Bruce and Company, n.d.

Carnell, E. J. *An Introduction to Christian Apologetics.* Grand Rapids, Mich.: Eerdmans Publishing Company, 1950.

Cline, Ted. *Questions for Jehovah's Witnesses.* Ventura: Gospel Light Publications, 1975.

Cole, Marley. *Jehovah's Witnesses, the New World Society.* New York: Vantage Press, 1955.

Comments From the Friends. *www.cftf.com,* 2003.

Cooper, Lee. "Publish or Perish: Negro Jehovah's Witnesses' Adaptation in the Ghetto," *Religious Movements in Contemporary America.* Irving Zaretsky and Mark P. Leone, eds. Princeton, N.J.: Princeton University Press, 1974.

Countess, Robert H. *The Jehovah's Witnesses New Testament.* Phillipsburg, N.J.: Presbyterian and Reformed Publishing Company, 1982.

Davies, Horton. *Christian Deviations.* New York: Philosophical Library, 1954.

Deissman, Adolf. *Light From the Ancient East.* New York: Harper, 1951.

Dencher, Ted. *The Watchtower Versus the Bible.* Chicago: Moody Press, 1961.

————. *Why I Left Jehovah's Witnesses.* Ft. Washington, Pa.: Christian Literature Crusade, 1966.

Finnegan, Jack. *Light From the Ancient Past.* Princeton, N.J.: Princeton Press, 1946.

Franz, Raymond. *Crisis of Conscience.* Atlanta: Commentary Press, 2002.

Gaebelein, Arno C. *The Hope of the Ages.* New York: Our Hope, n.d.

Gerstner, John H. *The Theology of the Major Sects.* Grand Rapids, Mich.: Baker Book House, 1963.

Gruss, Edmond C. *Apostles of Denial.* Nutley, N.J.: Presbyterian and Reformed Publishing Company, 1970.

———. *The Jehovah's Witnesses and Prophetic Speculation.* Nutley, N.J.: Presbyterian and Reformed Publishing Company, 1972.

Gruss, Edmond C., ed. *We Left Jehovah's Witnesses: A Non-Prophet Organization.* Nutley, N.J.: Presbyterian and Reformed Publishing Company, 1972.

Hamilton, Floyd E. *The Basis of Christian Faith.* New York: Harper, 1949.

Hoekema, Anthony A. *The Four Major Cults.* Grand Rapids, Mich.: Eerdmans Publishing Company, 1963.

———. *Jehovah's Witnesses.* Grand Rapids, Mich.: Eerdmans Publishing Company, 1972.

Irvine, William C. *Heresies Exposed.* Neptune, N.J.: Loizeaux Brothers, 1955.

Kauper, Paul G. *Religion and the Constitution.* Baton Rouge: Louisiana State University Press, 1964.

Knoch, Adolf E. *Concordant Version New Testament.* Los Angeles: Concordant Publishing Concern, 1931. Greek trans.

Knox, Ronald. *Translation of the Bible.* 3 vols. New York: Sheed & Ward, 1953.

Lewis, Gordon R. *The Bible, the Christian, and Jehovah's Witnesses.* Philadelphia: Presbyterian and Reformed Publishing Company, 1966.

Machen, J. G. *The Origin of Paul's Religion.* Grand Rapids, Mich.: Eerdmans Publishing Company, 1950.

———. *The Virgin Birth of Christ.* Grand Rapids, Mich.: Eerdmans Publishing Company, 1950.

MacMillan, A. H. *Faith on the March.* Englewood Cliffs, N.J.: Prentice Hall, 1957.

Magnani, Duane, and Arthur Barrett. *Dialogue With Jehovah's Witnesses.* 2 vols. Clayton, Calif.: Witness Inc., 1983.

Martin, Walter, and Norman Klann. *Jehovah of the Watchtower.* Minneapolis: Bethany House Publishers, 1981.

Mather, George A., and Larry A. Nichols. *Dictionary of Cults, Sects, Religions and the Occult.* Grand Rapids, Mich.: Zondervan Publishers, 1993.

Mayer, F. E. *Jehovah's Witnesses.* St. Louis: Concordia Publishing House, 1943.

McDowell, Josh, and Don Stewart. *A Handbook on Today's Religions.* Nashville: Thomas Nelson, 1993.

Metzger, Bruce M. "The Jehovah's Witnesses and Jesus Christ," *Theology Today,* April 1953.

Moulton, J. H. *A Grammar of the New Testament Greek.* 3rd ed. Edinburgh: Tavil T. Clark, n.d.

Newman, John Henry. *The Arians of the Fourth Century.* London: Longmans Green, 1911.

———. *St. Athanasius.* Vols. 1, 2. London: Longmans Green, 1911.

———. *Basic Writings of St. Augustine.* New York: Random House, 1950.

Pegis. *Basic Writings of St. Thomas Aquinas.* New York: Random House, 1950.

Reed, David A. *Jehovah's Witnesses Answered Verse by Verse.* Grand Rapids, Mich.: Baker, 1990.

Ross, Rev. J. J. *Some Facts and More Facts About the Self-Styled Pastor, Charles T. Russell.* Self-published, n.d.

Sanders, J. Oswald. *Heresies Ancient and Modern.* Edinburgh: Marshall, Morgan & Scott, 1954.

Schnell, W. J. *Into the Light of Christianity.* Grand Rapids, Mich.: Baker Book House, 1958.

———. *Thirty Years a Watchtower Slave.* Grand Rapids, Mich.: Baker Book House, 1956.

Souter, Alexander. *The New Testament in Greek.* Oxford: Oxford University Press, 1947.

Spittler, Russell P. *Cults and Isms.* Grand Rapids, Mich.: Baker Book House, 1962.

Stroup, Herbert Hewitt. *The Jehovah's Witnesses.* New York: Columbia University Press, 1945.

Thiessen, Henry. *An Introduction to the New Testament.* Grand Rapids, Mich.: Eerdmans Publishing Company, 1948.

Thomas, F. W. *Masters of Deception: An Exposé of the Jehovah's Witnesses.* Grand Rapids, Mich.: Baker Book House, 1970.

Van Baalen, Jan Karel. *Chaos of the Cults.* 4th Rev. ed. Grand Rapids, Mich.: Eerdmans Publishing Company, 1962.

Van Buskirk, Michael. *The Scholastic Dishonesty of the Watchtower.* Costa Mesa: CARIS, 1976.

Warfield, Benjamin B. *Christological Studies.* Princeton: Princeton University Press, 1950.

Watters, Randall. *Thus Saith the Governing Body of Jehovah's Witnesses.* Manhattan Beach: Bethel Ministries, 1982.

Westcott, B. F., and F. J. A. Hort. *The New Testament in the Original Greek.* New York: Macmillan, 1885, 1943.

Whalen, William J. *Armageddon Around the Corner.* New York: The John Day Company, 1962.

Wilson, Robert Dick. *A Scientific Investigation of the Old Testament.* Philadelphia: Sunday School Times, n.d.

Wright, J. Stafford. *Some Modern Religions.* Chicago: InterVarsity Press, 1956.

Wulfken, George W. *Let There Be Light.* Self-published, n.d.

Young, C. D. *An English Greek Lexicon.* London, n.p., 1859.

Young, E. J. *An Introduction to the Old Testament.* Rev. ed. Grand Rapids, Mich.: Eerdmans Publishing Company, 1958.

Young, G. Douglas. *Grammar of the Hebrew Language.* Grand Rapids, Mich.: Zondervan, 1951.

Young, Robert. *An Analytical Concordance to the Bible.* New York: Funk & Wagnalls Company, 1919.

Magazine and Newspaper Articles

The Brooklyn Daily Eagle, back issues, 1912, 1913, 1916, 1942.

The Brooklyn Daily Times, November 1, 1916, 4.

The Daily Standard Union, November 1, 1916, 5.

Davidson, Bill. "Jehovah's Traveling Salesman," *Reader's Digest,* 50:77–80, January 1947.

Dawn Bible Students Association. *When "Pastor" Russell Died.* n.d.

The New York Times, back issues, 1916.

Russell, Charles Taze. *Our Most Holy Faith: A Collection of Writings and Sermons of Pastor Charles Taze Russell.* Dawn Bible Students Association, 1948.

Stewart, E. D. "The Life of Charles Taze Russell," *Overland Monthly,* Los Angeles, 1917.

Watchtower Bible and Tract Society Publications

Awake! magazine.

The Emphatic Diaglott. Interlinear Greek-English Translation of the New Testament, n.d.

Let God Be True. Rev. ed. 1952.

Make Sure of All Things. 1953.

The New World Translation of the Hebrew Scriptures. Rev. ed. 1951.

The New World Translation of the Hebrew Scriptures. Vol. 1. 1953.

Russell, Charles Taze. *Studies in the Scriptures.* Vols. 1–7. n.d.

Rutherford, J. F. *The Harp of God; Creation; Religion; The Kingdom; Salvation; Deliverance; Children; Enemies; Light; Government; Why Serve Jehovah?; Jehovah's Witnesses—Why Persecuted?; Religious Intolerance—Why?.*

———. Pamphlets. Out of print. *A Great Battle in the Ecclesiastical Heavens* (1915); *Can the Living Talk With the Dead?* (1920); *Millions Now Living Will Never Die* (1920); *Prohibition and the League of Nations* (1920); *Talking With the Dead* (1920); *Comfort for the Jews* (1925); *Restoration* (1927); *The Last Days* (1928); *The Kingdom: The Hope of This World* (1931); *Causes of Death* (1932); *Final War* (1932); *Good News* (1932); *Health and Life*

(1932); *Hereafter* (1932); *Home and Happiness* (1932); *Keys of Heaven* (1932); *The Kingdom* (1932); *Liberty* (1932); *What Is Truth?* (1932); *What You Need* (1932); *Where Are the Dead?* (1932); *Who Is God?* (1932); *The Crisis* (1933); *Dividing the People* (1933); *Escape to the Kingdom* (1933); *Intolerance* (1933); *Angels* (1934); *Beyond the Grave* (1934); *Favored People* (1934); *His Vengeance* (1934); *His Works* (1934); *Righteous Ruler* (1934); *Supremacy* (1934); *World Recovery* (1934); *Government* (1935); *Loyalty* (1935); *Universal War Near* (1935); *Who Shall Rule the World?* (1935); *Choosing Riches or Ruin* (1936); *Protection* (1936); *Armageddon* (1937); *Safety and Comfort* (1937); *Uncovered* (1937); *Face the Facts* (1938); *Warning* (1938); *Fascism or Freedom* (1939); *Government and Peace* (1939); *Judge Rutherford Uncovers the Fifth Column* (1940); *Refugees* (1940); *God and the State* (1941). Published by the International Bible Students Association.

————. Pamphlets. Out of print. *Armageddon; Born of the Spirit; The Day of Judgment; Divine Healing; Does God Answer Prayer; Father, Son, and Holy Spirit; God and Reason; God's Plan, Creation; His Chosen People; Hope Beyond the Grave; Hope for a Fear-Filled World; Jesus the World Savior; Our Lord's Return; Spiritualism; The Truth About Hell; What Can a Man Pay; When a Man Dies.* The Dawn Bible Student Association.

The Watchtower magazine.

Christian Science

Writings of Mary Baker Eddy

Christ and Christmas.

Christian Healing.

Christian Science Hymnal, with five hymns written by Mary Baker Eddy. Christian Science Publishing House, 1909.

Christian Science Versus Pantheism.

The First Church of Christ, Scientist, and Miscellany.

Manual of the Mother Church.

Message to the Mother Church, June 1900.

Message to the Mother Church, June 1901.

Message to the Mother Church, June 1902.

Miscellaneous Writings.

No and Yes.

The People's Idea of God.

Poems.

Pulpit and Press.

Retrospection and Introspection.

Rudimental Divine Science.

Science and Health With Key to the Scriptures. (various editions).

Unity of Good.

General Bibliography

Armstrong, Joseph. *The Mother Church.* Boston, Mass.: Christian Science Publishing Society (CSPS), 1937.

Bates, Ernest Sutherland, and John V. Dittemore. *Mary Baker Eddy—The Truth and the Tradition.* New York: Alfred A. Knopf, Inc., 1932.

Beasley, Norman. *The Cross and the Crown: The History of Christian Science.* New York: Duell, Sloan & Pearce, 1952, 1963.

The Blight That Failed. New York: Charles Scribner's Sons, 1929.

Boa, Kenneth. *Cults, World Religions, and You.* Wheaton: Victor Books, 1977.

Boltzly, Rev. Oliver D. *The Death Plot in Christian Science.* Minneapolis: The Lutheran Literary Board, 1935.

Braden, Charles S. *Spirits in Rebellion.* Dallas: Southern Methodist University Press, 1963.

The Christian Science Journal.

The Christian Science Monitor.

The Christian Science Sentinel.

Christian Science Wartime Activities. Boston: CSPS, 1939–1947.

A Complete Concordance to Science and Health With Key to the Scriptures.

A Complete Concordance to the Writings of Mary Baker Eddy (other than *Science and Health*).

Dakin, Edwin Franden. *Mrs. Eddy.* New York: Charles Scribner's Sons, 1929.

Dickey, Adam. *Memoirs of Mary Baker Eddy.* London: Robert G. Carter, 1927.

Douglass, R. C. *Christian Science: A Defense.* n.p., n.d.

Dresser, Horatio W., ed. *The Quimby Manuscripts.* New York: Thomas Y. Crowell Company, 1921.

Gray, James M. *The Antidote to Christian Science.* Chicago: Moody Press, n.d.

Gruss, Edmond C. *Cults and Occult.* Grand Rapids, Mich.: Baker Book House, 1982.

Hadden, Robert A. *Christian Science and the Christian Scriptures Compared and Contrasted.* American Prophetic League, 1952.

Haldeman, Isaac Massey. *Christian Science in Light of Holy Scripture.* New York: Fleming H. Revell Company, 1909.

Hanna, Septimus J. *Christian Science History.* Boston: CSPS, 1899.

Haushalter, Walter M. *Mrs. Eddy Purloins From Hegel.* Boston: A. A. Beauchamp, 1936.

Hawkins, Ann Ballew. *Phineas Parkhurst Quimby.* Self-published, 1951.

Hoekema, Anthony A. *Christian Science.* Grand Rapids, Mich.: Eerdmans Publishing Company, 1974.

Johnston, Julia Michael. *Mary Baker Eddy: Her Mission and Triumph.* Boston: CSPS, 1946.

Judah, J. Stillson. *The History and Philosophy of the Legal Aspects of Christian Science.* Boston: CSPS, 1899.

———.*The History and Philosophy of the Metaphysical Movements in America.* Philadelphia: The Westminster Press, 1967.

Martin, Walter R. *Walter Martin Speaks Out on the Cults.* Ventura, Calif.: Vision House Publishers, 1983.

Martin, Walter R., and Norman H. Klann. *The Christian Science Myth.* Grand Rapids, Mich.: Zondervan, 1956.

Meekan, M. *Mrs. Eddy and the Late Suit in Equity.* Self-published, 1908.

Miller, Elliot. "Christian Science" in *Walter Martin's Cults Reference Bible.* Santa Ana: Vision House Publishers, 1981.

Milmine, Georgine. *The Life of Mary Baker G. Eddy and the History of Christian Science.* New York: Doubleday, Page & Company, 1909. Reprinted by Baker Book House, 1971.

Moore, Rev. A. Lincoln. *Christian Science—Its Manifold Attraction.* Theodore E. Schulte Publishing Company, 1906.

Paget, Stephen, M.D. *The Faith and Works of Christian Science.* London: Self-published, 1909.

Peabody, Frederick W. *The Religio-Medical Masquerade.* New York: Fleming H. Revell, 1910.

Peel, Robert. *Spiritual Healing in a Scientific Age.* San Francisco: Harper & Row, 1987.

Phillips, Jane. *Mary Baker Eddy's Early Writings Compared With the Quimby Manuscripts.* Pasadena, Calif.: Toujours Publishing Company, 1931.

Powell, Lyman P. *Mary Baker Eddy.* New York: Macmillan, 1930.

Ramsay, E. Mary. *Christian Science and Its Discoverer.* Boston: CSPS, 1935.

Riddle, T. Wilkinson. *Christian Science in the Light of Holy Scripture.* London: Marshall, Morgan and Scott, 1931.

Riley, Woodbridge, W. Frederick Peabody, and Charles E. Humiston. *The Faith, the Falsity, and the Failure of Christian Science.* Nutley, N.J.: Fleming H. Revell, 1925.

Sheldon, Henry C. *Christian Science So-Called.* Nashville: Abingdon Press, 1913.

Smith, Clifford P. *Historical Sketches.* Boston: CSPS, 1941.

Snowden, James H. *The Truth About Christian Science.* Philadelphia: Westminster Press, 1920.
Stewart, Herbert. *Christian Science—True or False.* Belfast: Graham L. Healy, Ltd., n.d.
Tenney, Rev. Herbert McIville. *Christian Science: Its Truths and Errors.* The Burrows Brothers Company, 1888.
Tomlinson, Irving C. *Twelve Years With Mary Baker Eddy.* Boston: CSPS, 1945.
Twain, Mark. *Christian Science.* New York: Harper, 1907.
Wilbur, Sybil. *The Life of Mary Baker Eddy.* Boston: CSPS, 1923.
Williamson, Margaret. *The Mother Church Extension.* Boston: CSPS, 1939.
Witmer, George W. *Christian Science in the Light of the Bible.* St. Louis, Mo.: Concordia Publishing House, 1949.
Woodbury, Josephine C. *War on Heaven.* Boston: S. Usher Printer, 1897.

Newspaper and Magazine Articles

Arena magazine. Selected copy regarding Mrs. Eddy and Christian Science.
Buckley, Dr. J. M. "Dr. J. M. Buckley on Christian Science," *North American Review,* July 1901.
Cabot, M.D., Richard C. "100 Christian Science Cures," *McClures* magazine, August 1908.
"The Deadly Parallel," *New York Times,* July 10, 1904.
Fishbein, M.D., Morris. "Mary Baker Eddy," *Plain Talk,* 1:2, November 1927:21–26.
McClures magazine. Selected copy regarding Mrs. Eddy and Christian Science.
The New York Herald Tribune. Article and editorial on Christian Science, December 12–13, 1951.
The New York Times. Selected material on Christian Science.
The New York World. Selected material on Christian Science.
Woodbury, Josephine C. "Quimbyism or the Paternity of Christian Science," *Arena,* May 1899.
Wright, Livingston. "How Reverend Wiggin Rewrote Mrs. Eddy's Book," *New York World,* n.d.

Mormonism

Anderson, Edward H. *A Brief History of the Church of Jesus Christ Latter-day Saints.* Jackson County, Mo.: Zion's Printing and Publishing Company, 1928.
Anderson, Einar. *Mormonism.* Chicago: Moody Press, 1956.
Argaugh, G. B. *Gods, Sex, and the Saints.* Rock Island: Augusta Press, 1957.
Arrington, Leonard J., and Davis Bitton. *The Mormon Experience.* New York: Alfred A. Knopf, Inc., 1979.
Bales, James D. *The Book of Mormon?* Rosemead, Calif.: Old Paths Book Club, 1958.
Baskin, R. N. *Reminiscences of Early Utah.* Self-published, 1914.
Beadle, J. H. *Polygamy or the Mysteries and Crimes of Mormonism.* Philadelphia: The National Publishing Company, 1882.
Bennett, Wallace Foster. *Why I Am a Mormon.* New York: T. Nelson, 1958.
Brewer, David I. *Utah Elites and Utah Racial Norms.* Salt Lake City: Modern Microfilm Company, n.d.
Brodie, Fawn M. *No Man Knows My History—The Life of Joseph Smith, the Mormon Prophet.* New York: Alfred A. Knopf, Inc., 1957, 1971.
Brooks, Juanita, ed. *On the Mormon Frontier: The Diary of Hosea Stout.* Salt Lake City: University of Utah Press, n.d.
Budvarson, Arthur. *The Book of Mormonism—True or False?* Grand Rapids, Mich.: Zondervan, 1941.
Call, Lamoni. *2,000 Changes in the Book of Mormon.* Salt Lake City: Modern Microfilm Company, n.d.

Cannon, Frank J. *Brigham Young and His Mormon Empire.* New York: Fleming H. Revell Company, 1913.

———. *Under the Prophet in Utah.* Boston: C. M. Clark, 1911.

Clark, J. A. *Gleanings by the Way.* n.p., 1842.

Codman, Jr. *The Mormon Country.* U.S. Publishing Company, 1874.

Corrill, John. *A Brief History of the Church of Christ of Latter-day Saints.* n.p.

Cowan, Marvin W. *Mormon Claims Answered.* Salt Lake City: Marvin W. Cowan, 1975.

Derby, and Miller, *History of the Mormons or Latter-day Saints.* New York: Auburn, 1852.

Draper, Maurice I. *Christ's Church Restored.* Independence, Mo.: Herald Publishing House, 1948.

Erickson, Ephraim D. *The Psychological and Ethical Aspects of Mormon Group Life.* Chicago: University of Chicago Press, 1922.

Etenhouser, R., and A. B. Phillips. *Three Bibles Compared.* Independence: Herald Publishing Company, 1954.

Evans, R. H. *One Hundred Years of Mormonism.* Salt Lake City: Deseret News, 1905.

Folk, Edgar E. *The Mormon Monster.* New York: Fleming H. Revell, 1900.

Fraser, Gordon H. *Is Mormonism Christian?* Chicago: Moody Press, 1957.

Gibbs, Josiah F. *The Mountain Meadows Massacre.* Salt Lake City: *Salt Lake Tribune,* 1910.

Goodspeed, Edgar J. *The New Testament—An American Translation.* Chicago: University of Chicago Press, 1923.

Hanson, Klaus. *Quest for Empire.* East Lansing, Mich.: Michigan State University Press, n.d.

Hickman, William A. *Brigham's Destroying Angel.* New York: G. A. Crofutt, 1872.

Hield, Charles R. *Baptism for the Dead.* Independence: Herald Publishing Company, 1953.

Hoekema, Anthony A. *Mormonism.* Grand Rapids, Mich.: Eerdmans Publishing Company, 1974.

Hougey, Hal. *Archaeology and the Book of Mormon.* Los Angeles: Pacific Press, 1973.

———. *Truth About the "Lehi Tree of Life" Stone.* Los Angeles: Pacific Press, 1973.

Howe, E. D. *Mormonism Unveiled.* 1834.

Hunter, Milton R. *The Gospel Through the Ages.* Salt Lake City: Melchizedek Priesthood Course of Study, 1945–1946.

Ivins, Stanley S. *The Moose Thatcher Case.* Salt Lake City: Modern Microfilm Company, n.d.

Jenson, Andrew. *Latter-day Saint Biographical Encyclopedia.* Salt Lake City: Self-published annual, 1901–1936.

———. *Plural Marriage.* Vol. 6. Salt Lake City: The Historical Record of the Church of Jesus Christ of Latter-day Saints. May 1887.

Jonas, Larry. *Mormon Claims Examined.* Salt Lake City: Modern Microfilm Company, n.d.

Kidder, Daniel P. *Mormonism and the Mormons.* New York: G. Lane & P. P. Sanford, 1842.

Lamb, M. T. *The Golden Bible.* New York: Ward and Drummond, 1887.

Lee, John Doyle. *A Mormon Chronicle.* San Marino, Calif.: Huntington Memorial Library, 1955.

Lewis, William. *The Church of Jesus Christ: How Shall I Know It?* Independence: Herald Publishing House, n.d.

Linn, William Alexander. *The Story of the Mormons.* New York: Macmillan, 1902.

Lyford, C. *The Mormon Problem.* New York: Hunt and Eaton, 1866.

Martin, Stuart. *The Mystery of Mormonism.* New York: E. P. Dutton and Company, n.d.

Martin, Walter. *Jehovah's Witnesses and the Trinity.* Audiotape. Walter Martin Ministries. *www.waltermartin.com.*

———. *The Maze of Mormonism.* Santa Ana: Vision House Publishers, 1978.

McConkie, Bruce R. *Mormon Doctrine.* Salt Lake City: Bookcraft, 1958, 1966, 1978.

———. *What the Mormons Think of Christ.* Salt Lake City: Bookcraft, n.d.

McElveen, Floyd C. *The Mormon Illusion.* Ventura: Gospel Light Publications, 1979.

McKeever, Bill, and Eric Johnson. *Mormonism 101: Examining the Religion of the Latter-day Saints.* Grand Rapids, Mich.: Baker Book House, 2000.

Meyer, Edward. *Ursprung und Geshichte der Mormonen mit Exkursen ueber Anfange des Islams und des Christentums.* n.p., 1912.

Mulder, William. *Among the Mormons.* New York: Alfred A. Knopf, Inc., 1958.

Nutting, J. D. *The Little Encyclopedia of Mormonism.* Cleveland: Utah Gospel Mission, 1927.

O'Dey, Thomas F. *The Mormons.* Chicago: University of Chicago Press, 1957.

Peck, Reed. *Reed Peck Manuscript.* Salt Lake City: Modern Microfilm Company, reprint, n.d.

Penrose, Charles W. *Mormon Doctrine Plain and Simple or Leaves From the Tree.* Salt Lake City: G. Q. Cannon, 1897.

Petersen, LaMar. *Problems in Mormon Text.* Salt Lake City: Modern Microfilm Company, n.d.

Petersen, Mark E. *Race Problems as They Affect the Church.* Salt Lake City: Modern Microfilm Company, n.d.

Pratt, Orson. *Pamphlets by Orson Pratt.* Liverpool: R. James, 1851.

Pratt, Parley P. *Key to the Science of Theology.* Liverpool: F. D. Richards, 1855.

Reed, David, and John Farkas. *Mormons.* Grand Rapids, Mich.: Answered Verse by Verse, Baker Book House, 1992.

Reiser, A. H., and Marian G. Merkley. *What It Means to Be a Latter-day Saint: Course of Study for the First Intermediates Department.* Salt Lake City: Bookcraft, 1946.

Richards, Le Grand. *A Marvelous Work and a Wonder.* Salt Lake City: Deseret Book Company, 1950.

Roberts, R. Phillip. *Mormonism Unmasked: Confronting the Contradictions Between Mormon Beliefs and True Christianity.* Broadman & Holman Publishers, 1998.

Rosten, Leo. *A Guide to the Religions of America.* New York: Simon and Schuster, 1963.

Rushton, John W. *The Apostasy and the Restoration.* Independence: Herald Publishing House, n.d.

Sackett, Charles C. *What's Going On in There?* Thousand Oaks, Calif.: Ex-Mormons for Jesus, 1982.

Schindler, Harold. *Orrin Porter Rockwell: Man of God, Son of Thunder.* Salt Lake City: University of Utah Press, n.d.

Shields, Stephen L. *Divergent Paths of the Restoration.* Bountiful, Utah: Restoration Research, 1982.

Shook, Charles A. *The True Origin of the Book of Mormon.* Cincinnati, Ohio: Self-published, 1914.

Smith, Elbert A. *Differences That Persist Between the Reorganized Church of Christ Latter-day Saints and the Utah Mormon Church.* Independence, Mo.: Herald Publishing House, 1943.

Smith, Ethan. *View of the Hebrews.* Poutney, Me.: Smith & Shute, 1823.

Smith, Joseph, Jr. *A Book of Commandments for the Government of the Church of Christ.* Reprinted by the *Salt Lake Tribune,* 1884.

———. *The Book of Mormon.* Salt Lake City: The Church of Jesus Christ of Latter-day Saints, various editions and publishers from 1830–1979.

Smith, Joseph Fielding, compiler. *Teachings of the Prophet Joseph Smith.* Salt Lake City: Deseret Book Company, 1976.

Smith, Lucy Mack. *Biographical Sketches of Joseph Smith.* Liverpool: S. W. Richards, 1853.

Snowden, James H. *The Truth About Mormonism.* New York: George H. Durant Company, 1926.

Spalding, F. S. *Why Egyptologists Reject the Book of Abraham.* Salt Lake City: The Arrow Press, n.d.

Spencer, Orson. *Letters Exhibiting the Most Prominent Doctrines of the Church of Jesus Christ of Latter-day Saints.* Liverpool: Self-published, 1848.

Starks, Arthur E. *A Complete Concordance to the Book of Mormon.* Independence: Herald Publishing House, 1950.

Stenhouse, T. B. *The Rocky Mountain Saints.* New York: B. Appleton Company, 1873.

Stewart, George. *Priesthood and Church Welfare.* Salt Lake City: Deseret Book Company, 1939.

Swartzell, William. *Mormonism Exposed.* Self-published, 1840.

Talmage, James E. *The Articles of Faith.* Salt Lake City: The Church of Jesus Christ of Latter-day Saints, 1952.

Tanner, Jerald. *Changes in Joseph Smith's History.* Salt Lake City: Modern Microfilm Company, n.d.

———. *Changes in the Key to Theology.* Salt Lake City: Modern Microfilm Company, n.d.

———. *Changes in The Pearl of Great Price.* Salt Lake City: Modern Microfilm Company, n.d.

———. *The Negro in Mormon Theology.* Salt Lake City: Modern Microfilm Company, n.d.

Tanner, Jerald, and Sandra Tanner. *The Case Against Mormonism.* Vol. 1. Salt Lake City: Modern Microfilm Company, n.d.

———. *The Changing World of Mormonism.* Chicago: Moody Press, 1981.

———. *Joseph Smith and Polygamy.* Salt Lake City: Modern Microfilm Company, n.d.

———. *Joseph Smith's Curse Upon the Negro.* Salt Lake City: Modern Microfilm Company, n.d.

———. *Joseph Smith's Strange Account of the First Vision.* Salt Lake City: Modern Microfilm Company, n.d.

———. *The Mormon Kingdom.* Salt Lake City: Modern Microfilm Company, n.d.

———. *The Mormon Papyri Question.* Salt Lake City: Modern Microfilm Company, n.d.

———. *Mormonism—Shadow or Reality?* Salt Lake City: Modern Microfilm Company, 1972, 1982.

———. *Revealing Statements by the Three Witnesses to the Book of Mormon.* Salt Lake City: Modern Microfilm Company, n.d.

———. *3,914 Changes in the Book of Mormon.* Salt Lake City: Modern Microfilm Company, n.d.

Taylor, Samuel W. *Rocky Mountain Empire: The Latter-day Saints Today.* New York: Macmillan, 1978.

Thayer, Joseph Henry. *Greek-English Lexicon.* Grand Rapids, Mich.: Zondervan, 1973.

Tope, Wallace W. *On the Frontlines.* La Canada-Flintridge, Calif.: Frontline Ministries, 1980, 1981.

Tucker, Pomeroy. *Origin, Rise, and Progress of Mormonism.* n.p., 1867.

Tullis, F. La Mond, ed. *Mormonism: A Faith for All Cultures.* Provo, Utah: Brigham Young University Press, 1978.

Turner, Wallace. *The Mormon Establishment.* Boston: Houghton Mifflin Co., 1966.

Van Gorden, Kurt. *Mormonism.* Grand Rapids, Mich.: Zondervan, 1995.

Van Wagoner, Richard S., and Steven C. Walker. *A Book of Mormons.* Salt Lake City: Signature Books, 1982.

Walters, Wesley P. *New Light on Mormon Origins From the Palmyra [N.Y.] Revival.* La Mesa, Calif.: Utah Christian Tract Society, 1973.

Wardle, James D. *Selected Changes in the Book of Mormon.* Salt Lake City: Modern Microfilm Company, n.d.

Weldon, Roy. *Other Sheep: Book of Mormon Evidences.* Independence, Mo.: Herald Publishing House, 1956.

White, James R. *Is the Mormon My Brother?* Minneapolis: Bethany House Publishers, 1997.

———. *Letters to a Mormon Elder.* Minneapolis: Bethany House Publishers, 1993.

Whitmer, John. *John Whitmer's History.* Salt Lake City: Modern Microfilm Company, reprint, n.d.

Widtsoe, John A. *Priesthood and Church Government.* Salt Lake City: Deseret Book Company, 1939.

Witte, Robert C. *Where Does It Say That?* Safety Harbor, Fla.: Ex-Mormons for Jesus, 1982.

Young, Brigham. *Journal of Discourses*. Salt Lake City: Church of Jesus Christ of Latter-day Saints, 1901.
Young, Eliza. *Wife No. 19: A Life in Bondage*. n.p., 1872.

Spiritism

Boa, Kenneth. *Cults, World Religions, and You*. Wheaton: Scripture Press, 1977.
Braden, Charles S. *These Also Believe*. New York: Macmillan, 1960.
———. *The World's Religions*. New York: Abingdon Press, 1954.
Butterworth, George W. *Spiritualism and Religion*. New York: Macmillan, 1944.
Doyle, A. Conan. *The History of Spiritualism*. 2 vols. Phineas Speaks: Direct Communications in the Family Circle. London, 1927.
Ferm, Vergilius. *Encyclopedia of Religion*. New York: Philosophical Library, 1945.
Fodor, Nandor. *Encyclopaedia of Psychic Science*. Secaucus, N.J.: The Citadel Press, 1966.
Gray, James M. *Spiritism and the Fallen Angels*. London: Fleming H. Revell, 1920.
Gruss, Edmond C. *Cults and the Occult*. Grand Rapids: Baker Book House, 1982.
Harding, Emma. *Modern American Spiritualism—A Twenty Year Record of the Communion of the World and Spirits*. New York, 1870.
Hill, Arthur J. *Spiritualism—Its History, Phenomena and Doctrine*. New York: George H. Doran & Co., 1919.
Hull, Moses. *Encyclopedia of Biblical Spiritualism*. Chicago: Moses Hull & Co., 1895.
Koch, Kurt E. *Christian Counseling and Occultism*. 21st ed. Grand Rapids: Kregel Publications, 1973.
Larson, Bob. *Larson's Book of Cults*. Wheaton: Tyndale House Publishers, 1982.
Lewis, Gordon R. *Confronting the Cults*. Grand Rapids: Baker Book House, 1966.
McCabe, Joseph. *Spiritualism—A Popular History From 1847*. London, 1920.
McKnight, Marcus. *Spiritualism*. London, 1950.
Melton, J. Gordon. *The Encyclopedia of American Religions*. Vol. 2. Wilmington, N.C.: McGrath Publishing Company, 1978.
Morrell, James Russell Lowell. *Spiritism and the Beginnings of Christianity*. Kila, Mont.: Kessinger Publishing Company, 1997.
Newton, Michael. *Destiny of Souls: New Case Studies of Life Between Lives*. St. Paul: Llewellyn Worldwide, Ltd., 2000.
Petersen, William J. *Those Curious New Cults*. New Canaan, Conn.: Keats Publishing Company, 1975.
Schofield, A. T. *Modern Spiritism—Its Science and Religion*. Philadelphia: P. Blakiston's Son & Co., 1920.
Spittler, Russell P. *Cults and Isms*. Grand Rapids: Baker Book House, 1962.
Stoddard, Jane T. *The Case Against Spiritualism*. New York: Houghton & Stoughton, 1919.
Unger, Merrill F. *Demons in the World Today*. Wheaton: Tyndale House Publishers, 1971.
Van Praagh, James. *Talking to Heaven: A Medium's Message of Life After Death*. Penguin, 1999.
Wade, Alda Madison. *Evidences of Immortality*. Boston: The Christopher Publishing House, 1956.
Walton, George S. *The Drama of Life After Death*. New York: A. H. Holt & Co., 1932.
Wilson, Clifford A., and John Weldon. *Occult Shock and Psychic Forces*. San Diego: Master Books, 1980.
Zaretsky, Irving I., and Mark P. Leone, eds. *Religious Movements in Contemporary America*. Princeton: Princeton University Press, 1974.

Pamphlets
Biederwolf, William E. *Spiritualism: Divine? Devilish? or Deception?* Grand Rapids: Wm. B. Eerdmans Publishing Co., 1952.

Froom, Leroy Edwin, *Spiritualism Today*. Washington, D.C.: Review and Herald, 1963.
Wright, The Rev. J. Stanford. *Spiritualism*. London: The Church Book Room Press, 1959.

The Theosophical Society

Ankerberg, John, and John Weldon. *Encyclopedia of Cults and New Religions*. Eugene, Ore.: Harvest House, 1999.

Arundale, George S. *Freedom and Friendship: The Call of Theosophy and the Theosophical Society*. Kessinger Publications, 2003.

Besant, Annie. *The Ancient Wisdom: An Outline of Theosophic Teaching*. London: The Theosophical Society, 1897.

———. *An Autobiography*. London: The Theosophical Society, 1893.

———. *The Changing World*. London: The Theosophical Publishing Society, 1901.

———. *Is Theosophy Anti-Christian?* London: The Theosophical Publishing Society, 1901.

———. *Karma*. London: The Theosophical Publishing Society, 1904.

———. *Man's Life in Three Worlds*. London: The Theosophical Publishing Society, 1899.

———. *The Seven Principles of Man*. London: The Theosophical Publishing Society, 1902.

Blavatsky, Helena Petrovna. *Isis Unveiled*. Wheaton: Theosophical Publishing House, 1972.

———. *The Key to Theosophy—An Abridgement*. Wheaton: Theosophical Publishing House, 1972.

———. *The Secret Doctrine*. London: The Theosophical Society, 1893.

———. *Theosophical Glossary*. Los Angeles: The Theosophical Company, 1892, 1973.

Braden, Charles S. *These Also Believe*. New York: Macmillan, 1960.

Butte, G. Baseden *Madame Blavatsky*. London: The Theosophical Society, 1926.

Cooper, Irving S. *Theosophy Simplified*. 7th ed. Wheaton: The Theosophical Press, 1964.

Davies, Horton. *The Challenge of the Sects*. Philadelphia: Westminster Press, 1961.

Ellwood, Robert S., Jr. *Alternative Altars*. Chicago: University of Chicago Press, 1979.

Ferguson, Charles. *Nehru Books of Revelation*. Garden City, N.J.: Doubleday, 1929.

Judah, J. Stillson. *The History and Philosophy of the Metaphysical Movements in America*. Philadelphia: The Westminster Press, 1967.

Kuhn, Alvin B. *Theosophy: A Modern Revival of Ancient Wisdom*. New York: H. Holt & Company, 1930.

Leadbeater, Charles W. *Textbook of Theosophy*. Chicago: The Theosophical Press, 1925.

McNiele, E. R. *From Theosophy to Christian Faith*. London: Longmans Green & Company, 1919.

Mills, Joy. *100 Years of Theosophy: A History of the Theosophical Society in America*. Theosophical Publishing House, 1994.

Olcott, Henry S. *Old Diary Leaves: An Authentic History of the Theosophical Society*. Madras, India: The Theosophical Publishing Society, 1935.

Rogers, L. W. *Elementary Theosophy*. 6th ed. Wheaton: The Theosophical Press, 1956.

Russell, J. H. "Theosophy," *The New Schaff-Herzog Encyclopedia of Religious Knowledge*. Grand Rapids, Mich.: Baker Book House, 1977, reprint.

Sheldon, H. C. *Theosophy and New Thought*. New York: Houghton Mifflin Co., 1916.

Sinnett, Alfred Percy. *The Theosophical Movement: 1875–1925: A History and a Survey*. New York: E. P. Dutton, 1925.

Sloan, Ellen M. *Modern Theosophy, Whence, What, Whither?* St. Paul: The Way Press, 1922.

Symonds, John. *Madame Blavatsky: Medium and Magician*. London: Odhams Press, 1959.

Van Baalen, Jan Karel. *The Chaos of the Cults*. 4th rev. ed. Grand Rapids, Mich.: Eerdmans Publishing Company, 1962.

Williams, Gertrude Leavenworth. *Priestess of the Occult, Madame Blavatsky*. New York: Alfred A. Knopf, Inc., 1946.

Wilson, Colin. *The Occult—A History*. New York: Random House, 1971.

Buddhism

Anderson, Norman J., ed. *The World's Religions,* Grand Rapids, Mich.: William B. Eerdmans Publishing Company, 1975.

Anderson, Walt. *Open Secrets: A Western Guide to Tibetan Buddhism.* New York: Viking Press, 1979.

Arvon, Henri. *Buddhism.* New York: Walker and Company, 1962.

Barrett, William. *Zen Buddhism: Selected Writings of D. T. Suzuki.* New York: Doubleday, 1956.

Beaver, R. Pierce, et al., eds. *Eerdmans Handbook to the World's Religions.* Grand Rapids, Mich.: Eerdmans Publishing Company, 1982.

Chan, Wing-Tist. "Buddhahood." Edited by Vergilius Ferm. *An Encyclopedia of Religion.* New York: Philosophical Library, 1945.

Chang, Lit-sen. *Zen-Existentialism: The Spiritual Decline of the West.* Nutley, N.J.: Presbyterian and Reformed Publishing Company, 1969.

Chen-Chi-Chang. *The Practice of Zen.* New York: Harper, 1959.

Conze, Edward. *Buddhism: Its Essence and Development.* New York: Harper & Row, 1951.

David-Neel, Alexandra. *Buddhism: Its Doctrines and Its Methods.* New York: Avon Books, 1977.

Fry, C. George, James R. King, Eugene R. Swanger, and Herbert C. Wolf. *Great Asian Religions,* n.p., n.d.

Gaer, Joseph. *What Great Religions Believe.* Signet, The New American Library: New York, 1963.

Geisler, Norman L., and Ytaka Amano. *The Reincarnation Sensation.* Wheaton: Tyndale House, 1987.

Guenther, Herbert V. *Buddhist Philosophy in Theory and Practice.* Middlesex: Penguin Books, 1971.

Halverson, Dean C., General Editor. *The Compact Guide to World Religions.* Minneapolis: Bethany House Publishers, 1996.

Humphreys, Christmas. *Zen Buddhism.* London: Allen and Unwin, 1957.

"Is Buddha Awakening the U.S.?" *Hinduism Today,* July 1994.

Jackson, Samuel Macauley, ed. *The New Schaff-Herzog Encyclopedia of Religious Knowledge.* Grand Rapids, Mich.: Baker Book House, 1977.

Johnson, David L. *A Reasoned Look at Asian Religions.* Minneapolis: Bethany House Publishers, 1985.

Kapleau, Philip, ed. *The Three Pillars of Zen.* Boston: Beacon Press, 1965.

Kung, Timothy. "Evangelizing Buddhists," *International Journal of Frontier Missions,* July 1993.

Layman, Emma McCloy. *Buddhism in America.* Chicago: Nelson-Hall, 1976.

Linssen, Robert. *Living Zen.* New York: Grove Press, 1958.

McDowell, Josh, and Don Stewart. *Handbook of Today's Religions.* San Bernardino, Calif.: Here's Life Publishers, 1981.

Martin, Walter. *The New Cults.* Santa Ana, Calif.: Vision House Publishers, 1980.

———. *Zen Buddhism, Hare Krishna, and Meher Baba.* Santa Ana, Calif.: One Way Libraries, 1976, side one.

Mather, George A., and Larry A. Nichols. "Hinduism History," *Dictionary of Cults, Sects, Religions and the Occult.* Grand Rapids, Mich.: Zondervan, 1993.

Mathison, Richard. *Faith, Cults, and Sects of America.* New York: The Bobbs-Merrill Company, Inc., 1960.

Melton, J. Gordon. *Encyclopedia of American Religions.* Vol. 2. Wilmington, N.C.: McGrath Publishing Company, 1978.

Nauman, St. Elmo. *Dictionary of Asian Philosophies.* Secaucus, N.J.: Citadel Press, 1978.

Nichiren Shoshu Buddhism Quarterly. Fall 1973; Spring 1974.

Ogata, Sohaku. *Zen for the West.* New York: Apollo, Williams, Morrow, 1962.

Parrinder, Geoffrey. *Avatar and Incarnation.* New York: Oxford University Press, 1982.
——. *A Dictionary of Non-Christian Religions.* Philadelphia: The Westminster Press, 1971.
Robinson, Richard H. *The Buddhist Religion.* Belmont, Calif.: Dickenson Publishing, 1970.
Seikyo Times, Oct. 1971; Nov. 1972; March 1973.
Stephens, James C. "Looking at Buddhist America: A Key to World Evangelization," *International Journal of Frontier Missions,* July 1993.
Suzuki, D. T. *Essays in Zen Buddhism.* 3 vols. London: n.p., 1949, 1951.
——. *An Introduction to Zen Buddhism.* New York: Philosophical Library, 1949.
——. *Manual of Zen Buddhism.* New York: Grove Press, 1960.
Watts, Alan. *The Spirit of Zen.* New York: Grove Press, 1958.
——. *The Way of Liberation in Zen Buddhism.* San Francisco: American Academy of Asian Studies, 1955.
——. *The Way of Zen.* New York: Pantheon Books, 1959.
Weerasingha, Tissa. "Karma and Christ: Opening Our Eyes to the Buddhist World," *International Journal of Frontier Missions,* July 1993.
Yamamoto, J. Isamu. "The Arrival of Theravad," *Christian Research Journal,* Fall 1994.
——. *Beyond Buddhism.* Downers Grove, Ill.: InterVarsity Press, 1982.
——. "The Buddha," *Christian Research Journal,* Spring/Summer 1994.
——. *Buddhism, Taoism, and other Far Eastern Movements.* Grand Rapids, Mich.: Zondervan, 1998.
——. "Tibetan Buddhists," *Christian Research Journal,* Spring 1995.
Zacharias, Ravi. *The Lotus and the Cross.* Sisters, Ore.: Multnomah Books, 2001.

The Baha'i Faith

Magazine Articles

Bach, Marcus. "Baha'i: A Second Look," *Christian Century,* April 10, 1957.
"We Love All Religions," *Time,* April 26, 1963.

Publications from the Baha'i Publishing Trust, Wilmette, Ill.

Abdu'l-Baha. *Some Questions Answered.*
Baha'u'llah. *Gleanings From the Writings of Baha'u'llah,* 1952.
Baha'u'llah and Abdu'l-Baha. *Baha'i World Faith.*
Principles of the Baha'i Faith.
Sears, William. *Release the Sun.*
Shoghi, Effendi. *Promised Day to Come.*
Star of the West. Wilmette: Baha'i Publishing Committee, December 31, 1913.
Townsend, George. *The Promise of All Ages.*
Willoughby, John. *All Things Made New.*
The Wisdom of Baha'u'llah. Wilmette: Baha'i Publishing Committee, n.d.

Additional Bibliography

Ankerberg, John, and John Weldon. *Encyclopedia of Cults and New Religions.* Eugene, Ore.: Harvest House, 1999.
Enroth, Ronald, et al. *A Guide to Cults and New Religions.* Downers Grove, Ill.: InterVarsity Press, 1983.
Esslemont, J. E. *Baha'u'llah and the New Era.* Wilmette, Ill.: Baha'i Publishing Trust, 1970. Reprinted from 1923.
Gruss, Edmond C. *Cults and Occult.* Grand Rapids, Mich.: Baker Book House, 1982.

House, H. Wayne. *Charts of Cults, Sects, and Religious Movements.* Grand Rapids: Zondervan Publishers, 2000.

Martin, Walter R, *Baha'i.* Audiotape. Walter Martin Ministries. *www.waltermartin.com.*

————. *Walter Martin Speaks Out on the Cults.* Ventura, Calif.: Vision House Publishers, 1983.

Mather, George A., and Larry A. Nichols. *Dictionary of Cults, Sects, Religions and the Occult.* Grand Rapids, Mich.: Zondervan Publishers, 1993.

Mathison, Richard. *Faith, Cults, and Sects in America.* New York: Scribners, 1952.

Miller, Elliot. "The Baha'i Faith" in *Walter Martin's Cults Reference Bible.* Santa Ana, Calif.: Vision House Publishers, 1981.

Miller, William McElwee. *What Is the Baha'i Faith?* Grand Rapids, Mich.: Eerdmans Publishing Company, 1977.

Van Baalen, Jan Karel. *Chaos of the Cults.* 4th ed. Revised. Grand Rapids, Mich.: Eerdmans Publishing Company, 1962.

Unitarian Universalism

Articles

Chandler, Russell. "Unitarians: Oneness in Diversity," *Los Angeles Times,* May 27, 1986.

Chethik, Neil. "The Saving Message: The New UU Evangelists," *The World,* 9:3, May/June 1995.

Doerr, Edd. Book Reviews: "The Quality of Religious Life in Unitarian Universalist Congregations: A Survey by the Commission on Appraisal and Our Chosen Faith: An Introduction to Unitarian Universalism," *The Humanist,* May/June 1990.

Gomes, Alan W. "De Jesu Christo Servatore: Faustus Socinus on the Satisfaction of Christ," *Westminster Theological Journal,* 55, 1993.

————."Winds of Change in the Worldwide Church of God: With Special Emphasis on the Doctrine of the Trinity," *Presbyterion* 20:2, 1994.

Gordon, Alexander. "The Sozzini and Their School," *Theological Review,* 65, 1879.

Gray, Duke T. "Letter to the Christians," *The Unitarian Universalist Christian,* 47, nos. 3–4 Fall/Winter 1992.

Klauber, Martin I., and Glenn S. Sunshine. "Jean-Alphonse Turrettini on Biblical Accommodation: Calvinist or Socinian?" *Calvin Theological Journal,* 25, 1990.

Kurtz, Paul, and Vern L. Bullough. "The Unitarian Universalist Association: Humanism or Theism?" *Free Inquiry* 11, no. 2, Spring 1991.

Lattin, Don. "Pagans to Light Up the Year's Longest Night," *San Francisco Chronicle,* December 21, 1991.

Neibuhr, Gustav. "With a New Spiritualism, Unitarians Welcome People of All Beliefs," *Washington Post,* July 6, 1993.

Olds, Mason, "Religious Humanism and Unitarianism," *Religious Humanism,* 12, no. 1, 1978.

Parke, David B., "Theological Directions of Unitarian Universalism for the Next Twenty-Five Years," *Unitarian Universalist Christian,* 44; 3–4, 1989.

Robb, Christina, "In Goddesses They Trust," *Boston Globe,* July 9, 1990.

White, Gayle, "Tide Turns for Unitarians As Scope Widens, Membership Grows," *Atlanta Journal and Constitution,* January 13, 1990.

Wilbur, Earl Morse, "Faustus Socinus, Pioneer," *Hibbert Journal,* 33, 1935.

Wilson, Craig, "Minister Preaches Gay Acceptance," *USA Today,* August 20, 1991.

Winston, Diane, "Unitarian 'Boomer' Following Growing," *Denver Post,* May 9, 1991.

Woodward, Kenneth L., et al., "And the Children Shall Lead Them: Young Americans Return to God," *Newsweek,* December 17, 1990.

Additional Bibliography

Alexander, Scott W., ed. *Salted With Fire: Unitarian Universalist Strategies for Sharing Faith and Growing Congregations.* Boston: Skinner House, 1995.

Braden, Charles S. *The World's Religions.* New York: Abingdon Press, 1954.

Channing, William Ellery. "Unitarian Christianity," *Three Prophets of Religious Liberalism: Channing, Emerson, Parker.* Edited and with an introduction by Conrad Wright. Boston: Beacon, 1961.

DeWolf, Harold F. *Present Trends in Christian Thought.* New York: Association Press, 1960.

Fields, Ann. "Continuous Creation," *Unitarian Universalist Views of God.* Edited by Doris Hunter. Boston: Unitarian Universalist Association, n.d.

Ferm, Vergilius. *Encyclopedia of Religion.* New York: Philosophical Library, 1945.

Gomes, Alan W. *Unitarian Universalism.* Grand Rapids, Mich., Zondervan Publishing Company, 1998.

James, Jacqui, ed. *Between the Lines: Sources for Singing the Living Tradition.* Boston: Unitarian Universalist Association, 1995.

Kegley, Charles W., and Robert W. Bretall. *The Theology of Paul Tillich.* New York: Macmillan, 1961.

Kimmel, William, and Geoffrey Clive. *Dimensions of Faith.* New York: Twayne Publishers, 1959.

Kosmin, Barry A., and Seymour P. Lachman. *One Nation Under God.* New York: Harmony Books, 1993.

Machen, John G. *Christianity and Liberalism.* New York: Macmillan, 1923.

———. *What Is Faith?* New York: Macmillan, 1935.

MacKintosh, Hugh Ross. *Types of Modern Theology From Schleiermacher to Barth.* New York: Charles Scribner and Sons, 1937.

Marshall, George N. *Challenge of a Liberal Faith.* New Canaan, Conn.: Keats Publishing, 1980.

———. "Unitarian Universalism," *Encounters With Eternity: Religious Views of Death and Life After Death.* Edited by Christopher Jay Johnson and Marsha G McGee. New York: The Philosophical Library, 1986.

McGiffert, Arthur Cushman. *Protestant Thought Before Kant.* New York: Charles Scribner's Sons, 1924.

Mendelsohn, Jack. *Meet the Unitarian Universalists.* Boston: Unitarian Universalist Association, 1993.

Nash, Arnold S. *Protestant Thought in the Twentieth Century.* New York: Macmillan, 1951.

Peers, Lawrence X. *The Congregational Handbook: How to Develop and Sustain Your Unitarian Universalist Congregation.* Boston: Unitarian Universalist Association, 1995.

Piepkorn, Arthur C. *Profiles in Belief.* Vol. 4. San Francisco: Harper & Row, 1979.

Rosten, Leo. *Religions in America.* New York: Simon & Schuster, 1963.

Schaff, Philip, and J. Herzog. *A Religious Encyclopedia or Dictionary of Biblical, Historical, Doctrinal, and Practical Theology.* New York: Funk and Wagnalls, 1891.

Scholefield, Harry, ed. *Unitarian Universalist Pocket Guide.* Boston: Beacon Press, 1963.

Schulz, William F. "About the Church of the Larger Fellowship," in *The Unitarian Universalist Pocket Guide.* Boston: Beacon, 1993.

———. *A Pocket Guide to Unitarianism.* Boston: Beacon Press, 1954.

Sias, John. From Interviews With Rev. Steve Edington, *One Hundred Questions That Non-Members Ask About Unitarian Universalism.* n.p.: Transition Publishing, 1994.

Spittler, Russell P. *Cults and Isms.* Grand Rapids, Mich.: Baker Book House, 1962.

Unitarian Universalist Association. *Singing the Living Tradition.* Boston: Beacon Press, 1993.

Wilbur, Earl Morse. *A History of Unitarianism.* Boston: Beacon Press, 1945.

Williams, George H. *The Radical Reformation.* Philadelphia: Westminster, 1962.

Scientology

Alexander, Brooks, and Dean C. Halverson, eds. *Scientology: The Technology of Enlightenment.* Berkeley: Spiritual Counterfeits Project, 1982.

Anderson, Kevin. *Report of the Board of Inquiry Into Scientology.* Melbourne: Australia Parliament Government Printer, 1965.

Atack, Jon. *A Piece of Blue Sky: Scientology, Dianetics, and L. Ron Hubbard Exposed.* New York: Carol Publishing Company, 1990.

Cooper, Paulette. *Scandal of Scientology.* New York: Tower Publications, 1971.

Corydon, Bent. *L. Ron Hubbard: Messiah or Madman?* Fort Lee, N.J.: Barricade Books, 1992.

Evans, Chris. *The Cults of Unreason.* New York: Dell Publishing Company, Inc., 1973.

"Federal Prosecutors Unveil the Astonishing Intrigues of the Scientology Church," *People Magazine,* August 14, 1978.

Foster, Sir John G. *Enquiry Into the Practice and Effects of Scientology.* London: Her Majesty's Stationery Office (report to the British government), n.d.

Gardner, Martin. *Fads and Fallacies in the Name of Science.* New York: Dover Publications, 1957.

Gruss, Edmund C. *Cults and the Occult.* Nutley, N.J.: Presbyterian and Reformed Publishing, 2002.

Hubbard, L. Ron. *The Aims of Scientology.* Hollywood: The Church of Scientology Celebrity Center, 1974, 1977.

———. *Axioms and Logics.* Los Angeles: American St. Hill Organization, 1973.

———. "Dianetics: The Evolution of a Science," *Astounding Science Fiction,* May 1950.

———. *Dianetics: The Modern Science of Mental Health.* Los Angeles: Bridge Publications, 1950.

———. *Dianetics and Scientology Technical Dictionary.* Los Angeles: American St. Hill Organization, 1975.

———. "Heaven," *Hubbard Communication Office Bulletin,* May 11, 1963.

———. *History of Man.* Los Angeles: American Hill Organization, 1968.

———. *Hymn of Asia.* Los Angeles: The Church of Scientology of California Publications Organization, 1974.

———. *The Phoenix Lectures.* Los Angeles: The Church of Scientology of California Publications Organization, 1969.

———. *Science of Survival.* Los Angeles: American Hill Organization, 1973.

———. *Scientology Abridged Dictionary.* Los Angeles: American Hill Organization, 1970.

———. *Scientology Clear Procedure.* Los Angeles: American Hill Organization, 1969.

———. *Scientology 8–008.* Los Angeles: American Hill Organization, 1967.

———. *Scientology: The Fundamentals of Thought.* Los Angeles: The Church of Scientology Publications Organization, 1972.

———. *Technical Bulletins.* Los Angeles: Scientology Publications, various issues.

———. *Volunteer Minister's Handbook.* Los Angeles: Church of Scientology, 1976.

Institute for Biblical Apologetics. *www.ibainfo.org.,* 2003.

Kaufman, Robert. *Inside Scientology.* New York: Olympia Publications, 1972.

McDowell, Josh, and Don Stewart. *The Deceivers.* Nashville, Tenn.: Thomas Nelson Publishers, 1992

Malko, George. *Scientology: The Now Religion.* New York: Dell Publishing, 1970.

Martin, Walter R. "Scientology." Audiotape. Ventura, Calif.: Vision House Publishers, 1976.

Methvin, Eugene H. "Scientology: Anatomy of a Frightening Cult," *Readers Digest,* May 1980.

———. "Scientology: The Sickness Spreads," *Readers Digest,* September 1981.

Miller, Russell. *Bare-Faced Messiah: The True Story of L. Ron Hubbard.* London: Michael Joseph/Penguin Books Ltd., 1987.

Sann, Paul. *Fads, Fallacies, and Delusions*. New York: Crown Publications, 1967.

———. *Scientology: An In-Depth Profile of a New Force in Clearwater*. Clearwater, Fla.: *St. Petersburg Times*, 1980.

———. *Scientology: A World Religion Emerges in the Space Age*. Los Angeles: Church of Scientology Information Service, 1974.

Schacter, Daniel L. *Stranger Behind the Engram*. Hillsdale, N.J.: Lawrence Erlbaum Associate, 1982.

Smith, Ralph Lee. "Scientology: Menace to Mental Health," *Today's Health*, December 1968.

Staff of Scientology. "The Scientology Catechism," *What Is Scientology?* Los Angeles: The Church of Scientology of California, 1979.

Wallis, Claudia. "Mystery of the Vanished Ruler," *Time*, January 31, 1983.

The Unification Church

Anonymous. *Outline of the Principle*. New York: The Holy Spirit Association for the Unification of World Christianity (HSAUWC), 1980.

Bjornstad, James. *Sun Myung Moon and the Unification Church*. Minneapolis: Bethany House Publishers, 1984.

Blake, Richard A. "The Attraction of the Moonies," *America Magazine*, June 12, 1982.

"Buses, Buses, and More Buses," *New Hope News*, October 21, 1976.

Byron, Christopher. "Seems Like Old Times," *New York Magazine*, n.d.

Coates, James. "Moon Church Traced From Sex Cult," *Chicago Tribune*, March 27, 1978.

Cooper, Nancy, and Mark Miller. "Rev. Moon's Rising Son," *Newsweek*, April 11, 1988.

Durham, Deanna. *Life Among the Moonies: Three Years in the Unification Church*. Plainfield, N.J.: Logos International, 1981.

Edwards, Christopher. *Crazy for God*. Englewood Cliffs, N.J.: Prentice-Hall, Inc., 1979.

Elkins, Chris. *Heavenly Deception*. Wheaton: Tyndale House, 1980.

———. *What Do You Say to a Moonie?* Wheaton: Tyndale House, 1981.

Geisler, Norman L. *Christian Apologetics*. Grand Rapids, Mich.: Baker Book House, 1976.

Holt, T. Harvey. "A View of the Moonrise," *Conservative Digest*, January/February 1989.

Hong, Nansook. *In the Shadow of the Moons: My Life in the Reverend Sun Myung Moon's Family*. New York: Little, Brown & Company, 1998.

Judis, John B. "Rev. Moon's Rising Political Influence," *U.S. News and World Report*, March 27, 1989.

Kemperman, Steve. *Lord of the Second Advent*. Ventura, Calif.: Gospel Light Publications, 1981.

Kim, Dr. Young Oon. *Speeches on Unification Teaching*. Barrytown, N.Y.: Unification Theological Seminary, 1986.

———. *Unification Theology*. New York: HSAUWC, 1987.

———. *Unification Theology and Christian Thought*. New York: Golden Gate Publishing Company, 1975.

Kim, Dr. Young Oon, ed. *The Divine Principles*. San Francisco: HSAUWC, 1960, 1963.

McDowell, Josh, and Don Stewart. *The Deceivers*. Nashville, Tenn.: Thomas Nelson Publishers, 1992.

Martin, Walter R. *The New Cults*. Ventura, Calif.: Vision House Publishers, 1981.

———. *Unification*. Audiotape. Walter Martin Ministries. *www.waltermartin.com*.

McCaughry, John. "The Uneasy Case Against Reverend Moon," *National Review*, December 23, 1983.

"Moon Pleads Not Guilty in Tax Case, Cites Discrimination," *Christianity Today*, November 20, 1981.

Moon, Sun Myung. *CAUSA Seminar Speech*. Washington, D.C.: HSAUWC, August 29, 1985.

———. *Christianity in Crisis*. Washington, D.C.: HSAUWC, 1974.

———. *God's Warning to the World.* New York: HSAUWC, 1985.

———. *Master Speaks,* various issues.

"Of Moon and Mammon," *Time,* October 26, 1981.

O'Hara, Jane. "Taxing Times for the Reverend," *McCleans Magazine,* April 5, 1982.

Sontag, Frederick. *Sun Myung Moon and the Unification Church.* Nashville: Abingdon Press, 1977.

Sudo, Dr. Kim. *120-Day Training Manual.* Washington, D.C.: HSAUWC, n.d.

Sun Myung Moon. Washington, D.C.: HSAUWC, 1969.

White, James H. "Unification Church's Anti-Communist Drive," *Christian Century,* August 28–September 4, 1985.

Woodward, Kenneth L., and Patrice Johnson. "Rev. Moon's New Friends," *Newsweek,* May 3, 1982.

Yamamoto, J. Isamu. *The Puppet Master.* Downers Grove, Ill.: InterVarsity Press, 1977.

———. *Unification Church.* Grand Rapids: Zondervan Publishing House, 1995.

Yoo, Kwang-Yol. "Unification Church History From the Early Days," *New Hope News,* Washington, D.C.: The Unification Church.

Eastern Religions

Anderson, J. N. D. *Christianity and Comparative Religion.* Downers Grove, Ill.: InterVarsity Press, 1970.

Anderson, Sir Norman, ed. *The World's Religions.* Rev. ed. Grand Rapids, Mich.: Eerdmans Publishing Company, 1975.

Bjornstad, James. *The Transcendental Mirage.* Minneapolis: Bethany House Publishers, 1976.

Bouquet, A. C. *Hinduism.* Rev. ed. London: Hutchinson University Library, 1962.

Carlson, Ron, and Ed Decker. *Fast Facts on False Teachings.* Eugene, Ore.: Harvest House, 1994.

Chandler, Russell, and Tyler Marshall, "Guru Brings His Ashram to Oregon," *The Los Angeles Times,* August 19, 1981.

Copan, Paul. *True for You But Not for Me.* Minneapolis: Bethany House Publishers, 1998.

Dietrich, Bill. "Conflict Over Rajneeshpuram," *Seattle Times,* September 9, 1984.

Goswam, Siddha Swarup Ananda. *Jesus Loves KRSNA.* Los Angeles: Vedic Christian Committee and Life Force, Krsna Yoga Viewpoint, 1975.

Haddon, David, and Gail Hamilton. *TM Wants You!* Grand Rapids, Mich.: Baker Book House, 1976.

Johansen, Jens. "The Master Will Not Speak Again," *New Religious Movements Update,* 5:5/4, December 1981.

Levine, Faye. *The Strange World of the Hare Krishnas.* New York: Fawcett Publications, 1974.

Lewis, Gordon R. *What Everyone Should Know About Transcendental Meditation.* Ventura, Calif.: Gospel Light Publications, 1975.

"Maharishi Ayur-Veda: Guru's Marketing Scheme Promises the World Eternal Perfect Health," *Journal of the American Medical Association (JAMA),* October 2, 1991.

Mangalwadi, Vishal. *The World of the Gurus.* Chicago: Cornerstone Books, 1977.

———. *Transcendental Meditation.* Audiotape. Walter Martin Ministries. *www.waltermartin.com.*

Martin, Walter. *The World of the Occult.* Audiotape. Walter Martin Ministries. *www.waltermartin.com.*

McCormack, Win, and Bill Driver, "Rajneeshpuram: Valley of Death?" *Oregon Magazine,* September 1984.

Miller, Elliot. "Inside ISKCON." Part One and Two. *Forward,* 4:1:1; 4:2:3.

"Pied Piper of Poona," *Eternity,* September 1981.

Prabhupada, A. C. Bhaktivedanta Swami. *Bhagavad-Gita As It Is.* New York: The Bhaktive-
danta Book Trust, 1968.
———. *The Nectar of Devotion.* New York: The Bhaktivedanta Book Trust, 1970.
Rajneesh, Bhagwan Shree. *Rajneeshism: An Introduction to Bhagwan Shree Rajneesh and His
Religion.* Rajneeshpuram, Ore.: Rajneesh Foundation International, 1985.
Ramacharaka, Yogi. *The Philosophies and Religions of India.* Chicago: The Yogi Publication
Society, 1930.
Singh, Chander Uday. "Sins of Bhagwan," *India Today,* June 15, 1982.
Smart, Ninan. *The Religious Experience of Mankind.* New York: Charles Scribner's Sons,
1976.
Spiritual Counterfeits Project. *TM in Court.* Berkeley: Spiritual Counterfeits Project,
1978.
Stillson, Judah J. *Hare Krishna and the Counterculture.* New York: John Wiley and Sons,
1974.
Weldon, John, and Zola Levitt. *The Transcendental Explosion.* Irvine, Calif.: Harvest House
Publishers, 1976.
Yamamoto, J. Isamu. *Hare Krishna Hare Krishna.* Downers Grove, Ill.: InterVarsity Press,
1978.
Yogi, Maharishi Mahesh. *Maharishi Mahesh Yogi on the Bhagavad-Gita.* New York: Penguin
Books, 1967.
———. *Meditation of Maharishi Mahesh Yogi.* New York: The New American Library, 1969.
———. *The Science of Being and the Art of Living.* New York: The New American Library,
1968.
Zacharias, Ravi. *Deliver Us from Evil: Restoring the Soul in a Disintegrating Culture.* Dallas:
Word Publishing, 1996.
———. *Jesus Among Other Gods.* Nashville: Word Publishing, 2000.
Zaehner, R. C. *Hinduism.* 2nd ed. Oxford: Oxford University Press, 1966.

The New Age

Alnor, William. *Heaven Can't Wait.* Grand Rapids, Mich.: Baker/Revell, 1996.
———. *UFOs in the New Age.* Grand Rapids, Mich.: Baker Book House, 1992.
Chandler, Russell. *Understanding the New Age.* Dallas: Word Books, 1988.
Creme, Benjamin. *Maitreya's Mission.* Amsterdam: Share International Foundation, 1986.
———. *The Reappearance of the Christ and the Masters of Wisdom.* London: Tara Press, 1980.
Downing, Levi. *The Aquarian Gospel of Jesus the Christ.* Marina del Rey, Calif.: DeVorss &
Company, 1981.
Dunphy, John. "A Religion for a New Age," *The Humanist,* January/February 1983.
Essene, Virginia. *New Teachings for an Awakening Humanity.* Santa Clara, Calif.: Spiritual
Education Endeavors Publishing, 1986.
Ferguson, Marilyn. *The Aquarian Conspiracy.* Los Angeles: J. P. Tarcher, 1980.
Goldstein, William. "Life on the Astral Plane," *Publishers Weekly,* March 8, 1983.
Groothuis, Douglas. *Revealing the New Age Jesus.* Downers Grove, Ill.: InterVarsity Press,
1990.
———. *Unmasking the New Age.* Downers Grove, Ill.: InterVarsity Press, 1986.
Lawren, Bill. "UFO Report," *OMNI,* October 1987.
Lewis, C. S. *Surprised by Joy.* New York: Harcourt, Brace, Jovanovich, 1955.
MacLaine, Shirley. *Dancing in the Light.* New York: Bantam Books, 1985.
Mahr, Douglas James. *Voyage to a New World.* Lopez, Wash.: Masterworks, Inc., Publishers,
1985.
Marty, Martin E. "An Old New Age in Publishing," *Christian Century,* November 18, 1987.
Melton, J. Gordon. *New Age Encyclopedia.* Detroit: Gale Research Inc., 1990.

Miller, Elliot. *A Crash Course on the New Age Movement.* Grand Rapids, Mich.: Baker Book House, 1989.

Spangler, David. *Emergence: Rebirth of the Sacred.* New York: Delta, 1984.

———. *Revelation: The Birth of a New Age.* San Francisco: Rainbow Bridge, 1976.

Steiger, Brad. *The Fellowship.* New York: Dolphin/Doubleday, 1988.

Strieber, Whitley. *Communion.* New York: William Morrow, 1987.

Weldon, John, and Zola Levitt. *Encounters With UFOs.* Irvine, Calif.: Harvest House Publishers, 1975.

Islam

Abdul-Haqq, Abdiyah Akbar. *Sharing Your Faith With a Muslim.* Minneapolis: Bethany House Publishers, 1980.

Accad, F. E. *Theological Principles in the Torah, the Zabur, the Injil, and the Qur'an.* Colorado Springs, Colo.: Navigators, n.d.

Ali, A. Yusuf. *The Holy Qur'an: Translation and Commentary.* Brentwood, Md.: Amana Corporation, 1983 (reprinted from 1934).

Bavinck, J. H. *The Church Between Temple and Mosque.* Grand Rapids, Mich.: Eerdmans Publishing Company, 1981 (reprint).

Beverley, James A. *Understanding Islam.* Nashville: Thomas Nelson, 2001.

Black's Law Dictionary, abridged 5th ed. St. Paul, Minn.: West Publishing Company, 1983.

Brackman, Harold. *Farrakhan's Reign of Historical Error: The Truth Behind the Secret Relationship Between Blacks and Jews.* Los Angeles: Simon Wiesenthal Center, 1992.

Braswell Jr., George W. *Islam.* Nashville: Broadman & Holman, 1996.

Bravmann, M. M. *The Spiritual Background in Early Islam: Studies in Ancient Arab Concepts.* Leiden, The Netherlands: E. J. Brill, 1972.

Bruce, F. F. *Jesus and Christian Origins Outside the New Testament.* Grand Rapids, Mich.: Eerdmans Publishing Company, 1974.

Christian Witness Among Muslims. Ghana, W. Africa: Africa Christian Press, 1971.

———. *The Sources of Islam.* Edinburgh: T. & T. Clark, n.d.

Cragg, Kenneth. *The Call of the Minaret.* New York: Oxford University Press, 1964.

Dashti, Ali. *Twenty-Three Years: A Study of the Prophetic Career of Mohammad.* London: George Allen & Unwin, 1985.

Davion, Edward, et al. *Unreached Peoples '80.* Elgin, Ill.: David C. Cook Publishing Company, 1980.

Davis, David Brion. *Slavery and Human Progress.* New York: Oxford University Press, 1984.

Dinnerstein, Leonard. *Antisemitism in America.* New York: Oxford University Press, 1994.

Early Islam: Collected Articles. Edinburgh: Edinburgh University Press, 1990.

Elder, John. *The Biblical Approach to the Muslim.* Fort Washington, Pa.: Worldwide Evangelism Crusade, 1974.

Epiphanius. *The Panarion of St. Epiphanius, Bishop of Slamis: Selected Passages.* Translated and edited by Philip R. Amidon. New York: Oxford University Press, 1990.

Esposito, John. *The Islamic Threat.* New York: Oxford University Press, 1993.

Evanzz, Karl. *The Judas Factor: The Plot to Kill Malcolm X.* New York: Thunder's Mouth Press, 1992.

Farah, Caesar E. *Islam.* New York: Barron's Educational Services, 1994.

"Farrakhan Attacks Jews and Whites," *Orange County Register,* March 13, 1994.

Fleischman, Janet. "Ethnic Cleansing," *Africa Reports,* January/February 1994.

Fry, C. George, and James R. King. *Islam: A Survey of the Muslim Faith.* Grand Rapids, Mich.: Baker Book House, 1980.

Gilchrist, John. *Christianity and Islam Series.* Durban, Republic of South Africa: Jesus to the Muslims, 1980.

Glasser, Carol A. *Muslim Awareness Seminar.* Altadena, Calif.: Samuel Zwemer Institute, 1981.

———. *Qur'an and Bible Series.* Durban: Jesus to the Muslims, 1981.

Goldsack, W. *The Origins of the Qur'an.* London: Christian Literature Society, 1907.

Goldsmith, Martin. *Islam and Christian Witness.* Downers Grove, Ill.: InterVarsity Press, 1982.

Haley, Alex, and Betty Shabazz. *The Autobiography of Malcolm X.* New York: Ballantine Books, 1965.

Hamada, Louis Bahjat. *Understanding the Arab World.* Nashville: Thomas Nelson Publishers, 1990.

Handbook for Christians Working With Iranians in North America. Altadena, Calif.: Samuel Zwemer Institute, 1980.

Hanna, Mark. *The Truth Path.* Colorado Springs, Colo.: International Doorways Publishers, 1975.

Hirji-Walji, Hass, and Jaryl Strong. *Escape From Islam.* Wheaton: Tyndale House, 1978.

Irvine, A. K. "The Arabs and Ethiopians," edited by J. D. Wiseman, *Peoples of Old Testament Times.* Oxford University Press, 1973.

Jeffery, Arthur, ed. *Material for the History of the Text of the Qur'an: The Old Codices.* New York: AMS, Inc., 1975.

Jones, L. Bevan. *Christianity Explained to Muslims.* Calcutta: Baptist Mission Press, 1937.

———. *The People of the Mosque.* London: Student Christian Movement Press, 1932.

Kateregga, Badru D., and David W. Shenk. *Islam and Christianity.* Grand Rapids, Mich.: Eerdmans Publishing Company, 1980.

Kershaw, R. Max. *How to Share the Good News With Your Muslim Friend.* Colorado Springs, Colo.: Fellowship of Faith for Muslims, 1978.

Lewis, Bernard. *The Arabs in History.* New York: Harper & Row, 1966.

———. *Race and Slavery in the Middle East: An Historical Inquiry.* New York: Oxford University Press, 1990.

Lincoln, C. Eric. *The Black Church Since Frazier.* New York: Schocken Books, 1974.

———. *The Black Muslims in America.* 3rd ed. Grand Rapids, Mich.: Eerdmans Publishing Company, 1994.

Lippman, Thomas W. *Understanding Islam: An Introduction to the Muslim World.* New York: Mentor Books, 1990.

"Malcolm X's Widow Accuses Farrakhan," *Orange County Register,* March 13, 1994.

Mansfield, Peter. *The Arabs.* New York: Penguin Books, 1978.

Marsh, Charles R. *Share Your Faith with a Muslim.* Chicago: Moody Press, 1975.

Marsh, Clifton E. *From Black Muslims to Muslims.* Metuchen, N.J. and London: The Scarecrow Press, 1984.

McCurry, Don M., ed. *The Gospel and Islam: A 1978 Compendium.* Monrovia, Calif.: Missions Advanced Research Communications Center, 1978.

———. *Sharing the Gospel With Iranians.* Altadena, Calif.: Samuel Zwemer Institute, 1982.

Mead, Frank S., and Samuel S. Hill. *Handbook of Denominations in the United States.* Nashville: Abingdon Press, 1990.

Morris, Leon. *The Gospel According to John.* Grand Rapids, Mich.: Eerdmans Publishing Company, 1971.

Muhammad, Elijah. *Message to the Black Man in America.* Newport News, Va.: United Brothers Communications, 1992.

Muslim/Christian Cross-Cultural Dating & Marriage. Altadena, Calif.: Samuel Zwemer Institute, 1981.

O'Brien, Joanne, and Martin Palmer. *The State of Religion Atlas.* New York: Touchstone Books, 1993.

Parrinder, Geoffrey. *Jesus in the Qur'an.* New York: Oxford University Press, 1977.

Parshall, Phil. *New Paths in Muslim Evangelism.* Grand Rapids, Mich.: Baker Book House, 1980.

Patterson, Orlando. *Slavery and Social Death: A Comparative Study.* Cambridge, Mass.: Harvard University Press, 1982.

Pfander, C. G. *The Mizanu'l Haqq: Balance of Truth.* London: Religious Tract Society, rev. 1910 (from original by St. Clair-Tisdall).

Plantinga, Alvin. *Does God Have a Nature?* Milwaukee, Wis.: Marquette University Press, 1980.

Raboteau, Albert J. "Afro-American Religions: Muslim Movements," edited by Mircea Eliade, *The Encyclopedia of Religion.* Vol. 1. New York: Macmillan, 1987.

Register, Ray G. *Dialogue and Interfaith with Muslims.* Kingsport: Moody Books, 1979.

St. Clair-Tisdall, Rev. W. *A Manual of the Leading Muhammadan Objections of Christianity.* London: Society for Promoting Christian Knowledge, 1904.

Sell, Canon. *Outlines of Islam.* London: Christian Literature Society for India, 1912.

Smith, Jane I. *An Historical and Semitic Study of the Term "Islam" as Seen in a Sequence of Quran Commentaries.* Missoula, Mt.: Scholars Press for Harvard Theological Review, 1975.

Spencer, H. *Islam and the Gospel of God.* Delhi, India: S.T.C.K., 1956.

Todd, Charles Burr. *Life and Letters of Joel Barlow.* New York: Da Capo Press, 1970.

Vander Werff, Lyle L. *Christian Mission to Muslims: The Record. Anglican and Reformed Approaches to India and the Near East, 1860–1938.* South Pasadena: William Carey Library, 1977.

Warraq, Ibn. *Why I Am Not a Muslim.* Amherst, N.Y.: Prometheus Books, 1995.

Watts Star Review, July 14, 1994.

Wilson, Christy J. *Today's Tentmakers: Self-Support—An Alternative Model for Worldwide Witness.* Wheaton: Tyndale House, 1979.

Wolf, Kenneth Baxter. "The Earliest Spanish Christian Views of Islam," *Church History.* 55:3, September 1986.

The World of Islam, Global Mapping International, 2001.

Your Muslim Guest: A Practical Guide to Friendship and Witness for Christians Who Meet Muslims in North America. Toronto: Fellowship of Faith for Muslims, 1975.

Zacharias, Ravi. *Light in the Shadow of Jihad.* Sisters, Ore.: Multnomah, 2002.

Zwemer, Samuel. *Islam: A Challenge to Faith.* New York: Student Volunteer Movement for Foreign Missions, 1907.

The Worldwide Church of God

Magazine Articles

Ambassador Report. P.O. Box 4068, Pasadena, Calif., 91106, various issues.

Campbell, Robert. "Herbert W. Armstrong: Does He Really Love the Plain Truth?" *Moody Monthly,* October 1972.

———. "Herbert W. Armstrong: Mr. Confusion," *The King's Business,* February 1962.

Flurry, Gerald. "Personal," *The Philadelphia Trumpet,* February 1997.

Flurry, Gerald, and Dennis Leap. "The Key of David Vision," *The Philadelphia Trumpet,* March 1997.

Hopkins, Joseph Martin. (no title cited). *Christianity Today,* December 17, 1971.

Knuteson, Darby, and Campbell Knuteson. *The Delusions of Herbert W. Armstrong.* A reprint of *The Discerner,* January/March 1962.

"Mr. Jones, Meet Herbert W. Armstrong," *Eternity,* October 1972.

The Plain Truth, various issues.

Tarr, Leslie, "Herbert W. Armstrong: Does He Really Love the Plain Truth?" *Moody Monthly*, September 1972.
The Worldwide News, various issues.

Additional Bibliography

Allen, J. H. *Judah's Scepter and Joseph's Birthright*. 6th ed. Boston: A. A. Beauchamp, Publisher, 1918.

Anderson, Stanley E. *Armstrongism's 300 Errors Exposed by 1300 Bible Verses*. Nashville: Church Growth Publications, 1973.

Anonymous. *God Is*. Pasadena: Worldwide Church of God, 1992.

———. *The Roadbuilder: God's Commonwealths, British and American*. Toronto: Commonwealth Publishers, Ltd., 1930.

———. *The United States and Britain in Prophecy: Study Paper*. Pasadena: Worldwide Church of God, November 1995.

Armstrong, Herbert W. *All About Water Baptism*. Pasadena: Ambassador College Press, 1972.

———. *The Autobiography of Herbert W. Armstrong*. Pasadena: Ambassador Press, 1967.

———. *Just What Do You Mean—Born Again!* Pasadena: Radio Church of God, 1962.

———. *Just What Do You Mean—Kingdom of God?* Pasadena: Ambassador Press, 1962.

———. *Mystery of the Ages*. Pasadena: Worldwide Church of God, 1985.

———. *1975 in Prophecy*. Pasadena: Radio Church of God, 1956.

———. *The United States and Britain in Prophecy*. Pasadena: Ambassador Press, 1980.

Armstrong, Herbert W., ed. *Ambassador College Bible Correspondence Course*. Pasadena: Ambassador College, 1966.

Benware, Paul N. *Ambassadors of Armstrongism: An Analysis of the History and Teachings of the Worldwide Church of God*. Philadelphia: Presbyterian and Reformed Publishing Company, 1975.

Buchner, J. L. F. *Armstrongism Bibliography*. Sydney, Australia: Self-published, 1983.

Chambers, Roger R. *The Plain Truth About Armstrongism*. Grand Rapids, Mich.: Baker Book House, 1972.

De Loach, Charles F. *The Armstrong Error*. Plainfield, N.J.: Logos International, 1971.

Feazell, J. Michael. *Liberation of the Worldwide Church of God*. Grand Rapids, Mich.: Zondervan, 2001.

Grant, Robert G. *The Plain Truth About the Armstrong Cult*. n.p., n.d.

Hopkins, Joseph M. *The Armstrong Empire*. Grand Rapids, Mich.: Eerdmans Publishing Company, 1974.

Kirban, Salem. *The Plain Truth About the Plain Truth*. Huntington Valley, Pa.: Salem Kirban, Inc., 1970.

Larson, Egon. *Strange Cults and Sects*. New York: Hart Publishing Company, 1972.

Leyendecker, Ruth, and Wayne Leyendecker, with Roger F. Campbell, "We Escaped From Armstrongism" in James R. Adair and Ted Miller, eds. *We Found Our Way Out*. Grand Rapids, Mich.: Baker Book House, 1965.

Lowe, Harry W. *Radio Church of God: How Its Teachings Differ From Those of Seventh-day Adventists*. Mountain View, Calif.: Pacific Press Publishing Association, 1970.

Marson, Richard A. *The Marson Report Concerning Herbert W. Armstrong*. Seattle: The Ashley-Calvin Press, 1970.

Meredith, Roderick. *The Inside Story of the World Tomorrow Broadcast*. Pasadena: Ambassador Press, n.d.

Nichols, Larry, and George Mather. *Discovering the Plain Truth: How the Worldwide Church of God Encountered the Gospel of Grace*. Downers Grove, Ill.: InterVarsity Press, 1999.

Ord, David R. *The Jet-Set Galatians*. Exeter, Devon, UK: The Paternoster Press, 1982.

Petersen, William J. *Those Curious New Cults*. New Canaan, Conn.: Keats Publishing, 1973.

Piepkorn, Arthur C. *Profiles in Belief*. Vol. 4. San Francisco: Harper & Row, 1979.

Roberts, Rev. Commander L. G. A. *Commentary on the Book of the Prophet Isaiah*. London: The Covenant Publishing Company, 1951.

Rutherford, Adam. *Israel-Britain or Anglo-Saxon Israel*. 3rd ed. London: Self-published, 1936.

Smith, Noel. *Herbert W. Armstrong and His World of Tomorrow*. Springfield, Mo.: Bible Baptist Tribune, 1964.

Smith, Paul B. *Other Gospels*. Denver: Gospel Advance Press, 1970.

Sumner, Robert L. *Herbert W. Armstrong: False Prophet*. Murfreesboro, Tenn.: Sword of the Lord Foundation, 1961.

Tkach, Joseph. *Transformed by Truth*. Sisters, Ore.: Multnomah Publishers, 1997.

Wilson, Paul. *The Armstrong Heresy: A Brief Examination*. Denver: Wilson Foundation, n.d.

Seventh-day Adventism

The Acts of the Apostles; Christian Experience and Teachings; The Desire of the Ages; The Great Controversy; Index to the Writings of Ellen G. White; Patriarchs and Prophets; Prophets and Kings; Testimonies for the Church, vols. 1–9; *Testimonies to Ministers; Thoughts From the Mount of Blessings*. Mountain View, Calif.: Pacific Press Publishing Association, n.d.

The Adventist Home; Child Guidance; Christ's Object Lessons; Counsels on Diets and Foods; Early Writings; Education; Evangelism; Messages to Young People; The Ministry of Healing; Steps to Christ. Takoma Park, Md.: Review and Herald Publishing Association, n.d.

Seventh-day Adventist Publications

Anderson, R. A. *The Shepherd Evangelist*. Takoma Park, Md.: Review and Herald Publishing Association, n.d.

———. *Unfolding the Revelation*. Mountain View, Calif.: Pacific Press Publishing Association, n.d.

Andreason, M. L. *The Book of Hebrews*. Takoma Park, Md.: Review and Herald Publishing Association, n.d.

———. *God's Holy Day*. Takoma Park, Md.: Review and Herald Publishing Association, n.d.

———. *The Sabbath*. Takoma Park, Md.: Review and Herald Publishing Association, n.d.

———. *The Sanctuary Service*. Takoma Park, Md.: Review and Herald Publishing Association, n.d.

———. *What Can a Man Believe?* Mountain View, Calif.: Pacific Press Publishing Association, n.d.

The Bible Made Plain: A Series of Short Bible Studies for the Home Circle Upon the Fundamentals of the Christian Faith. Takoma Park, Md.: Review and Herald Publishing Association, n.d.

Bible Readings for the Home. Takoma Park, Md.: Review and Herald Publishing Association, n.d.

Bollman, Calvin P. *Sunday: Origin of Its Observance in the Christian Church*. Takoma Park, Md.: Review and Herald Publishing Association, n.d.

Branson, W. H. *In Defense of the Faith*. Takoma Park, Md.: Review and Herald Publishing Association, n.d.

Bunch, Taylor G. *Behold the Man*. Nashville: Southern Publishing Association, n.d.

———. *The Ten Commandments*. Takoma Park, Md.: Review and Herald Publishing Association, n.d.

Christian, Lewis Harrison. *The Fruitage of Spiritual Gifts: The Influence and Guidance of Ellen G. White in the Advent Movement*. Washington, D.C.: Review and Herald Publishing Association, 1947.

Church Manual. Takoma Park, Md.: General Conference of Seventh-day Adventists, n.d.

Cottrell, Raymond F. *Perfection in Christ.* Washington, D.C.: Review and Herald Publishing Association, 1965.

———. *The True Sabbath.* Nashville: Southern Publishing Association, n.d.

Daniels, A. G. *The Abiding Gift of Prophecy.* Mountain View, Calif.: Pacific Press Publishing Association, n.d.

———. *Christ Our Righteousness.* Takoma Park, Md.: The Ministerial Association of Seventh-day Adventists, n.d.

Dixon, Louis J. *Law or Grace?* Nashville: Southern Publishing Association, n.d.

Everson, Charles T. *The Rich Man and Lazarus.* Nashville: Southern Publishing Association, n.d.

———. *Who Are the Angels?* Takoma Park, Md.: Review and Herald Publishing Association, n.d.

Froom, Leroy E. *The Coming of the Comforter.* Takoma Park, Md.: Review and Herald Publishing Association, n.d.

———. *Finding the Lost Prophetic Witness.* Takoma Park, Md.: Review and Herald Publishing Association, n.d.

———. *The Prophetic Faith of Our Fathers.* Vols. 1–4. Takoma Park, Md.: Review and Herald Publishing Association, n.d.

General Conference Young People's Department of Missionary Volunteers: Studies in Bible Doctrine. Takoma Park, Md.: Review and Herald Publishing Association, n.d.

Genesis-John. Takoma Park, Md.: Review and Herald Publishing Association, n.d.

Haskell, S. N. *Bible Handbook.* Takoma Park, Md.: Review and Herald Publishing Association, n.d.

Haynes, Carlyle B. *The Christian Sabbath: Is It Saturday or Sunday?* Nashville: Southern Publishing Association, n.d.

———. *From Sabbath to Sunday.* Takoma Park, Md.: Review and Herald Publishing Association, n.d.

———. *The Gift of Prophecy.* Nashville: Southern Publishing Association, n.d.

———. *Life, Death, and Immortality.* Nashville: Southern Publishing Association, n.d.

———. *Seventh-day Adventists: Their Work and Teachings.* Takoma Park, Md.: Review and Herald Publishing Association, n.d.

Horn, Sigfried H., and Lynn H. Wood. *The Chronology of Ezra Seven.* Takoma Park, Md.: Review and Herald Publishing Association, n.d.

How to Handle Objections. Prepared by the publishing department of the Secretaries of the Southern Union Conference. Nashville: Southern Publishing Association, n.d.

Jamison, T. Housel. *A Prophet Among You.* Mountain View, Calif.: Pacific Press Publishing Association, n.d.

Johns, Varner J. *The Secret Rapture and the Antichrist.* Mountain View, Calif.: Pacific Press Publishing Association, n.d.

Lickey, Arthur E. *Fundamentals of the Everlasting Gospel.* Takoma Park, Md.: Review and Herald Publishing Association, n.d.

Marsh, F. L. *Evolution, Creation, and Science.* Takoma Park, Md.: Review and Herald Publishing Association, n.d.

Maxwell, Arthur S. *The Coming King.* Mountain View, Calif.: Pacific Press Publishing Association, n.d.

———. *Your Friends the Adventists.* Mountain View, Calif.: Pacific Press Publishing Association, n.d.

Moseley, Calvin Edwin. *The Lord's Day.* Nashville: Southern Publishing Association, n.d.

Nichol, Francis D. *Answers to Objections.* Takoma Park, Md.: Review and Herald Publishing Association, n.d.

———. *The Certainty of My Faith.* Takoma Park, Md.: Review and Herald Publishing Association, n.d.

———. *Ellen G. White and Her Critics.* Takoma Park, Md.: Review and Herald Publishing Association, n.d.

———. *The Midnight Cry.* Takoma Park, Md.: Review and Herald Publishing Association.

Odom, Robert L. *The Final Crisis and Deliverance.* Nashville: Southern Publishing Association, n.d.

———. *How Did Sunday Get Its Name?* Nashville: Southern Publishing Association, n.d.

———. *Sunday in Roman Paganism.* Takoma Park, Md.: Review and Herald Publishing Association, n.d.

Problems in Bible Translation. Takoma Park, Md.: Review and Herald Publishing Association, n.d.

Reed, W. E. *The Bible, the Spirit of Prophecy, and the Church.* Takoma Park, Md.: Review and Herald Publishing Association, n.d.

Richards, H. M. S. *Hard Nuts Cracked.* Nashville: Southern Publishing Association, n.d.

Robinson, D. E. *The Story of Our Health Message.* Southern Publishing Association, n.d.

Washington, D.C.: Ministerial Association, General Conference of Seventh-day Adventists, 1988.

The Seventh-day Adventist Bible Commentary. Vols. 1–5. Takoma Park, Md.: Review and Herald Publishing Association, n.d.

Seventh-day Adventist Church Directory: United States and Canada. Takoma Park, Md.: Review and Herald Publishing Association, n.d.

Seventh-day Adventist Year Book, 1957. Takoma Park, Md.: Review and Herald Publishing Association.

Seventh-day Adventists Believe: A Biblical Exposition of Twenty-Seven Fundamental Doctrines.

Smith, Uriah. *Daniel and the Revelation.* Vols. 1–2. Takoma Park, Md.: Review and Herald Publishing Association, n.d.

Spalding, Arthur W. *Sister White.* Takoma Park, Md.: Review and Herald Publishing Association, n.d.

Spicer, W. A. *Our Day in the Light of Prophecy.* Takoma Park, Md.: Review and Herald Publishing Association, n.d.

Straw, W. E. *Origin of Sunday Observance.* Takoma Park, Md.: Review and Herald Publishing Association, n.d.

Walker, Allen. *The Law and the Sabbath.* Southern Publishing Association, n.d.

Werner, A. J. *Fundamentals of Bible Doctrine.* Takoma Park, Md.: Review and Herald Publishing Association, n.d.

Wheeler, Ruth. *His Messenger.* Takoma Park, Md.: Review and Herald Publishing Association, n.d.

Wilcox, F. M. *The Coming Crisis.* Takoma Park, Md.: Review and Herald Publishing Association, n.d.

———. *The Lord's Day, the Test of the Ages.* Mountain View, Calif.: Pacific Press Publishing Association, n.d.

———. *Questions Answered.* Mountain View, Calif.: Pacific Press Publishing Association, n.d.

Additional Bibliography

Biederwolf, William Edward. *Seventh-day Adventism: the Result of a Predicament.* Grand Rapids, Mich.: Eerdmans Publishing Company, n.d.

Bird, Herbert S. *Theology of Seventh-day Adventism.* Grand Rapids, Mich.: Eerdmans Publishing Company, 1961.

Bliss, Sylvester. *Memoirs of William Miller.* Boston, n.p., 1853.

Booth, A. E. *Seventh-day Adventism: What Is It?* n.p., n.d.

Buswell, J. Oliver, Jr. *The Length of Creative Days.* New York: Shelton College, 1950.

Canright, Dudley M. *Hard Nuts for Seventh-day Adventists.* n.p., n.d.

———. *Life of Mrs. E. G. White.* Nashville: B. C. Goodpasture, 1948.

————. *Seventh-day Adventism Renounced.* Grand Rapids, Mich.: Baker Book House, 1961 reprint from 1889.

Chafer, Louis Sperry. *Grace.* Van Kampen Press, 1947.

Davies, Horton. *Christian Deviations.* New York: Philosophical Library, 1954.

Deck, Norman C. *The Lord's Day or the Sabbath, Which?* Sydney, Australia: Bridge Printery, Ltd., n.d.

Dictionary of American Biography. New York: Charles Scribner's Sons, n.d.

Douty, Norman F. *Another Look at Seventh-day Adventism.* Grand Rapids, Mich.: Baker Book House, 1962.

Dugger, A. F. *The Bible Sabbath Defended.* Stanbury, Mo.: The Church of God Publishing House, n.d.

Dungan, D. R. *Sabbath or Lord's Day, Which?* Nashville: Harbinger Book Club, n.d.

Feinberg, Charles L. *The Sabbath and the Lord's Day.* Van Kampen Press, n.d.

Fletcher, W. W. *The Reasons for My Faith.* Sydney, Australia: William Brooks & Company, Ltd., n.d.

Hoekema, Anthony. *The Four Major Cults.* Grand Rapids, Mich.: Eerdmans Publishing Company, 1963.

Ironside, H. A. *What Think Ye of Christ?* New York: Loizeaux Brothers, n.d.

Irvine, William C. *Heresies Exposed.* New York: Loizeaux Brothers, n.d.

Jones, E. B. *The Answer and the Reasons: Eye-opening Information Regarding Seventh-day Adventism.* Oak Park: Designed Products, n.d.

————. *Forty Bible-Supported Reasons Why You Should Not Be a Seventh-day Adventist.* Oak Park: Designed Products, n.d.

————. *Free Indeed: The Author's Testimony Concerning His Deliverance From Seventh-day Adventism.* Oak Park: Designed Products, n.d.

Land, Gary, ed. *Adventism in America.* Grand Rapids, Mich.: Eerdmans Publishing Company, 1986.

————. *Seventh-day Adventism.* Audiotape. Walter Martin Ministries. *www.waltermartin.com.*

Martin, Walter R. *The Truth about Seventh-day Adventism.* Grand Rapids, Mich.: Zondervan, 1960.

McDowell, Josh, and Don Stewart. *A Handbook on Today's Religions.* Nashville: Thomas Nelson, 1993.

Miller, William. *Apology and Defense.* n.p., 1845.

————. *A Few Evidences of the Time of the Second Coming of Christ.* n.p., 1831.

Paxton, Geoffrey J. *The Shaking of Adventism.* Grand Rapids, Mich.: Baker Book House, 1977.

Pieper, Francis. *Christian Dogmatics.* Grand Rapids, Mich.: Zondervan, n.d. (reprint).

Pollock, A. J. *Seventh-day Adventism Briefly Tested by Scripture.* London: The Central Bible Truth Depot, n.d.

Putnam, C. E. *Legalism and the Seventh-day Question: Can Sinai Law and Grace Coexist?* Chicago: Moody Press, n.d.

Rea, Walter T. *The White Lie.* Turlock, Calif.: M & R Publications, n.d.

Rowell, J. B. *Seventh-day Adventism Examined.* Norwalk, Calif.: Challenge Publishing Company, n.d.

Smith, Oswald J. *Who Are the False Prophets?* Toronto: The People's Press, n.d.

————. *Who Are the Seventh-day Adventists and What Do They Teach?* Toronto: Hugh Warren, Wesley Press and Publishing House, n.d.

Talbot, Louis T. *What's Wrong With Seventh-day Adventism?* Grand Rapids, Mich.: Dunham Publishing House, n.d.

Tucker, Ruth. *Another Gospel: Alternative Religions and the New Age Movement.* Grand Rapids, Mich.: Zondervan, 1989.

Vincent, M. R. *Word Studies in the New Testament.* MacDill AFB, Fla.: MacDonald Publishing Company, n.d.

Vine, W. E. *An Expository Dictionary of New Testament Words.* Old Tappan, N.J.: Fleming H. Revell Company, 1940.

Magazine Articles

The Advent Herald magazine, various issues.
The Advent Shield and Review magazine, various issues.
Auchincloss, Douglas. "Peace With the Adventists," *Time* magazine, December 31, 1956.
Baer, James E. "The Seventh-day Adventists," from the series "The Bible and Modern Religions," *Journal of Theology*, January 1956.
Barnhouse, Donald Grey. "Are Seventh-day Adventists Christian?" *Eternity*, September 1956.
Bibliotheca Sacra, April 1956.
Bird, Herbert S. "Another Look at Adventism," *Christianity Today*, April 28, 1958.
Eternity, September 1956; June 1958.
Hulbert, Terry C. "Seventh-day Adventism Weighed in the Balances," *The Discerner Magazine*, October/December 1956.
Jones, E. B. "The Historical Background of Seventh-day Adventism," and "Seventh-day Adventism and the Gospel of Grace," *The Sunday School Times*, 1954.
———. "Seventh-day Adventists' Counterfeit Gospel," *Christian Victory*, February 1952.
King's Business, April 1957; March 1958.
Lindsell, Harold. "What of Seventh-day Adventism?" *Christianity Today*, March 31, 1958; April 14, 1958.
Martin, Walter R. "Are Seventh-day Adventists Evangelical?" *Christian Life*, October 1956.
———. "Seventh-day Adventism Today," *Our Hope*, November 1956.
Pickering, Ernest. "Can We Fellowship With Seventh-day Adventists?" *The Voice* of the Independent Fundamental Churches of America, October 1956.
Review and Herald magazine, various issues.
Sabbath-School Quarterly magazine, various issues.
Samples, Kenneth. "The Recent Truth About Seventh-day Adventism," *Christianity Today*, February 5, 1990.
"Seventh-day Adventists and the Date of Creation," *The Examiner* magazine, March/April 1952.
Signs of the Times magazine, various issues.
Sword of the Lord, various articles, August 2, 1957.
These Times magazine, various issues.
Yost, Frank H. "A Seventh-day Adventist Speaks Back," *Christianity Today*, July 21, 1958.

Swedenborgianism

Barrett, B. F. *The Science of Correspondences Elucidated.* Germantown, Pa.: Swedenborg Publishing Assoc., 1909.
Christian Apologetics & Research Ministry (CARM), *Swedenborg. www.carm.org/list/swedenborg.htm*, 2003.
Ferm, Vergilius, ed. *Encyclopedia of Religion.* New York: Philosophical Library, 1945.
Jackson, Samuel Macauley, ed. *The New Schaff Herzog Encyclopedia of Religious Knowledge.* Grand Rapids: Baker Book House, 1977 reprint.
Judah, J. Stillson. *The History and Philosophy of the Metaphysical Movements in America.* Philadelphia: The Westminster Press, 1967.
Larson, Bob. *Larson's Book of Cults.* Wheaton: Tyndale House Publishers, Inc., 1982.
New Church.org. *http://newchurch.newearth.org/gcncgb.php*, 2003.
Robertson, Irvine. *What the Cults Believe.* Chicago: Moody Press, 1981.
Sigstedt, Cyriel O. *The Swedenborg Epic, the Life and Works of Emmanuel Swedenborg.* New York: Twayne, 1952.

Smyth, Julian K., and Wunsch, William. *The Gist of Swedenborg.* Philadelphia: J. B. Lippincott, 1920.

Spittler, Russell P. *Cults and Isms.* Grand Rapids: Baker Book House, 1962.

Swedenborg, Emmanuel. *The Complete Works.* Boston: Houghton Mifflin Co., 1907.

Swedenborg.org. *Beliefs; Church Today. www.swedenborg.org/chtoday.cfm,* 2003.

Trobridge, G. *Swedenborg: Life and Teachings.* New York: Swedenborg Foundation, 1938.

Vrooman, Hiram. *Science and Theology Coordinated.* Pamphlet. Chicago: Swedenborg Philosophical Center.

Watchman Fellowship, Swedenborg. *www.watchman.org/profile/swedenborgpro.htm,* 2003.

Weaver, David. *Leaving Swedenborgianism: A Testimony.* Christian Apologetics & Research Ministry. *www.carm.org/testimonies/david_weaver.htm,* 2003.

Rosicrucianism

Ancient and Mystical Order of the Rosae Crucis (AMORC). *www.amorc.org,* 2003.

Braden, Charles S. "Rosicrucianism" in *Encyclopedia Britannica.* Vol. 9. 19th ed. Chicago: Benton Publishing, 1964.

Clymer, R. S. *The Book of Rosicruciae.* 3 vols. Quakerstown, Pa.: The Philosophical Publishing Co.

Gruss, Edmond C. *Cults and Occult.* Grand Rapids: Baker Book House, 1982.

Heindel, Max. *The Rosicrucian Cosmo-Conception.* Oceanside: The Rosicrucian Fellowship, 1922.

———. *The Rosicrucian Philosophy.* Oceanside, Calif.: The Rosicrucian Fellowship, 1922.

Howe, Ellic. "Rosicrucians" in *Man, Myth, & Magic.* Vol. 18. Edited by Richard Cavendish. New York: Marshall Cavendish Corp., 1970.

Lewis, H. Spencer. *Rosicrucian Questions and Answers With Complete History of the Rosicrucian Order.* 15th ed. San Jose, Calif.: Supreme Grand Lodge of AMORC, 1981.

———. *The Secret Doctrines of Jesus.* 10th ed. The Rosicrucian Press, Ltd., 1965.

Melton, J. Gordon. *The Encyclopedia of American Religions.* Vol. 2. Wilmington, N.C.: McGrath Publishing Co., 1978.

Rosicrucian Order. *www.rosicrucian.org,* 2003.

Van Baalen, Jan Karel. *Chaos of the Cults.* 4th ed., rev. Grand Rapids, Mich.: Wm. B. Eerdmans Publishing Co., 1962.

Wilson, Colin. *The Occult—A History.* New York: Random House, 1971.

Scripture Index

Subject Index